D0311526

Fodor's

ESSENTIAL
GREAT BRITAIN

Welcome to Great Britain

Great Britain packs spectacular landscapes and rich history into the borders of England, Wales, and Scotland. From the southern coast to the Highlands, its lush countryside and jagged mountains may surprise you. In London and other cities, explore iconic sights and museums—and also discover cutting-edge cultural scenes that tweak tradition. Ancient castles and pretty villages entice too. This book was produced in the middle of the COVID-19 pandemic. As you plan your upcoming travels to Great Britain, please confirm that places are still open and let us know when we need to make updates by writing to us at editors@fodors.com.

TOP REASONS TO GO

★ **Hip Cities:** London's celebrated landmarks, Edinburgh's innovative festivals, and more.

★ **History:** Sites from Stonehenge to Stirling Castle bring the nation's past to life.

★ **Pubs:** For a pint or a chat, a visit to one of "Britain's living rooms" is essential.

★ **Landscapes:** Wooded hills, sparkling lakes, rugged mountains, wide-open moors.

★ **Idyllic Towns:** Cozy cottages with flower beds, pastel-painted seaside charmers.

★ **Great Walks:** In England's Lake District, Scotland's Highlands, and along the Welsh coast.

Contents

1 EXPERIENCE GREAT BRITAIN............ 9
20 Ultimate Experiences 10
What's Where..18
Great Britain Today.................................22
What to Eat in Great Britain 24
What to Drink in Great Britain 26
What to Buy in Great Britain..................28
Best Museums in Great Britain 30
Best Castles in Great Britain.................32
Best Royal Sites in Great Britain..........34
Playing Golf in Scotland.........................36
What to Watch and Read 38

2 TRAVEL SMART 41
Know Before You Go 42
Getting Here and Around......................44
Essentials 53
Best Festivals and Events.....................59
Great Itineraries.....................................60
Contacts 67

3 LONDON 69
Welcome to London...............................70
Planning...72
Westminster and St. James's 78
Mayfair and Marylebone........................88
Soho and Covent Garden......................98
Bloomsbury and Holborn.....................109
The City...116
East London 122
South of the Thames 129
Kensington, Chelsea,
Knightsbridge, and Notting Hill..........138
Regent's Park and Hampstead 149
Up and Down the Thames...................154

4 OXFORD AND THE
THAMES VALLEY 159
Welcome to Oxford and the
Thames Valley 160
Planning...163
Windsor..164
Eton 169
Ascot..170
Cliveden...170
Marlow 171
Henley-on-Thames 172
Oxford..174
Woodstock...180
Aylesbury 182
St. Albans..183

5 CANTERBURY AND
THE SOUTHEAST 185
Welcome to Canterbury
and the Southeast................................186
Planning...189
Canterbury 191
Deal 197
Dover...198
Royal Tunbridge Wells 200
Hever...202
Tonbridge...204
Rochester..206
Rye...207
Hastings...210
Lewes..213
Brighton...216
Arundel..222
Chichester...223

6 STONEHENGE AND THE SOUTH 227
Welcome to Stonehenge
and the South 228
Planning...231
Winchester 234
Chawton 236
Portsmouth...238
Salisbury...241
Stonehenge...245
Avebury..247
Longleat House 249
Stourhead..249
Lyndhurst...251
Beaulieu 253
Corfe Castle 253
Dorchester 254
Sherborne 256
Weymouth..257
Lyme Regis 258

7 CORNWALL AND THE
WEST COUNTRY 261
Welcome to Cornwall and
the West Country 262
Planning...265
Bristol..268
Wells 271
Glastonbury...273
Dunster 274
Lynton and Lynmouth 275
Clovelly 276
Cornwall 277

Plymouth..................................287
Dartmoor National Park..............288
Tavistock and Around 289
Lydford..................................290
Chagford................................291
Exeter...................................292
Totnes...................................294
Dartmouth..............................295

8 BATH, THE COTSWOLDS, AND STRATFORD-UPON-AVON............. 297
Welcome to Bath, the Cotswolds,
and Stratford-upon-Avon 298
Planning.................................301
Bath.....................................304
Castle Combe..........................313
Lacock..................................314
Cheltenham.............................315
Broadway...............................318
Chipping Campden.....................319
Stow-on-the-Wold.....................321
Bourton-on-the-Water................323
Lower Slaughter and
Upper Slaughter......................324
Burford..................................325
Bibury...................................326
Cirencester.............................327
Painswick...............................328
Tetbury.................................329
Stratford-upon-Avon 331
Henley in Arden.......................340
Warwick.................................342
Kenilworth Castle.....................343

9 MANCHESTER, LIVERPOOL, AND THE PEAK DISTRICT 345
Welcome to Manchester,
Liverpool, and the Peak District 346
Planning.................................349
Manchester 352
Liverpool................................363
Buxton...................................372
Bakewell.................................374
Chester.................................376
Ironbridge Gorge......................379
Ludlow...................................381

10 THE LAKE DISTRICT 383
Welcome to The Lake District.............384
Planning.................................387
Kendal...................................390
Windermere and Bowness-on-
Windermere.............................392
Ambleside 395
Grasmere................................396

Elterwater and the Langdales............399
Coniston.................................400
Hawkshead..............................402
Ullswater................................404
Keswick..................................405
Borrowdale..............................408

11 CAMBRIDGE AND EAST ANGLIA.................... 409
Welcome to Cambridge
and East Anglia 410
Planning.................................413
Cambridge...............................415
Ely.......................................426
Long Melford 427
Lavenham................................428
Dedham..................................430
Woodbridge.............................432
Aldeburgh...............................433

12 YORKSHIRE AND THE NORTHEAST 435
Welcome to Yorkshire
and the Northeast.....................436
Planning.................................439
York......................................442
Harrogate...............................450
Castle Howard..........................452
Saltaire 452
Haworth.................................454
Durham..................................456
Hadrian's Wall..........................460
Hexham..................................462
Greenhead..............................463
Alnwick..................................466
Bamburgh................................468

13 WALES.................................... 469
Welcome to Wales 470
Planning.................................473
Cardiff (Caerdydd) 477
Abergavenny (Y Fenni) 485
Brecon (Aberhonddu) 488
Merthyr Mawr...........................492
Swansea (Abertawe) 492
Tenby (Dinbych-y-Pysgod) 496
St. Davids (Tyddewi) 498
Hay-on-Wye
(Y Gelli Gandryll) 500
Llandrindod Wells (Llandrindod) 503
Aberystwyth............................504
Dolgellau 508
Llangollen...............................500
Lake Vyrnwy (Llyn Efyrnwy) 512
Porthmadog 513

Contents

Betws-y-Coed................................516
Llanberis......................................518
Anglesey (Ynys Môn) 519
Conwy...520
Llandudno 522
Ruthin (Rhuthun) 523

14 EDINBURGH 525
Welcome to Edinburgh...............526
Planning......................................529
Old Town.....................................535
New Town 548
Haymarket...................................558
West End 559
South Side...................................563
Leith..565
The Lothians 568

15 GLASGOW 573
Welcome to Glasgow 574
Planning......................................577
City Centre..................................584
Merchant City.............................594
West End 599
Finnieston...................................605
East End 610
South Side...................................611
Side Trips from Glasgow:
Ayrshire, Clyde Coast, and
Robert Burns Country...............615

**16 THE BORDERS AND
THE SOUTHWEST 619**
Welcome to The Borders
and the Southwest.....................620
Planning......................................623
Jedburgh 626
Kelso 629
Melrose 631
Selkirk 633
Innerleithen................................634
Dumfries 635
North of Dumfries 638
Castle Douglas 640
Kirkcudbright..............................641
Whithorn.....................................643
Stranraer 643

**17 THE CENTRAL HIGHLANDS,
FIFE, AND ANGUS 645**
Welcome to The Central Highlands, Fife,
and Angus....................................646

Planning......................................650
Stirling..653
Callander.....................................656
The Trossachs 658
Aberfoyle 659
Loch Lomond 661
Perth..663
Dunkeld.......................................665
Pitlochry 666
Blair Atholl 668
Auchterarder...............................668
St. Andrews 669
Crail 673
Anstruther 674
Falkland 675
Dundee 676
The Angus Glens 681
Kirriemuir....................................681
Glamis 682

**18 ABERDEEN AND
THE NORTHEAST 683**
Welcome to Aberdeen
and the Northeast.......................684
Planning......................................687
Aberdeen.....................................689
Stonehaven..................................696
Banchory.....................................698
Ballater..699
Braemar.......................................701
Alford 702
Dufftown......................................705
Craigellachie...............................706
Aberlour.......................................708
Fochabers 709
Cullen 710
Banff..710
Fyvie Castle 711
Ellon..712

19 ARGYLL AND THE ISLES 713
Welcome to Argyll and the Isles 714
Planning......................................717
Oban..720
Appin 723
Loch Awe 724
Inveraray 725
Kintyre Peninsula.......................727
Arran 727
Islay and Jura.............................730
Isle of Mull and Iona..................734

20 INVERNESS, SKYE, AND THE NORTHERN HIGHLANDS 739
Welcome To Inverness, Skye, and the Northern Highlands 740
Planning 744
Inverness 747
Culloden Moor 751
Nairn 752
Forres 753
Aviemore 754
Kingussie 757
Drumnadrochit and Loch Ness 758
Fort William 760
Glenfinnan 763
Arisaig 764
Glencoe 764
Isle of Skye 765
Gairloch 775
Ullapool 776
Kylesku 777
Scourie 778
Durness 778
John O'Groats 780
Dornoch 781

INDEX 783

ABOUT OUR WRITERS 799

MAPS

Westminster and St. James's 80–81
Mayfair and Marylebone 90–91
Soho and Covent Garden 100–101
Bloomsbury and Holborn 112–113
The City 118–119
East London 124
South of the Thames 130–131
Kensington, Chelsea, Knightsbridge, and Notting Hill 140–141
Regent's Park and Hampstead 152
Up and Down the Thames 156
Windsor, Marlow, and Around 165
Oxford 176
Oxfordshire 181
Canterbury 194
Canterbury and the Kent Coast 199
Tunbridge Wells and West Kent 201
Rye and Lewes 208
Brighton 218
Brighton and the Sussex Coast 222
Winchester, Portsmouth, and Around 239
Salisbury, Stonehenge and Salisbury Plain 245

New Forest, Dorset, and the South Coast 252
Bristol, Wells, and North Devon 269
Cornwall 278
Plymouth, Exeter, and South Devon 288
Bath 306–307
Around Bath 314
The Cotswolds 316
Stratford-upon-Avon 332–333
Around Stratford-upon-Avon 341
Manchester 354–355
Liverpool 366–367
The Peak District 372
Chester, Ludlow, and Around 377
The Lake District 391
Cambridge 418–419
Suffolk 427
York 444
Around York 451
Brontë Country 454
Durham and Hadrian's Wall Country 460
The Far Northeast Coast 464
Cardiff 478–479
South Wales 486
Mid-Wales 501
North Wales 511
Old Town 536–537
New Town 550–551
Haymarket, West End, South Side, and Leith 560–561
The Lothians and the Forth Valley 569
City Centre and Merchant City 586–587
West End and Finniston 606–607
East End and South Side 612–613
Ayrshire 616
The Borders 628
Dumfries and Galloway 637
The Trossachs and Loch Lomond 658
Perthshire 664
St. Andrews and East Neuk 674
Dundee and Angus 680
Royal Deeside 697
The Northeast 704
Argyll and Arran 722
Islay and Jura 732
Isle of Mull and Iona 735
Inverness, Speyside, and the Cairngorms 748
Loch Ness, Fort William, and Nearby 759
Isle of Skye 766
The Northern Highlands 774

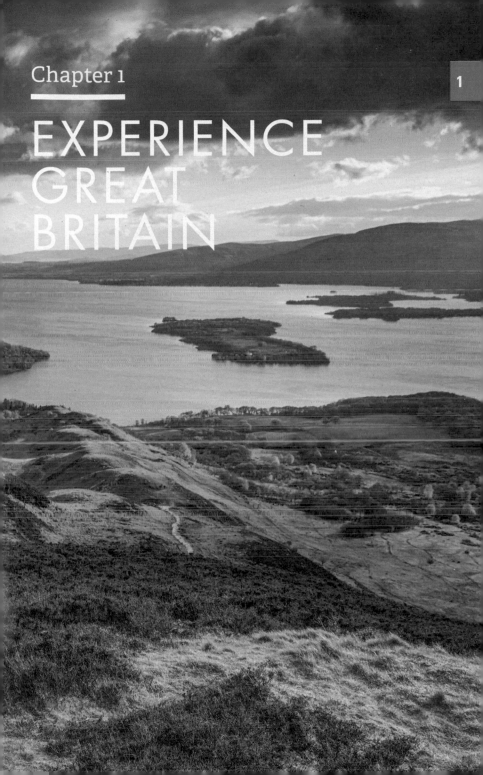

Chapter 1

EXPERIENCE GREAT BRITAIN

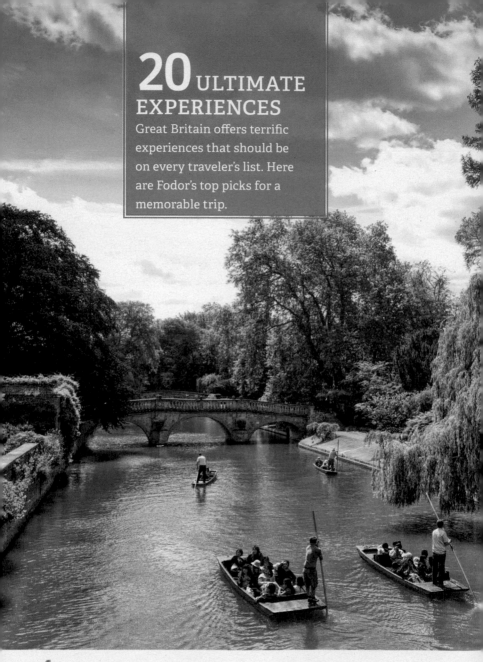

20 ULTIMATE EXPERIENCES

Great Britain offers terrific experiences that should be on every traveler's list. Here are Fodor's top picks for a memorable trip.

1 Oxford and Cambridge

England is home to these two prestigious universities, where you'll find centuries of history among ancient buildings and museums. Tour the accompanying towns via punting boats on local waterways. *(Ch. 4, 11)*

2 London

London is the beating heart of England, a world-class city with museums, palaces, and iconic sights that define the country for many. *(Ch. 3)*

3 Isle of Skye

With the misty Cuillin Mountains and rocky shores, Skye has few rivals among Scotland's islands for sheer loveliness. *(Ch. 20)*

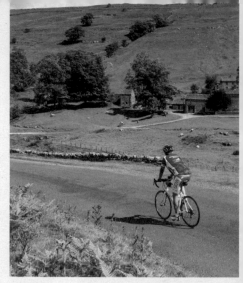

4 Seafood

From salmon to oysters, enjoy the delicious fish and seafood from Britain's rivers, lakes, and the sea. Fried fish-and-chips are the ultimate British comfort food. *(Ch. 7, 12, 18)*

5 Yorkshire

The stunning natural landscape of Yorkshire's moors and dales inspired the Brontës, and continues to attract hikers, cyclists, and nature-lovers. *(Ch. 12)*

6 Loch Lomond

The Trossachs are the essence of the Highlands. Clear water and access to Edinburgh and Glasgow make Loch Lomond a coveted retreat. *(Ch. 17)*

7 Glasgow

An urban renaissance has brought great shopping and nightlife to complement the city's rich architectural heritage and historic museums like the Kelvingrove. *(Ch. 15)*

8 The Cotswolds

Full of quaint English villages, the Cotswolds is one of the prettiest regions of the country, thanks to the stone cottages, famed gardens, and rural charm. *(Ch. 8)*

9 Castles

Castles dating from the medieval period to Victorian times are among Britain's glories, including Windsor in England, Dunnottar in Scotland, and Conwy in Wales. *(Ch. 13)*

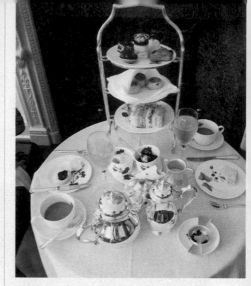

10 Stratford-upon-Avon

The birthplace of William Shakespeare offers plenty for fans of the Bard, including performances of his plays at the Royal Shakespeare Company. *(Ch. 8)*

11 Afternoon Tea

For a quintessential British ritual, enjoy a pot of tea served in bone china alongside finger sandwiches, fruit scones, and cakes. *(Ch. 3)*

12 Cardiff

As the capital of Wales, Cardiff is lively and charming, with a whole host of castles, museums, and pubs to explore. *(Ch. 13)*

13 Golf

The home of golf, Scotland claims some of the world's most challenging holes but has courses for all levels, many in beautiful settings. *(Ch. 14–20)*

14 Snowdonia National Park

Experience the Welsh countryside at its most gorgeous and dramatic at Snowdonia National Park, home to the country's highest mountain. *(Ch. 13)*

15 Glencoe

The wild beauty of Glencoe's craggy peaks and deep valley provided the background for a tragic massacre in 1692. Today the area is popular for outdoor activities. *(Ch. 20)*

16 Whisky Tours

From Speyside to Islay, whisky distilleries offer tours and tastings of Scotland's signature drink. Their often-spectacular settings are an added bonus. *(Ch. 18–20)*

17 Cathedrals

The cathedrals of Salisbury, Westminster, Canterbury, and York Minster, among others, are an essential part of England's urban landscapes and history. *(Ch. 3-12)*

18 Historic Pubs

The history of Britain's taverns and pubs is the history of the country itself. Grab a pint or a gin cocktail, and get to know how the locals live. London has some of the regon's best drinking holes. *(Ch. 3)*

19 Edinburgh

Scotland's capital charms with its Royal Mile and Old Town, and events such as the Edinburgh International Festival and the Fringe keep it lively. *(Ch. 14)*

20 Stonehenge

Awe-inspiring and mystical, Stonehenge is one of the most famous prehistoric sites in England, as well as one of history's most enduring mysteries. *(Ch. 6)*

WHAT'S WHERE

1 London. Not only Britain's financial and governmental center but also one of the world's great cities, London has mammoth museums, posh palaces, and iconic sights.

2 Oxford and the Thames Valley. London's commuter belt takes in Windsor, where the Queen spends most weekends. Then there are the spires of Oxford, peaceful river towns such as Henley and Marlow, and stately homes like Blenheim Palace.

3 Canterbury and the Southeast. This compact green and pleasant region takes in Canterbury and its cathedral, funky seaside Brighton, Dover's white cliffs, and gorgeous castles.

4 Stonehenge and the South. Hampshire, Dorset, and Wiltshire have quintessential English countryside. Explore the stone circles at Stonehenge and Avebury, take in Winchester and Salisbury, and discover Highclere Castle.

5 Cornwall and the West Country. Somerset, Devon, and Cornwall are sunnier and warmer than the rest of the country. Of the cities, Bristol is the largest and most vibrant.

6 Bath, the Cotswolds, and Stratford-upon-Avon. The grand Georgian town of Bath is one of England's highlights with its Roman baths. Nearby, the Cotswolds region is justly famous for tranquil, stone-built villages. Stratford-upon-Avon is the place to see Shakespeare's birthplace and watch his plays.

7 Manchester, Liverpool, and the Peak District. Liverpool rides the Beatles' coattails but, like Manchester, has transformed its warehouses and docks into sleek hotels, restaurants, and shops. The surrounding Peak District has great opportunities for walking and visiting stately homes.

8 The Lake District. A popular national park, this is a startlingly beautiful area of craggy hills, wild moorland, stone cottages, and glittering silvery lakes.

9 Cambridge and East Anglia. The biggest lure in this green, flat, low-key region is Cambridge, with its medieval halls of learning. The countryside is dominated by time-warp towns such as Lavenham and coastal spots like Aldeburgh.

WHAT'S WHERE

10 Yorkshire and the Northeast. This wilder part of England has great appeal for lovers of the outdoors, but the ancient walled city of York is also a center of attention. In the Northeast, medieval Durham, Hadrian's Wall, and coastal castles are highlights.

11 Wales. Clinging to the western edge of England, Wales is impossibly green and ruggedly beautiful, with soaring mountains, magnificent coastlines, and stunning castles.

12 Edinburgh. The captivating Scottish capital is the country's most popular city, famous for its high-perched castle, Old Town and 18th-century New Town, and the most celebrated arts festival in the world.

13 Glasgow. Scotland's largest city has evolved from prosperous Victorian hub to depressed urban center to thriving modern city with a strong artistic, architectural, and culinary reputation.

14 The Borders and the Southwest. The southern gateway from Scotland to England (or vice versa), the Borders offers a landscape of pretty moors, gentle hills, and river valleys.

15 The Central Highlands, Fife, and Angus. Convenient to both Edinburgh and Glasgow, this area encompasses some of Scotland's most beautiful terrain, including Loch Lomond and the Trossachs. In Fife, St. Andrews has world-famous golf courses.

16 Aberdeen and the Northeast. Malt-whisky buffs can use the prosperous port city of Aberdeen as a base for exploring the region's distilleries, including those on the Malt Whisky Trail. Aberdeen also makes a good starting point for touring Royal Deeside, with castles like Balmoral.

17 Argyll and the Isles. Remote and picturesque, this less visited region of Scotland's southwestern coastline has excellent gardens, religious sites, and distilleries.

18 Inverness, Skye, and the Northern Highlands. An awe-inspiring valley laced with rivers defines the Great Glen. Inverness, capital of the Highlands, is near Loch Ness. The beautiful Isle of Skye is a highlight for visitors, and the north's rugged highlands have wild moors.

Great Britain Today

Great Britain and the United Kingdom—what's the difference? Historically the United Kingdom (or U.K.) has consisted of the countries of England, Scotland, Wales, and Northern Ireland; the Channel Islands; and the Isle of Man. Great Britain, meanwhile, is the landmass occupied by England, Scotland, and Wales. Despite this precise definition, "Britain" is often used as a synonym of the U.K., and "the British" refer to all its citizens.

In a 2014 referendum, the Scottish people narrowly voted to remain as part of the U.K. However, a subsequent U.K.-wide vote in 2016 to leave the European Union (popularly termed "Brexit"), supported by a majority of voters in England and Wales, but only a minority in Scotland and Northern Ireland, has led to further debates about the future of the union.

It is important to note that neither Scotland nor Wales have ever been part of England, or vice versa, and each has their own unique heritage and culture. Get that wrong at your own peril—you haven't seen angry until you've seen a Scot referred to as English. That being said, all three countries (and the rest of the U.K.) still pledge loyalty to the British Royal Family, and, despite each having selected devolved powers, are generally governed by the Parliament of the United Kingdom centered in London.

THE ROYAL FAMILY

Essentially a figurehead monarchy with a symbolic political role, the Royal Family and each member of its four generations continue to exercise the public's fascination, both at home and abroad. Although taxpayer cost for supporting the family is estimated at £45 million (more than $61 million), many consider the tourists they bring worth the cost (tourism numbers have been helped along in recent years with the success of television shows like

The Crown and *Victoria*). The Queen, now the world's longest reigning monarch, celebrated her Sapphire Jubilee (65 years on the throne) in February 2017 and still maintains a full working schedule, although her husband, Prince Philip, has now retired from public life. Both are in their 90s.

Prince Charles remains in the wings, while his son, Prince William, is second in the line of succession. William's personal life has generated plenty of buzz, from his 2011 wedding to Kate Middleton (now known publicly as Catherine, Duchess of Cambridge) to the births of their three children; future king Prince George, Princess Charlotte, and Prince Louis. However, in the last few years, most of the headlines have gone to his younger brother Harry, first for his wedding to American actress Meghan Markle in May 2018, then for the birth of their son Archie in May 2019, and most recently for the couple's decison to step back as senior members of the Royal Family and split their time between the United States and the United Kingdom.

POLITICS

Since the general election of 2015, the United Kingdom's government has been in the hands of the Conservative Party. But the unexpected result of a June 2016 referendum, in which the country voted to leave the European Union (a decision known commonly as Brexit), led to the resignation of prime minister David Cameron, who was replaced by Theresa May. Following three turbulent years, which were dominated by Brexit negotiations but also marked by the loss of a parliamentary majority, cabinet resignations, tragic terrorist attacks in London and Manchester, the horrific Grenfell Tower fire disaster, and a crisis in the National Health Service (NHS), May was replaced by Boris Johnson in July 2019. Despite being seen as a deeply divisive figure, Johnson secured an overall parliamentary majority for the Conservatives at the December 2019 general election, and in January 2020 proceeded to finally take the U.K. out of the European Union under the terms of his Brexit withdrawal agreement.

BREXIT

The United Kingdom officially began to leave the European Union in January 2020, but despite this and Boris Johnson's election slogan of "Get Brexit Done," most experts agree that this issue is set to dominate British politics (and newspaper column inches) for years to come. The transition period, during which the U.K. remained in the single market, ended on December 31, 2020, and there is now a new trade deal in place between Great Britain and the E.U. For visitors to Great Britain, this means citizens of the E.U. still won't need a visa to enter the country for trips of less than 90 days, but they do now need a visa to work or live there (the exception being Irish citizens). Because of these changes, border checks might take longer than usual.

LONDON

Dynamic, complex, and cosmopolitan, London is undoubtedly a success story. Economically vibrant, it is Europe's financial hub—although whether it will maintain this position following Brexit remains to be seen. London also holds the nation's greatest concentration of arts, contains some of its most iconic attractions, and boasts its most vibrant restaurant and theater scenes. Consequently, it's also the U.K.'s top tourist draw, with ongoing debates about how to increase the capacity of its airports to meet visitor demand. However, London's extraordinary success has often come at the expense of the rest of the country, with many cities and towns still struggling with austerity measures imposed after the financial crash of 2008. Nor is London's preeminence always good news for Londoners, many of whom have been priced out of a skyrocketing property market by investors and foreign buyers (London is, by quite some distance, the most expensive British city to live in). London is in a category of its own—for better or worse.

SCOTLAND

At first glance, visitors to Scotland who have already been to its southern neighbor England will find much that is familiar. After all, the two countries have had a common history since their crowns were united in 1603 and their parliaments merged a hundred years later. Scotland's distinctiveness soon becomes apparent, however, as does the country's fiery pride in its own identity. It may only have 5.5 million people (to England's 56 million), but in modern history Scotland has had an extraordinary global influence in everything from art and literature to science and engineering. Today, it continues to have some big ideas about where it's headed socially, culturally, and economically.

This self-confidence is immediately evident in its thriving arts scene, with arts festivals proliferating and such companies as the National Theatre of Scotland continuing to enjoy international success. And it's just as evident when talking to locals, who will proudly proclaim their landscapes, their castles, and their food and drink to be the best in the world.

What to Eat in Great Britain

CULLEN SKINK
Cullen skink is a decadently creamy fish soup that's made with hearty smoked haddock, potatoes, onions, and cream. Think American chowder, but thicker, smokier, and served piping hot with bread. You'll find it on the menu in many Scottish pubs and restaurants, especially on the coasts.

HAGGIS, NEEPS, AND TATTIES
From the offal-heavy list of ingredients (minced heart, liver, and lungs mixed with onions, oatmeal, and spices) and the unconventional cooking method (the mixture is boiled in a sheep's stomach), haggis may not sound like the most appetizing of meals. But there's a very good reason for its status as Scotland's national dish: it's delicious. Travel the country and you'll see haggis all over menus. It's traditionally served with neeps (turnips) and tatties (potatoes), but is also found at breakfast, in sandwiches, and even on nachos.

FISH AND CHIPS
The U.K.'s most famous dish is available in almost every town and village. Best enjoyed out of a hot paper wrap from a typical fish and chip shop, or chippy, the meal should be eaten with a miniature wooden fork for extra authenticity. The fish is usually cod (but haddock, skate, and rock are not uncommon), covered in a crispy deep-fried batter. Chips are thick-cut fried potatoes and sides can include anything from pickled eggs to mushy peas. You can also opt for a sauce: regional English variations including tartare, curry sauce, and gravy while the Scots prefer "chippy sauce," a pungent mix of malt vinegar and brown sauce that's similar to American steak sauce).

WELSH RAREBIT
The ultimate grilled cheese sandwich, Welsh rarebit (originally Welsh rabbit) comprises slices of toasted bread smothered in a savory sauce of melted cheese and other ingredients that might include ale, mustard, cayenne pepper, and Worcestershire sauce. Add a fried egg on top and you get a "buck rarebit;" add tomatoes and it's a "blushing bunny."

CURRY
The 1970s saw a wave of South Asian immigrants arriving in the U.K. and setting up restaurants in big urban centers like London, Birmingham, and Manchester. These days, there's a mix of Indian, Bangladeshi, and Pakistani restaurants in almost every town and village, serving some of the finest curry anywhere outside of Asia. Aside from classics like vindaloo, madras, and tandoori meats, the range of sweet, salty, spicy, and sour curries makes it one of the country's best-loved cuisines.

SUNDAY ROAST
Roasted meat (chicken, beef, pork, or lamb), roast potatoes, assorted vegetables, cauliflower cheese, Yorkshire puddings, and condiments like mint sauce, bread sauce, English mustard, horseradish, and cranberry jelly make up some of the most important

Full English Breakfast

elements of a traditional Sunday roast, a meal that should leave you ready to sleep within 30 minutes of eating it. Almost every pub and restaurant in the U.K. serves a roast on a Sunday, and the quality ranges dramatically depending on the establishment. You'll also find "carveries" serving buffet-style roasts every day of the week.

CHEESE
The English stalwart Cheddar, Cheshire, Double Gloucester, and Stilton cheeses are complemented by traditional and experimental cheeses from small, local makers. Some cheeses come wrapped in nettles or vine leaves, others stuffed with apricots, cranberries, or herbs. Dairies are also producing more sheep and goat cheeses, yogurts, and ice creams.

BANGERS AND MASH
Simple but effective, this pub grub staple comprises sausages served on a bed of mashed potatoes and topped with onion gravy. The "bangers" are usually Cumberlands—long, coiled, and particularly meaty pork sausages—but they can also be made from lamb or beef.

BARA BRITH
Literally translated as "speckled bread," this tasty, fruity Welsh loaf is made with flour, yeast, butter, eggs, dried fruits (usually raisins, currants, and sultanas) soaked overnight in tea, and mixed spices. When slathered with salted butter, it's the perfect tea time treat.

FULL ENGLISH AND SCOTTISH BREAKFAST
A morning staple, the classic Full English breakfast consists of eggs

(usually fried, poached, or scrambled), sausages, bacon, fried tomatoes, black pudding, black beans, mushrooms, and toast. The full Scottish has all of the above, sometimes adding haggis and tattie (potato) scones to the mix.

SMOKED FISH
From Arbroath smokies to Finnan haddie, smoked fish is a staple of Scottish dining tables nationwide. Smokies are haddock, salted and dried overnight, then smoked in a barrel over a hardwood fire, while Finnan haddies are coldsmoked haddock, cooked over green wood and peat. And that's only the start of the many regional variations of smoked fish all over Scotland. Visitors will also find menus featuring smoked herring (kippers), smoked trout, and, of course, smoked salmon.

What to Drink in Great Britain

beer being served directly from the cask. The ales can be from kegs, bottles, or casks, and they range from pale amber to full-bodied. The Casque Mark outside pubs signals their availability.

PIMM'S CUP

Best enjoyed while outside in the sun, Pimm's is a gin-based liqueur typically mixed with lemonade and ice, then filled with sliced strawberries, cucumber, and mint. Popular at weddings, regattas, Wimbledon, horse-racing tracks, and cricket matches, it is the British version of the Aperol Spritz and even more refreshing than water.

IRN-BRU

After whisky, Irn-Bru is the drink most associated with Scotland. The luminous orange carbonated soda even outsells Coca-Cola in these parts. Nobody can quite agree exactly what the flavor is, and it famously isn't to everyone's taste, but you can't say you have truly experienced Scotland without a sip of Irn-Bru.

SCOTTISH WHISKY

No trip to Scotland is complete without trying a dram or two of Scotland's most famous tipple. There are several distinct Scotch whisky regions, each producing a single malt with its own complex character, from sweeter Speyside whiskies to smokier Islays.

AFTERNOON TEA

Typically enjoyed between an early lunch and late dinner, afternoon tea is a very British way to spend a few hours. A true afternoon tea consists of cakes, pastries, finger sandwiches, and scones with jam and clotted cream displayed on a tiered stand and served with steaming pots of loose-leaf tea. In many establishments, you can expect a tea menu (and the fanciest might even have a tea sommelier) where you can consider the likes of Earl Grey, Assam (the Queen's favorite teas), Darjeeling, and Ceylon.

REAL ALES

Also known as draught cask ale, real ale is unfiltered, unpasteurized beer that is served directly from a cask. The term was coined in the early 1970s to differentiate traditional English-style beers, containing live yeast and therefore naturally bubbly, from the highly processed, artificially carbonated beers made by big breweries of the time. Today real ales (from IPAs and stouts to golden ales and porters) are served in all good pubs throughout England, Scotland, and Wales; look for a traditional handpulled pump or for

ENGLISH CIDER

Sweet and refreshing, traditional English cider is made from pure apple juice and twice fermented. The drink is usually carbonated, though some variations—like West Country specialty *scrumpy*—can be still. Perry is a similar drink made from pear juice.

Pimm's Cup

GIN

Gin has had a big resurgence in recent years, and today you'll find a huge selection of gins available in pubs, clubs, and supermarkets across Great Britain. Opt for a stylishly-packaged, 21st-century gin like Curio, Sipsmith, or Hendrick's, or choose a classic, centuries-old spirit like Beefeater, Bloom, or Plymouth.

WINE

Believe it or not, wine-making in Southern England and Wales dates back to Roman times—and in recent years, there has been a major resurgence. There are now hundreds of vineyards producing internationally-acclaimed, awardwinning wines, including Chapel Down in Kent and Ancre Hill Estates in Monmouthshire.

ENGLISH BREAKFAST TEA

Even if you're not going the full afternoon tea route, tea is still a quintessential drink to sample in Great Britain, and English Breakfast is probably the country's most popular blend. It's a full-bodied, robust black tea that goes well with a splash of milk and a spoonful of sugar. You can pick up common brands like Twinings and PG Tips from any supermarket or treat yourself to superior blends from the likes of Harrods and Fortnum and Mason.

What to Buy in Great Britain

BISCUITS AND TEA CAKES

A "biscuit" here is a hard, sweet, baked treat that's akin to a cookie or a cracker in North America—and they're a cornerstone of British life, from English chocolate digestives to Scottish shortbread biscuits.

CADBURY CHOCOLATE

The country's best-selling chocolate bar is Cadbury Dairy Milk, which you'll find in every corner shop (and airport duty-free store) in the land. Along with Dairy Milk, Cadbury makes dozens of other popular chocolate bars, from the biscuit-filled Boost to the honeycomb-toffee Crunchie.

FOOTBALL GEAR

Football is Britain's favorite sport, so a soccer jersey—or any other item of football merchandise—makes the perfect souvenir. Take your pick from big-name Premier League clubs like Liverpool, Manchester United, and Chelsea, or opt for some merch from the England, Scotland, or Wales national teams.

ANYTHING TARTAN PRINT

Like the look of tartan but can't see yourself in a kilt? No problem. You'll find plenty of other tartan print products on sale in Scotland, from sweaters and scarves to coats and cushions to backpacks and bow ties. If you want to go the whole hog, you can even order yourself a statement tartan-clad armchair from ANTA in Edinburgh.

HARRIS TWEED

A traditional cloth handwoven from pure virgin wool by crofters in Scotland's Western Isles (not just Lewis and Harris, but also North Uist, Benbecula, South Uist, and Barra), Harris Tweed is world-famous for its warmth, softness, resilience, and breathability. From jackets to scarves to blankets, Harris Tweed items are for sale across the Western Isles but also on the mainland; simply look for the official orb trademark.

KILTS

These knee-length pleated skirts, usually made from woolen cloth in a tartan pattern, are the traditional dress of men in the Scottish Highlands. While no longer everyday wear for most modern Scots, you'll still see kilts worn on special occasions like weddings.

LAVERBREAD

This traditional Welsh delicacy is not bread at all; it's a gelatinous, iron-rich paste made from edible seaweed. Renowned Welsh actor Richard Burton memorably described it as

Kilts

"Welshman's caviar." Pick up a jar to take home; you can fry it with bacon, use it to make soups and sauces, or simply eat it cold as a salad.

ROYALTY-RELATED MEMORABILIA

From cheaply-made key rings and mugs to high-quality chinaware and jewelry, memorabilia celebrating the Royal Family comes in all shapes and sizes—and for all budgets. For the most authentic souvenirs, shop at the official Royal Collection stores, which you'll find at royal residences like Buckingham Palace and Windsor Castle.

QUAICH

An old Highland symbol of kinship and friendship, this shallow drinking vessel was the original whisky tumbler. Its distinctive two-handle design means it can be shared amicably between friends and loved ones (and it's still used to toast the bride at weddings). Though traditionally made of wood and modestly decorated, modern quaichs are commonly made from pewter and silver to allow for personalized engraving.

HP SAUCE

A true icon of British culture, this "brown sauce" has a tomato base, blended with malt vinegar, sugars, dates, and tamarind. HP stands for Houses of Parliament, which explains the Westminster illustration on the front of the bottle.

LOVE SPOONS

A Welsh tradition dating back to at least the 17th century, these intricately-carved wooden spoons would be gifted to young women by men to show romantic interest.

Best Museums in Great Britain

NATIONAL MUSEUM OF SCOTLAND, EDINBURGH
From Dolly the Sheep (the world's first cloned mammal) to the Lewis Chessmen (ivory-carved medieval chess pieces), the National Museum of Scotland has a host of fascinating, family-friendly exhibits. It also has one of Edinburgh's best city views; take the elevator to the rooftop terrace for a stunning panorama of the city.

KELVINGROVE ART GALLERY AND MUSEUM, GLASGOW
One of Scotland's most popular museums, Kelvingrove's collection includes works by Rembrandt, van Gogh, and Dali, an impressive collection of arms and armor, a gigantic concert pipe organ, and much more.

RIVERSIDE MUSEUM, GLASGOW
Set within an eye-catching, Zaha Hadid–designed building on the banks of the Clyde, the award-winning Riverside Museum has an exhaustive collection of transport exhibits, from skateboards to steam trains and everything in between. Also the *Tall Ship* at Riverside, a Victorian cargo ship, is moored outside.

TATE MODERN, LONDON
This spectacular contemporary art gallery starts with a bang, thanks to its entrance, Turbine Hall, filled with gigantic temporary installations from artists including Ai Weiwei, Abraham Cruzvillegas, and Kara Walker. Venture further inside for the Tate Modern's impressive permanent collection of works by the likes of Warhol, Picasso, Dalí, Rothko, and Gormley.

THE BRITISH MUSEUM, LONDON

Established in 1753, the British Museum has long been one of the world's most famous national museums. Today, the London landmark is home to a permanent collection of eight million works, including the Rosetta Stone and the Elgin Marbles.

The Roman Baths

ROMAN BATHS AND THE PUMP ROOM, BATH

The hot springs of Bath have drawn visitors to the city for thousands of years. Today, this museum displays relics from the Roman bath complex that used to stand on the site, as well as the Pump Room, a hang-out for 19th-century Bath society members.

INTERNATIONAL SLAVERY MUSEUM, LIVERPOOL

Tracing the shameful history and legacy of the transatlantic slave trade, in which the city of Liverpool played a significant role, this important dockside slavery museum recreates what life was like in West African compounds and aboard crammed slave ships bound for the Americas.

ASHMOLEAN MUSEUM, OXFORD

Known to locals simply as "The Ash," this extraordinary Oxford University museum was founded in 1683 (the first public museum in the United Kingdom). With a focus on art and archaeology, the collection spans everything from Egyptian mummies to Renaissance artwork.

NATIONAL MUSEUM, CARDIFF

Situated right in the heart of the cosmopolitan capital of Wales, this striking neoclassical building houses several different exhibitions. Step inside to find a world-class art gallery (featuring one of Britain's finest collections of Impressionist paintings), an interactive science discovery center, and more.

V&A DUNDEE

The V&A Dundee design museum is not only the first V&A outpost outside London but also the country's first design museum; it features permanent exhibits from designers across Scotland, including Charles Rennie Mackintosh.

Best Castles in Great Britain

STIRLING CASTLE

Magnificent Stirling Castle was at the heart of the Wars of Independence, and the biggest prize for Robert the Bruce's famous victory at Bannockburn. The castle's royal connections lasted for centuries; it was later the childhood home of Mary, Queen of Scots. Today, exhibits tell the story of the castle's roles as a battle site, royal palace, and tourism hot spot.

EDINBURGH CASTLE

Scotland's most famous medieval fortress, Edinburgh Castle is the capital's crowning glory, having played host to kings, queens, soldiers, and prisoners for close to a millennium.

ALNWICK CASTLE

Instantly recognizable to Harry Potter fans, Northumberland's beautiful Alnwick Castle—dubbed the "Windsor of the North"—is best known as the exterior of Hogwarts School of Witchcraft and Wizardry in the *Harry Potter* movie series.

HIGHCLERE CASTLE

This grand, Jacobean-style country house gained international fame during the 2010s as the main location for mega TV hit *Downton Abbey* and its 2019 movie adaptation. The house, gardens, and Egyptian exhibition are open to visit throughout the summer.

HEVER CASTLE

Arguably England's most picture-perfect castle, Hever Castle is a 700-year-old mass of romantic turrets, battlements, and manicured gardens, all enveloped by a moat. It was the ancestral home of Henry VIII's second wife Anne Boleyn until her 1536 execution.

CARDIFF CASTLE

Sitting pretty at the heart of the Welsh capital, Cardiff Castle is part Norman keep and part Victorian mansion, with ancient Roman roots. Admire it from afar or venture inside to explore its startlingly opulent interiors.

KENILWORTH CASTLE

Founded in the 12th century, this extraordinary fortification showcases five centuries of different English architectural styles. And these romantic ruins have seen a thing or two, from royal prisoners to civil wars.

Alnwick Castle

CAERNARFON CASTLE
This medieval fortress has watched over the Welsh town of Caernarfon for the best part of a millennium. Now a UNESCO World Heritage Site, its fascinating and bloody military history makes it one of the country's most visited tourist attractions.

GLAMIS CASTLE
Beautiful Glamis Castle has a long history of royal connections, from Macbeth, King of Scots (who was the Thane of Glamis, as well as Cawdor) to Princess Margaret (who was born within its four walls). Consequently, for any lovers of Shakespeare or the British royal family, Glamis Castle is a must-see sight.

SUDELEY CASTLE
It may officially be called a castle, but this Cotswolds icon is more akin to a Tudor palace. Once the home of Catherine Parr, Henry VIII's sixth and final wife (the only one who "survived"), it was used as a refuge by Charles I and besieged by Cromwell's army, reducing it to ruins.

FLOORS CASTLE
Built in the 1720s as the seat of the Duke of Roxburghe, the enormous Floors Castle remains the property of the duke to this day. That makes it the largest inhabited castle in Scotland; it has grand rooms decorated with plush furnishings, old portraits, and precious porcelain.

EILEAN DONAN
Scotland's most picture-perfect castle, Eilean Donan sits pretty on a loch islet en route to the Isle of Skye. Often obscured by rolling fog, the 14th-century fortification is a merry mess of imposing towers, timber-framed roofs, and crooked staircases.

Best Royal Sites in Great Britain

WESTMINSTER ABBEY

One of England's most famous buildings, Westminster Abbey has hosted 38 coronations (beginning with William the Conqueror in 1066) and 16 royal weddings. Fascinating royal sights include the Coronation Chair (used since 1308), Henry VII's Lady Chapel, and the tombs of Elizabeth I and her sister "Bloody" Mary I.

BALMORAL PALACE

This imposing estate house has been an official residence of the royal family since 1852 and remains the Queen's summer home of choice. Its 19th-century design is faux–Scottish baronial, but its grandiose ballroom, formal grounds, and fascinating exhibits make it a worthwhile stop.

SANDRINGHAM HOUSE

The Royal Family traditionally spends Christmas at Sandringham, a vast, red-brick Victorian mansion and estate near the coast in East Anglia. But for most of the rest of year, it's open to visitors. Along with the opulent Edwardian interiors and pretty formal gardens, you'll also find a superb transport museum.

TOWER OF LONDON

Dating back almost a millennium, the world-famous Tower of London has at times been a fortress, a mint, a palace, a zoo, and a prison. Today, it welcomes tourists to explore its historic attractions, from the Bloody Tower to the Crown Jewels.

WINDSOR CASTLE

Visible for miles around, this enormous fortification-cum-royal residence (the largest inhabited castle in the world) has been used by the Royal Family since the Middle Ages. Explore Windsor Castle's beautiful St. George's Chapel, home to the tombs of English kings including Charles I and Henry VIII, and the sumptuous State Apartments.

BUCKINGHAM PALACE

Probably the world's most famous royal residence, Buckingham Palace is the Queen's main home, and as such it is closed to the public for most of the year. However, every summer, when Her Majesty heads up to Balmoral Castle in Scotland, the palace's 19 State Rooms are open to visitors.

PALACE OF HOLYROODHOUSE

The official residence of the Queen in Scotland, the Palace of Holyroodhouse is located at the foot of Edinburgh's Royal Mile, opposite the modernist Scottish Parliament Building.

HAMPTON COURT PALACE

Situated 12 miles southeast of central London, this spectacular Tudor residence is one of England's most iconic royal buildings. Begun in 1515 by Cardinal Wolsey in order to curry favor with a young Henry VIII, Hampton Court's Great Hall and State Apartments provide a real insight into the lives of Tudor monarchs.

KENSINGTON PALACE

Kensington Palace has had some of the royal family's biggest names as residents, with William, Kate, and their three children continuing to call it home today. You can explore the Sunken Garden, the Queen's Apartments, and the King's State Apartments on a visit.

HIGHGROVE HOUSE

The personal home and estate of Prince Charles and Camilla, Duchess of Cornwall, Highgrove House is located 20 miles north of Bath. It's renowned for its exquisite gardens, orchards, and woodlands, which showcase Charles's enduring commitment to organic produce.

Playing Golf in Scotland

There are some 550 golf courses in Scotland for just 5.5 million residents, so the country has probably the highest ratio of courses to people anywhere in the world. If you're visiting Scotland, you'll probably want to play the "famous names" sometime in your career.

So by all means play the championship courses such as the Old Course at St. Andrews, but remember they *are* championship courses. You may enjoy the game itself much more at a less challenging course. Remember, too, that everyone else wants to play the big names, so booking can be a problem at peak times in summer. Reserving three to four months ahead is not too far for the famous courses, although it's possible to get a time up to a month (or even a week) in advance if you are relaxed about your timing. If you're staying in a hotel attached to a course, get the concierge to book a tee time for you.

Happily, golf has always had a peculiar classlessness in Scotland. It's a game for everyone, and for centuries Scottish towns and cities have maintained courses for the enjoyment of their citizens. Admittedly, a few clubs have always been noted for their exclusive air, and some newer golf courses are losing touch with the game's inclusive origins, but these are exceptions to the tradition of recreation for all. Golf here is usually a democratic game, played by ordinary folk as well as the wealthy.

TIPS ON PLAYING

Golf courses are everywhere in Scotland. Most courses welcome visitors with a minimum of formalities, and some at a surprisingly low cost. Other courses are very expensive, but a lot of great golf can be played for between about £30 to £100 a round. Online booking at many courses has made arranging a golf tour easier, too.

Be aware of the topography of a course. Scotland is where the distinction between "links" and "parkland" courses was first made. Links courses are by the sea and are subject to the attendant sea breezes—some quite bracing—and mists, which can make them trickier to play. The natural topography of sand dunes and long, coarse grasses can add to the challenge. A parkland course is in a wooded area and its terrain is more obviously landscaped. A "moorland" course is found in an upland area.

Here are three pieces of advice, particularly for North Americans: (1) in Scotland the game is usually played fairly quickly, so don't dawdle if others are waiting; (2) caddy carts are hand-pulled carts for your clubs and driven golf carts are rarely available; and (3) when they say "rough," they really mean "rough."

Unless specified otherwise, hours are generally sunrise to sundown, which in June can be as late as 10 pm. Note that some courses advertise the SSS, "standard scratch score," instead of par (which may be different). This is the score a scratch golfer could achieve under perfect conditions. Rental clubs, balls, and other gear are generally available from clubhouses, except at the most basic municipal courses. Don't get caught by the dress codes enforced at many establishments: in general, untailored shorts, round-neck shirts, jeans, and sneakers are frowned upon.

The prestigious courses may ask for evidence of your golf skills by way of a handicap certificate; check in advance and carry this with you.

COSTS AND COURSES

Many courses lower their rates before and after peak season—at the end of September, for example. It's worth asking about this. ■TIP➔ **Some areas offer regional golf passes that save you money. Check with the local tourist board.**

For a complete list of courses, contact local tourist offices or VisitScotland's official and comprehensive golf website, ⊕ *golf.visitscotland.com*. It has information about the country's golf courses, special golf trails, regional passes, special events, and tour operators, as well as on conveniently located accommodations. U.K. Golf Guide (⊕ *www.uk-golfguide.com*) has user-generated reviews. *For information about regional courses, also see individual chapters.*

BEST BETS AROUND SCOTLAND

If your idea of heaven is teeing off on a windswept links, then Scotland is for you. Dramatic courses, many of them set on sandy dunes alongside the ocean, are just one of the types you'll encounter. Highland courses that take you through the heather and moorland courses surrounded by craggy mountains have their own challenges.

Boat of Garten Golf Club, Inverness-shire. With the Cairngorm Mountain as a backdrop, this beautiful course has rugged terrain that requires even seasoned players to bring their A game. As an added bonus, a steam railway runs alongside the course.

Carnoustie Golf Links, Angus. Challenging golfers for nearly 500 years, Carnoustie is on many golfers' must-do list. The iconic Championship Course has tested many of the world's top players, while the Burnside and Buddon courses attract budding McIlroys, Spieths, and Koepkas.

Castle Stuart Golf Links, Inverness-shire. A more recent addition to Scotland's world-class courses offers cliff-top hazards, sprawling bunkers, and rolling fairways overlooking the Moray Firth.

Cruden Bay Golf Club, Aberdeenshire. This challenging and enjoyable links course was built by the Great North of Scotland Railway Company in 1894. Its remote location beside a set of towering dunes makes it irresistible.

Dunbar Golf Club, East Lothian. This classic and challenging links course has dramatic weather and scenery, with a backdrop of the Firth of Forth, Bass Rock, and a lighthouse.

Gleneagles, Perthshire. Host of the 2014 Ryder Cup championship, Gleneagles has three 18-hole courses that challenge the pros and a nine-hole course that provides a more laid-back game. It's also home to the PGA National Golf Academy.

Machrihanish Golf Club, Argyll. A dramatic location on the Mull of Kintyre and some exciting match play make these links well worth a journey.

Royal Dornoch Golf Club, Sutherland. Extending across a coastal shelf, Royal Dornoch has fast greens, pristine beaches, and mountain views. In spring yellow gorse sets the green hills ablaze.

St. Andrews Links, Fife. To approach the iconic 18th hole in the place where the game was invented remains the holy grail of golfers worldwide.

Western Gailes Golf Club, near Glasgow. This splendid links course is a final qualifying course for the British Open. Sculpted by Mother Nature, it's the country's finest natural links course.

What to Watch and Read

A HARD DAY'S NIGHT

This 1964 musical comedy film, which stars John Lennon, Paul McCartney, George Harrison, and Ringo Starr as themselves, portrays a fictionalized 36 hours in the life of the band at the very height of Beatlemania. *Time* magazine rated it one of the 100 greatest films of all time.

BEND IT LIKE BECKHAM

Offering insight into England's society-wide obsession with soccer—and with its prodigal son David Beckham—this 2002 romantic comedy sports film follows 18-year-old Jess as she defies her conservative Sikh parents to play for her local women's football team.

BRAVE

The first Pixar film directed by a woman (Brenda Chapman) and the first with a female main character, this 2012 animated film tells the story of Merida, the headstrong daughter of a Scottish king and queen who wishes to defy tradition in the name of her independence. Along with a heartwarming tale of mother and daughter love and acceptance, it portrays gorgeous animation of the Scottish Highlands and Highland traditions.

BRAVEHEART

This 1995 classic starring Mel Gibson was many a filmgoer's introduction to Scottish history and remains one of the most quoted movies ever. It tells a very embellished story of the real 13-century Scottish warrior, William Wallace, who did lead the Scots in the First War of Scottish Independence against England. While historians will be happy to point out the many historical inaccuracies, the film was nonetheless a commercial and critical success, earning several Academy Awards, including Best Picture.

THE CROWN

Since it debuted on Netflix in November 2016, this historical drama about the reign of Queen Elizabeth II has picked up a host of accolades and awards, from Emmys to Golden Globes. While you're unlikely to bump into Liz on your visit to England, you might well visit some of the many palaces, castles, and other locations featured in the show.

DOWNTON ABBEY

The hugely popular television series, which ran between 2010 and 2015, is one of England's most successful TV exports of recent years, while a movie adaptation was released in 2019. Most of the filming for the show takes place at Highclere Castle in the South of England; it's available to visit throughout the summer.

GAVIN & STACEY

This popular British sitcom, written by and starring Ruth Jones and James Corden (now of *The Late Late Show* fame), focuses on two families, one from Essex and one from Wales, who are brought together by the relationsip between the titular characters. First airing in 2007, the BAFTA-winning show was successfully revived in 2019 for a Christmas special.

THE GREAT BRITISH BAKE OFF

A quaint television baking competition has became an international phenomenon. Every season, a fresh-faced group of 10 amateur bakers are set a series of baking challenges over several weeks to determine the ultimate winner. The Bake Off has spawned dozens of international versions all over the world, including *The Great American Baking Show* on ABC, but the original—now 10 seasons in—remains the best.

OUTLANDER

If you're traveling to Scotland in the 21st century, chances are you're going to hear about the cultural phenomenon that is *Outlander*. The book series by Diana Gabaldon first captured the attention of the world in 1991, with many readers becoming dedicated fans of the time-traveling series through eight (and counting) novels. But then the television series debuted in 2014 on Starz and it seems the entire world fell in love with the love story between Claire Randall and Jamie Fraser amid a stunning Highlands backdrop. Both the book and the television show tell the same story: a nurse in 1946 finds herself sent back in time to 1743 Scotland, where she becomes entangled in the Jacobite uprising and falls in love with a Highland warrior. Many scenes are filmed on location, and you will find many a tour eager to take you to filming spots throughout the country.

POLDARK

Based on a series of historical novels by Winston Graham, this BBC drama series follows Captain Ross Poldark after his return to Cornwall following the 1783 American War of Independence. Poldark's developing romance with scullery maid Demelza, combined with regular shots of lead actor Aidan Turner's toned torso, sustained the show for 43 episodes over five seasons.

BRICK LANE BY MONICA ALI

Set on the eponymous Brick Lane, the heart of London's Bangladeshi community, this novel follows the life of Nazneen, an 18-year-old Bangladeshi woman who struggles to adapt to life in England after marrying an older man.

COMPLETE POEMS AND SONGS OF ROBERT BURNS BY ROBERT BURNS

You'll likely encounter Scotland's most famous poet in the form of Burns Nights or Burns Suppers, Scots get together to recite poetry, eat haggis, and drink whisky to celebrate the life of Robert Burns on his birthday each year. To brush up on your Scottish history, read some of his 18th-century poems (including his most beloved, "Auld Lang Syne") that helped spur Scotland's entrance into Romanticism.

THE HARRY POTTER SERIES BY J. K. ROWLING

The best-selling book series in history, J. K. Rowling's epic fantasy novels chronicle the lives of young wizard Harry Potter, along with his friends Hermione and Ron, as they attend the Hogwarts School of Witchcraft and Wizardry. Visitors to the Northeast can explore the real-life Hogwarts at Alnwick Castle.

HOW GREEN WAS MY VALLEY BY RICHARD LLEWELLYN

This classic 1939 novel may be heavy on sentimentality and Welsh clichés (so much singing!), but 80 years on from publication it remains an enthralling tale of a respectable mining family in the valleys of South Wales. It was a huge hit in the U.S., winning the National Book Award, and was adapted into a 1941 movie by John Ford.

OLIVER TWIST BY CHARLES DICKENS

Charles Dickens's second novel is perhaps his most famous, recounting the story of orphan Oliver Twist and his life as a juvenile pickpocket for the criminal Fagin. It offers a fascinating, unflinching insight into the criminal gangs and cruel treatment of orphans in London during the mid-19th century

THE POEMS OF DYLAN THOMAS

In his short life (he died at 39 in New York City), Welshman Dylan Thomas managed a level of fame and popularity that is rarely afforded poets. Many of his written works have spawned well-known lines, including "do not go gentle into that good night" and "though lovers be lost love shall not," while his seminal radio play *Under Milk Wood* is widely considered a masterpiece.

PRIDE AND PREJUDICE BY JANE AUSTEN

This romantic, Regency-era novel is one of the world's most enduring love stories. It follows 20-year-old Elizabeth Bennet and the course of her relationship with the older Mr. Darcy. There have been several film and television adaptations of the book, but perhaps the most loved is the BBC's 1995 adaptation starring Jennifer Ehle and Colin Firth.

WILLIAM SHAKESPEARE'S HISTORIES AND *MACBETH*

The Bard's series of historical plays chronicle the lives of four centuries of English monarchs, including King John, Henry V, and Richard III. Although widely regarded as Tudor propaganda (Shakespeare lived during the reign of Elizabeth I, the last Tudor monarch), the histories are hugely entertaining and informative, too. And one of his most famous plays tells a distinctly Scottish tale. The play is based on the lives of actual men who fought for power in 11th-century Scotland although the real life versions of Macbeth, Macduff, and Duncan were quite different. Nevertheless the fiction that the Bard weaves is one of the most powerful stories of ambition, power, and politics (and witchcraft) ever written.

WHITE TEETH BY ZADIE SMITH

This award-winning 2000 novel focuses on the lives of two best friends—Samad Iqbal and Archie Jones—and their families in North London. The novel, which was Zadie Smith's debut, deftly explores themes of cultural identity, faith, race, and gender in modern England.

WUTHERING HEIGHTS BY EMILY BRONTË

Originally published under the pen name Ellis Bell, this English literature classic from the third-eldest Brontë sibling was groundbreaking and controversial for its stark depiction of mental and physical cruelty, gender inequality, and religious hypocrisy.

Chapter 2

TRAVEL SMART

Updated by
Joseph Reaney

★ **CAPITAL:**
London

👥 **POPULATION:**
67,886,000

💬 **LANGUAGE:**
English

$ **CURRENCY:**
Pound

☎ **COUNTRY CODE:**
44

⚠ **EMERGENCIES:**
999 or 112

🚗 **DRIVING:**
On the left

⚡ **ELECTRICITY:**
240v/50 cycles; plugs have
three rectangular blades

🕐 **TIME:**
Five hours ahead of New
York

🌐 **WEB RESOURCES:**
www.visitbritain.com
www.visitengland.com
www.visitlondon.com
www.visitscotland.com
www.visitwales.com

ATLANTIC
OCEAN

Scotland

★ EDINBURGH

NORTH
SEA

GREAT
BRITAIN

Wales

CARDIFF ★

England

LONDON ★

Know Before You Go

Great Britain is a big place, with several distinct regions, cultures, and landscapes. Here are a few tips that will help your trip go as smoothly as possible no matter where you're going.

THE WEATHER IN GREAT BRITAIN IS ALWAYS TRICKY.

The summer months of June, July, and August give the best chance of good weather, although the crowds are at their largest. The start of August can be very busy for major tourist attractions and hot weather can make traveling on London's non-air-conditioned Tube uncomfortable. November through March is when you'll find Britain's best flight and hotel deals. Winter, while not generally frigid, can be dismal; the sun sets at 4 pm and it's pitch-dark by 5. Late spring is the time to see the countryside and the royal parks and gardens at their loveliest, while fall brings autumnal beauty and smaller crowds. Temperatures are usually mild at both times.

DON'T MIX UP YOUR SCOTS WITH YOUR WELSH.

Remember that although Scotland is part of the United Kingdom politically and does share many cultural links with England, Wales, and Northern Island, Scots do not take kindly to their country being called England or being called English. In recent years the Scottish have developed a burgeoning pride in their distinctive identity, which has even led to a waning sense of being British. So when in conversation, it's best not to associate Scottish people with the much maligned London-based Parliament and its English elite.

BREXIT IS STILL ON EVERYONE'S MINDS.

Although Britain voted to leave the European Union in June 2016 and officially left in January 2020, what this means in practice is still being worked out. Border arrangements, trade agreements, and participation in multinational organizations (including aviation safety regulation) all are still under discussion, and the country remains nearly as intractably divided on the issue, so approach with caution.

LEARNING SOME BRITISH IDIOMS CAN BE HELPFUL.

Nearly everyone knows that Britain and America are, in the phrase usually attributed to playwright George Bernard Shaw, "two countries separated by a common language," so you'll find some knowledge of British idioms very helpful for communicating with locals. An elevator is a lift; instead of waiting in line, you queue; the bathroom is known as the toilet, the loo, or the WC (for water-closet) so in public spaces you may see a W/C sign instead of a restroom sign; pants are trousers; underpants are pants or knickers; french fries are chips; potato chips are crisps; and soccer is football. Say "cheers" while clinking glasses or to say good-bye or thank you. The list is extensive, so if something a local is saying doesn't quite make sense to you, it's probably a matter of slang.

CHECK TO SEE IF YOUR TRIP FALLS DURING A BANK HOLIDAY.

In England and Wales, holidays are January 1, New Year's Day; Good Friday and Easter Monday; May Day (first Monday in May); spring and summer bank holidays (last Monday in May and August, respectively); December 25, Christmas Day; and December 26, Boxing Day (day after Christmas). In Scotland, locals also get January 2 and usually St. Andrews Day (November 30) off, but not Easter Monday. If these holidays fall on a weekend, the holiday is observed on the following Monday. Many stores and some attractions might be closed, and other restaurants and museums might be much busier than usual. During the Christmas holidays many restaurants, as well as museums and other attractions, may close for at least a week—call to verify hours. Book hotels for Christmas travel well in advance, and check whether the hotel restaurant will be open.

FOOTBALL FEVER IS REAL.

The Brits may not be known for their inclination to make small talk with strangers, but you can always strike up a conversation about football (aka soccer), especially in a pub. One word of warning: tribal loyalties run deep, so make sure you know what you're talking about. Otherwise, ask intelligent questions—fans love to express their opinions on a team's performance.

BE PREPARED TO NOT UNDERSTAND THE SCOTTISH ACCENT.

The Scots language, which borrows from Scandinavian, Dutch, French, and Gaelic, survives in various forms, with each region having its own dialect. In the northeast they speak Doric, while the Shetland and Orkney "tongue" is influenced by the now-extinct Norn. The Gaelic language, the indigenous language of those from the Western Isles and Highlands, has been given a new lease on life. Many primary schools in the region are teaching a new generation of Gaelic speakers. The language has its own TV channel, BBC Alba, and is being promoted in a huge signage campaign. Otherwise, Scots speak English, though often with a strong accent that can be hard for Americans (and even other Brits) to understand. Don't worry, after spending some time with Scots, your ears will soon come to terms with it.

TO SAVE MONEY, TRY A PASS.

If you plan to visit castles, gardens, and historic houses during your stay in England, look into discount passes or memberships that offer significant savings. Just be sure to match what the pass or membership offers against your itinerary to see if it's worthwhile.

The National Trust, English Heritage, Historic Scotland, the Historic Houses Association, and more each encompass hundreds of properties. English Heritage's Overseas Visitors Pass costs £35 for a nine-day pass and £42 for a 16-day pass for one adult. You can order it in advance by phone or online, or purchase it at a participating property in England. The National Trust Touring Pass, for overseas visitors, must be purchased in advance, either by phone or online. A seven-day pass is £33 per person; a 14-day pass is £38.

The Explorer Pass, available from any staffed Historic Scotland (HS) property as well as from many tourist information centers, allows visits to HS properties for three (£33), seven (£40), or 14 (£45) consecutive days. The Scottish Heritage pass gives free access from April through October to more than 120 Heritage Scotland– and National Trust for Scotland–run properties.

The London Pass gets you into more than 80 attractions and tours in the capital at a considerable saving, and can help you bypass some lines. Packages range from one day (£79) to 10 days (£201). A similar pass for Yorkshire, the York Pass, enables discounted entrance to more than 50 attractions and costs from £65 for two days to £130 for six days. Annual membership in the National Trust (through the Royal Oak Foundation, the U.S. affiliate) is $80 a year. English Heritage membership is £63, and the Historic Houses Association is £56. Memberships entitle you to free entry to properties, including free parking.

Getting Here and Around

Air

The least expensive airfares to the U.K. are often priced for round-trip travel and must usually be purchased in advance. Airlines generally allow you to change your return date for a fee; most low-fare tickets, however, are nonrefundable.

Flying time to London is about 6¾ hours from New York, 7¾ hours from Chicago, 9¼ hours from Dallas, 10½ hours from Los Angeles, and 20¾ hours from Sydney. From London, flights take an hour to Paris or Amsterdam, 1½ hours to Dublin or Frankfurt, 2 hours to Vienna or Prague, and 2½ hours to Rome or Madrid.

Scotland's main hubs are Glasgow, Prestwick (near Glasgow), Edinburgh, Inverness, and Aberdeen. Glasgow and Prestwick are the gateways to the west and southwest, Edinburgh the east and southeast, Aberdeen and Inverness the north. All these cities have excellent bus and train transportation services and well-maintained roads that link them with each other and other cities within Scotland. Taxis are also an efficient and reliable option, but they are three to four times the cost of going by public transport.

Flying time to Glasgow and Aberdeen is 6½ hours from New York, 7½ hours from Chicago, 9½ hours from Dallas, 10 hours from Los Angeles, and 21½ hours from Sydney. Flying time to Edinburgh is 7 hours from New York, 8 hours from Chicago, 10 hours from Dallas, 10½ hours from Los Angeles, and 22 hours from Sydney. Not all airlines offer direct flights to Scotland; many go via London. For those flights allow an extra four to five hours of travel (two to three for the layover in London plus an additional 1½ hours for the duration of the flight).

AIRPORTS

England: Most international flights to London arrive at either Heathrow Airport (LHR), 15 miles west of London, or at Gatwick Airport (LGW), 27 miles south of the capital. Most flights from the United States go to Heathrow, with Terminals 3, 4, and 5 handling transatlantic flights (British Airways uses Terminal 5). Gatwick is London's second gateway, serving many U.S. destinations. A third, much smaller airport, Stansted (STN), is 40 miles northeast of the city. It handles mainly European and domestic traffic.

London City Airport (LCY), a small airport inside the city near Canary Wharf, has a daily business-class-only flight to New York on British Airways, as well as flights to European destinations. Luton Airport (LLA), 32 miles north of the city, and London Southend (SEN), 42 miles east of the city, are both quite small, and serve British and European destinations. Luton is the hub for low-cost easyJet. Manchester (MAN) in northwest England handles some flights from the United States, as does Birmingham (BHX).

Heathrow and Gatwick are enormous and can seem like shopping malls (Heathrow even offers a personal shopping service). Both airports have bars and pubs and dining options. Several hotels are connected to each airport, and both Gatwick and Heathrow are near dozens of hotels that run free shuttles to the airports. Heathrow has a Hotel Hoppa service that runs shuttles between the airport and around 25 nearby hotels for £5.50 (online) or £6 (on bus) each way. A free, subsidized local bus service operates between the Central Bus Station serving Terminals 2 and 3 and nearby hotels. The bus also stops directly outside Terminals 4 and 5. You can find out more at the Central Bus Station or at the Transport for London (TfL)

Information Centre in the Underground station serving Terminals 2 and 3. Yotel has budget pod hotels in both Heathrow and Gatwick with cabin-size rooms to be booked in advance in four-hour blocks or overnight. Prices start from £40 for four hours in a standard cabin.

Scotland: The major international gateways to Scotland are Glasgow Airport (GLA), about seven miles outside Glasgow, and Edinburgh Airport (EDI), also about seven miles from the city center. Both offer connections for dozens of European cities and regular flights to London's Gatwick (LGW) and Heathrow (LHR) airports. Aberdeen Airport (ABZ) has direct flights to most major European cities. Prestwick (PIK) has direct flights to some European cities at discounted rates. Inverness (INV) offers direct flights in and around the United Kingdom.

Wales: Cardiff Airport is the busiest airport in Wales, but only flies to a small number of domestic and European destinations. Just across the border in England, Bristol Airport offers more international connections—though these are still limited to Europe.

Airport tax is included in the price of your ticket. Generally the tax for economy tickets within the United Kingdom from European Union countries is £13. For all other flights it is £78. The standard rate for flights from the United Kingdom and European Union is £26; for all other destinations it's £146.

LONDON GROUND TRANSPORTATION

London has excellent bus and train connections between its airports and the city center. Train service can be the fastest, but the downside is that you must get yourself and your luggage to the terminal, often via a series of escalators and connecting trams. Airport buses (generally run by National Express) may be located

From Heathrow to Central London		
Travel Mode	Time	Cost
Taxi	40–80 minutes	£45–£90
Heathrow Express Train	15 minutes	£27 one way
Underground	50 minutes	£6 one way
National Express Bus	45–80 minutes	£8–£12 one way

nearer to the terminals and drop you closer to central hotels, but they're subject to London traffic, which can be horrendous. Taxis can be more convenient than buses, but prices can go through the roof. Minicabs are more economical, but go with recommended companies. From London Heathrow Airport, it's also possible to take the Tube (Piccadilly line) to the city center, while a Crossrail (aka Elizabeth) Underground line is due to start operating a quick service in 2021.

The Transport for London website has helpful information, as does Airport Travel Line. The official sites for Gatwick, Heathrow, and Stansted are useful resources for transportation options.

Heathrow by Bus: National Express buses take around 45 minutes (longer at peak time) to reach the city center (Victoria Coach Station) and start from £6 one way. Buses leave every 5 to 75 minutes from 4:20 am to 10 pm. The National Express Hotel Hoppa service runs from all terminals to around 25 hotels near the airport (£5). Alternatively, nearly every hotel in London is served by the Heathrow Airport Hotel Shuttle service. Fares to central London begin at £21.33. The N9 night bus runs every 15 minutes from 11:35 pm to 4:55 am to Kensington, Hyde Park Corner, Trafalgar Square, and Aldwych; it takes about 75 minutes and costs £1.50. ■ **TIP→ Like all London buses,**

Getting Here and Around

the N9 takes cash, Visitor Oyster cards, Oyster cards, or contactless "tap and go" debit cards only.

Heathrow by Train: The cheap, direct route into London is via the Piccadilly Line of the Underground (London's extensive subway system, or "Tube"). Trains normally run every three to seven minutes from all terminals from around 5 am until just before midnight (a 24-hour service runs every 10 minutes to Terminals 2, 3, and 5 on Friday and Saturday). The 50-minute trip into central London costs £6 (cash), £5.10 (Oyster card peak times) or £3.10 (Oyster card off-peak). The Heathrow Express train is comfortable and very convenient, if costly, speeding into London's Paddington Station in 15 minutes. Standard one-way tickets cost £22 (off-peak), £25 (peak), or £32 for business class. All fares are substantially discounted if booked in advance online. If you arrive without tickets you should purchase them at a kiosk before you board, as they're more expensive on the train. There's daily service from 5:10 am (6:10 am on Sunday) to 11:25 pm, with departures every 15 minutes. The Crossrail (Elizabeth Line) Tube service will run from Terminals 2, 3, 4, and 5 to Paddington Station, takes about 25 minutes, and costs the same as the other Tube lines.

Gatwick by Bus: National Express buses run from Gatwick's north and south terminals to Victoria Coach Station (1½ to two hours, from £6 one way). Make sure you get on a direct bus not requiring a change, otherwise the journey could take much longer.

Gatwick by Train: There are three train services to Gatwick. The fast, nonstop Gatwick Express leaves for Victoria Station every 15 minutes 5 am–10:30 pm. The 30-minute trip costs £19.90 one way online. Tickets cost more on board. The Southern rail company's nonexpress

services are cheaper. Trains run regularly throughout the day until midnight to London Victoria, London Bridge, and Blackfriars stations; daytime departures are every 10–25 minutes (hourly between 1 am and 5 am), and the journey to London Victoria takes about 40 minutes. Tickets are from £11 one way and you can pay by Oyster card. You can also reach Gatwick by Southern trains coming from Brighton in the opposite direction. Thameslink offers a service similar to Southern but terminating at St. Pancras International instead of Victoria. The Thameslink and Southern services are on commuter trains, and during rush hour trains can be crowded, with little room for baggage and seats at a premium.

Stansted by Bus and Train: National Express Airport bus A6 (24 hours a day) to Victoria Coach Station via Waterloo Station and Southwark costs from £12 one way, leaves every 15 minutes (hourly 2:40 am to 5 am, then half hourly until 7:50 am), and takes about two hours. The Stansted Express train to Liverpool Street Station (with a stop at Tottenham Hale) runs every 15 minutes 5:30 am to 12:30 am daily. The 45-minute trip costs £19.40 each way if booked online. Tickets cost more on board.

Luton by Bus and Train: A free airport shuttle runs from Luton Airport to the nearby Luton Airport Parkway Station every 10 minutes, where you can take a train or bus into London. From there, the Thameslink train service runs to St. Pancras, Farringdon, Blackfriars, and London Bridge. The journey takes about 45 minutes. Trains leave every 10 minutes or so from 5 am until midnight, hourly at other times. One-way tickets begin at £15.50. The Green Line 757 bus service from Luton to Victoria Station runs every 30 minutes between 7 am and 12:35 am (hourly other times), takes 60 to 100 minutes, and costs from £11.50. National Express runs coaches from Victoria Coach Station to Luton from £6 one way.

Southend by Train: The train station right outside Southend Airport has six hourly trains to Liverpool Street Station in central London (via Stratford). The journey time is around 50 minutes and fares start from £16.70 one way. There is also a bus service, Jetlink X1, but it's only once a day in each direction.

Airports by Taxi: This is an expensive and time-consuming option. If your destination is within the city's congestion zone, £11.50 will be added to the bill during charging hours. If you get stuck in traffic, a taxi from the stand will be even more expensive; a cab booked ahead is a set price. A taxi trip from Heathrow to Victoria, for example, can take more than an hour and cost anything up to £90. Minicabs and private-hire cars may be the same price or even less—at this writing, the fee to Victoria Station is about £50 from Heathrow and £70 from Gatwick and Stansted, not including the congestion charge. Your hotel may also be able to recommend a car service. While the existence of Uber and other ride-sharing apps in London has been challenged in the courts over the last few years, they are still currently an option, but they are still subject to the same congestion charges and, of course, traffic.

SCOTLAND GROUND TRANSPORTATION

The best way to get to and from the airport based on speed and convenience is by taxi or ride-sharing apps. All airport taxi stands are just outside the airport's front doors and are well marked with clear signs. Most taxis have a set price when going to and from the airport to the city center but will turn on the meter at your request. Ask the driver to turn on the meter to confirm the flat-rate price.

If you're traveling with a large party, you can request a people carrier to transport everyone, luggage included. Luggage is included in the taxi fare; you should not be charged extra for it.

If you're traveling alone, a more economical transfer option is public transportation. Buses travel between city centers and Glasgow, Edinburgh, Aberdeen, and Inverness airports. Trams travel between Edinburgh Airport and the city center; Edinburgh Gateway station links the airport to the tram and rail network; trains go direct to Glasgow Prestwick Airport. All are fast, inexpensive, and reliable.

Boat

Ferries and other boats travel regular routes to Britain (mainly southeast England) from France, Spain, Ireland, and Scandinavia. P&O runs ferries from Belgium, France, Ireland, and the Netherlands. DFDS Seaways serves France, Denmark, Belgium, and the Netherlands, and Stena Line serves Ireland, Northern Ireland, France, and the Netherlands.

Low-cost airlines and Eurotunnel (which lets you take a car from France on the train) have cut into ferry travel, but companies have responded by cutting fares and upgrading equipment.

Prices vary; booking early ensures cheaper fares, but also ask about special deals. Seaview is a comprehensive online ferry- and cruise-booking portal for Britain and continental Europe. Ferry Cheap is a discount website.

WITHIN SCOTLAND

Because Scotland has so many islands, plus the great Firth of Clyde waterway, ferry services are of paramount importance. Most ferries transport vehicles as

Getting Here and Around

well as foot passengers, although a few smaller ones are for passengers only.

It's a good idea to make a reservation ahead of time, although reservations are not absolutely necessary. Most travelers show up on the day of departure and buy their tickets from the stations at the ports. Keep in mind that these are working ferries, not tourist boats. Although journeys are scenic, most people use these ferries as their daily means of public transportation to and from their hometowns.

The main operator is Caledonian MacBrayne, known generally as CalMac. Services extend from the Firth of Clyde in the south, where there's an extensive network, right up to the northwest of Scotland and all the Hebrides. CalMac offers 25 island-hopping itineraries, called Hopscotch, valid for 31 days, which can be combined for tailored exploration. Fares can range from £2 to £6 for a short trip to over £50 for a longer trip with several legs.

The Dunoon–Gourock route on the Clyde is served by Western Ferries.

Northlink Ferries operates a car ferry for Orkney between Scrabster, near Thurso, and Stromness, on the main island of Orkney; and between Aberdeen and Kirkwall, which is also on the mainland of Orkney. Northlink also runs an efficient ferry to Lerwick, Shetland, and Kirkwall, Orkney. The journey to Lerwick is overnight, but comfortable cabins are available. These ferries can be busy in summer, so book well in advance.

TRANSATLANTIC AND OTHER CRUISES

Most cruise ships leave from southern England—particularly Southampton and Portsmouth. Some ships leave from Liverpool and Dover, or from Harwich, near Cambridge.

Bus

Britain has a comprehensive bus (short-haul, multistop public transportation) and coach (more direct, plusher long-distance buses) network that offers an inexpensive way of seeing the country. National Express is the major coach operator, and Victoria Coach Station, near Victoria Station in central London, is its hub in the capital. The company serves more than 1,000 destinations within Britain (and, via Eurolines, 500 more in continental Europe). There are 2,000 ticket agents nationwide, including offices at London's Heathrow and Gatwick airport coach stations.

Green Line is the second-largest national service, serving airports and major tourist towns. A budget option for long-distance travel, Megabus has double-decker buses that serve cities across Britain, with seats that turn into bunk beds on routes to Scotland. In London, Megabus departs from Victoria Coach Station as well as other stops, while Green Line buses also stop at Baker Street and Hyde Park Corner.

Coach tickets can be much less than the price of a train ticket (even lower if you take advantage of special deals). For example, an Oxford Tube coach ticket from London to Oxford is £9, whereas a train ticket may be £28. Coaches are generally just as comfortable as trains, though they often take a while longer to reach their destinations. This disparity is particularly acute on long journeys—Glasgow to London by nonstop coach takes nine hours; by train it takes a little over five.

Double-decker buses, run by private companies, offer local bus service in cities and regions across Britain. Check with the local bus station or tourist information center for routes and schedules.

Most companies offer daylong or week-long unlimited-travel tickets, and those in popular tourist areas operate special scenic tours in summer. Sit on the top deck for the best views (and the novelty).

DISCOUNTS AND DEALS

National Express's Young Persons' Coach-Card for students age 16 to 26 costs £12.50 annually and gives a third off most fares—so as little as two journeys can make this worthwhile. Most companies also offer a discount for children under 15. A Senior CoachCard for the over-60s cuts many fares by a third. Apex tickets (advance-purchase tickets) save money on standard fares, and traveling off-peak during the week is cheaper than over weekends and holidays.

On Scottish Citylink, the Explorer Passes offer complete freedom of travel on all services throughout Scotland. Three permutations give three days of travel out of a five-day period, five days of travel out of 10, and eight days of travel out of 16. They're available from Scottish Citylink offices, and cost £49, £74, and £99 respectively.

 Car

Britain can be a challenging place for most foreigners to drive. After all, people drive on the left side of the often discon-certingly-narrow roads, many rental cars have standard transmissions, and the gearshift is on the "wrong" side entirely.

There's no reason to rent a car for a stay in London because the city and its sub-urbs are well served by public transporta-tion and traffic is desperately congested. Here, and in other major cities, it's best to rely on public transportation.

Outside the cities, a car can be very handy. Many sights aren't easily reached without one—castles, for example, are rarely connected to any public trans-portation system. Small villages might have only one or two buses a day pass through them. If you're comfortable on the road, the experience of driving between the tall hedgerows or on coun-try roads is a truly British experience.

As a short-term visitor, your own driver's license is enough to drive in the U.K. However, you may choose to get an International Driving Permit (IDP), which can be used only in conjunction with a valid driver's license and which translates your license into 10 languages. Check the Automobile Association of America website for more info as well as for IDPs ($20) themselves. These permits are universally recognized, and having one in your wallet may save you a problem with the local authorities.

PARKING

Parking regulations are strictly enforced, and fines are high. If there are no signs on a street, you can park there. Many streets have centralized "pay and dis-play" machines, in which you deposit the required money and get a ticket allowing you to park for a set period of time. In London's City of Westminster (⊕ *www.westminster.gov.uk*) and some other boroughs, parking machines have been replaced by a pay-by-phone plan, ena-bling you to pay by cell phone if you've preregistered. In town centers your best bet is to park in a public lot marked with a square blue sign with a white "P" in the center.

If you park on the street, follow these basic rules: Do not park within 15 yards of an intersection. Never park in bus lanes or on double yellow lines, and do not park on single yellow lines when parking meters are in effect. On busy roads with red lines painted on the street

Getting Here and Around

you cannot park or stop to let a passenger out of the car.

RENTALS

Rental rates are generally reasonable, and insurance costs are lower than in the United States. If you want the car only for country trips, consider renting outside London. Rates are cheaper, and you avoid traversing London's notoriously complex road system. Rental rates vary widely, beginning at £54 a day and £132 a week for a midsize car, usually with manual transmission. As in the United States, prices rise in summer and during holidays. Car seats for children cost around £8 per day, and GPS is usually around £10 per day. You can also arrange for cell phone hire or a portable Wi-Fi hot spot with your rental.

Major car-rental agencies are much the same in Britain as in the United States: Alamo, Avis, Budget, Enterprise, Hertz, Thrifty, and National all have offices in Britain. Europcar is another large company. Companies may not rent cars to people who are under 21. A few agencies have an upper age limit of 75.

ROAD CONDITIONS

There's a good network of major highways (motorways) and divided highways (dual carriageways) throughout most of Great Britain. Motorways (with the prefix "M"), shown in blue on most maps, are mainly two or three lanes in each direction. Other major roads (with the prefix "A") are shown on maps in green and red. Sections of fast dual carriageways (with black-edged, thick outlines on maps) have both traffic lights and traffic circles. Turnoffs are often marked by highway numbers, rather than place names. An exit is called a junction in Britain.

The vast network of lesser roads, for the most part old coach and turnpike roads, might make your trip twice as long but show you twice as much. Minor roads are drawn in yellow or white on maps, the former prefixed by "B," the latter unlettered and unnumbered. Should you take one of these, be prepared to back up into a passing place if you meet an oncoming car. These smaller roads are particularly prevalent in the Scottish Highlands.

RULES OF THE ROAD

Driving on the left side of the road might be easier than you expected, as the steering and mirrors on British cars are designed for driving on the left. If you have a standard transmission car, you have to shift gears with your left hand. Give yourself time to adjust before leaving the rental-car lot. Seat belts are obligatory in the front and back seats. It's illegal to talk on a handheld cell phone while driving.

Pick up a copy of the official Highway Code (£2.50) at a service station, newsstand, or bookstore, or check it out online by going to ⊕ www.gov.uk and putting "Highway Code" in the search bar. Besides driving rules and illustrations of signs and road markings, this booklet contains information for motorcyclists, cyclists, and pedestrians.

Speed limits are complicated, and there are speed cameras everywhere (yes, everywhere—don't even try it). The speed limit (shown on circular red signs) is generally 20 or 30 mph in towns and cities, 40 to 60 mph on two-lane highways, and 70 mph on motorways. At traffic circles (called roundabouts), you turn clockwise. As cars enter the circle, they must yield to those already in the circle or entering from the right. If you're taking an exit all the way around the circle, signal right as you enter, stay to the center, and then signal and move left just before your own exit.

Pedestrians have the right-of-way on "zebra" crossings (black-and-white-stripe crosswalks between two orange-flashing globe lights). At other crossings, pedestrians must yield to traffic, but they do have the right-of-way over traffic turning left.

Drunk-driving laws are strictly enforced. The legal limit is 80 milligrams of alcohol per 100 milliliters of blood, which means two units of alcohol—approximately one glass of wine, 1–1½ pints of beer, or two drams of whisky. However, these figures will vary according to the alcohol's strength, your size and weight (so women tend to reach the limit on less), and how much you've eaten that day.

🚆 Train

Operated by several different private companies, the train system in Britain is extensive and useful, though less than perfect. Some regional trains are old, and virtually all lines suffer from occasional delays, schedule changes, and periodic repair work that runs over schedule. The pricing structure is complex and prices tend to be high compared to the rest of Europe. While there are more than a dozen regional train companies operating in England and Wales, most of Scotland rail services are managed by just one: Scotrail.

All major cities and many small towns are served by trains—including some otherwise remote and hard-to-reach spots. Despite the difficulties, rail travel is the most pleasant way to cover long distances. Just keep in mind that rail service in rural areas is often limited on Sunday.

FARES AND SCHEDULES
National Rail Enquiries is a helpful, comprehensive, and free service that covers all the country's rail lines. National Rail

will help you choose the best train, and then connect you with the right ticket office. You can also book tickets online. A similar service is offered by the Trainline, which provides online train information and ticket booking for all rail services. The Man in Seat 61, a website, offers objective information along with booking facilities.

Ticket prices are more expensive during rush hour, so plan accordingly. For long-distance travel, tickets cost more the longer you wait. Book in advance and tickets can be half of what you'd pay on the day of departure. For example, a journey from London to Cardiff might cost £15 or £20 if you buy a ticket two weeks in advance, but the fare is likely to rise to £50 if you wait until the day of your trip.

■ TIP➔ **Ask the local tourist board about hotel and local transportation packages that include tickets to major events.**

PASSES
National Rail Enquiries has information about rail passes such as All Line Rovers, which offers unlimited travel on National Rail services for a week, with some restrictions, for £540. Children, seniors, and disabled Rovers are one-half to one-third less.

If you plan to travel a lot by train throughout Great Britain, consider purchasing a BritRail Pass, which gives unlimited travel over the entire British rail network and can save you money. If you don't plan to cover many miles, you may come out ahead by buying individual tickets. Buy your BritRail Pass before you leave home, as they are not sold in Britain. The passes are available from most U.S. travel agents or from ACP Rail International, Flight Centre, or VisitBritain. Note that Eurail Passes aren't honored in Britain.

BritRail passes come in two basic varieties: the Consecutive Pass and the

Getting Here and Around

England FlexiPass. You can get a Consecutive Pass good for two, three, four, eight, 15, or 22 consecutive days or one month starting at $119 standard and $180 first class for two days. The FlexiPass for two, three, four, or eight days of travel within one month, or 15 days within two months, costs from $151 standard and $224 first class for two days. If you're based in London, the BritRail London Plus pass offers access to southern England destinations such as Oxford, Cambridge, Bath, or Stratford-upon-Avon from $145 for standard class, $205 for first class. Tickets can be used for three, four, or eight days of travel within one month.

Don't assume that a rail pass guarantees you a seat on a particular train. You need to book seats even if you're using a rail pass, especially on trains that may be crowded, particularly in summer on popular routes.

CHANNEL TUNNEL

Short of flying, taking the Eurostar through the Channel Tunnel is the fastest way to cross the English Channel (and perhaps faster after factoring in airport travel time and security). Travel time is 2½ hours from London's St. Pancras Station to Paris's Gare du Nord. Trains also travel to Lille (1½ hours), Brussels (2 hours), and Disneyland Paris (2¾ hours) year-round, as well as Lyon (5¾ hours), Avignon (6½ hours), and Marseille (7¼ hours) on weekends from May through mid-September. On Friday (night train) and Saturday (day train) from late December through March, ski trains go to Moûtiers (9 hours) and four other nearby Alpine ski resorts.

Early risers can easily take a day trip to Paris if time is short. Book ahead, as Eurostar ticket prices increase as the departure date approaches. If purchased in advance, round-trip tickets to Paris start at £58 Monday–Thursday, £78 Friday–Sunday. Eurostar also offer last-minute "snap" tickets from £25 one way from London to Paris, and although you can specify the general time of day, the exact time of departure is potluck.

FROM ENGLAND TO SCOTLAND

There are two main rail routes to Scotland from the south of England. The first, the west-coast main line, runs from London Euston to Glasgow Central; it takes 5½ hours to make the 400-mile trip to central Scotland, and service is frequent and reliable. Useful for daytime travel to the Scottish Highlands is the direct train to Stirling and Aviemore, terminating at Inverness. For a restful route to the Scottish Highlands, take the overnight *Caledonian Sleeper* service, with comfortable ensuite sleeping carriages. It runs from London Euston, departing in late evening and arriving in its final destination (either Fort William, Aberdeen, or Inverness) the following morning.

The east-coast main line from London King's Cross to Edinburgh provides the quickest trip to the Scottish capital. Between 8 am and 6 pm there are usually trains every half hour to Edinburgh; three of them travel directly to Aberdeen. Connecting services to most parts of Scotland—particularly the Western Highlands—are often better from Edinburgh than from Glasgow.

Essentials

Lodging

Our local writers vet every hotel to recommend the best overnights in each price category, from budget to expensive. Unless otherwise specified, you can expect private bath, phone, and TV in your room.

APARTMENT AND HOUSE RENTALS

If you deal directly with local agents, get a recommendation from someone who's used the company. Unlike with hotels, there's no accredited system for apartment rental standards.

In the country your chances of finding a small vacation house are good; in the city you're more likely to find a flat (apartment) to let (rent). Either way, your best bet for finding these rentals is online. Individuals and large consortiums can own these properties, so it just depends on what you're looking for. Citybase Apartments is a handy resource for finding an apartment, from single studios to large apartments suitable for families and groups. Dreamhouse Apartments has swanky, serviced flats in Edinburgh, Glasgow, and Aberdeen. The National Trust for Scotland has many unique properties, from island cottages to castles, for rent. Mansley has 19 well-appointed, modern apartments in the heart of the Old Town, Edinburgh; it has 16 similarly smart apartments in Inverness, many with spectacular terrace views.

BED-AND-BREAKFASTS

B&Bs can be a good budget option, and will also help you meet the locals. Cottages, unlike B&Bs, usually do not provide breakfast.

FARMHOUSES AND COTTAGES

A popular option for families with children is a farmhouse or country cottage, combining the freedom of B&B accommodations with the hospitality of British family life. You'll need a car if you're staying deep in the countryside though. General information on rural stays is available from the Farm Stay UK website.

HOTELS

Most hotels have rooms with "ensuite" bathrooms—as private bathrooms are called—although some B&Bs may have only washbasins; in this case, showers and toilets are usually down the hall. Especially in London, rooms and bathrooms may be smaller than those you find in the United States.

Besides familiar international chains, Britain has some local chains that are worth a look. Opt for a less expensive city center option, like the basic but bargain Travelodge or the slightly more upscale Premier Inn and Jurys Inn. You can also choose a trendy boutique like ABode, Hotel du Vin, and Malmaison instead.

HOTEL GRADING SYSTEM

Hotels, guesthouses, inns, and B&Bs in the United Kingdom are all graded from one to five stars by the tourism board, VisitBritain. Basically, the more stars a property has, the more amenities it has, and the facilities will be of a higher standard. It's a fairly good reflection of lodging from small B&Bs up to palatial hotels. The most luxurious hotels will have five stars; a simple, clean, acceptable hostelry will have one star.

Dining

The stereotypical notion of British meals as parades of roast beef, overcooked vegetables, and stodgy desserts has largely been replaced—particularly in London, other major cities, and some country hot spots—with an evolving picture of the country as foodie territory. From trendy

Essentials

gastro-pubs to interesting ethnic-fusion restaurants to see-and-be-seen dining shrines, British food is now known for an innovative take on traditional dishes, with an emphasis on the local and seasonal. In less cosmopolitan areas, though, you're still looking at lots of offerings that are either stodgy, fried, sausages, or Indian.

Eating out in Britain's big cities in particular can be expensive, but you can do it cheaply. Try local cafes, more popularly known as "caffs," where heaping plates of British comfort food (bacon sandwiches and stuffed baked potatoes, for example) are served. Britain has plenty of the big names in fast food, as well as smaller places selling sandwiches, fish-and-chips, burgers, falafels, kebabs, and the like. For a local touch, check out Indian restaurants, which are found almost everywhere. Marks & Spencer, Sainsbury's, Morrison's, Tesco, Lidl, Aldi, and Waitrose are chain supermarkets with outlets throughout the country. They're good choices for groceries, premade sandwiches, or picnic fixings.

MEALS AND MEALTIMES

Cafes serving the traditional English breakfast (called a "fry-up") of eggs, bacon, sausage, beans, mushrooms, half a grilled tomato, toast, and strong tea are often the cheapest—and most authentic—places for breakfast. For lighter morning fare (or for real brewed coffee), try the Continental-style sandwich bars and coffee shops—the Pret-a-Manger chain being one of the largest—offering croissants and other pastries. In London, the Leon chain offers healthy alternatives.

At lunch you can grab a sandwich between sights, pop into the local pub, or sit down in a restaurant. Dinner, too, has no set rules, but a three-course meal is standard in most mid-range or high-end restaurants. Pre- or post-theater menus,

offering two or three courses for a set price, are usually a good value.

Note that most traditional pubs don't have any waitstaff and you're expected to go to the bar to order a beverage and your meal. Also, in cities many pubs don't serve food after 3 pm, so they're usually a better lunch option than dinner, unless they're gastro-pubs. In rural areas it's not uncommon for pubs to stop serving lunch after 2:30 and dinner after 9 pm.

Breakfast is generally served between 7:30 and 9, lunch between noon and 2, and dinner or supper between 7:30 and 9:30—sometimes earlier and seldom later except in large cities and tourist areas. These days high tea is rarely a proper meal anymore (it was once served between 4:30 and 6), and tearooms are often open all day in touristy areas (they're rarely found at all in nontouristy places). So you can have a cup and pastry or sandwich whenever you feel you need it. Sunday roasts at pubs last from 11 am or noon to 3 pm.

Smoking is banned in pubs, clubs, and restaurants throughout Britain.

PAYING

Credit cards are widely accepted in restaurants and pubs, though some require a minimum charge of around £10. Be sure that you don't double-pay a service charge. Many restaurants exclude service charges from the printed menu (which the law obliges them to display outside), and then add 10% to 15% to the check. Others will stamp "Service not included" along the bottom of the bill, in which case you should add 10% to 15%. You can also add to the included charge if the service was particularly good. Cash is always appreciated, as it's more likely to go to the specific waiter.

PUBS

A common misconception among visitors to Britain is that pubs are simply bars. Pubs are also community gathering places and even restaurants. In many pubs the social interaction is as important as the alcohol. Pubs are, generally speaking, where people go to meet their friends and catch up on one another's lives. In small towns pubs act almost as town halls. Traditionally pub hours are 11–11, with last orders called about 20 minutes before closing time, but pubs can apply for a license to stay open until midnight, 1 am, or even later.

It might seem that there's a pub on almost every corner in any given British town, but in fact pubs are becoming something of an endangered species, with regular closures of independent, non-chain pubs in smaller localities.

Most pubs tend to be child-friendly, but others have restricted hours for children. If a pub serves food, it'll generally allow children in during the day with adults. Some pubs are stricter than others, though, and won't admit anyone younger than 18. Some will allow children in during the day, but only until 6 pm. Family-friendly pubs tend to be packed with kids, parents, and all of their accoutrements.

RESERVATIONS

Regardless of where you are, it's a good idea to make a reservation if you can. For popular restaurants, book as far ahead as you can (often 30 days), and reconfirm as soon as you arrive. (Large parties should always call ahead to check the reservations policy.)

Online reservation services aren't as popular in Britain as in the United States, but OpenTable and SquareMeal have a fair number of listings in Britain.

WINES, BEER, AND SPIRITS

Although hundreds of varieties of beer are brewed around the country, the traditional brew is known as bitter and isn't carbonated; it's usually served at room temperature. Fizzy American-style beer is called lager. There are also plenty of other alternatives: stouts like Guinness are thick, pitch-black brews you'll either love or hate; ciders, made from apples, are alcoholic in Britain (Bulmer's and Strongbow are the big names, but look out for local microbrews); and shandies are a low-alcohol mix of lager and lemon soda. Real ales, which have a natural second fermentation in the cask, have a shorter shelf life (so many are brewed locally) but special flavor; these are worth seeking out. Craft beers are also now big business, especially in cities. Generally, the selection and quality of cocktails is higher in a wine bar or café than in a pub. The legal drinking age is 18.

You can order Scotland's most famous beverage—whisky (most definitely spelled without an *e*)—at any pub, but the selection of single malts is generally better north of the border. It's also possible to tour numerous distilleries in Scotland, where you can sample a dram and purchase a bottle. Most are concentrated in Speyside and Islay, but there are notable ones on Orkney and Skye. In recent years a new breed of craft gin producers have opened stills, many producing small batches of botanically infused tipples and offering tours, tastings, and lessons.

Activities

VisitBritain and local Tourist Information Centres can recommend places to enjoy your favorite sport.

Essentials

BIKING

The national body promoting cycle touring is the Cycling UK (£4 per month), which can organize cycling vacations. Members get free advice and route information and a magazine. Transport for London publishes maps of recommended routes across the capital, and British Cycling has online route maps of the United Kingdom.

BOATING

Boating—whether on bucolic rivers or industrial canals—can be a leisurely way to explore the English landscape. For boat-rental operators along Britain's several hundred miles of historic canals and waterways, from the Norfolk Broads to the Lake District, contact British Marine Inland Boating or Waterways Holidays. The Canal and River Trust has maps and other information. Waterways Holidays arranges boat accommodations from traditional narrow boats to wide-beam canal boats, motorboats, and sailboats.

WALKING

Walking and hiking, from the slowest ramble to a challenging mountainside climb, are enormously popular in Britain. National Trails, funded by Natural England and the Countryside Counsel for Wales, has great resources online. The Ramblers, a well-known charitable organization promoting walking and care of footpaths, has helpful information, including a list of B&Bs close to selected long-distance footpaths. Some of the best maps for walking are the Explorer Maps, published by the Ordnance Survey.

🌐 Customs and Duties

You're always allowed to bring goods of a certain value back home without having to pay any duty or import tax. But there's a limit on the amount of tobacco and liquor you can bring back duty-free, and some countries have separate limits for perfumes; for exact figures, check with your customs department. The values of so-called duty-free goods are included in these amounts. When you shop abroad, save all your receipts, as customs inspectors may ask to see them as well as the items you purchased. If the total value of your goods is more than the duty-free limit, you'll have to pay a tax (most often a flat percentage) on the value of everything beyond that limit.

Fresh meats, plants and vegetables, controlled drugs, and firearms (including replicas) and ammunition may not be brought into the United Kingdom, nor can dairy products from non-EU countries. Pets from the United States with the proper documentation may be brought into the country without quarantine under the U.K. Pet Travel Scheme (PETS). The process takes about four months to complete and involves detailed steps.

Once you are in the U.K., you'll face no customs formalities between England, Wales, and Scotland.

➕ Safety

Britain has a low incidence of violent crime. However, petty crime, mostly in urban areas, is on the rise, and tourists can be the targets. Use common sense: when in a city center, if you're paying at a shop or a restaurant, never put your wallet down or let your bag out of your hand. When sitting on a chair in a public place, keep your bag on your lap or between your feet. Don't wear expensive jewelry or watches, and don't flash fancy smart phones on the street in London, where there have been snatchings by moped-riding thieves. Store your passport in the hotel safe, and keep a copy with you. Don't leave anything in your car.

Although scams do occur in Britain, they aren't pervasive. If you're getting money out of an ATM, beware of someone bumping into you to distract you. You may want to use ATMs inside banks rather than those outside them. In London scams are most common at ATMs near tourist meccas like Oxford Street and Piccadilly Circus. Watch out for pickpockets, particularly in London. They often work in pairs, one distracting you in some way.

Always take a licensed black taxi or call a car service (sometimes called minicabs) recommended by your hotel. Avoid drivers who approach you on the street, as they may overcharge you. Always buy theater tickets from a reputable dealer. If you're driving in from a British port, beware of thieves posing as customs officials who try to "confiscate illegal goods."

While traveling, don't leave any bags unattended, as they may be viewed as a security risk and destroyed by the authorities. If you see an unattended bag on the train, bus, or Tube, find a worker and report it. Never hesitate to get off a Tube, train, or bus if you feel unsafe.

COVID-19

A new novel coronavirus brought all travel to a virtual standstill in the first half of 2020, and interruptions to travel have continued through 2020 and into 2021. Although the illness is mild in most people, some experience severe and even life-threatening complications. Once travel started up again, albeit slowly and cautiously, travelers were asked to be particularly careful about hygiene and to avoid any unnecessary travel, especially if they are sick.

Older adults, especially those over 65, have a greater chance of having severe complications from COVID-19. The same is true for people with weaker immune systems or those living with some types of medical conditions, including diabetes, asthma, heart disease, cancer, HIV/AIDS, kidney disease, and liver disease.

Starting two weeks before a trip, anyone planning to travel should be on the lookout for some of the following symptoms: cough, fever, chills, trouble breathing, muscle pain, sore throat, new loss of smell or taste. If you experience any of these symptoms, you should not travel at all.

And to protect yourself during travel, do your best to avoid contact with people showing symptoms. Wash your hands often with soap and water. Limit your time in public places, and, when you are out and about, wear a cloth face mask that covers your nose and mouth. Indeed, a mask may be required in some places, such as on an airplane or in a confined space like a theater, where you share the space with a lot of people.

You may wish to bring extra supplies, such as disinfecting wipes, hand sanitizer (12-ounce bottles were allowed in carry-on luggage at this writing), and a first-aid kit with a thermometer.

💲 Taxes

Air Passenger Duty (APD) is a tax included in the price of your ticket. The U.K.'s APD fees, currently among the highest in the world, are divided into two bands: short-haul destinations under 2,000 miles, £13 per person in economy, £26 in all first and business class, and £78 (private jets with fewer than 19 seats); long-haul destinations over 2,000 miles (including the United States), £78 economy, £156 first and business class (£172

Essentials

as of April 2019), and £468 (private jets with fewer than 19 seats).

The British sales tax (Value Added Tax, or VAT) is 20%. The tax is almost always included in quoted prices in shops, hotels, and restaurants. The most common exception is at high-end hotels, where prices often exclude VAT. Outside of hotels and rental-car agencies, which have specific additional taxes, there's no other sales tax in England.

Refunds apply for VAT only on goods being taken out of Britain. Many large stores provide a voluntary VAT–refund service, but only if you request it. You must ask the store to complete Form VAT 407, to be given to customs at departure along with a VAT Tax Free Shopping scheme invoice. If no customs official is on duty, there will be a customs post box where you can leave your forms. Fill in the form at the shop, have the salesperson sign it, have it stamped by customs when you leave the country, then mail the stamped form to the shop or to a commercial refund company. Alternatively, you may be able to take the form to an airport refund-service counter after you're through passport control for an on-the-spot refund. There is an extra fee for this service, and lines tend to be long.

Global Blue is a Europe-wide service with 270,000 affiliated stores. It has refund counters in the United Kingdom at Heathrow and Gatwick, at Harrods, in The City, Victoria, and Bloomsbury, and in the Westfield Shopping Centre. Outside London, counters are in Birmingham, Manchester, Oxford, and at Manchester airport. Its refund form, called a Tax Free Check, is the most common across the European continent.

Tipping

Tipping is done in Britain just as in the United States, but at a lower level than you would back home, generally 12.5% to 15%. You can tip more if service was exceptional. The server is likely to get more if you leave cash (employers can deduct administrative costs if it's left as a service charge or on a credit card.) Don't tip bar staff in pubs—although you can always offer to buy them a drink. There's no need to tip at clubs (it's acceptable at posher establishments, though) unless you're being served at your table. Rounding up to the nearest pound or 50p is appreciated. Always tip housekeepers at a hotel at least £2 per day.

Visitor Information

All of Britain's regions, along with most major towns and cities, have their own dedicated tourism websites providing information. VisitBritain (⊕ *www.visitbritain.com*), the official visitor website, focuses on general information for Britain-bound U.S. travelers, from practical tips to money-saving deals; you can even find out about movie locations.

For country-specific tourism websites, check out Visit England, Visit Wales, and Visit Scotland respectively. There are several regional and city visitor websites available too, most notably Visit London (⊕ *www.visitlondon.com*).

Many of England and Wales's historic sites are managed by one of two organizations: English Heritage and the National Trust. Scotland's sister organizations are called Historic Scotland and the National Trust for Scotland. In addition, the Royal Family has an official website with information about visiting royal homes.

Best Festivals and Events

SPRING

St. David's Day. Leeks and daffodils are ubiquitous on Wales' national day on March 1, with carnivals and processions in Cardiff and other places.

Shakespeare Birthday Celebrations. In late April, the Bard is celebrated with full pageantry and drama in his hometown of Stratford-upon-Avon. ⊕ *www.shakespearescelebrations.com.*

RHS Chelsea Flower Show. This five-day floral extravaganza in May is also a society event, held in London's upmarket Chelsea neighborhood. ⊕ *www.rhs.org.uk/chelsea.*

SUMMER

Highland Games. This annual shindig takes place in Highland locations between May and September, and includes hammer-throwing, caber-tossing, and traditional dancing. ⊕ *www.shga.co.uk.*

Trooping the Colour. Queen Elizabeth's official birthday is marked in majestic style in mid-June in London's Horse Guard Parade. ⊕ *www.royal.uk/trooping-colour.*

Glastonbury Festival. Iconic and idiosyncratic, this not-quite-annual music event sprawls across Somerset farmland and features hundreds of big-name bands over three days in late June or early July. ⊕ *www.glastonburyfestivals.co.uk.*

Royal Henley Regatta. High society lines the banks of the Thames River to cheer on rowers from around the world during this five-day event in early July. ⊕ *www.hrr.co.uk.*

Eisteddfod. The **International Musical Eisteddfod** is a gathering of choirs and dancers from around the world in the Welsh town of Llangollen in July. The **National Eisteddfod of Wales** in August focuses on Welsh culture, alternating between venues in north and south Wales. ⊕ *www.international-eisteddfod.co.uk* and ⊕ *www.eisteddfod.org.uk.*

Edinburgh's Festival. Taking over Scotland's capital every August, this cultural cornucopia is an amalgam of festivals running concurrently. Most prominent are the **Edinburgh International Festival** (⊕ *www.eif.co.uk*), featuring everything from opera to cutting-edge theater; the rowdier **Edinburgh Fringe** (⊕ *www.edfringe.com*), which highlights comedy and cabaret; and the **Royal Edinburgh Military Tattoo** (⊕ *www.edintattoo.co.uk*), a heady mix of music, dance, and military pageantry.

Notting Hill Carnival. West London's Caribbean community takes to the streets at the end of August, with spectacular floats, costumes, and steel bands.

The Proms. The main venue for this distinguished July–September series of classical music concerts is in London's Royal Albert Hall. ⊕ *www.bbc.co.uk/proms.*

FALL

Guy Fawkes Day. A foiled attempt in 1605 to blow up Parliament is remembered every November 5, when fireworks are set off all over the country. Lewes and York stage some of the biggest festivities.

Open House London. Taking place in late September, this popular weekend-long event gives the public free, behind-the-scenes access to some of the city's most famous, historic, and architecturally-interesting buildings.

WINTER

Hogmanay. Scotland's ancient, still-thriving New Year's bash extends over three days, with celebrations that are especially exuberant in Edinburgh. ⊕ *www.edinburghshogmanay.com.*

Burns Night. Ceremonial dinners are held throughout Scotland to celebrate poet Robert Burns on his birthday, January 25.

Great Itineraries

The Best of Scotland in 10 Days

DAYS 1 AND 2: EDINBURGH

The capital of Scotland is loaded with iconic sights in its Old Town and New Town. Visit **Edinburgh Castle** and the **National Gallery of Scotland,** and take tours of the **National Museum of Scotland** and the modern **Scottish Parliament** building. Walk along Old Town's **Royal Mile** and New Town's **George Street** for some fresh air and retail therapy. Later on, seek out a traditional pub with live music.

Logistics: Fly into Edinburgh Airport if you're flying via London. If you're flying directly into Glasgow from overseas, make your way from Glasgow Airport to Queen Street station via taxi or bus. It takes an hour to travel from Glasgow to Edinburgh by car or bus, about 45 minutes to an hour by train. Explore on foot or by public transportation.

DAY 3: STIRLING TO ST. ANDREWS

Rent a car in Edinburgh and drive to the historic city of **Stirling.** Spend the day visiting **Stirling Castle** and the **National Wallace Monument.** If you're eager to tour a distillery, make time for a stop at the **Glenturret Distillery** in **Crieff.** For your overnight stay, drive to the seaside town of St. Andrews, famous for golf.

Logistics: It's 35 miles or a one-hour drive to Stirling from Edinburgh, and 50 miles and 90 minutes from Stirling to St. Andrews. You can easily take a train or bus to these destinations.

DAY 4: ST. ANDREWS TO AVIEMORE

Spend the morning exploring **St. Andrews,** known for its castle and the country's oldest university as well as its golf courses.

If you've booked well in advance, play a round of golf. After lunch, drive to **Aviemore.** Along the way, either make a detour to **Dundee** and its spectacular V&A Dundee design museum or **Blair Castle** (just off the A9 and 10 miles north of **Pitlochry**). Head to Aviemore, gateway to the Cairngorm Mountains and Britain's largest national park, for two nights. The town is a center for outdoor activities and has many choices for accommodations, dining, and shopping, but you can also consider the more attractive surrounding villages and towns such as **Kingussie** for your stay.

Logistics: It's 120 miles from St. Andrews to Aviemore via the A9, a drive that will take 2½ hours. You can also take a train or bus.

DAY 5: THE CAIRNGORMS

For anyone who enjoys outdoor pursuits or dramatic scenery, the arctic plateau of the Cairngorms is a must. Hiking, biking, and climbing are options (Glenmore Lodge is a renowned outdoor-sports center), but so is visiting attractions such as the **Cairngorm Reindeer Centre** and **Highland Folk Museum.**

DAY 6: THE ISLE OF SKYE

Leave Aviemore early and head to Inverness, which has a busy center suited for a wander. **Inverness Castle** and the **Inverness Museum and Art Gallery** are worth seeing. The drive southwest to Skye is peaceful, full of raw landscapes and big, open horizons. Stop at **Eilean Donan Castle** on the way. Set on an island among three lochs, the castle is the stuff postcards are made of from the outside, although the interiors are comically underwhelming. Explore Skye: **Glen Brittle** is the perfect place to enjoy mountain scenery including the crystal clear **Fairy Pools** at the foot of the Black Cuillins;

and **Armadale** is a good place to go crafts shopping. End up in Portree for dinner and the night.

Logistics: It's 30 miles (a 40-minute drive) via the A9 from Aviemore to Inverness, and then it's 80 miles (a two-hour drive) from Inverness to Skye. Public transportation is possible but a car is best.

DAY 7: OBAN VIA BEN NEVIS

Leave Skye no later than 9 am and head for **Fort William** (get up an hour earlier and you can go via **Loch Ness**). The town isn't worth stopping for, but the view of Britain's highest mountain, the 4,406-foot Ben Nevis, is. If time permits, take a hike in **Glen Nevis,** and then continue on to **Oban,** a traditional Scottish resort town on the water, to overnight. Outside Oban, stop by the **Ocean Explorer Centre.** At night, feast on fish-and-chips in a local pub.

Logistics: It's nearly 100 miles from Skye to Oban; the drive is 3½ hours without stopping. Public transportation is challenging.

DAYS 8 AND 9: LOCH LOMOND AND GLASGOW

Enjoy a waterfront stroll in Oban. Midmorning set off for **Glasgow** via **Loch Lomond.** Arrive in Glasgow in time for dinner; take in a play or concert, or just relax in a pub on the first of your two nights in this rejuvenated city. Spend the next day visiting the sights; **Kelvingrove Art Gallery and Museum,** Charles Rennie Mackintosh's iconic buildings, and the **Riverside Museum** are a few highlights.

Logistics: It's 127 miles (a three-hour drive) from Oban to Glasgow via Balloch. Traveling by train is a possibility, but you won't be able to go via Balloch. Return your rental car in Glasgow.

DAY 10: GLASGOW AND HOME

On your final day, stow your suitcases at your hotel and hit Buchanan and Sauchiehall streets for some of Britain's best shopping. Clothes, whisky, and tartan items are good things to look for.

Logistics: It's less than 10 miles (15 minutes) by taxi to Glasgow's international airport in Paisley but more than 30 miles (40 minutes) to the international airport in Prestwick.

Great Itineraries

The Best of Wales in 5 Days

It may be smaller than New Hampshire, but Wales packs an awful lot into a compact space. This five-day itinerary takes in just some of its highlights, including the thriving cosmopolitan capital, gorgeous mountain and coastal scenery and, of course, historic castles. You can explore much of the country by public transport, but you will enjoy extra freedom with your own wheels.

DAY 1: CARDIFF

The Welsh capital is one of Britain's most interesting, cosmopolitan cities. Spend the day exploring its many sights, from its **hilltop castle** to its **National Museum**; go shopping in **St David's Dewi Sant** mall; or take in a game of rugby at the **Principality Stadium**. In the evening, head down to **Mermaid Quay** overlooking Cardiff Bay for some of the city's best bars and restaurants.

Logistics: Fly into Cardiff directly if possible. Otherwise, fly into London or Bristol and take a train to the Welsh capital. You can explore the city on foot or by public transport.

DAY 2: BRECON BEACONS

Slip on your walking boots and hop on a bus from Cardiff to Brecon. There are several points at which you can jump off the bus and start hiking, but the most popular trail is to **Corn Du** and **Pen y Fan**. Start from the Storey Arms bus stop and finish in the town of Brecon; the whole thing should take around four to six hours. In the evening, you can either take the bus back to Cardiff or to Wales's second city, **Swansea.**

Logistics: The T4 bus runs from Cardiff to Brecon every hour between 9 am and 7 pm; return buses are every two hours. The T6 bus runs from Brecon to Swansea five times a day.

DAY 3: PEMBROKESHIRE

If you don't already have a car, rent one today to explore the stunning shorelines of Wales's southwestern tip. There are dozens of beautiful beaches to choose from, including **Barafundle Bay, Tenby North Beach,** and **Freshwater West.** Spend the evening in pretty **St. Davids**, the U.K.'s smallest city (population 1,840), which has some fine sandy beaches of its own.

Logistics: It's a 2¼-hour drive from Cardiff to St. Davids at the far west of Pembrokeshire (or a 1¾-hour drive from Swansea).

DAY 4: SNOWDONIA

Drive up Wales's craggy west coast, passing through a number of pretty seaside towns and villages, and into **Snowdonia National Park.** Named for its headline mountain **Snowdon**—at 3,560 ft, the highest peak in England and Wales—the park is a staggering landscape of craggy peaks, glacial valleys, and glistening lakes. There are several different hiking trails up Snowdon, as well as a cog railway for those unable (or unwilling) to walk it.

Logistics: Start early today as it's a scenic, four-hour drive from St. Davids to Pen-y-Pass car park, a good starting point for a six-hour hike up and down Snowdon. If you take the railway, it's only one hour.

DAY 5: CASTLES

On your last morning, see some of northwest Wales's famous fortifications, including **Caernarfon Castle, Beaumaris,** and **Conwy.** Then, you can either drive back to Cardiff or Swansea to return the rental car, or cross the border into England to continue your journey (including an overnight stay in the beautiful Roman walled city of **Chester**).

Logistics: If you are returning the car to Cardiff or Swansea, factor in a four-hour drive back from Conwy. By comparison, Chester is less than an hour away.

Great Itineraries

The Best of England in 12 Days

DAY 1: LONDON

The capital is just the jumping-off point for this trip, so choose a few highlights for one day here. If it's the Changing of the Guard at **Buckingham Palace**, check the ceremony time to be sure you catch the pageantry. If **Westminster Abbey** appeals to your sense of history, arrive as early as you can. Pick a museum (many are free, so you needn't linger if you don't want to), whether it's the **National Gallery** in Trafalgar Square, the **British Museum** in Bloomsbury, or **Tate Modern** on the South Bank. Stroll through **Hyde Park** or take a boat ride on the Thames before you find a pub or Indian restaurant for dinner. End with a play; London's theater scene is world-renowned.

DAY 2: WINDSOR

Resplendent with centuries of treasures, **Windsor Castle** is the Queen's favorite residence, and has been home to many of her ancestors. A tour will give you an appreciation of the monarchy's history and power. The State Apartments are open if the Queen isn't in residence, and 10 kings and queens are buried in the magnificent St. George's Chapel on the grounds. Time permitting, take a walk in the adjacent **Great Park.** If you can splurge for a luxurious stay (as opposed to taking a day trip from London), head to **Cliveden,** the Thames Valley's most upscale hotel.

Logistics: Trains from Paddington and Waterloo stations leave about twice hourly and take less than one hour. Green Line buses depart from the Colonnades opposite London's Victoria Coach Station.

DAY 3: SALISBURY AND STONEHENGE OR STOURHEAD

The soaring spire of **Salisbury Cathedral** is visible for miles around and is a marvel of medieval engineering. The cathedral itself contains one of the original copies of the Magna Carta in its Chapter House. Walk through the town to the water meadows to see the view John Constable immortalized in his painting. While here, you shouldn't miss the opportunity to visit nearby **Stonehenge** (reachable by car or tour bus). Entry is by timed ticket, so make sure to book in advance to guarantee seeing this extraordinarily fascinating and evocative site. It's usually at its least crowded early or late in the day. If Stonehenge isn't your thing, visit the gardens of **Stourhead** instead, a superb example of the romantic, naturalistic 18th-century landscaping for which England is famous. Save some time to tour the grand Palladian mansion on the site as well.

Logistics: For trains to Salisbury from Windsor and Eton Riverside, head back to London's Waterloo to catch a train on the West of England line.

DAY 4: BATH

Bath's immaculately preserved, golden-stone Georgian architecture transports you back to the world of the late 18th century. Take time to explore the city on foot; check out the harmonious **Royal Crescent** (and the period interiors of No. 1) and sample the Pump Room's sulfuric "curative" water, just like Jane Austen's contemporaries would have. Originally established by the Romans when the city was an outpost of empire, the baths have been restored and expanded as the **Thermae Bath Spa** and today you can relax in the mineral waters fed by hot springs much like the Romans did. There's plenty to do here in the way of museums, shopping, and theater.

Logistics: Trains and buses leave hourly from Salisbury to Bath.

DAY 5: THE COTSWOLDS

Beloved for its mellow stone villages and dreamy green landscapes, the **Cotswolds** have much to offer a visitor, whether you're after antiques (try charming Stow-on-the-Wold) or just feeding ducks in a picturesque setting (the brook in Lower Slaughter). Choose a rainy or off-season day to visit lovely **Broadway** or risk being stuck in jams of tourist traffic. To really experience the bucolic landscape, take a walk on the **Cotswold Way** or any local path.

Logistics: You'll need a car to explore the beautiful countryside. Alternatively, opt for a guided tour bus.

DAY 6: OXFORD AND BLENHEIM PALACE

Join a guided tour to get the best access to **Oxford's** glorious, centuries-old quadrangles, chapels, and gardens. This leaves time for an excursion to **Blenheim**, a unique combination of baroque opulence and naturalistic parkland, the work of the great 18th-century landscape designer Capability Brown. For other classic Oxford experiences, rent a punt or go on a pub crawl around town.

Logistics: Hourly trains depart from Bath for Oxford. Buses frequently depart from Oxford's Gloucester Green for Blenheim Palace.

DAY 7: STRATFORD-UPON-AVON

A place of pilgrimage for Shakespeare enthusiasts, in **Stratford-upon-Avon** you can visit the **Bard's birthplace, Anne Hathaway's Cottage** where the future Mrs. S grew up (walking there is a delight), and then finish by taking in a memorable performance at the **Royal Shakespeare Company's** magnificently renovated main stage. Start the day early and be prepared for crowds.

Logistics: From Oxford, trains involve one or two changes; there is less-frequent Stagecoach bus service.

DAY 8: SHREWSBURY TO CHESTER

Head north to see the half-timber buildings of **Shrewsbury,** one of the best preserved of England's Tudor towns, and best experienced on foot. The architecture in **Chester** is very similar (if not always authentic), but don't miss the impressive **city walls** or the **Rows,** a terrace of two-story shops with medieval crypts beneath. You can walk part or all of the city walls for views of the town and surrounding area.

Great Itineraries

Tips

■ Train travelers should keep in mind that regional "Rovers" and "Rangers" offer unlimited train travel in one-day, three-day, or weeklong increments. See ⊕ *www.nationalrail.co.uk* for details. Also check out BritRail passes, which must be purchased before your trip.

■ Bus travel is time-consuming, but more scenic and cheaper than train travel. National Express offers discounts including fun fares—return fares from London to various cities (including Cambridge) for as low as £5 if booked more than 24 hours in advance. Or check out the low-cost Megabus.

■ To cut the tour short, consider skipping Chester and Shrewsbury and go directly to the Lake District from Stratford-upon-Avon on day eight. Likewise, you consider passing up a visit to Cambridge if you opt for Oxford. You can add the time to your London stay or anyplace else you'd like to linger.

■ Buy theater tickets well in advance for the Royal Shakespeare Company performances in Stratford-upon-Avon.

Logistics: For Shrewsbury, change trains at Birmingham. The train ride to Chester is less than an hour.

DAYS 9 AND 10: THE LAKE DISTRICT

The lakes and surrounding mountains extending north beyond Kendal and Windermere in the area known as the **Lake District** are renowned for their beauty and peacefulness despite the crowds of hikers in summer and on weekends; rent a car so you can seek out the more isolated destinations. Take a cruise on Lake Windermere or Coniston Water, or rent a boat for another classic Lakeland experience. If you have time for one Wordsworth-linked site, head for **Dove Cottage,** where you can have afternoon tea, too.

Logistics: Take the train to Oxenholme with a change at Warrington Bank Quay. At Oxenholme you can switch to Windermere.

DAY 11: YORK

The highlight of this historic cathedral city crammed with 15th- and 16th-century buildings (especially in the **Shambles**) is **York Minster** with its stunning stained glass and soaring Gothic architecture. Explore the city's Viking past in one of the many museums or unwind with afternoon tea at **Betty's** or a pint at a pub. A walk along the top of the medieval walls offers excellent views.

Logistics: By train from Oxenholme, switch at Manchester Piccadilly, or from Carlisle change at Newcastle or Leeds.

DAY 12: CAMBRIDGE

Spend the afternoon touring **King's College Chapel** and the gardens and sprawling meadows of the Backs, then refine your punting skills on the River Cam. A visit to the excellent **Fitzwilliam Museum,** full of art and antiquities, is another option, as is the **Polar Museum.**

Logistics: For train service, switch at Peterborough. Trains leave Cambridge for London frequently.

Contacts

Activities

BICYCLING
CONTACTS British Cycling. ☎ 0161/274–2010 ⊕ www.britishcycling.org.uk. Cycling UK. ☎ 01483/238301 ⊕ www.cyclinguk.org.

BOATING
CONTACTS British Marine Inland Boating. ☎ 01784/473377 ⊕ www.britishmarine.co.uk. Canal and River Trust. ☎ 0303/040–4040 ⊕ www.canalrivertrust.org.uk. Waterways Holidays. ☎ 01252/796400 ⊕ www.waterwaysholidays.com.

WALKING
CONTACTS National Trails. ⊕ www.nationaltrail.co.uk. Ordnance Survey. ☎ 03456/050505 ⊕ www.ordnancesurvey.co.uk. The Ramblers. ☎ 0203/961–3300 ⊕ www.ramblers.org.uk.

Air

ENGLAND
AIRPORT INFORMATION Birmingham Airport. (BHX). ☎ 0871/222–0072 ⊕ www.birminghamairport.co.uk. London City Airport. (LCY). ☎ 0207/646–0000 ⊕ www.londoncityairport.com. London Gatwick Airport. (LGW). ☎ 0844/892–0322 ⊕ www.gatwickairport.com. London Heathrow Airport. (LHR). ☎ 0844/335–1801 ⊕ www.heathrow.com. London Luton Airport. (LTN). ☎ 01582/405100 ⊕ www.london-luton.co.uk. London Stansted Airport. (STN). ☎ 0844/355–1803 ⊕ www.stanstedairport.com. Manchester Airport. (MAN). ☎ ⊕ www.manchesterairport.co.uk.

SCOTLAND
AIRPORT INFORMATION Aberdeen Airport. (ABZ). ☎ 0344/481–6666 ⊕ www.aberdeenairport.com. Edinburgh Airport. (EDI). ☎ 0844/448–8833 ⊕ www.edinburghairport.com. Glasgow Airport. (GLA). ☎ 0344/481–5555 ⊕ www.glasgowairport.com. Glasgow Prestwick Airport. (PIK). ☎ 0871/223–0700 ⊕ www.glasgowprestwick.com. Inverness Airport. (INV). ☎ 01667/464000 ⊕ www.invernessairport.co.uk.

WALES
AIRPORT INFORMATION Bristol Airport. (BRS). ☎ 0871/334–4444 ⊕ www.bristolairport.co.uk. Cardiff Airport. (CWL). ☎ 01446/711111 ⊕ www.cardiff-airport.com.

Boat

CONTACTS DFDS Seaways. ☎ 0871/522–9955 ⊕ www.dfds.com. P&O. ☎ 01304/863000 ⊕ www.poferries.com. Stena Line. ☎ 03447/707070 ⊕ www.stenaline.co.uk.

SCOTTISH CONTACTS Caledonian MacBrayne. ☎ 0800/066–5000 ⊕ www.calmac.co.uk. Northlink Ferries. ☎ 0845/6000–449 ⊕ www.northlinkferries.co.uk. Western Ferries. ☎ 01369/704452 ⊕ www.western-ferries.co.uk.

Bus

CONTACTS Green Line. ☎ 0344/801–7261 ⊕ www.greenline.co.uk. Megabus. ☎ 0141/352–4444 ⊕ uk.megabus.com. National Express. ☎ 0871/781–8181 ⊕ www.nationalexpress.com. Oxford Tube. ☎ 01865/772250 ⊕ www.oxfordtube.com. Scottish Citylink. ☎ 0871/266–3333 ⊕ www.citylink.co.uk. Traveline. ☎ 0871/200–2233 ⊕ www.traveline.info. Traveline Scotland. ☎ 0871/200–2233 ⊕ www.travelinescotland.com.

Contacts

🛏 Lodging

FARMHOUSES AND COTTAGES CONTACTS Farm Stay UK. ☎ 02476/696909 ⊕ www.farmstay. co.uk. **HolidayCottages. co.uk.** ☎ 01237/459888 ⊕ www.holidaycottages. co.uk. **Unique Home Stays.** ☎ 01637/881–183 ⊕ www. uniquehomestays.com.

HISTORIC BUILDINGS CONTACTS Celtic Castles. ☎ 01422/323200 ⊕ www. celticcastles.com. **English Heritage Holiday Cottages.** ☎ 0370/333–1187 ⊕ www. english-heritage.org.uk/ visit/holiday-cottages. **The Folly Fellowship.** ⊕ follies. org.uk. **Landmark Trust.** ☎ 01628/825925 ⊕ www. landmarktrust.org.uk. **National Trust Cottages.** ⊕ www.nationaltrust.org. uk/holidays.

HOTELS LOCAL CHAINS ABode Hotels. ☎ 01244/347000 ⊕ www.abodehotels. co.uk. **Apex Hotels.** ⊕ www.apexhotels.co.uk. **Hotel du Vin.** ☎ 0330/016– 0391 ⊕ www.hotelduvin. com. **Jurys Inn.** ⊕ www. jurysinns.com. **Malmaison.** ☎ 0330/016–0381 ⊕ www.malmaison.com. **Premier Inn.** ⊕ www.premierinn.com. **Travelodge.** ☎ 08719/848484 ⊕ www. travelodge.co.uk.

💲 Taxes

V.A.T. REFUNDS Global Blue. ☎ 866/706–6090 in U.S., 800/3211–1111 in U.K. ⊕ www.globalblue. com. **HM Revenue and Customs.** ☎ 0300/200– 3700 ⊕ www.gov.uk/ tax-on-shopping.

🚆 Train

FARE INFORMATION The Man in Seat 61. ⊕ www. seat61.com. **National Rail Enquiries.** ☎ 03457/484950 ⊕ www.nationalrail.co.uk. **ScotRail.** ☎ 0344/811–0141 ⊕ www.scotrail.co.uk. **Trainline.** ☎ 033/202–2222 ⊕ www.thetrainline.com.

DISCOUNT PASSES ACP Rail International. ☎ 866/938–7245 in U.S. and Canada ⊕ www. acprail.com. **BritRail.** ☎ 866/938–7245 in U.S. and Canada ⊕ www.britrail.com. **VisitBritain Shop.** ☎ ⊕ www.visitbritainshop.com.

CHANNEL TUNNEL CHANNEL TUNNEL CAR TRANSPORT Eurotunnel. ☎ 03457/353–535 in U.K. ⊕ www.eurotunnel.com.

CHANNEL TUNNEL PASSENGER SERVICE Eurostar. ☎ 03432/186–186 in U.K. ⊕ www.eurostar.com. **Rail Europe.** ☎ 800/622–8600 in U.S., 0847/916–1028 in U.K. ⊕ www.raileurope. com.

SPECIAL TRAINS Caledonian Sleeper. ☎ 0330/060– 0500 ⊕ www.sleeper.scot.

📍 Visitor Information

CONTACTS English Heritage. ☎ 0370/333–1181 ⊕ www.english-heritage. org.uk. **Historic Scotland.** ☎ 0131/668–8600 ⊕ www.historicenvironment.scot. **National Trust.** ☎ 0344/249–1895 ⊕ www.nationaltrust.org. uk. **National Trust for Scotland.** ☎ 0131/458–0200 ⊕ www.nts.org.uk. **The Royal Family.** ⊕ www. royal.uk/royal-art-and-residences. **VisitEngland.** ⊕ www.visitengland.com. **VisitScotland.** ⊕ www.visitscotland.com. **VisitWales.** ⊕ www.visitwales.com.

Chapter 3

LONDON

Updated by Jo Caird,
James O'Neill, Toby Orton,
Ellin Stein, and Alex Wijeratna

👁 Sights	🍴 Restaurants	🛏 Hotels	🛍 Shopping	🍸 Nightlife
★★★★★	★★★★★	★★★★★	★★★★★	★★★★★

WELCOME TO LONDON

TOP REASONS TO GO

★ **The abbey and the cathedral:** That Gothic splendor, Westminster Abbey, soars above the final resting place of several of Britain's most distinguished figures. To the east is St. Paul's, the beautiful English baroque cathedral.

★ **Buckingham Palace:** Although not the prettiest royal residence, this is the public face of the monarchy and the place to watch the culmination of the Changing the Guard ceremony.

★ **Tower of London:** Parts of this complex date back 11 centuries. The tower has been a prison, an armory, and a mint—now it houses the Crown Jewels.

★ **Majestic museums:** Discover the Old Masters at the National Gallery, the cutting-edge works at the Tate Modern, and the historical artifacts of the British Museum.

★ **A city of villages:** Each of London's dozens of neighborhoods has its own personality. Parks, shops, pubs: walk around and discover them for yourself.

1 Westminster and St. James's. Embrace your inner tourist. Take pictures of the mounted Horse Guards, and visit stacks of world-class art in the fantastic national galleries. It's well worth braving the crowds to visit historic Westminster Abbey.

2 Mayfair and Marylebone. You may not have the wallet for London's most prestigious shops, but remember window-shopping in historic Mayfair and chic Marylebone is free.

3 Soho and Covent Garden. More sophisticated than seedy these days, the heart of London puts Theatreland, strip joints, Chinatown, and notable restaurants side by side.

4 Bloomsbury and Holborn. The University of London dominates the city's historical intellectual center, Bloomsbury. Allow for long visits to the incomparable British Museum.

5 The City. London's Wall Street might be the oldest part of the capital, but thanks to the futuristic skyscrapers and a sleek Millennium Bridge, it looks like the newest. There's plenty for period architecture buffs as well, like St. Paul's Cathedral and the Tower of London.

6 East London. Once known for its slums immortalized by Charles Dickens and Jack the Ripper, today the area is home to London's contemporary art scene, along with Brick Lane's curry houses and Spitalfields Market.

7 South of the Thames. The National Theatre, Royal Festival Hall, BFI Southbank, Shakespeare's

Globe, and the Tate Modern make this area a cultural hub. Get a bird's-eye view of the whole city from the Shard or the London Eye.

8 Kensington, Chelsea, Knightsbridge, and Notting Hill. Although the many boutiques of King's Road have lost much of their heady '60s swagger, the free musuems are as inspiring

as ever, as are nearby Kensington Gardens and Hyde Park. Around Portobello Road, Notting Hill Gate is a trendsetting couple of square miles of galleries, bookshops, boutiques, and restaurants.

9 Regent's Park and Hampstead. London becomes noticeably calmer and greener as you head north from Euston

Road. Come here to experience just how laid-back moneyed Londoners can be.

10 Up and Down the Thames. Maritime Greenwich boasts the Royal Observatory and the Prime Meridian. Other river excursions take you to Kew Gardens and Hampton Court Palace.

If London's only attractions were its famous landmarks, it would still be unmissable. But London is so much more. Though its long history is evident at every turn, it's also one of the world's most modern and vibrant cities.

London beckons with great museums, royal pageantry, and historically significant buildings. Unique Georgian terraces perch next to cutting-edge modern skyscrapers, and parks and squares provide unexpected oases of greenery amid the dense urban landscape. Modern central London still largely follows its winding medieval street pattern.

As well as visiting landmarks like St. Paul's Cathedral and the Tower of London, set aside time for random wandering; the city repays every moment spent exploring its backstreets and mews on foot. Go to lesser-known but thoroughly rewarding sites such as Kensington Palace and the unique home of 19th-century architect Sir John Soane, which houses his outstanding collection of antiquities and art.

Today the city's art, style, fashion, and restaurant scenes make headlines around the world. London's chefs have become internationally influential, its fashion designers and art stars set global trends, its nightlife continues to produce exciting new acts, and its theater remains celebrated for superb classical and innovative productions.

Then there's that greatest living link with the past—the Royal Family. Don't let fear of looking like a tourist stop you from enjoying the pageantry of the Changing the Guard at Buckingham Palace, one of the greatest free shows in the world.

As the eminent 18th-century man of letters Samuel Johnson said, "When a man is tired of London, he is tired of life, for there is in London all that life can afford." Armed with energy and curiosity, you can discover its riches.

Planning

When to Go

The heaviest tourist season runs April through September, with another peak around Christmas. Late spring is the time to see the Royal Parks and gardens at their freshest; fall brings autumnal beauty and fewer people. Summer gives the best chance of good weather, although the crowds are intense. Winter can be dismal—it's dark by 5—but all the theaters, concerts, and exhibitions go full-speed ahead, and Christmas lights bring a major touch of festive magic. Weather-wise, winter is cold and wet with occasional light snow, and spring is colorful and fair. June through August can range from a total washout to a long hot summer and anything in between. Autumn ranges from warm to cool to mild. It's impossible to forecast London weather, but you can be certain that it will not be what you expect.

Getting Here and Around

AIR

Most international flights to London arrive at either Heathrow Airport (LHR), 15 miles west of London, or at Gatwick Airport (LGW), 27 miles south of the capital. Most flights from the United States go to Heathrow, which is divided into five terminals, with Terminals 3–5 handling transatlantic flights. Gatwick is London's second gateway. It has grown from a European airport into an airport that also serves dozens of U.S. destinations. A third airport, Stansted (STN), is 35 miles northeast of the city; it handles European and domestic traffic. Three smaller airports, Luton (LTN), 30 miles north of town, Southend (SEN), 40 miles to the east, and business-oriented London City (in east London, LCY) mainly handle flights to Europe.

BIKE

Nicknamed "Boris bikes" after the former mayor, dedicated cyclist, and current Prime Minister Boris Johnson, a 24-hour bike-rental program called Santander Cycles enables Londoners to pick up a bicycle at one of more than 750 docking stations and return it at another. The first 30 minutes are free, then it's £2 for every 30-minute period thereafter. There is also a £2-per-day access charge. You pay at the docking station, using credit or debit cards only (cash is not accepted)—simply follow the instructions on the touch screen and away you go.

BUS

Although London is famous for its double-decker buses, the old beloved rattletrap Routemasters, with the jump-on, jump-off back platforms, now only serve a single "heritage" route (No. 15H) and only on summer weekends and bank holidays. That route takes you from Trafalgar Square down Fleet Street and on to St. Paul's Cathedral and the Tower of London. Modernized Routemaster buses have taken to the streets on other routes.

Bus stops are clearly indicated; signs at bus stops feature a red TfL symbol on a plain white background. You must flag the bus down at some stops. Each numbered route is listed on the main stop, and buses have a large number on the front with their end destination. Not all buses run the full route at all times; check with the driver to be sure. You can pick up a free bus guide at a TfL Travel Information Centre (at Euston, Liverpool Street, Piccadilly Circus, King's Cross, and Victoria Tube stations, as well as at Heathrow Airport).

Buses are a good way of seeing the town, particularly if you plan to hop on and off to cover many sights, but don't take a bus if you're in a hurry, as traffic can really slow them down. To get off, press the red "Stop" buttons mounted on poles near the doors. You will usually see a "Bus Stopping" sign light up. Expect to get sardined during rush hours, 8–9:30 am and 4:30–6:30 pm.

Night buses, denoted by an "N" before their route numbers, run midnight–5 am on a more restricted route than day buses. However, some night-bus routes should be approached with caution, and the top deck avoided (the danger is that muggings are most likely to occur there, since it's farthest from both the exit doors and the driver). All night buses run by request stop, so flag them down if you're waiting, or push the button if you want to alight.

All London buses are now cash-free, which means you must buy your ticket *before* you board the bus. There are a number of ways to do this. One-day paper bus passes are available at Underground and rail stations as well as London Transport Visitor Centres and cost £5. An easier, and cheaper, option is to pay by prepaid Oyster card or "contactless" bank card. Visitor Oyster cards must be purchased before you arrive; they cost £5 (plus postage), but a day's bus travel is capped at £4.40. Normal Oyster cards (also £5) are available from ticket desks at all major airports or at any Tube station and are transferable if you have money left over. Contactless cards are increasingly being used for London travel: you touch a compatible debit or credit card on a bus or Tube station's reader, and the fare is automatically debited from your bank account.

One alternative is to buy a one- or seven-day Travelcard, which is good for both Tube and bus travel. Travelcards can be bought at Tube stations, rail stations, and travel information centers. However, note that seven-day Travelcards bought in London *must be loaded onto an Oyster card*. Although using a Travelcard may save you some money, it might be easier to just add additional money to your Oyster card as needed, since there are machines at all Tube stations and at lots of London newsagents. A seven-day paper Travelcard can only be purchased in advance, online. However you buy your ticket, just make sure you have one: traveling without a valid ticket makes you liable for a significant fine (£80). Buses are supposed to swing by most stops every five or six minutes, but in reality you often end up waiting a bit longer, although those in the city center are quite reliable.

CONTACTS Transport for London.
☎ *0343/222–1234* ⊕ *www.tfl.gov.uk.*

CAR

The best advice on driving in London is this: don't. London's streets are a winding mass of chaos, made worse by one-way roads. Parking is also restrictive and expensive, and traffic is tediously slow at most times of the day. During rush hours (8–9:30 am and 4:30–6:30 pm) it often grinds to a standstill, particularly on Friday, when everyone wants to leave town. Avoid city-center shopping areas, including the roads feeding Oxford Street, Kensington, and Knightsbridge. Other main roads into the city center are also busy, such as King's Cross and Euston in the north. Watch out also for cyclists and motorcycle couriers, who weave between cars and pedestrians that seem to come out of nowhere, and you may get a heavy fine for straying into a bus lane during its operating hours—check the signs.

If you are staying in London for the duration of your trip, there's virtually no reason to rent a car, because the city and its suburbs are widely covered by public transportation. However, you may want a car for day trips to castles or stately homes out in the countryside. Consider renting your car in a medium-size town in the area where you'll be traveling, and then journeying there by train and picking up the car once you arrive. Rental rates are generally reasonable, and insurance costs are lower than in comparable U.S. cities. Rates generally begin at £20 per day for a small economy car (such as a subcompact General Motors Vauxhall Corsa or a Renault Clio), usually with manual transmission. Air-conditioning and unlimited mileage generally come with the larger-size automatic cars.

Designed to reduce traffic through central London, a congestion charge has been instituted. Vehicles (with some exemptions) entering central London on weekdays 7 am–6 pm (excluding public holidays) have to pay £11.50 per day; it can be paid up to 90 days in advance, on the day of travel, or on the following "charging day," when the fee goes up to £14. Day-, month-, and yearlong passes are available on the Congestion Charging page of the Transport for London website, at gas stations, parking lots (car parks), by mail, by phone, and by SMS text message. Traffic signs designate the entrance to congestion areas, and cameras read car license plates and send the information to a database. Drivers who don't pay the congestion charge by midnight of the next charging day following the day of driving are penalized £160, which is reduced to £80 if paid within 14 days. On top of the congestion charge, the entire Greater London area has been designated a Low Emissions Zone, which means that all older and pollution-heavy vehicles will be levied with an extra daily charge of £12.50. However, this will almost certainly not apply to rented cars (which tend to be newer and therefore greener), but it's smart to check with the rental company first.

TAXI
Universally known as "black cabs" (even though many of them now come in other colors), the traditional big black London taxicabs are as much a part of the city's streetscape as red double-decker buses, and for good reason: the unique, spacious taxis easily hold five people, plus luggage. To earn a taxi license, drivers must undergo intensive training on the history and geography of London. The course, and all that the drivers have learned in it, is known simply as "the Knowledge." There's almost nothing your taxi driver won't know about the city. Partly because of lobbying efforts by the black cab industry, companies such as Uber have yet to make significant inroads into the London market, although the battle is ongoing.

TRAIN
London has eight major train stations, each serving a different area of the country, and all are accessible by Underground or bus. Various private companies operate trains, but National Rail Enquiries acts as a central rail information number.

CONTACTS National Rail Enquiries.
☎ 0345/748–4950 ⊕ www.nationalrail. co.uk.

UNDERGROUND (TUBE)
London's extensive Underground train system (the Tube) has color-coded routes, clear signage, and many connections. Trains run out into the suburbs, and all stations are marked with the London Underground circular symbol. (Do not be confused by similar-looking signs reading

"subway," which is British for "pedestrian underpass.") Trains are all one class; smoking isn't allowed on board or in the stations. There is also an Overground network serving the farther reaches of Inner London.

Some lines have multiple branches (Central, Circle, District, Northern, Metropolitan, and Piccadilly), so be sure to note which branch is needed for your particular destination. Do this by noting the end destination on the lighted sign on the platform, which also tells you how long you'll have to wait until the train arrives. Compare that with the end destination of the branch you want. When the two match, that's your train.

London is divided into six concentric zones (ask at Underground ticket booths for a map and booklet, which give details of the ticket options), so be sure to buy a ticket for the correct zone, or you may be liable for an on-the-spot fine of £80. Don't panic if you do forget to buy a ticket for the right zone: just tell a station attendant that you need to buy an "extension" to your ticket. Although you're meant to do that in advance, if you're an out-of-towner, they generally don't give you a hard time. You also can pay your fare using an Oyster card or a contactless debit or credit card.

Oyster cards are "smart cards" that can be charged with a cash value and then used for discounted travel throughout the city. A Visitor Oyster card, which you must buy before arriving in the United Kingdom, costs £5. Normal Oyster cards also cost £5 and you can open an Oyster account online or pick up an Oyster card at any London Underground station, and then prepay any amount you wish for your expected travel while in the city. Each time you take the Tube or bus, you place the blue card on the yellow readers at the entrance and the amount of your fare is deducted.

Passengers using Oyster cards pay lower rates. For one-way Tube fares paid in cash, a flat £4.90 price per journey now applies across all central zones (1–2), whether you're traveling 1 stop or 12. However, the corresponding Oyster card fare is £2.40 off-peak, £2.90 peak. One-day Travelcards used to be a good value for the money, but now, costing from £12.70 per card, they're a much less attractive option. If you're planning several trips in one day, it's much cheaper to buy an Oyster card: because of the system's daily "cap," you can make as many journeys as you want in Zones 1–2 for just £7 (or, in Zones 1–3 for £8.20). If you're going to be in town for several days, a seven-day Travelcard gives you the same value as an Oyster card (£35.10 for Zones 1–2, £64.20 for Zones 1–6). Children aged 11–15 can travel at discounted rates on the Tube and travel free on buses and trams with an Oyster photocard (must be ordered online at least four weeks before date of travel), while those under 11 travel free on all buses and on the Tube if accompanied by an adult or with an Oyster photocard. Young people aged 16–18 and students over 18 get discounted Tube fares with an Oyster photocard. Oyster card Tube fares start at £2 and go up depending on the number of zones you're covering, the time of day, and whether you're traveling into Zone 1.

However, although Oyster cards sound like the way of the future, they will soon be a thing of the past. Moves are underway to gradually phase out Oyster cards and to encourage passengers to move to a system of direct payments using their bank debit or credit cards instead. In practice, this means swiping a "contactless" bank card instead of your Oyster card at ticket barriers. The cheaper fares available to Oyster card holders are the same as those who pay by contactless cards.

Tube trains now run for 24 hours a day on weekends on five major lines: Piccadilly, Victoria, Northern, Central, and Jubilee. On all other lines the usual timetable still applies, with trains running from just after 5 am Monday to Saturday and with the last services leaving central London between midnight and 12:30 am. On Sunday, trains start an hour later and finish about an hour earlier. The frequency of trains depends on the route and the time of day, but normally you should not have to wait more than 10 minutes in central areas.

Tours

BOAT TOURS
★ City Cruises
BOAT TOURS | **FAMILY** | In nice weather, an open top-deck ride from Westminster, the London Eye, or Tower Piers to the ancient royal romping ground of Greenwich along the Thames River is one of the best ways to get acquainted with the city. You'll pass sights like Tower Bridge, the Tower of London, and St. Paul's Cathedral, all with a chirpy Cockney boatman running commentary. Lunch, Afternoon Tea, and nighttime cruises are also available. ✉ *Cherry Garden Pier, Cherry Garden St.* ☎ *020/7740–0400* ⊕ *www.citycruises.com* 🎫 *From £11.*

BUS TOURS
The Original London Sightseeing Tour
BUS TOURS | **FAMILY** | This one-day, hop-on-hop-off, open-top bus tour with over 80 stops along six different routes takes in major landmarks like the Houses of Parliament, Westminster Abbey, Trafalgar Square, the British Museum, the Tower of London, and, of course, Buckingham Palace, as well as more off-the-beaten-path sites like Lambeth Palace (home of the Bishop of London). Tickets are good for the entire day and for all routes. ✉ *London* ☎ *020/8877–1722* ⊕ *www. theoriginaltour.com* 🎫 *From £29.*

WALKING TOURS
City Guides
WALKING TOURS | The City Guides (or, to give them their full name, The City of London Guide Lecturers' Association) are the official guides to the City of London, the "City" being not the entire metropolis but the "Square Mile" historic financial district. They offer two highly informed daily walks at 11 am and 2 pm—some bookable but others just turn up on the day—that cover essential sights like Guildhall (the City's town hall), Mansion House, the Bank of England, and the Royal Exchange. More specialized walks offered by the Museum of London focus on topics like Samuel Johnson's London, the gardens of the City, the Great Fire of London, Roman London, or the churches of Christopher Wren, most notably his magnificent St. Paul's Cathedral ☎ 0207/606-3030 ⊕ www.cityoflondonguides.com ✉ From £7.

★ London Food Lovers Food Tours
GUIDED TOURS | **FAMILY** | London's a top global foodie city now, and the London Food Lovers walking tour of Soho is a fascinating way to explore the capital's gastro delights. Well-led and synchronized throughout, the four-hour walk kicks off with Hawaiian blueberry pancakes at burger bar Kua'Aina and takes in offbeat stops for truffle pumpkin ravioli at Soho's retro Italian delicatessen Lina Stores, a hot chocolate tasting at SAID artisanal Roman chocolatiers, and a sit-down lunch of fish-and-chips and Indian pale ale in quaint Soho pub the Dog and Duck. You'll also stop in Chinatown to sample steamed prawn dim sum at Beijing Dumpling and spot celebrities amid the Afternoon Tea crowds at the Maison Bertaux French patisserie and tearoom. The tour ends with a dessert and wine pairing in the Dickensian underground cellar vaults of the 1890s Gordon's Wine Bar. There are various versions of the Soho tour, as well as a Jack the Ripper Happy Hour Tasting Tour and a Borough Market tour. ✉ Islington ☎ 0777/4099-306 ⊕ www.londonfoodlovers.com ✉ £60.

★ London Walks
WALKING TOURS | **FAMILY** | With London's oldest established walking tours, there's no need to book ahead; instead, just turn up at the meeting point at the allotted hour and pay £10 for a first-rate, guided two-hour walk with themes like Secret London, Literary London, Harry Potter film locations, Haunted London, and much more. Top crime historian and leading Ripper authority Donald Rumbelow often leads the 7:30 pm Jack the Ripper walk in Whitechapel. As a bonus bargain, kids can come along for free. ☎ 020/7624-3070 ⊕ www.walks.com ✉ From £10.

Restaurants

For many years English food was a joke, especially to England's near neighbors, the French. But the days of steamed suet puddings and over-boiled brussels sprouts are long gone. For a good two decades London's restaurant scene has been booming, with world-class chefs—Jamie Oliver, Gordon Ramsay, Heston Blumenthal, and Jason Atherton among them—pioneering concepts that quickly spread overseas. Whether you're looking for bistros that rival their Parisian counterparts, five-star fine dining establishments, fantastic fried-chicken and burger joints (American diner food is a current trend), gastro-pubs serving "Modern British," or places serving Peruvian–Japanese fusion, gourmet Indian, or nouveau greasy spoon, you'll be spoiled for choice. And that's just as well because you'll be spending, on average, 25% of your travel budget on dining out.

The British now take pride in the best of authentic homegrown food—local, seasonal, regional, and foraged are the buzzwords of the day. But beyond reinterpretations of native dishes, London's dining revolution is built on its incredible ethnic diversity, with virtually every international cuisine represented.

Hotels

If your invitation from Queen Elizabeth still hasn't shown up in the mail, no worries: London's grande-dame hotels are the next best thing—and possibly better. If your budget won't stretch to five-star luxury, don't worry. There are plenty of comfortable, clean, friendly options available for a relatively reasonable price. The key word is relatively. In recent years, London has seen a welcome growth in the value-for-money sector, but overall, accommodations here still remain on the costly side.

If money is no object, London has some of the world's most luxurious hotels. Even these high-end places have deals, and you can sometimes find a bargain, particularly during January and February. Meanwhile, several mid-range hotels have dropped their average prices, which has made some desirable options more affordable. Large business-oriented hotels frequently offer weekend packages as well. Those on a budget should check out the stylish and supercheap hotels that have shaken up the lodging scene of late. The downside is that these places tend to be a little out of the way, but you may find this a price worth paying. Another attractive alternative includes hotels in the Premier and Millennium chains, which offer sleek, modern rooms, many up-to-date conveniences, and discount prices that sometimes fall below £100 a night.

Restaurant and hotel reviews have been shortened. For full information, visit Fodors.com. Restaurant prices are the average cost of a main course at dinner or, if dinner is not served, at lunch.

WHAT IT COSTS in Pounds

	$	$$	$$$	$$$$
RESTAURANTS				
	under £16	£16–£23	£24–£30	over £30
HOTELS				
	under £125	£125–£225	£226–£350	over £350

Visitor Information

You can get good information at the Travel Information Centres at Victoria Station and St. Pancras International train station. These are helpful if you're looking for brochures for London sights and if you need a hotel. Travel Information Centres can also be found at the Euston and Liverpool Street train stations, Heathrow Airport, St. Paul's Cathedral churchyard, and Piccadilly Circus, as well as in Greenwich and some other Outer London locations.

CONTACTS Visit London. ⊕ *www.visitlondon.com.*

Westminster and St. James's

This is postcard London at its best. Crammed with historic churches, grand state buildings, and some of the world's best art collections, the area unites politics and high culture. (Oh, and the Queen lives here, too.) World-class monuments such as Buckingham Palace, the Houses of Parliament, Westminster Abbey, and the National Gallery sit alongside lesser-known but lovingly curated museums redolent of British history. If you only have time to visit one part of London, this is it. This is concentrated sightseeing, so pace yourself.

GETTING HERE

Trafalgar Square—easy to access and in the center of the action—is a good place to start. Take the Tube to Embankment (District, Circle, Bakerloo, and Northern lines) and walk north until you cross the Strand, or exit to Northumberland Avenue at Charing Cross (Bakerloo and Northern lines). Buses are another great option, as almost all roads lead to Trafalgar Square.

 ## Sights

★ Buckingham Palace

CASTLE/PALACE | When the Queen heads off to Scotland on her annual summer holiday (you can tell because the Union Jack flies above the palace instead of the Royal Standard), the 19 State Rooms of her official residence, which was begun in 1702, plus the sprawling palace gardens, open up to visitors. However, the north wing's private apartments always remain behind closed doors. With fabulous gilt moldings and walls adorned with masterpieces by Rembrandt, Rubens, and other Old Masters, the State Rooms are the grandest of the palace's 775 rooms. Admission is by timed ticket with entry every 15 minutes throughout the day. Allow up to two hours.
■TIP→ Get there by 10:30 to grab a spot in the best viewing section for the ceremonial Changing the Guard—one of London's best free shows—that happens daily at 11 from May until the end of July (varies according to troop deployment requirements) and on alternate days for the rest of the year, weather permitting. ⊠ Buckingham Palace Rd., St. James's ☎ 030/3123–7300 ⊕ www.royalcollection.org.uk/visit ☎ From £25 ⊙ Closed Oct.–July except on selected dates Ⓜ Victoria, St. James's Park, Green Park.

★ Churchill War Rooms

MUSEUM | FAMILY | It was from this small warren of underground rooms—beneath the vast government buildings of the Treasury—that Winston Churchill and his team directed troops in World War II.

Designed to be bombproof, the whole complex has been preserved almost exactly as it was when the last light was turned off at the end of the war. Every clock shows almost 5 pm, and the furniture, fittings, and paraphernalia of a busy, round-the-clock war office are still in situ, down to the colored map pins.

During air raids, the leading government ministers met here, and the Cabinet Room is arranged as if a meeting were about to convene. In the Map Room, the Allied campaign is charted on wall-to-wall maps with a rash of pinholes showing the movements of convoys. In the hub of the room, a bank of differently colored phones known as the "Beauty Chorus" linked the War Rooms to control rooms around the nation. The Prime Minister's Room holds the desk from which Churchill made his morale-boosting broadcasts; the Telephone Room (a converted broom cupboard) has his hotline to FDR. You can also see the restored rooms that the PM used for dining and sleeping. Telephonists (switchboard operators) and clerks who worked 16-hour shifts slept in lesser quarters in unenviable conditions.

An excellent addition to the War Rooms is the Churchill Museum, a tribute to the great wartime leader himself. ⊠ Clive Steps, King Charles St., Westminster ☎ 020/7416–5000 ⊕ www.iwm.org. uk/visits/churchill-war-rooms ☎ £22 Ⓜ Westminster.

Downing Street

GOVERNMENT BUILDING | Were it not for the wrought-iron gates and armed guards that block the entrance, you'd probably miss this otherwise unassuming Georgian side street off Whitehall—but this is the location of the famous **No. 10**, London's modest equivalent of the White House. The Georgian entrance to the mid-17th-century mansion is deceptive, it's actually a huge complex of discreetly linked buildings. Since 1732 it has been the official home and office

Sights ▼

1 Buckingham Palace..... **C5**
2 Churchill War Rooms... **G4**
3 Downing Street **G4**
4 Houses of Parliament .. **H5**
5 National Gallery......... **G2**
6 National Portrait
   Gallery **G1**
7 St. James's Palace **D3**
8 St. James's Park **E4**
9 Tate Britain **G9**
10 Trafalgar Square........ **G2**
11 Westminster Abbey **G5**

Restaurants ▼

1 The Ritz Restaurant...... **C2**
2 Wiltons................... **D2**
3 The Wolseley............. **C2**

Hotels ▼

1 Artist Residence **B9**
2 The Corinthia **H2**
3 Hotel 41 .... **C6**
4 The Ritz **C2**
5 The Stafford London.... **D3**
6 Windermere Hotel...... **B9**

KEY

🟡 *Sights*
🟡 *Restaurants*
🟡 *Hotels*

A classic photo op: don't miss the view of Big Ben and Parliament over the River Thames.

of the prime minister—the last private resident was the magnificently named Mr. Chicken (the current prime minister actually lives in the private apartments above No. 11, traditionally the residence of the Chancellor of the Exchequer, the head of the Treasury). There are no public tours, but the famous black front door to No. 10 is clearly visible from Whitehall. Keep your eyes peeled for Larry the cat, whose official title is Chief Mouser to the Cabinet Office. Just south of Downing Street, in the middle of Whitehall, is the **Cenotaph,** a stark white monolith built to commemorate the 1918 armistice. On Remembrance Day (the Sunday nearest November 11), it's strewn with red poppy wreaths to honor the dead of both world wars and all British and Commonwealth soldiers killed in action since; the first wreath is always laid by the Queen. A hundred yards farther, toward Parliament, is the **Monument to the Women of World War II.** The prominent black marble sculpture uses a string of empty uniforms to symbolize the vital service of women in then-traditionally male jobs during the war, as well as in frontline roles, such as medics and auxiliary officers. ⊠ *Whitehall* Ⓜ *Westminster.*

★ **Houses of Parliament**

GOVERNMENT BUILDING | The Palace of Westminster, as the complex is called, was first established on this site by Edward the Confessor in the 11th century. William II built a new palace in 1097, and this became the seat of English power. Fire destroyed most of the palace in 1834; the current complex dates largely from the mid-19th century. The Clock Tower—renamed Elizabeth Tower in 2012—dates from 1858 and contains the 13-ton bell known as Big Ben. The Visitors' Galleries of the House of Commons are particularly popular during the Prime Minister's Questions at 12 pm every Wednesday when Parliament is sitting (tickets are free, but noncitizens can only line up and hope for no-shows). Westminster Hall, with its remarkable hammer-beam roof, was the work of William the Conqueror's son William Rufus and is one of the largest remaining Norman halls. ✉ *St. Stephen's Entrance, St. Margaret St., Westminster* ☎ *020/7219–4114 for public tours* ⊕ *www.parliament.uk/ visiting* 💷 *Free; tours from £20* ⊙ *Closed Sun.* Ⓜ *Westminster.*

★ National Gallery

MUSEUM | FAMILY | Standing proudly on the north side of Trafalgar Square is truly one of the world's supreme art museums, with more than 2,300 works on show. The collection includes masterpieces by Michelangelo, Leonardo, Turner, Monet, van Gogh, Picasso, and more—all for free. Watch out for outstanding temporary exhibitions, too, both free and ticketed. While you could allow a handful of paintings to fill your visit, there are hundreds of other paintings to see, enough to fill a full day, including important works by Van Eyck, Holbein, Velázquez, Caravaggio, and Sourat. One hour, free, guided tours start at the Sainsbury Wing every weekday at 2 pm. If you are eager for even more insight into the art, pick up a themed audio guide. ✉ *Trafalgar Sq., Westminster* ☎ *020/7747–2885* ⊕ *www.nationalgallery. org.uk* 💷 *Free; special exhibitions from £7; audio guide £5* Ⓜ *Charing Cross, Embankment, Leicester Sq.*

★ National Portrait Gallery

MUSEUM | FAMILY | The National Portrait Gallery was founded in 1856 with a single aim: to gather together portraits of famous (and infamous) Britons throughout history. More than 150 years and 200,000 portraits later, it is an essential stop for all history and literature buffs. If you visit with kids, ask at the desk about the excellent Family Trails, which make exploring the galleries with children much more fun. Galleries are arranged clearly and chronologically, from Tudor Times to the present. The huge permanent collections include portraits of all the British monarchs, Shakespeare, the Brontë sisters, and Jane Austen. Temporary exhibitions can be explored on the first three floors, particularly in the Wolfson and Porter galleries, on the ground floor. ⚠ **The National Portrait Gallery is currently closed for renovations until spring 2023.** ✉ *St. Martin's Pl., Westminster* ☎ *020/7306–0055* ⊕ *www.npg.org. uk* 💷 *Free; special exhibitions from £6; audiovisual guide £3* Ⓜ *Charing Cross, Leicester Sq.*

St. James's Palace

CASTLE/PALACE | Commissioned by Henry VIII, this Tudor brick palace was the residence of kings and queens for more than 300 years; indeed, while all monarchs have actually lived at Buckingham Palace since Queen Victoria's day, it is still one of the official residences of the Royal Family. (This is why foreign ambassadors are received by the "Court of St. James.") Today it contains various royal apartments and offices, including the working office of Prince Charles. The palace is not open to the public, but the surprisingly low-key Tudor exterior is well worth the short detour from the Mall. Friary Court out front is a splendid setting for Trooping the Colour, part of the Queen's official birthday celebrations. Everyone loves to take a snapshot of the scarlet-coated guardsman standing sentry outside the imposing Tudor gateway. Note that the Changing the Guard ceremony at St. James's Palace occurs only on days when the guard at Buckingham Palace is changed. ✉ *Friary Ct., St. James's* Ⓜ *Green Park.*

★ St. James's Park

CITY PARK | FAMILY | There is a story that, many years ago, a royal once inquired of a courtier how much it would cost to close St. James's Park to the public. "Only your crown, ma'am", came the reply. Bordered by three palaces—Buckingham, St. James's, and the governmental complex of the Palace of Westminster—this is one of London's loveliest public parks. It's also the oldest; the former marshland was acquired by Henry VIII in 1532 as a nursery for his deer. Later, James I drained the land and installed an aviary, which gave Birdcage Walk its name, and a zoo (complete with crocodiles, camels, and an elephant). When Charles II returned from exile in France, where he had been hugely impressed by the splendor of the gardens at the Palace of Versailles, he transformed the park into formal gardens, with avenues, fruit orchards, and a canal. Lawns were grazed by goats, sheep, and deer, and, in the 18th century, the park became a different kind of hunting ground, for wealthy lotharios looking to pick up nighttime escorts. A century later, John Nash redesigned the landscape in a more naturalistic, romantic style, and if you gaze down the lake toward Buckingham Palace, you could easily believe yourself to be on a country estate.

A large population of waterfowl—including pelicans, geese, ducks, and swans (which belong to the Queen)—breed on and around Duck Island at the east end of the lake. The pelicans are fed at 2:30 daily. From March to October, the deck chairs (charge levied) come out, crammed with office workers at midday, eating lunch while being serenaded by music from the bandstands. One of the best times to stroll the leafy walkways is after dark, with Westminster Abbey and the Houses of Parliament rising above the floodlit lake. ⊠ *The Mall or Horse Guards approach or Birdcage Walk, St. James's* ⊕ *www.royalparks.org.uk* Ⓜ *St. James's Park, Westminster.*

★ **Tate Britain**
MUSEUM | FAMILY | First opened in 1897, and funded by the sugar magnate Sir Henry Tate, this stately neoclassical institution is a great place to explore British art from 1500 to the present. The museum includes the Linbury Galleries on the lower floors, which stage temporary exhibitions, and a permanent collection on the upper floors. And what a collection it is—classic works by John Constable, Thomas Gainsborough, Francis Bacon, Duncan Grant, Barbara Hepworth, and

Vanessa Bell, and an outstanding display from J. M. W. Turner in the Clore Gallery. Sumptuous Pre-Raphaelite pieces are a major draw, while more recent art historical periods are represented with works by artists such as Rachel Whiteread, L.S. Lowry, Vanessa Bell, and David Hockney. There's a good little café, and the excellent Rex Whistler Restaurant has been something of an institution since it first opened in 1927. ■**TIP→ The Tate Boat (£8.60 one-way) offers a direct trip to the Tate Modern every 40 minutes.** ⊠ *Millbank, Westminster* ☎ *020/7887–8888* ⊕ *www. tate.org.uk/britain* ⊠ *Free; special exhibitions from £13; audio guide £5* Ⓜ *Pimlico.*

★ **Trafalgar Square**
PLAZA | This square is the official center of London: a plaque on the corner of the Strand and Charing Cross Road marks the spot from which distances on U.K. signposts are measured. (London's actual geographic center, as measured in 2014, is a rather dull bench on the Victoria Embankment.) Medieval kings once kept their aviaries of hawks and falcons here; today the humbler grey pigeons flock en masse to the open spaces around the ornate fountains (feeding them is banned). The square was designed in 1830 by John Nash, who envisaged a new public space with striking views of the Thames, the Houses of Parliament, and Buckingham Palace. It remains a magnet for open-air concerts, political demonstrations, and national celebrations. Dominating the square is the 168-foot **Nelson's Column**, erected as a monument to the great admiral in 1843. ⊠ *Westminster* Ⓜ *Charing Cross.*

★ **Westminster Abbey**
RELIGIOUS SITE | Steeped in hundreds of years of rich and occasionally bloody history, Westminster Abbey is one of England's most iconic buildings, most of which dates from the 1240s. It has hosted 38 coronations and no fewer than 16 royal weddings, but it is equally well known for its permanent residents,

from kings to writers, who are buried here—and many more who are memorialized. Highlights include the world's largest rose window, the Coronation Chair (dating from 1301), Grave of the Unknown Warrior, and the Poet's Corner. The adjoining medieval Chapter House is adorned with 14th-century frescoes and a magnificent 13th-century tiled floor. The **College Garden** of medicinal herbs is a delightful diversion. Climb the Weston Tower for historical artifacts and remarkable views from the Queen's Diamond Jubilee Galleries. Exact hours are long and complex (and can change), so it's important to check before setting out. ⚠ **Beware: lines can be long during peak hours.** ✉ Broad Sanctuary, Westminster ☏ 020/7222–5152 ⊕ www.westminster-abbey.org 🎫 £22 ⊘ Closed Sun., except for worship Ⓜ Westminster, St. James's Park.

Restaurants

The Ritz Restaurant
$$$$ | BRITISH | FAMILY | London's most opulent dining salon here at the Ritz would impress even Marie Antoinette with its sumptuous Gilded Age Rocco Revival trompe-l'oeil frescoes, tasseled silk drapery, and towering marble columns. Sit at the late Margaret Thatcher's favorite seat overlooking Green Park (Table 1) and luxuriate in unreconstructed British haute cuisine such as Bresse chicken with black Périgord truffles or beef Wellington carved table-side. **Known for:** luxurious dining made for the British elite; possibly London's best beef Wellington; legendary traditional Afternoon Tea in the Palm Court. ⑤ Average main: £47 ✉ The Ritz, 150 Piccadilly, St. James's ☏ 020/7493–8181 ⊕ www.theritzlondon.com 🎩 Jacket and tie Ⓜ Green Park.

Wiltons
$$$$ | BRITISH | Lords, ladies, and other assorted aristocrats blow the family bank at this Edwardian bastion of traditional English fine dining on Jermyn Street (the place first opened near the Haymarket as a shellfish stall in 1742). Posh patrons tend to order half a dozen oysters, followed by grilled Dover sole, Blythburgh pork from the carving trolley, or fabulous native game, such as roast partridge, grouse, or teal. **Known for:** traditional English dining focused on shellfish and game; waiter service that would put Jeeves to shame; Bordeaux-heavy wine menu. ⑤ Average main: £38 ✉ 55 Jermyn St., St. James's ☏ 020/7629 9955 ⊕ www.wiltons.co.uk ⊘ Closed Sun. and bank holidays. No lunch Sat 🎩 Jacket required Ⓜ Green Park.

The Wolseley
$$$ | AUSTRIAN | FAMILY | A glitzy procession of famous faces, media moguls, and hedge-funders comes for the spectacle, swish service, and soaring elegance at this bustling Viennese-style grand café on Piccadilly. Located in a former Wolseley Motors luxury-car showroom, this brasserie begins its long decadent days with breakfast at 7 am (8 am at weekends) and serves Dual Monarchy delights until 11:30 pm. **Known for:** old-country Austrian and Hungarian delights; Afternoon Tea with a Viennese twist; classic grand café ambience. ⑤ Average main: £25 ✉ 160 Piccadilly, St. James's ☏ 020/7499–6996 ⊕ www.thewolseley.com Ⓜ Green Park.

Hotels

★ Artist Residence
$$ | HOTEL | As packed with bohemian character as they come, this small boutique hotel oozes retro charm. **Pros:** quirky charm; excellent breakfasts; great staff. **Cons:** some rooms on the small side; stairs to upper floors; most rooms have a shower only. ⑤ Rooms from: £200 ✉ 52 Cambridge St., Pimlico ☏ 020/7931–8946 ⊕ www.artistresidencelondon.co.uk 🛏 10 rooms ⦿ Free breakfast Ⓜ Victoria, Pimlico.

★ The Corinthia

$$$$ | HOTEL | The London outpost of the exclusive Corinthia chain is design heaven-on-earth, with levels of service that make anyone feel like a VIP. **Pros:** so much luxury and elegance you'll feel like royalty; exceptional spa with indoor pool; excellent fine dining options. **Cons:** prices jump to the stratosphere once the least expensive rooms sell out; not many special offers; air-conditioning and lighting is difficult to use. ⑤ *Rooms from: £540* ✉ *Whitehall Pl., Westminster* ☎ *020/7930–8181* ⊕ *www.corinthia.com* ⤴ *283 rooms* ❑ *No meals* Ⓜ *Embankment.*

★ Hotel 41

$$$$ | HOTEL | With faultless service, sumptuous designer furnishings, and a sense of fun to boot, this impeccable hotel breathes new life into the cliché "thinks of everything," yet the epithet is really quite apt. **Pros:** impeccable service; beautiful and stylish; Buckingham Palace is on your doorstep. **Cons:** unusual design is not for everyone; expensive; the private bar can feel stuffy. ⑤ *Rooms from: £497* ✉ *41 Buckingham Palace Rd., Westminster* ☎ *020/7300–0041* ⊕ *www.41hotel.com* ⤴ *30 rooms* ❑ *No meals* Ⓜ *Victoria.*

The Ritz

$$$$ | HOTEL | If you're wondering if the *Downton Abbey*–style world of the old British upper class still exists, look no further than here; the Ritz is as synonymous with London's high society and decadence today as it was when it opened in 1906. **Pros:** historic luxury hotel; service at every turn; iconic restaurant and bar. **Cons:** sometimes snooty service; tediously old-fashioned dress code; located on a congested road. ⑤ *Rooms from: £555* ✉ *150 Piccadilly, St. James's* ☎ *020/7493–8181* ⊕ *www.theritzlondon.com* ⤴ *136 rooms* ❑ *No meals* Ⓜ *Piccadilly Circus.*

★ The Stafford London

$$$$ | HOTEL | This is a rare find: a posh hotel that's equal parts elegance and friendliness, and located in one of the few peaceful spots in the area, down a small lane behind Piccadilly. **Pros:** great staff; home to one of London's original "American Bars"; quiet location. **Cons:** traditional style of most rooms may not be to all tastes; perks in the more expensive rooms could be more generous (free airport transfer, but one-way only; free clothes pressing, but only one item per day); some rooms can feel small. ⑤ *Rooms from: £450* ✉ *16–18 St. James's Pl., St. James's* ☎ *020/7493–0111* ⊕ *www.thestaffordlondon.com* ⤴ *107 rooms* ❑ *No meals* Ⓜ *Green Park.*

Windermere Hotel

$$ | HOTEL | FAMILY | This sweet and rather elegant old hotel, on the premises of one of London's first B&Bs (1881), is a decent, well-situated option. **Pros:** good location close to Victoria Station; free Wi-Fi; good amenities for an old hotel of this size, including air-conditioning and an elevator. **Cons:** rooms and bathrooms are tiny; traditional decor might not suit all tastes; many major attractions are a 20-minute walk away. ⑤ *Rooms from: £185* ✉ *142–144 Warwick Way, Pimlico* ☎ *020/7834–5163* ⊕ *www.windermere-hotel.co.uk* ⤴ *19 rooms* ❑ *Free breakfast* Ⓜ *Victoria.*

Nightlife

BARS

★ American Bar

BARS/PUBS | FAMILY | Festooned with a chin-dropping array of old club ties, vintage signed celebrity photographs, sporting mementos, model airplanes, and baseball caps, this sensational hotel cocktail bar has superb martinis and Manhattans. The name dates from the 1930s, when hotel bars in London started to cater to growing numbers of Americans crossing the Atlantic in ocean liners. The collection of paraphernalia was started in the 1970s when a customer left a small carved wooden eagle. ✉ *The Stafford, 16–18 St. James's Pl.,*

St. James's ☎ 020/7493–0111 ⊕ www. thestaffordlondon.com Ⓜ Green Park.

★ Gordon's Wine Bar

BARS/PUBS | Nab a rickety candelit table in the atmospheric, 1890s, low-slung, brick vaulted cellar interior of what claims to be the oldest wine bar in London, or fight for standing room in the long pedestrian-only alley garden that runs alongside it. Either way, the mood is always cheery as a diverse crowd sips on more than 60 different wines, ports, and sherries. Tempting cheese and meat plates are great for sharing. ✉ 47 Villiers St., Westminster ☎ 020/7930–1408 ⊕ gordonswinebar.com Ⓜ Charing Cross, Embankment.

🎭 Performing Arts

Institute of Contemporary Arts (ICA)

ARTS VENUE | You would never suspect that behind the stately white John Nash–designed stucco facade in the heart of Establishment London, you'll find a champion of the avant-garde. Since 1947, the ICA has been pushing boundaries in visual arts, performance, theater, dance, and music. There are two movie theaters, a performance theater, three galleries, a highbrow bookstore, a reading room, a restaurant run by top chef Margot Henderson, and a café-bar. ✉ The Mall, St. James's ☎ 020/7930–3647 ⊕ www. ica.org.uk 🎟 Exhibitions £3, cinema tickets from £8 Ⓜ Charing Cross, Piccadilly Circus.

🛍 Shopping

ANTIQUES

The Armoury of St. James's

ANTIQUES/COLLECTIBLES | Besides fine toy soldiers in lead or tin representing conflicts ranging from the Crusades through World War II with prices starting at £15 and going into four figures, the shop has regimental brooches and drums, historic orders and medals, royal memorabilia, and military antiques. ✉ 17 Piccadilly Arcade, St. James's ☎ 020/7493–5082 ⊕ www.armoury.co.uk 🕒 Closed Sun. Ⓜ Piccadilly Circus.

BEAUTY

Floris

PERFUME/COSMETICS | What did Queen Victoria, Mary Shelley, and Marilyn Monroe have in common? They all used products from Floris, one of the most beautiful shops in London, with gleaming glass-and-Spanish-mahogany showcases salvaged from the Great Exhibition of 1851. In addition to scents for both men and women (including the current queen), Floris has been making its own shaving products—plus combs, brushes, and fragrances—since 1730 (and is still owned by the same family), reflecting its origins as a barbershop. Other gift possibilities include a famous rose scented mouthwash and beautifully packaged soaps and bath essences. ✉ 89 Jermyn St., St. James's ☎ 0330/134–0180 ⊕ www.florislondon.com Ⓜ Piccadilly Circus, Green Park.

BOOKS

★ Hatchards

BOOKS/STATIONERY | This is the United Kingdom's oldest bookshop, open since 1797 and beloved by writers themselves—customers have included Oscar Wilde, Rudyard Kipling, and Lord Byron. Despite its wood-paneled, "gentleman's library" atmosphere and eclectic selection of books, Hatchards is now owned by the large Waterstone's chain. Nevertheless, the shop still retains its period charm, aided by the staff's old-fashioned helpfulness and expertise. Look for the substantial number of books signed by notable contemporary authors on the well-stocked shelves. There's another branch in the St. Pancras International train station. ✉ 187 Piccadilly, St. James's ☎ 020/7439–9921 ⊕ www.hatchards. co.uk Ⓜ Piccadilly Circus.

CLOTHING
Turnbull & Asser

CLOTHING | The Jermyn Street store sells luxurious jackets, cashmere sweaters, suits, ties, pajamas, ready-to-wear shirts, and accessories perfect for the billionaire who has everything. The brand is best known for its superb custom-made shirts—worn by Prince Charles and every James Bond to appear in film, to name a few. These can be ordered at the nearby Bury Street or Davies Street branches, which are devoted to bespoke wear. At least 18 separate measurements are taken, and the cloth, woven to the company's specifications, comes in 1,000 different patterns—the cottons feel as good as silk. The first order must be for a minimum of four shirts, which start at £275 each. ⊠ 71–72 Jermyn St., St. James's ☎ 020/7808–3000 ⊕ www.turnbullandasser.co.uk ⊗ Closed Sun. Ⓜ Green Park.

FOOD
★ Berry Bros. & Rudd

WINE/SPIRITS | Nothing matches Berry Bros. & Rudd for rare offerings and a unique shopping experience. A family-run wine business since 1698 (Lord Byron was a customer), BBR stores more than 4,000 vintage bottles and casks in vaulted cellars that are more than 300 years old. The in-house wine school offers educational tasting sessions, while the dedicated spirits room also has an excellent selection of whiskeys, cognacs, rums, and more. The shop has a quirky charm, and the staff are extremely knowledgeable—and not snooty if you're on a budget. ⊠ 63 Pall Mall, St. James's ☎ 800/280–2440 ⊕ www.bbr.com ⊗ Closed Sun. Ⓜ Green Park.

★ Fortnum & Mason

DEPARTMENT STORES | Although F&M is jokingly known as "the Queen's grocer" and the impeccably mannered staff still wear traditional tailcoats, its celebrated food hall stocks gifts for all budgets, including irresistibly packaged luxury foods stamped with the gold "By Appointment" crest for under £5. Try the teas, preserves (including the unusual rose-petal jelly), condiments, or Gentleman's Relish (anchovy paste). The store's famous hampers are always a welcome gift. The gleaming food hall spans two floors and incorporates a sleek wine bar, with the rest of the store devoted to upscale housewares, men's and women's accessories and toiletries, a dedicated candle room, and a jewelry department featuring exclusive designs by breakthrough talent. If you start to flag, take a break in the tea salon, the Gallery café offering tastes of the food hall, the contemporary 45 Jermyn St. restaurant (the three-course set menu is good value), or an indulgent ice-cream parlor, where you can find decadent treats like a banana split or a less-traditional gin-and-tonic float. Gentlemen also can kick back at the traditional barbershop on the fourth floor. There's another branch at St. Pancras International train station. ⊠ 181 Piccadilly, St. James's ☎ 020/7734–8040 ⊕ www.fortnumandmason.com Ⓜ Green Park, Piccadilly Circus.

Mayfair and Marylebone

Mayfair forms the core of London's West End, the city's stylish central area. This neighborhood oozes class and old-school style. The sense of being in one of the world's most wealthy and powerful cities is palpable as you wander along its grand and graceful streets. Scoot across the district's one exception to all this elegance—Oxford Street—and you'll discover the pleasant thoroughfares of Marylebone, the most central of London's many "villages".

GETTING HERE

Three tube stations on the Central Line are handy for reaching these neighborhoods: Marble Arch, Bond Street (also on the Jubilee Line), and Oxford Circus (also on the Victoria and Bakerloo lines).

The best buses are the 22, which takes in Green Park, Berkeley Square, and New Bond Street, and the 9—London's oldest existing bus route—which runs along Piccadilly.

 Sights

Grosvenor Square

PLAZA | Pronounced "*Grove*-na," this leafy square was laid out in 1721–31 and is as desirable an address today as it was then. Americans have certainly always thought so—from John Adams, the second president, who as ambassador lived at No. 38, to Dwight D. Eisenhower, whose wartime headquarters was at No. 20. The entire west side of the square was home to the U.S. Embassy for more than 50 years until its relocation south of the river. In the square itself stand memorials to Franklin D. Roosevelt and those who died on September 11, 2001. Grosvenor Chapel, completed in 1730 and used by Eisenhower's men during World War II, stands a couple of blocks south of the square on South Audley Street, with the entrance to pretty **St. George's Gardens** to its left. ⊠ *Mayfair* ⊕ *www.royalparks.org.uk* Ⓜ *Bond St.*

★ Royal Academy of Arts

MUSEUM | Burlington House was built in 1664, with later Palladian additions for the 3rd Earl of Burlington in 1720. The piazza in front dates from 1873, when the Renaissance-style buildings around the courtyard were designed by Banks and Barry to house a gaggle of noble scientific societies, including the Royal Society of Chemistry and the Royal Astronomical Society.

The house itself is home to the Royal Academy of Arts and an ambitious redevelopment for the academy's 250th anniversary in 2018 has meant that even more of its 46,000 treasures are now on display. The statue of the academy's first president, Sir Joshua Reynolds, palette in hand, stands prominently in the piazza.

Free tours show off part of the collection and the excellent temporary exhibitions. Every June through August, the RA puts on its Summer Exhibition, a huge and eclectic collection of art by living Royal Academicians and many other contemporary artists. ⊠ *Burlington House, Piccadilly, Mayfair* ☎ *020/7300–8000* ⊕ *www.royalacademy.org.uk* ⊠ *Free –£18* Ⓜ *Piccadilly Circus, Green Park.*

Sherlock Holmes Museum

MUSEUM | FAMILY | Outside Baker Street Station, by the Marylebone Road exit, is a 9-foot-high bronze statue of Arthur Conan Doyle's celebrated detective, who "lived" around the corner at number 221B Baker Street—now a museum to all things Sherlock. Inside, Mrs. Hudson, Holmes's housekeeper, guides you into a series of Victorian rooms where the great man lived, worked, and played the violin. It's all carried off with such genuine enthusiasm and attention to detail that you could be forgiven for thinking that Mr. Holmes actually *did* exist. ⊠ *221B Baker St., Regent's Park* ☎ *020/7224–3688* ⊕ *www. sherlock-holmes.co.uk* ⊠ *£15* Ⓜ *Baker St.*

★ Wallace Collection

MUSEUM | FAMILY | With its Great Gallery stunningly refurbished, there's even more reason to visit this exquisite gem of an art gallery—although housing one of the world's finest collections of Old Master paintings is reason enough. This glorious collection and the 18th-century mansion in which it's located were bequeathed to the nation by Lady Julie-Amélie-Charlotte Wallace, the widow of Sir Richard Wallace (1818–90). Wallace's father, the 4th Marquess of Hertford, took a house in Paris after the French Revolution and set about snapping up paintings by what were then dangerously unpopular artists. Frans Hals's *Laughing Cavalier* is probably the most famous painting here, or perhaps Jean-Honoré Fragonard's *The Swing*. The full list of painters in the collection reads like a "who's who" of classical European art—from Rubens,

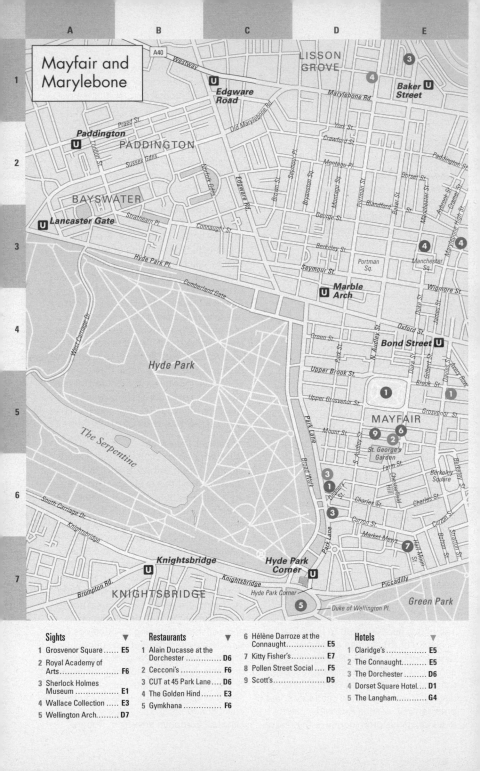

Mayfair and Marylebone

Sights ▼

1. Grosvenor Square **E5**
2. Royal Academy of Arts **F6**
3. Sherlock Holmes Museum **E1**
4. Wallace Collection **E3**
5. Wellington Arch **D7**

Restaurants ▼

1. Alain Ducasse at the Dorchester **D6**
2. Cecconi's **F6**
3. CUT at 45 Park Lane **D6**
4. The Golden Hind **E3**
5. Gymkhana **F6**
6. Hélène Darroze at the Connaught **E5**
7. Kitty Fisher's **E7**
8. Pollen Street Social **F5**
9. Scott's **D5**

Hotels ▼

1. Claridge's **E5**
2. The Connaught **E5**
3. The Dorchester **D6**
4. Dorset Square Hotel.... **D1**
5. The Langham **G4**

Rembrandt, and Van Dyck to Canaletto, Titian, and Velázquez. English works include paintings by Gainsborough and Turner. There are also fine collections of furniture, porcelain, Renaissance gold, and *majolica* (15th- and 16th-century Italian tin-glazed pottery). With craft activities, hands-on sessions, and the "Little Draw" drawing workshops, as well as the chance to try on a suit of armor in the "Arms and Armour" collection, there's plenty to keep kids occupied, too. The conditions of the bequest mean that no part of the collection can leave the building; this is the only place in the world you'll ever be able to see these works. ⊠ *Hertford House, Manchester Sq., Marylebone* ☎ *020/7563–9500* ⊕ *www. wallacecollection.org* ◪ *Free* Ⓜ *Bond St.*

Wellington Arch

BUILDING | Opposite the Duke of Wellington's mansion, Apsley House, this majestic stone arch surveys the traffic rushing around Hyde Park Corner. Designed by Decimus Burton and completed in 1828, it was created as a grand entrance to the west side of London and echoes the design of that other landmark gate, Marble Arch. Both were triumphal arches commemorating Britain's victory against France in the Napoleonic Wars. Atop the building, the Angel of Peace descends on the *quadriga*, or four-horse chariot of war. Inside the arch, three floors of permanent and temporary exhibits reveal the monument's history. From the balconies at the top of the arch you can peek into the Queen's back garden at across-the-road Buckingham Palace. ⊠ *Hyde Park Corner, Mayfair* ☎ *020/7930–2726* ⊕ *www.english-heritage.org.uk* ◪ *From £6* Ⓜ *Hyde Park Corner.*

🍴 Restaurants

★ Alain Ducasse at the Dorchester

$$$$ | **FRENCH** | One of only three three-Michelin-starred restaurants in the city, Alain Ducasse at the Dorchester achieves the pinnacle of classical French haute cuisine in a surprisingly fun, lively, and unstuffy salon. Diners feast on a blizzard of beautifully choreographed dishes including classic rum baba with Chantilly cream, sliced open and served in a silver domed tureen. **Known for:** impeccable five-star service; surprisingly unstarchy vibe; signature sautéed lobster with chicken quenelles. ⑤ *Average main: £45* ⊠ *The Dorchester, 53 Park La., Mayfair* ☎ *020/7629–8866 for reservations only* ⊕ *www.alainducasse-dorchester.com* ⊘ *Closed Sun. and Mon. No lunch Sat.* Ⓜ *Marble Arch, Green Park.*

Cecconi's

$$$ | **MODERN ITALIAN** | Revel with the A-listers in the glamorous buzz at this upscale Italian brasserie wedged between Cork Street, Savile Row, and the Royal Academy of Arts. It's perfect for a pit stop during a West End shopping spree or after browsing the nearby Mayfair galleries and auction houses, with diners spilling out onto pavement tables for breakfast, brunch, and *cicchetti* (Italian tapas)—and then returning later in the day for something more substantial. **Known for:** favorite of nearby Vogue House staff and Sotheby's clientele; popular veal Milanese; all-day jet-setter hangout. ⑤ *Average main: £29* ⊠ *5A Burlington Gardens, Mayfair* ☎ *020/7434–1500* ⊕ *www.cecconis.co.uk* Ⓜ *Green Park, Piccadilly Circus.*

CUT at 45 Park Lane

$$$$ | **STEAKHOUSE** | Austrian-born star chef Wolfgang Puck amps up the stakes at this ultraexpensive steak house on Park Lane. Set against a luxe backdrop of Damien Hirst artwork and globe lights, carnivores go crazy for the pricey prime cuts from England, Australia, Japan, and the United States. **Known for:** rare Kagoshima Wagyu beef steaks; celebrity chef hot spot; art gallery–like interior. ⑤ *Average main: £50* ⊠ *45 Park La., Mayfair* ☎ *020/7493–4545 for reservations only* ⊕ *www.dorchestercollection.com* Ⓜ *Marble Arch, Hyde Park Corner.*

The Golden Hind

$ | SEAFOOD | FAMILY | You'll land some of the best fish-and-chips in town at this British chippy in a retro 1914 art deco café. Marylebone locals and satisfied tourists alike hunker down for the neatly prepared and decidedly nongreasy deep-fried or steamed battered cod, haddock, and plaice, the classic hand-cut Maris Piper chips; and the traditional mushy peas and housemade tartare sauce. **Known for:** some of the city's best deep-fried battered cod and chips; hard-to-find traditional mushy peas; huge portions. ⑤ *Average main: £14 ⊠ 71A–73 Marylebone La., Marylebone* ☎ *020/7486–3644* ⊕ *www.goldenhindrestaurant.com* ☾ *Closed Sun. No lunch Sat.* Ⓜ *Bond St.*

★ Gymkhana

$$$ | MODERN INDIAN | The last days of the Raj are invoked here at one of London's finest Indian curry emporiums, where top choices include dosas with fennel-rich Chettinad duck or the famed suckling pig vindaloo. Diners admire the whirring ceiling fans, rattan chairs, and other decor inspired by the colonial-era gymkhana sporting clubs of yesteryear. **Known for:** unusual game curries; Indian punches in the basement private dining booths; signature kid goat methi keema. ⑤ *Average main: £28 ⊠ 42 Albemarle St., Mayfair* ☎ *020/3011–5900* ⊕ *www.gymkhanalondon.com* ☾ *Closed Sun.* Ⓜ *Green Park.*

Hélène Darroze at the Connaught

$$$$ | FRENCH | The city's wealthy flock to French virtuoso Hélène Darroze's restaurant at the Connaught for her dazzling regional French haute cuisine, served up in a stylish Edwardian wood-paneled dining salon. Taking inspiration from Les Landes in southwestern France, Darroze sallies forth with a procession of magnificent dishes, like Robert Dupérier foie gras with fig and port or Limousin sweetbreads with Jerusalem artichokes. **Known for:** sumptuous dining salon; classy French haute dishes; relatively affordable three-course set lunch. ⑤ *Average main:*

£38 ⊠ The Connaught, Carlos Pl., Mayfair ☎ *020/3147–7200 for reservations only* ⊕ *www.the-connaught.co.uk* 🎩 *Jacket required* Ⓜ *Green Park.*

Kitty Fisher's

$$$ | MODERN BRITISH | Named after an infamous 18th-century courtesan, Kitty Fisher's is situated in a tiny, creaky Georgian town house in Mayfair's Shepherd Market. Crammed with antique prints, portraits, and silver candelabras, here you can sample some of the finest wood-grill and smokehouse fare around. **Known for:** cozy and candlelit town-house setting; incredible steaks from the grill; high-end showbiz and politico diners. ⑤ *Average main: £29 ⊠ 10 Shepherd Market, Mayfair* ☎ *020/3302–1661* ⊕ *www.kittyfishers.com* ☾ *Closed Sun.* Ⓜ *Green Park.*

Pollen Street Social

$$$$ | MODERN EUROPEAN | Gastro god Jason Atherton may not man the stoves here anymore, but his flagship in a cute Dickensian alleyway off Regent Street still knocks the London dining scene for a loop. Fans can enjoy refined small and large dishes ranging from a "Fruits of the Sea" appetizer to sublime suckling pig belly with Spanish peach. **Known for:** Michelin-star riffs on classic British dishes; dedicated dessert bar; vegan and vegetarian tasting menus. ⑤ *Average main: £35 ⊠ 8–10 Pollen St., Mayfair* ☎ *020/7290–7600* ⊕ *www.pollenstreetsocial.com* ☾ *Closed Sun.* Ⓜ *Oxford Circus, Piccadilly Circus.*

Scott's

$$$$ | SEAFOOD | Imposing doormen in bowler hats greet visitors with a wee nod at this ever-fashionable seafood haven on Mount Street in Mayfair. Originally founded in 1851 in the Haymarket, and a former haunt of James Bond author Ian Fleming (he apparently enjoyed the potted shrimps), Scott's draws the wealthiest of London, who enjoy the fresh Lindisfarne oysters, Dover sole, and tasty shrimp burgers. **Known for:** possibly London's most magnificent crustacean bar; huge platters of fresh fruits de mer; extravagant prices. $ *Average main: £37* ✉ *20 Mount St., Mayfair* ☎ *020/7495-7309 for reservations only* ⊕ *www.scotts-restaurant.com* Ⓜ *Green Park, Bond St.*

Hotels

★ Claridge's

$$$$ | HOTEL | FAMILY | The well-heeled have been meeting—and eating—at Claridge's for generations, and the tradition continues in the original art deco public spaces of this superglamorous London institution. **Pros:** see-and-be-seen dining and drinking; serious luxury everywhere—this is an old-money hotel; famed history. **Cons:** better pack your designer wardrobe if you want to fit in with the locals; all that luxury means an expensive price tag; to protect the privacy of guests, photographs are prohibited in some areas. $ *Rooms from: £650* ✉ *Brook St., Mayfair* ☎ *020/7629-8860, 866/599-6991 in U.S.* ⊕ *www.claridges.co.uk* ☞ *203 rooms* ❦ *No meals* Ⓜ *Bond St.*

★ The Connaught

$$$$ | HOTEL | FAMILY | A huge favorite of the "we wouldn't dream of staying anywhere else" monied set since its opening in 1917, the Connaught has many dazzlingly modern compliments to its famously historic delights. **Pros:** legendary hotel; great for star-spotting; Michelin-starred dining. **Cons:** history comes at a price; bathrooms are small; the superior king room is small for the price. $ *Rooms from: £650* ✉ *Carlos Pl., Mayfair* ☎ *020/7499-7070, 866/599-6991 in U.S.* ⊕ *www.the-connaught.co.uk* ☞ *121 rooms* ❦ *No meals* Ⓜ *Bond St.*

★ The Dorchester

$$$$ | HOTEL | Few hotels this opulent manage to be as personable as the Dorchester, which opened in 1939 and boasts a prime Park Lane location with unparalleled glamour; gold leaf and marble adorn the public spaces, and guest quarters are awash in English country house–meets–art deco style. **Pros:** historic luxury in 1930s building; lovely views of Hyde Park; excellent spa. **Cons:** traditional look is not to all tastes; prices are sky-high; some rooms are disappointingly small. $ *Rooms from: £640* ✉ *53 Park La., Mayfair* ☎ *020/7629-8888* ⊕ *www.dorchestercollection.com* ☞ *250 rooms* ❦ *No meals* Ⓜ *Marble Arch, Hyde Park Corner.*

★ Dorset Square Hotel

$$$ | HOTEL | This fashionable boutique hotel occupies a charming old town house in one of London's most upscale neighborhoods. **Pros:** ideal location; lovely design; good afternoon tea. **Cons:** some rooms are small; no bathtub in some rooms; no gym. $ *Rooms from: £252* ✉ *39 Dorset Sq., Marylebone* ☎ *020/7723-7874* ⊕ *www.firmdalehotels.com* ☞ *38 rooms* ❦ *No meals* Ⓜ *Baker St.*

★ The Langham

$$$$ | HOTEL | Hotel pedigrees don't come much greater than this one: built in 1865, the Langham was *the* original luxury hotel in the city, all but inventing the very image of what a great London hotel looked like. **Pros:** beautiful historic building; gorgeous and peaceful pool; great restaurant and bar. **Cons:** price rises considerably once cheapest rooms sell out; need to book ahead for the wildly popular Artesian Bar; some modernized rooms don't share the building's historic charm. $ *Rooms from: £475* ✉ *1C Portland Pl., Mayfair* ☎ *020/7636-1000* ⊕ *www.langhamhotels.co.uk* ☞ *380 rooms* ❦ *No meals* Ⓜ *Oxford Circus.*

▼ Nightlife

Claridge's Bar

BARS/PUBS | This elegant Mayfair meeting place remains unpretentious even when it brims with beautiful people. The bar has an art deco heritage made hip by the sophisticated touch of designer David Collins. A library of rare Champagnes and brandies as well as a delicious choice of traditional and exotic cocktails—try the Flapper or the Black Pearl—will occupy your taste buds. Request a glass of vintage Cristal in the darkly moody, leather-walled, 36-seat Fumoir. ⊠ *Claridge's, 55 Brook St., Mayfair* ☎ *020/7629–0860* ⊕ *www.claridges.co.uk* Ⓜ *Bond St.*

★ Mr Fogg's Residence

BARS/PUBS | Explorers of all stripes will be captivated by this Jules Verne–inspired cocktail parlor, which is chock-full of the weathered maps, hunting trophies, taxidermy, suspended penny-farthings, and *Around the World in 80 Days* globe-trotting items of eccentric fictional Victorian British adventurer, Phileas J Fogg. Expect Victorian tipples and gin-based Afternoon "Tipsy teas" from staff in bow ties and other old-fashioned get-ups. ⊠ *15 Bruton La., Mayfair* ☎ *020/7036–0608* ⊕ *www. mr-foggs.com* Ⓜ *Green Park, Oxford Circus.*

Performing Arts

★ Wigmore Hall

CONCERTS | **FAMILY** | London's most beautiful venue for chamber music also happens to boast near-perfect acoustics. The hall has a rich history, including hosting the premieres of a number of works by the British composer Benjamin Britten, and today attracts leading ensembles from all over the world. The varied program contains lunchtime and Sunday morning concerts, plus workshops and concerts for babies and toddlers. ⊠ *36 Wigmore St., Marylebone* ☎ *020/7935–2141* ⊕ *www.wigmore-hall. org.uk* 🎫 *From £18* Ⓜ *Bond St.*

Shopping

ACCESSORIES

Mulberry

CLOTHING | Staying true to its rural Somerset roots, this luxury goods company epitomizes *le style anglais,* a sophisticated take on the earth tones

and practicality of English country style. Best known for highly desirable luxury handbags—such as the Lily, Chiltern, and Bayswater models—the company also produces gorgeous leather accessories, from wallets to luggage, as well as shoes and clothing for men and women. Aside from the New Bond Street flagship, there are branches in Knightsbridge, Covent Garden, Heathrow, and the Westfield centers, along with Mulberry concessions in most of the major upscale department stores. The small store on St. Christopher's Place in Marylebone stocks accessories only. ⊠ *50 New Bond St., Mayfair* ☎ *020/7491–3900* ⊕ *www. mulberry.com* Ⓜ *Bond St.*

★ Philip Treacy

JEWELRY/ACCESSORIES | Magnificent hats by Treacy are annual showstoppers on Ladies' Day at the Royal Ascot races and regularly grace the glossy magazines' party and catwalk pages. Part Mad Hatter, part Cecil Beaton, Treacy's creations always guarantee a grand entrance and are favorites with everyone from Lady Gaga to Kate Middleton. In addition to the extravagant, haute couture hats handmade in the atelier, less flamboyant ready-to-wear hats are also for sale, as are some bags. ⊠ *69 Elizabeth St., Belgravia* ☎ *020/7730–3992* ⊕ *www. philiptreacy.co.uk* Ⓜ *Sloane Sq.*

ANTIQUES

Alfies Antique Market

ANTIQUES/COLLECTIBLES | This four-story, bohemian-chic labyrinth is London's largest indoor antiques market, housing more than 75 dealers specializing in art, lighting, glassware, textiles, jewelry, furniture, and collectibles, with a particular strength in vintage clothing and 20th-century design. Come here to pick up vintage (1900–70) clothing, accessories, and luggage from Tin Tin Collectables; antique and vintage glassware and vases at Robinson Antiques; or a spectacular mid-20th-century Italian lighting fixture at Vincenzo Caffarella.

The atmosphere may be funky, but the prices are not. There's also a rooftop café with free Wi-Fi if you need a coffee break. In addition to the market, this end of Church Street is lined with excellent antiques shops. ⊠ *13–25 Church St., Marylebone* ☎ *020/7723–6066* ⊕ *www. alfiesantiques.com* ⊗ *Closed Sun. and Mon.* Ⓜ *Marylebone.*

BOOKS

★ Heywood Hill

BOOKS/STATIONERY | Open since 1936, this is considered by some to be the best small bookstore in the English-speaking world—John Le Carré, who set a scene in *Tinker Tailor Soldier Spy* here, was a long-standing customer. Browse for a leather-bound volume on architecture, gardening, natural history, or topography—just some of the topics in which the antiquarian collection specializes. The contemporary selection emphasizes literature, history, biography, travel, architecture, and children's books, and the knowledgeable staff is happy to provide advice. During World War II, author Nancy Mitford helped keep the bookstore going. Today, the 12th Duke of Devonshire, a descendant of her brother-in-law, the 11th Duke, is the owner. ⊠ *10 Curzon St., Mayfair* ☎ *020/7629–0647* ⊕ *www.heywoodhill.com* ⊗ *Closed weekends.* Ⓜ *Green Park.*

Smythson of Bond Street

BOOKS/STATIONERY | No hostess of any standing would consider having a leather-bound guest book made by anyone besides this elegant stationer, and the shop's social stationery and distinctive diaries with their pale-blue pages are the epitome of British good taste. These, along with other made-in-Britain leather goods including a small line of handbags, backpacks, and luggage tags, can be personalized. There are branches in Chelsea, Notting Hill, and Heathrow, plus concessions in leading department stores. ⊠ *131–132 New Bond St., Mayfair* ☎ *020/3535–8009* ⊕ *www.smythson. com* Ⓜ *Bond St., Oxford Circus.*

Waterstone's

BOOKS/STATIONERY | At this megabookshop (Europe's largest, with more than 8 miles of bookshelves) in a former art deco department store near Piccadilly Circus, browse for your latest purchase, attend one of the frequent meet-the-author events, or admire the view with a glass of wine at the 5th View Bar and Restaurant (open until 9.30); there's also a café in the basement. Waterstone's is the country's leading book chain, and it's pulled out all the stops to make its flagship as welcoming as a bookstore can be. There are several smaller branches throughout the city. ⊠ *203–206 Piccadilly, Mayfair* ☎ *0207/851–2400* ⊕ *www.waterstones.com* Ⓜ *Piccadilly Circus.*

CLOTHING

Browns

CLOTHING | A trendsetting boutique since it opened in the 1970s, this shop occupying interconnecting town houses has been reinvigorated after a purchase by luxury e-tailer Farfetch.com. Browns focuses on well-established international luxury designers such as Vetements, Valentino, Marques Almeida, or Saint Laurent. The menswear, footwear, and accessories collections are equally well chosen. A new Shoreditch branch showcases new design talent, and if you're about to go down the aisle, check out the appointment-only bridal boutique at 12 Hinde Street in Marylebone. ⊠ *23–27 S. Molton St., Mayfair* ☎ *020/7514–0016* ⊕ *www.brownsfashion.com* Ⓜ *Bond St.*

Ozwald Boateng

CLOTHING | The dapper menswear by Ozwald Boateng (pronounced "Bwateng") combines contemporary funky style with traditional Savile Row quality. His made-to-measure suits have been worn by the dandyish likes of Jamie Foxx, Mick Jagger, and Laurence Fishburne, who appreciate the sharp cuts, luxurious fabrics, and occasionally vibrant colors (even the more conservative choices have jacket linings in bright silk). ⊠ *30*

Savile Row, Mayfair ☎ 020/7437–2030
⊕ *www.ozwaldboateng.co.uk* ☯ *Closed
Sun.* Ⓜ *Piccadilly Circus.*

Vivienne Westwood
CLOTHING | From her beginnings as the
most shocking and outré designer
around, Westwood (now Dame Vivienne)
has become a standard-bearer for high-
style British couture. At the Chelsea
boutique where she first sold the lavish
corseted ball gowns, dandified nipped-
waist jackets, and tartan-meets-punk
daywear that formed the core of her
signature look, you can still buy ready-
to-wear—mainly items from the more
casual Anglomania diffusion line and the
exclusive Worlds End label, which draws
from her archives. The small Davies
Street boutique is devoted to couture
(plus bridal), while the flagship Conduit
Street store carries all of the above.
There's also a men's collection at 18
Conduit Street. ✉ *44 Conduit St., Mayfair*
☎ 020/7439–1109 ⊕ *www.viviennewest-
wood.com* Ⓜ *Oxford Circus.*

DEPARTMENT STORES
★ Selfridges
DEPARTMENT STORES | This giant bustling
store (the second largest in the United
Kingdom after Harrods) gives Harvey
Nichols a run for its money as London's
most fashionable department store.
Packed to the rafters with clothes
ranging from mid-price lines to the latest
catwalk names, the store continues to
break ground with its innovative retail
schemes, especially the ground-floor
Wonder Room (for extravagant jewelry
and luxury watches), a dedicated Denim
Studio, a Fragrance Bar where you can
create custom perfume, an array of pop-
ups ranging from spaces for designers
such as Jil Sander to a healthy shot
bar (if you need some colloidal silver to
keep you going) or a collaboration with
boutique boxing club BXR. The giant
accessories hall has miniboutiques
dedicated to top-end designers such as
Chanel, Gucci, and Vuitton while the new

Corner Shop offers U.K.-themed gifts and
souvenirs at all price points. There are so
many zones that merge into one another—from youth-oriented Miss Selfridge to
audio equipment to the large, comprehensive cosmetics department—that you
practically need a map. Don't miss the
Shoe Galleries, the world's largest shoe
department, which is filled with more
than 5,000 pairs from 120 brands, displayed like works of art under spotlights.
Take a break with a glass of wine at the
rooftop restaurant or pick up some tea
in the Food Hall as a gift. ✉ *400 Oxford
St., Marylebone* ☎ 0800/123400 ⊕ *www.
selfridges.com* Ⓜ *Bond St.*

JEWELRY
Asprey
JEWELRY/ACCESSORIES | The company's
"global flagship" store displays exquisite
jewelry—as well as silver and leather
goods, watches, china, and crystal—in
a discreet, very British setting that
oozes quality, expensive good taste, and
hushed comfort. If you're in the market
for an immaculate 1930s cigarette case,
a silver cocktail shaker, a pair of pavé diamond and sapphire earrings, or a ladylike
handbag, you won't likely be disappoint-
ed. And, for the really well-heeled, there's
custom service available as well (Ringo
Starr had a chess set made here). This
store has occupied the premises since
1847, some 66 years after Asprey was
established in 1781. ✉ *167 New Bond St.,
Mayfair* ☎ 020/7493–6767 ⊕ *www.asprey.
com* Ⓜ *Green Park.*

Kabiri
JEWELRY/ACCESSORIES | A carefully curated
array of exciting contemporary jewelry by
emerging and established designers from
around the world is packed into this small
shop. There is something to suit most
budgets and tastes, though understated
minimalism predominates. You can score
an elegant, one-of-a-kind piece here for
a very reasonable price. ✉ *94 Marylebone La., Marylebone* ☎ 020/7317–2150
⊕ *www.kabiri.co.uk* Ⓜ *Baker St.*

Soho and Covent Garden

A red-light district no more, today SoHo is more stylish than seedy and offers some of London's best bars, live music venues, restaurants, and theaters. By day, this hotbed of media production reverts to the business side of its late-night scene. If SoHo is all about showbiz, neighboring Covent Garden is devoted to culture. Both districts offer an abundance of narrow streets packed with one-of-a-kind shops and lots of antique character.

GETTING HERE

Almost all Tube lines cross the Covent Garden and Soho areas, so it's easy to hop off for a dinner or show in this lively part of London. For Soho, take any train to Piccadilly Circus, Leicester Square, Oxford Circus, or Tottenham Court Road. For Covent Garden, get off at the Covent Garden Station on the Piccadilly Line. It might be easier to exit the Tube at Leicester Square or Holborn and walk. Thirty buses connect to the Covent Garden area from all over London.

Sights

★ Covent Garden Piazza

HISTORIC SITE | FAMILY | Once home to London's main flower market, where *My Fair Lady's* Eliza Doolittle peddled her blooms, the square around which Covent Garden pivots is known as the Piazza. In the center, the fine old market building now houses stalls and shops selling expensive clothing, plus several restaurants and cafés, and knickknack stores that are good for gifts. One particular gem is Benjamin Pollock's Toyshop at No. 44 in the market. Established in the 1880s, it sells delightful toy theaters. The superior **Apple Market** has good crafts stalls on most days, too. On the south side of the Piazza, the indoor **Jubilee Market,** with its stalls of clothing, army-surplus gear, and more crafts and knickknacks, feels a bit like a flea market.

In summer it may seem that everyone in the huge crowds around you in the Piazza is a fellow tourist, but there's still plenty of office life in the area. Londoners who shop here tend to head for Neal Street and the area to the north of Covent Garden Tube station, rather than the market itself. In the Piazza, street performers—from global musicians to jugglers and mimes—play to the crowds, as they have done since the first English Punch and Judy Show, staged here in the 17th century. ⊠ *Covent Garden* ⊕ *www.coventgarden.london* Ⓜ *Covent Garden.*

Leicester Square

PLAZA | FAMILY | Looking at the neon of the major movie houses, the fast-food outlets, and the casino and disco entrances, you'd never guess that this square (pronounced "Lester") was a model of formality and refinement when it was first laid out around 1670. By the 19th century, the square was already bustling and disreputable, and although it's not a threatening place, you should still be on your guard, especially at night—any space so full of people is bound to attract pickpockets, and Leicester Square certainly does. Although there's a bit of residual glamour (major red-carpet film premieres often happen here), Londoners generally tend to avoid the place, though it's worth a visit for its hustle and bustle, its mime artists, and the pleasant modern fountain at its center. Also in the middle is a famous statue of a sulking Shakespeare, perhaps remembering the days when the movie houses were live theaters—burlesque houses, but live all the same. On the northeast corner, in Leicester Place, stands the church of **Notre Dame de France,** with a wonderful mural by Jean Cocteau in one of its side chapels. For more in the way of atmosphere, head north and west from here, through Chinatown and the narrow streets of Soho. ⊠ *Covent Garden* Ⓜ *Leicester Sq.*

London Transport Museum

MUSEUM | FAMILY | Housed in the old flower market at the southeast corner of Covent Garden, this stimulating museum is filled with impressive vehicle, poster, and photograph collections. As you watch the crowds drive a Tube-train simulation and gawk at the early Victorian steam locomotives and horse-drawn trams (and the piles of detritus that remained behind), it's unclear who's enjoying it more: children or adults. Best of all, the kid-friendly museum (under 18 admitted free, and there's a play area) has a multilevel approach to education, including information for the youngest visitor and the most advanced transit aficionado alike. Food and drink are available at the Upper Deck café, and the shop has lots of good options for gift-buying. ■ TIP→ Tickets are valid for unlimited entry for 12 months. ⊠ Covent Garden Piazza, Covent Garden ☎ 0343/222–5000 ⊕ www.ltmuseum. co.uk ⊠ £18 Ⓜ Covent Garden, Leicester Sq.

★ Newburgh Quarter

PEDESTRIAN MALL | Want to see the hip style of today's London? Find it one block east of Carnaby Street—where the look of the '60s "Swinging London" was born—in an adorable warren of cobblestone streets now lined with specialty boutiques, edgy stores, and young indie upstarts. A check of the ingredients reveals one part '60s London, one part futuristic fetishism, one part steampunk, and one part British street swagger. The new-bohemian look best flourishes in shops like Peckham Rye, a tiny boutique crowded with rockers and fashionistas who adore its grunge–meets– Brideshead Revisited vibe. Quality coffee shops abound—take a break at Department of Coffee and Social Affairs, where you can also browse for home coffee-making equipment. ⊠ Newburgh St., Foubert's Pl., Ganton St., and Carnaby St., Soho ⊕ www.carnaby.co.uk.

★ The Photographers' Gallery

MUSEUM | Britain's first and foremost public photography gallery programs cutting-edge and provocative exhibitions. The prestigious Deutsche Börse Photography Prize is exhibited and awarded here annually. The gallery also has a print sales room, a bookstore, an archive, and a café-bar—a great spot to escape the bustle of nearby Oxford Street. ⊠ 16–18 Ramillies St., Soho ☎ 020/7087–9300 ⊕ www.thephotographersgallery.org.uk ⊠ £5 for exhibitions Ⓜ Oxford Circus.

★ Somerset House

MUSEUM | FAMILY | This huge complex— the work of Sir William Chambers (1723–96) and built during the reign of George III to house offices of the Navy Board—has been transformed from dusty government offices to one of the capital's most buzzing centers of culture and the arts, often hosting several interesting exhibitions at one time. The cobblestone Italianate courtyard, where Admiral Nelson used to walk, makes a great setting for 55 playful fountains and is transformed into a romantic ice rink in winter; the grand space is the venue for music and outdoor movie screenings in summer. The Courtauld Gallery (currently closed for renovations) occupies most of the north building, facing the busy Strand. Across the courtyard are the barrell-vaulted Embankment Galleries, with a vibrant calendar of design, fashion, architecture, and photography exhibitions. The East Wing has another fine exhibition space, and events are sometimes also held in the atmospherically gloomy cellars below the Fountain Court. Fernandez & Wells is a great spot for an informal meal or snack. In summer, eating and drinking spills out onto the large terrace next to the Thames. ⊠ Strand, Covent Garden ☎ 020/7845– 4600 ⊕ www.somersethouse.org.uk ⊠ Embankment Galleries price varies, other areas free Ⓜ Charing Cross, Covent Garden, Holborn, Temple.

Soho and Covent Garden

FITZROVIA

Tottenham Court Road Ⓤ

Oxford St.

Soho Sq.

Sutton Row

Charing Cross Rd.

Wells St.

Poland St.

Noel St.

Dean St.

Carlisle St.

Greek St.

Frith St.

Ⓢ **5**

Gt. Marlborough St.

Foubert's Pl.

Marshall St.

Wardour St.

Berwick St.

Ⓡ **13**

Ⓡ **5** Ⓡ **2**

Ⓢ **3**

Ⓢ **6**

Newburgh Quarter ◆

Carnaby St.

Broadwick St.

Lexington St.

Ⓢ **1**

SOHO

Old Compton St.

Romilly St.

Ganton St.

Ⓢ **4** Newburgh St.

Regent St.

Beak St.

Golden Sq.

Brewer St.

Ⓡ **9**

Ⓡ **4**

Shaftesbury Ave.

Gerrard St.

CHINATOWN

Lisle St.

Warwick St.

Sherwood St.

Denman St.

Rupert St.

Saville Row

Old Burlington St.

Glasshouse St.

Viga St.

Regent St.

Piccadilly Circus

Coventry St.

Whitcomb St.

Leicester Sq.

Ⓡ **2**

St. Martin's

Cork St.

Ⓤ **Piccadilly Circus**

Sackville St.

Regent St.

Haymarket

Old Bond St.

Piccadilly

Jermyn St.

Duke of York St.

Charles II St.

Pall Mall

Cockspur St.

KEY
- Ⓢ **1** Sights
- Ⓡ **1** Restaurants
- Ⓗ **1** Hotels

ST. JAMES'S

Duke St.

St James's Sq.

| 0 | | 1/8 mi |
| 0 | | 200 m |

Sights ▼

1 Covent Garden Piazza **H4**
2 Leicester Square **E5**
3 London Transport Museum **H4**
4 Newburgh Quarter **B3**
5 The Photographers' Gallery **A2**
6 Somerset House **J4**

Restaurants ▼

1 Andrew Edmunds **C3**
2 Balthazar **H3**
3 Bancone **F6**
4 Blacklock **C4**
5 Dean Street Townhouse **D3**
6 Hoppers **D3**
7 The Ivy **F3**
8 J Sheekey **F4**
9 Kiln **C4**
10 Rules **H4**
11 Savoy Grill **I4**
12 Simpson's in the Strand **I4**

13 Social Eating
   House B3
14 Spring J4

Hotels ▼

1 Covent Garden Hotel ... F2
2 Dean Street
   Townhouse D3
3 Hazlitt's D2
4 ME London I4
5 The Savoy I4

Covent Garden is home to a charming variety of markets, shops, and cafés.

🍴 Restaurants

Andrew Edmunds

$$ | MEDITERRANEAN | Candlelit at night, with a haunting Dickensian vibe, Andrew Edmunds is a permanently packed, old-school dining institution. Tucked away behind Carnaby Street in an 18th-century Soho town house, it's a cozy favorite whose unpretentious and keenly priced dishes draw on the tastes of Ireland, the Mediterranean, and Middle East. **Known for:** deeply romantic, Georgian-era town-house setting; unpretentious daily changing handwritten menus; bargains galore on the acclaimed wine list. ⑤ *Average main: £18* ✉ *46 Lexington St., Soho* ☎ *020/7437–5708* ⊕ *www.andrewedmunds.com* Ⓜ *Oxford Circus, Piccadilly Circus.*

Balthazar

$$$ | BRASSERIE | FAMILY | British restaurateur Keith McNally re-creates his famed New York Parisian brasserie at this busy corner spot just off Covent Garden. The decor creates an enchanting backdrop to enjoy a classic French brasserie menu of few surprises, including flavor-packed dishes like macaroni and Gruyère cheese or ox cheek bourguignon. **Known for:** Parisian-style grand café; handy prix fixe, brunch, children's, and Afternoon Tea menus; vegan and vegetarian options. ⑤ *Average main: £24* ✉ *4–7 Russell St., Covent Garden* ☎ *020/3301–1155* ⊕ *www.balthazarlondon.com* Ⓜ *Covent Garden, Charing Cross, Holborn.*

★ Bancone

$ | ITALIAN | London's awash with New Wave, affordable, and fresh pasta joints, but Bancone in Covent Garden is one of the best options. Diners regularly pitch up at the white marble, porcelain, and bronze bar counter and marvel at the silkiness of the pastas and the outstandingly low prices. **Known for:** high-end pasta at cheap prices; slick urban Italian setting of olive greens, earth tones, and natural stones; location close to the National Portrait Gallery. ⑤ *Average main:*

£12 ✉ 39 William IV St., Covent Garden ☎ 020/7240–8786 ⊕ www.bancone. co.uk Ⓜ Charing Cross, Covent Garden, Leicester Sq.

Blacklock

$ | STEAKHOUSE | FAMILY | Set in a former basement brothel, this Soho meatopia cranks out £20 platters of delectable char-grilled lamb, beef, and pork skinny chops and juice-soaked flat bread, all served on retro antique pearlware. Supplied by master butchers Philip Warren from Cornwall, Blacklock's killer chops are charcoal-grilled under heavy antique blacklock irons from Tennessee. **Known for:** young and bubbly service with top '80s tunes; huge platters of skinny chops and flat bread; £18 Sunday roasts with all the trimmings. $ Average main: £12 ✉ The Basement, 24 Great Windmill St., Soho ☎ 020/3441 6996 ⊕ www.theblack-lock.com ⊗ No dinner Sun. Ⓜ Piccadilly Circus, Oxford Circus.

Dean Street Townhouse

$$$ | BRITISH | Everyone feels 10 times more glamorous just stepping inside this candlelit restaurant attached to the swanky Georgian-era hotel of the same name. Straightforward retro-British favorites include pea and ham soup, old-school mince and potatoes, smoked haddock soufflé, and tasty sherry trifle. **Known for:** classy candlelit dining salon with British art on the walls; super professional service; cheery High Tea and Afternoon Tea. $ Average main: £24 ✉ 69–70 Dean St., Soho ☎ 020/7434-1775 ⊕ www.deanstreettownhouse.com Ⓜ Oxford Circus, Tottenham Court Rd.

★ Hoppers

$ | SRI LANKAN | Sri Lankan curry fans have gone mad for the fermented rice-flour egg pancakes (a Sri Lankan specialty known as hoppers) and paper-thin griddled dosas at this highly spiced Frith Street snuggery. Diners gorge on chili mutton rolls, curried duck hearts, bone marrow curry, and piles of steamed string hoppers dipped in spicy broth, coconut chutney, or onion-and-Maldives-fish-flakes relish. **Known for:** crispy egg hopper pancakes with coconut sambol; authentic Colombo-style cabin atmosphere; signature goat or black pork kari curry. $ Average main: £9 ✉ 49 Frith St., Soho ⊕ www.hopperslondon.com ⊗ Closed Sun. Ⓜ Oxford Circus, Tottenham Court Rd.

★ The Ivy

$$$ | MODERN BRITISH | London's one-time most famous celebrity haunt and West End landmark is still so popular it receives over a thousand calls a day. Established as an Italian café in 1917, today it's still where London's wealthiest dine on haddock and chips, Thai-baked sea bass, and good ol' English classics like Shepherd's pie and sticky toffee pudding. **Known for:** celebrity-filled history; famed house staples like grilled calf's liver; great people-watching. $ Average main: £26 ✉ 1–5 West St., Covent Garden ☎ 020/7836-4751 ⊕ www.the-ivy.co.uk Ⓜ Covent Garden, Tottenham Court Rd.

J Sheekey

$$$ | SEAFOOD | This timelessly chic, 1896, seafood haven is a discreet alternative to the more celebrity-focused eateries in the neighborhood. J Sheekey charms with an inviting menu of snappingly fresh Atlantic prawns, pickled Arctic herring, scallop, shrimp, and salmon burgers, or the famous Sheekey fish pie. Better yet, sip Gaston Chiquet Champagne and down half a dozen Fine de Claire rock oysters at the antique mirrored oyster bar for the ultimate in true romance. **Known for:** low-key celebrity hideaway; old-school seafood menu and discreet service; glamorous art deco oyster bar. $ Average main: £27 ✉ 28–35 St. Martin's Ct., Covent Garden ☎ 020/7240-2565 ⊕ www.j-sheekey.co.uk Ⓜ Charing Cross, Leicester Sq.

Kiln

$ | THAI | Earthy northern Thai cuisine bursts out of the charcoal-fired kiln and clay pots at this barbecue-focused wonderland in Soho. Overlook the open kitchen and you'll see sizzling cumin-dusted hogget skewers and charcoal-grilled chicken thigh bites, along with other village-style dishes that show influences from Laos, Myanmar, and the Yunnan province of China. **Known for:** open kitchen counter setup with charcoal grill and hot clay pots; array of Cornish grown Thai, Burmese, and other Asian herbs and spices; popular cumin-dusted aged hogget skewers. ⑤ *Average main: £10* ✉ *58 Brewer St., Soho* ⊕ *www.kilnsoho. com* Ⓜ *Oxford Circus, Piccadilly Circus.*

★ Rules

$$$ | BRITISH | Opened by Thomas Rule in 1798, London's oldest restaurant is still arguably its most beautiful. Resembling a High Victoriana bordello, here you can dig into classic traditional British fare like jugged hare, steak-and-kidney pie, or roast beef and Yorkshire pudding. **Known for:** the oldest restaurant in London; fancy, high-class game-focused menu; famous diners from Charles Dickens to the Prince of Wales. ⑤ *Average main: £30* ✉ *35 Maiden La., Covent Garden* ☎ *020/7836–5314* ⊕ *www.rules.co.uk* 🏛 *Jacket required* Ⓜ *Covent Garden.*

Savoy Grill

$$$$ | BRITISH | You can feel the history at this 1889, art deco, hotel-dining powerhouse, which has wined and dined everyone from Oscar Wilde and Sir Winston Churchill to Elizabeth Taylor and Marilyn Monroe. Nowadays it caters to CEOs and wealthy West End tourists who come for the Grill's famed table-side serving trolley, which might trundle up laden with hulking great roasts like beef Wellington, Suffolk rack of pork, or saddle of lamb. **Known for:** ravishing old-school dining salon; beef Wellington from the daily carvery trolley service; signature glazed omelet Arnold Bennett. ⑤ *Average main: £40* ✉ *The Savoy, 100 Strand, Covent Garden* ☎ *020/7592–1600 for reservations only* ⊕ *www.gordonramsay-restaurants.com/savoy-grill* Ⓜ *Charing Cross, Covent Garden.*

Simpson's in the Strand

$$$ | BRITISH | Head straight for the 30-day roast rib of Scottish beef and Yorkshire puddings carved table-side at this magnificent 1828 dining institution. Originally a cigar lounge, coffeehouse, and later a famed chess venue, it was once frequented by the likes of Sir Arthur Conan Doyle, Charles Dickens, and Vincent van Gogh. **Known for:** one of the city's most grand and historic taverns; traditional Sunday roast dinner; roast beef and Welsh lamb served from the silver domed carving trolley. ⑤ *Average main: £28* ✉ *100 Strand, Charing Cross* ☎ *020/7420–2111 restaurant reservations only* ⊕ *www.simpsonsinthestrand.co.uk* Ⓜ *Charing Cross.*

Social Eating House

$$$ | FRENCH | At Jason Atherton's underrated but brilliant French *bistronomie* Soho hangout, witty dishes like smoked duck's ham (made from cured duck's breast) and Scotch egg-and-chips are served alongside complex classics like charred Cumbrian pork with mustard jelly. The moodily lit bare-brick salon is decorated with dark parquet floors, antique mirrored ceilings, and red leather banquettes. **Known for:** extravagant tasting menus at the open chef's table; popular set lunch menu; vintage cocktails at the speakeasy lounge upstairs. ⑤ *Average main: £29* ✉ *58 Poland St., Soho* ☎ *020/7993–3251* ⊕ *www.socialeatinghouse.com* ⊙ *Closed Sun.* Ⓜ *Oxford Circus, Tottenham Court Rd.*

★ Spring

$$$ | ITALIAN | Australian chef Skye Gyngell worships the four seasons at her wildflower-filled dining salon in majestic Somerset House off the Strand. Housed in the building's 1865 neoclassical New Wing, Spring offers healthy, root-to-stem, produce-driven, Italian dishes in a light-drenched room. **Known for:** housemade bread, butter, and ice cream; highly seasonal, sustainable, and ingredient-driven dishes; biodynamic Fern Verrow Farm salads. $ *Average main: £30* ⊠ *Somerset House, New Wing, Lancaster Pl., Covent Garden* ✢ *Turn right on entering courtyard at Somerset House from the Strand* ☎ *020/3011–0115* ⊕ *www.springrestaurant.co.uk* ☾ *Closed Sun.* Ⓜ *Charing Cross, Holborn.*

🛏 Hotels

★ Covent Garden Hotel
$$$$ | **HOTEL** | It's little wonder this is now the London home-away-from-home for off-duty celebrities, actors, and style mavens, with its Covent Garden location and guest rooms that are design-magazine stylish, using mix-and-match couture fabrics to stunning effect. **Pros:** great for star-spotting; supertrendy; basement cinema for movie buffs. **Cons:** you can feel you don't matter if you're not famous; location in Covent Garden can be a bit boisterous; only some rooms come with balcony views. $ *Rooms from: £320* ⊠ *10 Monmouth St., Covent Garden* ☎ *020/7806–1000, 888/559–5508 in U.S.* ⊕ *www.firmdalehotels.com/hotels/london/covent-garden-hotel* ⇥ *58 rooms* ❍ *No meals* Ⓜ *Covent Garden.*

Dean Street Townhouse
$$$ | **HOTEL** | Discreet and unpretentious—and right in the heart of Soho—this oh-so-stylish Georgian town house has a bohemian vibe and an excellent Modern British restaurant, hung with pieces by renowned artists like Peter Blake and Tracy Emin. **Pros:** ultracool vibe; resembles an upper-class pied-à-terre; great location in the heart of Soho. **Cons:** some rooms are extremely small; rooms at the front of the building can be noisy, especially on weekends; the crowd can often feel cooler-than-thou. $ *Rooms from: £330* ⊠ *69–71 Dean St., Soho* ☎ *020/7434–1775* ⊕ *www.deanstreettownhouse.com*

⇥ *39 rooms* ❍ *Free breakfast* Ⓜ *Leicester Sq., Tottenham Court Rd.*

★ Hazlitt's
$$$$ | **HOTEL** | This disarmingly friendly place, full of personality, robust antiques, Old Masters portraits, and claw-foot tubs, occupies three connected early 18th-century town houses, one of which was the last home of critic and essayist William Hazlitt (1778–1830). **Pros:** great for lovers of antiques and Old Masters art; historic atmosphere with lots of small sitting rooms and wooden staircases; truly beautiful and relaxed. **Cons:** no in-house restaurant; breakfast costs extra; no elevators. $ *Rooms from: £255* ⊠ *6 Frith St., Soho* ☎ *020/7434–1771* ⊕ *www.hazlittshotel.com* ⇥ *30 rooms* ❍ *No meals* Ⓜ *Tottenham Court Rd.*

★ ME London
$$$ | **HOTEL** | A shiny fortress of luxury, the ME brings a splash of modern cool to a rather stuffy patch of the Strand. **Pros:** sleek and fashionable; full of high-tech comforts; stunning views from rooftop bar. **Cons:** design can sometimes verge on form over function; very small closets and in-room storage areas; rooftop bar can get uncomfortably busy. $ *Rooms from: £280* ⊠ *336–337 The Strand, Covent Garden* ☎ *020/7395–3400* ⊕ *www.melia.com* ⇥ *157 rooms* ❍ *No meals* Ⓜ *Covent Garden, Charing Cross, Holborn.*

★ The Savoy
$$$$ | **HOTEL** | One of London's most iconic hotels maintains its status at the top with winning attributes of impeccable service, stunning decor, and a desirable location on the Strand. **Pros:** one of the top hotels in Europe; iconic pedigree; Thames-side location. **Cons:** everything comes with a price tag; street noise is surprisingly problematic, particularly on lower floors; street can be too busy for some. $ *Rooms from: £504* ⊠ *The Strand, Covent Garden* ☎ *020/7836–4343, 888/265–0533 in U.S.* ⊕ *www.thesavoylondon.com* ⇥ *268 rooms* ❍ *Free breakfast* Ⓜ *Covent Garden, Charing Cross.*

Nightlife

BARS

★ The Blind Pig

BARS/PUBS | Chances are you won't have heard of half the ingredients on the cocktail menu at this dark and sultry bar above Jason Atherton's smart casual restaurant, Social Eating House in Soho, but the sense of mystery only adds to the experience. So, too, do the antique mirrored ceilings and copper-topped bar, the delectable small plates (like black pepper prawn crackers and macaroni and cheese with shaved mushroom)—and the knowledge that you've nabbed a seat at one of the coolest spots in Soho. ✉ 58 Poland St., Soho ☎ 020/7993–3251 ⊕ www.socialeatinghouse.com Ⓜ Oxford Circus, Tottenham Court Rd.

The Dog and Duck

BARS/PUBS | **FAMILY** | A beautiful example of a late-19th-century London pub, the Dog and Duck has a well-preserved Heritage-listed interior furnished with glazed tiles, cut glass mirrors, and polished wood, though it's often so packed that it's hard to get a good look. There's a decent selection of real ales at the bar and a restaurant serving outstanding pale ale-battered fish-and-chips with mushy peas. Originally built in 1734 and patronized by artists John Constable and Dante Rossetti, the cozy upstairs dining room is named for writer George Orwell, who also frequented this spot. ✉ 18 Bateman St., Soho ☎ 020/7494–0697 ⊕ www.nicholsonspubs.co.uk Ⓜ Oxford Circus, Tottenham Court Rd.

Heaven

MUSIC CLUBS | With the best light show on any London dance floor, Heaven is unpretentious, loud, and huge, with a labyrinth of rooms, bars, and live-music parlors. Thursday through Saturday nights it's all about the G-A-Y club and comedy nights. Check in advance about live performances—they can take place any night of the week. If you go to just one gay club in London, Heaven should be it. ✉ Under the Arches, Villiers St., Covent Garden ☎ 0844/847–2351 24-hr ticket line ⊕ www.heavenlive.co.uk ✉ From £15 Ⓜ Charing Cross, Embankment.

Terroirs

WINE BARS—NIGHTLIFE | Specializing in low-intervention "natural wines" (organic, unfiltered, biodynamic, and sustainably produced with minimal added ingredients), Terroirs wine bar has an unusually large selection of 290 wines from small French and artisan winemakers. Red, white, sparkling and macerated orange and amber wines are served along with delicious, relatively simple wine-friendly dishes—charcuterie, tapas, cheese, and more substantial French-inspired dishes—at a bar and bare oak tables surrounded by whitewashed walls and wooden floors. ✉ 5 William IV St., Covent Garden ☎ 020/7036–0660 ⊕ www.terroirswinebar.com Ⓜ Charing Cross.

COMEDY AND CABARET

★ The Comedy Store

COMEDY CLUBS | Before heading off to prime time, some of the United Kingdom's funniest stand-ups cut their teeth here, at what's considered the birthplace of alternative comedy. The Comedy Store Players, a team with six comedians doing improvisation with audience suggestions, entertain on Wednesday and Sunday; The Cutting Edge steps in with a topical take every Tuesday; Thursday, Friday, and Saturday have the best stand-up acts. There's also a bar with food. Note you must be over 18 to enter. ✉ 1A Oxendon St., Soho ☎ 020/7024–2060 for tickets and booking ⊕ www.thecomedystore.co.uk ✉ From £12 Ⓜ Leicester Sq., Piccadilly Circus.

LIVE MUSIC

Pizza Express Jazz Club

MUSIC CLUBS | One of the United Kingdom's most ubiquitous pizza chains also runs a leading Soho jazz venue.

The Royal Opera House is simply dazzling inside and out.

Established in 1976, the dimly lit restaurant hosts both established and emerging top-quality international jazz acts every night, with food available in the downstairs venue (as opposed to the upstairs restaurant) around 90 minutes before stage time. The Italian-style thin-crust pizzas are popular, but they are about what you'd expect from a major chain. ⊠ *10 Dean St., Soho* ☎ *020/7439-4962 for jazz club, 020/7437-9595 for restaurant* ⊕ *www.pizzaexpresslive.com* ⊠ *From £16* Ⓜ *Tottenham Court Rd.*

Ⓝ Performing Arts

★ Royal Opera House

DANCE | Along with Milan's La Scala, New York's Metropolitan, and the Palais Garnier in Paris, this is one of the world's great opera houses. The resident troupe has mounted spectacular productions in the past, while recent productions have tended toward more contemporary operas. Whatever the style of the performance, the extravagant theater delivers a full dose of opulence. The famed Royal Ballet performs classical and contemporary repertoire here, too, and smaller-scale works of both opera and dance are presented in the Linbury Theatre and Clore Studio Upstairs. A small allocation of tickets for each performance of main stage productions for the week ahead—even those that are sold out—goes on sale online at 1 pm every Friday. ■**TIP**➜ **If you wish to see the famed auditorium but are not able to procure a ticket, you can join a backstage tour or one of the less frequent tours of the auditorium; they book up several weeks in advance.** BP Big Screens is the ROH's summer series of live relays of its opera and ballet productions. Screenings are free and take place outdoors in public spaces all over the country, including Trafalgar Square. ⊠ *Bow St., Covent Garden* ☎ *020/7304-4000* ⊕ *www.roh.org.uk* ⊠ *Performances from £4; tours from £10* Ⓜ *Covent Garden.*

Shopping

BOOKS

★ Foyles

BOOKS/STATIONERY | FAMILY | Founded in 1903 by the Foyle brothers after they failed the Civil Service exams, this family-owned bookstore is in a 1930s art deco building, once the home of the renowned art college Central Saint Martins. One of London's best sources for textbooks and the United Kingdom's largest retailer of foreign language books, with more than 200,000 titles on its four miles of bookshelves, Foyles also stocks everything from popular fiction to military history, sheet music, medical tomes, graphic novels, and handsome, illustrated fine arts books. It also offers the store-within-a-store Ray's Jazz (one of London's better outlets for music) and a cool café. Foyles also has branches in the Royal Festival Hall at the Southbank Centre and at Waterloo Station. ✉ *107 Charing Cross Rd., Soho* ☎ *020/7437–5660* ⊕ *www. foyles.co.uk* Ⓜ *Leicester Sq., Tottenham Court Rd.*

CLOTHING

Covent Garden Market

OUTDOOR/FLEA/GREEN MARKETS | FAMILY | This popular destination includes three separate market areas: the Apple Market, the East Colonnade Market, and the Jubilee Market. In the covered area originally designed by Inigo Jones and known as the Apple Market, 40 stalls sell handcrafted jewelry, prints, clothes (such as hand-painted dancewear), ceramics, and crafts Tuesday through Sunday, while Monday is given over to antiques, curios, and collectables. The East Colonnade Market has stalls with mostly handmade specialty items that include soaps and jewelry, as well as housewares, accessories, and magic tricks. The Jubilee Market, in Jubilee Hall toward Southampton Street, tends toward the more pedestrian (kitschy T-shirts, unremarkable household goods, and the like) Tuesday through Friday, but has vintage collectibles and antiques on Monday and worthwhile handmade goods on weekends. Largely aimed at the tourist trade in the past, Covent Garden Market continues its ascent, introducing a more sophisticated image (and correspondingly higher prices) with the opening of upscale restaurants and chains in the surrounding arcades, including the world's second largest Apple Store; beauty outlets for Chanel, M.A.C., and Dior; and boutiques for brands like Tumi, Mulberry, and N. Peal. ■**TIP→ Don't miss the magicians, musicians, jugglers, and escape artists who perform in the open-air piazza; the performances are free (though contributions are welcome).** ✉ *The Piazza, off Wellington St., Covent Garden* ⊕ *www.coventgarden.london* Ⓜ *Covent Garden.*

★ Paul Smith

CLOTHING | British classics with an irreverent twist define Paul Smith's collections for women, men, and children. Beautifully tailored suits for men and women take hallmarks of traditional British style and turn them on their heads with humor and color, combining exceptional fabrics with flamboyant linings or unusual detailing. Gift ideas abound—wallets, scarves, phone cases, and distinctive belts and socks—all in Smith's signature rainbow stripes. There are several branches throughout London, in Notting Hill, Soho, Marylebone, Southwark, and Canary Wharf, plus a Mayfair shop that includes vintage furniture. ✉ *40–44 Floral St., Covent Garden* ☎ *020/7379–7133* ⊕ *www. paulsmith.com* Ⓜ *Covent Garden.*

DEPARTMENT STORES

★ Liberty

DEPARTMENT STORES | FAMILY | The wonderful, black-and-white, mock-Tudor facade, created from the timbers of two Royal Navy ships, reflects this store's origins in the late-19th-century Arts and Crafts movement. Leading designers were recruited to create the classic art nouveau Liberty prints that are still a centerpiece of the brand, gracing everything from cushions and silk kimonos to embossed leather bags and photo albums. Inside, Liberty is a labyrinth of nooks and crannies stuffed with thoughtfully chosen merchandise, including niche beauty, perfume, footwear, and housewares lines such as Soho Home, which features furniture and textiles from the membership clubs. Clothes for both men and women focus on high quality and high fashion, with labels like Rixo and Roland Mouret. The store regularly commissions new prints from contemporary designers, and it sells both these and its classic patterns by the yard. If you're not so handy with a needle, an interior design service will create soft furnishings for you. There's also a florist, a hair salon, a traditional men's barber, branded beauty treatment rooms, a brow bar, a piercing studio, and a foot spa. ⊠ *Regent St., Soho* ☎ *020/7734–1234* ⊕ *www.libertylondon.com* Ⓜ *Oxford Circus.*

TOYS

★ Benjamin Pollock's Toyshop

TOYS | FAMILY | This landmark shop still carries on the tradition of its founder, who sold miniature theater stages made from richly detailed paper from the late 19th century until his death in 1937. Among his admirers was Robert Louis Stevenson, who wrote, "If you love art, folly, or the bright eyes of children, speed to Pollock's." Today the antique model theaters are expensive, but there are plenty of magical reproductions for less than £10. There's also an extensive selection of new but nostalgic puppets, marionettes, teddy bears, spinning tops, jack-in-the-boxes, and similar traditional children's toys from the days before batteries were required (or toys were even run on them). ⊠ *44 The Market Bldg., Covent Garden* ☎ *020/7379–7866* ⊕ *www.pollocks-coventgarden.co.uk* Ⓜ *Covent Garden.*

Bloomsbury and Holborn

With the British Library, the British Museum, and countless colleges of the University of London, Bloomsbury might appear all bookish and cerebral, but fear not, it's much more than that. There's a youthfulness about its buzzing thoroughfares, and this vitality extends from down-by-the-Thames Holborn—once Dickens territory, now the heartbeat of legal London—way up to the revamped King's Cross and classy Islington to the north, and cool Clerkenwell out east.

GETTING HERE

The Russell Square Tube stop on the Piccadilly Line leaves you right at the corner of Russell Square. Tottenham Court Road on the Northern and Central lines is best for the British Museum.

Sights

British Library

LIBRARY | FAMILY | With a collection totaling more than 150 million items, plus 3 million new additions every year, the British Library is a world-class repository of knowledge. Its greatest treasures are on view to the general public in the Sir John Ritblat Gallery: the Magna Carta, the Codex Sinaiticus (an ancient bible containing the oldest complete copy of the New Testament), Jane Austen's writings, and Shakespeare's First Folio, as well as musical manuscripts by Handel and Beethoven and original handwritten lyrics by the Beatles. ⊠ *96 Euston Rd., Bloomsbury* ☎ *0330/333–1144* ⊕ *www. bl.uk* ⊠ *Free, donations appreciated; charge for special exhibitions* Ⓜ *Euston, Euston Sq., King's Cross St. Pancras.*

★ British Museum

MUSEUM | FAMILY | The sheer scale and importance of the British Museum's many treasures is impossible to overstate or exaggerate; it truly is one of the world's great repositories of human civilization. Established in 1753 and initially

The massive, glass-roofed Great Court in the British Museum has a couple of cafés.

based on the library and "cabinet of curiosities" of the Royal Physician Sir Hans Sloane, the collection grew exponentially over the following decades, partly due to bequests and acquisitions, but also as a result of plundering by the burgeoning British Empire. Inside are some of the greatest relics of humankind: the Parthenon Sculptures (Elgin Marbles), the Rosetta Stone, the Sutton Hoo Treasure, Egyptian mummies, a colossal statue of Ramesses II, fragments of the Seven Wonders of the Ancient World—almost everything, it seems, but the original Ten Commandments. The museum's focal point is the **Great Court**, a brilliant modern design with a vast glass roof atop the museum's covered courtyard. The elegant **Reading Room**, with its gorgeous blue-and-gold dome, hosts temporary exhibitions. ■**TIP→ Free tours cover the highlights in an economical 30 or 40 minutes.** ⊠ *Great Russell St., Bloomsbury* ☎ *020/7323–8000* ⊕ *www.britishmuseum.org* 🎟 *Free; donations encouraged* Ⓜ *Russell Sq., Holborn, Tottenham Court Rd.*

Charles Dickens Museum

MUSEUM | This is one of the few London houses Charles Dickens (1812–70) inhabited that is still standing, and it's the place where he wrote *Oliver Twist* and *Nicholas Nickleby.* The house looks exactly as it would have in Dickens's day, complete with first editions, letters, and a tall clerk's desk (Dickens wrote standing up). Catch the fascinating Housemaid's Tour (£15) in which you're taken back in time to 1839 by Dickens's housemaid who reveals the private lives of the great author and his family; note that it's only available select Sunday mornings and must be booked in advance. ⊠ *48 Doughty St., Bloomsbury* ☎ *020/7405–2127* ⊕ *www.dickensmuseum.com* 🎟 *£10* ☉ *Closed Mon.* Ⓜ *Chancery La., Russell Sq.*

Lincoln's Inn

BUILDING | There's plenty to see at one of the oldest, best preserved, and most attractive of the Inns of Court—from the Chancery Lane Tudor brick gatehouse to the wide-open, tree-lined, atmospheric

Lincoln's Inn Fields and the 15th-century chapel remodeled by Inigo Jones in 1620. The chapel and the gardens are open to the public, but to see more you must reserve a place on one of the official tours. But be warned: they tend to prefer group bookings of 15 or more, so it's best to check the website or call for details. ⊠ *Chancery La., Holborn* ☎ *020/7405–1393* ⊕ *www.lincolnsinn.org.uk* ⌲ *Free* ⊙ *Closed weekends* Ⓜ *Chancery La.*

★ Sir John Soane's Museum

HOUSE | Sir John (1753–1837), architect of the Bank of England, bequeathed his eccentric house to the nation on one condition: that nothing be changed. It's a house full of surprises. In the Picture Room, two of Hogarth's famous *Rake's Progress* paintings swing away to reveal secret gallery recesses where you can find works by Canalotto and Turner. Everywhere, mirrors play tricks with light and space, and split-level floors worthy of a fairground fun house disorient you. Soane's lovingly restored private apartments are also open to the public, but they can only be viewed as part of a first-come, first-served tour at 1:15 pm and 2 pm daily. While entry to the house is free (with a suggested donation), you must book timed tickets at least a day in advance online or over the phone. ⊠ *13 Lincoln's Inn Fields, Bloomsbury* ☎ *020/7405–2107* ⊕ *www.soane.org* ⌲ *Free; guided tours £15* ⊙ *Closed Mon. and Tues.* Ⓜ *Holborn.*

🍴 Restaurants

Berners Tavern

$$$ | MODERN BRITISH | FAMILY | All the cool cats swing by this grand brasserie at Ian Schrager's insanely trendy London Edition hotel near Tottenham Court Road. Enter the monumental Edwardian dining salon, where you might swoon over a light lunch of hot smoked Loch Duart salmon or an evening dinner of Herdwick lamb rump with maitake mushrooms and salsa verde. **Known for:** knock-out dining

salon; cool back-lit cocktail bar; legendary Buccleuch Estate beef tartare. ⑤ *Average main: £30* ⊠ *The London Edition, 10 Berners St., Fitzrovia* ☎ *020/7908–7979* ⊕ *www.bernerstavern.com* Ⓜ *Oxford Circus, Tottenham Court Rd.*

★ Clipstone

$$$ | FRENCH | Flavorful, inventive dishes elevate this hipster casual joint to the top rank of London's mid-range gastro titans. With a focus on in-house curing, pickling, smoked meats, and heritage vegetables, expect a cavalcade of unlikely combinations and classic gastronomy specialties. **Known for:** fine dining without the fuss; lots of house-made, pickled, fermented, or cured extras; good value set lunches. ⑤ *Average main: £28* ⊠ *5 Clipstone St., Fitzrovia* ☎ *020/7637–0871* ⊕ *www.clipstonerestaurant.co.uk* ⊙ *Closed Sun.* Ⓜ *Great Portland St., Warren St.*

★ The Delaunay

$$$ | AUSTRIAN | FAMILY | It's all *fin de siècle* Vienna at this evocative art deco–style grand café on the Aldwych near Covent Garden. Dishes on the majestic 60-item menu would do the Austro Hungarian Empire proud—think Wiener schnitzel, Hungarian goulash, beef Stroganoff, and wonderful *würstchen* (frankfurters and hot dogs) served with sauerkraut and onions. **Known for:** elegant old-world Austro-Hungarian haunt; proper Holstein schnitzel and frankfurters; excellent wine list. ⑤ *Average main: £25* ⊠ *55 Aldwych, Holborn* ☎ *020/7499–8558* ⊕ *www.thedelaunay.com* Ⓜ *Covent Garden, Holborn.*

Noble Rot

$$$ | BRITISH | There's an old Amsterdam coffeehouse vibe at this dark and creaky wine bar and restaurant on historic Lamb's Conduit Street in Bloomsbury. Run by two wine buffs and cult wine magazine publishers, you'll find deceptively simple ingredient-driven British dishes like Whitstable oyster and Cornish turbot braised in oxidized 1998 Bâtard-Montrachet Grand Cru. **Known for:** paradise for oenophiles; unpretentious

Bloomsbury and Holborn

A **B** **C** **D** **E**

SOMERS TOWN

Ⓤ **Mornington Crescent**

King's Cross Station

King's Cross St. Pancras

Regent's Park

St. Pancras Station

The British Library ①

⑥

Euston Station

Euston Square Ⓤ

Warren Street Ⓤ

Great Portland Street Ⓤ

Regent's Park Ⓤ

University College London

②

Russell Square Ⓤ

Coram's Fields

BLOOMSBURY

University of London

Russell Sq.

British Museum ②

FITZROVIA

Holborn Ⓤ

①

③
①

Tottenham Court Rd Ⓤ

Oxford Circus Ⓤ

Oxford Circus

Covent Garden

Covent Garden Ⓤ

KEY

① Sights
① Restaurants
① Hotels

Sights ▼

1 British Library **D3**
2 British Museum **D5**
3 Charles Dickens Museum **F4**
4 Lincoln's Inn **F6**
5 Sir John Soane's Museum **F6**

Restaurants ▼

1 Berners Tavern **C6**
2 Clipstone................ **B5**
3 The Delaunay **F7**
4 Noble Rot **F5**
5 St. John **H5**

Hotels ▼

1 Charlotte Street Hotel.................... **C6**
2 Harlingford Hotel **D4**
3 The London Edition ... **C6**
4 The Rookery............ **H5**
5 Rosewood London.... **F6**

6 St. Pancras Renaissance **D3**
7 The Zetter.............. **H4**

seasonal British and French wine-friendly fare; neat combos like leeks vinaigrette and Brixham crab. $ *Average main: £26* ✉ *51 Lamb's Conduit St., Bloomsbury* ☎ *020/7242–8963* ⊕ *www.noblerot.co.uk* ⊘ *Closed Sun.* Ⓜ *Holborn.*

★ St. John

$$ | **MODERN BRITISH** | **FAMILY** | Global foodie fanatics join Clerkenwell locals for the pioneering nose-to-tail cuisine at this high-ceilinged, converted smoke-house near Smithfield Market. Here the chef uses all scraps of a carcass—from tongue and cheeks to tail and trotters—so brace for radically stark signatures like bone-marrow-and-parsley salad. **Known for:** ground zero of influential Modern British nose-to-tail dining; great wine list; crispy pig's-skin appetizer. $ *Average main: £23* ✉ *26 St. John St., Clerkenwell* ☎ *020/7251–0848* ⊕ *www.stjohnrestaurant.com* ⊘ *No dinner Sun.* Ⓜ *Farringdon, Barbican.*

Hotels

★ Charlotte Street Hotel

$$$ | **HOTEL** | Superstar London hotel designer Kit Kemp has taken the fabled Bloomsbury Group as her inspiration for this super stylish boutique hotel, which, if anything, feels more like a private members' club. **Pros:** elegant and luxurious; great attention to detail; excellent, lively location. **Cons:** the popular bar can be noisy; reservations essential for the restaurant; some rooms are small considering the price. $ *Rooms from: £320* ✉ *15–17 Charlotte St., Fitzrovia* ☎ *020/7806–2000, 888/559–5508 in U.S.* ⊕ *www.firmdalehotels.com* ↩ *52 rooms* ❢⃝ *No meals* Ⓜ *Goodge St.*

Harlingford Hotel

$$ | **HOTEL** | The most contemporary of the hotels around Bloomsbury's Cartwright Gardens offers sleek, quiet, and comfortable bedrooms and perfectly appointed public rooms. **Pros:** good location; free Wi-Fi; private garden. **Cons:** rooms are small; no air-conditioning; no elevator. $ *Rooms from: £140* ✉ *61–63 Cartwright Gardens, Bloomsbury* ☎ *020/7387–1551* ⊕ *www.harlingfordhotel.com* ↩ *43 rooms* ❢⃝ *Free breakfast* Ⓜ *Russell Sq.*

★ The London Edition

$$$ | **HOTEL** | Style and image are the draw at the London Edition Hotel, where Michelin-starred chefs and hip bars complement the boutique property's sleek, contemporary design. **Pros:** very trendy; great bars; beautifully designed bedrooms. **Cons:** rooms may feel small to some; lobby can get crowded with trendsetters descending upon the bars; can at times feel more like an events space than a hotel. $ *Rooms from: £333* ✉ *10 Berners St., Fitzrovia* ☎ *020/7781–0000* ⊕ *edition-hotels.marriott.com/london* ↩ *173 rooms* ❢⃝ *Free breakfast* Ⓜ *Oxford Circus.*

★ The Rookery

$$ | **HOTEL** | A stylish period masterpiece in the heart of laid-back Clerkenwell, the Rookery is a luxury boutique hotel with a hefty dollop of *Downton Abbey* charm. **Pros:** charming decor; free Wi-Fi; good deals in the off-season. **Cons:** breakfast costs extra; no restaurant in the hotel; the resident cat might put off guests with allergies. $ *Rooms from: £240* ✉ *12 Peter's La., at Cowcross St., Clerkenwell* ☎ *020/7336–0931* ⊕ *www.rookeryhotel.com* ↩ *33 rooms* ❢⃝ *No meals* Ⓜ *Farringdon.*

Rosewood London

$$$$ | **HOTEL** | So striking it was featured in the movie *Howards End,* this landmark structure (originally built by the Pearl Assurance Company in 1914) now houses a luxurious hotel with a clubby atmosphere, elegant decor and furnishings, and huge comfortable beds. **Pros:** gorgeous romantic space; excellent restaurant; great spa. **Cons:** luxury comes at a price; the area can be quiet on weekends; the rooms can't quite match the splendor of the public areas. $ *Rooms from: £500* ✉ *252 High Holborn, Holborn*

☎ 020/7781–8888, 888/767–3966 in U.S. ⊕ www.rosewoodhotels.com/en/london �']306 rooms ⎮❍⎮ No meals Ⓜ Holborn.

★ **St. Pancras Renaissance**
$$$ | HOTEL | This stunningly restored Victorian landmark—replete with gingerbread turrets and neo-Gothic flourishes—started as a love letter to the golden age of railways, and now it's one of London's most sophisticated places to stay. **Pros:** unique and beautiful; faultless service; close to the train station. **Cons:** very crowded bar and restaurant; streets outside are busy 24/7; free Wi-Fi only in the lobby and public areas. $ Rooms from: £270 ✉ Euston Rd., King's Cross ☎ 020/7041–3540 ⊕ www.marriott.com/hotels/travel/lonpr-st-pancras-renaissance-hotel-london ➷ 245 rooms ⎮❍⎮ No meals Ⓜ King's Cross St. Pancras. National Rail: Kings Cross, St. Pancras.

★ **The Zetter**
$$ | HOTEL | The five-story atrium, art deco staircase, and slick European restaurant hint at the delights to come in this converted warehouse—a breath of fresh air with its playful color schemes, elegant wallpapers, and wonderful views of the city from the higher floors. **Pros:** huge amounts of character; big rooms; free Wi-Fi. **Cons:** rooms with good views cost more; the contemporary style won't appeal to everyone; the property's best bar is across the street at the Zetter Townhouse. $ Rooms from: £140 ✉ 86–88 Clerkenwell Rd., Clerkenwell ☎ 020/7324–4444 ⊕ www.thezetter.com ➷ 59 rooms ⎮❍⎮ Free breakfast Ⓜ Farringdon.

 Nightlife

BARS
The Lamb
BARS/PUBS | FAMILY | Charles Dickens and his contemporaries drank here, but today's enthusiastic clientele make sure this intimate and eternally popular pub avoids the pitfalls of feeling too old-timey.

One interesting feature: for private chats at the bar, you can close a delicate etched-glass "snob screen" to the bar staff, opening it only when you fancy another pint. ✉ 94 Lamb's Conduit St., Bloomsbury ☎ 020/7405–0713 ⊕ www.thelamblondon.com Ⓜ Russell Sq.

Princess Louise
BARS/PUBS | FAMILY | This fine popular pub is an exquisite museum piece of a Victorian interior, with glazed tiles and intricately engraved glass screens that divide the bar area into cozy little annexes. It's not all show, either. There's a good selection of excellent-value Yorkshire real ales from Samuel Smith's brewery. ✉ 208 High Holborn, Holborn ☎ 020/7405–8816 ⊕ www.princesslouisepub.co.uk Ⓜ Holborn.

 Performing Arts

Almeida Theatre
THEATER | This Off West End venue, helmed by director Rupert Goold, premieres excellent new plays and exciting twists on the classics, often featuring high-profile actors. There's a good café and a licensed bar that serves "sharing dishes," as well as tasty main courses. ✉ Almeida St., Islington ☎ 020/7359–4404 ⊕ www.almeida.co.uk ☎ From £10 Ⓜ Angel, Highbury & Islington.

Little Angel Theatre
PUPPET SHOWS | FAMILY | Innovative puppetry performances for children and adults have been taking place in this adorable former temperance hall since 1961. ✉ 14 Dagmar Passage, Islington ☎ 020/7226–1787 ⊕ www.littleangeltheatre.com ☎ From £7 Ⓜ Angel, Highbury & Islington.

The Place
DANCE | This is London's only theater dedicated solely to contemporary dance, and with tickets under £20, it's good value, too. The Resolution Festival, held in January and February, is the United Kingdom's biggest platform event for new choreographers. There's also an

excellent bar and café. ⊠ *17 Duke's Rd., Bloomsbury* ☎ *020/7121–1100* ⊕ *www.theplace.org.uk* ◪ *From £10* Ⓜ *Euston.*

★ **Sadler's Wells**

DANCE | FAMILY | If you're into leading classical and contemporary dance companies, head to this purpose-built complex, which opened in 1998 and is the sixth theater on this site in its 300 year history. Choreographers like Matthew Bourne and Hofesh Shechter often bring their work here. The little Lilian Baylis Studio hosts avant-garde work. ⊠ *Rosebery Ave., Islington* ☎ *020/7863–8000* ⊕ *www.sadlerswells.com* ◪ *From £12* Ⓜ *Angel.*

 Shopping

ACCESSORIES

★ **James Smith & Sons Ltd.**

JEWELRY/ACCESSORIES | This has to be the world's ultimate umbrella shop (it is definitely Europe's oldest), and it's a must for anyone interested in real Victorian London. The family-owned shop has been in this location on a corner of New Oxford Street since 1857 and sells every kind of umbrella, parasol, cane, and walking stick imaginable (including some containing a small flask or a corkscrew or that fold out into a seat). The interior is unchanged since the 19th century; you will feel as if you have stepped back in time. Prices range from about £40 for a folding umbrella to more than £400 for a classic blackthorn root-knob solid stick umbrella to thousands for bespoke items. If the umbrella prices are too steep, smaller accessories like an oxhorn shoehorn or salt spoon make perfect gifts. ⊠ *Hazelwood House, 53 New Oxford St., Bloomsbury* ☎ *020/7836–4731* ⊕ *www.james-smith.co.uk* ☉ *Closed Sun.* Ⓜ *Tottenham Court Rd., Holborn.*

ANTIQUES

London Silver Vaults

ANTIQUES/COLLECTIBLES | Originally built in 1876 as Britain's first safe deposit building, this extraordinary space five floors beneath ground level has been converted to more than 30 small shops housing silver (plus a few jewelry) dealers, the majority of which are family businesses. Products range from 16th-century items to contemporary pieces (with everything in between), and from the spectacularly over-the-top costing thousands to smaller items—like teaspoons, candlesticks, or a set of Victorian cake forks—at £25. ⊠ *53–64 Chancery La., Holborn* ☎ *020/7242–3844* ⊕ *www.silvervaultslondon.com* ☉ *Closed Sun.* Ⓜ *Chancery La.*

The City

The capital's fast-beating financial heart, the City is associated with power and pomp, embodied in the three institutions at its epicenter: the Bank of England, the Royal Exchange, and Mansion House. The site of the original Roman settlement from which all of London grew, the "Square Mile" has statement skyscrapers cheek-by-jowl with some of London's most iconic historic buildings, from Wren's uplifting St. Paul's Cathdral to the Tower of London, a royal fortress, prison, and jewel house surrounded by a moat.

GETTING HERE

The City is well served by a concentration of Tube stations—St. Paul's and Bank on the Central Line, and Mansion House, Cannon Street and Monument on the District and Circle lines. Liverpool Street and Aldgate border the City's eastern edge, while Chancery Lane and Farringdon lie to the west. Barbican and Moorgate provide easy access to the theaters and galleries of the Barbican, and Blackfriars, to the south, leads to Ludgate Circus and Fleet Street.

◉ Sights

★ Museum of London

MUSEUM | FAMILY | If there's one place to absorb the history of London, from 450,000 BC to the present day, it's here. There are 7,000 objects to wonder at in all, including Oliver Cromwell's death mask, Queen Victoria's crinolines, Selfridges's art deco elevators, and an original door from the infamous Newgate Prison. The collection devoted to Roman London contains some extraordinary gems, including an astonishingly well-preserved floor mosaic uncovered just a few streets away. Innovative interactive displays abound, and there's also a fine schedule of temporary exhibitions. Don't miss the extraordinary Bronze Age and Roman artifacts unearthed during construction of the new Crossrail underground railway. ⊠ *150 London Wall, City of London* ☎ *020/7001-9844* ⊕ *www.museumoflondon.org.uk* ⊠ *Free* Ⓜ *Barbican, St. Paul's.*

★ St. Paul's Cathedral

RELIGIOUS SITE | For centuries, this iconic structure has represented London's spirit of survival and renewal, and it remains breathtaking, inside and out. The structure is Sir Christopher Wren's masterpiece, completed in 1710 after 35 years of building, and, much later, miraculously spared (mostly) by World War II bombs. It was actually Wren's third plan for the cathedral that was accepted, though he added the distinctive dome later. Up 163 spiral steps is the **Whispering Gallery**, with its incredible acoustic phenomenon; you whisper something to the wall on one side, and a second later it transmits clearly to the other side, 112 feet away. From the upper galleries you can walk outside for a spectacular panorama of London. As in Westminster Abbey, prominent people are buried inside the cathedral, including Wren himself, as well as the poet John Donne, the Duke of Wellington, and Admiral Lord Nelson. Free, 90-minute, guided tours take place

Monday to Saturday at 10, 11, 1, and 2; book a place at the welcome desk (on the day of only). ⊠ *St. Paul's Churchyard, City of London* ☎ *020/7246-8350* ⊕ *www.stpauls.co.uk* ⊠ *£20* ⊗ *Closed Sun. except for services* Ⓜ *St. Paul's.*

Tower Bridge

BRIDGE/TUNNEL | Despite its medieval appearance, Britain's most iconic bridge was actually built at the tail end of the Victorian age, first opening to traffic in 1894. Constructed of steel, then clothed in Portland stone, the Horace Jones masterpiece was built in the Gothic style that was highly popular at the time (and it nicely complements the Tower of London, next door). The bridge is famous for its enormous bascules—the 1,200-ton "arms" that open to allow large ships to glide beneath. This still happens several times per month (the website lists upcoming times), but when river traffic was dense, the bascules were raised up to 30 times a day. The **Tower Bridge Exhibition** is a family-friendly tour where you can discover how the bridge actually works before heading out onto the walkways for wonderful city views. ⊠ *Tower Bridge Rd., City of London* ☎ *020/7403-3761* ⊕ *www.towerbridge.org.uk* ⊠ *From £10* Ⓜ *Tower Hill.*

★ Tower of London

CASTLE/PALACE | FAMILY | Nowhere else does London's history come to life so vividly as it does in this minicity of 20 towers that have housed a palace, barracks, the Royal Mint, archives, an armory, and even the Royal Menagerie. Conceived in 1078 by William the Conqueror, the Tower has been a place of imprisonment, torture, and execution for the realm's most notorious traitors and a few innocents as well. Allow at least three hours for exploring, and take time to stroll along the battlements. Highlights include the **Crown Jewels**, the **White Tower** (the oldest structure here, which includes the Armouries), the Medieval Palace, and **Bloody Tower**. Free tours by

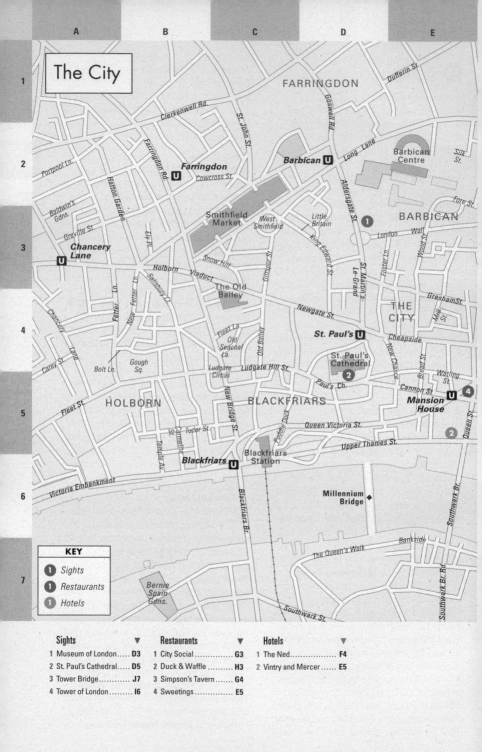

The City

FARRINGDON

Dufferin St.

Clerkenwell Rd.

Portpool Ln.

Baldwin's Gdns.

Hatton Garden

Greville St.

Farringdon U

Cowcross St.

St. John St.

Farringdon Rd.

Goswell Rd.

Long Lane

Barbican U

Barbican Centre

Silk St.

Fore St.

BARBICAN

Chancery Lane U

Ely Pl.

Elm Fetter Ln.

Salisbury Ct.

Holborn

Viaduct

Snow Hill

Smithfield Market

West Smithfield

Little Britain

King Edward St.

Aldersgate St.

St. Martin's Le-Grand

London Wall

Wood St.

Gresham St.

Milk St.

THE CITY

London Wall

Giltspur St.

The Old Bailey

Newgate St.

St. Paul's U

Cheapside

New Change

Fleet La.

Old Seacoal La.

Old Bailey

Chancery Lane

Carey St.

Bolt Ln.

Gough Sq.

Ludgate Circus

Ludgate Hill St.

St. Paul's Cathedral

Paul's Ch.

Bread St.

Watling St.

Cannon St.

Mansion House U

Queen St.

HOLBORN

Fleet St.

Tudor St.

Temple Av.

Carmelite St.

New Bridge St.

BLACKFRIARS

Puddle Dock

Queen Victoria St.

Upper Thames St.

Blackfriars U

Blackfriars Station

Victoria Embankment

Blackfriars Br.

Millennium Bridge ◆

Southwark Br.

Bankside

The Queen's Walk

Bernie Spain Gdns.

Southwark St.

Southwark Br. Rd.

KEY
- ① Sights
- ① Restaurants
- ① Hotels

Sights ▼	Restaurants ▼	Hotels ▼
1 Museum of London..... **D3**	1 City Social **G3**	1 The Ned................. **F4**
2 St. Paul's Cathedral..... **D5**	2 Duck & Waffle **H3**	2 Vintry and Mercer **E5**
3 Tower Bridge............. **J7**	3 Simpson's Tavern **G4**	
4 Tower of London......... **I6**	4 Sweetings **E5**	

Walking over the Millennium Bridge takes you to St. Paul's Cathedral, the Sir Christopher Wren–designed masterpiece that is one of the most beautiful cathedrals in England.

the Yeoman Warders, better known as the Beefeaters (who also mind the Tower's ravens), depart every half hour from the main entrance. ■TIP➔ **Buy tickets in advance whenever possible; write several months in advance to get free tickets to the 700-year-old Ceremony of the Keys (the nightly locking of main gates).** ⊠ *Tower Hill, City of London* ☎ *020/3166–6000* ⊕ *www.hrp.org.uk* ⌁ *£28 (£25 online)* Ⓜ *Tower Hill.*

🍴 Restaurants

City Social

$$$$ | **MODERN BRITISH** | A largely corporate crowd comes here for the Manhattan-esque views of the City and chef Jason Atherton's masterful but straightforward cuisine. Impressed diners look out from level 24 of Tower 42 on a majestic panorama that takes in iconic buildings like the Gherkin and the Walkie Talkie. **Known for:** majestic panoramas of the City; gutsy steak and fish standards; suited financiers and corporate deal-maker crowd. ⑤ *Average main: £34* ⊠ *Tower 42, 25 Old Broad St., City of London* ☎ *020/7877–7703* ⊕ *www.citysociallon-don.com* ⊙ *Closed Sun. No lunch Sat.* Ⓜ *Liverpool St.*

Duck & Waffle

$$ | **MODERN BRITISH** | **FAMILY** | Zoom up to the 40th floor of 110 Bishopsgate and head straight for the cult signature dish of confit duck leg, Belgium waffle, fried duck egg, and mustard maple syrup for a taste of foodie bliss. Open 24/7, with spectacular panoramas of the City, you might satisfy the munchies with a foie gras breakfast, served all day, alongside streaky bacon and housemade Nutella or an Elvis PB&J waffle with banana brûlée. **Known for:** rare-to-London 24-hour service; awe-inspiring panoramas of London's skyline; eponymous duck-and-waffle dish. ⑤ *Average main: £19* ⊠ *Heron Tower, 110 Bishopsgate, City of London* ☎ *020/3640–7310* ⊕ *www.duckandwaf-fle.com* Ⓜ *Liverpool St.*

Simpson's Tavern

$ | **BRITISH** | **FAMILY** | The City's oldest tavern and chop house was founded in 1757 and undoubtedly is every bit as raucous now as the day it opened. Approached via a cobbled alleyway, it draws diners who revel in the old boarding school surroundings and are eager to down oodles of claret and English tavern-style grub. **Known for:** lots of history, with past diners from diarist Samuel Pepys to Charles Dickens; signature stewed cheese on toast; charming but old-fashioned service. $ *Average main: £12* ✉ *Ball Court, 38½ Cornhill, City of London* ☎ *020/7626–9985* ⊕ *www.simpsonstavern.co.uk* ⊘ *Closed weekends. No dinner* Ⓜ *Bank.*

Sweetings

$$$ | SEAFOOD | Established in 1889 not far from St. Paul's Cathedral, little seems to have changed since the height of the British Empire at this quirky eatery. Although there are some things Sweetings doesn't do (dinner, reservations, coffee, or weekends), it does, mercifully, do great seafood. **Known for:** fresh Billingsgate fish served at raised linen-covered counters; tankards of "Black Velvet" Guinness and champagne; popular potted shrimp and Dover sole. $ *Average main: £30* ✉ *39 Queen Victoria St., City of London* ☎ *020/7248–3062* ⊕ *www.sweetingsrestaurant.co.uk* ⊘ *Closed weekends. No dinner* Ⓜ *Mansion House.*

 Hotels

★ The Ned

$$ | HOTEL | Bursting with eye-catching art deco design and achingly hip interiors, the Ned is as close to the glamour of the 1920s Jazz Age as you'll find in contemporary London. **Pros:** amazing variety of bars and restaurants, all of high quality; rooftop pool with views of St. Paul's Cathedral; beautiful interiors in all rooms. **Cons:** location in the City means public spaces get very busy after work; neighborhood is deserted on weekends; also doubles as a private members' clubs, so the vibe can get snooty. $ *Rooms from: £195* ✉ *27 Poultry, City of London*

☎ *020/3828–2000* ⊕ *www.thened.com* ⤶ *252 rooms* ⦿ *No meals* Ⓜ *Bank.*

Vintry and Mercer

$$ | HOTEL | Located close to the London Stock Exchange, merchant banks, hedgefunds, and the City's oldest guilds, the luxury boutique hotel Vintry and Mercer offers a nod to tradition then proceeds to deliver a chic, colorful, and contemporary experience that stands out in this neighborhood. **Pros:** rooms with gorgeous fabrics and chic wallpapers; excellent on-site izakaya restaurant; some rooms have stunning views of the City. **Cons:** predominantly business crowd dominates the bar and restaurant; neighborhood is extremely quiet on weekends; slightly removed from the sights of the West End. $ *Rooms from: £191* ✉ *19–20 Garlick Hill, City of London* ☎ *020/3908–8088* ⊕ *www.vintryandmercer.com* ⤶ *92 rooms* ⦿ *No meals* Ⓜ *Monument.*

 Nightlife

BARS

★ The Blackfriar

BARS/PUBS | FAMILY | A step from Blackfriars Tube station, this spectacular pub has an Arts and Crafts interior that is entertainingly, satirically ecclesiastical, with inlaid mother-of-pearl, wood carvings, stained glass, and marble pillars all over the place. Under finely lettered temperance tracts on view just below the reliefs of monks, fairies, and friars, there is a nice group of ales on tap from independent brewers. The 20th-century poet Sir John Betjeman once led a successful campaign to save the pub from demolition. ✉ *174 Queen Victoria St., City of London* ☎ *020/7236–5474* ⊕ *www.nicholsonspubs.co.uk* Ⓜ *Blackfriars.*

★ Jerusalem Tavern

BARS/PUBS | FAMILY | Loved by Londoners and owned by the well-respected St. Peter's Brewery in Suffolk, the Jerusalem Tavern is one-of-a-kind: small, historic, atmospheric, and endearingly eccentric.

Antique Delft-style tiles meld with wood and concrete in a converted watchmaker and jeweler's shop dating back to the 18th century. The beer, both bottled and on tap, is some of the best available anywhere in London. It's often busy, especially after work, but it's closed on weekends. ⊠ *55 Britton St., Clerkenwell* ☎ *020/7490–4281* ⊕ *www.stpetersbrewery.co.uk/london-pub* ⌚ *Closed weekends* Ⓜ *Farringdon.*

Ye Olde Mitre

BARS/PUBS | FAMILY | Hidden off the side of 8 Hatton Gardens (and notoriously hard to find), this cozy pub's roots go back to 1546, though it was rebuilt around 1782. Originally built for the staff of the Bishop of Ely, whose London residence was next door, it remained officially part of Cambridgeshire until the 20th century. Elizabeth I was once spotted dancing round a cherry tree here with a dashing young beau. Now it's a friendly little labyrinthine place, with a fireplace, well-kept ales, wooden beams, and traditional bar snacks. ⊠ *1 Ely Ct., City of London* ⊹ *Off 8 Hatton Gardens* ☎ *020/7405–4751* ⊕ *www.yeoldemitreholburn.co.uk* ⊙ *Closed weekends* Ⓜ *Chancery La.*

ⓧ Performing Arts

★ Barbican Centre

ART GALLERIES—ARTS | FAMILY | Opened in 1982, the Barbican is an enormous Brutalist concrete maze that Londoners either love or hate—but its importance to the cultural life of the capital is beyond dispute. At the largest performing arts center in Europe, you could listen to Elgar, see 1960s photography, and catch German animation with live accompaniment, all in one day. The main concert hall, known for its acoustics, is most famous as the home of the London Symphony Orchestra. The Barbican is also a frequent host to the BBC Symphony Orchestra. Architecture tours take place several times a week. ⊠ *Silk St., City of London* ☎ *020/7638–8891* ⊕ *www. barbican.org.uk* ✎ *Art exhibits free–£15, cinema from £6, theater and music from £10, tours £13* Ⓜ *Barbican.*

East London

Made famous by Dickens and infamous by Jack the Ripper, East London is one of London's most enduringly evocative neighborhoods, rich in popular history, architectural gems, and artists' studios. Since the early 1990s, hip gallerists, designers, and new-media entrepreneurs have colonized its handsome Georgian buildings and converted industrial lofts. Today, this collection of neighborhoods lays claim to being the city's hippest area.

GETTING HERE

The London Overground, with stops at Shoreditch High Street, Hoxton, Whitechapel, Dalston Junction, Dalston Kingsland, London Fields, Hackney Central, and Hackney Wick is the easiest way to reach East London. Alternatively, the best Tube stations to use are Old Street on the Northern Line, Bethnal Green on the Central Line, and Liverpool Street on the Metropolitan and Circle lines.

⊙ Sights

★ Christ Church, Spitalfields

RELIGIOUS SITE | This is the 1729 masterpiece of Sir Christopher Wren's associate Nicholas Hawksmoor, one of his six London churches and an example of English baroque at its finest. It was commissioned as part of Parliament's 1711 "Fifty New Churches" Act, passed in response to the influx of immigrants with the idea of providing for the religious needs of the "godless thousands"—and to help ensure they joined the Church of England, as opposed to such nonconformist denominations as the Protestant Huguenots. (It must have worked; you can still see gravestones with epitaphs in French in the crypt.) As the local silk industry declined, the church fell into disrepair, and by 1958 the structure was crumbling, with the looming prospect of demolition. But after 25 years—longer than it took to build the church—and a huge local fund-raising effort, the structure was meticulously restored and is a joy to behold, from the colonnaded Doric portico and tall spire to its soaring, heavily ornamented plaster ceiling. Its excellent acoustics make it a superb concert venue. Tours that take you "backstage" to the many hidden rooms and passages, from the tower to the vaults, are offered by appointment. There's also a café in the crypt. ⊠ *Commercial St., Spitalfields* ☎ *020/7377-2440* ⊕ *www.ccspits.org* ⌨ *Free, tours £50 per hr* ⊘ *Closed Sat.* Ⓜ *Overground: Shoreditch High St.*

★ Dennis Severs' House

HOUSE | The remarkable interiors of this extraordinary time machine of a house are the creation of Dennis Severs (1948–99), a performer-designer-scholar from Escondido, California, who dedicated his life to restoring this Georgian terraced house. More than that, he created "still life dramas" using sight, sound, and smell to evoke the world of a fictitious family of Huguenot silk weavers, the Jervises, who might have inhabited the house between 1728 and 1914. Each of the 10 rooms has a distinctive compelling atmosphere that encourages visitors to become lost in another time, deploying evocative design details like rose-laden Victorian wallpaper, Jacobean paneling, Georgian wing-back chairs, baroque carved ornaments, rich "Catholic" wall colors downstairs, and more sedate "Protestant" shades upstairs. The Silent Night candlelight tour offered Monday, Wednesday, and Friday evenings, a stroll through the rooms with no talking allowed, is the most theatrical and memorable way to experience the house. The Exclusive Silent Night visits, which conclude with champagne or mulled wine by the fire and a chat with the curators, are available one night per month (more

frequently near the Christmas holiday), and private group visits can also be arranged. ⊠ *18 Folgate St., Shoreditch* ☎ *020/7247-4013* ⊕ *www.dennissevershouse.co.uk* ⌨ *£10 Sun. and Mon., £15 Mon., Wed., and Fri. evenings* ⊘ *Closed Tues., Thurs., and Sat.* Ⓜ *Overground: Shoreditch High St.*

★ Queen Elizabeth Olympic Park

CITY PARK | FAMILY | Built for the London 2012 Olympic and Paralympic games, this 560-acre parkland still boasts some of the city's best sporting arenas. The Stadium, site of the London 2012 athletics competitions, is now home to local soccer team Westham United; it also hosts major athletic events. In addition, it's open for behind-the-scenes tours; check the website for dates. You can try four types of cycling (track, road racing, BMX, and mountain-biking) at the Lee Valley VeloPark or go for a swim in the magnificent pool within the London Aquatics Centre. The ArcelorMittal Orbit, an enormous sculpture, is well worth a visit—the views across London from the top are terrific. Thrill-seekers have a couple of options when it comes to getting back down: a gasp-inducing slide that twists its way around the outside of the structure (art buffs might recognize it as the work of Belgian artist Carsten Höller) or via vertical rappelling (available on selected dates, advance booking essential). ⊠ *East End* ☎ *080/0072-2110* ⊕ *www.queenelizabetholympicpark. co.uk* ⌨ *From £13, stadium tours £19* Ⓜ *Stratford, Hackney Wick, Pudding Mill Lane, Leyton.*

★ Regent's Canal

BODY OF WATER | The 19th-century waterway known as Regent's Canal officially starts in Little Venice in West London, but you'll find this quirky section east of City Road Basin. Join the towpath, where horses once walked as they pulled barges carrying all manner of cargo, at Wharf Road in Islington (N1) then head east on foot or by bike to experience the

East London

HAGGERSTON

SOUTH HACKNEY

Rosemary Gdns.

Shoreditch Park

HOXTON

Haggerston Park

BETHNAL GREEN

Cambridge Heath Station

Old Street

Columbia Road Flower Market

V & A Museum of Childhood

Bethnal Green

FINSBURY

Shoreditch High Street Station

Quaker St.

SPITALFIELDS

Bethnal Green Station

Moorgate

Liverpool Street Station

Spitalfields Market

Whitechapel

Liverpool Street

WHITECHAPEL

STEPNEY

Aldgate East

Bevis Marks Synagogue

Aldgate

Bank

THE CITY

Fenchurch St. Station

Swedenborg Gdns.

KEY

1 Sights
1 Restaurants
1 Hotels

Sights ▼

1 Christ Church, Spitalfields **C5**

2 Dennis Severs' House **B5**

3 Queen Elizabeth Olympic Park **E1**

4 Regent's Canal **A2**

5 Whitechapel Gallery **C6**

Restaurants ▼

1 E. Pellicci **D4**

2 Gunpowder **C6**

3 Lyle's **C4**

Hotels ▼

1 Andaz **D7**

2 The Hoxton Shoreditch **B4**

3 Town Hall Hotel and Apartments **E3**

East End from an unusual perspective. What was once a no-go area is now a route lined with trendy cafés, floating bookshops, and a distinct community of water-dwelling Londoners. The Regent's Canal runs through Hackney, before heading south through Bethnal Green and Mile End, ending up at Limehouse Basin and the River Thames. Or you can continue eastward by turning off along the Hertford Union Canal at Victoria Park, a route that eventually leads to the Queen Elizabeth Olympic Park. ⊠ *East End*.

★ Whitechapel Gallery

MUSEUM | Founded in 1901, this internationally renowned gallery mounts exhibitions that rediscover overlooked masters and showcase tomorrow's legends. Painter and leading exponent of abstract expressionism Jackson Pollock was exhibited here in the 1950s as was pop artist Robert Rauschenberg in the 1960s; the 1970s saw a young David Hockney's first solo show. The exhibitions continue to be on the cutting edge of contemporary art. The gallery also hosts talks, film screenings, workshops, and other events; tours of local galleries take place on the first Thursday of every month. Pick up a free East London art map to help you plan your visit to the area. ⊠ *77–82 Whitechapel High St., Whitechapel* ☎ *020/7522–7888* ⊕ *www. whitechapelgallery.org* ☉ *Closed Mon.* Ⓜ *Aldgate East.*

🍴 Restaurants

E. Pellicci

$ | CAFÉ | FAMILY | It's all Cockney banter and full English breakfasts at this tiny family-run café and onetime gangsters' lair near Brick Lane and Columbia Road markets. A rowdy hole-in-the-wall, it serves the greasy fry-ups Londoners still adore, like copious scrambled eggs, bacon, sausages, baked beans, toast, tomatoes, fried mushrooms, black pudding, cabbage 'n' mash, and scorching

hot tea. **Known for:** full cast of East End Cockney characters; copious full English breakfasts and builders' brew tea; cash-only cheap dishes. Ⓢ *Average main: £8* ⊠ *332 Bethnal Green Rd., Bethnal Green* ☎ *020/7739–4873* ⊕ *www.epellicci.com* ⊟ *No credit cards* ☉ *Closed Sun. and Aug. No dinner* Ⓜ *Bethnal Green.*

Gunpowder

$ | INDIAN | Eschew the myriad copy-and-paste curry houses of Brick Lane and opt instead for this broom cupboard–size Spitalfields restaurant serving flawless small plate Indian cuisine. The charming waitstaff is happy to offer guidance when it comes to the menu, with its highly original takes on authentic flavor combinations from the subcontinent. **Known for:** ingredients not normally found on Indian menus, such as duck or seabass; lines out the door, thanks to the no-reservations policy; rasam ke bomb snack, a puff of spiced potato served atop a flavorful Bloody Mary–style shot. Ⓢ *Average main: £11* ⊠ *11 White's Row, Spitalfields* ⊕ *www.gunpowderlondon.com* ☉ *Closed Sun.* Ⓜ *Liverpool St.*

★ Lyle's

$$ | MODERN BRITISH | Globally acclaimed Brit chef and co-owner James Lowe forsakes heavy sauces and sorcery at this stripped-back, informal British dining mecca in Shoreditch. Stark but highly inventive locally sourced dishes may include house-cured cod with radiant nasturtium flowers or 24-hour Cornish Helford Estuary monkfish with wood sorrel and pick-your-own East Sussex greengages. **Known for:** highly modern and airy dining space; serious new-wave British neo-bistronomy; excellent cheese plates and wines by the glass. Ⓢ *Average main: £19* ⊠ *Tea Bldg., 56 Shoreditch High St., East End* ⊕ *Entrance on Bethnal Green Rd.* ☎ *020/3011–5911* ⊕ *www. lyleslondon.com* ☉ *Closed Sun. and bank holiday Mon.* Ⓜ *Shoreditch High St.*

Afternoon Tea in London

So, what is Afternoon Tea, exactly? Well, it means real loose-leaf tea—Earl Grey, English Breakfast, Ceylon, Darjeeling, or Assam—brewed in a fine bone china or porcelain pot, and served with fine bone cups and saucers, milk or lemon, and silver spoons, taken between noon and 6 pm. Tea goers dress smartly (though not ostentatiously), and conversation by tradition should avoid politics and religion. Here are some top places in town to head:

Hands-down, the superglam **Savoy** on the Strand offers one of the most beautiful settings for tea. The Thames Foyer, a symphony of grays and golds centered around a winter garden wrought-iron gazebo, is just the place for the house pianist to accompany you as you enjoy the award-winning house teas along with finger sandwiches, housemade scones, and *yumptious* pastries.

Setting the standard in its English Tea Room for some of London's best-known traditional teas, **Brown's Hotel**, at 33 Albermarle Street—charmingly set in a classic Mayfair town house—offers Afternoon Tea for £55 or, if you wish to splash out, Champagne Tea for £65.

Moving west, you can sit looking out onto fab lawns amid mini potted orange trees at **The Orangery** in Prince William and Kate's London pad, Kensington Palace, inside resplendent Kensington Gardens. Afternoon Tea is £28 and a suitably Royal Afternoon Tea (with a glass of Laurent-Perrier) is £38.

Alternatively, add spice to your experience by trying a popular Moroccan-style Afternoon Tea at the souk-chic tearoom at **Momo** off Regent Street, where you'll enjoy sweet mint tea in colorful glass cups plus scones with fig jam, Maghrebian pastries, Moroccan chicken wraps, and honey-and-nut-rich Berber-style crêpes.

Finally, for frilly trompe l'oeil grandeur, few can compete with Afternoon Tea at **The Ritz** on Piccadilly. It's served in the impressive Palm Court, replete with marble tables, Louis XVI chaises, resplendent bouquets, and musical accompaniment: a true taste of Edwardian London in the 21st century. Afternoon Tea is £54 and Champagne Tea £81. Reserve a few months ahead and remember to wear a jacket and tie.

Hotels

Andaz

$$ | HOTEL | Swanky and upscale, this hotel sports a modern masculine design, and novel check-in procedure—instead of standing at a desk, guests sit in a lounge while a staff member with a tablet takes their information. **Pros:** nice attention to detail; no standing in line to check in; complimentary "healthy minibars" are stocked with nuts, fruit, and yogurt.

Cons: sparse interior design is not for all; rates rise significantly for midweek stays; busy, sometimes hectic neighborhood. $ *Rooms from: £240* ✉ *40 Liverpool St., East End* ☎ *020/7961–1234, 800/492–8804 in U.S.* ⊕ *www.andaz.hyatt.com* ⇥ *282 rooms* ⏸ *No meals* Ⓜ *Liverpool St.*

★ The Hoxton Shoreditch

$$ | HOTEL | The design throughout this trendy East London lodging is contemporary—but not so modern as to be absurd;

in keeping with a claim to combine a country-lodge lifestyle with true urban living, a fire crackles in the lobby. **Pros:** cool vibe; neighborhood known for funky galleries and boutiques; huge weekend discounts. **Cons:** price skyrockets during the week; away from major tourist sights; cheapest rooms are called "shoeboxes" for a reason. ⑤ *Rooms from: £149* ✉ *81 Great Eastern St., East End* ☎ *020/7550–1000* ⊕ *www.thehoxton.com* ⤳ *210 rooms* �’◯❘ *Free breakfast* Ⓜ *Shoreditch High St.*

Town Hall Hotel and Apartments
$$$ | **HOTEL** | An art deco town hall, abandoned in the early 1980s and turned into a chic hotel 30 years later, is now a lively and stylish place, with the best of the building's elegant original features intact. **Pros:** beautifully designed; lovely staff; big discounts on weekends. **Cons:** the area is far from the major sights; a 15-minute Tube ride from central London; some rooms choose style over function. ⑤ *Rooms from: £198* ✉ *Patriot Sq., Bethnal Green, East End* ☎ *020/7871–0460* ⊕ *www.townhallhotel.com* ⤳ *98 rooms* ❘◯❘ *Free breakfast* Ⓜ *Bethnal Green, Overground. Cambridge Heath.*

Nightlife

BARS
Callooh Callay
BARS/PUBS | Cocktails are tasty, well-executed classics, and there's also a selection of unique instant-classics at this eccentric Hoxton bar where the bells and whistles are left to the decor. ✉ *65 Rivington St., Hoxton* ☎ *020/7739–4781* ⊕ *www.calloohcallaybar.com* Ⓜ *Old St.*

The Ten Bells
BARS/PUBS | **FAMILY** | Although the number of bells in its name has varied between 8 and 12, depending on how many bells were used by neighboring Christ Church, Spitalfields, this pub retains it original mid-Victorian interior and original tiles, including a frieze depicting the area's

French Huguenot silk weaving tradition on the north wall and particularly fine floral tiling on two others. Urban legend says that Jack the Ripper's third victim, Annie Chapman, had a drink here before meeting her gory end. The pub is also depicted in Alan Moore's acclaimed graphic novel *From Hell.* ✉ *84 Commercial St., Spitalfields* ☎ *020/7247–7532* ⊕ *www.tenbells.com* Ⓜ *Liverpool St.*

DANCE CLUBS
★ Cafe Oto
MUSIC CLUBS | A relaxed café by day, and London's leading venue for experimental music by night, Cafe Oto is a Dalston institution. Its programming of free jazz, avant-garde electronica, and much more is enough of a draw that it regularly sells out, with music fans steaming up the windows and spilling out onto the pavement and road outside to smoke during breaks. Healthy Persian-inspired food is served in the daytime, before customers are kicked out at 5 pm to make way for sound checks. It's open as a bar (no cover) on nights when no concerts are taking place. ✉ *18–22 Ashwin St., Dalston* ⊕ *www.cafeoto.co.uk* Ⓜ *Overground: Dalston Junction.*

Shopping

CLOTHING
★ Blue Mountain School
CLOTHING | It's hard to think of somewhere more East London than Blue Mountain School, a building that comprises a fashion, furniture, and accessories archive (the focus at the boutique is slow fashion and homewares by the likes of Anecho, Geoffrey B. Small, and Amy Revier); a gallery with changing contemporary exhibits; a listening room; and a tiny chef's table restaurant from Nuno Mendes, of Chiltern Firehouse fame. Around the corner at 28 Old Nichol Street is Hostem, a more traditional format boutique selling men's and women's garments and footwear by brands such as P.R. Patterson, Casey Casey, and

Visvim. This might all sound offputtingly hip, but give it a chance; it's a beautifully curated shopping experience, albeit one that will make considerable demands on your wallet. The store also operates a three-bedroom guesthouse in a converted Georgian town house in Whitechapel. ⊠ *9 Chance St., Shoreditch* ☎ *020/7739–9733* ⊕ *www.bluemountain.school* Ⓜ *Overground: Shoreditch High St.*

Rokit

CLOTHING | Magazine and music stylists love these two premises along Brick Lane that carry everything from handbags and ball gowns to jeans, military garb, and Western wear. The ever-changing stock spans the 1930s to the 1990s. There are also branches in Camden and Covent Garden. ⊠ *101 and 107 Brick La., Spitalfields* ☎ *020/7375–3864* ⊕ *www.rokit.co.uk* Ⓜ *Overground: Shoreditch High St.*

HOUSEHOLD GOODS
Labour & Wait

HOUSEHOLD ITEMS/FURNITURE | Although mundane items like colanders and clothespins may not sound like ideal souvenirs, this shop (something of a hipster heaven selling both new and vintage items) will make you reconsider. The owners are on a mission to revive retro, functional British household goods, such as enamel kitchenware, genuine feather dusters, bread bins, bottle brushes, and traditional Welsh blankets. ⊠ *85 Redchurch St., Shoreditch* ☎ *020/7729–6253* ⊕ *www.labourandwait.co.uk* ⊘ *Closed Mon.* Ⓜ *Overground: Shoreditch High St.*

MUSIC
Rough Trade East

MUSIC STORES | Although many London record stores are struggling, this veteran indie-music specialist in the Old Truman Brewery seems to have gotten the formula right. The spacious surroundings are as much a hangout as a shop, complete with a stage for live gigs and a café. There's another branch on Talbot Road in Notting Hill. ⊠ *Dray Walk, Old Truman Brewery, 91 Brick La., Spitalfields* ☎ *020/7392–7788* ⊕ *www.roughtrade.com* Ⓜ *Liverpool St. Overground: Shoreditch High St.*

STREET MARKETS
★ Broadway Market

SHOPPING NEIGHBORHOODS | This parade of shops in hipster-centric Hackney (north of Regent's Canal) is worth visiting for the specialty bookshops, independent boutiques, organic cafés, neighborhood restaurants, and even a traditional (but now rare) pie-and-mash shop. But wait for Saturday (9–5), when it really comes into its own with a farmers' market and more than 100 street-food and produce stalls rivaling those of south London's famed Borough Market. Artisanal breads, cheeses, pastries, organic meats, waffles, fruit and vegetables, seafood, and international food offerings: this is foodie heaven. There are also stalls selling vintage clothes, crafts, jewelry, and more. ⊠ *Broadway Market, Hackney* ⊕ *www.broadwaymarket.co.uk* Ⓜ *London Fields.*

★ Columbia Road Flower Market

OUTDOOR/FLEA/GREEN MARKETS | London's premier flower market is about as pretty and photogenic as they come, with more than 50 stalls selling flowers, shrubs, bulbs, and trees—everything from bedding plants to 10-foot banana trees—as well as garden tools, pots, and accessories at competitive prices. The stallholders' patter is part of the fun. It's on Sunday only, and it's all over by 3 pm. Columbia Road itself is lined with 60 interesting independent shops purveying art, fashion, furnishings (most of which are only open on weekends), and the local cafés are superb. ⊠ *Columbia Rd., Hoxton* ⊕ *www.columbiaroad.info* ⊘ *Market closed Mon.–Sat.* Ⓜ *Old St. Overground: Hoxton.*

Old Spitalfields Market

OUTDOOR/FLEA/GREEN MARKETS | Once the East End's wholesale fruit and vegetable market and now restored to its original architectural splendor, this fine example of a Victorian market hall is at the center of the area's gentrified revival. The original building is largely occupied by shops (mostly upscale brands like Rag & Bone, Lululemon, and Superga, but some independents like trendy homeware-and-fashion purveyor the Mercantile), with traders' stalls in the courtyard. A modern shopping precinct under a Norman Foster–designed glass canopy adjoins the old building and holds approximately 70 traders' stalls. You may have to wade through a certain number of stalls selling cheap imports and tacky T-shirts to find the good stuff, which includes vintage and new clothing, handmade rugs and jewelry, hand-carved toy trains, vintage maps, unique baby clothes, rare vinyl, and cakes. Thursday is for antiques; Friday for a biweekly record fair; while weekends offer a little of everything. The Kitchens, 10 central dining venues showcasing small, independent chefs and restaurants, provide fresh takes on Mexican, Japanese, and other world cuisines. There are also indie street food stalls and some superior chain outlets. ⊠ *16 Horner Sq., Brushfield St., Spitalfields* ⊕ *www. oldspitalfieldsmarket.com* Ⓜ *Liverpool St. Overground: Shoreditch High St.*

South of the Thames

This area is a magnet for tourists and residents alike, with attractions that include the IWM London, the Southbank Centre (Europe's largest arts center), and the gastronomic delight that is Borough Market.

A borough of the City of London since 1327, Southwark first became well known for its inns (the pilgrims in Chaucer's *A Canterbury Tale* set off from one), theaters, prisons, tanneries, and brothels, as well as entertainments such as cockfighting. For four centuries, this was a sort of border town outside the city walls (and jurisdiction) where Londoners went to let their hair down and behave

badly. Originally, you were just as likely to see a few bouts of bearbaiting at the Globe as you were Shakespeare's most recent work. But now that south London encompasses a world-class museum, high-caliber art, music, film, and theater venues, as well as an aquarium, a historic warship, two popular food markets, and greatly improved transportation links, this neighborhood has become one of London's leading destinations.

GETTING HERE

For the South Bank, use Embankment on the District, Circle, Northern, and Bakerloo lines and walk across the Golden Jubilee Bridges; or Waterloo on the Northern, Jubilee, and Bakerloo lines, from where it's a 10-minute walk. London Bridge on the Northern and Jubilee lines is five minutes from Borough Market and Southwark Cathedral. The station also serves Bermondsey Street, although, confusingly, the next stop on the Jubilee Line is called Bermondsey. Brixton has its own stop on the Victoria Line.

Sights

★ Borough Market

MARKET | There's been a market in Borough since Roman times, and this latest incarnation, spread under the arches and railroad tracks leading to London Bridge Station, is where some of the city's best artisanal food producers set up stalls. Fresh coffees, gorgeous cheeses, chocolates, and baked goods complement the organically farmed meats, fresh fish, condiments, fruits, and vegetables.

Don't make any other lunch plans for the day; this is where celebrity chef Jamie Oliver's scallop man cooks them up fresh at Shellseekers, and Ginger Pig's rare-breed sausages sizzle on grills, while for the sweets lover there are chocolates, preserves, and Whirld's artisanal confectionery, as well as 18 restaurants and cafés, most above average. The Market Hall hosts workshops, tastings,

South of the Thames

Sights ▼

1 Borough Market **H4**
2 IWM London **C6**
3 London Eye **B3**
4 Shakespeare's Globe... **G2**
5 Southwark Cathedral... **H4**
6 Tate Modern............. **F3**
7 The View from
The Shard................ **H4**

Restaurants ▼

1 Casse-Croûte............. **I6**
2 José **I6**
3 Padella.................... **H4**

Hotels ▼

1 Church Street Hotel **G7**
2 Sea Containers
London **E2**
3 The Shangri-La
Hotel at the Shard **H4**

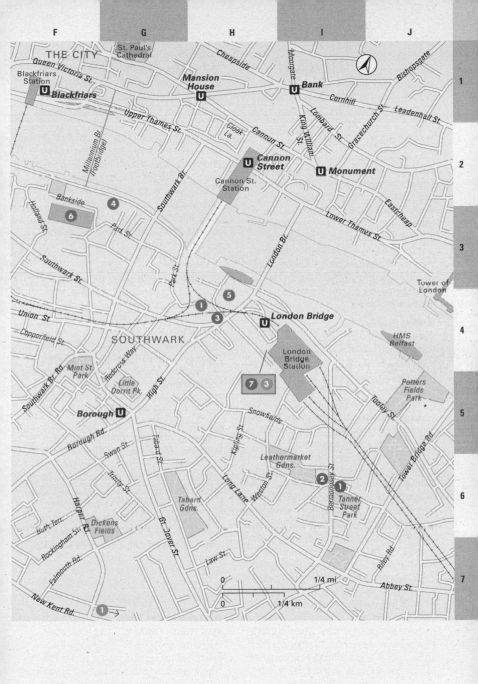

and demonstrations, and also acts as a greenhouse. The market is open Wednesday and Thursday 10–5, Friday 10–6, and Saturday 8–5, with only stalls for hot food and produce on Monday and Tuesday 10–5.

On weekends, a separate, highly regarded market specializing in produce and street food operates on nearby Maltby Street. It was originally established by eight breakaway Borough Market traders. Stalls include African Volcano, purveyors of Mozambique-style hot sauces and marinades, and Raclette Brothers' superb melted cheese. ⊠ 8 Southwark St., Borough ☎ 020/7402–1002 ⊕ www. boroughmarket.org.uk ⊙ Closed Sun. Ⓜ London Bridge.

★ IWM London

MUSEUM | FAMILY | Despite its name, the cultural venue formerly known as the Imperial War Museum (one of five IWM branches around the country) does not glorify either Empire or bloodshed but emphasizes understanding through conveying the impact of 20th- and 21st-century warfare on citizens and soldiers alike. A dramatic six-story atrium at the main entrance encloses an impressive amount of hardware—including a Battle of Britain Spitfire, a German V2 rocket, the remains of a car blown up in post-invasion Iraq, tanks, guns, and submarines—along with accompanying interactive material and a café. The First World War galleries explore the wartime experience on both the home and fighting fronts, with the most comprehensive collection on the subject in the world—some 1,300 objects ranging from uniforms, equipment, and weapons to letters and diaries. Three permanent exhibitions in the Second World War galleries shed light on that conflict: an extensive and haunting Holocaust exhibition; A Family In Wartime, which documents the story of one London family living through the Blitz; and Turning Points 1934–1945, which relates key moments in the conflict to objects on display. Peace and Security 1945–2015 looks at more contemporary hostilities, including the Cold War, Iraq, Afghanistan, and Kosovo. Other galleries are devoted to works relating to conflicts from World War I to the present day by painters, poets, documentary filmmakers, and photographers. James Bond fans won't want to miss the intriguing Secret War Gallery, which charts the work of secret agents. ⊠ Lambeth Rd., South Bank ☎ 020/7416–5000 ⊕ www.iwm.org.uk ☎ Free (charge for special exhibitions) Ⓜ Lambeth North.

★ London Eye

VIEWPOINT | FAMILY | To mark the start of the new millennium, architects David Marks and Julia Barfield devised an instant icon that allows Londoners and visitors alike to see the city from a completely new perspective. The giant Ferris wheel was the largest cantilevered observation wheel ever built at the time, and remains one of the city's tallest structures. The 25-minute slow-motion ride inside one of the enclosed passenger capsules is so smooth you'd hardly know you were suspended over the Thames. On a clear day you can see up to 25 miles, with a bird's-eye view of London's most famous landmarks as you circle 360 degrees. For an extra £10, you can save even more time with a Fast Track flight (check in 15 minutes before your "departure"). ■TIP➔ **Buy your ticket online to avoid the long lines and get a 15% discount.** ⊠ Jubilee Gardens, South Bank ☎ 0871/781–3000 ⊕ www.londoneye. com ☎ From £27; cruise package from £39 (online only) Ⓜ Waterloo.

★ Shakespeare's Globe

ARTS VENUE | FAMILY | This spectacular theater is a replica of Shakespeare's open-roof, wood-and-thatch Globe Playhouse (built in 1599 and burned down in 1613), where most of the Bard's greatest works premiered. American actor and director Sam Wanamaker worked ceaselessly for several decades to raise funds

At Shakespeare's Globe theater, you can watch the works of the Bard performed like they would've been in his day.

for the theater's reconstruction 200 yards from its original site, using authentic materials and techniques, a dream that was realized in 1997. "Ground-lings"—patrons with £5 standing-only tickets—are not allowed to sit during the performance. Fortunately, you can reserve an actual seat on any one of the theater's three levels, but you will want to rent a cushion for £2 (or bring your own) to soften the backless wooden benches. Forty-minute tours of the theater are offered every half-hour most days until 5 pm (unless there's a matinee performance or other major event, when they're offered until noon). ⌧ *21 New Globe Walk, Bankside* ☎ *020/7401–9919 general info* ⊕ *www.shakespearesglobe. com* ✉ *Globe Theatre tour £17; Bankside tour £14; Wanamaker tour £14; Globe performances £5 (standing), from £19 (seated); Wanamaker performances £10 (standing), from £20 (seated)* ⊙ *No Globe performances mid-Oct.–mid-Apr.; no Wanamaker Playhouse performances mid-Apr.–mid.-Oct.* Ⓜ *London Bridge;*

Mansion House, then cross Southwark Bridge.

Southwark Cathedral

RELIGIOUS SITE | Pronounced "Suth-uck," this is the oldest Gothic church in London, parts of it dating back to the 12th century. It remains off-the-beaten track, despite being the site of some remarkable memorials and a concert program that offers free half-hour organ recitals at 1:10 pm every Monday (except in August and December) and classical music at 3:15 pm every Tuesday during the school year. Originally the priory church of St. Mary Overie (as in "over the water," on the South Bank), it became a palace church under Henry VIII (when it became known as St Saviour's) until some merchant parishioners bought it from James I in 1611. It was only promoted to cathedral status in 1905. Look for the vivid 15th-century roof bosses (small ornamental wood carvings); the gaudily renovated 1408 tomb of John Gower, Richard II's poet laureate and a friend of Chaucer's; and the Harvard Chapel, where John Harvard, a local butcher's son who went on to found the American university, was baptized. Another notable buried here (between the choir stalls) is Edmund Shakespeare, brother of William. Free 45-minute tours are offered on Tuesday at 2 and 3 pm, Wednesday at 3 pm, Thursday at 11:30 am, and Friday at 11 am and 3 pm. ⊠ *London Bridge, Bankside* ☎ *020/7367–6700* ⊕ *cathedral. southwark.anglican.org* ⊠ *Free (suggested donation £4)* Ⓜ *London Bridge.*

★ Tate Modern

MUSEUM | This spectacular renovation of a mid-20th-century power station is one of the most-visited museums of modern art in the world. Its great permanent collection, which starts in 1900 and ranges from Modern masters like Matisse to the most cutting-edge contemporary artists, is arranged thematically (from In the Studio and Artist and Society to Materials and Society and Media Networks). Its blockbuster temporary exhibitions have showcased the work of such disparate artists as Gaugin, Roy Lichtenstein, and Dorothea Tanning. The vast **Turbine Hall** is a dramatic entrance point used to showcase big audacious installations that tend to generate a lot of publicity. Past highlights include Olafur Eliasson's massive glowing sun and Carsten Holler's huge metal slides. ⊠ *Bankside* ☎ *020/7887–8888* ⊕ *www.tate.org.uk/modern* ⊠ *Free (charge for special exhibitions)* Ⓜ *Southwark, Blackfriars, St. Paul's.*

The View from the Shard

BUILDING | At 800 feet, this addition to the London skyline currently offers the highest vantage point in Western Europe. Designed by the noted architect Renzo Piano, it has attracted both admiration and disdain. While the building itself is generally highly regarded, many felt it would have been better sited in Canary Wharf (or perhaps Dubai), as it spoils views of St. Paul's Cathedral from traditional vantage points such as Hampstead's Parliament Hill. No matter how you feel about the building, there's no denying that it offers a spectacular 360-degree view over London (extending 40 miles on a clear day) from viewing platforms on level 69, and the open-air skydeck on level 72—almost twice as high as any other viewpoint in the city. Digital telescopes provide information about 200 points of interest. There's a weather guarantee that lets you return on a more clement day if visibility is seriously impeded, and various themed events like silent discos or early morning yoga classes are offered at an extra charge. Admission is by timed ticket only. If you find the price as eye-wateringly high as the viewing platforms, there's a less dramatic but still very impressive (and free) view from the lobby of the Shangri-La hotel on the 35th floor, or, in the evenings, the hotel's chic Gong bar on the 52nd floor (over-18s only). ⊠ *Railway Approach, Borough* ☎ *0344/499–7222* ⊕ *www.theviewfromtheshard.com* ⊠ *From £32* Ⓜ *London Bridge.*

🍴 Restaurants

★ Casse-Croûte

$$ | **BISTRO** | This bistro on Bermondsey Street near the Shard is as French as a pack of Gauloises, from the yellow walls and red-and-white checked tablecloths to the perfectly executed classics like *lapin à la moutarde* (rabbit in a creamy mustard sauce), *suprême de volaille aux mousserons* (chicken breast stuffed with mushrooms), quiche Lorraine, and Paris-Brest (decadent choux pastry stuffed with praline and whipped cream). The daily changing menu offers three reasonably-priced options per course, and the wine list (French, of course) goes off-the-beaten path with discoveries from small local producers. **Known for:** beautifully prepared bistro classics; authentic French atmosphere in tight quarters; reservations necessary for dinner. ⑤ *Average main: £20* ⊠ *109 Bermondsey St., Bermondsey* ☎ *020/7407–2140* ⊕ *www.*

cassecroute.co.uk ⊗ *No dinner Sun.* Ⓜ *London Bridge.*

José
$$ | **TAPAS** | Renowned chef José Pizarro has managed to re-create an authentic, slightly rustic Spanish tapas-and-sherry bar. With just 30 seats and no reservations, it's always packed after 6 pm, but it's worth the wait for remarkably fresh, perfectly prepared classic tapas plates like *patatas bravas, croquetas*, flash-fried prawns with chili and garlic, and razor clams with chorizo. **Known for:** notoriously long waits and large crowds; daily changing menu of authentic tapas; unique sherry menu. ⑤ *Average main: £20* ⊠ *104 Bermondsey St., Southwark* ☎ *020/7103–4902* ⊕ *www.josepizarro. com/jose-tapas-bar* Ⓜ *Borough, London Bridge.*

★ Padella
$ | **ITALIAN** | Sit at the galley kitchen counter and you can watch the chefs toss hot pans of authentic handmade Italian pasta, generally considered among the best in London. The acclaimed but amazingly affordable dishes include a ravioli with Neal's Yard ricotta and sage butter, burrata with Puglian olive oil, papardelle with a slow-cooked beef-shin ragù, or Dorset crab tagliarini with chili and lemon. **Known for:** low priced, high-quality handmade Italian pasta; papardelle with eight-hour beef-shin ragù; no reservations and long waits. ⑤ *Average main: £7* ⊠ *6 Southwark St., Borough* ⊕ *www.padella.co* Ⓜ *Borough, London Bridge.*

 ## Hotels

★ Church Street Hotel
$$ | **HOTEL** | Like rays of sunshine in gritty south London, the rooms at this Camberwell hotel are decorated in rich colors that evoke Mexico, a theme enhanced by authentic touches like elaborately painted crucifixes, tiles handmade in Guadalajara, and handcrafted iron bed frames. **Pros:** individual and fun vibe; great breakfasts; closer to central London than it might appear. **Cons:** location very urban and busy; a mile from a Tube station (though bus connections are handier); some rooms have shared bathrooms. ⑤ *Rooms from: £115* ⊠ *29–33 Camberwell Church St., Camberwell, South East London* ☎ *020/7703–5984* ⊕ *www.churchstreethotel.com* ⤴ *31 rooms* ⦿I *Free breakfast* Ⓜ *Oval St.*

Sea Containers London
$$$ | **HOTEL** | The achingly hip Sea Containers started life as part of London's docklands, and is now a fun callback to the area's history. **Pros:** excellent bars and restaurants; beautiful river views; short riverside walk to Tate Modern and Shakespeare's Globe. **Cons:** river-view rooms are pricey (of course); public areas can be noisy; standard rooms are small. ⑤ *Rooms from: £256* ⊠ *Sea Containers House, 20 Upper Ground, Southwark* ☎ *020/3747–1000* ⊕ *www.seacontainerslondon.com* ⤴ *359 rooms* ⦿I *No meals* Ⓜ *Blackfriars, Southwark.*

★ The Shangri-La Hotel at the Shard
$$$$ | **HOTEL** | With its floor-to-ceiling windows, the city's highest cocktail bar and infinity pool, and unrivaled views of the London skyline from 1,016 feet above the South Bank of the Thames, the Shangri-La has become one of London's chicest addresses. **Pros:** perhaps the best views in the city; great infinity pool and spa; superb restaurants and cocktail bar. **Cons:** design flaw allows some guests to see into neighboring rooms at night; decor may be too understated for some; restaurant, bar, and elevator can be crowded due to popularity of the view. ⑤ *Rooms from: £468* ⊠ *31 St. Thomas St., South Bank* ☎ *0207/234–8000* ⊕ *www.theshard.com/shangri-la* ⤴ *202 rooms* ⦿I *No meals* Ⓜ *London Bridge Station.*

Nightlife

BARS

Aqua Shard

BARS/PUBS | This sophisticated bar on level 31 of the iconic Shard is worth a visit for the phenomenal views alone. The cocktail list is pretty special, too—big on fruit purees and unusual bitters. No reservations are taken in the bar, so be prepared to wait during busy periods. ⊠ *The Shard, 31 St. Thomas St., Level 31, London Bridge* ☎ *020/3011–1256* ⊕ *www. aquashard.co.uk* Ⓜ *London Bridge.*

Three Eight Four

BARS/PUBS | Epitomizing a new breed of Brixton bar, Three Eight Four is known for its innovative cocktails and tapas-style shared plates. The cocktail menu changes seasonally but always involves artisinal spirits and unusual mixing techniques—try the Nightshade, which comes with a pipette that you use to add the final ingredient (crème de cassis) yourself. The bare lightbulbs and stripped brick walls are a bit of a hipster bar cliché, but this place manages it with particular panache. ⊠ *384 Coldharbour La., Brixton* ☎ *020/3417–7309* ⊕ *www. threeeightfour.com* Ⓜ *Brixton.*

Performing Arts

★ Battersea Arts Centre (*BAC*)

ARTS CENTERS | Battersea Arts Centre has a reputation for producing innovative new work as well as hosting top alternative stand-up comics. Performances take place in quirky spaces all over this atmospheric former town hall. Check out Scratch events, low-tech theater where the audience provides feedback on works-in-progress. Entry for Scratch events is pay-what-you-can (minimum £3). The bar, which serves snacks and sharing plates, is open all day. ⊠ *176 Lavender Hill, Battersea* ☎ *020/7223–2223* ⊕ *www.bac.org.uk* 🎟 *Pay what you can (£3 suggested)–£30* Ⓜ *National Rail: Clapham Junction.*

BFI Southbank

FILM | With the best repertory programming in London, the four movie theaters here are effectively a national film center run by the British Film Institute. More than 1,000 titles are screened each year, with art-house, foreign, silent, overlooked, classic, noir, and short films favored over recent Hollywood blockbusters. The center also has a gallery, bookshop, and "mediatheque" where visitors can watch film and television from the National Archive for free (closed Monday). The Riverfront Bar and Kitchen offers dining with views while the Benugo BFI Bar and Kitchen is informal and buzzy. This is one of the venues for the BFI London Film Festival; throughout the year there are minifestivals, seminars, and guest speakers. ⊠ *Belvedere Rd., South Bank* ☎ *020/7928–3232* ⊕ *www. bfi.org.uk* 🎟 *From £10* Ⓜ *Waterloo.*

★ National Theatre

THEATER | FAMILY | When this complex designed by Sir Denys Lasdun opened in 1976, Londoners were slow to warm-up to the low-rise Brutalist block, with Prince Charles describing it as "a clever way of building a nuclear power station in the middle of London without anyone objecting." But whatever you think of the outside, the inside offers generally superb theatrical experiences at (relatively) friendly prices—several of which (like *War Horse* or *One Man, Two Guvnors*) have gone on to become long-running Broadway hits. Interspersed with the three theaters—the 1,150-seat Olivier, the 890-seat Lyttelton, and the 450-seat Dorfman—is a multilayered foyer with exhibitions, bars, restaurants, and free entertainment. Musicals, classics, and plays are performed by top-flight professionals, who you can sometimes catch giving foyer talks as well. Backstage, costume, and architecture tours are available daily at 9:45 am except Sunday. The Clore Learning Centre offers courses and events on different aspects of theater production, and you can watch staff at

London's Spectator Sports

Sport in the capital comes into its own when it's watched, rather than participated in. You'll most easily witness London's fervent sporting passions in front of a screen in a pub with a pint in hand. And those passions run deep.

Football

London's top teams—Chelsea, Arsenal, Tottenham Hotspur—are world-class (especially the first two) and often progress in the European Champions League. It's unlikely you'll be able to get tickets for anything except the least popular Premier League games during the August–May season, despite absurdly high ticket prices—as much as £41 for a standard, walk-up, match-day seat at Chelsea, and a whopping £126 for the match-day tickets at Arsenal.

Tennis

Wimbledon Lawn Tennis Championships The All England Club's Wimbledon Lawn Tennis Championships are famous for Centre Court, strawberries and cream, a gentle spot of rain, and a nostalgic old-school insistence on players wearing white. Thankfully, the rain has been banished on Centre Court by the nifty retractable roof, but whether you can get tickets for Centre Court all comes down to the luck of the draw—there's a ballot system for advance purchase (see website for more details). ⊠ *The All England Lawn Tennis Club, Church Rd.* ☎ *020/8971-2473 for general inquiries* ⊕ *www.wimbledon.com.*

work on set building and scenery painting from the Sherling High-Level Walkway. Each weekend in August, the free outdoor River Stage Festival presents live music, dance, family workshops, and DJ sets in front of the theater. ⊠ *Belvedere Rd., South Bank* ☎ *020/7452-3000* ⊕ *www.nationaltheatre.org.uk* ☏ *From £15, tours £13* Ⓜ *Waterloo.*

★ **Southbank Centre**
ART GALLERIES—ARTS | FAMILY | The general public has never really warmed to the Southbank Centre's hulking concrete buildings (beloved by architecture aficionados), products of the Brutalist style popular when the center was built in the 1950s and '60s—but all the same, the masses flock to the concerts, recitals, festivals, and exhibitions held here, Europe's largest arts center. The **Royal Festival Hall** is truly a People's Palace, with seats for 2,900 and a schedule that ranges from major symphony orchestras to pop stars. The smaller **Queen Elizabeth**

Hall is more classically oriented. It contains the **Purcell Room,** which hosts lectures and chamber performances. For art, head to the **Hayward Gallery,** which hosts shows on top contemporary artists such as Antony Gormley and Cy Twombly. The center's riverside street level has a terrific assortment of restaurants and bars, though you'll need to head to the Cut, just south of here, for independent eateries. ⊠ *Belvedere Rd., South Bank* ☎ *020/3879–9555* ⊕ *www.southbank-centre.co.uk* ☏ *Free–£120* Ⓜ *Waterloo, Embankment.*

Young Vic
THEATER | Just down the road from its elder sibling the Old Vic, this offshoot hosts big names performing alongside emerging talent, often in daring innovative productions of both new and classic plays that appeal to a more diverse audience than is traditionally found on the London scene. Good food is served all day at the bustling bar. ⊠ *66 The Cut,*

Waterloo, South Bank ☎ *020/7922–2922* ⊕ *www.youngvic.org* 🎫 *From £10* Ⓜ *Southwark, Waterloo.*

Kensington, Chelsea, Knightsbridge, and Notting Hill

The Royal Borough of Kensington & Chelsea (or K&C, as the locals call it) is where you'll find London at its richest, and not just in the moneyed sense. South Kensington offers a concentration of great museums near Cromwell Road, with historic Kensington Palace and Kensington Gardens nearby in Hyde Park. Once-raffish Chelsea, where the Pre-Raphaelites painted and Mick Jagger partied, is now a thoroughly respectable home for the discreetly wealthy, while flashier Knightsbridge has become a haven for international plutocrats, with shopping to match their tastes.

The center of London's West Indian community from the 1950s through the '70s, Notting Hill these days is the address of choice for the well-heeled, be they bankers, rock stars, media and advertising types, or rich hippies.

GETTING HERE

Several Tube stations are nearby: Sloane Square and High Street Kensington on the District and Circle lines; Knightsbridge and Hyde Park Corner on the Piccadilly Line; and South Kensington and Gloucester Road on the District, Circle, and Piccadilly lines. For Portobello Market and environs, the best Tube stops are Ladbroke Grove and Westbourne Park (Hammersmith and City Line); ask for directions when you emerge. The Notting Hill Gate stop on the District, Circle, and Central lines enables you to walk the length of Portobello Road while going slightly downhill.

Sights

Harrods

STORE/MALL | With an encyclopedic assortment of luxury brands, this Knightsbridge institution, currently owned by the Qatar Investment Authority, has more than 300 departments and 25 eating and drinking options, all spread over 1 million square feet on a 4½-acre site. Now populated more by window-shopping tourists and superrich visitors from abroad than by the bling-averse natives, Harrods is best approached as the world's largest, most upscale and expensive mall. After a two year redesign of the food hall, you can now find a variety of dining options on-site, including sushi, Indian, pasta, and more; all have counter seating so you can watch the chefs at work. At the center is the Wine Bar, with over a hundred wines by the glass and food by Caviar House and Prunier. There's also a giant coffee roasting station, ceiling-high shelves of fresh bread at the Bakery, a vegetable butchery, and an expanded deli counter. In addition, the revamped Beauty Hall now offers cult brands, innovative "Magic Mirrors" that allow shoppers to instantly see a new make-up look via digital technology, beauty master classes, and over 46,000 different lipsticks, as well as 13 treatment rooms where you can try on make-up in private. ✉ *87–135 Brompton Rd., Knightsbridge* ☎ *020/7730–1234* ⊕ *www.harrods.com* Ⓜ *Knightsbridge.*

★ Hyde Park

CITY PARK | **FAMILY** | Along with the smaller St. James's and Green parks to the east, the 350-acre Hyde Park started as Henry VIII's hunting grounds. Along its south side runs Rotten Row, once Henry's royal path to the hunt—the name is a corruption of *Route du Roi* (Route of the King). It's still used by the Household Cavalry, who live at the Hyde Park Barracks to the left. Hyde Park is wonderful for strolling, cycling, or just relaxing by the Serpentine, the long body of water near its southern border. On the south side, by the Lido Café and Bar at the 1930s **Serpentine Lido**, is the site of the **Princess Diana Memorial Fountain.** On Sunday, close to Marble Arch, you'll find the uniquely British tribute to free speech, Speakers' Corner. ⊠ *Hyde Park* ☎ *030/0061–2114* ⊕ *www.royalparks.org.uk* ⊠ *Free* Ⓜ *Hyde Park Corner, Knightsbridge, Lancaster Gate, Marble Arch.*

★ **Kensington Gardens**

GARDEN | FAMILY | Laid out in 1689 by William III, who commissioned Sir Christopher Wren to build Kensington Palace, the gardens are a formal counterpart to neighboring Hyde Park. Just to the north of the palace itself is the Dutch-style **Sunken Garden** . Nearby, the 1912 bronze statue *Peter Pan* commemorates the boy in J. M. Barrie's story who lived on an island in the Serpentine and who never grew up. Kids will enjoy the magical **Diana, Princess of Wales' Memorial Playground,** whose design was also inspired by Barrie's book. The **Elfin Oak** is a 900-year-old tree trunk that was carved with scores of tiny elves, fairies, and other fanciful creations in the 1920s. The **Italian Gardens,** an ornamental water garden commissioned by Prince Albert in 1860, comprise several ornamental ponds and fountains (there's also a nice café on-site), while the **Round Pond** attracts model-boat enthusiasts. ⊠ *Kensington* ☎ *030/0001–2000* ⊕ *www.royalparks.org.uk* ⊠ *Free* Ⓜ *High St. Kensington, Lancaster Gate, Queensway, South Kensington.*

★ **Kensington Palace**

CASTLE/PALACE | FAMILY | Neither as imposing as Buckingham Palace nor as charming as Hampton Court, Kensington Palace is something of a Royal Family commune, with various close relatives of the queen occupying large apartments in the private part of the palace. Bought in 1689 by Queen Mary and King William III, it was converted into a palace by Sir Christopher Wren and Nicholas Hawksmoor, and royals have been in residence ever since. Princess Diana lived here with her sons after her divorce, and this is where Prince William now lives with his wife, Catherine, Duchess of Cambridge and their children. The State Apartments are open to the public, with both permanent and temporary exhibitions. Look for the King's Staircase, with its panoramic trompe-l'oeil painting, and the King's Gallery, with royal artworks surrounded by rich red damask walls, intricate gilding, and a beautiful painted ceiling. Outside, the grounds are almost as lovely as the palace itself. ⊠ *The Broad Walk, Kensington Gardens, Kensington* ☎ *0207/482–7799 for advance booking in U.K., 0203/166–6000* ⊕ *www.hrp. org.uk* ⊠ *£18* Ⓜ *Queensway, High St. Kensington.*

★ **Natural History Museum**

MUSEUM | FAMILY | The ornate terracotta facade of this enormous Victorian museum is embellished with relief panels depicting living creatures to the left of the entrance and extinct ones to the right (although some species have subsequently changed categories). Most are represented inside the museum, which contains more than 70 million different specimens. Only a small percentage is on public display, but you could still spend a day here and not come close to seeing everything. The skeleton of a giant blue whale dominates the vaulted, cathedral-like entrance hall, affording you perhaps the most irresistible photo op in the building. The **Darwin Centre** houses some of the millions of items the museum itself doesn't have room to display. If you want to see some of the other thousands of specimens on the shelves, you must book a behind-the-scenes **Spirit Collection** tour on the day (space is limited). ⊠ *Cromwell Rd., South Kensington* ☎ *0207/942–5000* ⊕ *www. nhm.ac.uk* ⊠ *Free (some fees for special exhibitions)* Ⓜ *South Kensington.*

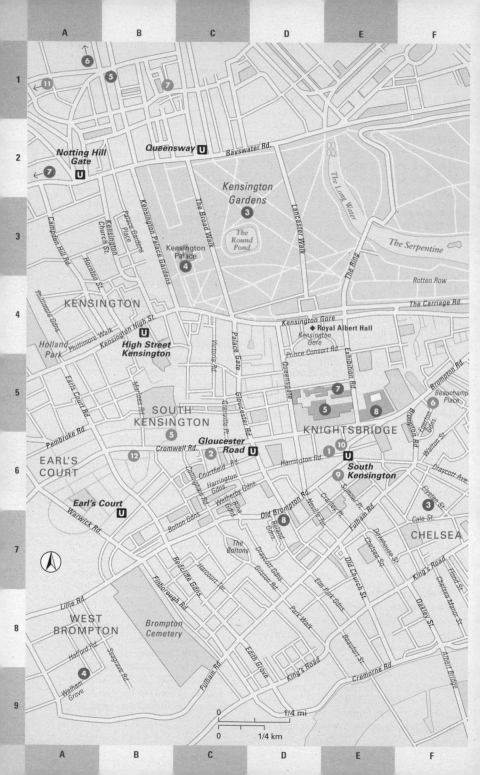

A   **B**   **C**   **D**   **E**   **F**

1

2   Notting Hill Gate Ⓤ   Queensway Ⓤ   Bayswater Rd.

3   Camden Hill Rd.   Kensington Church St.   Palace Gardens   Kensington Palace Gardens   The Broad Walk   Kensington Gardens   The Round Pond   Lancaster Walk   The Serpentine   Rotten Row

Kensington Palace

4   Holland Park   Phillimore Gdns.   Phillimore Walk   KENSINGTON   Hornton St.   Kensington High St.   High Street Kensington Ⓤ   Victoria Rd.   Palace Gate   Kensington Gore   Royal Albert Hall   Kensington Gore   Prince Consort Rd.   The Carriage Rd.   The Ring

5   Earls Court Rd.   Pembroke Rd.   SOUTH KENSINGTON   Marloes Rd.   Grenville Pl.   Gloucester Rd.   Queensgate   Exhibition Rd.   Brompton Rd.   Beauchamp Place   Egerton Gdns.   Walton St.   KNIGHTSBRIDGE

6   EARL'S COURT   Earl's Court Ⓤ   Cromwell Rd.   Gloucester Road Ⓤ   Courtfield Rd.   Harrington Rd.   Harrington Gdns.   Wetherby Gdns.   Bina Gdns.   Old Brompton Rd.   Harrington Rd.   South Kensington Ⓤ   Sumner Pl.   Cranley Pl.   Fulham Rd.   Draycott Ave.   Elystan St.   Cale St.   CHELSEA

7   Warwick Rd.   Bolton Gdns.   The Boltons   Harcourt Ter.   Redcliffe Gdns.   Draycott Gdns.   Roland Gdns.   Gilston Rd.   Newell Ter.   Elm Park Gdns.   Old Church St.   King's Road   Dovehouse St.   Chelsea St.   Oakley St.   Chelsea Manor St.   Flood St.   King's Road

8   Lillie Rd.   WEST BROMPTON   Halford Rd.   Seagrave Rd.   Finborough Rd.   Brompton Cemetery   Fulham Rd.   Edith Grove   Park Walk   Beaufort St.   King's Road   Cremorne Rd.   Albert Bridge

9   Walham Grove   0   1/4 mi   0   1/4 km

A   **B**   **C**   **D**   **E**   **F**

Kensington, Chelsea, Knightsbridge, and Notting Hill

Sights ▼

1 Harrods **G5**
2 Hyde Park **G3**
3 Kensington Gardens **C3**
4 Kensington Palace **C3**
5 Natural History Museum **E5**
6 Portobello Market **A1**
7 Science Museum **E5**
8 Victoria & Albert Museum **E5**

Restaurants ▼

1 Bar Boulud **G4**
2 Dinner by Heston Blumenthal **G4**
3 Elystan Street **F6**
4 The Harwood Arms **A9**
5 Hereford Road **B1**
6 Mari Vanna **G4**
7 Six Portland Road **A2**
8 Yashin Ocean House ... **D7**

Hotels ▼

1 Ampersand **E6**
2 Ashburn Hotel **C6**
3 The Berkeley **H4**
4 The Draycott **G6**
5 easyHotel South Kensington **B6**
6 Egerton House **F5**
7 London House Hotel **B1**
8 Mandarin Oriental Hyde Park **G4**
9 Number Sixteen **E6**
10 The Pelham Hotel **E6**
11 The Portobello Hotel ... **A1**
12 The Rockwell **B6**

Inside the Natural History Museum, you'll find a fascinating array of dinosaur fossils.

Portobello Market

OUTDOOR/FLEA/GREEN MARKETS | Still considered the best all-around market in town by many fans, and certainly the most famous, Portobello Market stretches almost 2 miles, from fashionable Notting Hill to the lively cultural melting pot of North Kensington, changing character as it goes. The southern end, starting at Chepstow Villas and going to Elgin Crescent, is lined with shops and stalls, and, on Saturday, arcades selling antiques, silver, and bric-a-brac. The middle, from Elgin Crescent to Talbot, is devoted to fruit and vegetables, interspersed with excellent hot food stalls. On Friday and Saturday, the area between Talbot Road and the elevated highway (called the Westway) becomes more of a flea market, specializing in new household and mass-produced goods sold at a discount. North of the Westway up to Goldborne Road are more stalls selling even cheaper secondhand household goods and bric-a-brac. Scattered throughout but mostly concentrated under the Westway are clothing stalls selling vintage pieces and items from emerging designers, custom T-shirts, and supercool baby clothes, plus jewelry. New and established designers are also found in the boutiques of the Portobello Green Arcade.

Some say Portobello Road has become a tourist trap, but if you acknowledge that it's a circus and get into the spirit, it's a lot of fun. Perhaps you won't find many bargains, but this is such a fascinating part of town that just hanging out is a good enough excuse to come. There are some food and flower stalls throughout the week (try the Hummingbird Bakery for delicious cupcakes), but Saturday is when the market in full swing. Serious shoppers avoid the crowds and go on Friday morning. Bring cash—several vendors don't take credit cards—but also be sure to keep an eye on it. ⊠ *Portobello Rd., Notting Hill* ⊕ *www.portobelloroad. co.uk* ⊗ *Closed Sun.* Ⓜ *Notting Hill Gate.*

★ Science Museum

MUSEUM | FAMILY | With attractions ranging from entertaining yet educational exhibits like an interactive gallery where kids can perform their own hands-on scientific experiments to an exhibition on the fight against superbugs, the Science Museum brings the subject alive for visitors of all ages. One of the three great South Kensington museums, it stands next to the Natural History Museum in a more modern, plainer building. Highlights include the Launch Pad gallery, which demonstrates basic laws of physics; *Puffing Billy,* the oldest steam locomotive in the world; and the actual Apollo 10 capsule. The six floors are devoted to subjects as diverse as the history of flight, space exploration, jet flight simulators, the large Hadron collider, 3-D printing, and the history of robots over the last 400 years. The museum also contains a 450-seat IMAX theater and a motion simulator ride. ⊠ *Exhibition Rd., South Kensington* ☎ *0870/870–4868* ⊕ *www.sciencemuseum.org.uk* ⊠ *Free (charge for special exhibitions, IMAX, Wonderlab, and simulator rides)* Ⓜ *South Kensington.*

★ Victoria & Albert Museum

MUSEUM | FAMILY | Known to all as the V&A, this huge museum is devoted to the applied arts of all disciplines, all periods, and all nationalities. First opened as the South Kensington Museum in 1857, it was renamed in 1899 in honor of Queen Victoria's late husband and has since grown to become one of the country's best-loved cultural institutions. Many collections at the V&A are presented not by period but by category—textiles, sculpture, jewelry, and so on. Nowhere is the benefit of this more apparent than in the **Fashion Gallery**, known for its high-profile temporary exhibitions. There are galleries devoted to Britain, Japan, China, Korea, and the Islamic Middle East. More recently installed areas include the Ceramics Gallery and the Medieval and Renaissance galleries, which have the largest collection of works from the period outside of Italy. The **Europe Gallery** (Rooms 1–7) brings together more than 1,100 objects from

1600 to 1800. ⊠ *Cromwell Rd., South Kensington* ☎ *020/7942–2000* ⊕ *www.vam.ac.uk* ⊠ *Free (charge for some special exhibitions, from £5)* Ⓜ *South Kensington.*

Restaurants

Bar Boulud

$$ | BRASSERIE | New York–based French superchef Daniel Boulud combines French brasserie classics like escargot, salade nicoise, and poule au pot with American-style gourmet burgers at this sophisticated but casual restaurant located within the Mandarin Oriental. The excellent grazing menu has something for everyone, and the professional but informal waitstaff enhances the convivial vibe. **Known for:** excellent foie gras/beef/short rib burgers; affordable set meals from noon until 6:30; superb take on French brasserie classics. Ⓢ *Average main: £25* ⊠ *Mandarin Oriental Hyde Park, 66 Knightsbridge, Knightsbridge* ☎ *020/7201–3899 for reservations only* ⊕ *www.barboulud.com/london* Ⓜ *Knightsbridge.*

★ Dinner by Heston Blumenthal

$$$$ | BRITISH | Medieval English cuisine meets molecular gastronomy in this reassuringly luxurious, two Michelin star Blumenthal flagship within the Mandarin Oriental. Try the signature "Meat Fruit" appetizer (last popular in the 18th century), a ball of ultrasmooth chicken liver parfait encased in a citrus-flavored gel "peel" or the much-more-appetizing-than-it-sounds "Rice and Flesh", a 15th-century dish of yellow saffron rice with veal sweetbreads and wild smoked eel. **Known for:** handsome dining room with Hyde Park views; creative reinterpretations of historical dishes; pineapple Tipsy cake for dessert. Ⓢ *Average main: £44* ⊠ *Mandarin Oriental Hyde Park, 66 Knightsbridge, Knightsbridge* ☎ *020/7201–3833* ⊕ *www.dinnerbyheston.com* Ⓜ *Knightsbridge.*

★ Elystan Street

$$$ | MODERN BRITISH | Chef Phil Howard is committed to seasonality, bringing together well-matched ingredients in this relaxed, loftlike space that leans toward the modernist and minimalist. The dishes are deeply flavored and accomplished, earning the restaurant a Michelin star (the vegetarian game is especially strong). **Known for:** Michelin-level cuisine in a relaxed setting; roast grouse with celeriac and pear puree; convivial vibe enhanced by a smart wine list. ⑤ *Average main: £30 ⊠ 43 Elystan St., Chelsea ☎ 020/7628–5005 ⊕ www.elystanstreet. com Ⓜ South Kensington.*

The Harwood Arms

$$$$ | MODERN BRITISH | Despite a Michelin star and a co-owner who's also the chef at one of Britain's (and indeed the world's) top restaurants, this is a relaxed neighborhood gastropub with an unusually fine kitchen. It specializes in British produce, wild food, and especially game, with dishes like crab royale with peas and lovage and game pie with Somerset cider jelly, all served via set menus only. **Known for:** Michelin-starred food in a gastropub setting; seasonal venison from the pub's own hunting estate; good value set menus. ⑤ *Average main: £38 ⊠ 27 Walham Grove, Chelsea ☎ 020/7386–1847 ⊕ www.harwoodarms.com ⊙ No lunch Mon. Ⓜ Fulham Broadway.*

Hereford Road

$ | MODERN BRITISH | FAMILY | A Bayswater favorite with the well-connected Notting Hill set, Hereford Road is renowned for its pared-down, pomp-free, and ingredient-driven seasonal British fare, with an emphasis on well-sourced regional British produce. Work your way through uncluttered combos like steamed mussels with cider and thyme, lemon sole with roast cauliflower and capers, or chilled English rice pudding with a dollop of strawberry jam. **Known for:** pared-back Modern British nose-to-tail dining; deceptively simple-sounding dishes like duck livers with green beans; famously affordable two- and three-course set lunches. ⑤ *Average main: £15 ⊠ 3 Hereford Rd., Bayswater ☎ 020/7727–1144 ⊕ www.herefordroad.org ⊙ No lunch Mon.–Wed. Ⓜ Bayswater, Queensway.*

Mari Vanna

$$ | RUSSIAN | London's sizeable, well-heeled Russian community flocks to this maximalist evocation of a pre-Revolution *babushka's* living room, overflowing with vintage chandeliers, porcelain figurines, tapestries, and nested Russian dolls. The menu leans toward traditional old-country comfort food like Siberian *pelmeni* (dumplings) filled with pork and beef, smoked salmon blinis, creamy beef Stroganoff with wild mushrooms, and, of course, borscht, finished off with a 12-layer honey cake. **Known for:** over-the-top nostalgic Russian décor; borscht, blinis, and beef Stroganoff; flavored vodka shot selection. ⑤ *Average main: £24 ⊠ The Wellington Court, 116 Knightsbridge, Knightsbridge ☎ 020/7225–3122 ⊕ www. marivanna.ru/london Ⓜ Knightsbridge.*

★ Six Portland Road

$$ | FRENCH | FAMILY | The ultimate neighborhood restaurant in west London's wealthy Holland Park section draws diners with its brilliant-but-understated French and Mediterranean classics, relaxed service, and interesting, largely French Caves de Pyrene–sourced wines. Treat yourself to sea trout with romesco and saffron or some superdelicate nettle and ricotta ravioli. **Known for:** intimate seating; unpretentious but pitch-perfect service; winning boutique wine list. ⑤ *Average main: £22 ⊠ 6 Portland Rd., Notting Hill ☎ 020/7229–3130 ⊕ www. sixportlandroad.com ⊙ Closed Sun. No lunch Sat. Ⓜ Holland Park.*

Yashin Ocean House

$$$ | JAPANESE | Here at one of London's top Japanese restaurants, head chef and cofounder Yasuhiro Mineno creates fresh, colorful, and exquisite sushi, sashimi, salads, and carpaccios. Tofu-topped miso cappuccino comes in a Victorian cup and saucer, while *nigiri* might include signature flourishes such as truffle shavings on fatty tuna. **Known for:** exquisite sushi and sashimi with creative twists; 5- to 15-piece chef-decides omakase sets; head-to-tail seafood dishes. $ *Average main: £30 ⌧ 117–119 Old Brompton Rd., Kensington ☎ 020/7373–3990 ⊕ www.yashinocean.com Ⓜ High St. Kensington.*

Hotels

Ampersand
$$ | HOTEL | A sense of style emanates from every surface of this stylish hotel in the heart of Kensington, and the playful vintage vibe lends the property a refreshingly down-to-earth feel in a neighborhood that can feel stodgy. **Pros:** flawless design; great service; good restaurant. **Cons:** ground-floor rooms can be noisy; breakfast is not included in the price of a room; the area swarms with tourists visiting the museums on weekends. $ *Rooms from: £234 ⌧ 10 Harrington Rd., Kensington ☎ 020/7589–5895 ⊕ www.ampersandhotel.com ⌁ 111 rooms ⦿ No meals Ⓜ Gloucester Rd.*

Ashburn Hotel
$$ | HOTEL | A short walk from Gloucester Road Tube station and within walking distance of Harrods and the Kensington museums, the Ashburn is one of the better "boutique" hotels in this part of town. **Pros:** friendly atmosphere; free Wi-Fi; different turndown gift every night. **Cons:** summer prices sometimes hike the cost; some rooms on the small side; on very busy road. $ *Rooms from: £144 ⌧ 111 Cromwell Rd., Kensington ☎ 020/7244–1999 ⊕ www.ashburn-hotel.co.uk ⌁ 38 rooms ⦿ Free breakfast Ⓜ Gloucester Rd.*

★ The Berkeley
$$$$ | HOTEL | FAMILY | Convenient for Knightsbridge shopping, the very elegant Berkeley is known for its excellent restaurants, splendid rooftop swimming pool and garden, and an excellent, if pricey, Bamford spa. **Pros:** lavish and elegant; attentive service; great drinking and dining options. **Cons:** you'll need your best designer clothes to fit in; even the cheapest rooms are expensive; while beautiful, the style is very traditional luxury. $ *Rooms from: £450 ⌧ Wilton Pl., Knightsbridge ☎ 020/7235–6000, 800/637–2869 in U.S. ⊕ www.the-berkeley.co.uk ⌁ 190 rooms ⦿ Free breakfast Ⓜ Knightsbridge.*

★ The Draycott
$$$ | HOTEL | FAMILY | This elegant yet homey boutique hotel near Sloane Square is the stuff London dreams are made on—if your dream is to live like a pleasantly old-fashioned, impeccably mannered, effortlessly stylish Chelsea lady or gentleman. **Pros:** lovely traditional town house; attentive service; access to garden square. **Cons:** no restaurant or bar; single rooms are very small; elevator is tiny. $ *Rooms from: £286 ⌧ 26 Cadogan Gardens, Chelsea ☎ 020/7730–0236 ⊕ www.draycotthotel.com ⌁ 35 rooms ⦿ Free breakfast Ⓜ Sloane Sq.*

easyHotel South Kensington
$ | HOTEL | London's original "pod hotel" has tiny rooms with a double bed, private shower room, and little else—each brightly decorated in the easyGroup's trademark orange and white (to match their budget airline easyJet). **Pros:** amazing rates; safe and decent-enough space; good location. **Cons:** not for the claustrophobic—rooms are truly tiny and most have no windows; six floors and no elevator; Wi-Fi is not included in the price of rooms. $ *Rooms from: £48 ⌧ 14 Lexham Gardens, Kensington ☎ 07951/440134 ⊕ www.easyhotel.com ⌁ 34 rooms ⦿ No meals Ⓜ Gloucester Rd.*

★ Egerton House
$$$ | HOTEL | FAMILY | This welcoming boutique hotel is an oasis of understated country house chic in glitzy Knightsbridge, with guest rooms that don't stint on design touches, like bold, rich textiles.

Pros: personalized, attentive service; luxurious but comfortable design; striking art. **Cons:** some may find rooms over-decorated; the traditional elegance won't appeal to everyone; on the pricier side. $ *Rooms from: £330* ✉ *17–19 Egerton Terr., Knightsbridge* ☎ *020/7589–2412, 877/955–1515 in U.S.* ⊕ *www.redcarnationhotels.com* ☞ *29 rooms* ⑪ *Free breakfast* Ⓜ *Knightsbridge, South Kensington.*

London House Hotel

$ | **HOTEL** | Set in a row of white Georgian town houses, this excellent budget option in hit-or-miss Bayswater is friendly, well run, and spotlessly clean. **Pros:** friendly and efficient; emphasis on value; good location. **Cons:** basement rooms lack sunlight; smallest rooms are tiny; the area isn't quite as vibrant as neighboring Notting Hill. $ *Rooms from: £110* ✉ *81 Kensington Garden Sq., Bayswater* ☎ *020/7243–1810* ⊕ *www.londonhousehotels.com* ☞ *103 rooms* ⑪ *No meals* Ⓜ *Queensway, Bayswater.*

★ Mandarin Oriental Hyde Park

$$$$ | **HOTEL** | Following an extensive postfire renovation, this ultraluxe hotel on the edge of Hyde Park welcomes you with one of the most exuberantly Edwardian facades in town, then fast-forwards you to high-trend modern London, thanks to striking and luxurious guest rooms filled with high-tech gadgets. **Pros:** several rooms have balconies or terraces overlooking Hyde Park; spacious rooms and bathrooms; excellent service. **Cons:** nothing comes cheap; rooms on lower floors on Knightsbridge side may have traffic noise; street outside often very busy. $ *Rooms from: £720* ✉ *66 Knightsbridge, Knightsbridge* ☎ *020/7235–2000* ⊕ *www.mandarinoriental.com/london* ☞ *181 rooms* ⑪ *Free breakfast* Ⓜ *Knightsbridge.*

★ Number Sixteen

$$$$ | **HOTEL** | Rooms at this lovely boutique hotel, just around the corner from the Victoria & Albert Museum, look like they come from the pages of *Architectural Digest,* and the delightful garden is an added bonus. **Pros:** just the right level of helpful service; interiors are gorgeous; the afternoon tea is excellent. **Cons:** no restaurant; elevator doesn't go to third floor; intimacy of a small boutique hotel may not be for everyone. $ *Rooms from: £336* ✉ *16 Sumner Pl., South Kensington* ☎ *020/7589–5232, 888/559–5508 in U.S.* ⊕ *www.firmdale.com* ☞ *41 rooms* ⑪ *Free breakfast* Ⓜ *South Kensington.*

The Pelham Hotel

$$ | **HOTEL** | One of the first boutique hotels ever in London, this still-stylish choice is just a short stroll away from the Natural History, Science, and Victoria & Albert museums. **Pros:** great location for museum-hopping; elegant interior design; lovely staff. **Cons:** taller guests will find themselves cursing the top-floor rooms with sloping ceilings; some rooms are on the small side given the price; some suites are only accessible via the stairs. $ *Rooms from: £200* ✉ *15 Cromwell Pl., South Kensington* ☎ *020/7589–8288, 888/757–5587 in U.S.* ⊕ *www.starhotelscollezione.com/en/our-hotels/the-pelham-london* ☞ *52 rooms* ⑪ *Free breakfast* Ⓜ *South Kensington.*

The Portobello Hotel

$$ | **HOTEL** | One of London's quirkiest hotels, the little Portobello (formed from two adjoining Victorian houses) has attracted scores of celebrities to its small but stylish rooms over the years, and the decor reflects these hip credentials with joyous abandon. **Pros:** stylish and unique; pets are allowed; guests have use of nearby gym and pool. **Cons:** all but the priciest rooms are quite small; may be too eccentric for some; a continental breakfast is included in the price but cooked breakfasts are extra. $ *Rooms from: £195* ✉ *22 Stanley Gardens, Notting Hill* ☎ *020/7727–2777* ⊕ *www.portobellohotel.com* ☞ *21 rooms* ⑪ *Free breakfast* Ⓜ *Notting Hill Gate.*

The Rockwell

$ | HOTEL | Despite being on the notoriously traffic-clogged Cromwell Road, the Rockwell is one of the best boutique hotels in this part of London—and windows have triple-soundproofing. **Pros:** large bedrooms; good value for neighborhood; helpful staff. **Cons:** on busy road; no bathtubs; decor a bit tired in places. *$ Rooms from: £108 ⊠ 181 Cromwell Rd., South Kensington ☎ 020/7244–2000 ⊕ www.therockwell.com ⌇ 40 rooms ⧊ Free breakfast M Earl's Ct.*

Nightlife

BARS

The Blue Bar at the Berkeley Hotel

BARS/PUBS | With its Lutyens blue walls, Edwardian plasterwork, white onyx bar, and black crocodile-print leather floor, this hotel bar oozes sultry sophistication. Immaculate service, an excellent seasonal cocktail list, and a glass extension make this an ideal spot for a romantic tête-à-tête, complete with a background soundtrack of lounge and deep house music. *⊠ The Berkeley, Wilton Pl., Knightsbridge ☎ 020/7235–6000 ⊕ www.the-berkeley.co.uk M Knightsbridge, Hyde Park Corner.*

LIVE MUSIC

606 Club

MUSIC CLUBS | This Chelsea jazz club has been doing things speakeasy-style since long before it became a nightlife trend. Buzz the door near the far end of King's Road and you'll find a basement venue showcasing mainstream and contemporary jazz by well-known U.K.-based musicians. You must eat a meal in order to consume alcohol, so allow for an extra £30. Reservations are advisable. Lunchtime jazz takes place on select Sundays; call ahead. *⊠ 90 Lots Rd., Chelsea ☎ 020/7352–5953 ⊕ www.606club.co.uk ☑ From £10 music charge added to bill M Fulham Broadway. Overground: Imperial Wharf.*

Performing Arts

★ Royal Albert Hall

CONCERTS | Opened in 1871, this splendid iron-and-glass-domed auditorium hosts everything from pop and classical headliners to Cirque du Soleil, awards ceremonies, and sumo wrestling championships, but it is best known for the annual July–September BBC Promenade Concerts. Bargain-price standing-room (or promenading or sitting-on-the-floor) tickets for "the Proms" are sold on the night of the concert. The circular 5,272-seat auditorium has a terracotta exterior surmounted by a mosaic frieze depicting figures engaged in cultural pursuits. The hall is open most days for daytime guided tours Tuesday through Sunday for afternoon tea. *⊠ Kensington Gore, Kensington ☎ 0207/589–8212 ⊕ www.royalalberthall.com ☑ From £7; tours £14 M South Kensington.*

Royal Court Theatre

THEATER | For decades, the Royal Court was one of Britain's leading showcases for exciting new theatrical voices and premieres of groundbreaking works, and it still continues to produce important British and international dramas. For some productions, four 10-pence standing tickets go on sale one hour before each performance (but the view is severely restricted), and £12 tickets are available at 9 am Mondays for that night's performance. Monthly backstage and building tours are offered occasionally (check website for more information). *⊠ Sloane Sq., Chelsea ☎ 020/7565–5000 ⊕ www.royalcourttheatre.com ☑ From £12; tours £10 M Sloane Sq.*

Shopping

BOOKS

★ Books for Cooks

BOOKS/STATIONERY | It may seem odd to describe a bookshop as delicious-smelling, but on several days you can't but notice the aromas wafting out of the tiny

Royal Albert Hall is not only host to the acclaimed Proms performances, but it's also one of the city's most beautiful buildings.

café in the back of the shop—where the resident chef cooks a three-course set lunch for only £7, served from noon to 1 pm Tuesday through Friday (but be sure to get there early). The dishes are drawn from recipes in the 8,000 cookbooks on the shelves. Just about every world cuisine is represented, along with a complete lineup of works by celebrity chefs. Before you come to London, visit the shop's website to sign up for a specialized cooking workshop in the upstairs demonstration kitchen. ⊠ *4 Blenheim Crescent, Notting Hill* ☎ *020/7221–1992* ⊕ *www.booksforcooks.com* Ⓜ *Notting Hill Gate, Ladbroke Grove.*

CLOTHING

Jigsaw

CLOTHING | The quality of fabrics and detailing belie the reasonable prices here, where clothes are classic yet trendy and elegant without being dull—and where cuts are kind to the womanly figure. The style is epitomized by the Duchess of Cambridge, who, as Kate Middleton before her marriage, was a buyer for the company. Although there are numerous branches across London, no two stores are the same. Preteens have their own line, Jigsaw Junior. ⊠ *The Chapel, 6 Duke of York Sq., Chelsea* ☎ *020/730–4404* ⊕ *www.jigsaw-online.com* Ⓜ *Sloane Sq.*

Rigby & Peller

SPECIALTY STORES | Many of London's most affluent women find their luxury lingerie (plus swimwear) here because the quality is excellent and the service impeccably knowledgeable—and perhaps because it's the Queen's favored underwear supplier and has provided maternity wear to the Duchess of Cambridge. Despite the upscale clientele, it's much friendlier than you might expect. Brands include Primadonna and Aubade as well as R&P's own line, and if the right fit eludes you, there's a made-to-measure service that starts at around £300. There are also branches in Mayfair, Chelsea, St. John's Wood, and the City. ⊠ *2 Hans Rd., Knightsbridge* ☎ *020/7225–4760* ⊕ *www. rigbyandpeller.com* Ⓜ *Knightsbridge.*

DEPARTMENT STORES
Harvey Nichols

DEPARTMENT STORES | While visiting tourists flock to Harrods, local fashionistas shop at Harvey Nichols, aka "Harvey Nicks." The womenswear and accessories departments are outstanding, featuring top designers like Tom Ford, Loewe, Roland Mouret, Valentino, Tory Burch, and just about every fashionable name you can think of. The furniture and housewares are equally gorgeous (and pricey), although they become somewhat more affordable during the biannual sales in January and July. The Fifth Floor bar is the place to see and be seen, but if you're in search of food, the same floor also has an all-day Modern European café, a branch of Burger & Lobster, the carnivore-friendly Zelman Meats, or sushi-to-go from Yo! Sushi. To keep you looking as box-fresh as your purchases, the Beauty Lounge features a rotating menu of treatments from brands such as Elemis, La Mer, and Dermalogia, plus makeovers, LED facials, IV vitamin infusions, and blow-dry, nail, and brow bars. ⊠ 109–125 Knightsbridge, Knightsbridge ☎ 020/7235–5000 ⊕ www.harveynichols. com Ⓜ Knightsbridge.

JEWELRY
Butler & Wilson

JEWELRY/ACCESSORIES | Specialists in bold costume jewelry and affordable glamour, Butler & Wilson attracts fans including the Duchess of Cambridge. Semiprecious stones have been added to its foundation diamanté, colored rhinestone, and crystal collections. The British sense of humor is reflected in items like Champagne-bottle earrings or crystal studs in the shape of an eye. ⊠ 189 Fulham Rd., South Kensington ☎ 020/7352–3045 ⊕ www.butlerandwilson.co.uk ☉ Closed Sun. Ⓜ South Kensington.

MUSIC
Music & Video Exchange

MUSIC STORES | This store is a music collector's treasure trove, with a constantly changing stock refreshed by customers selling and exchanging as well as buying. The ground floor focuses on rock, pop, indie, and punk, both mainstream and obscure, in a variety of formats ranging from vinyl to CD, cassette, and even minidisk. Don't miss the classical music in the basement and the soul, jazz, house, techno, reggae, and more upstairs. Like movies? There's a wide variety of Blu-ray and DVD box sets, as well as bargain classic and cult films. Keep an eye out for rarities—including first pressings and one-offs—in all departments. Similar exchanges for comics (No. 32) and books (No. 30) are on nearby Pembridge Road (also a destination for vintage clothing for men [No. 34] and women [No. 20], plus more clothing, accessories, and retro homewares [No. 28]). Note: stock depends on what customers bring in to exchange, so you'll surely find many more DVDs with European (PAL) formatting than the North American–friendly NTSC format, but the store does get the latter occasionally. ⊠ 38 Notting Hill Gate, Notting Hill ☎ 020/7243–8573 ⊕ www.mgeshops. com Ⓜ Notting Hill Gate.

Regent's Park and Hampstead

Regent's Park, Primrose Hill, Belsize Park, and Hampstead are four of London's prettiest and most genteel neighborhoods. The city becomes noticeably calmer and greener as you head uphill from Marylebone Road through Regent's Park to the refreshing greenery of Primrose Hill and the handsome Georgian houses and Regency villas of Hampstead. To the west, the less bucolic but equally elegant St. John's Wood and Little Venice also provide a taste of moneyed London.

GETTING HERE

To get to Hampstead by Tube, take the Northern Line (the Edgware branch) to Hampstead or Golders Green Station, or take the London Overground to Hampstead Heath Station. The south side of Hampstead Heath can also be reached by the London Overground Gospel Oak Station. To get to Regent's Park, take the Bakerloo Line to Regent's Park Tube station or, for Primrose Hill, the Chalk Farm stop on the Northern Line. Little Venice is reachable by the Warwick Avenue stop on the Bakerloo Line, and St. John's Wood has its own stop on the Jubilee Line.

Sights

★ Hampstead Heath

NATURE PRESERVE | FAMILY | For generations, Londoners have headed to Hampstead Heath to escape the dirt and noise of the city. A unique expanse of *rus in urbe* ("country in the city"), its 791 acres encompass a variety of wildlife as well as habitats: grassy meadows, woodland, scrub, wetlands, and some of Europe's most venerable oak forests. Be aware that, aside from the southern slope of Parliament Hill and Golders Hill Park, it is more like countryside than a park, with signs and facilities in short supply. Pick up a map at Kenwood House or at the "Enquiries" window of the Staff Yard near the tennis courts off Highgate Road, where you can also get details about the history of the Heath and the flora and fauna growing there. An excellent alfresco café near the Athletics Field serves Italian food.

Coming onto the Heath from the South End Green entrance, walk east past the children's **Playground** and **Paddling Pool,** turn left, and head to the top of **Parliament Hill.** At 321 feet above sea level, it's one of the highest points in London. You'll find a stunning panorama over the city. On clear days you can see all the way to the South Downs, the hills beyond southern London.

If you keep heading east from the playground instead, you'll come to the **Lido,** an Olympic-size, outdoor, unheated swimming pool that gets packed on all-too-rare hot summer days. ⊠ *Hampstead* ☎ *020/7332–3322* ⊕ *www.cityoflondon. gov.uk/hampstead* ⊠ *Free* Ⓜ *Overground: Hampstead Heath for west of Heath or Gospel Oak for south and east of Heath and Lido. Northern Line: Golders Green, then Bus 210 or 268 to Whitestone Pond for north and west of Heath and Golders Hill Park.*

Highgate Cemetery

CEMETERY | Highgate is not the oldest cemetery in London, but it is probably the best known, both for its roster of famous "inhabitants" and the quality of its funerary architecture. After it was consecrated in 1839, Victorians came from miles around to appreciate the ornate headstones, the impressive tombs, and the view. Such was its popularity that 19 acres on the other side of the road were acquired in 1850, and this additional East Cemetery is the final resting place of numerous notables, including the most visited, Karl Marx (1818–83), as well as George Eliot and, a more recent internment, George Michael. At the summit is the **Circle of Lebanon,** a ring of vaults built around an ancient cypress tree, a legacy of the 17th-century gardens that formerly occupied the site. Leading from the circle is the **Egyptian Avenue,** a subterranean stone tunnel lined with catacombs, itself approached by a dramatic colonnade that screens the main cemetery from the road. Both sides are impressive, with a grand (locked) iron gate leading to a sweeping courtyard built for the approach of horses and carriages. By the 1970s the cemetery had become unkempt and neglected until a group of volunteers, the Friends of Highgate Cemetery, undertook the huge upkeep. Tours are conducted by the Friends, who will show you the most interesting graves among the numerous statues and memorials once hidden by overgrowth. The West side can only be seen during a one-hour tour. Booking is essential for weekdays but not permitted for weekends; tours of the East side on Saturday are first-come, first-served. You're expected to dress respectfully, so skip the shorts and the baseball cap; children under eight are not admitted and neither are dogs, tripods, or video cameras. Note that unless you book online in advance, admission and tour fees are cash-only. ⊠ Swains La., Highgate ☎ 020/8340–1834 ⊕ www. highgatecemetery.org ✉ East Cemetery £4, tours f8; West Cemetery tours £12, includes admission to East Cemetery Ⓜ Archway, then Bus 210, 271, or 143 to Waterlow Park; Belsize Park, then Bus C11 to Brookfield Park.

★ Kenwood House

HOUSE | This largely Palladian villa offers an escape to a gracious country house with a magnificent collection of Old Masters and beautiful grounds, all within a short Tube ride from central London. Originally built in 1616, Kenwood was expanded by Robert Adam starting in 1767 and later by George Saunders in 1795. Adam refaced most of the exterior and added the splendid library, which, with its vaulted ceiling and Corinthian columns, is the highlight of the house's interior. A major renovation restored four rooms to reflect Adam's intentions as closely as possible, incorporating the furniture he designed for them and his original color schemes. Kenwood is also home to the **Iveagh Bequest,** a world-class collection of some 60 paintings that includes masterworks like Rembrandt's *Self-Portrait with Two Circles* and Vermeer's *The Guitar Player,* along with major works by Reynolds, Van Dyck, Hals, Gainsborough, Turner, and more. The grounds, designed by Humphry Repton and bordered by Hampstead Heath, are equally elegant and serene, with lawns sloping down to a little lake crossed by a trompe-l'oeil bridge. All in

all, it's the perfect home for an 18th-century gentleman. In summer, the grounds host a series of popular and classical concerts, culminating in fireworks on the last night. The Brew House café, occupying part of the old coach house, has outdoor tables in the courtyard and a terraced garden. ⊠ Hampstead La., Highgate ☎ 0870/333–1181 ⊕ www. english-heritage.org.uk/visit/places/kenwood ✉ Free, house and estate tour £18 Ⓜ Golders Green or Archway, then Bus 210. Overground: Gospel Oak.

★ Regent's Park

CITY PARK | FAMILY | The formal cultivated Regent's Park, more country-house grounds than municipal amenity, began life in 1812, when John Nash was commissioned by the Prince Regent (later George IV) to create a master plan for the former royal hunting ground. Nash's original plan included a summer palace for the prince and 56 villas for friends, none of which were realized except for 8 villas (only 2 survive). However, the grand neoclassical terraced houses on the south, east, and west edges of the park were built by Nash and reflect the scope of his ambitions. Queen Mary's Gardens, which has some 30,000 roses and is a favorite spot for weddings, was created in the 1930s. Today the 395-acre park, with the largest outdoor sports area in central London, draws the athletically inclined from around the city.

At the center of the park is the **Queen Mary's Gardens,** a fragrant 17-acre circle containing more than 400 varieties of roses. Just to the east of the gardens is the **Regent's Park Open-Air Theatre** and the **Boating Lake,** which you can explore by renting a pedalo (paddleboat) or rowboat. Heading east from the rose gardens along Chester Road past the **Broad Walk** will bring you to Nash's iconic white-stucco **Cumberland Terrace,** with its central Ionic columns surmounted by a triangular Wedgwood-blue pediment. At the north end of the Broad Walk you'll find the

Regent's Park and Hampstead

A B C D E

1 HIGHGATE

0   1/4 mi

0   1/4 km

Hampstead Ln

HIGHGATE

2 Kenwood House

Waterlow Park

Hampstead Heath

Ladies Bathing Pond

2 Highgate Cemetery

1 Hampstead Heath

Mixed Bathing Pond

Parliament Hill

Oakeshott Ave.
Makepeace Ave.
Langbourne Ave.
Swains Ln
St. Albans Rd.

Chester Rd.

Dartmouth

Croftdown Rd

Dartmouth Park

Dartmouth Pk Rd.

3 HAMPSTEAD

Hampstead U

Flask Wk.
Willow Rd.
Church Row

Oak Hill

Frognal

Hampstead High St.

Keats Gr.

Hampstead Heath Station

Gospel Oak Station

Mansfield Rd

Highgate Rd

Tufnell Park U

4 Finchley Road & Frognal Station

Belsize Park U

Haverstock Hill

1 Haverstock Hotel

KENTISH TOWN

Kentish Town Station

Wates Rd.

5 Swiss Cottage

PRIMROSE HILL

Chalk Farm U

CHALK FARM

KILBURN

Primrose Hill

Camden Town U

6 St. Johns Wood U

ST. JOHN'S WOOD

Regent's Park

2 York & Albany

CAMDEN TOWN

Camden High Street

7

5 ZSL London Zoo

4 Regent's Park

Chester Rd.

KEY

① Sights

① Hotels

Sights ▼

1 Hampstead Heath **B2**
2 Highgate Cemetery..... **D1**
3 Kenwood House **C1**
4 Regent's Park **D7**
5 ZSL London Zoo......... **D6**

Hotels ▼

1 Haverstock Hotel **C4**
2 York & Albany **E6**

London Zoo, while to the northwest of the central circle is **The Hub** (*0300/061–2323*), a state-of-the-art community sports center that has changing rooms, exercise classes, and a café with 360-degree views of the surrounding sports fields, used for soccer, rugby, cricket, field hockey, and softball contests. There are also tennis courts toward the park's southeast (Baker Street) entrance, and the park is a favorite north–south route for cyclists. ✉ *Chester Rd., Regent's Park* ☎ *0300/061–2300* ⊕ *www.royalparks. org.uk* ✉ *Free* Ⓜ *Baker St., Regent's Park, Great Portland St.*

★ ZSL London Zoo

ZOO | FAMILY | With an emphasis on education, wildlife conservation, and the breeding of endangered species, London Zoo offers visitors the chance to see tigers, gorillas, meerkats, and more in something resembling a natural environment rather than a cage. Operated by the nonprofit Zoological Society of London, the zoo was begun with the royal animals collection, moved here from the Tower of London in 1828; the zoo itself did not open to the public until 1847. Big attractions include Land of the Lions, a walk-through re-creation of an Indian forest where you can see three resident Asiatic lions relaxing at close range; Gorilla Kingdom, which provides a similar re-created habitat (in this case an African rain forest) for its colony of six Western Lowland Gorillas; and the Attenborough Komodo Dragon House, renamed to honor the renowned naturalist. The zoo also offers the chance to get up close and personal with 15 ring-tailed lemurs. The huge B.U.G.S. pavilion (Biodiversity Underpinning Global Survival) is a self-sustaining, contained ecosystem for 140 less-cuddly species, including invertebrates such as spiders and millipedes, plus some reptiles and fish. Rainforest Life is an indoor tropical rain forest (complete with humidity) inhabited by the likes of armadillos, monkeys, and sloths. A special nighttime section offers glimpses of nocturnal creatures like slow lorises and bats. The Animal Adventures Children's Zoo allows kids to closely observe coatis, as well as to interact with llamas, donkeys, small pigs, sheep, and goats. Two of the most popular attractions are Penguin Beach, especially at feeding time (1:30 and 4:30), and meerkat snack time (11:15), where you can see the sociable animals keeping watch over their own sandy territory.

If you're feeling flush, try to nab one of the six daily "Meet the Penguins" VIP tickets (1:45 pm) that offer a 20-minute guided close encounter with the locals (£54); there are similar VIP encounters with giraffes, meerkats, and various denizens of the rain forest. Other zoo highlights include Butterfly Paradise and Tiger Territory, an enclosure for four beautiful endangered Sumatran tigers (including two cubs born at the zoo). Adults-only Zoo Nights held Friday nights in June and July offer street food, alcoholic drinks, and entertainment. You can also experience the zoo after-hours by booking an overnight stay in one of the cozy cabins near (not in) the lion enclosure. Check the website or the information board out front for free events, including creature close encounters and "ask the keeper" sessions. ✉ *Outer Circle, Regent's Park* ☎ *0844/225–1826* ⊕ *www.zsl.org* ✉ *From £27* Ⓜ *Camden Town, then Bus 274.*

🛏 Hotels

Haverstock Hotel

$$ | HOTEL | Just down the hill from Hampstead Village is this stylish boutique hotel located in a converted pub. **Pros:** cool, minimalist decor; convenient to Hampstead, Belsize Park, and Primrose Hill; free Wi-Fi and buffet breakfast. **Cons:** no elevator; rooms on the small side; some rooms can be noisy. ⑤ *Rooms from. £135* ✉ *154 Haverstock Hill, Hampstead* ☎ *020/7722–5097* ⊕ *www.*

A Trip to Abbey Road

The black-and-white crosswalk (known as a "zebra crossing") near the Abbey Road Studios at No. 3, where the Beatles recorded their entire output from "Love Me Do" onward, is a place of pilgrimage for Beatles' fans from around the world, many of them teenagers born long after the band split up. They converge here to re-create the cover of the Beatles' 1969 *Abbey Road* album, posing on the crossing despite the onrushing traffic. ■TIP→ Be careful if you're going to attempt this; traffic on Abbey Road is busy. One of the best ways to explore landmarks in the Beatles' story is to take one of the excellent walking tours offered by **Original London Walks** (☎ *020/7624–3978* ⊕ *www. walks.com*). Try **The Beatles In-My-Life Walk** (Saturday and Tuesday at 11 am outside Marylebone Railway station) or **The Beatles Magical Mystery Tour** (Wednesday at 2 pm and Thursday except for December and January and Sunday at 11 am, at Underground Exit 1, Tottenham Court Road).

haverstockhotel.com *22 rooms* ⊚ *Free breakfast* Ⓜ *Belsize Park.*

York & Albany
$$ | HOTEL | Located on the northern edge of Regent's Park opposite the zoo entrance, this town house hotel with stylish, individually decorated rooms is owned by noted chef Gordon Ramsay, who also operates the restaurant on the ground floor. **Pros:** location close to Regent's Park and Camden town; excellent restaurant on-site; charming decor that is both traditional and modern. **Cons:** some traffic noise from outside road; hotel located at busy intersection; rooms not spacious for the price. Ⓢ *Rooms from: £210* ✉ *127–129 Parkway* ☎ *207/387–5700* ⊕ *www.gordonramsay-restaurants.com/york-and-albany* ⌁ *9 rooms* ⊚ *No meals* Ⓜ *Camden Town.*

🎭 Performing Arts

Open Air Theatre
THEATER | FAMILY | Works by Shakespeare have been performed here every summer (from mid-May to mid-September) since 1932, with casts including luminaries such as Vivien Leigh, Dame Judi Dench, and Damien Lewis. Today the theater also mounts productions of classic plays, musicals, and shows for family audiences among its four annual productions. *A Midsummer Night's Dream* is the one to catch, if it's on— never has that enchanted Greek wood been better evoked, especially when enhanced by genuine birdsong and a rising moon. There's a covered restaurant for pretheater dining, an informal café, and, of course, a bar. You also can order picnic hampers in advance. The park can get chilly, so bring a blanket. Performances proceed rain or shine (umbrellas aren't allowed) with refunds only in case of a very heavy downpour. ✉ *Inner Circle, Regent's Park* ☎ *0844/826–4242* ⊕ *www. openairtheatre.com* 🎟 *From £25* Ⓜ *Baker St., Regent's Park.*

Up and Down the Thames

Downstream—meaning seaward, or east—from central London, Greenwich will require a day to explore, especially if you have any interest in maritime history or technology. Upstream to the west are the royal palaces and grand houses that were built as country residences with easy access to London by river. Hampton Court Palace, with its famous maze, is the most notable.

GREENWICH

8 miles east of central London.

About 8 miles downstream (meaning seaward, to the east) from central London, Greenwich is a small borough that looms large across the world. Once the seat of British naval power, it is not only home to the Old Royal Observatory, which measures time for our entire planet, but also the Greenwich Meridian, which divides the world into two—you can stand astride it with one foot in either hemisphere.

The Docklands Light Railway (DLR) is a zippy way to get to Cutty Sark Station from Canary Wharf or Bank Tube station in the City. Or take the DLR to Island Gardens and walk the old Victorian Foot Tunnel under the river. (Sitting at the front of a train can be disconcerting, as you watch the controls in the fully automated driver's cab move about as if a ghost were at the helm.) The best way to arrive, however—time and weather permitting—is like a sea captain of old: by water (it takes an hour from central London).

Sights

★ *Cutty Sark*

HISTORIC SITE | FAMILY | This sleek, romantic clipper was built in 1869, one among a vast fleet of tall-masted wooden ships that plied the oceanic highways of the 19th century, trading in exotic commodities—in this case, tea. *Cutty Sark* (named after a racy witch in a Robert Burns poem) was the fastest in the fleet, sailing the London–China route in 1871 in only 107 days. The clipper has been preserved in dry dock as a museum ship since the 1950s, but was severely damaged in a

devastating fire in 2007. Yet up from the ashes, as the song goes, grow the roses of success: after a major restoration project, the visitor facilities are now better than ever. Not only can you tour the ship in its entirety, but the glittering visitor center (which the ship now rests directly above) allows you to view the hull from below. There's plenty to see here, and the cramped quarters form a fantastic time capsule to walk around in—this boat was never too comfortable for the 28-strong crew (as you'll see). Don't forget to take in the amusing collection of figureheads. The ship also hosts comedy, cabaret, and theater shows. ⊠ *King William Walk, Greenwich* ☎ *020/8858–4422* ⊕ *www.rmg.co.uk/cuttysark* ⛴ *From £15* Ⓜ *DLR: Cutty Sark.*

★ National Maritime Museum

MUSEUM | FAMILY | From the time of Henry VIII until the 1940s, Britain was the world's preeminent naval power, and the collections here trace half a millennia of that seafaring history. The story is as much about trade as it is warfare: *Atlantic: Slavery, Trade, Empire* gallery explores how trade in goods (and people) irrevocably changed the world, while *Traders: The East India Company and Asia* focuses on how the epoch-defining company shaped trade with Asia for 250 years. One gallery is devoted to Admiral Lord Nelson, Britain's most famous naval commander, and among the exhibits is the uniform he was wearing, complete with bloodstains, when he died at the Battle of Trafalgar in 1805. ⊠ *Romney Rd., Greenwich* ☎ *020/8312–6608* ⊕ *www.rmg.co.uk/national-maritime-museum* ⛴ *Free; tours £10; fee for special exhibitions* Ⓜ *DLR: Greenwich.*

★ Royal Observatory

MUSEUM | FAMILY | Greenwich is on the prime meridian at 0° longitude, and the ultimate standard for time around the world has been set here since 1884, when Britain was the world's maritime superpower.

Up and Down the Thames

Prime Meridian 0°
(Greenwich Mean Line)

Sights ▶

1 Cutty Sark................**G1**
2 Hampton Court Palace...**A3**
3 Kew Gardens.............**B1**
4 National Maritime
   Museum.................**G1**
5 Richmond Park..........**B2**
6 Royal Observatory.......**G1**

Restaurants ▶

1 Chez Bruce..............**D2**

The observatory is actually split into two sites, a short walk apart—one devoted to astronomy, the other to the study of time. The enchanting **Peter Harrison Planetarium** is London's only planetarium, its bronze-clad turret glinting in the sun. Shows on black holes and how to interpret the night sky are enthralling and enlightening. Even better for kids are the high-technology rooms of the **Astronomy Centre,** where space exploration is brought to life through cutting-edge interactive programs and fascinating exhibits—including the chance to touch a 4.5-billion-year-old meteorite.

Across the way is **Flamsteed House,** designed by Christopher Wren in 1675 for John Flamsteed, the first Astronomer Royal. A climb to the top of the house reveals a **28-inch telescope,** built in 1893 and now housed inside an onion-shape fiberglass dome. It doesn't compare with the range of modern optical telescopes, but it's still the largest in the United Kingdom. Regular wintertime viewing evenings reveal startlingly detailed views of the lunar surface. In the **Time Galleries,** linger over the superb workmanship of John Harrison (1693–1776), whose famous **Maritime Clocks** won him the Longitude Prize for solving the problem of accurate timekeeping at sea, which paved the way for modern navigation. ✉ *Romney Rd., Greenwich* ☏ *020/8858-4422* ⊕ *www.rmg.co.uk/royal-observatory* ⌨ *Royal Observatory £16, planetarium shows £10; combined ticket with Cutty Sark £27* Ⓜ *DLR: Greenwich.*

RICHMOND
20 miles southwest of central London.

Named after the (long-vanished) palace Henry VII started here in 1500, Richmond is still a welcoming suburb with a small-town feel, marred only by choking levels of traffic. Duck away from the main streets to find many handsome Georgian and Victorian houses, antiques shops, a Victorian theater, a grand stately home—and, best of all, the largest of London's royal parks.

Sights

★ Hampton Court Palace
CASTLE/PALACE | **FAMILY** | The beloved seat of Henry VIII's court, sprawled elegantly beside the languid waters of the Thames, Hampton Court is steeped in more history than virtually any other royal building in England. Begun in 1515 by Cardinal Wolsey to curry favor with the young Henry, the Tudor palace actually conceals a larger 17th-century baroque building partly designed by Christopher Wren. George II moved the royal household closer to London in the early 18th century. Wander through the State Apartments before taking in the strikingly azure ceiling of the Chapel Royal. Well-handled reconstructions of Tudor life take place all year. Latter-day masters of the palace, the joint rulers William and Mary (reigned 1689–1702), were responsible for the beautiful King's and Queen's Apartments and the elaborate baroque of the Georgian Rooms. Don't miss the famous hedge maze and the Lower Orangery Garden, which shows off thousands of exotic species that William and Mary gathered from around the globe. ✉ *Hampton Court Rd., East Molesey* ☏ *020/3166–6000* ⊕ *www.hrp.org.uk/hamptoncourtpalace* ⌨ *£24 palace, maze, and gardens; £5 maze only; £8 maze and gardens* Ⓜ *Richmond, then Bus R68. National Rail: Hampton Court, 35 mins from Waterloo (most trains require change at Surbiton).*

★ Richmond Park
CITY PARK | **FAMILY** | This enormous park was enclosed in 1637 for use as a royal hunting ground—like practically all other London parks. Unlike the others, however, Richmond Park still has wild red and fallow deer roaming its 2,500 acres (three times the size of New York's Central Park) of grassland and heath. Its ancient oaks are among the last

3

London UP AND DOWN THE THAMES

remnants of the vast, wild forests that once encroached on London in medieval times. The Isabella Plantation (near the Ham Gate entrance) is an enchanting and colorful woodland garden, first laid out in 1831. There's a splendid protected view of St. Paul's Cathedral from King Henry VIII's Mound, the highest point in the park; find it, and you have a piece of magic in your sights. The park is also home to White Lodge, a 1727 hunting lodge that now houses the Royal Ballet School. ⊠ *Richmond* ☎ *030/0061–2200* ⊕ *www. royalparks.org.uk* ✉ *Free* Ⓜ *Richmond, then Bus 371 or 65.*

🍴 Restaurants

Chez Bruce

$$$ | **MODERN FRENCH** | Top-notch French and Mediterranean cuisine, faultless service, and a winning wine list make this one of London's all-star favorite restaurants. At this cozy haunt overlooking Wandsworth Common, prepare for unfussy grown-up gastro wonders ranging from housemade charcuterie to lighter, simply grilled fish dishes. **Known for:** elegant neighborhood salon; luxe classics like lobster and scallop ravioli; impressive sommelier. Ⓢ *Average main: £27* ⊠ *2 Bellevue Rd., Wandsworth Common, Battersea* ☎ *020/8672–0114* ⊕ *www.chezbruce.co.uk* Ⓜ *Overland: Wandsworth Common.*

KEW

6 miles southwest of central London.

A leafy suburb, Kew offers little to see except for its two big attractions: the lovely Kew Palace and the Royal Botanic Gardens—anchored in the landscape for several miles around by a towering, mock-Chinese pagoda.

👁 Sights

★ Kew Gardens

GARDEN | **FAMILY** | Enter the Royal Botanic Gardens, as Kew Gardens are officially known, and you are enveloped by blazes of color, extraordinary blooms, hidden trails, and lovely old follies. Beautiful though it all is, Kew's charms are secondary to its true purpose as a major center for serious research: over 200 academics are consistently hard at work here on projects spanning 110 countries. First opened to the public in 1840, this 326-acre site has been supported by royalty and nurtured by landscapers, botanists, and architects since the 1720s. Today the gardens, now a UNESCO World Heritage Site, hold more than 30,000 species of plants from every corner of the globe. Although the plant houses make Kew worth visiting even in the depths of winter (there's also a seasonal garden), the flower beds are, of course, best enjoyed in the fullness of spring and summer.

Architect Sir William Chambers built a series of temples and follies, of which the crazy 10-story **Pagoda,** visible for miles around, is the star. The Princess of Wales Conservatory houses 10 climate zones, and the Xstrata Treetop Walkway takes you 59 feet up into the air. Two great 19th-century greenhouses—the **Palm House** and the **Temperate House**—are filled with exotic blooms, and many of the plants have been there since the final glass panel was fixed into place, including the largest greenhouse plant in the world, a Chilean wine palm planted in 1846 (and so big that you have to climb the spiral staircase to the roof to get a proper view of it). ⊠ *Kew Rd. at Lichfield Rd., for Victoria Gate entrance, Kew* ☎ *020/8332–5000* ⊕ *www.kew. org* ✉ *£17, Explorer Land Train £5* Ⓜ *Kew Gardens. National Rail: Kew Gardens, Kew Bridge.*

Chapter 4

OXFORD AND THE THAMES VALLEY

4

Updated by
Toby Orton

 Sights
★★★★☆

 Restaurants
★★★★☆

 Hotels
★★★★☆

 Shopping
★★★☆☆

 Nightlife
★★★☆☆

WELCOME TO OXFORD AND THE THAMES VALLEY

TOP REASONS TO GO

★ **Oxford:** While scholars' noses are buried in their books, you get to sightsee among Oxford University's ancient stone buildings and memorable museums.

★ **Windsor Castle:** The mystique of eight successive royal houses of the British monarchy permeates Windsor and its famous castle, where a fraction of the current Queen's vast wealth is displayed.

★ **Blenheim Palace:** The only British historic home to be named a World Heritage Site has magnificent baroque architecture, stunning parkland, and remembrances of Winston Churchill.

★ **Boating on the Thames:** Life is slower on the river, and renting a boat or taking a cruise is an ideal way to see verdant riverside pastures and villages. Windsor, Marlow, Henley, and Oxford are good options.

An ideal place to begin any exploration of the Thames Valley is the town of Windsor, about an hour's drive west of central London. From there you can follow the river to Marlow and to Henley-on-Thames, site of the famous regatta, and then make a counterclockwise sweep west to the area around Henley-on-Thames. To the north is Oxford, with its pubs, colleges, and museums; it can make a good base for exploring some of the area's charming towns and notable stately homes. If you're extending your itinerary, west of the region but still nearby are the Cotswolds and Stratford-upon-Avon.

1 Windsor. A gorgeous town with one of England's most famous castles.

2 Eton. Home to England's most prestigious secondary school.

3 Ascot. A posh town famous for horse racing.

4 Cliveden. A stately mansion and one of the country's grandest hotels.

5 Marlow. A lovely Thames-side village.

6 Henley-on-Thames. A village famed for its rowing regatta.

7 Oxford. One of the world's oldest and greatest centers of learning.

8 Woodstock. Home to extraordinary Blenheim Palace, Winston Churchill's birthplace.

9 Aylesbury. A good base for exploring the area's grand manor houses.

10 St. Albans. A historical town that's close to the popular Harry Potter Studio Tour.

Easy proximity to London has made the Thames Valley a favored hangout for the wealthy, just as it has been for centuries. The rich and powerful of centuries past built the lavish country estates and castles, including Windsor, that today form the area's most popular tourist attractions.

Many of these are easy day trips from London, as is Oxford and its famed university. Consider exploring this stretch of the River Thames by boat, either jumping aboard a cruiser or getting behind the oars. Windsor, Henley, and Marlow all make good starting points.

Once an aquatic highway connecting London to the rest of England and the world, the Thames was critical to the power of the city when the sun never set on the British Empire. By the 18th century the Thames was one of the world's busiest water systems, declining in commercial importance only when the 20th century brought other means of transportation to the forefront. Traditionally, the area west of London is known as the Thames Valley, and the area to the east is called the Thames Gateway.

Anyone who wants to understand the mystique of the British monarchy should visit Windsor, home to the medieval and massive Windsor Castle. Farther upstream, the green quadrangles and graceful spires of Oxford are the hallmarks of one of the world's most famous universities. Within 10 miles of Oxford the storybook village of Woodstock and gracious Blenheim Palace, one of the grandest houses in England, are both well worth your time.

The railroads and motorways carrying traffic to and from London have turned much of this area into commuter territory, but you can still find timeless villages and miles of relaxing countryside. The stretches of the Thames near Marlow and Henley-on-Thames are lovely, with rowing clubs, piers, and sturdy waterside cottages and villas. It all conspires to make the Thames Valley a wonderful find, even for experienced travelers.

MAJOR REGIONS

Windsor, Marlow, and Nearby. Windsor Castle is one of the jewels of the area known as Royal Windsor, but a journey around this section of the Thames has other pleasures. The town of Eton holds the eponymous private school, Ascot has its famous racecourse, and Cliveden is a stately home turned into a grand hotel.

The stretch of the Thames Valley from Marlow to Henley-on-Thames is enchanting. Walking through its fields and along its waterways, it's easy to see how it inspired Kenneth Grahame's classic 1908 children's book, The Wind in the Willows. Whether by boat or on foot, you can discover some of the region's most delightful scenery. On each bank are fine wooded hills with spacious homes, greenhouses, flower gardens, and neat lawns that stretch to the water's edge. Grahame wrote his book in Pangbourne, and his illustrator, E. H. Shepard, used the great house at Mapledurham as the model for Toad Hall. It all still has the power to inspire.

Oxford. Wonderfully walkable, this university town has handsome, golden-stone buildings and museum after museum to explore. Take a punt on the local waterways for a break. Oxford's good bars, pubs, and restaurants keep you going late at night as well.

Oxfordshire The River Thames takes on a new graciousness as it flows along the borders of Oxfordshire for 71 miles; with each league it increases in size and importance. Three tributaries swell the river as it passes through the landscape: the Windrush, the Evenlode, and the Cherwell. Tucked among the hills and dales are one of England's most impressive stately homes, an Edenic little town, and a former Rothschild estate. Closer to London in Hertfordshire is St. Albans, wtih its cathedral and Roman remains.

Planning

When to Go

High summer is lovely, but droves of visitors have the same effect on some travelers as bad weather. Consider visiting in late spring or early fall, when the weather isn't too bad and the crowds have headed home. Book tickets and accommodations well in advance for Henley's Royal Regatta at the cusp of June and July and Ascot's Royal Meeting in mid-June. Visiting Eton and the Oxford colleges is much more restricted during term time (generally September to late March and late April to mid-July). Most stately homes are open March through September or

October only—call in advance. Avoid any driving in the London area during morning and afternoon rush hours.

FESTIVALS
★ **Oxford Literary Festival**
FESTIVALS | The festival takes place during the last week of March at Christ Church College, the Sheldonian, and other university venues. Leading authors come to give lectures and interviews, and there's plenty to entertain children. ⊠ *Christ Church College, St. Aldate's, Oxford* ☎ *07444/318986* ⊕ *www.oxfordliteraryfestival.org.*

Planning Your Time

The major towns of the Thames Valley are easy to visit on a day trip from London A train to Windsor, for example, takes about an hour, and you can fully explore Windsor and its environs in a day. Base yourself in Oxford for a couple of days, though, if you want to make a thorough exploration of the town and the surrounding countryside. To visit the great houses and the rural castles you need to either rent a car or join an organized tour. Blenheim Palace and Waddesdon Manor require at least half a day to do them justice, as does Stowe Landscape Gardens.

Getting Here and Around

BUS
Oxford and the area's main towns are convenient by bus from London, as is Windsor (although trains are faster), but St. Albans is best reached by train.

You can travel between the major towns by local bus, but it's complicated and can require changing more than once. For information, contact Traveline. If you want to see more than one town in this area in a day, it's best to rent a car or join a tour.

CONTACTS Arriva. ⊕ *www.arrivabus. co.uk.* **First.** ☎ *01224/650100* ⊕ *www.firstgroup.com.* **Megabus.** ☎ *0900/160–0900*

booking line, calls cost £0.60 per min ⊕ *uk.megabus.com.* **Oxford Bus Company.** ☎ *01865/785400* ⊕ *www.oxfordbus. co.uk.* **Reading Buses.** ☎ *0118/959–4000* ⊕ *www.reading-buses.co.uk.* **Stagecoach Oxford Tube.** ☎ *01865/772250* ⊕ *www. oxfordtube.com.* **Traveline.** ☎ *0871/200– 2233* ⊕ *www.traveline.info.*

CAR

Most towns in this area are within a one- or two-hour drive of central London—except during rush hour, of course. Although the roads are good, this wealthy section of the commuter belt has heavy traffic, even on the secondary roads. Parking in towns can be a problem, so take advantage of public parking lots near the outskirts of town centers.

TRAIN

Trains to Oxford (one hour) and the region depart from London's Paddington Station. Trains bound for Ascot (50 minutes) leave from Waterloo every 30 minutes. Trains to St. Albans (20 minutes) leave from St. Pancras Station. A number of lines, including Chiltern and First Great Western, serve the area; National Rail Enquiries has information.

CONTACTS National Rail Enquiries. ☎ *0845/748–4950* ⊕ *www.nationalrail. co.uk.*

Restaurants

Londoners weekend here, and where they go, stellar restaurants follow. Bray (near Windsor), Marlow, and Great Milton (near Oxford) claim some excellent tables; you need to book months ahead for these. Simple pub food, as well as classic French cuisine, can be enjoyed in waterside settings at many restaurants beside the Thames. Even in towns away from the river, well-heeled commuters and Oxford professors support top-flight establishments. Reservations are often not required but are strongly recommended, especially on weekends.

Hotels

From converted country houses to refurbished Elizabethan inns, the region's accommodations are rich in history and distinctive in appeal. Many hotels cultivate traditional gardens and retain a sense of the past with impressive collections of antiques. Book ahead, particularly in summer; you're competing for rooms with many Londoners in search of a getaway.

Restaurant and hotel reviews have been shortened. For full information, visit Fodors.com. Restaurant prices are the average cost of a main course at dinner, or if dinner is not served, at lunch. Hotel prices are the lowest cost of a standard double room in high season, including 20% V.A.T.

WHAT IT COSTS in Pounds			
$	$$	$$$	$$$$
RESTAURANTS			
under £16	£16–£23	£24–£30	over £30
HOTELS			
under £125	£125–£225	£226–£350	over £350

Visitor Information

CONTACTS Tourism Southeast. ☎ *02380/625400* ⊕ *www.visitsoutheastengland.com.* **Visit Thames.** ⊕ *www. visitthames.co.uk.*

Windsor

21 miles west of London.

Only a small part of old Windsor—the settlement that grew up around the town's famous castle in the Middle Ages—has survived. The town isn't what it was in the time of Sir John Falstaff and

Windsor, Marlow, and Around

the Merry Wives of Windsor, when it was famous for its convivial inns—in 1650, it had about 70 of them. Only a handful remain today, with the others replaced, it seems, by endless cafés. Windsor can feel overrun by tourists in summer, but even so, romantics appreciate cobbled Church Lane and noble Queen Charlotte Street, opposite the castle entrance.

GETTING HERE AND AROUND

Fast Green Line buses leave from the Colonnades opposite London's Victoria Coach Station every half hour for the 70-minute trip to Windsor. First Group has frequent service from Heathrow Airport's Terminal 5; the journey takes less than an hour. First Group also runs regional bus service to small towns and villages near Windsor.

Trains travel from London Waterloo every 30 minutes, or you can catch a more frequent train from Paddington and change at Slough. The trip takes less than an hour from Waterloo and around 30 minutes from Paddington. If you're driving, the M4 from London takes around an hour. Park in one of the public lots near the edge of the town center.

TOURS

City Sightseeing

Hop-on, hop-off tours of Windsor and Eton are offered by City Sightseeing, though it's easy to explore compact Windsor on foot. ☎ 01789/299123 ⊕ www.city-sightseeing.com ✉ From £12.

ESSENTIALS

BUS CONTACTS First Group. ☎ 0175/352–4144 ⊕ www.firstgroup.com. **Green Line.** ☎ 0344/801–7261 ⊕ www.greenline. co.uk.

VISITOR INFORMATION Royal Windsor **Information Centre.** ⊠ *Old Booking Hall, Windsor Royal Station, Thames St.* ☏ *01753/743900, 01753/743907 for accommodations* ⊕ *www.windsor.gov. uk.*

Sights

Savill Garden
GARDEN | The main horticultural delight of Windsor Great Park, the exquisite Savill Garden is about 4 miles from Windsor Castle. The 35 acres of ornamental gardens contain an impressive display of 2,500 rosebushes and a tremendous diversity of trees and shrubs. The Savill Building, easily recognizable by its undulating roof in the shape of a leaf, holds a visitor center, restaurant, and terrace where you can dine overlooking the garden, as well as a large shopping area with plenty of gifts, cards, and original artwork. ⊠ *Wick Rd., Egham* ☏ *01753/860222* ⊕ *www.windsorgreatpark.co.uk* ⊠ *£12 Mar.–Oct., £6 Nov.–Feb.*

★ Windsor Castle
CASTLE/PALACE | From William the Conqueror to Queen Victoria, the kings and queens of England have added towers and wings to this brooding, imposing castle, visible for miles and now the largest inhabited castle in the world. Most of England's kings and queens have demonstrated their undying attachment to the castle, the only royal residence in continuous use by the Royal Family since the Middle Ages. The State Apartments are open to the public most days and contain priceless furniture and works of art; high points of the tour include the Throne Room, the Waterloo Chamber, and the speculator collection of arms and armor. A visit between October and March also includes the Semi-State rooms, the private apartments of George IV. You can also wander the expansive grounds. ■**TIP**→ **Entrance lines can be long in season, and you're likely to spend at** least half a day here, so come early. ⊠ *Castle Hill* ☏ *0303/123–7304 for tickets* ⊕ *www.rct.uk/visit/windsor-castle* ⊠ *£23.50 for Precincts, State Apartments, Gallery, St. George's Chapel, and Queen Mary's Dolls' House; £12.90 when State Apartments are closed.*

★ Windsor Great Park
CITY PARK | The remains of an ancient royal hunting forest, this park stretches for some 5,000 acres south of Windsor Castle. Much of it is open to the public and can be explored by car or on foot. Its chief attractions are clustered around the southeastern section, known (or at least marketed) as the **Royal Landscape.** These include **Virginia Water,** a 2-mile-long lake that forms the park's main geographical focal point. More than anything, however, the Royal Landscape is defined by its two beautiful gardens. **Valley Gardens,** located on the north shore of Virginia Water, is particularly vibrant in April and May, when the dazzling multicolor azaleas are in full bloom. If you're feeling fit, the romantic **Long Walk** is one of England's most photographed footpaths—the 3-mile-long route, designed by Charles II, starts in the Great Park and leads all the way to Windsor Castle.

Divided from the Great Park by the busy A308 highway, the smaller **Windsor Home Park,** on the eastern side of Windsor Castle, is the private property of the Royal Family. It contains **Frogmore House,** a lavish royal residence. Completed in 1684, Frogmore was bought by George III as a gift for his wife, Queen Charlotte. The sprawling white mansion later became a beloved retreat of Queen Victoria. It was also formerly home to the Duke and Duchess of Sussex, otherwise known as Prince Harry and Meghan Markle, and can still only be visited by guided tour on a handful of days throughout August; see ⊕ www.rct.uk for more information. ⊠ *Entrances on A329, A332, B383, and Wick La.* ☏ *01753/860222* ⊕ *www.windsorgreatpark.co.uk* ⊠ *£12.50* ☉ *Windsor*

Boating on the Thames

Whether you're drifting lazily along in your own boat or taking a sight-seeing cruise past crucial points of English history, you'll see the River Thames from a new and delightful vantage point out on the water. It's hard to beat gliding peacefully on the river, water meadows on either side of you, and then tying up for a picnic or lunch at a riverside pub. You can just putter about in a rowboat for an hour or so, or hire a boat and organize your own itinerary for a few days. If this doesn't appeal, go on a romantic lunch cruise or take one of the many organized trips. There are 125 miles of navigable water to explore, quieter nearer the source of the Thames in the Cotswolds, perhaps most picturesque between Pangbourne and Marlow, and busiest nearer London. Wherever you go, your pace of life will slow right down: boats aren't allowed to travel above 5 mph.

Choosing a Boat
Most boats rented by the hour accommodate four people. Motorboats are noisy, but you can opt for electric canoes or launches that have the benefit of canopies. Punts (flat-bottom wooden boats) require a strong arm so you can maneuver the long wooden pole and push the boat along. Narrow boats carried freight on canals but are now well equipped for pleasure trips.

Renting Boats
The main hubs for boat rental are at Windsor, Henley-on-Thames, Oxford, and Lechlade. The costs are £15 an hour for a rowboat, £25 for an electric boat, £60 for half a day with a punt, and £175 a day for a motor cruiser. A short trip for four on a narrow boat from Oxfordshire Narrowboats ranges from around £160 to £1,000.

Hobbs of Henley ⊠ *Station Rd., Henley-on-Thames* ☎ *01491/572035* ⊕ *www.hobbsofhenley.com.*

Oxford River Cruises ⊠ *Folly Bridge, Oxford* ☎ *01865/987147, 0845/226–9396* ⊕ *www.oxfordrivercruises.com.*

Oxfordshire Narrowboats ⊠ *Heyford Wharf, Station Rd., Lower Heyford* ☎ *01869/340348* ⊕ *www.oxfordshire-narrowboats.co.uk.*

Hiring Boats
Hire a private boat with its own skipper to take you on a leisurely cruise. Compleat Angler in Marlow will take you on 1- or 2½-hour-long cruises down the river as far as Cliveden or even Windsor. The shortest trips available take about one hour.

Compleat Angler ⊠ *Marlow Bridge, Bisham Rd., Marlow* ☎ *0344/879–9210* ⊕ *www.macdonaldhotels.co.uk/compleatangler.*

Cruises
Windsor Castle, Runnymede, Henley (where you can stop for the River & Rowing Museum), and Mapledurham all lie on the banks of the Thames. Salter's Steamers runs short round-trips out of Windsor, Henley, Oxford, and Marlow, and French Brothers runs round-trips from Windsor.

French Brothers ⊠ *The Promenade, Barry Ave.* ☎ *01753/851900* ⊕ *www.frenchbrothers.co.uk.*

Salter's Steamers ⊠ *Folly Bridge, Oxford* ☎ *01865/243421* ⊕ *www.salterssteamers.co.uk.*

Home Park closed Sept.–July and Mon. and weekends in Aug.

🍴 Restaurants

Bel and the Dragon

$$ | **MODERN BRITISH** | Sit street side and watch as village life streams by, or cozy up in the oak-beamed bar of this historic inn dating from the 11th century. Rotisserie-cooked beef, pork, and chicken are specialties, and they do an exceptionally fine fish pie. **Known for:** excellent dishes right off the grill; perfect fish pie; hip and friendly staff. ⑤ *Average main: £18* ✉ *Thames St.* ☎ *01753/866056* ⊕ *www. belandthedragon-windsor.co.uk.*

★ Fat Duck

$$$$ | **MODERN BRITISH** | One of the top restaurants in the country, and ranked by many food writers among the best in the world, this extraordinary place packs in fans of hypercreative, hyper-expensive cuisine, who enjoy it for the theater as much as for the food. Culinary alchemist Heston Blumenthal is famed for the so-called molecular gastronomy he creates in his laboratory-like kitchen, and his name has become synonymous with weird and funky taste combinations. **Known for:** creative and immersive dining experience; strict booking process and long waiting list for reservations; famed strange dishes like bacon-and-egg ice cream. ⑤ *Average main: £325* ✉ *High St., Bray* ☎ *01628/580333* ⊕ *www.thefatduck.co.uk* ⊗ *Closed Sun. and Mon.*

★ Two Brewers

$$ | **BRITISH** | Locals congregate in a pair of low-ceiling rooms at this tiny 17th-century establishment by the gates of Windsor Great Park. Those under 18 aren't allowed inside the pub (although they can be served at a few outdoor tables), but adults will find a suitable collection of wine, espresso, and local beer, plus an excellent menu with dishes like roasted cod with butter sauce and samphire or steak frites with brandy and peppercorn.

Known for: classic, adults-only British pub; traditional lunchtime roast on Sunday; historic setting. ⑤ *Average main: £16* ✉ *34 Park St.* ☎ *01753/855426* ⊕ *www. twobrewerswindsor.co.uk.*

Hotels

Langton House

$ | **B&B/INN** | **FAMILY** | A former residence for representatives of the crown, this Victorian mansion on a quiet, leafy road is a 10-minute walk from Windsor Castle. **Pros:** soothing decor; family-friendly environment; friendly hosts. **Cons:** may hear some airplane noise; a little out of town; cheaper rooms have shared bathrooms. ⑤ *Rooms from: £102* ✉ *46 Alma Rd.* ☎ *01753/858299* ⊕ *www.langtonhouse. co.uk* ⋺ *5 rooms* ⍟ *Free breakfast.*

MGallery Windsor Castle Hotel

$$$ | **HOTEL** | You're treated to an exceptional view of Windsor Castle's Changing the Guard ceremony from this former coaching inn, parts of which date back to the 16th century. **Pros:** excellent location; wonderful afternoon tea; great view of the castle. **Cons:** older rooms are small; furniture is faux antique; a bit pricey. ⑤ *Rooms from: £320* ✉ *18 High St.* ☎ *01753/851577* ⊕ *www.castlehotelwindsor.com* ⋺ *112 rooms* ⍟ *Free breakfast.*

★ Stoke Park

$$$$ | **HOTEL** | On a 350-acre estate, Stoke Park's neoclassical grandeur can make Windsor Castle, visible in the distance, seem almost humble in comparison. **Pros:** luxurious rooms; sweeping grounds; great spa. **Cons:** not for those lukewarm about golf; old-school atmosphere not for everyone; very pricey, even for what you get. ⑤ *Rooms from: £350* ✉ *Park Rd., Stoke Poges* ☎ *01753/717171* ⊕ *www.stokepark.com* ⋺ *77 rooms* ⍟ *No meals.*

🛍 Shopping

Windsor Royal Station
SHOPPING CENTERS/MALLS | Set within a handsome building that was once a Victorian-era train station, Windsor Royal Station is home to fashion outlets like Mint Velvet, Jigsaw, Whistles, and Vanilla. ⊠ *5 Goswell Hill* ☎ *01753/797070* ⊕ *www.windsorroyalstation.co.uk.*

Eton

23 miles west of London.

Some observers may find it symbolic that almost opposite Windsor Castle—which embodies the continuity of the royal tradition—stands Eton, a school that for centuries has educated many leaders of the country. With High Street, its single main street, leading from the river to the famous school, the old-fashioned town of Eton is much quieter than Windsor.

GETTING HERE AND AROUND
Eton is linked to Windsor by a footbridge across the Thames. Most visitors barely notice passing from one to the other.

👁 Sights

★ Eton College
COLLEGE | Signs warn drivers of "Boys Crossing" as you approach the splendid Tudor-style buildings of Eton College, the distinguished boarding school for boys ages 13–18 founded in 1440 by King Henry VI. It's all terrifically photogenic—during the college semester students still dress in pinstripe trousers, swallowtail coats, and stiff collars. Rivaling St. George's at Windsor in terms of size, the Gothic **Chapel** contains superb 15th-century grisaille wall paintings juxtaposed with modern stained glass by John Piper. Beyond the cloisters are the school's playing fields where, according to the Duke of Wellington, the Battle of Waterloo was really won, since so many of his officers had learned discipline and strategy during their school days. Boris Johnson is the most recent of the country's many prime ministers to have been educated here. The **Museum of Eton Life** has displays on the school's history and vignettes of school life. The school gives public tours on Friday afternoon from early April through August, bookable online. ⊠ *Brewhouse Yard* ☎ *01753/370100* ⊕ *www.etoncollege.com* 💷 *£10* ◷ *Closed Sept.–early Apr.*

🍴 Restaurants

Gilbey's Eton
$$ | **MODERN BRITISH** | Just over the bridge from Windsor, this restaurant at the center of Eton's Antiques Row serves a changing menu of imaginative fare, from potted ham hock and rhubarb with sweet onion and mustard seed to crayfish and dill hot-smoked trout fish cakes. Well priced wines, both French and from the restaurant's own English vineyard, are a specialty, as are the savories—meat, fish, and vegetarian pâtés. **Known for:** traditional English food; old-school charm; bargain fixed-price lunches. ⑤ *Average main: £19* ⊠ *82–83 High St.* ☎ *01753/854921* ⊕ *www.gilbeygroup.com/restaurants/gilbeys-eton.*

🛏 Hotels

Christopher Hotel
$$ | **HOTEL** | This former coaching inn on the village's main shopping street has spacious rooms in the handsome main building as well as in the courtyard mews. **Pros:** a nice mix of modern and historic; good restaurant; great location. **Cons:** steep stairs; courtyard rooms can be noisy; rooms could use a little sprucing up. ⑤ *Rooms from: £160* ⊠ *110 High St.* ☎ *01753/852359* ⊕ *www.thechristopher.co.uk* ⇆ *34 rooms* ⦿ *Free breakfast.*

Ascot

8 miles southwest of Windsor, 28 miles southwest of London.

The posh town of Ascot (pronounced as-cut) has for centuries been famous for horse racing and for style. Queen Anne chose to have a racecourse here, and the first race meeting took place in 1711. The impressive show of millinery for which the Royal Meeting (or Royal Ascot, as it is also known) is famed was immortalized in My Fair Lady, in which a hat with osprey feathers and black-and-white silk roses transformed Eliza Doolittle into a grand lady. Betting on the races at England's most prestigious course is as important as dressing up; it's all part of the fun.

GETTING HERE AND AROUND

If you're driving, leave M4 at Junction 6 and take A332. Trains from London leave Waterloo Station every half hour, and the journey takes 50 minutes. The racecourse is a seven-minute walk from the train station.

 ## Sights

Ascot Racecourse

SPORTS—SIGHT | The races run regularly throughout the year, and Royal Ascot takes place annually in mid-June.
■ **TIP→ Tickets for Royal Ascot generally go on sale in November, so buy them well in advance.** Prices range from £26 for standing room on the heath to around £90 for seats in the stands. Car parking costs £40 in advance or £45 on the day. ⊠ *A329* ☎ *0844/346–3000* ⊕ *www.ascot. co.uk.*

 ## Hotels

★ Coworth Park

$$$ | HOTEL | FAMILY | Much imaginative and thoughtful renovation has transformed this 18th-century mansion, set on 240 acres of parkland, into a playful and contemporary lodging. **Pros:** country-house atmosphere; attentive and friendly service; free activities for kids. **Cons:** not for traditionalists; eye-wateringly expensive; some bedrooms are small. ⑤ *Rooms from: £350* ⊠ *Blacknest Rd.* ☎ *01344/876600* ⊕ *www.dorchestercollection.com/en/ascot/coworth-park* ⤴ *70 rooms* ❍ *Free breakfast.*

Cliveden

8 miles northwest of Windsor, 16 miles north of Ascot, 26 miles west of London.

This grand stately home, designed by Charles Barry, the architect of the Houses of Parliament, and the setting of the notorious Profumo affair in the 1960s, has spectacular gardens and sweeping views to the Thames.

GETTING HERE AND AROUND

If you're driving, take the M4 to the A4, where brown signs lead you to the entrance off the A4094.

 ## Sights

Cliveden

HOUSE | FAMILY | Described by Queen Victoria as a "bijou of taste," Cliveden (pronounced *Cliv*-dn) is a magnificent country mansion that, for more than 300 years, has lived up to its Georgian heritage as a bastion of aesthetic delights. The house, set on 376 acres of gardens and parkland above the River Thames, was rebuilt in 1851; but it was the rich and powerful Astor family, who purchased it in 1893, that made Cliveden famous. In the 1920s and 1930s this was the meeting place for the influential salon known as the "Cliveden Set"—a group of strongly conservative thinkers who many accused of being Nazi sympathizers. Its doyenne was Nancy Astor, an American by birth, who became the first woman to sit in the British Parliament. The ground-floor rooms of the house are open, as is

Watching the horse races at Royal Ascot is a posh British tradition.

the Octagon Chapel, with its beautiful gilt-painted ceiling and wall panels. You can wander the lovely grounds, which include a water garden, miles of woodland and riverbank paths, a kids' play area, and a yew-tree maze. Book your timed ticket for the house beforehand or early on the day. Boat hire and trips are available daily in July and August. Note that opening times of the house can be unpredictable, even at the busiest times of the year; always call before setting out. ⊠ *Cliveden Rd., Taplow* ✛ *Near Maidenhead* ☎ *01628/605069* ⊕ *www. nationaltrust.org.uk/cliveden* 🎫 *Garden and woodland £16, house £2.*

 Hotels

★ Cliveden House

$$$$ | HOTEL | If you've ever wondered what it would feel like to be an Edwardian grandee, then sweep up the drive to this stately home, one of Britain's grandest hotels. **Pros:** like stepping back in time; outstanding sense of luxury; beautiful grounds. **Cons:** airplanes fly overhead;

two-night minimum on weekends; you'll need deep pockets. $ *Rooms from: £500* ⊠ *Cliveden Rd., Taplow* ☎ *01628/668561* ⊕ *www.clivedenhouse.co.uk* 🛏 *47 rooms* ○ *Free breakfast.*

Marlow

7 miles west of Cliveden, 15 miles northwest of Windsor.

Just inside the Buckinghamshire border, Marlow and the surrounding area overflow with Thames-side prettiness. The unusual suspension bridge was built in the 1830s by William Tierney Clark, architect of the bridge in Hungary linking Buda and Pest. Marlow has a number of striking old buildings, particularly the privately owned Georgian houses along Peter and West streets. In 1817, the Romantic poet Percy Bysshe Shelley stayed with friends at 67 West Street and then bought **Albion House** on the same street. His second wife, Mary, completed her Gothic novel *Frankenstein* here. Ornate **Marlow Place,** on Station Road, dating from 1721, is reputedly the finest building in town.

Marlow hosts its own one-day regatta in mid-June. The town is a good base from which to join the **Thames Path** to Henley-on-Thames. On summer weekends tourism can often overwhelm the town.

GETTING HERE AND AROUND

Trains leave London from Paddington every half hour and involve a change at Maidenhead; the journey takes an hour. By car, leave M4 at Junction 8/9, following A404 and then A4155. From M40, join A404 at Junction 4.

Sights

Swan-Upping

FESTIVAL | This traditional event, which dates back 800 years, takes place in Marlow during the third week of July. By bizarre ancient laws, the Queen owns every single one of the country's swans, so each year swan-markers in skiffs start from Sunbury-on-Thames, catching the new cygnets and marking their beaks to establish ownership. The Queen's Swan Marker, dressed in scarlet livery, presides over this colorful ceremony. ⊠ *Marlow* ☎ *01628/523030* ⊕ *www.royal.uk.*

🍴 Restaurants

Vanilla Pod

$$$$ | **FRENCH** | Discreet and intimate, this restaurant is a showcase for the French-inspired cuisine of chef Michael Macdonald, who, as the restaurant's name implies, holds vanilla in high esteem. The fixed-price menu borrows the flavor of a French bistro and shakes it up a bit, so you might have filet mignon with polenta or something more adventurous, such as fennel escabeche with mackerel and vanilla. **Known for:** French-inspired cooking; a flair for vanilla; great value set lunch. 💲 *Average main: £45* ⊠ *31 West St.* ☎ *01628/898101*

⊕ *www.thevanillapod.co.uk* ⊘ *Closed Sun. and Mon.*

🛏 Hotels

Macdonald Compleat Angler

$$ | **HOTEL** | Although fishing aficionados consider this luxurious, 17th-century, Thames-side inn the ideal place to stay, the place is stylish enough to attract those with no interest in casting a line. **Pros:** gorgeous rooms; great views of the Thames; legendary fishing spot. **Cons:** river views cost more, except Rooms 9 and 10; need a car to get around; rooms could use some updating. 💲 *Rooms from: £180* ⊠ *Marlow Bridge, Bisham Rd.* ☎ *0844/879–9128, 01628/484444 international* ⊕ *www.macdonaldhotels.co.uk/our-hotels/south-england/marlow/macdonald-compleat-angler* ⤳ *64 rooms* 🍽 *Free breakfast.*

Henley-on-Thames

7 miles southwest of Marlow, 8 miles north of Reading, 36 miles west of central London.

Henley's fame is based on one thing: rowing. The Henley Royal Regatta, held at the cusp of June and July on a long, straight stretch of the River Thames, has made the little riverside town famous throughout the world. Townspeople launched the Henley Regatta in 1839, initiating the Grand Challenge Cup, the most famous of its many trophies. The best amateur oarsmen from around the globe compete in crews of eight, four, or two, or as single scullers. For many spectators, the event is on par with Royal Ascot and Wimbledon.

The town is set in a broad valley between gentle hillsides. Henley's historic buildings, including half-timber Georgian cottages and inns (as well as one of Britain's oldest theaters, the Kenton), are all within a few minutes' walk. The river near Henley is alive with boats of every shape and size, from luxury cabin cruisers to tiny rowboats.

GETTING HERE AND AROUND
Frequent First Great Western trains depart for Henley from London Paddington; the journey time is around an hour. If you're driving from London or from the west, leave M4 at Junction 8/9 and follow A404(M) and then A4130 to Henley Bridge. From Marlow, Henley is a 7-mile drive southwest on A4155.

ESSENTIALS
VISITOR INFORMATION Henley Visitor Information Centre. ✉ Henley Town Hall, Market Pl., Henley ☎ 01491/578034 ⊕ www.henleytowncouncil.gov.uk/information-centre-including-tourism.aspx.

Sights

River & Rowing Museum
MUSEUM | FAMILY | Focusing on the history and sport of rowing, this absorbing museum built on stilts includes exhibits devoted to actual vessels, from a Saxon log boat to an elegant Victorian steam launch to Olympic boats. One gallery tells the story of the Thames as it flows from its source to the ocean, while another explores the history of the town and its famed regatta. A charming Wind in the Willows walk-through exhibit evokes the settings of the famous children's book. ✉ Mill Meadows, Henley ☎ 01491/415600 ⊕ www.rrm.co.uk ✆ £9.

St. Mary's Church
RELIGIOUS SITE | With a 16th-century "checkerboard" tower, St. Mary's is a stone's throw from the bridge over the Thames. The adjacent, yellow-washed **Chantry House,** built in 1420, is one of England's few remaining merchant houses from the period. It's an unspoiled example of the rare timber-frame design, with upper floors jutting out. You can enjoy tea here on Sunday afternoon in summer.

✉ Hart St., Henley ☎ 01491/577340 ⊕ www.stmaryshenley.org.uk ✆ Free.

Restaurants

The Three Tuns
$$ | MODERN BRITISH | Walk past the cozy bar in this traditional 17th-century pub to eat in the snug dining room with the clutch of locals who come nightly for the traditional British comfort food. Plates such as beer-battered fish-and chips or local butcher's sausages and mashed potatoes are easy crowd-pleasers. **Known for:** excellent traditional savory pies; lovely old pub atmosphere; delicious desserts. $ Average main: £16 ✉ 5 Market Pl., Henley on Thames ☎ 01491/410138 ⊕ www.threetunshenley.co.uk ⊗ Closed Mon.

Hotels

The Row Barge
$ | B&B/INN | This historic, 15th-century pub certainly looks the part, with low-beamed ceilings and a fire crackling in the grate. **Pros:** historic inn with lots of character; friendly owners; good food. **Cons:** entrance to guest rooms through bar and up a staircase with very low ceiling; room No. 1 has no door to the bathroom; quirks of historic building not for everyone. $ Rooms from: £05 ✉ West St. ☎ 01491/572649 ➟ 4 rooms ⦿ Free breakfast.

Activities

Henley Royal Regatta
CANOEING/ROWING/SKULLING | A series of rowing competitions attracting participants from many countries, the annual Henley Royal Regatta takes place over five days in late June and early July. Large tents are erected along both sides of a straight stretch of the river known as Henley Reach, and every surrounding field becomes a parking lot. There's

plenty of space on the public towpath from which to watch the early stages of the races. ■TIP➔ **If you want to attend, book a room months in advance. After all, 500,000 people turn out for the event.** ✉ *Henley* ☎ *01491/571900 for ticket line, 01491/572153 for inquiries* ⊕ *www.hrr. co.uk.*

Oxford

With arguably the most famous university in the world, Oxford has been a center of learning since 1167, with only the Sorbonne preceding it. It doesn't take more than a day or two to explore its winding medieval streets, photograph its ivy-covered stone buildings and ancient churches and libraries, and even take a punt down one of its placid waterways. The town center is compact and walkable, and at its heart is Oxford University. Alumni of this prestigious institution include 48 Nobel Prize winners, 26 British prime ministers (including Boris Johnson), and 28 foreign presidents (including Bill Clinton), along with poets, authors, and artists such as Percy Bysshe Shelley, Oscar Wilde, and W. H. Auden.

Oxford is 55 miles northwest of London, at the junction of the rivers Thames and Cherwell. The city is more interesting and more cosmopolitan than Cambridge, and although it's also bigger, its suburbs aren't remotely interesting to visitors. The charm is all at the center, where the old town curls around the grand stone buildings, good restaurants, and historic pubs. Victorian writer Matthew Arnold described Oxford's "dreaming spires," a phrase that has become famous. Students rush past you on the sidewalks on the way to their exams, clad with marvelous antiquarian style in their requisite mortar caps, flowing dark gowns, stiff collars, and crisp white bow ties. ■TIP➔ **Watch your back when crossing roads, as bikes are everywhere.**

GETTING HERE AND AROUND

Megabus, Oxford Bus Company, and Stagecoach Oxford Tube all have buses traveling from London 24 hours a day; the trip takes between one hour 40 minutes and two hours. In London, Megabus departs from Victoria Coach Station, while Oxford Bus Company and Stagecoach Oxford Tube have pickup points on Buckingham Palace Road, Victoria; Oxford Tube also picks up from the Marble Arch underground station. Oxford Bus Company runs round-trip shuttle service from Gatwick (£37) every hour and Heathrow (£30) every half hour. Most of the companies have multiple stops in Oxford, with Gloucester Green, the final stop, being the most convenient for travelers. You can easily traverse the town center on foot, but the Oxford Bus Company has a one-day ticket (£4.30) for unlimited travel in and around Oxford.

Trains to Oxford depart from London's Paddington Station for the one-hour trip. Oxford Station is at the western edge of the historic town center on Botley Road.

To drive, take the M40 northwest from London. It's an hour's drive, except during rush hour, when it can take twice as long. In-town parking is notoriously difficult, so use one of the five free park-and-ride lots and pay for the bus to the city. The Thornhill Park and Ride and the St. Clement's parking lot before the roundabout that leads to Magdalen Bridge are convenient for the M40.

ESSENTIALS

BUS CONTACTS Megabus. ☎ *0871/266–3333 for inquiries, 0900/160–0900 booking line* ⊕ *www.megabus.com.* **Oxford Bus Company.** ☎ *01865/785400* ⊕ *www. oxfordbus.co.uk.* **Stagecoach Oxford Tube.** ☎ *01865/772250* ⊕ *www.oxfordtube. com.*

TOURS

City Sightseeing
ORIENTATION | This company runs hop-on, hop-off bus tours with 20 stops

around Oxford. Your ticket, purchased from the driver, is good for 24 hours. ☎ 01865/790522 ⊕ www.citysightseeingoxford.com ☒ From £16.

 Sights

Oxford University isn't one easily identifiable campus, but a sprawling mixture of 38 colleges scattered around the city center, each with its own distinctive identity and focus. Oxford students live and study at their own college, and also use the centralized resources of the overarching university. The individual colleges are deeply competitive. Most of the grounds and magnificent dining halls and chapels are open to visitors, though the opening times (displayed at the entrance gates) vary greatly.

★ **Ashmolean Museum**

MUSEUM | What might be Britain's greatest museum outside London is also the oldest public museum in the United Kingdom. "The Ash," as locals call it, displays its rich and varied collections from the Neolithic to the present day over five stunning floors. Innovative and spacious galleries explore connections between priceless Greek, Roman, and Indian artifacts, as well as Egyptian and Chinese objects, all of which are among the best in the country. In the superb art collection, don't miss drawings by Raphael, the shell-encrusted mantle of Powhatan (father of Pocahontas), the lantern belonging to Guy Fawkes, and the Alfred Jewel, set in gold, which dates from the reign of King Alfred the Great (ruled 871–899). ☒ Beaumont St. ☎ 01865/278000 ⊕ www.ashmolean.org ☒ Free.

The Bodleian Library and Radcliffe Camera

LIBRARY | A vast library, the domed Radcliffe Camera is Oxford's most spectacular building, built in 1737–49 by James Gibbs in Italian baroque style. It's usually surrounded by tourists with cameras trained at its golden-stone walls. The Camera contains part of the Bodleian Library's enormous collection, begun in 1602 and one of six "copyright libraries" in the United Kingdom. It also contains valuable treasures such as a Gutenberg Bible and a Shakespeare First Folio. Guided tours reveal the magnificent Duke Humfrey's Library, which was completed in 1488, and the spots used for Hogwarts School in the Harry Potter films. Arrive early to secure tickets for the three to six daily tours. The standard tours can be prebooked, as can the extended tours on Wednesday and Saturday; otherwise, tours are first-come, first-served. Audio tours don't require reservations. ☒ Broad St. ☎ 01865/287400 ⊕ www.bodleian. ox.ac.uk ☒ From £4 ⊙ Sometimes closed for events; call to confirm.

Christ Church

COLLEGE | Built in 1546, the college of Christ Church is referred to by its members as "The House." This is the site of Oxford's largest quadrangle, Tom Quad, named after the huge bell (6¼ tons) that hangs in the Sir Christopher Wren–designed gate tower and rings 101 times at 9:05 every evening in honor of the original number of Christ Church scholars. The vaulted, 800-year-old chapel in one corner has been Oxford's cathedral since the time of Henry VIII. The college's medieval dining hall contains portraits of many famous alumni, including 13 of Britain's prime ministers, but you'll recognize it from its recurring role in the Harry Potter movies (although they didn't actually film here, the room was painstakingly re-created in a studio). ■TIP→ **Plan carefully, as the dining hall is often closed between noon and 2 during term time.** Lewis Carroll, author of Alice in Wonderland, was a teacher of mathematics here for many years; a shop opposite the meadows on St. Aldate's sells Alice paraphernalia. ☒ St. Aldate's ☎ 01865/276492 ⊕ www.chch.ox.ac.uk ☒ £15 ⊙ Sometimes closed for events; check website to confirm.

Sights ▼

1 Ashmolean Museum ... **A3**
2 The Bodleian Library and Radcliffe Camera ... **C4**
3 Christ Church **B5**
4 Christ Church Picture Gallery **C4**
5 Magdalen College **E5**
6 Oxford University Museum of Natural History........... **C1**
7 Pitt Rivers Museum..... **B1**
8 Sheldonian Theatre **C3**
9 St John's College **B2**
10 University of Oxford Botanic Garden **E5**

Restaurants ▼

1 Brasserie Blanc.......... **A1**
2 CuttleFish **E5**
3 Gee's **A1**
4 Le Manoir aux Quat'Saisons **E5**

Hotels ▼

1 Le Manoir aux Quat'Saisons............. **E5**
2 Malmaison Oxford...... **A5**
3 Newton House.......... **B5**
4 Old Bank Hotel **C4**
5 Old Parsonage **A1**

Christ Church Picture Gallery

MUSEUM | This connoisseur's delight in Canterbury Quadrangle exhibits works by the Italian masters as well as Hals, Rubens, and Van Dyck. Drawings in the 2,000-strong collection are shown on a changing basis. ⊠ *Oriel Sq.* ☎ *01865/276172* ⊕ *www.chch.ox.ac.uk/ gallery* ⊠ *f4* ⊘ *Closed Tues. Oct.–June.*

★ Magdalen College

COLLEGE | Founded in 1458, with a handsome main quadrangle and a supremely monastic air, Magdalen (pronounced *maud*-lin) is one of the most impressive of Oxford's colleges and attracts its most artistic students. Alumni include such diverse people as P. G. Wodehouse, Oscar Wilde, and John Betjeman. The school's large, square tower is a famous local landmark. ■ TIP→ **To enhance your visit, take a stroll around the Deer Park and along Addison's Walk; then have tea in the Old Kitchen, which overlooks the river.** ⊠ *High St.* ☎ *01865/276000* ⊕ *www. magd.ox.ac.uk* ⊠ *£7* ⊘ *Closed mornings Oct.–June.*

Oxford University Museum of Natural History

MUSEUM | FAMILY | This highly decorative Victorian Gothic creation of cast iron and glass, more a cathedral than a museum, is worth a visit for its architecture alone. Among the eclectic collections of entomology, geology, mineralogy, and zoology are the towering skeleton of a *Tyrannosaurus rex* and casts of a dodo's foot and head. There's plenty for children to explore and touch. ⊠ *Parks Rd.* ☎ *01865/272950* ⊕ *www.oumnh.ox.ac. uk* ⊠ *Free.*

★ Pitt Rivers Museum

MUSEUM | FAMILY | More than half a million intriguing archaeological and anthropological items from around the globe, based on the collection bequeathed by Lieutenant-General Augustus Henry Lane Fox Pitt Rivers in 1884, are crammed into a multitude of glass cases and drawers. In an eccentric touch that's surprisingly thought-provoking, labels are handwritten, and items are organized thematically rather than geographically—a novel way to gain perspective. Give yourself plenty of time to wander through the displays of shrunken heads, Hawaiian feather cloaks, and fearsome masks. ⊠ *S. Parks Rd.* ☎ *01865/270927* ⊕ *www.prm.ox.ac.uk* ⊠ *Free (donations welcome).*

Sheldonian Theatre

ARTS VENUE | This fabulously ornate theater is where Oxford's impressive graduation ceremonies are held, conducted almost entirely in Latin. Dating from 1663, it was the first building designed by Sir Christopher Wren when he served as professor of astronomy. The D-shaped auditorium has pillars, balconies, and an elaborately painted ceiling. The stone pillars outside are topped by 18 massive stone heads. Climb the stairs to the cupola for the best view of the city's "dreaming spires." Guided tours take place a few times per week; call in advance for details. ⊠ *Broad St.* ☎ *01865/277299* ⊕ *www.sheldon.ox.ac. uk* ⊠ *£3.80; tours £8.*

St. John's College

COLLEGE | One of Oxford's most attractive campuses, St. John's has seven quiet quadrangles surrounded by elaborately carved buildings. You enter the first through a low wooden door. This college dates to 1555, when Sir Thomas White, a merchant, founded it. His heart is buried in the chapel (it's a tradition for students to curse as they walk over it). The Canterbury Quad represented the first example of Italian Renaissance architecture in Oxford, and the Front Quad includes the buildings of the old St. Bernard's Monastery. ⊠ *St. Giles'* ☎ *01865/277300* ⊕ *www.sjc.ox.ac.uk* ⊠ *Free.*

University of Oxford Botanic Garden

GARDEN | Founded in 1621 as a healing garden, this is the oldest of its kind in the British Isles. Set on the river, the diverse garden displays 6,000 species ranging from lilies to citrus trees. There is a spacious walled garden, six luxuriant glass houses, including insectivorous and lily houses, and interesting medicinal, rock, and bog gardens to explore. Picnics are allowed, but you must bring your own food and drinks, as there's nowhere to buy them inside. ✉ *Rose La.* ☎ *01865/286690* ⊕ *www.obga.ox.ac.uk* ✉ *£5.45.*

Restaurants

Brasserie Blanc

$$ | FRENCH | Raymond Blanc's sophisticated brasserie in the Jericho neighborhood is the more affordable chain restaurant cousin of Le Manoir aux Quat'Saisons in Great Milton. The changing menu always lists a good selection of steaks and innovative adaptations of bourgeois French fare, sometimes with Mediterranean or Asian influences. **Known for:** French classics like beef bourguignonne; affordable prix-fixe lunch menu; good wine selection. ⑤ *Average main: £17* ✉ *71–72 Walton St.* ☎ *01865/510999* ⊕ *www.brasserieblanc.com.*

CuttleFish

$ | SEAFOOD | The clue's in the name here—this popular local restaurant specializes in fresh, upscale seafood. Dishes are prepared with a European touch and frequently come with butter, cream, and other sauces, such as sardines served with lemon and parsley butter. **Known for:** excellent seafood; nautical surroundings; good-value lunches. ⑤ *Average main: £14* ✉ *36–37 St. Clement's St.* ☎ *01865/243003* ⊕ *www.cuttlefishoxford.co.uk.*

Gee's

$$ | MODERN BRITISH | With its glass-and-steel framework, this former florist's shop just north of the town center makes a charming conservatory dining room, full of plants and twinkling with lights in the evening. The menu concentrates on the best of Oxfordshire produce and changes daily, but you can expect to find the likes of delicate seafood linguine, farm-fresh roasted vegetables, and wood-fired guinea fowl. **Known for:** sophisticated British dishes with local produce; chocolate nemesis and pistachio ice cream dessert; affordable lunch and early dinner menus. ⑤ *Average main: £18* ✉ *61 Banbury Rd.* ☎ *01865/553540* ⊕ *www.geesrestaurant.co.uk.*

★ Le Manoir aux Quat'Saisons

$$$$ | FRENCH | One of the original gastronomy-focused hotels, Le Manoir was opened in 1984 by chef Raymond Blanc, whose culinary talents have earned the hotel's restaurant two Michelin stars—now held for an incredible 29 years and running. Decide from among such innovative French creations as spiced cauliflower velouté with langoustines, beef fillet with braised Jacob's ladder, or Dover sole with brown butter and rosemary. **Known for:** one of the top restaurants in the country; flawless French-style fine dining; beautiful surroundings. ⑤ *Average main: £170* ✉ *Church Rd., Great Milton* ☎ *01844/278881* ⊕ *www.belmond.com/hotels/europe/uk/oxfordshire/belmond-le-manoir-aux-quat-saisons/.*

Hotels

★ Le Manoir aux Quat'Saisons

$$$$ | HOTEL | FAMILY | Standards are high at this 15th-century stone manor house, the ultimate place for a gourmet getaway, where master-chef Raymond Blanc's epicurean touch shows at every turn, including one of the country's finest kitchens. **Pros:** design is plush, but not stuffy; perfect for romance, but also accommodates kids; famous on-site cooking school and amazing food. **Cons:** every room is different, so if you have specific requirements, let them know when booking; all the food is tough on the waistline; price is even tougher on the wallet. ⑤ *Rooms from: £550* ✉ *Church Rd., Great Milton* ☎ *01844/278881* ⊕ *www.belmond.com/hotels/europe/uk/oxfordshire/*

belmond-le-manoir-aux-quat-saisons ⟿ *32 rooms* |◎| *Free breakfast.*

Malmaison Oxford

$$$ | **HOTEL** | Housed in what was a 19th-century prison, this high-concept boutique hotel remains true to its unusual history by showing off the original metal doors and exposed-brick walls. **Pros:** modern luxury in a beautifully converted building; unique setting; great bar and restaurant. **Cons:** no matter how comfortable they make it, the prison ambience can still be weird; expensive parking; no elevator and lots of stairs. $ *Rooms from: £230* ⊠ *3 Oxford Castle* ☎ *01865/689944* ⊕ *www.malmaison.com/locations/oxford* ⟿ *95 rooms* |◎| *Free breakfast.*

Newton House

$$ | **B&B/INN** | This handsome Victorian mansion, a five-minute walk from all of Oxford's action, is a sprawling, friendly place on three floors. **Pros:** great breakfasts; handy parking lot; excellent value for the location. **Cons:** on a main road; no elevator; some may be disappointed with the contemporary look. $ *Rooms from: £127* ⊠ *82 Abingdon Rd.* ☎ *01865/240561* ⊕ *www.newtonhouseoxford.co.uk* ⟿ *14 rooms* |◎| *Free breakfast.*

Old Bank Hotel

$$ | **HOTEL** | From the impressive collection of modern artwork throughout the hotel to the sleek furnishings in the guest rooms, this stately converted bank building displays contemporary style in a city that favors the traditional. **Pros:** excellent location; interesting artwork at every turn; good restaurant. **Cons:** standard rooms can be small; breakfast costs extra; location a bit noisy. $ *Rooms from: £220* ⊠ *91–94 High St.* ☎ *01865/799599* ⊕ *www.oldbankhotel.co.uk* ⟿ *43 rooms* |◎| *No meals.*

Old Parsonage

$$$ | **HOTEL** | A 17th-century gabled stone house in a small garden next to St.

Giles Church, the Old Parsonage is a dignified retreat. **Pros:** beautiful vine-covered building; complimentary walking tours; free parking. **Cons:** pricey; some guest rooms are small; cool, contemporary look favored over period charm. $ *Rooms from: £300* ⊠ *1 Banbury Rd.* ☎ *01865/310210* ⊕ *www.oldparsonagehotel.co.uk* ⟿ *35 rooms* |◎| *Free breakfast.*

 Nightlife

Head of the River

BARS/PUBS | Near Folly Bridge, the terrace at the Head of the River is the perfect place to watch life on the water. It gets very crowded on sunny afternoons, but there's a great, quintessentially Oxford atmosphere. The pub also offers 20 comfortable guest rooms if you want to stay and appreciate the views a little longer. ⊠ *St. Aldate's* ☎ *01865/721600* ⊕ *www.headoftheriveroxford.co.uk.*

★ Raoul's

BARS/PUBS | This hip cocktail bar was named one of the 100 best cocktail bars in the world by the *Times* of London, and the bartenders can prove it with their encyclopedic knowledge of mixology and creative flair. The crowd is generally as bright and young as you'd expect. ⊠ *32 Walton St.* ☎ *01865/553732* ⊕ *www.raoulsbar.com.*

Turf Tavern

BARS/PUBS | Off Holywell Street, the Turf Tavern has a higgledy-piggledy collection of little rooms and outdoor spaces where you can enjoy a quiet drink and inexpensive pub food. ⊠ *Bath Pl.* ☎ *01865/243235* ⊕ *www.greenekingpubs.co.uk/pubs/oxfordshire/turf-tavern.*

White Horse

BARS/PUBS | This cozy pub, dating from at least 1823, serves real ales and traditional food all day. ⊠ *52 Broad St.* ☎ *01865/204801* ⊕ *www.whitehorseoxford.co.uk.*

Shopping

Blackwell's

BOOKS/STATIONERY | Family owned and run since 1879, Blackwell's stocks an excellent selection of books. Inquire about the literary and historic walking tours that run from late April through October. ⊠ *48–51 Broad St.* ☎ *01865/792792* ⊕ *blackwell. co.uk.*

★ Covered Market

OUTDOOR/FLEA/GREEN MARKETS | This is a fine place for a cheap sandwich and a leisurely browse; the smell of pastries and coffee follows you from cake shop to jeweler to cheesemonger. ⊠ *High St.* ⊕ *www.oxford-coveredmarket.co.uk.*

Scriptum

GIFTS/SOUVENIRS | Cards, stationery, handmade paper, and leather-bound journals can be purchased here, alongside marvelously arcane stuff you didn't know you needed—like quills, sealing wax, and even Venetian masks. ⊠ *3 Turl St.* ☎ *01865/200042* ⊕ *www.scriptum.co.uk.*

University of Oxford Shop

GIFTS/SOUVENIRS | Run by the university, the University of Oxford Shop sells authorized clothing, ceramics, and tea towels, all emblazoned with university crests. ⊠ *106 High St.* ☎ *01865/247414* ⊕ *www.oushop.com.*

Activities

PUNTING

You may choose, like many an Oxford student, to spend a summer afternoon punting, while dangling your champagne bottle in the water to keep it cool. Punts—shallow-bottom boats that are poled slowly up the river—can be rented in several places, including at the foot of the Magdalen Bridge.

Cherwell Boathouse

LOCAL SPORTS | From mid-March through mid-October, Cherwell Boathouse rents boats and, if you call ahead, someone to punt it. Rentals cost £18 per hour weekdays (£20 on weekends) or £90 (£100 on weekends) per day and should be booked ahead. The facility, a mile north of the heart of Oxford, also includes a stylish restaurant. ⊠ *Bardwell Rd.* ☎ *01865/515978* ⊕ *www.cherwellboathouse.co.uk.*

Salter's Steamers

LOCAL SPORTS | At the St. Aldates Road end of Folly Bridge, Salter's Steamers rents out punts and skiffs (rowboats) for £20 per hour, £60 per half day, and £100 per day. Chauffeured punts are £60 per hour, booked in advance. Day cruises are also run from Christ Church meadows to nearby Abingdon. ⊠ *Folly Bridge* ☎ *01865/243421* ⊕ *www.salterssteamers.co.uk.*

SPECTATOR SPORTS

Eights Week

BOATING | At the end of May, during Oxford's Eights Week (also known as Summer Eights), men and women from the university's colleges compete to be "Head of the River." This is a particularly fun race to watch because the shape of the river provides an added element of excitement. It's too narrow for the eight-member teams to race side by side, so the boats set off one behind another. Each boat tries to catch and bump the one in front. ⊠ *Oxford* ⊕ *www.ourcs.co.uk.*

Woodstock

8 miles northwest of Oxford.

Handsome 17th- and 18th-century houses line the trim streets of Woodstock, at the eastern edge of the Cotswolds. It's best known for nearby Blenheim Palace, and in summer tour buses clog the village's ancient streets. On a quiet fall or spring afternoon, however, Woodstock is a sublime experience: a mellowed 18th-century church and town hall mark the central square, and along its backstreets, you can find flower-bedecked houses and quiet lanes right out of a 19th-century etching.

GETTING HERE AND AROUND

The public bus service S3 runs (usually every half hour) between Oxford and Woodstock and costs £3.30 one way. It can drop you at the gates of Blenheim Palace.

Sights

★ Blenheim Palace

CASTLE/PALACE | This magnificent palace has been called England's Versailles, and with good reason—it's still the only historic house in Britain to be named a World Heritage Site. Designed by Sir John Vanbrugh in the early 1700s in collaboration with Nicholas Hawksmoor, Blenheim was given by Queen Anne and

the nation to General John Churchill, first duke of Marlborough. The exterior is nothing short of sumptuous. Inside, lavishness continues in extremes: you can join a free guided tour or simply walk through on your own. Book a tour of the current duke's private apartments for a more intimate view of ducal life. For some visitors, the most memorable room is the small, low-ceiling chamber where Winston Churchill was born in 1874. He's buried in nearby Bladon. Its 2,000 acres of grounds, the work of Capability Brown, 18th-century England's best-known landscape gardener, are arguably the best example of the "cunningly natural" park in the country. The Pleasure Gardens, reached by a miniature train that stops outside the palace's main entrance, contain a butterfly house, a hedge maze, and a giant chess set. ⊠ Off A4095, Woodstock ☎ 01993/810530

Fountains and formal Italian gardens set off the monumental baroque pile that is Blenheim Palace.

⊕ www.blenheimpalace.com ✉ Palace, park, and gardens £28.50; park and gardens £18.50.

Aylesbury

22 miles east of Oxford, 46 miles north-west of London.

Aylesbury makes a good base for exploring the surrounding countryside, including stately homes and gardens. It's a pretty, historic place with a 13th-century church surrounded by small Tudor lanes and cottages. This market town has been associated with the Aylesbury duck since the 18th century, when flocks were walked 40 miles to the London markets. Kids appreciate a visit to the Roald Dahl's Children's Gallery, which is open all year.

GETTING HERE AND AROUND
From London, Chiltern Railways runs frequent trains from Marylebone Station (one hour). The town is easily accessible from Oxford by Arriva Bus 280, which runs every 30 minutes; travel time is 80

minutes. If you're driving from Oxford, take A40 and A418. From London, follow M1 and A41 and allow 90 minutes.

Sights

★ Stowe Landscape Gardens
GARDEN | This exquisite example of a Georgian garden was created for the Temple family by the most famous gardeners of the 18th century. Capability Brown, Charles Bridgeman, and William Kent all worked on the land to create 980 acres of trees, valleys, and meadows. More than 40 striking monuments, follies, and temples dot the landscape of lakes, rivers, and pleasant vistas. This is a historically important place, but it's not for those who want primarily a flower garden. Allow at least half a day to explore the grounds. Stowe House, at the center, is now a fancy school with some magnificently restored rooms. It's open for tours most afternoons, but the actual schedule is notoriously changeable, so do call ahead or check ⊕ www. stowe.co.uk for more information. The

gardens are about 3 miles northwest of Buckingham, which is 14 miles north-west of Aylesbury. You enter through the New Inn visitor center, where there are period parlor rooms to explore.
✉ *New Inn Farm, off A422, Stowe* ☎ *01280/817156, 01280/818002 for tours* ⊕ *www.nationaltrust.org.uk/stowe-gardens* 🎫 *£14; house only £7.*

★ **Waddesdon Manor**

HOUSE | Many of the regal residences created by the Rothschild family through-out Europe are gone now, but this one is still a vision of the 19th century at its most sumptuous. G. H. Destailleur built the house in the 1880s for Baron Ferdinand de Rothschild in the style of a 16th-century French château, with perfectly balanced turrets and towers and walls of creamy stone. Although intended only for summer weekend house parties, it was lovingly furnished over 35 years with Savonnerie carpets; Sèvres porcelain; furniture made by Riesener for Marie Antoinette; and paintings by Guardi, Gainsborough, and Reynolds. The collection is brought into the 21st century by an extraordinary broken porcelain chandelier, by artist Ingo Maurer, located in the Blue Dining Room. The gardens are equally extraordi-nary, with an aviary, colorful plants, and winding trails that provide panoramic views. In the restaurant you can dine on English or French fare and order excellent Rothschild wines. Admission is by timed ticket; arrive early or book in advance. The annual Christmas fairs and light festivals held here are well worth seeing; check the website in advance for details.
✉ *Silk St., Waddesdon* ✛ *On A41 west of Aylesbury* ☎ *01296/820414* ⊕ *www.waddesdon.org.uk* 🎫 *House and gardens £21; gardens only £11.50* 🕑 *Closed Mon. and Tues.*

St. Albans

25 miles east of Aylesbury, 20 miles northwest of London.

A lively town on the outskirts of London, St. Albans is known for its historic cathedral, and it also holds reminders of a long history. From AD 50 to 440, the town, then known as Verulamium, was one of the largest communities in Roman Britain. You can explore this past in the Verulamium Museum and splendid Roman sites around the area. For activi-ties more focused on the present, every Wednesday and Saturday, the Market Place on St. Peter's Street bustles with traders from all over England selling everything from fish and farm produce to clothing. A 20-minute drive away from St. Albans is Warner Bros. Harry Potter Studio Tour, which has sets and props from the successful films.

GETTING HERE AND AROUND

About 20 miles northwest of London, St. Albans is off the M1 and M25 highways, about an hour's drive from the center of the capital. Thameslink has frequent trains from London's St. Pancras Station, arriving at St. Albans City Station in 30 minutes. The main train station is on Victoria Street, in the town center. A sec-ond station on the south side of town, St. Albans Abbey Station, serves smaller towns in the surrounding area. Trains on this line are operated by London Midland. Bus service is slow and not direct. Central St. Albans is small and walkable. There's a local bus service, but you're unlikely to need it. Taxis usually line up outside the train stations.

ESSENTIALS

TRAIN CONTACTS Southern Railway. ☎ *0345/1272920* ⊕ *www.southernrail-way.com.*

VISITOR INFORMATION St. Albans Tourist and Information Centre. ✉ *Town Hall, Market Pl.* ☎ *01727/864511* ⊕ *www.enjoystalbans.com.*

Sights

★ Warner Bros. Harry Potter Studio Tour

MUSEUM | **FAMILY** | Attention all Muggles: this spectacular attraction just outside Watford immerses you in the magical world of Harry Potter for hours. From the Great Hall of Hogwarts—faithfully re-created, down to the finest detail—to magical props beautifully displayed in the vast studio space, each section of this attraction showcases the real sets, props, and special effects used in the eight movies. Visitors enter the Great Hall, a fitting stage for costumes from each Hogwarts house. You can admire the intricacies of the huge Hogwarts Castle model, ride a broomstick, try butterbeer, explore the Forbidden Forest, and gaze through the shop windows of Diagon Alley. The Hogwarts Express section—at a faithfully reproduced Platform 9¾—allows you to walk through a carriage of the actual steam train and see what it's like to ride with Harry and the gang. Tickets, pegged to a 30-minute arrival time slot, must be prebooked online. The studio tour is a 20-minute drive from St. Albans. You can also get here by taking a 20-minute train ride from London's Euston Station to Watford Junction (then a 15-minute shuttle-bus ride; £3 round-trip, cash only). Via car from London, use M1 and M25—parking is free. ⊠ *Studio Tour Dr., Leavesden Green* ☎ *0345/084–0900* ⊕ *www.wbstudiotour.co.uk* 🎫 *£47.*

Chapter 5

CANTERBURY AND THE SOUTHEAST

Updated by
Joseph Reaney

⊙ **Sights**
★★★★☆

🍽 **Restaurants**
★★☆☆☆

🛏 **Hotels**
★★☆☆☆

🛍 **Shopping**
★★☆☆☆

🍸 **Nightlife**
★★★☆☆

WELCOME TO CANTERBURY AND THE SOUTHEAST

TOP REASONS TO GO

★ **Castles galore:** From Dover to Herstmonceux, these fortresses will dazzle with their architecture and fascinate with their histories.

★ **Brighton:** With its great bars and restaurants, top-notch nightlife, and sunbathing-friendly shoreline, this is the quintessential modern English seaside city.

★ **Canterbury Cathedral:** This enormous House of God, a masterpiece of medieval architecture, inspires awe with its soaring towers and flagstone corridors.

★ **Manors and Mansions:** West Kent is home to one of England's richest concentrations of historic homes, including the medieval moated Ightham Mote and the sprawling Jacobean-style Knole.

★ **Gardens:** Gardens of all kinds are an English specialty, and at Sissinghurst and Wisley, as well as in the gardens of Hever Castle and Chartwell, you can easily spend an entire afternoon wandering through acres of exotic flora.

The eastern part of the region takes in the cathedral town of Canterbury and the Kent coast, right down to the port city of Dover with its famous white cliffs. The next section heads inland to the pretty spa town of Royal Tunbridge Wells and the surrounding area of West Kent, where stately homes and castles dot the farmland. A third part encompasses the county of East Sussex, which includes the medieval hill town of Rye, the 1066 battlefield near Hastings, and the cool coastal city of Brighton. And the fourth section covers the western part of the region: coast-hugging West Sussex—including its county town of Chichester—and Surrey.

1 Canterbury. A UNESCO-listed medieval town dominated by a massive cathedral founded more than 1,000 years ago.

2 Deal. A quiet seaside town home to two famous coastal castles built during the reign of Henry VIII.

3 Dover. A busy port town, famed for its striking white cliffs.

4 Royal Tunbridge Wells. An ideal base for exploring nearby regal homes and gardens.

5 Hever. Home to Hever Castle—seat of Anne Boleyn's family—and close to Winston Churchill's residence Chartwell.

6 Tonbridge. A little market town within easy reach of renowned country houses like Knole and Ightham Mote.

7 Rochester. A historic cathedral city best known for its Norman castle and Georgian dockyard.

8 Rye. A pretty hill town popular with London day-trippers.

9 Hastings. A once-popular Victorian spa town, famed for the nearby 1066 battefield.

10 Lewes. A gem of a town with a crumbling medieval castle, a famous opera festival, and a penchant for bonfires.

11 Brighton. A funky and lively city that blends Victorian architecture with the best shopping and dining on the coast.

12 Arundel. A little hilltop town with an impressive castle, a neo-Gothic cathedral, and a medieval priory church.

13 Chichester. The charming capital of West Sussex, which once played an important role in ancient Rome.

Surrey, Kent, and Sussex form the breadbasket of England, where bucolic farmland stretches as far as the eye can see. Once a favorite destination of English nobility, this region is rich with history, visible in the great castles and stately homes that dot the countryside.

Its cities are similarly historic, especially ancient Canterbury, with its spectacular cathedral and medieval streets. Along the coast, funky seaside towns have a more relaxed attitude, especially artsy Brighton, where artists and musicians use the sea as inspiration for their work.

Although it's close to London (both Surrey and Kent reach all the way to London's suburbs) and is one of the most densely populated areas of Britain, the Southeast feels far away from the big city. In Kent, acres of orchards burst into a mass of pink-and-white blossoms in spring, while Dover's white cliffs and brooding castle have become symbols of coastal Britain. Historic mansions, such as Petworth House and Knole, are major draws for travelers, and lush gardens—such as Vita Sackville-West's Sissinghurst and the Royal Horticultural Society's Wisley—attract thousands to their vivid floral displays.

Because the English Channel is at its narrowest here, a great deal of British history has been forged in the Southeast. The Romans landed in this area and stayed to rule Britain for four centuries. So did the Saxons—*Sussex* means "the land of the South Saxons." The biggest invasion of them all took place here when William ("the Conqueror") of Normandy defeated the Saxons at a battle near Hastings in 1066, changing the island forever.

MAJOR REGIONS

Canterbury and the Kent Coast. The cathedral city of Canterbury is an ancient place that has attracted travelers since the 12th century. Its magnificent cathedral, the Mother Church of England, remains a powerful draw. Even in prehistoric times, this part of England was relatively well settled. Saxon settlers, Norman conquerors, and the folk who lived here in late-medieval times all left their mark. From Canterbury there's rewarding wandering to be done in the gentle Kentish countryside between the city and the busy port of Dover. Here the landscape ravishes the eye in spring with apple blossoms and in autumn with lush fields ready for harvest. In addition to orchards and market gardens, the county contains round oast houses. These buildings with tilted, pointed roofs were once used for drying hops; now many are expensive homes.

Tunbridge Wells and West Kent. England is world-renowned for its magnificent stately homes and castles, but many of them are scattered across the country, presenting a challenge for travelers. Within a 15-mile radius of Tunbridge Wells, however, in the area of hills and hidden dells known as the Weald, lies a wealth of architectural wonder in the historic homes, castles, and gardens found here: Penshurst Place, Hever Castle, Chartwell, Knole, Ightham Mote, Leeds Castle, and lovely Sissinghurst Castle Garden.

Rye and Lewis. From Dover the coast road winds west through Folkestone (a genteel resort, small port, and Channel Tunnel terminal), across Romney Marsh (famous for its sheep and, at one time, its ruthless smugglers), and on to the delightful medieval town of Rye. The region along the coast is noted for Winchelsea, the history-rich sites of Hastings, Herstmonceux, and Bodiam, and the Glyndebourne Opera House festival, based outside Lewes, a town celebrated for its architectural heritage. One of the three steam railroads in the Southeast services part of the area: the Romney, Hythe, and Dymchurch Railway.

Brighton and the Sussex Coast. The self-proclaimed belle of the coast, Brighton is upbeat, funky, and endlessly entertaining. Outside town the soft green downs of Sussex and Surrey hold stately homes you can visit, including Arundel Castle and Petworth House. Along the way, you'll discover the largest Roman villa in Britain and the city of Chichester, whose cathedral is a poem in stone.

Planning

When to Go

It's best to visit in spring, summer, or early fall. Many privately owned castles and mansions are open only between April and September or October, though the parks surrounding the stately houses may be open all year. If crowds tend to spoil your fun, avoid August, Sunday, and national holidays, particularly in Canterbury and the seaside towns.

FESTIVALS
Brighton Festival
FESTIVALS | The three-week-long Brighton Festival, one of England's biggest and liveliest arts festivals, takes place every May in venues around Brighton. The more than 600 events include drama, music, dance, and visual arts. ✉ Brighton ☎ 01273/709709 ⊕ www.brightonfestival. org.

★ Brighton Fringe
FESTIVALS | One of the largest fringe festivals in the world—and second only to the Edinburgh Fringe in Scotland—this four-week-long arts extravaganza sees hundreds of stand up, sketch comedy, music, dance, and circus acts descend on the city every May. ✉ Brighton ☎ 01273/917272 ⊕ www.brightonfringe. org.

Broadstairs Dickens Festival
FESTIVALS | In 1937, Gladys Waterer, the then-resident of Dickens House in Broadstairs, put on a commemorative production of Charles Dickens's *David Copperfield* and had people about the town dress in Victorian clothing to publicize it. Since then, the town has hosted a Dickens Festival every June, incorporating everything from film screenings and walking tours to country fairs and dress-up mini golf. ✉ Broadstairs ☎ 01843/863701 ⊕ www.broadstairsdickensfestival.co.uk.

Planning Your Time

With the exception of Brighton, you can easily see the highlights of each of the towns in less than a day. Brighton has more to offer, and you should allot at least two days to take it all in. Consider basing yourself in one town while exploring a region. For example, you could stay in Brighton and take in Lewes on a day trip. Base yourself in Rye for a couple of days while exploring Winchelsea, Battle, Hastings, and Herstmonceux Castle. Royal Tunbridge Wells is a great place to overnight if you plan on exploring the many stately homes and castles nearby.

Getting Here and Around

AIR

Although Heathrow isn't too far away, Gatwick Airport is the most convenient gateway for the Southeast. The rail station inside Gatwick has trains to Brighton and other major towns, and you can also take a taxi from Heathrow to Guildford for around £50.

BUS

National Express buses serve the region from London's Victoria Coach Station. Most of the larger towns can be reached this way; journey times vary from less than two hours (Canterbury) to more than three (Chichester). Megabus runs buses at budget prices from Victoria Coach Station to many of the same destinations as National Express and can be cheaper, although luggage limits are strict.

Bus service between towns can be useful but is often intermittent. Out in the country, don't expect buses more often than once every half hour or hour. Traveline is the best central place to call for bus information, and local tourist information centers cán be a big help.

CONTACTS Megabus. ☎ 0900/160–0900 ⊕ uk.megabus.com. **National Express.** ☎ 0871/781–8181 ⊕ www.nationalex-press.com. **Traveline.** ☎ 0871/200–2233 ⊕ www.traveline.info.

CAR

While larger towns in the area can be easily reached by public transport (and having a car can be a bit of a nuisance), you will need your own wheels to visit most castles, grand country homes, and quiet villages. Major routes radiating outward from London to the Southeast are, from east to west, the A2/M2 via Canterbury (60 miles) to Dover (76 miles); the A21, passing by Royal Tunbridge Wells (42 miles) to Hastings (66 miles); the

M23/A23 to Brighton (53 miles); and the A3 via Guildford (32 miles) to Chichester (72 miles).

TRAIN

Trains are the fastest and most efficient way to travel to major cities in the region, but they don't stop in many small towns. From London, Southeastern trains serve Sussex and Kent from Victoria and Charing Cross stations, and South Western Railway travels to Surrey from Waterloo Station. Getting to Brighton can take as little as one hour, Canterbury about 1½ hours, and Dover around two hours. A Network Railcard costing £30, valid throughout the Southeast for a year, entitles you and three companions to one-third off many off-peak rail fares.

CONTACTS National Rail Enquiries. ☎ 03457/484950 ⊕ www.nationalrail. co.uk. **Network Railcard.** ☎ 0345/300–0250 ⊕ www.network-railcard.co.uk.

Restaurants

If you're in a seaside town, look for that great British staple, fish-and-chips. Perhaps "look" isn't the word—just follow your nose. On the coast, locally caught seafood is the specialty. Try local smoked fish (haddock and mackerel) or the succulent local oysters. If you're inland, sample fresh local lamb and beef. In cities such as Canterbury, Brighton, and Tunbridge Wells, there are numerous restaurants and cafés, but out in the countryside the best options are often pubs.

Hotels

All around the coast, resort towns stretch along beaches, their hotels standing cheek by jowl. Not all of the smaller hotels and guesthouses remain open year-round; many do business only from mid-April to September or October. Some hotels have all-inclusive rates for a week's stay. Prices rise in July and

August, when the seaside resorts can get solidly booked, especially Brighton. On the flip side, hotels may drop rates by up to 40% off-season. Places in Brighton may not take a booking for a single night in summer or on weekends.

Restaurant and hotel reviews have been shortened. For full information, visit Fodors.com. Restaurant prices are per person for a main course at dinner, or if dinner is not served, at lunch. Hotel prices are the lowest cost of a standard double room in high season, including 20% V.A.T.

WHAT IT COSTS in Pounds

	$	$$	$$$	$$$$
RESTAURANTS				
	under £16	£16–£23	£24–£30	over £30
HOTELS				
	under £125	£125–£225	£226–£350	over £350

Visitor Information

Tourist boards in the main towns can help with information, and many will also book local accommodations.

CONTACTS Southeast England Tourist Board. ⊕ *www.visitsoutheastengland. com.*

Canterbury

56 miles southeast of London.

Just mention Canterbury, and most people are taken back to memories of high-school English classes and Geoffrey Chaucer's *Canterbury Tales,* about medieval pilgrims making their way to Canterbury Cathedral. Judging from the tales, however, in those days Canterbury was as much a party town as it was a spiritual center.

The city has been the seat of the Primate of All England, the archbishop of Canterbury, since Pope Gregory the Great dispatched St. Augustine to convert the pagan hordes of Britain in 597. The height of Canterbury's popularity came in the 12th century, when thousands of pilgrims flocked here to see the shrine of the murdered archbishop Thomas Becket. This southeastern town became one of the most visited in England, if not Europe. Buildings that served as pilgrims' inns (and that survived World War II bombing of the city) still dominate the streets of Canterbury's center, though it's tourists, not pilgrims, who flock to this city of about 40,000 people today.

Prices at city museums are higher than average, so if you plan to see more than one, ask at the tourist office if a combination ticket might be cheaper.

GETTING HERE AND AROUND

The fastest way to reach Canterbury from London is by train. Southeastern trains to Canterbury run every half hour in peak times from London's Charing Cross Station. The journey takes around 1½ hours. Canterbury has two centrally located train stations, Canterbury East and Canterbury West; both are about a 10-minute walk from the cathedral.

National Express and Megabus buses bound for Canterbury depart several times a day from London's Victoria Coach Station. Trips to Canterbury take around two hours and drop passengers at the bus station right in the center. If you're driving, take the A2/M2 to Canterbury from London (60 miles). Park in one of the signposted lots at the edge of the town center.

Canterbury has a small, walkable town center (there's also a good local bus service, but you're unlikely to need it). Most major tourist sites are on one street, though it changes name three times— from St. George's Street, to High Street, to St. Peter's Street.

Impressive both inside and out, ancient Canterbury Cathedral dominates the town.

ESSENTIALS

VISITOR INFORMATION Canterbury Visitor Information Centre. ✉ *The Beaney House of Art & Knowledge, 18 High St.* ☎ *01227/862162* ⊕ *www.canterbury. co.uk.*

TOURS

Canterbury Guided Tours

Expert guides lead 90-minute walking tours at 11 am daily, with an additional tour at 2 pm on weekends from November to March and daily April through October. Tours start outside Christchurch Gate (the main cathedral gate) opposite the Buttermarket, and they cost £10. You can buy a ticket in advance online or during the tour. ✉ *Christchurch Gate, The Precincts* ☎ *01227/459779* ⊕ *www. canterburyguidedtours.com* 🎫 *From £8.*

 Sights

The Beaney House of Art & Knowledge

MUSEUM | The medieval Poor Priests' Hospital is the site of this quirky local museum, where exhibits provide an overview of the city's history and architecture from Roman times to World War II. It covers everything and everyone associated with the town, including the mysterious death of the 16th-century writer Christopher Marlowe and the British children's book and TV characters Rupert the Bear and Bagpuss. One recent acquisition is a beautiful gold dragon pendant, made in Kent during the Anglo-Saxon era (410–1066). ✉ *18 High St.* ☎ *01227/862162* ⊕ *www.canterburymuseums.co.uk/ beaney* 🎫 *Free.*

★ Canterbury Cathedral

RELIGIOUS SITE | The focal point of the city was the first of England's great Norman cathedrals. Nucleus of worldwide Anglicanism, the Cathedral Church of Christ Canterbury (its formal name) is a living textbook of medieval architecture. The building was begun in 1070, demolished, begun anew in 1096, and then systematically expanded over the next three centuries. When the original choir section burned to the ground in 1174, another replaced it, designed in the new Gothic style, with tall, pointed arches.

The cathedral was only a century old, and still relatively small, when Thomas Becket, the archbishop of Canterbury, was murdered here in 1170. Becket, as head of the church, had been engaged in a political struggle with his old friend Henry II. Four knights supposedly overheard Henry scream, "Will no one rid me of this turbulent priest?" (although there is no evidence that those were his actual words—the only contemporary record has him saying, "What miserable drones and traitors have I nourished and brought up in my household, who let their lord be treated with such shameful contempt by a low-born cleric?").

Thinking they were carrying out the king's wishes, the knights went immediately to Canterbury and hacked Becket to pieces in one of the side chapels. Henry, racked with guilt, went into deep mourning. Becket was canonized, and Canterbury's position as the center of English Christianity was assured.

For almost 400 years, Becket's tomb was one of the most extravagant shrines in Christendom, until it was destroyed by Henry VIII's troops during the Reformation. In **Trinity Chapel,** which held the shrine, you can still see a series of 13th-century stained-glass windows illustrating Becket's miracles. (The actual site of Becket's murder is down a flight of steps just to the left of the nave.) Nearby is the tomb of Edward, the Black Prince (1330–76), warrior son of Edward III and a national hero. In the corner of Trinity Chapel, a second flight of steps leads down to the enormous Norman **undercroft,** or vaulted cellar, built in the early 12th century. A row of squat pillars engraved with dancing beasts (mythical and otherwise) supports the roof.

To the north of the cathedral are the **cloisters** and a small compound of monastic buildings. The 12th-century

octagonal water tower is still part of the cathedral's water supply. The Norman staircase in the northwest corner of the Green Court dates from 1167 and is a unique example of the architecture of the times. Another highlight is the almost Disney-like stained glass window "'Salvation" by Hungarian artist Ervin Bossányi. Look out for a little padlock with a swastika, a reference to the atrocities that occured during World War II.

At the entrance to the cathedral, by Christchurch Gate, is a free-to-enter visitor center, which has more information on the history (and myth) of Canterbury Cathedral. ■ **TIP) The cathedral is popular, so arrive early or late in the day to avoid the crowds.** ✉ The Precincts ☎ 01227/762862 ⊕ www.canterbury-cathedral.org ⟟ £12.50; free for services; £5 tour; £4 audio guide.

Canterbury Roman Museum
MUSEUM | Below ground, at the level of the remnants of Roman Canterbury, this small but informative museum tells the story of the area's distant Roman past. Highlights of the collection include a hypocaust (the Roman version of central heating) and two colorful floor mosaics dating from around the year 270 that were unearthed in the aftermaths of the bombs that fell on Canterbury during World War II. Displays of excavated objects—some of which you can hold in the **Touch the Past** area—and computer-generated reconstructions of Roman buildings and the marketplace help recreate the past. ✉ Butchery La. ☎ 01227/785575 ⊕ www.canterburymuseums.co.uk/romanmuseum ⟟ £9.

Christchurch Gate
RELIGIOUS SITE | This huge gate, built in 1517, leads into the cathedral close. As you pass through, look up at the sculpted heads of two young figures: Prince Arthur, elder brother of Henry VIII, and the young Catherine of Aragon, to whom Arthur was married in 1501 (when he was just 15). He died shortly afterwards,

Canterbury

KEY

- **1** Exploring Sights
- **1** Restaurants
- **1** Hotels
- **i** Tourist information

Sights ▼

1 The Beaney House of
Art & Knowledge **C3**

2 Canterbury Cathedral ...**C3**

3 Canterbury
Roman Museum **C3**

4 Christchurch Gate **C3**

5 Medieval City Walls **C4**

6 Westgate Towers **B2**

Restaurants ▼

1 City Fish Bar **C3**

2 The Corner House **C4**

3 The Goods Shed **B2**

4 The Old Buttermarket ...**C3**

Hotels ▼

1 ABode Canterbury **B3**

2 Canterbury Cathedral
Lodge....................**D3**

3 Ebury Hotel **E5**

4 House of Agnes.........**A2**

and Catherine married Henry. Jump forward 25 years, and Henry was king. But they had produced no male children, a fact Henry attributed to God's wrath for marrying his sister-in-law. The Pope refused to grant him a divorce, but Henry went ahead and did it anyway, creating an irrevocable breach with the Roman Catholic Church and altering the course of English history forever.

Outside the gate is the tiny Buttermarket, an old dairy market square with a sweet name and a dark past. Before the 16th century, it was called "the Bullstake," because animals were tied here and tortured (a popular activity of the time known as "baiting") before they were slaughtered. Today, it's surrounded by bars and restaurants and leads onto pretty Mercery Lane, with its medieval-style cottages and massive, overhanging timber roofs. ⊠ The Precincts, Off Sun St. ⊕ www.canterbury-cathedral.org.

Medieval City Walls
ARCHAEOLOGICAL SITE | For an essential Canterbury experience, follow the circuit of the 13th- and 14th-century walls, built on the line of the Roman walls. Roughly half survive; those to the east are intact, towering some 20 feet high and offering a sweeping view of the town. You can access these from a number of places, including Castle Street and Broad Street, but perhaps the most photo-worthy section is by Canterbury East Station Bridge. ⊠ Canterbury E. Station Bridge.

Westgate Towers
LOCAL INTEREST | In medieval times, Canterbury had seven gatehouses guarding entry to the city, but today only this one survives. Still, with its twin castellated towers, it's one of England's finest. Currently under renovation but still open to the public, Westgate Towers contains a small museum with exhibits on the gate's history, including medieval armaments once used by the city guard and artifacts related to the city jail that was here from the 14th century. There are

also some surprising links to the United States: one of the prisoners held here, Robert Cushman, was an organizer of the Mayflower voyage in 1620. Climb to the roof for a panoramic view of the city. The entrance is via a bar called The Pound Bar & Kitchen. Be aware that a trip to the top requires climbing five sets of narrow stairs. ⊠ The Pound Bar & Kitchen, 1 Pound La. ☎ 01227/458629 ⊕ www.one-poundlane.co.uk/westgate-towers ☞ £4 (£2 during renovation).

🍴 Restaurants

City Fish Bar
$ | **BRITISH** | Long lines and lots of satisfied finger licking attest to the deserved popularity of this excellent fish-and-chip shop in the center of town, where all orders are takeout. Everything is freshly fried, the batter crisp, and the fish tasty; the fried mushrooms are also surprisingly good. **Known for:** fresh fish in crispy batter; chunky chips; good-quality fast food. ⑤ Average main: £7 ⊠ 30 St. Margaret's St. ☎ 01227/760873 ⊕ www.facebook.com/cityfishbar.

★ The Corner House
$$ | **BRITISH** | Set just outside the medieval city walls, this historic pub turned restaurant serves locally sourced British produce with creative culinary twists. Mains include confit pork belly with creamed kale and bacon and herb-crumbed cod loin with mash and cockles, but it's the "nibbles" (snacks) that are really inventive—try the sausage roll, served as three thick slices with housemade mushroom ketchup. **Known for:** building that dates back to 1574; to-die-for treacle bread; four guest rooms available on-site. ⑤ Average main: £19 ⊠ 1 Dover St. ☎ 01227/780793 ⊕ www.cornerhouserestaurants.co.uk.

The Goods Shed
$$ | **BRITISH** | Next to Canterbury West Station, this farmers' market restaurant with wooden tables is well known for

offering fresh, seasonal Kentish food—think monkfish with parsley dumplings and broccoli or guinea fowl with lentils and black pudding. Whatever is freshest that day appears on the menu, whether it's quail eggs, John Dory, or duck breast. **Known for:** fresh local produce; great seafood, including a catch of the day; cool historic design. $ *Average main: £18* ✉ *Station Rd. W* ☎ *01227/459153* ⊕ *www.thegoodsshed.co.uk* ⊘ *Closed Mon. No dinner Sun.*

The Old Buttermarket

$ | BRITISH | A colorful, friendly old pub near the cathedral, the Old Buttermarket is a great place to grab a hearty lunch and sample some traditional English fare with a modern inflection. You can sip a pint of fresh English ale from the ever-changing selection while sampling a wild boar and chorizo pie or perhaps a warming bowl of Applewood-smoked mac and cheese. **Known for:** great selection of ales; excellent savory pies; interesting history (there's been a pub in this spot for 500 years). $ *Average main: £13* ✉ *39 Burgate* ☎ *01227/462170* ⊕ *www.nicholsonspubs.co.uk/theoldbuttermarketcanterbury* ▭ *No credit cards.*

Hotels

ABode Canterbury

$ | HOTEL | This glossy boutique hotel inside the old city walls offers up-to-date style in traditional Canterbury, with good-size rooms—modern but not minimal—classed as Comfortable, Desirable, Enviable, and Most Enviable. **Pros:** central location; luxurious handmade beds; tasty afternoon tea. **Cons:** one of the pricier hotels in town; bar gets quite crowded; breakfast is extra. $ *Rooms from: £110* ✉ *30–33 High St.* ☎ *01227/766266* ⊕ *www.abodecanterbury.co.uk* ⤴ *72 rooms* ¶⊙¶ *No meals.*

★ Canterbury Cathedral Lodge

$ | HOTEL | There is no more peaceful place to stay in Canterbury then at this small and modern hotel tucked away within the grounds of the famous cathedral. **Pros:** outstanding location; incredible cathedral views; free entry to the cathedral (worth £12.50). **Cons:** no lunch or dinner served in restaurant; double beds are small; gets booked up during conferences. $ *Rooms from: £120* ✉ *The Precincts* ☎ *01227/865350* ⊕ *www.canterburycathedrallodge.org* ⤴ *35 rooms* ¶⊙¶ *Free breakfast.*

Ebury Hotel

$$ | HOTEL | Family run, this hotel earns rave reviews for its laid-back attitude and comfortable accommodations inside two big Victorian buildings. **Pros:** cozy lounge; lovely indoor pool; three- and four-bedrooms good value for families. **Cons:** a bit of a walk to the town center; no elevator; pet-friendly ethos is great for dog lovers, not allergy sufferers. $ *Rooms from: £130* ✉ *65–67 New Dover Rd.* ☎ *01227/768433* ⊕ *www.ebury-hotel.co.uk* ⤴ *15 rooms* ¶⊙¶ *Free breakfast.*

★ House of Agnes

$ | B&B/INN | This historic B&B, which dates back 600 years and was written about by Dickens, offers unique and stylish accommodations not far from Canterbury West Station. **Pros:** historic building; just enough modern touches; honesty bar. **Cons:** rooms vary quite a bit in size; no elevator; quirky design not for everyone. $ *Rooms from: £95* ✉ *71 St. Dunstans St.* ☎ *01227/472185* ⊕ *www.houseofagnes.co.uk* ⤴ *17 rooms* ¶⊙¶ *Free breakfast.*

Nightlife

Alberry's Wine Bar

BARS/PUBS | With late-night jazz and hip-hop and a trendy crowd, Alberry's Wine Bar is one of Canterbury's coolest nightspots. At lunchtime they serve a fine burger, too. ✉ *38 St. Margaret's St.* ☎ *01227/452378* ⊕ *www.alberrys.co.uk.*

Parrot

BARS/PUBS | Built in 1370 on Roman foundations, the Parrot is an atmospheric old pub known for its ever-changing selection of real ales. They also do good food; Sunday lunch here is particularly popular. ⊠ *1–9 Church La.* ☎ *01227/454170* ⊕ *www.parrotcanterbury.co.uk.*

Thomas Becket

BARS/PUBS | A traditional English pub, with bunches of hops hanging from the ceiling and a fire crackling in the hearth on a cold winter's day, the Thomas Becket is a convivial kind of place. There is food available, but most people just come for the ale and the atmosphere. ⊠ *21 Best La.* ☎ *01227/464384* ⊕ *www.facebook.com/thethomasbecketpubrestaurant.*

🛍 Shopping

★ Catching Lives Charity Bookshop

BOOKS/STATIONERY | One of Canterbury's most photographed buildings (and that's saying something), this wonderfully crooked half-timbered house dates back to the 17th century. Inside, volunteers sell a wide range of secondhand and collectable books, with all profits going to the local homeless charity Catching Lives. ⊠ *28 Palace St.* ☎ *07899/458961* ⊕ *www.catchinglives.org/catching-lives-bookshop.*

Crowthers of Canterbury

MUSIC STORES | Behind the delightfully old-style red shop front, Crowthers of Canterbury carries an extensive selection of musical instruments, gifts, and other souvenirs for music lovers. ⊠ *1 Borough* ☎ *01227/763965* ⊕ *www.crowthersof-canterbury.co.uk.*

925 Silver

JEWELRY/ACCESSORIES | This little shop has a great selection of handmade silver jewelry. ⊠ *57 Palace St.* ☎ *01227/785699* ⊕ *www.925-silver.co.uk.*

Deal

18 miles southeast of Canterbury, 9 miles north of Dover.

The large seaside town of Deal, known for its castle, is famous in history books as the place where Caesar's legions landed in 55 BC, and it was from here that William Penn set sail in 1682 on his first journey to the American colony he founded, Pennsylvania.

GETTING HERE AND AROUND

Southeastern trains travel to Deal twice an hour from London's St. Pancras Station and once an hour from London's Charing Cross. The journey takes between 1½ and two hours. You can also get a National Express bus from London's Victoria Coach Station, but there's only one bus per day (late evening), and the trip takes around three hours. From Canterbury, drive east on the A258 to Sandwich, then south on the A258 into Deal. Direct bus number 12 (45 minutes) is the best public transport option from Canterbury; trains take longer, cost more, and require a change in Ashford.

👁 Sights

Deal Castle

CASTLE/PALACE | Erected in 1540 and intricately built to the shape of a Tudor rose, Deal Castle is the largest of the coastal defenses constructed by Henry VIII. A moat surrounds its gloomy passages and austere walls. The castle museum has exhibits about prehistoric, Roman, and Saxon Britain. ⊠ *Victoria Rd., Deal* ☎ *0370/333–1181* ⊕ *www.english-heritage.org.uk/deal* ⊠ *£7.60* ⊙ *Closed Mon. and Tues. in Mar. and weekdays Nov.–mid-Feb.*

Dickens House Museum

MUSEUM | This house was originally the home of Mary Pearson Strong, on whom Dickens based the character of Betsey Trotwood, David Copperfield's aunt. Dickens lived here from 1837 to 1839 while writing *The Pickwick Papers* and *Oliver Twist*. Some rooms have been decorated to look as they would have in Dickens's day, and there's a reconstruction of Miss Trotwood's room as described by Dickens. The house is in Broadstairs, 18 miles up the coast from Deal. ⊠ *2 Victoria Parade* ☎ *01843/861232* ⊕ *www.dickensmuseumbroadstairs.co.uk* ⊠ *£3.75* ⊙ *Closed Dec.–Mar. and weekdays in Nov.*

Dover

8 miles south of Deal, 78 miles east of London.

The busy passenger port of Dover has for centuries been Britain's gateway to Europe, famed for its pretty white cliffs. The town itself is, sadly, not a pretty place; the savage bombardments of World War II and the shortsightedness of postwar developers left the city center in something of a mess. Mostly Dover town is a place you go through to get to the ferry. However, there are a couple of notable exceptions, including the Roman-era legacy of a lighthouse adjoining a stout Anglo-Saxon church.

GETTING HERE AND AROUND
National Express buses depart from London's Victoria Coach Station for Dover about every 90 minutes. The journey takes between 2½ and 3 hours. Drivers from London take the M20, which makes a straight line southeast to Dover. The journey should take around two hours. Southeastern trains leave London's Charing Cross, Victoria, and St. Pancras stations about every 30 minutes for Dover Priory Station in Dover. Direct trains take around two hours; a slightly quicker (but usually more expensive) service changes in Ashford.

To get to Dover from Deal, drive south on the A258. There are also regular direct trains (16 minutes) and buses (40 minutes).

For the best views of the cliffs, you need a car or taxi; it's a long way to walk from town.

ESSENTIALS
VISITOR INFORMATION Dover Visitor Information Centre. ⊠ *Dover Museum, Market Sq.* ☎ *01304/201066* ⊕ *www.whitecliffscountry.org.uk.*

 Sights

★ Dover Castle
CASTLE/PALACE | FAMILY | Spectacular and with plenty to explore, Dover Castle, towering high above the ramparts of the white cliffs, is a mighty medieval castle that has served as an important strategic center over the centuries.

Most of the castle, including the keep, dates to Norman times. It was begun by Henry II in 1181 but incorporates additions from almost every succeeding century. The **Great Tower** re-creates how the opulent castle would have looked in Henry's time, complete with sound effects, interactive displays, and courtly characters in medieval costume.

History jumps forward the better part of a millennium (and becomes rather more sober in the telling) as you venture down into the labyrinthine **Secret Wartime Tunnels.** The castle played a surprisingly dramatic role in World War II, the full extent to which remained unknown for years afterward. These well-thought-out interactive galleries tell the complete story. The tunnels themselves, originally built during the Napoleonic Wars, were used as a top-secret intelligence-gathering base in the fight against Hitler. ⊠ *Castle Hill Rd.* ☎ *0370/333–1181* ⊕ *www.english-heritage.org.uk/dover* ⊠ *£20.90* ⊙ *Closed weekdays Nov.–mid-Feb. and Mon. and Tues. mid-Feb.–Mar.*

Canterbury
and the Kent Coast

Roman Painted House

ARCHAEOLOGICAL SITE | Believed to have been a hotel, the remains of this nearly 2,000-year-old structure were excavated in the 1970s. It includes some Roman wall paintings (mostly dedicated to Bacchus, the god of revelry), along with the remnants of an ingenious heating system. ⊠ *25 New St.* ☎ *01304/203279* ⊕ *karu.org.uk/roman_painted_house.html* ⊡ *£4* ⊙ *Closed Sun., Mon., Oct.–Mar., and Wed.–Fri. in May.*

★ White Cliffs

NATURE SITE | Plunging hundreds of feet into the sea, Dover's startlingly white cliffs are a spectacular sight, and one of the most iconic symbols of England. The cliffs, which are composed mainly of chalk with slivers of flint, are eroding at a rather alarming rate: more than a foot (30 cm) a year on average. Because of this, you must be cautious when walking along the cliffs—experts recommend staying at least 20 feet from the edge. The cliffs stretch for around eight miles altogether, but the most popular section to visit is the one managed by the National Trust, about two miles east of town. The visitor center has five miles of walking trails heading farther east to the 19th-century South Foreland Lighthouse and St. Margaret's Bay, with spectacular views along the way. There are also some lovely coastal walks to the west of Dover with good views of the cliffs, inclduing Samphire Hoe, Folkestone East Cliff, and Warren Country Park. Signs will direct you from the roads to scenic spots. ⊠ *Visitor Centre, Upper Rd., Guston* ⊕ *www.nationaltrust.org.uk/the-white-cliffs-of-dover* ⊡ *Free; parking £5.*

Restaurants

The Allotment

$ | **BRITISH** | This charming, slightly quirky restaurant in the center of Dover doesn't look like much from the outside, but don't be fooled—delicious, creative Modern British meals are served within. The menu is jam-packed with local and regional ingredients; try the pan-seared scallops to start, followed by Kentish venison steak or, even better, the bouillabaisse (a French seafood stew made with seasonal fish, shrimp, calamari, and clams in a garlic, white wine, and tomato sauce). **Known for:** house special fisherman's pie; lots of local produce; charming and quirky character. $ *Average main: £15* ⌂ *9 High St.* ☎ *01304/214467* ⊕ *www.theallotmentrestaurant.com.*

🛏 Hotels

White Cliffs Hotelwhite

$$ | **B&B/INN** | Situated near St. Margaret's Bay, four miles east of town along the famous White Cliffs of Dover, this colorful little hotel is attached to a friendly pub that serves good food. **Pros:** tons of character; beautiful cliff-top location; good food. **Cons:** a little way from central Dover; Wi-Fi comes and goes; quite pricey for what you get. $ *Rooms from: £180* ⌂ *High St., St. Margaret's-at-Cliffe* ☎ *01304/852229* ⊕ *www.thewhitecliffs. com* ⇥ *17 rooms* ⦿ *Free breakfast.*

Royal Tunbridge Wells

39 miles southeast of London.

Nobody much bothers with the "Royal" anymore, but Tunbridge Wells is no less regal because of it. Because of its wealth and political conservatism, this historic bedroom community has been the subject of (somewhat envious) British humor for years. Its restaurants and lodgings make it a convenient base for exploring the many homes and gardens nearby.

The city owes its prosperity to the 17th- and 18th-century passion for spas and mineral baths. In 1606, a mineral-water spring was discovered here, drawing legions of royal visitors looking for eternal health. Tunbridge Wells reached its zenith in the mid-18th century, when Richard "Beau" Nash presided over its social life. The buildings at the lower end of High Street are mostly 18th century, but as the street climbs the hill north, changing its name to Mount Pleasant Road, structures become more modern.

GETTING HERE AND AROUND
Southeastern trains leave from London's Charing Cross Station every 15 to 20 minutes. The journey to Tunbridge Wells takes just under an hour. If you're traveling by car from London, head here on the A20/M25/A21; travel time is about an hour.

To get to Tunbridge Wells from Dover, drive west on the A20/M20, switching to the A228 heading south; the journey typically takes 1½ to two hours. You can also take an hourly train from Dover (1½ hours, with a change in Tonbridge).

Tunbridge Wells sprawls in all directions, but the historic center is compact. None of the sights is more than a 10-minute walk from the main train station. You can pick up a town map at the station.

ESSENTIALS
VISITOR INFORMATION Tunbridge Wells Tourist Information Centre. ⌂ *The Corn Exchange, The Pantiles* ☎ *01892/515675* ⊕ *www.visittunbridgewells.com.*

Sights

★ Church of King Charles the Martyr

RELIGIOUS SITE | This important parish church dates from 1678, when the area was little more than a mineral spring surrounded by fields; the modern town of Tunbridge Wells grew up around it. Dedicated to Charles I, who had been executed by Parliament in 1649—and

Tunbridge Wells
and West Kent

whose son, Charles II, was restored 11 years later—the church's plain exterior belies its splendid interior, with a particularly beautiful plastered baroque ceiling. The entrance is on the corner of the A26 and the A267, across the road from the Pantiles. ⊠ *Chapel Pl.* ☎ *01892/511745* ⊕ *www.kcmtw.org* ⊠ *Free; donations welcome* ⊘ *Closed Sun. except for services.*

Pantiles

PROMENADE | A good place to begin a visit to Tunbridge Wells is at the Pantiles, a famous promenade with colonnaded shops near the spring on one side of town. Its odd name derives from the Dutch "pan tiles" that originally paved the area. Now sandwiched between two busy main roads, the Pantiles remains an elegant, tranquil oasis, and the site of the actual well. ■**TIP→ You can still drink**

the waters when a "dipper" (the traditional water dispenser) is in attendance, from Easter through September. ⊠ *Royal Tunbridge Wells.*

🍽 Restaurants

★ Kitsu

$ | **JAPANESE** | This tiny, unassuming restaurant might seem like an unlikely venue for exceptional sushi, but it's the best for miles. Everything is fresh and delicious, from the fragrant miso soup to the light tempura to the sushi platters that are big enough to share. **Known for:** excellent sushi; good casual dining; BYOB and cash-only policies. ⑤ *Average main: £13* ⊠ *82a Victoria Rd.* ☎ *07425/900016* ⊕ *www.kitsu.co.uk* ⊟ *No credit cards*

★ Thackeray's

$$$$ | FRENCH | Once the home of Victorian novelist William Makepeace Thackeray, this mid-17th-century tile-hung house is now an elegant restaurant known for creative French cuisine, with à la carte dishes like monkfish "on the bone" with barbecued celeriac or saddle of venison with roast sweet potatoes. A starter, main (plus side), and dessert will set you back £60, so if you're feeling hungry, opt for one of the prix fixe menus instead: there's the five-course seasonal tasting menu (£59 per person, plus £30 for wine pairing) or the seven-course "Chef's Tasting Menu" (£78 per person, plus £95 for premium wine pairing). **Known for:** fine dining experience; extravagant wine list; very expensive prices. ⑤ *Average main: £34 ⌧ 85 London Rd.* ☎ *01892/511921* ⊕ *www.thackerays-restaurant.co.uk* ☾ *Closed Mon. No dinner Sun.*

Hotels

Hotel du Vin

$$ | HOTEL | An elegant sandstone house dating from 1762 has been transformed into a chic boutique hotel with polished wood floors and luxurious furnishings. **Pros:** historic building; cute old-school elevator with mesh door; reliably good service. **Cons:** some rooms are small; bar can get crowded; big price hike in summer. ⑤ *Rooms from: £170 ⌧ Crescent Rd.* ☎ *01892/320749* ⊕ *www.hotelduvin.com/locations/tunbridge-wells* ⤵ *34 rooms* ❍❘ *Free breakfast.*

★ The Mount Edgcumbe

$$ | HOTEL | Perched on a hill overlooking the town below, this charming family-run boutique hotel has spacious, individually designed rooms that combine home comforts like Hypnos beds, walk-in showers, and roll-top baths, with quirky touches like bold print cushions, pineapple-shaped lamps, and antique chairs. **Pros:** excellent cellar restaurant; private parking available; delicious eggs royale at breakfast. **Cons:** an uphill walk from town; quirky touches not for everyone; no staffed reception. ⑤ *Rooms from: £170 ⌧ Off A264* ☎ *01892/618854* ⊕ *www.themountedgcumbe.com* ⤵ *6 rooms* ❍❘ *Free breakfast.*

Spa Hotel

$$ | HOTEL | The country-house flavor of this 1766 Georgian mansion has been beautifully maintained by luxurious furnishings and preserved period details. **Pros:** lap-of-luxury feel; gorgeous countryside views; pony-riding lessons for kids. **Cons:** breakfast is extra; quite formal atmosphere; uphill walk from the town center. ⑤ *Rooms from: £190 ⌧ Off Langton Rd.* ☎ *01892/520331* ⊕ *www.spahotel.co.uk* ⤵ *70 rooms* ❍❘ *No meals.*

Hever

10 miles northwest of Royal Tunbridge Wells.

The pretty village of Hever is best known for its romantic, history-layered castle—a fairy-tale medieval fortification on the outside and a Tudor mansion within. However, it's also within easy reach of two other famous heritage properties: Chartwell, the beloved home of Winston Churchill and magnificent views across rolling Kentish hills; and Penshurst Place, an Elizabethan manor house with one of the oldest and grandest medieval halls in England.

GETTING HERE AND AROUND

Southern trains leave from London Bridge Station every hour. The journey to Hever takes around 40 minutes. If you're traveling by car from London, take the A2/M25/B2042; travel time is one to 1½ hours. If driving from Tunbridge Wells, take the A264 east then follow signs directing you north on the B2026 toward Hever. Bus 234 runs between Tunbridge Wells and Hever three times a day (there's no convenient train connection).

◉ Sights

Chartwell

HOUSE | A grand Victorian mansion with a pond-dotted estate offering views over the surrounding countryside, Chartwell was the beloved private home of Sir Winston Churchill from 1924 until his death in 1965. Virtually everything has been kept as it was when he lived here, with his pictures, books, photos, and maps. There's even a half-smoked cigar that the World War II prime minister never finished. Churchill was an amateur artist, and his paintings show a softer side of the stiff-upper-lipped statesman; outdoor art trails show his work displayed at the points where he likely sat to paint them. Admission to the house is by timed ticket available only the day of your visit. To get here from Hever, head north on the B2027 and follow signs. ■TIP→ **Be sure to explore the rose gardens and take a walk in the surrounding countryside.** ⊠ Mapleton Rd., Westerham ☎ 01732/868381 ⊕ www.nationaltrust.org.uk/chartwell ☑ £19; garden and studio only £11; parking £4 ⊙ House closed Nov.–Feb.

★ Hever Castle

CASTLE/PALACE | It's hard to imagine a more romantic castle than this: nestled within rolling hills, all turrets and battlements, the whole encircled by a water lily–bound moat filled with fabulous beasts (enormous Japanese koi carp). Here, at her childhood home, Anne Boleyn, second wife of Henry VIII and mother of Elizabeth I, was courted by Henry. He loved her dearly for a time, but had her beheaded in 1536 after she failed to give birth to a son. He then gifted Boleyn's home to his fourth wife, Anne of Cleves.

Famous though it was, the castle fell into disrepair in the 19th century. When American millionaire William Waldorf Astor acquired it in 1903, he needed additional space to house his staff. His novel solution was to build a replica Tudor village, using only methods, materials, and even tools appropriate to the era. The result is more or less completely indistinguishable from the genuine Tudor parts.

Astor also created the stunning gardens, which today include an excellent yew maze, ponds, playgrounds, tea shops, gift shops, plant shops—you get the picture. There's a notable collection of Tudor portraits, and, in summer, activities are nonstop here, with jousting, falconry exhibitions, and country fairs, making this one of southern England's most rewarding castles to visit. In one of the Victorian wings, B&B rooms go for upwards of £145 per night for a basic room; there's also a four-bedroom holiday cottage available for £3,250 a week. ⊠ Off B2026, Hever ☎ 01732/865224 ⊕ www.hevercastle.co.uk ☑ £18.80; grounds only £15.55 ⊙ Closed Jan.–mid-Feb. and Mon. and Tues. in late Nov.–late Dec.

Penshurst Place

HOUSE | At the center of the adorable hamlet of Penshurst stands this fine medieval manor house, hidden behind tall trees and walls. Although it has a 14th-century hall, Penshurst is mainly Elizabethan and has been the family home of the Sidneys since 1552. The most famous Sidney is the Elizabethan poet Sir Philip, author of *Arcadia*. The **Baron's Hall**, topped with a chestnut roof, is the oldest and one of the grandest halls to survive from the early Middle Ages. Family portraits, furniture, tapestries, and armor help tell the story of the house, which was first inhabited in 1341 by Sir John de Pulteney, the very wealthy four-time London mayor. On the grounds are a toy museum, a gift shop, and the enchanting 11-acre walled Italian Garden, which displays tulips and daffodils in spring and roses in summer. Take time to study the village's late-15th-century half-timber structures adorned with soaring brick chimneys. To get here from Hever, take the B2027 east then follow signs to Penshurst. ⊠ *Rogues*

Hill, Penshurst ☎ 01892/870307 ⊕ www.penshurstplace.com ✎ £12.50; grounds only £10.50 ⊙ Closed Nov.–mid-Feb. and weekdays mid-Feb.–Mar.

🍴 Restaurants

The Spotted Dog

$ | BRITISH | One mile south of Penshurt, this historic pub first opened its doors in 1520 and in many ways hardly appears to have changed today. Its big ingle-nook fireplace and heavy beams give it character, the views from the hilltop are lovely, and the good food (a mixture of traditional pub grub and slightly more sophisticated fare) make it a pleasure to relax inside. **Known for:** mixture of casual and formal dining; atmospheric old pub; lovely beer garden in summer. ⑤ Average main: £13 ⊠ 6 Saint's Hill, Penshurst ☎ 01892/870253 ⊕ www.spotteddogpub.com.

Tonbridge

9 miles east of Hever.

This Kentish market town is a great base for exploring two magnificent Tudor properties. The first is Knole, perhaps the quintessential Tudor mansion, as famous for its literary connections and impressive collection of furniture and tapestries as it is for its elegant 15th- and 16th-century architecture. The second is Ightham Mote, a captivating, unreal-looking place that's almost unique among medieval manor houses in that it still has a moat (although that has nothing to do with the name).

GETTING HERE AND AROUND

Southeastern trains leave several times an hour from London Charing Cross to Tonbridge (40 minutes). Driving, via the A2/M25/A21, takes a little longer (one to 1½ hours). If driving from Hever, head east on the B2027 to reach Tonbridge. The town is five miles north of Tunbridge

Wells; drive on the A26 or take one of the regular trains (10 minutes) or buses (25 minutes).

◉ Sights

All Saints Church

RELIGIOUS SITE | Situated two miles east of Tonbridge in the little village of Tudeley, this modest 13th-century church holds one of the glories of 20th-century church art. The building is awash with the luminous yellows and blues of 12 windows by Marc Chagall (1887–1985), commissioned as a tribute by the family of a young girl who drowned in a sailing accident in 1963. To get here, take the A26 from Tonbridge, then continue a mile or so east along B2017. ⊠ Off B2017, Tudeley ☎ 01892/833241 ⊕ www.tudeley.org/allsaintstudeley.htm ✎ Free; £3 donation requested.

★ Ightham Mote

HOUSE | This wonderful, higgledy-pig-gledy, timber-framed medieval manor house looks like something out of a fairy tale. Even its name is a bit of an enigma—"Ightham" is pronounced "Item" (we can't quite figure that out either) and "Mote" doesn't refer to the kind of moat you get in a castle, but an old English word for meeting place. Perhaps it's also fitting, then, that finding the place takes careful navigation down tiny, winding country lanes, and then even to reach the front door you must first cross a narrow stone bridge over the moat (yes, it has one of those, too). But it's all worth the effort to see a fanciful vision right out of the Middle Ages.

Built nearly 700 years ago, Ightham's magical exterior has hardly changed since the 14th century, but within you'll find that it encompasses styles of several periods, from Tudor to Victorian. The Great Hall, the Tudor chapel, and the drawing room are all highlights of the main property. Nearby is the smaller but equally pretty Laundry Hall, home to a

One of England's most notable stately homes, sprawling Knole displayed the power of the Sackvilles.

second-hand bookshop and exhibition, as well as shaded woodland walks (awash with bluebells in spring), a pretty pond, and a natural play area for little ones. Ightham Mote is six miles north of Tonbridge on the A227. ✉ Mote Rd., off A227, Sevenoaks ☎ 01732/810378 ⊕ www.nationaltrust.org.uk/ightham-mote ☜ £15.50 Mar.–Oct.; £5.40 Nov.–Feb. ⊙ House closed Nov., Jan., and Feb.

⚑ Knole

HOUSE | The pleasant but workaday town of Sevenoaks, seven miles northwest of Tonbridge, lies in London's commuter belt, a world away from the baronial air of its premier attraction: Knole, the grand, beloved estate of the Sackville family since the 16th century.

Begun in the 1400s and enlarged in 1603 by Thomas Sackville, Knole's sprawling complex of courtyards and outbuildings resembles a small town. In fact, with more that 300 rooms, 51 chimneys (count them!), and a total footprint covering five acres—the equivalent to almost four football fields—it's England's

largest house. Factor in the supremely stroll-worthy (and free-roaming deer-filled) 1,000-acre park surrounding the property, and you'll need at least an afternoon to explore Knole thoroughly.

The house is noted for its wonderful tapestries, embroidered furnishings, and an extraordinary set of 17th-century silver furniture. Most of the salons are in the pre-baroque model, rather dark and armorial. The magnificently florid staircase was a novelty in its Elizabethan heyday. Vita Sackville-West grew up here and used it as the setting for her novel *The Edwardians,* a witty account of life among the gilded set.

Also on the property is the Conservation Studio, which showcases the work that the National Trust does at Knole and other local properties (you can also see the conservators in action), as well as the beautiful private garden, though this is only open on rare occasions.

In contrast to the property itself, the entrance is surprisingly low-key; look for the signposted track opposite St. Nicholas Church. ⊠ *Knole La., off A225, Sevenoaks* ☎ *01732/462100* ⊕ *www. nationaltrust.org.uk/knole* ⊠ *£15.50; gatehouse tower £5; parking £5* ⊙ *House closed Nov.–early Mar.*

Rochester

20 miles northeast of Tonbridge.

Positioned near the confluence of the Thames and the River Medway, this posh town has a history of Roman, Saxon, and Norman occupation, all of which have left architectural remains, including the vast castle at the town center. Novelist Charles Dickens called Rochester home for more than a decade, until his death in 1870, and would sometimes walk here all the way from London.

South of Rochester, in the corridor between Canterbury and Tunbridge Wells, lies a number of interesting historic sights, including Leeds Castle and Sissinghurst Castle Gardens.

GETTING HERE AND AROUND
From London, Rochester is a 45-minute drive via the M2/A2. Regular Southeastern trains from several London stations—including St. Pancras, Victoria, and Charing Cross—take a similar amount of time. To reach Rochester from Tonbridge, take the A26 and A228 northeast. The journey takes about 45 minutes. Southeastern trains run regular services from Tonbridge to Strood (one hour), which is a 15-minute walk from Rochester town center.

⊙ Sights

★ Leeds Castle
CASTLE/PALACE | Every inch the grand medieval castle, Leeds is more like a storybook illustration of what an English castle should look like, from the fortress-like exterior to the breathtaking rooms within. Ramparts and battlements? Check. Moat? Check. Ancient stone walkways on which you just know a knight in shining armor might pass by at any second? Pretty much.

Leeds—not to be confused with the city in the north of England; the name comes from its mention as "Esledes" (meaning "hill" or "slope") in the Domesday Book of 1086—has all this and more. One of England's finest castles, it commands two small islands on a peaceful lake. Dating to the 9th century and rebuilt by the Normans in 1119, the castle became a favorite home of many medieval English queens. Henry VIII liked it so much he had it converted from a fortress into a grand palace.

The interior doesn't match the glories of the much-photographed exterior, although there are fine paintings and furniture, including many pieces from the 20th-century refurbishment by the castle's last private owner, Lady Baillie. The outside attractions are more impressive and include a surprisingly tricky maze (made from 2,400 yew trees), which leads to an atmospheric rock-carved grotto, as well as two adventure playgrounds, an aviary of native and exotic birds, and woodland gardens. There are also several dining options, including the informal but excellent Castle View Restaurant (try the haddock-and-chips).

Leeds Castle is 12 miles southeast of Rochester, off the M20 highway. ■TIP→ **All tickets are valid for a year, in case you don't manage to see everything in one day.** ⊠ *Off A20, Maidstone* ☎ *01622/765400* ⊕ *www.leeds-castle. com* ⊠ *£27.*

★ Sissinghurst Castle Garden
GARDEN | One of the most famous gardens in the world, unpretentiously beautiful and quintessentially English, Sissinghurst rests deep in the Kentish countryside. The gardens, with their many different themed "rooms," were laid out in the 1930s around the remains of part of a moated Tudor castle by writer

Vita Sackville-West (one of the Sackvilles of Knole, her childhood home) and her husband, diplomat Harold Nicolson. The relationship was clearly loving but also complicated, as both had a string of extramarital same-sex affairs; Vita, famously, had a decade-long romance with Virginia Woolf.

Climb the tower for a wonderful overview of the gardens—as well as a peek inside Vita's study en route—then descend to see them up close. There's the stunning White Garden, filled with snow-color flowers and silver-gray foliage; the herb and cottage gardens, which showcase Sackville-West's encyclopedic knowledge of plants; and the Delos Garden, which brings a slice of the Mediterranean to the heart of Kent (as well as finally realizing a dream of Vita and Harold's following their visit to Greece in 1935). As well as the gardens, there are woodland and lake walks all around, making it easy to spend a half day or more here.

If you love it all so much you want to stay, you can—the National Trust rents the Priest's House on the property for a minimum stay of three nights; prices start at around £700 and rise to upwards of £1,600 in midsummer. See the National Trust website for details (but be warned, you'll need to book well ahead).

Sissinghurst Castle Garden is 22 miles south of Rochester on the A229, and 16 miles east of Tunbridge Wells on the A262. ⊠ Off A262, Cranbrook ☎ 01580/710700 ⊕ www.nationaltrust. org.uk/sissinghurst-castle ⊴ £14.50; parking £4 ⊘ Closed weekdays Nov.–mid-Mar.

🛏 Hotels

★ Sissinghurst Castle Farmhouse
$$ | B&B/INN | This lovely, larger-than-you-expect farmhouse on the grounds of Sissinghurst Castle was originally built in 1885 and lovingly restored by the National Trust in 2009. **Pros:** beautiful location on the grounds of a historic home; delicious breakfast; barbecues on the lawn in summer. **Cons:** patchy TV signal in the rooms; need a car to get here; no restaurant for dinner. ⑤ Rooms from: £160 ⊠ Off A262, Sissinghurst ☎ 01580/720992 ⊕ www. sissinghurstcastlefarmhouse.com ⟿ 9 rooms ⦿ Free breakfast.

Rye

68 miles southeast of London, 34 miles southwest of Dover.

With cobbled streets and ancient timbered dwellings, Rye is an artist's dream. It was an important port town until the harbor silted up and the waters retreated more than 150 years ago; now the nearest harbor is two miles away. Virtually every building in the little town center is intriguingly historic. Rye is known for its many antiques stores and also for its sheer pleasantness. This place can be easily walked without a map, but if you need some direction, Campion Frames (71 The Mint) sells a fact-packed walking tour map for £2.

GETTING HERE AND AROUND
If you're driving to Rye from London, take the A2, followed by M2, M20, and A2070/A259. Trains from London's St. Pancras leave once an hour and take just over one hour, including a change in Ashford. Driving from Rochester is the same route as from London (though starting with the M2), while getting to Rye from Rochester by train means going via London.

👁 Sights

★ Bodiam Castle
CASTLE/PALACE | FAMILY | Immortalized in paintings, photographs, and films, Bodiam Castle (pronounced *Boe*-dee-um) rises out of the distance like a piece of medieval legend. From the outside it's one of Britain's most impressive castles,

Rye and Lewes

with turrets, battlements, a glassy moat (one of the very few still in use), and two-foot-thick walls. However, once you cross the drawbridge to the interior there's little to see but ruins, albeit on an impressive scale. Built in 1385 to withstand a threatened French invasion, it was partly demolished during the English Civil War of 1642–46 and has been uninhabited ever since. Still, you can climb the intact towers to take in sweeping countryside views, and kids love running around the keep. The castle, 12 miles northwest of Rye, schedules organized activities for kids during school holidays. **■ TIP→ For a unique way to approach Bodiam Castle, take a 45-minute river cruise through the pretty Sussex countryside. Boats leave from the riverbank in Newenden; find more information and sailing times at www. bodiamboatingstation.co.uk.** ⊠ *Off Main Rd., Bodiam* ☎ *01580/830196* ⊕ *www.*

nationaltrust.org.uk/bodiamcastle ⊞ *£11.40.*

Church of St. Mary

RELIGIOUS SITE | At the top of the hill at the center of Rye, this classic English village church is more than 900 years old and encompasses a number of architectural styles. The turret clock dates to 1561 and still keeps excellent time. Its huge pendulum swings inside the church nave. **■ TIP→ Climb the tower for amazing views of the surrounding area.** ⊠ *Church Sq.* ☎ *01797/222318* ⊕ *www.ryeparish-church.org.uk* ⊞ *Free.*

Mermaid Street

NEIGHBORHOOD | One of the town's original cobbled streets, and perhaps its most quintessential view, heads steeply from the top of the hill to the former harbor. Its name supposedly came from the night a drunken sailor swore he heard a mermaid call him down to the sea (back when Rye was still a seaside town). The houses here date from between the medieval and Georgian periods; a much-photographed pair have the delightfully fanciful names "The House with Two Front Doors" and "The House Opposite." ⚠ **Be careful on your feet—the cobbles are very uneven.** ✉ *Rye.*

Ypres Tower

BUILDING | Down the hill past Church Square, Ypres Tower (pronounced "Wipers" by locals) was originally built as part of the town's fortifications (now all but disappeared) in 1249; it later served as a prison. A row of defensive cannons is fixed to the rampart overlooking the (disappointingly industrial) edge of Rye and several miles of flatland beyond. When they were installed, however, the canons pointed directly out to sea. Inside the tower is the Rye Castle Museum, which has displays on the city's history, from medieval floor tiles to 15th-century suits of armor, as well an interesting exhibition on 1830s life as a female prisoner in the "women's tower."

A second (free to enter) outpost of the RCM on nearby East Street has even more exhibits, including examples of Rye pottery for which the town was famous and a fire engine that was built in 1745 and served the town for 120 years. ✉ *Gungarden* ☎ *01797/226728* ⊕ *www. ryemuseum.co.uk* 🎫 *£4.*

🍴 Restaurants

★ Webbes at the Fish Café

$$ | **SEAFOOD** | One of Rye's most popular restaurants, where most of the seafood is freshly caught nearby, occupies a brick building that dates to 1907, but the interior has been redone in a sleek, modern style. Sample the salt and Sichuan pepper squid with soy and sherry dressing or the pan-fried Rye Bay scallops with pancetta and chive vermouth sauce. **Known for:** top-quality and locally caught seafood; fast and friendly service; dinner reservations recommended. ⑤ *Average main: £17* ✉ *17 Tower St.* ☎ *01797/222210* ⊕ *www.webbesrestaurants.co.uk.*

Whitehouse

$ | **CAFÉ** | **FAMILY** | This chic, contemporary café serves delectable baked goods, all-day breakfasts, and tapas-style light bites. Come for the Turkish eggs, poached with yogurt and dill, or, if you're in the mood for something heartier, try the coconut red lentil dal with chili salsa. **Known for:** perfectly brewed coffee; healthful light bites; delicious cakes. ⑤ *Average main: £9* ✉ *24 High St.* ☎ *01797/224748* ⊕ *www.whitehouserye. co.uk* 🌙 *No dinner.*

 ## 🛏 Hotels

★ The Mermaid Inn

$$ | **HOTEL** | Steeped in a history of smuggling—look for Rudyard Kipling's atmospheric poem *A Smuggler's Song* on the wall outside—the 600-year-old Mermaid is Rye's most historic inn; its sloping floors, oak beams, low ceilings, and huge open hearth look like a film set, but it's all totally authentic. **Pros:** dripping in atmosphere; good restaurant; one of England's oldest inns. **Cons:** price is high for what's on offer; small bedrooms; allegedly haunted. ⑤ *Rooms from: £160* ✉ *Mermaid St.* ☎ *01797/223065* ⊕ *www. mermaidinn.com* 🍽 *31 rooms* ⭐ *Free breakfast.*

★ Rye Windmill

$ | **HOTEL** | One of the Southeast's most unique B&Bs, this 450-year-old white-washed windmill overlooking the River Tillingham is home to 10 lovely bedrooms with large en suite bathrooms, including walk-in showers. **Pros:** unique and luxurious Windmill Suite; central location but feels rural; welcoming hosts. **Cons:** tap water not drinkable (refillable bottled water provided); no restaurant; two-night minimum in summer. ⑤ *Rooms*

*from: £95 ⊠ Ferry Rd., Off B2089
☏ 01797/224027 ⊕ www.ryewindmill.
co.uk ⇌ 10 rooms ◯ Free breakfast.*

Nightlife

★ Rye Waterworks

BARS/PUBS | This cozy little micropub, set
within a 17th-century pump house, offers
eight (mostly local) beers on tap. The bar
staff is friendly and chatty, and there's
a real communal vibe to the place, with
most drinkers sharing tables. If you get
peckish, there are tasty pub snacks
available; try the pork pie with mustard
and chutney. ■**TIP→ If you like the pub
furnishings, you can pick some up for yourself at the Waterworks Curios antiques shop
next door.** ⊠ *Tower St.* ☏ *01797/224110*
⊕ *www.ryewaterworks.co.uk.*

Shopping

Britcher & Rivers

FOOD/CANDY | This traditional sweet shop
is like something out of a bygone age.
Choose from row upon row of tall jars
packed with every imaginable type of
candy, measured out into little paper
bags. ⊠ *109 High St.* ☏ *01797/227152.*

Glass Etc

CERAMICS/GLASSWARE | A glorious col-
lection of quality antique glass can be
found in this colorful, friendly shop near
the train station. ⊠ *18–20 Rope Walk*
☏ *01797/226600* ⊕ *www.decanterman.
com.*

Hastings

*12 miles southwest of Rye, 68 miles
southeast of London.*

In the 19th century, Hastings became
one of England's most popular spa
resorts. Tall Victorian row houses painted
in lemony hues still cover the cliffs
around the deep blue sea, and the views
from the hilltops are extraordinary. The
pretty Old Town, on the east side of
the city, offers a glimpse into the city's
16th-century past. Hastings has been
through difficult times in recent decades,
and the town developed a reputation as
a rough place. It's currently trying hard
to reinvent itself—a clutch of trendy
new boutique bed-and-breakfasts have
opened, as well as an important new art
gallery—but the town center can still be
quite rowdy after dark. Expect a handsome but tattered town, with a mix of
traditional English seaside amusements:
miniature golf, shops selling junk, fish-
and-chips stands, and a rocky beach that
stretches for miles.

Of course, Hastings is also known for
the famous battle that took place on
October 14, 1066, when William of
Normandy and his troops trounced King
Harold's Anglo-Saxon army (although the
battle itself actually took place six miles
northwest of Hastings). Today, you can
visit the battlefield and the abbey built in
its honor, as well as the sweet little town
around it (called, fittingly, Battle).

GETTING HERE AND AROUND

If you're driving to Hastings from London,
take the A21. Trains travel to Hastings
three or four times an hour from London's Victoria and St. Pancras stations.
The journey takes between 1½ and two
hours; some trains involve a change in
Brighton or Ashford. The main station
is within easy walking distance of most
sights, though a second station—the
more grandly titled St Leonards Warrior
Square—may be more convenient if
you're staying farther west. National
Express buses travel from London Victoria Coach Station to Hastings once or
twice a day in around 2½ hours.

From Rye, there are direct trains every
hour to Hastings (20 minutes). It's a
30-minute drive along the A259.

ESSENTIALS
VISITOR INFORMATION Hastings Tourist Information Centre. ✉ *Muriel Matters House, 2 Breeds Pl.* ☎ *01424/451111* ⊕ *www.visit1066country.com.*

⊙ Sights

★ Battle Abbey
ARCHAEOLOGICAL SITE | Situated six miles northwest of Hastings, this great Benedictine abbey was erected by William the Conqueror on the site of the Battle of Hastings—one of the most decisive turning points in English history and the last time the country was successfully invaded. All of this meant little to Henry VIII, of course, who didn't spare the building from his violent dissolution of the monasteries. Today the abbey is just a ruin, but a very pretty one.

Start at the visitor center to get the full story through a series of films and interactive exhibits before taking a walk around the abbey site, including up to the first floor. A memorial stone marks the high altar, which in turn was supposedly laid on the spot where Harold II, the last Saxon king, was killed.

You can also follow a trail around the 1066 battlefield, lined with a series of intricately carved wooden sculptures of Norman and Saxon soldiers, or climb the gatehouse for an exhibiton on the site's post-invasion history as well as spectacular rooftop views of the town. For a potted history of Battle, head to nearby St. Mary's Church, where the three-meter-long Battle Tapestry artfully illustrates how the town developed around the abbey. ✉ *High St., Battle* ☎ *01424/775705* ⊕ *www.english-heritage.org.uk/battle-abbey* ☜ *£12.30; parking £4* ⊘ *Closed weekdays early Nov.–mid-Feb. and Mon. and Tues. mid-Feb.–Apr.*

Hastings Castle
CASTLE/PALACE | FAMILY | Take a thrilling ride up the West Hill Cliff Railway from George Street precinct to the atmospheric ruins of the thousand-year-old fortress now known as Hastings Castle. It was built by William the Conqueror in 1066, before he had even won the Battle of Hastings and conquered England—that's confidence for you. Today all that remains of the country's first Norman castle are mere fragments of the fortifications, some ancient walls, and a number of gloomy dungeons. Nevertheless, you get an excellent view of the chalky cliffs, the rocky coast, and the town below. You can buy a joint ticket that covers admission to Smuggler's Adventure and the nearby Blue Reef aquarium for £19; you then have seven days to see the other attractions. ✉ *West Hill, Off Castle Hill Rd.* ☎ *01424/422964* ☜ *£5.25* ⊘ *Closed Nov.–Mar.*

Hastings Contemporary
MUSEUM | A symbol of Hastings's slow but growing regeneration after decades of neglect, this spruced-up exhibition space in the Old Town has become one of the most talked-about contemporary art galleries outside London. Formerly known as the Jerwood Gallery, Hastings Contemporary's collection includes works by Walter Sickert, Stephen Lowry, and Augustus John, while temporary exhibitions change every couple of months. The glazed-tile building on the seafront was designed to reflect the row of distinctive old, blackened fishing sheds it sits alongside. ✉ *Rock-a-Nore Rd.* ☎ *01424/728377* ⊕ *www.hastings-contemporary.org* ☜ *£9* ⊘ *Closed Mon. except bank holidays.*

★ Herstmonceux Castle
CASTLE/PALACE | FAMILY | With a banner waving from one tower and a glassy moat crossed by what was once a drawbridge, this fairy-tale castle has everything except knights in shining armor. Situated 13 miles northwest of Hastings, the redbrick structure was originally built by Sir Roger Fiennes (ancestor of actor Ralph Fiennes) in 1444, although it was altered in the Elizabethan age and

again early in the 20th century after it had largely fallen to ruin. Canadian Queen's University owns the castle, so only part of it is open for guided tours, usually once or twice a day except on Saturday; call in advance to schedule a tour in high season.

Highlights include the magnificent ballroom, a medieval room, and the stunning Elizabethan-era staircase. Explore the formal walled garden, lily-covered lakes, and miles of woodland—the perfect place for a picnic on a sunny afternoon. There's also a hands-on science center for kids.

When school isn't in session, the castle rents out its small, plain guest rooms from £40 per night. On the last weekend of August, the castle hosts a large **Medieval Festival,** complete with jousting, falconry shows, and around 100 craft stalls. ✉ *Off Wartling Rd., Herstmonceux* ☎ *01323/833816* ⊕ *www.herstmonceux-castle.com* 🎫 *Castle, grounds, and science center £14.50; grounds only £7; castle tours £3* ⊙ *Closed Nov.–mid-Feb.*

🍴 Restaurants

★ Blue Dolphin Fish Bar
$ | SEAFOOD | The crowds line up all day to make their way into this small fish-and-chip shop just off the seafront, down near the fish shacks. Although the decor is humble, reviewers consistently rank the battered fish and huge plates of double-cooked chips (chunky fries) as among the best in the country. **Known for:** popularity across Britain; beachside location; tasty traditional fish-and-chips. ⑤ *Average main: £7* ✉ *61A High St.* ☎ *01424/547150.*

★ Sundial
$$$ | MODERN FRENCH | A 17th-century brick farmhouse with wood-beamed ceilings and lovely views of the South Downs is home to an excellent modern French restaurant. Situated near the castle in Herstmonceux, it features an imaginative three-course "Gourmet Menu" (£48 per

person) that changes regularly but may include pan-fried wild turbot with truffle butter or beef fillet steak with a sauce of port and shallot. **Known for:** sophisticated Modern French cooking; lovely views; delicious pineapple tarte tatin dessert. ⑤ *Average main: £25* ✉ *Gardner St., Herstmonceux* ☎ *01323/832217* ⊕ *www.sundialrestaurant.co.uk* ⊙ *Closed Mon. No dinner Sun.*

White's Seafood & Steak Bar
$$ | SEAFOOD | FAMILY | Great seafood in simple, unpretentious surroundings is the order of the day at this popular place in Hastings Old Town. Fresh-as-can-be seafood, huge platters of shellfish, creamy fish pies, and delicious plates of fish-and-chips are the epitome of unfussy local flavor. **Known for:** huge seafood platters; fresh catch of the day; hot-rock cooking at your table. ⑤ *Average main: £16* ✉ *44-45 George St.* ☎ *01424/719846* ⊕ *www.whitesbar.co.uk.*

Hotels

The Cloudesley
$ | B&B/INN | No TVs and a general Zen vibe at this boutique B&B in the quieter St. Leonard's district of Hastings make it a thoroughly relaxing place to stay. **Pros:** oasis of calm; great spa treatments; impeccable eco credentials. **Cons:** chill vibe won't be for everyone; two-night minimum at certain times; 20-minute walk into Hastings. ⑤ *Rooms from: £85* ✉ *7 Cloudesley Rd., St. Leonards-on-Sea* ☎ *01424/722759* ⊕ *www.thecloudesley.co.uk* 🛏 *5 rooms* ⦿ *Free breakfast.*

★ Swan House
$ | B&B/INN | Originally a bakery, this extraordinary 15th-century building has been beautifully converted into an elegant and welcoming B&B, where the light and airy guest rooms are decorated in neutral modern tones and retain original features such as exposed wood beams. **Pros:** beautiful and historic building; welcoming hosts; seriously delicious

breakfasts. **Cons:** some bathrooms have shower only; two-night minimum on summer weekends; gets booked up. $ *Rooms from: £120* ✉ *1 Hill St.* ☎ *01424/430014* ⊕ *www.swanhouse-hastings.co.uk* ↩ *4 rooms* ⃝ *Free breakfast.*

Lewes

24 miles east of Battle, 8 miles northeast of Brighton, 54 miles south of London.

The town nearest to the celebrated Glyndebourne Opera House, Lewes is so rich in history that the Council for British Archaeology named it one of the 50 most important English towns. A walk is the best way to appreciate its steep streets and appealing jumble of building styles and materials—flint, stone, brick, tile—and the secret lanes (called "twittens") behind the castle, with their huge beeches. Here and there are smart antiques shops, good eateries, and secondhand-book dealers. Most of the buildings in the center date to the 18th and 19th centuries.

Something about this town has always attracted rebels. It was once the home of Thomas Paine (1737–1809), whose pamphlet *Common Sense* advocated that the American colonies break with Britain. It was also favored by Virginia Woolf and the Bloomsbury Group, early-20th-century countercultural artistic innovators.

Today Lewes's beauty and proximity to London mean that the counterculture crew can't really afford to live here anymore, but its rebel soul still peeks through, particularly on Guy Fawkes Night (November 5), the anniversary of Fawkes's foiled attempt to blow up the Houses of Parliament in 1605. Flaming tar barrels are rolled down High Street and into the River Ouse, while costumed processions fill the streets.

GETTING HERE AND AROUND

If you're driving to Lewes from London, take the M23 south. The journey takes around an hour and 45 minutes. Southern trains run direct to Lewes from Victoria Station about three times an hour (the journey takes an hour), but there's no good bus connection. To get to Lewes from Hastings, it's an hour drive west along the A259 and A27 or an hour by train (there are four Southern services an hour).

ESSENTIALS

VISITOR INFORMATION Lewes Information Centre. ✉ *187 High St.* ☎ *01273/483448* ⊕ *www.visitlewes.co.uk.*

 ## Sights

Anne of Cleves House

HOUSE | FAMILY | This 16th-century structure, a fragile-looking, timber-frame building, holds a small collection of Sussex ironwork and other items of local interest, such as Sussex pottery. The house was part of Anne of Cleves's divorce settlement from Henry VIII, although she never lived in it. There are medieval dress-up clothes for kids. To get to the house, walk down steep, cobbled Keere Street, past lovely Grange Gardens, to Southover High Street. ✉ *52 Southover High St.* ☎ *01273/474610* ⊕ *www.sussexpast.co.uk/anneofcleves* ⌨ *£6.50; combined ticket with Lewes Castle £13.40* ⊘ *Closed Nov.–mid-Feb.*

★ Charleston

HOUSE | Art and life mixed at Charleston, the farmhouse that Vanessa Bell—sister of Virginia Woolf—bought in 1916 and fancifully decorated, along with Duncan Grant (who lived here until 1978). The house, which is seven miles east of Lewes, soon became a refuge for the writers and artists of the Bloomsbury Group. On display are colorful ceramics and textiles of the Omega Workshop—in which Bell and Grant participated—and paintings by Picasso and Renoir, as well

A mixture of architectural styles and good shops makes Lewes a wonderful town for a stroll.

as by Bell and Grant themselves. Entry to the house is by guided tour; you can buy tickets when you arrive (first come, first served) or book in advance online. It's also possible to book private, themed tours that focus on different aspects of Charleston's heritage, such as its groundbreaking LGBTQ+ history or the influence French culture had on the Bloomsbury Group. ■TIP➔ **The house isn't suitable for those with mobility issues, although reduced-price ground-floor-only tickets are available.** ⊠ *Off A27, Firle* ☎ *01323/811626* ⊕ *www.charleston.org. uk* ✉ *£14.50* ◔ *Closed Mon. and Tues.*

Lewes Castle

CASTLE/PALACE | High above the valley of the River Ouse stand the majestic ruins of Lewes Castle, begun in 1100 by one of the country's Norman conquerors and completed 300 years later. The castle's barbican holds a small museum with archaeology collections, a changing temporary exhibition gallery, and a bookshop. There are panoramic views of the town and countryside. ⊠ *92 High St.* ☎ *01273/486290* ⊕ *www.sussexpast. co.uk/properties-to-discover/lewes-castle* ✉ *£8.50; combined ticket with Anne of Cleves House £13.40* ◔ *Closed Mon. in Jan.–Mar.*

Restaurants

The Limetree Kitchen

$ | BRITISH | Elegant, imaginative menus and a commitment to locally sourced produce is at the heart of this popular restaurant in the center of Lewes. Menus are heavily influenced by what's in season, with just a few, well-chosen options available each day—examples might include tempura of Devonshire hake with tartare sauce or local rib-eye steak with parsley and shallot. **Known for:** excellent value main courses; seasonal menus; locally sourced produce. ⑤ *Average main: £11* ⊠ *14 Station St.* ☎ *01273 /478636* ⊕ *www.limetreekitchen.co.uk* ◔ *Closed Mon. and Tues.*

Robson's of Lewes

$ | CAFÉ | Good coffee, fresh produce, and delicious pastries make this coffee shop one of the best places in Lewes to drop by for an afternoon pick-me-up. A light-filled space with wood floors and simple tables creates a pleasant, casual spot to enjoy a cup of coffee with breakfast, a scone, or a light sandwich or salad lunch. **Known for:** great coffee; tasty light bites; good to-go options. ⑤ *Average main: £6* ⊠ *22A High St.* ☎ *01273/480654* ⊕ *www. robsonsoflewes.co.uk* ⊗ *No dinner.*

 ## Hotels

Horsted Place

$$ | B&B/INN | On 1,100 acres, this luxurious Victorian manor house was built as a private home in 1850; it was owned by a friend of the current Queen until the 1980s, and she was a regular visitor. **Pros:** historic country manor; delicious food; lovely gardens. **Cons:** too formal for some; creaky floors bother light sleepers; the English manor lifestyle doesn't come cheap. ⑤ *Rooms from: £200* ⊠ *Off A26, Little Horsted* ☎ *01825/750581* ⊕ *www. horstedplace.co.uk* ⇄ *20 rooms* ⧾ *Free breakfast.*

The Ram Inn

$$ | B&B/INN | Roaring fires, cozy rooms, and friendly locals give this 500-year-old inn its wonderful feeling of old-world authenticity. **Pros:** proper village pub atmosphere; excellent breakfast (try the croissants); well-designed rooms. **Cons:** you need a car to get here; rooms over the bar can be noisy; Wi-Fi is patchy. ⑤ *Rooms from: £150* ⊠ *The St., West Firle* ☎ *01273/858222* ⊕ *www.raminn. co.uk* ⇄ *5 rooms* ⧾ *Free breakfast.*

 ## Nightlife

The Brewers Arms

BARS/PUBS | On High Street, this is a good pub with a friendly crowd. While the half-timbered building only dates from 1906, a pub has stood on this spot since the 16th century. ⊠ *91 High St.* ☎ *01273/475524* ⊕ *www.thebrewersarmslewes.com.*

King's Head

BARS/PUBS | A contemporary pub dating back to 1891, the King's Head has a good menu with locally sourced fish and meat dishes. There are also three quirky boutique rooms available. ⊠ *9 Southover High St.* ☎ *01273/474628* ⊕ *www.kingsheadlewes.co.uk.*

 ## Performing Arts

★ Glyndebourne Opera House

OPERA | Nestled beneath the Downs, three miles east of Lewes, this world-famous opera house combines first-class productions, a state-of-the-art auditorium, and a beautiful setting. Tickets are *very* expensive (the cheapest start at around £85, though for many productions it's twice that, rising to around £250), and you have to book months in advance. But it's worth every penny to aficionados, who traditionally wear evening dress and bring a hamper to picnic on the grounds. The main season runs from mid-May to the end of August. ■ **TIP➜ Save money by booking standing-room tickets (from £10), or look out for special nights when adults under 30 pay just £30.** ⊠ *New Rd., Ringmer* ☎ *01273/813321* ⊕ *www.glyndebourne. com.*

Shopping

Cliffe Antiques Centre

ANTIQUES/COLLECTIBLES | This packed-to-the-rafters shop carries a fine mix of vintage English prints, estate jewelry, and art at reasonable prices. ⊠ *47 Cliffe High St.* ☎ *01273/473266* ⊕ *www.cliffeantiques.co.uk.*

The Fifteenth Century Bookshop

BOOKS/STATIONERY | A wide collection of rare and vintage books can be found at this ancient, timber-framed building in the center of Lewes. Antique children's

books are a specialty. ✉ *99–100 High St.*
☎ *01273/474160* ⊕ *www.oldenyoung-
books.co.uk.*

Louis Potts & Co.
CERAMICS/GLASSWARE | From frivolous
knickkacks to full-on formal dining sets,
Louis Potts specializes in stylish bone
china and glassware. ✉ *43 Cliffe High St.*
☎ *01273/472240* ⊕ *www.louispotts.com.*

Brighton

*9 miles southwest of Lewes, 54 miles
south of London.*

For more than 200 years, Brighton
has been England's most interesting
seaside city, and today it's more vibrant,
eccentric, and cosmopolitan than ever. A
rich cultural mix—Regency architecture,
specialty shops, sidewalk cafés, lively
arts, and a flourishing gay scene—makes
it unique and unpredictable.

In 1750, physician Richard Russell published a book recommending seawater
treatment for glandular diseases. The
fashionable world flocked to Brighton to
take Dr. Russell's "cure," and sea bathing
became a popular pastime. Few places in
the south of England were better for it,
since Brighton's broad beach of smooth
pebbles stretches as far as the eye can
see. It's been popular with sunbathers
ever since.

The next windfall for the town was
the arrival of the Prince of Wales (later
George IV). "Prinny," as he was called,
created the Royal Pavilion, a mock-Asian
pleasure palace that attracted London
society. This triggered a wave of villa
building, and today the elegant terraces
of Regency houses are among the town's
greatest attractions. The coming of the
railway set the seal on Brighton's popularity: the *Brighton Belle* brought Londoners
to the coast in an hour.

Londoners still flock to Brighton. Add
them to the many local university

students, and you have a trendy, young,
and laid-back city that does, occasionally,
burst at its own seams. Property values
have skyrocketed, but all visitors may
notice is the good shopping and restaurants, attractive (if pebbly) beach, and
wild nightlife. Brighton is also the place
to go if you're looking for hotels with
offbeat design and party nights.

GETTING HERE AND AROUND
Southeastern trains leave from London's
Victoria and London Bridge stations
several times per hour. The journey takes
about an hour, and the trains stop at
Gatwick Airport. Brighton-bound National
Express buses depart from London's
Victoria Coach Station every day on the
hour and half hour. The direct buses take
around 2½ hours. By car from London,
head to Brighton on the M23/A23. The
journey should take between 1½ and 2
hours, depending on traffic.

From Lewes, Southern train services
leave every 10 minutes for Brighton
(15 minutes). Otherwise, it's a simple
drive down the A27 and A270 (20 to 30
minutes).

Brighton (and the adjacent Hove) sprawls
in all directions, but the part of interest to
travelers is fairly compact. All the major
sights are within a 10-minute walk of the
train station, where you can pick up a
town map. City Sightseeing has a hop-
on, hop-off tour bus that leaves Brighton
Pier every 20 to 30 minutes. It operates
April through October and costs £14.

ESSENTIALS
**VISITOR AND TOUR INFORMA-
TION Brighton Visitor Information Point.**
✉ *The Brighton Centre, King's Rd.*
☎ *01273/290337* ⊕ *www.visitbrighton.
com.* **City Sightseeing.** ☎ *01789/299123*
⊕ *www.city-sightseeing.com.*

👁 Sights

Brighton Beach

BEACH—SIGHT | Brighton's most iconic landmark is its famous beach, which sweeps smoothly from one end of town to the other. In summer, sunbathers, swimmers, and ice cream–sellers pack the shore; in winter, people stroll at the water's stormy edge, walking their dogs and searching for seashells. The water is bracingly cold, and the beach is covered in a thick blanket of large, smooth pebbles (615 billion of them, according to the tourism office). ■ **TIP→ Bring a pair of rubber swimming shoes if you're taking a dip—the stones are hard on bare feet.** **Amenities:** food and drink; lifeguards; toilets; parking (fee); water sports. **Best for:** partiers; sunset; swimming. ⊠ *Brighton.*

Brighton Museum and Art Gallery

MUSEUM | The grounds of the Royal Pavilion contain this museum, in a former stable block designed for the Prince Regent (1762–1830), son of George III. The museum has particularly interesting art nouveau and art deco collections. Look out for a tiny replica of Salvador Dalí's famous sofa in the shape of Mae West's lips. The Fashion & Style Gallery has clothes from the Regency period to the present day, and the Performance gallery has a collection of masks, puppets, and other theatrical curiosities. ⊠ *Royal Pavilion Gardens, Off Church St.* ☎ *0300/029–0900* ⊕ *brightonmuseums. org.uk/brighton* ⊡ *£6* ⊗ *Closed Mon. except holidays.*

Brighton Pier

MARINA | **FAMILY** | Opened in 1899, the pier is an amusement park set above the sea. In the early 20th century it had a music hall and entertainment; today it has roller coasters and other carnival rides, as well as game arcades, clairvoyants, candy stores, and greasy-food stalls. In summer it's packed with children by day and (on weekends) teenagers by night. There's no fee to enter the pier, although the individual kiosks have their own charges. Alternatively, a wristband (£20 adults, £12 children) allows blanket entry, which can amount to a big savings if you're making the rounds of what's on offer. The skeletal shadow of a pier you can see off in the water is all that's left of the old West Pier. ⊠ *Off Madeira Dr.* ☎ *01273/609361* ⊕ *www. brightonpier.co.uk.*

★ i360

VIEWPOINT | **FAMILY** | Designed by the same people who made the London Eye, this seaside viewing platform ascends 531 feet into the air, allowing an incredible view of the coastline and the South Downs. On clear days you can see the Isle of Wight. The ride (or "flight" as sponsor British Airways insists on calling it) lasts about 25 minutes. Booking is advisable, especially in summer; it's also 10% cheaper if you reserve online. Check out the website for special packages that include dinner. i360 stays open in all weather, other than exceptionally strong winds. It's so peaceful inside the doughnut-shaped pods, you'd never guess the storm that raged over the £43 million structure, ahead of its eventual opening in 2016. Locals worried it would ruin the character of the promenade. After you take in the sweeping view, you've got the leisurely descent back to street level to decide if you agree with them. ⊠ *Lower King's Rd.* ☎ *0337/720360* ⊕ *www.britishairwaysi360.com* ⊡ *£13.50.*

The Lanes

NEIGHBORHOOD | This maze of tiny alleys and passageways was once the home of fishermen and their families. Closed to vehicular traffic, the area's narrow cobbled streets are filled with interesting restaurants, boutiques, and antiques shops. Fish and seafood restaurants line the heart of the Lanes, at Market Street and Market Square. ⊠ *Bordered by (clockwise) North St., Market St., Prince Albert St., and Ship St.*

Brighton

NORTH LAINE

KEY

- 1 *Exploring Sights*
- 1 *Restaurants*
- 1 *Hotels*

West Pier

Tourist Information

English Channel

| 0 | 1,000 ft |
| 0 | 250 m |

Sights ▼

1 Brighton Beach **D5**
2 Brighton Museum and
   Art Gallery **D3**
3 Brighton Pier **D5**
4 i360 .... **A4**
5 The Lanes **C4**
6 Royal Pavilion **D3**

Restaurants ▼

1 Gelato Gusto **D3**
2 Riddle & Finns
   The Lanes **C3**
3 Terre à Terre **D4**
4 The Witchez **E4**

Hotels ▼

1 Brightonwave **E4**
2 Drakes **E4**
3 The Grand Brighton **B4**
4 Granville Hotel **A4**
5 Hotel du Vin **C4**
6 Nineteen Brighton **E4**
7 Oriental Brighton **A3**

Brighton and the Regent

The term "Regency" comes from the last 10 years of the reign of George III (1811–20), who was ultimately deemed unfit to rule because of his mental illness. Real power was officially given to the Prince of Wales, also known as the Prince Regent, who became King George IV and ruled until his death in 1830.

Throughout his regency, George IV spent grand sums indulging his flamboyant tastes in architecture and interior decorating—while failing in affairs of state.

The distinctive architecture of the Royal Pavilion is a prime, if extreme, example of the Regency style, popularized by architect John Nash (1752–1835) in the early part of the 19th century. The style is characterized by a diversity of influences—French, Greek, Italian, Persian, Japanese, Chinese, Roman, Indian... you name it. Nash was George IV's favorite architect, beloved for his interest in Indian and Asian art and for his neoclassical designs, as evidenced in his other most famous work: Regent's Park and its terraces in London.

★ Royal Pavilion

MUSEUM | The city's most remarkable building is this delightfully over-the-top domed and pinnacled fantasy. Built as a simple seaside villa in the fashionable classical style of 1787 by architect Henry Holland, the Pavilion was rebuilt between 1815 and 1822 by John Nash for the Prince Regent (later George IV). The result was an exotic, foppish Eastern design with opulent Chinese interiors. The two great set pieces are the **Music Room,** styled in the form of a Chinese pavilion, and the **Banqueting Room,** with its enormous flying-dragon "gasolier," or gaslight chandelier, a revolutionary invention in the early 19th century. The gardens, too, have been restored to Regency splendor, following John Nash's naturalistic design of 1826. For an elegant time-out, a tearoom serves snacks and light meals. ⊠ *Off Church St.* ☎ *0300/029–0900* ⊕ *brightonmuseums. org.uk/royalpavilion* 🎫 *£15.*

🍴 Restaurants

★ Gelato Gusto

$ | **CAFÉ** | **FAMILY** | No seaside town would be complete without an ice-cream store, and the delicious, housemade, artisanal gelato on sale here is a real treat. Everything is made fresh daily; try the cherry cheesecake flavor or maybe a scoop of the delicious chocolate and sea salt. **Known for:** delicious Italian ice cream; indulgent desserts; essential part of the Brighton seafront experience. ⑤ *Average main: £9* ⊠ *2 Gardner St.* ☎ *01273/673402* ⊕ *www.facebook.com/ gelatogustobtn.*

★ Riddle & Finns The Lanes

$$ | **SEAFOOD** | White tiles, bare metal tables, and sparkling chandeliers set the tone as soon as you walk through the door of this casually elegant restaurant. The house specialty is oysters, fresh and sustainably sourced, served with or without a foaming tankard of black velvet (champagne and Guinness) on the side. **Known for:** romantic atmosphere; supremely fresh seafood; no reservations policy so be prepared to wait. $ *Average main: £22* ✉ *12B Meeting House La.* ☎ *01273/721667* ⊕ *www.riddleandfinns. co.uk.*

Terre à Terre

$$ | **VEGETARIAN** | This inspiring vegetarian restaurant is incredibly popular, so come early for a light lunch or later for a more sophisticated evening meal. Dishes have a pan-Asian influence, so you may have steamed rice buns stuffed with ginger pak choi or battered halloumi with the pleasingly tongue-twistery side of lemony Yemeni relish. **Known for:** Asian-influenced cooking; excellent vegetarian dishes; great wine list. $ *Average main: £17* ✉ *71 East St.* ☎ *01273/729051* ⊕ *www.terreaterre.co.uk.*

The Witchez

$ | **EASTERN EUROPEAN** | Owned by talented graphic designers and photo artists, the Witchez Photo Design Restaurant is certainly a unique concept: delicious German- and Polish-influenced comfort food served in the middle of a design studio (which means you can have your passport photo taken while you wait). Never mind the weirdness of the concept; this place is a whole lot of fun, and the food is good to boot—schnitzel, pierogi, German sausage, potato dumplings, and pizzas. **Known for:** truly unique concept; tasty German and Polish dishes; great atmosphere. $ *Average main: £14* ✉ *16 Marine Parade* ☎ *01273/673652* ⊕ *www.thewitchez.co.uk* ⊗ *Closed Sun. No lunch.*

 Hotels

★ Brightonwave

$$ | **B&B/INN** | Chic and sleek, this hotel a little off the seafront (three minutes' walk from Brighton Pier) is all about relaxation. **Pros:** big and comfortable beds; beautiful design; lovely hosts. **Cons:** rooms on the small side; few extras; limited parking.

$ *Rooms from: £130* ✉ *10 Madeira Pl.* ☎ *01273/676794* ⊕ *www.brightonwave. com* ⇌ *8 rooms* ❑ *Free breakfast.*

★ Drakes

$$ | **HOTEL** | It's easy to miss the low-key sign for this elegant, modern hotel tucked away amid the frilly houses on Marine Parade, but it's worth the trouble of finding, because everything is cool, calm, and sleekly designed. **Pros:** attention to detail; well-designed bathrooms; excellent restaurant. **Cons:** two-night minimum on weekends; breakfast is extra; limited parking. $ *Rooms from: £160* ✉ *43–44 Marine Parade* ☎ *01273/696934* ⊕ *www.drakesofbrighton.com* ⇌ *20 rooms* ❑ *No meals.*

The Grand Brighton

$$ | **HOTEL** | The city's most famous hotel and a seafront landmark, the Grand Brighton is a huge, Victorian wedding cake of a building dating from 1864. **Pros:** as grand as its name; lovely sea views; luxurious spa. **Cons:** a bit impersonal; prices can rise sharply on weekends; cheaper rooms are small. $ *Rooms from: £220* ✉ *97–99 Kings Rd.* ☎ *01273/224300* ⊕ *www.grandbrighton.co.uk* ⇌ *201 rooms* ❑ *Free breakfast.*

Granville Hotel

$$ | **HOTEL** | Three grand Victorian buildings facing the sea have been combined to create one great boutique hotel. **Pros:** creative design; friendly staff; rambunctious atmosphere. **Cons:** decor too quirky for some; sea-facing rooms can be noisy; not wheelchair accessible. $ *Rooms from: £125* ✉ *124 King's Rd.* ☎ *01273/326302* ⊕ *www.granvillehotel. co.uk* ⇌ *24 rooms* ❑ *Free breakfast.*

Hotel du Vin

$$ | **HOTEL** | In the Lanes area, this outpost of a snazzy boutique chain has chic, modern rooms. **Pros:** gorgeous rooms; comfortable beds; excellent restaurant. **Cons:** bar can get crowded;

big price fluctuations in summer; often gets booked up. **$** *Rooms from: £185* ✉ *2 Ship St.* ☎ *01273/855221* ⊕ *www. hotelduvin.com* ⇄ *49 rooms* ❖ *Free breakfast.*

Nineteen Brighton

$ | **B&B/INN** | A calm oasis in the heart of Brighton, this guesthouse is filled with contemporary art and designer accessories. **Pros:** innovative design; close to the beach; three nights for the price of two. **Cons:** not on the nicest street; two-night minimum on weekends; breakfast not included. **$** *Rooms from: £95* ✉ *19 Broad St.* ☎ *07426/043930* ⊕ *www.nineteen-brighton.com* ⇄ *7 rooms* ❖ *No meals.*

Oriental Brighton

$$ | **HOTEL** | With a casual elegance that typifies Brighton, this Regency-era boutique hotel sits close to the seafront. **Pros:** close to the beach; chic and colorful rooms; tasty cooked breakfasts. **Cons:** lacking a restaurant; bar can get rowdy; no free parking. **$** *Rooms from: £150* ✉ *9 Oriental Pl.* ☎ *01273/205050* ⊕ *www. orientalbrighton.co.uk* ⇄ *9 rooms* ❖ *Free breakfast.*

Nightlife

Patterns

MUSIC CLUBS | One of Brighton's foremost venues, in an art deco building east of Brighton Pier, Patterns is the latest incarnation of a string of popular nightclubs that have occupied this spot. Expect to hear live acts during the week, including a regular local slot (this being Brighton, the quality is generally quite high) and techno and house on the weekend. ✉ *10 Marine Parade* ☎ *01273/894777* ⊕ *www. patternsbrighton.com.*

The Plotting Parlour

BARS/PUBS | This ultrahip nightclub on Stein Street feels like a glamorous speakeasy. Cocktails are a specialty, and the bar staff certainly know what they're doing (try the fierce ginger and chili margarita). It's extremely popular with the cooler brand of local partygoer, and it's fabulously good fun to boot. ✉ *6 Steine St.* ☎ *01273/621238* ⊕ *www. theplottingparlour-brighton.co.uk.*

Proud Cabaret

CABARET | A mixture of vintage and avant-garde cabaret and burlesque is on offer at this stylish nightclub, which has a distinctly 1920s flavor. It's only open Friday and Saturday and can get very busy, so booking ahead is advisable. ✉ *83 St. Georges Rd.* ☎ *01273/605789* ⊕ *proud-cabaret.com.*

Shopping

The Great Frog Paterson and Curiouser & Curiouser

JEWELRY/ACCESSORIES | A two-for-one of funky jewelry stores sharing the same premises, the Great Frog Paterson specializes in jewelry with a rock 'n' roll theme (the owners claim to be the creators of the original skull ring) while Curiouser & Curiouser is filled with unique handmade pieces (the shop made several pieces of jewelry for the Harry Potter movies). ✉ *2 Sydney St.* ☎ *01273/673120* ⊕ *www.thegreatfrogpaterson.com.*

Lavender Room

JEWELRY/ACCESSORIES | This relaxing boutique tempts with scented calendars, glittery handmade jewelry, and little things you just can't live without. ✉ *16 Bond St.* ☎ *01273/220380* ⊕ *www.lavender-room. co.uk.*

Royal Pavilion Shop

GIFTS/SOUVENIRS | Next door to the Royal Pavilion, this little shop sells well-designed toys, trinkets, books, and cards, all with a loose Regency theme. There are also high-quality fabrics, wallpapers, and ceramics based on material in the pavilion itself. ✉ *4–5 Pavilion Parade* ☎ .

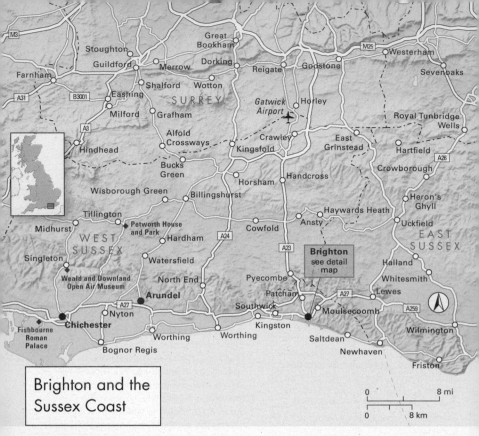

Brighton and the Sussex Coast

Arundel

23 miles west of Brighton, 60 miles south of London.

The little hilltop town of Arundel is dominated by three oversized landmarks. First, a great—and greatly restored—castle, which has been home of the dukes of Norfolk for more than 700 years. Second, an imposing neo-Gothic Roman Catholic cathedral (the duke is Britain's leading Catholic peer). And third, a spectacular medieval priory church. The town center, which spreads down the hill towards the river, is also full of interesting old buildings, the vast majority of which are either pubs, tea shops, or antiques dealers.

GETTING HERE AND AROUND

Arundel is located at the point where the A27 meets the A824, about a two-hour drive south of central London. Trains from London's Victoria Station leave every half hour and take 1½ hours. No direct buses run from London, and while it's possible to take a National Express bus to Worthing or Chichester and change to a local bus to Arundel, the journey is likely to take five hours or more.

From Brighton, there are regular Southern trains to Arundel (one to 1½ hours, changing in Barnham), or it's a 45-minute drive west along the A27.

ESSENTIALS

VISITOR INFORMATION Arundel Visitor Information Centre. ⊠ *Arundel Museum, River Rd.* ☎ *01903/885866* ⊕ *www. sussexbythesea.com.*

👁 Sights

★ Arundel Castle

CASTLE/PALACE | FAMILY | You've probably already seen Arundel Castle without knowing it, at least on screen. Its striking resemblance to Windsor means that it's frequently used as a stand-in for its more famous cousin in movies and television.

Begun in the 11th century, this vast castle remains rich with the history of the Fitzalan and Howard families and holds paintings by Van Dyck, Gainsborough, and Reynolds. During the 18th century and in the Victorian era it was reconstructed in the fashionable Gothic style—although the keep, rising from its conical mound, is as old as the original castle (climb its 130 steps for great views of the River Arun), and the barbican and the Barons' Hall date from the 13th century. Among the treasures here are the rosary beads and prayer book used by Mary, Queen of Scots, in preparing for her execution.

The formal garden, a triumph of order and beauty, is also worth a visit. Special events happen year-round, including a week of jousting, usually in late July. (Ticket prices rise slightly during event weeks.) Although the castle's ceremonial entrance is at the top of High Street, you enter at the bottom, close to the parking lot. ⊠ *Off High St.* ☎ *01903/882173* ⊕ *www.arundelcastle.org* 🎫 *£23; gardens only £13* ⏱ *Closed Mon. and Nov.–Mar.*

🍴 Restaurants

★ The Town House

$$$ | BRITISH | This small but elegant restaurant in a beautifully converted Regency town house (look above you—the dining room ceiling is quite something) serves top-notch British and European cuisine. The fixed-price lunch and dinner menus change regularly but could include roast breast of local partridge with red-currant jelly or trout with a chive butter sauce. **Known for:** local meats and fish; seasonal menus; beautiful dining room. 💲 *Average main: £30* ⊠ *65 High St.* ☎ *01903/883847* ⊕ *www.thetownhouse.co.uk.*

🛏 Hotels

★ Amberley Castle

$$$ | HOTEL | Enter under the portcullis of this genuine medieval castle, where across the moat, present-day luxury dominates. **Pros:** sleep in a real castle; lovely gardens and grounds; good afternoon tea. **Cons:** you have to dress up for dinner; five miles outside Arundel; incredibly expensive. 💲 *Rooms from: £295* ⊠ *Church St., Off B2139, Amberley* ☎ *01798/831992* ⊕ *www.amberleycastle.co.uk* 🛏 *19 rooms* 🍴 *Free breakfast.*

Norfolk Arms Hotel

$$ | HOTEL | The best accommodation option in the town center, this 18th-century coaching inn on the main street was, like Arundel's cathedral and castle, built by one of the dukes of Norfolk (during the Napoleonic Wars, it was used to house soldiers). **Pros:** charming old building; good pub food and craft beer; friendly and welcoming staff. **Cons:** older rooms on the small side; underpowered and slow-to-heat showers; no elevator. 💲 *Rooms from: £130* ⊠ *22 High St.* ☎ *01903/882101* ⊕ *www.norfolkarmsarundel.com* 🛏 *37 rooms* 🍴 *Free breakfast.*

Chichester

10 miles west of Arundel, 66 miles southwest of London.

The Romans founded Chichester, the capital city of West Sussex, on the low-lying plains between the wooded South Downs and the sea. The city walls and major streets follow the original Roman plan to this day. This cathedral

A visit to Chichester Cathedral isn't complete without exploring the surrounding lovely cloisters.

town, a good base for exploring the area, is a well-respected theatrical hub, with a reputation for attracting good acting talent during its summer repertory season. North of town is Petworth House, one of the region's finest stately homes.

GETTING HERE AND AROUND

From London, take the A3 south and follow exit signs for Chichester. The journey takes around two hours, as much of it is on smaller highways. Southern trains run to Chichester at least twice-hourly from London Victoria Station, with a travel time of around 1½ hours. Buses leave from London's Victoria Coach Station a handful of times per day and take between 3½ and 4 hours with a change at Gatwick Airport.

From Arundel, it's a 25-minute drive west along the A27 to Chichester. There's also a regular 85A bus service (35 minutes), as well as trains via Barnham (25 minutes).

ESSENTIALS

VISITOR INFORMATION Chichester Tourist Information Centre. ⊠ *The Novium, Tower St.* ☎ *01243/775888* ⊕ *www.visitchichester.org.*

Sights

★ Chichester Cathedral

RELIGIOUS SITE | Standing on Roman foundations, 900-year-old Chichester Cathedral has a glass panel that reveals Roman mosaics uncovered during restorations. Other treasures include the wonderful Saxon limestone reliefs of the raising of Lazarus and Christ arriving in Bethany, both in the choir area. Among the outstanding contemporary artworks are a stained-glass window by Marc Chagall and a colorful tapestry by John Piper. Keep an eye out, too, for the memorial to Gustav Holst: the composer's ashes were interred here as he wished to be close to his favorite Tudor musician, Thomas Weelkes.

Entrance to the cathedral is free—as are the guided tours that begin every day except Sunday at 11:15 and 2:30—though donations are very welcome, particularly as the roof is in the midst of an €8 million restoration. You can also prebook tours that concentrate on subjects including the English Civil War and the cathedral's art collection; call or go online for details. After visiting the cathedral's interior, be sure to walk around its pretty cloisters, where you'll also find a lovely café and shop. ⊠ Off West St. ☎ 01243/782595 ⊕ www.chichestercathedral.org.uk ⊠ Free; £5 suggested donation.

Fishbourne Roman Palace
MUSEUM | In 1960, workers digging a water-main ditch uncovered a Roman wall; so began nine years of archaeological excavation of this site, the remains of the largest, grandest Roman villa in Britain. Intricate mosaics (including Cupid riding a dolphin) and painted walls lavishly decorate what is left of many of the 100 rooms of the palace, built in the 1st century AD, possibly for local chieftain Tiberius Claudius Togidubnus. You can explore the sophisticated bathing and heating systems, along with the only example of a Roman garden in northern Europe. An extension has added many modern attributes, including a video reconstruction of how the palace might have looked. The site is 1½ miles west of Chichester, a 30-minute walk. ⊠ Roman Way, Fishbourne ☎ 01243/785859 ⊕ www.sussexpast.co.uk/fishbourne ⊠ £10 ☉ Closed weekdays Dec.–mid-Feb.

★ Pallant House Gallery
MUSEUM | This small but important collection of mostly modern British art includes work by Henry Moore and Graham Sutherland. It's in a modern extension to Pallant House, a mansion built for a wealthy wine merchant in 1712 and considered one of the finest surviving examples of Chichester's Georgian past. At that time, its state-of-the-art design showed the latest in complicated brickwork and superb wood carving. Appropriate antiques and porcelains furnish the faithfully restored rooms. Temporary and special exhibitions (usually around three at once) invariably find new and interesting angles to cover. ⊠ 9 N. Pallant ☎ 01243/774557 ⊕ www.pallant.org.uk ⊠ Ground-floor galleries free; rest of museum £12.50 (£6.50 Tues. and Thurs. evening) ☉ Closed Mon.

Petworth House and Park
HOUSE | One of the National Trust's greatest treasures, Petworth is the imposing 17th-century home of Lord and Lady Egremont and holds an outstanding collection of English paintings by Gainsborough, Reynolds, and Van Dyck. There are also 19 oil paintings by J. M. W. Turner, the great proponent of romanticism who often visited Petworth and immortalized it in luminous drawings.

A 13th-century chapel is all that remains of the original manor house. The celebrated landscape architect Capability Brown (1716–83) added a 700-acre deer park; today, it has the largest herd of fallow deer in England. Other highlights include Greek and Roman sculpture and Grinling Gibbons wood carvings, such as those in the spectacular Carved Room. Six rooms in the servants' quarters, among them the old kitchen, are also open to the public.

You can reach Petworth off the A285/A283; the house is 14 miles northeast of Chichester. ⊠ A283, Petworth ☎ 01798/343929 ⊕ www.nationaltrust.org.uk/petworth ⊠ £10.90; parking £4.

Weald and Downland Open Air Museum
MUSEUM | FAMILY | On the outskirts of Singleton, a secluded village five miles north of Chichester, is this sanctuary for historical buildings dating from the 13th through 19th century. Among the 45 structures moved to 50 acres of pretty wooded meadows are a cluster of medieval houses, a working water mill, a Tudor market hall, and a Victorian schoolhouse.

Look carefully, and you might recognize some of the structures from the hit Amazon/BBC TV show *Good Omens*. The buildings are brought to life with regular tours, talks, and demonstrations. ⌧ *Town La., Off A286, Singleton* ☎ *01243/811363* ⊕ *www.wealddown.co.uk* ⌧ *£14.*

Restaurants

Purchases

$$ | **BRITISH** | This excellent bistro is popular with locals for a special-occasion dinner and with the pre-theater crowd, who enjoy the fixed-price early-bird menus. The food strikes a nice balance between hearty, traditional fare and contemporary stylings. **Known for:** bargain pre-theater menus; traditional cooking with a contemporary edge; tasty beef Wellington with spinach and tarragon sauce. ⑤ *Average main: £23* ⌧ *31 North St.* ☎ *01243/771444* ⊕ *www.purchases-restaurant.co.uk.*

Hotels

Chichester Harbour Hotel

$$ | **HOTEL** | This handsome 18th-century house, known for its flying (partially freestanding) staircase and colonnade, was once the residence of Admiral George Murray, one of Admiral Nelson's right-hand men. **Pros:** beautifully restored building; stylish design; great city center location. **Cons:** street-facing rooms can be noisy; prices are a little high; gets booked up during Glorious Goodwood horse racing season. ⑤ *Rooms from: £160* ⌧ *North St.* ☎ *01243/778000* ⊕ *www.harbourhotels.co.uk/chichester* ⤴ *37 rooms* ⦿ *Free breakfast.*

★ Nightingale Cottage

$$ | **B&B/INN** | Located in Boxgrove, a village just northeast of Chichester, this charming B&B offers space, comfort, and personalized service within a gorgeous, 17th-century thatched cottage. **Pros:** attractive 400-year-old property; spacious suites with armchairs and desks; location opposite a lovely ruined priory. **Cons:** limited space means it's often full; low ceilings can be a hazard; a little way out of town. ⑤ *Rooms from: £125* ⌧ *The St.* ☎ *01243/926389* ⊕ *www.nightingalecottagebedandbreakfast.com* ⤴ *2 suites* ⦿ *Free breakfast.*

Performing Arts

Chichester Festival Theatre

THEATER | The modernist, hexagonal Chichester Festival Theatre presents classics and modern plays from May through September and is a venue for touring companies the rest of the year. Built in 1962, it has an international reputation for innovative performances and attracts theatergoers from across the country. ⌧ *Oaklands Park, Off A286* ☎ *01243/781312* ⊕ *www.cft.org.uk.*

Chapter 6

STONEHENGE AND THE SOUTH

6

Updated by
Ellin Stein

⊙ Sights	🍴 Restaurants	🛏 Hotels	🛍 Shopping	🍸 Nightlife
★★★★★	★★★☆☆	★★★★☆	★★★☆☆	★★☆☆☆

WELCOME TO STONEHENGE AND THE SOUTH

TOP REASONS TO GO

★ **Salisbury Cathedral:** Crowned with England's tallest church spire, this impressive cathedral offers spectacular views of the surrounding countryside from the roof and spire, accessible by daily tours.

★ **Stonehenge:** The power and mystery of this Neolithic stone circle on Salisbury Plain is still spellbinding.

★ **House and garden at Stourhead:** The cultivated English landscape at its finest, with an 18th-century Palladian stately home and beautiful gardens adorned with neoclassical temples.

★ **The New Forest:** Get away from it all in the South's most extensive woodland, crisscrossed by myriad trails ideal for horseback riding, hiking, and biking.

★ **Literary trails:** Jane Austen, Thomas Hardy, John Fowles, and Ian McEwan have made this area essential for book buffs, with a concentration of sights with literary associations in Chawton, Dorchester, Chesil Beach, and Lyme Regis.

The south of England's contrasting landscapes range from Salisbury Plain and the sheltered villages of coastal Hampshire and Dorset to the port cities of Southampton and Portsmouth and the woodlands of the New Forest. Culture-rich towns like Salisbury and Winchester are great places to spend the night. Salisbury puts you within easy reach of Stonehenge and the equally ancient stone circles at Avebury. The southern coast of Dorset has a couple of popular vacation resorts, Bournemouth and Weymouth, and historic sites like Corfe Castle. Lyme Regis is the gateway to the Jurassic Coast, a fossil-packed World Heritage Site.

1 Winchester. One of the region's most culturally and historically significant towns.

2 Chawton. A genteel village once home to Jane Austen.

3 Portsmouth. A historically significant south-coast port town.

4 Salisbury. A great cathedral city often used as a home base for Stonehenge visits.

5 Stonehenge. One of the world's greatest and most enigmatic prehistoric monuments.

6 Avebury. A village home to the largest stone circles in the world.

7 Longleat House. A popular Elizabethan estate.

8 Stourhead. Wiltshire's most beautiful garden.

9 Lyndhurst. The hub of the rustic New Forest area.

10 Beaulieu. A classic English village.

11 Corfe Castle. An atmospheric ruined castle.

12 Dorchester. The heart of Thomas Hardy country.

13 Sherborne. A market town with a beautiful abbey.

14 Weymouth. West Dorset's main coastal resort town.

15 Lyme Regis. A seaside town on the Jurassic Coast.

With cathedrals, stately homes, and stone circles, the South—consiting of the counties of Hampshire, Dorset, and Wiltshire—contains a variety of significant attractions, as well as several quieter pleasures. Two important cathedrals, Winchester and Salisbury (pronounced *sawls*-bree), are here, as are classic stately homes such as Longleat, Stourhead, and Wilton House, along with remarkable prehistoric sites like Avebury and Stonehenge.

And these are just the tourist-brochure highlights. Anyone spending time in the region should rent a bike or a car and set out to discover the back-road villages and larger market towns. Close to London, the green fields of Hampshire separate the cliffs and coves of the West Country from the sprawl of the suburbs. Even if you have a coastal destination in mind, slow down on your way there—there's plenty to see. Originally a Roman town, historic Winchester was made capital of the ancient kingdom of Wessex in the 9th century by Alfred the Great, a pioneer in establishing the rule of law and considered to be the first king of a united England. The city is dominated by its imposing cathedral, the final resting place of notables ranging from Saxon kings to the son of William the Conqueror to Jane Austen. It's a good base for visiting Austen's home village of Chawton, as well as other locations associated with

several British literary greats such as Thomas Hardy.

North of Hampshire and the New Forest lies the somewhat harsher terrain of Salisbury Plain, part of it owned by the British army and used for training and weapons testing. Two monuments, millennia apart, dominate the plain. One is the 404-foot-tall stone spire of Salisbury Cathedral, the subject of one of John Constable's finest paintings. Not far away is the best-known prehistoric structure in Europe, the dramatic Stonehenge. The many theories about its construction and purpose only add to its otherworldly allure.

Other subregions have their own appeal, and many are of literary or historical interest. The Dorset countryside of grass-covered chalk hills known as the Dorset Downs—the wooded valleys, meandering rivers, and meadows immortalized in the novels of Thomas

Hardy—is interspersed with unspoiled market towns and villages. Busy beach resorts such as Lyme Regis perch next to hidden coves on the fossil-rich Jurassic Coast. Just off Hampshire is the Isle of Wight—Queen Victoria's favorite getaway—where colorful flags flutter from the many sailboats anchored at Cowes, home of the famous regatta.

The South has been quietly integral to England's history for well over 4,000 years, occupied successively by prehistoric people, the Celts, the Romans, the Saxons, the Normans, and the modern British. Though short on historic buildings due to wartime bombing, the port cities of Southampton and Portsmouth are rich in history itself. The *Mayflower* departed from the former, and the latter is home to the oldest dry dock in the world— Henry VIII's navy built its ships here. Portsmouth was also the departure point for Nelson to the Battle of Trafalgar, Allied forces to Normandy on D-Day, and British forces to the Falklands.

MAJOR REGIONS

Winchester and Portsmouth. From the cathedral city of Winchester, 70 miles southwest of London, you can meander southward to the coast, stopping at the bustling port of Portsmouth to explore its maritime heritage.

Salisbury, Stonehenge, and Salisbury Plain. Filled with sites of cultural and historical interest, this area includes the handsome city of Salisbury, renowned for its spectacular cathedral, and the iconic prehistoric stone circles at Stonehenge and Avebury. A trio of nearby stately homes displays the ambitions and wealth of their original aristocratic inhabitants—Wilton House with its Inigo Jones–designed state rooms, Stourhead and its exquisite neoclassical gardens, and the Elizabethan splendor of Longleat. Your own transportation is essential to get to anything beyond Salisbury other than Stonehenge or Avebury.

New Forest, Dorset, and the South Coast. The New Forest, a woodland southwest of Southampton, was once a hunting preserve of William the Conqueror, so he could pursue his favorite sport close to the royal seat at Winchester. Thus protected from the worst of the deforestation that has befallen most of southern England's other forests, this relatively undeveloped, scenic national park has great possibilities for walking, riding, and biking. West of here stretches the largely unspoiled county of Dorset, which encompasses the beaches, coves, rolling hills, and lush fields that were the setting for most of Thomas Hardy's books, including *Far from the Madding Crowd*, and other classic Victorian-era novels. "I am convinced that it is better for a writer to know a little bit of the world remarkably well than to know a great part of the world remarkably little," Hardy wrote, and the bit he chose to know was the towns, villages, and countryside of this rural area, not least the county capital, Dorchester, an ancient agricultural center. North of here is the picturesque market town of Sherborne, with its impressive abbey. You may find Lyme Regis (associated with 20th-century novelist John Fowles) and the villages along the route closer to your ideal of coastal England. Fossil enthusiasts should head for the Jurassic Coast.

Planning

When to Go

In summer, the coastal resorts of Bournemouth and Weymouth are crowded; it may be difficult to find the accommodations you want. The Isle of Wight gets its fair share of summer visitors, too, especially during the weeklong Cowes Regatta in late July or early August. Because ferries fill up to capacity, you may have to wait for the next one. The New Forest is most alluring in spring and early summer (for the foaling season) and fall (for the colorful foliage), whereas summer can be busy with walkers and campers. In all seasons, take waterproof boots for the mud and puddles. Major attractions such as Stonehenge and Longleat House attract plenty of people at all times; bypass such sights on weekends, public holidays, or school vacations. Don't plan to visit the cathedrals of Salisbury and Winchester on a Sunday, when your visit will be restricted, or during services, when it won't be appreciated by worshippers.

FESTIVALS
Salisbury International Arts Festival
FESTIVALS | Held from late May through early June, the festival has outstanding classical recitals, plays, author talks, international cinema, dance, comedy, and family events. ⊠ *87 Crane St., Salisbury* ☎ *01722/332241* ⊕ *www.wiltshirecreative.co.uk.*

Planning Your Time

The South has no obvious hub, though many people base themselves in one or both of the cathedral cities of Winchester and Salisbury and make excursions to nearby destinations. The coastal cities of Portsmouth and Southampton have their charms, but neither of these large urban centers is particularly attractive as an overnight stop. Busy Bournemouth, whose major sight is a Victorian-era museum, has quieter areas that are more conducive to relaxation. To escape the bustle, the New Forest, southwest of Southampton, has space and semi-wilderness. It's easy to take a morning or afternoon break to enjoy the available activities, whether on foot, bike, or horseback. The Isle of Wight needs more time and is worth exploring at leisure over at least a couple of days.

Getting Here and Around

BUS
National Express buses at London's Victoria Coach Station on Buckingham Palace Road depart every 60–90 minutes for Bournemouth (2¾ hours), Southampton (2½ hours), and Portsmouth (2¼ hours), and every two hours for Winchester (2 hours). There are three buses daily to Salisbury (about 3 hours). Bluestar operates a comprehensive service in the Southampton and Winchester areas, as well as buses to the New Forest. Stagecoach South operates services in Portsmouth and around Hampshire. Salisbury Reds serves Salisbury; More travels to Bournemouth and Poole; First Bus serves Portsmouth, Southampton, and Dorset locations such as Weymouth and Dorchester; and Southern Vectis covers the Isle of Wight. More, Bluestar, Salisbury Reds, and Southern Vectis sell one-day (and two-day, five-day, and 15-day from Southern Vectis) passes as well as seven-, 30-, and 90-day passes for all routes. Ask about the Megarider tickets sold by Stagecoach South. Contact Traveline for all information on routes and tickets.

BUS CONTACTS Bluestar.
☎ *01202/338421* ⊕ *www.bluestarbus. co.uk.* **First Bus.** ☎ *0345/646–0707* ⊕ *www.firstgroup.com.* **More.** ☎ *01202/338420* ⊕ *www.morebus. co.uk.* **National Express.** ☎ *0871/781–8181* ⊕ *www.nationalexpress.com.* **Salisbury Reds.** ☎ *01202/338420* ⊕ *www. salisburyreds.co.uk.* **Southern Vectis.** ☎ *0330/053–9182* ⊕ *www.islandbuses. info.* **Stagecoach South.** ☎ *0345/121–0190* ⊕ *www.stagecoachbus.com.* **Traveline.** ☎ *0871/200–2233* ⊕ *www.traveline.info.*

CAR
On the whole, the region is easily negotiable using public transportation. But for rural spots, especially the grand country estates, a car is useful. The well-developed road network includes

M3 to Winchester (70 miles from London) and Southampton (77 miles); A3 to Portsmouth (77 miles); and M27 along the coast, from the New Forest and Southampton to Portsmouth. For Salisbury, take M3 to A303, then A30. A35 connects Bournemouth to Dorchester and Lyme Regis, and A350 runs north to Dorset's inland destinations.

TRAIN

South Western Railway serves the South from London's Waterloo Station. Travel times average 1 hour to Winchester, 1½ hours to Southampton, 2 hours to Bournemouth, and 2¾ hours to Weymouth. The trip to Salisbury takes 1½ hours and that to Portsmouth about 1¾ hours. A yearlong Network Railcard, valid throughout the South and Southeast, entitles you and up to three accompanying adults to one-third off most train fares and up to four accompanying children ages 5–15 to a 60% discount off each child fare. It costs £30. Weekend First tickets, available on weekends and public holidays, let you upgrade to first class from £5–£25, depending on the train operator.

TRAIN CONTACTS National Rail Enquiries. ☎ 0845/748–4950 ⊕ www.nationalrail.co.uk. **South Western Railway.** ☎ 0345/600–0650 ⊕ www.southwesttrains.co.uk.

Restaurants

In summer, and especially on summer weekends, visitors can overrun the restaurants in small villages, so either book a table in advance or prepare to wait. The more popular or upscale the restaurant, the more critical a reservation is. For local specialties, try fresh-grilled river trout or sea bass poached in brine, or dine like a king on New Forest's renowned venison. Hampshire is noted for its pig and sheep farming, and you might zero in on pork and lamb dishes on local restaurant menus. The region places a strong emphasis

on seasonal produce, so venison, for example, is best between September and February.

Hotels

Modern hotel chains are well represented, and in rural areas you can choose between elegant country-house hotels, traditional coaching inns (updated to different degrees), and modest guesthouses. Some seaside hotels don't accept one-night bookings in summer. If you plan to visit Cowes on the Isle of Wight during Cowes Week, the annual yachting jamboree in late July or early August, book well in advance.

Restaurant and hotel reviews have been shortened. For full information, visit Fodors.com. Restaurant prices are the average cost of a main course at dinner, or if dinner is not served, at lunch. Hotel prices are the lowest cost of a standard double room in high season, including 20% V.A.T.

WHAT IT COSTS in Pounds			
$	$$	$$$	$$$$
RESTAURANTS			
under £16	£16–£23	£24–£30	over £30
HOTELS			
under £125	£125–£225	£226–£350	over £350

Tours

British Guild of Tourist Guides
This organization maintains a directory of qualified Blue Badge guides who can meet you anywhere in the region for private tours. Tours are tailored to your particular interests or needs and generally start around £290 per full day, £180 per half day. ☎ 020/7403–1115 ⊕ www.britainsbestguides.org.

Visitor Information

CONTACTS Tourism South East.
☎ *023/8062–5400* ⊕ *www.tourismsouth-east.com.* **Visit South West .** ☎ *0203/117–0664* ⊕ *www.swtourismalliance.org.uk.*

Winchester

70 miles southwest of London.

Winchester is among the most historic of English cities, and as you walk the graceful streets and wander the many public gardens, a sense of the past envelops you. Although it's now merely the county seat of Hampshire, for more than four centuries Winchester served first as the capital of the ancient kingdom of Wessex and then of England. The first king of England, Egbert, was crowned here in AD 827, and the court of his successor Alfred the Great was based here until Alfred's death in 899. After the Norman Conquest in 1066, William I ("the Conqueror") had himself crowned in London, but took the precaution of repeating the ceremony in Winchester. William also commissioned the local monastery to produce the Domesday Book, a land survey begun in 1085. The city remained the center of ecclesiastical, commercial, and political power until the 13th century, when that power shifted to London. Despite its deep roots in the past, Winchester is also a thriving market town living firmly in the present, with numerous shops and restaurants on High Street.

GETTING HERE AND AROUND

On a main train line and on the M3 motorway, Winchester is easily accessible from London. The train station is a short walk from the sights; the bus station is in the center, opposite the tourist office. The one-way streets are notoriously confusing, so find a parking lot as soon as possible. The city center is very walkable, and most of the High Street is closed to vehicular traffic. A walk down High Street and Broadway brings you to St. Giles Hill, which has a panoramic view of the city.

ESSENTIALS

VISITOR INFORMATION Winchester Tourist Information Centre. ⊠ *Winchester Guildhall, High St.* ☎ *01962/840500* ⊕ *www.visitwinchester.co.uk.*

 Sights

★ The Great Hall

HISTORIC SITE | A short walk west of the cathedral, this outstanding example of early English Gothic architecture, and one of Britain's finest surviving 13th-century halls, is all that remains of the city's original Norman castle built by William the Conqueror (later razed by Oliver Cromwell). It's also the site of numerous historically significant events: the English Parliament is thought to have had one of its first meetings here in 1246, Sir Walter Raleigh was tried for conspiracy against King James I in 1603, and Dame Alice Lisle was sentenced to death by the brutal Judge Jeffreys for sheltering fugitives after Monmouth's Rebellion in 1685. Hanging on the west wall is the hall's greatest artifact, a huge oak table, which, legend has it, was King Arthur's original Round Table. In fact, it was probably created around 1290 at the beginning of the reign of Edward I for a tournament. It is not clear when the green and white stripes that divide the table into 24 places, each with the name of a knight of the mythical Round Table, were added, but it is certain that the Tudor Rose in the center surmounted by a portrait of King Arthur was commissioned by Henry VIII. Take time to wander through the garden—a re-creation of a medieval shady retreat, named for two queens: Eleanor of Provence and Eleanor of Castile. ⊠ *Castle Ave.* ☎ *01962/846476* ⊕ *www. hants.gov.uk/greathall* ⊠ *£3* ☞ *May be closed for events—check website.*

★ Highclere Castle

CASTLE/PALACE | Set in 1,000 acres of parkland designed by Capability Brown, this is the historic home of the actual earls of Carnarvon—as opposed to the imaginary earls of Grantham that are portrayed living within it in the television drama *Downton Abbey*. Victorian Gothic rather than actual Gothic, this huge country house was designed by Sir Charles Barry, architect of the similar Houses of Parliament. Commissioned by the third earl in 1838 to transform a simpler Georgian mansion, Barry used golden Bath stone to create this fantasy castle bristling with turrets. Like its fictional counterpart, it served as a hospital during World War I. There's also an exhibit of Egyptian antiquities collected by the fifth earl, known for his pivotal role in the 1920s excavation of ancient Egyptian tombs, notably Tutankhamun's. The house is 25 miles north of Winchester and 5 miles south of Newbury. There's train service from London and Winchester to Newbury, and taxis can take you the 5 miles to Highclere. ⊠ *Highclere Castle, Highclere Park, Newbury* ✛ *Off A34* ☎ *01635/253204* ⊕ *www.highclere-castle.co.uk* ☞ *£24 castle, exhibition, and gardens; £17 castle or exhibition plus gardens; £7 gardens only* ⊗ *Closed June.*

King's Gate

HISTORIC SITE | One of two surviving gateways in the city's original ancient walls, this structure to the south of the Close is thought to have been built in the 12th century as a remodeling of a Roman gate on the site. The tiny 13th-century church of St. Swithun-upon-Kingsgate, a rare surviving example of a "gateway church" (built into the walls of medieval cities), is on the upper floor. Nearby, 8 College Street is the house where Jane Austen died on July 18, 1817, three days after writing a comic poem about the legend of St. Swithun's Day (copies are usually available in the cathedral). ⊠ *St. Swithun St.*

★ Winchester Cathedral

RELIGIOUS SITE | The imposing Norman exterior of the city's greatest monument, begun in 1079 and consecrated in 1093, makes the Gothic lightness within even more breathtaking. It's one of the largest cathedrals in Europe, and throughout it you will find outstanding examples of every major architectural style from the 11th to 16th century: the transepts and crypt are 11th-century Romanesque; the great nave, the longest in Europe, is 14th- and 15th-century Perpendicular Gothic; and the presbytery (behind the choir, holding the high altar) is 14th-century Decorated Gothic. Free tours are run year-round. The Library's Winchester Bible, one of the finest remaining 12th-century illuminated manuscripts, is on display in the South Transept. Among the other well-known people buried here are William the Conqueror's son, William II ("Rufus"), mysteriously murdered in the New Forest in 1100, and Jane Austen, whose grave lies in the north aisle of the nave. ⊠ *The Close, Cathedral Precincts* ☎ *01962/857200* ⊕ *www.winchester-cathedral.org.uk* ☞ *Cathedral £9.50; tower tour £7.50.*

🍴 Restaurants

The Black Rat

$$$$ | **MODERN BRITISH** | This former pub retains relatively reasonable prices despite being Winchester's only Michelin-starred restaurant. The Black Rat specializes in hearty Modern British dishes that use locally sourced, seasonal ingredients, several from the restaurant's own kitchen garden. **Known for:** imaginative flavor combinations; four huts for outdoor dining; extensive wine list. ⑤ *Average main: £45* ⊠ *88 Chesil St.* ☎ *01962/844465* ⊕ *www.theblackrat.co.uk.*

Chesil Rectory

$$ | **MODERN BRITISH** | The timbered and gabled building may be venerable—it dates back to the mid-15th century—but the cuisine is Modern British, using locally sourced ingredients. The small but well-executed menu is particularly strong on game dishes, like pressed duck with golden raisins, a Sauternes gel, and brioche or vegetarian options like a King Oyster mushroom with miso butter, puffed black rice, and a confit egg yolk. **Known for:** historic, romantic ambience; fresh takes on British classics like the roast beef traditional Sunday lunch; good-value set-price lunches. $ *Average main: £20* ⊠ *1 Chesil St.* ☎ *01962/851555* ⊕ *www.chesilrectory.co.uk.*

★ Rick Stein, Winchester

$$$ | SEAFOOD | Renowned as Britain's finest seafood chef, Rick Stein chose Winchester for his first venture away from the Cornish coast. The menu is largely focused on fish and crustaceans, but carnivores and vegetarians are catered to as well. **Known for:** simply but confidently prepared classics like turbot hollandaise; exotic choices like spicy Indonesian curry with prawn and squid; good-value set menus for lunch and early evening dinner. $ *Average main: £27* ⊠ *7 High St.* ☎ *01962/353535* ⊕ *www.rickstein.com.*

 Hotels

★ Lainston House

$$$ | HOTEL | The 63 acres surrounding this elegant 17th-century country house retain many original features, including the walls of the kitchen garden (still in use), the apple trees in the former orchard, and a mile-long avenue of linden trees, the longest in Europe. **Pros:** beautiful setting; period detail in guest and public rooms; excellent bar and restaurant. **Cons:** lower-priced modern rooms small; noise from functions can bleed into some rooms; restaurant service can be erratic. $ *Rooms from: £230* ⊠ *Woodman La., off B3049, Sparsholt* ☎ *01962/776088* ⊕ *www.exclusive.co.uk/lainston-house* ⤴ *50 rooms* ⊙ *No meals.*

Wykeham Arms

$$ | B&B/INN | A watering hole since 1755, this pub with rooms near the cathedral and the college wears its Britishness proudly, with depictions of national heroes like Nelson and Churchill, military artifacts, and an assortment of pewter mugs hanging from the ceiling. **Pros:** quirky charm; lively bar; central location. **Cons:** rooms above bar can be noisy; not for those looking for luxury; housekeeping erratic. $ *Rooms from: £149* ⊠ *75 Kingsgate St.* ☎ *01962/853834* ⊕ *wykehamarmswinchester.co.uk* ⤴ *14 rooms* ⊙ *Free breakfast* ⟲ *No children under 14.*

 Shopping

Kingsgate Books and Prints

ART GALLERIES | Located under the medieval Kingsgate Arch, this atmospheric shop is filled with drawings, prints, and engravings (many by local artists); rare antique county maps; and secondhand books. ⊠ *1 Kingsgate St.* ☎ *01962/864710* ⊕ *www.kingsgatebooksandprints.co.uk.*

P&G Wells

BOOKS/STATIONERY | The oldest bookshop in the country (in business for more than 250 years), P&G Wells has numerous books by and about Jane Austen, who had an account here and, in 1817, died almost next door. It also has the region's largest selection of children's books. ⊠ *11 College St.* ☎ *01962/852016* ⊕ *bookwells.co.uk.*

Chawton

16 miles northeast of Winchester.

In Chawton you can visit the home of Jane Austen (1775–1817), who lived the last eight years of her life in the village, moving to Winchester only during her final illness. The site has always drawn literary pilgrims, but with the ongoing

In Search of Jane Austen

Jane Austen country—verdant countryside interspersed with relatively unspoiled villages—still bears traces of the decorous early-19th-century life she described with wry wit in novels such as *Emma, Persuasion, Sense and Sensibility,* and *Pride and Prejudice.* Serious Janeites will want to retrace her life in Bath, Chawton, Winchester, and Lyme Regis.

Bath

Bath provided the elegant backdrop for the society Austen observed with such razor sharpness. Austen lived in Bath between 1801 and 1806, and although she wrote relatively little during this time, it provided the setting for *Northanger Abbey* and *Persuasion.* The Jane Austen Centre in Bath explores her relationship to the city.

Chawton

About 83 miles southeast of Bath is the heart of Jane Austen country, where you'll find the tiny Hampshire village of Chawton. Here you will find the tastefully understated house, a former bailiff's cottage on her brother's estate, where Austen worked on three of her novels. It's now a museum that sensitively evokes her life there.

Winchester

Driving southwest from Chawton, take the A31 for about 15 miles to Winchester, where you can visit Austen's austere grave within the cathedral and view an exhibit about her life. Then see the commemorative plaque on No. 8 College Street, where Addison's disease ended her life on July 18, 1817.

Lyme Regis

Lyme Regis, 110 miles southwest of Winchester, is the 18th-century seaside resort on the Devon border where Austen spent the summers of 1804 and 1805. It's home to the Cobb, the stone jetty that juts into Lyme Bay, where poor Louisa Musgrove jumps off the steps known as Granny's Teeth—a turning point in *Persuasion.*

release of successful films based on her novels, the town's popularity among visitors has grown enormously.

GETTING HERE AND AROUND
Hourly Stagecoach Bus 64 service connects Winchester and Alresford with Chawton. It's a 10-minute walk from the bus stop to Jane Austen's House. By car, take A31. Alternatively, take a 40-minute stroll along the footpath from Alton.

◉ Sights

★ Chawton House Library
LIBRARY | Located in an Elizabethan country house on a 275-acre estate (part of the South Downs National Park), this library specializes in works by English women writers from 1600 to 1830, including authors such as Mary Shelley, Mary Wollstonecraft, and Frances Burney. It also houses the Knight Collection, the private library of the family who owned the house for over 400 years. Jane Austen's brother, Edward, eventually inherited the property and added the walled kitchen garden, shrubberies, and parkland. You can see the dining room table where Austen joined her family for meals and the library collection that contains a manuscript written in her own hand ✉ *Chawton* ☎ *01420/541010* ⊕ *www.chawtonhouse.org* ✉ *Library and gardens £10; gardens only £6; gardens*

238

free Jan.–mid-Feb. ⊗ *House closed Jan., Feb., and some Sat. in June and July (check website).*

★ Jane Austen's House Museum

HOUSE | This unassuming redbrick house is where Jane Austen spent the last eight years of her life, writing *Emma, Persuasion,* and *Mansfield Park,* and revising *Sense and Sensibility, Northanger Abbey,* and *Pride and Prejudice.* Now a museum, the house retains a modest but genteel atmosphere suitable for the home of a clergyman's widow and her unmarried daughters. The drawing room contains a piano similar to the one Jane would play every morning before retiring to a small writing table in the family dining parlor—leaving her sister, Cassandra, to do the household chores ("I find composition impossible with my head full of joints of mutton and doses of rhubarb," Jane wrote). In the early 19th century, the road near the house was a bustling thoroughfare, and although Jane was famous for working through interruptions, she retained one protection against the outside world—the famous creaking door, its hinges deliberately unoiled to better warn her when someone was entering her workspace. ■TIP→ **The museum is often closed for special events, so call ahead.** ⊠ *Winchester Rd., signed off A31/A32 roundabout* ☎ *01420/83262* ⊕ *www.jane-austens-house-museum.org.uk* 🖾 *£9* ⊗ *Closed Jan.*

Hotels

Four Seasons Hotel Hampshire

$$$$ | HOTEL | FAMILY | Although deep in the peaceful British countryside, this country-house hotel on a 500-acre estate is only a half hour from Heathrow. **Pros:** peaceful location; great spa; plenty of activities. **Cons:** pricey; pool dominated by children at some times; inconsistent dining service. ⑤ *Rooms from: £450* ⊠ *Dogmersfield Park, Chalky La., Hook* ☎ *01252/853000* ⊕ *www.fourseasons.com/hampshire* 🗗 *133 rooms* ⦙⦙ *No meals.*

★ Heckfield Place

$$$$ | HOTEL | Because this property reflects the owner's precise vision and attention to detail, a stay here is like a stay at a friend's home, if your friend has an exquisitely tasteful but comfortable, eco-friendly Georgian house on a 400-acre estate an hour from London. **Pros:** understatedly luxurious decor; imaginative menus using ingredients from property; dedicated eco-friendly ethos. **Cons:** ubiquitous "relaxing" music in public rooms may not be for everyone; some rooms don't have phone reception; complicated AV system. ⑤ *Rooms from: £500* ⊠ *Heckfield Place, Hook* ☎ *0118/932–6868* ⊕ *www.heckfieldplace.com* 🗗 *44 rooms, 1 cottage* ⦙⦙ *Free breakfast.*

Portsmouth

24 miles south of Chawton, 77 miles southwest of London.

In addition to a historic harbor and revitalized waterfront, Portsmouth has the energy of a working port. At Gunwharf Quays is the soaring Spinnaker Tower, as well as shops, restaurants, bars, and a contemporary art gallery. The main attractions for many visitors are the HMS *Victory,* the well-preserved flagship from which Nelson won the Battle of Trafalgar, on view at the Portsmouth Historic Dockyard; the extraordinary record of seafaring history at the National Museum of the Royal Navy; and the D-Day Museum (Operation Overlord embarked from Portsmouth). For others, Portsmouth is primarily of interest for the ferries that set off from here to the Isle of Wight and more distant destinations.

GETTING HERE AND AROUND

The M27 motorway from Southampton and the A3 from London take you to Portsmouth. There are also frequent

Winchester, Portsmouth, and Around

buses and trains that drop you off at the Hard, the main transport terminus. It's only a few steps from the Historic Dockyard and Gunwharf Quays. Regular passenger ferries cross Portsmouth Harbour from the Hard for Gosport's Royal Navy Submarine Museum. Attractions in the nearby town of Southsea are best reached by car or by buses departing from the Hard.

ESSENTIALS

VISITOR INFORMATION Portsmouth Visitor Information Centre. ⊠ *Portsmouth Museum, Museum Rd.* ☎ *023/9282–6722* ⊕ *www.visitportsmouth.co.uk.*

 Sights

The D-Day Story

MUSEUM | FAMILY | Here three galleries tell the absorbing story of the planning and preparation for the invasion of Europe during WWII and the actual landings on D-Day—June 6, 1944—through an eclectic range of exhibits including maps, uniforms, and even actual landing craft, as well as filmed testimonies from those who were there. The museum's centerpiece is the Overlord Embroidery ("Overlord" was the invasion's code name), a 272-foot-long embroidered cloth with 34 panels illustrating the history of the operation, from the Battle of Britain in 1940 to victory in Normandy in 1944. ⊠ *Clarence Esplanade* ☎ *023/9288–2555* ⊕ *www.theddaystory.com* 🎫 *£10.*

★ The Mary Rose

MUSEUM | FAMILY | An on-site museum houses the *Mary Rose,* the former flagship of Henry VIII's navy and the world's only 16th-century warship on display. Built in this same dockyard more than 500 years ago, the ship sank in the harbor in 1545 and remained there until raised in 1982. In an accompanying exhibition, you can see artifacts retrieved from the seabed ranging from the ship's large guns to personal possessions like surgeon's tools, tankards, bowls, combs, and games. ✉ *Main Rd.* ☎ *023/9281– 2931* ⊕ *www.maryrose.org* 🎫 *£18 (£14.40 online), includes admission to the Portsmouth Historic Dockyard.*

★ Portsmouth Historic Dockyard

HISTORIC SITE | FAMILY | The city's most impressive attraction includes an unrivaled collection of historic ships, including the HMS *Warrior* (1860), Britain's first iron-clad battleship and perhaps the Royal Navy's best-known warship, the HMS *Victory.* It served as the flagship of Vice-Admiral Lord Nelson, Britain's most celebrated naval hero at the Battle of Trafalgar (1805) and is still the ceremonial flagship of Britain's First Sea Lord. You can inspect the cramped gun decks, visit the cabin where Nelson met his officers, and stand on the spot where he was mortally wounded by a French sniper. There's also an interactive gallery that explores the ship's history and audio guides to take along your visit.

The **National Museum of the Royal Navy** has extensive exhibits about Nelson and the Battle of Trafalgar, a fine collection of painted figureheads, and galleries of paintings and mementos recalling naval history from King Alfred to the present. **Action Stations,** an interactive attraction, gives insight into life in the modern Royal Navy and tests your sea legs with tasks such as piloting boats through gales. **Boathouse 4** explores the role of smaller wooden boats in the Navy's history and challenges the adventurous to a "Mast and Rigging" experience. You should allow one or two days to tour all the attractions in the Historic Dockyard. The entrance fee includes a boat ride around the harbor, and the all-attractions ticket is valid for one year. ✉ *Victory Gate, HM*

Naval Base ☎ *023/9283–9766* ⊕ *www. historicdockyard.co.uk* 🎫 *£18 for one attraction; £27 for any two attractions; £36 for any three attractions; Full Navy Ticket £39 (includes HMS Warrior, HMS Victory, Horrible Histories Pirates, Action Stations, National Museum of the Royal Navy, HMS M.33, Harbour Tours, Waterbus, Boathouse 4, Dockyard Apprentice, Royal Navy Submarine Museum, and Explosion Museum).*

Royal Navy Submarine Museum

MILITARY SITE | FAMILY | Here you can learn about submarine history and the rigors of life below the waves with the help of family-friendly interactive games. The highlight is a tour of the only surviving World War II submarines in the United Kingdom, the HMS *Alliance* and the midget-class HMS *X24,* from the cramped living quarters to the engine rooms. Also on the large site is the first Royal Navy sub, *Holland 1,* built in 1901, and a *Biber,* a German WWII midget submarine. From Portsmouth Harbour, take the ferry to Gosport and walk along Millennium Promenade past the huge sundial clock. From April to October, an hourly free water bus runs from the Historic Dockyard. ✉ *Haslar Jetty Rd., Gosport* ☎ *023/9251–0354* ⊕ *www.submarine-museum.co.uk* 🎫 *£18* 🕐 *Closed Nov.–Mar., Mon., and Tues. except bank holidays.*

Spinnaker Tower

VIEWPOINT | The focal point of the lively Gunwharf Quays development of shops and bars, the Spinnaker Tower is a striking addition to Portsmouth's skyline. The slender structure evokes a mast with a billowing sail, and rises to a height of 558 feet. An elevator whisks you to three viewing platforms 330 feet high for thrilling all-around views of the harbor and up to 23 miles beyond. ✉ *Gunwharf Quays* ☎ *023/9285–7520* ⊕ *www.spinnakertower.co.uk* 🎫 *£11.50; £43 with Portsmouth Historic Dockyard all-attraction ticket;*

You can tour Admiral Nelson's famous flagship, the HMS *Victory*, at Portsmouth's Historic Dockyard.

£34.90 with PHD two-attraction ticket; £26.55 with Mary Rose Museum ticket.

Restaurants

Abarbistro

$$ | MODERN BRITISH | A relaxed, modern bistro midway between Old Portsmouth and Gunwharf Quays, this place is ideal for a snack, meal, or glass of wine from the thoughtfully chosen wine list. The changing Modern British menu specializes in seafood dishes like seared scallops with butternut squash puree or beer-battered fish-and-chips, mostly sourced from Portsmouth's fish market directly opposite. **Known for:** super fresh seafood; friendly service; extensive wine list. ⑤ *Average main: £16* ⊠ *58 White Hart Rd.* ☎ *023/9281–1585* ⊕ *www.abarbistro. co.uk* ⊟ *No credit cards.*

🛏 Hotels

Fortitude Cottage

$ | B&B/INN | With sleek, modern bedrooms, this friendly B&B provides top-class waterside accommodation in two buildings in the center of Old Portsmouth, within walking distance of the Historic Dockyard via the Millennium Promenade just across the street. **Pros:** central but quiet location; helpful, friendly owners; great view from penthouse suite. **Cons:** a good amount of stairs; not all rooms have great views; some rooms on small side. ⑤ *Rooms from: £99* ⊠ *51 Broad St.* ☎ *023/9282–3748* ⇨ *6 rooms* �� *Free breakfast.*

Salisbury

24 miles northwest of Southampton, 44 miles southeast of Bristol, 79 miles southwest of London.

The silhouette of Salisbury Cathedral's majestic spire signals your approach to this historic city long before you arrive. Although the cathedral is the principal focus of interest here, and its Cathedral Close is one of the country's most atmospheric spots (especially on a foggy night), Salisbury has much more to see, not least its largely unspoiled—and relatively traffic-free—old center. Here are stone shops and houses that over the centuries grew up in the shadow of the great church. You're never far from any of the five rivers that meet here or from the bucolic water meadows that stretch out to the west of the cathedral and provide the best views of it. Salisbury didn't become important until the early 13th century, when the seat of the diocese was transferred here from Old Sarum, the original settlement 2 miles to the north, of which only ruins remain. In the 19th century, novelist Anthony Trollope based his tales of ecclesiastical life, notably *Barchester Towers,* on life here, although his fictional city of Barchester is really an amalgam of Salisbury and Winchester. The local tourist office organizes walks—of differing lengths for varying stamina—to guide you to the must-sees. And speaking of must-sees, prehistoric Stonehenge is less than 10 miles away and easily visited from the city.

GETTING HERE AND AROUND

Salisbury is on main bus and train routes from London and Southampton; regular buses also connect Salisbury with Winchester. The bus station is centrally located on Endless Street. Trains stop west of the center. After negotiating a ring-road system, drivers will want to park as soon as possible. The largest of the central parking lots is by Salisbury Playhouse. The city center is compact, so you won't need to use local buses for most sights. For Wilton House, take Bus Red 3 or Red 8 from Salisbury town center.

ESSENTIALS

VISITOR INFORMATION Salisbury Information Centre. ⊠ *Fish Row, off Market Pl.* ☎ *01722/342860* ⊕ *www.visitwiltshire. co.uk/explore/salisbury.*

 Sights

Cathedral Close

HISTORIC SITE | Eighty acres of rolling lawns and splendid period architecture provide one of Britain's finest settings for a cathedral. The Close, the largest in the country, contains three museums: historic Mompesson House, the Salisbury Museum, and the Rifles Museum devoted to the county's infantry regiments. ⊠ *The Close* ✠ *Bounded by West Walk, North Walk, and Exeter St.* ⊕ *www. salisburycathedral.org.uk.*

Long Bridge

LOCAL INTEREST | For a classic view of Salisbury, head to Long Bridge and Town Path. From the main street, walk west to Mill Road, which leads you across the Queen Elizabeth Gardens. Cross the bridge and continue on Town Path through the water meadows, from which you can see the vista that inspired John Constable's 1831 *Salisbury Cathedral from the Meadows,* one of Britain's most iconic paintings, now on view in London's Tate Britain. ⊠ *Salisbury.*

Market Place

MARKET | The Charter Market, one of southern England's most popular markets, fills this square on Tuesday and Saturday. Permission to hold an annual fair here was granted in 1221, and that right is still exercised for three days every October, when the Charter Fair takes place. A narrow side street links Poultry Cross to Market Place. ⊠ *Salisbury.*

Old Sarum

ARCHAEOLOGICAL SITE | Massive earthwork ramparts on a bare sweep of Wiltshire countryside are all that remain of this impressive Iron Age hill fort, which was successively taken over by Romans, Saxons, and Normans (you can still see the ruins of a castle built by William the Conqueror in 1070 within the earthworks). The site was still fortified in Tudor times, though the population had mostly decamped in the 13th century to New

With its art and gilded furniture, the Double Cube Room at Wilton House may well be one of England's most beautiful interiors.

Sarum, or Salisbury. Clamber over the huge banks to take in the far-reaching views to Salisbury Cathedral. ⊠ *Castle Rd.* ✛ *Off A345* ☎ *01722/335398* ⊕ *www. english-heritage.org.uk* 🖭 *£5.40.*

★ Salisbury Cathedral

RELIGIOUS SITE | Salisbury is dominated by the towering cathedral, a soaring hymn in stone. It is unique among cathedrals in that it was conceived and built as a whole in the amazingly short span of 38 years (1220–58). The spire, added in 1320, is the tallest in England and a miraculous feat of medieval engineering—even though the point, 404 feet above the ground, is 2½ feet off vertical. For all their sophistication, the height and immense weight of the great spire have always posed structural problems. In the late 17th century, Sir Christopher Wren was summoned from London to strengthen the spire, and in the mid-19th century Sir George Gilbert Scott, a leading Victorian Gothicist, undertook a major program of restoration. Next to the cathedral model in the north aisle is a medieval clock—probably the oldest working mechanism in Europe, if not the world—made in 1386. ■TIP➔ **Join a free one-hour tour of the cathedral, leaving two or more times a day.** ⊠ *Cathedral Close* ☎ *01722/555120* ⊕ *www.salisburyca-thedral.org.uk* 🖭 *Cathedral and Chapter House free, suggested donation £7.50; tower tour £13.50.*

The Salisbury Museum

MUSEUM | Opposite the cathedral's west front, this excellent museum is in the King's House, parts of which date to the 15th century (James I stayed here in 1610 and 1613). The history of the area from prehistoric times through the Norman Conquest is explored in the Wessex gallery, which houses some of Britain's most important archaeological finds and where Stonehenge-related exhibits provide helpful background information for a visit to the famous megaliths. Also on view are collections of local costumes dating back 250 years, outstanding British ceramics, and Turner watercolors, all dwarfed by the 12-foot Salisbury

Giant, a 13-century pageant figure, and his companion hobbyhorse, Hob Nob. A cozy café is in one of the oldest sections of the building. ⊠ *The King's House, 65 The Close* ☎ *01722/332151* ⊕ *www. salisburymuseum.org.uk* ✉ *£8 (tickets good for 1 year).*

★ Wilton House

CASTLE/PALACE | This is considered to be one of the loveliest stately homes in England and, along with its grounds, a fine example of the English Palladian style. The seat of the earls of Pembroke since Tudor times, the south wing of the current building was rebuilt in the early 17th century by Isaac de Caus, with input from Inigo Jones, Ben Jonson's stage designer and the architect of London's Banqueting House. Most noteworthy are the seven state rooms in the south wing, among them the Single Cube Room (built as a perfect 30-foot cube) and, one of the most extravagantly beautiful rooms in the history of interior decoration, the aptly named Double Cube Room. The room's headliner is the spectacular Van Dyck portrait of the Pembroke family. Elsewhere at Wilton House, the art collection includes several other Old Master paintings, including works by Rembrandt and members of the Brueghel family. ⊠ *Off A36, Wilton* ✛ *The town of Wilton is 3 miles west of Salisbury. Buses Red 3 and Red 8 from Salisbury depart every 10 to 15 mins and stop outside Wilton House.* ☎ *01722/746728* ⊕ *www.wiltonhouse.co.uk* ✉ *£15.50; grounds only £6.50* ۞ *Closed early Sept.–early May, Fri., and Sat.*

🍴 Restaurants

★ Allium

$$ | MODERN BRITISH | This family-run, centrally located restaurant has been winning rave reviews for both the taste and presentation of its creative Modern British dishes. Produce is largely fresh and local while meats and poultry are free-range and sustainably farmed. **Known for:** high quality, creative dishes; pork belly confit with curry-spiced scallops; reasonable prices. ⑤ *Average main: £20* ⊠ *6–7 Ox Row* ☎ *01722/326057* ⊕ *alliumsalisbury.restaurant* ۞ *Closed Sun. and Mon.*

★ Anokaa

$$ | INDIAN | For a refreshingly modern take on Indian cuisine, try this bustling restaurant a few minutes from the center. Classic recipes are taken as starting points for the artistically presented dishes, which include tandoori-seared rack of lamb, cinnamon-glazed duck breast stuffed with garlicky spinach, and a seasonal (and local) vegetable curry. **Known for:** creative, well-executed Indian dishes; excellent service; buffet lunch. ⑤ *Average main: £16* ⊠ *60 Fisherton St.* ☎ *01722/414142* ⊕ *www.anokaa.com.*

Howard's House

$$$$ | MODERN BRITISH | If you're after complete tranquility, head for this early-17th-century house surrounded by two acres of grounds in the Nadder Valley. The excellent restaurant has fixed-price menus specializing in contemporary English cooking using local and seasonal ingredients, such as a butter-baked fillet of wild brill or roast loin of Wiltshire venison. **Known for:** excellent five-course tasting menu; relaxed and romantic atmosphere; terrace dining in the summer. ⑤ *Average main: £42* ⊠ *Teffont Evias, Teffont Evias* ✛ *Off B3089* ☎ *01722/716392* ⊕ *www. howardshousehotel.co.uk.*

🛏 Hotels

Cricket Field House

$ | B&B/INN | Located halfway between Wilton and Salisbury, this comfortable ex-gamekeeper's cottage overlooks a cricket ground and has a large, peaceful garden of its own. **Pros:** efficient, helpful management; well-maintained rooms; good breakfasts. **Cons:** 20-minute walk from town; on a busy road; no restaurant on-site. ⑤ *Rooms from: £110* ⊠ *Wilton*

Salisbury, Stonehenge, and
Salisbury Plain

Rd. ☎ 01722/322595 ⊕ www.cricket-
fieldhouse.co.uk ⇌ 18 rooms ⏹️ Free
breakfast.

Mercure Salisbury White Hart Hotel

$ | HOTEL | Behind the pillared portico and
imposing 17th-century classical facade of
this city center hotel (part of the Mercure
chain) are modern bedrooms (of various
sizes) with a muted cream-and-brown
color scheme. **Pros:** central location;
cozy public areas; friendly service. **Cons:**
some rooms are small; impersonal,
corporate feel; tired decor in rooms.
$ Rooms from: £120 ⊠ 1 St. John St.
☎ 01722/312801 ⊕ www.mercure.com
⇌ 68 rooms ⏹️ Free breakfast.

Wyndham Park Lodge

$ | B&B/INN | This simple Victorian house
in a quiet part of town (off Castle Street)
provides an excellent place to rest and a
delicious breakfast, as well as a garden.

Pros: efficient and hospitable owners;
good breakfast; handy parking. **Cons:**
spotty Wi-Fi; furnishings a bit dated;
books up quickly. $ Rooms from: £85
⊠ 51 Wyndham Rd. ☎ 01722/416517
⊕ www.wyndhamparklodge.co.uk ⇌ 4
rooms ⏹️ Free breakfast.

Stonehenge

*8 miles north of Salisbury, 20 miles south
of Avebury.*

Almost five millennia after their construction, these stone circles on the Salisbury Plain continue to pose fascinating
questions. How were the giant stones,
some weighing as much as 45 tons,
brought here, possibly from as far away
as Wales? What was the site used for?
Why were the stones aligned with the

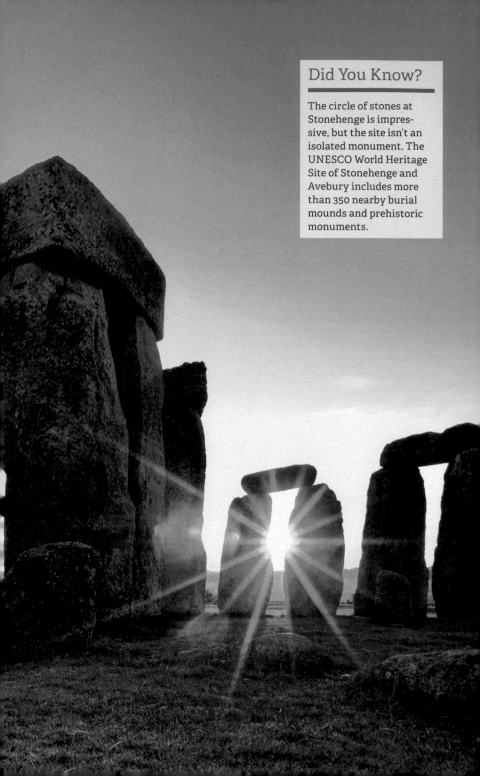

midsummer sunrise and the midwinter sunset? But Stonehenge is more than just the megaliths; the surrounding landscape is dotted with ancient earthworks, remains of Neolithic settlements, and processional pathways, creating a complex of ceremonial structures that testifies to the sophisticated belief system of these early Britons.

GETTING HERE AND AROUND

Stonehenge Tour buses leave from Salisbury's train and bus stations every half hour from 9:30 to 2:30, and then hourly from 3 to 5, from early June to August; hourly from 10 to 4 from April to early June and September through October; and 10 to 2 in November through March. Tickets cost £16 or £31.50 (includes Stonehenge and a visit to Old Sarum). Other options are a taxi or a custom tour. Drivers can find the monument near the junction of A303 with A344.

★ Stonehenge

ARCHAEOLOGICAL SITE | FAMILY | Mysterious and ancient, Stonehenge has baffled archaeologists, not to mention the general public, for centuries. One of England's most visited monuments and a UNESCO World Heritage Site, the circle of giant stones standing starkly against the wide sweep of Salisbury Plain still has the capacity to fascinate and move those who view it. The stone circle itself was completed in stages, beginning around 2500 BC. You can no longer walk among the stones, so bring a pair of binoculars to help make out the details on the monoliths. To fully engage your imagination, or to get that magical photo, it's worth exploring all aspects of the site, both near and far. An informative visitor center is located 1½ miles away (access to the stone circle is via a frequent shuttle). To best experience the awe and mystery of Stonehenge, visit the circle in the early morning or in the evening, when the crowds have dispersed. Visits are by timed admission slots only. ⊠ Amesbury ✛ Junction of A360 and Airman's Corner

☎ 0370/333–1181 ⊕ www.english-heritage.org.uk ⌨ £21.10 (walk-up); £19 (advance).

Avebury

24 miles north of Stonehenge, 34 miles north of Salisbury, 25 miles northeast of Longleat, 27 miles east of Bath.

The village of Avebury was built much later than its famous stone circles; it has an informative museum with an outstanding collection of Bronze Age artifacts from the area around here and Stonehenge. You can also explore a cluster of other prehistoric sites nearby.

GETTING HERE AND AROUND

From Salisbury, follow A345 north to Upavon and take the A342 to Devizes; then continue 7 miles northeast on the A361. You can also take the hourly Stagecoach bus No. 49 from Swindon to Avebury (30 minutes).

Sights

Alexander Keiller Museum

MUSEUM | FAMILY | The Avebury Stone Circles are put into context by this collection of Neolithic and Bronze Age artifacts from the site, one of the most important prehistoric archaeological collections in Britain. The museum contains charts, photos, models, and home movies taken by its namesake, archaeologist Alexander Keiller. It has been suggested that Keiller, responsible for the excavation of Avebury in the 1930s, may have adapted the site's layout to highlight presentation more than authenticity. The exhibits are divided between the 17th-century **Stables Gallery,** which displays finds from Keiller's excavations, the child-friendly **Barn Gallery**, where you find interactive exhibits about the history of Avebury, and an activity area where kids can dress up in Bronze Age clothes. You can also visit the **Manor House**, where Keiller lived, and its surrounding gardens. The Tudor-era build-ing received several subsequent (Queen Anne, Regency, and art deco) additions, and the rooms have been filled with acquired or commissioned period-appro-priate furniture to illustrate how previous occupants lived. ⊠ *High St. ⊹ Off A4361* ☎ *01672/539250 ⊕ www.nationaltrust. org.uk ✉ Museum £4.40; manor house and gardens £9 ☉ Manor House and gardens closed Jan.–mid-Feb.*

★ Avebury Stone Circles

ARCHAEOLOGICAL SITE | Surrounding part of Avebury village, the Avebury Stone Circles, the largest in the world, are one of England's most evocative prehistoric monuments—not as famous as Stone-henge, but all the more powerful for their lack of commercial exploitation. The stones were erected around 2600 BC, about the same time as the better-known monument. As with Stonehenge, the purpose of this stone circle has never been ascertained, although it most likely was used for similar ritual purposes. Unlike Stonehenge, however, there are no certain astronomical alignments at Avebury, at least none that have sur-vived. The main site consists of a wide, circular ditch and bank, about 1,400 feet across and more than half a mile around. Entrances break the perimeter at roughly the four points of the compass, and inside stand the remains of three stone circles. The largest one originally had 98 stones, although only 27 remain. Many stones on the site were destroyed centuries ago, especially in the 14th cen-tury when they were buried for unclear reasons, possibly religious fanaticism. Others were later pillaged in the 18th century to build the thatched cottages you see flanking the fields. You can walk around the circles, a World Heritage Site, at any time; early morning and early evening are recommended. As with Stonehenge, the summer solstice tends to draw the crowds. ⊠ *Avebury ⊹ 1 mile north of A4* ☎ *01672/539–250 ⊕ www. english-heritage.org.uk ✉ Free.*

★ West Kennet Long Barrow

ARCHAEOLOGICAL SITE | One of the largest Neolithic chambered tombs in Britain, West Kennet Long Barrow was built around 3400 BC. You can explore all around the site and also enter the tomb, which was used for more than 1,000 years before the main passage was blocked and the entrance closed, around 2000 BC. More than 300 feet long, it has an elevated position with a great view of Silbury Hill and the surrounding countryside. It's about 1 mile east of Avebury. ⊠ *Avebury ⊹ ¾ mile southwest of West Kennett, along footpath off A4* ☎ *01672/539250 ⊕ www.english-herit-age.org.uk ✉ Free.*

🍴 Restaurants

Waggon and Horses

$ | BRITISH | A 17th-century thatched-roof building with foundations made from sarsen stones, this traditional inn and pub (Dickens mentions the building in the *Pickwick Papers)*is a two-minute drive from the Avebury stone circles. With a beer garden that has views of Silbury Hill, it's something of a tourist hub in high season, but lunches and dinners are still excellent. **Known for:** cozy atmosphere with open fire; housemade food using locally sourced ingredients; crowds in high season. ⑤ *Average main: £15 ⊠ Beckhampton ⊹ A4, 300 feet east of junction with A361* ☎ *01672/539418 ⊕ www.waggonandhorsesbeckhampton. co.uk.*

🛏 Hotels

The Lodge

$$ | B&B/INN | With their eclectic design, rare prints, and antique furnishings, the two spacious guest rooms of this charm-ing B&B are full of character. **Pros:** unique location and views; comfortable rooms; vegetarian breakfasts. **Cons:** can book up; expensive; early 10 am checkout. ⑤ *Rooms from: £195 ⊠ Rawlings Park*

⚓ *Off A4361* ☎ *01672/539023* ⊕ *www. aveburylodge.co.uk* ⇥ *2 rooms* †⊙† *Free breakfast.*

Longleat House

31 miles southwest of Avebury, 6 miles north of Stourhead, 19 miles south of Bath, 27 miles northwest of Salisbury.

With its popular safari park and a richly decorated High Elizabethan house to explore, Longleat can provide a day of diversions.

GETTING HERE AND AROUND
Longleat House is off A36 between Bath and Salisbury. The nearest train station is Warminster, about 5 miles away. Your best option is to take a taxi from there.

⊙ Sights

★ Longleat House
CASTLE/PALACE | **FAMILY** | The family seat of the Marquesses of Bath, Longleat House is one of southern England's most famous stately homes, and possibly the most ambitiously, even eccentrically, commercialized, as evidenced by the presence of a drive-through safari park (open since 1966) with giraffes, zebras, gorillas, monkeys, rhinos, and lions. The house, considered to be one of the finest remaining examples of High Elizabethan, was largely completed in 1580 for more than £8,000, an astronomical sum at the time. It contains outstanding tapestries, paintings, porcelain, furniture, and one of the largest private collections of books in England (more than 40,000 volumes housed in seven libraries). Notable period features include Victorian kitchens, an Elizabethan minstrels' gallery, painted ceilings, and a great hall with massive wooden beams. You can wander at will or take one of the specialized guided tours (such as the "Rooftop" tour or the "Scandalous History" tour). In addition to 900 acres of parkland designed by Capability

Brown, plus formal and pleasure gardens and the safari park, the property has a miniature railway, a petting zoo, an extensive (and fairly fiendish) hedge maze, and an "adventure castle," all of which make it extremely popular, particularly in summer and during school vacations. A first-come, first-served safari bus service is available (£5) for those arriving without their own transport. ⊠ *Warminster* ⚓ *Off A362* ☎ *01985/844400* ⊕ *www.longleat. co.uk* ✉ *£34.90, £29.70 online* ⊙ *Closed Jan.–mid-Feb., Mon.–Thurs. in Mar., and Mon.–Wed. in Nov.*

Hotels

Bishopstrow Hotel and Spa
$$ | **HOTEL** | This ivy-covered Regency manor house set on 27 acres has been converted into a relaxed country-house hotel that combines well-chosen antiques with modern amenities. **Pros:** country-house ambience; impressive suites; friendly staff. **Cons:** drink prices high; dinner service can be understaffed and slow; maintenance needs more attention. ⑤ *Rooms from: £150* ⊠ *Boreham Rd., Warminster* ☎ *01985/212312* ⊕ *www.bishopstrow.co.uk* ⇥ *32 rooms* †⊙† *Free breakfast.*

Stourhead

9 miles southwest of Longleat, 15 miles northeast of Sherborne, 30 miles west of Salisbury.

England has many memorable gardens, but Stourhead is one of the most glorious. Its centerpiece is a magnificent artificial lake surrounded by neoclassical temples, atmospheric grottos, and rare trees. The Palladian stately home is also worth a look.

GETTING HERE AND AROUND
By car, you can reach Stourhead via B3092. It's signposted off the main road. From London, board a train to Gillingham

The gardens of Stourhead are perhaps the most beautiful in all of England.

and take a five-minute cab ride to Stourton.

 Sights

★ **Stourhead**

GARDEN | Close to the village of Stourton lies one of Wiltshire's most breathtaking sights—Stourhead, a Palladian mansion whose gardens are the most celebrated example of the English 18th-century taste for "natural" landscaping. Both house and grounds have few parallels for beauty anywhere in Europe. Stourhead was built between 1721 and 1725 by wealthy banker Henry Hoare, popularly known as "Good Henry" (he died the same year as the mansion's completion), with his descendants adding the portico and wings (a fire gutted the building in 1902 shortly after a restoration, but it was able to be largely reconstructed unaltered). Henry's grandson added a wing for the elegant Regency library and a picture gallery built to house his collections of paintings and books. There are also significant collections of Chippendale furniture and Chinese and French porcelain collected by the early Hoares on their Grand Tours. Still, Stourhead's greatest masterpiece is its gardens, designed by Henry Hoare II. Influenced by the neoclassical dream landscapes of 17th century painters Claude Lorrain and Nicolas Poussin, Henry "the Magnificent" used hills, water (notably the central lake), and a remarkable collection of trees and shrubs—interspersed with classically inspired temples, grottoes, follies, and bridges—to create the effect of a three-dimensional oil painting. Discover the changing vistas on a walk around the artificial lake (1½ miles; walk counterclockwise for the best views). ■**TIP→ The best times to visit are early summer when the massive banks of rhododendrons are in full bloom or mid-October for autumn color, but the gardens are beautiful at any time of year.** You can get a fine view of the surrounding area from King Alfred's Tower, a 1772 folly (a structure built for picturesque effect). ✉ *Stourton ✛ Off B3092, near Mere* ☎ *01747/841152* ⊕ *www.nationaltrust.*

org.uk ⌂ *House and gardens £20.40;
King Alfred's Tower £5* ⊗ *House closed
mid-Dec.–mid-Mar. and mid–late Nov.;
King Alfred's Tower closed late Oct.–mid-
Mar. and weekdays mid-Mar.–late Oct.*

Hotels

The Spread Eagle Inn

$$ | B&B/INN | You can't stay at Stourhead,
but you can stay at this popular inn built
at the beginning of the 19th century just
inside the main entrance. **Pros:** period
character; lovely rooms; free access to
Stourhead. **Cons:** needs some moderniza-
tion; food can be disappointing; handheld
shower attachments as opposed to real
showers. ⑤ *Rooms from: £125* ⊠ *Church
Lawn, near Warminster, Stourton*
☎ *01747/840587* ⊕ *www.spreadeagleinn.
com* ↝ *5 rooms* ⓘ◎ *Free breakfast.*

Lyndhurst

*26 miles southeast of Stonehenge, 18
miles southeast of Salisbury, 9 miles
west of Southampton.*

Lyndhurst is famous as the capital of
the New Forest. Although some popular
spots can get crowded in summer, there
are ample parking lots, picnic areas, and
campgrounds. Miles of trails crisscross
the region.

GETTING HERE AND AROUND

From Salisbury, follow A36, B3079, and
continue along A337 another 4 miles or
so. To explore the New Forest, take A35
out of Lyndhurst (the road continues
southwest to Bournemouth) or A337
south. The New Forest Tour is a hop-
on, hop-off open-top bus. Regular bus
services are operated by Bluestar and
Wilts & Dorset. Many parts of the New
Forest are readily accessible by train
from London via the centrally located
Brockenhurst Station.

⊙ Sights

★ New Forest

NATIONAL/STATE PARK | FAMILY | This nation-
al park, still largely owned by the Crown,
consists of 150 square miles of woodland, heaths, grassland, bogs, and the
remains of coppices and timber planta-
tions established in the 17th to 19th century. Residents have had grazing rights
since the 12th century, and you can still
encounter free-roaming cattle, and, most
famously, the hardy New Forest ponies.
An extensive network of trails makes it a
wonderful place for biking, walking, and
horseback riding. ⊠ *Lyndhurst* ⊕ *www.
thenewforest.co.uk* ⌂ *Free.*

New Forest Heritage Centre

INFO CENTER | FAMILY | This visitor complex
with a gallery, museum, and reference
library devoted to the New Forest
contains displays and activities related
to the area's geology, history, wildlife,
and culture. The museum is packed with
quizzes and other interactive elements
that keep children engaged. There's also
a café. ⊠ *Main Car Park, Avenue Rd.*
☎ *023/8028-3444* ⊕ *www.newforesther-
itage.org.uk* ⌂ *Free.*

⑪ Restaurants

★ The Pig

$$ | MODERN BRITISH | Funkier sister
of glamorous Lime Wood, this New
Forest "restaurant with rooms" puts the
emphasis on localism and seasonality
and is a local favorite. Lunch and dinner
are served in a large Victorian greenhouse overlooking lawns, and the frequently changing menu may include dishes like pork belly with oyster mushrooms
and a basil-and-sunflower-seed salsa
verde or poached silver mullet with fen-
nel, Dorset olives, and samphire. **Known
for:** nearly all ingredients come from their
own garden or other sources within 25
miles; porcine dishes, as the name suggests; foraging expeditions with the staff.
⑤ *Average main: £20* ⊠ *Beaulieu Rd.,*

New Forest, Dorset, and the South Coast

Brockenhurst ☎ 01590/622354 ⊕ www.
thepighotel.com.

 ## Hotels

Chewton Glen Hotel and Spa

$$$$ | HOTEL | This grand early-19th-century
country-house hotel and spa on extensive
manicured grounds ranks among Britain's
most acclaimed—and most expensive—
lodgings. **Pros:** classic English luxury; top-
notch leisure facilities; high staff-to-guest
ratio. **Cons:** expensive rates; somewhat
lacking in atmosphere; service not always
up to five-star expectations. ⑤ *Rooms
from: £370* ⊠ *Christchurch Rd., New
Milton* ☎ *01425/275341, 800/344–5087
in U.S.* ⊕ *www.chewtonglen.com* ⤳ *70
rooms* ⦿❘ *No meals.*

★ Lime Wood

$$$$ | HOTEL | If you're looking for a dis-
creet, luxurious hideaway in a woodland
setting with uninterrupted views and
an excellent spa, this hugely relaxing
country-house hotel is hard to beat. **Pros:**
great location; stylish yet comfortable
design; friendly staff. **Cons:** hard to reach
without a car; breakfast not included;
pricey. ⑤ *Rooms from: £395* ⊠ *Beaulieu
Rd.* ☎ *023/8028–7177* ⊕ *www.limewood-
hotel.co.uk* ⤳ *29 rooms* ⦿❘ *No meals.*

Activities

Largely unspoiled and undeveloped, yet
accessible even to those not normally
given to long walks or bike rides, the
New Forest provides numerous opportunities to explore the outdoors. Bike rental
and horseback riding are widely available.
Numerous trails lead through thickly

wooded country, across open heaths, and through the occasional bog. With very few hills, it's fairly easy terrain, and rich with wildlife. You're almost guaranteed to see wild ponies and deer, and occasionally free-roaming cattle and pigs.

BIKING
Cycle Experience
BICYCLING | Bike rentals from £18.50 per day allow you to explore a range of trails weaving through the New Forest, one of Britain's best terrains for off-road biking. ⊠ *2 Brookley Rd., Brockenhurst* ☎ *01590/624808* ⊕ *www.cyclex.co.uk.*

HORSEBACK RIDING
Brockenhurst Riding Stables
HORSEBACK RIDING | **FAMILY** | The stable offers rides on forest trails for all levels. Hour-long treks are £38, and two-hour outings are £76. ⊠ *Warren Farm, Balmer Lawn Rd., Brockenhurst* ☎ *01590/624717* ⊕ *www.brockenhurstridingstables.co.uk.*

Beaulieu

7 miles southeast of Lyndhurst.

The unspoiled village of Beaulieu (pronounced *byoo*-lee) has three major attractions in one at Beaulieu Abbey and is near the museum village of Buckler's Hard.

GETTING HERE AND AROUND
Beaulieu is best reached by car on B3056 from Lyndhurst or B3054 from Lymington. It's signposted off A326 from Southampton. Bus 112 has a limited service (three times daily on Tuesday and Thursday) between Beaulieu and Lymington and Hythe, and runs daily. During the summer, the New Forest Tour bus extends to Beaulieu.

Sights

Beaulieu
TOWN | **FAMILY** | With a ruined 13th-century abbey, a stately home, and an automobile museum, Beaulieu appeals to several different interests. **Beaulieu Abbey** was founded in 1204 by Cistercian monks on land given to them by King John (the name means "beautiful place" in French). You can still see the ruins of the cloister and the herb garden, as well as two remaining buildings, one containing an exhibition re-creating daily life in the monastery. **Palace House and Gardens** incorporates the abbey's original 14th-century gatehouse and has been the home of the Montagu family since they purchased it in 1538, after the dissolution of the monasteries, when the abbey was badly damaged. You can explore the drawing rooms, dining halls, fine family portraits, and the beautiful grounds. The father of the present Lord Montagu established the **National Motor Museum,** which traces the history of British motoring. The collection contains more than 280 classic cars and motorcycles, from late-19th-century vehicles to futuristic F1 racing cars, rally cars, and luxury cars, plus famous film cars like the flying Ford Anglia from *Harry Potter and the Chamber of Secrets.* Other museum attractions include interactive experiences, audiovisual displays, a World of *Top Gear* attraction devoted to the popular British TV show (complete with test track), and rides in vehicles ranging from a monorail to a 1912 London bus. ⊠ *Beaulieu* ✛ *Off B3056* ☎ *01590/612345* ⊕ *www.beaulieu.co.uk* ⊠ *Abbey, Palace House, World of Top Gear, and Motor Museum £24.75 (£19.50 in advance).*

Corfe Castle

25 miles south of Wimborne Minster, 15 miles south of Poole, 5 miles southeast of Wareham.

The village of Corfe Castle is best known for the ancient, ruined castle that overlooks it.

ESSENTIALS

VISITOR INFORMATION Discover Purbeck Information Centre. ✉ *Wareham Library, South St.* ☎ *01929/552740* ⊕ *www. visit-dorset.com.*

 Sights

Corfe Castle

ARCHAEOLOGICAL SITE | One of the most dramatic ruins in Britain, Corfe Castle overlooks the picturesque gray limestone village of the same name. The present ruins are of the castle built in 1086, when the great central keep was erected by William the Conqueror to guard the principal route through the surrounding Purbeck Hills. The outer walls and towers were added in the 1270s. Cromwell's soldiers blew up the castle in 1646 during the Civil War, after a long siege during which its Royalist chatelaine, Lady Bankes, led its defense. ✉ *Off A351* ☎ *01929/481294* ⊕ *www.nationaltrust. org.uk* 🎫 *£12 Apr.–Oct. weekends and bank holidays; £11 all other times.*

Swanage Railway

SCENIC DRIVE | **FAMILY** | Train enthusiasts love this largely volunteer-run railroad that makes 25-minute, 6-mile scenic trips, with steam (and some diesel) locomotives pulling vintage train carriages across the Isle of Purbeck—actually a peninsula. Trips begin from Norden in the center and go to the seaside town of Swanage via Corfe Castle. Small, pretty stations with flower baskets, painted signs, and water bowls for dogs add to the excursion's charm. Trains leave approximately every 80 to 120 minutes in low season, and every 40 minutes in high season. ✉ *Station House, Springfield Rd., Swanage* ☎ *01929/425800* ⊕ *www.swanage-railway.co.uk* 🎫 *£3–£15* 🕐 *Closed Jan., Nov., Feb. except school midterm holiday, Sun.–Fri. in Mar., and weekdays in Dec. except school Christmas holiday.*

 Hotels

★ The Pig on the Beach

$$$ | **HOTEL** | The latest outpost of the Hampshire luxury minichain is in a Victorian Gothic former private residence in an unspoiled village on the scenic, peaceful Studland Peninsula. **Pros:** beautiful location; comfortable bedrooms and welcoming public rooms; excellent restaurant. **Cons:** on the pricey side; breakfast not included; ubiquitous piped music not for everyone. 💲 *Rooms from: £230* ✉ *Manor House, Manor Rd., Swanage* ☎ *01929/450288* ⊕ *www.thepighotel.com/on-the-beach* 🛏 *23 rooms, 2 cottages, 1 hut* 🍴 *No meals.*

Dorchester

21 miles west of Corfe, 30 miles west of Bournemouth, 43 miles southwest of Salisbury.

The traditional market town of Dorchester was immortalized as Casterbridge by Thomas Hardy in his 19th-century novel *The Mayor of Casterbridge.* In fact, the whole area around here, including a number of villages tucked away in the rolling hills of Dorset, has become known as "Hardy country" because of its connection with the author. Hardy was born in a cottage in the hamlet of Higher Bockhampton, about 3 miles northeast of the town, and his bronze statue looks westward from a bank on Colliton Walk. Two important historical sites, as well as the author's birthplace and a former residence, are a short drive from Dorchester.

Dorchester has many reminders of its Roman heritage. A stroll along Bowling Alley Walk, West Walk, and Colliton Walk follows the approximate line of the original Roman town walls, part of a city plan laid out around AD 70. On the north side of Colliton Park is an excavated Roman villa with a marvelously preserved mosaic floor. While the high street in the center of town can be busy with vehicular traffic, the tourist office has walking itineraries that cover the main points of interest along quieter routes and help you appreciate the character of Dorchester today.

GETTING HERE AND AROUND
Dorchester can be reached from Corfe Castle via A351 and A352. From Salisbury take A354. Park wherever you can (pay parking lots are scattered around the center) and explore the town on foot.

ESSENTIALS
VISITOR INFORMATION Dorchester Tourist Information Centre. ⊠ *Dorchester Library and Learning Centre, Charles St.* ☎ *01305/267992* ⊕ *www.visit-dorset. com.*

Sights

Athelhampton House and Gardens
HOUSE | Largely unchanged since it was built in 1485, this outstandingly well-preserved example of domestic Tudor architecture (with 16th- and 20th-century additions) turns up as "Athelhall" in some of Thomas Hardy's writings (Hardy was a frequent visitor and his father, a stonemason, worked on roof repairs here). Don't miss the Great Hall, still with its original linenfold paneling, heraldic stained glass, and vaulted timber roof. The paneled Library contains more than 3,000 books. Outside, 20 acres of grounds include eight formal walled gardens created in the 19th century and 12 yew pyramids, each 30 feet high. ⊠ *Dorchester ✛ A35, 5 miles east of Dorchester* ☎ *01305/848363* ⊕ *www. athelhampton.com* ⊠ *House and garden £14.50; garden only £10* ۞ *Closed Sat. year-round and weekdays Nov.–mid-Feb.*

Hardy's Cottage
HOUSE | Thomas Hardy's grandfather built this small thatch-and-cob cottage, where the writer was born in 1840, and little has changed since the family left. Here Hardy grew up and wrote many of his early works, including *Far from the Madding Crowd*, at a desk you can still see. Access is by foot only, via a walk through woodland or down a country lane from the parking lot. There's a visitor center with information about the surrounding landscape and trails that let you follow in Hardy's footsteps. ⊠ *Brockhampton La., Higher Bockhampton ✛ ½ mile south of Blandford Rd.* ☎ *01305/262366* ⊕ *www. nationaltrust.org.uk* ⊠ *£7.90* ۞ *Closed Nov.–mid-Feb. and Mon.–Wed.*

Maiden Castle
ARCHAEOLOGICAL SITE | Although called a castle, this is actually one of the most important pre-Roman archaeological sites in England and the largest, most complex Iron Age hill fort in Europe, made of stone and earth with ramparts that enclose about 45 acres. England's Neolithic inhabitants built the fort some 4,000 years ago, and many centuries later it was a Celtic stronghold. In AD 43 invading Romans, under the general (later emperor) Vespasian, stormed the fort. Finds from the site are on display in the Dorset County Museum in Dorchester. To experience an uncanny silence and sense of mystery, climb Maiden Castle early in the day. Leave your car in the lot at the end of Maiden Castle Way, a 1½-mile lane. ⊠ *Winterborne Monkton ✛ Off A354, 2 miles southwest of Dorchester* ☎ *0370/333–1181* ⊕ *www.english-heritage.org.uk.*

Restaurants

Yalbury Cottage
$$$$ | MODERN FRENCH | Oak-beamed ceilings, exposed stone walls, and inglenook fireplaces add to the charm of this restaurant in a 300-year-old cottage across the road from where Thomas Hardy went to school. It specializes in set menus featuring superior modern French cooking using locally sourced produce, with dishes like Portland crab fritter with Lyme Bay scallop, beef brisket with Dorset black garlic, and Cornish

brill in phyllo pastry. **Known for:** French cuisine with an English twist; good-value fixed-price two- or three-course dinner menus; booking up quickly so making reservations is a good idea. ⑤ *Average main: £43* ⊠ *Bockhampton La., Lower Bockhampton* ☎ *01305/262382* ⊕ *www. yalburycottage.com* ⊗ *No dinner Sun. No lunch Tues.–Sat.*

Hotels

The Casterbridge

$$ | B&B/INN | Small but full of character, this family-owned inn in a Georgian building dating from 1790 is elegantly decorated with period antiques. **Pros:** central location; hospitable owners; good breakfasts. **Cons:** traffic noise in front rooms; water pressure could be better; Wi-Fi not in all bedrooms. ⑤ *Rooms from: £140* ⊠ *49 High East St.* ☎ *01305/264043* ⊕ *www.thecasterbridge.co.uk* ⇥ *11 rooms* ⑩ *Free breakfast.*

Activities

Thomas Hardy Society

HIKING/WALKING | From April through October, the Thomas Hardy Society organizes guided walks to sites that inspired locations in Hardy's novels. Readings and discussions accompany the walks, which range from a couple of hours to most of a day. ⊠ *Dorset County Museum, 19 North Sq.* ☎ *01305/251501* ⊕ *www. hardysociety.org.*

Sherborne

20 miles north of Dorchester, 15 miles west of Shaftesbury, 40 miles west of Wilton, 43 miles west of Salisbury.

Originally the capital of Wessex (the actual Saxon kingdom, not Hardy's retro conceit), this unspoiled market town is populated with medieval buildings built using the local honey-colored stone. The focal point of the winding streets is Sherborne Abbey, where King Alfred's older brothers are buried. Also worth visiting are the ruins of Sherborne Castle, a Tudor mansion originally built by Sir Walter Raleigh, and its Capability Brown–designed gardens.

GETTING HERE AND AROUND

Hourly trains from Salisbury take 45 minutes to reach Sherborne. The station is at the bottom of Digby Road, near the abbey. Drivers should take A30, passing through Shaftesbury.

ESSENTIALS

VISITOR INFORMATION Sherborne Tourist Information Centre. ⊠ *3 Tilton Ct., Digby Rd.* ☎ *01935/815341* ⊕ *www.visit-dorset. com.*

Sights

Shaftesbury

TOWN | This small market town, the model for "Shaston" in Thomas Hardy's *Jude the Obscure*, sits on a ridge overlooking Blackmore Vale—you can catch a sweeping view of the surrounding countryside from the top of Gold Hill, a steep street lined with cottages so picturesque it was used in an iconic TV commercial to evoke the quintessential British village of yore. Shaftesbury is 20 miles west of Salisbury and 15 miles east of Sherborne. ⊠ *Sherborne* ✛ *Intersection of A30 and A350* ⊕ *www.shaftesburytourism.co.uk.*

Sherborne Abbey

RELIGIOUS SITE | As much as the golden hamstone exterior, majestic tower, and fine flying buttresses impress, the glory of Sherborne Abbey is the delicate 15th-century fan vaulting that extends the length of the soaring nave and choir. Some features from the original 8th-century cathedral, like a Saxon doorway in the northwest corner, still remain. If you're lucky, you might hear "Great Tom," one of the heaviest bells in the world, pealing out from the bell tower. Guided tours are run from April through September on Tuesday (10:30) and Friday (2:30), or by prior arrangement. ⊠ *3 Abbey Close* ☎ *01935/812452* ⊕ *www.sherborneabbey.com.*

★ Sherborne Castle

CASTLE/PALACE | After building this castle in 1594, Sir Walter Raleigh made it his home for 10 years before it passed into the custodianship of the Digby family. The castle's interiors cover a variety of periods, including Tudor, Jacobean, and Georgian. The Victorian Gothic rooms are notable for their splendid plaster ceiling moldings. After admiring the extensive collections of Meissen and Asian porcelain, stroll around the lake and 45 acres of landscaped grounds (a designated English Heritage Grade I site), the work of Capability Brown. The house is less than a mile southeast of town. ⊠ *New Rd.* ☎ *01935/812072* ⊕ *www.sherbornecastle.com* 🎟 *Castle and gardens £13.50; gardens only £9* ⏱ *Closed Nov.–early Apr. and Mon. and Fri. except bank holidays.*

 ## Hotels

The Alders

$ | **B&B/INN** | This homey B&B, a secluded stone house set in an old walled garden opposite a 13th-century church, is in a quiet, unspoiled village 3 miles north of Sherborne. **Pros:** peaceful setting; hospitable owners; excellent breakfasts. **Cons:** a bit remote; unlit walk to dinner; small towels. ⑤ *Rooms from: £85* ⊠ *Off B3145, Sandford Orcas* ☎ *01963/220666* ⊕ *www.thealdersbb.com* ⇆ *3 rooms* ⊙⫘ *Free breakfast.*

Weymouth

8 miles south of Dorchester, 28 miles south of Sherborne.

West Dorset's main coastal resort, Weymouth, is known for its sandy and pebble beaches and its royal connections. King George III began seawater bathing here for his health in 1789, setting a trend among the wealthy and fashionable of the day. The legacy of this popularity is Weymouth's many fine buildings, including the Georgian row houses lining the Esplanade. Striking historical details command attention: a wall on Maiden Street holds a cannonball that was embedded in it during the English Civil War, while a nearby column commemorates the embarkation of U.S. forces from Weymouth on D-Day.

Weymouth and its lively harbor provide the full bucket-and-spade seaside experience: donkey rides, sand castles, and plenty of fish-and-chips. Weymouth and Portland hosted the 2012 Olympic sailing events.

GETTING HERE AND AROUND

You can reach Weymouth on frequent local buses and trains from Dorchester or on less frequent services from Bourne mouth. The bus and train stations are close to each other near King's Statue, on the Esplanade. If you're driving, take A354 from Dorchester and park on or near the Esplanade—an easy walk from the center—or in a lot near the harbor.

 ## Sights

★ Chesil Beach

BEACH—SIGHT | The unique geological curiosity known as Chesil Beach (official slogan: "18 miles and 180 billion pebbles") is in fact not a beach but a tombolo, a thin strip of sand and shingle that joins two bits of land together. Part of the Jurassic Coast World Heritage Site, Chesil, 18 miles long, is remarkable for its pebbles that decrease in size from east to west. It's also known as the setting for Ian McEwan's novel and its 2018 film adaptation, *On Chesil Beach.* You can access the eastern section leading to the Isle of Portland (a peninsula) and the western section beyond Abbotsbury year-round. However, access to the central section is restricted, with its environmentally sensitive eastern side facing the

Sunrise is lovely at the Cobb, the harbor wall built by Edward I in Lyme Regis.

shallow saltwater Fleet Lagoon entirely off-limits and its western side closed April to August to protect nesting birds. The entire beach is better suited to walking and fossil hunting than sunbathing and swimming since powerful undertows make the water dangerous (plus it's cold). There are walking and cycle trails along the rugged coastline. **Amenities:** parking (at five access points, £6–£8 per day); toilets (at five access points). **Best for:** walking; windsurfing. ⊠ *Portland Beach Rd., Portland* ☎ *03108/807000* ⊕ *www.jurassiccoast.org.*

🍴 Restaurants

Pascal's Brasserie

$ | **BISTRO** | Tucked away from the busy harbor, this French-owned local favorite serves classic Gallic dishes such as onion soup, eggs Benedict, and croque monsieur, plus pastas and salads. If you're looking for an afternoon pit stop, try the substantial, and very English, cream tea selection and other superlative baked goods. **Known for:** delicious housemade

cakes and scones; gluten-free options; excellent breakfasts. ⑤ *Average main: £9* ⊠ *8 Cove St.* ☎ *01305/777500* ▭ *No credit cards* ⊗ *No dinner.*

Lyme Regis

19 miles west of Abbotsbury.

"A very strange stranger it must be, who does not see the charms of the immediate environs of Lyme, to make him wish to know it better," wrote Jane Austen in *Persuasion.* Judging from the summer crowds, many people agree with her. The scenic seaside town of Lyme Regis and the so-called Jurassic Coast are highlights of southwest Dorset. The crumbling Channel-facing cliffs in this area are especially fossil rich.

GETTING HERE AND AROUND

Lyme Regis is off the A35, extending west from Bournemouth and Dorchester. Drivers should park as soon as possible—there are lots at the top of town—and explore the town on foot. First buses run here from Dorchester and Axminster, 6 miles northwest; the latter town is on the main rail route from London Waterloo and Salisbury, as is Exeter, from which you can take the X53 bus.

ESSENTIALS
VISITOR INFORMATION Lyme Regis Tourist Information Centre. ✉ *Guildhall Cottage, Church St.* ☎ *01297/442138* ⊕ *www. visit-dorset.com.*

Sights

The Cobb
MARINA | Lyme Regis is famous for its curving stone harbor breakwater, the Cobb, built by King Edward I in the 13th century to improve the harbor. The Duke of Monmouth landed here in 1685 during his ill-fated attempt to overthrow his uncle, James II, and the Cobb figured prominently in the movie of John Fowles's novel *The French Lieutenant's Woman*, as well as in the 1995 film version of Jane Austen's *Persuasion.* There's a sweeping coastal view to Chesil Beach to the east. ✉ *Lyme Regis* ⊕ *www. lymeregis.org/the-cobb.aspx.*

Dinosaurland Fossil Museum
MUSEUM | **FAMILY** | Located in a former church, this compact private museum run by a paleontologist has an excellent collection of local fossils with more than 12,000 specimens dating back 200 million years. It also provides information on regional geology, how fossils develop, and guided fossil-hunting walks. There are more fossils for sale in the shop on the ground floor along with minerals. ✉ *Coombe St.* ☎ *01297/443541* ⊕ *www. dinosaurland.co.uk* 🎫 *£5* ⊙ *Closed mid-Oct.–mid-Feb.*

Lyme Regis Museum
MUSEUM | A gabled and turreted Edwardian building on the site of fossilist Mary Anning's former home, this lively museum is devoted to the town's maritime and domestic history, geology, local artists, writers (John Fowles was

an honorary curator for a decade), and, of course, fossils. The museum also leads fossil-hunting and local history walks throughout the year. ✉ *Bridge St.* ☎ *01297/443370* ⊕ *www.lymeregismuseum.co.uk* 🎫 *£4.95* ⊙ *Closed Mon. and Tues. in Nov.–late Mar.*

🍴 Restaurants

The Bell Cliff Restaurant and Tea Rooms
$ | **BRITISH** | This cozy, child-and-dog-friendly restaurant in a 17th-century building at the bottom of Lyme Regis's main street makes a great spot for a light lunch or a cream tea with views over the bay. Apart from hot drinks and sandwiches (including fresh crab), you can order more substantial dishes like sausages and mashed potatoes, mac-and-cheese, or mussels with bacon and cider. **Known for:** large portions; vegan full English breakfast; noisy and cramped ambience. 🅢 *Average main: £11* ✉ *5–6 Broad St.* ☎ *01297/442459* ⊙ *No dinner Nov.–Mar.*

★ Hix Oyster & Fish House
$$ | **SEAFOOD** | This coastal outpost of one of London's trendiest restaurants combines stunning views overlooking the Cobb with the celebrity-chef's trademark high standards and originality. Simply cooked and beautifully presented seafood rules here, including fillet of pollock with wild garlic, grilled fish on the bone, and, of course, local oysters. **Known for:** expertly prepared and locally sourced seafood; great views of the coast; extensive dessert menus. 🅢 *Average main: £19* ✉ *Cobb Rd.* ☎ *01297/446910* ⊕ *www.hixoysterandfishhouse.co.uk* ⊙ *No lunch Mon. and Tues. No dinner Sun.*

Hotels

Coombe House
$ | **B&B/INN** | Tucked away in a stone house one minute from the seafront on one of the oldest lanes in Lyme, this uncluttered, stylish B&B has genial hosts

and airy, modern guest rooms decorated in maritime blue and white. **Pros:** friendly owners; pleasant rooms; central location. **Cons:** books up fast; simple amenities; relaxed atmosphere not for everyone. Ⓢ *Rooms from: £72* ✉ *41 Coombe St.* ☎ *01297/443849* ⊕ *www.coombe-house. co.uk* ⇆ *3 rooms* �‖ *Free breakfast.*

Activities

Dorset Coast Path

HIKING/WALKING | This 95-mile path—a section of the 630-mile-long South West Coast Path National Trail—runs east from Lyme Regis to Old Harry Rocks near Studland, bypassing Weymouth and taking in the quiet bays, shingle beaches, and low chalk cliffs of the coast. Some highlights are Golden Cap, the highest point on the South Coast; the Swannery at Abbotsbury; Chesil Beach; Durdle Door; and Lulworth Cove (between Weymouth and Corfe Castle). Villages and isolated pubs dot the route, as do many rural B&Bs. ✉ *Lyme Regis* ☎ *01752/896237* ⊕ *www.southwest-coastpath.org.uk.*

Chapter 7

CORNWALL AND THE WEST COUNTRY

Updated by
Robert Andrews

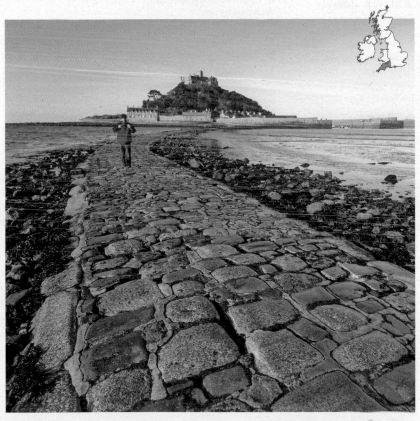

◉ Sights	🍴 Restaurants	🛏 Hotels	🛍 Shopping	🍸 Nightlife
★★★★☆	★★★★☆	★★★☆☆	★★☆☆☆	★★☆☆☆

WELCOME TO CORNWALL AND THE WEST COUNTRY

TOP REASONS TO GO

★ **Coastal walks:** For high, dramatic cliff scenery, choose the Exmoor coast around Lynmouth or the coast around Tintagel. The South West Coast Path is 630 miles long.

★ **Riding or hiking on Dartmoor:** Escape to southern England's greatest wilderness—a treeless expanse dotted with rocky outcrops; there are many organized walks and pony-trekking operations.

★ **Tate St. Ives Gallery:** There's nowhere better to absorb the local arts scene than this offshoot of London's Tate Museum in the pretty seaside town of St. Ives. A rooftop café claims views over Porthmeor Beach.

★ **A visit to Eden:** It's worth the journey west for Cornwall's Eden Project alone—a wonderland of plant life in a former clay pit. Two gigantic geodesic "biomes" are filled with flora.

★ **Wells Cathedral:** A perfect example of medieval craftsmanship, the building is a stunning spectacle.

1 Bristol. The region's biggest city.

2 Wells. A town with a mighty cathedral.

3 Glastonbury. A cathedral town connected to the mythical Avalon.

4 Dunster. A charming village.

5 Lynton and Lynmouth. A charming pair of Devonshire villages.

6 Clovelly. A picture-perfect English town.

7 Cornwall. Britain's famed Western peninsula.

8 Plymouth. A modern city with some important historical sights.

9 Dartmoor National Park. Open heath and wild moorland.

10 Tavistock and Around. A good base for Dartmoor.

11 Lydford. Home to a spectacular gorge.

12 Chagford. A village with plenty of history.

13 Exeter. A historic city with a sturdy cathedral.

14 Totnes. A relaxed market town.

15 Dartmouth. A port town.

0 _____ 12 mi
0 _____ 12 km

Padstow Bay

Padstow

Newquay

Perranporth

Camborne · A30 · Truro

St. Ives

St. Mawes

Penzance

Falmouth

Mousehole

7

Clevedon

Bristol

Weston
Super Mare

Bristol Channel

Lynmouth 5   Porlock
Lynton   4 Dunster

Exmoor
National Park

Wells 2

Glastonbury
3

Bridgwater

Barnstaple

Taunton

SOMERSET

Barnstaple
Bay

6
Clovelly

DEVON

A361

A303

Boscastle

Tintagel

Okehampton

Honiton

DORSET

Port Isaac

Launceston

11

Lydford

12

Chagford

Exeter 13

Topsham

Beer

A30

CORNWALL

Bodmin

Tavistock

10

Dartmoor
National Park

9

Exmouth

Torquay
Torbay

Paignton

Fowey

St Austell

St Austell
Bay

Plymouth 8

Totnes 14

Brixham

15

Dartmouth

English Channel

England's West Country is a land of granite promontories, windswept moors, hideaway hamlets, and—above all—the sea. Leafy, narrow country roads lead through miles of buttercup meadows and cider-apple orchards to heathery heights and mellow villages. With their secluded beaches and dreamy backwaters, Somerset, Devon, and Cornwall can be some of England's most relaxing regions to visit.

The counties of the West Country each have their own distinct flavor, and each comes with a regionalism that borders on patriotism. Somerset is noted for its rolling green countryside; Devon's wild and dramatic moors—bare, boggy, upland heath dominated by heathers and gorse—contrast with the restfulness of its many sandy beaches and coves; and Cornwall has managed to retain a touch of its old insularity, despite the annual invasion of thousands of people lured by the Atlantic waves or the ripples of the English Channel.

The historic port of Bristol is where you come across the first unmistakable burrs of the western brogue. Its Georgian architecture and a dramatic gorge create a backdrop to what has become one of Britain's most dynamic cities. To the south lie the cathedral city of Wells and Glastonbury, with its ruined abbey and Arthurian associations. Abutting the north coast is heather-covered Exmoor National Park.

There's more wild moorland in Devon, where Dartmoor is famed for its ponies roaming amid an assortment of strange tors (rocky outcroppings eroded into weird shapes). Devon's coastal towns are as interesting for their cultural and historical appeal—many were smuggler havens—as for their scenic beauty. Parts of south Devon resemble some balmy Mediterranean shore—hence its sobriquet, the English Riviera.

Cornwall, England's westernmost county, has always regarded itself as separate from the rest of Britain, and the Arthurian legends really took root here, not least at Tintagel Castle, the legendary birthplace of Arthur. The south coast is filled with sandy beaches, delightful coves, and popular resorts.

MAJOR REGIONS

Bristol, Wells, and North Devon. On the eastern side of this region is the vibrant city of Bristol. From here you might head south to the pretty cathedral city of Wells and continue on via Glastonbury, which just might be the Avalon of Arthurian legend. Proceed west along the Somerset coast into Devon, skirting the moorlands of Exmoor and tracing the northern shore via Clovelly.

Cornwall. You're never more than 20 miles from the sea in this western outpost of Britain, and the maritime flavor imbues such port towns as Padstow and Falmouth. A string of good beaches and resort towns such as St. Ives pull in the summer crowds.

Plymouth and Dartmoor. Just over the border from Cornwall is Plymouth, an unprepossessing city but one with a historic old core and splendid harbor that recall a rich maritime heritage. North of Plymouth, you can explore the vast, boggy reaches of hilly Dartmoor, the setting for the Sherlock Holmes classic *The Hound of the Baskervilles*. This national park is a great place to hike or go horseback riding away from the crowds.

Exeter and South Devon. The ancient city of Exeter, Devon's county seat, has preserved some of its historical character despite wartime bombing. From Exeter you can explore southeast to the estuary village of Topsham. Sheltered by the high mass of Dartmoor to the west, the coastal resort area of Torbay, known as the English Riviera, enjoys a mild, warm climate that allows for subtropical vegetation, including palm trees. Between the two, on the banks of the River Dart, is the pretty market town of Totnes, while the well-to-do yachting center of Dartmouth lies south of Torbay at the river's estuary.

Planning

When to Go

In July and August, traffic chokes the roads leading into the West Country. Somehow the region squeezes in all the "grockles," or tourists, and the chances of finding a remote oasis of peace and quiet are severely curtailed. The beaches and resort towns are either bubbling with zest or unbearably tacky, depending on your point of view. In summer, your best option is to find a secluded hotel and make brief excursions from there. Avoid traveling on Saturday, when weekly rentals start and finish, and the roads are jammed. Most properties that don't accept business year-round open for Easter and close in late September or October. Those that remain open have reduced hours. Winter has its own appeal: the Atlantic waves crash dramatically against the coast, and the austere Cornish cliffs are at their most spectacular.

The most notable festivals are Padstow's Obby Oss, a traditional celebration of the arrival of summer that takes place around May 1; the Cornish-themed Golowan Festival in Penzance in late June; and the St. Ives September Festival of music and art in mid-September. In addition, many West Country maritime towns host regattas over summer weekends. The best times to visit Devon are late summer and early fall, during the end-of-summer festivals, especially popular in the coastal towns of east Devon.

FESTIVALS
Glastonbury Festival
FESTIVALS | Held in Pilton (a few miles from the town of Glastonbury), the Glastonbury Festival is England's biggest and perhaps best annual rock festival. For five days over the last weekend in June, it hosts hundreds of bands—established and up-and-coming—on three main stages and myriad smaller venues. Tickets are steeply priced—around £270—and sell out months in advance; they include entertainment, a camping area, and service facilities. ✉ *Pilton* ⊕ *www.glastonburyfestivals.co.uk*.

Planning Your Time

The elongated shape of Britain's south-western peninsula means that you may well spend more time traveling than seeing the sights. The key is to base yourself in one or two places and make day trips to the surrounding region. The cities of Bristol, Exeter, and Plymouth make handy bases from which to explore the region, but they can also swallow up a lot of time, at the expense of smaller, less demanding places. The same is true of the resorts of Torquay, Newquay, and Falmouth, which can get very busy. Choose instead towns and villages such as Wells, Lynmouth, Port Isaac, St. Mawes, and Fowey to soak up local atmosphere. If you stick to just a few towns in Somerset and Devon (Bristol, Wells, and Exeter) you could get a taste of the area in four or five days. If you intend to cover Cornwall, at the end of the peninsula, you'll need at least a week. Allow time for aimless rambling—the best way to explore the moors and the coast—and leave enough free time for doing nothing at all.

Getting Here and Around

AIR
Bristol International Airport, a few miles southwest of the city, has frequent flights from London, as well as from Dublin, Amsterdam, and other international cities. Exeter International Airport, 5 miles east of the city, and Cornwall Airport Newquay, 5 miles northeast of town, both have daily flights to London.

AIRPORT INFORMATION Bristol International Airport. ✉ *A38, Lulsgate Bottom* ☎ *0371/334–4444* ⊕ *www.bristolairport. co.uk.* **Cornwall Airport Newquay.** ✉ *Off A3059, St. Mawgan* ☎ *01637/860600* ⊕ *www.cornwallairportnewquay.com.* **Exeter International Airport.** ✉ *A30, Clyst Honiton* ☎ *01392/367433* ⊕ *www.exeter-airport.co.uk.*

BUS
National Express buses leave London's Victoria Coach Station for Bristol (2½ hours), Exeter (4–5 hours), Plymouth (5–6 hours), and Penzance (8–10 hours). Megabus offers cheap service to Bristol, Exeter, Plymouth, Newquay, Bodmin, and Falmouth (book online to avoid premium-line costs). There's also a good network of regional bus services. First buses serve Somerset, Devon, and Cornwall, and Stagecoach South West covers mainly south Devon and the north Devon coast. Dartline Coaches has a small network in Devon, and Plymouth Citybus operate around Plymouth and north and east Cornwall. First and Stagecoach South West offer money-saving one- or seven-day passes good for unlimited bus travel. Traveline can help you plan your trip.

BUS CONTACTS Dartline Coaches. ☎ *01392/872900* ⊕ *www.dartline-coaches.co.uk.* **First.** ☎ *0345/602–0121* ⊕ *www. firstgroup.com.* **Megabus.** ☎ *0900/160–0900 for booking, 0141/352–4444 for general inquiries* ⊕ *uk.megabus.com.* **National Express.** ☎ *0871/781–8181* ⊕ *www.nationalexpress.com.* **Plymouth Citybus.** ☎ *01752/662271* ⊕ *www.plymouthbus.co.uk.* **Stagecoach South West.** ☎ *01392/427711* ⊕ *www.stagecoachbus.com.* **Traveline.** ☎ *0871/200–2233* ⊕ *www.travelinesw.com.*

CAR
Unless you confine yourself to a few towns—for example, Exeter, Penzance, and Plymouth—you'll be at a huge disadvantage without your own transportation. The region has a few main arteries, but you should take minor roads whenever possible, if only to see the real West Country at a leisurely pace.

The fastest route from London to the West Country is via the M4 and M5 motorways. Allow at least two hours to drive to Bristol, three to Exeter. The main roads heading west are the A30 (burrowing through the center of Devon and Cornwall all the way to the tip of Cornwall), the A39 (near the northern shore), and the A38 (near the southern shore, south of Dartmoor and taking in Plymouth).

TRAIN

Rail travelers can make use of a fast service connecting Exeter, Plymouth, and Penzance. Great Western Railway and South Western Railway serve the region from London's Paddington and Waterloo stations. Average travel time to Exeter is 2½ hours, to Plymouth 3¼ hours, and to Penzance about 5½ hours. Once you've arrived, however, you'll find trains to be of limited use in the West Country, as only a few branch lines leave the main line between Exeter and Penzance.

Freedom of the South West tickets provide three days of unlimited travel throughout the West Country in any seven-day period or eight days in any 15-day period. Localized Ranger passes cover Devon or Cornwall.

TRAIN CONTACTS National Rail Enquiries. ☎ 0345/748 4950 ⊕ www.nationalrail. co.uk.

Restaurants

The last several years have seen a food renaissance in England's West Country. In the top restaurants the accent is firmly on local and seasonal products. Seafood, from Atlantic pollock to Helford River oysters, is the number one choice along the coasts, and it's available in places from haute restaurants to harborside fish shacks. Celebrity chefs have marked their pitch all over the region, including Michael Caines outside Exeter, Mitch Tonks in Dartmouth, Nathan Outlaw in Port Isaac, and Rick Stein and Paul Ainsworth in Padstow. Better-known establishments are often completely booked on Friday or Saturday, so reserve well in advance.

Hotels

Accommodations include national hotel chains, represented in all of the region's principal centers, as well as ancient inns and ubiquitous bed-and-breakfast places. Availability can be limited on the coasts during August and during the weekend everywhere, so book well ahead. Many farmhouses also rent out rooms—offering tranquil rural surroundings—but these lodgings are often difficult to reach without a car. If you have a car, though, renting a house or cottage with a kitchen may be ideal. It's worth finding out about the weekend and winter deals that many hotels offer.

Restaurant and hotel reviews have been shortened. For full information, visit Fodors.com. Restaurant prices are the average cost of a main course at dinner, or if dinner is not served, at lunch. Hotel prices are the lowest cost of a standard double room in high season, including 20% V.A.T.

WHAT IT COSTS in Pounds

	$	$$	$$$	$$$$
RESTAURANTS				
	under £16	£16–£23	£24–£30	over £30
HOTELS				
	under £125	£125–£225	£226–£350	over £350

VISITOR INFORMATION

CONTACTS Visit Cornwall. ✉ 30 Boscawen St., Truro ☎ 01872/261735 ⊕ www. visitcornwall.com Ⓜ . **Visit Devon.** ⊕ www.visitdevon.co.uk. **Visit Somerset.** ☎ 01749/835416 ⊕ www.visitsomerset. co.uk.

Bristol

120 miles west of London, 46 miles south of Birmingham, 45 miles east of Cardiff, 13 miles northwest of Bath.

The West Country's biggest city (population 430,000), Bristol has, in recent years, become one of the country's most vibrant centers, with a thriving cultural scene encompassing some of the best contemporary art, theater, and music. Buzzing bars, cafés, and restaurants, and a largely youthful population make it an attractive place to spend time.

Now that the city's industries no longer rely on the docks, the historic harbor along the River Avon has been given over to recreation. Arts and entertainment complexes, museums, and galleries fill the quayside. The pubs and clubs here draw the under-25 set and make the area fairly boisterous (and best avoided) on Friday and Saturday nights.

Bristol also trails a great deal of history in its wake. It can be called the "birthplace of America" with some confidence, for John Cabot and his son Sebastian sailed from the old city docks in 1497 to touch down on the North American mainland, which he claimed for the English crown. The city had been a major center since medieval times, but in the 17th and 18th centuries it became the foremost port for trade with North America, and it played a leading role in the Caribbean slave trade. Bristol was the home of William Penn, developer of Pennsylvania, and a haven for John Wesley, whose Methodist movement played an important role in colonial Georgia.

GETTING HERE AND AROUND

Bristol has good connections by bus and train to most cities in the country. From London, calculate about 2½ hours by bus or 1¾ hours by train. From Cardiff it's about 50 minutes by bus or train. By train, make sure you get tickets for Bristol Temple Meads Station (not Bristol Parkway), which is a short bus, taxi, or river-bus ride from the center. The bus station is more central, near the Broadmead shopping center. Most sights can be visited on foot, though a bus or a taxi is necessary to reach the Clifton neighborhood.

ESSENTIALS

VISITOR INFORMATION Bristol Tourist Information Centre. ⊠ *E Shed, Canon's Rd.* ☎ *0117/929–9205* ⊕ *www.visitbristol. co.uk.*

Sights

Church of St. Mary Redcliffe

RELIGIOUS SITE | Built by Bristol merchants who wanted a place in which to pray for the safe (and profitable) voyages of their ships, the rib-vaulted, 14th-century church was called "the fairest in England" by Queen Elizabeth I. High up on the nave wall hang the arms and armor of Sir William Penn, father of the founder of Pennsylvania. The church is a five-minute walk from Temple Meads train station toward the docks. ⊠ *Redcliffe Way* ☎ *0117/231–0060* ⊕ *www. stmaryredcliffe.co.uk* 🖾 *Free.*

Clifton Suspension Bridge

BRIDGE/TUNNEL | **FAMILY** | A monument to Victorian engineering, this 702-foot-long bridge spans the Avon Gorge. Work began on Isambard Kingdom Brunel's design in 1831, but the bridge wasn't completed until 1864. Free hour-long guided tours usually take place on weekends at 3 between Easter and October or 2 from November to Easter, departing from the tollbooth at the Clifton end of the bridge. At the far end of the bridge, the **Clifton Suspension Bridge Visitor Centre** has an engaging exhibition on the bridge and its construction, including a range of videos and hands-on experiences. Near the bridge lies **Clifton Village,** studded with boutiques, antiques shops, and smart crafts shops in its lanes and squares. Bus No. 8 from Bristol Temple

Bristol, Wells, and North Devon

Meads Station and the city center stops in Clifton Village. ⊠ *Bridge Rd., Leigh Woods* ☎ *0117/974–4664* ⊕ *www.clifton-bridge.org.uk* ⌨ *Free.*

★ M Shed

MUSEUM | FAMILY | In a refurbished transit shed on the harborside, this museum is dedicated to the city's history. The collection comprises three main galleries—Bristol People, Bristol Places, and Bristol Life—that focus on everything from the slave trade to scientific inventions to recent cultural innovations associated with the city. Check out the artifacts, photos, and sound and video recordings of and by Bristolians, all jazzed up with the latest interactive technology. Don't forget to take in the magnificent harbor views from the top-floor terrace. ⊠ *Princes Wharf, Wapping Rd.* ☎ *0117/352–6600* ⊕ *www.mshed.org* ⌨ *Free* ⊘ *Closed*

Mon., except bank holidays and school vacations.

★ SS *Great Britain*

MILITARY SITE | FAMILY | On view in the harbor is the first iron ship to cross the Atlantic. Built by the great English engineer Isambard Kingdom Brunel in 1843, it remained in service until 1970, first as a transatlantic liner and ultimately as a coal storage hulk. Everything from the bakery to the officers' quarters comes complete with sounds and smells of the time, and there are even shadowy glimpses of rats in the galley. You can try on typical garments of the time, descend into the ship's dry dock for a view of the hull and propeller, and climb the ship's rigging (daily between Easter and October and during school vacations, or weekends at other times; £10, or free for under-18s). Your entry ticket also admits you to engrossing exhibits on the ship's history and to Being Brunel, a separate museum dedicated to the life of Isambard Brunel. A short walk east along the harborside from here will bring you to a replica of the *Matthew*, the tiny craft that carried John Cabot to North America in 1497, moored here when it is not sailing on the high seas. ■TIP→ **Tickets are valid for one year. Buy online for a 5% discount.** ⊠ *Great Western Dockyard, Gas Ferry Rd.* ☎ *0117/926–0680* ⊕ *www.ssgreatbritain. org* ⊠ *£17.*

★ **Tyntesfield**
HOUSE | This extravagant, 35-bedroom Victorian–Gothic Revival mansion has been magnificently restored to reveal a showcase of the decorative arts where every ornate detail compels attention. Besides magnificent woodwork, stained glass, tiles, and original furniture and fabrics, the house contains the modern conveniences of the 1860s, such as a heated billiards table; the servants' quarters are equally absorbing. There's a restaurant and family play area, too. You can see the house, garden, and chapel at your own pace, or join a free garden tour. ■TIP→ **Arrive early in the day to avoid the crowds competing for timed tickets—Monday and Tuesday are the quietest days.** Tyntesfield is 7 miles southwest of Bristol; the daily bus service X6 is the most convenient public transport from the city (present your ticket for a 20% discount in the café and shop). The house is a 15-minute walk from the bus stop. ⊠ *B3128, Wraxall* ☎ *01275/461900* ⊕ *www.nationaltrust.org.uk* ⊠ *£17.40; gardens only £10.75.*

★ **We The Curious**
MUSEUM | FAMILY | One of the country's top family-friendly science centers, this multimedia attraction provides a "hands-on, minds-on" exploration of science and technology in more than 300 interactive exhibits and displays. "All About Us" is dedicated to the inner workings of the human body. Another section allows you to create your own animations. A 3D planetarium in a gleaming stainless-steel sphere takes you on a 30-minute voyage through the galaxy. There are up to 10 shows a day, bookable when you buy your ticket (£2.50–3.50). A popular exhibit lets kids test their skills at creating animations. Allow at least three hours to see it all. ■TIP→ **Buy tickets onlne for a 5% discount.** ⊠ *Anchor Rd., Harbourside* ☎ *0117/915–1000* ⊕ *www.wethecurious. org* ⊠ *£14.50.*

🍴 Restaurants

★ **Riverstation**
$$ | MODERN BRITISH | Occupying a former police station, this modern, clean-lined restaurant affords serene views over the passing swans and boats. Upstairs, the more formal restaurant serves delicately cooked dishes like pigeon breast with date puree and smoked bacon in a madeira jus, and trout with new potatoes, baby leek, and samphires, while the irresistible desserts include coconut and blood orange mousse, and caramel and apple cheesecake with honey ice cream. **Known for:** warm, friendly environment; soothing river views; good fixed-price menus. ⑤ *Average main: £18* ⊠ *The Grove, Harbourside* ☎ *0117/914–4434* ⊕ *www.riverstation.co.uk* ☉ *No dinner Sun.*

Source Food Hall & Café
$ | MODERN BRITISH | In the heart of the old city, this trendy eatery benefits from its location in the St. Nicholas Market by offering a range of fresh seasonal produce, either to eat in or take out from the deli, meat, and fish counters. The wholesome lunch menu might feature Italian cold meats, spiced aubergine with almond couscous and mint yogurt, or Bavette steak with fries. **Known for:** quality local ingredients; great breakfast and coffee; microbrewery beers and ciders. ⑤ *Average main: £11* ⊠ *St. Nicholas Market, 1–3 Exchange Ave.* ☎ *0117/927–2998*

⊕ *www.source-food.co.uk* ⊘ *Closed Sun.*
No dinner.

 Hotels

★ Hotel du Vin
$$ | HOTEL | This hip chain has brought
high-tech flair to six former sugar-refining
warehouses, built in 1728 when the River
Frome ran outside the front door. **Pros:**
tastefully restored old building; great
bathrooms; excellent bar and bistro. **Cons:**
traffic-dominated location; dim lighting in
rooms; limited parking ⑤ *Rooms from:*
£129 ⊠ *The Sugar House, Narrow Lewins*
Mead ☎ *0117/403 2979* ⊕ *www.hoteldu-*
vin.com ➡ *40 rooms* ⦿| *No meals.*

★ Thornbury Castle
$$ | HOTEL | An impressive lodging,
Thornbury has everything a genuine
16th-century Tudor castle needs: huge
fireplaces, moody paintings, mullioned
windows, and a large garden. **Pros:** grand
medieval surroundings; sumptuous
rooms; doting service. **Cons:** many steps
to climb; some rooms and bathrooms
are relatively small; unexciting location.
⑤ *Rooms from: £199* ⊠ *Castle St., off*
A38, Thornbury ☎ *01454/281182* ⊕ *www.*
thornburycastle.co.uk ➡ *28 rooms*
⦿| *Free breakfast.*

⊛ Performing Arts

Arnolfini
ARTS CENTERS | In a converted warehouse
on the harbor, the Arnolfini is one of the
country's most prestigious contempo-
rary-art venues, known for uncovering
innovative yet accessible art. There are
galleries, a cinema, a bookshop, and
a lively café-bar. ⊠ *16 Narrow Quay*
☎ *0117/917–2300* ⊕ *www.arnolfini.org.uk.*

Wells

22 miles south of Bristol, 132 miles west
of London.

England's smallest cathedral city, with a
population of 10,000, lies at the foot of
the Mendip Hills. Although set in what
feels like a quiet country town, the great
cathedral is a masterpiece of Gothic
architecture—the first to be built in the
Early English style. The city's name refers
to the underground streams that bubble
up into St. Andrew's Well within the
grounds of the Bishop's Palace. Spring
water has run through High Street since
the 15th century. Seventeenth-century
buildings surround the ancient mar-
ketplace, which hosts market days on
Wednesday and Saturday.

GETTING HERE AND AROUND
Regular First buses from Bristol take one
hour to reach Wells; the bus station is a
few minutes south of the cathedral. Drivers should take A37, and park outside the
compact and eminently walkable center.

ESSENTIALS
VISITOR INFORMATION Wells Visitor
Information Service. ⊠ *Wells Museum,*
8 Cathedral Green ☎ *01749/671770*
⊕ *www.wellssomerset.com.*

Sights

Bishop's Palace
CASTLE/PALACE | The Bishop's Eye gate
leading from Market Place takes you to
the magnificent, moat-ringed Bishop's
Palace, which retains parts of the original
13th-century residence. The peaceful
grounds command the most attention,
including the gatehouse, the ramparts, and the impressive remains of a
late-13th-century great hall that fell into
ruin after the lead in its roof was sold in
the 16th century. Most rooms of the palace are closed to the public, but you can
see the undercroft, the private chapel,
and the sumptuously decorated Long

Harmonious and stately, Wells Cathedral has a monumental west front decorated with medieval statues of kings and saints.

Gallery. In summer, ticket-holders can join a free tour of the palace and chapel at 11 am and 2 pm, and of the grounds at noon and 3 pm; in winter there are tours of the palace and gardens at noon. ⊠ *Market Pl.* ☎ *01749/988111* ⊕ *www. bishopspalace.org.uk* ⊠ *£9.10.*

Wells Cathedral

RELIGIOUS SITE | The great west towers of the Cathedral Church of St. Andrew, the oldest surviving English Gothic church, can be seen for miles. Dating from the 12th century, Wells Cathedral (as it's more commonly known) derives its beauty from the perfect harmony of all of its parts, the glowing colors of its original stained-glass windows, and its peaceful setting among stately trees and majestic lawns. To appreciate the elaborate west-front facade, approach the building from the cathedral green, accessible from Market Place through a great medieval gate called "penniless porch" (named after the beggars who once waited here to collect alms from worshippers). The cathedral's west front is twice as wide as

it is high, and some 300 statues of kings and saints adorn it. Inside, vast inverted arches—known as scissor arches—were added in 1338 to stop the central tower from sinking to one side.

The cathedral has a rare and beautiful medieval clock, the second-oldest working clock in the world, consisting of the seated figure of a man called Jack Blandifer, who strikes a bell on the quarter hour while mounted knights circle in a joust. Near the clock is the entrance to the Chapter House—a small wooden door opening onto a great sweep of stairs worn down on one side by the tread of pilgrims over the centuries. Free guided tours lasting approximately one hour begin at the back of the cathedral; the website also has details of "High Parts" tours (taking in the galleries and roof spaces) and chained library tours, which need booking and are charged, as well as free tours exploring the cathedral's stained glass, stone carvings, and embroidery (usually on Wednesday and Saturday mornings in summer). A cloister restaurant serves snacks and teas. ✉ *Cathedral Green* ☎ *01749/674483* ⊕ *www.wellscathedral.org.uk* 🕮 *£6 suggested donation.*

Restaurants

The Fountain Inn
$ | **MODERN BRITISH** | Slightly off the tourist track but only a few minutes from the cathedral, this classic gastro-pub offers a winning combination of traditional decor lightened with tasteful modern touches and great, locally sourced food. The eclectic menu includes such standout dishes as Madras chicken curry, confit of duck, and beer-battered haddock. **Known for:** warm, intimate atmosphere; extensive menu with some good English classics; great range of beers, including local ales. ⑤ *Average main: £15* ✉ *1 St. Thomas St.* ☎ *01749/672317* ⊕ *www.fountaininn.co.uk* ◷ *No lunch Mon. No dinner Sun.*

🛏 Hotels

Swan Hotel
$ | **HOTEL** | A former coaching inn built in the 15th century, the Swan has an ideal spot facing the cathedral. **Pros:** friendly and helpful service; some great views; good restaurant. **Cons:** dated in places; occasional noise issues; parking lot tricky to navigate. ⑤ *Rooms from: £103* ✉ *11 Sadler St.* ☎ *01749/836300* ⊕ *www.swan-hotelwells.co.uk* ⇨ *55 rooms* ⁍ *Free breakfast.*

Glastonbury

5 miles southwest of Wells, 27 miles south of Bristol, 27 miles southwest of Bath.

A town steeped in history, myth, and legend, Glastonbury lies in the lea of Glastonbury Tor, a grassy hill rising 520 feet above the drained marshes known as the Somerset Levels. The Tor is supposedly the site of crossing ley lines (hypothetical alignments of significant places), and, in legend, Glastonbury is identified with Avalon, the paradise into which King Arthur was reborn after his death.

Partly because of these associations but also because of its world-class rock-music festival, the town has acquired renown as a New Age center, mixing crystal gazers with druids, yogis, and hippies, variously in search of Arthur, Merlin, Jesus—and even Elvis. ■**TIP→ Between April and September, a shuttle bus runs every half hour between all of Glastonbury's major sights. Tickets are £3.50 and are valid all day.**

GETTING HERE AND AROUND
Frequent buses link Glastonbury to Wells and Bristol, pulling in close to the abbey. Drivers should take the A39. You can walk to all the sights or take the shuttle bus, though you'll need a stock of energy for ascending the Tor.

ESSENTIALS
VISITOR INFORMATION Glastonbury Tourist Information Centre. ✉ *St. Dunstan's House, 1 Magdalene St.* ☎ *01458/832954* ⊕ *www.glastonburytic.co.uk.*

Sights

Glastonbury Abbey
RELIGIOUS SITE | The ruins of this great abbey, in the center of town, are on the site where, according to legend, Joseph of Arimathea built a church in the 1st century. A monastery had certainly been erected here by the 9th century, and the site drew many pilgrims. The ruins are those of the abbey completed in 1524 and destroyed in 1539, during Henry VIII's dissolution of the monasteries. A sign south of the Lady Chapel marks the sites where Arthur and Guinevere were supposedly buried. Between April and October, guides in period costumes are on hand to point out some of the abbey's most interesting features. The visitor center has a scale model of the abbey

as well as carvings and decorations salvaged from the ruins. ■TIP→ **Tickets bought online are cheaper.** ✉ *Magdalene St.* ☎ *01458/832267* ⊕ *www.glastonbury-abbey.com* 🎟 *£8.60.*

★ Somerset Rural Life Museum

MUSEUM | **FAMILY** | Occupying a Victorian farmhouse and a 14th-century abbey tithe barn, this museum tells the story of life in Somerset throughout the ages. Exhibits in the six galleries illustrate farming practices and daily life in the 19th century using sound recordings and projections as well as an array of tools and domestic objects. The barn, more than 90 feet in length, once stored the one-tenth portion of the town's produce that was owed to the church and now holds exhibitions. Soups and crusty sandwiches are available at the Grain Store Café, which has tables in the yard. The grounds also contain an apple cider orchard. For a good walk, take the scenic footpath from the museum that leads up to the Tor, a half mile east. ✉ *Chilkwell St.* ☎ *01458/831197* ⊕ *www.swheritage.org.uk/rural-life-museum* 🎟 *£7.50* ⊘ *Closed Mon. year-round and Sun. Nov.–Easter.*

 Restaurants

Who'd a Thought It

$ | **BRITISH** | As an antidote to the natural-food cafés of Glastonbury's High Street, try this traditional backstreet inn for some more down-to-earth fare that doesn't compromise on quality. Bar classics such as beer-battered fish-and-chips and Somerset sausages appear alongside chicken curry, vegan dishes, and sizzling steaks. **Known for:** fast and friendly service; quirky interior crammed with memorabilia; traditional dishes served alongside local beers and ciders. ⑤ *Average main: £15* ✉ *17 Northload St.* ☎ *01458/834460* ⊕ *www.whodathought-it.co.uk.*

 Hotels

★ Melrose House

$ | **B&B/INN** | Superbly situated at the base of Glastonbury Tor, this elegant B&B on the edge of town is surrounded by lush gardens with far-reaching views over the Vale of Avalon. **Pros:** tranquil setting; easy access to Glastonbury Tor; superb breakfasts. **Cons:** not very central; one-night stays not always possible; does not accept credit cards. ⑤ *Rooms from: £90* ✉ *Coursing Batch* ☎ *01458/834706* ⊕ *www.melrose-bandb.co.uk* 🛏 *3 rooms* ❙◯❙ *Free breakfast* ⊟ *No credit cards.*

Dunster

35 miles west of Glastonbury, 43 miles north of Exeter.

Lying between the Somerset coast and the edge of Exmoor National Park, Dunster is a picture-book village with a broad main street. The eight-sided yarn-market building on High Street dates from 1589.

GETTING HERE AND AROUND

To reach Dunster by car, follow the A39. By bus, there are frequent departures from nearby Minehead and Taunton. Dunster Castle is a brief walk from the village center. In the village is the Exmoor National Park Visitor Centre, which can give you plenty of information about local activities.

ESSENTIALS

VISITOR INFORMATION Exmoor National Park Visitor Centre. ✉ *Dunster Steep* ☎ *01643/821835* ⊕ *www.exmoor-nation-alpark.gov.uk.*

 Sights

★ Dunster Castle

CASTLE/PALACE | A 13th-century fortress remodeled in 1868, Dunster Castle dominates the village from its site on a hill. Parkland and unusual gardens with subtropical plants surround the building, which has fine plaster ceilings, stacks of family portraits (including one by Joshua Reynolds), 17th-century Dutch leather hangings, and a magnificent 17th-century oak staircase. The climb to the castle from the parking lot is steep. In winter, visits are by guided tour only, on a first-come-first-served basis and at a reduced price ⊠ Off A39 ☎ 01643/821314 ⊕ www.nationaltrust.org.uk ☜ £12.90.

🛏 Hotels

Luttrell Arms

$ | B&B/INN | In style and atmosphere, this classic inn harmonizes perfectly with Dunster village and castle; it was used as a guesthouse by the abbots of Cleeve in the 14th century. **Pros:** central location; historic trappings; good dining options. **Cons:** some standard rooms are small and viewless, no parking; heavy presence of dogs in the bar not great for allergy sufferers. ⑤ *Rooms from: £102* ⊠ *High St.* ☎ *01643/821555* ⊕ *www.luttrellarms.co.uk* ⌲ *29 rooms* ⦿ *Free breakfast.*

Lynton and Lynmouth

13 miles west of Porlock, 60 miles north-west of Exeter.

A steep hill separates this pretty pair of Devonshire villages, which are linked by a Victorian cliff railway you can still ride. Lynmouth, a fishing village at the bottom of the hill, crouches below 1,000-foot-high cliffs at the mouths of the East and West Lyn rivers; Lynton is higher up. The poet Percy Bysshe Shelley visited Lynmouth in 1812, in the company of his 16-year-old bride, Harriet Westbrook. During their nine-week sojourn, the poet found time to write his polemical *Queen Mab.* The grand landscape of Exmoor lies all about, with walks to local beauty spots: Watersmeet, Hollerday Hill, or the Valley of Rocks, where rare feral goats graze.

GETTING HERE AND AROUND

These towns are best reached via the A39. Lynton is a stop on Quantock Heritage Bus 300, which runs Monday through Saturday from Minehead. It's a steep and winding ascent to Lynton from Lynmouth; take the cliff railway to travel between them.

ESSENTIALS

VISITOR INFORMATION Lynton and Lymouth Tourist Information Centre. ⊠ *26 Lee Rd., Lynton* ☎ *01598/752225* ⊕ *www.visitlyntonandlynmouth.com.*

👁 Sights

Coleridge Way

TRAIL | The 51-mile Coleridge Way runs between Nether Stowey (site of Coleridge's home) and Lynmouth, passing through the northern fringes of the Quantock Hills, the isolated villages of the Brendon Hills, and along the Exmoor coast. ⊠ *Lynmouth* ⊕ *www.visit-exmoor.co.uk/coleridge-way.*

Lynton and Lynmouth Cliff Railway

TRANSPORTATION SITE (AIRPORT/BUS/FERRY/TRAIN) | Water and a cable system power the 862-foot cliff railway that connects these two towns. As it ascends a rocky cliff, you are treated to fine views over the harbor. Inaugurated in 1890, it was the gift of publisher George Newnes, who also donated Lynton's imposing town hall, near the top station on Lee Road. ⊠ *The Esplanade, Lynmouth* ☎ *01598/753908* ⊕ *www.cliffrailwaylynton.co.uk* ☜ *£4 round-trip* ⊗ *Closed early Nov.–early Feb.*

🍽 Restaurants

Rising Sun

$$ | MODERN BRITISH | A 14th-century inn and a row of thatched cottages make up this pub-restaurant with great views over the Bristol Channel. The kitchen specializes in local cuisine with European influences, so expect dishes like roast

quail with black garlic gnocchi. **Known for:** traditional pub decor and ambience; good range of local ales; delicious seafood like lobster risotto and bouillabaisse. ⑤ *Average main: £21* ✉ *Riverside Rd., Lynmouth* ☎ *01598/753223* ⊕ *www. risingsunlynmouth.co.uk.*

Hotels

Highcliffe House

$$ | B&B/INN | As the name suggests, this luxury Victorian B&B in Lynton occupies a lofty position with spectacular vistas over the Bristol Channel. **Pros:** romantic ambience; inspiring views; generous and wide-ranging breakfasts. **Cons:** design not for everyone; unsightly parking lot directly below; relatively high room rates. ⑤ *Rooms from: £150* ✉ *Sinai Hill, Lynton* ☎ *01598/752235* ⊕ *www.highcliffehouse. co.uk* ⌖ *6 rooms* ⍟ *Free breakfast* ☞ *No guests under 18 allowed.*

Activities

West of Lynton, the Atlantic-facing beaches of Saunton Sands, Croyde Bay, and Woolacombe Bay are much beloved by surfers, with plenty of outlets renting equipment and offering lessons. Croyde Bay and Woolacombe Bay are more family-friendly.

Clovelly

40 miles southwest of Lynton, 60 miles northwest of Exeter.

Lovely Clovelly always seems to have the sun shining on its flower-lined cottages and stepped and cobbled streets. Alas, its beauty is well-known, and day-trippers can overrun the village in summer. Perched precariously among cliffs, a steep, cobbled road—tumbling down at such an angle that it's closed to cars—leads to the toylike harbor with its 14th-century quay. Allow about two hours

(more if you stop for a drink or a meal) to take in the village. Hobby Drive, a 3-mile cliff-top carriageway laid out in 1829 through thick woods, gives scintillating views over the village and coast.

GETTING HERE AND AROUND

To get to Clovelly by bus, take Stagecoach service 319 from Barnstaple or Bideford. If you're driving, take the A39 and park at the Clovelly Visitor Centre for £7.75. The center of town is steep and cobbled. The climb from the harbor to the parking lot can be exhausting, but from Easter through October a reasonably priced shuttle service brings you back.

Sights

Clovelly Visitor Centre

INFO CENTER | Here you'll see a 25-minute film that puts Clovelly into context. In the village you can visit a 1930s-style fisherman's cottage and an exhibition about Victorian writer Charles Kingsley, who lived here as a child. The admission fee includes parking, and you can book walking tours of the village at the Visitor Centre (£5). To avoid the worst crowds, arrive early or late in the day. ✉ *Off A39* ☎ *01237/431781* ⊕ *www.clovelly.co.uk* ☞ *£7.95.*

Hotels

Red Lion Hotel

$$ | HOTEL | You can soak up the tranquility of Clovelly after the day-trippers have gone at the 18th-century Red Lion, located right on the harbor in this coastal village. **Pros:** superb location; clean and comfortable; friendly staff. **Cons:** some rooms and bathrooms are small; bar lacks character; steep walk to get anywhere. ⑤ *Rooms from: £170* ✉ *The Quay* ☎ *01237/431237* ⊕ *www.clovelly.co.uk* ⌖ *17 rooms* ⍟ *Free breakfast.*

Clovelly may have it all. cobbled streets, quaint houses, and the endless blue sea.

Cornwall

Cornwall stretches west into the sea, with plenty of magnificent coastline to explore, along with tranquil towns and some bustling resorts. One way to discover it all is to travel southwest from Boscastle and the cliff-top ruins of Tintagel Castle, the legendary birthplace of Arthur, along the north Cornish coast to Land's End. This predominantly cliff-lined coast, interspersed with broad expanses of sand, has many tempting places to stop, including Padstow (for a seafood feast), Newquay (a surfing and tourist center), or St. Ives (a delightful artists' colony).

From Land's End, the westernmost tip of Britain, known for its savage land- and seascapes and panoramic views, return to the popular seaside resort of Penzance, the harbor town of Falmouth, and the river port of Fowey. The Channel coast is less rugged than the northern coast, with more sheltered beaches. Leave time to visit the excellent Eden Project, with its surrealistic-looking conservatories in an abandoned clay pit, and to explore the boggy, heath-covered expanse of Bodmin Moor.

Tintagel

3 miles southwest of Boscastle.

The romance of Arthurian legend thrives around Tintagel's ruined castle on the coast. Ever since the somewhat unreliable 12th-century chronicler Geoffrey of Monmouth identified Tintagel as the home of Arthur, son of Uther Pendragon and Ygrayne, devotees of the legend cycle have revered the site. In the 19th century Alfred, Lord Tennyson described Tintagel's Arthurian connection in *The Idylls of the King.* Today the village has its share of tourist junk—including Excaliburgers—but the headland around Tintagel is still splendidly scenic.

GETTING HERE AND AROUND

To drive to Tintagel, take the A39 to the B3263. Numerous parking lots are found in the village center. There's a bus stop

Cornwall

0 ⸺ 10 mi
0 ⸺ 10 km

DEVON

CORNWALL

Wainhouse Corner
Boscastle
Tintagel Castle
Tintagel
Hallworthy
Launceston
Port Isaac Bay
Port Isaac
Padstow Bay
Padstow
Wadebridge
Bodmin
Dobwalls
Carkeel
Newquay
Quintrell Downs
Trevarren
Summercourt
Trevarren
Eden Project
Trerule Foot
Plymouth
Perranporth
St. Austell
Fowey
Charlestown
St Austell Bay
Blackwater
Lost Gardens of Heligan
St Ives Bay
Redruth
Truro
Trelissick
St. Ives
Camborne
Pendeen
Whitecross
Falmouth
St. Mawes
Penzance
St. Michael's Mount
Pendennis Castle
Mousehole
Helston
St Keveme
Land's End
Pothcurno
Kynance Cove
Lizard Peninsula
Lizard

A39 · A30 · A395 · A39 · A30 · A388 · A390 · A38 · A39 · A30 · A3078 · A393 · A394 · B3306 · B3315 · B3293

near the tourist office for First Kernow buses from Wadebridge, which has connections from Bodmin Parkway, the nearest train station. Between April and October, a shuttle service brings mobility impaired passengers to the castle.

VISITOR INFORMATION Tintagel Visitor Centre. ⊠ *Bossiney Rd.* ☎ *01840/779084* ⊕ *www.tintagelparishcouncil.gov.uk.*

👁 Sights

★ Tintagel Castle
CASTLE/PALACE | Although all that remains of the ruined cliff-top Tintagel Castle, legendary birthplace of King Arthur, is the outline of its walls, moats, and towers, it requires only a bit of imagination to conjure up a picture of Sir Lancelot and Sir Galahad riding out in search of the Holy Grail over the narrow causeway

above the seething breakers. Archaeological evidence, however, suggests that the castle dates from much later—about 1150, when it was the stronghold of the earls of Cornwall. Long before that, Romans may have occupied the site. The earliest identified remains here are of Celtic (AD 5th century) origin, and these may have some connection with the legendary Arthur. Legends aside, nothing can detract from the castle ruins, dramatically set off by the wild, windswept Cornish coast, on an island joined to the mainland by a narrow isthmus. Paths lead down to the pebble beach and a cavern known as **Merlin's Cave.** Exploring Tintagel Castle involves some arduous climbing on steep steps, but even on a summer's day, when people swarm over the battlements and a westerly Atlantic wind sweeps through Tintagel, you can feel the proximity of the distant past.

⊠ Castle Rd., ½ mile west of the village ☎ 01840/770328 ⊕ www.english-heritage.org.uk ⊠ £13 ⊙ Closed Mon. and Tues. in Nov.; closed Mon.–Thurs. in Dec.–mid-Feb. (except week after Christmas).

Padstow

10 miles southwest of Port Isaac.

A small fishing port at the mouth of the River Camel, Padstow attracts attention and visitors as a center of culinary excellence, largely because of the presence here since 1975 of pioneering seafood chef Rick Stein. Stein's empire includes two restaurants, a café, a fish-and-chips joint, a delicatessen, a patisserie, and a cooking school where classes fill up months in advance.

Even if seafood isn't your favorite fare, Padstow is worth visiting. The cries of seagulls fill its lively harbor, a string of fine beaches lies within a short ride—including some choice strands highly prized by surfers—and two scenic walking routes await: the Saints Way across the peninsula to Fowey and the Camel Trail, a footpath and cycling path that follows the river as far as Bodmin Moor. If you can avoid peak visiting times—summer weekends—so much the better.

GETTING HERE AND AROUND

Regular buses connect Padstow with Bodmin, the main transportation hub hereabouts, and on the main Plymouth–Penzance train line. To get here from Port Isaac, change buses at Wadebridge. Alternatively, take the bus to Rock and the passenger ferry across the river. There are numerous direct buses on the Newquay–Padstow route. Drivers should take A39/A389 and park in the waterside parking lot before reaching the harbor.

FERRY CONTACTS Padstow Rock

Ferry. ☎ 01841/532239 Harbour Office, 0777/308–1574 Ferry Office ⊕ www.padstow-harbour.co.uk.

VISITOR INFORMATION Padstow Tourist Information Centre. ⊠ The Mariner's Clock Building, South Quay ☎ 01841/533449 ⊕ www.padstowlive.com Ⓜ.

🍴 Restaurants

★ Paul Ainsworth at no6

$$$$ | MODERN BRITISH | Paul Ainsworth is gradually expanding his culinary presence in Padstow to rival that of Rick Stein, and for many foodies, Ainsworth offers the better experience. His innovative creations can best be sampled at this intimate bistro that was his original foothold in the town, where diners seated in a series of small, stylish rooms feast on ingeniously concocted dishes that make the most of local and seasonal produce. **Known for:** exciting, creative cuisine like black truffle with morels and chicken tournedos Rossini; affordable set-price lunches; vivacious atmosphere. $ *Average main: £85* ⊠ 6 Middle St. ☎ 01841/532093 ⊕ www.paul-ainsworth.co.uk ⊙ Closed Sun., Mon., and mid-Jan.–early Feb.

★ The Seafood Restaurant

$$$ | SEAFOOD | Just across from where the lobster boats and trawlers unload their catches, Rick Stein's flagship restaurant has built its reputation on the freshest fish and the highest culinary artistry. The exclusively fish and shellfish menu includes everything from grilled Padstow lobster with herbs to stir-fried Singapore chili crab. **Known for:** top-quality, eclectic seafood dishes creatively prepared; famous regional chef; attentive service. $ *Average main: £30* ⊠ Riverside ☎ 01841/532700 ⊕ www.rickstein.com.

🛏 Hotels

St. Edmund's House

$$$$ | B&B/INN | The most luxurious Rick Stein lodgings in town are distinguished by their sophisticated and minimalist style. **Pros:** stylish and spacious bedrooms; top-notch service; central but

secluded. **Cons:** short walk to breakfast; extravagant prices; some noise issues. ⑤ *Rooms from: £320* ✉ *St. Edmund's La.* ☎ *01841/532700* ⊕ *www.rickstein.com* ⌗ *6 rooms* ⦿ *Free breakfast.*

 Activities

SURFING
Harlyn Surf School

SURFING | This school can arrange two-hour to three-day surfing courses at its base in Harlyn Bay, 3 miles west of Padstow. ✉ *Harlyn Bay Beach* ☎ *07757/779008* ⊕ *www.harlynsurf-school.co.uk.*

WALKING
Saints Way

HIKING/WALKING | This 30-mile inland path takes you between Padstow and the Camel Estuary on Cornwall's north coast to Fowey on the south coast. It follows a Bronze Age trading route, later used by Celtic pilgrims to cross the peninsula. Several relics of such times can be seen along the way. ✉ *Padstow.*

Newquay

14 miles southwest of Padstow, 30 miles southwest of Tintagel.

The biggest, most developed resort on the north Cornwall coast is a fairly large town established in 1439. It was once the center of the trade in pilchards (a small herringlike fish), and on the headland you can still see a white hut where a lookout known as a "huer" watched for pilchard schools and directed the boats to the fishing grounds. Newquay has become Britain's surfing capital, and, in summer, young California-dreamin' devotees often pack the wide, cliff-backed beaches.

GETTING HERE AND AROUND
A branch line links Newquay with the main Plymouth–Penzance train line at Par, and there are regular buses from Padstow, Bodmin, and St. Austell. Train and bus stations are both in the center of town. Newquay has good road connections with the rest of the peninsula via the A30 and A39 and is linked to the rest of the country by its airport. The best beaches are a long walk or a short bus ride from the center.

VISITOR INFORMATION Newquay Tourist Information Centre. ✉ *Marcus Hill* ☎ *01637/838516* ⊕ *www.visitnewquay.org.*

 Hotels

★ The Scarlet
$$$$ | **HOTEL** | The pampering begins the moment you enter this adults-only beachside hotel when you are greeted with a drink by the enthusiastic and highly professional staff, followed by a tour of the facilties. **Pros:** impeccable service; inspiring sea views; excellent dining. **Cons:** staff can be over-zealous; no children; some rooms only accessible by stairs. ⑤ *Rooms from: £340* ✉ *Tredragon Rd.* ☎ *01637/861800* ⊕ *www.scarlethotel.co.uk* ⌗ *37 rooms* ⦿ *Free breakfast.*

Activities

Surfing is Newquay's raison d'être for many of the enthusiasts who flock here throughout the year. Great Western and Tolcarne beaches are most suitable for beginners, while Fistral Beach is better for those with more experience. There are dozens of surf schools around town, many offering accommodation packages, and rental outlets are also ubiquitous.

SURFING
Extreme Academy

SURFING | One of the West Country's water-sports specialists, Extreme Academy based at Watergate Bay offers courses in wave skiing, kite surfing, kite buggying, paddle surfing, and just plain old surfing. It also has equipment for hire. ✉ *Trevarrian Hill, Watergate Bay* ☎ *01637/860840* ⊕ *www.extremeacademy.co.uk.*

St. Ives

25 miles southwest of Newquay, 10 miles north of Penzance.

James McNeill Whistler came here to paint his landscapes, Barbara Hepworth to fashion her modernist sculptures, and Virginia Woolf to write her novels. Today sand, sun, and superb art continue to attract thousands of vacationers to the fishing village of St. Ives, named after Saint Ia, a 5th-century female Irish missionary said to have arrived on a floating leaf. Many come to St. Ives for the sheltered beaches; the best are Porthmeor, on the northern side of town, and, facing east, Porthminster—the choice for those seeking more space to spread out.

GETTING HERE AND AROUND

St. Ives has good bus and train connections with Bristol, Exeter, and Penzance. Train journeys usually involve a change at St. Erth (the brief St. Erth–St. Ives stretch is one of the West Country's most scenic train routes). The adjacent bus and train stations are within a few minutes' walk of the center. Drivers should avoid the center—parking lots are well marked in the higher parts of town.

VISITOR INFORMATION Visit St. Ives Information Centre. ✉ *St. Ives Library, Gabriel St.* ☎ *01736/796297* ⊕ *www.stives-cornwall.co.uk* .

⦿ Sights

Barbara Hepworth Museum and Sculpture Garden

GARDEN | The studio and garden of Dame Barbara Hepworth (1903–75), who pioneered abstract sculpture in England, are now a museum and sculpture garden, managed by Tate St. Ives. The artist lived here for 26 years. ✉ *Trewyn Studio, Barnoon Hill* ☎ *01736/796226* ⊕ *www.tate.org.uk* ✄ *£7, £13 combined ticket with Tate St. Ives* ⊘ *Closed Mon. Nov.–Mar.*

★ Tate St. Ives

MUSEUM | The most spectacular branch of the renowned London gallery displays the work of artists who lived and worked in St. Ives, mostly from 1925 to 1975. The collection occupies a modernist building—a fantasia of seaside art deco-period architecture with panoramic views of the rippling ocean. Works of other international artists who influenced the St. Ives school—Picasso, Braque, and Mondrian among them—are exhibited alongside the local figures, and there are frequent exhibitions of contemporary art connected to West Cornwall. A four-story extension has significantly increased the exhibition space, and the rooftop café provides excellent food and views. ✉ *Porthmeor Beach* ☎ *01736/796226* ⊕ *www.tate.org.uk* ✄ *£9.50, £13 combined ticket with Barbara Hepworth Museum and Sculpture Garden* ⊘ *Closed Mon. Nov.–Mar.*

Restaurants

★ Gurnard's Head

$$ | MODERN BRITISH | This pub with bright, homey furnishings and a relaxed ambience looks past green fields to the ocean beyond. The frequently changing menu features fresh, inventively prepared meat and seafood dishes; look for spiced lamb parcel with harissa hummus, cucumber, and mint or red gurnard with tomato, anchovy, olive, and samphire—and leave room for some stupendous desserts. **Known for:** unusual dishes alongside old English favorites; remote coastal location; good set-price deals. ⑤ *Average main: £19* ✉ *B3306, near Zennor, Treen* ☎ *01736/796928* ⊕ *www.gurnardshead.co.uk.*

Porthminster Café

$$ | SEAFOOD | Unbeatable for its location alone—on the broad, golden sands of Porthminster Beach—this sleek, modern eatery prepares imaginative breakfasts, lunches, teas, and evening meals that you can savor while you

take in the marvelous vista across the bay. The accent is on Mediterranean and Asian seafood dishes, and typical choices include tuna sashimi, fried whole sea-bass with tempura prawns and a sweet and sour chili sauce, and seafood curry. **Known for:** beachside location; consistently high quality of food; famous seafood curry. ⑤ *Average main: £22* ✉ *Porthminster Beach* ☎ *01736/795352* ⊕ *www.porthminstercafe.co.uk.*

Hotels

★ Cornerways

$$ | B&B/INN | Everything in St. Ives seems squeezed into the tiniest of spaces, and this cottage B&B in the quiet Downalong quarter is no exception. **Pros:** friendly owners; tasteful decor; excellent breakfast choices. **Cons:** rooms are mostly small; narrow stairways to climb; very limited parking. ⑤ *Rooms from: £140* ✉ *1 Bethesda Pl.* ☎ *01736/796706* ⊕ *www.cornerwaysstives.co.uk* ▭ *No credit cards* ⌁ *6 rooms* ⦿| *Free breakfast.*

Land's End

17 miles southwest of St. Ives, 9 miles southwest of Penzance.

The coastal road, B3306, ends at the western tip of Britain at what is, quite literally, Land's End.

GETTING HERE AND AROUND
Frequent buses serve Land's End from Penzance (around one hour). There is no direct service from St. Ives in winter, but, in summer, an open-top double-decker tracks the coast between St. Ives and Penzance, taking in Land's End en route.

Sights

Land's End
VIEWPOINT | The sea crashes against the rocks at Land's End and lashes ships battling their way around the point.

■ **TIP→ Approach from one of the coastal footpaths for the best panoramic view.**
Over the years, sightseers have caused some erosion of the paths, but new ones are constantly being built, and Cornish "hedges" (granite walls covered with turf) have been planted to prevent erosion. The scenic grandeur of Land's End remains undiminished. The Land's End Hotel here is undistinguished, though the restaurant has good views. ✉ *Sennen.*

⚙ Activities

Sennen Cove
BEACHES | Located in the aptly named Whitesand Bay, Sennen Cove is a gorgeous expanse of creamy soft sand on the western tip of Cornwall. When the tide is coming in, the waves attract legions of surfers. When the tide's out, kids paddle in the tidal pools, and the sand stretches as far as you can see. Cafés are nearby, and surfing equipment is for rent on the beach. Sennen is off A30 less than 2 miles north of Land's End, and can be reached on foot on the South West Coast Path. **Amenities:** food and drink; lifeguards; parking (fee); toilets; water sports. **Best for:** sunset; surfing; swimming; walking. ✉ *Off A30, Whitesand Bay.*

Penzance

3 miles north of Mousehole, 1½ miles north of Newlyn, 10 miles south of St. Ives.

Superb views over Mount's Bay are one lure of this popular, unpretentious seaside resort. Even though it does get very crowded in summer, Penzance makes a good base for exploring the area. The town's isolated position has always made it vulnerable to attacks from the sea. During the 16th century, Spanish raiders destroyed most of the original town, and the majority of old buildings date from as late as the 18th century. The main street is Market Jew Street, a folk mistranslation of the Cornish expression Marghas Yow, which means "Thursday Market." Where Market Jew Street meets Causeway Head is Market House, an impressive, domed granite building constructed in 1837, with a statue of locally born chemist Humphry Davy in front.

In contrast to artsy St. Ives, Penzance is a no-nonsense working town. Though lacking the traffic-free lanes and quaint cottages of St. Ives, Penzance preserves pockets of handsome Georgian architecture.

GETTING HERE AND AROUND
The main train line from Plymouth terminates at Penzance, which is also served by National Express buses. Bus and train stations are next to each other at the east end of town. A car is an encumbrance here, so use one of the parking lots near the tourist office or the bus and train stations.

VISITOR INFORMATION Penzance Welcome Centre. ⊠ *Station Approach* ☎ *01736/335530* ⊕ *www.lovepenzance. co.uk.*

Sights

St. Michael's Mount
ISLAND | FAMILY | Rising out of Mount's Bay just off the coast, this spectacular granite-and-slate island is one of Cornwall's greatest natural attractions. The 14th-century castle perched at the highest point—200 feet above the sea—was built on the site of a Benedictine chapel founded by Edward the Confessor. In its time, the island has served as a church (Brittany's island abbey of Mont St. Michel was an inspiration), a fortress, and a private residence. The castle rooms you can tour include the Chevy Chase Room—a name probably associated with the Cheviot Hills or the French word *chevaux* (horses), after the hunting frieze that decorates the walls of this former monks' refectory. Family portraits include

works by Reynolds and Gainsborough. Don't miss the wonderful views from the castle battlements. Around the base of the rock are buildings from medieval to Victorian times, but they appear harmonious. Fascinating gardens surround the Mount, and many kinds of plants flourish in its microclimate.

To get to the island, walk the cobbled causeway from the village of Marazion or, when the tide is in, take the £2 ferry during summer or the £3 amphicraft in winter. There are pubs and restaurants in the village, but the island also has a café and restaurant. ■ TIP→ **Wear stout shoes for your visit, which requires a steep climb.** Visits may be canceled in severe weather. ⊠ *A394, Marazion* ✛ *3 miles east of Penzance* ☎ *01736/710265* ⊕ *www. stmichaelsmount.co.uk* ✍ *£17.50, castle only £11.50; garden only £8.50* ☉ *Closed Sat., Nov.–mid-Feb., and Thurs.–Sun. in late Feb.–mid-Mar.*

🎭 Performing Arts

Minack Theatre
THEATER | The open-air Minack Theatre perches high above a beach 3 miles southeast of Land's End and about 6 miles southwest of Penzance. The slope of the cliff forms a natural amphitheater, with bench seats on the terraces and the sea as a magnificent backdrop. Different companies present everything from classic dramas to modern comedies, as well as operas and concerts, on afternoons and evenings between late March and late September. An exhibition center tells the story of the theater's creation. Note that this center is closed afternoons when matinee performances are scheduled. ⊠ *Off B3315, Porthcurno* ☎ *01736/810181* ⊕ *www.minack.com* ✍ *Exhibition center £6, performances £12–£17.*

Lizard Peninsula

23 miles southeast of Penzance.

The southernmost point on mainland Britain, this peninsula is a government-designated Area of Outstanding Natural Beauty, named so for the rocky, dramatic coast rather than the flat and boring interior. The huge, eerily rotating dish antennae of the Goonhilly Satellite Earth Station are visible from the road as it crosses Goonhilly Downs, the backbone of the peninsula. There's no coast road, unlike Land's End, but the coastal path offers marvelous opportunities to explore on foot—and is often the only way to reach the best beaches. With no large town (Helston at the northern end is the biggest but isn't a tourist center), it's far less busy than the Land's End peninsula.

GETTING HERE AND AROUND

If you're driving, take A394 to reach Helston, gateway town to the Lizard Peninsula. From Helston, A3083 heads straight down to Lizard Point. Helston is the main public transport hub, but bus service to the villages is infrequent.

 Sights

Kynance Cove

BEACH—SIGHT | A path close to the tip of the peninsula plunges down 200-foot cliffs to this tiny cove dotted with a handful of pint-size islands. The sands here are reachable only during the 2½ hours before and after low tide. The peninsula's cliffs are made of greenish serpentine rock, interspersed with granite; souvenirs of the area are carved out of the stone. ⊠ *Lizard.*

Falmouth

8 miles northeast of Lizard Peninsula.

The bustle of this resort town's fishing harbor, yachting center, and commercial port only adds to its charm. In the 18th century, Falmouth was the main mail-boat port for North America, and in Flushing, a village across the inlet, you can see the slate-covered houses built by prosperous mail-boat captains. A ferry service now links the two towns. On Custom House Quay, off Arwenack Street, is the King's Pipe, an oven in which seized contraband was burned.

GETTING HERE AND AROUND

Falmouth can be reached from Truro on a branch rail line or by frequent bus service, and is also served by local and National Express buses from other towns. Running parallel to the seafront, the long, partly pedestrianized main drag links the town's main sights. Visitors to Pendennis Castle traveling by train should use Falmouth Docks Station, from which it's a short walk. Alternatively, drive or take a local bus to the castle to save legwork.

VISITOR INFORMATION Fal River Visitor Information Centre. ⊠ *Prince of Wales Pier, 11 Market Strand* ☎ *01326/741194* ⊕ *www.falmouth.co.uk.*

 Sights

National Maritime Museum Cornwall

MUSEUM | FAMILY | The granite-and-oak-clad structure by the harbor is an excellent place to come to grips with Cornish maritime heritage, weather lore, and navigational science. You can view approximately 30 of the collection of 140 or so boats, examine the tools associated with Cornish boatbuilders, and gaze down from the lighthouselike lookout, which is equipped with maps, telescopes, and binoculars. In the glass-fronted Tidal Zone below sea level, you come face-to-face with the sea itself. Between May and September, hour-long boat tours of the harbor and nearby coast depart from the museum three times daily. ■**TIP**→ **Buy museum tickets online for a 10% discount.** ⊠ *Discovery Quay* ☎ *01326/313388* ⊕ *www.nmmc.co.uk* 💷 *£14.50.*

★ Pendennis Castle

CASTLE/PALACE | FAMILY | At the end of its own peninsula stands this formidable castle, built by Henry VIII in the 1540s and improved by his daughter Elizabeth I. You can explore the defenses developed over the centuries. In the Royal Artillery Barracks, the Pendennis Unlocked exhibit explores the castle's history and its connection to Cornwall and England. The castle has sweeping views over the English Channel and across to St. Mawes Castle, designed as a companion fortress to guard the roads. There are free tours of the Half Moon Battery and regular performances, historical reenactments, and shows for kids. ⊠ *Pendennis Head* ☎ *01841/316594* ⊕ *www.english-heritage.org.uk* ⊠ *£10.90* ⊘ *Closed Mon. and Tues. in late Feb.–late Mar. and weekdays in Nov.–mid-Feb.*

 Restaurants

Rick Stein's Fish

$$ | SEAFOOD | Celebrity-chef Rick Stein has expanded his seafood empire to Falmouth, where this spruced-up takeaway and restaurant opposite the National Maritime Museum makes a welcome addition to the local dining scene. The hake, plaice, and haddock are grilled, fried to a golden hue, or charcoal roasted and served with salad. **Known for:** celebrity-chef status; down-to-earth ambience; perfect seafood including classic fish-and-chips. ⑤ *Average main: £16* ⊠ *Discovery Quay* ☎ *01841/532700* ⊕ *www.rickstein.com* ⊘ *No dinner Sun. and Mon. Oct.–Easter.*

 Hotels

St. Michaels Resort

$$ | HOTEL | A cool, contemporary ambience pervades this seaside hotel overlooking Falmouth Bay and fronted by a lush, subtropical garden. **Pros:** excellent facilities; good restaurants; attentive and amiable staff. **Cons:** spa facilities can be busy; cheapest rooms are small and viewless; some rooms are noisy. ⑤ *Rooms from: £191* ⊠ *Gyllyngvase Beach* ☎ *01326/312707* ⊕ *www.stmichaelshotel.co.uk* ⊅ *61 rooms* ❍ *Free breakfast.*

Fowey

25 miles northeast of St. Mawes.

Nestled in the mouth of a wooded estuary, Fowey (pronounced Foy) is still very much a working china-clay port as well as a focal point for the sailing fraternity. Increasingly, it's also a favored home of the rich and famous. Good and varied dining and lodging options abound, and these are most in demand during Regatta Week in mid- to late August and the annual Fowey Festival of Words and Music in mid-May. The Bodinnick and Polruan ferries take cars as well as foot passengers across the river for the coast road on to Looe.

A few miles west of Fowey are a pair of very different gardens: the Eden Project, a futuristic display of plants from around the world, and the Lost Gardens of Heligan, a revitalized reminder of the Victorian age.

GETTING HERE AND AROUND

Fowey isn't on any train line, but the town is served by frequent buses from St. Austell. Don't attempt to drive into the steep and narrow-lane town center, which is ideal for strolling around. Parking lots are signposted on the approach roads.

VISITOR INFORMATION Fowey Tourist Information. ⊕ *www.fowey.co.uk.*

 Sights

★ Eden Project

GARDEN | FAMILY | Spectacularly set in a former china-clay pit, this garden presents the world's major plant systems in microcosm. The crater contains more than 70,000 plants—many of them rare or endangered species—from three climate zones. Plants from the temperate zone are outdoors, and those from other zones are housed in hexagonally paneled geodesic domes. In the Mediterranean Biome, olive and citrus groves mix with cacti and other plants indigenous to warmer climates. The Rainforest Biome steams with heat, resounds to the gushing of a waterfall, and blooms with exotic flora; the elevated Canopy Walkway enables you to experience a monkey's-eye view of all of it. The emphasis is on conservation and ecology, but is free of any editorializing. A free shuttle helps the footsore, and well-informed guides provide information. An entertaining exhibition in the visitor center gives you the lowdown on the project, and the Core, an education center, provides amusement and instruction for children—if you can drag them away from the zipwire and giant swing. ■TIP→ **Buy tickets online at least a day before your visit for a discounted entry.** There are open-air concerts in summer and an ice-skating rink in winter. The Eden Project is 3 miles northeast of Charleston and 5 miles northwest of Fowey. There's frequent bus service from Fowey to St. Austell and from St. Austell train station to Eden. ⊠ *Bodelva Rd., off A30, A390, and A391, St. Austell* ☎ *01726/811911* ⊕ *www.edenproject. com* ☜ *£28.50; £24.50 if arriving by bike, on foot, or on public transport; £39.50 combined ticket with Lost Gardens of Heligan (available online in advance only)* ⊗ *Usually closed Mon. and Tues. Jan.–mid-Feb.*

Lost Gardens of Heligan

GARDEN | These sprawling grounds have something for all garden lovers, as well as an intriguing history. Begun by the Tremayne family in the late 18th century, they were rediscovered and spruced up in the early 1990s by former rock music producer Tim Smit (the force behind the Eden Project). In Victorian times the gardens displayed plants from around the British Empire. The Jungle area contains surviving plants from this era, including a lone Monterey pine, as well as giant redwood, clumps of bamboo, and a wobbly rope bridge crossing the subtropical valley. The Italian Garden and walled Flower Gardens are delightful, but don't overlook the fruit and vegetable gardens or Flora's Green, bordered by a ravine. It's easy to spend half a day here. Guided tours can be arranged for groups. ■**TIP→ Travel via St. Austell to avoid confusing country lanes, then follow signs to Mevagissey.** ⊠ *B3273, Pentewan* ☎ *01726/845100* ⊕ *www.heligan.com* ☜ *£15, £39.50 combined ticket with Eden Project (when bought online at least one day before visit).*

Restaurants

Sam's

$ | **AMERICAN** | **FAMILY** | This small and buzzing bistro has a rock-and-roll flavor, thanks to the walls adorned with posters of music icons. Diners squeeze onto benches and into booths to savor dishes made with local seafood, including a majestic bouillabaisse, or just a simple "Samburger". **Known for:** convivial atmosphere; best burgers in Cornwall; long waits for a table. ⑤ *Average main: £13* ⊠ *20 Fore St.* ☎ *01726/832273* ⊕ *www. samscornwall.co.uk.*

Hotels

St. Michaels Resort

$$ | **HOTEL** | A cool, contemporary ambience pervades this seaside hotel overlooking Falmouth Bay and fronted by a lush, subtropical garden. **Pros:** excellent facilities; good restaurants; attentive and amiable staff. **Cons:** spa facilities can be busy; cheapest rooms are small and viewless; some rooms are noisy. ⑤ *Rooms from: £191* ⊠ *Gyllyngvase Beach, Falmouth* ☎ *01326/312707* ⊕ *www.stmichaelshotel.co.uk* ⇄ *61 rooms* ⦿ *Free breakfast.*

Plymouth

48 miles southwest of Exeter, 124 miles southwest of Bristol, 240 miles southwest of London.

Devon's largest city has long been linked with England's commercial and maritime history. The Pilgrims sailed from here to the New World on the *Mayflower* in 1620. Although much of the city center was destroyed by air raids in World War II and has been rebuilt in an uninspiring style, there are worthwhile sights. A harbor tour is also a good way to see the city.

GETTING HERE AND AROUND

Frequent trains arrive from Bodmin, Penzance, and Exeter. From London Paddington, trains take three to four hours; Megabus and National Express buses from London's Victoria Coach Station take five or six hours. The train station is 1 mile north of the seafront, connected by frequent buses. Long-distance buses stop at the centrally located bus station off Royal Parade. Drivers can leave their cars in one of the numerous parking lots, including a couple right by the harbor. The seafront and central city areas are best explored on foot.

ESSENTIALS

VISITOR INFORMATION Plymouth Tourism Information Centre. ⊠ *Mayflower Museum, 3–5 The Barbican* ☎ *01752/306330* ⊕ *www.visitplymouth.co.uk.*

Sights

Mayflower Museum

MUSEUM | FAMILY | On three floors, this interactive exhibition narrates the story of Plymouth, from its beginnings as a fishing and trading port to the modern industrial city it is today. Along the way, you'll take in the stories of various expeditions that embarked from here to the New World, including the *Mayflower* itself. The city's tourist office is also in this building. ⊠ *3–5 The Barbican* ☎ *01752/306330.*

⊕ *www.visitplymouth.co.uk* 🖾 *£3.50* 🕙 *Closed Sun. Nov.–Mar.*

Plymouth Gin Distillery

WINERY/DISTILLERY | At the Black Friars Distillery, Plymouth's most famous export, gin, has been distilled since 1793. You can purchase bottles of sloe gin, damson liqueur, fruit cup, or the fiery "Navy Strength" gin that traditionally was issued to the Royal Navy. Learn the full story on walking tours around the distillery, ending with a sampling in the wood-paneled Refectory Bar. The building originally housed a friary and was where the Pilgrims spent their last night on English soil in 1620. ⊠ *Black Friars Distillery, 60 Southside St.* ☎ *01752/665292* ⊕ *www.plymouthgin.com* 🚶 *Tours £12.50–£55.*

Saltram

HOUSE | An exquisite 18th-century home with many of its original furnishings, Saltram was built around the remains of a late-Tudor mansion. Its jewel is one of Britain's grandest neoclassical rooms—a vast, double-cube salon designed by Robert Adam and hung with paintings by Sir Joshua Reynolds, first president of the Royal Academy of Arts, who was born nearby in 1723. Fine plasterwork adorns many rooms, and three have original Chinese wallpaper. The outstanding garden includes rare trees and shrubs, and there's a restaurant and a cafeteria. Saltram is 3½ miles east of Plymouth city center. ⊠ *South of A38, Plympton* ☎ *01752/333500* ⊕ *www.nationaltrust. org.uk* 🖾 *£12.80* 🕙 *House may close for a few weeks in Jan. and Nov.*

Restaurants

Quay 33

$$ | MODERN BRITISH | Fresh seafood landed at the nearby quays, such as sea bass and hake, features high on the menu at this Barbican eatery, but you will also find pastas, risottos, steaks, and slow-cooked duck-leg confit. Exmouth mussels or

Plymouth, Exeter, and South Devon

grilled scallops make an ideal light lunch, while desserts include crème brûlée and housemade cheesecake. **Known for:** first-class service; creative and delicious food; tasty desserts. $ *Average main: £16* ✉ *33 Southside St.* ☎ *01752/229345* ⊕ *www.quay33.co.uk* ⊙ *Closed Sun.*

 Hotels

Boringdon Hall Hotel
$$ | HOTEL | One of the foremost manor houses in the West Country during Tudor times, this battlemented pile oozes historic character. **Pros:** country house splendor; quality restaurant; luxury spa facilities. **Cons:** cheaper rooms are very ordinary; no elevator; remote from Plymouth's center. $ *Rooms from: £146* ✉ *Colebrook* ☎ *01752/546196* ⊕ *www. boringdonhall.co.uk* 🛏 *42 rooms* ❙○❙ *Free breakfast.*

Dartmoor National Park

10 miles north of Plymouth, 13 miles west of Exeter.

Devon presents no greater contrast to the country's quaint and picturesque image than the bleak, deserted expanses of Dartmoor. Southern England's greatest natural wilderness is largely a treeless landscape of sometimes alarming emptiness, though it also harbors surprises in the form of hidden lakes, abandoned quarries, and the dramatically wind-sculpted tors, or craggy peaks, that puncture the horizon in every direction. Sudden mists and above-average rainfall levels add to the simultaneously inhospitable and alluring scene.

GETTING HERE AND AROUND

Public transport services are extremely sparse on Dartmoor, making a car indispensable for anywhere off the beaten track. The peripheral towns of Okehampton and Tavistock are well served by bus from Exeter and Plymouth, and Chagford also has direct connections to Exeter, but central Princetown has only sporadic links with the outside world.

ESSENTIALS

VISITOR INFORMATION National Park Visitor Centre. ✉ *Tavistock Rd., Princetown* ☎ *01822/890414* ⊕ *www.dartmoor.gov.uk.*

Sights

Dartmoor National Park

NATIONAL/STATE PARK | Even on a summer's day, the brooding hills of this sprawling wilderness appear a likely haunt for such monsters as the hound of the Baskervilles, and it seems entirely fitting that Sir Arthur Conan Doyle set his Sherlock Holmes thriller in this landscape. Sometimes the wet, peaty wasteland of Dartmoor National Park vanishes in rain and mist, although in clear weather you can see north to Exmoor, south over the English Channel, and west far into Cornwall. Much of Dartmoor consists of open heath and moorland, unspoiled by roads—wonderful walking and horseback-riding territory but an easy place to lose your bearings. Dartmoor's earliest inhabitants left behind stone monuments and burial mounds that help you envision prehistoric man roaming these pastures. Ponies, sheep, and birds are the main animals to be seen.

Several villages scattered along the borders of this 368-square-mile reserve—one-third of which is owned by Prince Charles—make useful bases for hiking excursions. Accommodations include simple inns and some elegant havens. **Okehampton** is a main gateway, and **Chagford** is a good base for exploring north Dartmoor. Other scenic spots include **Buckland-in-the-Moor,** a hamlet with thatch-roof cottages; **Widecombe-in-the-Moor,** whose church is known as the Cathedral of the Moor; and **Grimspound,** the Bronze Age site featured in Conan Doyle's most famous tale. Transmoor Link buses connect many of Dartmoor's towns and villages. The **National Park Visitor Centre** in Princetown is a good place to start your trip, as are centers in Postbridge and Haytor. You can also pick up information in Ivybridge, Ashburton, Okehampton, Moretonhampstead, Bovey Tracey, Tavistock, and Buckfastleigh. ✉ *National Park Visitor Centre, Tavistock Rd., Princetown* ☎ *01822/890414* ⊕ *www.dartmoor.gov.uk.*

Activities

Hiking is extremely popular in Dartmoor National Park. The areas around Widgery Cross, Becky Falls, and the Bovey Valley, as well as the short but dramatic walk along Lydford Gorge, have wide appeal, as do the many valleys around the southern edge of the moors. Guided hikes, typically costing £3 to £8, are available through the park's visitor information centers. Reservations are usually not necessary. Longer hikes in the bleak, less-populated regions—for example, the tors south of Okehampton—are appropriate only for most experienced walkers. Dartmoor is a great area for horseback riding; many towns have stables for guided rides.

Tavistock and Around

13 miles north of Plymouth.

On the River Tavy, the ancient town of Tavistock historically owed its importance to its Benedictine abbey (dissolved by Henry VIII in the 16th century) and to its status as a stannary town, where tin was weighed, stamped, and assessed. Today the town of 11,000 preserves a prosperous, predominantly Victorian appearance, especially at the bustling indoor Pannier Market off central Bedford Square. Tavistock makes a useful base for exploring a scattering of nearby sights—Buckland Abbey, Cotehele House, and Morwellham Quay—and for touring Dartmoor's western reaches.

GETTING HERE AND AROUND

Tavistock, on A386 and A390, is easily accessed via the frequent buses from Plymouth, which take about an hour. You'll need your own transportation to visit the attractions scattered around it, however.

Sights

Cotehele House and Quay

HOUSE | About 4 miles west of Buckland Abbey and 9 miles southwest of Tavistock, Cotehele House and Quay was formerly a busy port on the River Tamar, but it is now usually visited for the well-preserved, atmospheric late-medieval manor, home of the Edgcumbe family for centuries. The house has original furniture, tapestries, embroideries, and armor, and you can also visit the impressive gardens, a quay museum, and a restored mill (usually in operation on Sunday and Thursday—call for other days). A limited number of visitors are allowed per day, so arrive early and be prepared to wait during busy periods. Choose a bright day, because the rooms have no electric light. Shops, crafts studios, a gallery, and a restaurant provide other diversions. ■ TIP➔ Take advantage of the shuttle bus that runs every half hour between the house, quay, and mill. ✉ Off A390, St. Dominick ☎ 01579/351346 ⊕ www.nationaltrust. org.uk ✍ £12.80, £8.80 Jan.–early Mar. ⊘ Restricted access and mill closed Nov.–Dec.

Restaurants

★ The Horn of Plenty

$$$$ | MODERN BRITISH | The restaurant within this Georgian house has magnificent views across the wooded, rhododendron-filled Tamar Valley and a sophisticated menu featuring traditional British cuisine with French and Asian elements. A typical starter and main course might be seared scallops with cauliflower, cumin, and mango followed by Creedy Carver duck with baby leeks and Jerusalem artichokes, while desserts include warm rum baba with marinated pineapple, banana, and coconut. **Known for:** extravagant and exceptional fine dining; stunning views; affordable potluck set-menu on Monday night. ⑤ *Average main: £52.50* ✉ *A390, Gulworthy* ☎ *01822/832528* ⊕ *www.thehornofplenty.co.uk.*

Hotels

★ Hotel Endsleigh

$$$ | HOTEL | Under the auspices of hotelier Olga Polizzi, the Endsleigh has risen to be one of the country's best-loved hotels, nestled in a fold of the Tamar Valley with the river itself rolling serenely by at the bottom of the garden. **Pros:** elegant without being pompous; discreet but ever-present staff; beautiful rural setting. **Cons:** few leisure facilities; a bit rickety in places; remote location. ⑤ *Rooms from: £295* ✉ *Milton Abbot* ☎ *01822/870000* ⊕ *www.hotelendsleigh.com* ⤸ *19 rooms* ❚◯❚ *Free breakfast.*

Lydford

7 miles north of Tavistock, 24 miles north of Plymouth.

The sequestered hamlet of Lydford packs a lot into a small area: there's the dramatic scenery of the gorge just outside the village, the remains of a medieval castle, and some attractive options for eating and sleeping. The Granite Way cycle and walking track, much of it running along a disused railway route, connects Lydford with Okehampton.

GETTING HERE AND AROUND

The gorge is easily accessed on Stagecoach South West buses from Plymouth to Tavistock, then Dartline Coaches to Lydford, and on Dartline Coaches from Okehampton (connected to Exeter). By car, take A386 between Tavistock and Okehampton.

Sights

★ Lydford Gorge

NATURE SITE | The River Lyd carved a spectacular 1½-mile-long chasm through the rock at Lydford Gorge, outside the pretty village of Lydford, midway between Okehampton and Tavistock. Two paths follow the gorge past gurgling whirlpools and waterfalls with evocative names such as the Devil's Cauldron and the White Lady Waterfall. ■ **TIP→ Sturdy footwear is recommended.** Although the walk can be quite challenging, the paths can still get congested during busy periods. Two tearooms are open early March through October. In winter, access is restricted to the waterfall and the top of the gorge. ⊠ *Off A386, Lydford* ☎ *01822/820320* ⊕ *www.nationaltrust.org.uk* ⊠ *£10.50; £5 in winter.*

Restaurants

Dartmoor Inn

$$ | MODERN BRITISH | Locals and visitors alike make a beeline for this gastro-pub in a 16th-century building with a number of small dining spaces done in spare, contemporary country style. The elegantly presented dishes may include dry-aged moorland sirloin in a peppercorn sauce, beer-battered hake, or venison with celeriac, cavolo nero, and quince. **Known for:** cozy ambience; fresh, locally sourced food; affordable lunch menu. ⑤ *Average main: £18* ⊠ *Moorside, on A386, Lydford* ☎ *01822/820221* ⊕ *www.dartmoorinn. com.*

Hotels

Castle Inn

$ | B&B/INN | In the heart of Lydford village, this 16th-century inn sits next to Lydford Castle. **Pros:** antique character; tasty pub food; peaceful rural setting. **Cons:** shabby in places; some small rooms; occasionally sloping floors and low ceilings. ⑤ *Rooms from: £75* ⊠ *School Rd., off A386, Lydford* ☎ *01822/820242* ⊕ *www.castleinnlydford.com* ⇨ *9 rooms* ⑩ *Free breakfast.*

★ Lewtrenchard Manor

$$ | HOTEL | Paneled rooms, stone fireplaces, leaded-glass windows, and handsome gardens outfit this spacious 1620 manor house on the northwestern edge of Dartmoor. **Pros:** beautiful Jacobean setting; conscientious service; outstanding food. **Cons:** rooms in outbuildings have less atmosphere; restaurant service sometimes slow; not very child-friendly. ⑤ *Rooms from: £180* ⊠ *Off A30, Lewdown* ☎ *01566/464077* ⊕ *www.lewtrenchard.co.uk* ⇨ *14 rooms* ⑩ *Free breakfast.*

Chagford

9 miles southeast of Okehampton, 30 miles northeast of Plymouth.

Once a tin-weighing station, Chagford was an area of fierce fighting between the Roundheads and the Cavaliers during the English Civil War. Although officially a "town" since 1305, Chagford is more of a village, with taverns grouped around a seasoned old church and a curious "pepper-pot" market house on the site of the old Stannary Court. With a handful of cafés and shops to browse around, it makes a convenient base from which to explore north Dartmoor.

GETTING HERE AND AROUND

Infrequent local buses connect Chagford with Okehampton and Exeter (except on Sunday, when there's no service). The village is off A382; a car or bicycle is the best way to see its far-flung sights.

Sights

Castle Drogo

CASTLE/PALACE | Northeast of Chagford, this castle looks like a stout medieval fortress, complete with battlements, but construction actually took place between 1910 and 1930. Designed by noted architect Sir Edwin Lutyens for Julius Drewe, a wealthy grocer, the castle is only half finished (funds ran out). Inside, medieval grandeur is combined with early-20th-century comforts, and there are awesome views over Dartmoor's Teign Valley. The grounds are well worth a prolonged wander, with paths leading down to the river at Fingle Bridge. Turn off the A30 Exeter–Okehampton road at Whiddon Down to reach the castle. ⊠ *Off A30 and A382, Drewsteignton* ☎ *01647/433306* ⊕ *www.nationaltrust. org.uk* ☜ *£12.80* ⊗ *Castle closed Nov. and late Dec.–Feb.*

Devon Guild of Craftsmen

MUSEUM | One of the Southwest's most important contemporary arts and crafts centers, the Devon Guild is in a converted 19th-century coach house in the village of Bovey Tracey, 10 miles southeast of Chagford and 14 miles southwest of Exeter. The center has excellent exhibitions of local, national, and international crafts, as well as a shop and café. ⊠ *Riverside Mill, Fore St., Bovey Tracey* ☎ *01626/832223* ⊕ *www. crafts.org.uk* ☜ *Free.*

Restaurants

★ Gidleigh Park

$$$$ | **MODERN BRITISH** | One of England's foremost country-house hotels, Gidleigh Park occupies an enclave of landscaped gardens and streams, reached via a lengthy, winding country lane and private drive at the edge of Dartmoor. The extremely pricey contemporary restaurant, directed by chef Chris Ede, has been showered with culinary awards. **Known for:** top-notch dining experience; prix-fixe menus with multicourse options; excellent wine menu. ⑤ *Average main: £125* ⊠ *Gidleigh Park* ☎ *01647/432367* ⊕ *www.gidleigh.co.uk.*

Hotels

★ Bovey Castle

$$ | **HOTEL** | **FAMILY** | With the grandeur of a country estate and the amenities of a modern hotel, Bovey Castle, built in 1906 for Viscount Hambledon, has it all. **Pros:** baronial splendor; range of activities; good for families. **Cons:** spa facilities not always up to expectations; overpriced drinks and extras; remote location. ⑤ *Rooms from: £184* ⊠ *Off B3212, North Bovey* ☎ *01647/445000* ⊕ *www.bovey-castle.com* ⟿ *82 rooms* ⫶○⫶ *No meals.*

Exeter

18 miles east of Chagford, 48 miles northeast of Plymouth, 85 miles southwest of Bristol, 205 miles southwest of London.

Exeter has been the capital of the region since the Romans established a fortress here 2,000 years ago, and evidence of the Roman occupation remains in the city walls. Although it was heavily bombed in 1942, Exeter retains much of its medieval character, as well as examples of the gracious architecture of the 18th and 19th centuries. It's convenient to both Torquay and Dartmoor.

GETTING HERE AND AROUND

Once- or twice-hourly train service from London Paddington takes about 2¼ hours; the less frequent service from London Waterloo via Salisbury takes just under 3½ hours. From London's Victoria Coach Station, National Express buses leave every two hours, and Megabus has four daily departures, all taking between

4½ and 5¼ hours. With its own airport, Exeter is a major transportation hub for Devon. Trains from Bristol, Salisbury, and Plymouth stop at Exeter St. David's and connect to the center by frequent buses. Some trains also stop at the more useful Exeter Central. The bus station is off Paris Street near the tourist office. Cars are unnecessary in town, so park yours as soon as possible—all the sights are within an easy walk.

ESSENTIALS

VISITOR INFORMATION Exeter Visitor Information and Tickets. ⊠ *Dix's Field* ☎ *01392/665700* ⊕ *www.visitexeter.com.*

◉ Sights

★ Cathedral of St. Peter

RELIGIOUS SITE | At the heart of Exeter, the great Gothic cathedral was begun in 1275 and completed almost a century later. Its twin towers are even older survivors of an earlier Norman cathedral. Rising from a forest of ribbed columns, the nave's 300-foot stretch of unbroken Gothic vaulting is the longest in the world. Myriad statues, tombs, and memorial plaques adorn the interior. In the minstrels' gallery, high up on the left of the nave, stands a group of carved figures singing and playing musical instruments, including bagpipes. Guided tours of the interior (up to four a day Monday through Saturday), roof, chapel, garden, and precinct are available, as are audio tours. Outside in Cathedral Close, don't miss Mol's Coffee House at No. 1 (now a gift shop), whose half-timber facade bearing the coat of arms of Elizabeth I is redolent of bygone times, and the 400-year-old door to No. 10, the bishop of Crediton's house, is ornately carved with angels' and lions' heads. ⊠ *Cathedral Close* ☎ *01392/285983* ⊕ *www.exeter-cathedral.org.uk* ☜ *£7.50, cathedral tours free, audio tours £2.50, other tours £14 (including admission).*

Guildhall

GOVERNMENT BUILDING | On the city's main shopping street, this is said to be the oldest municipal building in the country still in use. The current hall, with its Renaissance portico, dates from 1330, although a guildhall has occupied this site since at least 1160. The walls are adorned with imposing portraits of royal figures and noteworthy locals, and its timber-braced roof, one of the earliest in England, dates from about 1460. ⊠ *High St.* ☎ *01392/665500* ⊕ *www.exeter.gov. uk* ☜ *Free* ⊙ *Closed Sun. and during municipal functions.*

★ Royal Albert Memorial Museum

MUSEUM | FAMILY | This family-friendly museum is housed in a recently refurbished Victorian building. The centerpiece is the extensive Making History gallery, a giddy mix of objects imaginatively illustrating the city's history and covering everything from Roman pottery to memorabilia from World War II. The geology section is thrillingly enhanced by the latest video technology, and there are also excellent ethnography and archaeological collections, natural-history displays, and works by West Country artists. ⊠ *Queen St.* ☎ *01392/265858* ⊕ *www.rammuseum.org.uk* ☜ *Free* ⊙ *Closed Mon.*

Underground Passages

ARCHAEOLOGICAL SITE | FAMILY | Exeter's Underground Passages, which once served as conduits for fresh water, are the only medieval vaulted passages open to the public in Britain. They date to the mid-14th century, although some were enlarged by the Victorians. An exhibition and video precede the 25-minute guided tour. Many of the passages are narrow and low: be prepared to stoop. The tours often sell out during school vacations, so come early. Children under five are not permitted in the tunnels. ⊠ *2 Paris St.* ☎ *01392/665887* ⊕ *www.exeter.gov.uk* ☜ *£7* ⊙ *Closed Mon. Oct.–May.*

🍴 Restaurants

Lympstone Manor

$$$$ | MODERN BRITISH | Exeter-born master chef Michael Caines has breathed new life into this elegant Georgian mansion overlooking the Exe estuary 5 miles south of Exeter, where he has installed three separate dining rooms to showcase his highly original recipes. The wow-factor starts the moment you arrive, with unforgettable estuary views forming a fitting prelude to the gastronomic feast to follow. **Known for:** fabulous location; stylishly presented and eclectic gourmet cuisine; frequently changing fixed-price menus and multicourse tasting menus. ⑤ *Average main: £140* ⊠ *Courtlands La., Exmouth* ☎ *01395/202040* ⊕ *www. lympstonemanor.co.uk.*

Ship Inn

$ | BRITISH | Here you can lift a tankard of stout in the very rooms where Sir Francis Drake and Sir Walter Raleigh enjoyed their ale. The pub dishes out casual bar fare, from sandwiches to grills and steak and ale pie, either in the bar or in the beamed and paneled upstairs restaurant. **Known for:** famous former patrons; traditional English pub fare; lively and welcoming environment. ⑤ *Average main: £9* ⊠ *1–3 St. Martin's La.* ☎ *01392/272040* ⊕ *www.greeneking-pubs.co.uk.*

🛏 Hotels

★ Hotel du Vin

$ | HOTEL | This former hospital has been reimagined as a modish hotel with a zippy, happening vibe and add-ons that include a heated indoor-outdoor pool, a fitness room, and spa treatments. **Pros:** contemporary style; great food; nice wellness facilities. **Cons:** rooms on the small side; tiny gym and pool; limited parking. ⑤ *Rooms from: £115* ⊠ *Magdalen St.* ☎ *0330/016–0391* ⊕ *www.hotelduvin. com* ⟿ *59 rooms* ⦿ *Free breakfast.*

The Pig-at Combe

$$ | HOTEL | Rolling parkland surrounds this stately Elizabethan manor house, which is 16 miles east of Exeter and has been converted into a hipster retreat run with energy and enthusiasm. **Pros:** beautiful rural surroundings; relaxed ambience; attentive but informal staff. **Cons:** rather remote; defiantly untraditional; crowded tables in restaurant. ⑤ *Rooms from: £199* ⊠ *Off A30, Gittisham* ☎ *01404/540400* ⊕ *www.thepighotel. com* ⟿ *30 rooms* ⦿ *No meals.*

★ Raffles

$ | B&B/INN | A 10-minute walk from the center, this quirky B&B in a quiet neighborhood makes an ideal base for a night or two in town. **Pros:** peaceful location; plenty of character; great breakfasts. **Cons:** single room is small; parking costs £5; no elevator. ⑤ *Rooms from: £95* ⊠ *11 Blackall Rd.* ☎ *01392/270200* ⊕ *www. raffles-exeter.co.uk* ⟿ *6 rooms* ⦿ *Free breakfast.*

🛍 Shopping

Some of Exeter's most interesting shops are along Gandy Street, off the main High Street drag, with several good food and clothes outlets. Exeter was the silver-assay office for the West Country, and the earliest example of Exeter silver (now a museum piece) dates from 1218; Victorian pieces are still sold. The Exeter assay mark is three castles.

Totnes

8 miles west of Torquay, 28 miles southwest of Exeter.

This busy market town on the banks of the River Dart preserves plenty of its medieval past, and, on summer Tuesdays, vendors dress in period costume for the Elizabethan Market. Market days are Friday and Saturday, when the town's status as a center of alternative medicine and culture becomes especially clear, and on the third Sunday of the month, when there's a local produce market on Civic Square. The historic buildings include a guildhall and St. Mary's Church.

GETTING HERE AND AROUND

Totnes is on a regular fast bus route between Plymouth and Torbay and is a stop for main-line trains between Plymouth and Exeter. Buses pull into the center, and the train station is a few minutes' walk north of the center. Drivers should take A38 and A385 from Plymouth or A385 from Torbay.

ESSENTIALS

VISITOR INFORMATION Visit Totnes.
01803/411183 Telephone service available Apr.–Oct. ⊕ www.visittotnes.co.uk.

Sights

Brixham

TOWN | At the southern point of Tor Bay, Brixham has kept much of its original charm, partly because it still has an active fishing harbor. Much of the catch goes straight to restaurants as far away as London. Sample fish-and-chips on the quayside, where there's a (surprisingly petite) full-scale reproduction of the vessel on which Sir Francis Drake circumnavigated the world. The village is 10 miles southeast of Totnes by A385 and A3022. *Brixham.*

South Devon Railway

TRANSPORTATION SITE (AIRPORT/BUS/ FERRY/TRAIN) | **FAMILY** | Steam trains of this railway run through 7 miles of the wooded Dart Valley between Totnes and Buckfastleigh, on the edge of Dartmoor. Call about special trips around Christmas. ■**TIP→** **Keep your train tickets to receive discounts at local English Heritage sites.** *Dart Bridge Rd., Buckfastleigh 01364/644370 ⊕ www.southdevon-railway.co.uk £16 round-trip ☉ Closed Nov., part of Dec., Jan., most of Feb., and early Mar.*

Hotels

★ **Royal Seven Stars Hotel**

$ | **HOTEL** | Conveniently located at the bottom of the main street, this centuries-old coaching inn has counted Daniel Defoe and Edward VII among its former guests. **Pros:** central location; friendly staff; spotless rooms. **Cons:** standard accommodations and bathrooms are small; rooms over bars can be noisy; busy public areas. *$ Rooms from: £120 The Plains 01803/862125 ⊕ www. royalsevenstars.co.uk 21 rooms ❍ Free breakfast.*

Dartmouth

13 miles southeast of Totnes, 35 miles east of Plymouth, 35 miles south of Exeter, 5 miles southwest of Brixham.

An important port in the Middle Ages, Dartmouth is today a favorite haunt of yacht owners. Traces of its past include the old houses in Bayard's Cove at the bottom of Lower Street, where the *Mayflower* made a stop in 1620, the 16th-century covered Butterwalk, and the two castles guarding the entrance to the River Dart. The Royal Naval College, built in 1905, dominates the heights above the town. A few miles south of Dartmouth on Start Bay there are a number of pretty beaches including Blackpool Sands, popular with families.

GETTING HERE AND AROUND

Frequent buses connect Dartmouth with Plymouth and Totnes. Drivers coming from the west should follow A381 and A3122. Approaching from the Torbay area via A3022 and A379, you can save mileage by using the passenger and car ferries crossing the Dart. Travelers on foot can take advantage of a vintage steam train service operating between Paignton and Kingswear, where there are ferry connections with Dartmouth. River ferries also link Dartmouth with Totnes.

ESSENTIALS

VISITOR INFORMATION Dartmouth Visitor Centre. ⊠ *The Engine House, Mayors Ave.* ☎ *01803/834224* ⊕ *www.discoverdartmouth.com.*

⊙ Sights

Greenway

HOUSE | A rewarding way to experience the River Dart is to join a cruise from Dartmouth's quay to visit Greenway, the 16th-century riverside home of the Gilbert family (Sir Humphrey Gilbert claimed Newfoundland on behalf of Elizabeth I), more famous today for its association with the crime writer Agatha Christie. Mrs. Mallowan (Christie's married name) made it her holiday home beginning in 1938, and the house displays collections of archaeological finds, china, and silver. The gorgeous gardens are thickly planted with magnolias, camellias, and rare shrubs and are richly endowed with panoramic views. Beware, however, that the grounds are steeply laid out, and those arriving by boat face a daunting uphill climb. Allow three hours to see everything; in busy periods, timed tickets for the house are given on arrival. Parking spaces here are restricted and must be booked in advance. Alternatively, ask at the tourist office about walking and cycling routes to reach the house, as well as about the bus service from Greenway Halt (a stop on the Dartmouth Steam Railway). A round-trip ticket between Dartmouth and Greenway costs £9.50 on the Greenway Ferry (⊕ *www.greenway-ferry.co.uk*). ⊠ *Greenway Rd., Galmpton* ☎ *01803/842382* ⊕ *www.nationaltrust.org.uk* ⊡ *£12.80* ⊗ *Closed Jan.–early Feb., and weekdays early Nov.–late Dec.*

⊙ Restaurants

The Seahorse

$$$ | SEAFOOD | In a prime riverside location, this seafood restaurant epitomizes the region's ongoing food revolution. The knowledgeable staff guides diners through the Italian-inspired menu, which primarily depends on the day's catch: look for scallops with garlic and white port, *zuppa di pescatore* (seafood soup), or Dover sole or gurnard grilled over charcoal with rosemary. **Known for:** relaxed and convivial atmosphere; good set-price menus; charming and attentive staff. *Average main: £30* ⊠ *5 S. Embankment* ☎ *01803/835147* ⊕ *www.seahorserestaurant.co.uk* ⊗ *Closed Sun. and Mon.*

⊟ Hotels

★ Royal Castle Hotel

$ | HOTEL | Part of Dartmouth's historic waterfront (and consequently a hub of activity), this hotel has truly earned the name "Royal"—several monarchs have slept here. **Pros:** historical resonance; superb central location; professional staff. **Cons:** some cheaper rooms are nondescript; many steps, no elevator; noise intrusion in some rooms. ⑤ *Rooms from: £115* ⊠ *11 The Quay* ☎ *01803/833033* ⊕ *www.royalcastle.co.uk* ⇆ *24 rooms* ⏐○⏐ *No meals.*

Chapter 8

BATH, THE COTSWOLDS, AND STRATFORD-UPON-AVON

Updated by Sophie Ibbotson
and Sally Coffey

8

☉ Sights	🍴 Restaurants	🛏 Hotels	🛍 Shopping	🍸 Nightlife
★★★★☆	★★★★☆	★★★★☆	★★★★☆	★★☆☆☆

WELCOME TO BATH, THE COTSWOLDS, AND STRATFORD-UPON-AVON

TOP REASONS TO GO

★ **Bath's architecture:** Bath is perhaps the most perfectly preserved and harmonious English city. Close up, the elegance and finesse of the Georgian buildings is a perpetual delight.

★ **Roman baths:** Take a break from Bath's Georgian elegance and return to its Roman days on a tour around this ancient bath complex.

★ **Shakespeare in Stratford:** To see a play by Shakespeare in the town where he was born—and perhaps after you've visited his birthplace or other sights—is a magical experience.

★ **Hidcote Manor Garden:** In a region rich with imaginative garden displays, Hidcote lays good claim to eminence. Exotic shrubs from around the world and the famous "garden rooms" are the highlights of this Arts and Crafts masterpiece.

★ **Perfect villages:** With their stone cottages, Cotswold villages tend to be improbably picturesque; the hamlets of Upper and Lower Slaughter are among the most charming.

1 Bath. Home to the famous Roman baths.

2 Castle Combe. The prettiest village in England.

3 Lacock. A charming village.

4 Cheltenham. A hub of the Cotswolds.

5 Broadway. The ultimate Cotswold village.

6 Chipping Camden. A beautiful town.

7 Stow-on-the-Wold. The highest town in the Cotswolds.

8 Bourton-on-the-Water. A classic village.

9 Lower Slaughter and Upper Slaughter. Two quieter villages.

10 Burford. A village known for antiques.

11 Bibury. A small village.

12 Cirencester. The area's largest market town.

13 Painswick. A picture-postcard town.

14 Tetbury. Home to Prince Charles's country house.

15 Stratford-upon-Avon. Shakespeare's famous hometown.

16 Henley-in-Arden. A sleepy village.

17 Warwick. Home to a historic castle.

18 Kenilworth Castle. A romantic ruined castle.

The rolling uplands of the Cotswolds represent all the beauty and charm rural England has to offer, as immortalized in countless books, paintings, and films.

In eloquently named settlements from Bourton-on-the-Water to Stow-on-the-Wold, you can taste the glories of the old English village—its stone slate roofs, low-ceiling rooms, and gardens; the atmosphere is as thick as honey, and equally as sweet. On the edge of the Cotswolds is Bath, among the most alluring small cities in Europe, and nothing evokes the England of the imagination more vividly than Stratford-upon-Avon, birthplace of perhaps the nation's most famous son, William Shakespeare.

Bath rightly boasts of being the best-planned town in England. Although the Romans founded the city when they discovered here the only true hot springs in England, its popularity during the 17th and 18th centuries luckily coincided with one of Britain's most creative architectural eras. Today people come to walk in the footsteps of Jane Austen, visit Bath Abbey and the excavated Roman baths, shop in an elegant setting, or have a modern spa experience at the stunning Thermae spa.

North of Bath are the Cotswolds—a region that more than one writer has called the very soul of England. This idyllic region, which from medieval times grew prosperous on the wool trade, remains a vision of rural England. Here are time-defying churches, sleepy hamlets, sequestered ancient farmsteads, and such fabled abodes as Sudeley Castle. The Cotswolds can hardly claim to be undiscovered, but the area's poetic appeal has survived the tour buses and gift shops.

Visits to Strartford-upon-Avon, William Shakespeare's birthplace, and the surrounding areas yield insights into the great playwright's life and inspirations. The sculpted, rolling farmland of Warwickshire may look nothing like the forested countryside of the 16th century, but plenty of sturdy Tudor buildings that Shakespeare knew survive to this day (including his birthplace). There's beauty in this—but also the possibility of tourist overkill. Stratford itself, with its Shakespeare sites and the theaters of the Royal Shakespeare Company, sometimes can get to feel like "Shakespeare World." And while Shakespeare himself would recognize plenty of the ancient, timber-framed buildings that line the main shopping streets, the same cannot be said of the bland, cookie-cutter chain stores that occupy most of these buildings today. Still, there's much more to see—magnificent castles, pastoral churches, and gentle countryside—in this famously lovely part of England. Stop in at Charlecote Park, a grand Elizabethan manor house, and moated Baddesley Clinton, a superb example of late-medieval domestic architecture. The huge fortresses of Warwick Castle and Kenilworth Castle provide glimpses into the past.

MAJOR REGIONS

Bath and Nearby. On the eastern edge of the county of Somerset, the city of Bath has strong links with the Cotswolds stretching north, the source of the wool that for centuries underpinned its economy. The stone mansions and cottages of that region are recalled in Bath's Georgian architecture and in the mellow stone that it shares with two of the villages across the Wiltshire border, Lacock and Castle Combe.

The Cotswolds. A gently undulating area of limestone uplands, the Cotswolds are among England's best-preserved rural districts, and the quiet but lovely grays and ambers of the stone buildings here are truly unsurpassed. Much has been written about the area's age-mellowed towns, but the architecture of the villages actually differs little from that of villages elsewhere in England. Their distinction lies in their surroundings: the valleys are lush and rolling, and cozy hamlets appear covered in foliage from church tower to garden gate. Beyond the town limits, you can explore, on foot or by car, the "high wild hills and rough uneven ways" that Shakespeare wrote about.

Over the centuries, quarries of honey-color stone have yielded building blocks for many Cotswold houses and churches and have transformed little towns into realms of gold. Make Chipping Campden or Stow-on-the-Wold your headquarters and wander for a few days. Then ask yourself what the area is all about. Its secret seems shared by two things—sheep and stone. These were once the great sheep-rearing areas of England, and during the peak of prosperity in the Middle Ages, Cotswold wool was in demand far and wide. This made the local merchants rich, but many gave back to the Cotswolds by restoring old churches (the famous "wool churches" of the region) or building rows of limestone almshouses now seasoned to a glorious golden-gray. These days the wool merchants have gone but the wealth remains—the region includes some of the most exclusive real estate in the country.

One possible route is to begin with Cheltenham—the largest town in the area and a gateway to the Cotswolds, but slightly outside the boundaries and more of a small city in atmosphere—then move on to the beauty spots in and around Winchcombe. Next are Sudeley Castle, Stanway House, and Snowshill Manor, among the most impressive houses of the region; the oversold village of Broadway; Chipping Campden, the Cotswold cognoscenti's favorite; and Hidcote Manor, one of the most spectacular gardens in England. Then circle back south, down through Stow-on-the-Wold, Upper Slaughter, Lower Slaughter, and Bourton-on-the-Water, and end with Bibury and Tetbury. This is definitely a region where it pays to go off the beaten track to take a look at that village among the trees.

Stratford-upon-Avon and Around. The countryside around Stratford is marked by gentle hills, green fields, slow-moving rivers, quiet villages, and time-burnished halls, churches, and castles (Warwick and Kenilworth are the best examples and well worth visiting). Historic houses such as moated Baddesley Clinton and Packwood House Court are another reason to explore. All the sights are close enough to Stratford-upon-Avon that you can easily use the town as a base if you wish.

Planning

When to Go

This area contains some of England's most popular destinations, and it's best to avoid weekends in the busier areas of the Cotswolds. During the week, even in summer, you may hardly see a soul in the more remote spots. Bath is particularly congested in summer, when students flock to its language schools. On the other hand, Cheltenham is a relatively workaday place that can absorb many tour buses comfortably. The Shakespeare sights get very crowded on weekends and school vacations; Warwick Castle usually brims with visitors, so arrive early in the day.

Book your room well ahead if you visit during the two weeks in May and June, when the Bath Festival hits town, or if you visit Cheltenham during the National Hunt Festival (horse racing) in mid-March. Note that the private properties of Hidcote Manor, Snowshill Manor, and Sudeley Castle close in winter; Hidcote Manor Garden is at its best in spring and fall.

FESTIVALS
★ Bath Festival
FESTIVALS | Held over 17 days in May, the Bath Festival is a multi-arts celebration of literature and music in and around the city. Events include classical, jazz, and world-music concerts, dance performances, literary talks, and exhibitions, many in the Assembly Rooms and Bath Abbey. ⊠ Bath Box Office, 2 Terrace Walk, Bath ☎ 01225/463362 ⊕ www.bathfestivals. org.uk.

Jane Austen Festival
FESTIVALS | Celebrating the great writer with films, plays, walks, and talks over nine days in mid-September, the Jane Austen Festival is a feast for Janeites. ⊠ Bath ☎ 01225/443000 ⊕ www. janeaustenfestivalbath.co.uk.

★ Shakespeare Birthday Celebrations
CULTURAL FESTIVALS | These festivities have taken place on and around the weekend closest to April 23, the Bard's birthday, since 1824. Over several days, the streets are filled with performers, impromptu concerts, and pageantry, and special events are held at various venues. The celebrations culminate with a spectacular procession. ⊠ Stratford-upon-Avon ☎ 01789/269332 ⊕ www. shakespearescelebrations.com.

Planning Your Time

You can get a taste of Bath and the Cotswolds in three hurried days; a weeklong visit gives you plenty of time for the slow wandering this small region deserves. Near Bath, it's an easy drive to Lacock and Castle Combe, two stately villages on the southern edge of the Cotswolds, and Winchcombe makes a good entry into the area from Cheltenham. At the heart of the Cotswolds, Stow-on-the-Wold, Bourton-on-the-Water, and Broadway should on no account be missed. Within a short distance of these, Chipping Campden and Moreton-in-Marsh are less showy, with a more relaxed feel. Northleach is fairly low-key but boasts a fine example of a Cotswold wool church, while Bibury and Upper and Lower Slaughter are tiny settlements that can easily be appreciated on a brief passage. On the southern fringes of the area, Burford, Tetbury, and Cirencester have antiques and tea shops galore while avoiding the worst of the crowds.

Stratford-upon-Avon is ideal for day visits from London or as a base for exploring nearby, but even ardent Shakespeare lovers probably won't need more than a day or two here. Warwick can be explored in an hour or two, but allow half a day to tackle the many lines at busy Warwick Castle. A drive through the area's country lanes is a pleasant way to spend a day; a stop at any stately home will take a few hours. You're also near the northern Cotswolds if you want to explore the countryside further.

Getting Here and Around

AIR
This area is about two hours from London; Bristol and Birmingham have the closest regional airports.

CONTACTS Birmingham International Airport. ⊠ A45, off M42, Birmingham

☎ 0871/222–0072 ⊕ www.birmingha-mairport.co.uk.

BUS

National Express buses head to the region from London's Victoria Coach Station. Megabus, a budget bus company best booked online, also serves Cheltenham and Bath from London. Bus service between some towns can be extremely limited. The First company covers the area around Bath. Stagecoach, Johnson's Coaches, Cotswold Green, Swanbrook, Marchants, and Pulham's Coaches operate in the Cotswolds region. Stagecoach serves local routes throughout the Stratford area. Traveline has comprehensive information about all public transportation.

CONTACTS Cotswold Green.
☎ 01453/835153 ⊕ www.bustimes. org/operators/cotswold-green. **First.** ☎ 0871/2002233 ⊕ www.firstgroup. com. **Johnson's Coaches.** ☎ 01564/797000 ⊕ www.johnsonscoaches.co.uk. **Marchants.** ☎ 01242/257714 ⊕ www. marchants-coaches.com. **Megabus.** ☎ 0141/352–4444 for general inquiries, 0900/160–0900 for bookings ⊕ www.megabus.com. **National Express.** ☎ 0871/781–8181 ⊕ www. nationalexpress.com. **Pulham's Coaches.** ☎ 01451/820369 ⊕ www.pulhamscoaches.com. **Stagecoach.** ☎ 0871/200–2233 ⊕ www.stagecoachbus.com. **Swanbrook.** ☎ 01452/712386 ⊕ www.swanbrook. co.uk. **Traveline.** ☎ 0871/200–2233 ⊕ www.traveline.info.

CAR

A car is the best way to make a thorough tour of the area, given the limitations of public transportation. M4 is the main route west from London to Bath and southern Gloucestershire; expect about a two-hour drive. From London you can also take M40 and A40 to the Cotswolds, where a network of minor roads links the villages. The M40 serves Stratford and Warwick as well.

TRAIN

First Great Western trains serve the region from London's Paddington Station; First Great Western and CrossCountry trains connect Cheltenham and Birmingham. Travel time from Paddington to Bath is about 90 minutes. Most trains to Cheltenham (two hours and 20 minutes) involve a change at Swindon or Bristol Parkway. Train service within the Cotswold area is extremely limited, with Kemble (near Cirencester) and Moreton-in-Marsh being the most useful stops, both serviced by regular trains from London Paddington. A three-day or seven-day Heart of England Rover pass is valid for unlimited travel within the region. National Rail Enquiries can help with schedules and other information.

Stratford has good train connections and can be seen as a day trip from London if your time is limited (a matinee is your best bet if you want to squeeze in a play). Chiltern Railways trains leave from London Marylebone Station and take two hours direct or 2½–3 hours with transfers. They also go to Warwick.

CONTACTS Chiltern Railways.
☎ 03456/005165 ⊕ www.chilternrailways.co.uk. **National Rail Enquiries.** ☎ 03457/484950 ⊕ www.nationalrail. co.uk. **West Midlands Rail.** ☎ 0344/811–0133 ⊕ www.westmidlandsrailway.co.uk.

Restaurants

Good restaurants dot the region, thanks to a steady flow of fine chefs seeking to cater to wealthy locals and waves of demanding visitors. The country's food revolution is in full evidence here. Restaurants have never had a problem with a fresh food supply: excellent regional produce; salmon from the rivers Severn and Wye; local lamb and pork; venison from the Forest of Dean; and pheasant, partridge, quail, and grouse in season. Also look for Gloucestershire Old Spot pork, bacon (try a delicious Old Spot bacon sandwich), and sausage on area menus. Stratford has many reasonably priced bistros and unpretentious eateries offering a broad choice of international fare; Warwick and Kenilworth both have good restaurant options.

Hotels

The hotels of this region are among Britain's most highly rated—from bed-and-breakfasts in village homes and farmhouses to luxurious country-house hotels. Many hotels present themselves as deeply traditional rural retreats, but some have opted for a sleeker, fresher style, with boldly contemporary or minimalist furnishings. Spas are becoming increasingly popular at these hotels. Book ahead whenever possible, and brace yourself for some high prices. B&Bs are a cheaper alternative to the fancier hotels, and most places offer two- and three-day packages. Note that the majority of lodgings in Bath and many in the Cotswolds require a two-night minimum stay on weekends and holidays; rates are often higher on weekends. Accommodation in Cheltenham and the Cotswolds is especially hard to find during the week of Cheltenham's National Hunt Festival in March. Stratford and Warwick have accommodations to suit every price range. Because Stratford is so popular with theatergoers, you need to book well ahead. Most hotels offer discounted two- and three-day packages. Near Stratford, a number of top-notch country hotels guarantee discreet but attentive service—at fancy prices.

Restaurant and hotel reviews have been shortened. For full information, visit Fodors.com. Restaurant prices are the average cost of a main course at dinner or, if dinner is not served, at lunch. Hotel prices are the lowest cost of a standard double room in high season, including 20% V.A.T.

WHAT IT COSTS in Pounds

	$	$$	$$$	$$$$
RESTAURANTS				
	under £16	£16–£23	£24–£30	over £30
HOTELS				
	under £125	£125–£225	£226–£350	over £350

Visitor Information

The South West Tourism website has information about the entire region; the Cotswolds site is a government one that has a useful section on tourism. The major towns have Tourist Information Centres that provide advice and help with accommodations. Shakespeare's England offers the Explorer Pass, available for one, two, or three days (£39, £50, and £60 respectively), which allows entry to 18 attractions, including the five Shakespeare family homes, plus Kenilworth and Warwick castles. Local tourist offices can recommend day or half-day tours of the region and will have the names of registered Blue Badge guides—a mark of prestige among tour companies.

CONTACTS The Cotswolds. ⊕ *www. cotswolds.com.* **Shakespeare's England.** ☏ *01789/260677* ⊕ *www.shakespeares-england.co.uk.* **South West Tourism.** ⊕ *www.visitsouthwest.co.uk.*

Bath

13 miles southeast of Bristol, 115 miles west of London.

In Bath, a UNESCO World Heritage Site, you're surrounded by magnificent 18th-century architecture, a lasting reminder of a vanished world often described by the likes of Jane Austen. In the 19th century, the city lost its fashionable luster and slid into a refined gentility that still remains. Bath is no museum, though: it's lively, with good dining and shopping; excellent art galleries and museums; the remarkable excavated Roman baths; and theater, music, and other performances all year. Many people rush through Bath in a day, but there's enough to do to merit an overnight stay—or more. In summer, the sheer volume of sightseers may hamper your progress.

The Romans put Bath on the map in the 1st century when they built a temple here, in honor of the goddess Minerva, and a sophisticated network of baths to make full use of the mineral springs that gush from the earth at a constant temperature of 116°F (46.5°C). ■ TIP→ Don't miss the remains of the baths, one of the city's glories. Visits by Queen Anne in 1702 and 1703 brought attention to the town, and soon 18th-century "people of quality" took it to heart. Assembly rooms, theaters, and pleasure gardens were built to entertain the rich and titled when they weren't busy attending the parties of Beau Nash (the city's master of ceremonies and chief social organizer, who helped increase Bath's popularity) and having their portraits painted by Gainsborough.

GETTING HERE AND AROUND

Frequent trains from Paddington and National Express buses from Victoria connect Bath with London. The bus and train stations are close to each other south of the center. By car from London, take M4 to Exit 18, from which A46 leads 10 miles south to Bath.

Drivers should note that parking is extremely limited within the city, and any car illegally parked will be ticketed. Fees for towed cars can be hundreds of pounds. Public lots in the historic area fill up early, but the park-and-ride lots on the outskirts provide inexpensive shuttle service into the center, which is pleasant to stroll around.

TOURS

Mayor of Bath's Honorary Guides

Free two-hour walking tours of Bath are offered year-round by the Mayor of Bath's Honorary Guides. Individuals can just show up outside the Roman Baths. Tours are Sunday through Friday at 10:30 am and 2 pm, Saturday at 10:30 am, and there's an additional tour at 7 pm Tuesday and Thursday from May to August. Note that unlike many other free tours, these guides don't accept tips. ☎ *01225/477411* ⊕ *www.bathguides.org.uk.*

ESSENTIALS

VISITOR INFORMATION Bath Tourist Information Centre. ✉ *Bridgwater House, 2 Terrace Walk* ☎ *01225/614420* ⊕ *www.visitbath.co.uk.*

Sights

Bath Abbey

RELIGIOUS SITE | Dominating Bath's center, this 15th-century edifice of golden, glowing stone has a splendid west front, with carved figures of angels ascending ladders on either side. Notice, too, the miter, olive tree, and crown motif, a play on the name of the building's founder, Bishop Oliver King. More than 50 stained-glass windows fill about 80% of the building's wall space, giving the interior an impression of lightness. The abbey was built in the Perpendicular (English late-Gothic) style on the site of a Saxon abbey, and the nave and side aisles contain superb fan-vaulted ceilings. Look for the 21st-century expressively carved angels on the choir screens. The building's heating comes from the adjacent Roman baths. There are four services on Sunday, including choral evensong at 3 pm. **Tower tours** (45 minutes; on the hour every hour daily except Sunday) allow close-up views of the massive bells and panoramic cityscapes from the roof; the 212 dizzying steps demand a level of fitness. ✉ *Abbey Churchyard* ☎ *01225/422462* ⊕ *www.bathabbey.org*

Sights ▼

1 Bath Abbey **F5**
2 Bath Skyline Walk **J6**
3 Circus **D3**
4 Fashion Museum and
   Assembly Rooms **D3**
5 Holburne Museum................. **H3**
6 Jane Austen Centre **D4**
7 Museum of Bath Architecture **E3**
8 Number 1 Royal Crescent **C3**
9 Prior Park Landscape Garden.... **H9**
10 Pulteney Bridge................... **F5**
11 Roman Baths and the
    Pump Room **E6**
12 Thermae Bath Spa................. **E6**

Restaurants ▼

1 The Grand Eastern................. **E5**
2 Menu Gordon Jones **C9**
3 The Pig Near Bath................. **A6**
4 Pump Room **E6**
5 Rustico............................. **C3**
6 Sally Lunn's........................ **F6**

Hotels ▼

1 The Albany **D4**
2 The Gainsborough Bath Spa **E6**
3 Marlborough House.............. **A4**
4 Queensberry Hotel **D3**
5 The Royal Crescent............... **C2**

⌖ *Abbey £4 suggested donation, tower tours £6* ⊙ *No tower tours Sun.*

Bath Skyline Walk

TRAIL | An excellent way to appreciate the beauty and uniqueness of Bath is through the Bath Skyline Walk. One of England's most popular walks, it is 6 miles of greenery that encircles the city and includes woodlands, valleys, meadows, and trails with captivating views of the city's architecture. Grab a picnic and some strong shoes and head out on the waymarked path. The starting point is on Bathwick Hill near the entrance to the National Trust Bathwick Fields; you can download a free walking guide from the National Trust website. ■ **TIP→ If you don't have the time (or energy) for the full walk, take the 3-mile "Walk to the View" waymarked from Bath Abbey.** ⌖ *Bathwick Hill* ☎ *01225/833977* ⊕ *www.nationaltrust.org.uk/bath-skyline/trails/bath-skyline-walk* ⌖ *Free.*

Circus

PLAZA | John Wood designed the masterful Circus, a circle of curving, perfectly proportioned Georgian houses interrupted just three times for intersecting streets. Wood died shortly after work began; his son, the younger John Wood, completed the project. Notice the carved acorns atop the houses: Wood nurtured the myth that Prince Bladud founded Bath, ostensibly with the help of an errant pig rooting for acorns (this is one of a number of variations of Bladud's story). A garden with large plane trees fills the center of the Circus. The painter Thomas Gainsborough (1727–88) lived at No. 17 from 1760 to 1774. ⌖ *Intersection of Bennett, Brock, and Gay Sts.*

★ Fashion Museum and Assembly Rooms

MUSEUM | In its role as the **Assembly Rooms,** this neoclassical building was one of the leading centers for social life in 18th-century Bath. Jane Austen came here often, and it's in the Ballroom that Catherine Morland has her first, disappointing encounter with Bath's beau monde in *Northanger Abbey*; the Octagon Room is the setting for an important encounter between Anne Elliot and Captain Wentworth in *Persuasion*. Built by John Wood the Younger in 1771, the building was badly damaged by wartime bombing in 1942 but was faithfully restored. Its stunning chandeliers are the 18th-century originals. Throughout the year, classical concerts are given here, just as they were in bygone days. The Assembly Rooms are also known today for the entertaining **Fashion Museum,** displaying apparel from Jacobean times up to the present. You can see examples of what would have been worn in the heydays here, as well as glamorous frocks from the 20th century—a dress of the year is an annual addition. Besides admiring the changing exhibits, you can have fun trying on corsets and crinolines. An audio guide and daily guided tours at noon and 3:30 are included in the admission. ⌖ *Bennett St.* ☎ *01225/477789* ⊕ *www.fashionmuseum.co.uk* ⌖ *Assembly Rooms free; Fashion Museum £9.50; £26 combined ticket includes Roman Baths and the Victoria Art Gallery.*

★ Holburne Museum

MUSEUM | One of Bath's gems, this elegant 18th-century building and its modern extension house a superb collection of 17th- and 18th-century decorative arts, ceramics, and silverware. Highlights include paintings by Gainsborough (*The Byam Family*, on indefinite loan) and George Stubbs (*Reverend Carter Thelwall and Family*), and a hilarious collection of caricatures of the Georgian city's fashionable elite. In its original incarnation as the Sydney Hotel, the house was one of the pivots of Bath's high society, which came to perambulate in the pleasure gardens (Sydney Gardens) that still lie behind it. One visitor was Jane Austen, whose main Bath residence was No. 4 Sydney Place, a brief stroll from the museum. There's also an excellent café and tea garden on-site. ⌖ *Great Pulteney*

St. ☎ 01225/388569 ⊕ www.holburne.org ✉ £12.50.

Jane Austen Centre

MUSEUM | The one place in Bath that gives Austen any space provides a briefly diverting exhibition about the influence of Bath on her writings; *Northanger Abbey* and *Persuasion* are both set primarily in the city. The center is brought to life by characters in costume, and displays and a short film give a pictorial overview of life in Bath around 1800. Immerse yourself further by dressing up in costume; assistants are on hand to take your photo. The cozy Georgian house, a few doors up from where the writer lived in 1805 (one of several addresses she had in Bath), also includes the Austen-themed Regency Tea Rooms, open to the public. ✉ 40 Gay St. ☎ 01225/443000 ⊕ www. janeausten.co.uk ✉ £12.

Museum of Bath Architecture

MUSEUM | This absorbing museum in the Georgian Gothic–style Countess of Huntingdon's Chapel is an essential stop on any exploration of Bath, particularly for fans of Georgian architecture. It illustrates the evolution of the city, with examples of everything from window design and wrought-iron railings to marbling and other interior decoration, while an informative film puts what you see into context. ✉ The Paragon ☎ 01225/333895 ⊕ www.museumofbatharchitecture.org.uk ✉ £6.90; joint ticket with Number 1 Royal Crescent, Herschel Museum of Astronomy, and Beckford's Tower £16 ⊙ Closed Dec. and Jan.

★ Number 1 Royal Crescent

BUILDING | The majestic arc of the Royal Crescent, much used as a film location, is the crowning glory of Palladian architecture in Bath. The work of John Wood the Younger, these 30 houses fronted by 114 columns were laid out between 1767 and 1774. The first house to be built, on the corner of Brock Street and the Royal Crescent, was Number 1 Royal Crescent.

The museum now crystallizes a view of the English class system in the 18th century—the status, wealth, and elegance of the upstairs in contrast with the extensive servants' quarters and kitchen downstairs. You can witness the predilections of the first resident, Henry Sandford, in the cabinet of curiosities and the electrical machine, as well as a Georgian love of display in the sumptuous dessert table arrangement in the dining room. Several varieties of historic mousetraps make their appearance downstairs. Everything is presented with elegant attention to authenticity and detail. ✉ Royal Crescent ☎ 01225/428126 ⊕ no1royalcrescent.org. uk ✉ £10.90; joint ticket with Museum of Bath Architecture, Herschel Museum, and Beckford's Tower £16 ⊙ Closed Jan.

Prior Park Landscape Garden

GARDEN | A vision to warm Jane Austen's heart, Bath's grandest house lies a mile or so southeast of the center, with splendid views over the Georgian townscape. Built around 1738 by John Wood the Elder, the Palladian mansion was the home of quarry owner and philanthropist Ralph Allen (1693–1764), whose guests included such luminaries as poet Alexander Pope and novelists Henry Fielding and Samuel Richardson. Today it's a school, and the interior is not open to the public, but you may wander through the beautiful grounds, designed by Capability Brown and embellished with a Palladian bridge and lake. A leisurely circuit of the park should take around an hour. ■TIP➔ **The parking here is reserved for people with disabilities, so take a taxi or bus from the center. The City Sightseeing bus also calls here.** ✉ Ralph Allen Dr. ☎ 01225/833977 ⊕ www. nationaltrust.org.uk ✉ £8.40 ⊙ Closed weekdays Nov.–Jan.

Pulteney Bridge

BRIDGE/TUNNEL | Florence's Ponte Vecchio inspired this 18th-century span, one of the most famous landmarks in the city and the only work of Robert Adam in

Bath. It's unique in Great Britain because shops line both sides of the bridge. ⊠ Between Bridge St. and Argyle St.

★ **Roman Baths and the Pump Room**
MUSEUM | The hot springs have drawn people here since prehistoric times, so it's quite appropriate to begin an exploration of Bath at this excellent museum on the site of the ancient city's primary "watering hole." Roman patricians would gather to immerse themselves, drink the mineral waters, and socialize. With the departure of the Romans, the baths fell into disuse. When bathing again became fashionable at the end of the 18th century, this magnificent Georgian building was erected.

Almost the entire Roman bath complex was excavated in the 19th century, and the museum displays relics that include a memorable mustachioed, Celtic-influenced Gorgon's head, fragments of colorful curses invoked by the Romans against their neighbors, and information about Roman bathing practices. The **Great Bath** is now roofless, and the statuary and pillars belong to the 19th century, but much remains from the original complex (the Roman characters strutting around, however, are 21st century) and the steaming, somewhat murky waters are undeniably evocative. Tours take place hourly for no additional charge, and you can visit after 6:30 pm in July and August to experience the baths lighted by torches. Wear sensible shoes as the ancient stones are uneven and can be slippery. The ongoing Archway project will see new educational spaces and more of the Roman site being opened up to the public starting in 2021.

Adjacent to the Roman bath complex is the famed **Pump Room,** built in 1792–96, a rendezvous for members of 18th- and 19th-century Bath society. Here Catherine Morland and Mrs. Allen "paraded up and down for an hour, looking at everybody and speaking to no one," to quote from Jane Austen's *Northanger*

Abbey. Today you can take in the elegant space—or you can simply, for a small fee, taste the fairly vile mineral water. Charles Dickens described it as tasting like warm flatirons. ⊠ *Abbey Churchyard* ☎ *01225/477785* ⊕ *www.romanbaths. co.uk* ⊠ *£18.50; £26 combined ticket includes the Fashion Museum and Assembly Rooms and the Victoria Art Gallery.*

Thermae Bath Spa
HOT SPRINGS | One of the few places in Britain where you can bathe in natural hot-spring water, and in an open-air rooftop location as well, this striking complex designed by Nicholas Grimshaw consists of a Bath-stone building surrounded by a glass curtain wall. The only difficulty is in deciding where to spend more time—in the sleekly luxurious, light-filled Minerva Bath, with its curves and gentle currents, or in the smaller, open-air rooftop pool for the unique sensation of bathing with views of Bath's operatic skyline (twilight is particularly atmospheric here). Two 18th-century thermal baths, the Cross Bath and the Hot Bath, are back in use, too (the latter for treatments only). End your session in the crisp third-floor café and restaurant. ■TIP➜ **It's essential to book spa treatments ahead of time.** Towels, robes, and slippers are available for rent. Note that changing rooms are co-ed. Weekdays are the quietest time to visit. You must be 16 to bathe here and 18 to book a spa treatment. A separate, free **Visitor Centre** (April through October, Monday through Saturday 10–5, Sunday 11–4) opposite the entrance gives an overview of the project and provides audio guides (£2) for a brief tour of the exterior. ⊠ *Hot Bath St.* ☎ *01225/331234* ⊕ *www.thermaebathspa.com* ⊠ *£37 for 2 hrs (£42 on weekends) and £10 for each additional hr.*

🍴 Restaurants

The Grand Eastern

$ | INDIAN | Delicious Indian dishes are the main draw, but the three magnificent glass domes of the large Georgian interior and the arresting South Asian murals mean that a meal here becomes an event. Specialties of the house include *mughlai* chicken (flavored with egg, ginger, and garlic and fried in a sauce of yogurt, coconut, and poppy seeds) and salmon *bhaja* (panfried with Bengali spices and served with diced potatoes). **Known for:** classic Indian and Bengali cuisine; elaborate setting; long menu with lots of options. $ *Average main: £13* ✉ *8a Quiet St.* ☎ *01225/422323* ⊕ *grandeastern.co.uk.*

Menu Gordon Jones

$$$$ | MODERN BRITISH | Step away from the center of town to sample the ingenious cuisine that Michelin-trained chef Gordon Jones conjures up in his open kitchen. There is no set menu, but each course is carefully explained before it's served; there might be smoked eel with maple syrup and purple potatoes, a crisp haggis, roasted turbot with giant raisins and caper dressing, and blackberry sorbet with marinated cucumber. **Known for:** imaginative cuisine served with style; tasting menus that change every single day (so it's always a surprise); reservations required far in advance. $ *Average main: £65* ✉ *2 Wellsway* ☎ *01225/480871* ⊕ *www.menugordonjones.co.uk* ⊙ *Closed Mon.*

★ The Pig Near Bath

$$ | MODERN BRITISH | The Bath outpost of the growing Pig empire is a funky but chic "restaurant with rooms" in a converted country house in the Mendip Hills. It's all about the local and seasonal here (everything comes from within a 25-mile radius): kale, arugula, and other leaves and veggies are sourced from the Pig's kitchen garden; apples, pears, and apricots come from its orchard; and pork, chicken, quail, and venison are provided by animals raised on the property. **Known for:** salmon, bacon, and pancetta smoked on-site; relaxed atmosphere in a quaint deer park setting; alfresco dining in summer. $ *Average main: £18* ✉ *Hunstrete House, Pensford* ☎ *01761/49049* ⊕ *www.thepighotel.com.*

Pump Room

$$ | BRITISH | The 18th-century Pump Room, with views over the Roman baths, serves morning coffee, lunches, and afternoon tea, to music by a pianist or string trio who play every day. The stately setting is the selling point rather than the food, but do sample the West Country cheese board and the housemade cakes and pastries. **Known for:** gorgeous setting from a bygone era; classic afternoon tea, coffee, and cakes; long waits during the day and reservations required for dinner. $ *Average main: £16* ✉ *Abbey Churchyard* ☎ *01225/444477* ⊕ *www.thepumproombath.co.uk* ⊙ *No dinner Sept.–Jan. and Mar.–June.*

Rustico

$ | ITALIAN | Serving old-fashioned Italian country fare along with a dash of dolce vita, this delightful restaurant has a cozy, intimate atmosphere. The welcoming staff gladly serves you housemade pastas like grandma used to make, quantities of seafood casserole, handsome steaks, and pork in sage and white wine sauce, for instance. **Known for:** traditional Italian home-cooking; the area's best tiramisu; cozy outdoor seating. $ *Average main: £15* ✉ *2 Margaret's Buildings* ☎ *01225/310064* ⊕ *www.rusticobistroitaliano.co.uk* ⊙ *Closed Mon.*

Sally Lunn's

$ | BRITISH | Small and slightly twee, this tourist magnet near Bath Abbey occupies the oldest house in Bath, dating from 1482. It's famous for the Sally Lunn bun, a semisweet bread served here since 1680. **Known for:** famed Sally Lunn buns with sweet and savory toppings; lots of tourists; tiny but interesting on-site museum. $ *Average main: £12* ⊠ *4 N. Parade Passage* ☎ *01225/461634* ⊕ *www.sallylunns.co.uk.*

Hotels

The Albany

$ | **B&B/INN** | Homey and friendly, this Edwardian house close to the Royal Crescent has simply furnished rooms decorated with neutral shades of beige and cream. **Pros:** spotless rooms; convenient location; excellent breakfasts. **Cons:** some rooms are very small; limited parking; on a main road so can get noisy. $ *Rooms from: £85* ⊠ *24 Crescent Gardens* ☎ *01225/313339* ⊕ *www.albanybath. co.uk* ☞ *6 rooms* ⦿️ *Free breakfast.*

★ The Gainsborough Bath Spa

$$$ | **HOTEL** | As the only hotel in the United Kingdom with access to Bath's natural thermal waters, thanks to its location in a custom-designed Spa Village, the Gainsborough has a unique appeal. **Pros:** spectacular Georgian setting in a central location; exclusive spa facilities; flawless service. **Cons:** only showers in some rooms; a little pricey; spa not always accessible without booking a treatment. $ *Rooms from: £250* ⊠ *Beau St.* ☎ *01225/358888* ⊕ *www.thegainsboroughbathspa.co.uk* ☞ *98 rooms* ⦿️ *Free breakfast.*

Marlborough House

$$ | **B&B/INN** | A warm, informal welcome greets all who stay at this Victorian establishment not too far from the Royal Crescent, where each room charms with period furniture, fresh flowers, and antique beds. **Pros:** obliging and helpful hosts; immaculate rooms; parking available. **Cons:** walk to the center is along a busy road; minimum two-night stay on weekends; gets booked up quickly at peak times. $ *Rooms from: £145* ⊠ *1 Marlborough La.* ☎ *01225/318175* ⊕ *www.marlborough-house.net* ☞ *6 rooms* ⦿️ *Free breakfast.*

Queensberry Hotel

$ | **HOTEL** | Intimate and elegant, this boutique hotel on a residential street near the Circus occupies three 1772 town houses built by John Wood the Younger for the Marquis of Queensberry; it's a perfect marriage of chic sophistication, homey comforts, and attentive service. **Pros:** efficient service; tranquil ambience; valet parking. **Cons:** occasional street noise; no tea/coffee-making facilities in rooms; slight uphill walk from the city center. $ *Rooms from: £110* ⊠ *7 Russell St.* ☎ *01225/447928* ⊕ *www.thequeensberry.co.uk* ☞ *29 rooms* ⦿️ *Free breakfast.*

The Royal Crescent

$$$$ | **HOTEL** | You can't get a more prestigious address in Bath than the Royal Crescent, and this hotel, discreetly plumb center, overlooks parkland and the town. **Pros:** historic building; total comfort; great location. **Cons:** most bedrooms are very modern in feel; some rooms have no views; some bathrooms are small. $ *Rooms from: £360* ⊠ *16 Royal Crescent* ☎ *01225/823333* ⊕ *www. royalcrescent.co.uk* ☞ *45 rooms* ⦿️ *Free breakfast.*

Nightlife

The Bell

BARS/PUBS | Owned by a co-op and a favorite among locals, the Bell has live music—jazz, blues, and folk—on Monday, Wednesday, and Sunday, as well as a selection of real ales, good food, computer access, and even self-service laundry. ⊠ *103 Walcot St.* ☎ *01225/460426* ⊕ *www.thebellinnbath.co.uk.*

Circo

WINE BARS—NIGHTLIFE | The buzzing circular bar whips up a sassy cocktail or glass of champagne in this popular venue. There are movie nights on Wednesday, Cuban Thursdays, and even a gin high tea. Circo also serves tapas-style

food. ✉ *16 George St.* ☎ *01225/465905*
⊕ *www.circobar.co.uk.*

Raven

BARS/PUBS | Pub aficionados will relish
the friendly, unspoiled ambience of the
Raven, a great spot for a pie and a pint.
There are regular arts, science, and storytelling nights upstairs. ✉ *6-7 Queen St.*
☎ *01225/425045* ⊕ *www.theravenofbath.*
co.uk.

Shopping

Bath Christmas Market

CRAFTS | For 18 days in late November
and early December, the outdoor Bath
Christmas Market sells gift items and
regional specialties—from handcraft-
ed toys to candles, cards, and edible
delights—in over 200 chalet-style stalls
concentrated in the area just south of
the Abbey. ✉ *York St.* ☎ *0844/8475256*
⊕ *www.bathchristmasmarket.co.uk.*

Bath Sweet Shop

FOOD/CANDY | The city's oldest candy
store, Bath Sweet Shop boasts of
stocking some 350 different varieties,
including traditional licorice torpedoes,
pear drops, and aniseed balls. Sugar-free
treats are available. ✉ *8 N. Parade Pas-*
sage ☎ *01225/428040.*

Beaux Arts Bath

CERAMICS/GLASSWARE | This gallery,
close by the Abbey, carries the work of
prominent artists, potters, sculptors,
painters, and printmakers. ✉ *12–13 York*
St. ☎ *01225/464850* ⊕ *www.beauxarts-*
bath.co.uk.

Guildhall Market

OUTDOOR/FLEA/GREEN MARKETS | The
covered Guildhall Market, open Monday
through Saturday 9–5, is the place for
everything from jewelry and gifts to delicatessen food, secondhand books, bags,
and batteries. There's a café, too. ✉ *En-*
trances on High St. and Grand Parade
⊕ *www.bathguildhallmarket.co.uk.*

Castle Combe

12 miles northeast of Bath, 5 miles north-
west of Chippenham.

This Wiltshire village lived a sleepy
existence until 1962, when it was voted
the "prettiest village" in England—without any of its inhabitants knowing that it
had even been a contender. The village's
magic is that it's so delightfully toylike,
you can see almost the whole town at
one glance from any one position. Castle
Combe consists of little more than a
brook, a pack bridge, a street (which is
called the Street) of simple stone cottages, a market cross from the 13th century,
and the Perpendicular-style church of
St. Andrew. The grandest house in the village (on its outskirts) is the Upper Manor
House, which was built in the 15th
century by Sir John Fastolf and is now
the Manor House Hotel. If you're coming
by car, use the village parking lot at the
top of the hill and walk down.

GETTING HERE AND AROUND

Regular buses and trains go to Chippenham, where you can pick up a bus for
Castle Combe, but it's easier to drive or
join a tour.

Hotels

★ Manor House Hotel

$$$ | HOTEL | Secluded in a 23-acre park
on the edge of the village, this partly
14th-century manor house has guest
rooms—some in mews cottages—
that brim with antique character. **Pros:**
romantic getaway; rich historical setting;
good golf course. **Cons:** some rooms not
in main house; not for those who dislike
sound of constant running water; might
be too stuffy for some. ⑤ *Rooms from:*
£240 ✉ *Castle Combe* ☎ *01249/782206*
⊕ *www.exclusive.co.uk/the-manor-house*
⤻ *48 rooms* ⑩ *Free breakfast.*

Around Bath

Lacock

8 miles southeast of Castle Combe, 12 miles east of Bath.

Owned by the National Trust, this lovely Wiltshire village is the victim of its own charm, its unspoiled gabled and stone-tile cottages drawing tour buses aplenty. Off-season, however, Lacock slips back into its profound slumber, the mellow stone and brick buildings little changed in 500 years and well worth a wander. Besides Lacock Abbey, there's the handsome church of St. Cyriac (built with money earned in the wool trade), a 14th-century tithe barn, and, in the village, a few antiques shops and a scattering of pubs that serve bar meals in atmospheric surroundings.

GETTING HERE AND AROUND

All buses from Bath to Lacock involve a change and take 60 to 110 minutes, so it's best to drive or join a tour.

◉ Sights

Lacock Abbey

HOUSE | Well-preserved Lacock Abbey reflects the fate of many religious establishments in England—a spiritual center became a home. The abbey, at the town's center, was founded in the 13th century and closed down during the dissolution of the monasteries in 1539, when its new owner, Sir William Sharington, demolished the church and converted the cloisters, sacristy, chapter house, and monastic quarters into a private dwelling. The house passed to the Talbot family, the most notable descendant of whom was William Henry Fox Talbot (1800–77), who developed the world's first photographic negative. You can see the oriel window, the subject of this photograph in the upper rooms of the abbey, along with a rare 16th-century purpose-built strong room in the octagonal tower. Look for the sugar lump on the goat's nose in the Great Hall. The last descendant, Matilda Talbot, donated the property as well as Lacock itself to the National Trust in the 1940s. The abbey's grounds and Victorian woodland are also worth a wander. Harry Potter fans, take note: Lacock Abbey was used for some scenes at Hogwarts School in the film *Harry Potter and the Sorcerer's Stone.*

The **Fox Talbot Museum,** in a 16th-century barn at the gates of Lacock Abbey, commemorates the work of Fox Talbot as well as other pioneers and contemporary artists in this field. ✉ High St. ☎ 01249/730459 ⊕ www.nationaltrust. org.uk ☒ £15.20; excluding Abbey rooms £11.60.

Cheltenham

50 miles north of Bath, 13 miles east of Gloucester, 99 miles west of London.

Although Cheltenham has acquired a reputation as snooty—the population (around 110,000) is generally well-heeled and conservative—it's also cosmopolitan. The town has excellent restaurants and bars, fashionable stores, and a thriving cultural life. Its primary claim to renown, however, is its architecture, rivaling Bath's in its Georgian elegance, with wide, tree-lined streets, crescents, and terraces with row houses, balconies, and iron railings.

Like Bath, Cheltenham owes part of its fame to mineral springs. By 1740 the first spa was built, and after a visit from George III and Queen Charlotte in 1788, the town dedicated itself to idleness and enjoyment. "A polka, parson-worshipping place"—in the words of resident

Lord Tennyson—Cheltenham gained its reputation for snobbishness when stiff-collared Raj majordomos returned from India to find that the springs—the only purely natural alkaline waters in England—were the most effective cure for their "tropical ailments."

Great Regency architectural set pieces—Lansdown Crescent, Pittville Spa, and the Lower Assembly Rooms, among them—were built solely to adorn the town. The Rotunda building (1826) at the top of Montpellier Walk—now a bank—contains the spa's original "pump room," in which the mineral waters were on tap. More than 30 statues adorn the storefronts of Montpellier Walk. Wander past Imperial Square, with its ironwork balconies, past the ornate Neptune's Fountain, and along the Promenade. In spring and summer, lush flower gardens enhance the town's buildings, attracting many visitors.

GETTING HERE AND AROUND

Trains from London Paddington and buses from London Victoria head to Cheltenham. The train station is west of the center, and the bus station is centrally located off Royal Well Road. Drivers should leave their vehicles in one of the numerous parking lots. The town center is easily negotiable on foot.

◉ Sights

★ Gloucester Cathedral

RELIGIOUS SITE | In the center of Gloucester, magnificent Gloucester Cathedral, with its soaring, elegant exterior, was originally a Norman abbey church, consecrated in 1100. Reflecting different periods, the cathedral mirrors perfectly the slow growth of ecclesiastical taste and the development of the Perpendicular style. The interior has largely been spared the sterilizing attentions of modern architects and is almost completely Norman, with the massive pillars of the nave left untouched since their completion. The fan-vaulted roof of

The Cotswolds

the 14th-century cloisters is the finest in Europe, and the cloisters enclose a peaceful garden (used in the filming of *Harry Potter and the Sorcerer's Stone*).

■**TIP→ Don't miss the Whispering Gallery, which has a permanent exhibition devoted to the splendid, 14th-century stained glass of the Great East Window.** Tours of the tower (269 steps up) are available, as are guided tours. Gloucester is 13 miles southwest of Cheltenham and reachable from there on frequent buses and trains. ✉ *12 College Green* ☎ *01452/528095* ⊕ *www.gloucestercathedral.org.uk* ✉ *£5 requested donation, photography permit £3, tower tours £5* ☉ *Whispering Gallery closed during services.*

★ Sudeley Castle

CASTLE/PALACE | One of the grand showpieces of the Cotswolds, Sudeley Castle was the home and burial place of Catherine Parr (1512–48), Henry VIII's sixth and last wife, who outlived him by one year. Here Catherine undertook, in her later years, the education of the ill-fated Lady Jane Grey and the future queen, Princess Elizabeth. Sudeley, for good reason, has been called a woman's castle. The term "castle" is misleading, though, for it looks more like a Tudor-era palace, with a peaceful air that belies its turbulent history. In the 17th century Charles I took refuge here, causing Oliver Cromwell's army to besiege the castle. It remained in ruins until the Dent-Brocklehurst family stepped in with a 19th-century renovation.

The 14 acres of gardens, which include the roses of the Queen's Garden (best seen in June) and a Tudor knot garden, are the setting for Tudor fun days in summer. Inside the castle, visitors see the

West Wing, with the Long Room where exhibitions illustrate the castle's history, and the East Wing, which contains the private apartments of Lord and Lady Ashcombe, where you can see paintings by Van Dyck, Rubens, Turner, and Reynolds. Art tours can also be booked in advance. Rare and exotically colored birds strut in the pheasantry. The 11 cottages and apartments on the grounds are booked for a minimum of three-night stays. The castle is a mile southeast of Winchcombe. ⊠ *Off B4632, Winchcombe* ☎ *01242/604244, 01242/609481 cottages* ⊕ *www.sudeleycastle.co.uk* ✉ *£17.25* ⊗ *Closed mid-Dec.–mid-Feb.*

★ The Wilson, Cheltenham Art Gallery and Museum

MUSEUM | From the 1880s onward, Cheltenham was at the forefront of the Arts and Crafts movement, and this is still demonstrated by the fine displays of William Morris textiles, furniture by Charles Voysey, and wood and metal pieces by Ernest Gimson at this museum and art gallery. Decorative arts, such as Chinese ceramics, are also well represented, and British artists, including Stanley Spencer, Vanessa Bell, and Jake and Dinos Chapman, make their mark. The Summerfield Galleries demonstrate life through the ages in easily digestible chunks. Exhibits on Cheltenham's history complete the picture; one is devoted to Edward Wilson, who traveled with Robert Scott to the Antarctic on Scott's ill-fated 1912 expedition. ⊠ *Clarence St.* ☎ *01242/237431* ⊕ *www.cheltenhammuseum.org.uk* ✉ *Suggested donation £4* ⊗ *Galleries closed Mon.*

🍴 Restaurants

The Coffee Dispensary

$ | BRITISH | Located in a former pharmacy, the Coffee Dispensary is a small independent café that sources its beans from single estates, aiming to bring the best flavors to the people of Cheltenham. It also serves cakes and savory snacks.

Known for: the best coffee in Cheltenham; friendly vibe; sourcing from single-estate coffee producers. ⑤ *Average main: £3* ⊠ *18 Regent St.* ☎ *01242/260597* ⊕ *www.the-coffee-dispensary.co.uk.*

The Daffodil

$$ | MODERN BRITISH | Housed in a former art deco cinema, the Daffodil is themed along 1920s lines with a touch of glamour and an enticing menu. The menu features dishes like twice-baked Double Gloucester soufflé, calves' liver with mustard mash, and curry spiced chicken breast. **Known for:** 1920s decor and style; great cocktail menu; live jazz on Monday nights and Saturday afternoons. ⑤ *Average main: £19* ⊠ *18–20 Suffolk Parade* ☎ *01242/700055* ⊕ *www.thedaffodil.com* ⊗ *Closed Mon. and Tues.*

 ## Hotels

The Bradley

$ | B&B/INN | The thoughtful and hospitable owners take great pride in this town house, near the town center, that has been in the same family for more than 100 years. **Pros:** good value; attentive hosts; well-designed rooms. **Cons:** lots of stairs to top rooms; no private parking; some bathrooms are very small. ⑤ *Rooms from: £115* ⊠ *19 Bayshill Rd.* ☎ *01242/519077* ⊕ *www.thebradleyhotel. co.uk* ⌨ *10 rooms* ⦙⦙ *Free breakfast* ⌨ *No children under 11 are allowed.*

Malmaison Cheltenham

$ | HOTEL | Just around the corner from the calming Montpelier Gardens, the Malmaison's classic white building blends with the local architecture. **Pros:** quiet, beautiful rooms; short walk to Montpellier and the Suffolks; very relaxed atmosphere. **Cons:** limited parking; restaurant is sometimes closed for private functions; gets booked quickly at peak times. ⑤ *Rooms from: £110* ⊠ *Bayshill Rd.* ☎ *01242/370655* ⊕ *www.malmaison. com/locations/cheltenham* ⌨ *60 rooms* ⦙⦙ *Free breakfast.*

As enchanting as the house, the gardens at Sudeley Castle provide a perfect spot for summer meanderings.

🛍 Shopping

Cavendish House

DEPARTMENT STORES | The town's oldest department store, now run by House of Fraser, stocks designer fashions. ✉ 32–48 The Promenade ☎ 01242/521300 ⊕ www.houseoffraser. co.uk/cheltenham-hof-store-2013.

Martin & Co

JEWELRY/ACCESSORIES | This shop carries a good stock of classic and modern jewelry. ✉ 19 The Promenade ☎ 01242/522821 ⊕ www.martin-and-co.com.

Q and C Militaria

SPECIALTY STORES | A treasure trove for military buffs, Q and C Militaria offers badges and medals, breastplates, helmets, coats of arms, and books. It's run by ex-soldiers. ✉ 22 Suffolk Rd. ☎ 01242/519815 ⊕ www.qcmilitaria.com.

Broadway

8 miles north of Winchcombe, 17 miles northeast of Cheltenham.

The Cotswold town to end all Cotswold towns, Broadway has become a favorite of day-trippers. William Morris first discovered the delights of this village, and J. M. Barrie, Vaughan Williams, and Edward Elgar soon followed. Today you may want to avoid Broadway in summer, when it's clogged with cars and buses. Named for its handsome, wide main street (well worth a stroll), the village includes numerous antiques shops, tea parlors, and boutiques. Step into Broadway's back-roads and alleys and you can discover any number of honey-color houses and colorful gardens.

GETTING HERE AND AROUND

Broadway can be reached by car via A44; park in one of the lots signposted from the main street. Johnson's Coaches connects the town with Stratford-up-on-Avon, Chipping Campden, and

Moreton-in-Marsh; Marchants connects Broadway with Winchcombe and Cheltenham. No buses run on Sunday. You'll need a car to reach Broadway Tower, Stanway House, and Snowshill Manor.

ESSENTIALS

VISITOR INFORMATION Broadway Tourist Information Centre. ⊠ *Russell Sq.* ☎ *01386/852037* ⊕ *www.broadway-cotswolds.co.uk/tourist-information-centre.*

Sights

★ Snowshill Manor

HOUSE | FAMILY | Three miles south of Broadway and 13 miles northeast of Cheltenham, Snowshill is one of the most unspoiled of all Cotswold villages. Snuggled beneath Oat Hill, with little room for expansion, the hamlet is centered on an old burial ground, the 19th-century St. Barnabas Church, and Snowshill Manor, a splendid 17th-century house that brims with the collections of Charles Paget Wade, gathered between 1919 and 1956. Over the door of the house is Wade's family motto, *Nequid pereat* ("Let nothing perish"). The rooms are bursting with Tibetan scrolls, spinners' tools, ship models, Persian lamps, and bric-a-brac; the Green Room displays 26 suits of Japanese samurai armor. Outside, an imaginative terraced garden provides an exquisite frame for the house. ■**TIP**→ **Admission is by timed tickets issued on a first-come, first-served basis, so arrive early in peak season.** ⊠ *Off A44, Snowshill* ☎ *01386/852410* ⊕ *www.nationaltrust.org.uk/snowshill-manor-and-garden* ☞ *£12.80; garden only £7.60* ☽ *Closed Nov.–mid-Mar.*

Restaurants

Russell's

$$$ | MODERN BRITISH | With a courtyard at the back and a patio at the front, this chic "restaurant with rooms" is perfect for a light lunch at midday or a full meal in the evening. Menus concentrate on Modern British dishes and change seasonally. **Known for:** good-value fixed-price menu; fresh local produce; stylish setting. ⑤ *Average main: £25* ⊠ *20 High St.* ☎ *01386/853555* ⊕ *www.russellsofbroadway.co.uk* ☽ *No dinner Sun.*

Hotels

Mill Hay House

$$ | B&B/INN | If the rose garden, trout-filled pond, and sheep on the hill at this 18th-century Queen Anne house aren't appealing enough, then the stone-flagged floors, leather sofas, and grandfather clocks should satisfy. **Pros:** delightful owners; beautifully landscaped gardens; gourmet breakfasts. **Cons:** books up quickly; two-night minimum stay for most of the year; entrance can be hard to find. ⑤ *Rooms from: £195* ⊠ *Snowshill Rd.* ☎ *01386/852498* ⊕ *www.millhay.co.uk* ☞ *3 rooms* ⏐◎⏐ *Free breakfast* ☞ *No young children allowed.*

Chipping Campden

4 miles east of Broadway, 18 miles northeast of Cheltenham.

Undoubtedly one of the most beautiful towns in the area, Chipping Campden, with its population of about 2,500, is the Cotswolds in a microcosm. It has St. James, the region's most impressive church; frozen-in-time streets; a silk mill that was once the center of the Guild of Handicraft; and pleasant, untouristy shops. One of the area's most seductive settings unfolds before you as you travel on B4081 through sublime English countryside and happen upon the town, tucked in a slight valley. North of town is lovely Hidcote Manor Garden. ■**TIP**→ **Chipping Campden can easily be reached on foot along a level section of the Cotswold Way from Broadway Tower, outside Broadway; the walk takes about 75 minutes.**

GETTING HERE AND AROUND

By car, Chipping Campden can be reached on minor roads from A44 or A429. There's a small car park in the center and spaces on the outskirts of the village. By bus, take Johnson's Coaches from Stratford-upon-Avon, Broadway, and Moreton-in-Marsh, or Pulham's Coaches from Bourton-on-the-Water and Cheltenham, changing at Moreton-in-Marsh (no Sunday service).

ESSENTIALS

VISITOR INFORMATION Chipping Campden Tourism Information Centre. ⊠ *The Old Police Station, High St.* ☎ *01386/841206* ⊕ *www.chippingcampdenonline.org.*

Sights

★ Hidcote Manor Garden

GARDEN | Laid out around a Cotswold manor house, Hidcote Manor Garden is arguably the most interesting and attractive large garden in Britain. Crowds are large at the height of the season, but it's worthwhile anytime. A horticulturist from the United States, Major Lawrence Johnston, created the garden in 1907 in the Arts and Crafts style. Johnston was an imaginative gardener and avid traveler who brought back specimens from all over the world. The formal part of the garden is arranged in "rooms" separated by hedges and often with fine topiary work and walls. Besides the variety of plants, what's impressive are the different effects created, from calm open spaces to areas packed with flowers. ■TIP→ **Look for one of Johnston's earliest schemes, the red borders of dahlias, poppies, fuchsias, lobelias, and roses; the tall hornbeam hedges; and the Bathing Pool garden, where the pool is so wide there's scarcely space to walk.** The White Garden was probably the forerunner of the popular white gardens at Sissinghurst and Glyndebourne. If you have time, explore the tiny village of Hidcote Bartrim with its thatched stone houses; it borders the garden and fills a storybook dell. The garden is 4 miles northeast of Chipping Campden. ⊠ *Hidcote Bartrim* ☎ *01386/438333* ⊕ *www.nationaltrust. org.uk/hidcote* 🖾 *£14.20* ⊗ *Closed late Dec.–mid-Feb. and weekdays Nov.–mid-Dec.*

Kiftsgate Court Gardens

GARDEN | While not as spectacular as Hidcote Manor Garden, this intimate, privately-owned garden, just a five-minute stroll away, still captivates. It's skipped by the majority of visitors to Hidcote, so you won't be jostled by the crowds. The interconnecting flower beds present harmonious arrays of color, and the contemporary formal water garden adds an elegant contrast. Don't miss the prized Kiftsgate rose, supposed to be the largest in England, flowering gloriously in mid-July. ⊠ *Off B4081, Mickleton* ☎ *01386/438777* ⊕ *www.kiftsgate.co.uk* 🖾 *£9* ⊗ *Closed Oct.–Mar., Thurs. and Fri. year-round, and Sat. and Tues. Apr. and Sept.*

St. James

RELIGIOUS SITE | The soaring pinnacled tower of St. James, a prime example of a Cotswold wool church (it was rebuilt in the 15th century with money from wool merchants), announces Chipping Campden from a distance; it's worth stepping inside to see the lofty, light-filled nave. The church recalls the old saying, which became popular because of the vast numbers of houses of worship in the Cotswolds, "As sure as God's in Gloucestershire." ⊠ *Church St.* ☎ *01386/841927* ⊕ *www.stjameschurchcampden.co.uk* 🖾 *£3 donation suggested.*

🍴 Restaurants

★ Churchill Arms

$$ | MODERN BRITISH | FAMILY | With chef Neil Deverell-Smith at the helm, this is the epitome of cozy Cotswolds fine dining. In the small country pub just outside Chipping Campden, plain wooden tables and benches, a flagstone floor, light-colored walls, and a roaring fire provide the backdrop for excellent food. **Known for:** British classics reimagined; family-run atmosphere; a focus on local produce and gin. $ *Average main: £16* ✉ *Paxford, Off B4479* ☎ *01386/593159* ⊕ *www.churchillarms.co.*

Eight Bells

$ | **BRITISH** | Close to St. James Church, this traditional tavern has low beams, a flagstone floor, and a small courtyard. The long menu includes daily specials, local ales, and enticing dishes like confit duck and deep-fried fish-and-chips. **Known for:** historic pub with lots of character; affordable ciabatta sandwich lunches; local beers. $ *Average main: £14* ✉ *Church St.* ☎ *01386/840371* ⊕ *www. eightbellsinn.co.uk.*

 Hotels

Cotswold House Hotel and Spa

$$ | **HOTEL** | This luxury hotel in the heart of Chipping Campden injects contemporary design into a stately 18th-century manor house, and from the swirling staircase in the entrance to the individually designed guest rooms studded with contemporary art, it's a winning formula. **Pros:** plenty of pampering; pleasant garden; personalized service. **Cons:** some bathrooms are small; additional charge to use spa; no swimming pool. $ *Rooms from: £150* ✉ *The Square* ☎ *01386/840330* ⊕ *www.bespokehotels. com/cotswoldhouse* ➟ *28 rooms* ❖ *Free breakfast.*

Noel Arms Hotel

$$ | **HOTEL** | Dating to the 14th century, Chipping Campden's oldest inn was built to accommodate foreign wool traders, and even though it's been enlarged, the building retains its exposed beams and stonework. **Pros:** traditional character; friendly staff; excellent curries at restaurant. **Cons:** rooms can be noisy and overheated; annex overlooks car park; some rooms are small. $ *Rooms from: £125* ✉ *High St.* ☎ *0844/8159833* ⊕ *www.*

bespokehotels.com/noelarmshotel ➟ *28 rooms* ❖ *Free breakfast.*

 Shopping

Hart

JEWELRY/ACCESSORIES | Descendants of an original member of the Guild of Handicraft specialize in fashioning lovely items from silver at this shop. ✉ *Guild of Handicraft, Sheep St.* ☎ *01386/841100* ⊕ *www.hartsilversmiths.co.uk.*

Stuart House Antiques

ANTIQUES/COLLECTIBLES | Three bay windows filled with silverware and copperware, porcelain, Doulton figurines, and Staffordshire figures show you only a fraction of what's available here over two floors overflowing with antiques. ✉ *High St.* ☎ *01386/840995* ⊕ *www.antiques-atlas.com/stuarthouseantiques.*

Stow-on-the-Wold

5 miles south of Moreton-in-Marsh, 15 miles east of Cheltenham.

At an elevation of 800 feet, Stow is the highest town in the Cotswolds—"Stow-on-the-Wold, where the wind blows cold" is the age-old saying. Built around a wide square, Stow's imposing golden stone houses have been discreetly converted into high-quality antiques stores, shops, and tea parlors. The Square, as it's known, has a fascinating history. In the 18th century, Daniel Defoe wrote that more than 20,000 sheep could be sold here on a busy day. Such was the press of livestock that sheep runs, known as "tures," were used to control the sheep, and these narrow streets still run off the main square. Today pubs and antiques shops fill the area.

Also here are St. Edward's Church and the Kings Arms Old Posting House, its wide entrance still seeming to wait for the stagecoaches that used to stop here on their way to Cheltenham.

GETTING HERE AND AROUND

Stow-on-the-Wold is well connected by road (A429, A424, and A436) and bus (from Moreton-in-Marsh, Bourton-on-the-Water, Northleach, Cirencester, and Cheltenham). There are parking lots off Sheep Street and Fosseway (A429). Chastleton House is reachable only by car.

Sights

Chastleton House

HOUSE | One of the most complete Jacobean properties in Britain opts for a beguilingly lived-in appearance, taking advantage of almost 400 years' worth of furniture and trappings accumulated by many generations of the single family that owned it until 1991. The house was built between 1605 and 1612 for William Jones, a wealthy wool merchant, and has an appealing authenticity: bric-a-brac is strewn around, wood and pewter are unpolished, upholstery is uncleaned. The top floor is a glorious, barrel-vaulted long gallery, and throughout the house you can see exquisite plasterwork, paneling, and tapestries. The gardens include rotund topiaries and the first croquet lawn (the rules of croquet were codified here in 1865). During busy periods, admission is by timed ticket on a first-come, first-served basis. Note that there is no tearoom or shop here, but the church next door sells tea and snacks when the house is open. Chastleton is 6 miles northeast of Stow, signposted off A436 between Stow and A44. ⊠ Off A436, Stow on the Wold ☎ 01608/674355 ⊕ www.nationaltrust.org.uk/chastleton-house ⊠ £10.50; garden only £5 ⊙ Closed Nov.–Feb., Mon., and Tues.

Restaurants

★ Feathered Nest Inn

$$$$ | **BRITISH** | A ten-minute drive from Stow-on-the-Wold, this popular gastro-pub is as cozy and comforting as the name would suggest. The food here is exceptional, and the products so local that the staff can usually point to the farm the meat was sourced from, contributing to a generous prix-fixe menu, or, for those who brought their appetites, a superb tasting menu. **Known for:** locally sourced produce; high-end presentation; lovely valley views. $ Average main: £45 ⊠ Nether Westcote ☎ 01993/833030 ⊕ www.thefeatherednestinn.co.uk.

Hotels

Number Nine

$ | **B&B/INN** | Beyond the traditional Cotswold stone exterior of this former coaching inn—now a bed-and-breakfast—are unfussy, spacious bedrooms done in soothing white and pale colors. **Pros:** helpful and amiable hosts; close to pubs and restaurants; delicious breakfasts. **Cons:** two bathrooms have tubs, not showers; low ceilings; steps to climb. $ Rooms from: £75 ⊠ 9 Park St., Stow on the Wold ☎ 01451/870333 ↘ 3 rooms ⫟⊙⫠ Free breakfast.

Stow Lodge

$$ | **HOTEL** | A former rectory, this stately, family-run hotel couldn't be better placed, separated from Stow's main square by a tidy garden. **Pros:** central location; hospitable service; good breakfasts. **Cons:** chiming church clock can be disturbing; steep steps to top-floor rooms; minimum stay on weekends. $ Rooms from: £150 ⊠ The Square, Stow on the Wold ☎ 01451/830485 ⊕ www.stowlodge.co.uk ↘ 20 rooms ⫟⊙⫠ Free breakfast ⫸ No children under 5.

💼 Shopping

Stow-on-the-Wold is the leading center for antiques stores in the Cotswolds, with dealers centered on the Square, Sheep Street, and Church Street.

Baggott Church St. Limited

ANTIQUES/COLLECTIBLES | This shop displays fine old furniture, portraits and landscape paintings, silver, and toys, with their price tags tied on with ribbon. ⊠ *Church St., Stow on the Wold* ☎ *01451/830370* ⊕ *www.baggottantiques.com.*

Durham House Antiques

ANTIQUES/COLLECTIBLES | Showcases of jewelry, silver items, and ceramics, along with antiquarian books and period furniture, are on display over two floors. ⊠ *48 Sheep St., Stow on the Wold* ☎ *01451/870404* ⊕ *www.durhamhouse-antiques.co.uk.*

Tudor House

ANTIQUES/COLLECTIBLES | Three floors of showcases contain the finds of 20 antiques dealers presenting anything from tiny mother-of-pearl pieces and beaded bags to wooden dressers full of plates and jugs. ⊠ *40 Sheep St., Stow on the Wold* ☎ *01451/830021.*

Bourton-on-the-Water

4 miles southwest of Stow-on-the-Wold, 12 miles northeast of Cheltenham.

Off A429 on the eastern edge of the Cotswolds, Bourton-on-the-Water is deservedly famous as a classic Cotswold village. Like many others, it became wealthy in the Middle Ages because of wool. The little River Windrush runs through Bourton, crossed by low stone bridges; it's as pretty as it sounds. This village makes a good touring base and has a collection of quirky small museums, but in summer it can be overcrowded. A stroll through Bourton takes you past stone cottages, many converted to small stores and fish-and-chips and tea shops.

GETTING HERE AND AROUND

Bourton-on-the-Water is served by Pulham's Coaches from Stow-on-the-Wold, Moreton-in-Marsh, Cirencester, and Cheltenham. By car, take A40 and A436 from Cheltenham. You may find parking in the center, but if not, use the lot outside the village.

ESSENTIALS

VISITOR INFORMATION Bourton-on-the-Water Visitor Information Centre. ⊠ *Victoria St.* ☎ *01451/820211* ⊕ *www.bourtoninfo.com.*

Sights

Cotswold Motoring Museum and Toy Collection

MUSEUM | **FAMILY** | Housed in an old mill and marked by a topiary vintage Mini car, this museum has seven rooms crammed to the rafters with more than 30 shiny vintage and classic cars, delightful caravans from the 1920s and 1960s, ancient motorbikes and bicycles, road signs from past times, and a shepherd's hut on wheels. If this and the assortment of motoring memorabilia is not enough, there are also children's toys, pedal cars, models, and board games. ⊠ *The Old Mill, Sherborne St.* ☎ *01451/821255* ⊕ *www.cotswoldmotoringmuseum.co.uk* ☞ *£6.50* ⏱ *Closed mid-Dec.–mid-Feb.*

Model Village

MUSEUM | **FAMILY** | Built in 1937, this knee-high model of Bourton-on-the-Water took five years to complete. As you walk down its tiny lanes, you'll see how little has changed over the past decades. The small exhibition at Miniature World shows miniature scenes and rooms; some you can make come to life. Particularly entertaining is the model village within the model village, which, much like an infinity mirror, is perpetuated to an increasingly smaller scale. ⊠ *Old New Inn, High St.* ☎ *01451/820467* ⊕ *www.themodelvillage.com* ☞ *£4.25.*

Restaurants

Rose Tree

$ | **BRITISH** | Plain wooden tables and understated decor are the setting for the wholesome British dishes served in this traditional restaurant beautifully sited on the banks of the Windrush with a large outdoor area. Sip a cocktail on the riverside terrace while you wait for your order. **Known for:** beautiful riverside setting; classic ploughman's lunches; locally sourced food. ⑤ *Average main: £15* ✉ *Victoria St.* ☎ *01451/820635* ⊕ *www. therosetreeinbourton.co.uk* ⊙ *Closed Mon. No dinner Sun.*

Hotels

Chester House Hotel
$ | HOTEL | Just steps from the River Windrush, this traditional stone building has been tastefully adapted with contemporary fittings and style. **Pros:** friendly staff; stylish rooms; ideal location for exploring the area. **Cons:** busy on weekends; coach-house rooms overlook car park; limited parking. ⑤ *Rooms from: £120* ✉ *Victoria St.* ☎ *01451/820286* ⊕ *www. chesterhousehotel.com* ⌁ *22 rooms* ⑩ *Free breakfast.*

Shopping

Cotswold Perfumery
PERFUME/COSMETICS | This popular, family-owned shop carries many perfumes that are manufactured on the premises by hand, and also stocks perfume bottles, diffusers, and essential oils, as well as jewelry. Classes are also available on-site for those who want to learn to mix their own perfume. ✉ *Victoria St.* ☎ *01451/820698* ⊕ *www.cotswold-perfumery.co.uk* ⌁ *Factory tour £5.*

Lower Slaughter and Upper Slaughter

2 miles north of Bourton-on-the-Water, 15 miles east of Cheltenham.

To see the quieter, more typical Cotswold villages, seek out the evocatively named Lower Slaughter and Upper Slaughter

(the names have nothing to do with mass murder, but come from the Saxon word *sloh,* which means "a marshy place"). Lower Slaughter is one of the "water villages," with Slaughter Brook running down the center road of the town. Little stone footbridges cross the brook, and the town's resident gaggle of geese can often be seen paddling through the sparkling water. Nearby, Lower and Upper Swell are two other quiet towns to explore.

GETTING HERE AND AROUND
The Slaughters are best explored by car.

Sights

Warden's Way
TRAIL | Connecting the two Slaughters is the Warden's Way, a mile-long pathway that begins in Upper Slaughter at the town-center parking lot and passes stone houses, green meadows, ancient trees, and a 19th-century corn mill with a waterwheel and brick chimney. The Warden's Way continues south to Bourton-on-the-Water; the full walk from Winchcombe to Bourton is 14 miles. You can pick up maps from local tourist offices. ✉ *Lower Slaughter.*

Hotels

Lords of the Manor Hotel
$$ | HOTEL | You'll find refinement and a warm welcome in this rambling 17th-century manor house with Victorian additions, tucked away in a quintessential Cotswold village. **Pros:** heavenly setting; understated elegance; outstanding food. **Cons:** some rooms on the small side; limited Wi-Fi; packages book up quickly. ⑤ *Rooms from: £192* ✉ *Off A429, Upper Slaughter* ☎ *01451/820243* ⊕ *www.lordsofthemanor.com* ⌁ *26 rooms* ⑩ *Free breakfast.*

Blue skies, stone buildings, a peaceful brook: villages such as Upper Slaughter demonstrate the enduring appeal of the Cotswolds.

Burford

9 miles east of Northleach, 18 miles north of Swindon, 18 miles west of Oxford.

Burford's broad main street leads steeply down to a narrow bridge across the River Windrush. The village served as a stage-coach stop for centuries and has many historic inns; it's now a popular stop for tour buses and seekers of antiques.

GETTING HERE AND AROUND

Burford can be easily reached by bus from Oxford and Northleach. Once here, it's easy to stroll around. Drivers should park as soon as possible; there are possibilities on and off High Street.

ESSENTIALS

VISITOR INFORMATION Burford Visitor Information Centre. ⌧ *33A High St.* ☎ *01993/823558* ⊕ *www.oxfordshirecotswolds.org.*

Sights

St. John the Baptist

RELIGIOUS SITE | Hidden away at the end of a lane at the bottom of High Street is the splendid parish church of St. John the Baptist, its interior a warren of arches, chapels, and shrines. The church was remodeled in the 15th century from Norman beginnings. Among the monuments is one dedicated to Henry VIII's barber, Edmund Harman, that depicts four Amazonian Indians; it's said to be the first depiction of native people from the Americas in Britain. Also look for the elaborate Tanfield monument and the grave of Christopher Kempster, master mason to Christopher Wren during the rebuilding of St. Paul's Cathedral in London. ⌧ *Church Green* ☎ *01993/823788* ⊕ *www.burfordchurch.org* ✉ *Suggested donation £2.*

Restaurants

The Angel at Burford

$ | **MODERN BRITISH** | At this informal eatery in a 16th-century coaching inn, the farmhouse-style tables are filled with traditional dishes with locally sourced ingredients. The secluded garden is the perfect place to enjoy lunchtime baguettes or sandwiches in nice weather. **Known for:** fantastic steaks and other meats; relaxed and informal atmosphere; beautiful garden. $ *Average main: £15* ✉ *14 Witney St.* ☎ *01993/822714* ⊕ *www.theangelatburford.co.uk.*

Hotels

The Lamb Inn

$$ | **HOTEL** | Step through the door of this ancient coaching inn and be greeted by huge flagstones, gateleg tables, armchairs, and a roaring fire, then wind your way along the tartan carpet through creaking passages and stairways to the immaculate and cozy bedrooms. **Pros:** idyllic location; attentive service; historical building. **Cons:** some rooms are small; some street parking; very pet-friendly, so not for non-dog lovers. $ *Rooms from: £205* ✉ *Sheep St.* ☎ *01993/823155* ⊕ *www.cotswold-inns-hotels.co.uk/the-lamb-inn* ⇌ *17 rooms* ⊚ *Free breakfast.*

Bibury

10 miles southwest of Burford, 6 miles northeast of Cirencester, 15 miles north of Swindon.

The tiny town of Bibury, with a population of less than 1,000, sits idyllically beside the little River Coln on B4425. It was famed Arts and Crafts designer William Morris's choice for Britain's most beautiful village. Fine old cottages, a river meadow, and the church of St. Mary's are some of the delights here.

GETTING HERE AND AROUND

There are a few buses to Bibury operated on weekdays only by Pulham's Coaches from Cirencester which continue on to Bourton-on-the-Water. You'll need a car to reach Chedworth Roman Villa.

Sights

Arlington Row

NEIGHBORHOOD | The town has a famously pretty and much-photographed group of 17th-century weavers' cottages made of stone. ✉ *Bibury.*

Chedworth Roman Villa

ARCHAEOLOGICAL SITE | **FAMILY** | The remains of a mile of walls are what's left of one of the largest Roman villas in England, beautifully set in a wooded valley on the eastern fringe of the Cotswolds. Thirty-two rooms, including two complete bath suites, have been identified, and covered walkways take you over the colorful mosaics, some of the most complete in England. Audio guides are available, and there's a small museum. Look out for the rare large snails, fattened on milk and herbs during Roman times, in the grounds; they come out on warm, wet days. There's a café here, but it's also an ideal place for a picnic. ■**TIP**→ **Look carefully for the signs for the villa: from Bibury, go across A429 to Yanworth and Chedworth. The villa is also signposted from A40. Roads are narrow.** The site is 6 miles northwest of Bibury and 10 miles southeast of Cheltenham. ✉ *Off A429, Yanworth* ☎ *01242/890256* ⊕ *www.nationaltrust.org.uk/chedworth-roman-villa* 🎟 *£11.50* ⊗ *Closed mid-Nov.–mid-Feb.*

Hotels

Swan Hotel

$$ | **HOTEL** | Few inns can boast of a more idyllic setting than this mid-17th-century coaching inn, originally a row of cottages on the banks of the gently flowing River Coln. **Pros:** idyllic spot; helpful staff; tasty

local food. **Cons:** busy with day-trippers, and wedding parties on weekends; most standard rooms lack views; not enough electrical plugs in rooms. ⑤ *Rooms from: £180* ✉ *B4425* ☎ *01285/740695* ⊕ *www. cotswold-inns-hotels.co.uk/the-swan-hotel* ⇌ *22 rooms* ⓘ◎ⓘ *Free breakfast.*

Cirencester

6 miles southwest of Bibury, 9 miles south of Chedworth, 14 miles southeast of Cheltenham.

A hub of the Cotswolds since Roman times, when it was called Corinium, Cirencester (pronounced *siren-sester*) was second only to London in importance. Today this old market town is the area's largest, with a population of 19,000. It sits at the intersection of two major Roman roads, the Fosse Way and Ermin Street (now A429 and A417). In the Middle Ages, Cirencester grew rich on wool, which funded its 15th-century parish church. It preserves many mellow stone buildings dating mainly from the 17th and 18th centuries and bow-fronted shops that still have one foot in the past.

GETTING HERE AND AROUND
Cirencester has hourly bus service from Cheltenham and less frequent service from Moreton-in-Marsh, Tetbury, and Kemble (for rail links). By road, the town can be accessed on A417, A419, and A429. Its compact center is easily walkable.

ESSENTIALS
VISITOR INFORMATION Cirencester Visitor Information Centre. ✉ *Corinium Museum, Park St.* ☎ *01285/654180* ⊕ *www.cirencester.co.uk/ visitorinformationcentre.*

 Sights

★ **Corinium Museum**
MUSEUM | FAMILY | Not much of the Roman town remains visible, but the museum displays an outstanding collection of Roman artifacts, including jewelry and coins, as well as mosaic pavements and full-scale reconstructions of local Roman interiors. Spacious and light-filled galleries that explore the town's history in Roman and Anglo-Saxon times and in the 18th century include plenty of hands-on exhibits for kids. ✉ *Park St.* ☎ *01285/655611* ⊕ *www.coriniummuseum.org* ⓢ *£5.80.*

St. John the Baptist
RELIGIOUS SITE | At the top of Market Place is this magnificent Gothic parish church, known as the cathedral of the "woolgothic" style. Its gleaming, elaborate, three-tier, three-bay south porch is the largest in England and once served as the town hall. The chantry chapels and many coats of arms bear witness to the importance of the wool merchants as benefactors of the church. A rare example of a delicate 15th-century wineglass pulpit sits in the nave. ✉ *Market Pl.* ☎ *01285/659317* ⊕ *www.cirenparish.co.uk* ⓢ *£3 donation suggested.*

 Restaurants

The Fleece
$$ | BRITISH | This 17th-century inn retains its historic past while serving fabulous modern food, real ales, and gin cocktails. Choose from a wide range of dishes including venison, steak, and seafood, or the varied selections on the daily specials board. **Known for:** lots of locals; real ales on tap; cool history with plenty of famous guests. ⑤ *Average main: £17* ✉ *Market Pl.* ☎ *01285/ 658507* ⊕ *www.thefleece-cirencester.co.uk.*

 Hotels

Barnsley House
$$$ | HOTEL | A honey-and-cream Georgian mansion, the former home of garden designer Rosemary Verey, has been discreetly modernized and converted into a luxurious retreat without sacrificing its

essential charm. **Pros:** romantic setting; great attention to detail; beautiful gardens. **Cons:** some rooms at the top of three flights of stairs; no kids under 14; farm next door not for everyone. ⑤ *Rooms from: £350 ⊠ Off the B4425, Barnsley ☎ 01285/740000 ⊕ www. barnsleyhouse.com ⌖ 18 rooms* ❍❙ *Free breakfast.*

Ivy House

$ | **B&B/INN** | Delicious breakfasts, hospitable owners, and reasonable rates enhance a stay at this stone Victorian house, close to the center of town. **Pros:** housemade granola at breakfast; child-friendly atmosphere; easy 10-minute walk to town center. **Cons:** on a main road; rooms can be on the small side; some ground-floor rooms can be viewed by passing pedestrians. ⑤ *Rooms from: £100 ⊠ 2 Victoria Rd. ☎ 01285/656626 ⊕ www.ivyhousecotswolds.com ⌖ 4 rooms* ❍❙ *Free breakfast.*

Shopping

Corn Hall
ANTIQUES/COLLECTIBLES | This is the venue for a home, garden, and fashion market Monday through Thursday; an antiques market on Friday; and a crafts market on Saturday. ⊠ *Market Pl. ⊕ www.cornhall-cirencester.com.*

Makers and Designers Emporium
JEWELRY/ACCESSORIES | Better known as m.a.d.e., this shop is a cornucopia of unusual designer items, including stationery, textiles, housewares, toys, and jewelry. ⊠ *9 Silver St. ☎ 01285/658225 ⊕ www.made-gallery.com.*

Market Place
OUTDOOR/FLEA/GREEN MARKETS | Every Monday and Friday, Cirencester's central Market Place is packed with stalls selling a motley assortment of goods, mainly household items but some local produce and crafts, too. A farmers' market takes place here every second and fourth

Saturday of the month. ⊠ *Cirencester ⊕ www.cirencester.gov.uk/markets.*

Painswick

16 miles northwest of Cirencester, 8 miles southwest of Cheltenham, 5 miles south of Gloucester.

An old Cotswold wool town of around 2,000 inhabitants, Painswick has become a chocolate-box picture of quaintness, attracting day-trippers and tour buses. But come during the week and you can discover the place in relative tranquility. The huddled gray-stone houses and inns date from as early as the 14th century and include a notable group from the Georgian era. It's worth a stroll through the churchyard of St. Mary's, renowned for its table tombs and monuments and its 100 yew trees planted in 1792. The Cotswold Way passes near the center of the village, making it easy to take a pleasant walk in the countryside.

GETTING HERE AND AROUND
Painswick is on A46 between Stroud and Cheltenham. Stagecoach runs hourly bus connections with Stroud (15 minutes) and Cheltenham (35 minutes), with reduced service on Sunday.

ESSENTIALS
VISITOR INFORMATION Painswick Visitor Information Centre. ⊠ *Grave Diggers Hut, St. Mary's Church ☎ 01452/812278 ⊕ www.painswicktouristinfo.co.uk.*

◉ Sights

Painswick Rococo Garden
GARDEN | Half a mile north of town, this delightful garden is a rare survivor from the exuberant rococo period of English garden design (1720–60). After 50 years in its original form, the 6-acre garden became overgrown. Fortunately, the rediscovery of a 1748 painting of the garden by local artist Thomas Robins sparked a full-scale restoration in the

1980s. Now you can view the original structures—such as the pretty Gothic Eagle House and curved Exedra—take in the asymmetrical vistas, and try the modern maze, which, unusually, has three centers you can discover. It's also famous for the snowdrops that bloom in January and February. There's a restaurant and a shop, too ⊠ B4073 ☎ 01452/813204 ⊕ www.rococogarden.org.uk ⊠ £10 ⊙ Closed Oct.–mid-Jan.

Restaurants

Falcon Inn

$$ | BRITISH | With views of the church of St. Mary's, this historic pub dating from 1554 offers a reassuringly traditional and charming milieu for food and refreshment. Light meals are available at lunchtime, teas in the afternoon, and for the evening meal you might start with deep-fried calamari and whitebait with caper sauce, then try the rump of lamb with minted mashed potato for your main course. **Known for:** traditional British food; beautiful views; plenty of history. $ Average main: £17 ⊠ New St. ☎ 01452/814222 ⊕ www.falconpainswick.co.uk.

Hotels

Cardynham House

$ | HOTEL | In the heart of the village, this 15th- to 16th-century former wool merchant's house, which retains its beamed ceilings, Jacobean staircase, and Elizabethan fireplace, has four-poster beds in almost all of its rooms. **Pros:** romantic and quirky; great food in restaurant; tasty breakfasts. **Cons:** some low ceilings; mainly small bathrooms; no Wi-Fi in rooms. $ Rooms from: £110 ⊠ The Cross, Tibbiwell La. ☎ 01452/814006 guesthouse, 01452/810030 restaurant ⊕ www.cardynham.co.uk ⤴ 9 rooms ⦿ Free breakfast.

Tetbury

12 miles south of Painswick, 8 miles southwest of Cirencester.

With about 5,300 inhabitants, Tetbury claims royal connections. Indeed, the soaring spire of the church that presides over this Elizabethan market town is within sight of Highgrove House, the Prince of Wales's abode. The house isn't open to the public, but you can book well in advance for a tour of the gardens. Tetbury is known as one of the area's antiques centers.

GETTING HERE AND AROUND

Tetbury is connected to Cirencester by buses operated by Cotswold Green. There is no Sunday service. It's easy to stroll around the compact town.

ESSENTIALS

VISITOR INFORMATION Tetbury Tourist Information Centre. ⊠ 33 Church St. ☎ 01666/503552 ⊕ www.visittetbury.co.uk.

Sights

Chavenage

HOUSE | Tall gate piers and spreading trees frame the family-owned Chavenage, a gray Cotswold-stone Elizabethan manor house. The tour includes a room with fine tapestries, where Cromwell lodged during the Civil War, and a main hall with minstrels' gallery and spy holes. The house is 2 miles northwest of Tetbury. It has recently been used as a filming location for the popular television show *Poldark*. ⊠ Between B4104 and A4135 ☎ 01666/502329 ⊕ www.chavenage.com ⊠ £10 ⊙ Closed Oct.–Apr., Mon.–Wed., and Sat.

★ Highgrove House

GARDEN | Highgrove House is the much-loved country home of Prince Charles and Camilla, Duchess of Cornwall. Here the prince has been making the 37-acre estate his personal showcase for traditional and organic growing methods and conservation of native plants and animals since 1980. Joining a tour of 26 people, you can appreciate the amazing industry on the part of the royal gardeners who have created the orchards, kitchen garden, and woodland garden almost from nothing. Look for the stumpery, the immaculate and quirky topiaries, and the national collection of hostas. You can sample the estate's produce in the restaurant and shop or from its retail outlet in Tetbury. Tickets go on sale in February and sell out quickly, though extra dates are released through the year via a mailing list. Be sure to book well ahead. Allow three to four hours for a visit to the garden, which is 1½ miles southwest of Tetbury. Those under 12 aren't permitted. ⊠ *Highgrove House, Off A433, Doughton* ☎ *0300/1237310 tours* ⊕ *www.high-grovegardens.com* ⊠ *£27.50, prebooked only* ⊙ *Closed late Oct.–early Apr.*

Rodmarton Manor

HOUSE | One of the last English country houses constructed using traditional methods and materials, Rodmarton Manor (built 1909–29) is furnished with specially commissioned pieces in the Arts and Crafts style. Ernest Barnsley, a follower of William Morris, worked on the house and gardens. The notable gardens—wild, winter, sunken, and white— are divided into "rooms" bounded by hedges of holly, beech, and yew. The manor is 5 miles northeast of Tetbury. Admission is cash-only. ⊠ *Off A433, Rodmarton* ☎ *01285/841442* ⊕ *www.rod-marton-manor.co.uk* ⊠ *£10; garden only £7.50* ⊙ *Closed Oct.–Mar., Sun.–Tues., Thurs., and Fri.*

Westonbirt National Arboretum

GARDEN | FAMILY | Spread over 600 acres and with 17 miles of paths, this arboretum contains one of the most extensive collections of trees and shrubs in Europe. A lovely place to spend an hour or two, it's 3 miles southwest of Tetbury and 10 miles north of Bath. The best times to come for color are in late spring, when the rhododendrons, azaleas, and magnolias are blooming, and in fall, when the maples come into their own. Open-air concerts take place in summer, and there are exhibitions throughout the year. A gift shop, café, and restaurant are on the grounds. ⊠ *Off A433* ☎ *0300/0674890* ⊕ *www.forestryengland.uk/weston-birt-the-national-arboretum* ⊠ *£11 Mar.– Nov.; £7 Dec.–Feb.*

Restaurants

The Royal Oak

$ | MODERN BRITISH | This mellow-stone gabled pub, located in the snug village of Leighterton just five miles west of Tetbury, likes to satisfy the crowds that assemble here with the best local fare in the area. Draw up a stool at the bar or take a seat at one of the many wooden tables to try the squid, chorizo, and tomato stew or cauliflower, squash, and chickpea tagine. **Known for:** traditional English country pub; huge desserts; walled garden for summer dining. ⑤ *Average main: £14* ⊠ *1 The Street, Leighterton* ☎ *0166/890250* ⊕ *www.royaloakleighter-ton.co.uk* ⊙ *No dinner Sun.*

Hotels

★ Calcot Manor

$$$ | HOTEL | FAMILY | In an ideal world everyone would sojourn in this oasis of opulence at least once; however, the luxury never gets in the way of the overall air of relaxation, a tribute to the warmth and efficiency of the staff. **Pros:** delightful rural setting; excellent spa facilities; children love it. **Cons:** all but 12 rooms are separate from main building; some traffic noise; steep prices. ⑤ *Rooms from: £310* ⊠ *A4135* ☎ *01666/890391* ⊕ *www.calcot. co* ⇆ *35 rooms* ⑩ *Free breakfast.*

🛍 Shopping

Highgrove Shop
GIFTS/SOUVENIRS | This pleasant, though pricey, shop sells organic products and gifts inspired by Prince Charles's gardens. ✉ 10 Long St. ☎ 01666/505666 ⊕ www. highgrovegardens.com/collections.

House of Cheese
FOOD/CANDY | Farm-produced cheeses, all wonderfully fresh and flavorsome, are on offer at the House of Cheese. Pâtés, preserves, and olive-wood cheese boards are other goodies at this tiny shop. ✉ 13 Church St. ☎ 01666/502865 ⊕ www. houseofcheese.co.uk.

Stratford-upon-Avon

Even under the weight of busloads of visitors, Stratford, on the banks of the slow-flowing River Avon, has somehow hung on to much of its ancient character and, on a good day, can still feel like a traditional English market town. It doesn't take long to figure out who's the center of attention here. Born in a half-timber, early-16th-century building in the center of Stratford on April 23, 1564, William Shakespeare died on April 23, 1616, his 52nd birthday, in a more imposing house at New Place, also in the center of Stratford. Although he spent much of his life in London, the world still associates him with his hometown, so much so that the town's river is sometimes referred to as "Shakespeare's Avon."

Here, in the years between his birth and 1587, he played as a young lad, attended grammar school, and married Anne Hathaway; and here he returned as a prosperous man. You can see Shakespeare's whole life here: his birthplace on Henley Street; his burial place in Holy Trinity Church; the home of his wife, Anne Hathaway's Cottage; the home of his mother, Mary Arden's Farm, at Wilmcote; New Place; and Hall's Croft,

the home of Shakespeare's daughter, Susanna; her husband, Dr. John Hall; and their daughter, Elizabeth.

By the 16th century, Stratford was a prosperous market town with thriving guilds and industries. Half-timber houses from this era have been preserved, and they're set off by later architecture, such as the elegant Georgian storefronts on Bridge Street, with their 18th-century porticoes and arched doorways.

Most sights cluster around Henley Street (off the roundabout as you come in on the A3400 Birmingham road), the High Street, and Waterside, which skirts the public gardens through which the River Avon flows. Bridge Street and the parallel Sheep Street are Stratford's main thoroughfares and where you will find mostly banks, shops, and restaurants. Bridgefoot, between the canal and the river, is next to Clopton Bridge, built in the 15th century by Sir Hugh Clopton, once lord mayor of London and one of Stratford's richest and most philanthropic residents.

GETTING HERE AND AROUND
Stratford lies about 100 miles northwest of London; take the M40 to Junction 15. The town is 35 miles southeast of Birmingham by the A38, M6, M42, and M40 (Junction 16).

Chiltern Railways serves the area from London's Marylebone Station, with trains taking an average of two hours; some are direct, but most have one change. West Midlands Railway operates direct routes from Birmingham's Snow Hill Station (journey time under an hour). Stratford has two stations, Stratford-upon-Avon Parkway, northwest of the center at Bishopston, and Stratford-upon-Avon at the edge of the town center on Alcester Road, from where it is a short walk into town.

TOURS
★ City Sightseeing
GUIDED TOURS | Running from early April to early November, these double-decker

Stratford-upon-Avon

Sights ▼

1 Anne Hathaway's Cottage........ **A3**
2 Charlecote Park.................... **J4**
3 Guild Chapel........................ **D5**
4 Hall's Croft......................... **D7**
5 Holy Trinity Church **D9**
6 MAD Museum **D3**
7 Mary Arden's Farm................ **A3**
8 Royal Shakespeare Theatre....... **F5**
9 Shakespeare's Birthplace **D2**
10 Shakespeare's New Place **D5**
11 Shakespeare's Schoolroom
    and Guildhall **D5**
12 Stratford-upon-Avon
    Butterfly Farm..................... **H6**

Restaurants ▼

1 The Black Swan/
   The Dirty Duck **E6**
2 Hobsons Patisserie **E3**
3 Hussain's **D5**
4 Lambs of Sheep Street........... **E4**
5 33 The Scullery................... **B3**
6 The Townhouse................... **D5**
7 The Vintner **E4**

Hotels ▼

1 Arden Hotel........................ **F5**
2 Arden House **B5**
3 The Bell Alderminster............. **H9**
4 Ettington Park Hotel **H9**
5 Hotel Indigo
   Stratford-upon-Avon **C5**
6 Macdonald Alveston Manor **J5**
7 Mercure Stratford-upon-Avon
   Shakespeare Hotel................ **D5**
8 White Swan **C3**

Bancroft
Gardens

Avon River

Warwick Road
Bridgeway
Birmingham Road
Clopton Bridge
Tiddington Road
Swan's Nest Lane
Shipston Road
Banbury Road
A422
A3400
Shipston Road

0 500 ft
0 100 m

KEY

1 Exploring Sights
1 Restaurants
1 Hotels

tour buses offer two options: a hop-on, hop-off bus tour that allows you to create your own itinerary around 11 landmarks in and around the town or a ticket that includes entry to each of the five Shakespeare family homes. ☎ *01789/299123* ⊕ *www.city-sightseeing.com/en/100/ stratford-upon-avon* 🖾 *From £15.*

★ **Shakespeare Birthplace Trust**
The main places of Shakespearean interest (Anne Hathaway's Cottage, Hall's Croft, Mary Arden's Farm, Shakespeare's New Place, and Shakespeare's Birthplace) are run by the Shakespeare Birthplace Trust, an independent charity that aims to preserve and promote the properties. By far the most economical way to visit the properties is to get a Full Story ticket (£23), which gives unlimited access to all five houses for a year. ☎ *01789/204016* ⊕ *www.shakespeare. org.uk.*

ESSENTIALS
VISITOR INFORMATION Stratford-upon-Avon Tourist Information Centre. ⊠ *Bridgefoot* ☎ *01789/264293* ⊕ *www.visitstratfordu- ponavon.co.uk.*

 Sights

★ **Anne Hathaway's Cottage**
BUILDING | The most picturesque of the Shakespeare Birthplace Trust properties, this thatched cottage on the western outskirts of Stratford is the family home of the woman Shakespeare married in 1582. The "cottage," actually a substantial Tudor farmhouse with latticed windows, is astonishingly beautiful. Inside, it is surprisingly cozy with lots of period furniture, including the loveseat on which Shakespeare reputedly conducted his courtship and a rare carved Elizabethan bed. The cottage garden is planted in lush Edwardian style with herbs and flowers. Wildflowers are grown in the adjacent orchard (a nod to what was grown in the garden in the Hathaways' time), and the neighboring arboretum has trees, shrubs,

and roses mentioned in Shakespeare's works. ■**TIP➜ The best way to get here is on foot, especially in late spring when the apple trees are in blossom.** The signed path runs from Evesham Place (an extension of Grove Road) opposite Chestnut Walk. Pick up a leaflet with a map from the tourist office; the walk takes 25–30 minutes. ⊠ *Cottage La.* ☎ *01789/338532* ⊕ *www.shakespeare.org.uk* 🖾 *£13; Full Story ticket (includes entry to Hall's Croft, Mary Arden's Farm, Shakespeare's New Place, and Shakespeare's Birthplace) £23.*

Charlecote Park
HISTORIC SITE | A celebrated house in the village of Hampton Lucy just outside Stratford, Charlecote Park is a Prodigy house, built in 1558 by Sir Thomas Lucy to impress Queen Elizabeth I (the house is even shaped like the letter "E" in her honor). Shakespeare knew the house—he was supposedly even caught poaching deer here. Overlooking the River Avon, the redbrick manor is striking and sprawling. It was renovated in neo-Elizabethan style by the Lucy family, represented here by numerous portraits, during the mid-19th century. A carved ebony bed is one of many spectacular pieces of furniture. The Tudor gatehouse is unchanged since Shakespeare's day, and a collection of carriages, a Victorian kitchen, and a small brewery occupy the outbuildings. Indulge in a game of croquet near the quirky, thatched, Victorian-era summer hut, or explore the deer park landscaped by Capability Brown. Interesting themed tours and walks take place in summer—call in advance to find out what's on offer. The house is five miles northeast of Stratford; by car it is reached via the B4086 or it costs around £15 in a taxi from Stratford-upon-Avon. ⊠ *Wellesbourne, Warwick* ☎ *01789/470277* ⊕ *www.nationaltrust. org.uk* 🖾 *£14.80; winter admission to grounds and outbuildings £11* ☉ *House closed Nov.–mid-Feb.*

With its thatched roof, half-timbering, and countryside setting, Anne Hathaway's Cottage is a vision from the past.

Guild Chapel

RELIGIOUS SITE | This historic chapel is the noble centerpiece of Stratford's Guild buildings, including the Guildhall, the Grammar School, and the almshouses—all well known to Shakespeare. It also houses some of the finest surviving medieval wall paintings in Europe. The ancient structure was rebuilt in the late Perpendicular style in the 5th century. The paintings were covered with limewash during the Reformation on orders given to Shakespeare's father, who was mayor at the time. Some of the most impressive paintings, rediscovered hundreds of years later, have now been restored and can be viewed, including an ornate painting known as *The Doom* above the chancel arch. Restoration on other paintings continues. ⊠ *Chapel La.* ☎ *01789/207111* ⊕ *www.guildchapel.org. uk* 🖂 *Free, donations welcome.*

Hall's Croft

HISTORIC SITE | One of the finest surviving Jacobean (early-17th-century) town houses in England, this impressive residence (one of the best preserved of the Shakespeare family homes) has a delightful walled garden and was once the home of Shakespeare's eldest daughter, Susanna, and her husband, Dr. John Hall. John Hall was a wealthy physician who, by prescribing an herbal cure for scurvy, was well ahead of his time. One room is furnished as a medical dispensary of the period, and throughout the building are fine examples of heavy oak Jacobean furniture, including a child's high chair and some 17th-century portraits. The café serves light lunches and afternoon teas. ⊠ *Old Town* ☎ *01789/338533* ⊕ *www. shakespeare.org.uk* 🖂 *£9; Full Story ticket (includes Anne Hathaway's Cottage and Gardens, Shakespeare's Birthplace, Shakespeare's New Place, and Mary Arden's Farm) £23.*

★ Holy Trinity Church

RELIGIOUS SITE | This 13th-century church on the banks of the River Avon is the final resting place of William Shakespeare. He was buried here not because he was a famed poet but because he was a lay rector of Stratford, owning a portion of the township tithes. On the north wall of the sanctuary, over the altar steps, is the famous marble bust created by Gerard Jansen in 1623 and thought to be a true likeness of Shakespeare. The bust offers a more human, even humorous, perspective when viewed from the side. Also in the chancel are the graves of Shakespeare's wife, Anne; his daughter, Susanna; his son-in-law, John Hall; and his granddaughter's first husband, Thomas Nash. Also here is the christening font in which Shakespeare was baptized. ⊠ *Old Town* ☎ *01789/266316* ⊕ *www. stratford-upon-avon.org* ✉ *£4 donation requested.*

MAD Museum

MUSEUM | FAMILY | Push buttons and pedals to your heart's content to make the exhibits in the Mechanical Art & Design Museum come alive. Witty, beautiful, and intricate automata and examples of kinetic art will clank, whir, and rattle away. Marbles and Ping-Pong balls thread and bounce through looping runs, a typewriter plays tunes on glasses and bottles, and two trains chuff around high up on the walls. Kids will love constructing their own marble run, and grown-ups will marvel at the Kitchenator display. There's also a shop full of weird and wonderful things to buy. Tickets last all day so you can come and go as you please. ⊠ *4–5 Henley St.* ☎ *01789/269356* ⊕ *themad-museum.co.uk* ✉ *£7.80.*

★ Mary Arden's Farm

HOUSE | FAMILY | This charming working farm was the childhood home of Shakespeare's mother, Mary Arden, and offers great insight into the farming methods employed in Tudor England. The rural heritage attraction, just three miles outside Stratford, is great for kids, who can try their hand at basket weaving and gardening, listen as the farmers explain their work in the fields, watch the cooks prepare food in the Tudor farmhouse kitchen, or play in the amazing timber-framed adventure playground. There are also daily falconry and archery displays and opportunities to meet the farm animals, as well as a good café. ⊠ *Station Rd., Wilmcote* ☎ *01789/338535* ⊕ *www.shakespeare.org.uk* ✉ *Adult £15.50; Full Story ticket (includes Anne Hathaway's Cottage and Gardens, Hall's Croft, Shakespeare's New Place, and Shakespeare's Birthplace) £23* ☾ *Closed Nov.–mid-Mar.*

★ Royal Shakespeare Theatre

ARTS VENUE | FAMILY | Overlooking Bancroft Gardens and with views along the River Avon, the Stratford home of the world-renowned Royal Shakespeare Company is undoubtedly one of the best places in the world to watch a Shakespearean play. The company has existed since 1879 and today boasts three Stratford venues: the Royal Shakespeare Theatre, the Swan Theatre (on the site of the original Shakespeare Memorial Theatre), and The Other Place. There's a great rooftop restaurant at the Royal Shakespeare Theatre, plus a popular Behind the Scenes tour. You can also ascend to the theater's tower, for a panoramic view of Stratford. ⊠ *Waterside* ☎ *01789/331111* ⊕ *www.rsc.org.uk* ✉ *Behind the Scenes tour £9; tower £3.*

★ Shakespeare's Birthplace

MUSEUM | A half-timber house typical of its time, the playwright's birthplace is a much-visited shrine that has been altered and restored since Shakespeare lived here. Passing through the modern visitor center, you are immersed in the world of Shakespeare through a state-of-the-art exhibition that includes evocative audio and visuals from contemporary stagings of his plays. The house itself is across the garden from the visitor center. Colorful wall decorations and furnishings reflect comfortable, middle-class Elizabethan domestic life. You can view his father's workshop and you can see the very room where Shakespeare was born. Mark Twain and Charles Dickens were both pilgrims here, and you can see the signatures of Thomas Carlyle and Walter Scott scratched into the windowpanes. In the garden, actors present excerpts from his plays. There's also a café and bookshop on the grounds. ✉ Henley St. ☎ 01789/204016 ⊕ www.shakespeare. org.uk 🎫 £18; Full Story ticket (includes Anne Hathaway's Cottage and Gardens, Hall's Croft, Shakespeare's New Place, and Mary Arden's Farm) £23.

★ Shakespeare's New Place

HOUSE | This is the spot where Shakespeare lived for the last 19 years of his life and where he wrote many of his plays, including The Tempest. Though the actual 15th-century building he inhabited was torn down in the 18th century, the site was imaginatively reinterpreted in 2016 as an outdoor space where the footprint of the original house can be traced. Each of his 38 plays is represented by a pennant in the Golden Garden, and his sonnets are engraved into the stone paving. Highlights include a mulberry tree that some believe was given to Shakespeare by King James I and a restored Elizabethan knot garden. A permanent exhibition inside the neighboring Nash's House tells the story of the New Place and Shakespeare's family life within it; there's also a roof terrace, which provides views of the gardens. Nash's House was once home to Thomas Nash, the husband of Shakespeare's granddaughter, Elizabeth Hall. ✉ 22 Chapel St. ☎ 01789/338536 ⊕ www.shakespeare. org.uk 🎫 £13; Full Story ticket (includes Anne Hathaway's Cottage and Gardens, Shakespeare's Birthplace, Hall's Croft, and Mary Arden's Farm) £23.

Shakespeare's Schoolroom and Guildhall

HISTORIC SITE | Dating from the early 15th century, the Guildhall is where a young Shakespeare went to school and where he was allegedly first introduced to the world of theater. Once the administrative center of the town, it now serves as a heritage center where visitors can see newly discovered medieval wall paintings, including two of the oldest surviving Tudor roses in England, plus take part in a lesson in the very room where Shakespeare was once taught. In the 16th century, the Guildhall was where the city council once sat, including John Shakespeare, Shakespeare's father, who was town mayor in the 1560s. Around this time it also became home to the King's New School, and shortly afterwards William Shakespeare attended as a pupil. On the first floor is the Guildhall proper, where traveling acting companies performed to obtain their licenses. Many historians believe that it was after seeing the troupe known as the Earl of Leicester's Men in 1587 that Shakespeare got the acting bug and set off for London. Today the building is still home to a school, and lessons take place on weekday mornings during term time before the attraction opens at 11 am. ✉ Church St. ☎ 01789/203170 ⊕ www. shakespearesschoolroom.org 🎫 £8.50.

Stratford-upon-Avon Butterfly Farm

NATURE PRESERVE | **FAMILY** | The United Kingdom's largest exotic butterfly collection is housed in a tropical greenhouse, a two-minute walk past the Bridgefoot footbridge (spiders, caterpillars, and insects from all over the world also make their home here). Kids can watch as butterflies emerge from pupae, search for caterpillars among the plants, or take a look at a toxic black widow spider. The ant colony is another highlight. There is also a fantastic shop, plus places to picnic in the lovely garden. ✉ Swan's Nest La. ☎ 01789/299288 ⊕ www.butterfly-farm.co.uk 🎫 £7.25.

🍴 Restaurants

The Black Swan/The Dirty Duck

$ | **BRITISH** | The only pub in Britain to be licensed under two names (the more informal one came courtesy of American GIs who were stationed here during World War II), this is one of Stratford's most celebrated and consistently rated pubs, attracting actors since the 18th-century days of thespian David Garrick. Along with your pint of bitter, you can choose from the extensive pub-grub menu of fish-and-chips, steaks, burgers, and grills; there are also good-value light bites. **Known for:** classic English pub atmosphere; reservations-only for dinner; veranda overlooking the river. $ *Average main: £10* ✉ *Waterside* ☎ *01789/297312* ⊕ *www.greeneking-pubs.co.uk.*

★ Hobsons Patisseries

$ | **BRITISH** | Visitors and locals alike head for the half-timber Hobsons Patisseries to indulge in the famous savory pies or scrumptious afternoon teas. Just a couple of minutes walk from Shakespeare's Birthplace, it's an almost obligatory lunch stop. **Known for:** delicious cakes and pies; cheap eats; low-key afternoon tea. $ *Average main: £7* ✉ *1 Henley St.* ☎ *01789/293330* ⊕ *www.hobsonspatisseries.com.*

Hussain's

$ | **INDIAN** | The luxuriant marigolds in the window might draw you in, but locals will tell you it's the Indian dishes that are the real appeal here. The extensive menu lists plenty of balti and rogan josh choices; for a little less heat, try the tandoori chicken with mild spices, cream, ground almonds, and mixed fruits, or increase the heat a bit with *jhinga bhuna* (king-size prawns in a spicy tomato sauce with onions, green peppers, and coriander). **Known for:** range of tandoori specialties; local curry-house atmosphere; prompt, friendly service. $ *Average main: £12* ✉ *6A Chapel St.* ☎ *01789/267506* ⊕ *www.hussains-restaurant.com* ⊗ *No lunch Mon.–Wed.*

★ Lambs of Sheep Street

$$ | **BRITISH** | Sit downstairs to appreciate the hardwood floors and oak beams of this local epicurean favorite; upstairs, the look is a bit more contemporary. The updates of tried-and-true dishes include herb-crusted rack of English lamb and panfried calf's liver with creamed potato, wilted spinach, pancetta, and crisp shallot. **Known for:** good-value set meals; one of the oldest buildings in Stratford; modern twists on British classics. $ *Average main: £19* ✉ *12 Sheep St.* ☎ *01789/292554* ⊕ *www.lambsrestaurant.co.uk* ⊗ *No lunch Mon. and Sun.*

★ 33 The Scullery

$$ | **BRITISH** | This small restaurant has attracted quite a following thanks to its fresh, seasonal ingredients. This is British cooking at its best and includes good options for seafood, game, and vegetarian dishes. **Known for:** buzzy atmosphere; seasonal ingredients; high-quality British dishes. $ *Average main: £18* ✉ *33a Greenhill St.* ☎ *01789/205–700* ⊕ *www.33scy.co.uk* ⊗ *Closed Mon.*

★ The Townhouse

$$ | **MODERN BRITISH** | Theatergoers tucking into an early supper to the strains of the piano in the bar, grandmothers enjoying afternoon tea, and couples lingering over candlelit suppers can all happily be found at this restaurant with rooms, which is part of the Brakspear Brewery. Chefs source the best ingredients locally where possible and serve up dishes such as oven-roasted duck breast and whole grilled plaice. **Known for:** good-value pretheater menus; chic decor; Sunday roast with all the trimmings. $ *Average main: £16* ✉ *16 Church St.* ☎ *01789/262222* ⊕ *www.stratfordtownhouse.co.uk.*

The Vintner

$$ | **BISTRO** | The imaginative, bistro-inspired menu varies each day at this café and wine bar set in a 15th-century building. Tempting British and European-style dishes include confit leg of duck bigarade with dauphinoise potatoes and seared beef fillet Stroganoff. **Known for:** inventive pretheater menu; historic setting; excellent wine list. $ *Average main: £18* ✉ *4 and 5 Sheep St.* ☎ *01789/297259* ⊕ *www.the-vintner.co.uk.*

🛏 Hotels

★ Arden Hotel

$$ | HOTEL | Bedrooms are spacious and discreet with splashes of green, violet, and dark crimson in this redbrick boutique hotel across the road from the Royal Shakespeare Theatre. **Pros:** convenient for theatergoers; crisp and modern style; gorgeous guest areas. **Cons:** gets booked up quickly; may be too noisy for some; can be popular with business travelers. $ *Rooms from: £200* ✉ *Waterside* ☎ *01789/298682* ⊕ *www. theardenhotelstratford.com* ⤳ *15 rooms* ⭐ *Free breakfast.*

★ Arden House

$$ | B&B/INN | This luxury guesthouse, sister property to the nearby Arden Hotel, offers a first-class stay, with a help-yourself pantry, books to borrow, afternoon tea, and a daily gin o'clock **Pros:** welcoming atmosphere; free afternoon tea and gin; amazing breakfast selection. **Cons:** hosts can seem overeager to please; no tea and coffee-making facilities in rooms; you may feel obliged to chat with other guests. $ *Rooms from: £169* ✉ *58–59 Rother St.* ☎ *01789/298682* ⊕ *www. theardenhotelstratford.com* ⤳ *10 rooms* ⭐ *Some meals.*

The Bell Alderminster

$$ | B&B/INN | Just a few miles south of Stratford, this pub with rooms oozes imagination and individuality. **Pros:** rural setting; close to the Cotswolds; excellent food; housemade biscuits and fresh milk in the rooms. **Cons:** on a loud main road; bar can get busy; a bit inconvenient for the Shakespeare attractions. $ *Rooms from: £125* ✉ *Shipston Rd., Alderminster* ☎ *01789/335671* ⊕ *www.brunningand-price.co.uk/bell* ⤳ *8 rooms* ⭐ *Free breakfast.*

★ Ettington Park Hotel

$ | HOTEL | This Victorian Gothic mansion, featuring arched windows and romantic turrets, is approached along a private avenue and is a soothing retreat for theatergoers who want to escape Stratford's crowds. **Pros:** gorgeous building; spacious rooms; relaxing lounge. **Cons:** a bit too formal for some; well outside Stratford; a lot of wedding guests on weekends. $ *Rooms from: £105* ✉ *Off A3400, Alderminster* ☎ *0845/072–7454 reservations, 01789/451401 inquiries* ⊕ *www.handpickedhotels.co.uk/hotels/ ettington-park-hotel* ⤳ *48 rooms* ⭐ *Free breakfast.*

★ Hotel Indigo Stratford-upon-Avon

$ | HOTEL | This hotel in a black-and-white timber-frame building in the center of town has a great location just opposite Shakespeare's New Place and a gorgeous, stripped-back feel that works well within the confines of a historic building. **Pros:** great location; excellent restaurant; plenty of character that combines old and new. **Cons:** part of a chain; neighborhood can be a little busy; some rooms on the small side. $ *Rooms from: £95* ✉ *Chapel St.* ☎ *0330/102–7244* ⊕ *stratford.hotelindigo.com* ⤳ *93 rooms* ⭐ *Free breakfast.*

Macdonald Alveston Manor

$ | HOTEL | This redbrick Elizabethan manor house across the River Avon has plenty of historic features, as well as a modern spa with a long list of treatments. **Pros:** a nice mix of the modern and historic; award-winning restaurant; interesting theatrical history. **Cons:** a lack of charm; no elevator and lots of stairs; fee for parking. $ *Rooms from: £113* ✉ *Clopton Bridge* ☎ *0344/879–9138, 01789/205478 for international calls* ⊕ *www.macdonald-hotels.co.uk/our-hotels/alveston* ⤳ *113 rooms* ⭐ *Free breakfast.*

Mercure Stratford-upon-Avon Shakespeare Hotel

$ | HOTEL | Built in the 1400s, this Elizabethan town house in the heart of Stratford is a vision right out of *The Merry Wives of Windsor,* with its nine gables and long, stunning, black-and-white, half-timber facade. **Pros:** historic building; relaxing lounge; great food. **Cons:** some very small bedrooms; parking fee; a bit dated in places. [$] *Rooms from: £105* ✉ *Chapel St.* ☎ *01789/294997* ⊕ *www.mercure. com* ⇨ *78 rooms* ⏴⏵*No meals.*

★ White Swan

$ | **HOTEL** | None of the character of this black-and-white timbered hotel, in one of Stratford's most historic buildings, has been lost in its swanky but sympathetic update. **Pros:** great sense of history; large bathrooms; friendly service. **Cons:** fee for parking, which is not on-site; food not impressive; Shakespeare motif can feel a bit overdone. [$] *Rooms from: £107* ✉ *Rother St.* ☎ *01789/297022* ⊕ *www. white-swan-stratford.co.uk* ⇨ *41 rooms* ⏴⏵ *Free breakfast.*

🎭 Performing Arts

★ Royal Shakespeare Company

THEATER | One of the finest repertory troupes in the world and long the backbone of England's theatrical life, the Royal Shakespeare Company (RSC) performs plays year-round in Stratford and at venues across Britain. The stunning Royal Shakespeare Theatre, home of the RSC, has a thrust stage based on the original Globe Theater in London. The Swan Theatre, part of the theater complex and also built in the style of Shakespeare's Globe, stages plays by Shakespeare and his contemporaries such as Christopher Marlowe and Ben Jonson. Contemporary works are staged at The Other Place nearby. Prices start from £5 for rehearsals and previews. ■**TIP**➜ **Seats book up fast, but day-of-performance and returned tickets are sometimes available.** ✉ *Waterside* ☎ *01789/403493* ⊕ *www.rsc.org.uk* 🎟 *General tickets from £16.*

🛍 Shopping

Antiques Centre

ANTIQUES/COLLECTIBLES | This building set in a Tudor courtyard contains around 50 stalls displaying jewelry, silver, linens, porcelain, and memorabilia. There's also a lovely tearoom next door. ✉ *59–60 Ely St.* ☎ *01789/204180.*

B&W Thornton

CERAMICS/GLASSWARE | Above Shakespeare's Birthplace, B&W Thornton stocks Moorcroft pottery and glass along with Shakespearean figurines. ✉ *23 Henley St.* ☎ *01789/269405* ⊕ *www. bwthornton.co.uk.*

★ Chaucer Head Bookshop

BOOKS/STATIONERY | This is the best of Stratford's many secondhand bookshops and a great place to pick up books on British history and travel. ✉ *21 Chapel St.* ☎ *01789/204330* ⊕ *www.chaucerhead. com.*

★ Shakespeare Bookshop

BOOKS/STATIONERY | Run by the Shakespeare Birthplace, the Shakespeare Bookshop carries Elizabethan plays, Shakespeare studies, children's books, and general paraphernalia. ✉ *Shakespeare's Birthplace, Henley St.* ☎ *01789/292176* ⊕ *www.shakespeare. org.uk/shop/bookshop.*

Henley-in-Arden

8 miles northwest of Stratford.

A brief drive out of Stratford will take you under the Stratford-upon-Avon Canal aqueduct to pretty Henley-in-Arden, whose wide main street is an architectural pageant of many periods. This area was once the Forest of Arden, where Shakespeare set one of his greatest comedies, *As You Like It.* Among the buildings to look for are the former Guild Hall, dating from the 15th century, and the White Swan pub, built in the early 1600s. Near Henley-in-Arden are two stately homes worth a stop, Packwood House and Baddesley Clinton.

GETTING HERE AND AROUND

The town is on the A3400. West Midlands trains for Henley-in-Arden depart every hour from Stratford; the journey takes about 15 minutes. Train service from Birmingham Moor Street takes about 35 minutes, and trains leave every hour. The town heritage center is open from April through October.

ESSENTIALS

VISITOR INFORMATION Henley-in-Arden Heritage Centre. ✉ *Joseph Hardy House, 150 High St., Henley in Arden* ☎ *01564/795919* ⊕ *www.heritagehenley. org.uk.*

◉ Sights

★ Baddesley Clinton

HOUSE | The eminent architectural historian Sir Nikolaus Pevsner described this as "the perfect late medieval manor house," and it's hard to argue with that assessment. The Tudor mansion, with its elegant Queen Anne brick bridge

reaching over the moat, is like something out of a period drama. Set off a winding back-road, this grand manor dating from the 15th century retains its great fireplaces, 17th-century paneling, and three priest holes (secret chambers for Roman Catholic priests, who were hidden by sympathizers when Catholicism was banned in the 16th and 17th centuries). Admission to the house is by timed ticket. Baddesley Clinton is two miles east of Packwood House and 15 miles north of Stratford-upon-Avon. ✉ *Rising La., Knowle, Henley in Arden* ⊕ *Off A4141 near Chadwick End* ☎ *01564/783294* ⊕ *www.nationaltrust.org.uk/baddesley-clinton* 🎟 *£12.60.*

Packwood House

HOUSE | Garden enthusiasts are drawn to Packwood's re-created 17th-century gardens, highlighted by an ambitious topiary Tudor garden in which yew trees represent Jesus's Sermon on the Mount. With tall chimneys, the house combines redbrick and half-timbering. Exquisite collections of 16th-century furniture and tapestries in the interior's 20th-century version of Tudor architecture make this one of the area's finest historic houses open to the public. It's five miles north of Henley-in-Arden and 12 miles north of Stratford-upon-Avon. ⊠ *Packwood La., Lapworth, Henley in Arden* ⊕ *Off B4439, 2 miles east of Hockley Heath* ☎ *01564/782024* ⊕ *www.nationaltrust. org.uk/packwood-house* 🖾 *£12.60; £8.40 in winter.*

Warwick

8 miles east of Henley-in-Arden, 4 miles south of Kenilworth, 9 miles northeast of Stratford-upon-Avon.

Most famous for Warwick Castle—that vision out of the feudal ages—the town of Warwick (pronounced *war*-ick) is an interesting architectural mix of Georgian redbrick and Elizabethan half-timbered buildings.

GETTING HERE AND AROUND
Frequent trains to Warwick leave London's Marylebone Station; travel time is about 90 minutes. The journey between Stratford-upon-Avon and Warwick takes around 40 minutes by train or bus. Stagecoach Bus X18 is more frequent, running every half hour.

ESSENTIALS
VISITOR INFORMATION Warwick Tourist Information Centre. ⊠ *Court House, Jury St.* ☎ *01926/492212* ⊕ *www.visitwarwick.co.uk.*

Sights

Collegiate Church of St. Mary
RELIGIOUS SITE | Crowded with gilded, carved, and painted tombs, the Beauchamp Chantry within this church is considered one of the finest medieval chapels in England. Despite the wealth of late-medieval and Tudor chivalry, the chapel was built in the 15th century in honor of the somewhat-less-than-chivalrous Richard de Beauchamp, who consigned Joan of Arc to burn at the stake. Alongside his impressive effigy in gilded bronze lie the fine tombs of Robert Dudley, Earl of Leicester, adviser and favorite of Queen Elizabeth I, and Dudley's brother, Ambrose. The church's chancel, distinguished by its flying ribs, houses the alabaster table tomb of Thomas Beauchamp, one of the first knights of the Order of the Garter, and his wife.

In the Norman crypt, look for the rare ducking stool (a chair in which people were tied for public punishment). You can also climb St. Mary's Tower for views of Warwick Castle, just a five-minute walk away. ⊠ *Old Sq.* ☎ *01926/403940* ⊕ *www.stmaryswarwick.org.uk* 🖾 *£2 donation suggested; tower £3.*

★ Warwick Castle
CASTLE/PALACE | FAMILY | The vast bulk of this medieval castle rests on a cliff overlooking the Avon River and is considered "the fairest monument of ancient and chivalrous splendor which yet remains uninjured by time," to use the words of Sir Walter Scott. Today, the company that runs the Madame Tussauds wax museums owns the castle, and it has become more theme park than authentic heritage site, but it is still a lot of fun. Warwick's two soaring towers, bristling with battlements, can be seen for miles: the 147-foot-high Caesar's Tower, built in 1356, and the 128-foot-high Guy's Tower, built in 1380. Warwick Castle's monumental walls enclose an impressive armory of medieval weapons, as well as state rooms with historic furnishings and paintings. Other exhibits explore the castle's history through the ages, display the sights and sounds of a great medieval household as it prepares for an important battle, and tell the story of a princess's

fairy-tale wedding. Be prepared both to play your part and be spooked in the gruesome dungeon experience (50 minutes and not recommended for under-10s) as you travel through scenes of torture, poisonings, and death sentences. Elsewhere, a working trebuchet (a kind of catapult), falconry displays, and rat-throwing (stuffed, not live) games add to the atmosphere. Below the castle, strutting peacocks patrol the 64 acres of grounds elegantly landscaped by Capability Brown in the 18th century. ■ TIP→ **Arrive early to beat the crowds. If you book online, you save 30% on ticket prices.** Lavish medieval banquets take place throughout the year, and plenty of food stalls serve lunch. For the ultimate castle experience, you can "glamp" (glamorously camp) in a medieval tent, stay in a wooden lodge in the Knight's Village, or spend the night in your own luxury suite in the 14th-century Caesar's Tower. ⊠ *Castle La. off Mill St.* ☎ *0371/265–2000* ⊕ *www.warwick-castle.com* ✇ *Castle £20, £13 in advance; castle and dungeon £18 (in advance only).*

🍴 Restaurants

★ Rose & Crown

$$ | MODERN BRITISH | Plain wood floorboards, comfy sofas, sturdy wooden tables, and solidly good food and drink set the tone at this contemporary gastro-pub with rooms on the town's main square. It's popular with locals, and the owners take pride in offering seasonal food that mixes British and international influences with only the best ingredients. **Known for:** seasonal produce; great pub; warm atmosphere. ⑤ *Average main: £16* ⊠ *30 Market Pl.* ☎ *01926/411117* ⊕ *www. roseandcrownwarwick.co.uk.*

 ## Hotels

★ Mallory Court Country House Hotel and Spa

$$ | HOTEL | This elegant country-house hotel four miles southeast of Warwick makes for a quiet, luxurious getaway; it has 43 rooms but still manages to make you feel like you're visiting friends (albeit very wealthy ones). **Pros:** good for pampering; excellent restaurant; real English country-house experience. **Cons:** outside town; lots of weekend weddings; some traffic noise. ⑤ *Rooms from: £220* ⊠ *Harbury La., Bishops Tachbrook* ☎ *01926/330214* ⊕ *www.mallory.co.uk* ⇗ *43 rooms* ❍ *Free breakfast.*

Kenilworth Castle

5 miles north of Warwick.

The sprawling, graceful red ruins of Kenilworth Castle loom over the green fields of Warwickshire, surrounded by the low grassy impression of what was once a lake.

GETTING HERE AND AROUND

The local Stagecoach company offers bus services to and from Stratford and Warwick on the X17 and X18 routes. The castle is 1½ miles from the town center.

ESSENTIALS

VISITOR INFORMATION Kenilworth Library and Information Centre. ⊠ *Kenilworth Library, 11 Smalley Pl., Kenilworth* ☎ *0300/555–8171* ⊕ *www.warwickshire. gov.uk/kenilworthlibrary.*

 ## Sights

★ Kenilworth Castle & Elizabethan Garden

CASTLE/PALACE | The romantic ruins of Kenilworth give some sense of the turbulent times the castle has witnessed in its 900-year history. In 1326, King Edward II was imprisoned here and forced to renounce the throne before he was transferred to Berkeley Castle in

Gloucestershire and allegedly murdered with a red-hot poker. Here the ambitious Robert Dudley, Earl of Leicester, one of Elizabeth I's favorites, entertained the queen four times, most notably in 1575 with 19 days of revelry. It was for this extended visit that Dudley created the elaborate Elizabethan garden in which to woo the queen; the garden has since been restored to its original splendor with arbors, an aviary, and an 18-foot-high Carrara marble fountain. The top of the keep has commanding views of the countryside, one good indication of why this was such a formidable fortress from 1120 until it was dismantled by Oliver Cromwell after the English Civil War in the mid-17th century. Still intact are its keep, with 20-foot-thick walls; its great hall built by John of Gaunt in the 14th century; and its curtain walls, the low outer walls forming the castle's first line of defense. You can climb the stairs to the viewing platforms for the vista that Queen Elizabeth would have had when she stayed and visit the restored gatehouse where an excellent exhibition explores her relationship with Dudley. The fine gift shop sells excellent replicas of tapestries and swords. ✉ *Castle Green, off A452, Kenilworth* ☎ *01926/852078* ⊕ *www.english-heritage.org.uk* ✉ *£11.80* ⊘ *Closed weekdays Jan.–mid-Feb.*

🍴 Restaurants

Clarendon Arms

$ | **BRITISH** | **FAMILY** | A location close to Kenilworth Castle and some good hand-pulled ales helps make this pub a nice spot for lunch. You can order home-cooked food, including steaks and grills from the bar or the ever-classic fish-and-chips. **Known for:** classic pub grub; good kids' menu; closed kitchen from 3 to 5:30 pm on weekdays. ⑤ *Average main: £11* ✉ *44 Castle Hill, Kenilworth* ☎ *01926/852017* ⊕ *www.clarendonarms-pub.co.uk.*

Chapter 9

MANCHESTER, LIVERPOOL, AND THE PEAK DISTRICT

Updated by Rhonda Carrier
and Sally Coffey

⊙ Sights   🍴 Restaurants   🛏 Hotels   🛍 Shopping   🍸 Nightlife

★★★★☆   ★★★★☆   ★★★★☆   ★★★★☆   ★★★★☆

WELCOME TO MANCHESTER, LIVERPOOL, AND THE PEAK DISTRICT

TOP REASONS TO GO

★ **Manchester theater and nightlife:** The city's theater scene keeps getting more exciting, while bustling café-bars and pubs, together with ornate Victorian-era beer houses, mean there are plenty of ways to continue your night out in style.

★ **Liverpool culture, old and new:** This once-run-down merchant city, already a must-see for fans of the Fab Four, has reinvented itself as a cultural hub with plenty of dining, lodging, and nightlife hot spots.

★ **Outdoor activities in the Peak District:** Even a short hike in Edale or High Peak reveals the craggy, austere beauty for which the area is famous, but cycling, caving, and other sports make the Peaks a veritable natural playground.

★ **Grand country houses:** The stately Chatsworth House and the Tudor manor Haddon Hall will enchant fans of both *Downton Abbey* and quintessentially English architecture alike.

Manchester lies at the heart of a tangle of motorways in the northwest of England, about a half hour across the Pennines from Yorkshire. It's 70 miles from the southern edge of the Lake District. The city spreads west toward the coast and the mouth of the River Mersey and Liverpool. To see any great natural beauty, you must head east to the Peak District, a national park less than an hour's drive southeast of Manchester. It's also where you'll find two of the grandest and best-preserved historic homes in all of Britain: Chatsworth and Haddon Hall. The southwestern part of the region, bordering Wales, is a gentler landscape; the medieval city of Chester is here, along with Ironbridge and its stunning industrial heritage museums.

1 Manchester. England's second city and the main setting of the Industrial Revolution.

2 Liverpool. A waterfront city famous for its maritime history and as the birthplace of the Beatles.

3 Buxton. A good base for the Peak District, Britain's first national park.

4 Bakewell. The commercial hub of the Peak District.

5 Chester. The thriving historical center of Cheshire.

6 Ironbridge Gorge. A World Heritage Site considered the cradle of the Industrial Revolution.

7 Ludlow. An old market town with an impressive food scene.

Southport

Chorley

Horwich

Bolton   Bury   Rochdale

M62

Formby

Ormskirk

M6

Wigan

Whitefield   Chadderton

Crosby

Kirkby

M58

Hindley   Salford   Failsworth   Penistone   M1

St Helens   Astley   Eccles   Manchester   A628   A61

Bootle

Prescot

Irlam   Hadfield

Liverpool

Huyton   Stretford   Hyde   Sheffield

M62   Stockport

M53   2   Warrington   Newall   New Mills

Spital   Widnes   Green

Bromborough   Whaley Bridge   Chapel-en-le-Frith   A61

Frodsham   M6   A6   Chatsworth   A1

Flint   PEAK   Buxton   3   House

M56   DISTRICT   4

Ewloe   Chester   Middlewich   Dakewell   Haddon   Hall

5   Congleton   A53   A6

Tarporley   Sandbach   Thurlwood   Leek   Matlock

Wrexham   Nantwich   Longport   A53   A52   Ashbourne

WALES   A49   Newcastle-under-Lyme   Stoke-on-Trent

Chirk   Whitchurch   Longton   A50   Derby

A5   Stone   A518

Oswestry   Wem   Market Drayton   M6   Uttoxeter   A50

A483   A5   A53   Eccleshall   A518   Burton-on-Trent

Newport   Stafford   Rugeley   A38

Shrewsbury   Wellington   Penkridge   Lichfield   A42

A458   Oakengates   Shifnal   M54   Bloxwich

A49   6 ◆ Ironbridge Gorge   Wolverhampton   M6   Walsall   Kingsbury

Much   A454   Erdington   Coleshill

Wenlock   Bridgnorth   Dudley   M6   Aston   M6

Church   A458   Smethwick   Birmingham   A45

Stretton   Stourbridge   Halesowen

Craven Arms   A442   Hagley   M5   M42

A49   Kidderminster   Northfield   Shirley   Coventry

7   Ludlow   Rowley

A456   0   10 mi

0   10 km   M40

For those looking for picture-postcard England, the northwest region of the country might not top many sightseeing lists, but it has plenty to offer. Manchester, Britain's third-largest city by size and second by cultural significance, bustles with redevelopment, and Liverpool is undergoing similar revitalization.

Yes, the 200 years of smokestack industry that abated only in the 1980s have taken a toll on the landscape, but the region does have some lovely scenery inland in Derbyshire (pronounced *Dar*-be-sha)—notably the spectacular Peak District, a national park at the southern end of the Pennine range.

Manchester and Liverpool, the economic engines that propelled Britain in the 18th and 19th centuries, have sloughed off their mid-20th-century decline and celebrate their rich industrial and maritime heritage through some excellent museums—either in converted Victorian edifices, strikingly modern buildings, or, in the case of the Manchester Art Gallery and Whitworth Art Gallery, a stunning combination of the two.

The cities, each with a population of about 500,000, have reestablished themselves as centers of sporting and musical excellence, as well as hot spots for culture and nightlife. Since 1962, the Manchester United, Manchester City, Everton, and Liverpool football (soccer) clubs have between them won everything worth winning in Britain and Europe. The Beatles launched the Mersey sound of the '60s; contemporary Manchester groups and acts from the Smiths to Bugzy Malone still punch above their weight on both sides of the Atlantic. On the classical side of music, Manchester is the home of Britain's oldest leading orchestra, the Hallé (founded in 1857)—just one legacy of 19th-century industrialists' investments in culture.

As you head inland to the Peak District, nature comes to the forefront in the form of crags that rear violently out of the plains. The Pennines, a line of hills that begins in the Peak District and runs as far north as Scotland, are sometimes called the "backbone of England." In this landscape of rocky outcrops and undulating meadowland you'll see nothing for miles but sheep, drystone walls (built without mortar), and farms, interrupted—spectacularly—by 19th-century villages and stately homes. In and around this area are Victorian-era spas such as Buxton, pretty towns such as Bakewell, and magnificent houses such as Chatsworth and Haddon Hall. The delight of the Peak District is being able to ramble for days in rugged countryside but still enjoy the pleasures of civilization.

To the west, some of England's prettiest countryside lies along the 160-mile border with Wales in the counties of Herefordshire, Worcestershire, and Shropshire. The Welsh borders are remote and tranquil, dotted with small villages and market towns full of 13th- and 14th-century black-and-white half-timber buildings, the legacy of a forested countryside. The Victorians were responsible for the more recent fashion of painting these structures black and white. The more elaborately decorated half-timber buildings in market towns such as Shrewsbury and Chester are monuments to wealth, dating mostly from the early 17th century. More half-timbered structures are found in Ludlow, now a culinary center nestled in the lee of its majestic ruined castle.

MAJOR REGIONS

Manchester. This vibrant city mixes a compelling industrial heritage with cutting-edge urban design and thriving music and club scenes. Great museums and art galleries justify its blossoming status as the United Kingdom's second city of culture.

Liverpool. The imposing waterfront, the pair of cathedrals, and the grand architecture make it clear that this city—now undergoing a postindustrial rebirth—is more than just the Beatles. Even so, the many museums don't leave out the city's place in rock-and-roll history.

The Peak District. Heading southeast, away from the urban congestion of Manchester and Liverpool, it's not far to the southernmost contortions of the Pennine Hills. Here, about an hour southeast of Manchester, sheltered in a great natural bowl, is the spa town of Buxton: at an elevation of more than 1,000 feet, it's the second-highest town in England. Buxton makes a convenient base for exploring the 540 square miles of the Peak District, Britain's oldest—and, its fans say, most beautiful—national park. About 38,000 people live in the towns throughout the park.

"Peak" is perhaps misleading; despite being a hilly area, it contains only gentle rises that don't reach much higher than 2,000 feet. Yet a trip around destinations such as Bakewell, Matlock, Castleton, and Edale, as well as around the grand estates of Chatsworth House and Haddon Hall, involves negotiating fairly perilous country roads, each of which repays the effort with enchanting views.

Outdoor activities are popular in the Peaks, particularly caving (or "potholing"), walking, and hiking. Bring all-weather clothing and waterproof shoes.

Chester, Ludlow, and Around. Rural Shropshire, one of the least populated English counties, is far removed from most people's preconceptions of the industrial Midlands. Within its spread are towns long famed for their beauty, such as Ludlow. Chester, one of the region's most important cities, is renowned for its medieval heritage and wealth of half-timber buildings. The 6-mile stretch of the Ironbridge Gorge, however, gives you the chance to experience the cradle of the Industrial Revolution with none of the reeking smoke that gave this region west of Birmingham its name—the Black Country—during the mid-19th century. Now taken over by the Ironbridge Gorge Museum Trust, the bridge, the first in the world to be built of iron and opened in 1781, is the centerpiece of this vast museum complex.

Planning

When to Go

Manchester has a reputation as one of the wettest cities in Britain, and visiting in summer won't guarantee dry weather. Nevertheless, the damp or cold shouldn't spoil a visit because of the many indoor sights and cultural activities here and in Liverpool. Summer is the optimal time to see the Peak District, especially because traditional festivities take place in many villages. The only time to see the great houses of Derbyshire's Wye Valley is from spring through fall.

Planning Your Time

It's possible to see the main sights of Manchester or Liverpool in two days, but you'd have to take the museums at a real gallop. In Manchester, the Museum of Science and Industry and the Imperial War Museum North could easily absorb a day by themselves, as could the Albert Dock and waterfront area of Liverpool, where the Beatles Story's main venue, the Tate Liverpool, and the Merseyside Maritime and International Slavery museums, as well as the neighboring Museum of Liverpool, all vie for your attention. In Liverpool, an additional half day is needed to see the homes of John Lennon and Paul McCartney. The excellent nightlife of each city demands at least an overnight stay at each. You can explore the Peak District on a day trip from Manchester in a pinch, but allow longer to visit the stately homes or to hike. In the south of the region, Ironbridge Gorge demands a full day. You could do Ludlow and Chester in a half day each, though it would be a shame to leave Ludlow without sampling its fine dining.

FESTIVALS

★ **Manchester International Festival**

FESTIVALS | This biennial multi-arts festival has played a major role in Manchester's cultural development since it launched in 2007. With international artists such as Björk and Marina Abramović making appearances, it often premieres events that go on to tour nationally or globally. Events take place in some of the city's most popular performing arts spaces, as well as obscure locations such

as disused buildings. ✉ *Manchester* ⊕ *www.mif.co.uk.*

Getting Here and Around

AIR

Both Manchester and Liverpool are well served by their international airports. Manchester, the third-largest airport in the country (and the busiest outside London), has the greater number of flights, including some from the United States. East Midlands Airport southwest of Derby also provides an alternative international air route into the region.

AIRPORTS East Midlands Airport. ✉ *Castle Donington* ☎ *0808/169–7032* ⊕ *www.eastmidlandsairport.com.* **Liverpool John Lennon Airport.** ✉ *Hale Rd., Liverpool* ☎ *0871/521–8484* ⊕ *www.liverpoolairport.com.* **Manchester Airport.** ☎ *0808/169–7030* ⊕ *www.manchesterairport.co.uk.*

BUS TRAVEL

National Express buses serve the region from London's Victoria Coach Station. Average travel time to Manchester or Liverpool is five hours. To reach Matlock, Bakewell, and Buxton, you can take a bus from London to Derby and change to the TransPeak bus service, though you might find it more convenient to travel first to Manchester.

BUS CONTACTS National Express. ☎ *0871/781–8181* ⊕ *www.nationalexpress.com.* **TransPeak.** ☎ *0844/351–1120* ⊕ *www.highpeakbuses.com.*

CAR

If you're traveling by road, expect heavy traffic out of London on weekends. Travel time to Manchester or Liverpool from London via the M6 is 3 to 3½ hours. Although a car may not be an asset in touring the centers of Manchester and Liverpool, it's helpful in getting around the Peak District. Bus service is quite good, but a car allows the most flexibility.

Roads within the region are generally very good, but the deeper you get into the countryside, the more likely you are to encounter narrow, one-lane farm roads once you turn off the main routes. In summer, Peak District traffic is very heavy; watch out for speeding motorbikes, especially on the A6. In winter, know the weather forecast, as moorland roads can quickly become impassable. To reach Ludlow and Chester from London, take M40.

In Manchester and Liverpool, try to sightsee on foot to avoid parking issues. In the Peak District, park in signposted parking lots whenever possible.

TRAIN

Virgin Trains serves the region from London's Euston Station. Direct services to Manchester and Liverpool take between 2 and 2½ hours. There are trains between Manchester's Piccadilly Station and Liverpool's Lime Street roughly four times an hour during the day; the trip takes 50 minutes. (Trains also go less frequently from Manchester's Victoria and Oxford Road stations.) Get schedules and other information through National Rail Enquiries.

To reach Buxton in the Peak District from London, take the train to Manchester that stops at Stockport and change there; to Buxton it's another 45-minute ride. The local service—one train an hour (more at peak times)—from Manchester Piccadilly to Buxton takes just under one hour.

TRAIN CONTACTS National Rail Enquiries. ☎ 03457/484950 ⊕ www.nationalrail. co.uk.

TRANSPORTATION DISCOUNTS AND DEALS

A Greater Manchester Wayfarer ticket (£14.40; £28.80 for groups of up to two adults and two children) covers a day's travel on all forms of transport in Manchester and parts of Lancashire, Cheshire, Staffordshire, Derbyshire, and the Peak District. See ⊕ www.tfgm.com or call ☎ 0161/244–1000 for information.

Restaurants

Dining options in Manchester and Liverpool vary from smart cafés offering Modern British, Continental, or global fare to world-class international restaurants for all budgets. Manchester has one of Britain's biggest Chinatowns, as well as its "Curry Mile" of 40-odd Bangladeshi, Pakistani, and Indian restaurants a mile south of the city center (although delicious modern Indian restaurants certainly exist in the city center, too).

One local dish that has survived is Bakewell pudding (never called "tart" in these areas, as its imitations are elsewhere in England). Served with custard or cream, the pudding—a pastry covered with jam and a thin layer of almond-flavor filling—can't be missed if visiting Bakewell.

Hotels

Because the larger city-center hotels in Manchester and Liverpool rely on business travelers during the week, they may markedly reduce their rates on weekends. Smaller hotels and guesthouses abound, often in nearby suburbs, many just a short bus ride from downtown. The Manchester and Liverpool visitor information centers operate room-booking services. Also worth investigating are serviced apartments, which are becoming more popular in the cities. The Peak District has inns, bed-and-breakfasts, and hotels, as well as a network of youth hostels and campsites. Local tourist offices have details; reserve well in advance for Easter and summer.

Restaurant and hotel reviews have been shortened. For full information, visit Fodors.com. Restaurant prices are the average cost of a main course at dinner, or if dinner is not served, at lunch. Hotel prices are the lowest cost of a standard double room in high season, including 20% V.A.T.

WHAT IT COSTS in Pounds			
$	$$	$$$	$$$$
RESTAURANTS			
under £16	£16–£23	£24–£30	over £30
HOTELS			
under £125	£125–£225	£226–£350	over £350

Manchester

Central Manchester is alive with the vibe of cutting-edge popular music and a swank, often fancy café, cocktail bar, and restaurant culture that keeps evolving at a dizzying speed. The city's once-grim industrial landscape, redeveloped since the late 1980s, includes tidied-up canals, cotton mills transformed into loft apartments, and stylish contemporary architecture that has pushed the skyline ever higher. Beetham Tower, the 12th-tallest building in Britain (the second tallest outside London since the addition of the Deansgate Square South Tower to the Manchester cityscape), stands proud and prominent. Since 2020, over £300 million of investment has unleashed another cultural boom that includes or will include several major city projects, including the expansion of several museums and music venues, the reopening of the Contact Theatre and the Manchester Jewish Museum, the launch of the OMA/Rem Koolhas-designed Factory cultural space (which will serve as the permanent home to the Manchester International Festival), and the opening of the RHS Garden Bridgewater. Manchester's imposing Town Hall is closed until 2024, but you can still admire its 280-foot-tall clock tower from the outside.

The now-defunct Haçienda Club marketed the 1980s rock band New Order to the world, and Manchester became the clubbing capital of England. Other Manchester-based bands like Joy Division, the Smiths, Stone Roses, Happy Mondays, and Oasis also rose to the top of the charts throughout the '70s, '80s, and '90s. The extraordinary success of the Manchester United and Manchester City football clubs has kept the eyes of sports fans around the world fixed firmly on Manchester.

GETTING HERE AND AROUND

Manchester Airport has many international flights, so you might not even have to travel through London. There are frequent trains from the airport to Piccadilly Railway Station (15–20 minutes), Metrolink trams to the city center (50 minutes), and buses to Piccadilly Gardens Bus Station (70-80 minutes). A taxi from the airport to Manchester city center costs around £30. For details about public transportation in Manchester, see ⊕ *www.tfgm. com* or call ☎ *0161/244–1000.*

Driving to Manchester from London (3 to 3½ hours), take the M1 north to the M6, then the M62 east, which becomes the M602 as it enters Greater Manchester.

Trains from London's Euston Station drop passengers at the centrally located Piccadilly railway station. The journey takes just over two hours. Manchester Central (Chorlton Street) Coach Station, a five-minute walk west of Piccadilly railway station, is the main bus station for regional and long-distance buses.

Most local buses leave from Piccadilly Gardens bus station, the hub of the urban bus network. Metroshuttle operates three free circular routes around the city center; frequency and times vary by route.

The ever-expanding Metrolink electric tram service runs through the city center and out to the suburbs and the airport. The Eccles extension has a stop for the

Lowry (Harbour City) and the Altrincham line a stop for Manchester United Stadium (Old Trafford). Buy a ticket from the platform machine before you board.

SystemOne Travelcards are priced according to the times of day, number of days, and modes of transport you want to include (for example: unlimited buses, trams, and trains after 9:30 am cost £10); buy from the bus driver or a train- or tram-stop ticket machine.

TOURS
City Centre Cruises
Take a three-hour round-trip cruise (prices starting from £18) on a barge to the Manchester Ship Canal; some include a traditional Sunday lunch or afternoon tea. Another includes entry to the Manchester United football stadium tour. Times vary; call or go online for departure schedule. ☎ *0161/902–0222* ⊕ *www.citycentrecruises.com* ✉ *From £25.*

Manchester Guided Tours
Group tours run by this tourism board–recommended firm include daily Discover Manchester walks. Prices start at £10. ☎ *07505/685942* ⊕ *www.manchesterguidedtours.com.*

ESSENTIALS
TRANSPORTATION CONTACTS Metrolink. ☎ *0161/205–2000* ⊕ *www.tfgm.com.* **Transport for Greater Manchester.** ☎ *0161/244–1000* ⊕ *www.tfgm.com.*

VISITOR INFORMATION Manchester Visitor Information Centre. ✉ *Manchester Central Library, St Peter's Sq., City Centre* ☎ ⊕ *www.visitmanchester.com.*

Sights

Castlefield Urban Heritage Park
ARCHAEOLOGICAL SITE | FAMILY | Site of an early Roman fort, the district of Castlefield was later the center of the city's industrial boom, which resulted in the building of Britain's first modern canal in 1764 and the world's first railway station in 1830. It has been beautifully restored

into an urban park with canal-side walks, landscaped open spaces, and refurbished warehouses. The 7-acre site contains the reconstructed gate to the Roman fort of Mamucium, the buildings of the **Museum of Science and Industry,** and several bars and restaurants, many with outdoor terraces. You can easily spend a day here. ✉ *Liverpool Rd., Castlefield.*

★ Central Library
LIBRARY | This 1930s structure was once the biggest municipal library in the world, and today its circular exterior, topped by a line of Doric columns and a massive Corinthian portico facing St. Peter's Square, is a major focus for Manchester's most prestigious civic quarter. Notable sights within the library are the **British Film Institute Mediatheque,** a free-to-view collection of 2,000 films and TV programs relating to the United Kingdom and its people, the Media Lounge with creative software and gaming stations; the Music Library with a DJ-mixing desk and instrument collection that is free to use; and the Children's Library, as well as free Wi-Fi, displays on local history, and a convenient café. ✉ *St. Peter's Sq., City Centre* ☎ *0161/234–1983* ⊕ *www.manchester.gov.uk/centrallibrary* ⊙ *Closed Sun.*

★ IWM North
MUSEUM | FAMILY | The thought-provoking exhibits in this striking, aluminum-clad building, which architect Daniel Libeskind described as representing three shards of an exploded globe, present the reasons for war and show its effects on society. Hourly Big Picture audiovisual shows envelop you in the sights and sounds of conflicts while a time line from 1914 to the present examines objects and personal stories from veterans showing how war changes lives. Excellent special exhibitions cover everything from life in Britain during the Blitz to artistic responses to conflict. The museum is on the banks of the Manchester Ship Canal in The Quays, across the footbridge

Sights ▼

1 Castlefield Urban
   Heritage Park C5
2 Central Library E4
3 IWM North A5
4 John Rylands Library D3
5 The Lowry A5
6 Manchester Art Gallery F4
7 Manchester Museum H9
8 Museum of Science and
   Industry B1
9 National Football Museum F1
10 People's History Museum C3
11 RHS Garden Bridgewater A2
12 Whitworth Art Gallery I9

Restaurants ▼

1 Bundobost H3
2 The Creameries E9
3 Hispi Bistro E9
4 Mackie Mayor H1
5 The Refuge by Volta F6
6 TAST D3
7 Where the Light Gets In I9

Hotels ▼

1 Abel Heywood G2
2 Dakota I3
3 The Edwardian Manchester, a
   Radisson Collection Hotel D4
4 Hyatt Regency Manchester and
   Hyatt House Manchester G9
5 Native I4
6 Roomzzz Aparthotel Manchester
   Corn Exchange F1

Manchester was an industrial powerhouse; learn all about this history at the engaging Museum of Science and Industry.

from the Lowry. It's a five-minute walk from the MediaCityUK stop of the Metrolink tram. ✉ *Trafford Wharf Rd.* ☎ *0161/836–4000* ⊕ *www.iwm.org.uk/ visits/iwm-north.*

★ John Rylands Library

LIBRARY | Owned by the University of Manchester, this Gothic Revival masterpiece designed by Alfred Waterhouse was built by Enriqueta Augustina Rylands as a memorial to her husband, a cotton magnate. Constructed of red sandstone in the 1890s, the library resembles a cathedral and contains some outstanding collections of illuminated manuscripts and beautifully illustrated books. Among the many highlights are the oldest known fragment of the New Testament in existence, dating from around AD 100; an original Gutenberg Bible; and several works by William Caxton (c.1417–92), who introduced the printing press to the English-speaking world. A lively temporary exhibition and events program includes printing press demonstrations, photography tours, and

family crafts based on elements of the building's decor or other related objects. ✉ *150 Deansgate, Millennium Quarter* ☎ *0161/306–0555* ⊕ *www.library.manchester.ac.uk* ✉ *Free.*

The Lowry

ARTS VENUE | **FAMILY** | Clad in perforated steel and glass, this arts center is one of the highlights of the Salford Quays waterways. L. S. Lowry (1887–1976) was a local artist, and one of the few who painted the industrial landscape; galleries here showcase his work alongside that of contemporary artists. The theater has three spaces showcasing everything from West End musicals and new works by up-and-coming theater companies to some of the U.K.'s most popular stand-up comedians. The nearest Metrolink tram stop is Harbour City, a 10-minute walk away. ✉ *Pier 8, Salford* ☎ *0343/235–8888* ⊕ *www.thelowry.com* ✉ *Galleries free, performances vary.*

Manchester Art Gallery

MUSEUM | **FAMILY** | Behind an impressive classical portico, this splendid museum and its sparkling modern atrium houses an outstanding collection of paintings by the Pre-Raphaelites and their circle, notably Ford Madox Brown's masterpiece *Work* and Holman Hunt's *The Hireling Shepherd* . British artwork from the 18th and the 20th centuries is also well represented. The second-floor Craft and Design Gallery shows off the best of the decorative arts in ceramics, glass, metal-work, and furniture. The Clore Art Studio is a creative space for families. ⊠ *Mosley St., City Centre* ☎ *0161/235–8888* ⊕ *www.manchesterartgallery.org* ☜ *Free.*

★ **Manchester Museum**
MUSEUM | FAMILY | Run by the University of Manchester and located in a superb Gothic Revival building with modern add-ons, this museum is currently undergoing a £13½ million transformation that will culminate in a new South Asia gallery, a Chinese culture gallery, and the world's first center for age-friendly culture. Embracing anthropology, natural history, and archaeology, it features one of the U.K.'s largest ancient Egyptian collections as part of the extensive Ancient Worlds galleries, a beautiful Living Worlds gallery designed to raise questions about our attitude towards nature, and a vivarium complete with live frogs and other amphibians and reptiles. A lively events program for all ages helps lure in repeat visitors. ⊠ *Oxford Rd., University Quarter* ☎ *0161/275–2648* ⊕ *www.museum.manchester.ac.uk.*

★ **Museum of Science and Industry**
HISTORIC SITE | FAMILY | The venue's historic buildings, one of which is the world's oldest passenger rail station (1830), hold marvelous collections relating to the city's industrial past and present, although conservation, restoration, and expansion over the next few years will mean certain areas are off-limits or obscured by scaffolding. You can walk through a reconstructed Victorian sewer, be blasted by the heat and noise of working steam engines, see cotton

looms whirring in action, and watch a planetarium show. The Air and Space Gallery fills a graceful cast-iron-and-glass building, constructed as a market hall in 1877. ■ TIP➔ **Allow at least half a day to get the most out of all the sites, temporary exhibitions, talks, and events.** ⊠ *Castlefield Urban Heritage Park, Liverpool Rd., main entrance on Lower Byrom St., Castlefield* ☎ *0161/832–2244* ⊕ *www.scienceandindustrymuseum.org.uk* ☜ *Free, charges vary for special exhibits.*

National Football Museum
MUSEUM | FAMILY | This striking, glass-skinned triangle of a building includes a galaxy of footballing (soccer) memorabilia, from historic trophies, souvenirs, and shirts (many of them match-worn and signed by legends of the sport) to such near-sacred items as the ball from the 1966 World Cup—the last time England won the sport's ultimate prize. There's also lots of interactive fun to be had, like in the penalty shoot-out area, the Performance section that looks at how football affects the body, and the under-5s discovery zone. ⊠ *Urbis Bldg., Cathedral Gardens, City Centre* ☎ *0161/605–8200* ⊕ *www.nationalfootballmuseum.com* ☜ *£10.*

People's History Museum
MUSEUM | Not everyone in 19th-century Manchester owned a cotton mill or made a fortune on the trading floor. This museum recounts powerfully the struggles of working people in the city and in the United Kingdom as a whole since the Industrial Revolution. Displays include the story of the 1819 Peterloo Massacre—when the army attacked a crowd of civil rights protesters in Manchester's St. Peter's Square, killing 15 and almost sparking revolution—together with an unrivaled collection of trade-union banners, tools, toys, utensils, and photographs, all illustrating the working lives and pastimes of the city's people. ⊠ *Left Bank, City Centre* ☎ *0161/838–9190* ⊕ *www.phm.org.uk* ☜ *Free.*

★ RHS Garden Bridgewater

GARDEN | FAMILY | This 154-acre garden has transformed the heritage grounds of Worsley New Hall into a delightful green space for both locals and visitors. There's a kitchen garden, a stream-side Chinese garden, community growing spaces, a learning garden, and a play area. ⊠ *Worsley New Hall, Off Leigh Rd., Salford* ✛ *About a 15-min drive west of city center* ☎ *020/7821–3187* ⊕ *www. rhs.org.uk/gardens.*

★ Whitworth Art Gallery

MUSEUM | FAMILY | This University of Manchester–owned art museum is beautifully—and uniquely—integrated into the surrounding parkland through its art garden, sculpture terrace, orchard garden, and landscape gallery. Some of the free events and activities take you into the park itself, including children's outdoor art clubs. The renowned collections inside the gallery embrace British watercolors, Old Master drawings, postimpressionist works, wallpapers, and an outstanding textile gallery befitting a city built on textile manufacturing. There's also a learning studio for families and a "café in the trees" overlooking the art garden, with a seasonal British menu. ⊠ *University of Manchester, Oxford Rd., University Quarter* ☎ *0161/275–7450* ⊕ *www.whitworth. manchester.ac.uk* ⤢ *Free.*

Restaurants

Bundobost

$ | INDIAN | Tasty Gujrat-inspired vegetarian street food lures the budget-conscious to this colorful and vivacious canteen-style restaurant tucked away in a basement on Piccadilly Gardens. Order from the bar, and watch chefs get busy in a semi-open kitchen on Indian dishes both classic and modern. **Known for:** sociable Indian sharing dishes; local and global craft beers; inventive cocktails. ⑤ *Average main: £6* ⊠ *61 Piccadilly, City Centre* ☎ *0161/359–6757* ⊕ *www. bundobust.com.*

The Creameries

$$$$ | MODERN BRITISH | An exciting venture by seasoned local chef Mary-Ellen McTague (who cooked under Heston Blumenthal at the legendary Fat Duck for many years), this airy suburban dining room in a former bakery offers great-value three-course lunch and five-course supper menus. This is contemporary comfort food at its finest; you can sample the likes of home-smoked mackerel, goat cheese beignets, and treacle tart. **Known for:** ethically sourced produce including wild meats; zero-waste policy; on-site wine bar and shop offering low-intervention wines. ⑤ *Average main: £35* ⊠ *406 Wilbraham Rd., Chorlton, South Manchester* ☎ *0161/312–8328* ⊕ *www. thecreameries.co.uk.*

★ Hispi Bistro

$$ | MODERN EUROPEAN | Part of a small group of famously crowd-funded (yup, people liked the owner-chef so much they raised money so he could open a place in their 'hood) restaurants found across northwest England, this neighborhood bistro offers ambitious dining at remarkably fair prices. In pared-back surroundings, expect the likes of torched mackerel, cured cod loin, and crottin cheese baked in truffle honey, plus wonderful accompaniments including hard-to-find vegetables. **Known for:** great-value early dinners; exceptional kids' menu; Sunday lunch. ⑤ *Average main: £20* ⊠ *1C School La., Didsbury* ☎ *0161/445–3996* ⊕ *www.hispi.net.*

Mackie Mayor

$ | INTERNATIONAL | Located in a 19th-century market building, this food court brings together several casual dining experiences under one stunningly restored roof. Choose from sourdough pizza, rotisserie chicken, fish-and-chips, rare cuts of beef, Thai street food, and tortillas, tacos, and nachos, all ordered from the counters and delivered to long shared tables. **Known for:** convivial atmosphere; local artisanal produce; fabulous breakfasts and brunches. $ *Average main: £7* ✉ *1 Eagle St., Northern Quarter* ⊕ *www.mackiemayor.co.uk* ⊗ *Closed Mon. No dinner Sun.*

★ The Refuge by Volta

$ | **INTERNATIONAL** | This glamorous spot serves eclectic global food amidst the original features of a stunning Victorian Gothic building that's been given new life as the Principal Hotel. Expect dishes from Spanish salt cod croquettes and Asian-inspired ceviche to Middle Eastern *mutabal* (an eggplant dish similar to baba ghanoush) and lamb shawarma. **Known for:** Sunday lunches; local ingredients; buzzy atmosphere. $ *Average main: £9* ✉ *The Principal Hotel, Oxford St., City Centre* ☎ *0161/233–5151* ⊕ *www. refugemcr.co.uk.*

★ TAST

$$$ | **CATALAN** | Financed by one-time Barcelona soccer legend and Manchester City FC manager Pep Guardiola, this Catalonian restaurant pulls no punches when it comes to contemporary cooking, with dishes courtesy of two Michelin-star chef Paco Pérez. The unifying overall concept is "tastets": small tastes of food with greater complexity than tapas. **Known for:** groundbreaking cuisine; quirky, theatrical presentation; special occasion dining. $ *Average main: £30* ✉ *20–22 King St., City Centre* ☎ *0161/806–0547* ⊕ *www.tastcatala.com* ⊗ *Closed Mon.*

★ Where the Light Gets In

$$$$ | **MODERN BRITISH** | Much-loved by food critics, this groundbreaking "New Northern" restaurant in a former coffee warehouse offers a no-choice tasting menu (£90) that depends on "the day's catch, harvest, and slaughter." Regular ingredients include Macclesfield trout, cured Middle White pork, and salt-baked beets in delicious combinations; much of the produce comes from the restaurant's own farm. **Known for:** immense creativity; excellent wine flights; hip atmosphere. $ *Average main: £90* ✉ *7 Rostron Brow* ⊹ *7 miles southeast of central*

Manchester in Stockport ☎ *0161/477–5744* ⊕ *www.wtlgi.co* ⊗ *Closed Sun.– Tues. No lunch Wed.–Fri.*

Hotels

Abel Heywood

$ | **HOTEL** | Ideal for those who want a true Mancunian feel to their accommodation, this well-priced boutique hotel and bar in the funky Northern Quarter was named for a local mayor, radical, and publisher. **Pros:** in room visitor guide to the Northern Quarter and Manchester; historic ambience and local charm; great location for nightlife. **Cons:** rooms are small; some rooms have noise from the kitchen; tempermamental/noisy air-conditioning. $ *Rooms from: £85* ✉ *38 Turner St., Northern Quarter* ☎ *0161/819–1441* ⊕ *www.abelheywood.co.uk* ⇨ *15 rooms* ⦙◯⦙ *No meals.*

Dakota

$ | **HOTEL** | This boutique hotel has brought some glamorous decadence to the Manchester hotel scene, with its low-lit vibe, bold palette of mainly pale and chocolate browns, and sumptuous fabrics mixing well with the champagne bar and cigar garden. **Pros:** just a five-minute walk from Piccadilly Station; outdoor terraces in some rooms; great cocktails. **Cons:** room service is not 24 hours; building a bit severe; not all rooms have robes. $ *Rooms from: £120* ✉ *29 Ducie St., City Centre* ☎ *0161/674–9180* ⊕ *www. dakotahotels.co.uk/manchester* ⇨ *137 rooms* ⦙◯⦙ *No meals.*

★ The Edwardian Manchester, a Radisson Collection Hotel

$$ | **HOTEL** | In the heart of the city, this elegant option invites you to unwind with its atmospheric spa (complete with a urban subterranean swimming pool, sauna, steam rooms and cutting-edge gym), luxurious afternoon teas, and memorable dining including contemporary Japanese and Mexican small plates in Peter Street Kitchen. **Pros:** great central location;

highly attentive staff; some suites with private verandas. **Cons:** spa can get very busy; some rooms small by city standards; bars sometimes fully booked for private events. ⑤ *Rooms from: £144* ✉ *Free Trade Hall, Peter St., City Centre* ☎ *0161/835–9929* ⊕ *www.radissonhotels.com/en-us/hotels/radisson-collection-edwardian-manchester* ↝ *263 rooms* ❢❘ *Free breakfast.*

Hyatt Regency Manchester and Hyatt House Manchester

$$ | HOTEL | This sleek upscale hotel and its sister apart-hotel (the U.K.'s very first Hyatt House property) are located within the same modern building and are ideal for those who like to be away from the fray of the city center with all its nightlife noise. It's also very handy for visiting the University of Manchester campus, Manchester Museum, and The Whitworth. **Pros:** floor-to-ceiling windows with city or university green views; nice amenities including gym; 24-hour H Market for snacks and groceries. **Cons:** a walk away from the city's best restaurants and bar areas; strange layout (Hyatt House reception on 18th floor); hotel may feel corporate to some. ⑤ *Rooms from: £135* ✉ *55 Booth St. West, University Quarter* ☎ *0161/359–5550* ⊕ *www.hyatthouse-manchester.com* ↝ *328 rooms* ❢❘ *Free breakfast.*

★ Native

$ | RENTAL | A charming reincarnation of a one-time cotton warehouse, Native retains its impressive original brick barrelled ceilings, exposed beams, and wrought-iron girders (now painted a hip powder-blue). **Pros:** unique historic building with gorgeous wooden floors; sociable community hub on-site; just steps from Piccadilly Station. **Cons:** early check-out time if not booked direct; some rooms a bit dark; can suffer from outside noise. ⑤ *Rooms from: £95* ✉ *Ducie Street Warehouse, Ducie St., City Centre* ☎ *0161/503–9551* ⊕ *www.nativeplaces.com* ↝ *166 rooms* ❢❘ *No meals.*

Roomzzz Aparthotel Manchester Corn Exchange

$$ | RENTAL | The architecture and the original features of the iconic Manchester Corn Exchange—which also has served as a shopping mall and is now largely a dining hub—are the stars at this apartment hotel. **Pros:** free grab-and-go breakfasts and 24-hour coffee; on-site gym; round-the-clock essentials shop. **Cons:** specific rooms can be requested but not booked; not all rooms have bathtubs; water pressure not reliably powerful. ⑤ *Rooms from: £130* ✉ *Corn Exchange, Exchange Sq., City Centre* ☎ *0203/504–5555* ⊕ *www.roomzzz.com* ↝ *114 apartments* ❢❘ *Free breakfast.*

⦿ Nightlife

Manchester vies with London as Britain's capital of youth culture, but it has vibrant nightlife and entertainment options for all ages. Spending time at a bar, pub, or club is an essential part of any trip. For event listings, check out the free *Manchester Evening News,* widely available throughout the city or as a website or app. Other helpful websites include ⊕ *www.manchesterconfidential.co.uk,* ⊕ *www.manchesterwire.co.uk,* and ⊕ *creativetourist.com.*

The neighborhood of Gay Village lines up stylish bars and cafés along the Rochdale Canal; Canal Street is its heart. There are several gay bars, but most attract a mixed crowd.

BARS

Cloud 23

BARS/PUBS | This dressy champagne and cocktail bar in the city's tallest building has stunning 360-degree views. Some of its inventive concoctions make a playful nod to local culture. You can also get afternoon tea or dine from a small menu of tacos, flatbreads, and desserts. ✉ *Hilton Manchester Deansgate, Beetham Tower, 303 Deansgate, City Centre*

☏ 0161/870–1670 ⊕ www.cloud23bar.com.

Folk

BARS/PUBS | Bars and restaurants come and go on trendy, ever-evolving Burton Road, but this bar and café has stood the test of time thanks to its heated terrace (complete with palm trees), eclectic tunes by live DJs, chic interiors, and good food. ✉ 169 Burton Rd., West Didsbury ☏ 0161/445–2912 ⊕ www.folkcafebar.co.uk.

Kosmonaut

BARS/PUBS | With stripped-down decor of exposed brick walls, old tiles, and leather benches, this bar exudes a hipster vibe. There's a Ping-Pong table and changing art exhibitions, as well as a wine list and beer selection, although it's the inventive cocktails that draw the crowds. ✉ 10 Tariff St., Northern Quarter ☏ 07496/977443 ⊕ www.kosmonaut.co.

The Liars Club

BARS/PUBS | This self-described "tiki dive bar" serves up generously sized cocktails in its kitschy Polynesian beach–style bar. Order a Zombie if you like your drinks set on fire. They also serve a hundred types of rum. ✉ 19A Back Bridge St., City Centre ☏ 0161/834–5111 ⊕ www.theliarsclub.co.uk.

PUBS
The Angel

BARS/PUBS | You won't find any televisions in this atmospheric real ale pub that serves beers from small independent breweries. British comfort food (sometimes with a modern twist like Lancashire cheese croquettes) is also offered in both the bar and its cozy restaurant, which comes with a log fire and grand piano. ✉ 6 Angel St., Northern Quarter ☏ 0161/833–4786.

The Briton's Protection

BARS/PUBS | You can sample more than 230 whiskies and bourbons at this gorgeous pub with stained-glass windows, cozy back rooms, a spacious

beer garden, and a mural of the Peterloo Massacre. ✉ 50 Great Bridgewater St. ☏ 0161/236–5895.

The Oast House

BARS/PUBS | This unique pub is surrounded by a large terrace andoccupies a 16th century oasthouse (where brewers roasted hops) that was brought here, brick by brick, from Kent. The emphasis here is on craft beers and ales, accompanied by food like hanging kebabs and grilled meats. ✉ The Avenue Courtyard, Crown Sq. ☏ 0161/829–3830 ⊕ www.theoasthouse.uk.com.

DANCE CLUBS
★ Depot at Mayfield

GATHERING PLACES | This vast cultural venue in the historic former Mayfield railway station showcases the city's industrial past alongside a lively roster of arts, music, industry, culture, and community events. Its atmospheric spaces include the old concourse and the roof-top, open-air platform. ✉ Baring St., City Centre ☏ 0161 /806–0161 ⊕ www.depotmayfield.com.

42's

DANCE CLUBS | Off Deansgate, this venue plays retro, indie, singalong anthems, and classic rock, with Manchester's proud musical heritage at the fore. ✉ 2 Bootle St., City Centre ☏ 0161/831–7108 ⊕ www.42s.co.uk.

Gorilla

MUSIC CLUBS | Nestled under old railway arches, Gorilla is a live-music venue and gin parlor with an intimate vibe. ✉ 54–56 Whitworth St., University Quarter ☏ 0161/826–2998 ⊕ www.thisisgorilla.com.

LIVE MUSIC
★ Albert Hall

MUSIC CLUBS | One of the city's most exciting venues, this former Wesleyan chapel was abandoned and forgotten about for over four decades; it's now a superb indie music hall and clubbing venue retaining many of the site's original features, including an organ and stained-glass windows. ⊠ *27 Peter St., City Centre* ☎ *0161/817–3490* ⊕ *www. alberthallmanchester.com.*

★ The Deaf Institute

MUSIC CLUBS | Good acoustics characterize the intimate domed music hall of this landmark building (a onetime institute for those with hearing and speech impairments) that regularly hosts cutting-edge indie acts. There are also club nights, open mics, and quiz nights. ⊠ *135 Grosvenor St., University Quarter* ☎ *0161/276–9350* ⊕ *www.thedeafinstitute.co.uk.*

Manchester Arena

MUSIC CLUBS | Europe's largest indoor arena by capacity hosts shows by major rock and pop stars, as well as large-scale sporting events. ⊠ *21 Hunts Bank* ☎ *0845/337–0717 box office* ⊕ *www. manchester-arena.com.*

🎫 Performing Arts

★ HOME

ARTS CENTERS | This cutting-edge contemporary arts venue houses a main 450-seat theater, a studio theater space, a gallery, five cinema screens, and digital production and broadcast facilities, as well as a bar, a café, and a bookshop. ⊠ *2 Tony Wilson Pl., University Quarter* ☎ *0161/200–1500* ⊕ *homemcr.org.*

★ Royal Exchange Theatre

THEATER | Housed in the city's one-time cotton exchange, this innovative venue for classic and contemporary works includes a glass-and-metal structure cradling a theater-in-the-round, plus a studio space. ⊠ *St. Ann's Sq., City Centre* ☎ *0161/833–9833* ⊕ *www.royalexchange. co.uk.*

👜 Shopping

Afflecks

CLOTHING | With a collection that ranges from top hats to punk skinny jeans and skate wear, this emporium has been purveying indie fashion and lifestyle paraphernalia to its many fans for decades. ⊠ *52 Church St., Northern Quarter* ☎ *0161/839–0718* ⊕ *www.afflecks.com.*

Barton Arcade

SHOPPING CENTERS/MALLS | This charming Victorian arcade houses various specialty stores selling fashion and shoes, as well as bars and restaurants. ⊠ *51–63 Deansgate, City Centre* ⊕ *www.barton-arcade. co.uk.*

★ Manchester Craft and Design Centre

CRAFTS | This vibrant, airy space in a onetime Victorian fish-market building houses two floors of studios for resident artists and craft makers selling to the public. Crafts workshops are hosted, too, and there's a wonderful café. ⊠ *17 Oak St., Northern Quarter* ☎ *0161/832–4274* ⊕ *www.craftanddesign.com.*

🏃 Activities

FOOTBALL

Football (soccer in the United States) is *the* reigning passion in Manchester. Locals tend to be torn between Manchester City and Manchester United, the two local clubs. Matches for both are usually sold out months in advance; stadium tours can be a good alternative if you can't snag match tickets.

Manchester City Etihad Stadium

SOCCER | This is the place to see Manchester City in action and also to inspect club memorabilia, visit the changing rooms, and explore the pitch. There are also daily tours, including on match days. ⊠ *Etihad Campus, Rowsley St., Sportcity* ☎ *0161/444–1894* ⊕ *www.mancity.com* 💷 *£25.*

Old Trafford

SOCCER | Matches at Manchester United's home stadium attract fans of one of the biggest names in soccer from near and far. The museum and tour take you behind the scenes into the changing rooms and players' lounge, as well as down the tunnel. ⊠ *Sir Matt Busby Way, Trafford Park* ☎ *0161/868–8000* ⊕ *www. manutd.com* 🎫 *£25.*

Liverpool

A city lined with one of the most famous waterfronts in England, celebrated around the world as the birthplace of the Beatles, and still the place to catch that "Ferry 'Cross the Mersey," Liverpool reversed a downturn in its fortunes with late 1980s developments, such as the impressively refurbished Albert Dock area. In 2004, UNESCO named six historic areas in the city center together as one World Heritage Site, in recognition of the city's maritime and mercantile achievements during the height of Britain's global influence. The city's heritage, together with famous attractions and a legacy of cultural vibrancy that includes an ever-growing events program, draws an increasing number of visitors each year—in turn impacting its growing hotel and dining scenes.

The 1960s produced Liverpool's most famous export: the Beatles. The group was one of hundreds influenced by the rock and roll they heard from visiting American GIs and merchant seamen in the late 1950s and one of many that played local venues such as the Cavern Club (demolished but rebuilt nearby). All four Beatles were born in Liverpool, but the group's success dates from the time they left for London. Nevertheless, the city has milked the group's Liverpool connections for all they're worth, with a multitude of local attractions such as Paul McCartney's and John Lennon's childhood homes.

GETTING HERE AND AROUND

Liverpool John Lennon Airport, about 5 miles southeast of the city, receives mostly domestic and European flights. The Arriva 500 bus service runs to the city center up to every 30 minutes; other buses to the center are the 80 and 80A. A taxi to the center of Liverpool costs around £30.

Long-distance National Express buses, including a service from London, use the Liverpool One bus station, as do some local buses. Other local bus terminals are Sir Thomas Street and Queen Square. Train service on Virgin Trains from London's Euston Station takes 2½ hours.

If you're walking (easier than driving), you'll find the downtown sights well signposted. Take care when crossing the busy inner ring road separating the Albert Dock from the rest of the city.

TOURS
Magical Mystery Tours

This ever-popular tour departs daily from the Albert Dock's Anchor Courtyard. The bus—decked out in full psychedelic colors—takes you around all the Beatles-related high points, including Penny Lane and Strawberry Fields, in two hours. The ticket price includes entry to the Cavern Club on the evening of your tour day. The firm also offers private tours. ⊠ *City Centre* ☎ *0151/703–9100* ⊕ *www. cavernclub.org/the-magical-mystery-tour* 🎫 *£18.95.*

Mersey Guides

PERSONAL GUIDES | This is your point of contact for dozens of different tours of the city, bringing together professional local guides with in-depth knowledge on topics as diverse as Manchester's maritime or wartime histories. ⊕ *www. showmeliverpool.com.*

ESSENTIALS
BUS CONTACTS Merseytravel.

☎ *0151/330–1000* ⊕ *www.merseytravel. gov.uk.*

VISITOR INFORMATION Visit Liverpool.

⊠ *Central Library, William Brown St., City Centre*

Sights

Albert Dock

MARINA | To understand the city's prosperous maritime past, head for these 7 acres of restored waterfront warehouses built in 1846. Named after Queen Victoria's consort, Prince Albert, the dock provided storage for silk, tea, and tobacco from the Far East until it was closed in 1972. Today the fine colonnaded brick buildings contain the **Merseyside Maritime Museum,** the **International Slavery Museum, Tate Liverpool,** and the main venue of the **Beatles Story.** When weather allows, you can sit at an outdoor café overlooking the dock; there are also bars, restaurants, and even hotels on the site. For a bird's-eye view of the Albert Dock area, take the rotating Liverpool Wheel—a 60-meter-tall version of the London Eye. ■**TIP→ Much of the pedestrian area of the Albert Dock and waterfront area is cobblestone, so wear comfortable shoes.** ⊠ *Off Strand St. (A5036), Waterfront* ☎ ⊕ *www.albertdock.com.*

★ Another Place

PUBLIC ART | A hundred naked, life-size, cast-iron figures by sculptor Antony Gormley stand proudly on the 2 miles of foreshore at Crosby Beach, weathered by sand and sea. Unlike most other statues, you are permitted to interact with these and even clothe them if you wish. Check tide times before you go, and be aware that it's not safe to walk out to the farthest figures. The site is 6 miles north of downtown Liverpool; to get here, take the Merseyrail train to Blundellsands or Crosby from Liverpool Central or Moorfields Stations. A taxi will cost around £30. ⊠ *Mariners Rd., Crosby Beach* ☎ *0845/140–0845 for tide times* ⊕ *www.visitliverpool.com* ⊠ *Free.*

★ The Beatles' Childhood Homes

HOUSE | A must-see for Beatles pilgrims, this tour takes you to Mendips, the 1930s middle-class, semidetached house that was the home of John Lennon from 1946 to 1963, and 20 Forthlin Road, Paul McCartney's childhood home. After his parents separated, John joined his aunt Mimi at Mendips; she gave him his first guitar but banished him to the porch, saying, "The guitar's all very well, John, but you'll never make a living out of it." Meanwhile, Forthlin Road is a modest 1950s council house where a number of the Beatles' songs were written. The tour leaves from Jury's Inn hotel next to Albert Dock (mornings) or Speke Hall (afternoons). ■**TIP→ Advanced bookings are essential—places are strictly limited to 15.** ⊠ *City Centre* ☎ *0344/249–1985* ⊕ *www.nationaltrust.org.uk/beatles-childhood-homes* ⊠ *From £27.50* ⊗ *Closed Dec.–Feb.*

★ Beatles Story

MUSEUM | Entertaining scenes at this popular attraction in the Albert Dock complex re-create stages in the Beatles' story (and their later careers as solo artists). You'll find everything from the enthusiastic early days in Germany and the Cavern Club to the White Room, where "Imagine" seems to emanate from softly billowing curtains. A second location at the Mersey Ferries Terminal at Pier Head is included in the admission price; here you can see changing exhibitions. On-site shops sell every conceivable kind of souvenir a Fab Four fan could wish for. ⊠ *Britannia Vaults, Albert Dock* ☎ *0151/709–1963* ⊕ *www.beatlesstory.com* ⊠ *£17.*

Casbah Coffee Club

MUSEUM | A coffee shop owned by original drummer Pete Best's mother, this is where The Beatles played some of their earliest gigs. Decorated by the band themselves, it's now a museum offering an authentic taste of those exciting early days. Entry is by guided tour only. ⊠ *8 Hayman's Green, West Derby* ⊹ *Take bus No. 11 or 12 from Queen's Sq. to West Derby; it's 3½ miles from the city center.* ☎ *0787/201–7473* ⊕ *www.petebest.com/casbah-coffee-club* ⊠ *From £15.*

★ International Slavery Museum

MUSEUM | In the same building as the Merseyside Maritime Museum, this museum's four dynamic galleries recount the history of transatlantic slavery and trace its significance in contemporary society. "Life in West Africa" reproduces a Nigerian Igbo compound; life aboard slave ships bound for the Americas is revealed in the "Enslavement and the Middle Passage" section; and "Legacy" examines the effect of the African diaspora on contemporary society. ✉ *Albert Dock, Hartley Quay, Waterfront* ☎ *0151/478–4499* ⊕ *www.liverpoolmuseums.org.uk* ✉ *Free.*

★ Merseyside Maritime Museum

MUSEUM | This wonderful museum captures the triumphs and tragedies of Liverpool's seafaring history over five floors. Besides exhibits of maritime paintings, models, ceramics, and ships in bottles, it brings to life the ill-fated stories of the *Titanic* and *Lusitania;* the Battle of the Atlantic; and the city's role during World War II. Seized, the gallery for the Border Force National Museum, explores the heroes and villains of the world of smuggling, together with the story of mass emigration from the port in the 19th century, while the Life on Board gallery looks at everyone from merchant sailors to leisure cruise-liner passengers. ✉ *Albert Dock, Hartley Quay, Waterfront* ☎ *0151/478–4499* ⊕ *www.liverpoolmuseums.org.uk* ✉ *Free.*

Museum of Liverpool

MUSEUM | FAMILY | Clad in Jura stone and shaped like a ship, with a spectacular spiral staircase running from the atrium to each floor, this ambitious museum tells the story of the city from its earliest settlement in the Neolithic Age. Highlights include an extraordinary 3D map with different perspectives of the city as you move around it, an engrossing film about soccer culture, and an interactive time line peeling away layers of Liverpool's history. There's a children's gallery and family museum trails, too. ✉ *Pier Head, Waterfront* ☎ *0151/478–4545* ⊕ *www.liverpoolmuseums.org.uk* ✉ *Free.*

Royal Liver Building

BUILDING | The 322-foot-tall Royal Liver (pronounced *lie-ver*) Building with its twin towers is topped by two 18-foot-high copper birds representing the mythical Liver Birds, the town symbol; local legend has it that if they fly away, Liverpool will cease to exist. For decades Liverpudlians looked to the Royal Liver Society for assistance—it was originally a burial club to which families paid contributions to ensure a decent send-off. ■TIP→ **The building, now offices, can best be seen from one of the Mersey ferries.** ✉ *Water St., Waterfront.*

★ Tate Liverpool

MUSEUM | FAMILY | This offshoot of the London-based art galleries of the same name occupies a handsome conversion of Albert Dock warehouses by the late James Stirling, one of Britain's leading 20th-century architects. There is no permanent collection; challenging exhibitions of modern and contemporary art change every couple of months. There are children's activities, an excellent gift shop, and a dockside café-restaurant. ✉ *Albert Dock, Waterfront* ☎ *0151/702–7400* ⊕ *www.tate.org.uk* ✉ *Free; charges for certain special exhibitions vary.*

★ Walker Art Gallery

MUSEUM | FAMILY | With a superb display of British art and some outstanding Italian and Flemish works, this is one of the best British art collections outside London. Don't miss the unrivaled collection of paintings by 18th-century Liverpudlian equestrian artist George Stubbs or works by J. M. W. Turner, Claude Monet, Frederic Lord Leighton, and the Pre-Raphaelites. Modern artists are included, too; on display is one of David Hockney's typically Californian pool scenes. Other excellent exhibits showcase classical Greek and Roman sculptures as well as china, silver, and furniture that once adorned

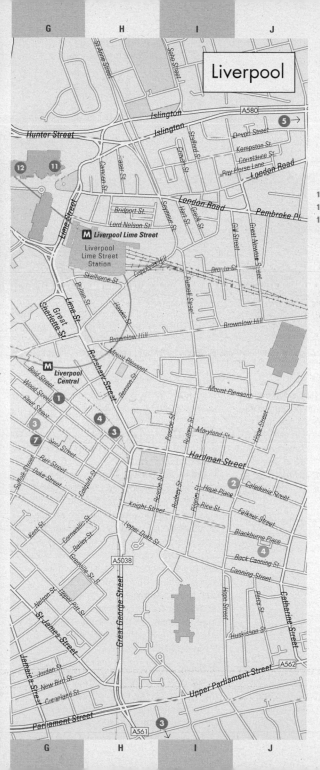

Liverpool

Sights

1 Albert Dock........................D7
2 Another Place.....................B1
3 The Beatles'
Childhood Homes.................I9
4 Beatles Story....................C7
5 Casbah Coffee Club J2
6 International Slavery Museum....C6
7 Merseyside Maritime Museum...C6
8 Museum of Liverpool..............C5
9 Royal Liver Building B4
10 Tate Liverpool C6
11 Walker Art Gallery................G2
12 World Museum Liverpool.........G2

Restaurants

1 Bakchich...........................G5
2 Lunya..............................F5
3 Maray.............................H6
4 Mowgli............................H5
5 Panoramic 34......................B2
6 Salt House Bacaro D4
7 Wreckfish.........................C6

Hotels

1 Aloft Liverpool....................D3
2 Hope Street Hotel.................J6
3 The Resident G5
4 2 Blackburne Terrace J7
5 Z Liverpool........................D3

Once a major shipping center and now transformed with museums, restaurants, and shops, the Albert Dock has views of the green dome of the Royal Liver Building.

the mansions of Liverpool's industrial barons. There are temporary exhibitions, including those focusing on photography, and a dedicated children's art space. The café holds center stage in the airy museum lobby. ⊠ *William Brown St., City Centre* ☎ *0151/478–4199* ⊕ *www. liverpoolmuseums.org.uk* ⊠ *Free; charge for temporary exhibitions.*

World Museum Liverpool

MUSEUM | FAMILY | Travel from the prehistoric to the space age through the stunning displays in these state-of-the-art galleries. Ethnology, the natural and physical sciences, and archaeology all get their due over five floors. Highlights include a collection of Egyptian mummies and a beautiful assemblage of Japanese arms and armory in the World Cultures Gallery. There's plenty to keep kids amused, like fish and other sea creatures in the Aquarium, monster bugs in the Bug House, and life-size casts of prehistoric monsters in the Dinosaurs and Natural World Gallery, plus a planetarium and a busy program of events

and activities. ⊠ *William Brown St., City Centre* ☎ *0151/478–4393* ⊕ *www.liverpoolmuseums.org.uk* ⊠ *Free.*

🍴 Restaurants

★ Bakchich

$ | LEBANESE | FAMILY | Those who like good food at great prices head to Bakchich, a Lebanese street-food joint featuring a large communal table with smaller tables dotted around it for convivial or more intimate dining. On offer are delicious hot and cold meze, *meshawi* charcoal grills (chicken, lamb, and seafood), wraps, salads, and a small but tasty kids' menu. **Known for:** Middle Eastern breakfasts; fresh juices and mocktails; huge portions. ⑤ *Average main: £8* ⊠ *54 Bold St., City Centre* ☎ *0151/707–1255* ⊕ *www.bakchich.co.uk.*

★ Lunya

$ | CATALAN | FAMILY | An 18th-century warehouse on the edge of the Liverpool One shopping district houses this impressive Catalan fusion restaurant and deli, where you can feast on classic and creative tapas dishes. An extensive breakfast menu makes this a great place to start your day, while the children's menu tempts those with junior foodies. **Known for:** wine, cheese, and sherry tastings along with other events; Catalan breakfasts and brunches; deli platters to share. $ *Average main: £9* ⊠ *55 Hanover St., City Centre* ☎ *0151/706–9770* ⊕ *www.lunya.co.uk.*

Maray

$ | **INTERNATIONAL** | Tapping into Liverpool's love affair with the sharing experience, this tiny bistro serves eclectic and inventive dishes with global inspirations, ranging from the Middle East and the southern United States to Scandinavia. The place—all bare bricks, upcycled furniture, and edgy artwork—takes its name from the Marais district of Paris, though it's actually inspired more by the falafel joints of the French capital's less scenic Bastille district. **Known for:** falafel (homemade daily); member of the Sustainable Restaurant Association; luscious after-dinner cocktails. $ *Average main: £7* ⊠ *91 Bold St., City Centre* ☎ *0151/709–5820* ⊕ *www.maray.co.uk.*

★ Mowgli

$ | **INDIAN** | **FAMILY** | Indian street food is the draw at this fun and colorful spot that has lights upcycled from old birdcages and a bar created from former railway sleepers. Many of the vibrant dishes, such as the hugely popular yogurt chat bombs (crispy, filled bread puffs), are served in tiffin boxes (traditional Indian lunch containers) to charming effect. **Known for:** innovative cocktails; enthusiastic, informative staff; handmade ice-cream cones. $ *Average main: £7* ⊠ *69 Bold St., City Centre* ☎ *0151/708–9356* ⊕ *www.mowglistreetfood.com.*

Panoramic 34

$$$$ | **MODERN EUROPEAN** | For some, the waterfront and city views through the floor-to-ceiling windows of this 34th-floor restaurant might outdo the food, but there's no denying the ambition and love that's gone into the Modern European set menus. You can also just come here to soak up that vista over afternoon tea or a cocktail. **Known for:** best views in town; fantastic seven-course tasting menu; dressed-up atmosphere. $ *Average main: £34* ⊠ *West Tower, Brook St., 34th fl., Waterfront* ☎ *0151/236–5534* ⊕ *www.panoramic34.com* ⊗ *Closed Mon.*

★ Salt House Bacaro

$ | **ITALIAN** | This stylish place—a lively take on the workingmen's canteens of backstreet Venice, known as *bacaros*—offers highly creative small plates and charcuterie. Options include croquettes, fried mixed fish, and *pizzette* (mini-pizzas). **Known for:** cicchetti (sharing plates); casual eating at the bar—great for solo diners; fabulous cocktails, some with Italian bitters. $ *Average main: £8* ⊠ *47 Castle St., City Centre* ☎ *0151/665–0047* ⊕ *www.salthousebacaro.com.*

★ Wreckfish

$$ | **MODERN BRITISH** | Part of the same crowd-funded group as Manchester's Hispi Bistro and KALA Bistro, this hip spot serves up seriously good modern global cuisine from an open kitchen in a once derelict building in the Ropewalks district. As with its sister restaurants, think excellent local ingredients—duck's heart or featherblade of beef—taken to the next level through the use of ingredients such as orange blossom vinegar, 'nduja butter, and truffles. **Known for:** great value lunch and early dinner menu; fantastic service; choice of communal and private tables. $ *Average main: £20* ⊠ *Slater St., City Centre* ☎ *0151/707–1960* ⊕ *www.wreckfish.co.*

 ## Hotels

Aloft Liverpool

$ | **HOTEL** | It's a lot about the architecture and the original features at this hotel in the landmark Victorian Royal Insurance

Building, with green-marble wall tiles, sleek dark-wood paneling, and a grand staircase winding up to a domed rotunda. **Pros:** central location near the Cavern Club; good snack bar; hip Bliss Spa toiletries. **Cons:** noise from bar can transfer to rooms; some rooms have odd layout due to historic building; some rooms are in basement. ⑤ *Rooms from: £83 ⌧ No. 1 North John St., City Centre ☎ 0151/294–3970 ⊕ www.marriott.com/hotels/travel/lplal-aloft-liverpool ⤳ 116 rooms* ⦿⃝ *No meals.*

Hope Street Hotel

$ | **HOTEL** | In Liverpool's Georgian Quarter, this chic but relaxed hotel happily blends old (an 1890s building inspired by Venetian palazzos) and new (a contemporary steel-and-glass facade fitted over part of the frontage) with rooms with minimalist, Scandinavian-esque decor. **Pros:** lovely spa; frequent upgrades; very good deals in off-season. **Cons:** reception can be very busy; food in restaurant not as impressive as the rooms; rooms can be noisy due to wooden floors. ⑤ *Rooms from: £92 ⌧ 40 Hope St., City Centre ☎ 0151/709–3000 ⊕ www.hopestreethotel.co.uk ⤳ 89 rooms* ⦿⃝ *No meals.*

★ The Resident

$ | **HOTEL** | **FAMILY** | This hip hotel brand focuses on the guest experience and growing its visitors' connections with the city by offering hosted evening drinks (with a wine list curated by renowned oenologist Joe Flatiron) where guests can socialize while getting insider tips on what to see and do during their stay. **Pros:** focus on local artisan produce; room-service drinks and snacks; immersive city experience. **Cons:** no restaurant; small doubles may be too cozy for some; soundproofing not 100%. ⑤ *Rooms from: £59 ⌧ 29 Seel St., City Centre ☎ 0151/705–2626 ⊕ www.residenthotels.com/the-resident-liverpool ⤳ 106 rooms* ⦿⃝ *No meals* ⊟ *No credit cards.*

★ 2 Blackburne Terrace

$$ | **B&B/INN** | On a cobbled lane in Liverpool's charming Georgian Quarter, this boutique town house B&B is an intimate haven within a hectic city. **Pros:** complimentary in-room treats such as bath oils and artisan gin; personal coffee machines; free parking. **Cons:** no restaurant; hilltop setting not great for those with mobility issues; one of the city's pricer options. ⑤ *Rooms from: £207 ⌧ 2 Blackburne Terr., City Centre ☎ 0151/708–5474 ⊕ 2blackburneterrace.com ⤳ 4 rooms* ⦿⃝ *Free breakfast.*

Z Liverpool

$ | **HOTEL** | Modern urban style on a budget and a supercentral location make the Z a superb option; rooms are all clean and simple, with bespoke beds, crisp linen, and flat-screen TVs. **Pros:** free wine and cheese in the evening; thoughtful design features; great views from some rooms. **Cons:** street noise in some rooms; not all rooms have windows; glassed-in shower rooms and toilets don't feel private enough for some guests. ⑤ *Rooms from: £35 ⌧ 2 N. John St., City Centre ☎ 0151/ 556–1770 ⊕ www.thezhotels.com ⤳ 92 rooms* ⦿⃝ *Free breakfast.*

Nightlife

Alma de Cuba

BARS/PUBS | A church transformed into a luxurious bar, Alma de Cuba has a huge mirrored altar and hundreds of dripping candles. They also serve a popular Sunday brunch with a live gospel choir. ⌧ *St. Peter's Church, Seel St., City Centre ☎ 0151/305–3744 ⊕ www.alma-de-cuba.com.*

Berry and Rye

BARS/PUBS | Hidden away behind an unassuming and umarked facade, Berry and Rye is a Prohibition-era speakeasy that brings together expertly mixed cocktails and cakes in a stylish candlelit space. ⌧ *48 Berry St., City Centre.*

Camp and Furnace

MUSIC CLUBS | This huge bar, live music venue, and restaurant complex in a former Edwardian foundry and blade-making factory retains a suitably industrial vibe. ⊠ *67 Greenland St., City Centre* ☎ *0151/708–2890* ⊕ *www.campandfurnace.com.*

Cavern Club

MUSIC CLUBS | While not the original venue—that was demolished years ago—this is still a popular music spot, drawing in rock-and-roll fans with its live acts including Beatles tribute bands. ⊠ *10 Mathew St., City Centre* ☎ *0151/236–9091* ⊕ *www.cavernclub.com.*

★ LEAF on Bold Street

CAFES—NIGHTLIFE | Tea shop meets bar and live music venue (with club nights) at this bohemian spot in a former art deco cinema. ⊠ *65–67 Bold St., City Centre* ☎ *0161/707 7747* ⊕ *www.thisisleaf.co.uk.*

The Shipping Forecast

MUSIC CLUBS | Big-name acts mean this intimate venue often gets packed to the rafters, but that only adds to the clubby vibe. There are also club nights that range from hip-hop to indie, vintage fairs, plus a menu of well-executed American comfort food classics. ⊠ *15 Slater St., City Centre* ☎ *0151/709–6901* ⊕ *www.theshippingforecastliverpool.com.*

⊙ Performing Arts

★ Bluecoat

ART GALLERIES—ARTS | The city center's oldest building is now a creative hub encompassing contemporary visual arts, live art, literature, music, and dance, along with a café and bistro. ⊠ *School La., City Centre* ☎ *0151/702–5324* ⊕ *www.thebluecoat.org.uk.*

⊙ Shopping

The Beatles Shop

GIFTS/SOUVENIRS | All the mop-top knick-knacks of your dreams are available at this hugely popular, official Beatles souvenir shop. ⊠ *31 Mathew St., City Centre* ☎ *0151/236–8066* ⊕ *www.thebeatlesonline.co.uk.*

★ Liverpool One

SHOPPING CENTERS/MALLS | The city's largest shopping complex comprises four districts (Peter's Lane, South John Street, Paradise Street, and Hanover Street) totaling more than 160 stores, from small independent shops to international chains, plus restaurants and leisure amenities. ⊠ *Paradise St., City Centre* ☎ *0151/232–3100* ⊕ *www.liverpool-one.com.*

Metquarter

SHOPPING CENTERS/MALLS | This luxury shopping district is the place for upscale boutiques, designer names, and cutting-edge fashions. ⊠ *35 Whitechapel, City Centre* ☎ *0151/224–2390* ⊕ *www.metquarter.com.*

⊙ Activities

FOOTBALL

Football matches are played on weekends and, increasingly, some weekdays. Tickets for Liverpool sell out months in advance; you should have more luck with Everton.

Anfield Stadium

SOCCER | If you can't get tickets to a match at the stadium of Liverpool FC, one of England's top teams, take a trip into the dressing rooms and down the tunnel of Anfield Football Stadium as part of a tour. You can also visit the interactive museum, on the tour or separately. ⊠ *Anfield Rd., Anfield* ☎ *0151/260–2500* ⊕ *www.liverpoolfc.com* 🎟 *£20 tour.*

The Peak District

Goodison Park

SOCCER | Home to Everton, one of Liverpool's two great football teams, this 40,000-capacity stadium now also hosts tours. ✉ *Goodison Rd.* ☎ *0151/556–1878* 🌐 *www.evertonfc.com* 🎟 *£15 tours.*

Buxton

25 miles southeast of Manchester.

Just outside the Peak District National Park yet almost entirely surrounded by it, Buxton makes a good base for park excursions but it has its own attractions as well. The town's spa days left a notable legacy of 18th- and 19th-century buildings, parks, and open spaces that give the place an air of faded grandeur. The Romans arrived in AD 79 and named Buxton Aquae Arnemetiae, loosely translated as "Waters of the Goddess of the Grove." The mineral springs, which emerge from 3,500 to 5,000 feet below-ground at a constant 82°F, were believed to cure assorted ailments. In the 18th century, the town became established as a popular spa, a minor rival to Bath. You can still drink water, which is also sold throughout Britain, from the ancient St. Ann's Well. The architecturally revered semicircular 18th-century Crescent Building houses heritage displays in the Pump Room where the 7th Duke of Devonshire used to "take the waters," and several major thermal hotel and spa openings are planned, putting Buxton back in contention for the title of England's leading spa town.

GETTING HERE AND AROUND

Some National Express bus services to and from London stop at Buxton, departing from Manchester's Central Coach Station. There are also Skyline buses between Buxton and Manchester Airport and buses between Buxton and Chatsworth House. If you're driving to Buxton from Manchester, take the A6 southeast to Buxton. The journey takes one hour, as does the hourly train from Manchester.

ESSENTIALS

VISITOR INFORMATION Buxton Visitor Centre & Crescent Heritage Experience.
⊠ *The Pump House, The Crescent* 🕾 *01298/214577* ⊕ *www.visitpeakdistrict. com.*

Sights

Buxton Museum and Art Gallery

MUSEUM | The highlight of this venue is its "Wonders of the Peak" gallery with displays on Derbyshire's geology, archaeology, history, and art. It's a good place to see Blue John, a colorful, semiprecious mineral found only in the Peak District (the name comes from *bleu jaune*—literally "blue yellow"—a term supposedly coined by visiting French mine workers). ⊠ *Terrace Rd.* 🕾 *01629/533540* ⊕ *www. derbyshire.gov.uk/leisure/buxton-museum* 🖅 *Free* ⊙ *Closed Mon.*

Buxton Opera House

ARTS VENUE | Built in 1903, this lovely Edwardian edifice is one of England's best examples of Frank Matcham theater design, with its marble columns, carved cherubs, and gold leaf. A varied performance program includes classical music, opera, dance, drama, and comedy, and it's also host to the Buxton Festival. ⊠ *Water St.* 🕾 *01298/72190* ⊕ *www. buxtonoperahouse.org.uk.*

Pavilion Gardens

GARDEN | These 23 acres are home to a miniature train, a boating lake, a play area, and the 1870s Pavilion building. With its ornate iron-and-glass roof, the latter was originally a concert hall and ballroom, but it's now the setting for an arts center, three cafés, an ice-cream parlor, a market hall, and a gift boutique. ⊠ *St. John's Rd.* 🕾 *01298/23114* ⊕ *www. paviliongardens.co.uk.*

★ Poole's Cavern and Buxton Country Park

ARCHAEOLOGICAL SITE | FAMILY | The Peak District's extraordinary geology can be seen up close in this large limestone cave far beneath the 100 acres of Buxton Country Park. Inhabited in prehistoric times, the cave contains, in addition to the standard stalactites and stalagmites, the source of the River Wye, which flows through Buxton. The Country Park paths take you up to Grin Low, home to the Victorian fortified hill marker Solomon's Tower, the remains of several Bronze Age burial chambers, and views of Mam Tor and Kinder Scout. There's also a fun Go Ape! treetop adventure course on site. Admission to the cave includes a guided tour lasting nearly an hour. ⊠ *Green La.* 🕾 *01298/26978* ⊕ *www.poolescavern. co.uk* 🖅 *£11.*

Restaurants

Columbine

$$$ | MODERN BRITISH | In a town blessed with good cafés but few noteworthy restaurants, this option run by a husband-and-wife team has a somewhat old-fashioned feel but stands out for its fine use of local ingredients, including High Peak lamb and beef, in the inventive cuisine. The cozy venue, with upstairs and downstairs cellar seating, is especially good for pre- and post-theater meals. **Known for:** produce from small local producers; advance booking needed outside festival and Christmas seasons; proximity to opera house. ⑤ *Average main: £24* ⊠ *7 Hall Bank* 🕾 *01298/78752* ⊕ *www.columbinerestaurant.co.uk* ⊙ *Closed Tues. No lunch Sun. and late Dec.–mid-Jan.*

Hotels

Old Hall

$ | **B&B/INN** | **FAMILY** | In a refurbished 16th-century building claiming to be England's oldest hotel and rumored to have once accommodated Mary, Queen of Scots, this hotel overlooks the ornate Buxton Opera House. **Pros:** family-friendly, with picnics to take to the Pavilion Gardens; good food in the restaurant; historic ambience. **Cons:** no private parking; rooms may be a bit chintzy for some; bathrooms are uninspiring. ⑤ *Rooms from: £69* ⊠ *The Square* ☎ *01298/22841* ⊕ *www.oldhallhotelbuxton.co.uk* ⇄ *35 rooms* ⦿❘ *Free breakfast.*

Roseleigh Guesthouse

$ | **B&B/INN** | This prize-winning B&B overlooking Pavilion Gardens has comfortable, classic rooms that chime well with the Victorian atmosphere. **Pros:** adventurous hosts who can advise on local activities; some rooms with lake views; private parking. **Cons:** no family rooms; one room has private but not en suite bathroom; some of the quirkier decorative elements might not be to everyone's taste. ⑤ *Rooms from: £78* ⊠ *19 Broad Walk* ☎ *01298/24904* ⊕ *www. roseleighhotel.co.uk* ⊙ *Closed Dec.–mid-Jan.* ⇄ *13 rooms* ⦿❘ *Free breakfast.*

Shopping

Buxton has a wide variety of stores, especially around Spring Gardens, the main shopping street.

Cavendish Arcade

SHOPPING CENTERS/MALLS | The independent stores in this beautifully tiled building on the site of the old thermal baths sell handmade chocolates, fashion, housewares, pottery, and gifts. ⊠ *The Crescent* ⊕ *www.cavendisharcade.co.uk.*

Bakewell

12 miles southeast of Buxton.

In Bakewell, a medieval bridge crosses the winding River Wye in five graceful arches. A 9th-century Saxon cross that stands outside the parish church reveals the town's great age. Narrow streets and houses built out of the local gray-brown stone also make the town extremely appealing. Ceaseless traffic can take the shine off—though there's respite down on the quiet riverside paths.

This market town is the commercial hub of the Peak District, for locals and visitors. The crowds are really substantial on market day (Monday), attended by area farmers. For a self-guided hour-long stroll, pick up a map at the tourist office, where the town trail begins.

GETTING HERE AND AROUND

TransPeak buses to Derby from Manchester's Central Coach Station stop at Bakewell, as do some National Express buses to London. By car, Bakewell is a 1½-hour drive southeast on the A6 from Manchester.

ESSENTIALS

VISITOR INFORMATION Bakewell Visitor Centre. ⊠ *Old Market Hall, Bridge St.* ☎ *01629/813227* ⊕ *www.peakdistrict. gov.uk.*

Sights

★ Chatsworth House

HOUSE | **FAMILY** | One of England's greatest country houses, the "Palace of the Peak" is the ancestral home of the dukes of Devonshire and stands in vast parkland grazed by deer and sheep. Originally an Elizabethan house, it was altered over several generations starting in 1686 and now has a hodge-podge look, though the Palladian facade remains untouched. It's surrounded by woods, elaborate gardens, greenhouses, rock gardens, and a beautiful water cascade—all designed by Capability Brown in the 18th century and, in the 19th, Joseph Paxton, an engineer as well as a brilliant gardener. ■TIP→ **Plan on at least a half day to explore the grounds; avoid Sunday if you can as it gets very crowded.** Inside are intricate carvings, superb furniture, Van Dyck portraits, Sir Joshua Reynolds's *Georgiana, Duchess of Devonshire and Her Baby,* John Singer Sargent's enormous *Acheson Sisters,* and fabulous rooms, including the Sculpture Gallery, the library, and the Painted Hall. On the estate, you'll also find a working farm with milking demonstrations, an adventure playground, cafés, restaurants, a tea shop, and a farm shop: you can even stay in several cottages scattered throughout the grounds. ⊠ *Off B6012* ⬧ *4 miles northeast of Bakewell* ☎ *01246/565300* ⊕ *www.chatsworth.org* ⊠ *House, gardens, farm, and adventure playground £24; house and gardens £22; gardens only £13; farmyard and adventure playground £7; parking £4 (free with online tickets)* ⊗ *Closed 2nd wk of Jan.– late Mar.*

Eyam Plague Village

HISTORIC SITE | After a local tailor died of the plague in this tiny, idyllic, gray-stone village in 1665, locals isolated themselves from the outside world rather than risk the spread of Black Death (the area had hitherto been spared). They succeeded in containing the disease, but at huge cost; by the time it had run its course, most of the residents were dead. Their heroism is commemorated in florid memorials in the village churchyard. The small **Eyam Museum** puts everything into context, while **Eyam Hall and Craft Centre**, run by the National Trust, hosts history walks on the topic. ⊠ *Hawkhill Rd., Eyam* ⬧ *6 miles north of Bakewell off A623* ☎ *01433/631371 museum* ⊕ *www. eyam-museum.org.uk* ⊠ *Museum £3* ⊗ *Museum closed Mon. and Nov.–late Mar.*

★ Haddon Hall

HOUSE | One of England's finest stately homes, and perhaps the most authentically Tudor of all the great houses, Haddon Hall bristles with intricate period detail. Built between 1180 and 1565, the house passed into the ownership of the dukes of Rutland and remained largely untouched until the early 20th century, when the ninth duke undertook a superlative restoration that revealed a series of early decorative 15th-century frescoes in the chapel. The finest of the intricate plasterwork and wooden paneling is best seen in the superb Long Gallery on the first floor. A popular filming location, Haddon's starring roles include *The Princess Bride* (1985), *Pride and Prejudice* (2005), and *The Other Boleyn Girl* (2008). ⊠ *A6* ☎ *01629/812855* ⊕ *www.haddonhall. co.uk* ⊠ *£18.50, parking £3* ⊗ *Closed Nov. and late Dec.–early Apr.*

★ Peak District National Park

NATIONAL/STATE PARK | The United Kingdom's first-ever national park (inaugurated in 1951, paving the way for a further nine parks), the Peak District provides a wild green space for the estimated 20 million people who live within an hour's journey of it, including the inhabitants of Manchester and Stoke-on-Trent, as well as to the millions people who visit each year. Located mostly in northern Derbyshire but including parts of Greater Manchester, Staffordshire, Cheshire, and Yorkshire, the national park is generally divided into the Dark Peak (gritstone moorlands) and the White Peak (limestone), but it has a remarkable diversity of landscapes that make it popular with hikers, cyclists, climbers, and cavers. It's also much-loved for the spa towns, country houses, and heritage sites that are found within the park itself. Visitor centers with information on outdoor activities in the region can be found in Bakewell, Castleton, Derwent, and Edale. Public transport is patchy, it's best explored by car. ☎ *1629/816200* ⊕ *www. peakdistrict.gov.uk.*

Restaurants

The Old Original Bakewell Pudding Shop

$ | BRITISH | Given the plethora of local rivals, it takes a bold establishment to claim its Bakewell puddings as "original," but those served here are among the best. The "pudding" in question is actually a dense, sugary pie with a jam and almond filling and a puff pastry crust, eaten cold or hot with custard or cream. **Known for:** breakfast sandwiches; afternoon teas ("All Things Bakewell" includes both pudding and tart); on-site deli counter. $ Average main: £12 ⊠ The Square ☎ 01629/812193 ⊕ www.bakewellpuddingshop.co.uk ⊗ No dinner.

Hotels

Bagshaw Hall

$ | HOTEL | This characterful 17th-century property offers upscale suites with kitchenettes or full kitchens as well as luxury touches including bathrobes and slippers. **Pros:** a short stroll from the center of Bakewell; self-catering facilities; attractive grounds. **Cons:** no restaurant (breakfast can be brought to rooms); no reception (need to call on arrival); early checkout (10 am). $ Rooms from: £80 ⊠ Bagshaw Hill ☎ 01629/810333 ⊕ www.bagshawhall.com ⇆ 12 rooms ⦿ No meals.

Chester

75 miles north of Ludlow, 46 miles north of Shrewsbury.

Cheshire's thriving center is Chester, a city similar in some ways to Shrewsbury, though it has many more black-and-white half-timber buildings (some built in Georgian and Victorian times), and its medieval walls still stand. History seems more tangible in Chester than in many other ancient cities, as modern buildings haven't been allowed to intrude on the center. A negative result of this perfection is that Chester has become a favorite tour bus destination, with gift shops, noise, and crowds aplenty.

Chester has been a prominent city since the late 1st century, when the Roman Empire expanded north to the banks of the River Dee. The original Roman town plan is still evident: the principal streets, Eastgate, Northgate, Watergate, and Bridge Street, lead out from the Cross—the site of the central area of the Roman fortress—to the four city gates. The partly excavated remains of what is thought to have been the country's largest Roman amphitheater lie to the south of Chester's medieval castle.

GETTING HERE AND AROUND

There's a free shuttle bus to the center if you arrive by train, and buses pull up at Vicar's Lane in the center (Monday to Saturday). Chester is 180 miles from London and about two hours by train; some trains change at Crewe. If you're driving and here for a day only, use the city's Park and Ride lots, as central parking lots fill quickly, especially in summer.

Guided walks leave the town hall daily at 10:30 am with an additional tour at 2 pm from Easter to October (£8). In summer, the 10:30 am tour ends with a proclamation from the Town Crier, who is dressed in traditional attire.

ESSENTIALS

VISITOR AND TOUR INFORMATION Chester Tourist Information Centre. ⊠ Town Hall, Northgate St. ☎ 01244/405340 ⊕ www.visitcheshire.com/chester. **City Sightseeing.** ☎ 01244/347452 ⊕ www.city-sightseeing.com/en/89/chester.

Sights

★ Chester Cathedral

RELIGIOUS SITE | Tradition has it that, in Roman, times a church of some sort stood on the site of what is now Chester Cathedral, but records date construction to around AD 900. The earliest work traceable today, mainly in the north transept, is that of the 11th-century Benedictine abbey. After Henry VIII dissolved the monasteries in the 16th century, the abbey church became the cathedral church of the new diocese of Chester. The misericords in the choir stalls reveal carved figures of people and animals, both real and mythical, and above is a gilded and colorful vaulted ceiling. Cathedral at Height tours (£8) take you to parts of the building usually off-limits to visitors, including the roof—from which you can see two countries (England and Wales) and five separate counties. ⊠ St. Werburgh St., off Market Sq. ☎ 01244/500959 ⊕ www.chesterca-thedral.com ⊘ No tours Sun.

Chester Rows

BUILDING | Chester's unique Rows, which originated in the 12th and 13th centuries, are essentially double rows of stores, one at street level and the other on the second floor with galleries overlooking the street. The Rows line the junction of the four streets in the old town. They have medieval crypts below them, and some reveal Roman foundations ⊠ Ches-ter ⊕ www.visitchester.com/things-to-do/chester-rows-p22731.

City Walls

BUILDING | Accessible from several points, the city walls provide splendid views of Chester and its surroundings. The whole circuit is two miles, but if your time is short, climb the steps at Newgate and walk along toward Eastgate to see the great ornamental **Eastgate Clock,** erected to commemorate Queen Victoria's Diamond Jubilee in 1897. Lots of small shops near this part of the walls sell old books, old postcards, antiques, and jewelry. Where the **Bridge of Sighs** (named after the enclosed bridge in Venice that it closely resembles) crosses the canal, descend to street level and walk up Northgate Street into Market Square. ⊠ *Chester.*

Restaurants

Albion Inn
$ | **BRITISH** | You feel as if you're stepping back in time at this Victorian pub; the posters, advertisements, flags, and curios tell you the idiosyncratic landlord keeps it as it would have been during World War I. The candlelit restaurant forms one of the three snug rooms and, unsurprisingly, serves up traditional fare such as lamb's liver, corned beef hash, and gammon (thick-sliced ham) with pease pudding. **Known for:** old-fashioned British food; historic, old-school ambience; local hangout. $ *Average main: £10* ⊠ *Park St.* ☎ *01244/340345* ⊕ *www. albioninnchester.co.uk* ⊗ *No dinner Sun.*

Chez Jules
$$ | **BISTRO** | Once a fire station, this bustling bistro is now unashamedly French and rustic, with red-and-white-check tablecloths and a menu chalked up on the blackboard. Start perhaps with some *moules marinières* (mussels cooked in a white-wine-and-onion sauce) or French onion soup, followed by grilled sea bass or a classic rib-eye steak with Café du Paris butter. **Known for:** rural French cooking; dishes that change daily; good value set menus. $ *Average main: £18* ⊠ *71 Northgate St.* ☎ *01244/400014* ⊕ *www. chezjules.com.*

Simon Radley at the Chester Grosvenor
$$$$ | **FRENCH** | Named for its noted chef, this Michelin-starred restaurant has a sophisticated panache and prices to match. Expect the seasonal but not the usual: the Two Hens features black-leg chicken alongside lobster, while the wild halibut comes with shaved octopus and seaweed dumplings. **Known for:**

unexpected flavor combinations; smart dress code and no children under 12; reservations needed for weekend. $ *Average main: £45* ⊠ *Chester Grosvenor Hotel, Eastgate St.* ☎ *01244/324024* ⊕ *www.chestergrosvenor.com/ simon-radley-restaurant* ⊗ *Closed Sun. and Mon.* 🍴 *Jacket required.*

Hotels

★ Chester Grosvenor Hotel
$$ | **HOTEL** | Handmade Italian furniture and swaths of French silk fill this deluxe downtown hotel in a Tudor-style building, which was established in 1865. **Pros:** pampered luxury; superb food; excellent service and facilities. **Cons:** no private parking; spa is small; extra for cooked breakfast. $ *Rooms from: £162* ⊠ *Eastgate* ☎ *01244/324024* ⊕ *www.chestergrosvenor.com* ⇌ *80 rooms* ❣ *Free breakfast.*

Grove Villa
$ | **B&B/INN** | This family-run B&B—in a charming Victorian building with antique furnishings on the banks of the River Dee—has just three guest rooms to choose from, two of which overlook the river. **Pros:** beautiful river location; breakfast around a communal table; friendly and welcoming hosts. **Cons:** no credit cards; no Internet connection; 15 minutes to town center. $ *Rooms from: £90* ⊠ *18 The Groves* ☎ *01244/349713* ⊕ *www.grovevillachester.co.uk* ▭ *No credit cards* ⇌ *3 rooms* ❣ *Free breakfast.*

Shopping

Chester Market
SHOPPING CENTERS/MALLS | This indoor market, near the Town Hall, has more than 50 stalls, including Chester's only fishmonger. It's a great place to try local food delicacies. It's open Monday through Saturday from 8 am until 5 pm (except for bank holidays). ⊠ *6 Princess St.* ⊕ *www.chester.market.*

A literal iron bridge leads to the town of Ironbridge and its museums highlighting the area's industrial history.

Ironbridge Gorge

4 miles east of Much Wenlock, 15 miles east of Shrewsbury, 28 miles northwest of Birmingham.

The River Severn and its tree-cloaked banks make an attractive backdrop to this cluster of villages; within a mile of the graceful span of the world's first substantial iron bridge are fascinating museums exploring the area's industrial past and the reasons why it's been described as the "cradle of the Industrial Revolution."

GETTING HERE AND AROUND

To drive here from Shrewsbury, take the A5 east, A442 south, and then the A4169 west before following the brown signs for Ironbridge. On weekends and bank holidays from Easter to late October, the Gorge Connect Bus shuttles passengers between Ironbridge's museums every 30 minutes; it's just £2 for museum passport holders and £2.50 for anyone else.

ESSENTIALS

VISITOR INFORMATION Ironbridge Visitor Information Centre. ⊠ *The Museum of the Gorge, The Wharfage, Telford* ☎ *01952/433424* ⊕ *www.ironbridge.org. uk.*

👁 Sights

★ Ironbridge Gorge Museum

MUSEUM | FAMILY | The 10 sites that make up the Ironbridge Gorge Museum—a World Heritage Site spread over 6 square miles—preserve the area's fascinating industrial history in spectacular fashion. The best starting point is the **Museum of the Gorge,** which has a good selection of literature and an audiovisual show on the history of the area. In nearby Coalbrookdale, the **Museum of Iron** explains the production of iron and steel. You can see the blast furnace built by Abraham Darby, who developed the original coke process in 1709. The adjacent **Enginuity** exhibition is a hands-on, feet-on interactive exploration of engineering that's good for kids. From here, drive the few miles along the river until the arches of the **Iron Bridge** come into view. Designed by T. F. Pritchard, smelted by Darby, and erected between 1777 and 1779, this graceful arch spanning the River Severn can best be seen—and photographed—from the towpath, a riverside walk edged with wildflowers and shrubs. The tollhouse on the far side houses an exhibition on the bridge's history and restoration.

A mile farther along the river is the **Jackfield Tile Museum,** a repository of decorative tiles from the 19th and 20th centuries. Another half mile brings you to the **Coalport China Museum.** Exhibits show some of the factory's most beautiful wares, and craftspeople give demonstrations; visit the restrooms for the unique communal washbasins. A short walk from Coalport is the **Tar Tunnel,** part of a 1787 tar mine; note the black bitumen still seeping through the walls. Nearby is Ironbridge's star attraction: **Blists Hill Victorian Town,** where you can see old mines, furnaces, and a wrought-iron works. The main draw is the re-creation of the "town" itself, with its doctor's office, bakery, grocer, candle maker, sawmill, printing shop, and candy store. At the entrance you can change some money for specially minted pennies and make purchases from the shops. Shopkeepers, the bank manager, and the doctor's wife are on hand to give you advice. If you don't fancy the refreshments at the Fried Fish Dealers, you could drop into the **New Inn** pub (in Blists Hill) for a traditional ale or ginger beer and join one of the singalongs around the piano that take place a couple of times every afternoon; or, for something more formal, try the **Club Room** restaurant next door. Allow at least a full day to appreciate all the major sights and perhaps to take a stroll around the famous Iron Bridge or hunt for Coalport china in the stores clustered near it. On weekends and national holidays from April through October, a shuttle bus takes you between sites. ✉ B4380, Telford ☎ 01952/433424 ⊕ www.ironbridge.org.uk ✈ Passport ticket (all attractions, valid 1 year) £25.15. Individual sites: Blists Hill £18.50; Enginuity, Coalport China Museum, Jackfield Tile Museum, and Museum of Iron £9.50 each; Museum of the Gorge £4.50.

Restaurants

Restaurant Severn

$$$ | **MODERN BRITISH** | At this discreet restaurant set back from the main road in the center of Ironbridge, the concept is simple: locally sourced produce and modern techniques are combined to serve up a twist of British classics and European favorites. Start with a Scotch egg with brown sauce and pancetta before moving on to pork belly stuffed with black pudding, kale, and spiced red cabbage. **Known for:** British classics with a modern slant; personal service; fabulous wines. ⑤ Average main: £29 ✉ 33 High St., Ironbridge ☎ 01952/432233 ⊕ www.restaurantsevern.co.uk ⊗ Closed Mon. and Tues.

🏨 Hotels

★ Library House

$ | **B&B/INN** | Built in 1740 and at one time the village's library, this small guesthouse sits on the hillside near the Ironbridge museums and just a few steps from the bridge. **Pros:** welcoming hosts; good location; elegant bedrooms. **Cons:** no restaurant; books up quickly; might be too personable for some. ⑤ Rooms from: £100 ✉ 11 Severn Bank, Telford ☎ 01952/432299 ⊕ www.libraryhouse.com ⇱ 3 rooms ⑩ Free breakfast.

Ludlow

25 miles south of Ironbridge Gorge, 27 miles south of Shrewsbury, 24 miles north of Hereford.

Medieval, Georgian, and Victorian buildings jostle for attention in pretty Ludlow, which has a finer display of black and white half-timber buildings than even Shrewsbury. Dominating the center is the Church of St. Laurence, its extravagant size a testimony to the town's prosperous medieval wool trade. Cross the River Teme and climb Whitcliffe Common for a spectacular view of the church and the Norman castle.

Several outstanding restaurants have given the town of just 11,000 a reputation as a culinary hot spot. Ludlow is a proponent of the Slow Food movement, which focuses on food traditions and responsible production with the aim of protecting forgotten foods, such as the Shropshire prune, from being lost forever.

GETTING HERE AND AROUND

From London Paddington; the journey time by train is 3½ hours (changing at Newport in southern Wales), from Shrewsbury 30 minutes, and from Birmingham just under two hours with a change in Shrewsbury. From the train station, it's less than a 10-minute walk to the city center. Driving from London, take the M40, M42, and A448 to Kidderminster, then the A456 and A4117 to Ludlow. The town has good parking and is easily walkable.

ESSENTIALS

VISITOR INFORMATION Ludlow Visitor Information Centre. ✉ *Ludlow Assembly Rooms, 1 Mill St.* ☎ *01584/875053* ⊕ *www.ludlow.org.uk.*

◉ Sights

★ Ludlow Castle

CASTLE/PALACE | FAMILY | The "very perfection of decay," according to author Daniel Defoe, the ruins of this red sandstone castle date from 1085. No wonder the massive structure dwarfs the town: it served as a vital stronghold for centuries and was the seat of the Marcher Lords who ruled "the Marches," the local name for the border region. The two sons of Edward IV—the little princes of the Tower of London—spent time here before being dispatched to London and before their death in 1483. Follow the terraced walk around the castle for a lovely view of the countryside. ✉ *Castle Sq.* ☎ *01584/873355* ⊕ *www.ludlowcastle.com* ▢ *£7* ⊗ *Closed weekdays early Jan.–early Feb.*

🍴 Restaurants

The Cliffe at Dinham

$$ | BRITISH | Although there are lovely rooms in this 1850s redbrick inn near Ludlow Castle, the main draw is the food. The dining room serves up good quality local dishes, but what really makes the modern British menu standout are its special evenings, such as Fish Night, in which fresh oysters and langoustines are cooked to perfection. **Known for:** classic British cuisine; nice cocktail menu and wine list; castle views. ⑤ *Average main: £18* ✉ *Dinham* ☎ *01584/872063* ⊕ *www.thecliffeatdinham.co.uk.*

🛏 Hotels

The Feathers

$$ | HOTEL | Even if you're not staying here, take time to admire the extravagant half-timber facade of this hotel, built in the early 17th century and described by many as one of the most beautiful inns in the world. **Pros:** ornate plasterwork; unpretentious feel; some four-poster beds. **Cons:** most guest rooms lack traditional feel; can be very tourist heavy; it's an old building and sometimes this shows. ⑤ *Rooms from: £129* ✉ *21 Bullring* ☎ *01584/875261* ⊕ *www.feathersatludlow.co.uk* ⇨ *42 rooms* ⑩ *Free breakfast.*

★ Fishmore Hall
$$ | **HOTEL** | Saved from dereliction in the late 2000s, Fishmore Hall has been beautifully converted from a crumbling old mansion into a relaxing, contemporary lodge. **Pros:** lovely location; well-designed rooms; serene, luxurious spa. **Cons:** restaurant is pricey; a little out of town; outdoor hot tub is not to everyone's liking. ⑤ *Rooms from: £145* ✉ *Fishmore Rd.* ☎ *01584/875148* ⊕ *www.fishmore-hall.co.uk* ⇨ *15 rooms* ⑩ *Free breakfast.*

★ Timberstone
$ | **B&B/INN** | **FAMILY** | The Read family has turned a rambling stone cottage in the Clee Hills into a welcoming haven with rooms furnished in neutral tones in a soothing, contemporary style. **Pros:** relaxing and hospitable; geared to families; great food. **Cons:** far from the center of Ludlow; rustic living may not appeal to everyone; dinner menu is limited. ⑤ *Rooms from: £120* ✉ *B4363, Cleestanton* ☎ *01584/823519* ⊕ *www.timberstoneludlow.co.uk* ⇨ *5 rooms* ⑩ *Free breakfast.*

Chapter 10

THE LAKE DISTRICT

Updated by
Sophie Ibbotson

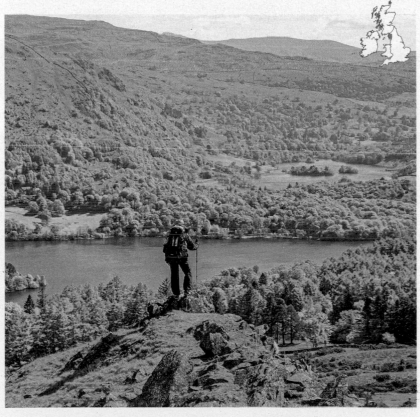

⊙ **Sights**   🍴 **Restaurants**   🛏 **Hotels**   🛍 **Shopping**   🍸 **Nightlife**
★★★☆☆   ★★★☆☆   ★★★☆☆   ★★☆☆☆   ★☆☆☆☆

WELCOME TO THE LAKE DISTRICT

TOP REASONS TO GO

★ **Hiking:** Whether it's a demanding trek or a gentle stroll, walking is the way to see the Lake District at its best.

★ **Boating:** There's nowhere better for renting a small boat or taking a cruise. The Coniston Boating Centre and Derwent Water Marina near Keswick are possible places to start.

★ **Literary landscapes:** The Lake District has a rich literary history, in the children's books of Beatrix Potter, in the writings of John Ruskin, and in the poems of William Wordsworth. Stop at any of the writers' homes to enrich your experience.

★ **Pints and pubs:** A pint of real ale in one of the region's inns, such as the Drunken Duck near Hawkshead, may never taste as good as after a day of walking.

★ **Sunrise at Castlerigg:** The stone circle at Castlerigg, in a hollow ringed by peaks, is a reminder of the region's ancient history.

The Lake District is in northwest England, some 70 miles north of the industrial belt that stretches from Liverpool to Manchester and south of Scotland. The major gateway from the south is Kendal, and from the north, Penrith. Both are on the M6 motorway. Main-line trains stop at Oxenholme, near Kendal, with a branch linking Oxenholme to Kendal and Windermere. Windermere, in the south, is the most obvious starting point and has museums, cafés, and gift shops. But the farther (and higher) you can get from the southern towns, the more you'll appreciate the area's spectacular landscapes. Lake District National Park breaks into two reasonably distinct sections: the gentler, rolling south and the craggier, wilder north.

1 **Kendal.** The southern gateway to the Lake District.

2 **Windermere and Bowness-on-Windermere.** The region's largest body of water.

3 **Ambleside.** A quintessential Lakeland town.

4 **Grasmere.** A romantic village with literary connections.

5 **Elterwater and the Langdales.** Beautiful upland country great for hikers.

6 **Coniston.** A small lake resort and boating center.

7 **Hawkshead.** A market town in the Vale of Esthwaite.

8 **Ullswater.** The region's second largest lake.

9 **Keswick.** A good base to explore the less crowded northern lakes.

10 **Borrowdale.** Challenging, spectacular walking country.

"Let nature be your teacher." Wordsworth's ideal comes true in this popular national park of jagged mountains, waterfalls, wooded valleys, and stone-built villages.

No mountains in Britain give a greater impression of majesty; deeper and bluer lakes can be found, but none that fit so readily into the surrounding scene. Outdoors enthusiasts flock to this region for boating or hiking, while literary types visit the homes of Beatrix Potter, William Wordsworth, and other classic writers.

In 1951, the Lake District National Park was created here from parts of the old counties of Cumberland, Westmorland, and Lancashire. The Lake District is a contour map come to life, covering an area of approximately 885 square miles and holding 16 major lakes and countless smaller stretches of water. The scenery is key to all the park's best activities: you can cross it by car in about an hour, but this is an area meant to be walked or boated or climbed. The mountains aren't high by international standards—Scafell Pike, England's highest peak, is only 3,210 feet above sea level—but they can be tricky to climb. In spring, many summits remain snowcapped long after the weather below has turned mild.

The poets Wordsworth and Coleridge, and other English writers, found the Lake District an inspiring setting for their work, and visitors have followed ever since, to walk, go boating, or just relax and take in the views. Seeing the homes and other sights associated with these writers can occupy part of a trip.

This area can be one of Britain's most appealing reservoirs of calm, though, in summer, the lakeside towns can lose their charm when cars and tour buses clog the narrow streets. Similarly, the walks and hiking trails that crisscross the region seem less inviting when you share them with a crowd. Despite the challenges of popularity, the Lake District has managed tourism and the landscape in a manner that retains the character of the villages and the natural environment. Explore beyond Windermere and Keswick to discover little farming communities eking out a living despite the occasionally harsh conditions.

Today, too, a new generation of hotel and restaurant owners is making more creative use of the local foods and other assets of the Lakeland fells, and chic modern or foodie-oriented establishments are springing up next to traditional tearooms and chintz-filled inns.

Off-season visits can be a real treat. All those inns and bed-and-breakfasts that turn away crowds in summer are eager for business the rest of the year (and their rates drop accordingly). It's not an easy task to find a succession of sunny days in the Lake District—some malicious statisticians allot to it about 250 rainy days a year—but when the sun breaks through and brightens the surfaces of the lakes, it's an away-from-it-all place to remember.

MAJOR REGIONS

The Southern Lakes. The southern lakes and valleys contain the park's most popular destinations and, thus, those most overcrowded in summer. Among the many attractions here are the small resort towns clustered around Windermere, England's largest lake, and the area's hideaway valleys, rugged walking centers, and monuments rich in literary associations. This is the easiest part of the Lake District to reach, with Kendal, the largest town, just a short distance from the M6 motorway. An obvious route from Kendal takes in Windermere, the area's natural touring center, before moving north through Ambleside to Grasmere. Some of the loveliest Lakeland scenery is to be found by then turning south, through Elterwater, Hawkshead, and Coniston.

The North Lakes. The scenery of the northern lakes is considerably more dramatic—some would say bleaker—than much of the landscape to the south, a change that becomes apparent on your way north from Kendal to Penrith. A 30-mile drive on the A6 takes you through the wild and desolate Shap Fells, which rise to a height of 1,304 feet. This is one of the most notorious moorland crossings in the country: even in summer it's a lonely place to be, and in winter, snow on the road can be dangerous. From Penrith the road leads to Ullswater, possibly the grandest of all the lakes; then there's a winding route west past Keswick, south through the marvelous Borrowdale Valley, and on to Cockermouth. Outside the main towns such as Keswick it can be easier to escape the summer crowds in the northern lakes.

Planning
When to Go

The Lake District is one of the rainiest areas in Britain, but June, July, and August hold the best hope of fine weather, and summer is the time for all the major festivals. You will, however, be sharing the lakes with thousands of other people. If you travel at this time, turn up early at popular museums and attractions, and expect to work to find parking. April and May, as well as September and October, are good alternatives. Later and earlier in the year there'll be even more space and freedom, but many attractions close, and from December to March, snow and ice can sometimes block high passes and may preclude serious hill walking without heavy-duty equipment.

Planning Your Time

You could spend months tramping the hills, valleys, and fells of the Lake District, or, in three days you could drive through the major towns and villages. The key is not to do too much in too short a time. If you're traveling by public transportation, many places will be off-limits. As a base, Windermere has the best transport links, but it can be crowded, and it has less character than some of the smaller towns like Ambleside and Keswick, which also have plenty of sleeping and eating options. For a more intimate version of village life, try Coniston, Hawkshead, or Grasmere. Keep in mind that the northern and western lakes have the most dramatic scenery and offer the best opportunity to escape the summertime hordes.

The Lake District may be compact, but it's not a place to hurry. Allow plenty of time for walking: paths can be steep and rocky, and, in any case, you'll want to stop frequently to look at the great views. A good day's walking with a picnic can be done from nearly anywhere. Driving brings its own speed inhibitors, from sheep on the roads to slow tractors.

You're likely to be based down near lake level, but try to experience the hills, too. If you're short of time, a drive over one of the high passes such as Honister will give you a glimpse of the enormity of the landscape.

Getting Here and Around

AIR

Manchester Airport has its own rail station with direct service to Carlisle, Windermere, and Barrow-in-Furness. Manchester is 70 miles from the southern part of the Lake District.

CONTACT Manchester Airport. ✉ M56, Near Junctions 5 and 6 ☎ 0808/169–7030 ⊕ www.manchesterairport.co.uk.

BOAT

Whether you rent a boat or take a ride on a modern launch or vintage vessel, getting out on the water is a fun (and often useful) way to see the Lake District. Windermere, Coniston Water, and Derwentwater all have boat rental facilities.

BUS

National Express serves the region from London's Victoria Coach Station and from Manchester's Chorlton Street Station. Average travel time to Kendal is just over 7 hours from London; to Windermere, 7½ hours; and to Keswick, 8¼ hours. From Manchester there's one bus a day to Windermere via Ambleside, Grasmere, and Keswick. There's direct bus service to the Lake District from Carlisle, Lancaster, and York.

Stagecoach in Cumbria provides local service between Lakeland towns and through the valleys and high passes. Bus service between main tourist centers is fairly frequent on weekdays, but much reduced on weekends and bank holidays. Don't count on reaching the more remote parts of the area by bus. Off-the-beaten-track touring requires a car or strong legs. A one-week Cumbria Megarider ticket (£28), available on the bus, is valid on all routes. Dayrider tickets (£6–£8) are valid for a day; the price varies depending on how far you wish to travel. Contact Traveline for up-to-date timetables.

CONTACTS National Express. ☎ 0871/781–8181 ⊕ www.nationalexpress.com.

Stagecoach. ☎ 01539/722217 ⊕ www.stagecoachbus.com. **Traveline.** ☎ 0871/200–2233 ⊕ www.traveline.info.

CAR

A car is almost essential in the Lake District; bus service is limited and trains can get you to the edge of the national park but no farther. You can rent cars in Penrith and Kendal. Roads within the region are generally good, although minor routes and mountain passes can be steep and narrow. Warning signs are often posted if snow or ice has made a road impassable; check local weather forecasts in winter before heading out. In July and August and during the long public holiday weekends, expect heavy traffic. The Lake District has plenty of parking lots; use them to avoid blocking narrow lanes. Most parking lots require payment; it's smart to keep some change on hand.

To reach the Lake District by car from London, take M1 north to M6, getting off either at Junction 36 and joining A590/A591 west (around the Kendal bypass to Windermere) or at Junction 40, joining A66 direct to Keswick and the northern lakes region. Travel time to Kendal is about four to five hours, to Keswick five to six hours. Expect heavy traffic out of London on weekends.

TRAIN

There are direct trains from Manchester and Manchester airport to Windermere. For schedule information, call National Rail Enquiries. Two train companies serve the region from London's Euston Station: take an Avanti West Coast or Northern Rail train bound for Carlisle, Edinburgh, or Glasgow and change at Oxenholme for the branch line service to Kendal and Windermere. Average travel time from London to Windermere (including the change) is 3¼ hours. If you're heading for Keswick, you can either take the train to Windermere and continue from there by Stagecoach bus (Bus 554/555/556; 70 minutes) or stay on the main London–Carlisle train to Penrith Station (4 hours), from which Stagecoach buses (Bus X5) also run to Keswick (45 minutes). Direct trains from Manchester depart for Windermere five times daily (travel time 2 hours). First North Western runs a local service from Windermere and Barrow-in-Furness to Manchester Airport. National Rail can handle all questions about trains.

Train connections are good around the edges of the Lake District, but you must take the bus or drive to reach the central Lakeland region. Trains are sometimes reduced, or nonexistent, on Sunday.

CONTACTS Avanti West Coast.
☎ 0344/556–1394 ⊕ www.avantiwest-coast.co.uk. **National Rail Enquiries.**
☎ 03457/484950 ⊕ www.nationalrail.co.uk. **Northern Rail.** ☎ 0800/200–6060 ⊕ www.northernrailway.co.uk.

The Lake District National Park

The Lake District National Park head office (and main visitor center) is at Brockhole, north of Windermere. Helpful regional national-park information centers sell books and maps, book accommodations, and provide walking advice.

CONTACTS Bowness Bay Information Centre. ✉ Glebe Rd., Bowness-on-Windermere ☎ 0845/901–0845 ⊕ www.lakedistrict.gov.uk. **Keswick Information Centre.** ✉ Moot Hall, 12-14 Main St., Keswick ☎ 0845/901–0845 ⊕ www.keswick.org. **Lake District Visitor Centre.** ✉ Brockhole, Ambleside Rd., Windermere ☎ 015394/46601 ⊕ www.brockhole.co.uk. **Ullswater Information Centre.** ✉ Beckside Car Park, off Greenside Rd., Glenridding ☎ 0845/901–0845 ⊕ www.lakedistrict.gov.uk.

Tours

Cumbria Tourist Guides

This organization of Blue Badge–accredited guides, who are all experts on the area, offers a large range of customized tours, from low impact country ambles to brewery crawls. From £175 for a half day. ☎ 01228/562096 ⊕ www.cumbriatourist-guides.org.

★ Swim the Lakes

ADVENTURE TOURS | With more than 80 lakes, meres, and tarns, Cumbria is a great place for open-water swimming. Swim the Lakes has specialized swimming wet suits and a wealth of knowledge and enthusiasm about the best places to swim. Guided trips range from a couple of hours to weekends with accommodation and food included. As a way to see the lakes, the view and the experience from the water is hard to beat. ✉ 2 Compston Rd., Ambleside ☎ 015394/33826 ⊕ www.swimthelakes.co.uk ⌖ From £30 for guided short wild swims.

Restaurants

Lakeland restaurants increasingly reflect a growing British awareness of good food. Local sourcing and international influences are common, and even old Cumberland favorites are being creatively reinvented. Pub dining in the Lake District can be excellent—the hearty fare often makes use of local ingredients such as Herdwick lamb, and real ales are a good accompaniment. If you're going walking, ask your hotel or B&B about making you a packed lunch. Some local delicatessens also offer this service.

Hotels

Your choices include everything from small country inns to grand lakeside hotels. Many hotels offer the option of paying a higher price that includes dinner as well as breakfast. The regional mainstay is the bed-and-breakfast, from the house on Main Street to an isolated farmhouse. Most country hotels and B&Bs gladly cater to hikers and can provide on-the-spot information. Wherever you stay, book well in advance for summer visits, especially those in late July and August. In winter, many accommodations close for a month or two. On weekends and in summer it may be hard to get a reservation for a single night. Internet access is improving, and an increasing number of hotels and cafés offer Wi-Fi.

Restaurant and hotel reviews have been shortened. For full information, visit Fodors.com. Restaurant prices are the average cost of a main course at dinner, or if dinner is not served, at lunch. Hotel prices are the lowest cost of a standard double room in high season, including 20% V.A.T.

WHAT IT COSTS in Pounds			
$	$$	$$$	$$$$
RESTAURANTS			
under £16	£16–£23	£24–£30	over £30
HOTELS			
under £125	£125–£225	£226–£350	over £350

Visitor Information

CONTACTS Cumbria Tourism. ⊠ *Windermere Rd., Staveley* ☎ *01539/822222* ⊕ *www.golakes.co.uk.*

Kendal

70 miles north of Manchester.

The southern gateway to the Lake District is the "Auld Gray Town" of Kendal, outside the national park and less touristy than the towns to the northwest. You may want to stay closer to the action, but the town has some worthwhile sights. Nearby hills frame Kendal's gray stone houses and provide some delightful walks; you can also explore the ruins of Kendal Castle. ■TIP→ **Pack a slab of Kendal mint cake, the local peppermint candy that British walkers and climbers swear by. It's for sale around the region.**

The town's motto, "Wool Is My Bread," refers to its importance as a textile center in northern England before the Industrial Revolution. It was known for manufacturing woolen cloth, especially Kendal Green, which archers favored. Away from the main road are quiet courtyards and winding medieval streets known as "ginnels." Wool merchants used these for easy access to the River Kent.

GETTING HERE AND AROUND
Kendal is just off the M6, about 70 miles north of Manchester. It has train service via a branch line from Oxenholme and National Express bus service from London as well. It's the largest town in the area but is still plenty small enough to walk around.

ESSENTIALS
VISITOR INFORMATION Kendal Tourist Information Centre. ⊠ *Fantastic Kendal, 26-28 Finkle St.* ☎ *01539/725139* ⊕ *www.exploresouthlakeland.co.uk.*

 Sights

Levens Hall
GARDEN | FAMILY | An Elizabethan house and the home of the Bagot family since 1590, Levens Hall is famous for its topiary garden, probably the most distinctive in the world. Laid out in 1694, the garden retains its original design, and the yew and beech hedges, cut into complex shapes that resemble enormous chess pieces, rise among a profusion of flowers. The house contains a stunning medieval hall with oak paneling, ornate

The Lake District

plasterwork, Jacobean furniture, and Cordova goat-leather wallpaper. You can easily spend a couple of hours here admiring the place or getting lost in the living willow labyrinth. There's a play area for children. Levens Hall is 4 miles south of Kendal. ✉ Off A590, Levens ☎ 01539/560321 ⊕ www.levenshall.co.uk ⌨ £14.50; gardens only £10.50 ☾ Closed early Oct.–mid-Apr. and Fri.–Sat.

🍴 Restaurants

The Moon Highgate

$$ | **MODERN BRITISH** | Small but sleek, this restaurant with an open fire and artfully battered floorboards has won a good local reputation for high-quality dishes. The vegetarian selections are always worthwhile, and the sometimes adventurous Modern British cooking shows Mediterranean flourishes. **Known**

for: imaginative British menu; seasonal ingredients; fixed-price early dinners. ⑤ Average main: £17 ✉ 129 Highgate ☎ 01539/729254 ⊕ www.themoonhighgate.com ☾ Closed Sun. and Mon.

🛏 Hotels

Kendal Hostel

$ | **HOTEL** | Right on Kendal's main street, this upscale hostel is located in an attractive building with plenty of character. **Pros:** central location; friendly staff; self-catering facilities. **Cons:** shared bathrooms; can get noisy with large groups; no free parking. ⑤ Rooms from: £40 ✉ 118–120 Highgate ☎ 01539/724066 ⊕ www.kendalhostel.com ⤳ 14 rooms ⑩ No meals.

🎭 Performing Arts

★ **Brewery Arts Centre**

ARTS CENTERS | A contemporary complex in a converted brewery, the Brewery Arts Centre includes a gallery, theater, cinemas, and workshop spaces. The Vats Bar, an on-site freehouse, serves up a tasty selection of pizzas and hearty mains, as well as a variety of craft beers and wine. In November, the Mountain Film Festival presents productions aimed at climbers and walkers. ⊠ *122A Highgate* 🕾 *01539/725133* ⊕ *www.breweryarts.co.uk* ✆ *Free* ☞ *Kitchen closed Sun.–Mon.*

Windermere and Bowness-on-Windermere

10 miles northwest of Kendal.

For a natural touring base for the southern half of the Lake District, you don't need to look much farther than Windermere, though it does get crowded in summer. The resort became popular in the Victorian era when the arrival of the railway made the remote and rugged area accessible. Wordsworth and Ruskin opposed the railway, fearing an influx of tourists would ruin the tranquil place. Sure enough, the railway terminus in 1847 brought with it Victorian day-trippers, and the original hamlet of Birthwaite was subsumed by the new town of Windermere, named after the lake.

Windermere has continued to flourish, despite being a mile or so from the water. The development now spreads to envelop the slate-gray lakeside village of Bowness-on-Windermere. Bowness is the more attractive of the two, but they're so close that it doesn't matter where you stay.

GETTING HERE AND AROUND

Windermere is easily reached by car, less than a half hour off the M6. There's also a train station at the eastern edge of town; change at Oxenholme for the branch line to Kendal and Windermere.

Bus 599, leaving every 20 minutes in summer (hourly the rest of the year) from outside the Windermere train station, links the town with Bowness.

The Windermere Ferry, which carries cars and pedestrians, crosses from Ferry Nab on the Bowness side of the lake to reach Far Sawrey and the road to Hawkshead. With year-round ferry service between Ambleside, Bowness, Brockhole, and Lakeside, Windermere Lake Cruises is a pleasant way to experience the lake.

ESSENTIALS

CONTACTS Windermere Ferry. 🕾 *01228/227653* ⊕ *www.cumbria.gov. uk/roads-transport/highways-pavements/ windermereferry.asp.* **Windermere Lake Cruises.** 🕾 *015394/43360* ⊕ *www.windermere-lakecruises.co.uk.*

👁 Sights

★ **Blackwell**

HOUSE | From 1898 to 1900, architect Mackay Hugh Baillie Scott (1865–1945) designed Blackwell, a quintessential Arts and Crafts house with carved paneling, delicate plasterwork, and a startling sense of light and space. Originally a retreat for a Manchester brewery owner, the house is a refined mix of modern style and the local vernacular. Lime-washed walls and sloping slate roofs make it fit elegantly into the landscape above Windermere, and the artful integration of decorative features into stained glass, stonework, friezes, and wrought iron gives the house a sleekly contemporary feel. Accessibility is wonderful here: nothing is roped off, and you can even play the piano. There's some Baillie Scott furniture, too, and an exhibition space upstairs. Peruse the shop, and try the honey-roast ham in the excellent tea-room. The grounds are also worth a visit; they often host contemporary sculpture installations. ⊠ *Off the B5360, Windermere* ☎ *01539/446139* ⊕ *www.blackwell.org.uk* ⧖ *f9*

Brockhole

GARDEN | FAMILY | A lakeside 19th-century mansion with 30 acres of terraced gardens sloping down to the water, Brockhole serves as the park's official visitor center and has some exhilarating activities. Among them are "treetop trek"—a rope bridge and zipline route high up through oak trees—and the U.K.'s only "treetop nets," allowing everyone over the age of three to climb and bounce around safely among the twigs and leaves more than 25 feet up, supported by elastic ropes. There's also a 30-foot climbing wall. The gardens, designed in the Arts and Crafts style by Thomas Mawson, are at their best in spring, when daffodils punctuate the lawns and azaleas burst into bloom. There's an adventure playground, pony rides, minigolf, and rowboats for rent. The bookstore carries hiking guides and maps, and you can picnic here or eat at the café-restaurant. Bus 555/559 goes to the visitor center from Windermere, and boats from Waterhead stop at a pier. Windermere Lake Cruises has seasonal ferry service to Brockhole from Waterhead in Ambleside. ⊠ *Ambleside Rd., Windermere* ☎ *015394/46601* ⊕ *www.brockhole.co.uk* ⧖ *Free; treetop trek £22; treetop nets from £13.*

★ Lakes Aquarium

ZOO | FAMILY | On the quayside at the southern end of Windermere, this excellent aquarium has wildlife and waterside exhibits. One highlight is an underwater tunnel walk along a re-created lake bed, complete with diving ducks and Asian short-clawed otters. Piranhas, rays, and tropical frogs also have their fans, and there are some unexpected treats such as marmosets. A friendly, knowledgeable staff is eager to talk about the animals. ■ TIP➜ **Animal handling takes place daily at 1 pm in the rain-forest areas.** Tickets are cheapest if booked in advance online. ⊠ *C5062, Newby Bridge* ☎ *01539/430153* ⊕ *www.lakesaquarium.co.uk* ⧖ *£7.50.*

Lakeside & Haverthwaite Railway Company

TRANSPORTATION SITE (AIRPORT/BUS/FERRY/TRAIN) | FAMILY | Vintage steam trains chug along on the 18-minute, 4-mile branch line between Lakeside and Haverthwaite, giving you a great view of the lake's southern tip. You can add on a lake cruise for another perspective on the region's natural beauty. Departures from Lakeside coincide with ferry arrivals from Bowness and Ambleside. See the website for timetables. ⊠ *Haverthwaite Railway Station, A590, Haverthwaite* ☎ *01539/531594* ⊕ *www.lakesiderailway.co.uk* ⧖ *£7.10 round-trip; £12 unlimited 1-day travel.*

Windermere Jetty

MARINA | Right beside the lake, the center houses the world's finest collection of Victorian and Edwardian steam- and motor-powered yachts and launches. Displays about Windermere's nautical history include the famous names of motorboat racing on the lake. The *Dolly*, built around 1850, is one of the two oldest mechanically powered boats in the world. Among the many other vessels on view are Beatrix Potter's rowing boat and a dinghy that belonged to Arthur Ransome. ■ TIP➜ **For £14, you can take a boat ride on Windermere in an antique vessel—if the weather is good.** ⊠ *Rayrigg Rd., Bowness-on-Windermere* ☎ *01539/445565* ⊕ *windermerejetty.org* ⧖ *£9* ⊗ *Closed mid-Jan. for maintenance.*

World of Beatrix Potter

MUSEUM | FAMILY | A touristy attraction aimed at kids interprets the author's 23 tales with three-dimensional scenes of Peter Rabbit and more. Skip it if you can, and visit Potter's former home at Hill Top and the Beatrix Potter Gallery in Hawkshead. ⊠ *The Old Laundry,*

Crag Brow, Bowness-on-Windermere ☎ 01539/488444 ⊕ www.hop-skip-jump. com ✉ £8.20.

Restaurants

Angel Inn

$ | **BRITISH** | Up the steep slope from the water's edge in Bowness, this spacious, stylish pub serves good home-cooked fare as well as a fine collection of beers that includes its own Hawkshead brew. Specials, chalked on a board, may include dishes such as roasted cod with bok choy or goat cheese and fig tart. **Known for:** draft beers and ciders; landscaped gardens; local, seasonal food. $ *Average main: £14* ✉ *Helm Rd., Bowness-on-Windermere* ☎ *01539/444080* ⊕ *www. angelbowness.com.*

Masons Arms

$ | **BRITISH** | **FAMILY** | With fabulous views over the rolling countryside of the Winster Valley to the east of Windermere, the Masons Arms is a slate-floored traditional old inn serving local ales and good pub food. Old mirrors and tankards decorate the walls, and there's a speciality gin list as well as a menu showcasing the best local ingredients. **Known for:** locally farmed meats; housemade desserts; popular children's menu. $ *Average main: £15* ✉ *Strawberry Bank, Windermere* ☎ *01539/568486* ⊕ *www.masonsarmsstrawberrybank.co.uk.*

Hotels

★ Gilpin Hotel and Lake House

$$$ | **HOTEL** | Hidden among 22 acres of grounds with meandering paths leading to sleek, spacious lodges, this rambling country house provides the ultimate pampering. **Pros:** plenty of pampering; notable food; a policy of no weddings or conferences. **Cons:** a little out of the way; expensive rates; might be too posh for some. $ *Rooms from: £295* ✉ *Crook Rd., Bowness-on-Windermere* ✛ *2 miles east of Windermere* ☎ *01539/488818*

⊕ *thegilpin.co.uk* ↬ *20 rooms, 5 lodges* ⦿| *All-inclusive* ☞ *No children under 7.*

★ 1 Park Road

$ | **B&B/INN** | On a quiet corner, this upscale boutique B&B has spacious guest rooms with carefully chosen fabrics and wallpaper, comfortable mattresses, and contemporary touches. **Pros:** welcoming and stylish; hosts will pick guests up from the station; good food, wine, and beer. **Cons:** a 15-minute walk to the lake; limited car parking; not handicap accessible. $ *Rooms from: £90* ✉ *1 Park Rd., Windermere* ☎ *01539/442107* ⊕ *1parkroad.co.uk* ↬ *6 rooms* ⦿| *Free breakfast.*

Shopping

★ More? The Artisan Bakery

FOOD/CANDY | Between Kendal and Windermere, this bakery is the place to stop for mouthwatering, award-winning bread, cakes, and sandwiches, including an unforgettable bright green matcha tea blondie. It also brews fine coffee. Proximity to the neighboring Hawkshead Brewery makes for a couple of hours of true indulgence. ✉ *Mill Yard, Staveley* ☎ *01539/822297* ⊕ *www.moreartisan. co.uk.*

Peter Hall & Son

CRAFTS | This woodcraft workshop, between Kendal and Windermere, sells bespoke furniture and finely honed boxes and bowls, among other items. ✉ *Danes Rd., Staveley* ☎ *01539/821633* ⊕ *www. peter-hall.co.uk.*

Activities

BIKING

Country Lanes Cycle Hire

BICYCLING | This shop rents a variety of bikes from £26 per day. Helmets and a number of other useful accessories are included in the price. ✉ *Windermere Railway Station, off A591, Windermere* ☎ *01539/444544* ⊕ *www.countrylaneslakedistrict.co.uk.*

Ambleside

7 miles northwest of Windermere.

Unlike Kendal and Windermere, Ambleside seems almost part of the hills and fells. Its buildings, mainly of local stone and many built in the traditional style that forgoes the use of mortar in the outer walls, blend perfectly into their setting. The small town sits at the northern end of Windermere along A591, making it a popular center for Lake District excursions. It has recently seen a sharp rise in quality restaurants, and the numerous outdoor shops are handy for walkers. Ambleside does, however, suffer from overcrowding in high season. Wednesday, when the local market takes place, is particularly busy.

GETTING HERE AND AROUND

An easy drive along A591 from Windermere, Ambleside can also be reached by ferry.

ESSENTIALS

VISITOR INFORMATION Ambleside Tourist Information Centre. ⊠ *In the Post Office, Central Bldgs., 8-9 Market Pl.* ☎ *01539/432582 Post Office/Tourist Information, 0844/225–0544 Ambleside Online* ⊕ *www.visitcumbria.com/amb/ambleside, www.amblesideonline.co.uk.*

 Sights

Armitt Museum

MUSEUM | Ambleside's fine local museum is a scholarly place, focusing on influential German artist Kurt Schwitters and Beatrix Potter. Schwitters lived out his final years in Ambleside, and the museum now has a room filled with his art. The museum also shows the less well-known aspects of Beatrix Potter, revealing her work as an important scientific and intellectual figure. Exhibits shed light on her as a naturalist, mycologist, sheep breeder, and conservationist. A large collection of her natural-history watercolors

and a huge number of photographic portraits can be viewed by appointment in the excellent library upstairs. ⊠ *Rydal Rd.* ☎ *01539/431212* ⊕ *www.armitt.com* ☞ *£5.*

Bridge House

BUILDING | This tiny 17th-century stone building, once an apple store, perches on an arched stone bridge spanning Stone Beck. It may have been built here to avoid land tax. This much-photographed building, which is cared for by the National Trust, holds a shop and an information center. ⊠ *Rydal Rd.* ☎ *015394/32617* ⊕ *www.nationaltrust.org.uk/ambleside/features/bridge-house—a-17th-century-survivor* ☞ *Free.*

 Restaurants

★ Fellinis

$ | VEGETARIAN | Billing itself as "vegeterranean" to reflect its Mediterranean culinary influences, Fellinis is one of Cumbria's finest foodie destinations and a particular treat for vegetarians. Upstairs is a plush studio cinema screening arthouse releases, while downstairs the restaurant rustles up sumptuous concoctions for a sophisticated crowd. **Known for:** unpretentious fine dining; vegetarian and vegan dishes; romantic dinner-and-a-movie ambience. ⑤ *Average main: £14* ⊠ *Church St.* ☎ *01539/432487* ⊕ *www.tellinisambleside.com* ⊗ *No lunch.*

Lake Road Kitchen

$$$$ | MODERN BRITISH | Cuttlefish shells piled in the window and a Nordic-style wood-paneled interior give a clue as to the culinary style of Lake Road Kitchen, quite possibly the most awarded restaurant in Ambleside. About 80% of everything green on the menu is foraged; the remainder comes from the highest-quality, mainly local suppliers. **Known for:** homegrown and foraged produce; mouthwatering set menu with wine pairings; small space so reservations necessary. ⑤ *Average main: £65* ⊠ *Lake Rd.*

☎ 01539/422012 ⊕ www.lakeroadkitchen. co.uk ⊗ Closed Mon. and Tues. No lunch.

★ Old Stamp House

$$$ | BRITISH | The quality of locally sourced and foraged food has been raised to a new level by this startlingly good restaurant, which, together with the Lake Road Kitchen, has given Ambleside unexpected status on the British gastro map. Chef Ryan Blackburn has created a menu anchored to Cumbrian traditions but at the same time mouthwateringly creative and contemporary. **Known for:** creative seasonal menu; celebrity chef; excellent wine list. Ⓢ Average main: £26 ⊠ Church St. ☎ 01539/432775 ⊕ www.oldstamphouse.com ⊗ Closed Sun. and Mon. No lunch Tues.

Rattle Ghyll

$ | VEGETARIAN | Hidden away up a winding lane past the old mill waterwheel, homey Rattle Ghyll is a deservedly popular little café serving great housemade cakes, soups, sandwiches, and salads. The tasting plate of cakes is an especially good option. **Known for:** housemade soups; tasting plates of cakes; outdoor seating. Ⓢ Average main: £7 ⊠ 2 Bridge St. ☎ 07975/912990 ⊕ www.rattleghyll. com ⊗ Closed Mon. and Tues. No dinner.

 Hotels

Rooms at the Apple Pie

$ | B&B/INN | Converted from what were once the offices of Beatrix Potter's solicitor husband, this Ambleside café has branched out into accommodations, with eight simple but stylishly furnished rooms decorated with photos of delights from the café next door. **Pros:** scrumptious breakfasts; central location; stylish rooms. **Cons:** not staffed 24 hours a day; breakfast is extra; limited parking. Ⓢ Rooms from: £56 ⊠ Rydal Rd., Keswick ☎ 01539/433679 ⊕ www. applepieambleside.co.uk ⤸ 8 rooms ⏐○⏐ No meals.

★ Rothay Manor

$$ | HOTELHOTEL | One of the original luxury hotels of the Lakes, Rothay Manor was recently purchased from previous owners, a family who owned it for most of a century and gave it a loving facelift. **Pros:** spectacular, experimental cuisine; spacious rooms; quiet location. **Cons:** can feel a little intimidating; on the more expensive end; not all bathrooms have tubs. Ⓢ Rooms from: £220 ⊠ Off the A593 ☎ 01539/433605 ⊕ www. rothaymanor.co.uk ⤸ 18 rooms ⏐○⏐ Free breakfast.

The Samling

$$$ | HOTEL | On its own sculpture-dotted 67 acres not far from Ambleside and Windermere, this place oozes exclusivity from the moment you enter the long, winding drive. **Pros:** set on gorgeous private estate; superb restaurant; celebrity guest list. **Cons:** exclusivity doesn't come cheap; steep climb up from the lake; outside Ambleside. Ⓢ Rooms from: £330 ⊠ Ambleside Rd. ☎ 015394/431922 ⊕ www.thesamlinghotel.co.uk ⤸ 12 rooms ⏐○⏐ Free breakfast.

 Activities

The fine walks in the vicinity include routes north to Rydal Mount or southeast over Wansfell to Troutbeck. Each walk will take up to a half day, there and back. Ferries from Bowness-on-Windermere dock at Ambleside's harbor, called Waterhead. ■TIP➔ **To escape the crowds, rent a rowboat at the harbor for an hour or two.**

Grasmere

3 miles north of Rydal, 4 miles northwest of Ambleside.

Lovely Grasmere, on a tiny, wood-fringed lake, is made up of crooked lanes in which Westmorland slate–built cottages hold shops and galleries. The village is

Children's writer Beatrix Potter used details from her house at Hill Top, near Hawkshead, in the illustrations for her stories.

a focal point for literary and landscape associations because this area was the adopted heartland of the Romantic poets, notably Wordsworth and Coleridge. The Vale of Grasmere has changed over the years, but many features Wordsworth wrote about are still visible. Wordsworth lived on the town's outskirts for almost 50 years and described the area as "the loveliest spot that man hath ever known."

GETTING HERE AND AROUND
On the main A591 between Ambleside and Keswick, Grasmere is easily reached by car.

ESSENTIALS
VISITOR INFORMATION Grasmere Tourist Information Centre. ⊠ *Church Stile* ☏ *01539/435665* ⊕ *www.nationaltrust. org.uk/allan-bank-and-grasmere.*

Sights

★ Allan Bank
HOUSE | FAMILY | Rope swings on the grounds, picnics in atmospheric old rooms, free tea and coffee, and huge blackboards you can write on: Allan Bank is unlike most other historic houses cared for by the National Trust. On a hill above the lake near Grasmere village, this grand house was once home to poet William Wordsworth as well as to Canon Rawnsley, the founder of the National Trust. Seriously damaged by fire in 2011, it has been partially restored but also left deliberately undecorated. It offers a much less formal experience than other stops on the Wordsworth trail. There are frequent activities for both children and adults: arts and crafts but also music and astronomy. Red squirrels can be seen on the 30-minute woodland walk through the beautiful grounds. ⊠ *Off A591* ☏ *01539/435143* ⊕ *www.nationaltrust. org.uk/allan-bank-and-grasmere* 🎫 *£7.90* ⊗ *Closed Jan.–mid-Feb.*

Dove Cottage and Wordsworth Museum
HOUSE | William Wordsworth lived in Dove Cottage from 1799 to 1808, a prolific and happy time for the poet. During this

time he wrote some of his most famous works, including "Ode: Intimations of Immortality" and *The Prelude*. Built in the early 17th century as an inn, this tiny, dim, and, in some places, dank house is beautifully preserved, with an oak-paneled hall and floors of Westmorland slate. It first opened to the public in 1891 and remains as it was when Wordsworth lived here with his sister, Dorothy, and wife, Mary. Bedrooms and living areas contain much of Wordsworth's furniture and many personal belongings. Coleridge was a frequent visitor, as was Thomas De Quincey, best known for his 1822 autobiographical masterpiece *Confessions of an English Opium-Eater*. De Quincey moved in after the Wordsworths left. You visit the house on a timed guided tour, and the ticket includes admission to the spacious, modern **Wordsworth Museum,** which documents the poet's life and the literary contributions of Wordsworth and the Lake Poets. The museum includes space for major art exhibitions. The **Jerwood Centre,** open to researchers by appointment, houses 50,000 letters, first editions, and manuscripts. Afternoon tea is served at a café next to the parking lot. ✉ *A591, south of Grasmere* ☎ *01539/435544* ⊕ *www.wordsworth. org.uk* 🎫 *£8.95* ⊗ *Closed Jan.*

St. Oswald's

RELIGIOUS SITE | William Wordsworth, his wife Mary, his sister Dorothy, and four of his children are buried in the churchyard of this historical church with a curious split interior on the River Rothay. The poet planted eight of the yew trees here, including the one under which he was interred. As you leave the churchyard, stop at the Gingerbread Shop, in a tiny cottage, for a special local treat. ✉ *Stock La.* ⊕ *www.stoswaldsgrasmere.uk.*

Restaurants

★ The Jumble Room

$$ | BRITISH | A small stone building dating to the 18th century, Grasmere's first shop is now a friendly, fashionable, and colorful restaurant, with children's books, bold animal paintings, and hanging lamps. The food is an eclectic mix of international and traditional British; think porcini mushroom arancini, beetroot and pumpkin ravioli, or Lebanese chicken with clementine and fennel. **Known for:** freshly baked bread; lively atmosphere; imaginative menu. ⑤ *Average main: £16* ✉ *Langdale Rd.* ☎ *01539/435188* ⊕ *www. thejumbleroom.co.uk* ⊗ *No lunch, closed Mon. and Tues.*

Tweedies Bar & Lodge

$$ | MODERN BRITISH | One of the region's best gastro-pubs, Tweedies attracts many locals as well as visitors. Delicious updated British classics include beer-battered Fleetwood haddock, braised ox cheek with lardons, and an 8-ounce burger with roasted shallots. **Known for:** live music; classic British menu including great burgers; awesome local ales. ⑤ *Average main: £16* ✉ *Langdale Rd.* ☎ *01539/435300* ⊕ *www.tweediesgrasmere.com.*

Hotels

★ Heidi's Grasmere Lodge

$ | B&B/INN | Small but sumptuous, this lodging has a distinctly feminine sensibility, with floral wallpaper, curly steel lamps, and painted woodwork. **Pros:** chic bathrooms with whirlpool tubs; warm welcome; some rooms have mountain views. **Cons:** no children allowed; so pristine you may worry about your muddy boots; rooms vary in size. ⑤ *Rooms from: £99* ✉ *Red Lion Sq.* ☎ *01539/435248* ⊕ *www.heidisgrasmerelodge.co.uk* ⇨ *6 rooms* ⏿ *Free breakfast.*

Moss Grove Organic

$ | B&B/INN | A Victorian building in the heart of Grasmere, the chic and spacious Moss Grove Organic puts an emphasis on its environmental credentials. **Pros:** roaring fire in the evenings; housemade marmalade at breakfast; modern design with a conscience. **Cons:** tight parking; not the place for a big fry-up breakfast; service can be slow. $ *Rooms from: £124* ⊠ *Red Lion Sq.* ☎ *01539/435251* ⊕ *www.mossgrove.com* ↝ *11 rooms* ⍥ *Free breakfast.*

Shopping

★ Grasmere Gingerbread Shop

FOOD/CANDY | The smells wafting across the churchyard draw many people to the Grasmere Gingerbread Shop. Since 1854, Sarah Nelson's gingerbread has been sold from this cramped 17th-century cottage, which was once the village school. The delicious treats, still made from a secret recipe, are sold by costumed ladies and packed into attractive tins for the journey home or to eat right away. ⊠ *Church Cottage* ☎ *01539/435428* ⊕ *www.grasmeregingerbread.co.uk.*

Activities

Loughrigg Terrace

HIKING/WALKING | The most panoramic views of lake and village are from the south of Grasmere, from the bare slopes of Loughrigg Terrace, reached along a well-signposted track on the western side of the lake or through the woods from parking lots on the A591 between Grasmere and Rydal Water. It's less than an hour's walk from the village, though your stroll can be extended by continuing around Rydal Water, passing Rydal Mount, detouring onto White Moss Common before returning to Dove Cottage and Grasmere, a 4-mile (three-hour) walk in total. ⊠ *Grasmere.*

Elterwater and the Langdales

2½ miles south of Grasmere, 4 miles west of Ambleside.

The delightful village of Elterwater, at the eastern end of the Great Langdale Valley on B5343, is a good stop for hikers. It's barely more than a cluster of houses around a village green, but from here you can choose from a selection of excellent circular walks. Great Langdale winds up past hills known as the Langdale Pikes towards Great End and England's highest hill, Scafell Pike. To the south, Little Langdale is another of Cumbria's most beautiful valleys with walks aplenty. At its head, the high passes of Wrynose and Hardknott lead west across wild fells to Eskdale and one of the most beautiful and remote lakes, Wast Water. Beyond that, at Ravenglass, the national park reaches all the way to the Cumbrian coast. Between the two Langdales are plenty more great walking opportunities over fells and past far-flung beauty spots such as Blea Tarn.

🍴 Restaurants

Britannia Inn

$ | BRITISH | At this 500-year-old pub, restaurant, and inn in the heart of superb walking country, antiques, comfortable chairs, and prints and oil paintings furnish the cozy, beamed public rooms. The hearty traditional British food—from grilled haggis with housemade plum jam to pan-seared sea bass and wild-mushroom stroganoff—is popular with locals, as are the many whiskies and ales, including a specially brewed Britannia Gold beer. **Known for:** specialty beers; traditional oak-beamed interior; annual beer festival in November. $ *Average main: £14* ⊠ *B5343* ☎ *01539/437210* ⊕ *www. thebritanniainn.com.*

Hotels

Old Dungeon Ghyll Hotel

$ | HOTEL | There's no more comforting stop after a day outdoors than the Hiker's Bar of this 300-year-old hotel at the head of the Great Langdale Valley. **Pros:** ideally situated for walking; wonderfully isolated; spectacular views all around. **Cons:** no-nonsense approach not to everyone's taste; busy in summer; remote location. ⑤ *Rooms from: £116* ✉ *Off B5343, Great Langdale* ☎ *01539/437272* ⊕ *www.odg. co.uk* ⤴ *12 rooms* ❍❘ *Some meals.*

Activities

There are access points to Langdale Fell from several spots along B5343, the main road; look for information boards at local parking places. You can also stroll up the river valley or embark on more energetic hikes to Stickle Tarn or to one of the summits of the Langdale Pikes. Beyond the Old Dungeon Ghyll Hotel, the Great Langdale Valley splits in two around a hill known as the Band—a path up its spine has particularly good views back down over the valley and can be continued to the summit of Scafell Pike.

Coniston

5 miles south of Elterwater.

This small lake resort and boating center attracts climbers to the steep peak of the **Old Man of Coniston** (2,635 feet), which towers above the slate-roof houses. It also has sites related to John Ruskin. Quieter than Windermere, Coniston is a good introduction to the pastoral and watery charms of the area, though the small town itself can get crowded in summer.

GETTING HERE AND AROUND

The Coniston Launch connects Coniston Pier with Ruskin's home at Brantwood and some other stops around the lake, offering hourly service (£11.25 for a daylong, hop-on, hop-off ticket; £18.25 including entry to Brantwood) on its wooden Ruskin and Ransome launches.

ESSENTIALS

VISITOR INFORMATION Coniston Launch. ☎ *01768/775753* ⊕ *www.conistonlaunch. co.uk.* **Coniston Tourist Information Centre.** ✉ *Ruskin Ave.* ☎ *01539/441533.*

Sights

★ Brantwood

HOUSE | On the eastern shore of Coniston Water, Brantwood was the cherished home of John Ruskin (1819–1900), the noted Victorian artist, writer, critic, and social reformer, after 1872. The rambling 18th-century house (with Victorian alterations) is on a 250-acre estate that stretches high above the lake. Here, alongside mementos such as his mahogany desk, are Ruskin's own paintings, drawings, and books. On display is art that this great connoisseur collected, and in cerebral corners such as the Ideas Room visitors are encouraged to think about meaning and change. Ruskin's Rocks explores his fascinations with stones and music with a brilliant bit of modern technology. A video on Ruskin's life shows the lasting influence of his thoughts, and the Severn Studio has rotating art exhibitions. Ruskin himself laid out the extensive grounds. Take time to explore the gardens and woodland walks, which include some multilayered features: Ziggy Zaggy, for example, originally a garden built by Ruskin to reflect Dante's Purgatorial Mount, is now an allegory of the seven deadly sins. Brantwood hosts a series of classical concerts on some Saturdays, as well as talks, guided walks, and study days. ✉ *Off B5285* ☎ *01539/441396* ⊕ *www. brantwood.org.uk* ⌷ *£8.70; gardens only £6.20* ⊘ *Closed Mon. and Tues. in Nov.–mid-Mar.*

Coniston Boating Centre

TRANSPORTATION SITE (AIRPORT/BUS/FERRY/TRAIN) | The National Trust's restored Victorian steam yacht and the slightly more utilitarian Coniston Launch both leave from the town's spruced-up waterside satellite, a 15-minute stroll from the center. There's a parking lot, a smart café, and various boat- and bike-hire options, too. Originally launched in 1859 and restored in the 1970s, the Steam Yacht (⊕ *www.nationaltrust.org.uk/gondola*) runs between Coniston Pier, Brantwood, and Park-a-Moor at the south end of Coniston Water daily from late March through October (half-lake cruise £11; 10% discount for National Trust members). The Coniston Launch (⊕ *www.conistonlaunch.co.uk*) runs similar routes and is marginally cheaper, though also a little less romantic. Both will get you across the lake to Brantwood, and a stop at Monk Coniston jetty, at the lake's northern tip, connects to the footpaths through the Monk Coniston Estate and the beauty spot of Tarn Hows. ⊠ *Coniston Pier* ☎ *01539/441366* ⊕ *www.conistonboatingcentre.co.uk.*

Coniston Water

BODY OF WATER | The lake came to prominence in the 1930s when Arthur Ransome made it the setting for *Swallows and Amazons,* one of a series of novels about a group of children and their adventures. The lake is about 5 miles long, a tempting stretch that drew Donald Campbell here in 1959 to set a water-speed record of 260 mph. He was killed when trying to beat it in 1967. His body and the wreckage of *Bluebird K7* were retrieved from the lake in 2001. Campbell is buried in St. Andrew's church in Coniston, and a stone memorial on the village green commemorates him. ⊠ *Coniston.*

Ruskin Museum

MUSEUM | This repository of fascinating and thought-provoking manuscripts, personal items, and watercolors by John Ruskin illuminates his thinking and influence. There is also a focus on speedboat racer Donald Campbell; his *Bluebird K7,* dragged up from Coniston Water, will eventually rest here once it has been painstakingly put back together. Good local-interest exhibits include copper mining, geology, lace, and more. Upstairs, the Dawson Gallery occasionally hosts high-profile artists. ⊠ *Yewdale Rd.* ☎ *01539/441164* ⊕ *www.ruskinmuseum.com* 💷 *£6.50* 🕙 *Closed Mon. in mid-Nov.–mid-Mar.*

Restaurants

Black Bull Inn

$ | **BRITISH** | Attached to the Coniston Brewing Company, whose ales are on tap here, the Black Bull is an old-fashioned pub in the heart of the village. It can feel a little dated, but it's a good pick for simple, hearty food such as fried whitebait, housemade leek-and-potato soup, and a tasty steak-and-ale pie. **Known for:** locally sourced ingredients; large range of real ales; old-fashioned decor. 💲 *Average main: £13* ⊠ *Coppermines Rd.* ☎ *01539/441335* ⊕ *www.blackbullconiston.co.uk.*

Hotels

★ Bank Ground Farm

$$ | **HOTEL** | Used by Arthur Ransome as the setting for *Swallows and Amazons,* 15th-century Bank Ground is beautifully situated on the eastern shore of Coniston Water, opposite the village of Coniston on the western shore. **Pros:** stunning lake views; homey atmosphere; traditional welcome. **Cons:** a fair walk from the village; some rooms are cramped; low ceilings in the cottage. 💲 *Rooms from: £150* ⊠ *Off B5285* ☎ *01539/441264* ⊕ *www.bankground.com* 🕙 *Guesthouse closed Nov.–Easter* 🛏 *6 rooms, 4 cottages* 🍽 *Free breakfast.*

Lakeland House

$ | B&B/INN | In the middle of Coniston, Lakeland House has smart, modern rooms with bold wallpaper, beamed ceilings, and slate-floored bathrooms. **Pros:** café downstairs; good value; open fire for cozy evenings. **Cons:** not as homey as a traditional B&B; on a main road; attic rooms have low ceilings. ⑤ *Rooms from: £80* ✉ *Tilberthwaite Ave., Keswick* ☎ *01539/441303* ⊕ *www.lakelandhouse. co.uk* ⤳ *12 rooms* ◯ *Free breakfast.*

Activities

HIKING

Steep tracks lead up from the village to the **Old Man of Coniston.** The trail starts near the Sun Hotel on Brow Hill and goes past an old copper mine to the peak, which you can reach in about two hours. It's one of the Lake District's most satisfying hikes—not too arduous, but high enough to feel a sense of accomplishment and get fantastic views (west to the sea, south to Morecambe Bay, and east to Windermere). Experienced hikers include the peak in a seven-hour circular walk from the village, also taking in the heights and ridges of Swirl How and Wetherlam.

Hawkshead

3 miles east of Coniston.

In the Vale of Esthwaite, this small market town is a pleasing hodgepodge of tiny squares, cobbled lanes, and whitewashed houses. There's a good deal more history here than in most local villages, however. The Hawkshead Courthouse, just outside town, was built by the monks of Furness Abbey in the 15th century. Hawkshead later derived much wealth from the wool trade, which flourished here in the 17th and 18th centuries.

As a thriving market center, Hawkshead could afford to maintain the **Hawkshead Grammar School,** at which William Wordsworth was a pupil from 1779 to 1787; he carved his name on a desk inside, now on display. In the village, Ann Tyson's House claims the honor of having provided the young William with lodgings. The twin draws of Wordsworth and Beatrix Potter—apart from her home, Hill Top, there's a Potter gallery—conspire to make Hawkshead crowded year-round.

GETTING HERE AND AROUND

Hawkshead is east of Coniston on B5285 and south of Ambleside via B5286. An alternative route is to cross Windermere via the car ferry from Ferry Nab, south of Bowness. Local buses link the village to others nearby.

ESSENTIALS

VISITOR INFORMATION Hawkshead Tourist Information Centre. ✉ *Main St.* ☎ *01539/436946* ⊕ *www.hawksheadtour-istinfo.org.uk.*

Sights

★ Beatrix Potter Gallery

MUSEUM | FAMILY | In the 17th-century solicitor's offices formerly used by Potter's husband, the Beatrix Potter Gallery displays a selection of the artist-writer's original illustrations, watercolors, and drawings. There's also information about her interest in conservation and her early support of the National Trust. The house looks almost as it would have in her day, though with touch screens in wooden frames and a children's play area upstairs. Admission is by timed ticket when the place gets busy. ✉ *Main St.* ☎ *01539/436355* ⊕ *www.nationaltrust. org.uk/beatrix-potter-gallery-and-hawks-head* ▭ *£8* ⊘ *Closed Jan.–mid-Feb.*

★ Hill Top

HOUSE | Children's author and illustrator Beatrix Potter (1866–1943), most famous for her *Peter Rabbit* stories, called this place home. The house looks much the same as when Potter bequeathed it to the National Trust, and fans will recognize details such as the porch and garden gate, old kitchen range, Victorian dollhouse, and four-poster bed, which were depicted in the book illustrations. ■ **TIP→** Admission to this often-crowded spot is by timed ticket; book in advance and avoid summer weekends and school vacations. Hill Top lies 2 miles south of Hawkshead by car or foot, though you can also approach via the car ferry from Bowness-on-Windermere. ⊠ *Off B5285, Near Sawrey* ☎ *01539/436269* ⊕ *www. nationaltrust.org.uk/hill-top* ⊒ *£12.60* ☉ *Closed mid-Feb. and weekdays in Nov.–Dec.*

Restaurants

★ Tower Bank Arms

$ | BRITISH | With a porch that appears in a Beatrix Potter story and a location just a rabbit's hop from the author's home, you might expect this pub to be something of a tourist trap, but luckily it's anything but. The meals are tasty and copious, making use of local ingredients. **Known for:** literary influences; standard pub fare; some of the area's best ales. Ⓢ *Average main: £12* ⊠ *Off B5285, Near Sawrey* ☎ *01539/436334* ⊕ *www. towerbankarms.co.uk* ☉ *Closed Mon. in winter.*

🛏 Hotels

★ Drunken Duck Inn

$$ | HOTEL | After four centuries, this friendly old coaching inn remains an outstanding place for both food and lodging. **Pros:** superchic rural style; excellent dining and drinking; exceptionally friendly staff. **Cons:** chic interior at odds with the rustic setting; can feel isolated; standard rooms are small. Ⓢ *Rooms from: £125* ⊠ *Off B5286, Ambleside*

☎ *01539/436347* ⊕ *www.drunkenduck-inn.co.uk* ⇄ *16 rooms* ❑ *Free breakfast.*

★ Yewfield Vegetarian Guesthouse

$ | B&B/INN | With the laid-back friendliness of a B&B and the sophisticated style of a country house, Yewfield is a very good value—especially if you can score one of the rooms at the front of the house with a great view across the valley. **Pros:** good location to begin walks; pretty garden; apartments are great for weeklong stays. **Cons:** not good for families with young kids; remote; closed in winter. Ⓢ *Rooms from: £110* ⊠ *Hawkshead Hill* ☎ *01539/436765* ⊕ *www.yewfield.co.uk* ☉ *Closed Dec. and Jan.* ⇄ *19 rooms, 2 apartments* ❑ *Free breakfast.*

🏃 Activities

Grizedale Forest Park

BICYCLING | Stretching southwest from Hawkshead and blanketing the hills between Coniston and Windermere, Grizedale Forest Park has a thick mix of oak, pine, and larch woods crisscrossed with biking and walking paths. Forty permanent outdoor sculptures are scattered beside the trails and more are planned. The **visitor center** has information, maps, a café, and an adventure playground. ⊠ *Off B5286* ☎ *0300/067–4495* ⊕ *www. forestryengland.uk/grizedale.*

Grizedale Mountain Bikes

BICYCLING | If you have the urge to explore the trails of the national park, Grizedale Mountain Bikes rents all the right equipment, with bicycles from £35 per day. They also have a workshop staffed by mechanics if you need to service or repair your own bike. ⊠ *Grizedale Forest Park Visitor Centre, off B5286* ☎ *01229/860335* ⊕ *www.grizedalemountainbikes.co.uk.*

Ullswater

6 miles southwest of Penrith.

Hemmed in by towering hills, Ullswater, the region's second-largest lake, is one of the least developed, drawing people for its calm waters and good access to the mountain slopes of Helvellyn. The A592 winds along the lake's pastoral western shore, through the adjacent hamlets of Glenridding and Patterdale at the southern end. Lakeside strolls, great views, tea shops, and rowboat rentals provide the full Lakeland experience.

ESSENTIALS

VISITOR INFORMATION Ullswater Tourist Information Centre. ⊠ *Beckside Car Park, off A592, Glenridding* ☏ *017684/82414* ⊕ *www.lakedistrict.gov.uk.*

Sights

Aira Force

BODY OF WATER | A spectacular 65-foot waterfall pounds under a stone bridge and through a wooded ravine to feed into Ullswater. From the parking lot it's a 10-minute walk to the falls, with more serious walks on Gowbarrow Fell and to the village of Dockray beyond. A new 1¼-mile footpath allows visitors to leave their cars at Glencoyne Bay, to the south, and walk through a deer park. ■**TIP→ Bring sturdy shoes, especially in wet or icy weather, when the paths can be treacherous.** Just above Aira Force in the woods of Gowbarrow Park is the spot where, in 1802, William Wordsworth's sister, Dorothy, observed daffodils that, as she wrote, "tossed and reeled and danced and seemed as if they verily laughed with the wind that blew upon them." Two years later, Wordsworth transformed his sister's words into the famous poem "I Wandered Lonely as a Cloud." Two centuries later, national park wardens patrol Gowbarrow Park in season to prevent tourists from picking the few remaining daffodils. ⊠ *A592, near A5091* ⊕ *www.nationaltrust.org.uk/aira-force-and-ullswater* ⊠ *Parking £5 for 2 hrs.*

Helvellyn

MOUNTAIN—SIGHT | West of Ullswater's southern end, the brooding presence of Helvellyn (3,118 feet), one of the Lake District's most formidable mountains and England's third highest, recalls the region's fundamental character. It's an arduous climb to the top, especially via the challenging ridge known as Striding Edge, and the ascent shouldn't be attempted in poor weather or by inexperienced hikers. Signposted paths to the peak run from the road between Glenridding and Patterdale and pass by **Red Tarn,** which is the highest small mountain lake in the region at 2,356 feet. ⊠ *Glenridding.*

★ Ullswater Steamers

TRANSPORTATION SITE (AIRPORT/BUS/FERRY/TRAIN) | These antique vessels, including a 19th-century steamer that is said to be the oldest working passenger ship in the world, run the length of Ullswater between Glenridding in the south and Pooley Bridge in the north, via Howtown on the eastern shore. It's a pleasant tour, especially if you combine it with a lakeside walk. One-way trips start at £6.50, or you can sail the entire day for £16.80 with the Cruise All Piers Pass. ⊠ *Pier House, off A592, Glenridding* ☏ *017684/82229* ⊕ *www.ullswater-steamers.co.uk.*

Hotels

Inn on the Lake

$$$ | **HOTEL** | With some of the best lake views in the Lake District, Inn on the Lake is a large Victorian property right on the edge of Ullswater, with only its own terrace and lawns separating it from the water. **Pros:** right on the lakeshore; beautiful scenery; plenty of parking. **Cons:** very busy in summer; can be noisy if there's a wedding; decor in the rooms is a bit fussy. ⑤ *Rooms from: £250* ⊠ *Ullswater, Glenridding* ☏ *0800/840–1245 reservations, 017684/82444 reception* ⊕ *www. lakedistricthotels.net/innonthelake* ⤴ *47 rooms* ❍❘ *Free breakfast.*

Keswick

14 miles west of Ullswater.

The great mountains of Skiddaw and Blencathra brood over the gray slate houses of Keswick (pronounced *kezz*-ick), on the scenic shores of Derwentwater. The town is a natural base for exploring the rounded, heather-clad Skiddaw range to the north, while the hidden valleys of Borrowdale and Buttermere (the latter reached by stunning Honister Pass) take you into the rugged heart of the Lake District. Nearby, five beautiful lakes are set among the three highest mountain ranges in England. The tourist information center here has regional information and is the place to get fishing permits for Derwentwater.

Keswick's narrow, cobbled streets have a grittier charm compared to the refined Victorian elegance of Grasmere or Ambleside. However, it's the best spot in the Lake District to purchase mountaineering gear and outdoor clothing. There are also many hotels, guesthouses, restaurants, and pubs.

GETTING HERE AND AROUND
Keswick is easily reached along A66 from Penrith, though you can get there more scenically via Grasmere in the south. Buses run from the train station in Penrith to Keswick. The town center is pedestrianized.

■ **TIP**➔ **Traffic can be horrendous in summer, so consider leaving your car in Keswick.** The open-top Borrowdale bus service between Keswick and Seatoller (to the south) runs frequently, and the Honister Rambler minibus is perfect for walkers aiming for the high fells of

the central lakes; it makes stops from Keswick to Buttermere. The Keswick Launch service on Derwentwater links to many walks as well as the Borrowdale bus service.

ESSENTIALS
VISITOR INFORMATION Keswick Information Centre. ⊠ *Moot Hall, Market Sq.* ☏ *0845/9010845* ⊕ *www.lakedistrict.gov. uk.*

Sights

★ Castlerigg Stone Circle
ARCHAEOLOGICAL SITE | A Neolithic monument about 100 feet in diameter, this stone circle was built around 3,000 years ago on a hill overlooking St. John's Vale. The brooding northern peaks of Skiddaw and Blencathra loom to the north, and there are views of Helvellyn to the south. The 38 stones aren't large, but the site makes them particularly impressive. Wordsworth described them as "a dismal cirque of Druid stones upon a forlorn moor." The site, always open to visitors, is 4 miles east of Keswick. There's usually space for cars to park beside the road that leads along the northern edge of the site: head up Eleventrees off Penrith Road at the eastern edge of Keswick. ⊠ *Off A66* ⊕ *www.english-heritage.org. uk* ⤴ *Free.*

Derwent Pencil Museum
MUSEUM | **FAMILY** | Legend has it that shepherds found graphite on Seathwaite Fell after a storm uprooted trees in the 16th century. The Derwent company still makes pencils here, and the museum contains the world's longest colored pencil (it takes 28 men to lift it), a pencil produced for World War II spies that contains a rolled-up map, and displays about graphite mining. There's a café and plenty of opportunities for kids to draw, so it's a good, family-friendly option on a rainy day. ⊠ *Southey Works, Carding Mill La.* ☏ *01768/773626* ⊕ *www.pencilmuseum. co.uk* ⤴ *£4.95.*

Derwentwater

BODY OF WATER | To understand why Derwentwater is considered one of England's finest lakes, take a short walk from Keswick's town center to the lakeshore and past the jetty, and follow the **Friar's Crag** path, about a 15-minute level walk from the center. This pine-tree-fringed peninsula is a favorite vantage point, with its view of the lake, the ring of mountains, and many tiny islands. Ahead, crags line the **Jaws of Borrowdale** and overhang a mountain ravine—a scene that looks as if it emerged from a Romantic painting. ⊠ *Keswick.*

Keswick Launch Company

TOUR—SIGHT | For the best lake views, take a wooden-launch cruise around Derwentwater. Between late March and November, circular cruises set off every half hour in alternate directions from a dock; there's a more limited (roughly hourly) winter timetable. You can also rent a rowboat here in summer. Buy a hop-on, hop-off Around the Lake ticket (£10.50) and take advantage of the seven landing stages around the lake that provide access to hiking trails, such as the two-hour climb up and down Cat Bells, a celebrated lookout point on the western shore of Derwentwater. ■**TIP**➔ **Buy slightly discounted tickets at the Moot Hall information office in the center of town.** ⊠ *Lake Rd.* ☎ *017687/72263* ⊕ *www. keswick-launch.co.uk* ✉ *From £2.35* ⊙ *Closed mid-Dec.–early Feb.*

Restaurants

★ Fellpack

$ | **BRITISH** | Created by four friends who have returned home to the Lakes, the menu at Fellpack is designed as a celebration of Cumbria's ingredients and traditional recipes, albeit with a quirky twist. Fellpack has a gallery of incredible landscape images shot by photographer James Appleton, as well as a collection of fell running jerseys from clubs across the United Kingdom. **Known for:** food

served in handmade dishes; delicious, hearty cuisine; awesome landscape photography. ⑤ *Average main: £15* ⊠ *Lake Rd.* ☎ *01768/771177* ⊕ *www.fellpack. co.uk* ⊙ *No lunch.*

Square Orange Café Bar

$ | **CAFÉ** | Young locals and windblown walkers gather in Keswick's liveliest café for excellent coffee or tea, fruit-flavored cordials, and some serious hot chocolate. The music is laid-back; the staff is undeniably cool; the walls are hung with paintings and photos; and there are housemade pizzas, tapas, and pints of local beer for long rainy days or cold winter nights. **Known for:** decadent chocolate orange cake; ethically sourced tea and coffee; live music on Wednesday evening. ⑤ *Average main: £10* ⊠ *20 St. John's St.* ☎ *017687/73888* ⊕ *www. thesquareorange.co.uk.*

Hotels

Ferndene

$ | **B&B/INN** | **FAMILY** | Exceptionally friendly, this spotless B&B a 10-minute walk from the lake is carefully tended by its kindly owners, who offer plenty of advice on walking and local sights when you want it. **Pros:** family-focused; good value; bicycle storage. **Cons:** lacks style of more expensive lodgings; road busy in summer; limited parking. ⑤ *Rooms from: £90* ⊠ *6 St. John's Terr.* ☎ *017687/74612* ⊕ *www.ferndene-keswick.co.uk* ✈ *6 rooms* ❍ *Free breakfast.*

★ Howe Keld

$ | **B&B/INN** | In a town that overflows with B&Bs, this comfortable town house stands out because of its contemporary flair and pampering touches. **Pros:** famously filling breakfasts; good ecological practices; one room accessible for people with disabilities. **Cons:** a short distance from the heart of town; backs onto a busy road; some rooms have low ceilings. ⑤ *Rooms from: £120* ⊠ *5–7 The Heads* ☎ *017687/72417* ⊕ *www.*

The setting of the Castlerigg Stone Circle, ringed by stunning mountains, makes this Neolithic monument deeply memorable.

howekeld.co.uk ⊙ Closed Jan. ⤴ 14 rooms ⦿ Free breakfast.

 Performing Arts

Theatre by the Lake
ARTS CENTERS | In one of Cumbria's most vibrant cultural settings, the company at the Theatre by the Lake presents classic and contemporary productions year round. The Keswick Music Society season runs from September through January, and the Words by the Water literary festival takes place here in March. ✉ Lake Rd. ☎ 017687/74411 ⊕ www.theatrebythelake.com.

 Shopping

George Fisher
SPORTING GOODS | The area's largest and best outdoor equipment store, George Fisher sells sportswear, travel books, and maps. The staff is faultlessly friendly, helpful, and well informed. Daily weather information is posted in the window, and there's a children's play den. ✉ 2 Borrowdale Rd. ☎ 017687/72178 ⊕ www.georgefisher.co.uk.

Needle Sports
SPORTING GOODS | This company stocks all the best equipment for mountaineering and for rock and ice climbing. They also provide information about local climbing and fell running clubs. ✉ 56 Main St. ☎ 01768/772227 ⊕ www.needlesports.com.

Thomasons
FOOD/CANDY | A butcher and delicatessen, Thomasons sells some very good meat pies—just the thing for putting in your pocket before you climb a Lakeland fell. The housemade sausages are fantastic if you're planning a barbecue. ✉ 8–10 Station St. ☎ 017687/80169 ⊙ Closed Sun.

 Activities

BIKING
Keswick Bikes
BICYCLING | This company rents bikes (from £30 per day) and provides information on all the nearby trails. Guided tours

can be arranged with advance notice.
⊠ *133 Main St.* ☎ *017687/73355* ⊕ *www.
keswickbikes.co.uk.*

WATER SPORTS

Derwent Water Marina

WATER SPORTS | Rental boats in all shapes
and sizes and instruction in canoeing,
sailing, and windsurfing can be had at
Derwent Water Marina. Other water-re-
lated activities include ghyll scram-
bling—the fine art of walking up or down
a steep Lakeland stream. A two-day
sailing or windsurfing course costs £230
(⊕ *www.getonthelake.co.uk/tuition-cours-
es*). ⊠ *Portinscale* ☎ *017687/72912*
⊕ *www.derwentwatermarina.co.uk.*

Borrowdale

7 miles south of Keswick.

South of Keswick and its lake lies the
valley of Borrowdale, whose varied
landscape of green valley floor and surrounding crags has long been considered
one of the region's most magnificent
treasures. **Rosthwaite,** a tranquil farming
village, and **Seatoller,** the southernmost
settlement, are the two main centers
(both are accessible by bus from Keswick), though they're little more than
clusters of aged buildings surrounded by
glorious countryside.

GETTING HERE AND AROUND

The valley is south of Keswick on B5289.
The Borrowdale bus service between
Keswick and Seatoller runs frequently.

Sights

★ Borrowdale Fells

MOUNTAIN—SIGHT | These steep fells rise
up dramatically behind Seatoller. Get out
and walk whenever inspiration strikes.
Trails are well signposted, or you can
pick up maps and any gear in Keswick.
⊠ *Seatoller.*

Scafell Pike

MOUNTAIN—SIGHT | England's highest
mountain at 3,210 feet, Scafell (pronounced *scar*-fell) Pike is visible from
Seatoller. One route up the mountain, for
experienced walkers, is from the hamlet
of Seathwaite, a mile south of Seatoller.
⊠ *Seatoller.*

Hotels

★ Hazel Bank Country House

$$ | B&B/INN | Though this stately, carefully
restored home retains original elements
from its days as a grand Victorian country
pile, its welcoming owners have invested
in handsome local furniture and stripped
away some of the chintz, opening up
inspiring views across the pristine lawns
to the valley and the central Lakeland
peaks beyond. **Pros:** serene location;
immaculate gardens; attentive staff. **Cons:**
not near many amenities; car required to
get here; deposit required for bookings.
⑤ *Rooms from: £160* ⊠ *Off B5289,
Rosthwaite* ☎ *017687/77248* ⊕ *www.
hazelbankhotel.co.uk* ⤴ *7 rooms* ⦿ *Free
breakfast.*

CAMBRIDGE AND EAST ANGLIA

Updated by
Toby Orton

Sights ★★★☆☆　　Restaurants ★★★☆☆　　Hotels ★★★☆☆　　Shopping ★★★☆☆　　Nightlife ★★★☆☆

WELCOME TO
CAMBRIDGE AND EAST ANGLIA

TOP REASONS TO GO

★ **Cambridge:** A walk through the colleges is grand, but the best views of the university's buildings and immaculate lawns (and some famous bridges) are from a punt on the river.

★ **Constable country:** In the area where Constable grew up, you can walk or row downstream from Dedham straight into the setting of one of the English landscape painter's masterpieces at Flatford Mill.

★ **Ely Cathedral:** The highlight of Ely, north of Cambridge, is its beautiful cathedral, known for its octagonal Lantern Tower.

★ **Lavenham:** This old town is the most comely of the tight-knit cluster of places that prospered from the medieval wool trade, with architecture including timber-frame houses gnarled into crookedness by age.

★ **Aldeburgh:** A trip to Suffolk isn't complete without a stop by the seaside. Aldeburgh fills the bill and is also home to the famous Aldeburgh Festival, which includes music and more.

East Anglia, in southeastern England, can be divided into distinct areas for sightseeing. The central area surrounds the ancient university city of Cambridge and includes Ely, with its magnificent cathedral rising out of the flatlands, and the towns of inland Suffolk. The Suffolk Heritage Coast is home to historic small towns and villages.

1 Cambridge. Home to one of the world's most famous universities.

2 Ely. A village with a lofty cathedral that dominates the surrounding flatlands.

3 Long Melford. A charming wool town.

4 Lavenham. A perfectly preserved Tudor village.

5 Dedham. An idyllic village in the heart of Constable Country.

6 Woodbridge. An atmospheric seaside town.

7 Aldeburgh. A quiet seaside resort.

One of those beautiful English inconsistencies, East Anglia has no spectacular mountains or rivers to disturb the quiet, storied land of rural delights. Occupying an area of southeastern England that pushes out into the North Sea, its counties of Essex, Norfolk, Suffolk, Lincolnshire, and Cambridgeshire feel cut off from the pulse of the country.

Among its highlights is Cambridge, a lovely and ancient university city. East Anglia also has four of the country's greatest stately homes: Holkham Hall, Blickling Hall, Houghton Hall, and Sandringham—where the Queen spends Christmas.

In times past, East Anglia was one of the most important centers of power in northern Europe. Towns like Lincoln were major Roman settlements, and the medieval wool trade brought huge prosperity to the higgledy-piggledy streets of tiny Lavenham. Thanks to its relative lack of thoroughfares and canals, however, East Anglia was mercifully untouched by the Industrial Revolution. The area is rich in idyllic, quintessentially English villages: sleepy, sylvan settlements in the midst of otherwise deserted lowlands. Even the towns feel small and manageable; the biggest city, Norwich, has a population of just 130,000. Cambridge, with its ancient university, is the area's most famous draw, along with incomparable cathedrals, at Ely and Lincoln particularly, and one of the finest Gothic buildings in Europe, King's College Chapel.

And yet, despite all of these treasures, the real joy of visiting East Anglia is making your own discoveries. Spend a couple of days exploring the hidden byways of the fens or just taking in the subtle beauties of the many England-like-it-looks-in-the-movies villages. If you find yourself driving down a small country lane and an old church or mysterious, ivy-covered ruin peeks out from behind the trees, give in to your curiosity and look inside. Such places are East Anglia's best-kept secrets.

MAJOR REGIONS

Cambridge. The home of the ancient university is East Anglia's liveliest town. The city center is perfect for ambling around the colleges, museums, and King's College Chapel, one of England's greatest monuments.

Suffolk. The central area of towns and villages within easy reach of Cambridge is testament to the amazing changeability of the English landscape. The town of Ely is set in an eerie, flat, and apparently endless marsh, or fenland. (A medieval term, "the fens," is still used informally to describe the surrounding region.) Only a few miles south and east into Suffolk, however, all this changes to pastoral landscapes of gently undulating hills and clusters of villages including pretty Lavenham.

Further east, the 40-mile Suffolk Heritage Coast, which wanders northward from Felixstowe up to Kessingland, is one of the most unspoiled shorelines in the country. The lower part of the coast is the most impressive; however, some of the loveliest towns and villages, such as Dedham and the older part of Flatford, are inland. The best way to experience the countryside around here is to be willing to get lost along its tiny, ancient back roads. Try to avoid the coastal area between Lowestoft and Great Yarmouth; it has little to offer but run-down beach resorts.

Planning

When to Go

Summer and late spring are the best times to visit East Anglia. Late fall and winter can be cold, windy, and rainy, though this is England's driest region and crisp, frosty days here are beautiful. To escape crowds, avoid the popular Norfolk Broads in late July and August. You can't visit most of the Cambridge colleges during exam period (late May to mid-June), and the competition for hotel rooms heats up during graduation week (late June). The Aldeburgh Festival of Music and the Arts, one of the biggest events on the British classical music calendar, takes place in June.

Planning Your Time

Cambridge is the region's most interesting city, and ideally you should allow two days to absorb its various sights. (In a

pinch, you could do it as a day trip from London but only with an early start and a good pair of walking shoes.) You could easily use the city as a base for exploring Ely, Bury St. Edmunds, Lavenham, Long Melford, and Sudbury, although accommodations are available in these towns as well. The Suffolk Coast has enticing overnight stops in such small towns as Dedham and Aldeburgh.

FESTIVALS
★ **Aldeburgh Festival**
FESTIVALS | East Anglia's most important arts festival, and one of the best known in Britain, is the Aldeburgh Festival. It's held for two weeks in June in the small village of Snape, 5 miles west of Aldeburgh. Founded by Benjamin Britten, the festival concentrates on music but includes exhibitions, poetry readings, and lectures. A handful of events are aimed specifically at children. ✉ Snape ☎ 01728/687100 for inquiries, 01728/687110 for box office ⊕ www.snapemaltings.co.uk/season/aldeburgh-festival.

Getting Here and Around

AIR
Norwich International Airport serves a limited number of domestic and international destinations, though not the United States. London Stansted Airport, 30 miles south of Cambridge, is used mainly for European flights. The vast majority of travelers to the region arrive by train, car, or bus.

AIRPORTS London Stansted Airport.
✉ Bassingbourn Rd., Bishop's Stortford ☎ 0808/169–7031 ⊕ www.stanstedairport.com. **Norwich International Airport.**
✉ Amsterdam Way, off A140, Norwich ☎ 01603/411923 ⊕ www.norwichairport.co.uk.

BUS

National Express buses serve the region from London's Victoria Coach Station. Average travel times are 3 hours to Cambridge and Norwich, 2½ hours to Bury St. Edmunds, and 4½ hours to Lincoln.

Long-distance buses are useful for reaching the region and traveling between its major centers, but for smaller hops, local buses are best. First and Stagecoach buses cover the Cambridge, Lincolnshire, and Norwich areas. Traveline can answer public transportation questions.

BUS CONTACTS Stagecoach.
☎ 01223/433250 ⊕ www.stagecoachbus. com/about/east. **Traveline.** ☎ 0871/200– 2233, 84268 text "Traveline" from mobile phone for link to bus finder ⊕ www. traveline.info.

CAR

If you're driving from London, Cambridge (54 miles) is off M11. East Anglia has few fast main roads besides those mentioned here. Once off the A roads, traveling within the region often means taking country lanes that have many twists and turns. Going even just a few miles can take much longer than you think.

TRAIN

The entire region is well served by trains from London's Liverpool Street and King's Cross stations. The quality and convenience of these services varies enormously, however. Cambridge trains leave from King's Cross and Liverpool Street, take about 45 minutes to an hour, and cost about £26. A good way to save money on local trains in East Anglia is to buy an Anglia Plus Ranger Pass. It costs £24.70 for one day or £49.40 for three days and allows unlimited rail travel in Norfolk, Suffolk, and part of Cambridgeshire. You can add up to four kids for an extra £4 each.

TRAIN CONTACTS Abellio Greater Anglia. ☎ 0345/600–7245 ⊕ www. greateranglia.co.uk. **East Midlands Trains.** ☎ 03457/125678 ⊕ www.eastmid-landsrailway.co.uk. **Great Northern Rail.**

☎ 0345/026–4700 ⊕ www.greatnorthernrail.com. **National Rail Enquiries.** ☎ 03457/484950 ⊕ www.nationalrail. co.uk.

Restaurants

In summer, the coast gets so packed with people that reservations are essential at restaurants. Getting something to eat at other than regular mealtime hours isn't always possible in small towns; head to cafés if you want a midmorning or after-lunch snack. Look for area specialties, such as crab, lobster, duckling, Norfolk black turkey, hare, and partridge, on menus around the region. In Norwich there's no escaping the hot, bright-yellow Colman's mustard, which is perfect smeared gingerly on some sausage and mash.

Hotels

The region is full of centuries-old, half-timber inns with rooms full of roaring fires and cozy bars. Bed-and-breakfasts are a good option in pricey Cambridge. It's always busy in Cambridge and along the coast in summer, so reserve well in advance.

Restaurant and hotel reviews have been shortened. For full information, visit Fodors.com. Restaurant prices are the average cost of a main course at dinner, or if dinner is not served, at lunch. Hotel prices are the lowest cost of a standard double room in high season, including 20% V.A.T.

WHAT IT COSTS in Pounds

	$	$$	$$$	$$$$
RESTAURANTS				
	under £16	£16–£23	£24–£30	over £30
HOTELS				
	under £125	£125–£225	£226–£350	over £350

Visitor Information

CONTACTS East of England Tourism.
✉ Dettingen House, Dettingen Way, Bury St. Edmunds ☎ 0333/320–4202 ⊕ www. visiteastofengland.com.

Cambridge

With the spires of its university buildings framed by towering trees and expansive meadows, and its medieval streets and passages enhanced by gardens and riverbanks, the city of Cambridge is among the loveliest in England. The city predates the Roman occupation of Britain, but there's confusion over exactly how and when the university was founded. The most widely accepted story is that it was established in 1209 by a pair of scholars from Oxford, who left their university in protest over the wrongful execution of a colleague for murder.

Keep in mind there's no recognizable campus: the scattered colleges *are* the university. The town reveals itself only slowly, filled with tiny gardens, ancient courtyards, imposing classic buildings, alleyways that lead past medieval churches, and wisteria-hung facades. Perhaps the best views are from the Backs, the green parkland that extends along the River Cam behind several colleges. This sweeping openness, a result of the larger size of the colleges and lack of industrialization in the city center, is what distinguishes Cambridge from Oxford.

This university town may be beautiful, but it's no museum. Well-preserved medieval buildings sit cheek by jowl with the latest in modern architecture (for example, the William Gates Building, which houses Cambridge University's computer laboratory) in this growing city dominated culturally and architecturally by its famous university (students make up around one-fifth of the city's 109,000 inhabitants), and beautified by parks, gardens, and the quietly flowing River Cam.

The exquisite King's College choir defines the traditional English Christmas, when the *Festival of Nine Lessons and Carols* is broadcast live on Christmas Eve. On top of all its tradition and history, Cambridge remains a lively city and an extraordinary center of learning and research where innovation and discovery still happen behind its ancient walls.

GETTING HERE AND AROUND

Good bus (three hours) and train (one hour) services connect London and Cambridge. The long-distance bus terminal is on Drummer Street, very close to Emmanuel and Christ's colleges. Several local buses connect the station with central Cambridge, including the frequent Citi 7 and 8 services, although any bus listing City Centre or Emmanuel Street among its stops will do. The journey takes just under 10 minutes. If you're driving, don't attempt to venture very far into the center—parking is scarce and pricey. The center is amenable to explorations on foot, or you could join the throng by renting a bicycle.

Stagecoach sells Dayrider (£4.50) tickets for all-day bus travel within Cambridge, and Megarider tickets (£15) for seven days of travel within the city. You can extend these to cover the whole county of Cambridgeshire (£7 and £25, respectively), or even an extension to a week as far as Oxford (£42.40). Buy any of them from the driver.

TOURS

Visit Cambridge

WALKING TOURS | Walking tours are led by official Blue or Green Badge guides. The 1½- or 2-hour tours leave from the tourist information center at Peas Hill. Hours vary according to the tour, with the earliest leaving at 11 am and the latest at 2 pm. ⊠ *The Guildhall, Peas Hill* ☎ *01223/791501* ⊕ *www.visitcambridge. org/official-tours* 🎫 *From £8.*

ESSENTIALS

VISITOR INFORMATION Cambridge Visitor Information Centre. ⊠ *The Guildhall, Peas Hill* ☎ *01223/791500* ⊕ *www.visitcambridge.org.*

 Sights

Exploring the city means, in large part, exploring the university. Each of the 25 oldest colleges is built around a series of courts, or quadrangles, framing manicured, velvety lawns. Because students and fellows (faculty) live and work in these courts, access is sometimes restricted, and you're asked not to picnic in the quadrangles at any time.

Visitors aren't normally allowed into college buildings other than chapels, dining halls, and some libraries; some colleges charge admission for certain buildings. Public visiting hours vary from college to college, depending on the time of year, and it's best to call or to check with the city tourist office. Colleges close to visitors during the main exam time, late May to mid-June. Term time (when classes are in session) means roughly October to December, January to March, and April to June; summer term, or vacation, runs from July to September. ■TIP➔ **Bring a pair of binoculars, as some college buildings have highly intricate details, such as the spectacular ceiling at King's College Chapel.** When the colleges are open, the best way to gain access is to join a walking tour led by an official Blue Badge guide—many areas are off-limits unless

you do. The 90-minute and two-hour tours (£8 to £18) leave up to four times daily from the city tourist office. The other traditional view of the colleges is gained from a punt—the boats propelled by pole on the River Cam.

Audley End House and Gardens

HOUSE | **FAMILY** | A famous example of early-17th-century architecture, Audley End was once owned by Charles II, who bought it as a convenient place to break his journey on the way to the Newmarket races. Although the palatial building was remodeled in the 18th and 19th centuries, the Jacobean style is still on display in the magnificent Great Hall. You can walk in the park, landscaped by Capability Brown in the 18th century, and the fine Victorian gardens. Exhibitions focus on the lives of domestic servants in the late 19th century. A recent renovation opened up the Nursery Suite, bedecked in the style of the 1830s, and the Coal Gallery, which once provided hot water for the family upstairs (though not the servants). The Service Wing lets you look "below stairs" at the kitchen, scullery (where fish were descaled and chickens plucked), and game larder (where pheasants, partridges, and rabbits were hung), while the Stable Yard gives kids the chance to see old saddles and tack and don Victorian riding costumes. The house is in Saffron Waldon, 14 miles south of Cambridge. ⊠ *Audley End Road, Off London Rd., Saffron Walden* ☎ *01799/522842* ⊕ *www.english-heritage.org.uk/visit/ places/audley-end-house-and-gardens* 🎫 *£18.50 Apr.–Oct., £13 Nov.–Mar.* ⊘ *House closed Nov.–Mar.*

Christ's College

COLLEGE | To see the way a college has grown over the centuries you could not do better than a visit here. The main gateway bears the enormous coat of arms of its patroness, Lady Margaret Beaufort, mother of Henry VII, who established the institution in 1505. It leads into a fine courtyard, with the chapel framed

Cricket, anyone? Audley End, a 17th-century house, serves as an idyllic backdrop for a cricket match.

by an ancient magnolia. In the dining hall hang portraits of John Milton and Charles Darwin, two of the college's most famous students. Next, walk past a fellows' building credited to Inigo Jones, who transformed English architecture in the early 17th century, to the spacious garden (once a favorite haunt of Milton's), and finally to a modern ziggurat-like confection from the 1960s. ⊠ *St. Andrew's St.* ☎ *01223/334900* ⊕ *www.christs.cam. ac.uk* 🖃 *Free* ⊙ *Gardens closed weekends. Closed during exam periods.*

Emmanuel College

COLLEGE | The master hand of architect Sir Christopher Wren (1632–1723) is evident throughout much of Cambridge, particularly at Emmanuel, built on the site of a Dominican friary, where he designed the chapel and colonnade. A stained-glass window in the chapel has a likeness of John Harvard, founder of Harvard University, who studied here. The college, founded in 1584, was an early center of Puritan learning; a number of the Pilgrims were Emmanuel alumni, and they remembered their alma mater in naming Cambridge, Massachusetts. ⊠ *St. Andrew's St.* ☎ *01223/334200* ⊕ *www.emma.cam.ac.uk* 🖃 *Free* ⊙ *Closed during exam periods.*

★ Fitzwilliam Museum

MUSEUM | In a classical-revival building renowned for its grand Corinthian portico, "The Fitz," founded by the 7th Viscount Fitzwilliam of Merrion in 1816, has one of Britain's most outstanding collections of art and antiquities. Highlights include two large Titians, an extensive collection of French impressionist paintings, and many works by Matisse and Picasso. The opulent interior displays these treasures to marvelous effect, from Egyptian pieces like inch-high figurines and painted coffins to sculptures from the Chinese Han dynasty of the 3rd century BC. Other collections of note here include a fine collection of flower paintings, an assortment of medieval illuminated manuscripts, and a fascinating room full of armor and muskets. ⊠ *Trumpington St.* ☎ *01223/332900*

Sights ▼

1 Audley End
House and Gardens **G9**

2 Christ's College...................... **E5**

3 Emmanuel College.................. **E6**

4 Fitzwilliam Museum **D7**

5 Great St. Mary's.................... **D5**

6 Imperial War Museum
Duxford **G9**

7 Kettle's Yard **C3**

8 King's College **C6**

9 King's College Chapel **C5**

10 Museum of Archaeology
and Anthropology................. **D6**

11 Polar Museum **F7**

12 Queens' College **C6**

13 Trinity College **C5**

Restaurants ▼

1 Loch Fyne.......................... **D7**

2 Midsummer House **F3**

3 The Oak............................. **F7**

4 Pickerel Inn........................ **C4**

5 Restaurant 22 .... **E2**

6 River Bar
Steakhouse & Grill................ **D4**

7 Three Horseshoes................ **A2**

Hotels ▼

1 Duke House **F5**

2 5 Chapel Street..................... **H1**

3 Regent Hotel **E7**

4 University Arms.................... **E6**

5 The Varsity......................... **D4**

KEY

1 *Exploring Sights*

1 *Restaurants*

1 *Hotels*

⊕ *www.fitzmuseum.cam.ac.uk* ☟ *Free*
⊘ *Closed Mon. except bank holidays.*

Great St. Mary's
RELIGIOUS SITE | Known as the "university church," Great St. Mary's has its origins in the 11th century, although the current building dates from 1478. The main reason to visit is to climb the 113-foot tower, which has a superb view over the colleges and marketplace (though it may be closed in bad weather). Also here is the Michaelhouse Centre, a small café, gallery, and performing arts venue with frequent free lunchtime concerts. Tours must be booked in advance. ☒ *Market Hill, King's Parade* ☏ *01223/747273* ⊕ *www.gsm.cam.ac.uk* ☟ *Free; tower £5; guided tours £10.*

Imperial War Museum Duxford
MUSEUM | Europe's leading aviation museum houses a remarkable collection of 180 aircrafts from Europe and the United States. The former airfield is effectively a complex of several museums under one banner. The **Land Warfare Hall** features tanks and other military vehicles. The striking **American Air Museum** honors the 30,000 Americans killed in action flying from Britain during World War II. It contains the largest display of American fighter planes outside the United States. **AirSpace** holds a vast array of military and civil aircraft in a 3-acre hangar. Directly underneath is the **Airborne Assault Museum,** which chronicles the history of airborne forces, such as the British Parachute Regiment, which played a pivotal role in the Normandy Landings. One of the most popular exhibits is a Spitfire plane that was shot down over Calais during World War II and recovered in 1986. After a massive restoration project, the plane was restored to full airworthiness in 2014. There are also hangars where you can see restoration work taking place on other WWII planes and exhibitions on maritime warfare and the Battle of Britain. See the planes in action with the historic air shows that are held on a handful of dates every summer; check the website for details. ☒ *A505, Duxford* ☏ *01223/835000* ⊕ *www.iwm. org.uk/visits/iwm-duxford* ☟ *£17.10.*

★ Kettle's Yard
MUSEUM | Originally a private house owned by a former curator of London's Tate galleries, Kettle's Yard contains a fine collection of 20th-century art, sculpture, furniture, and decorative arts, including works by Henry Moore, Barbara Hepworth, and Alfred Wallis. The museum reopened in 2018 after a two-year renovation project. A separate gallery shows changing exhibitions of modern art and crafts, and weekly concerts and lectures attract an eclectic mix of enthusiasts. Ring the bell for admission. ☒ *Castle St.* ☏ *01223/748100* ⊕ *www.kettlesyard. co.uk* ☟ *Free* ⊘ *Closed Mon. except bank holidays.*

King's College
COLLEGE | Founded in 1441 by Henry VI, King's College has a magnificent late-15th-century chapel that is its most famous landmark. Other notable architecture includes the neo-Gothic Porters' Lodge, facing King's Parade, which was a comparatively recent addition in the 1830s, and the classical Gibbs building. ■**TIP**→ **Head down to the river, from where the panorama of college and chapel is one of the university's most photographed views.** Past students of King's College include the novelist E. M. Forster, the economist John Maynard Keynes, and the World War I poet Rupert Brooke. ☒ *King's Parade* ☏ *01223/331100* ⊕ *www.kings. cam.ac.uk* ☟ *£9, includes chapel.*

★ King's College Chapel
RELIGIOUS SITE | Based on Sainte-Chapelle, the 13th-century royal chapel in Paris, this house of worship is perhaps the most glorious flowering of Perpendicular Gothic in Britain. Henry VI, the king after whom the college is named, oversaw the work. From the outside, the most prominent features are the massive flying buttresses and the fingerlike spires that

A must-see at Cambridge is King's College Chapel, a masterpiece of Perpendicular Gothic style.

line the length of the building. Inside, the most obvious impression is of great space—the chapel was once described as "the noblest barn in Europe"—and of light flooding in from its huge windows. The brilliantly colored bosses (carved panels at the intersections of the roof ribs) are particularly intense, although hard to see without binoculars. An exhibition in the chantries, or side chapels, explains more about the chapel's construction. Behind the altar is *The Adoration of the Magi,* an enormous painting by Peter Paul Rubens. ■ **TIP→ The chapel, unlike the rest of King's College, stays open during exam periods.** Every Christmas Eve, a festival of carols is sung by the chapel's famous choir. It's broadcast on national television and considered a quintessential part of the traditional English Christmas. To compete for the small number of tickets available, join the line at the college's main entrance in the early hours—doors open at 7 am. ⊠ *King's Parade* ☎ *01223/331212* ⊕ *www.kings. cam.ac.uk* ✉ *£9, includes college and* grounds ⊙ *Sometimes closed for events; check ahead to confirm.*

★ Museum of Archaeology and Anthropology

MUSEUM | Cambridge University maintains some fine museums in its research halls on Downing Street—the wonder is that they're not better known to visitors. At the recently renovated Museum of Archaeology and Anthropology, highlights include an array of objects brought back from Captain Cook's pioneering voyages to the Pacific; Roman and medieval-era British artifacts; and the oldest human-made tools ever discovered, from the African expeditions of British archaeologist Louis Leakey (1903–72). ⊠ *Downing St.* ☎ *01223/333516* ⊕ *maa.cam.ac.uk* ✉ *Free* ⊙ *Closed Mon.*

★ Polar Museum

MUSEUM | Beautifully designed, this museum at Cambridge University's Scott Polar Research Institute chronicles the history of polar exploration. There's a particular emphasis on the British expeditions of the 20th century, including the ill-fated attempt by Robert Falcon Scott to be the first to reach the South Pole in 1912. Norwegian explorer Roald Amundsen reached the pole first; Scott and his men perished on the return journey, but their story became legendary. There are also collections devoted to the science of modern polar exploration; the indigenous people of northern Canada, Greenland, and Alaska; and frequently changing art installations. ⊠ *Scott Polar Research Institute, Lensfield Rd.* ☎ *01223/336540* ⊕ *www.spri.cam.ac.uk/museum* ✉ *Free* ⊘ *Closed Mon. except bank holidays.*

Queens' College

COLLEGE | One of the most eye-catching colleges, with a secluded "cloister court" look, Queens' is named after Margaret, wife of Henry VI, and Elizabeth, wife of Edward IV. Founded in 1448 and completed in the 1540s, the college is tucked away on Queens' Lane, next to the wide lawns that lead down from King's College to the Backs. The college's most famed piece of architecture is the wooden lattice Mathematical Bridge, first built in 1749. The original version is said to have been built without any fastenings, though the current bridge (reconstructed in 1902) is securely bolted. ⊠ *Queens' La.* ☎ *01223/335500* ⊕ *www.quns.cam.ac.uk* ✉ *£3.50* ⊘ *Closed weekends Jan. and Feb. and during exam periods, certain wks Apr.–July; call to confirm.*

Trinity College

COLLEGE | Founded in 1546 by Henry VIII, Trinity replaced a 14th-century educational foundation and is the largest college in either Cambridge or Oxford, with nearly 1,000 undergraduates. In the 17th-century great court, with its massive gatehouse, is **Great Tom,** a giant clock that strikes each hour with high and low notes. The college's true masterpiece is Sir Christopher Wren's **library,** colonnaded and seemingly constructed with as much light as stone. Among the things you can see here is A. A. Milne's handwritten manuscript of *The House at Pooh Corner.*

Trinity alumni include Sir Isaac Newton, William Thackeray, Lord Byron, Lord Tennyson, and 31 Nobel Prize winners. ⊠ *St. John's St.* ☎ *01223/338400* ⊕ *www.trin. cam.ac.uk* ✉ *£3* ⊘ *College and chapel closed exam period and event days; Wren library closed Sun.*

Restaurants

Loch Fyne

$$ | SEAFOOD | Part of a Scottish chain that harvests its own oysters, this airy, casual place across from the Fitzwilliam Museum is deservedly popular. The seafood is fresh and well prepared, served in a traditional setting with a modern ambience. **Known for:** Bradan Rost smoked salmon; Scottish oysters; great Scotch whiskey menu. ⑤ *Average main: £17* ⊠ *37 Trumpington St.* ☎ *01223/362433* ⊕ *www. lochfyneseafoodandgrill.co.uk.*

★ Midsummer House

$$$$ | FRENCH | Beside the River Cam on the edge of Midsummer Common, this gray-brick 19th-century villa holds a two–Michelin star restaurant set in a comfortable conservatory. Fixed-price menus for lunch and dinner (with five to eight courses) present innovative French and Mediterranean-influenced dishes that often include apples from the trees in the garden. **Known for:** great river views; beautiful historic setting; special-occasion dining. ⑤ *Average main: £135* ⊠ *Midsummer Common* ☎ *01223/369299* ⊕ *www.midsummerhouse.co.uk* ⊘ *Closed Sun.–Tues.*

The Oak

$$ | BRITISH | This charming, intimate restaurant is a local favorite. It's near an uncompromisingly busy intersection, but the friendliness of the staff and classic bistro food more than make up for it. **Known for:** bistro-style menus; excellent steaks; delicious, regional seafood. ⑤ *Average main: £20* ⊠ *6 Lensfield Rd.* ☎ *01223/323361* ⊕ *www.theoakbistro. co.uk* ⊘ *Closed Sun.*

Pickerel Inn

$ | **BRITISH** | This 600-year-old inn is home to one of the city's oldest pubs, making it a good stop for an afternoon pint of real ale and bowl of doorstop-sized potato wedges. Watch for the low beams. **Known for:** traditional pub atmosphere; excellent steak pie; classsic English pints. $ *Average main: £10* ✉ *30 Magdalene St.* ☎ *01223/355068* ⊕ *www. greeneking-pubs.co.uk/pubs/cambridge-shire/pickerel-inn* ▭ *No credit cards.*

Restaurant 22

$$$$ | **BRITISH** | Pretty stained-glass windows separate this sophisticated little restaurant from bustling Chesterton Road. The setting, in a terrace of houses, is low-key, but the food is creative and eye-catching. **Known for:** low-key setting; creative approach to classics; delicious desserts. $ *Average main: £50* ✉ *22 Chesterton Rd.* ☎ *01223/351880* ⊕ *www. restaurant22.co.uk* ☾ *Closed Sun. and Mon. No lunch.*

River Bar Steakhouse & Grill

$$ | **MODERN BRITISH** | Across the river from Magdalene College, this popular waterfront bar and grill serves delicious steak, burgers, and pies, plus specialties such as lobster mac and cheese or salmon steak with molasses and spices. There's an extensive cocktail menu as well. **Known for:** classic British mains; rooftop terrace dining; huge cocktail menu. $ *Average main: £23* ✉ *Quayside, 3 Thompsons La., off Bridge St.* ☎ *01223/307030* ⊕ *www.riverbarsteakhouse.com.*

Three Horseshoes

$$ | **MEDITERRANEAN** | This early-19th-century pub and restaurant in a thatched cottage has an elegant dining space in the conservatory and more casual tables in the airy bar. Sourcing of ingredients is taken seriously here—the menu lists not only the suppliers, but specific reasons for choosing them—and this is all put to good use in Modern British dishes with hints of the Mediterranean. **Known for:** local ingredients; seafood board; excellent wine. $ *Average main: £19* ✉ *High St., Madingley* ☎ *01954/210221* ⊕ *www. threehorseshoesmadingley.co.uk.*

 ## Hotels

★ Duke House

$$ | **B&B/INN** | This beautifully converted town house (home of the Duke of Gloucester when he was a student) is forever cropping up in British newspaper articles about the best B&Bs in the country. **Pros:** beautiful house; great location; suites are quite spacious. **Cons:** books up fast; two-night minimum on weekends; cheaper rooms are small. $ *Rooms from: £150* ✉ *1 Victoria St.* ☎ *01223/314773* ⊕ *www.dukehousecambridge.co.uk* ⤜ *5 rooms* ⑩ *Free breakfast.*

5 Chapel Street

$ | **B&B/INN** | This sweet Georgian town house and B&B in the northeastern corner of the city is a beautiful 20-minute walk along the river from central Cambridge. **Pros:** quiet location; wonderful host; excellent breakfast. **Cons:** some rooms are small; suburban location; 20-minute walk to the center. $ *Rooms from: £110* ✉ *5 Chapel St., Chesterton* ☎ *01223/514856* ⊕ *www.5chapelstreet. com* ⤜ *3 rooms* ⑩ *Free breakfast.*

Regent Hotel

$$ | **HOTEL** | A rare small hotel in central Cambridge, this handsome Georgian town house has wooden sash windows that look out over a tree-lined park called Parker's Piece. **Pros:** good view from top rooms; close to bars and restaurants; cozy atmosphere. **Cons:** no parking; a tad scruffy; no breakfast. $ *Rooms from: £140* ✉ *41 Regent St.* ☎ *01223/351470* ⊕ *www.regenthotel.co.uk* ⤜ *22 rooms* ⑩ *No meals.*

University Arms

$$ | **HOTEL** | Decorated with a chic, contemporary flair that contributes to its rich historical status as Cambridge's oldest hotel, the University Arms is a welcome

luxurious option on the city's hotel scene. **Pros:** beautiful historic building; charming, contemporary interior design; lively bar and dining room. **Cons:** prices are high in peak season; parking is limited; busy location on one of the city's main thoroughfares. ⑤ *Rooms from: £170* ✉ *Regent St.* ☎ *01223/606066* ⊕ *www.universityarms.com* ⇆ *192 rooms* ⦿ *No meals.*

★ The Varsity

$$$ | HOTEL | This stylish boutique hotel with an adjoining spa has wide windows that flood the place with light. **Pros:** beautiful location; gorgeous views; stylish design. **Cons:** not such great views in the less expensive rooms; prices are a bit high (particularly on weekdays); not much choice at breakfast. ⑤ *Rooms from: £250* ✉ *Thompson's La., off Bridge St.* ☎ *01223/306030* ⊕ *www.thevarsityhotel.co.uk* ⇆ *44 rooms* ⦿ *No meals.*

Nightlife

The Eagle

BARS/PUBS | This 16th-century coaching inn with a cobbled courtyard has lost none of its old-time character. It also played a walk-on part in scientific history when, on February 28, 1953, a pair of excited Cambridge scientists announced to a roomful of rather surprised lunchtime patrons that they'd just discovered the secret of life: DNA. (Unfortunately they forgot to mention their third colleague, Rosalind Franklin, who has been largely erased from the history of their discovery). A plaque outside commemorates the event. ✉ *8 Benet St.* ☎ *01223/505020* ⊕ *www.greeneking-pubs.co.uk/pubs/cambridgeshire/eagle.*

Fort St. George

BARS/PUBS | Overlooking the university boathouses, this lovely old pub gets honors for its riverside views. ✉ *Midsummer Common* ☎ *01223/354327* ⊕ *www.greeneking-pubs.co.uk/pubs/cambridgeshire/fort-st-george.*

Free Press

BARS/PUBS | A favorite of student rowers, this small pub has an excellent selection of traditional ales. ✉ *7 Prospect Row* ☎ *01223/368337* ⊕ *www.freepresscambridge.com.*

Performing Arts

★ Cambridge Folk Festival

FESTIVALS | Spread over four days in late July or early August at Cherry Hinton Hall, the Cambridge Folk Festival attracts major international folk singers and groups. ✉ *Cambridge* ☎ *01223/357851* ⊕ *www.cambridgelive.org.uk/folk-festival.*

King's College Chapel

CONCERTS | During regular terms, King's College Chapel has evensong services Monday through Saturday at 5:30 and Sunday at 10:30 and 3:30. ■**TIP➔ Your best chance of seeing the full choir is Thursday to Sunday.** ✉ *King's Parade* ☎ *01223/331212* ⊕ *www.kings.cam.ac.uk.*

🔖 Shopping

Head to the specialty shops in the center of town, especially in and around Rose Crescent and King's Parade. Bookshops, including antiquarian stores, are Cambridge's pride and joy.

BOOKS

Cambridge University Press Bookshop

BOOKS/STATIONERY | In business since at least 1581, the Cambridge University Press runs this store on Trinity Street. ✉ *1 Trinity St.* ☎ *01223/333333* ⊕ *www.cambridge.org/about-us/visit-bookshop.*

David's

BOOKS/STATIONERY | Near the Arts Theatre, G. David (known locally as just David's) sells antiquarian books. ✉ *16 St. Edward's Passage* ☎ *01223/354619.*

Haunted Bookshop

BOOKS/STATIONERY | This shop carries a great selection of old, illustrated books

Punting on the Cam

To punt is to maneuver a flat-bottom, wooden, gondolalike boat—in this case, through the shallow River Cam along the verdant Backs behind the colleges of Cambridge. One benefit of this popular activity is that you get a better view of the ivy-covered walls from the water. Mastery of the sport lies in your ability to control a 15-foot pole, used to propel the punt. With a bottle of wine, some food, and a few friends, you may find yourself saying things such as, "It doesn't get any better than this." One piece of advice: if your pole gets stuck, let go. You can use the smaller paddle to go back and retrieve it. Hang on to a stuck punt for too long and you'll probably fall in with it.

The lazier-at-heart may prefer chauffeured punting, with food supplied. Students from Cambridge often do the work, and you get a fairly informative spiel on the colleges. For a romantic evening trip, there are illuminated punts.

One university punting society once published a useful "Bluffer's Guide to Punting" featuring detailed instructions and tips on how to master the art. It has been archived online at ⊕ *duramecho.com/Misc/HowToPunt. html*.

11

Cambridge and East Anglia **CAMBRIDGE**

and British classics. And (the clue's in the name) apparently it has a ghost, too. ⊠ *9 St. Edward's Passage* ☏ *01223/312913* ⊕ *www.sarahkeybooks.co.uk.*

Heffers
BOOKS/STATIONERY | Filled with rare and imported books, Heffers' boasts a particularly fine arts section. ⊠ *20 Trinity St.* ☏ *01223/463200* ⊕ *heffersbookshop. business.site.*

CLOTHING
Ryder & Amies
CLOTHING | Need a straw boater? This shop is the official outlet for Cambridge University products, from hoodies to ties to cuff links. ⊠ *22 King's Parade* ☏ *01223/350371* ⊕ *www.ryderamies. co.uk.*

MARKETS
All Saints Garden Art & Craft Market
CRAFTS | This market displays the wares of local artists outdoors on Saturday. It's also open Fridays in July and August and some weekends in December (weather permitting). ⊠ *Trinity St.* ⊕ *www.visitcambridge.org/shopping/ all-saints-garden-art-and-craft-market.*

Activities

BIKING
City Cycle Hire
BICYCLING | This shop charges supercheap rates of £8 per half day, £15 per day, and £25 for a week. All bikes are mountain or hybrid bikes. Reservations are essential in July and August. ⊠ *61 Newnham Rd.* ☏ *01223/365629* ⊕ *www.citycyclehire. com.*

PUNTING
You can rent punts at several places, notably at Silver Street Bridge–Mill Lane, at Magdalene Bridge, and from outside the Rat and Parrot pub on Thompson's Lane on Jesus Green. Hourly rental costs around £16 to £25. Chauffeured punting, usually by a Cambridge student, is also popular. It costs upwards of £15 to £20 per person.

★ **Scudamore's Punting Co.**
BOATING | This company rents chauffeured and self-drive punts. Daily, 45-minute tours start at around £20 per person (less if booked online). Scudamore's also runs various special tours—for afternoon tea

or Halloween, for example. Private tours and punting lessons are also available. High-stakes romantics can even arrange a "Proposal Tour," which includes champagne and roses if your beloved says yes. ⊠ Granta Place, Mill La. ☎ 01223/359750 ⊕ www.scudamores.com.

Ely

16 miles north of Cambridge.

Known for its magnificent cathedral, Ely is the "capital" of the fens, the center of what used to be a separate county called the Isle of Ely (literally "island of eels"). Until the land was drained in the 17th century, Ely was surrounded by treacherous marshland, which inhabitants crossed wearing stilts. Today Wicken Fen, a nature reserve 9 miles southeast of town (off A1123), preserves the sole remaining example of fenland in an undrained state.

Enveloped by fields of wheat, sugar beets, and carrots, Ely is a small, dense town that somewhat fails to live up to the high expectations created by its big attraction, its magnificent cathedral. The shopping area and market square lie to the north and lead down to the riverside, and the medieval buildings of the cathedral grounds and the King's School (which trains cathedral choristers) spread out to the south and west. Ely's most famous resident was Oliver Cromwell, whose house is now a museum.

GETTING HERE AND AROUND

The 9 and 12 buses leave twice an hour from the Drummer Street bus station in Cambridge. The journey to Ely takes around an hour. To drive there from Cambridge, simply take the A10 road going north out of the city. Ely is quite small, so find somewhere to park and walk to the center. Trains from Cambridge to Ely leave three times an hour and take 15 minutes.

ESSENTIALS

VISITOR INFORMATION Visit Ely. ⊠ *Oliver Cromwell's House, 29 St. Mary's St.* ☎ *01353/662062* ⊕ *www.visitely.org.uk.*

 Sights

★ Ely Cathedral

RELIGIOUS SITE | Known affectionately as the Ship of the Fens, Ely Cathedral can be seen for miles, towering above the flat landscape on one of the few ridges in the fens. In 1083, the Normans began work on the cathedral, which stands on the site of a Benedictine monastery founded by the Anglo-Saxon princess Etheldreda in 673. In the center of the cathedral you see a marvel of medieval construction—the unique octagonal **Lantern Tower,** a sort of stained-glass skylight of colossal proportions, built to replace the central tower that collapsed in 1322. The cathedral's **West Tower** is even taller; the view from the top (if you can manage the 288 steps) is spectacular. Tours of both towers run daily. The cathedral is also notable for its 248-foot-long **nave,** with its simple Norman arches and Victorian painted ceiling. Much of the decorative carving of the 14th-century **Lady Chapel** was defaced during the Reformation (mostly by knocking off the heads of the statuary), but enough traces remain to show its original beauty.

The cathedral also houses the wonderful **Stained Glass Museum** (⊕ *www.stainedglassmuseum.com*). Exhibits trace the history of stained glass from medieval to modern times, including some stunning contemporary pieces. Ely Cathedral is a popular filming location; it doubled for Westminster Abbey in *The King's Speech* (2010) and *The Crown* (2015).

■**TIP➔ There are guided tours of the cathedral from Monday to Saturday (and Sunday in summer). Generally they start at 10:45, noon, and 2, with extra tours in the summer, but times vary so it's a good idea to call**

ahead. ✉ *The Gallery* ☎ *01353/667735*
🌐 *www.elycathedral.org* 💲 *£8–£19.*

🍴 Restaurants

★ Old Fire Engine House

$$ | BRITISH | Scrubbed pine tables fill the
main dining room of this converted fire
station near Ely Cathedral; another room,
used when there's a crowd, has an open
fireplace and a polished wood floor, and
also serves as an art gallery. The menu
could include fenland recipes like sea
bass with shrimp and dill sauce, as well
as more familiar English fare, such as
steak and kidney pie. **Known for:** seasonal
produce; regularly changing menus;
afternoon tea. 💲 *Average main: £18* ✉ *25
St. Mary's St.* ☎ *01353/662582* 🌐 *www.
theoldfireenginehouse.co.uk* 🕐 *No dinner
Sun.*

Long Melford

*2 miles north of Sudbury, 14 miles south
of Bury St. Edmunds.*

It's easy to see how this village got its
name, especially if you walk the full
length of its 2-mile-long main street,
which gradually broadens to include
green squares and trees and finally
opens into a large triangular green on the
hill. Long Melford grew rich on its wool
trade in the 15th century, and the town's
buildings are an appealing mix, mostly
Tudor half-timber or Georgian. Many
house antiques shops. Away from the
main road, Long Melford returns to its
resolutely late-medieval roots.

GETTING HERE AND AROUND

Long Melford is just off the main A134. If you're driving from Sudbury, take the smaller B1064; it's much quicker than it looks on the map. There are several bus connections with Sudbury, Bury St. Edmunds, and Ipswich.

 Sights

Holy Trinity Church

RELIGIOUS SITE | This largely 15th-century church, founded by the rich clothiers of Long Melford, stands on a hill at the north end of the village. Close up, the delicate flint flush-work (shaped flints set into a pattern) and huge Perpendicular Gothic windows that take up most of the church's walls have great impact, especially because the nave is 150 feet long. The Clopton Chapel, with an ornate (and incredibly rare) painted medieval ceiling, predates the rest of the church by 150 years. The beautiful Lady Chapel has an unusual cloister; the stone on the wall in the corner is an ancient multiplication table, used when the chapel served as a school in the 17th and 18th centuries. ■**TIP**➜ **Tours can be arranged in advance; email alisonewbankis@gmail.com for more details and to make reservations.** ⊠ Main St. ☎ 01787/310845 ⊕ www.longmelford-church.com 🖾 Free.

Melford Hall

HOUSE | Distinguished from the outside by its turrets and topiaries, Melford Hall is an Elizabethan house with its original banqueting room, a fair number of 18th-century additions, and pleasant gardens. Much of the porcelain and other fine pieces here come from the *Santisima Trinidad,* a ship loaded with gifts from the emperor of China and bound for Spain that was captured in the 18th century. Children's writer Beatrix Potter, related to the owners, visited often; there's a small collection of Potter memorabilia. ⊠ Off A134 ☎ 01787/379228 ⊕ www. nationaltrust.org.uk/melfordhall 🖾 £9.50 🕙 Closed Nov.–Mar.

 Hotels

The Bull

$ | **HOTEL** | This half-timber Elizabethan building reveals its long history with stone-flagged floors, bowed and twisted oak beams, and heavy antique furniture. **Pros:** historic atmosphere; comfortable bedrooms; friendly staff. **Cons:** minimum stay on summer weekends; popular with wedding parties; small bathrooms. ⑤ *Rooms from: £110* ⊠ *Hall St.* ☎ *01787/378494* ⊕ *www.greenekinginns. co.uk/hotels/bull-hotel-sudbury* ⤳ *25 rooms* ⦿| *Some meals.*

Lavenham

4 miles northeast of Long Melford.

Virtually unchanged since the height of its wealth in the 15th and 16th centuries, Lavenham is one of the most perfectly preserved examples of a Tudor village in England. The weavers' and wool merchants' houses occupy not just one show street but most of the town. The houses are timber-frame in black oak, the main posts looking as if they could last another 400 years, although their walls are often no longer entirely perpendicular to the ground. The town has many examples of so-called "Suffolk pink" buildings—actually a catch-all term for brightly painted colors, including rose, yellow, and apricot; many of these house small galleries selling paintings and crafts.

GETTING HERE AND AROUND

Lavenham is on the A1141 and B1071. Take the latter if possible, as it's a prettier drive. There are hourly buses from Sudbury and Bury St. Edmunds and slightly less frequent buses from Ipswich.

ESSENTIALS

VISITOR INFORMATION Lavenham Tourist Information Centre. ⊠ *Lady St.* ☎ *01787/247983* ⊕ *www.lovelavenham. co.uk.*

Colorful and ancient, the timbered houses in pretty towns such as Lavenham recall the days when these buildings housed weavers and wool merchants.

Sights

Church of St. Peter and St. Paul
RELIGIOUS SITE | Set apart from the village on a hill, this grand 15th-century church was built between 1480 and 1520 by cloth merchant Thomas Spring. The height of its tower (141 feet) was meant to surpass those of the neighboring churches—and perhaps to impress rival towns. The rest of the church is perfectly proportioned, with intricately carved wood. ⊠ *Church St.* ☎ *01787/247244* ⊕ *www. lavenhamchurch.onesuffolk.net* ☐ *Free.*

Lavenham Guildhall
BUILDING | Also known as the Guildhall of Corpus Christi, this higgledy-piggledy timber-framed building dating from 1529 dominates Market Place, an almost flawlessly preserved medieval square. Upstairs is a rather dull exhibition on local agriculture and the wool trade, although looking around the building itself is worth the admission charge. ⊠ *Market Pl.* ☎ *01787/247646* ⊕ *www.nationaltrust. org.uk/lavenham-guildhall* ☐ *£8* ⊙ *Closed*

weekdays in Jan. and Feb., and Tues.– Thurs. in early Nov.–late Dec.

Little Hall
BUILDING | This timber-frame wool merchant's house (brightly painted on the outside, in the local custom) contains a display showing the building's progress from its creation in the 14th century to its subsequent "modernization" in the 17th century. It also has a beautiful garden at the back. ⊠ *Market Pl.* ☎ *01787/247019* ⊕ *www.littlehall.org.uk* ☐ *£4.50* ⊙ *Closed Nov.–Mar.*

Restaurants

★ Great House
$$$ | **FRENCH** | This excellent "restaurant with rooms" on the medieval Market Square takes deeply traditional flavors of the British countryside and updates them with a slight French twist in dishes like grilled salmon with spinach fondue or lamb with onion and thyme pie. Served in an elegant, whitewashed dining room, the three-course, fixed-price menus use

a reassuring amount of local and regional ingredients. **Known for:** elegant, refined menus; local ingredients; a French touch. ⑤ *Average main: £25* ✉ *Market Pl.* ☎ *01787/247431* ⊕ *www.greathouse. co.uk* ⊘ *Closed Mon. and Jan. No dinner Sun. No lunch Tues.*

★ **Memsaab**

$ | INDIAN | In a town ready to burst with cream teas, it's a bit of a surprise to find an Indian restaurant, let alone such an exceptional one. Among the classics one would expect from a curry house—from mild kormas to spicy *madrases* and *jalfrezies* (traditional curries made with chili and tomato)—are some finely executed specialties, including Nizami chicken (a fiery dish prepared with yogurt and fresh ginger) and king prawn *bhuna* (with ginger, garlic, and spring onion). **Known for:** top-notch Indian food; diverse choices; lively atmosphere. ⑤ *Average main: £11* ✉ *2 Church St.* ☎ *01787/249431* ⊕ *www. memsaaboflavenham.co.uk.*

 Hotels

Lavenham Priory

$$$$ | RENTAL | You can immerse yourself in Lavenham's Tudor heritage at this sprawling house, one of the most widely photographed in the village. **Pros:** historic building; charming rooms; lovely garden. **Cons:** minimum two-night stay; no amenities; traffic noise in side rooms. ⑤ *Rooms from: £365* ✉ *Water St.* ☎ *01787/247404* ⊕ *www.lavenhampriory.co.uk* 🛏 *2 rooms* �“◎❙ *No meals* ☞ *2-night minimum.*

Swan Hotel

$$$ | HOTEL | This half-timber 14th-century lodging has rambling public rooms, roaring fireplaces, and corridors so low that cushions are strategically placed on beams. **Pros:** lovely old building; atmospheric rooms; beautiful spa. **Cons:** creaky floors; lots of steps to climb; popular wedding venue. ⑤ *Rooms from: £235* ✉ *High St.* ☎ *01787/247477* ⊕ *www.theswanatlavenham.co.uk* 🛏 *49 rooms* ❙◎❙ *Some meals.*

Dedham

62 miles southeast of Cambridge.

Dedham is the heart of Constable country. Here, gentle hills and the cornfields of Dedham Vale, set under the district's delicate, pale skies, inspired John Constable (1776–1837) to paint some of his most celebrated canvases. He went to school in Dedham, a picture-book village that did well from the wool trade in the 15th and 16th centuries and has retained a prosperous air ever since. The 15th-century church looms large over handsomely sturdy, pastel-color houses.

Nearby towns have several other sites of interest to Constable fans. About 2 miles from Dedham is Flatford, where you can see Flatford Mill, one of the two water mills owned by Constable's father. Northeast of Dedham, off A12, the Constable trail continues in East Bergholt, where Constable was born in 1776. Although the town is mostly modern, the older part has some atmospheric buildings like the church of St. Mary-the-Virgin.

GETTING HERE AND AROUND

From the main A12 road, Dedham is easily reached by car via B1029. Public transportation is extremely limited; there's no nearby train station.

 Sights

Bridge Cottage

HOUSE | On the north bank of the Stour, this 16th-century home in East Bergholt has a shop, an exhibition about Constable's life, and a pleasant tearoom overlooking the river. You can also rent rowboats here. ✉ *Off B1070, East Bergholt* ☎ *01206/298260* ⊕ *www.nationaltrust.org.uk/flatford* 🖾 *Free* ⊘ *Closed mid-Dec.–late Dec. and weekdays Jan., Feb., and Nov.–mid-Dec.*

★ St. Mary-the-Virgin

RELIGIOUS SITE | One of the most remarkable churches in the region, St. Mary-the-Virgin was started just before the Reformation. The doors underneath the ruined archways outside (remnants of a much older church) contain a series of mysterious symbols—actually a coded message left by Catholic sympathizers of the time. The striking interior contains a mini-museum of treasures, including an ancient wall painting of the Virgin Mary in one of the rear chapels, a 14th-century chest, and an extraordinary series of florid memorial stones on the nave wall opposite the main entrance. A unique feature of the church is that its bells are rung from a cage in the graveyard; this was erected as a temporary measure, pending the construction of a tower in 1531 that was never completed. ⊠ *Flatford Rd., East Bergholt* ☎ *01206/392646* 🖾 *Free.*

Willy Lott's House

HOUSE | A five-minute stroll down the path from Bridge Cottage brings you to this 16th-century structure that is instantly recognizable from Constable's painting *The Hay Wain* (1821). Although the house is not usually open to the public, the road is a public thoroughfare, so you can just walk right on up to see the famous—and completely unchanged—view for yourself. Just stand across from the two trees on the far bank, with the mill on your right, and look upstream. On the outside wall of the mill is a handy reproduction of the painting to help you compose your own photo. ⊠ *Flatford Rd., off B1070, East Bergholt.*

🍴 Restaurants

★ Le Talbooth

$$$ | BRITISH | This sophisticated restaurant serving excellent British-French fare is set in a Tudor house beside the idyllic River Stour. Outside, there are lighted terraces where food and drinks are served on warm evenings and jazz and steel bands play on Sunday evening in summer; inside, original beams, leaded-glass windows, and a brick fireplace add to the sense of history. **Known for:** superb British-French cooking; excellent service; summer barbecues. ⑤ *Average main: £28* ⊠ *Gun Hill* ☎ *01206/323150* ⊕ *www.milsomhotels.com/letalbooth* ⊙ *No dinner Sun. mid-Sept.–early June.*

Marlborough Head

$ | BRITISH | This friendly, 300-year-old pub across from Constable's school in Dedham serves traditional English pub food. Dishes such as bangers and mash (sausages and mashed potatoes) and roast chicken share the menu with fish-and-chips and burgers. **Known for:** traditional pub food; proper village "local" feel; good old-school comfort eating. ⑤ *Average main: £11* ⊠ *Mill La.* ☎ *01206/323250* ⊙ *No dinner Sun.*

Hotels

★ Maison Talbooth

$$$ | HOTEL | Constable painted the rich meadowlands in which this luxurious Victorian country-house hotel is set. **Pros:** good food; lovely views over Dedham Vale; some private hot tubs. **Cons:** restaurant books up fast; prices are high; need a car to get here. ⑤ *Rooms from: £300* ⊠ *Stratford Rd.* ☎ *01206/322367* ⊕ *www.milsomhotels.com/maison-talbooth* 🛏 *12 rooms* ⦿ *Free breakfast.*

🏃 Activities

Boathouse Restaurant

BOATING | FAMILY | From Dedham, on the banks of the River Stour, you can rent a rowboat from the Boathouse Restaurant. They're available daily, April through October (depending on weather). The cost is £16 per hour, although you can rent for 30 minutes for £8 if you only want a brief sojourn in the water. ⊠ *Mill La.* ☎ *01206/323153* ⊕ *www.dedham-boathouse.com.*

Woodbridge

18 miles northeast of Dedham.

One of the first good ports of call on the Suffolk Heritage Coast, Woodbridge is a town whose upper reaches center on a fine old market square, site of the 16th-century Shire Hall. Woodbridge is at its best around its old quayside, where boatbuilding has been carried out since the 16th century. The most prominent building is a white-clapboard mill, which dates from the 18th century and is powered by the tides.

GETTING HERE AND AROUND

Woodbridge is on A12. There are a few local buses, but they mostly serve commuters. By train, Woodbridge is 1½ hours from London and just under 2 hours from Cambridge (with connections).

ESSENTIALS

VISITOR INFORMATION Woodbridge Tourist Information Centre. ⊠ *Station Building, Station Rd.* ☎ *01394/383789* ⊕ *choosewoodbridge.co.uk/listings/ tourist-information-centre.*

Sights

★ Sutton Hoo

INFO CENTER | The visitor center at Sutton Hoo tells the story of one of Britain's most significant Anglo-Saxon archaeological sites. In 1938, a local archaeologist excavated a series of earth mounds and discovered a 7th-century burial ship, probably that of King Raedwald of East Anglia. A complete replica of the 90-foot-long ship stands in the visitor center, which has artifacts and displays about Anglo-Saxon society. Nothing can quite make up for the fact that the best finds have been moved to the British Museum in London, but it is, nonetheless, all quite fascinating. Trails around the 245-acre site explore the area along the River Deben. ⊠ *Off B1083* ☎ *01394/389700* ⊕ *www. nationaltrust.org.uk/suttonhoo* 🎫 *£15.*

Restaurants

★ Butley Orford Oysterage

$ | SEAFOOD | What started as a little café that sold oysters and cups of tea is now a bustling restaurant, with a nationwide reputation. It has no pretenses of grandeur but serves some of the best smoked fish you're likely to taste anywhere. **Known for:** legendary fish pie; traditional, local flavors; great, simple seafood. ⑤ *Average main: £13* ⊠ *Market Hill, Orford* ☎ *01394/450277* ⊕ *www. pinneysoforford.co.uk* ⊗ *No dinner Sun.– Tues. in Apr.–July, Sept., and Oct. No dinner Sun.–Thurs. in Nov.–Mar.*

🛏 Hotels

★ Crown and Castle

$$ | B&B/INN | Artsy, laid-back, and genuinely friendly, this little gem occupies an 18th-century building in the village of Orford, 10 miles east of Woodbridge. **Pros:** warm service; relaxed atmosphere; good restaurant. **Cons:** need a car to get around; not great for families; not close to major sights. ⑤ *Rooms from: £160* ⊠ *Market Hill, Orford* ☎ *01394/450205* ⊕ *www.crownandcastle.co.uk* ⤳ *21 rooms* ⛾ *Free breakfast.*

Seckford Hall

$$ | HOTEL | The sense of history at this delightfully old-school hotel comes from more than just the magnificent Tudor architecture; several pieces of furniture are castoffs from Buckingham Palace, and one of the beds was supposedly slept in by Elizabeth I. Rooms are large and comfortable, with modern bathrooms (some have whirlpool tubs). **Pros:** antique charm; lovely setting; great atmosphere. **Cons:** no elevator; antique beds are creaky; minimum stay on weekends. ⑤ *Rooms from: £150* ⊠ *Off A12* ☎ *01394/385678* ⊕ *www.seckford.co.uk* ⤳ *32 rooms* ⛾ *Free breakfast.*

Aldeburgh

15 miles northeast of Woodbridge.

Aldeburgh (pronounced *orl*-bruh) is a quiet seaside resort, except in June, when the town fills with people attending the noted Aldeburgh Festival. Its beach is backed by a promenade lined with candy-color dwellings. The 20th-century composer Benjamin Britten lived here for some time. He was interested in the story of Aldeburgh's native son, poet George Crabbe (1754–1832), and turned his life story into *Peter Grimes*, a celebrated opera that perfectly captures the atmosphere of the Suffolk Coast.

GETTING HERE AND AROUND

You have little choice but to drive to Aldeburgh; turn off A12 near Farnham and follow signs. There's no train station and no bus service.

ESSENTIALS

VISITOR INFORMATION Aldeburgh Tourist Information Centre. ⊠ *51 High St.* ☎ *01728/454884* ⊕ *www.thesuffolkcoast.co.uk/things-to-do/attractions/aldeburgh-visitor-information.*

👁 Sights

★ Aldeburgh Beach Lookout

ARTS VENUE | This tiny, disused lookout tower is in the middle of the main beachfront in Aldeburgh and has been converted into a bijou space for contemporary art and performances. Artists take up weekly residences here, welcoming the public each Saturday to observe what they've created during the week. This isn't just a space for local talent, however; some big names in the British arts world have taken part in recent years, including the poet Michael Horovitz and painter Eileen Cooper, the first female head of the Royal Academy. They also sometimes show art films projected on the side of the building—an arresting sight against a backdrop of dark seas lapping on the nighttime shore. ⊠ *31 Crag Path* ☎ *01728/452754* ⊕ *www.aldeburghbeachlookout.com* 🖻 *Free* ⊘ *Closed Sun.–Fri. Sometimes closed in winter.*

Moot Hall and Aldeburgh Museum

BUILDING | Moot Hall was the place where local elders met to debate and make decisions about the locality. Built of flint and timber, the 16th-century building once stood in the center of a thriving town; the fact that it's now just a few steps from the beach is testament to the erosive powers of the North Sea. Today, it contains the Aldeburgh Museum, a low-key collection that includes finds from an Anglo-Saxon ship burial. ⊠ *Moot Hall, Market Cross Pl.* ☎ *01728/454666* ⊕ *www.aldeburghmuseum.org.uk* 🖻 *£3* ⊘ *Closed Nov.–Feb. and weekdays in Mar.*

🍴 Restaurants

★ Aldeburgh Fish and Chip Shop

$ | **BRITISH** | A frequent (and deserving) entry on "best fish-and-chips in Britain" lists, Aldeburgh's most celebrated eatery always has a long line of eager customers come frying time. The fish is fresh and local, the batter melts in your mouth, and the chips (from locally grown potatoes) are satisfyingly chunky. **Known for:** one of the most famous fish-and-chips shops in Britain; BYO wine or beer if you sit upstairs; long lines. Ⓢ *Average main: £6* ⊠ *226 High St.* ☎ *01728/452250* ⊕ *www.aldeburghfishandchips.co.uk* ⊘ *Closed Mon. No dinner Sun., Tues., and Wed.*

🛏 Hotels

Brudenell

$$ | **HOTEL** | With its good food, modest but comfortable rooms, and sweeping views of the sea, Brudenell is the very definition of an English seaside hotel. **Pros:** laid-back atmosphere; the beach is

literally a stone's throw away; pleasant and quiet bedrooms. **Cons:** rooms are small for the price; car park is tiny; beach bar gets full early. Ⓢ *Rooms from: £160* ✉ *The Parade* ☎ *01728/452071* ⊕ *www. brudenellhotel.co.uk* ⮌ *44 rooms* ⏋⨀⏋ *Free breakfast.*

ⓣ Performing Arts

★ Snape Maltings

ARTS CENTERS | It's worth a stop to take in the peaceful River Alde location of this cultural center. It includes nine art galleries and crafts shops in distinctive large brick buildings once used to malt barley, plus a café and tearoom. There's a farmers' market on the first Saturday of the month, a major food festival in September, and a Benjamin Britten festival in October. Leisurely 45-minute river cruises (£7.50) leave from the quayside in spring and summer. From the Maltings, you can stroll out along an elevated trail through some reed marshes for beautiful views—just watch for uneven ground. ✉ *Off B1069, Snape* ☎ *01728/688303* ⊕ *www.snapemaltings.co.uk.*

Chapter 12

YORKSHIRE AND THE NORTHEAST

Updated by Ellin Stein
and Joseph Reaney

12

⊙ Sights	🍴 Restaurants	🛏 Hotels	🛍 Shopping	🍸 Nightlife
★★★★☆	★★★☆☆	★★★☆☆	★★☆☆☆	★★☆☆☆

WELCOME TO YORKSHIRE AND THE NORTHEAST

TOP REASONS TO GO

★ **York Minster:** The largest Gothic cathedral in Northern Europe helps make York one of the country's most visited cities. An interactive exhibit in the undercroft explores the site's history from Roman times onward.

★ **Haworth:** Looking as if it were carved from stone, this picture-perfect hillside town where the Brontë sisters lived is a lovely place to learn about them.

★ **Hadrian's Wall:** The ancient Roman wall is a wonder, as much for the wild countryside around it as for its stones and forts, such as Housesteads and Vindolanda.

★ **Castles:** Fought over by the Scots and the English, and prey to Viking raiders, the Northeast was heavily fortified. Bamburgh, Durham, and Alnwick castles are spectacular remnants of this history.

★ **Medieval Durham:** A splendid Norman cathedral that dates back to the 11th century is just one of the city's charms. Take a stroll along its ancient winding streets.

Yorkshire is the largest of England's historic counties. At its heart is the ancient city of York, with its Gothic cathedral and medieval city walls while to the west are the unspoiled hills that form what the tourist office calls Brontë Country—Haworth, where the Brontë family lived, and the valleys and villages of the Yorkshire Dales. The southernmost part of the Northeast region is County Durham, which is centered around the beautiful and historic cathedral city of the same name. To the west of Newcastle is Hadrian's Wall country, where the remains of the famous Roman fortification snake through rugged scenery. Then, it's up to the Far Northeast, where towering castles and misty islands punctuate the stunning, final miles of England's eastern shoreline.

1 York. Yorkshire's major city with its famous Gothic cathedral.

2 Harrogate. An elegant Georgian and Victorian spa town.

3 Castle Howard. A baroque masterpiece near York.

4 Saltaire. A planned village that's also a UNESCO World Heritage Site.

5 Haworth. The heart of Brontë country.

6 Durham. A historic city set on a rocky spur, home to one of England's most spectacular cathedrals.

7 Hadrian's Wall. The famous wall that once marked the northern border of the Roman Empire.

8 Hexham. This pretty town is a useful base for visiting Hadrian's Wall and the wild countryside surrounding it.

9 Greenhead. A town surrounded on all sides by Roman history, including the Housesteads Roman Fort.

10 Alnwick. A small town with some big sights, including a Harry Potter-featured castle and spectacular gardens.

11 Bamburgh. Another stunning castle ruin on the Northumberland coast; best viewed from the Farne Islands.

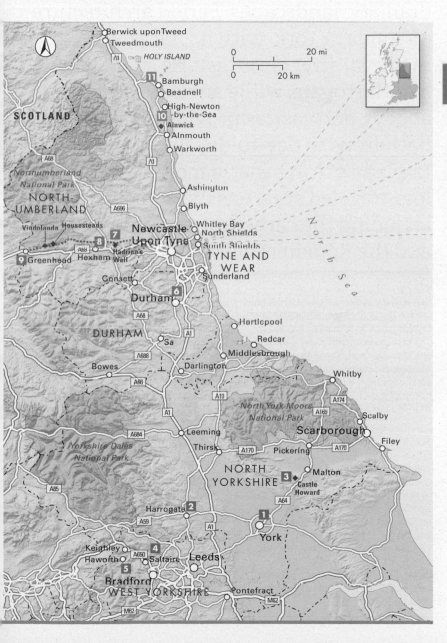

Berwick upon Tweed
Tweedmouth
A1
HOLY ISLAND
0   20 mi
0   20 km

SCOTLAND

11 Bamburgh
Beadnell
High-Newton
-by-the-Sea
10 Alnwick
Alnmouth
Warkworth

A68

Northumberland
National Park

NORTH-
UMBERLAND

A696

Ashington

Blyth

Vindolanda Housesteads
Whitley Bay
Newcastle North Shields
Upon Tyne South Shields

8 **7**
A69
9 Greenhead Hexham Hadrian's
Wall
TYNE AND
WEAR
Sunderland

Consett

Durham
6

A1

A68

DURHAM
Sa
A1
A688

Hartlepool
Redcar

Bowes
Darlington
Middlesbrough

A66

Whitby

A19

A1

North York Moors
National Park
A174
A169
Scalby

A684
Leeming
Scarborough
Filey

Thirsk
A170
Pickering
A170

NORTH
YORKSHIRE
3 Malton
Castle
Howard
A64

A65

Harrogate **2**

1

A59
A1
York

Keighley
Haworth **4**
A650 Saltaire
Leeds

5
Bradford
WEST YORKSHIRE
Pontefract

M62
M62

North Sea

A hauntingly beautiful region, Yorkshire is known for its wide-open spaces and dramatic landscapes. Period architecture abounds in York, with its narrow medieval streets, or historic spa towns like Harrogate, while ancient cathedrals, abbeys, and castles provide majestic backdrops to day-to-day life in the area. England's Northeast, a more remote and less-traveled area, has its own appeal, including the cathedral city of Durham and the Roman remains of Hadrian's Wall.

Some of the region's biggest attractions are the result of human endeavor: York's towering Gothic cathedral, created by unknown master craftsmen; Castle Howard, Vanbrugh and Hawksmoor's baroque masterpiece near York; and the Georgian parsonage (now a museum), in the small hilltop village of Haworth, where the Brontë sisters changed literature.

For many Britons, the words "the Northeast" provoke a vision of near-Siberian isolation. But although there are wind-hammered, wide-open spaces and empty roads threading the wild high moorland, the Northeast also has simple fishing towns, small villages of remarkable charm, and historic abbeys and castles that are all the more romantic for their often-ruinous state. This is also where you'll find two of England's most iconic sights: the medieval city of Durham and the stark remains of Hadrian's Wall.

Mainly composed of the two large counties of Durham and Northumberland, the Northeast includes English villages adjacent to the Scottish border area, renowned in ballads and romantic literature for feuds, raids, and battles. Fittingly, Durham Cathedral, the seat of bishops for nearly 800 years, was once described as "half church of God, half castle 'gainst the Scot." Hadrian's Wall, which marked the northern limit of the Roman Empire, stretches across prehistoric remains and moorland.

MAJOR REGIONS

York. Still enclosed within its medieval city walls, this beautifully preserved city makes the perfect introduction to Yorkshire. Its towering Minster and narrow streets are alive with history.

Around York. West and north of York a number of sights make easy, appealing day trips from the city, including the spa town of Harrogate and Castle Howard, a magnificent stately home.

Brontë Country. Rocky and bleak, this windswept stretch of country provides an appropriate setting for the dark, dramatic narratives penned by the Brontë sisters in Haworth. From the city of Leeds, you can strike out for the traditional wool towns, such as Saltaire, a UNESCO-protected gem. But the main thrust of many visits to West Yorkshire is to the west of Leeds, where the stark hills north of the Calder Valley and south of the River Aire form the landscape immortalized in the equally unsparing novels of the Brontë sisters. The gray-stone village of Haworth might have faded into obscurity were it not for the enduring fame of the literary sisters. Every summer, thousands toil up the steep main street to visit their former home. To truly appreciate the setting that inspired their books, though, you need to go farther afield to the ruined farm of Top Withens, which, in popular mythology, if not in fact, was the model for *Wuthering Heights*.

County Durham. Durham—the first major Northeastern town on the main road up from London—is by far the region's most interesting historic city. Its cobblestone streets and towering cathedral make it a charming place to visit. The city is surrounded on all sides by scenic countryside, ruined castles, and isolated villages.

Hadrian's Wall Country. A formidable line of Roman fortifications, Hadrian's Wall was the Romans' most ambitious construction in Britain. The land through which the old wall wanders is wild and inhospitable in places, but that only adds to the powerful sense of history it evokes. Museums and information centers along the wall make it possible to learn as much as you want about the Roman era, while nearby market towns like Hexham make a great base for exploration.

The Far Northeast. Extraordinary medieval fortresses and monasteries line the final 40 miles of the Northeast coast before England gives way to Scotland. Northumbria was an enclave where the flame of learning was kept alive during Europe's Dark Ages, most notably at Lindisfarne, home of saints and scholars. Castles abound, including the spectacularly sited Bamburgh. The region also has some magnificent beaches, though because of the cold water and rough seas they're far better for walking than swimming.

Planning

When to Go

To see the Yorkshire heather at its most vibrant, visit in summer (but despite the season, be prepared for some chilly days). It's also the best time to see the coast, as colorful regattas and arts festivals are underway. York Minster makes a splendidly atmospheric focal point for the prestigious York Early Music Festival in early July. Spring and fall bring their own rewards: far fewer crowds and crisp, clear days, although there's an increased risk of rain and fog. The harsh winter is tricky: while the moors and dales are beautiful covered in snow and the coast sparkles on a clear, bright day, storms and blizzards can set in quickly, making the moorland roads impassable and villages at risk of being cut off entirely. In winter, stick to York and the main towns.

The best time to see the Northeast is in summer. This ensures that the museums—and the roads—will be open, and you can take advantage of the countryside walks that are one of the region's greatest pleasures. Rough seas and inclement weather make it dangerous to swim at any of the beaches except in July and August; even then, don't expect warm water. Winter here isn't for the fainthearted. The weather is terrible, but there are few places in England so beautiful and remote.

FESTIVALS
Viking Festival

FESTIVALS | FAMILY | Held every February in York, this weeklong commemoration of the conquest of England by the Great Viking Army in 866 (only the British would hold a festival celebrating a losing battle) has more than 60 events, including a longship regatta and workshops for kids ranging from Viking-era crafts to fighting skills like archery and swordplay, as well as historical lectures, a banquet, and a beard competition. It ends with the Jorvik Viking Centre combat reenactment, where the invading Norsemen confront the Anglo-Saxon defenders. ⊠ *Jorvik Viking Centre, Coppergate, York* ☎ *01904/615505* ⊕ *www.jorvikvikingfestival.co.uk.*

Planning Your Time

Yorkshire is a vast region and difficult to explore in a short amount of time. If you're in a hurry, you could see the highlights of York as a day trip from London; the fastest trains take just two hours. But it's an awful lot to pack into one day, and you're bound to leave out places you'll probably regret missing. Proper exploration—especially of the countryside—requires time and effort. If you're interested in exploring Hadrian's Wall and the Roman ruins, you'll probably want to base yourself at a guesthouse in or around Hexham. From there you can easily take in Housesteads and the other local landmarks. Anywhere in this area is within easy reach of Durham, with its lovely ancient buildings.

Getting Here and Around

AIR

Leeds Bradford Airport, 11 miles northwest of Leeds, has frequent flights from other cities in England and Europe. Look for cheap fares on British Airways, Jet2, or Ryanair. Another good choice for this region is Manchester Airport, about 40 miles southwest of Leeds. This larger airport is well served by domestic and international carriers.

AIRPORTS Leeds Bradford International Airport. ⊠ *Whitehouse Lane, Yeadon, Leeds* ✛ *Off A658* ☎ *0871/288–2288* ⊕ *www.leedsbradfordairport.co.uk.* **Manchester Airport.** ⊠ *M56, near Junctions 5 and 6, Manchester* ☎ *0808/169–7030* ⊕ *www.manchesterairport.co.uk.*

BUS

National Express and Megabus have numerous daily departures from London's Victoria Coach Station to major cities in Yorkshire and to Durham. Once you're in the region, local bus companies take over the routes. There are Metro buses from Leeds and Bradford into the more remote parts of the Yorkshire Dales. Other companies are Harrogate Bus Company and Keighley Bus Company for services to Harrogate and Haworth, and Coastliner for Castle Howard. In York the main local bus operator is Transdev. Traveline has route information. The Network One Explorer North East ticket (£10.90, or £20.60 for families of up to five) allows unlimited one-day travel on most local bus and Metro train services in the Northeast. It's available from most bus and Metro stations or through the Go North East app.

CONTACTS Coastliner. ☎ *01653/692556* ⊕ *www.transdevbus.co.uk/coastliner.* **Explorer Northeast Pass.** ☎ *0191/276–3706* ⊕ *www.networkonetickets.co.uk.* **The Harrogate Bus Company.** ☎ *01423/566061* ⊕ *www.transdevbus.co.uk/harrogate.* **Keighley Bus Company.** ☎ *01535/603284* ⊕ *www.transdevbus.co.uk/keighley.* **Megabus.** ☎ *0141/352–4444* ⊕ *uk.megabus.com.* **Metro.** ☎ *0113/245–7676* ⊕ *www.wymetro.com.* **National Express.** ☎ *0871/781–8181* ⊕ *www.nationalexpress.com.* **Traveline.** ☎ *0871/200–2233* ⊕ *www.traveline.info.*

CAR

If you're driving, the M1 is the principal route north from London. This major highway gets you to Leeds in about four hours. For York (215 miles), stay on M1 to Leeds (197 miles), and then take A64. For the Yorkshire Dales, take M1 to Leeds, then A65 north and west to Skipton. The trans-Pennine motorway, the M62 between Liverpool and Hull, crosses the bottom of this region. North of Leeds, the A1 is the major north–south road, although narrow stretches, roadworks, and heavy traffic make this route slow going at times.

Some of the steep, narrow roads in the countryside off the main routes are difficult drives and can be perilous (or closed altogether) in winter. Main roads often closed by snowdrifts are the moorland A169 and the coast-and-moor A171. If you plan to drive in the dales or moors in winter, check the weather forecast in advance.

If you're headed to small villages in the Northeast, remote castles, or Hadrian's Wall, traveling by car is the best option. The A1 highway links London and Newcastle (five to six hours). The scenic route is the A697, which branches west off A1 north of Morpeth. For the coast, leave the A1 at Alnwick and follow the minor B1340 and B1339 for Craster, Seahouses, and Bamburgh.

TRAIN

London North Eastern Railway (LNER) trains travel to York, Leeds, and the Northeast from London's King's Cross Station. Grand Central trains head to York, Bradford, and Thirsk. Average travel times from King's Cross are two hours to York and three hours to Durham. Northern Rail trains also operate throughout the region. Contact National Rail for train times, and to find out if any discounted Rover tickets are available for your journey.

CONTACTS Grand Central Trains.
☎ 0345/603–4852 ⊕ www.grandcentral-rail.com. **London North Eastern Railway.** ☎ 03457/225333 ⊕ www.lner.co.uk. **National Rail Enquiries.** ☎ 0345/748–4950 ⊕ www.nationalrail.co.uk. **Northern Rail.** ☎ 0800/200–6060 ⊕ www.northernrail-way.co.uk.

Restaurants

Yorkshire is known for hearty food, though bacon-based breakfasts and lunches of pork pies do tend to get old fairly quickly. Increasingly, the larger towns and cities, particularly Leeds, have developed a foodie scene of sorts. Indian restaurants (often called curry houses) can be very good in northern cities. Out in the countryside, pubs are your best bet for dining. Many serve excellent home-cooked food and locally reared meat (especially lamb) and vegetables. Roast beef dinners generally come with Yorkshire pudding, the tasty, puffy, oven-baked dish made from egg batter, similar to a popover in the United States. It's generally served with lots of gravy. Be sure to sample local cheeses, especially Wensleydale, which has a delicate flavor and honey aftertaste.

The Northeast has some very fine local meats and produce. Look for restaurants that serve game from the Kielder Forest; local lamb from the hillsides; salmon and trout from the rivers; and shellfish, crab, and oysters from the coast. Outside the cities, the region lags somewhat behind other parts of England in terms of exceptional places to eat, although there are special spots to be found. Aside from the ubiquitous chains, the best bets are often small country pubs that serve the traditional, hearty fare associated with the region. Don't wait until too late to have dinner, though, as most places stop serving between 9 and 10 pm

Hotels

Traditional hotels are limited primarily to major towns and cities; those in the country tend to be guesthouses, inns, bed-and-breakfasts, or pubs with rooms, plus the occasional luxurious country-house hotel. Many of the better guesthouses are at the edge of town, but some proprietors will pick you up at the main station if you're relying on public transportation—verify before booking. Rooms fill quickly at seaside resorts in July and August, and some places in the moors and dales close in winter. Always call ahead to make sure a hotel is open and has space available.

The large hotel chains don't have much of a presence in the Northeast outside Durham and Newcastle. Instead, you can expect to find country houses converted into welcoming hotels, old coaching inns that still greet guests after 300 years, and cozy bed-and-breakfasts convenient to hiking trails. And if you've ever dreamed of staying in a castle, the Northeast delivers in spades.

Restaurant and hotel reviews have been shortened. For full information, visit Fodors.com. Restaurant prices are the average cost of a main course at dinner or, if dinner is not served, at lunch. Hotel prices are the lowest cost of a standard double room in high season, including 20% V.A.T.

WHAT IT COSTS in Pounds

	$	$$	$$$	$$$$
RESTAURANTS				
	under £16	£16–£23	£24–£30	over £30
HOTELS				
	under £125	£125–£225	£226–£350	over £350

Visitor Information

CONTACT Durham Visitor Contact Center. ☎ *03000/262626* ⊕ *www.thisisdurham. com.* **Hadrian's Wall Country.** ☎ ⊕ *www. hadrianswallcountry.co.uk.* **Welcome to Yorkshire.** ☎ *0113/322–3500* ⊕ *www. yorkshire.com.*

York

For many people, the first stop in Yorkshire is the historic cathedral city of York. Much of the city's medieval and 18th-century architecture has survived, making it a delight to explore. It's one of the most popular short-stay destinations in Britain and only three hours by train from London's King's Cross Station.

York was the military capital of Roman Britain, when it was known as Eboracum, and traces of Roman garrison buildings survive throughout the city. After the Empire's collapse in the 5th century, the Saxons built Eoforwic on the ruins of a fort, but were soon defeated by Vikings, who called the city Jorvik and used it as a base from which to subjugate the countryside. When the Normans arrived in the 11th century, they emulated the Vikings by using the city as a military base. They also established the foundations of York Minster, the largest Gothic cathedral in northern Europe. The timber-frame buildings on the medieval street known as the Shambles suggest what the city looked like in Tudor times.

GETTING HERE AND AROUND

If you're driving, take the M1 north from London. Stay on it to Leeds, and then take the A64 northeast for 25 miles to York. The journey should take around 4 to 5 hours. Megabus coaches leave from Victoria Coach Station 7 times a day (6–7½ hours) and National Express buses depart from London's Victoria Coach Station approximately 11 times a day (5½–8 hours). Grand Central and London

North East Line trains run from London's King's Cross Station every 6–30 minutes during the week (2 hours). York Station, just outside the city walls, has a line of taxis out front to take you to your hotel. If you don't have bags, the walk to town takes 8 minutes.

York's city center is mostly closed to traffic and very walkable. The old center is a compact, dense web of narrow streets and tiny medieval alleys called "snickelways." These provide shortcuts across the city center, but they're not on maps, so you never quite know where you'll end up, which in York is often a pleasant surprise.

TOURS

Association of Voluntary Guides to the City of York

Established more than 60 years ago, this organization arranges short walking tours around the city, taking in two medieval gateways, a walk along the ancient walls, and a visit to a medieval church, in addition to well-known sights. The tours are free, but tips are appreciated. Tours happen three times a day in June through August and two times a day the rest of the year. ☒ 1 Museum St. ☎ 01904/550098 ⊕ www.avgyork.co.uk ☜ Free.

Ghost Trail of York

TOUR—SIGHT | FAMILY | Still going strong after 21 years, the Ghost Trail of York has guides well versed in local lore, combining traditional spooky tales, Victorian tragedies, and more recent reports of modern ghostly phenomena. The 70-minute tours start at 7:30 pm at the west doors of the Minster. ☒ York ⊹ By west doors of the Minster ☎ 01904/633276 ⊕ www.ghosttrail.co.uk ☜ £4.

Original Ghost Walk of York

TOUR—SIGHT | FAMILY | Claiming to be the world's first Ghost Walk, the Original Ghost Walk of York presents the city's ghost tales as a combination of "history and mystery," with an emphasis

on accuracy and authenticity. The tours depart at 8 pm from in front of the King's Arms Pub near Ouse Bridge. ☒ Kings St. ⊹ In front of King's Arms Pub ☎ 01759/373090 ⊕ www.theoriginal-ghostwalkofyork.co.uk ☜ £5.

ESSENTIALS

VISITOR INFORMATION Visit York. ☒ 1 Museum St. ☎ 01904/555670 ⊕ www.visityork.org.

 Sights

City of York Walls

HISTORIC SITE | Almost 3 miles of original medieval town walls remain around York, more than any other city in England. In the 9th century, invading Vikings buried the original Roman defensive walls, built some 1,900 years ago, under earthen ramparts topped with wooden stakes. These in turn were replaced by the current stone walls in the 13th and 14th centuries. In the mid-19th century, the walls, which had fallen into disrepair, were restored and maintained for public access, and you can now walk along a narrow paved path at the top and enjoy outstanding views (the whole circuit takes about two hours). In spring, the remains of the Viking embankment at the base are alive with daffodils. The walls are crossed periodically by York's distinctive "bars," or fortified gates: the portcullis on Monk's Bar on Goodramgate is still in working order, and Walmgate Bar in the east is the only gate in England with an intact barbican, although one scarred by the cannonballs fired during the Civil War. Bootham Bar in Exhibition Square was the defensive bastion for the north road, and Micklegate Bar, in the city's southwest corner, was traditionally the monarch's entrance. To access the path and lookout towers, find a staircase at one of the many breaks in the walls. ☒ York ☎ 01904/551550 ⊕ www.yorkwalls.org.uk.

York

KEY

- 1 Exploring Sights
- 1 Restaurants
- 1 Hotels
- *i* Tourist information

Sights ▼

1 City of York Walls **E2**
2 DIG **E4**
3 Jorvik Viking Centre **C4**
4 National
  Railway Museum **A1**
5 The Shambles........... **D3**
6 Stonegate................ **D2**
7 York Minster............ **D2**
8 Yorkshire
  Air Museum **E4**
9 Yorkshire Museum....... **E4**

Restaurants ▼

1 Betty's Cafe
  Tea Rooms................ **C2**
2 The Blue Barbakan..... **D5**
3 Café Concerto........... **D2**
4 Melton's.................. **A5**

Hotels ▼

1 Dairy Guest House...... **A5**
2 The Grand Hotel
  and Spa **B2**
3 Grange Hotel **D1**
4 Gray's Court Hotel **E2**
5 Hotel du Vin **A3**
6 Middlethorpe
  Hall & Spa **C5**

DIG

ARCHAEOLOGICAL SITE | FAMILY | This reproduction of an archaeological dig in and beneath an old church is a great way to inspire an interest in history and archaeology in young people. A venture by the people behind the Jorvik Viking Centre, DIG is supervised by knowledge-able experts. Kids dig in the dirt to "find" Roman or Viking artifacts, and everyone heads to the lab afterwards to learn what previous archaeological finds discovered on the site have revealed about former inhabitants. ⊠ *St. Saviour's Church, St. Saviourgate* 🕾 *01904/615505* ⊕ *digyork. com* ⊐ *£7; joint admission with Jorvik Viking Centre £15.50.*

Jorvik Viking Centre

ARCHAEOLOGICAL SITE | FAMILY | This kid-fo-cused exhibition re-creates, based on extensive research, a 10th-century Viking village, with everything from the blind storyteller to the slaughter yard awash in offal. The olfactory element is especially popular with children (even the open sewer), as is the Disneyesque "travel through time" machine that propels you above straw huts and mannequins wear-ing Viking dress. Commentary is provided in six languages. Kids get a lot out of it, but adults are unlikely to learn anything new. A small collection of Viking-era arti-facts is on display at the end of the ride. ⊠ *Coppergate* 🕾 *01904/615505* ⊕ *www. jorvikvikingcentre.co.uk* ⊐ *£12.50; joint admission with DIG £15.50.*

★ National Railway Museum

MUSEUM | FAMILY | A must for train lovers, Britain's biggest railway museum houses part of the national collection of rail vehicles. Don't miss such gleaming giants of the steam era as the *Mallard*, holder of the world speed record for a steam engine (126 mph), and a replica of the prototype steam engine, the *Rocket*. Passenger cars used by Queen Victoria are on display, as is the only Japanese bullet train to be seen outside Japan, along with railway-related art, posters, and memorabilia. You can climb aboard some of the trains and occasionally take a short trip on one. There's also a little tourist train that makes the short journey to York Minster (£3). ⊠ *Leeman Rd.* 🕾 *03330/161010* ⊕ *www.railwaymuse-um.org.uk.*

The Shambles

NEIGHBORHOOD | York's best-preserved medieval street has shops and resi-dences in half-timber buildings with overhangs so massive you could almost reach across the narrow gap from one second-floor window to another. Once a hub of butchers (meat hooks are still fastened outside some of the doors), today it's mostly filled with independent shops and remains highly atmospheric. ⊠ *York* ✛ *Off The Stonebow* ⊕ *www. insideyork.co.uk.*

Stonegate

NEIGHBORHOOD | This narrow, pedes-trian-only street lined with Tudor and 18th-century storefronts retains consid-erable charm. First paved during Roman times (the original Roman road lies six feet below), it's been a central thorough-fare for almost 2,000 years. Today it's lined with interesting independent shops including upscale boutiques, jewelers, and quirky one-offs. A passage just off Stonegate, at 52A, leads to the remains of a 12th century Norman stone house attached to a more recent structure. You can still see the old Norman wall and window. ■**TIP→ Look out for the little red "printer's devil" at No. 33, a medieval symbol of a printer's premises. And above the doorway of No. 35 at the intersection of Stonegate and High Petergate, Minerva reclines on a stack of books, indicating they were once sold within.** ⊠ *Stonegate between Petergate and Davygate.*

★ York Minster

BUILDING | The city's focal point, this vast cathedral is the largest Gothic building north of the Alps and attracts almost as many visitors as London's Westminster Abbey. Inside, the effect created by its

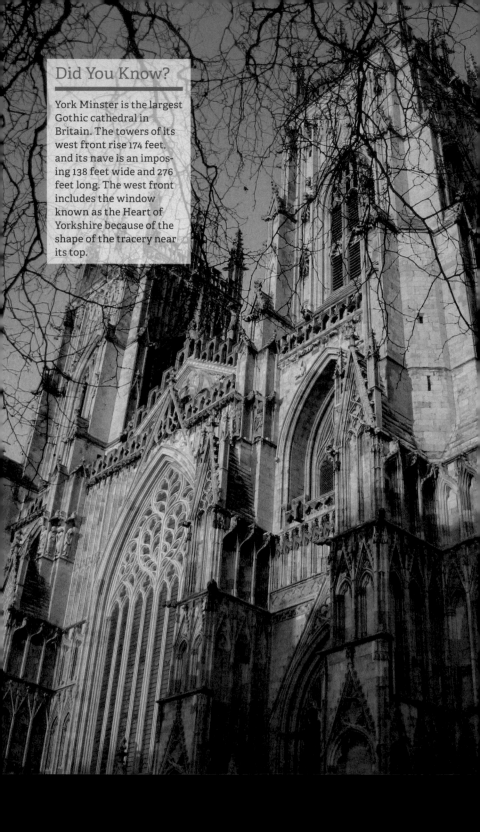

Did You Know?

York Minster is the largest
Gothic cathedral in
Britain. The towers of its
west front rise 174 feet,
and its nave is an impos-
ing 138 feet wide and 276
feet long. The west front
includes the window
known as the Heart of
Yorkshire because of the
shape of the tracery near
its top.

soaring pillars and lofty vaulted ceilings is almost overpowering. Binoculars may be helpful for viewing the loftiest of the 128 dazzling stained-glass windows. While mere numbers can't convey the scale of the building, the central towers are 200 feet high while the Minster itself is 519 feet long, 249 feet across its transepts, and 90 feet from floor to roof. Among the especially notable contributions to the building's uplifting splendor is the ornamentation of the 14th-century nave: the east window, one of the greatest pieces of medieval glazing in the world; the north transept's Five Sisters windows, five tall lancets of gray-tinged 13th-century glass; the enormous choir screen depicting stylized images of every king of England from William the Conqueror to Henry VI; and the masterful tracery of the Rose Window, with elements commemorating the 1486 marriage of Henry VII and Elizabeth of York, a union which ended the Wars of the Roses and started the Tudor dynasty. Don't miss the exquisite 13th-century **Chapter House,** with its superb medieval ribbed wooden roof and fine traceried stained-glass windows; the **Treasury;** the **Crypt;** and the interactive Revealing York Minster exhibition in the **undercroft,** where you can see the remains of a Roman barracks, the Minster's Norman foundations, stained glass, and the 10th-century Horn of Ulf carved from an elephant tusk and donated by a Viking nobleman. After exploring the cathedral at ground level, climb the 275 winding steps to the roof of the great **Central Tower**, which offers both close-up glimpses of the cathedral's detailed carvings and panoramic views of the city. Allow 45 minutes for the Tower tour, which is by timed admission only. Don't miss the newly restored great east window, Britain's largest expanse of medieval stained glass with its 311 stained-glass panels dating back to the 15th century. ■ TIP→ **To experience the cathedral at its most atmospheric, attend one of the evensong services**

with organ and choir. ⊠ *Minster Yard* ☎ *01904/557200* ⊕ *www.yorkminster. org* ▨ *Minster £11.50, Minster and Tower £16.50.*

Yorkshire Air Museum

MILITARY SITE | FAMILY | Located on 22 acres of parkland, this is the country's largest World War II airfield that's open to the public. The independent museum showcases more than 60 historic vehicles and aircraft, many of which are still in working condition and are certain to delight aviation enthusiasts. Planes range from early-20th-century biplanes and gliders, such as the Eastchurch Kitten (the only surviving one in the world), to Spitfires, other World War II–era planes, and contemporary fighter jets. There are also exhibits devoted to military vehicles, aircraft weaponry, and Royal Air Force uniforms. The museum is home to a memorial and gardens commemorating British and Allied service members who lost their lives in conflict. ⊠ *Halifax Way, Elvington* ☎ *01904/608595* ⊕ *www. yorkshireairmuseum.org* ▨ *£12.*

Yorkshire Museum

MUSEUM | The ecological and archaeological history of the county is the focus of this museum in an early-19th-century Greek Revival–style building with massive Doric columns. Themed galleries focus mostly on Roman, Anglian, Viking, and medieval periods, with nearly 1 million objects, including the 15th-century Middleham Jewel, a pendant gleaming with a large sapphire; a Paleolithic hand axe; and an extremely rare copperplate helmet, a 1,200-year-old Viking artifact. Another exhibition documents Yorkshire during the Jurassic period. ⊠ *St. Mary's Lodge, Museum Gardens* ☎ *01904/687687* ⊕ *www.yorkshiremu-seum.org.uk* ▨ *Museum £7.27; gardens and observatory free.*

Restaurants

Betty's Cafe Tea Rooms

$ | CAFÉ | Betty's has been a York institution since 1936. The decor—inspired by the art deco ocean liner the *Queen Mary*—the dessert trolleys, and the solicitous white-aproned staff all contribute to an impression of stepping back in time to a more genteel era. **Known for:** charming afternoon tea; cool World War II history; pastries and old-fashioned sweets. ⑤ *Average main: £12* ✉ *6–8 Helen's Sq., off Stonegate* ☏ *01904/659142* ⊕ *www.bettys.co.uk* ☉ *Closed Sun.*

The Blue Barbakan

$ | EASTERN EUROPEAN | This cozy independent restaurant receives rave reviews for its hearty Eastern European fare. You'll find largely Polish dishes, including favorites like pierogi, bigos (a hunter's stew made with cabbage, wild mushroom, and sausage), pancetta-wrapped rabbit leg, and schnitzel, as well as vegetarian options. **Known for:** excellent Polish-inspired dishes; big crowds; good value. ⑤ *Average main: 15* ✉ *34 Fossgate* ☏ *01904/672474* ⊕ *www.bluebarbakan.co.uk.*

Café Concerto

$$ | BRITISH | Wallpaper made from sheet music reiterates the musical theme at this relaxed, intimate bistro in sight of York Minster. The kitchen serves simple, house-made café classics with an emphasis on local ingredients. **Known for:** hearty portions; vegan and gluten-free options; friendly atmosphere. ⑤ *Average main: £16* ✉ *21 High Petergate* ☏ *01904/610478* ⊕ *www.cafeconcerto.biz.*

Melton's

$$$$ | MODERN BRITISH | This family-run restaurant in what was once a Victorian shop uses locally sourced Yorkshire produce to create a seasonal, highly imaginative take on Modern British cuisine. Selections include slow-cooked duck egg with Jerusalem artichoke and oyster mushrooms; venison with celeriac and damson plums; and cod in smoked cream, apples, dates, and raisins. **Known for:** informal atmosphere despite Michelin star; friendly, involved owners; lots of extras like amuse-bouches and palate cleansers. ⑤ *Average main: £38* ✉ *7 Scarcroft Rd.* ☏ *01904/634341* ⊕ *www.meltonsrestaurant.co.uk* ☉ *Closed Sun., Mon., and 3 wks at Christmas. No lunch Tues.*

Hotels

Dairy Guest House

$$ | B&B/INN | This former dairy in a Victorian town house near the city walls retains atmospheric original features like stained or etched glass, period fireplaces, and ornate plaster cornices. **Pros:** nice period details; comfortable rooms; good breakfast. **Cons:** small bathrooms; two-night minimum stay; few amenities. ⑤ *Rooms from: £160* ✉ *3 Scarcroft Rd.* ☏ *01904/639367* ⊕ *www.dairyguesthouse.co.uk* ⇥ *6 rooms* ⏃⃝ *Free breakfast.*

The Grand Hotel and Spa

$$ | HOTEL | This handsome, comfortable hotel near the train station—not surprising, considering it was formerly the headquarters of the regional railroad—was built in 1906 and retains many original features, such as solid mahogany doors, beautiful tilework on the stairwells, and art nouveau ironwork. **Pros:** beautiful building; spacious rooms; good location. **Cons:** continental breakfast is average; occasional lapses in service; some unexpected charges. ⑤ *Rooms from: £162* ✉ *Station Rise* ☏ *01904/380038* ⊕ *www.thegrandyork.co.uk* ⇥ *207 rooms* ⏃⃝ *Free breakfast.*

Grange Hotel

$ | HOTEL | Built in the early 19th century as the home for two wealthy members of the York clergy, this luxurious boutique hotel decorated with racing memorabilia goes in for traditional country house style, with tastefully decorated bedrooms boasting lovely period textiles, mantel-pieces, and four-poster beds. **Pros:** nice ambience; some on-site parking; helpful staff. **Cons:** some rooms small; restaurant food uneven; no elevator. $ *Rooms from: £116* ✉ *1 Clifton* ☎ *01904/644744* ⊕ *www.grangehotel.co.uk* ⤳ *41 rooms* ❘❉❘ *Free breakfast.*

Gray's Court Hotel

$$ | **HOTEL** | Close to York Minster yet with its own half-acre garden, Gray's Court is an oasis of countryhouse peacefulness in the city center and the oldest inhabited house in York. **Pros:** peaceful but central location; lovely period decor; access to City Walls. **Cons:** expensive parking; breakfast service slow; decor not for everyone. $ *Rooms from: £170* ✉ *Chapter House St.* ☎ *01904/612613* ⊕ *www.grayscourtyork.com* ⤳ *11 rooms* ❘❉❘ *Free breakfast.*

Hotel du Vin

$$ | **HOTEL** | A converted 19th-century orphanage, the York outpost of this boutique hotel mini-chain has preserved the exposed brick walls and arched doorways of the original building. **Pros:** makes great use of the space; good-sized rooms; comfortable beds. **Cons:** some rooms can be damp; low bathroom lighting; on outskirts of city. $ *Rooms from: £129* ✉ *89 The Mount* ☎ *0844/748-9268* ⊕ *www.hotelduvin.com* ⤳ *44 rooms* ❘❉❘ *Free breakfast.*

Middlethorpe Hall & Spa

$$$ | **HOTEL** | Aimed at visitors who prize period details like oak-paneled walls, four-poster beds, carved wood bannisters, and window seats, and whose idea of luxury is a bowl of fresh daffodils, this splendidly restored Queen Anne building with mid-18th-century additions feels less like a country-house hotel than an actual country house. **Pros:** period luxury; gorgeous grounds; attentive staff. **Cons:** poor water pressure; outside city center; might be too formal for some. $ *Rooms from: £229* ✉ *Bishopthorpe Rd.*

☎ *01904/641241* ⊕ *www.middlethorpe. com* ⤳ *29 rooms* ❘❉❘ *Free breakfast.*

Nightlife

The Black Swan

BARS/PUBS | Located in a half-timber 15th-century building complete with wood paneling, flagstone floors, and mullioned windows, this pub (there's been one here since the 16th century) serves home-cooked bar food and hosts folk and acoustic music nights. There are three rooms upstairs if you wish to spend the night. ✉ *Peasholme Green* ☎ *01904/679131* ⊕ *www.blackswanyork. com.*

Old White Swan

BARS/PUBS | Spreading across five half-timber 16th-century buildings on busy Goodramgate, the Old White Swan is known for its good pub lunches and its ghosts—it claims to have more than the equally venerable Black Swan. ✉ *80 Goodramgate* ☎ *01904/540911* ⊕ *www. nicholsonspubs.co.uk.*

Snickleway Inn

BARS/PUBS | With its wood paneling and open brick fireplaces, the allegedly haunted Snickleway Inn provides a real sense of stepping back into the 15th century (when it was built). Its colorful past includes being used by Royalists during the English Civil War to store ammunition and explosives. ✉ *47 Goodramgate* ☎ *01904/656138.*

Shopping

The Antiques Centre York

ANTIQUES/COLLECTIBLES | With five showrooms spread over three floors of a Georgian town house, this antiques mecca sells furniture, jewelry, ceramics, coins, vintage fashion, and collectibles—Roman, Georgian, Victorian, Edwardian, and art deco—from more than 120 dealers, who display their wares in "cabinets." ✉ 41 Stonegate ☎ 01904/635888 ⊕ www.theantiquescentreyork.co.uk.

Minster Gate Bookshop

BOOKS/STATIONERY | This bookshop in a Georgian town house has been in the trade since 1580 and sells secondhand and antiquarian books as well as new children's books, illustrated editions, old maps, and prints, largely of Yorkshire in general and York in particular. ✉ 8 Minster Gate ☎ 01904/621812 ⊕ www.minstergatebooks.co.uk.

Harrogate

21 miles west of York, 11 miles south of Ripon, 16 miles north of Leeds.

During the Regency and early Victorian periods, it became fashionable for the aristocratic and wealthy to "take the waters" at British spa towns, combining the alleged health benefits with socializing. In Yorkshire, the most elegant spa destination was Harrogate, and today its mainly Victorian buildings, parks, and spas still provide a relaxing getaway.

GETTING HERE AND AROUND

Trains from York leave every hour or so, and the journey takes about 40 minutes. There's at least one direct train daily from London. National Express buses leave from York every 30 minutes most days; the journey takes about 35 minutes. By car, Harrogate is off A59 and well marked. It's a walkable town, so you can park in one of its central lots and explore on foot.

Within and around Harrogate, the Harrogate & District bus company provides area services, and taxis are plentiful.

ESSENTIALS

VISITOR INFORMATION **Harrogate Tourist Information Centre.** ✉ Royal Baths, Crescent Rd. ☎ 01423/537300 ⊕ www.visitharrogate.co.uk.

 Sights

Royal Pump Room Museum

LOCAL INTEREST | Built in 1842 over the original sulfur well that made Harrogate a destination, the Pump Room housed in this octagonal structure sold 1,500 glasses of water to spa goers each morning in its heyday (so no, designer water is not a modern phenomenon). The pungent odor of Europe's strongest sulfuric well is still very much present. The museum has displays of bygone spa treatment paraphernalia alongside a somewhat eccentric collection of 19th-century clothes, fine china, and bicycles. ✉ Crown Pl. ☎ 01423/556188 ⊕ www.harrogate.gov.uk ☑ £3.50.

The Stray

CITY PARK | These 200 acres of grassy parkland wrapped around Harrogate's Old Town become a riot of color in spring. Many of the mineral springs that made the town famous bubble below. ✉ Harrogate ☎ 01423/841097 ⊕ www.harrogate.gov.uk.

Turkish Baths Harrogate

HOT SPRINGS | Dating from 1897, these Moorish-inspired, fully restored Turkish baths look virtually the same as they would have to the many Victorians who visited them. After changing into your bathing suit, relax on luxurious lounge chairs in the stunning mosaic-tile warming room. Move on to the increasingly hot sauna rooms, and then soak up eucalyptus mist in the steam room before braving the icy plunge pool. You can also book a massage or facial. Open hours are divided into single-sex and mixed sessions, so book in advance. ✉ Royal Baths, Parliament St. ☎ 01423/556746 ⊕ www.turkishbathsharrogate.co.uk ☑ £19–£32 per session; 45-minute guided tour £3.80.

Valley Gardens

CITY PARK | FAMILY | Southwest of the town center, these 17 acres of formal gardens include a children's boating lake,

Around York

North York Moors Nat'l Park

tennis courts, skate park, adventure playground, paddling pool, and a little café.
✉ *Valley Dr.* ✛ *Junction with Cornwall Rd. and Royal Parade* ☎ *01423/500600*
⊕ *www.harrogate.gov.uk.*

🍴 Restaurants

★ Betty's Cafe Tea Rooms

$ | **CAFÉ** | This celebrated Yorkshire tearoom began life in Harrogate in 1919, when a Swiss restaurateur brought his Alpine pastries and chocolates to England. The welcoming interior has changed little since it first opened, and the extensive array of teas not at all. **Known for:** classic English afternoon tea; traditional cakes, pastries, and sandwiches; nightly live piano music. **$** *Average main: £14*
✉ *1 Parliament St.* ☎ *01423/814070*
⊕ *www.bettys.co.uk.*

★ The Yorke Arms

$$$ | **MODERN BRITISH** | The peaceful rural location of this restaurant with rooms in the scenic Nidderdale Valley belies the sophistication of its distinctive cooking: it has been consistently rated as one of the top five dining spots not only in Yorkshire, but in the United Kingdom. It won its Michelin star with an emphasis on seasonal ingredients, creative combinations of flavors, and elegant presentations. **Known for:** daily changing menu of high-quality Modern British dishes; fabulous dessert selection; historic building in a peaceful setting. **$** *Average main: £30*
✉ *Ramsgill-in-Nidderdale, Pateley Bridge*
☎ *01423/755243* ⊕ *www.theyorkearms.co.uk* ☾ *Closed Sun.–Tues.*

Hotels

Hotel du Vin

$$ | **HOTEL** | This boutique hotel may sprawl through eight Georgian houses, but the public rooms, with their stripped-wood floors and clubby leather sofas, combine a contemporary, relaxed atmosphere with period charm. **Pros:** knowledgeable spa therapists; wonderful wine list; good breakfasts. **Cons:** some rooms tired; toilet maintenance could be better; bistro food uneven. ⑤ *Rooms from: £134* ✉ *Prospect Pl.* ☎ *01423/608121* ⊕ *www.hotelduvin.com* ⟿ *52 rooms* ⦿ *No meals.*

Castle Howard

15 miles northeast of York.

The baroque grandeur of Castle Howard is without equal in northern England. The grounds, enhanced by groves of trees, a twinkling lake, and a perfect lawn, add to the splendor.

GETTING HERE AND AROUND

There's daily scheduled bus service between Malton and Castle Howard, which is well outside any town and several miles off any public road. The nearest train stop is Malton, and you can take a taxi from there. By car, follow signs off A64 from York.

⦿ Sights

★ Castle Howard

CASTLE/PALACE | Standing in the Howardian Hills to the west of Malton, Castle Howard is an outstanding example of English baroque architecture, with a distinctive roofline punctuated by a magnificent central dome. It served as Brideshead, the home of the fictional Flyte family in *Brideshead Revisited,* Evelyn Waugh's tale of aristocratic woe, in both its 1981 TV and 2008 film adaptations. The house was the first commission for playwright-turned-architect Sir John Vanbrugh, who, assisted by Nicholas Hawksmoor, designed it for the third Earl of Carlisle, a member of the Howard family. The central structure was started in 1701 and took 25 years to complete (with a Palladian wing added subsequently), but the end result was a stately home of audacious grandeur.

A spectacular central hallway with soaring columns supports a hand-painted ceiling that dwarfs all visitors, and there's no shortage of splendor elsewhere: vast family portraits, intricate marble fireplaces, immense tapestries, Victorian silver on polished tables, and a great many marble busts. Outside, the neoclassical landscape of carefully arranged woods, lakes, and lawns led 18th-century bon vivant Horace Walpole to comment that a pheasant at Castle Howard lived better than a duke elsewhere. Hidden throughout the 1,000 acres of formal and woodland gardens are temples, statues, fountains, and a grand mausoleum—even a fanciful children's playground. There's also a restaurant, two cafés, and three shops. Hourly tours of the grounds, included in the admission price, fill you in on more background and history. ✉ *Castle Howard, Malton* ✛ *A64 past York, then B1257* ☎ *01653/648333* ⊕ *www.castlehoward.co.uk* ✉ *House and gardens £19.95; gardens only £9.95 in winer, £12.95 in high season* ⦿ *House closed Nov.–late Mar.*

Saltaire

12 miles east of Leeds, 8 miles east of Haworth.

This planned community, built by a philanthropic Victorian industrialist in the wool trade to house his workers, perfectly preserves the architecture—both residential and industrial—of the period.

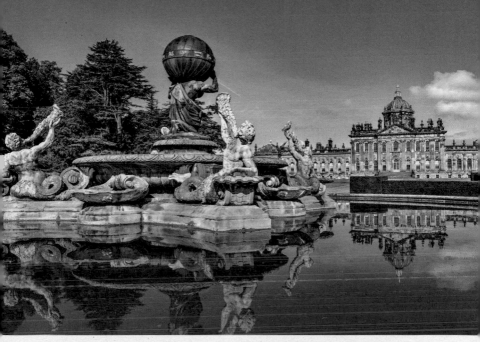

At Castle Howard, a baroque masterpiece, the splendor of the grounds matches the opulence of the sprawling house.

GETTING HERE AND AROUND

Saltaire has regular bus and train services from the nearby town of Bradford. Drivers should take A650 from Bradford and follow the signs.

ESSENTIALS

VISITOR INFORMATION Saltaire Visitor Information Centre. ⊠ *Victoria Hall, Victoria Rd., Shipley* ☎ *01274/433678* ⊕ *www. saltairevillage.info.*

Sights

Hockney 1853 Gallery

MUSEUM | Housed in a historic mill building that dates back to 1853, this gallery is devoted to a remarkable exhibition of over 300 works by Bradford-born artist David Hockney. The gallery also sells art materials and art books, plus there's a shopping complex and two restaurants in the building. ⊠ *Salt's Mill, Victoria Rd., Shipley* ☎ *01274/531163* ⊕ *www.saltsmill. org.uk.*

Saltaire

FACTORY | A UNESCO World Heritage Site, Saltaire was built as a model village in the mid-19th century by textile magnate Sir Titus Salt, who, aspiring to create the ideal industrial community, decided to relocate his factories from the dark mills of Bradford to the countryside. The Italianate village (the main building resembles a palazzo) is remarkably well preserved, with its former mills and houses now turned into shops, restaurants, and galleries, as well as private homes. The largest factory in the world when it was built in 1853, today it contains an art gallery, along with crafts and furniture shops. ⊠ *Saltaire Rd., Shipley* ☎ *01274/433678* ⊕ *www.saltairevillage. info.*

Haworth

8 miles west of Saltaire.

Whatever Haworth might have been in the past, today it's Brontë country. This old stone-built textile village on the edge of the Yorkshire Moors long ago gave up its own personality and allowed itself to be taken over by the literary sisters, their powerful novels, and legions of fans. In 1820, when Anne, Emily, and Charlotte were very young, their father relocated them and their other three siblings away from their old home in Bradford to Haworth. The sisters—Emily (author of *Wuthering Heights,* 1847), Charlotte (*Jane Eyre,* 1847), and Anne (*The Tenant of Wildfell Hall,* 1848) were all influenced by the stark, dramatic landscape.

These days, it seems that every building they ever glanced at has been turned into a memorial, shop, or museum. The Haworth Visitor Center has good information about accommodations, maps, books on the Brontës, and inexpensive leaflets to help you find your way to such outlying *Wuthering Heights* sites as Ponden Hall (Thrushcross Grange) and Ponden Kirk (Penistone Crag).

GETTING HERE AND AROUND

To reach Haworth by bus or train, buy a Metro Day Rover for bus and rail (£8.40), take the Metro train from Leeds train station to Keighley, and walk to the bus stop, where you change to a Keighley & District bus to Haworth. On weekends and bank holidays you can opt to take the old-school steam-engined Keighley and Worth Valley Railway to continue on to Haworth.

The streets and houses of Haworth look much as they did when the Brontë sisters lived and wrote their famous novels in this village near the moors.

By car, Haworth is an easy 25-mile drive on A629 from Leeds; it's well signposted, and there's plenty of cheap parking in town.

ESSENTIALS

VISITOR INFORMATION Haworth Visitor Information Centre. ⊠ *2–4 West La., Haworth* 🕾 *01535/642329* ⊕ *www.visit-bradford.com.*

 Sights

★ Brontë Parsonage Museum

HOUSE | The most evocative of Haworth's Brontë sights is this somber Georgian (1778) house, the sisters' family home, where you can see original furniture (some bought by Charlotte after the success of *Jane Eyre*), portraits, and books. The Brontës moved here when the Reverend Patrick Brontë was appointed vicar of the local church, but tragedy soon struck—his wife, Maria, and their two eldest children died within five years. The museum explores the family's tragic story, bringing it to life with a strong collection of enchanting mementos of the four children. These include tiny books they made when they were still very young; Charlotte's wedding bonnet; and the sisters' spidery, youthful graffiti on the nursery wall. Branwell, the Brontës' only brother, painted several of the portraits on display. ⊠ *Church St., Haworth* 🕾 *01535/642323* ⊕ *www.bronte.org.uk* 🎫 *£9.50* ⊗ *Closed Jan.*

Brontë Waterfall

BODY OF WATER | If you have the time, pack a lunch and walk for 2¾ miles or so from Haworth along a field path, lane, and moorland track to the lovely, isolated waterfall that has, inevitably, been renamed in honor of the sisters. It was one of their favorite haunts, which they wrote about in poems and letters. ⊠ *Haworth* ✛ *From Haworth Church on Main St., follow signs* ⊕ *www.bronteadventures.co.uk/moors/bronte-waterfall.*

Keighley and Worth Valley Railway

TOUR—SIGHT | FAMILY | Haworth is one stop along the route of this scenic 5-mile heritage railway between Keighley and Oxenhope through the picturesque Worth Valley, as seen in numerous film and television shows including *Peaky Blinders*. Many of the trains are pulled by handsome steam engines. Frequent themed special events add to the fun. ⊠ *Haworth Station, Station Rd., Haworth* ☎ *01535/645214* ⊕ *www.kwvr.co.uk* 🎫 *£13 round-trip, £18 Day Rover ticket* ⊘ *Closed Jan.; weekdays Feb.–early Apr., late Apr.–mid-May, and Nov.–Dec.; Mon., Tues., Thurs., and Fri. mid-May–late May and mid-Sept.–late Oct.; and Mon. and Tues. mid-June–mid-July.*

Main Street

NEIGHBORHOOD | Haworth's steep, cobbled high street has changed little in outward appearance since the early 19th century, but it now acts as a funnel for crowds heading for points of interest: the **Black Bull** pub, where the reprobate Branwell Brontë drank himself into an early grave (his stool is kept in mint condition); the former **post office** (now a bookshop) from which Charlotte, Emily, and Anne sent their manuscripts to their London publishers; and the **church,** with its atmospheric graveyard (Charlotte and Emily are buried in the family vault inside the church; Anne is buried in Scarborough). ⊠ *Haworth.*

Top Withens

LOCAL INTEREST | The foreboding ruin of a mansion perched on a bleak hilltop three miles from Haworth, Top Withens is often assumed to be the inspiration for the fictional Wuthering Heights. Brontë scholars say it probably isn't; even in its heyday, the house never fit the book's description of Heathcliff's domain. Still, it's an inspirational walk across the moors. There and back from Haworth is a 3½-hour walk along a well-marked footpath that goes past the Brontë waterfall. If you've read *Wuthering Heights*, you don't need to be reminded to wear sturdy shoes and protective clothing. ⊠ *Haworth* ⊕ *www.haworth-village.org.uk.*

Restaurants

Haworth Old Hall

$ | BRITISH | This 16th-century building with two magnificent stone fireplaces is now a welcoming gastro-pub, and the friendly and efficient service gets high marks. The menu is hearty British food, with mains like pan-fried chicken breast in a creamy mushroom and brandy sauce as well as modern lighter options like jackfruit croquettes or a winter vegetable pot pie, plus sandwiches and burgers. **Known for:** good beer selection; filling portions of classic British dishes; atmospheric setting. ⑤ *Average main: £13* ⊠ *Sun St., Haworth* ☎ *01535/642709* ⊕ *www.hawortholdhall.co.uk.*

Hotels

The Apothecary Guest House

$ | B&B/INN | Built in 1640, this family-run B&B is located at the top of the cobbled main street, opposite the Brontë church. **Pros:** scenic views; town center location; helpful hosts. **Cons:** rooms at front may have noise from pub; limited time to order breakfast; decor may be too basic for some. ⑤ *Rooms from: £60* ⊠ *86 Main St., Haworth* ☎ *01535/643642* ⊕ *www. theapothecaryguesthouse.co.uk* ⤸ *7 rooms* ⦿❘ *Free breakfast.*

Durham

250 miles north of London, 15 miles south of Newcastle.

The great medieval city of Durham, seat of County Durham, stands dramatically on a rocky spur overlooking the countryside. Its cathedral and castle, a UNESCO World Heritage Site, rise together on a wooded peninsula almost entirely encircled by the River Wear (rhymes with "beer"). For centuries, these two ancient structures have dominated Durham, a thriving university town that's the Northeast's equivalent of Oxford or Cambridge. Steep, narrow streets overlooked by perilously angled medieval houses and 18th-century town houses make for fun exploring. In the most attractive part of the city, near the Palace Green and along the river, people go boating, anglers cast their lines, and strollers walk along the shaded paths. For great views, take a short stroll along the River Wear, and cross the 17th-century Prebends Footbridge. You can return to town via the 12th-century Framwellgate Bridge.

Despite the military advantages of its location, Durham was founded surprisingly late, probably in about the year 1000, growing up around a small Saxon church erected to house the remains of St. Cuthbert. It was the Normans, under William the Conqueror, who put Durham on the map, building the first defensive castle and beginning work on the cathedral. From here, Durham's prince-bishops, granted almost dictatorial local powers by William in 1072, kept a tight rein on the county, coining their own money and maintaining their own laws and courts. It wasn't until 1836 that these rights were restored to the English Crown.

GETTING HERE AND AROUND

East Coast trains from London's King's Cross Station arrive at the centrally located Durham Station once an hour during the day. The journey takes about three hours. There are even more regular non-direct trains via York, with a similar journey time. A handful of National Express and Megabus buses make the seven-hour trip from London daily. The Durham Cathedral Bus (Route 40) links parking lots and the train and bus stations with the cathedral, castle, and university. Between 10 am and 4 pm Monday through Saturday, cars are subject to a "congestion charge" of

£2 (on top of parking charges) to enter the Palace Green area. You can pay the charge at the Parking Shop or over the phone. Payment must be made by 6 pm on the day of usage, or you'll be subject to a £50 fine.

ESSENTIALS

VISITOR INFORMATION World Heritage Site Visitor Centre. ⊠ *7 Owengate* ☎ *0191/334–3805* ⊕ *www.durhamworldheritagesite.com.* **The Parking Shop.** ⊠ *3-10 Old Pit Ln.* ☎ *0191/384–6633* ⊕ *www.durham.gov.uk.*

Sights

★ **Beamish, the Living Museum of the North**
MUSEUM VILLAGE | FAMILY | Made up of buildings found on-site or moved from elsewhere in the region, this sprawling, award-winning complex—which celebrated its 50th year in 2020—explores the way people in the Northeast lived and worked from the early 1800s to the mid-1900s. A vintage bus and a streetcar take you around the site to various points of interest, including a farm estate; a pit village and colliery; and an entire 1920s town complete with a bank, convenience store, and Masonic hall. Everything is staffed by workers in period costumes, and you can buy era-appropriate food and drinks in the pub, bakery, and "sweet shop" (candy store). As well as the permanent exhibits, there are special events year-round, from weekend-long festivals, where you're encouraged to come in old-style fancy dress, to traditional English celebrations such as May Day and Harvest Festival. Beamish is nine miles northwest of Durham. ■**TIP→ You can spend at least half a day here, and tickets are valid for a whole year in case you want to return.** ⊠ *Off A693, Beamish* ☎ *0191/370–4000* ⊕ *www.beamish.org. uk* ☎ *£19.50* ⊘ *Closed Mon. and Fri. in mid-Jan.–mid-Feb.*

Durham Castle

CASTLE/PALACE | Facing the cathedral across Palace Green, Durham's stately, manorlike castle commands a strategic position above the River Wear. For almost 800 years the castle was the home of the enormously powerful prince-bishops; from here they ruled large tracts of the countryside and acted as the main line of defense against Scottish raiders from the north. Henry VIII was the first to curtail the bishops' autonomy, although it wasn't until the 19th century that they finally had their powers annulled. At that point, the castle was given over to the University of Durham, the third oldest university in England after Oxford and Cambridge (albeit more than 600 years younger; it was founded in 1832). The castle interior can only be seen on a 45-minute guided tour. These are usually available four times a day but are not held when the building is hired out for private events, so it's best to check the website or call ahead. ■TIP➔ **During university vacation times, the castle also offers bed-and-breakfast accommodations in the state rooms for around £200 per night; call or check the website for details.** ⊠ *Palace Green* ☎ *0191/334–2932* ⊕ *www.dur. ac.uk/durham.castle* 🖾 *£5.*

★ Durham Cathedral

RELIGIOUS SITE | A Norman masterpiece in the heart of the city, Durham Cathedral is a vision of strength and fortitude, a far cry from the airy lightness of later Gothic cathedrals. Construction began about 1090, and the main body was finished around 1150. The round arches of the nave and the deep zigzag patterns carved into them typify the heavy, gaunt style of Norman, or Romanesque, building. The technology of Durham, however, was revolutionary; this was the first European cathedral to be given a stone, rather than a wooden, roof.

Note the enormous bronze **Sanctuary Knocker,** shaped like the head of a ferocious mythological beast, mounted on the massive northwestern door. By grasping the ring clenched in the animal's mouth, medieval felons could claim sanctuary; cathedral records show that 331 criminals sought this protection between 1464 and 1524. An unobtrusive tomb at the western end of the cathedral, in the Moorish-influenced **Galilee Chapel,** is the final resting place of the Venerable Bede, an 8th-century Northumbrian monk whose contemporary account of the English people made him the country's first reliable historian. In good weather, and if you're feeling up to it, you can climb the 325 steps up to the tower, which has spectacular views of Durham.

The impressive £10 million **Open Treasure** exhibition displays priceless artifacts from the cathedral's own collection. The exhibition also allows visitors to see parts of the cathedral that were previously closed to the public, including the **Monks Dormitory** and the **Great Kitchen,** with its breathtaking octagonal roof. Treasures on display include Anglo-Saxon art, gold and garnet crosses, elaborate vestments, illuminated manuscripts, and the original coffin of St. Cuthbert. Together it represents one of the most significant single collections of Anglo-Saxon artifacts in the world.

For a more modern take on this ancient monument, check out the elaborate LEGO model of Durham Cathedral, situated between the Undercroft Restaurant and shop. It's made up of more than 300,000 bricks.

Guided tours of the cathedral (one hour) are available Monday through Saturday at 10:30 am, 11 am, and 2 pm, though times can change if there's a special service going on. A choral evensong service takes place Tuesday through Saturday at 5:15 pm and Sunday at 3:30 pm. ⊠ *Palace Green* ☎ *0191/386–4266* ⊕ *www.dur-hamcathedral.co.uk* 🖾 *Free (requested donation £3); Open Treasure £7.50; tower £5; guided tours £5; combined tour and Open Treasure £10* ☉ *No tours Sun.*

Oriental Museum

MUSEUM | A 15-minute walk from the cathedral, this Durham University–owned museum displays fine art and craftwork from all parts of Asia and the Middle East. Galleries are ordered by culture, including Ancient Egypt, Japan, China, and Korea. Among the highlights are some exquisite Qing dynasty jade and lacquer ornaments, ancient tapestries and embroideries from the Himalayas, and a collection of Japanese woodblock prints from the Edo period. ⊠ *Off Elvet Hill Rd.* ☎ *0191/334–5691* ⊕ *www.dur.ac.uk/oriental.museum* ⊠ *£1.50.*

Restaurants

Cafedral

$ | **CAFÉ** | **FAMILY** | Ignore the dad-joke pun—this is a really good, modern, vegetarian- and celiac-friendly café. Mismatched, shabby-chic furniture fills the cozy dining room, where you can enjoy delicious, fresh scones, cakes, gluten-free desserts, and tasty panini and wraps. **Known for:** fantastic gluten-free treats; vegetarian food; good coffee. ⑤ *Average main: £6* ⊠ *Owengate House, 1st fl., Owengate.*

Finbarr's

$$ | **EUROPEAN** | Excellent seafood and indulgent desserts are the specialties at this popular bistro, but there are steaks and a few veggie options on the menu as well. Order the fishcakes with buttered spinach or the jumbo shrimp grilled Tandoori style (with a hint of Indian spice), and save room for the Knickerbocker Glory, an old-fashioned concoction of ice cream, sponge cake, fruit, and chocolate, served in a tall glass. **Known for:** intimate atmosphere; great seafood; heavenly desserts. ⑤ *Average main: £20* ⊠ *Aykley Heads House, Aykley Heads* ☎ *0191/307–7033* ⊕ *www.finbarrsrestaurant.co.uk.*

Hotels

Georgian Town House

$ | **B&B/INN** | At the top of a cobbled street overlooking the cathedral and castle, this family-run guesthouse has small, snug bedrooms with pleasant city views. **Pros:** great city center location; jovial owners; tasty pancakes right downstairs. **Cons:** most rooms are small; decor won't please everyone; some noise from nearby pubs. ⑤ *Rooms from: £95* ⊠ *11 Crossgate* ☎ *0191/386–8070* ⊕ *www.thegeorgiantownhousedurham.co.uk* ⤴ *8 rooms* ⦿⊙ *Free breakfast.*

★ Lumley Castle Hotel

$$ | **HOTEL** | This is a real Norman castle, right down to the dungeons and maze of dark flagstone corridors—one room even has a bathroom hidden behind a bookcase. **Pros:** great for antiques lovers; gorgeous high-ceilinged restaurant; good value out of high season. **Cons:** easy to get lost among winding corridors; a little way out of Durham; (verily) ye banquet is cheesy. ⑤ *Rooms from: £190* ⊠ *Off B1284, Chester-le-Street* ☎ *0191/389–1111* ⊕ *www.lumleycastle.com* ⤴ *73 rooms* ⦿⊙ *No meals.*

Nightlife

The Half Moon Inn

BARS/PUBS | This handsome old pub is popular for its excellent range of traditional ales, as well as for its old-school atmosphere that reminds you pubs like this are a dying breed. ⊠ *86 New Elvet* ☎ *0191/374–1918* ⊕ *www.thehalfmoonindurham.co.uk.*

Market Tavern

BARS/PUBS | Fans of real ales are drawn to the Market Tavern, which has been in business since the late 18th century. Today, it's a Greene King pub, serving a good range of drinks and decent pub food. ⊠ *27 Market Pl.* ☎ *0191/386–2069* ⊕ *www.greeneking-pubs.co.uk.*

Durham and Hadrian's Wall Country

🛍 Shopping

Bramwells Jewellers
JEWELRY/ACCESSORIES | The specialty here is a pendant copy of the gold-and-silver cross of St. Cuthbert. ⊠ 24 Elvet Bridge ☎ 0191/386–8006 ⊕ www.bramwellsjewellers.co.uk.

Durham Indoor Market
SHOPPING CENTERS/MALLS | The food and bric-a-brac stalls in Durham Indoor Market, a Victorian arcade, are open Monday through Saturday, 9 am to 4:30 pm. An excellent farmers' market is held in Market Place in Mar-ket Place on the third Thursday of every month. ⊠ Market Pl. ☎ 0191/384–6153 ⊕ www.durhammarkets.co.uk.

Hadrian's Wall

73 miles from Wallsend, north of New-castle, to Bowness-on-Solway, beyond Carlisle.

The most important Roman relic in Britain extends across the countryside and can be accessed at many different points. Committed hikers can tackle the full, 73-mile-long Hadrian's Wall Path. The Sill National Landscape Discovery Centre, about a mile northwest of Vindolanda, reveals more about the local landscape.

GETTING HERE AND AROUND
The A69 roughly follows Hadrian's Wall, although sometimes it's a few miles in either direction. The best sections of the wall are near the narrower B6318, including Vindolanda, Housesteads Roman Fort, and Chesters Roman Fort. There's

a small railway station at Hexham, with frequent trains from Newcastle.

The aptly named AD122 Hadrian's Wall Country bus runs between Newcastle and Carlisle during the summer months, stopping near all the major destinations along the way. A special "rover ticket" pass gives you unlimited travel on the route for one (£12.50), three (£25), or seven (£50) days. You can extend the tickets to cover any bus operating on the same route for a few extra pounds. Several other local buses depart from Newcastle and other towns in the region to various parts of the wall.

ESSENTIALS

VISITOR INFORMATION AD112 Hadrian's Wall Country Bus. ☎ ⊕ *www.hadrianswall-country.co.uk/travel/bus.*

 Sights

★ Hadrian's Wall

ARCHAEOLOGICAL SITE | Dedicated to the Roman god Terminus, the massive span of Hadrian's Wall once marked the northern frontier of the Roman Empire. Today, remnants of the wall wander across pastures and hills, stretching 73 miles from Wallsend in the east to Bowness-on-Solway in the west. The wall is a UNESCO World Heritage Site, and excavating, interpreting, repairing, and generally managing it remains a Northumbrian growth industry.

At Emperor Hadrian's command, three legions of soldiers began building the wall in AD 122 and finished it in four years. It was constructed by soldiers and masons after repeated invasions by Pictish tribes from what is now Scotland. During the Roman era it was the most heavily fortified wall in the world, with walls 15 feet high and 9 feet thick; behind it lay the vallum, a ditch about 20 feet wide and 10 feet deep. Spaced at 5-mile intervals along the wall were massive forts (such as those at Housesteads and Chesters), which could house up to

1,000 soldiers. Every mile was marked by a thick-walled milecastle (a fort that housed about 30 soldiers), and between each milecastle were two turrets, each lodging four men who kept watch. For more than 250 years the Roman army used the wall to control travel and trade and to fortify Roman Britain against the barbarians to the north.

During the Jacobite Rebellion of 1745, the English army dismantled much of the Roman wall and used the stones to pave what is now the B6318 highway. The most substantial stretches of the remaining wall are between Housesteads and Birdoswald (west of Greenhead). Running through the southern edge of Northumberland National Park and along the sheer escarpment of Whin Sill, this section is also an area of dramatic natural beauty. The ancient ruins, rugged cliffs, dramatic vistas, and spreading pastures make it a great area for hiking. ⊕ *www.hadrianswallcountry.co.uk.*

 Activities

BIKING

Hadrian's Cycleways

BICYCLING | Between Tynemouth and Whitehaven, Hadrian's Cycleway follows the River Tyne from the east coast until Newcastle, where it traces the entire length of Hadrian's Wall. It then continues west to the Irish Sea. Maps and guides are available at the Tourist Information Centre in Newcastle. ⊕ *www.cyclenorthumberland.org.uk/listing/hadrians-cycleway.*

HIKING

Hadrian's Wall Path

HIKING/WALKING | One of Britain's national trails, Hadrian's Wall Path runs the entire 73-mile length of the wall. If you don't have time for it all, take one of the less-challenging circular routes. One of the most scenic (but also most difficult) sections is the 12-mile western stretch between Sewingshields and Greenhead. ⊕ *www.nationaltrail.co.uk/hadrianswall.*

Hexham

22 miles west of Newcastle, 31 miles northwest of Durham.

The busy market town of Hexham is a popular base for visiting Hadrian's Wall. Just a few miles from the most significant remains, it's a bustling working town, but it has enough historic buildings and winding medieval streets to warrant a stop in its own right. First settled in the 7th century, around a Benedictine monastery, Hexham later became a byword for monastic learning, famous for its book painting, sculpture, and singing.

GETTING HERE AND AROUND
The A1 and A69 highways link London and the region (five to six hours). No major bus companies travel here, but the AD122 Hadrian's Wall Country Bus from Newcastle and Carlisle does. East Coast trains take about three hours to travel from London's King's Cross to Newcastle. From there, catch a local train.

Hexham is a small, walkable town. It has infrequent local bus service, but you're unlikely to need it. If you're driving, park in the lot by the tourism office and walk into town. The tourism office has free maps and will point you in the right direction.

ESSENTIALS
VISITOR INFORMATION Hexham Tourist Information Centre. ⊠ *Queens Hall, Beaumont St.* ☏ *01670/620450* ⊕ *www. visithexham.net.*

 ## Sights

Chesters Roman Fort
MILITARY SITE | In a wooded valley on the banks of the North Tyne River, 4 miles north of Hexham, this cavalry fort was known as Cilurnum in Roman times,

when it protected the point where Hadrian's Wall crossed the river. Although the setting is not as dramatic as the nearby Housesteads Roman Fort, this mazelike layout of surviving fortifications is said to be Britain's most complete Roman cavalry fort, while the military bathhouse by the river is the best-preserved Roman structure of its kind in the British Isles. The Museum of Roman Finds includes a fascinating array of artifacts including statues of river and water gods and Roman jewelry. ⊠ *B6318, Chollerford* ☏ *01434/681379* ⊕ *www.english-heritage.org.uk/chesters* ⌷ *£7.20* ⊙ *Closed weekdays in Nov.–Feb.; closed Mon.–Tues. in Mar.*

★ Corbridge Roman Town
ARCHAEOLOGICAL SITE | The foundations of this important Roman garrison town (the farthest north in the entire Roman Empire) are brought to life with a lively audio commentary, plus occasional reenactments during the summer. The recently renovated visitor center houses the Corbridge Hoard, a surprisingly well-preserved collection of tools and personal possessions left behind by Roman soldiers in the 2nd century, as well as other objects found in and around the site. In particular, look out for three items: the Corbridge Lion, a free-standing sandstone sculpture depicting a male lion on top of a deer; the Corbridge Lanx, a large silver dish intricately engraved with mythological scenes; and a gambling soldier's "cheat's dice," which on close inspection features two ones and no six. Corbridge Roman Town is around four miles east of Hexham. ⊠ *Corchester La., Corbridge* ☏ *01434/632349* ⊕ *www. english-heritage.org.uk* ⌷ *£7.90* ⊙ *Closed weekdays Nov.–Feb.*

★ Hexham Abbey
RELIGIOUS SITE | A site of Christian worship for more than 1,300 years, ancient Hexham Abbey forms one side of the town's main square. Most of the current building dates from the 12th and 13th centuries,

and much of the stone, including that of the Anglo-Saxon crypt, was taken from the nearby Roman fort at Corbridge. Inside, you can climb the 35 worn stone "night stairs," which once led from the main part of the abbey to the canon's dormitory, to overlook the whole ensemble—look out for the drop of lead on the sixth step, a remnant from when the roof was set alight by a Scottish army in 1286. Also of note inside are the portraits on the 16th-century wooden rood screen and the four panels from a 15th-century *Dance of Death* in the sanctuary. You can find out more about the history of the abbey in the free, interactive exhibition The Big Story. ⊠ *Beaumont St.* ☎ *01434/602031* ⊕ *www.hexhamabbey. org.uk* ⊠ *Free; requested donation £3.*

Old Gaol

MUSEUM | FAMILY | England's oldest purpose-built prison, dating from 1330, Hexham's Old Gaol houses fascinating exhibits about the history of the borderlands, including tales of the terrifying "reivers" and their bloodthirsty raids into Northumberland from Scotland during the 16th and 17th centuries. Photographs, weapons, and a reconstructed house interior give a full account of what the region was like in medieval times. A glass elevator takes you up and down four floors, including to the dungeon. ⊠ *Hallgate* ☎ *01670/624523* ⊕ *museumsnorthumberland.org.uk/hexham-old-gaol* ⊠ *£5* ⊗ *Closed Nov.—Mar.*

Restaurants

The Corbridge Larder

$ | DELI | Located near Corbridge Roman Town and the best deli for miles around, this place is filled with all manner of local produce, as well as specialty foods from small-time artisans across Europe. Try the delicious but alarmingly colored Delfts Blauw cheese from Holland; its almost fluorescent blue hue is entirely natural. **Known for:** local and international artisanal produce; lovely upstairs café; village-shop atmosphere. ⑤ *Average main: £10* ⊠ *18 Hill St., Corbridge* ☎ *01434/632948* ⊕ *www.corbridgelarder.co.uk.*

Hotels

★ Langley Castle

$$ | HOTEL | Close your eyes and picture an English castle, you're probably seeing Langley, a lavish 14th-century fortification complete with turrets and battlements. **Pros:** romantic and historic setting; lavish afternoon tea; full movies and sports TV packages in rooms. **Cons:** breakfast hit or miss; decor a little tired in places; service can be slow. ⑤ *Rooms from: £175* ⊠ *Off A686* ☎ *01434/688888* ⊕ *www. langleycastle.co.uk* ⊅ *27 rooms* ⑩ *Free breakfast.*

Activities

The Bike Place

This cycle-hire place in Kielder is the nearest to this part of Hadrian's Wall, despite being 34 miles northwest of Hexham. Still, it's a great excuse to head up into Northumberland National Park. Rental prices start at £30 per day, or £50 for e-bikes, and they can arrange delivery and collection for an extra fee. The main store is in Kielder village, though there's a second on Kielder Waterside, which is marginally closer. ⊠ *Kielder Cycle Centre, Station Garage, Kielder* ✛ *Take A6079 from the main A69 road. The shop is signposted on the main road through the village* ☎ *01434/250457* ⊕ *www.thebikeplace.co.uk.*

Greenhead

18 miles west of Hexham, 49 miles northwest of Durham.

Greenhead may be small, but it's a good base for exploring some of the Hadrian's Wall sites that lie farther west, including the Housesteads Roman Fort, the Roman Army Museum, and Vindolanda.

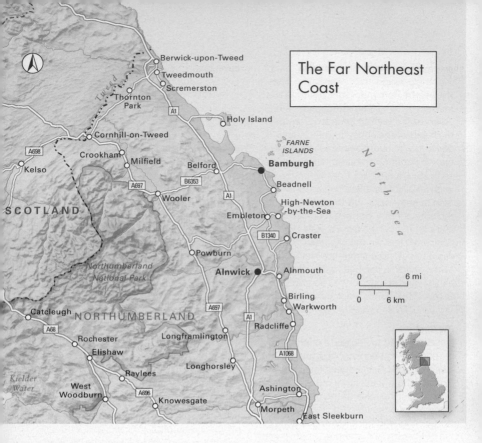

FARNE ISLANDS

North Sea

SCOTLAND

NORTHUMBERLAND

Berwick-upon-Tweed
Tweedmouth
Scremerston
Thornton Park
Holy Island
Cornhill-on-Tweed
Crookham
Milfield
Belford
Bamburgh
Kelso
Beadnell
Wooler
High-Newton-by-the-Sea
Embleton
Craster
Powburn
Alnwick
Alnmouth
Birling
Warkworth
Catcleugh
Rochester
Elishaw
Longframlington
Radcliffe
Raylees
Longhorsley
West Woodburn
Knowesgate
Ashington
Morpeth
East Sleekburn
Northumberland National Park
Kielder Water

0   6 mi
0   6 km

In Northumberland National Park, around 6 miles northest of Greenhead, The Sill National Landscape Discovery Centre has informative displays about Hadrian's Wall and can advise about local walks.

GETTING HERE AND AROUND
Greenhead is on the A69 and B6318. The nearest train station is 3 miles east, in Haltwhistle.

ESSENTIALS
VISITOR INFORMATION The Sill National Landscape Discovery Centre. ⊠ *North-umberland National Park, Bardon Mill* ☎ *01434/341200* ⊕ *www.thesill.org.uk.*

 Sights

Birdoswald Roman Fort
ARCHAEOLOGICAL SITE | Beside the longest unbroken stretch of Hadrian's Wall, Birdoswald Roman Fort reveals the remains of gatehouses, a granary, and a parade ground. You can also see the line of the original turf wall, later rebuilt in stone. Birdoswald has a unique historical footnote: unlike other Roman forts along the wall, it was maintained by local tribes long after being abandoned by the Romans. The small visitor center has artifacts discovered at the site, a full-scale model of the wall, and a good café. ⊠ *Wallace Dr.* ☎ *0370/333–1181* ⊕ *www. english-heritage.org.uk/birdoswald* 🎫 *£8.60* ⊙ *Closed weekdays in Nov.–Feb.; closed Mon.–Tues. in Mar.*

★ Housesteads Roman Fort
MUSEUM | If you have time to visit only one Hadrian's Wall site, Housesteads Roman Fort is your best bet. Britain's most complete example of a Roman fort also features long sections of the wall, with an informative visitor center

showcasing a collection of artifacts discovered at the site and computer-generated images of what the fort originally looked like. The site is a 10-minute walk uphill from the parking lot (not for those with mobility problems), but the effort is more than worth it to see the surprisingly extensive ruins, dating from around AD 125. Excavations have revealed the remains of granaries, gateways, barracks, a hospital, and the commandant's house ◾TIP→ **Come for the history, stay for the views: the northern tip of the fort offers sweeping vistas of Hadrian's Wall as it winds up and over distant hills and crags.** ⊠ *Off B6318, Haydon Bridge* ☎ *01434/344363* ⊕ *www.english-heritage.org.uk/housesteads* ⊠ *£8.10; parking £3.*

Roman Army Museum
MUSEUM | FAMILY | At the garrison fort of Carvoran, this museum makes an excellent introduction to Hadrian's Wall. Full-size models and excavations bring this remote outpost of the empire to life, with a host of historic artifacts including authentic Roman graffiti adorning the walls of an excavated barracks. There's also a flashy 3D film that puts it all into historical context. Opposite the museum, at Walltown Crags on the Pennine Way (one of Britain's long-distance national hiking trails), are 400 yards of the best-preserved section of the wall. The museum is 1 mile northeast of Greenhead. ⊠ *Off B6318* ☎ *01697/747485* ⊕ *www.vindolanda.com* ⊠ *£7.25; £12.60 combined with Vindolanda* ⊙ *Closed mid-Nov.–mid-Feb.*

★ Vindolanda
ARCHAEOLOGICAL SITE | About 8 miles east of Greenhead, this archaeological site—which celebrated its 50th anniversary in 2020—holds the remains of eight successive Roman forts and civilian settlements, providing an intriguing look into the daily life of a military compound. Most of the visible remains date from the 2nd and 3rd centuries, and new excavations are constantly under way. A reconstructed Roman temple, house, and shop provide context, and the museum displays rare artifacts, such as a handful of extraordinary wooden tablets with messages about everything from household chores to military movements. A full-size reproduction of a section of the wall gives a sense of its sheer scale. ⊠ *Off B6318, Bardon Mill* ☎ *01434/344277* ⊕ *www.vindolanda.com* ⊠ *£8.50; £12.60 combined with Roman Army Museum* ⊙ *Closed mid-Nov.–mid-Feb.*

Restaurants

Milecastle Inn
$ | BRITISH | The snug bar and restaurant of this remote, peaceful, 17th-century pub make an excellent place to dine. Fine local meat goes into its famous savory pies; take your pick from wild boar and duckling pie or maybe a plate of Whitby scampi with chips. **Known for:** tasty house specialty meat pies; traditional pub food; 17th-century building. Ⓢ *Average main: £12* ⊠ *B6318, Haltwhistle* ☎ *01434/321372* ⊕ *www.milecastle-inn.co.uk.*

🛏 Hotels

Holmhead Guest House
$ | B&B/INN | Talk about a feel for history—this former farmhouse in open countryside, graced with stone arches and exposed beams, is not only built *on* Hadrian's Wall but also partly *from* it. **Pros:** full of atmosphere; close to Hadrian's Wall; reasonable rates. **Cons:** rooms are a bit of a squeeze; out of the action; you need a car to get around. Ⓢ *Rooms from: £72* ⊠ *Off B6318* ☎ *01697/747402* ⊕ *bandb-hadrianswall.co.uk* ▭ *No credit cards* ⇆ *5 rooms* ❍ *Free breakfast.*

The romantic grounds of Alnwick Castle are filled with flowers and rolling fields.

Alnwick

30 miles north of Newcastle, 46 miles north of Durham.

Dominated by a grand castle, the little market town of Alnwick (pronounced *ahn*-ick) is the best base from which to explore the dramatic coast and countryside of northern Northumberland.

GETTING HERE AND AROUND

If you're driving, Alnwick is just off the A1. Buses X15 and X18 connect Alnwick with Newcastle, Morpeth, and Lindisfarne. The nearest train station is 4 miles away in Alnmouth (pronounced *alun*-mowth); trains travel between here and Newcastle roughly every hour and take 25 minutes.

ESSENTIALS

VISITOR INFORMATION Alnwick Tourist Information Centre. ⊠ *The Playhouse, Bondgate Without* ☎ *01670/622152* ⊕ *www.visitalnwick.org.uk.*

Sights

Alnwick Castle

CASTLE/PALACE | FAMILY | Sometimes called the "Windsor of the North," the imposing Alnwick Castle will likely provoke cries of "Hogwarts!" from younger visitors as it comes into view over the hill; the grounds appear as the exterior of the famous School of Witchcraft and Wizardry in the *Harry Potter* movies. Older visitors might also recognize it as Brancaster Castle from the TV series *Downton Abbey*. In reality, the castle is the ancestral home to the dukes of Northumberland, whose family, the Percys, dominated in the Northeast for centuries.

Head inside to find family photos and other knickknacks scattered around the lavish state rooms, a subtle but pointed reminder that this is a family home rather than a museum. Highlights include the extraordinary gun room, lined with hundreds of antique pistols arranged in swirling patterns; the formal dining room, its table set as if guests are due at any minute; and the magnificent galleried library, containing 14,000 books in floor-to-ceiling cases.

There's plenty here for younger visitors: **Knights' Quest** lets kids dress up and complete interactive challenges; **Dragon's Quest** is a labyrinth designed to teach a bit of medieval history; and for the very young, there are Harry Potter–style events on certain dates, including **Broomstick Lessons** on the exact spot used in the movie (check the website for the schedule). Spooky ghost stories are told by costumed actors in the **Lost Cellars**. In addition, staff members hide a toy owl somewhere in each room of the castle, and kids get a certificate if they spot them all. Tickets are valid for one year, so you can come back if you don't see everything in a day. ⊠ *Off B6431* ☎ *01665/511100* ⊕ *www.alnwickcastle. com* ⊠ *£16.75; combined ticket with Alnwick Gardens £28.70* ⊙ *Closed Nov.–Mar.*

★ Alnwick Garden
GARDEN | FAMILY | A marvelous flight of fancy, Alnwick Garden celebrated its 20-year anniversary at the turn of this decade and remains one of the area's most beautiful, unusual, and kid-friendly attractions. Alongside traditional features like perfectly manicured lawns, shaded woodland walks, and a charming rose garden are more unusual elements like the enormous Grand Cascade water feature, a Poison Garden with everything from hemlock to cannabis, and a labyrinth of towering bamboo. The grounds are also home to the largest "Tai-haku" cherry orchard in the world, as well as a recently spruced up shop and a number of excellent dining and drinking options, including one of the area's most unique restaurants, the Treehouse. ■TIP→ **You can buy clippings of the unique varieties of roses in the shop.** ⊠ *Denwick La.*

☎ *01665/511350* ⊕ *www.alnwickgarden. com* ⊠ *£14.30; combined ticket with Alnwick Castle £28.70* ⊙ *Closed Jan.; closed midweek mid-Nov.–mid-Dec.*

Restaurants

★ The Treehouse
$ | MODERN BRITISH | The treetop location may sound gimmicky, but the effect at this extraordinary restaurant is quite magical and unexpectedly romantic, especially when the place is lit up at night. Here, an enormous complex of buildings spreads out over more than 550 square meters, with a roaring log fire at its center and furniture made from fallen branches. **Known for:** unique setting; Northeastern flavors and ingredients; inoffensive acoustic music on a loop. $ *Average main: £15* ⊠ *Alnwick Garden, Denwick La.* ☎ *01665/660320* ⊕ *www. alnwickgardenhospitality.com* ⊙ *No dinner Sun.*

🛏 Hotels

★ The Cookie Jar
$$$ | HOTEL | With sumptuously appointed rooms, a popular bistro restaurant, and convenient location right by the castle, this historic convent-turned-boutique-hotel is Alnwick's most luxurious town-center stay. **Pros:** delicious cooked breakfast; spacious and comfortable rooms; housemade cookies in rooms. **Cons:** superior rooms are expensive; no dinner served midweek; unrelentingly blue decor. $ *Rooms from: £165* ⊠ *12 Bailiffgate* ☎ *01665/510465* ⊕ *www.cook-iejaralnwick.com* ⊅ *11 rooms* ❧ *Free breakfast.*

Bamburgh

14 miles north of Alnwick.

Tiny Bamburgh has a splendid castle, and several beaches are just a few minutes' walk away.

GETTING HERE AND AROUND

Bamburgh can be reached by car on the B3140, B3141, or B3142. Buses X18 and 418 run from Alnwick to Bamburgh a few times per day. The nearest train station is in Chathill, about 7 miles away.

Sights

★ Bamburgh Castle

CASTLE/PALACE | You'll see Bamburgh Castle long before you reach it: a solid, weather-beaten, clifftop fortress that dominates the coastal view for miles around. A fortification of some kind has stood here since the 6th century, but the Norman castle was damaged during the 15th century, and the central tower is all that remains intact. Much of the structure—the home of the Armstrong family since 1894—was restored during the 18th and 19th centuries. The interior is mostly late Victorian (most impressively, the Great Hall), although a few rooms, such as the small but alarmingly well-stocked armory, have a more authentically medieval feel. The breathtaking view across the North Sea is worth the steep climb up from the main road; bring a picnic if the weather's good (or order to-go sandwiches at the café). ⊠ *Off B1340* ☎ *01668/214515* ⊕ *www.bamburghcastle.com* ☜ *£11.75* ⊗ *Closed weekdays Nov.–mid-Feb.*

Restaurants

★ Grays Restaurant

$$ | **BRITISH** | Located on a quiet bay between Bamburgh and Lindisfarne and surrounded by 6 acres of woodland, this elegant, award-winning restaurant sits within the historic Waren House Hotel. The fixed-price dinners (one course for £22.50, two for £33.95, three for £42.50) feature local flavors, with options like the steamed Berwick white crab and apple tian, Northumberland beef fillet with shallot confit, and Alnwick rum and chocolate ganache torte. **Known for:** picturesque surroundings; elegant, traditional menus; short serving time (from 6:30 pm to 8:30 pm). ⑤ *Average main: £22.50* ⊠ *Off B1342* ☎ *01668/214581* ⊕ *www.warenhousehotel.co.uk.*

Hotels

Lord Crewe Hotel

$ | **HOTEL** | This cozy, stone-walled inn with oak beams sits in the heart of the village and has simple, modern guest rooms decorated with pine furnishings; some of them date back to the 1600s. **Pros:** in the center of the village; good seafood restaurant; close to Bamburgh Castle. **Cons:** pub can get quite crowded; some uninspiring room decor; pet-friendly bar is ideal for dog lovers but not for allergy sufferers. ⑤ *Rooms from: £110* ⊠ *Front St.* ☎ *01668/214243* ⊕ *www.lord-crewe.co.uk* ☜ *7 rooms* ⧄ *Free breakfast.*

WALES

Updated by
Victoria Trott

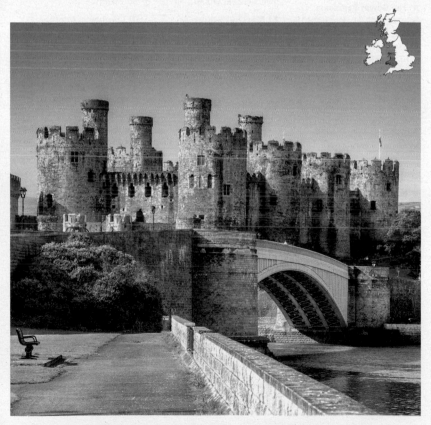

👁 Sights	🍴 Restaurants	🏨 Hotels	🛍 Shopping	🍸 Nightlife
★★★★☆	★★★☆☆	★★★☆☆	★★★☆☆	★★☆☆☆

WELCOME TO WALES

TOP REASONS TO GO

★ **Castle country:** Wales doesn't quite have a castle in each town, but there is a greater concentration than almost anywhere else in Europe—more than 600 in all.

★ **The Gower Peninsula:** This stretch of coastland near Swansea includes some of the region's prettiest beaches, as well as spectacular coastal views and ancient sites.

★ **Snowdonia:** The biggest of the country's three national parks contains its highest mountain, Snowdon, as well as picture-perfect villages.

★ **Brecon Beacons:** Moorlands, mountains, and valleys make up this rough and wild stretch of the Welsh midlands, as popular with hikers as it is with those who are just happy to take in the stunning views from the road.

★ **Hay-on-Wye:** This pretty village on the Welsh-English border has become world famous as a book lover's paradise; every street is lined with secondhand bookstores.

1 Cardiff. The largest and most important city in Wales.

2 Abergavenny. A market town, renowned for its food festival and location just outside Brecon Beacons National Park.

3 Brecon. The gateway to Brecon Beacons.

4 Merthyr Mawr. An idyllic village with thatched cottages.

5 Swansea. The birthplace of poet and playwright Dylan Thomas.

6 Tenby. A popular 19th-century coastal resort.

7 St. Davids. Britain's smallest city and the resting place of the patron saint of Wales.

8 Hay-on-Wye. A bookstore-centric town with a famous Literary Festival.

9 Llandrindod Wells. A charming old spa town.

10 Aberysthwyth. The largest town in mid-Wales, home to the National Library of Wales.

11 Dolgellau. The southern gateway to Snowdonia National Park.

12 Llangollen. A charming Welsh town famous for its international music festival.

13 Lake Vyrnwy. An attractive man-made reservoir surrounded by woodland.

14 Porthmadog. The gateway to the Llŷn Peninsula and the quirky resort of Portmeirion.

15 Betws-y-Coed. A popular base for Snowdonia.

16 Llanberis. Another gateway to Snowdonia and home to the National Slate Museum.

17 Anglesey. A charming island with glorious beaches and coastal walks.

18 Conwy. A medieval walled town with one of the finest castles in Wales.

19 Llandudno. A charming seaside town.

20 Ruthin. A market town that's home to plenty of artisans.

ISLE OF ANGLESEY

Holyhead
A5
Beaumaris
A55
Caernarfon
Llanberis
A5
Pant Glas
A496
Portmeirion
Porthmadog
Pwllheli

Irish Sea

Hells Mouth

BARDSEY ISLAND

Cardigan Bay

Llandudno
Conwy Bay
Pensarn
Conwy
A55

Prestatyn
Dee
M53

Ruthin
A494

Betws-y-Coed

Blaenau Ffestiniog
Snowdonia National Park
Bala
Tv..v cefn

Llangollen
Chirk
Oswestry
A5

A470
A494
Dolgellau
Barmouth
Mallwyd
Machynlleth
Cemmaes Road
A487
Caersws
Newtown

ENGLAND

Lake Vyrnwy
A450
Welshpool
A483

Aberystwyth
A44
Llangurig
Llanrhystud
Rhayader
Aberaeron
A470
Crossgates
A407
Llandrindod Wells
Synod Inn
Builth Wells

Hay-on-Wye

Mynydd Preseli

Cardigan
Fishguard
St. David's
Pembrokeshire Coast National Park
St. Brides Bay
A487
Haverfordwest
A40
Milford Haven
Pembroke
Tenby

Carmarthen Bay

Gower Peninsula

Llanelli

A483
Llandovery
Llandeilo
A40
A40
Brecon
Brecon Beacons National Park
A465
Carmarthen
Laugharne

Llyswen
Crickhowell
Abergavenny
Merthyr Tydfil
A470

M4
Swansea
Swansea Bay
Merthyr Mawr
Pontypridd
Newport
M4

Bristol Channel

Barry

CARDIFF

0   10 mi
0   10 km

17 18 19 16 15 14 11 13 12 10 9 8 7 6 5 4 3 2 1 20

Wales is a land of dramatic national parks, plunging, unspoiled coastlines, and awe-inspiring medieval castles. Its ancient history and deep-rooted Celtic culture make Wales similar in many ways to its more famous neighbors, Scotland and Ireland; and yet it doesn't attract the same hordes of visitors, which is a big part of the appeal.

Vast swaths of Wales were untouched by the industrial boom of the 19th century. Although pockets of the country were given over to industries such as coal mining and manufacturing (both of which have all but disappeared), most of Wales remained unspoiled. The country is largely rural, and there are more than 10 million sheep—but only 3 million people. It has a Britain-as-it-used-to-be feel that can be hugely appealing.

The country has been politically autonomous since 1997 and Welsh culture is flourishing. Cardiff has the most successful creative economy in the U.K. outside of London, with a burgeoning television and film industry, as well as thriving art scenes in most towns and cities. Welsh produce is constantly being celebrated and championed by a passionate new generation of chefs and artisan foodies. And of course, national rugby matches still bond the nation together. Simply put, Wales loves being Wales, and that enthusiasm is infectious to visitors. It also means that the tourism industry has grown by leaps and bounds, including some truly unique and special places to stay.

Although Wales is a small country—on average, about 60 miles wide and 170 miles north to south—looking at it on a map is deceptive. It's quite a difficult place to get around, with a distinctly old-fashioned road network and poor public transportation connections. To see it properly, you really need a car. The good news is that along the way you'll experience some beautiful drives. There are rewards to be found in the gentle folds of its valleys and in the shadow of its mountains.

Were some of the more remote attractions in Wales in, say, the west of Ireland, they'd be world famous and overrun with millions of visitors. Here, if you're lucky, you can almost have them to yourself.

MAJOR REGIONS
South Wales. Cardiff, the lively young capital city, is here, as are two very different national parks: the green, swooping hills of the Brecon Beacons and, in the far west, the sea cliffs, beaches, and estuaries of the Pembrokeshire Coast. Both are excellent for outdoor activities such as walking and mountain biking. Swansea and Laugharne are essential stops for fans of poet Dylan Thomas.

The most diverse of Wales's three regions, the south covers the area around Cardiff that stretches southwest as far as the rugged coastline of Pembrokeshire. It's the most accessible part of the country, as the roads are relatively good and the rail network is more extensive than it is elsewhere in Wales. Pleasant seaside towns such as Tenby are within a four- to five-hour drive of London; from Cardiff and Swansea you're never more than a half hour away from some gorgeous small villages.

Mid-Wales. Traditional market towns and country villages, small seaside resorts, quiet roads, and rolling landscapes filled with sheep farms, forests, and lakes make up Mid-Wales, the country's green and rural heart. There are no cities here—the area's largest town is barely more than a big village. Outside of one or two towns, such as Aberystwyth and Llandrindod Wells, accommodations are mainly country inns, small hotels, and rural farmhouses. This area also has some splendid country-house hotels.

There are no motorways through Mid-Wales either, and the steam railways that once linked this area with Cardiff are long gone. Getting around requires a bit of advance planning, but it's worth the trouble. The bibliophilic charms of Hay-on-Wye have made the town world famous, while the countryside around Aberystwyth is peppered with peaceful sandy beaches and dramatic beauty spots.

North Wales. Wales masses its most dramatic splendor and fierce beauty in the north. Dominating the area is Snowdon, at 3,560 feet the highest peak in England and Wales. The peak gives its name to 823-square-mile Snowdonia National Park, which extends southward all the way to Machynlleth in Mid-Wales. As in other British national parks, much of the land is privately owned, so inside the park are towns, villages, and farms, in addition to some spectacular mountain scenery.

The mock-Italianate village of Portmeirion is an extraordinary architectural flight of fancy, and the seaside resort of Llandudno is as popular today as it was during its Victorian heyday. And scattered across the countryside are a ring of mighty medieval castles, built by King Edward I (1239–1307) at the end of a bloody war to bring the population under English rule. The cream of the crop is Caernarfon, a medieval palace dominating the waterfront on the Menai Strait. Conwy (castle and town) is popular, too.

Although North Wales is more popular with travelers than Mid-Wales, the road network is even more tortuous. In fact, you haven't really experienced North Wales until you've spent a maddening hour snaking along a narrow mountain road, all the while with your destination in plain view.

Planning

When to Go

The weather in Wales, as in the rest of Britain, is a lottery. It can be hot in summer or never stop raining. Generally it's cool and wet in spring and autumn, but could also be surprisingly warm and sunny. The only surefire rule is that you should be prepared for the unexpected.

Generally speaking, southwest Wales tends to enjoy a milder climate than elsewhere in Britain, thanks in part to the moderating effects of the Gulf Stream. In contrast, mountainous areas like Snowdonia and the Brecon Beacons can be chilly at any time of the year. Book far ahead for major festivals such as the literary Hay Festival, Brecon Jazz, Llangollen International Musical Eisteddfod, and the Abergavenny Food Festival.

FESTIVALS

★ Abergavenny Food Festival

FESTIVALS | FAMILY | Held on the third weekend in September, the Abergavenny Food Festival is a celebration for foodies and a symbol of the growing interest in Welsh cuisine, regularly attracting leading figures from the British food scene. There are demonstrations, lectures, special events, and, of course, a huge indoor and outdoor food market. Be sure to sample the delicious local cheese called Y Fenni, flavored with a piquant combination of mustard seeds and ale. ⊠ *Abergavenny* ☎ *01873/851643* ⊕ *www. abergavennyfoodfestival.com.*

★ International Musical Eisteddfod

FESTIVALS | FAMILY | The six-day International Musical Eisteddfod, held in early July, brings together amateur choirs and dancers—more than 12,000 participants in all—from all corners of the globe for a colorful folk festival. The tradition of the eisteddfod, held throughout Wales, goes back to the 12th century. Originally gatherings of bards, the *eisteddfodau* of today are more like national festivals. ⊠ *Llangollen* ☎ *01978/862001* ⊕ *www. international-eisteddfod.co.uk.*

★ Victorian Festival

FESTIVAL | FAMILY | For a week in late August, the Victorian Festival takes over Llandrindod Wells. Everyone from shopkeepers to hotel clerks dresses up in period costume for events from tea dances to street parades. ⊠ *Llandrindod Wells* ☎ *01597/825012* ⊕ *www.victorian-festival.co.uk* 🎫 *Free; special events £8–£25.*

Getting Oriented

Wales has three main regions: South, Mid-, and North. South Wales is the most varied, and in just a few miles you can travel from Wales's bustling and cosmopolitan capital city, Cardiff, to the most enchanting old villages and historical sights. Mid-Wales is almost entirely rural

(its largest town has a population of just 16,000), and it's fringed on its western shores by the arc of Cardigan Bay. Here you'll find mountain lakes, quiet roads, hillside sheep farms, and traditional market towns. North Wales is a mixture of mountains, popular sandy beaches, and coastal hideaways. Although dominated by rocky Snowdonia National Park, the north has a gentler, greener side along the border with England. You can walk the entire length of the coast on the 870-mile Wales Coast Path.

Planning Your Time

First-time visitors often try to cover too much ground in too little time. It's not hard to spend half your time traveling between points that look close on the map but take the better part of a day to reach. From Cardiff, it's easy to visit the Wye Valley, Brecon Beacons, and the Gower Peninsula. Along the North Wales coast, Llandudno and Lake Vyrnwy make good bases for Snowdonia National Park.

The location of Wales lends itself to a border-hopping trip—in both directions. Well-known locations like Bath (near South Wales) and Chester (near North Wales) are no more than an hour from the Welsh border, and you can even take a ferry to Ireland if you want to go farther afield.

Getting Here and Around

AIR

If you're arriving from the United States, London's Heathrow and Gatwick airports are generally the best options because of their large number of international flights. Heathrow (2 hours) is slightly closer than Gatwick (2½ hours), but both have excellent motorway links with South Wales. For North Wales, the quickest access is via Manchester Airport, with a travel time of less than an hour to the Welsh border.

Cardiff Airport, 12 miles from downtown Cardiff, is the only airport in Wales with international flights, but these are mostly from Europe. The T9 bus service runs from the airport to Cardiff's central train station.

AIRPORTS Cardiff Airport. ✉ *A4226, Rhoose* ☎ *01446/711111* ⊕ *www.cardiff-airport.com.*

BUS

Most parts of Wales are accessible by bus, but long-distance bus travel takes a long time. National Express travels to all parts of Wales from London's Victoria Coach Station and also direct from London's Heathrow and Gatwick airports. The company also has routes into Wales from many major towns and cities in England and Scotland. Average travel times from London are 3½ hours to Cardiff, 4 hours to Swansea, 7 hours to Aberystwyth, and 4½ hours to Llandudno.

Many of Wales's national parks run summer bus services. In the North, the excellent Snowdon Sherpa runs into and around Snowdonia and links with main rail and bus services. The Pembrokeshire Coastal Bus Service operates in Pembrokeshire Coast National Park.

CONTACTS National Express. ☎ *0871/781–8181* ⊕ *www.nationalexpress.com.* **Pembrokeshire Coastal Bus.** ☎ *0800/464–0000 Travcline* ⊕ *www.pembrokeshirecoast. wales.* **Snowdon Sherpa.** ☎ *0800/464–0000* ⊕ *www.gwynedd.llyw.cymru/en.*

CAR

To explore the Welsh heartland properly, you really need a car. Be prepared to take the scenic route: there are no major highways north of Swansea (which means virtually all of Wales). For the most part it's all back-roads, all the way. There are some stunning routes to savor: the A487 road runs along or near most of the coastline, while the A44 and A470 both wind through mountain scenery with magnificent views.

FERRY

Three ferry ports that connect Britain with Ireland are in Wales. Regular daily ferries with Stena Line and Irish Ferries sail from Fishguard and Pembroke, in the southwest, and Holyhead, in the northwest.

CONTACTS Irish Ferries. ☎ *08717/300400* ⊕ *www.irishferries.com.* **Stena Line.** ☎ *0344/770–7070* ⊕ *www.stenaline. co.uk.*

TRAIN

Travel time on the Great Western Railway service from London's Paddington Station is about 1 hour, 50 minutes to Cardiff and 2 hours, 45 minutes to Swansea; an electrified rail line between London Paddington and Cardiff, which opened in 2020, shaved 14 minutes off the traditional journey. Trains connect London's Euston Station with Mid-Wales and North Wales, often involving changes in cities such as Birmingham. Travel times average between three and five hours. Regional train service covers much of South and North Wales but, frustratingly, there are virtually no direct connections between these regions. For example, to make the 73-mile trip between Cardiff and Aberystwyth you have to make a connection in Shrewsbury, doubling the trip to 147 miles. North Wales has a cluster of steam railways, but these are tourist attractions rather than a practical way of getting around. The mainline long-distance routes can be very scenic indeed, such as the Cambrian Coast Railway, running between Machynlleth and Pwllheli, and the Heart of Wales Line, linking Swansea with Shrewsbury on the Welsh-English border.

CONTACTS National Rail Enquiries. ☎ *0345/748–4950* ⊕ *www.nationalrail. co.uk.*

Discounts and Deals

For travel within Wales, ask about money-saving unlimited-travel tickets (such as the Explore Wales Pass, the North and Mid-Wales Pass, and the South Wales Pass), which include the use of bus services. A discount card offering a 20% reduction on each of the steam-driven Great Little Trains of Wales is also available. It costs £15, is valid for 12 months, and can be purchased online.

The Cadw/Welsh Historic Monuments Explorer Pass is good for unlimited admission to most of Wales's historic sites. The seven-day pass costs £33.60 per person, £53.55 per couple, or £65.10 per family; the three-day pass costs £23.10, £35.70, and £47.25, respectively. Passes are available at any site covered by the Cadw program. All national museums and galleries in Wales are free.

INFORMATION Cadw/Welsh Historic Monuments. ✉ *Plas Carew, Unit 5–7 Cefn Coed, Nantgarw* ☎ *0300/025–6000* ⊕ *cadw.gov.wales.* **Explore Wales Pass Information.** ☎ *0333/3211–202* ⊕ *www. tfwrail.wales/ticket-types/explore-wales.* **Great Little Trains of Wales.** ☎ ⊕ *www. greatlittletrainsofwales.co.uk.*

Restaurants

Wales has developed a thriving restaurant scene over the last 20 years or so, and not just in major towns. Some truly outstanding food can be found in rural pubs and hotel restaurants. More and more restaurants are creating dishes using fresh local ingredients—Welsh lamb, Welsh Black beef, Welsh cheeses, and seafood from the Welsh coast—that show off the best of the region's cuisine.

Hotels

A 19th-century dictum, "I sleeps where I dines," still holds true in Wales, where good hotels and good restaurants often go together. Castles, country mansions, and even disused railway stations are being transformed into interesting hotels and restaurants. Traditional inns with low, beamed ceilings, wood paneling, and fireplaces are often the most appealing places to stay. The best ones tend to be off the beaten track. Cardiff and Swansea have some large chain hotels, and, for luxury, some excellent spas have cropped up in the countryside. An added bonus is that prices are generally lower than they are for equivalent properties in the Cotswolds, Scotland, or southeast England.

Restaurant and hotel reviews have been shortened. For full information, visit Fodors.com. Restaurant prices are the average cost of a main course at dinner, or if dinner is not served, at lunch. Hotels prices are the lowest cost of a standard double room in high season, including 20% V.A.T.

WHAT IT COSTS in Pounds			
$	$$	$$$	$$$$
RESTAURANTS			
under £16	£16–£23	£24–£30	over £30
HOTELS			
under £125	£125–£225	£226–£350	over £350

Tours

In summer there are all-day and half-day tour-bus excursions to most parts of the country. In major resorts and cities, ask for details at a tourist information center or bus station.

Wales Best Guides

GUIDED TOURS | The country's official guide organization will set you up only with guides recognized by VisitWales. You can book a driver-guide or someone to accompany you as you drive, or you can take a tailor-made tour. ☎ ⊕ *www. walesbestguides.com.*

Visitor Information

CONTACTS Visit Wales. ☎ *0333/006–3001* ⊕ *www.visitwales.com.* **Wales in Style.** ⊕ *www.walesinstyle.com.*

Cardiff (Caerdydd)

30 miles southwest of the Second Severn Bridge.

With a population of around 360,000, Cardiff is the largest and most important city in Wales. It's also one of the youngest capitals in Europe: although a settlement has existed here since Roman times, Cardiff wasn't declared a city until 1905, and didn't become the capital until 50 years later. This is an energetic, youthful place, keen to show its newfound cosmopolitanism to the world. Cardiff has experienced something of a cultural renaissance since the opening of the Wales Millennium Centre in Cardiff Bay.

For all its urban optimism, however, Cardiff is still a rather workaday town, with little to detain you for more than a couple of days. See Cardiff Castle and the National Museum, wander Cardiff Bay, and maybe catch a show. Otherwise, it's a convenient base for exploring the nearby countryside.

GETTING HERE AND AROUND

The capital is a major transportation hub with good connections to other parts of South Wales and with England. Getting to Mid-Wales and North Wales is more difficult, as there's no direct north–south

train route (you'll have to connect in Bristol or Shrewsbury) and north–south buses are painfully slow. From London, trains from Paddington to Cardiff Central take 1 hour and 50 minutes on average; National Express coaches take about three hours. Cardiff is easily accessible by the M4 motorway.

ESSENTIALS
VISITOR AND TOUR INFORMATION
Cardiff Tourist Information Centre. ⊠ *Cardiff Castle, Castle St.* ☎ *029/2087–2167* ⊕ *www.visitcardiff.com.*

Sights

★ Caerphilly Castle

CASTLE/PALACE | **FAMILY** | The largest and most impressive fortress in Wales, and one of the few still to be surrounded by its original moat, Caerphilly must have been awe-inspiring at the time of its construction in the 13th century. Built by an Anglo-Norman lord, the concentric fortification contained powerful inner and outer defenses. It was badly damaged during the English Civil War (check out the leaning tower), although extensive 20th-century renovations have restored much of its former glory. The original Great Hall is still intact, and near the edge of the inner courtyard there's a replica of a trebuchet—a giant catapult used to launch rocks and other projectiles at the enemy. Additionally, an interesting collection of modern interpretive sculptures has been placed around the castle, both inside and outside. To celebrate the town's famous cheese, a free festival, The Big Cheese, is held here every year at the end of July. Caerphilly is 7 miles north of Cardiff. ⊠ *Castle St., Caerphilly* ☎ *029/2088–3143* ⊕ *cadw.gov.wales* 🎫 *£9.40.*

Cardiff Bay

NEIGHBORHOOD | Perhaps the most potent symbol of Cardiff's 21st-century rebirth, this regenerated district is a 15-minute bus ride from St. Mary Street. It's the

Sights ▼

1 Caerphilly Castle E1
2 Cardiff Bay I9
3 Cardiff Castle E2
4 Castell Coch E1
5 Llandaff Cathedral B1
6 Museum of Cardiff F3
7 National Museum Cardiff F1
8 National Roman Legion
   Museum ,,,,,,,,,,,,,,,,,,,,,,,,,,,,,,,,J1
9 Pierhead J8
10 St. Fagans National Museum
   of History A1
11 Tredegar House J1
12 Wales Millennium Centre I8

Restaurants ▼

1 Bayside Brasserie I9
2 The Classroom F6
3 The Clink H2
4 Madame Fromage E3
5 Park House F1
6 Pottigrew Tea Rooms D3
7 The Potted Pig E3

Hotels ▼

1 Hotel Indigo F2
2 Jolyon's Boutique Hotel I8
3 Lincoln House Private Hotel B1
4 Maltsters' Arms Hotel B1
5 voco St. David's Hotel H9
6 West Usk Lighthouse J7

Castell Coch looks medieval, but don't be fooled: it's a delightful Victorian-Gothic fantasy.

location of Senedd Cymru, the Welsh Parliament, and Wales Millennium Centre, as well as a good selection of restaurants and bars. Don't miss the Norwegian Church Arts Centre, where children's author Roald Dahl was baptized; you can also take a boat trip around the bay. It was from Roath Dock in 1910 that Captain Robert Falcon Scott and his crew left aboard the SS *Terra Nova* for their ill-fated British Antarctic Expedition. ✉ *Between Stuart St. and Harbour Dr.* ⊕ *www.visit-cardiffbay.info.*

★ Cardiff Castle

CASTLE/PALACE | **FAMILY** | A mishmash of styles, from austere Norman keep to over-the-top Victorian mansion, Cardiff Castle is an odd but beguiling place, located right in the middle of the city. Take the tour of the Victorian portion to discover the castle's exuberant side. William Burges (1827–81), an architect obsessed by the Gothic period, transformed the castle into an extravaganza of medieval color for the third marquess of Bute. The result was the Moorish-style ceiling in the Arab Room, the intricately carved shelves lining the Library, and gold leaf murals everywhere. Look for the painting of the Invisible Prince in the Day Nursery; on first glance it's just a tree, but stare long enough and a man takes shape in the branches. Note the not-so-subtle rejection of Darwin's theory of evolution, represented by monkeys tearing up his book around the library's doorway. Fans of military history shouldn't miss "Firing Line," an exhibition tracing the history of Welsh regiments. The vast castle grounds, which include beautiful rhododendron gardens and a habitat for owls and falcons, are also the setting for an open-air cinema and music concerts in the summer. A visitor center houses the ticket office, a gift shop, bistro, and an information center focusing on the city. Tours, including of the clock tower and evening ghost tours, are held on certain dates year-round; call or check the website for schedule and booking information. ✉ *Castle St.* ☎ *029/2087–8100* ⊕ *www.cardiffcastle. com* ✉ *£14.50.*

★ Castell Coch

CASTLE/PALACE | FAMILY | Perched on a hillside is this fairy-tale castle, built on the site of a medieval stronghold in the 1870s, about the time that the "Fairy-Tale King" Ludwig II of Bavaria was creating his castles in the mountains of Germany. This turreted Victorian fantasy wouldn't look out of place among them. The castle was another collaboration of the third marquess of Bute and William Burges, who transformed Cardiff Castle. Burges created everything, including the whimsical furnishings and murals, in a remarkable exercise of Victorian-Gothic whimsy. ✉ *A470, 4 miles north of Cardiff, Tongwynlais* ☎ *029/2081–0101* ⊕ *cadw. gov.wales* 💷 *£7.70.*

Llandaff Cathedral

RELIGIOUS SITE | In a suburb that retains its village feeling, you can visit this cathedral, which was repaired after serious bomb damage in World War II. The cathedral includes the work of a number of Pre-Raphaelites as well as *Christ in Majesty*, a 15-foot-tall aluminum figure by sculptor Jacob Epstein (1880–1959). From Cardiff, cross the River Taff and follow Cathedral Road for about 2 miles. Buses 25, 61, and 63 from Westgate Street in Cardiff stop in Llandaff. ✉ *Cathedral Close, Llandaff* ☎ *029/2056–4554* ⊕ *www.llandaffcathedral.org.uk* 💷 *Free.*

Museum of Cardiff

MUSEUM | FAMILY | This well-executed museum tells the story of Cardiff and its people from the city's medieval origins to the present day. There's a particularly interesting exhibit on the old docks (now Cardiff Bay), one of the biggest ports in the world in the early 1900s. It's also worth a visit to see the building itself, formerly the Cardiff Free Library, which was built in the 1880s and is now a recognized historic building; note the lovely green ceramic tiles. ✉ *The Old Library, The Hayes* ☎ *029/2034–6214* ⊕ *www. cardiffmuseum.com* 💷 *Free.*

★ National Museum Cardiff

MUSEUM | FAMILY | This splendid neoclassical museum in Cardiff's civic center houses the National Museum of Art and the National Museum of Natural History. It is renowned for its exquisite collection of impressionist and modern art, featuring many of the art world's major players as well as one of the world's best collections of British silverware. This is also the main venue of the biannual Artes Mundi, the United Kingdom's largest arts prize. The Evolution of Wales gallery, showing the country's history from the Big Bang onward, uses inventive robotics and audiovisual effects. Kids, however, will be more interested in the dinosaurs and the enormous, 9-meter (29-foot) skeleton of a humpback whale that washed ashore near Cardiff in 1982. ✉ *Cathays Park* ☎ *0300/111–2333* ⊕ *www.museum. wales* 💷 *Free* 🕐 *Closed Mon.*

National Roman Legion Museum

MUSEUM | FAMILY | Located within the remains of one of only three permanent Roman fortresses in Britain (built AD 75), this fascinating museum looks at all aspects of Roman life, and includes an exquisite collection of gemstones and a coffin complete with male remains. Of particular note are the ruins of the amphitheater, the baths, and the only Roman barracks on view in Europe. On Saturdays, families can meet with costumed Roman soldiers and dress up themselves; there are also occasionally reenactments of battles. The reconstructed Roman garden is particularly attractive. Caerleon is 4 miles northeast of Newport. ✉ *High St., Newport* ☎ *0300/111–2333* ⊕ *www.museum. wales* 💷 *Free.*

Pierhead

MUSEUM | Topped by a distinctive redbrick clock tower, the Victorian Gothic Pierhead contains a good exhibition on Welsh history, including a few artifacts relating to the medieval struggle for independence from England. They have an occasional but eclectic program of public events here, including art exhibitions, talks, and debates; call or check the website for the upcoming schedule. ⊠ *Pierhead St., Cardiff Bay* ☎ *0300/200–6565* ⊕ *www. pierhead.org* ⊠ *Free.*

★ **St. Fagans National Museum of History**

MUSEUM | **FAMILY** | On 100 acres of gardens, this excellent open-air museum celebrates the region's architectural history with a collection of farmhouses, cottages, shops, chapels, a school, and a 16th-century manor house. All but two of the structures were brought here from around Wales. Of special note are the string of ironworkers' cottages, each reflecting a different era from 1805, 1855, 1925, 1955, and 1985, from the decor to the technology to the gardens. Craftspeople work at the museum using traditional methods; most of the work is for sale. Galleries display clothing and other articles from daily life, and special events highlight local customs. The native animal breeds are popular with kids. ⊠ *Off A4232, St. Fagans* ☎ *0300/111–2333* ⊕ *www.museum.wales* ⊠ *Free; parking £6.*

Tredegar House

HOUSE | Bought by the National Trust in 2011, Tredegar House is one of the grandest stately homes in Wales. Highlights of the self-guided tour include the grand baroque Jacobean New Hall and the enormous Victorian kitchens, both restored to their former glory. Don't miss the lavish Victorian Side Hall, lined with portraits of the Morgan family, which owned Tredegar until the 1950s. The grounds include immaculately laid-out formal gardens and an orangery. Tredegar is just outside Newport, 12 miles northwest of Cardiff. ⊠ *Tredegar House Dr., off A48, Newport* ☎ *01633/815880* ⊕ *www. nationaltrust.org.uk/tredegar-house* ⊠ *£11.35; gardens free.*

Wales Millennium Centre

ARTS VENUE | Inviting comparisons to Bilbao's Guggenheim, Cardiff's main arts complex (known locally as "The Armadillo", for its coppery, shingled exterior) is an extraordinary building, inside and out. The materials used in the construction are intended to represent "Welshness." (Slate is for the rocky coastline, for example, while wood is for its ancient forests.) The massive words carved into the curving facade read "In These Stones Horizons Sing" in English and Welsh. Inside there's a maritime feel, from the curving wooden stairs to balconies evoking the bow of a ship. A broad range of cultural programs take place on the various stages, from ballet and opera to major touring shows. You might be lucky enough to catch a production by the innovative National Theatre Wales. There are often free daily musical performances in the foyer along with cafés, a restaurant, and a shop selling Welsh gifts. ⊠ *Bute Pl., Cardiff Bay* ☎ *029/2063–6464* ⊕ *www.wmc.org.uk* ⊠ *Free (event tickets vary).*

🍴 Restaurants

Bayside Brasserie

$$ | **FRENCH** | With its gorgeous view over Cardiff Bay, this undeniably romantic restaurant is a popular choice. The classic French bistro menu is jazzed up with international influences like tempura tiger prawns and classic mac-and-cheese, but it's the steaks, especially the Chateaubriand, that diners come here for. **Known for:** waterside views; delicious steaks; French-fusion food. ⑤ *Average main: £16* ⊠ *Mermaid Quay, Bute Pl.* ☎ *029/2035–8444* ⊕ *www.baysidebrasserie.com.*

The Classroom

$$ | **MODERN EUROPEAN** | On the top floor of Cardiff and Vale College's City Centre Campus, this smart restaurant is run by catering and hospitality students with panoramic views from the floor-to-ceiling windows. The menus, which change with the seasons, are overseen by some of the top Welsh chefs working in the U.K. **Known for:** panoramic views; Modern

British cuisine; creative use of Welsh produce. $ *Average main: £17* ✉ *CAVC City Centre Campus, Dumballs Rd.* ☎ *029/2025–0377* ⊕ *www.theclassroom. wales* ⊘ *Closed Sun. and Mon.*

★ The Clink

$$ | BRITISH | Well, this is unusual: a trendy restaurant in which all the food is prepared by prisoners; the idea behind The Clink (British slang for jail) is that those serving time for minor crimes are given the chance to turn their lives around by gaining experience as gourmet chefs. The restaurant (just outside the prison grounds) is a bright, modern space, and the Modern British food, made with local, seasonal produce, is genuinely delicious. **Known for:** unique atmosphere and concept; local, seasonal produce; no alcohol policy. $ *Average main: £16* ✉ *Knox Rd., in front of Cardiff Prison* ☎ *029/2092–3130* ⊕ *www.the-clinkcharity.org/restaurants/cardiff* ⊘ *No dinner Sun.–Tues.*

Madame Fromage

$ | EUROPEAN | In one of Cardiff's most atmospheric Victorian arcades, this café-deli has a Welsh-French menu, where cheese features heavily. The daily specials usually include salads, quiches, and soups—all with a Welsh-Continental feel. **Known for:** Welsh and French cheeses; famed cawl (lamb stew); delicious cakes. $ *Average main: £8* ✉ *21-25 Castle Arcade* ☎ *029/206–4888* ⊕ *www. madamefromage.co.uk* ⊘ *Closed Sun. No dinner.*

★ Park House

$$$ | FRENCH | In a building designed by William Burges (the same architect who helped design Cardiff Castle and Castell Coch), this upscale restaurant with a Welsh-French menu is one of the city's top eateries. Its grand surroundings make it a popular venue for afternoon tea, and there's also a simple bar menu featuring cheese and charcuterie. **Known for:** one of the best wine lists in the United Kingdom; charming building; local

produce. $ *Average main: £28* ✉ *20 Park Pl.* ☎ *029/2022–4343* ⊕ *www.parkhous-erestaurant.co.uk* ⊘ *Closed Mon. No dinner Sun.*

★ Pettigrew Tea Rooms

$ | BRITISH | In a crenellated former park lodge a short walk west of the entrance to Cardiff Castle, this cozy tearoom is the place to go for superb cakes such as Victoria Sandwich or Lemon Drizzle. There's a good range of sandwiches and around 20 teas on the menu, but the splendid Afternoon Tea is the real draw here (reservations advised). **Known for:** mouthwatering cakes; traditional Welsh breakfast; quaint building. $ *Average main: £8* ✉ *West Lodge, Castle St.* ☎ *02920/235 486* ⊕ *www.pettigrew-tea-rooms.com.*

The Potted Pig

$$ | BRITISH | Vaulted ceilings and exposed brick walls provide a dramatic backdrop to this restaurant down the block from Cardiff Castle. Formerly a bank vault, today the Potted Pig turns out superb Welsh dishes. **Known for:** pork in various forms; extensive gin menu; romantic dining room. $ *Average main: £21* ✉ *27 High St.* ☎ *029/2022–4817* ⊕ *www. thepottedpig.com* ⊘ *No dinner Sun.*

🛏 Hotels

Hotel Indigo

$ | HOTEL | Housed in an art deco shopping arcade on one of the city's main shopping streets, Hotel Indigo is the stylish hotel Cardiff has been waiting for. **Pros:** stylish decor; city center location; excellent roof terrace. **Cons:** rooms are spread between two buildings; no parking on-site; can feel a bit impersonal. $ *Rooms from: £62* ✉ *Dominions Arcade, Queen St.* ☎ *0871/942–9104* ⊕ *www.hotelindigo.com/cardiff* ⇱ *122 rooms* ⦿ *No meals.*

★ Jolyon's Boutique Hotel

$ | B&B/INN | This town house, a hop and a skip from the Wales Millennium Centre in Cardiff Bay, bucks the trend in a city where big, modern hotels are usually a safer bet than boutique lodgings. **Pros:** loads of character; eco-friendly toiletries; cozy lounge. **Cons:** 10-minute drive from the city center; no elevator; no parking. $ *Rooms from: £89* ⊠ *5 Bute Crescent* ☎ *029/2048–8775* ⊕ *www.jolyons.co.uk* ⤶ *7 rooms* ⍤ *Free Breakfast.*

Lincoln House Private Hotel
$ | **B&B/INN** | Perhaps the best of the many B&Bs on Cathedral Road—a handsome enclave of Victorian houses—this place close to the city center is a great find. **Pros:** good service; handy location; free parking. **Cons:** attractive road is spoiled by traffic; no restaurant; no elevator. $ *Rooms from: £99* ⊠ *118 Cathedral Rd.* ☎ *029/2039–5558* ⊕ *www. lincolnhotel.co.uk* ⤶ *24 rooms* ⍤ *Free Breakfast.*

Maltsters' Arms Hotel
$ | **B&B/INN** | This pub has spent a small fortune renovating its superb bedrooms, which combine cool design and true comfort. **Pros:** combines luxury and informality; great food; attractive suburb location. **Cons:** not a quiet retreat; on a busy road; a 10-minute drive into the city center. $ *Rooms from: £88* ⊠ *42 Cardiff Rd., Llandaff* ☎ *029/2033–3096* ⊕ *www.sabrain.com* ⤶ *5 rooms* ⍤ *Free Breakfast.*

voco St. David's Hotel
$ | **HOTEL** | Natural light from a glass atrium floods this starkly modern luxury hotel overlooking Cardiff Bay. **Pros:** great food; award-winning spa; good deals. **Cons:** out-of-the-way location; price fluctuates wildly; not as plush as you'd expect for 5-star lodging. $ *Rooms from: £80* ⊠ *Havannah St.* ☎ *029/2045–4045* ⊕ *stdavids.vocohotels.com* ⤶ *132 rooms* ⍤ *No meals.*

West Usk Lighthouse
$$ | **B&B/INN** | **FAMILY** | Overlooking the Severn Estuary, this extraordinary bed-and-breakfast is one of the most romantic places to stay in Wales. **Pros:** unique and beautiful decor; amazing location; charming hosts. **Cons:** no restaurant; too quirky for some tastes; full price charged if canceled within one week of stay. $ *Rooms from: £165* ⊠ *Green La., Newport* ☎ *01633/810126* ⊕ *www.westusklighthouse.co.uk* ⤶ *5 rooms* ⍤ *Free Breakfast.*

 Nightlife

Clwb Ifor Bach
MUSIC CLUBS | This hot spot, whose name means "Little Ivor's Club" in Welsh, has three floors of eclectic music from funk to folk to rock. They also regularly host gigs by hip, young (usually Welsh) bands. ⊠ *11 Womanby St.* ☎ *029/2023–2199* ⊕ *www.clwb.net.*

St. Canna's Ale House
BARS/PUBS | Situated in an end-of-terrace house just opposite Chapter Arts Centre, this friendly "micropub" is the place to go to try a wide range of Welsh craft beers. There's usually live music on weekends. ⊠ *42 Llandaff Rd.* ☎ *07890/106–449.*

 Performing Arts

★ Chapter Arts Centre
ARTS CENTERS | In the suburb of Canton, a 10-minute cab ride from Cardiff's center, Chapter is the hippest place in town to hang out. There's a cinema showing art-house and independent films; an auditorium for theater and comedy; a contemporary art gallery; and a bar serving food and Welsh craft beer. ⊠ *Market Rd.* ☎ *029/2030–4400* ⊕ *www.chapter.org.*

Motorpoint Arena Cardiff
CONCERTS | This huge venue is Cardiff's premier location for big-ticket music acts and other touring shows. ⊠ *Mary Ann St.* ☎ *029/2022–4488* ⊕ *www.motorpointarenacardiff.co.uk.*

New Theatre

THEATER | FAMILY | This refurbished Edwardian playhouse presents touring plays, musicals, ballet performances, and kids' shows. ⊠ *Park Pl.* ☎ *029/2087–8889* ⊕ *www.newtheatrecardiff.co.uk.*

St. David's Hall

CONCERTS | This popular venue presents the Welsh Proms in July, attracting major international orchestras and soloists. It also stages rock, pop, jazz, and folk events as well as comedy and dance shows. ⊠ *The Hayes* ☎ *029/2087–8444* ⊕ *www.stdavidshallcardiff.co.uk.*

🛍 Shopping

Canopied Victorian and Edwardian shopping arcades lined with specialty stores weave in and out of the city's modern shopping complexes.

Cardiff Antiques Centre

ANTIQUES/COLLECTIBLES | Located in an 1858 arcade, the Cardiff Antiques Centre is a good place to buy vintage jewelry and accessories. ⊠ *Royal Arcade* ☎ *029/2039–8891.*

Cardiff Market

OUTDOOR/FLEA/GREEN MARKETS | The traditional Cardiff Market sells tempting fresh foods beneath its Victorian glass canopy. Be sure to try the Welshcakes at Cardiff Bakestones. ⊠ *St. Mary St.* ☎ *029/2087–1214* ⊕ *www.cardiffcouncilproperty.com/cardiff-market.*

★ Craft in the Bay

CRAFTS | Located opposite Wales Millennium Centre, this shop stocks tasteful arts and crafts from makers around Wales. ⊠ *The Flourish, Lloyd George Ave.* ☎ *029/2048–4611* ⊕ *www.makersguildin-wales.org.uk.*

Spillers Records

MUSIC STORES | The world's oldest record store stocks vinyl and CDs in every genre and occasionally hosts live gigs on the tiny premises. Established in 1894, it originally sold phonographs and shellac. ⊠ *27 Morgan Arcade* ☎ *029/2022–4905* ⊕ *www.spillersrecords.com.*

Abergavenny (Y Fenni)

32 miles northeast of Cardiff.

The market town of Abergavenny, just outside Brecon Beacons National Park, is a popular base for walkers and hikers. It has a ruined castle and is near the industrial history sites at Blaenavon. It's also a foodie hot spot.

GETTING HERE AND AROUND
Abergavenny is on the A40 road, about an hour's drive from Cardiff. Direct trains connect with Cardiff about every half hour and take around 40 minutes.

ESSENTIALS
VISITOR INFORMATION Abergavenny Tourist Information Centre. ⊠ *Tithe Barn, Monk St.* ☎ *01873/853254* ⊕ *www.visitaberga-venny.co.uk.*

👁 Sights

Abergavenny Castle and Museum

MUSEUM | FAMILY | Built early in the 11th century, this castle witnessed a tragic event on Christmas Day, 1176: the Norman knight William de Braose invited the neighboring Welsh chieftains to a feast, and in a crude attempt to gain control of the area, had them all slaughtered as they sat to dine. The Welsh retaliated and virtually demolished the castle. Most of what now remains dates from the 13th and 14th centuries. The castle's 19th-century hunting lodge houses an excellent museum of regional history. There's a re-created saddler's shop and a World War II air-raid shelter, but the Victorian Welsh farmhouse kitchen, with its old utensils and butter molds, is perhaps the most diverting exhibit. ⊠ *Castle St.* ☎ *01873/854282* ⊕ *www.abergavenny-museum.co.uk* 🎫 *Free* ⊗ *Closed Wed.*

★ Big Pit National Coal Museum

MUSEUM | FAMILY | For hundreds of years, South Wales has been famous for its mining industry. Decades of decline—particularly during the 1980s—left only a handful of mines in business. The mines around Blaenavon, a small town 7 miles northeast of Abergavenny, have been designated a UNESCO World Heritage Site, and this fascinating museum is the centerpiece. Ex-miners lead you 300 feet underground into a coal mine. You spend just under an hour examining the old stables, machine rooms, and exposed coalfaces. Afterward you can look around an exhibition housed in the old Pithead Baths, including an extraordinary section on child labor in British mines. ■TIP→ **Children under 3½ feet tall are not allowed on the underground portion of the tour.** ⊠ *Off A4043, Blaenavon*

☎ *0300/111–2333* ⊕ *www.museum. wales* ⊠ *Free; £5 parking.*

Blaenavon Ironworks

FACTORY | A UNESCO World Heritage Site, the 1789 Blaenavon Ironworks traces the entire process of iron production in the late 18th century. Well-preserved blast furnaces, a water-balance lift used to transport materials to higher ground, and a terraced row of workers' cottages show how the business operated. ⊠ *A4043, Blaenavon* ☎ *01495/792615* ⊕ *cadw.gov.wales* ⊠ *£6.10* ⊘ *Closed Sun.–Wed. in Nov.–Mar.*

Raglan Castle

CASTLE/PALACE | FAMILY | Impressively complete from the front, majestically ruined within, Raglan was built in the 15th century and was the childhood home of Henry Tudor (1457–1509), who seized the throne of England in 1485 and became Henry VII. Raglan's heyday was relatively short-lived. The castle was attacked by Parliamentary forces in 1645, during the English Civil War, and has lain in ruins ever since. The hexagonal Great Tower survives in reasonably good condition (you can climb to the top), as do a handful of rooms on the ground floor. ✉ *A40, Raglan* ☎ *01291/690228* ⊕ *cadw. gov.wales* ✆ *£7.70.*

Tintern Abbey

RELIGIOUS SITE | Literally a stone's throw from the English border, Tintern is one of the region's most romantic monastic ruins. Founded in 1131 by the Cistercians and dissolved by Henry VIII in 1536, it has inspired its fair share of poets and painters over the years—most famously J. M. W. Turner, who painted the transept covered in moss and ivy, and William Wordsworth, who idolized the setting in his poem "Lines Composed a Few Miles Above Tintern Abbey." Come early or late to avoid the crowds. The abbey, 5 miles north of Chepstow and 19 miles southeast of Abergavenny, is on the banks of the River Wye. ✉ *A466, Tintern* ☎ *01291/689251* ⊕ *cadw.gov.wales* ✆ *£7.70.*

Tretower Court

HOUSE | An extremely rare surviving example of a fortified medieval manor house, Tretower Court was built in the early 1300s and expanded in the 15th century. The atmospheric interior contains a large hall, which was probably used for public business, and a solar, a private space used for working and relaxing. Buildings such as these were huge status symbols in their day, as they combined the security of a castle with the luxury of a manor house. On the grounds are the ruins of an earlier Norman castle. Tretower Court, restored in the 1930s, is signposted from the idyllic village of Crickhowell, which is 5 miles northwest of Abergavenny. ✉ *A479,*

Crickhowell ☎ *01874/730279* ⊕ *cadw. wales* ✆ *£7.70* ⊙ *Closed Sun.–Wed. in Nov.–Mar.*

Restaurants

Cripple Creek Inn

$$ | BRITISH | This charming whitewashed inn serves elegant Welsh cuisine in a rustic dining room. Fish is a specialty, underlined with plenty of regional flavors—grilled hake encrusted with Tintern cheese, for instance—and the beef and lamb are locally sourced. **Known for:** tasty local produce; intimate dining room; great Sunday lunch. ⑤ *Average main: £17* ✉ *Old Abergavenny Rd. , Bryngwyn, Raglan* ☎ *01291/690256* ⊕ *www.thecripplecreek.com.*

★ The Walnut Tree

$$$ | MODERN BRITISH | Regarded as one of the best chefs in the United Kingdom, Shaun Hill has been at the helm of this rustic-chic restaurant 3 miles northeast of Abergavenny since 2008. The focus here is on local, seasonal produce with international influences; lunch is an accessible £27 for two courses. **Known for:** superb cooking; attractive dining room; peaceful location. ⑤ *Average main: £29* ✉ *Llanddewi Skirrid* ✢ *Along the B4521 northeast of Abergavenny* ☎ *01873/852797* ⊕ *www.thewalnuttree-inn.com* ⊙ *Closed Sun. and Mon.*

Hotels

★ Angel Hotel

$ | HOTEL | This country-chic hotel in the town center is renowned for its excellent food, especially the afternoon tea. **Pros:** stylish decor; delicious afternoon tea; friendly, professional staff. **Cons:** not all rooms are in the main building; limited, pricey parking; very busy on weekends. ⑤ *Rooms from: £95* ✉ *15 Cross St.* ☎ *01873/857121* ⊕ *www.angelabergavenny.com* ⤳ *35 rooms* ⦿ *No meals* Ⓜ *NP7 5EN.*

Bear Hotel

$ | **HOTEL** | In the middle of town, this refurbished coaching inn is full of character; the low-beamed bar, decorated with memorabilia from the days when stagecoaches stopped here, has a log fire in winter. **Pros:** friendly bar; good food; some rooms have spa baths. **Cons:** some rooms overlook the road; rooms vary in size; can get busy on weekends. ⑤ *Rooms from: £99* ✉ *High St., Crickhowell* ☎ *01873/810408* ⊕ *www.bearhotel.co.uk* ↪ *35 rooms* ⧉ *Free Breakfast.*

Tintern Old Rectory

$ | **B&B/INN** | **FAMILY** | Set on a hill overlooking the Wye Valley, this black-and-white, 18th-century rectory offers period charm and a warm welcome. **Pros:** river views; comfortable beds; housemade Welsh cakes. **Cons:** off-site parking; steep steps up to rectory; owners have dogs so not very allergy-friendly. ⑤ *Rooms from: £100* ✉ *Tintern* ☎ *01291/689–920* ⊕ *www.tintern-oldrectory.co.uk* ↪ *4 rooms* ⧉ *Free Breakfast.*

Brecon (Aberhonddu)

19 miles northwest of Abergavenny, 41 miles north of Cardiff.

The historic market town of Brecon is known for its Georgian buildings, narrow passageways, and pleasant riverside walks. It's also the gateway to Brecon Beacons National Park. The town is particularly appealing on the second Saturday of each month, when the farmers' market takes place. A smaller market is also held every Tuesday and Friday. Brecon is also renowned for its jazz festival in August.

GETTING HERE AND AROUND

Brecon is easily accessible from Swansea and Cardiff, as well as many other towns, by direct buses. The nearest railway stations are at Merthyr Tydfil and Abergavenny (both about 19 miles away). Brecon is a handsome town to explore on foot—especially the riverside walk along the Promenade.

ESSENTIALS

VISITOR INFORMATION Visit Brecon. ✉ *11 Lion Yard* ☎ *01874/620–860* ⊕ *www.breconbeacons.org.*

 Sights

Brecknock Museum & Art Gallery

MUSEUM | **FAMILY** | In the colonnaded Shire Hall, built in 1842, this museum stages art exhibitions and holds artifacts of Welsh rural life, including a large collection of carved love spoons and a perfectly preserved 19th-century law court. It is also now a community center for the town and houses its library. ✉ *Captain's Walk* ☎ *01874/624121* ⧉ *Free.*

★ Brecon Beacons National Park

NATIONAL/STATE PARK | **FAMILY** | About 5 miles southwest of Brecon you encounter mountains and wild, windswept uplands that are tipped by shafts of golden light when the weather's fine, or fingers of ghostly mist when it's not. This 519-square-mile park is one of Wales's most breathtaking areas, perfect for a hike or scenic drive; it's also one of the world's few accredited International Dark Sky Reserves, which means it's an excellent location for star-gazing. Start at the visitor center on Mynydd Illtyd, a grassy stretch of upland west of the A470. Also known as the Mountain Centre, it's an excellent source of information about the park, including maps and advice on the best routes (guided or self-guided). There's also an excellent tearoom where you can fuel up for the journey or reward yourself with an indulgent slice of cake afterward. If you want to see it all from your car, any road that crosses the Beacons will offer you beautiful views, but the most spectacular is the high and undulating A4069, between Brynamman and Llangadog in the park's western end. ■ **TIP→ To explore the moorlands on foot, come prepared. Mist and rain descend**

One of three national parks in Wales, Brecon Beacons offers some panoramic mountain views, whether you're on foot or in a car.

quickly, and the summits are exposed to high winds. ⊠ Off A470, Brecon Beacons National Park ☎ 01874/623366 ⊕ www. breconbeacons.org ☜ Free; parking £1 for 2 hrs, £2 for 4 hrs, £3 all-day.

Brecon Cathedral

RELIGIOUS SITE | Modest on the outside but surprisingly cavernous on the inside, this cathedral stands on the hill above the middle of town. The cathedral was built on the site of an 11th-century priory, which was destroyed during Henry VIII's dissolution of the monasteries in the 1530s. It was rebuilt as a parish church fairly soon after and was remodeled in the 1860s. It became an Anglican Cathedral in 1923. The heritage center does a good job of telling the building's history, and there's also a handy café. Local choirs perform concerts here regularly; check the website for event listings. ⊠ Cathedral Close ☎ 01874/623857 ⊕ www.breconcathedral.org.uk ☜ Free.

★ Carreg Cennen Castle

CASTLE/PALACE | FAMILY | On the edge of Brecon Beacons National Park, about 30 miles west of Brecon, this decaying clifftop fortress was built in the 12th century, and remains of earlier defenses have been found dating back to the Iron Age. The castle, though a ruin, has a partially intact barbican (fortified outer section) and some inner chambers hewn dramatically from the bedrock. The climb to get there is somewhat punishing—you have to trudge up a steep, grassy hill—but the views of the valley, with its patchwork of green fields framed by the peaks of the Black Mountains, are enough to take away whatever breath you have left. Thankfully, there's a tearoom in the farm below the castle to take a breather after the climb. Kids will love the Longhorn cattle, Welsh Mountain ponies, and sheep on the owners' farm. ⊠ Off Derwydd Rd., Llandeilo ☎ 01558/822291 ⊕ www.carregcennencastle.com ☜ £5.50.

National Show Caves of Wales

CAVE | FAMILY | This underground cave system was discovered by two local men in 1912—make that rediscovered, as one of

Hiking and Biking in Wales

The Wales Coast Path is an 870-mile walking path that snakes along the entire coastline. Linking existing routes like the Pembrokeshire Coast Path in southeast Wales with newer sections, it passes as close to the coastline as possible. Managed by the Welsh government, the route can be pretty wild in places and there isn't always a guardrail, so keep a close eye on small children. Work is currently underway to link it up with other popular routes, which should create an unbroken system of walking trails extending for more than 1,000 miles within a few years.

Other long-distance paths include north–south Offa's Dyke Path, based on the border between England and Wales established by King Offa in the 8th century, and Glyndwr's Way, a 135-mile-long highland route that traverses Mid-Wales from the border town of Knighton via Machynlleth to Welshpool. Signposted footpaths in Wales's forested areas are short and easy to follow. Dedicated enthusiasts might prefer the wide-open spaces of Brecon Beacons National Park or the mountains of Snowdonia.

Wales's reputation as both an on-road and off-road cycling mecca is well established. There's an amazing choice of scenic routes and terrain from challenging off-road tracks (⊕ www. mbwales.com is for the serious cyclist) to long-distance road rides and gentle family trails; VisitWales has information to get you started.

Contacts and Resources

Cycling Wales ⊠ Brecon ⊕ www.visit-wales.com/things-to-do/activities/biking/cycling.

Offa's Dyke Centre ⊠ West St., Knighton ☎ 01547/528753 ⊕ www.offasdyke.org.uk/offas-dyke-association/offas-dyke-centre.

Pembrokeshire Coast Path ⊠ Pembroke ☎ 01646/624800 ⊕ www.pembrokeshire-coast.wales/coast-path.

Ramblers' Association in Wales ⊠ Cardiff ☎ 0203/961–3310 ⊕ www.ramblers.org.uk/wales.aspx.

Wales Coast Path ⊠ Brecon ⊕ www.walescoastpath.gov.uk.

the caves contained 42 human skeletons that had lain undisturbed for around 7,000 years. The main cave system, Dan Yr Ogof (Welsh for "beneath the cave"), is an impressive natural wonder, particularly the Cathedral Cave with natural stone archways and a dramatic waterfall. The whole thing is pitched at kids, with "dramatic" piped music to "enhance" the atmosphere, and a park featuring 200 life-size models of dinosaurs and other prehistoric creatures. There's also a playground, shire horse center, and a Victorian farm where kids can pet the animals. The caves are 17 miles southwest of Brecon. ⊠ Off A48 or B4310, Abercraf ☎ 01639/730284 ⊕ www.showcaves.co.uk 🎫 £15.50 🕙 Closed Nov.–Mar.

The Regimental Museum of the Royal Welsh
MUSEUM | The military exhibits here span centuries of conflict; some relate to battles in which this famous regiment and its Welsh predecessors participated. There's a vast collection of militaria, which will be of interest mostly to fans of military history. The 3,000 or so medals on display include copies of 16 Victoria Crosses (the British equivalent of the Purple Heart) owned by the regiment. The

Zulu Room recalls the defense of Rorke's Drift in the Anglo-Zulu war of 1879, an action dramatized in the 1964 film *Zulu*. ⊠ *The Barracks* ☎ *01874/613310* ⊕ *www. royalwelsh.org.uk* 🎫 *£5* 🕙 *Closed Sat. Oct.–Mar. and Sun. Sept.–July.*

Restaurants

★ Felin Fach Griffin
$$ | MODERN BRITISH | This excellent "restaurant with rooms" is renowned for its creative use of local products and the rustic-chic vibe. Fruit and vegetables come from the Griffin's own organic kitchen garden, while meat is sourced from surrounding estates such as the Welsh Venison Centre. **Known for:** great Sunday lunch; delicious local produce and meat; cozy atmosphere. ⑤ *Average main: £19* ⊠ *A470, Felin Fach* ☎ *01874/620111* ⊕ *www.eatdrinksleep.ltd.uk.*

Hotels

Coach House
$ | B&B/INN | This former coach house in the center of Brecon has been converted into a luxurious place to stay, and the friendly hosts—a wealth of information about the local area—can arrange transport to and from the best walking paths in the Beacons. **Pros:** lovely staff; central location; private parking. **Cons:** on a main road; minimum two-night stay most weekends; not very family-friendly. ⑤ *Rooms from: £99* ⊠ *12 Orchard St.* ☎ *01874/620043* ⊕ *www.coachhouse-brecon.com* 🛏 *6 rooms* ⧪ *Free Breakfast* ☞ *No children under the age of 16.*

Felin Glais
$ | B&B/INN | FAMILY | In the 17th century Felin Glais was a barn; today it provides spacious and comfortable accommodations but still hasn't lost its ancient character. **Pros:** beautiful building; spacious rooms; delicious breakfast. **Cons:** dog-friendly environment won't please everyone; cash or check only; cancellations within 72 hours are charged

in full. ⑤ *Rooms from: £100* ⊠ *Abersycir* ☎ *01874/623107* ⊕ *www.felinglais.co.uk* 🚫 *No credit cards* 🛏 *4 rooms* ⧪ *Free Breakfast.*

Performing Arts

Brecon Jazz Festival
MUSIC FESTIVALS | For a weekend every August, Brecon Jazz, an international music festival, takes over the town. Although the headliners perform at various venues in the evenings, roads are usually closed to traffic to make way for street entertainment, a market, and a kids' fair. ⊠ *Brecon* ⊕ *www.breconjazz. org.*

Theatr Brycheiniog
ARTS CENTERS | On the canal, Theatr Brycheiniog is the town's main venue for plays, live music, and comedy shows. It also has a café (lunch only) and a bar. ⊠ *Canal Wharf* ☎ *01874/611622* ⊕ *www. brycheiniog.co.uk.*

Shopping

★ The Hours
BOOKS/STATIONERY | This lovely little building on the main shopping street sells a good selection of books by Welsh writers as well as guides to the area. It also has a very nice café serving sandwiches and salads made with local ingredients. Local artwork adorns the walls. ⊠ *15 Ship St.* ☎ *01874/622800* ⊕ *www.thehours-brecon.co.uk.*

Activities

Biped Cycles
BICYCLING | FAMILY | The Brecon Beacons contain some of the best mountain biking routes in Britain. Biped Cycles will rent you the right bike and equipment. ⊠ *10 Ship St.* ☎ *01874/622296* ⊕ *www. bipedcycles.co.uk.*

Merthyr Mawr

45 miles south of Brecon, 22 miles west of Cardiff.

As you cross over an ancient stone bridge into Merthyr Mawr, you feel as if you've entered another world. From stone cottages with beehive-shape thatched roofs to the Victorian-era Church of St. Teilo, with the pieces of its long-gone 5th-century predecessor lined up in its churchyard, it's an idyllic place to wander around. The picturesque ruin of Ogmore Castle is just off the B4524, but the most memorable way to reach it is via the walking path that starts in the car park at the very southern tip of the village. The mile-long route goes through a farm and past a Shetland pony stable.

GETTING HERE AND AROUND
Merthyr Mawr is signposted from the A48 and B4524, 7 miles southwest of junction 35 on the M4. The nearest train station is in Bridgend. There's no bus service to the village, but you can take bus 303 from Bridgend to Ogmore, just south of the river.

Sights

★ Nash Point
VIEWPOINT | FAMILY | Just a few miles south of Merthyr Mawr is this stunning promontory overlooking the Bristol Channel. Twin lighthouses stand guard against the elements; one is still operational, but the other is open for tours (by prior arrangement). This is also a popular picnic spot, and a small snack kiosk is open during summer months. Nothing beats this place at sunset, when the evening sky ignites in a riot of color. It's one of the most romantic spots in South Wales. ⚠ **There's no guardrail on the cliff, so keep a close eye on children.** ⊠ *Marcross* ☎ *07866/767707* ⊕ *www.nashpoint. co.uk* ⌕ *Free; lighthouse £5* ☉ *Closed Nov.–Feb.*

Ogmore Castle
CASTLE/PALACE | FAMILY | Just south of the village are these atmospheric ruins, nestled by a river that can only be crossed via stepping-stones. A number of legends are associated with the castle, one concerning a ghost that supposedly forces passersby to embrace a large rock known as the "Goblin Stone." When you try to draw back, so the story goes, you find that your hands and feet have become part of the rock. ⊠ *Ogmore Rd.* ⌕ *Free.*

Restaurants

The Plough and Harrow
$ | BRITISH | FAMILY | A short drive from Nash Point is this historic pub, on the edge of the tiny clifftop village of Monknash. The food is delicious and unfussy; the menu changes regularly, but features tasty pub classics like burgers and fish-and-chips. **Known for:** craft beer and cider; delicious pies; lively atmosphere. ⑤ *Average main: £10* ⊠ *Off Heol Las, Monknash* ☎ *01656/890209.*

Swansea (Abertawe)

22 miles northwest of Merthyr Mawr, 40 miles west of Cardiff.

The birthplace of poet Dylan Thomas (1914–53), Swansea adores its native son. Every year the poet is honored with his own day: May 14th, the anniversary of when *Under Milk Wood* was first read onstage. For many years, Swansea wasn't a place that inspired much poetry; heavily bombed in World War II, it was clumsily rebuilt. However, now times are changing and a cultural renaissance is taking place, with a thriving arts-and-music scene developing in recent years. There are also several good museums. In the surrounding area, the National Botanic Gardens and Laugharne make for interesting diversions, and the stunning

Gower Peninsula contains some of the country's best beaches.

GETTING HERE AND AROUND

There's an hourly rail service from London's Paddington Station. The city has direct National Express bus connections to other parts of Wales, as well as to London and other cities

ESSENTIALS

VISITOR INFORMATION Swansea Tourist Information. ⊕ *www.visitswanseabay. com.*

Sights

Dylan Thomas Centre

MUSEUM | Situated on the banks of the Tawe in the Maritime Quarter, the Dylan Thomas Centre celebrates the life of the writer with an excellent permanent exhibition as well as literary events and activities. In summer, guided tours showcasing Dylan's Swansea start from here. There's also a cozy little café serving locally sourced products. Fans of the poet can buy a booklet here that outlines the Dylan Thomas Trail around South Wales. It includes the Boathouse (now a museum) in Laugharne, where the poet lived and wrote for the last four years of his life. ✉ *Somerset Pl.* ☎ *01792/463980* ⊕ *www.dylanthomas.com* ✉ *Free.*

Egypt Centre

MUSEUM | **FAMILY** | A substantial collection of ancient Egyptian artifacts is on display here, including bead necklaces from the time of Tutankhamun and the beautiful painted coffin of a Theban musician. ✉ *University of Wales–Swansea, Singleton Park* ☎ *01792/295960* ⊕ *www.egypt. swan.ac.uk* ✉ *Free* ⊙ *Closed Sun. and Mon.*

★ 5 Cwmdonkin Drive

HOUSE | Dylan Thomas was born in this suburban Edwardian house, which remains a place of pilgrimage for the poet's devotees. You can wander the house with no restrictions (they're proud of the fact that nothing is roped off), or prebook tours that are tailored according to how much time you want to spend here. You can also arrange tours of other Thomas-related sites in Swansea and farther afield in the region. The house can be rented as self-catering accommodation for around £150 per night. You can also book lunch, afternoon tea, or dinner. ✉ *5 Cwmdonkin Dr.* ☎ *01792/472555* ⊕ *www.dylanthomasbirthplace.com* ✉ *£8.*

★ Glynn Vivian Art Gallery

MUSEUM | **FAMILY** | Founded in 1911 by a bequest from Richard Glynn Vivian (1835–1910), an art collector and philanthropist whose family were prominent industrialists in the city, the public gallery is one of Swansea's highlights. Exhibits include an internationally important collection of Swansea china as well as works by acclaimed local artists. There is usually a busy calendar of events, including regular temporary exhibitions; check the website for more details. The contemporary, airy café serves good coffee, cakes, salads, and sandwiches. ✉ *Alexandra Rd.* ☎ *01792/516900* ⊕ *www.swansea.gov.uk/glynnvivian* ✉ *Free* ⊙ *Closed Mon.*

★ Gower Peninsula

BEACH—SIGHT | **FAMILY** | This peninsula, which stretches westward from Swansea, was the first part of Britain to be designated an Area of Outstanding Natural Beauty. Its shores are a succession of sheltered sandy bays and awesome headlands. The seaside resort of Mumbles, on the outskirts of Swansea, is the most famous town along the route. It's a pleasant place to wander on a sunny afternoon, with a Norman castle, an amusement pier, and a seaside promenade, as well as a variety of independent cafés and boutiques. Farther along the peninsula, the secluded Pwlldu Bay can only be reached on foot from nearby villages like Southgate. A few miles westward is the more accessible (and very popular) Three Cliffs Bay, with its sweeping views and wide, sandy beach. At the far western tip of the peninsula, Rhossili has perhaps the best beach of all. Its unusual, snaking causeway—known locally as the Worm's Head—is inaccessible at high tide. Gower is a popular destination with surfers and you'll find many other water sports offered here. ⊠ Swansea ⊕ www.explore-gower.co.uk.

Laugharne

TOWN | According to Dylan Thomas, this attractive estuary town 39 miles west of Swansea was the "strangest town in Wales"; nonetheless, he spent the last four years of his adult life here and is buried in the graveyard at St. Martin's Church. Visitors should first head to the Boathouse, where Dylan lived with his family from 1949 to 1953 and where he wrote *Do Not Go Gentle* and *Under Milk Wood*. Then head for a drink at Brown's, his local pub. Be sure to also check out the ruined castle, browse the second-hand bookshop, and enjoy a coastal walk. Laugharne buzzes in April when the arts festival, Laugharne Weekend, takes place. ⊠ Laugharne ⊕ www.laugharne-lines.wales.

★ National Botanic Garden of Wales

GARDEN | FAMILY | This 568-acre, 18th-century estate is dotted with lakes, fountains, and a Japanese garden. The centerpiece is the Norman Foster–designed Great Glass House, the largest single-span greenhouse in the world, which blends into the curving landforms of the Tywi Valley. The greenhouse's interior landscape includes a 40-foot-deep ravine and thousands of plants from all over the world. The Ghost Forest is a stunning art installation, made from the carved stumps of 10 giant hardwood trees—a powerful statement on how rapidly the world's forests are being destroyed. Also here is the British Bird of Prey Centre, where you can watch native raptors flying daily, including a golden eagle. The grounds have lovely views

across the Carmarthenshire countryside, especially from the Paxton's View lookout point. It's marked by Paxton's Tower, a Gothic folly built to honor Horatio Nelson, now owned by the National Trust (it's free to wander, though there's nothing to see inside). The garden, 20 miles northwest of Swansea, is signposted off the main road between Swansea and Carmarthen. ⊠ Off A48 or B4310, Llanarthne ☎ 01558/667149 ⊕ www.gardenofwales.org.uk ⊠ £11.50.

National Waterfront Museum

MUSEUM | FAMILY | Housed in a construction of steel, slate, and glass grafted onto a historic redbrick building, the National Waterfront Museum's galleries have 15 theme areas, presenting Welsh maritime and industrial history through state-of-the-art interactive technology and a host of artifacts. Highlights of the collection include a monoplane built by amateur aviation enthusiasts in the early 1900s, one of the oldest British aircraft in existence, as well as one of the last carriages from the Mumbles Train, the world's first passenger rail service (1807–1960). You'll also learn about Swansea's important international role in copper smelting in the 19th century. ⊠ Oystermouth Rd., Maritime Quarter ☎ 0300/111–2333 ⊕ www.museum.wales/swansea ⊠ Free.

Swansea Market

MARKET | Swansea's covered market, part of the Quadrant Shopping Centre, is one of the best fresh-foods markets in Wales. In 2020, it was even voted Best Large Indoor Market at The Great British Market Awards. You can buy cockles from the Penclawdd beds on the nearby Gower Peninsula, and laverbread, that unique Welsh delicacy made from seaweed, which is usually served with bacon and eggs. ⊠ Oxford St. ☎ 01792/654296 ⊕ www.swanseaindoormarket.co.uk ⊙ Closed Sun.

Swansea Museum

MUSEUM | FAMILY | Founded in 1841, this museum contains a quirky and eclectic collection that includes an Egyptian mummy, local archaeological exhibits, and the intriguing Cabinet of Curiosity, which holds artifacts from Swansea's past. In 2016, a forgotten Flemish masterpiece by Jacob Jordaens (1593–1678) was discovered in the museum's storeroom and is now on show. ⊠ Victoria Rd. ☎ 01792/653763 ⊕ www.swanseamuseum.co.uk ⊠ Free ⊘ Closed Mon.

🍴 Restaurants

★ Beach House
$$$ | MODERN BRITISH | On the beach at Oxwich, this stylish Michelin-starred eatery is considered one of the best in all of Wales. The beautifully presented dishes are made using excellent local ingredients, particularly seafood. **Known for:** beachside location; creative fish dishes; interesting wine list. $ Average main: £25 ⊠ Oxwich Beach ☎ 01792/390965 ⊕ www.beachhouseoxwich.co.uk ⊘ Closed Mon. and Tues.

The Cliff
$ | BRITISH | After a bracing walk around Three Cliffs Bay, head to this restaurant on the top floor of Three Cliffs Coffee Shop. The emphasis here is on showcasing local produce, including cured meats and salt-marsh lamb. **Known for:** dishes with local produce; delicious cakes and other desserts; coastal location. $ Average main: £15 ⊠ 68 Southgate Rd. ☎ 01792/399030 ⊕ www.the-cliff.co.uk ⊘ No dinner Sun.–Tues.

Hanson at the Chelsea
$$ | MODERN BRITISH | Tucked down a lane off Wind Street, the town's main nightlife area, this cozy restaurant is the most consistently reliable for good food in the city center. The London Ritz–trained chef deftly turns out delicious dishes made with the best local ingredients. **Known for:** one of the city's best restaurants; delicious fish dishes; affordable two course lunch menu. $ Average main: £18 ⊠ 17 St. Mary St. ☎ 01792/464068 ⊕ www.hansonatthechelsea.co.uk ⊘ Closed Sun.

La Braseria
$ | SPANISH | Lively and welcoming, this spot resembles a Spanish bodega (wine cellar), with its flamenco music, oak barrels, and whitewashed walls. Among the house specialties are sea bass in rock salt, roast suckling pig, and steak. **Known for:** delicious grills; good selection of champagne; fresh fish dishes. $ Average main: £15 ⊠ 28 Wind St. ☎ 01792/469683 ⊕ www.labraseria.com.

Pant-y-Gwydr
$$ | BISTRO | This excellent little bistro in the center of Swansea has an air of retro sophistication. The menu is traditionally French; you might start with a half dozen escargots served with garlic butter before moving on to steak frites. **Known for:** authentic French cuisine with some vegan options; French wine options; rustic-chic dining room. $ Average main: £17 ⊠ Pantygwydr Hotel, Oxford St. ☎ 01792/455498 ⊕ www.pantygwydr.co.uk ⊘ Closed Mon. No dinner Sun.

Verdi's
$ | ITALIAN | FAMILY | This family run ice-cream parlor, café, and restaurant sits right on the seafront. Housemade pizza is a specialty, or you could just join the queue for the delicious fresh gelato. **Known for:** tasty Italian food; good selection of ice creams; great sea views. $ Average main: £10 ⊠ Knab Rock, Mumbles Rd., The Mumbles ☎ 01792/369135 ⊕ www.verdis-cafe.co.uk.

Hotels

Langland Cove
$ | B&B/INN | FAMILY | This stylish B&B is a ten-minute walk to the village of Mumbles and a stone's thrown from a couple of lovely beaches on the southeastern edge of the Gower Peninsula. **Pros:** attractive decor; delicious breakfast; beach-friendly location. **Cons:** steep stairs; suburb location; no sea views.

⑤ *Rooms from: £100* ✉ *4 Rotherslade Rd.* ☎ *07411/5450–685* ⊕ *www.langland-cove.co.uk* ⇄ *4 rooms* ⑩ *Free Breakfast.*

★ Morgans
$$ | **HOTEL** | **FAMILY** | Now a hotel, the Victorian-era Port Authority building in the Maritime Quarter has lost none of its period features: moldings, pillars, stained glass, and wood floors. **Pros:** free parking; short walk to shops; historic building. **Cons:** no room service in Townhouse; on the busy main road into Swansea; bar gets crowded. ⑤ *Rooms from: £125* ✉ *Somerset Pl.* ☎ *01792/484848* ⊕ *www.morganshotel.co.uk* ⇄ *42 rooms* ⑩ *Free Breakfast.*

Three Cliffs Bay Holiday Park
$ | **RENTAL** | **FAMILY** | Not only is this five-star campsite in an Area of Out-standing Natural Beauty (aka the Gower Peninsula), it overlooks what has been voted one of Britain's best beaches. **Pros:** stunning location; on-site shop selling local produce; free guide for walks. **Cons:** minimum stay on weekends and school holidays; payments are non-refundable; sea view pitches can't be reserved in advance. ⑤ *Rooms from: £43* ✉ *North Hills Farm* ☎ *01792/371–218* ⊕ *www.threecliffsbay.com* ⇄ *20 yurts, 23 caravan pitches, 90 tent pitches* ⑩ *No meals.*

Tenby (Dinbych-y-Pysgod)

53 miles west of Swansea.

Pastel-color Georgian houses cluster around a harbor in this seaside town, which became a fashionable resort in the 19th century and is still popular. Two golden sandy beaches stretch below the hotel-lined cliff top. Medieval Tenby's ancient town walls still stand, enclosing narrow streets and passageways full of shops, inns, and places to eat. From the harbor you can take a short boat trip to Caldey Island, with its active Cistercian community.

GETTING HERE AND AROUND
Tenby is on the southwest Wales rail route from London's Paddington Station. You have to change trains at Swansea or Newport. The center of Tenby, a maze of narrow medieval streets, has parking restrictions. In summer, downtown is closed to traffic, so park in one of the lots and take the shuttle buses.

ESSENTIALS
VISITOR INFORMATION Tenby Tourist Information Centre. ✉ *Upper Park Rd.* ☎ *01437/775603* ⊕ *www.visitpembroke-shire.com.*

 ## Sights

Caldey Island
RELIGIOUS SITE | **FAMILY** | This beautiful little island off the coast at Tenby has whitewashed stone buildings that lend it a Mediterranean feel. The island is best known for its Cistercian order, whose black-and-white-robed monks make a famous perfume from the local plants. You can visit tiny St. Illtyd's Church to see the Caldey Stone, an early Christian arti-fact from circa AD 600, engraved in Latin and ancient Celtic. St. David's Church, on a hill above the village, is a simple Nor-man chapel noted for its art-deco stained glass. The monastery itself isn't open to the public, but its church has a public viewing gallery if you want to observe a service. Boats to Caldey Island leave from Tenby's harbor every 20 minutes or so between Easter and October. ✉ *Caldey Island* ☎ *01834/844453* ⊕ *www.caldeyislandwales.com* ⬚ *Free; boats £14 round-trip* ☉ *Closed Sun.*

Pembroke Castle
CASTLE/PALACE | **FAMILY** | About 10 miles east of Tenby is this remarkably com-plete Norman fortress dating from 1199, and where Henry VII was born in 1457. Its walls remain stout, its gatehouse mighty, and the enormous cylindrical

keep proved so impregnable to cannon fire in the Civil War that Cromwell's men had to starve out its Royalist defenders. Climb the towers and walk the walls for fine views. A well-stocked gift shop sells faux-medieval knickknacks. ✉ *Westgate Hill, Pembroke* ☎ *01646/681510* ⊕ *www. pembrokecastle.co.uk* 🎟 *£7.*

Tenby Museum and Art Gallery
MUSEUM | FAMILY | Close to the castle, this small but informative museum recalls the town's maritime history and its growth as a fashionable resort. Kids will appreciate the section on Tenby's role in the golden age of piracy. Two art galleries feature works by local artists, including Augustus John. ✉ *Castle Hill* ☎ *01834/842809* ⊕ *www.tenbymuseum.org.uk* 🎟 *£4.95* ⊗ *Closed Sun. and Mon.*

Town Trails of Tenby
TOUR—SIGHT | Learn more about Tenby's storied past with guide Marion Davies, who offers general tours as well as thematic tours on local poets and painters, the harbor, pirates and smuggling, and ghosts. ✉ *Tenby* ☎ *01834/845841, 07970/420734* ⊕ *guidedtourswales. co.uk.*

Tudor Merchant's House
HOUSE | FAMILY | This late-15th-century home shows how a prosperous trader would have lived in Tudor times. Kids can try on Tudor-style costumes. The gift shop sells handmade pottery based on unique, original designs found at the house. ✉ *Quay Hill* ☎ *01834/842279* ⊕ *www. nationaltrust.org.uk/tudor-merchants-house* 🎟 *£6* ⊗ *Closed Tues.*

🍽 Restaurants

★ Coast
$$$ | BRITISH | FAMILY | Located right next to the beach, this unassuming restaurant is one of the best in south Wales. Local produce like Welsh Wagyu beef is turned into a work of art, served on the terrace in summer. **Known for:** fantastic coastal views; excellent seafood; superb

seven-course tasting menu. ⑤ *Average main: £24* ✉ *Coppet Hall Beach, Saundersfoot* ☎ *01834/810–800* ⊕ *coastsaundersfoot.co.uk* ⊗ *Closed Mon. and Tues.*

★ Plantagenet House
$$$ | BRITISH | Flickering candles, open fireplaces, exposed stone walls, and top-notch locally sourced food are hallmarks of this restaurant and bar, which dates back to the 10th century. The menu contains a selection of Welsh-reared steaks and other meat dishes, but outstanding seafood is the real specialty. **Known for:** romantic setting; extensive menu with local produce; great seafood dishes. ⑤ *Average main: £25* ✉ *Quay Hill* ☎ *01834/842650* ⊕ *www.plantagenettenby.co.uk* ⊗ *Closed Jan.–mid-Feb.*

🛏 Hotels

Ivy Bank Guest House
$ | B&B/INN | FAMILY | This comfortable and immaculate Victorian house sits across from the train station, a five-minute stroll from the sea. **Pros:** cozy and simple; close to beach; welcoming host. **Cons:** you have to park at the train station; first night must be paid in advance (nonrefundable and nonchangeable); gets booked up in advance. ⑤ *Rooms from: £76* ✉ *Harding St.* ☎ *01834/842311* ⊕ *www.ivybankguesthouse.co.uk* 🛏 *5 rooms* 🍽 *Free Breakfast.*

★ Penally Abbey
$$ | HOTEL | Built on the site of a 6th-century abbey in 5 acres of lush forest overlooking Camarthen Bay, this dignified 18th-century house is awash with period details. **Pros:** informal luxury; great views; friendly hosts. **Cons:** cheaper rooms are in the Coach House; seven-day cancellation rule; no elevator. ⑤ *Rooms from: £155* ✉ *Off A4139, 2 miles west of Tenby, Penally* ☎ *01834/843033* ⊕ *www.penally-abbey.com* ⊗ *Closed Jan.* 🛏 *12 rooms* 🍽 *Free Breakfast*

★ St. Brides Spa Hotel

$$ | HOTEL | FAMILY | Between Amroth and Tenby, this luxury hotel has a breathtaking location perched above Carmarthen Bay; most of the superbly appointed rooms have stunning sea views. **Pros:** amazing views; wonderful spa; good restaurant. **Cons:** steep walk from the beach; minimum stay on weekends; pricey for the area. $ *Rooms from: £200* ✉ *St. Brides Hill, Saundersfoot* ☎ *01834/812304* ⊕ *www.stbridesspahotel.com* ⤳ *34 rooms* ❖ *Free Breakfast.*

 Nightlife

Harbwr

BREWPUBS/BEER GARDENS | Housed in a charming 18th-century warehouse overlooking the beach, Tenby Harbour Brewery was the town's first craft brewery. You can sample the award-winning ales in the shabby-chic surroundings, tuck into good pub food including fresh fish, and even book a tour (minimum four people). ✉ *Sergeant's Lane, St. Julian St.* ☎ *01834/845–797* ⊕ *www.harbwr.wales.*

 Activities

The town's beaches are hugely popular in summertime. North Beach is the busiest, with shops and a little café along the promenade. The adjoining Harbour Beach is prettier and more secluded. Castle Beach is in a little cove where you can walk out to a small island at low tide. Past that is South Beach, which stretches for more than a mile.

St. Davids (Tyddewi)

35 miles northwest of Tenby.

Despite its minuscule size, this community of fewer than 1,800 people isn't a village or a town—it's actually Britain's smallest city. Historically, little St. Davids has punched above its weight due to the presence of St. Davids Cathedral,

the resting place of the patron saint of Wales and once a major destination for pilgrims. These days, visitors with time on their hands might want to consider approaching the city via the Wales Coast Path, around the St. Davids headland from St. Justinian to Caerfai Bay. You might also consider a wildlife-watching boat trip or an afternoon surfing at Whitesands Beach. In May and June the town's hedgerows and coastal paths are ablaze with wildflowers. The Pembrokeshire Coast National Park Visitor Centre is also here and features an exhibition of works by Pembrokeshire artists, notably Graham Sutherland.

GETTING HERE AND AROUND

St. Davids is on the A487. The nearest train station is 14 miles southeast in Haverfordwest. Bus 411 travels from Haverfordwest to St. Davids every hour or so.

ESSENTIALS

VISITOR INFORMATION Oriel y Parc Gallery and Visitor Centre. ✉ *The Grove, St. Davids* ☎ *01437/720392* ⊕ *www. orielyparc.co.uk.*

⦿ Sights

Last Invasion Tapestry

MEMORIAL | The 100-foot-long Last Invasion Tapestry, on display in the Town Hall in Fishguard, is modeled on the famous Bayeux Tapestry depicting the Norman invasion of 1066. This modern version marks a lesser known and certainly less successful assault on the country. In 1797, a unit of French soldiers, led by an Irish-American general, landed in Fishguard Harbour. They were defeated by a hastily assembled local militia, which included many women. The impressive tapestry, commissioned to mark the event's 200th anniversary, took 70 local women more than 40,000 hours to complete. Fishguard is 16 miles northeast of St. Davids off the A487. ✉ *Fishguard Town Hall, Market Sq., Fishguard*

St. Davids Cathedral was originally founded by St. David himself around 600 AD.

☎ 01437/776638 ⊕ *lastinvasiontapestry. co.uk* ✉ *Free* ☉ *Closed Sun.*

★ **Pembrokeshire Coast National Park**
NATIONAL/STATE PARK | FAMILY | By far the smallest of the country's three national parks, Pembrokeshire Coast is no less strikingly beautiful than the other two. The park has several Blue Flag beaches and a host of spectacular cliff-top drives and walks, including some of the most popular stretches of the Wales Coast Path. The park has a smattering of historic sites, including the impossibly picturesque St. Davids Cathedral, built in a Viking-proof nook by the Irish Sea. The information center in St. Davids is a good place to start. ✉ *Oriel Y Parc Gallery and Visitor Centre, The Grove, St. Davids* ☎ 01437/720392 ⊕ *www.pembrokeshire-coast.wales* ✉ *Free.*

★ **St. Davids Cathedral**
RELIGIOUS SITE | The idyllic valley location of this cathedral helped protect the church from Viking raiders by hiding it from the view of invaders who came by sea. Originally founded by St. David himself around AD 600, the current building dates from the 12th century, although it has been added to at various times since. You must climb down 39 steps (known locally as the Thirty-Nine Articles) to enter the grounds; then start at the Gatehouse, with its exhibition on the history of the building. In the cathedral itself, the 15th-century choir stalls still have their original floor tiles, while the Holy Trinity Chapel contains an intricate fan-vaulted ceiling and a casket said to contain the patron saint's bones.
■ **TIP→ Don't miss the Treasury and its illuminated gospels, silver chalices, and 700-year-old golden bishop's crosier.** At the rear of the grounds of St. Davids Cathedral are the ruins of the 13th-century Bishop's Palace, particularly beautiful at dusk. The cathedral has a good café serving lunch made with local produce. ✉ *The Close, St. Davids* ☎ 01437/720202 ⊕ *www.stdavidscathedral.org.uk* ✉ *Free.*

Hotels

★ Twr-Y-Felin Hotel

$$ | HOTEL | This luxury hotel on the southeast edge of the city features spacious, contemporary rooms, a restaurant with delicious Welsh produce, and a strong contemporary art collection. **Pros:** contemporary luxury; good restaurant; excellent art collection. **Cons:** brown/grey decor might not appeal to some; limited facilities; on the pricier side. $ *Rooms from: £190* ⊠ *Ffordd Caerfai, St. Davids* ☎ *01437/725555* ⊕ *www.twryfelinhotel. com* ↪ *21 rooms* ⧖ *Free Breakfast* ↷ *No children under 12.*

Nightlife

★ The Dyffryn Arms (*Bessie's*)

BARS/PUBS | Most commonly referred to by the name of its 90-year-old landlady (Bessie), this traditional pub, in an attractive rural location 5 miles east of Fishguard, is a real step back in time. Jugs of Bass beer are served through a hatch in the antique-filled parlor, which is warmed by a coal fire in winter. ⊠ *Pontfaen Rd., Pontfaen, Fishguard.*

Hay-on-Wye (Y Gelli Gandryll)

57 miles north of Cardiff, 25 miles north of Abergavenny.

With its crumbling old castle and low-slung buildings framed by lolloping green hills, Hay-on-Wye is a beautiful little place. In 1961 the late Richard Booth established a small secondhand bookshop here. Other booksellers soon got in on the act, and now there are dozens of shops. It's now the largest secondhand bookselling center in the world, and priceless 14th-century manuscripts rub spines with "job lots" selling for a few pounds.

For 10 days every May and June, Hay-on-Wye is taken over by its Literary Festival, a celebration of literature that attracts famous writers from all over the world. (Bill Clinton, himself an attendee, once called it "the Woodstock of the mind.") Plan ahead if you want to attend, as hotels get booked several months in advance.

GETTING HERE AND AROUND

You'll need a car to get to Hay. Use one of the public lots on the outskirts of town and walk—the whole town is accessible on foot. The nearest train stations are Builth Wells in Wales (19 miles) and Hereford in England (22 miles).

ESSENTIALS

VISITOR INFORMATION Hay-on-Wye Tourist Information Bureau. ⊠ *Chapel Cottage, Oxford Rd., Hay-on-wye* ☎ *01497/820144* ⊕ *www.hay-on-wye.co.uk/tourism.*

Sights

Gospel Pass

SCENIC DRIVE | FAMILY | About 5 miles south of Hay on the B4350 is the highest mountain pass in Wales (1,801 feet). Park your car at the top, and take a walk along part of Offa's Dyke. ⊠ *Hay-on-wye* ⧉ *Free.*

Restaurants

Chapters

$$$$ | BRITISH | Seasonal, local produce is what it's all about at this sustainable restaurant located in an attractive old stone building in the town center. The five-course set menu features beautifully crafted dishes like Heirloom tomato with Ragstone goat's cheese, nasturtiums, and pickled shallots; there's also a separate vegetarian menu. **Known for:** creative use of local produce; excellent service; stylish dining room. $ *Average main: £35* ⊠ *Lion St., Hay-on-wye* ☎ *07855/783–799* ⊕ *www.chaptershayonwye.co.uk* ⊗ *Closed Sun.–Wed. No lunch.*

Mid-Wales

Shepherd's Parlour

$ | BRITISH | FAMILY | Sheep's-milk ice cream, delicious cakes, and local produce mixed with international flavors are offered at this little café. Many customers come just for the coffee, especially the Lebanese variety. **Known for:** variety of ice-cream flavors; interesting sandwich fillings; artisan coffee. *$ Average main: £7 ⊠ 9 High Town, Hay-on-wye ☎ 01497/821–898 ⊕ www.shepherdsparlour.com.*

 ## Hotels

★ Llangoed Hall

$$ | HOTEL | This magnificent Jacobean mansion on the banks of the River Wye, about 7 miles west of Hay-on-Wye, has beautiful fabrics and furnishings, open fireplaces, a sweeping carved staircase, and a paneled library dating back to 1632. **Pros:** secluded setting by River Wye; wonderful art collection; regular special events and offers. **Cons:** often filled with wedding parties; minimum stay sometimes required; no attractions within walking distance. *$ Rooms from: £160 ⊠ A470, Llyswen ☎ 01874/754525 ⊕ www.llangoedhall.co.uk ⤶ 23 rooms ⊦⊙⊦ Free Breakfast.*

The Swan

$$ | HOTEL | Once a coaching inn, this sophisticated lodging on the edge of town retains its sense of history. **Pros:** gorgeous building; popular bar; good food. **Cons:** wedding parties dominate in summer; some rooms are small; narrow, steep staircases. *$ Rooms from: £130 ⊠ Church St., Hay-on-wye ☎ 01497/821188 ⊕ www.swanathay.co.uk ⤶ 19 rooms ⊦⊙⊦ No meals.*

The annual Royal Welsh Show in Llanelwedd features old-school livestock competitions.

Shopping

The Thursday Market takes over much of the town center every Thursday morning. Traders sell everything from antiques to home-baked cakes.

Addyman Books

BOOKS/STATIONERY | The second best-known bookshop in Hay (after Richard Booth's) has a warren of rooms devoted to different genres, from steampunk to vintage Penguin editions. Relax in one of the upstairs armchairs while you browse. ⊠ *39 Lion St., Hay-on-wye* ☏ *01497/821–136* ⊕ *www.hay-on-wyebooks.com.*

Hay Cinema Bookshop

BOOKS/STATIONERY | A former movie theater, Hay Cinema Bookshop isn't the prettiest place, but its collection of books about cinema is unrivaled. That's just a fraction of the 200,000 or so titles on offer. ⊠ *Castle St., Hay-on-wye* ☏ *01497/820071* ⊕ *www.haycinemabookshop.co.uk.*

Murder and Mayhem

BOOKS/STATIONERY | True to its name, this shop specializes in crime and horror. Head upstairs for a cheaper and more eclectic selection, including old pulp novellas. ⊠ *5 Lion St., Hay-on-wye* ☏ *01497/821613.*

The Old Electric Shop

SPECIALTY STORES | FAMILY | This shop features a mixed bag of local crafts, internationally-sourced vintage home decor, and a curated collection of non-fiction books. The on-site café is the place to go for vegetarian food and good coffee in town, and even its chairs and tables are for sale. ⊠ *10 Broad St., Hay-on-wye* ☏ *01497/821–194* ⊕ *www.oldelectric.co.uk.*

★ Richard Booth Books

BOOKS/STATIONERY | Founder Richard Booth once tried to declare Hay an independent kingdom—with himself as king. Richard died in 2019 but his bookstore lives on and has a huge collection from all over the world, piled haphazardly across two labyrinthine floors. There's also a tiny cinema (around the corner on Brook Street) and a café along with regular events. ⊠ *44 Lion St., Hay-on-wye* ☎ *01497/820322* ⊕ *www.boothbooks. co.uk.*

Llandrindod Wells (Llandrindod)

27 miles north of Hay-on-Wye, 67 miles north of Cardiff.

Also known as Llandod, the old spa town of Llandrindod Wells preserves its Victorian look with turrets, cupolas, loggias, and balustrades everywhere. Cross over to South Crescent, passing the Glen Usk Hotel with its wrought-iron balustrade and the Victorian bandstand in the gardens opposite, and you reach Middleton Street, a Victorian thoroughfare. From there, head to Rock Park and the path that leads to the Pump Room. This historic building is now an alternative health center, but visitors can freely "take the waters."

GETTING HERE AND AROUND
There are about half a dozen trains daily from Cardiff Central Station, and the journey takes around three to four hours. Direct trains from Swansea and Shrewsbury also stop here, but they're less frequent.

ESSENTIALS
VISITOR INFORMATION Llandrindod Wells Tourist information Centre. ⊠ *The Old Town Hall, Temple St.* ☎ *01597/822600* ⊕ *www. llandrindod.co.uk.*

Sights

The National Cycle Museum
MUSEUM | FAMILY | This quirky museum, housed in an art-deco building, has a collection of more than 260 bicycles dating from 1818 to the present day.

⊠ *The Automobile Palace, Temple St.* ☎ *01597/825531* ⊕ *www.cyclemuseum. org.uk* ⊠ *£5* ⊗ *Closed Mon., Thurs., and most weekends (check website).*

★ Powis Castle
CASTLE/PALACE | FAMILY | Continuously occupied since the 13th century, Powis Castle rises above the town of Welshpool. One of the most elegant residential castles in Britain, Powis is equally renowned for its magnificent terraced gardens. The interior contains an outstanding art collection, from Greek vases to paintings by Thomas Gainsborough and Joshua Reynolds. The **Clive of India Museum** contains perhaps the most extensive private collection of antique Indian art in Britain. Powis Castle is north of Llandrindod Wells on the A483. ⊠ *A483, Welshpool* ☎ *01938/551944* ⊕ *www.nationaltrust.org.uk/powis-castle-and-garden* ⊠ *£14.20.*

Radnorshire Museum
MUSEUM | In Memorial Gardens, this museum tells the story of the town's development from prehistory onwards and includes a small collection of Roman and medieval artifacts. The largest and most interesting section is devoted to the town's Victorian heyday, with some of the "cures" at the spa explained in detail. ⊠ *Temple St.* ☎ *01597/824513* ⊕ *en.powys.gov.uk/article/1703/Radnorshire-Museum* ⊠ *Free* ⊗ *Closed Sun. and Mon.*

★ Royal Welsh Show
FESTIVAL | FAMILY | The town of Llanelwedd, 7 miles south of Llandrindod, comes to life in late July for the Royal Welsh Show. The old-school livestock judging, sheepdog competitions, and craft demonstrations are spiced up with events such as vintage air displays and motorbike stunt shows. And don't miss the food pavilion, filled with tasty local options. ⊠ *Llanelwedd* ☎ *01982/553683* ⊕ *rwas.wales/royal-welsh* ⊠ *£27.*

Restaurants

Sugar and Spice
$ | **MEDITERRANEAN** | **FAMILY** | This sweet and friendly little bistro looks unassuming from the outside, but its pan-Mediterranean, locally-sourced fare has won over legions of local fans. Choose from the selection of tapas (Spanish with a hint of Greek), fresh pasta or pizza, a Mediterranean salad, or just a tasty hamburger; there are also vegan options. **Known for:** good selection of tapas; creative cocktails; Mediterranean flavors. *Average main: £14* ✉ *Park Crescent* ☎ *01597/824442* ⊕ *www.sugarandspice-bistro.co.uk* ☾ *No dinner Sun.–Thurs.*

Hotels

Brynhir Farm
$ | **B&B/INN** | A friendly welcome awaits at this cozy 17th-century farmhouse 2 miles outside Llandrindod. **Pros:** lovely house; peaceful location; charming hosts. **Cons:** lacks modern extras; remote location is not walking distance to town; old-fashioned decor. *Rooms from: £75* ✉ *Chapel Rd.* ☎ *01597/822425* ⊕ *www.brynhirfarm.co.uk* ☞ *5 rooms* ❍⧵ *Free Breakfast.*

Lake Country House Hotel & Spa
$$ | **HOTEL** | The place to go for total Victorian country elegance, Lake Country and its 50 acres of sloping lawns contain a trout-filled lake bordered by an impressive spa. **Pros:** superb grounds; good food; luxurious spa. **Cons:** remote location; dress code in evenings; dinner is a bit pricey. *Rooms from: £165* ✉ *Off B4519, Llangammarch Wells* ☎ *01591/620202* ⊕ *www.lakecountryhouse.co.uk* ☞ *30 rooms* ❍⧵ *Free Breakfast.*

The Metropole Hotel & Spa
$ | **HOTEL** | This grand-looking hotel from 1896 is surprisingly contemporary on the inside, with modern furnishings that complement the original architectural flourishes. **Pros:** very central; good service; inexpensive spa. **Cons:** lacks character; can be taken over by conferences; popular meeting place for vintage car and motorbike owners. *Rooms from: £119* ✉ *Temple St.* ☎ *01597/823700* ⊕ *www.metropole.co.uk* ☞ *120 rooms* ❍⧵ *Free Breakfast.*

Squirrel's Nest Treehouse Retreat
$$$ | **RENTAL** | **FAMILY** | These well-equipped wooden treehouses on a working sheep farm six miles from the nearest town offer a wonderful luxury retreat. **Pros:** peaceful location; comfortable glamping; good walking trails. **Cons:** no Wi-Fi; two-night minimum stay; not easily accessible for all. *Rooms from: £295* ✉ *Nantygelli, Llanbister Rd.* ☎ *01597/840–506* ⊕ *www.squirrels-nest.co.uk* ☞ *2 treehouses* ❍⧵ *No meals.*

Aberystwyth

41 miles northwest of Llandrindod Wells via A44, 118 miles northwest of Cardiff.

A pleasingly eccentric combination of faded Victorian seaside resort and artsy college town, Aberystwyth is the largest community in Mid-Wales, with a population of barely 16,000. When the weather's fine, the beaches along the bay fill up with sunbathers; when it's not, waves crash so ferociously against the seawall that even the hotels across the street get soaked. To the east of the town are the Cambrian Mountains and the Veil of Rheidol, which can be visited by steam train.

GETTING HERE AND AROUND
All journeys from South Wales are routed through Shrewsbury and take four to five hours. From London, the trip here takes five to six hours. Long-distance buses are infrequent and painfully slow, though the local bus system is good. There are two roads to Aberystwyth, both of them among the most scenic in Wales: the coastal A487 and the mountainous A44.

ESSENTIALS
VISITOR INFORMATION Aberystwyth
Tourist Information Centre. ⊠ *Ceredigion Museum, Terrace Rd.* ☎ *019/0/612125* ⊕ *www.visitmidwales.co.uk.*

Sights

Aberystwyth Castle
ARCHAEOLOGICAL SITE | The British writer Caitlin Moran once wrote fondly of Aberystwyth's "Glitter-glue sea and smashed-cake castle," and these crumbling ruins at the southern end of the bay do have an endearing quality. Built in 1277, the castle was one of the key strongholds captured in the early 15th century by Owain Glyndwr, a Welsh prince who led the country's last serious bid for independence from England. Today it's a romantic, wind-swept ruin, rather incongruously used as a cut-through walking path by locals for whom it's nothing out of the ordinary at all. To find the ruins, just walk along the bay, away from the town center; they are located just after the small pier. ⊠ *New Promenade* ⚲ *Free.*

Aberystwyth Cliff Railway
TRANSPORTATION SITE (AIRPORT/BUS/FERRY/TRAIN) | **FAMILY** | The Victorian-era Aberystwyth Cliff Railway deposits you at the top of Constitution Hill. Opened in 1896, it's the longest electric cliff railway in Britain. ⊠ *Cliff Terr.* ☎ *01970/617642* ⊕ *www.aberystwythcliffrailway.co.uk* ⚲ *£5.50 round-trip* ⚲ *Closed Nov.–Easter.*

Ceredigion Museum
MUSEUM | **FAMILY** | Housed on the upper floor of a flamboyant 1905 Edwardian theater, the Ceredigion Museum has collections related to folk history and the building's own music hall past. Highlights include a reconstructed mud-walled cottage from 1850 and items illustrating the region's seafaring, lead-mining, and farming history. There's a nice café here selling local products, and the tourist information center is downstairs. ⊠ *Terrace Rd.* ☎ *01970/633088* ⊕ *www.ceredigionmuseum.wales* ⚲ *Free* ⚲ *Closed Sun.*

Constitution Hill
VIEWPOINT | **FAMILY** | At the northern end of the beach promenade, Constitution Hill dominates the skyline. From the top you can see much of the Welsh coastline (and, on *exceptionally* clear days, Ireland). There's a small cafe at the top and plenty of space for a picnic. If you're feeling hale and hearty, there's a long footpath that zigzags up to the 430-foot summit. From there, a 5-mile-long coastal path stretches to the village of Borth, a smaller, sleepier resort north of Aberystwyth where the remains of a 3,000-year-old petrified forest may be seen on the beach at low tide. ⊠ *Aberystwyth.*

Great Aberystwyth Camera Obscura
OBSERVATORY | **FAMILY** | A modern version of a Victorian amusement, Great Aberystwyth Camera Obscura is a massive 14-inch lens that gives you a bird's-eye view of Cardigan Bay and 26 Welsh mountain peaks. It's reached via the Aberystwyth Cliff Railway. ⊠ *Cliff Terr.* ☎ *01970/617642* ⊕ *www.aberystwythcliffrailway.co.uk* ⚲ *Free* ⚲ *Closed Nov.–Easter.*

Llanerchaeron
HOUSE | **FAMILY** | This late-18th-century Welsh gentry estate in the Aeron Valley, 17 miles south of Aberystwyth, is a superb example of the early work of John Nash (1752–1835). Nash was the leading architect of the Regency period and the designer of Brighton's Royal Pavilion. The estate survived with few changes until the present; it is a self-contained world with stables, barns, a dairy, and a brewery. The walled gardens are particularly beautiful. ⊠ *Off A482, Ciliau Aeron* ☎ *01545/570200* ⊕ *www.nationaltrust.org.uk/llanerchaeron* ⚲ *£8.49.*

National Library of Wales
LIBRARY | This massive neoclassical building next to the University of Wales houses notable Welsh and other Celtic

literary works among its more than 4.5 million volumes. The cache of public records makes it an invaluable tool if you're tracing your family tree. Also here is the **National Screen and Sound Archive of Wales**, which hosts lunchtime and evening film screenings. ✉ *Off Penglais Rd.* ☎ *01970/632800* ⊕ *www.library. wales* ☞ *Free* ☉ *Closed Sun.*

Silver Mountain Experience

MINE | FAMILY | Outside the village of Ponterwyd, 10 miles east of Aberystwyth, this 200-year-old silver-lead mine is now a museum where you can tour reproductions of mining buildings and some original machinery, including working waterwheels. Kids over the age of eight can also enjoy a few harmless scares on the Black Chasm ghost tour, though very young ones will be better off sticking to the Woo Hoo Woods adventure playground. ■**TIP→ It's cold in the mine, even on hot days, so bring a jacket or sweater.** Times can vary; call to check, especially in off-season. ✉ *Off A44, Pont-erwyd* ☎ *01970/890620* ⊕ *www.silvermountain-experience.co.uk* ☞ *£14.95.*

Vale of Rheidol Railway

TRANSPORTATION SITE (AIRPORT/BUS/FERRY/ TRAIN) | FAMILY | At Aberystwyth Station you can hop on the steam-powered Vale of Rheidol Railway for an hour-long ride to the **Devil's Bridge** (*Pont y Gwr Drwg,* or, literally, "the Bridge of the Evil One"), where the rivers Rheidol and Mynach meet in a series of spectacular falls. Clamped between two rocky cliffs where a torrent of water pours unceasingly, there are actually three bridges, one built on top of the other. The oldest bridge is about 800 years old. ✉ *Park Ave.* ☎ *01970/625819* ⊕ *www.rheidol-railway.co.uk* ☞ *£26 round-trip* ☉ *Closed Nov.–mid-Feb.*

Ynyslas Beach

BEACH—SIGHT | FAMILY | About 9 miles up the coast from Aberystwyth is Ynyslas Beach (pronounced "*Inn*-iss-lass"), a popular local beauty spot. Where the River Dyfi flows into the sea at Cardigan Bay, enormous dunes undulate from the sandy beach in a network of hillocks crisscrossed by wooden bridges. Ynyslas Beach is part of a nature reserve that is home to several species of butterfly and—unusual for the British Isles—lizards. The strong currents make the sea here unsuitable for swimming. Ynyslas is 8 miles north of Aberystwyth on the B4572. **Amenities:** food and drink; parking on the sand (£2). **Best for:** sunsets. ✉ *Ynyslas* ☎ *01970/872901* ⊕ *www. naturalresources.wales.*

🍴 Restaurants

Ultracomida

$ | SPANISH | This lively, modern Spanish eatery brings a splash of Mediterranean color to the Mid-Wales coastline. The lunch menu is served tapas-style: hake with lentils and Serrano ham, squid fried in garlic with salsa verde, or maybe just some fresh hummus and toast. **Known for:** delicious tapas; Spanish wine list; convivial atmosphere. ⑤ *Average main: £12* ✉ *31 Pier St.* ☎ *01970/630686* ⊕ *www.ultracomida.co.uk* ☉ *No dinner Sun. and Mon.*

★ Ynyshir Restaurant and Rooms

$$$$ | MODERN BRITISH | FAMILY | This Michelin-starred restaurant, housed in a Georgian mansion set among parkland, is one of the best eateries in Wales thanks to its wonderful dishes featuring local meats. The restaurant has just five tables next to the open kitchen and only serves a tasting menu featuring a whopping 20 dishes. **Known for:** tasting menu featuring creative meat dishes; award-winning wine list; stylish dining room. ⑤ *Average main: £180* ✉ *Eglwys Fach, Eglwys-fach* ☎ *01654/781209* ⊕ *www.ynyshir.co.uk* ☉ *Closed Sun.–Tues. No lunch Fri. and Sat.*

Hotels

★ Harbourmaster Hotel

$$ | HOTEL | A drive south on the coast road from Aberystwyth brings you to this early19th-century Georgian-style, bright blue building right on the harbor, among many other colorfully painted structures. **Pros:** good food; stunning harbor location; friendly hosts. **Cons:** difficult parking; often booked up; minimum stay on weekends. $ *Rooms from: £190 ✉ Pen Cei, 15 miles south of Aberystwyth, Aberaeron ☎ 01545/570755 ⊕ www. harbour-master.com ⇆ 13 rooms ⦙O⦙ Free Breakfast.*

Nanteos Mansion

$$ | HOTEL | FAMILY | This historic Georgian mansion, now a luxury hotel which also offers self-catering accommodations, was for many years the home of the Nanteos Cup (alleged to be the Holy Grail and now in the National Library of Wales). **Pros:** sumptuous decor; 30 acres of parkland; food and music evenings. **Cons:** popular wedding venue; need a car to stay here; deposit of one night's stay taken at booking. $ *Rooms from: £132 ✉ Rhydyfelin ☎ 01970/600–522 ⊕ www.nanteos. com ⇆ 23 rooms ⦙O⦙ Free Breakfast.*

Yr Hafod

$ | B&B/INN | In the shadow of Aberystwyth Castle, this cozy B&B is just far enough from the town center to qualify as peaceful. **Pros:** short walk from town center; pleasant hosts; most rooms have sea views. **Cons:** cheaper rooms have shared bathrooms; no restaurant; limited parking. $ *Rooms from: £94 ✉ 1 S. Marine Terr. ☎ 01970/617579 ⊕ www. yrhafod.co.uk ⇆ 6 rooms ⦙O⦙ Free Breakfast.*

Nightlife

Rummers Wine Bar

BARS/PUBS | Opposite the harbor, Rummers Wine Bar is a lively, easygoing place with sawdust on the floor and live music on weekends. The bar stays open until 2 am on Fridays and Saturdays. ✉ *Bridge St. ☎ 01970/625177.*

Scholars

BARS/PUBS | Filled with Victorian knick-knacks and lots of nooks and crannies, Scholars hosts live music on Thursdays and Saturdays and a popular pub quiz on Sunday nights. ✉ *8 Queen's Rd. ☎ 01970/615241.*

Ship and Castle

BARS/PUBS | An inn since the 1700s, the Ship and Castle draws a mix of chatty locals and students and has a selection of ales unrivaled in the region. ✉ *1 High St. ☎ 07773/778785.*

Performing Arts

Aberystwyth Arts Centre

ARTS CENTERS | In addition to a cinema, the lively Aberystwyth Arts Centre has a theater, a gallery, shops, and a good café and bar. The list of movies is varied, including an international horror movie festival every fall (the rather brilliantly named "Abertoir"). ✉ *Aberystwyth University, Penglais Rd. ☎ 01970/623232 ⊕ www.aberystwytharteentre.co.uk.*

Activities

Glyndwr's Way

HIKING/WALKING | FAMILY | To the east of Aberystwyth, the 135-mile Glyndwr's Way walking route passes through the Cambrian Mountains before turning north through the town of Machynlleth. From there it veers east to climb above the River Dovey, with wonderful views north to Cadair Idris. ✉ *Aberystwyth ⊕ www.nationaltrail.co.uk/en_GB/trails/ glyndwrs-way.*

Dolgellau

34 miles northeast of Aberystwyth.

A solidly Welsh town with dark stone buildings and old coaching inns made of the local gray dolerite and slate, Dolgellau (pronounced dol- *geth*-lie) thrived with the wool trade until the mid-19th century. Prosperity left striking architecture with buildings of different eras side by side on crooked streets that are a legacy from Norman times.

Dolgellau has long been a popular base for people eager to walk the surrounding countryside, which forms the southern tip of Snowdonia National Park. To the south of Dolgellau rises the menacing bulk of 2,927-foot Cadair Idris. The name means "the Chair of Idris," a reference to a giant from ancient Celtic mythology.

GETTING HERE AND AROUND
Dolgellau's nearest railway station is at the town of Barmouth, about 10 miles away. The town is small and full of interesting nooks and crannies easily explored on foot. To discover the surrounding area you'll need a car.

Sights

Ty Siamas
ARTS VENUE | FAMILY | The National Centre for Welsh Folk Music is in the converted Victorian Market Hall and Assembly Rooms. It has a fascinating interactive folk music exhibition, performance auditorium, and café and bar. ⊠ *Neuadd Idris, Eldon Sq.* ☎ *01341/421800* ⊕ *www. tysiamas.cymru* 🎟 *Free.*

Llangollen

23 miles southwest of Chester, 60 miles southwest of Manchester.

Llangollen's setting in a deep valley carved by the River Dee gives it a typically Welsh appearance. The bridge over the

Dee, a 14th-century stone structure, is named in a traditional Welsh folk song as one of the "Seven Wonders of Wales." In July the very popular International Musical Eisteddfod brings crowds to town.

For a particularly scenic drive in this area, head for the Horseshoe Pass. For other views, follow the marked footpath from the north end of the canal bridge up a steep hill to see Castell Dinas Bran, the ruins of a 13th-century castle built by a native Welsh ruler. The views of the town and the Vale of Llangollen are worth the 45-minute (one-way) walk.

GETTING HERE AND AROUND
You'll need a car to get here, but once you arrive you can take a trip on the Llangollen Railway. Along the Llangollen Canal longboat tours head both west and east. The town itself is easy to explore on foot.

ESSENTIALS
VISITOR INFORMATION Llangollen Tourist Information Centre. ⊠ *Y Capel, Castle St.* ☎ *01978/860828* ⊕ *www.llangollen.org. uk.*

Sights

Castell Dinas Brân
CASTLE/PALACE | This romantic hilltop ruin looks out over a breathtaking patchwork of green fields and mountains. The fortress was built in the 1260s on the site of an earlier castle, which was an Iron Age fort before that. Its heyday was incredibly short lived; by the end of the 13th century it had been captured and abandoned by English forces after which it gradually fell into ruin. The castle is located on top of a hill just north of Llangollen town center. There are no roads to the summit; the best walking path starts at Canal Bridge in Llangollen and zigzags up the side of the hill. The rather punishing hike is a little over a mile long. ⊠ *Llangollen* 🎟 *Free.*

Welsh: A Short Primer

The native language of Wales, Welsh (or *Cymraeg*, as it's properly called) is spoken fluently by around 19% of the country's population (most Welsh people do know a little of the language, however). Not legally recognized in Britain until the 1960s, it was suppressed beginning in the time of Henry VIII and blamed for poor literacy during the reign of Queen Victoria. Today Welsh children under 17 are required to take classes to learn the language.

Welsh may look daunting, with its complicated words and confusing double consonants, but it's a phonetic language, so pronunciation is actually quite easy once the alphabet is learned. A quick primer to get you started: "dd" is sounded like "th" in they, "f" sounds like "v" in save, and "ff" is the equivalent of the English "f" in forest. The "ll" sound has no English equivalent; the closest match is the "cl" sound in "close."

Terms that crop up frequently in Welsh are *bach* or *fach* (small; also a common term of endearment similar to "dear"), *craig* or *graig* (rock), *cwm* (valley; pronounced coom), *dyffryn* (valley), *eglwys* (church), *glyn* (glen), *llyn* (lake), *mawr* or *fawr* (great, big), *pentre* (village, homestead), *plas* (hall, mansion), and *pont* or *bont* (bridge).

★ Chirk Castle

CASTLE/PALACE | This impressive medieval fortress has evolved from its 14th-century origins into a grand home complete with an 18th-century servants' hall and interiors furnished in 16th- to 19th-century styles. However, it still looks satisfyingly medieval from the outside—and also belowground, where you tour the original dungeons. Surrounding the castle are beautiful formal gardens and parkland. Chirk Castle is 5 miles southeast of Llangollen. ⊠ *Off B4500, Chirk* ☎ *01691/777701* ⊕ *www.nationaltrust.org.uk/chirk-castle* ☞ *£15.*

Llangollen Railway

TRANSPORTATION SITE (AIRPORT/BUS/FERRY/TRAIN) | FAMILY | This restored standard-gauge steam line runs for 10 miles along the scenic Dee Valley. The terminus is near the town's bridge. ⊠ *Abbey Rd.* ☎ *01978/860979* ⊕ *www.llangollen-railway.co.uk* ☞ *£16 round-trip.*

Pistyll Rhaeadr

BODY OF WATER | FAMILY | The peat-brown water of Pistyll Rhaeadr, the highest waterfall in Wales, thunders down a 240-foot double cascade. When you're driving on the B4500 between Llangollen and Llanwddyn, take the road leading northwest from the town of Llanrhaeadr ym Mochnant in the peaceful Tanat Valley. There's also a pretty 18th-century restaurant and tearoom, along with camping and self-catering accommodations, on-site. It was near here that, in 1588, the Bible was translated into Welsh—one of the key moments that helped to ensure the survival of the language. ⊠ *Llanrhaeadr-ym-Mochnant* ☎ *01691/780392* ⊕ *www.pistyllrhaeadr.co.uk* ☞ *Parking £5; £4 in winter.*

★ Plas Newydd

HOUSE | From 1778 to 1828 Plas Newydd (not to be confused with the similarly named Isle of Anglesey estate) was the home of Lady Eleanor Butler and Sarah Ponsonby, the eccentric Ladies of Llangollen, who set up a then-scandalous single-sex household, collected curios and magnificent carvings, and made it into a tourist attraction even during their lifetimes. You can take tea there, as did

Charming Plas Newydd was home to the most famous same-sex couple in Wales from 1778 to 1828.

Wordsworth and the Duke of Wellington, and stroll in the attractively terraced gardens. ⊠ *Hill St.* ☎ *01978/862834* ⊕ *www.plasnewyddllangollen.co.uk* ✉ *£6* ⊗ *Closed Nov.–Mar.*

★ Pontcysyllte

TRANSPORTATION SITE (AIRPORT/BUS/FERRY/TRAIN) | FAMILY | From the Llangollen Canal Wharf you can take a two-hour trip on a narrow boat (a slender barge) along the canal to the world's longest and highest navigable cast-iron aqueduct: Pontcysyllte (Welsh for "the bridge that connects"), a UNESCO World Heritage Site. The aqueduct is more than 1,000 feet long. Pontcysyllte is 3 miles east of Llangollen. ⊠ *Llangollen Canal Wharf, Wharf Hill* ☎ *01978/860702 Llangollen Wharf* ⊕ *www.pontcysyllte-aqueduct.co.uk* ✉ *£14.50* ⊗ *No boat trips Nov.–mid-Mar.*

Vale of Ceiriog

SCENIC DRIVE | Near Llangollen is this verdant valley, known locally as "Little Switzerland." The B4500 road, running between Chirk and the village of Glyn Ceiriog, at the foothills of the Berwyn Mountains, is one of the region's great drives. It's just remote enough that you can often have the road to yourself. ⊠ *Llangollen.*

★ Valle Crucis Abbey

ARCHAEOLOGICAL SITE | The last abbey of the Cistercian order to be founded in Wales, Valle Crucis was built in 1201 and abandoned in 1537—a victim of Henry VIII's violent dissolution of the monasteries. Today it's a highly picturesque ruin beside a glassy lake. Surprisingly large sections survive relatively intact—particularly the sacristy and more or less complete chapter house, with its intricate vaulted ceiling. In its day Valle Crucis was one of the richest and most powerful abbeys in Wales; despite half a millennium of decay, this is still an impressive site to wander. ⊠ *Off A542* ☎ *01639/651931* ⊕ *cadw.gov.wales* ✉ *£3.80; free Nov.–Mar.*

North Wales

🍴 Restaurants

The Corn Mill

$ | BRITISH | In a converted mill on the River Dee, this pub and restaurant has an old waterwheel that turns behind the bar. Dine on the open-air deck or in the cozy dining room, sampling stylishly updated pub fare, such as grilled sea bass with potato and shallot terrine. **Known for:** attractive riverside location; good pub food; good selection of beers, including Welsh ales. [$] *Average main: £14* ⊠ *Dee La.* ☎ *01978/869555* ⊕ *www.brunningandprice.co.uk/cornmill.*

Pontcysyllte Chapel Tearoom

$ | BRITISH | FAMILY | This 19th-century chapel has been successfully converted into a café, complete with its original features. The owners are trained baristas and roast the coffee beans themselves.

Known for: good coffee; quirky surroundings; friendly service. [$] *Average main: £6* ⊠ *Bryn Seion Chapel, Station Rd.* ☎ *01978/812–786* ⊕ *www.pontcysylltechapeltearoom.com.*

🛏 Hotels

Manorhaus-Townhaus

$ | B&B/INN | Most of the stylish, contemporary rooms in this Victorian town house have their own lounge, but the real highlight here is the rooftop hot tub with panoramic views. **Pros:** stylish decor; great views, especially from the rooftop; self-catering cottage available. **Cons:** reached via steps; no elevator; off-site parking. [$] *Rooms from: £85* ⊠ *Hill St.* ☎ *01824/704830* ⊕ *www.manorhaus. com* 🛏 *8 rooms* ⦿❙ *Free Breakfast.*

Activities

Offa's Dyke Path
HIKING/WALKING | There are easy walks along the banks of the River Dee or along part of the Offa's Dyke Path, which passes through hills, river valleys, and lowlands. This 177-mile-long National Trail follows the line of an ancient earthen wall, still surviving in parts, which was built along the border with England in the 8th century by King Offa of Mercia to keep out Welsh raiders. ⊠ *Llangollen* ⊕ *www.nationaltrail.co.uk/en_GB/trails/offas-dyke-path.*

Lake Vyrnwy (Llyn Efyrnwy)

27 miles southwest of Llangollen.

This beautiful lake has a sense of tranquillity that doesn't entirely befit its history. Lake Vyrnwy was created in the 1880s to provide water for the people of Liverpool, 80 miles north. Unfortunately, this meant forcibly evicting the residents of a small town—an act that's still controversial in Wales. Today it's a peaceful spot surrounded by a thriving nature reserve. The closest settlement is tiny Llanwddyn, and a bit farther away is Bala, a pretty town with an almost-as-lovely natural lake of its own.

GETTING HERE AND AROUND
Rural bus service is infrequent, so you need a car to explore the area. The B4393 circles Lake Vyrnwy itself; from here, Bala is a 14-mile drive over hair-raising Bwlch y Groes pass or a circuitous drive along the B4391. Llangollen is 27 miles northeast of Lake Vyrnwy on the B4396.

Sights

Bala Lake Railway
TRANSPORTATION SITE (AIRPORT/BUS/FERRY/TRAIN) | **FAMILY** | The steam-powered train runs along the southern shores of Bala Lake (Llyn Tegid, or "Lake of Beauty"), a large natural reservoir just northeast of Lake Vyrnwy. Bala Lake is also popular for kayaking and other water sports. Look on the website for departure times. ⊠ *Off B4403, Llanuwchllyn* ☎ *01678/540666* ⊕ *www.bala-lake-railway.co.uk* 🌐 *£12 round-trip* ⊗ *Closed Nov.–Mar.*

Bwlch y Groes
SCENIC DRIVE | One of the great drives of North Wales, the sweeping, vertiginous panoramas of Bwlch y Groes (Pass of the Cross) form the second-highest mountain pass in the country at 1,788 feet. From Lake Vyrnwy, drive for a mile on B4393 before heading west on the mountain road. ⊠ *Bwlch y Groes.*

★ Lake Vyrnwy Nature Reserve
NATURE PRESERVE | **FAMILY** | Bordered by lush forest and emerald green hills, Lake Vyrnwy is a haven for wildlife. It's rich in rare bird species, from falcons to siskins and curlews. Stretching out along the shores of the lake near the visitor center, the Lake Vyrnwy Sculpture Park is a collection of pieces by talented local artist Andy Hancock. Arranged along a paved walking trail, many of the wooden sculptures resemble oversize versions of the lake's wildlife, including a 15-foot-long dragonfly. It's an extremely popular cycling route, and there's a bike shop and coffee shop near the visitor center. ⊠ *Visitor Centre, Off B4393 via southwest side, Llanwddyn* ☎ *01691/870278* ⊕ *www.lake-vyrnwy.com* 🌐 *Free.*

Hotels

Bron Heulog
$ | **B&B/INN** | **FAMILY** | Carefully restored in period style as a guesthouse, this former Victorian home (pronounced *haylog*, which means "sunny bank") is nestled at the foot of the Berwyn Mountains. **Pros:** good views; discounts for two nights or more; packed lunches available. **Cons:** no evening meal; check-in

times quite restrictive; limited parking. $ *Rooms from: £65* ✉ *Waterfall St., Llanrhaeadr-ym-Mochnant* ☎ *01691/780521* 🌐 *www.bronheulog.co.uk* ⇆ *3 rooms* ⋈ *Free Breakfast.*

★ Lake Vyrnwy Hotel & Spa

$$ | **HOTEL** | Awesome views of mountain-ringed Lake Vyrnwy are just one asset of this country mansion on a 24,000-acre estate. **Pros:** perfect for outdoor pursuits; luxurious spa; excellent package deals. **Cons:** too remote for some; minimum stay on some summer weekends; decor could use updating. $ *Rooms from: £149* ✉ *Off B4393, Llanwddyn* ☎ *01691/870692* 🌐 *www.lakevyrnwy.com* ⇆ *52 rooms* ⋈ *Free Breakfast.*

Porthmadog

35 miles southeast of Lake Vyrnwy, 16 miles southeast of Caernarfon.

The little seaside town of Porthmadog, built as a harbor to export slate from nearby Blaenau Ffestiniog, stands at the gateway to the Llŷn Peninsula (pronounced like "lean," with your tongue touching your palate), with its virtually unspoiled coastline and undulating wildflower-covered hills. It's also near the town of Harlech, which contains one of the great castles of Wales, and the weird and wonderful Portmeirion.

GETTING HERE AND AROUND

The picturesque Cambrian Coast Railway runs from Machynlleth, near Aberystwyth, up the coast to Porthmadog. When you arrive you can take a scenic trip on the town's "little railways." Porthmadog is a stop on the excellent Snowdon Sherpa bus service. The town itself is totally walkable and has good access to coastal trails.

◉ Sights

Criccieth Castle

CASTLE/PALACE | In the Victorian seaside resort of Criccieth, a few miles west of Porthmadog on the A497, a medieval castle with sweeping views crowns the headland. Criccieth was the scene of the last real uprising against English rule in Wales, in the early 1400s, when it was attacked and burned by rebel prince and latter-day folk hero Owain Glyndwr (1359–1416). David Lloyd George, who was prime minister of Britain for most of the First World War, grew up in Wales and lived in the town; a small museum in his childhood home honors him. ✉ *Castle St., Criccieth* ☎ *01766/522227* 🌐 *cadw.gov.wales* ⌹ *£5.10* ⊘ *Closed Mon. and Tues. Nov.–Mar.*

Ffestiniog Railway

TRANSPORTATION SITE (AIRPORT/BUS/FERRY/TRAIN) | **FAMILY** | Founded in the early 19th century to carry slate, the Ffestiniog Railway starts at the quayside and climbs up 700 feet through a wooded vale, past a waterfall, and across the mountains. The northern terminus is in Blaenau Ffestiniog, where you can visit an old slate mine. The Ffestiniog Railway is perhaps the best of several small steam lines in this part of the country. Porthmadog gets very crowded in summer, and parking is limited, so you might want to make this journey from Blaenau Ffestiniog to Porthmadog instead. Check the website for the daily timetable. ✉ *Harbour Station, High St.* ☎ *01766/516024* 🌐 *www.festrail.co.uk* ⌹ *£25 round-trip* ⊘ *Closed Nov.–Jan.*

★ Harlech Castle

CASTLE/PALACE | **FAMILY** | A wealth of legend, poetry, and song is conjured up by the 13th-century Harlech Castle, built by Edward I to help subdue the Welsh. Its mighty ruins, visible for miles, are as dramatic as its history (though you have to imagine the sea, which used to crash against the rocks below but receded in the 19th century). Harlech was occupied by the Welsh Prince Owain Glyndwr from 1404 to 1408 during his revolt against the English. The music of the traditional folk song "Men of Harlech" refers to the heroic defense of this castle in 1468 by Dafydd ap Eynion, who, summoned to surrender, is alleged to have replied: "I held a castle in France until every old woman in Wales heard of it, and I will hold a castle in Wales until every old woman in France hears of it." On a clear day you can climb the battlements for a spectacular view of the surrounding countryside. A helpful visitor center explains the castle's history; you can also arrange to stay overnight in the castle in one of five luxury apartments. The castle dominates the coastal town of Harlech, 12 miles south of Porthmadog. ⊠ *Off B4573, Harlech* ☎ *01766/780552* ⊕ *cadw. wales.gov.uk* ⊠ *£6.50.*

★ Llechwedd Slate Caverns

MINE | FAMILY | At these caverns you can descend 500 feet on Britain's deepest underground railway to a mine where you walk by an eerie underground lake. Here Victorian working conditions have been re-created, and the tour gives a good idea of the difficult lives the miners had to endure. Above are a re-created Victorian village and slate-splitting demonstrations. Wear sturdy footwear when visiting the mine—during busy times you may have to climb 70 steps as part of the tour. ⊠ *Off A470, Blaenau-Ffestiniog* ☎ *01766/830306* ⊕ *www.llechwedd.co.uk* ⊠ *£20.*

Nant Gwrtheyrn

LOCAL INTEREST | This is a worthwhile stop—for awesome views of Caernarfon Bay as well as cultural information—if you're exploring the Llŷn Peninsula. A former village for granite-quarry workers serves as the Welsh Language and Heritage Centre, offering Welsh-language classes and cultural courses (in Welsh). There's a tourist information center, a café that serves good sandwiches, and

a modest exhibit of historical items, including an old quarryman's cottage fitted out exactly as it would have been in 1910. Some of the other cottages have been turned into B&Bs and self-catering accommodations. ⊠ *Off B4417, Llithfaen* ☎ *01758/750334* ⊕ *www.nantgwrtheyrn. org* ⊠ *Free.*

Porthdinllaen

BEACH—SIGHT | On the very tip of a thumb-shape bay jutting out into the Irish Sea, this miniscule but gorgeous little harbor community is 20 miles from Porthmadog. There's a wide, sheltered beach where the sand is so fine that it squeaks underfoot, and whitewashed cottages line the curving seafront. Park at the nearby visitor center, one mile from the beach. ⊠ *Porthdinllaen* ⊕ *www. nationaltrust.org.uk/porthdinllaen.*

★ Portmeirion

TOWN | One of the true highlights of North Wales is Portmeirion, a tiny fantasy-Italianate village on a private peninsula surrounded by hills; it's said to be loosely modeled after Portofino in Italy. Designed in the 1920s by architect Clough Williams-Ellis (1883–1978), the village has a hotel and restaurant among its multicolored buildings, and gift shops sell a distinctive local pottery. On the edge of town is a peaceful woodland trail punctuated here and there by such flourishes as a red iron bridge and a miniature pagoda. Williams-Ellis called it his "light-opera approach to architecture," and the result is magical, though distinctly un-Welsh. Portmeirion is about 2 miles east of Porthmadog. ⊠ *Off A487, Portmeirion* ☎ *01766/772409* ⊕ *www. portmeirion.wales* ⊠ *£13.*

★ Tre'r Ceiri

ARCHAEOLOGICAL SITE | Remote, atmospheric, and astoundingly little-known, Tre'r Ceiri is one of the most impressive ancient monuments in Wales. Today parts of the 4th-century fort's outer walls are still intact (rising more than 18 feet in places), and within are the ruins of 150 stone huts. They were inhabited by a Celtic tribe known as the Ordovices, and may have survived as a settlement for up to 700 years. From Porthmadog, take the A497 west, then turn left onto the A499 just before Pwllheli. At the village of Llanaelhaearn, turn left onto the B4417. Less than a mile down this road is an unmarked footpath on the right leading straight up a hill to Tre'r Ceiri. ⊠ *B4417, Llanaelhaearn* ⌑ *Free*.

Tremadog

TOWN | North of Porthmadog is Tremadog, a handsome village that was the birthplace of T. E. Lawrence (1888–1935), better known as Lawrence of Arabia. ⊠ *Tremadog*.

Welsh Highland Heritage Railway

TRANSPORTATION SITE (AIRPORT/BUS/FERRY/ TRAIN) | **FAMILY** | You can take a short rail ride on this narrow-gauge railway, tour the engine sheds, and clamber onto the locomotives housed here. If the train looks small, wait until you see the miniature version that's a hit with kids. ⊠ *Tremadog Rd.* ☎ *01766/513402* ⊕ *www.whr.co.uk* ⌑ *f10.25* ⊙ *Closed Nov.–Mar.*

🍴 Restaurants

★ Castle Cottage

$$$$ | **BRITISH** | Close to Harlech's mighty castle, this friendly "restaurant with rooms" is a wonderful find. Chef-proprietor Glyn Roberts uses locally sourced ingredients from lobster to lamb to create imaginative, beautifully presented contemporary dishes. **Known for:** excellent Welsh menu featuring local produce; good wine list; historic building. ⑤ *Average main: £39* ⊠ *Y Llech, Harlech* ☎ *01766/780479* ⊙ *No lunch*.

Ty Coch Inn

$ | **BRITISH** | In a seafront building in picture-postcard Porthdinllaen, this pub has what is undoubtedly one of the best locations in Wales. The lunches are honest and unpretentious: pies, sandwiches,

or perhaps a plate of local mussels in garlic butter. **Known for:** stunning beach location; local craft beers; laid-back vibe. ⑤ *Average main: £8* ⊠ *Off B4417, Porthdinllaen* ☎ *01758/720498* ⊕ *www.tycoch. co.uk* ⊙ *No dinner.*

🛏 Hotels

★ Hotel Portmeirion

$$$ | **HOTEL** | One of the most elegant and unusual places to stay in Wales, this waterfront mansion is located at the heart of Portmeirion. **Pros:** unique location; beautiful building; woodland walks. **Cons:** gets crowded with day-trippers; minimum stay on weekends; expensive food. ⑤ *Rooms from: £289* ⊠ *Off A487, Portmeirion* ☎ *01766/772440* ⊕ *www. portmeirion.wales* ⌑ *42 rooms* ⊙l *Free Breakfast.*

Plas Weunydd

$ | **HOTEL** | **FAMILY** | The former quarry owner's house on the Llechwedd Slate Caverns site has been turned into this stylish boutique hotel. **Pros:** good location for an active break; tasty pub food; stylish decor. **Cons:** slate mountain views might not appeal to some; need a car to stay here; reception desk has limited hours. ⑤ *Rooms from: £120* ⊠ *Blaenau-Ffestiniog* ☎ *01766/830–306* ⊕ *www. plasweunydd.co.uk* ⌑ *24 rooms* ⊙l *Free Breakfast.*

Y Branwen

$$ | **B&B/INN** | Located in the shadow of Harlech Castle, Y Branwen is a homey restaurant with rooms and a friendly place for an overnight stay. **Pros:** cozy and comfortable; close to Harlech Castle; good food. **Cons:** some rooms are small; inevitable noise from the bar; on the main road. ⑤ *Rooms from: £125* ⊠ *Fford Newydd, Harlech* ☎ *01766/780477* ⊕ *www.branwenhotel.co.uk* ⌑ *7 rooms* ⊙l *Free Breakfast.*

Activities

★ Zipworld

ZIP LINING | FAMILY | Not only can you go on a tour of Llechwedd Slate Caverns, but you can take part in some breath-taking activities there too. The highlight is Europe's largest zipwire zone, which includes the world's fastest and highest (and Europe's longest) zipline along with several calmer zipline paths. Then head into the mine for Bounce Below, where you can enjoy a few hours on a trampoline adventure course within the former slate cavern, accompanied by the perfect soundtrack. Zipworld offers 13 exhilarating activities across three sites in North Wales (Blaenau-Ffestiniog, Betws-y-Coed, and Bethesda), which are detailed on the website. ⊠ *Blaenau-Ffestiniog* ☎ *01248/601–444* ⊕ *www.zipworld.co.uk.*

Betws-y-Coed

25 miles northeast of Porthmadog, 19 miles south of Llandudno.

The rivers Llugwy and Conwy meet at Betws-y-Coed, a popular village surrounded by woodland with excellent views of Snowdonia. It can be used as a base to explore the national park, although its diminutive size means that it can get overcrowded in summer. The most famous landmark in the village is the ornate iron Waterloo Bridge over the River Conwy, designed in 1815 by Thomas Telford.

GETTING HERE AND AROUND

The town is easy to reach on the Conwy Valley Railway that runs from Llandudno to Blaenau Ffestiniog. Betws-y-Coed is also a hub for the excellent Snowdon Sherpa bus service that covers most of Snowdonia's beauty spots, so it's feasible to explore this part of Wales without a car.

ESSENTIALS

VISITOR INFORMATION Snowdonia National Park Visitor Centre. ⊠ *Royal Oak Stables, Station Rd.* ☎ *01690/710426* ⊕ *www.snowdonia.gov.wales.*

 Sights

Gwydyr Forest and Swallow Falls

BODY OF WATER | Betws-y-Coed is bordered by Gwydyr Forest, which has several well-marked walking trails. The forest also contains a half dozen or so mines, the last of which was abandoned in the 1940s. On the western approach to the village you'll find Swallow Falls, where the River Llugwy tumbles down through a wooded chasm. ■TIP➔ **Be careful on the footpath: there's no guardrail.** ⊠ *Off A5.*

★ Snowdonia National Park

NATIONAL/STATE PARK | FAMILY | Stretching from the Welsh midlands almost to its northern coast, Snowdonia National Park covers a vast swath of North Wales. The park consists of 823 square miles of rocky mountains, valleys clothed in oak woods, moorlands, lakes, and rivers, all guaranteeing natural beauty and, to a varying extent, solitude. Its most famous attraction, by far, is the towering peak of Mt. Snowdon, the highest mountain in Wales. The view from the top is jaw-dropping: to the northwest you can see the Menai Strait and Anglesey; to the south, Harlech Castle and the Cadair Idris mountain range. To the southwest, on an exceedingly clear day, you can make out the distant peaks of Ireland's Wicklow Mountains. There are six different walking paths to the top, but a far less punishing way is via the Snowdon Mountain Railway in nearby Llanberis.

Perched at the top of Snowdon is Hafod Eryri, an eco-friendly replacement for the previous visitor center (once described by Prince Charles as "the highest slum in Wales"). The granite-roof building, which blends beautifully into the rocky landscape, has a café and exhibitions about

Snowdonia National Park is perhaps one of the most beautiful places in all of Great Britain.

the mountain, its ecology, and its history. If you're planning to make the ascent, the visitor center in Betws-y-Coed is the best place to stop for information. ⊠ *Royal Oak Stables, Station Rd.* ☎ *01690/710426* ⊕ *www.snowdonia.gov.wales.*

Restaurants

Ty Gwyn

$ | BRITISH | This coaching inn, built in 1636, is one of the best places to eat in Snowdonia. The food is traditional Welsh fare, beautifully prepared with local ingredients. **Known for:** charming, historic building in a beautiful setting; good choice of seafood dishes; nice options for vegetarians. $ *Average main: £14* ⊠ *A5* ☎ *01690/710383* ⊕ *www.tygwyn-hotel.co.uk.*

Hotels

Aberconwy House

$ | B&B/INN | This luxurious Victorian house has panoramic views over Betws-y-Coed. **Pros:** breathtaking countryside

views; great breakfasts; charge for kids under two only £5 per night. **Cons:** no bar or evening meal; climbing stairs required; minimum stay in high season. $ *Rooms from: £85* ⊠ *Lôn Muriau, off A470* ☎ *01690/710202* ⊕ *www.aberconwy-house.co.uk* ➦ *9 rooms* ⦿ *Free Breakfast.*

★ Pengwern Country House

$ | B&B/INN | Hosts Ian and Gwawr Mowatt are charmingly adept at making their guests feel at home in this former Victorian artists' colony. **Pros:** woodland location; wealth of Victorian details; lovely hosts. **Cons:** close to main road; car is essential; minimum two-night stay on weekends and in high season. $ *Rooms from: £84* ⊠ *A5* ☎ *01690/710480* ⊕ *www. snowdoniaaccommodation.co.uk* ➦ *3 rooms* ⦿ *Free Breakfast.*

Tan-y-Foel Country House

$$ | B&B/INN | Hidden away on a wooded hillside outside Betws-y-Coed, this quiet, contemporary hideaway has views over the Conwy Valley. **Pros:** bold decor; cushy bathrobes; lovely location. **Cons:**

no restaurant; too far to walk into town; minimum two-night stay at weekends. $ *Rooms from: £125* ✉ *Off A5, Capel Garmon* ☎ *01690/710507* ⊕ *www. tanyfoelcountryhouse.co.uk* ⌁ *6 rooms* ⦿ *Free Breakfast* ☞ *No children under 12.*

Llanberis

17 miles west of Betws-y-Coed.

Like Betws-y-Coed, Llanberis is a focal point for people visiting Snowdonia National Park.

GETTING HERE AND AROUND

Llanberis is accessible by bus. The most convenient service, targeted at visitors, is the Snowdon Sherpa bus route.

◉ Sights

★ Caernarfon Castle

CASTLE/PALACE | The grim, majestic mass of Caernarfon Castle, a UNESCO World Heritage Site, looms over the waters of the River Seiont. Numerous bloody encounters were witnessed by these sullen walls, erected by Edward I in 1283 as a symbol of his determination to subdue the Welsh. The castle's towers, unlike those of Edward I's other castles, are polygonal and patterned with bands of different-color stone. In 1284 the monarch thought of a scheme to steal the Welsh throne. Knowing that the Welsh chieftains would accept no foreign prince, Edward promised to designate a ruler who could speak no word of English. Edward presented his infant son to the assembled chieftains as their prince "who spoke no English, had been born on Welsh soil, and whose first words would be spoken in Welsh." The ruse worked, and on that day was created the first prince of Wales of English lineage. In the Queen's Tower, a museum charts the history of the local regiment, the Royal Welch Fusiliers. More recently,

the castle was also the location of the investiture of Prince Charles in 1969, an event featured in the third season of the hit Netflix series *The Crown*. The castle is currently undergoing renovation and not all of the building is accessible. The castle is in the town of Caernarfon, 7 miles west of Llanberis. ✉ *Castle Hill, Caernarfon* ☎ *01286/677617* ⊕ *cadw.gov. wales* ✉ *£5.20.*

Llanberis Pass

CANYON | The town of Llanberis stands beside twin lakes at the foot of the rocky Llanberis Pass, which cuts through the highest mountains in the park and is lined with slabs popular with rock climbers. There are trails from the top of the pass, but the going can be rough for the inexperienced. Ask for local advice before starting any hike. ✉ *Llanberis.*

National Slate Museum

MUSEUM | In Padarn Country Park, this museum in the old Dinorwig Slate Quarry is dedicated to what was once an important industry for the area. The museum has quarry workshops and slate-splitting demonstrations, as well as restored worker housing, all of which convey the development of the industry and the challenges faced by those who worked in it. The narrow-gauge Llanberis Lake Railway departs from here. ✉ *Padarn Country Park, A4086* ☎ *0300/111–2333* ⊕ *www.museum.wales/slate* ✉ *Free* ⊗ *Closed Sat. Nov.–Easter.*

★ Snowdon Mountain Railway

TRANSPORTATION SITE (AIRPORT/BUS/FERRY/TRAIN) | FAMILY | One of the region's most famous attractions is the rack-and-pinion Snowdon Mountain Railway, with some of its track at a thrillingly steep grade. The 3,560-foot-high Snowdon—*Yr Wyddfa* in Welsh—is the highest peak south of Scotland and lies within the 823-square-mile national park. Weather permitting, trains go all the way to the summit; on a clear day you can see as far as the Wicklow Mountains in Ireland, about 90 miles away. You can take two types of train: a modern diesel-driven version, or "heritage" version, complete with restored carriages and working steam engine. From mid-March to May, or in times of high winds, the journey is truncated so you don't get all the way up to the summit; if so, tickets are a few pounds cheaper. ■**TIP→ Tickets can sell out early on busy days, so try to book in advance.** ✉ *A4086* ☎ *01286/870223* ⊕ *www.snowdonrailway.co.uk* ⊠ *Diesel service, £31 round-trip; heritage service, £40 round-trip* ⊘ *Closed Nov.–mid-Mar.*

Welsh Highland Railway

TRANSPORTATION SITE (AIRPORT/BUS/FERRY/TRAIN) | FAMILY | You can take a trip on a coal-fired steam locomotive at this narrow-gauge line that operates on the scenic route of a 25-mile abandoned railway line from Caernarfon to Porthmadog, linking with the Ffestiniog Railway. First-class afternoon tea trips for two are a fun way to spend a special occasion (£175 per couple). ✉ *St. Helens Rd., Caernarfon* ☎ *01766/516024* ⊕ *www.festrail.co.uk* ⊠ *£10.25 round-trip* ⊘ *Closed Jan.*

Restaurants

Gallt y Glyn

$ | PIZZA | FAMILY | This laid-back restaurant is popular with locals, drawn by the delicious, fresh pizza made entirely to order. They also serve salads, burgers, and other comfort food. **Known for:** delicious pizza; craft beer (including one free pint with each main course); lively atmosphere. ⑤ *Average main: £8* ✉ *A4086* ☎ *01286/870370* ⊕ *www.galltyglyn.com* ⊘ *Closed Sun.–Tues. No lunch.*

Hotels

Dolafon Guest House

$ | B&B/INN | This cozy, traditional B&B in the center of Llanberis makes no pretense to contemporary style, and that's precisely the appeal. **Pros:** characterful house; charming owner; central location. **Cons:** style may be a bit fussy for some;

one room has a bathroom down the hall; full cooked breakfast (as opposed to Continental-style) is £7.99 extra. ⑤ *Rooms from: £65* ✉ *High St.* ☎ *01286/870993* ⊕ *www.dolafon.com* ⊠ *7 rooms* ○| *Free Breakfast.*

★ Ty Castell

$ | B&B/INN | This former wine bar dating from the 18th century has been turned into a chic B&B. **Pros:** Welsh-inspired decor and ambience; good food; friendly owners. **Cons:** no elevator; no on-site parking; children not allowed. ⑤ *Rooms from: £85* ✉ *18 Stryd Fawr, Caernarfon* ☎ *01286/674–937* ⊕ *www.tycastell.cymru* ⊠ *4 rooms* ○| *No meals.*

Anglesey (Ynys Môn)

14 miles north of Llanberis.

Elegant Beaumaris is on the Isle of Anglesey, the largest island directly off the shore of Wales. It's linked to the mainland by the Britannia road and rail bridge and by Thomas Telford's remarkable chain suspension bridge, built in 1826 over the Menai Strait. Though its name means "beautiful marsh," Beaumaris has become a town of pretty cottages, Georgian houses, and bright shops; it also has Plas Newydd, one of the grandest stately homes in Wales.

Around 70% of Anglesey's 70,000 or so inhabitants speak Welsh, so you'll probably hear it more than English.

GETTING HERE AND AROUND

Anglesey is linked to the mainland by the A55 and A5. The roads on the island are in good condition, and there's a relatively extensive bus network. Ferries and catamarans to Ireland leave from Holyhead, on the island's western side.

Sights

★ Beaumaris Castle

CASTLE/PALACE | FAMILY | The town of Beaumaris dates from 1295, when Edward I commenced work on this impressive castle, the last and largest link in an "iron ring" of fortifications around North Wales built to contain the Welsh. Guarding the western approach to the Menai Strait, the unfinished castle (a World Heritage Site) is solid and symmetrical, with concentric lines of fortification, arrow slits, and a moat: a superb example of medieval defensive planning. ⊠ *Castle St., Beaumaris* ☎ *01248/810361* ⊕ *cadw.gov.wales* ✈ *£6.50.*

Bryn Celli Ddu

ARCHAEOLOGICAL SITE | Dating from around 3000 BC, this megalithic passage tomb is the most complete site of its kind in Wales. You enter via a narrow opening built into a burial mound. The passage extends for around 25 feet before opening out into a wider burial chamber. The far wall, made of quartz, is illuminated at dawn on the summer solstice. Bring a flashlight, as the tomb has no artificial lighting. Next to the entrance is a replica of a stone pillar carved with Celtic spirals, found here in 1928. The original is in the National Museum in Cardiff. The site is 7 miles southwest of Beaumaris. ⊠ *Off A4080, Llanddaniel Fab* ⊕ *cadw.gov. wales* ✈ *Free.*

★ Plas Newydd

HOUSE | Some historians consider Plas Newydd to be the finest mansion in Wales. Remodeled in the 18th century by James Wyatt (1747–1813) for the marquesses of Anglesey (whose descendants still live here), it stands on the Menai Strait about 7 miles southwest of Beaumaris. The interior has some fine 18th-century Gothic Revival decorations. Between 1936 and 1940 the society artist Rex Whistler (1905–44) painted the mural in the dining room. A museum commemorates the Battle of Waterloo, where the first marquess led the cavalry. The woodland walk and rhododendron gardens are worth exploring, and it's sometimes possible to take boat trips on the strait. Plas Newydd is not to be confused with the Gothic mansion of the same name in Llangollen. ⊠ *Off A4080, southwest of Britannia Bridge, Llanfairpwllgwyngyll* ☎ *01248/714795* ⊕ *www.nationaltrust.org.uk/plas-newydd* ✈ *£13.26.*

Hotels

The Bull and Townhouse

$$ | HOTEL | These twin hotels, a stone's throw away from each other, could hardly be more different: one is a restored 15th-century coaching inn, the other a contemporary lodging. **Pros:** lovely blend of historic and contemporary; good food; luxury bedding. **Cons:** the Bull has low ceilings; no on-site parking; breakfast portions are small for some. ⑤ *Rooms from: £135* ⊠ *Castle St., Beaumaris* ☎ *01248/810329* ⊕ *www.bullsheadinn. co.uk* ⇆ *13 rooms* ⏹ *No meals.*

Activities

Isle of Anglesey Coastal Path

HIKING/WALKING | Extending 130 miles around the island, this path leads past cliffs, sandy coves, and plenty of scenic variety. Pick up information at any of the regional tourist offices and choose a section; the west coast has the most dramatic scenery. ⊠ *Beaumaris* ⊕ *www. visitanglesey.co.uk.*

Conwy

23 miles east of Beaumaris, 48 miles northwest of Chester.

The still-authentic medieval town of Conwy grew up around its castle on the west bank of the River Conwy. A ring of ancient but well-preserved walls, built in the 13th century to protect the English merchants who lived here, enclose the old town and add to the pervading sense of history. Sections of the walls, with their 21 towers, can still be walked. The impressive views from the top take in the castle and the estuary, with mountains in the distance.

GETTING HERE AND AROUND

The A55 expressway links Conwy into the central U.K. motorway system via the M56. The town is also on the North Wales coast rail route, which ends at Holyhead on Anglesey. The town itself—surrounded by its wonderfully preserved walls—is perfect for pedestrians.

ESSENTIALS

VISITOR INFORMATION Conwy Tourist Information Centre. ⊠ *Muriau Bldgs., Rosehill St.* ☎ *01492/577566* ⊕ *www. visitconwy.org.uk.*

Sights

Aberconwy House

HOUSE | FAMILY | Thought to be the oldest complete medieval house in Wales, Aberconwy House's rooms have been restored to reflect three distinct periods in its history: medieval, Jacobean, and Victorian. It's a diverting and atmospheric little place, which also holds the distinction of (supposedly) being one of the most haunted buildings in North Wales. ⊠ *Castle St.* ☎ *01492/592246* ⊕ *www. nationaltrust.org.uk/aberconwy-house* ⊠ *£5.*

★ Bodnant Garden

GARDEN | Undoubtedly one of the best gardens in Wales, Bodnant Garden is something of a pilgrimage spot for horticulturists from around the world. Laid out in 1875, the 87 acres are particularly famed for rhododendrons, camellias, and magnolias. ■TIP➜ **Visit in late May to see the laburnum arch that forms a huge tunnel of golden blooms.** The mountains of Snowdonia form a magnificent backdrop to the Italianate terraces, rock and rose gardens, and pinetum. The gardens

are about 5 miles south of Conwy. ⊠ *Off A470, Tal-y-Cafn* ☎ *01492/650460* ⊕ *www.nationaltrust.org.uk/bodnant-garden* ⊠ *£8.*

★ Conwy Castle

CASTLE/PALACE | FAMILY | Of all Edward I's Welsh strongholds, it is perhaps Conwy Castle that best preserves a sheer sense of power and dominance. The eight large round towers and tall curtain wall, set on a rocky promontory, provide sweeping views of the area and the town walls. Although the castle is roofless (and floorless in places), the signage does a pretty good job of helping you visualize how rooms such as the Great Hall must once have looked. Conwy Castle can be approached on foot by a dramatic suspension bridge completed in 1828; engineer Thomas Telford designed the bridge with turrets to blend in with the fortress's presence. ⊠ *Rose Hill St.* ☎ *01492/592358* ⊕ *cadw.gov.wales* ⊠ *£8.80.*

Plas Mawr

HOUSE | Dating from 1576, Plas Mawr is one of the best preserved Elizabethan town houses in Britain. Richly decorated with ornamental plasterwork, it gives a unique insight into the lives of the Tudor gentry and their servants. ⊠ *High St.* ☎ *01492/580167* ⊕ *cadw.gov.wales* ⊠ *£6.50* ⊘ *Closed Nov.–Feb.*

Smallest House in Great Britain

HOUSE | What is said to be Britain's smallest house is furnished in mid-Victorian Welsh style. The house, which is 6 feet wide and 10 feet high, was reputedly last occupied in 1900 by a fisherman who was more than 6 feet tall. ⊠ *Lower Gate St.* ☎ *01492/573965* ⊕ *www.thesmallesthouse.co.uk* ⊠ *£1* ⊘ *Closed Nov.–Mar.*

Restaurants

★ Bodnant Welsh Food Centre

$$ | BRITISH | FAMILY | Wales has undergone something of a culinary renaissance in the last decade and a half, and

this fantastic center is a great place to explore why. Traditional cheeses, house-made ice creams, and other artisanal food products are for sale in the farm shop and deli; there's also a bakery, a coffee bar, and a wineshop where you can pick up Welsh malt whisky. **Known for:** one-stop farm shop for all things Welsh; delicious cuisine made with local produce; cooking classes. ⑤ *Average main: £20* ⊠ *Furnace Farm, Tal-y-Cafn* ☎ *01492/651100* ⊕ *www.bodnant-welsh-food.co.uk.*

Groes Inn

$ | **MODERN BRITISH** | Beamed ceilings, log fires, and rambling rooms abound at this old inn dating back to the 15th century. The menu consists of pub classics done well—think Welsh beef burger with local Bodnant cheese, or sea bass with potato and asparagus salad. **Known for:** charming, historic building; lovely garden; traditional Welsh pub cuisine. ⑤ *Average main: £14* ⊠ *B5106* ☎ *01492/650545* ⊕ *www.groesinn.com.*

Watson's Bistro

$$ | **BRITISH** | This popular bistro in central Conwy combines traditional Welsh flavors with accents of the Mediterranean. In the rustic dining room, try the crab fritters to start followed by slow-roast shoulder of lamb with minted port wine jus and potato gratin. **Known for:** local produce with a Mediterranean twist; delicious desserts; friendly service. ⑤ *Average main: £17* ⊠ *Chapel St.* ☎ *01492/596326* ⊕ *www.watsonsbistro-conwy.co.uk* ⊗ *Closed Mon.–Wed. No lunch Thurs., Fri,. and Sun.*

 Hotels

Castle Hotel

$$ | **HOTEL** | Nestled within Conwy's medieval walls, this former coaching inn has wood beams, stone fireplaces, and plenty of antiques. **Pros:** plenty of history; in the heart of Conwy; good food. **Cons:** small rooms; noisy seagulls; allegedly

one of the most haunted buildings in Wales. ⑤ *Rooms from: £150* ⊠ *High St.* ☎ *01492/582800* ⊕ *www.castlewales. co.uk* ⇄ *29 rooms* ⦿ *No meals.*

 Activities

Adventure Parc Snowdonia

SURFING | **FAMILY** | Surrounded by green hills, this lake is the world's first inland surf lagoon. All ages and abilities can ride the man-made waves, but there are other activities as well like rock-climbing. There's even a spa and on-site accom-modations. Adventure Parc Snowdonia is 7 miles south of Conwy in Dolgarrog. ⊠ *Conway Rd.* ☎ *01492/353–123* ⊕ *www.adventureparcsnowdonia.com.*

Llandudno

3 miles north of Conwy, 50 miles north-west of Chester.

This engagingly old-fashioned North Wales seaside resort has a wealth of well-preserved Victorian architecture and an ornate amusement pier with entertainments, shops, and places to eat. Grand-looking small hotels line the wide promenade with a view of the deep-blue waters of the bay. The shopping district beyond retains its original canopied walkways.

GETTING HERE AND AROUND

Llandudno is on the North Wales railway line with fast access from London and other major cities. By road, it's connect-ed to the motorway system via the A55 expressway. The scenic Conwy Valley rail line runs to Blaenau Ffestiniog, and the town is also on the network covered by the Snowdon Sherpa bus service.

ESSENTIALS

VISITOR INFORMATION Llandudno Tourist Information Centre. ⊠ *Victoria Centre, Mostyn St.* ☎ *01492/577577* ⊕ *www. visitconwy.org.uk.*

◉ Sights

Great Orme

VIEWPOINT | FAMILY | Named for the Norse word meaning "sea monster," the 679-foot headland called Great Orme towers over Llandudno, affording extraordinary views over the bay. The Llandudno Cable Car (North Parade) zips you one mile to the top of Great Orme. At the summit there's a visitor center (Easter through October only), an artificial ski slope, and a toboggan run. The most picturesque way to reach the summit is the Great Orme Tramway (Victoria Station, Church Walks). Trips depart about every 20 minutes. The summit is a sylvan spot, with open grassland, fields of wildflowers, and rare butterflies. Also look out for a wild herd of Kashmir goats. ✉ Llandudno ☎ 01492/877205 cable car, 01492/577877 tramway, 01492/874151 visitor center ⊕ www.greatormetramway.co.uk ⛝ Cable car £11 round-trip; tramway £8.10 round-trip ⊘ Closed Nov.–Easter.

Great Orme Mines

MINE | FAMILY | Discovered in 1987, these mines date back 4,000 years to when copper was first mined in the area. You can take a tour and learn about the technology that ancient people used to dig the tunnels, which are thought to be the largest surviving prehistoric mines in the world. ✉ Pyllau Rd. ☎ 01492/870447 ⊕ www.greatormemines.info ⛝ £8 ⊘ Closed Nov.–Easter.

Mostyn Art Gallery

MUSEUM | Housed in a restored Edwardian building, this is the leading contemporary art gallery in Wales. Six spaces host temporary exhibitions along with a shop and café. ✉ 12 Vaughan St. ☎ 01492/879201 ⊕ www.mostyn.org ⛝ Free ⊘ Closed Mon.

🛌 Hotels

★ Bodysgallen Hall

$$ | HOTEL | Tasteful antiques, polished wood, and comfortable chairs by cheery fires distinguish one of Wales's most luxurious country-house hotels. **Pros:** superb spa and pool; rare 17th-century knot garden; elegant dining and after noon tea. **Cons:** too formal for some; hard to get to without a car; lots of steps and stairs. $ Rooms from: £200 ✉ Off A470 ☎ 01492/584466 ⊕ www.bodysgallen. com ⛝ 31 rooms ⦿ Free Breakfast.

Bryn Derwen Hotel

$ | HOTEL | FAMILY | This immaculate, impeccably run Victorian hotel is traditional in style, but has a contemporary edge. **Pros:** historic building; charming decor; close to the beach. **Cons:** no sea views; one-night nonrefundable deposit required; minimum two-night stay. $ Rooms from: £88 ✉ 34 Abbey Rd. ☎ 01492/876804 ⊕ www.bryn-derwen. co.uk ⛝ 9 rooms ⦿ Free Breakfast ⛝ No children under 12.

St. Tudno Hotel

$ | HOTEL | FAMILY | Perfectly situated on the seafront promenade overlooking the beach and pier, this hotel has been run by the same family for nearly 40 years. **Pros:** ocean views; free on-site parking; good food. **Cons:** some rooms are snug; overly fussy decor; popular wedding venue. $ Rooms from: £90 ✉ Promenade ☎ 01492/874411 ⊕ www.st-tudno.co.uk ⛝ 18 rooms ⦿ Free Breakfast.

Ruthin (Rhuthun)

33 miles southeast of Llandudno, 23 miles southwest of Chester.

Once a stronghold of the rebel Welsh prince Owain Glyndwr (c. 1354–1416), Ruthin is a delightful market town with elegant shops, good inns, and a fascinating architectural mix of medieval, Tudor, and Georgian buildings. The town also has a crafts complex with displays of the artisans' creations.

GETTING HERE AND AROUND

Ruthin is on the A494 and A525 roads. The nearest railway stations are Rhyl and Wrexham, both about 20 miles away. Local bus connections are reasonably good; most useful bus connections go through Rhyl.

 ## Sights

The Myddelton Grill on the Square

BUILDING | This distinctive 16th-century building in the town square has seven Dutch-style dormer windows, known as the "eyes of Ruthin," set into its red-tile roof. Inside, you'll find a pub serving decent food. ⊠ *St. Peter's Sq.*

Nantclwyd y Dre

HOUSE | Dating from 1435, the oldest known timbered house in Wales offers visitors the opportunity to see how its inhabitants lived throughout the centuries; there's a useful interactive display, too. A colony of Lesser Horseshoe bats lives in the attic and you can watch them via a bat cam. Outside, the original medieval garden has been restored. ⊠ *Castle St.* ☎ *01824/706868* ⊠ *£7* ⊘ *Closed Oct.–Mar.; weekdays Apr., May, and Sept.; and Thurs. and Fri. June–Aug.*

Ruthin Gaol

JAIL | **FAMILY** | You can tour the local jail, where from 1654 to 1916 thousands of prisoners were incarcerated, and learn about prison conditions in Victorian times. ⊠ *Clwyd St.* ☎ *01824/708281* ⊠ *£7* ⊘ *Closed Tues. and Nov.–Mar.*

 ## Hotels

Eyarth Station

$ | **B&B/INN** | **FAMILY** | This Victorian railway station 2 miles south of Ruthin has been converted into an outstanding B&B, with spacious modern bedrooms with large windows looking out over the Vale of Clwyd. **Pros:** unique building; packed lunches and evening meals available; great views. **Cons:** decor a little dated in the public areas; need a car to get around; slow Wi-Fi. $ *Rooms from: £85* ⊠ *Off A525, Llanfair Dyffryn Clwyd* ☎ *01824/703643* ⊕ *www.eyarthstation. com* ⊃ *6 rooms* ⦿| *Free Breakfast.*

manorhaus

$ | **B&B/INN** | A Georgian town house in the heart of Ruthin has been converted into a gorgeous boutique hotel. **Pros:** cutting-edge design; local art in each room; trendy bistro. **Cons:** small rooms; limited parking; two-night minimum on some dates. $ *Rooms from: £85* ⊠ *Well St.* ☎ *01824/704830* ⊕ *www.manorhaus. com* ⊃ *8 rooms* ⦿| *No meals.*

 ## Shopping

Ruthin Craft Centre

CRAFTS | Along with exhibitions and artist residencies, this Center for the Applied Arts sells works by leading artists and craftspeople from around Wales. There's also a nice café. ⊠ *Park Rd.* ☎ *01824/704774* ⊕ *www.ruthincraftcentre.org.uk.*

Chapter 14

EDINBURGH

Updated by
Joseph Reaney

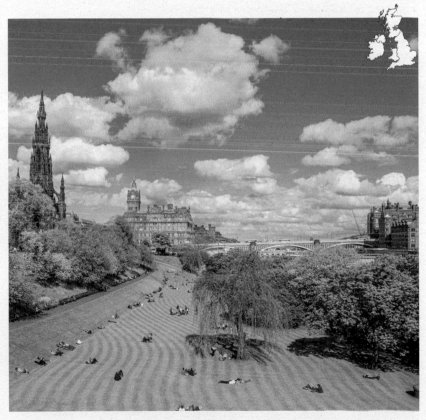

⦿ Sights	🍽 Restaurants	🛏 Hotels	🛍 Shopping	🍸 Nightlife
★★★★★	★★★★★	★★★★★	★★★★★	★★★★★

WELCOME TO EDINBURGH

TOP REASONS TO GO

★ **Culture:** From floor-stomping *ceilidhs* to avant-garde modern dance, the city's calendar of cultural festivals, including the remarkable Edinburgh Festival Fringe—the world's largest arts festival by a mile—is truly outstanding.

★ **The Royal Mile:** History plays out before your eyes in this centuries-old capital along the Royal Mile. Edinburgh Castle and the Palace of Holyroodhouse were the locations for some of the most important struggles between Scotland and England.

★ **Architecture:** From the Old Town's labyrinthine medieval streets to the neoclassical orderliness of the New Town to imaginative modern developments like the Scottish Parliament, the architecture of Auld Reekie spans the ages.

★ **Food:** The city's ever-expanding restaurant scene attracts celebrity chefs that serve up international dishes and genuine Scottish cuisine, like Cullen skink and haggis with neeps and tatties.

For all its steep roads and hidden alleyways, Edinburgh is not a difficult place to navigate. Most newcomers gravitate to two areas, the Old Town and the New Town. The former funnels down from the castle on either side of High Street, better known as the Royal Mile. Princes Street Gardens and Edinburgh Waverley station separate the oldest part of the city from the stately New Town, known for its neoclassical architecture and verdant gardens. To the north the city sweeps down to the Firth of Forth. It is here you will find the port of Leith, replete with trendy pubs and fine-dining restaurants. The southern and western neighborhoods are mainly residential, but are home to a few attractions, such as Edinburgh Zoo.

1 **Old Town.** The focal point of Edinburgh for centuries, the Old Town is a picturesque jumble of medieval tenements. Here are prime attractions such as Edinburgh Castle and the newer symbol of power, the Scottish Parliament. Here you will find everything from buzzing bars and nightclubs to

ghostly alleyways and vaults.

2 **New Town.** Built in the 18th and 19th centuries to prevent the wealthier residents of overcrowded Old Town from decamping to London, the neoclassical sweep of the New Town is a masterpiece of city planning. Significant sights include the National Gallery of Scotland and Calton Hill, which offers some of the best views of the city from its summit.

3 Haymarket. West of the Old Town and south of the West End is Haymarket, a district with its own down-to-earth character and well-worn charm. It's close to Edinburgh's second train station.

4 West End. Edinburgh's commercial center has boutiques aplenty as well as the Edinburgh Zoo.

5 South Side. Mostly residential, the South Side makes a good base for budget-conscious travelers. It's where most of the city's students live.

6 Leith. On the southern shore of the Firth of Forth, Edinburgh's port of Leith is where you'll find the now-retired Royal Yacht *Britannia*, along with some of the city's smartest restaurants and bars.

7 The Lothians. Known collectively as the Lothians, the areas of green countryside and seafront villages around Edinburgh are replete with historic houses, castles, museums, and world-renowned golf courses.

Edinburgh is "a city so beautiful it breaks the heart again and again," as Alexander McCall Smith once wrote. One of the world's stateliest cities and proudest capitals, it is—like Rome—built on seven hills, making it a striking backdrop for the ancient pageant of history.

In a skyline of sheer drama, Edinburgh Castle looks out over the city, frowning down on Princes Street's glamour and glitz. But despite its rich past, the city's famous festivals, excellent museums and galleries, and the modernist Scottish Parliament are all reminders that Edinburgh has its feet firmly in the 21st century.

Nearly everywhere in Edinburgh (the *burgh* is always pronounced *burra* in Scotland) are spectacular buildings, whose Doric, Ionic, and Corinthian pillars add touches of neoclassical grandeur to the largely Presbyterian backdrop. Large gardens are a strong feature of central Edinburgh, while Arthur's Seat, a craggy peak of bright green-and-yellow furze, rears up behind the spires of the Old Town. Even as Edinburgh moves through the 21st century, its tall guardian castle remains the focal point of the city and its venerable history.

Modern Edinburgh has become a cultural capital, staging the Edinburgh International Festival and the Festival Fringe in every possible venue each August. The stunning National Museum of Scotland complements the city's wealth of galleries and artsy hangouts. Add Edinburgh's growing reputation for food and nightlife and you have one of the world's most beguiling cities.

Today, Edinburgh is the second-most-important financial center in the United Kingdom, and is widely renowned for its exceptional (and ever-expanding) dining and nightlife scenes—some of the reasons it regularly ranks near the top of quality-of-life surveys.

Edinburgh's Old Town, which bears a great symbolic weight as the "heart of Scotland's capital," is a boon for lovers of atmosphere and history. In contrast, if you appreciate the unique architectural heritage of the city's Enlightenment, then the New Town's for you. If you belong to both categories, don't worry—the Old and New Towns are only yards apart. Explore the city's main thoroughfares—peopled by the spirits of Mary, Queen of Scots, Sir Walter Scott, and Robert Louis Stevenson—then get lost among the tiny *wynds* and *closes* (old medieval alleys that connect the winding streets). And remember: you haven't earned your porridge until you've climbed Arthur's Seat.

Head out of the city center and you'll find smaller communities with an abundance of charm. Dean Village, with its cobbled streets and 19th-century water mills, has a character all its own. Duddingston, just southeast of Arthur's Seat, has all the bucolic charm of a country village. Then there's Edinburgh's port, Leith, home to some of Scotland's smartest bars and restaurants. Visible beyond them all, across the Firth of Forth, is the patchwork of fields that is the county of Fife—a reminder, like the mountains to the northwest that can be glimpsed from Edinburgh's highest points, that the rest of Scotland lies within easy reach.

Planning

When to Go

Scotland's reliably unreliable weather means that you could visit at the height of summer and be forced to wear a winter coat. Conversely, conditions can be balmy in early spring and late autumn. You may choose to avoid the crowds (and hotel price hikes) of July and August, but you'd also miss some of the greatest festivals on Earth. May, June, and September are probably the most hassle free months in which to visit, while still offering hope of good weather. Short days and grim conditions make winter less appealing, though there are few better New Year's Eve celebrations than Edinburgh's Hogmanay.

FESTIVALS

★ Edinburgh Festival Fringe

ARTS FESTIVALS | FAMILY | During the world's largest arts festival in August, most of the city center becomes one huge performance area, with fire eaters, sword swallowers, unicyclists, jugglers, string quartets, jazz groups, stand-up comedians, and magicians all thronging into High Street and Princes Street. Every available performance space—church halls, community centers, parks, sports fields, nightclubs, and more—is utilized for every kind of event, with something for all tastes. There are even family-friendly shows. Many events are free; others start at a few pounds and rise to £15 or £20. There's so much happening in the three weeks of the festival that it's possible to arrange your own entertainment program from early morning to after midnight. ■ TIP→ Be aware that hotels get booked up months in advance during the Fringe and bargains are virtually impossible to come by, so plan your trip as far in advance as possible. ⊠ Edinburgh Festival Fringe Office, 180 High St., Old Town ☎ 0131/226–0026 ⊕ www. edfringe.com.

Edinburgh International Book Festival

FESTIVALS | FAMILY | This two-week-long event held every August pulls together a heady mix of authors from around the world, from Nobel laureates to best-selling fiction writers, and gets them talking about their work in a magnificent tent village. There are more than 750 events in total, with the workshops for would-be writers and children proving hugely popular. ⊠ Edinburgh International Book Festival Admin Office, 5 Charlotte Sq., New Town ☎ 0131/718–5666 ⊕ www edbookfest.co.uk.

Edinburgh International Festival

ARTS FESTIVALS | FAMILY | Running throughout August, this flagship traditional arts festival attracts international performers and audiences to a celebration of music, dance, theater, opera, and art. Programs, tickets, and reservations are available from the Hub, set within the impressive Victorian-Gothic Tolbooth Kirk. Tickets for the festival go on sale in April, and the big events sell out within the month. Nevertheless, you'll still be able to purchase tickets for some events during the festival; prices range from around £4 to £60. ⊠ The Hub, 348–350 Castlehill, Old Town ☎ 0131/473–2015 ⊕ www.eif.co.uk.

Edinburgh International Film Festival

FESTIVALS | One of Europe's foremost film festivals, promoting the best of global independent cinema since 1947, this event takes place from mid-June to early July each year. It's a great place for a first screening of a new film—movies from Billy Elliot to Little Miss Sunshine to The Hurt Locker have premiered here. ⊠ Edinburgh Film Festival Office, 88 Lothian

Rd., West End ☎ 0131/228–4051 ⊕ *www.
edfilmfest.org.uk.*

★ **Edinburgh's Hogmanay**

FESTIVALS | Nowadays most capital cities
put on decent New Year's celebrations,
but Edinburgh's three-day-long Hogmanay festivities are on a whole other
level. There's a reason this city is famous
around the world as the best place to
ring in the New Year. Yes, it's winter and
yes, it's chilly, but joining a crowd of
80,000 people in a monster street party,
complete with big-name rock concerts,
torchlight processions, ceilidh dancing,
and incredible fireworks, is something
you won't forget in a hurry. The headline
city center events are ticketed (and can
be pricey), but there are free parties
happening all over the city. ⊠ *Princes St.,
Old Town* ⊕ *www.edinburghshogmanay.
com* ⊠ *From £20.*

Planning Your Time

One of Edinburgh's greatest virtues is
its compact size, which means that it is
possible to pack a fair bit into even the
briefest of visits. The two main areas of
interest are the Old Town and the New
Town, where you'll find Edinburgh Castle,
the Scottish Parliament, Princes Street
Gardens, and the National Gallery of
Scotland. You can cover the major attractions in one day, but to give the major
sights their due, you should allow at least
two. You can also choose between the
Palace of Holyroodhouse and the important museums of Edinburgh, or explore
the Royal Botanic Garden and Holyrood
Park. Head down to leafy, villagelike
Stockbridge, then immerse yourself in
the greenery along the Water of Leith,
visiting the Scottish National Gallery of
Modern Art along the way.

Getting out of town is also an option
for longer stays. Hop on a bus out to Midlothian to see the magnificent Rosslyn
Chapel (even if you're not a fan of *The
Da Vinci Code*, it's still interesting), and

Crichton Castle, parts of which date back
to the 14th century. Head west along the
Firth of Forth to explore South Queensferry, with its three Forth bridges (including the iconic red railway bridge) and
palatial Hopetoun House, or head east
for the beautiful beaches, bird-watching,
and golf courses in and around North
Berwick.

■TIP→ **Some attractions have special
hours during August, due to the large influx
of festivalgoers. If you want to see something special, be sure to check the hours
ahead of time.**

Getting Here and Around

AIR

Edinburgh Airport is 7 miles west of the
city center. Flights bound for Edinburgh
depart virtually every hour from London's
Gatwick, Heathrow, and City airports.

Airlines serving Edinburgh, Scotland's
busiest airport, include Air France, Aer
Lingus, American Airlines, British Airways, Delta Virgin, easyJet, Iberia, Jet2,
KLM, Lufthansa, and Ryanair.

Delta flies direct to Edinburgh from
New York's JFK airport, while United
flies direct from Newark. There are also
direct flights from Boston and Wash-
ington, D.C., (Delta), Chicago (United),
and Philadelphia (American). Otherwise,
your airline is likely to require a change
somewhere in Europe. You could also fly
into Glasgow Airport, 50 miles away, or
the smaller Glasgow Prestwick, another
30 miles south, but these will add about
an hour and a half to your journey.

There are no rail links to the city center,
so the most efficient way to do the
journey on public transport is by tram;
the service runs every 8 to 12 minutes
and takes about half an hour. Tickets cost
£6 one-way and £8.50 for a round-trip.
By bus or car you can usually make it
to Edinburgh in a half hour, unless you
hit the morning (7:30 to 9) or evening

(4 to 6) rush hours. Lothian Buses runs an Airlink express service to Waverley railway station via Haymarket that usually takes around half an hour, depending on traffic. Buses run every 10 minutes (every 30 minutes throughout the night); tickets cost £4.50 one way or £7.50 round-trip and can be purchased from the booth beside the bus. Local buses also run between Edinburgh Airport and the city center every 15 minutes or so from 9 to 5, and roughly every hour during off-peak hours; they are far cheaper—just £1.70 one-way—but can take twice as long.

You can arrange for a chauffeur-driven limousine to meet your flight at Edinburgh Airport through Transvercia Chaffeur Drive, Little's, or W L Sleigh Ltd, for upwards of £50.

Taxis are readily available outside the terminal. The trip takes 20 to 30 minutes to the city center, 15 minutes longer during rush hour. The fare is roughly £25. Note that airport taxis picking up fares from the terminal are any color, not the typical black cabs.

AIRPORT CONTACTS Edinburgh Airport. ✉ *Glasgow Rd., Ingliston* ☎ *0844/448–8833* ⊕ *www.edinburghairport.com.* **Little's.** ✉ *1282 Paisley Rd. W, Glasgow* ☎ *0131/334–2177* ⊕ *www.littles. co.uk.* **Transvercia Chaffeur Drive.** ✉ *The Harland Bldg., Unit 6, Suite 19, Pilrig Heights, Leith* ☎ *0131/555–0459* ⊕ *www. transvercia.co.uk.* **W L Sleigh.** ✉ *Unit 11A West Craigs, Turnhouse Rd., Edinburgh* ☎ *0131/339–9607* ⊕ *sleigh.co.uk.*

BUS

National Express provides a coach service to and from London and other major towns and cities. The main terminal, Edinburgh Bus Station, is a short walk north of Edinburgh Waverley station, immediately east of St. Andrew Square. Long-distance coaches must be booked in advance online, by phone, or at the terminal. Edinburgh is approximately eight hours by bus from London.

Lothian Buses provides most of the services between Edinburgh and the Lothians and conducts day tours around and beyond the city. First Bus runs additional buses out of Edinburgh into the surrounding area. Megabus offers dirt-cheap fares to selected cities across Scotland.

Lothian Buses is the main operator within Edinburgh. You can buy tickets from the driver on the bus, though you will need the exact fare. Alternatively, you can buy tickets in advance at a Lothian Buses store or on your phone through the Lothian Buses M-Tickets app. On a limited (but ever-increasing) number of routes, contactless card payment is also available. In all cases, it's £1.70 for a single ticket or £4 for a day ticket, which allows unlimited one-day travel on the city's buses. A single night ticket costs £3, or you can get unlimited travel from 6 pm to 4:30 am with a DAY&NIGHT ticket (£3.50). ■ **TIP→ Buses can be packed on Friday and Saturday nights, so you may want to consider a taxi instead.**

CONTACTS First Bus. ☎ *0871/200–2233* ⊕ *www.firstgroup.com.* **Lothian Buses.** ☎ *0131/554–4494* ⊕ *www.lothianbuses.com.* **Megabus.** ☎ *0900/160–0900* ⊕ *uk.megabus.com.* **National Express.** ☎ *0871/781–8181* ⊕ *www.nationalexpress.co.uk.*

CAR

It's not necessary to have a car in Edinburgh, as the city is quite walkable and has an extensive and efficient public transport system. Driving in Edinburgh has its quirks and pitfalls—particularly at the height of festival season. Metered parking in the city center is scarce and expensive, and the local traffic wardens are an unforgiving lot. Note that illegally parked cars are routinely towed away, and getting your car back will be expensive. After 6 pm, the parking situation improves considerably, and you may manage to find a space quite near your hotel, even downtown. If you park on a yellow line or in a resident's parking bay, be prepared to move your car by 8 the following morning. Parking lots are clearly signposted; overnight parking is expensive and not always permitted.

TAXI

Taxi stands can be found throughout the city, mostly in the New Town. The following are the most convenient: the west end of Princes Street, South Street, David Street, and North Street, Andrew Street (both just off St. Andrew Square), Waverley Mall, Waterloo Place, and Lauriston Place. Alternatively, hail any taxi displaying an illuminated "for hire" sign.

TRAIN

Edinburgh's main train hub, Edinburgh Waverley station, is downtown, below Waverley Bridge and around the corner from the unmistakable spire of the Scott Monument. Travel time from Edinburgh to London by train is as little as 4½ hours for the fastest service.

Edinburgh's other main station is Haymarket, about four minutes (by rail) west of Edinburgh Waverley. Most Glasgow and other western and northern services stop here.

CONTACTS National Rail Enquiries. ☏ 08457/484950 ⊕ www.nationalrail. co.uk. **ScotRail.** ☏ 0344/811–0141 ⊕ www.scotrail.co.uk.

TRAM

Absent since 1956, trams returned to the streets of Edinburgh in 2014. The 8½-mile stretch of track currently runs between Edinburgh Airport in the west to York Place in the east, although work is under way to extend it up Leith Walk and to The Shore. Useful stops for travelers include Haymarket, Princes Street, and St. Andrew Square (for Edinburgh Waverley station). Tickets are £1.70 for a single journey in the "City Zone" (which is every stop excluding the airport), or £6 for a single to/from the airport (£8.50 return). Day tickets, allowing unlimited travel,

cost £4 in the City Zone and £9 including the airport.

CONTACTS Edinburgh Trams. ☏ 0131/338–5780 ⊕ www.edinburghtrams.com.

Restaurants

Edinburgh's eclectic restaurant scene has attracted a brigade of well-known chefs, including the award-winning trio of Martin Wishart, Tom Kitchin, and Paul Kitching, who have abandoned the tried-and-true recipes for more adventurous cuisine. Of course, you can always find traditional fare, which usually means the Scottish-French style that harks back to the historical "Auld Alliance" of the 13th century. The Scottish element is the preference for fresh and local foodstuffs; the French supplies the sauces. In Edinburgh you can sample anything from Malaysian *rendang* (a thick, coconut-milk stew) to Kurdish kebabs, while the long-established French, Italian, Chinese, Pakistani, and Indian communities ensure that the majority of the globe's most treasured cuisines are well represented. It's possible to eat well in Edinburgh without spending a fortune. Multicourse prix-fixe options are common, and almost always less expensive than ordering à la carte. Even at restaurants in the highest price category, you can easily spend less than £35 per person. People tend to eat later in Scotland than in England—around 8 pm on average—and then drink on in leisurely Scottish fashion.

Hotels

From stylish boutique hotels to homey bed-and-breakfasts, Edinburgh has a world-class array of accommodation options to suit every taste. Its status as one of Britain's most attractive and fascinating cities ensures a steady influx of visitors, but the wealth of overnight options means there's no need to compromise on where you stay. Grand old hotels are rightly renowned for their regal bearing and old-world charm, but if your tastes are a little more contemporary, the city's burgeoning contingent of chic design hotels offers an equally alluring alternative. For those on a tighter budget, the town's B&Bs are the most obvious choice. If you've previously found B&Bs to be restrictive, keep in mind that Scots are trusting people—many proprietors provide front-door keys and very few impose curfews.

Space is at a premium in August and September, when the Edinburgh International Festival and the Festival Fringe take place, so reserve your room at least three months in advance. B&Bs may prove trickier to find in the winter months (with the exception of Christmas and New Year), as this is when many proprietors choose to close up shop and go on vacation themselves.

To save money and see how local residents live, stay in a B&B in one of the areas away from the city center, such as Pilrig to the north, Murrayfield to the west, or Sciennes to the south. Public buses can whisk you to the city center in 10 to 15 minutes.

Restaurant and hotel reviews have been shortened. For full information, visit Fodors.com. Restaurant prices are the average cost of a main course at dinner or, if dinner is not served, at lunch. Hotel prices are the lowest cost of a standard double room in high season, including 20% V.A.T.

WHAT IT COSTS in Pounds

	$	$$	$$$	$$$$
RESTAURANTS				
	under £15	£15–£19	£20–£25	over £25
HOTELS				
	under £125	£125–£200	£201–£300	over £300

Tours

The Cadies and Witchery Tours

WALKING TOURS | Spooky tours tracing Edinburgh's ghouls, murders, and other grisly happenings start outside the Witchery Restaurant. The Cadies and Witchery Tours has built an award-winning reputation for combining entertainment and historical accuracy in its lively and enthusiastic Murder and Mystery and (in summer only) Ghosts and Gore tours. Both take you through the narrow Old Town lanes and closes, with costumed guides and other theatrical characters popping up along the route. ⊠ *The Witchery, 352 Castlehill, Old Town* ☎ *0131/225–6745* ⊕ *www.witcherytours.com* ⊡ *£10.*

Edinburgh Bus Tours

BUS TOURS | Explore every corner of Edinburgh with this company's range of bus tours. The most popular are the Edinburgh Tour, which mainly covers Old Town sights including Edinburgh Castle, the Royal Mile, and the Palace of Holyroodhouse; and the Majestic Tour, which explores the New Town and farther corners of the city, including the Royal Yacht *Britannia* at Leith and the Royal Botanic Garden. Buses depart from Waverley Bridge, with each tour lasting an hour. ■ **TIP➔ If you plan more than one bus tour during a weekend, buy a money-saving Grand 48 ticket.** ⊠ *Waverley Bridge, New Town* ☎ *0131/220–0770* ⊕ *www.edinburghtour.com* ⊡ *From £16.*

The Edinburgh Literary Pub Tour

WALKING TOURS | Professional actors invoke local literary characters while taking you around some of the city's most hallowed watering holes on these lively and informative tours. The experience is led by "Clart and McBrain"—one a bohemian, the other an intellectual—who regale you with witty tales of the literary past of Edinburgh's Old and New Towns. Tours run daily from May to September and meet outside the Beehive Inn. ⊠ *The Beehive Inn, 18–20 Grassmarket,*

Edinburgh ☎ 0800/169–7410 ⊕ www. edinburghliterarypubtour.co.uk ⊠ £14.

★ The Tartan Bicycle Company

BICYCLE TOURS | Cycling enthusiast and Edinburgh native Johann offers a range of guided and self-guided bike tours in and around the capital. Each half-day or full-day tour includes hotel pickup and your choice of standard or e-bikes. For a relaxed half-day introduction to Edinburgh, including some lesser-visited neighborhoods, opt for the Sky to Sea tour; it starts at leafy Union Canal, passes by The Meadows and Arthur's Seat, visits Portobello Beach, The Shore, and the Water of Leith, and ends in the New Town. *⊠ Edinburgh ☎ 0797/394–0924 ⊕ www.tartanbiketours.co.uk ⊠ From £45.*

Visitor Information

The VisitScotland Edinburgh iCentre, located close to St. Giles' Cathedral on the Royal Mile, offers an accommodation-booking service, along with regular tourist information services.

VISITOR INFORMATION VisitScotland Edinburgh iCentre. *⊠ 249 High St., Old Town ☎ 0131/473–3868 ⊕ www.visitscotland.com.*

 Activities

FOOTBALL

Like Glasgow, Edinburgh is mad for football (soccer in the United States), and there's an intense rivalry between the city's two professional teams.

Heart of Midlothian Football Club

SOCCER | Better known simply as "Hearts," the Heart of Midlothian Football Club plays in maroon and white and is based at Tynecastle. The club's crest is based on the Heart of Midlothian mosaic on the Royal Mile. *⊠ Tynecastle Stadium, McLeod St., Edinburgh ☎ 0333/043–1874 ⊕ www.heartsfc.co.uk.*

Hibernian Football Club

SOCCER | Known to most as simply "Hibs," the green-and-white-bedecked Hibernian Club was founded in 1875—one year after Hearts—and plays its home matches at Easter Road Stadium in Leith. *⊠ Easter Road Stadium, 12 Albion Pl., Leith ☎ 0131/661–2159 ⊕ www. hibernianfc.co.uk.*

GOLF

Edinburgh is widely considered to be the birthplace of modern golf, as its first official rules were developed at Leith Links. Naturally, there are a number of great courses in the city. For more information, the VisitScotland website has an extensive, searchable guide to Scottish courses.

Braid Hills

GOLF | This golf course is beautifully laid out over a rugged range of small hills in the southern suburbs of Edinburgh. The views in each direction—the Pentland Hills to the south, the city skyline and Firth of Forth to the north—are worth a visit in themselves. The city built this course at the turn of the 20th century after urban development forced golfers out of the city center. There's also a nine-hole "Wee Braids" course for beginners and younger players. Reservations are recommended for weekend play. *⊠ 27 Braids Hill Approach, Edinburgh ☎ 0131/447–6666 ⊕ www.edinburghleisure.co.uk ⊠ Braids: £26.50 weekday, £27.50 weekends; Wee Braids: £15 weekdays, £16 weekends ⅃. Braids: 18 holes, 5865 yards, par 71; Wee Braids: 9 holes, 2232 yards, par 31.*

Royal Burgess Golfing Society

GOLF | Edinburgh's other Victorian courses are newcomers when compared to Royal Burgess, which opened in 1735. Its members originally played on Bruntsfield Links; now they and their guests play on elegantly manicured parkland in the city's northwestern suburbs. It's a challenging course with fine, beautifully maintained greens. There's a fairly conservative dress code—no denim or T-shirts allowed, and you must wear a jacket and tie in the clubhouse. ☒ *181 Whitehouse Rd., Barnton* ☎ *0131/339–2075* ⊕ *www.royalburgess.co.uk* ✉ *£100 for 1 round; £150 day ticket* ⚐. *18 holes, 6511 yards, par 71* ⚑ *Reservations essential.*

RUGBY

Edinburgh is the home of Scottish rugby, with national stadium Murrayfield hosting regular international matches. It's also home to several amateur clubs and the professional club Edinburgh Rugby, who compete in the international Pro14 League.

★ Murrayfield Stadium

RUGBY | Home of the Scottish Rugby Union, Murrayfield Stadium hosts rugby matches in early spring and fall, as well as prestigious Six Nations tournament games in February and March. Crowds of good-humored rugby fans from all over the world add greatly to the sense of excitement in the streets of Edinburgh. Stick around after the game as there's often live music, food, and drinks to enjoy in the stadium grounds. Outside of the rugby season, you can still see Murrayfield with a stadium tour; tickets are £12 for adults. ☒ *Roseburn St., Murrayfield* ☎ *0131/346–5000* ⊕ *www. scottishrugby.org.*

Old Town

East of Edinburgh Castle, the historic castle esplanade becomes the street known as the Royal Mile, leading down through Old Town to the Palace of Holyroodhouse. The Mile, as it's known locally, is actually made up of one thoroughfare that bears, in consecutive sequence, different names—Castlehill, Lawnmarket, Parliament Square, High Street, and Canongate. This thoroughfare, and the streets and passages that wind off it on both sides, really *were* Edinburgh until the 18th century saw expansions to the south and north. Everybody lived here: the richer folk on the lower floors of houses; the less well-to-do families on the middle floors; and the poor highest up.

Time and progress (of a sort) have swept away some of the narrow closes and tall tenements of the Old Town, but enough survive for you to be able to imagine the original profile of Scotland's capital. There are many guided tours of the area, or you can simply stroll around at your leisure. The latter is often a better choice in summer, when tourists pack the area and large guided groups have trouble making their way through the crowds.

◉ Sights

Arthur's Seat

VIEWPOINT | The high point of 640-acre Holyrood Park is this famously spectacular viewpoint. You'll have seen it before—countless photos have been snapped from this very spot. The "seat" in question is actually the 822-foot-high plateau of a small mountain. A ruined church—the 15th century Chapel of St. Anthony—adds to its impossible picturesqueness. There are various starting points for the walk, but one of the most pleasant begins at the Scottish Parliament building. Cross the road from Parliament, skirt around the parking lot, cross a second road, and join the gently rising path to the left (rather than the steeper fork to the right). At a moderate pace, this climb takes around 45 minutes up and 30 minutes down, and is easy so long as you're reasonably fit. Even if you aren't, there are plenty of places to stop for a rest and to admire the views along the way. A faster—though less beautiful—way to reach the summit is to drive to the small parking area at Dunsapie Loch, on Queen's Road, then follow the footpath up the hill; this walk takes about 20 minutes. ☒ *Queen's Dr., Old Town.*

Old Town

NEW TOWN

OLD TOWN

TOLLCROSS

St. James Centre

Edinburgh Waverley Station

Queen St.

Hanover St.

St. David St.

St. Andrew St.

George St.

St Andrews Square

Scott Monument

St. Tram.

Castle St.

Frederick St.

Hanover St.

Princes St.

Princes Street Gardens

Ross Fountain

The Mound

Market St.

Cockburn St.

Waverley Bridge

North Bridge

High St.

Mercat Cross

New College-University of Edinburgh

Parliament Sq.

Edinburgh Castle

Cowgate

South Bridge

Guthrie St.

Chambers St.

Old College

Johnston Terrace

King's Stables Rd.

Grassmarket

Candlemaker Row

Greyfriars Kirk

West Port

Spittal St.

University of Edinburgh-Lauriston Campus

Flodden Wall

George Heriot's School

Forrest Rd.

Teviot Pl.

University of Edinburgh

E. Fountainbridge

Heriot Pl.

Lauriston Place

George Square Gardens

Lauriston Gdns.

Chalmers St.

Nightingale Way

Simpson Loan

Buccleuch Pl.

The Meadows

KEY

- 🔵 Exploring Sights
- 🟠 Restaurants
- 🟢 Hotels

Sights ▼

1 Arthur's Seat **J5**

2 Camera Obscura and World of Illusions **C4**

3 Canongate Tolbooth and People's Story Museum **G3**

4 Dynamic Earth **I3**

5 Edinburgh Castle........ **B4**

6 George IV Bridge **D5**

7 Gladstone's Land **C4**

8 Grassmarket............ **B5**

9 Greyfriars Kirkyard **D5**

10 High Kirk of St. Giles.... **D4**

11 High Street **E3**

12 Museum of Edinburgh................ **G3**

13 National Museum of Scotland **E5**

14 Palace of Holyroodhouse........... **I2**

15 The Real Mary King's Close **D3**

16 The Scottish Parliament............... **H2**

17 Scotch Whisky Experience **C4**

18 Scottish Storytelling Centre and John Knox House.. **F3**

19 Writers' Museum **C4**

Restaurants ▼	7 Lovecrumbs **A5**	**Hotels** ▼
1 Checkpoint **E5**	8 Michael's **E4**	1 Radisson Collection
2 Cannonball Restaurant. **C4**	9 Oink....................... **C4**	Royal Mile Edinburgh .. **D4**
3 David Bann **F4**	10 Ondine **D4**	2 Hotel du Vin **E5**
4 Hanam's................. **C4**	11 Timberyard **A5**	3 The Inn on the Mile..... **E3**
5 Howies.................. **D4**	12 Wedgwood the	4 The Scotsman........... **E3**
6 La Garrigue............. **F3**	Restaurant............. **F3**	5 The Witchery by the
		Castle **C4**

An emblem of the city's history, the rock where Edinburgh Castle stands has been inhabited as far back as 1,000 BC.

Camera Obscura and World of Illusions

OBSERVATORY | FAMILY | View Edinburgh like a Victorian at the city's 19th-century camera obscura. Head up Outlook Tower for the headline attraction—an optical instrument that affords live bird's-eye views of the city, illuminated onto a concave table. It's been wowing visitors since 1853, and yet it retains a magical quality that can captivate even the most cynical smartphone-toting teen. After you've seen the camera obscura and enjoyed the rooftop views, head down to explore five more floors of interactive optical illusions. They are guaranteed to keep the kids entertained and educated for an hour or two. ⊠ *549 Castlehill, Old Town* ☎ *0131/226–3709* ⊕ *www.cam-era-obscura.co.uk* ▱ *£16.*

Canongate Tolbooth and People's Story Museum

MUSEUM | Nearly every city and town in Scotland once had a tolbooth. Originally a customhouse, where tolls were gathered, it soon came to mean town hall and later prison, as there were detention cells in the cellar. The building where Canongate's town council once met now has a museum, the **People's Story Museum,** which focuses on the lives of everyday folk from the 18th century to today. Exhibits describe how Canongate once bustled with the activities of the tradespeople needed to supply life's essentials. There are also displays on the politics, health care, and leisure time (such as it was) in days of yore. Other exhibits leap forward in time to show, for example, a typical 1940s kitchen. ⊠ *163 Canongate, Old Town* ☎ *0131/529–4057* ⊕ *www.edinburghmuseums.org.uk.*

Dynamic Earth

MUSEUM | FAMILY | Using state-of-the-art technology, the 11 theme galleries at this interactive science museum educate and entertain as they explore the wonders of the planet, from polar regions to tropical rain forests. Geological history, from the big bang to the unknown future, is also examined, all topped off with a 360-degree Showdome movie-theater experience. Book tickets online for a

10% discount. ✉ *112–116 Holyrood Rd., Old Town* ☎ *0131/550–7800* ⊕ *www. dynamicearth.co.uk* ✉ *£15.95 at door; £14.50 online* ⏱ *Closed Mon. and Tues. Nov.–Feb.*

★ Edinburgh Castle

CASTLE/PALACE | **FAMILY** | The crowning glory of the Scottish capital, Edinburgh Castle is popular not only for its pivotal role in Scottish history, but also because of the spectacular views from its battlements: on a clear day the vistas stretch all the way to Fife. You'll need at least three hours to see everything it has to offer (even longer if you're a military history buff), though if you're in a rush, its main highlights can be squeezed into an hour and a half. You enter across the Esplanade, the huge forecourt built in the 18th century as a parade ground, then proceed to the curvy ramparts of the Half-Moon Battery, which give Edinburgh Castle its distinctive silhouette. Highlights include the tiny 11th-century St. Margaret's Chapel, the oldest part of the castle; the Crown Room, which contains the crown, scepter, and sword that once graced the Scottish monarch, as well as the Stone of Scone, where Scottish monarchs once sat to be crowned; and the famous 15th-century Belgian-made cannon Mons Meg. ✉ *Castle Esplanade and Castlehill, Old Town* ☎ *0131/225–9846* ⊕ *www.edinburghcastle.scot* ✉ *£18.*

George IV Bridge

BRIDGE/TUNNEL | Here's a curiosity—a bridge that most of its users don't ever realize is a bridge. With buildings closely packed on both sides, George IV Bridge can feel to many like a regular Edinburgh street, but for those forewarned, the truth is plain to see. At the corner of the bridge stands one of the most photographed sculptures in Scotland, *Greyfriars Bobby*. This statue pays tribute to the legendarily loyal Skye terrier who kept vigil beside his master's grave for 14 years after he died in 1858. The 1961 Walt Disney film *Greyfriars Bobby* tells a

version of the heartrending tale. ✉ *Bank St. and Lawnmarket, Old Town.*

Gladstone's Land

HOUSE | This narrow, six-story tenement, situated next to the Assembly Hall, is one of the oldest buildings on the Royal Mile. It's a survivor from the early 17th century, and now stands as a re-creation of the living conditions of the time. Rooms are decorated in authentic period furnishings, and the sense of how cramped life must have been, even for the moderately successful, is deftly portrayed. Typical Scottish architectural features are evident on two floors, including an arcaded ground floor (even in the city center, livestock sometimes inhabited the ground floor) and some magnificent painted ceilings. Look out for the lovely spinet in the drawing room; the ingeniously designed instrument, resembling a space-saving piano, plucks strings rather than strikes them, producing a resonantly baroque sound. ✉ *477B Lawnmarket, Old Town* ☎ *0131/226–5856* ⊕ *www.nts. org.uk* ✉ *£7.*

Grassmarket

PLAZA | For centuries an agricultural marketplace, Grassmarket is now the site of numerous shops, bars, and restaurants, making it a hive of activity at night. Sections of the Old Town wall can be traced on the north side by a series of steps that ascend from Grassmarket to Johnston Terrace. The best-preserved section of the wall can be found by crossing to the south side and climbing the steps of the lane called the Vennel. The 16th-century **Flodden Wall** comes in from the east and turns south at Telfer's Wall, a 17th-century extension.

From the northeast corner of the Grassmarket, **Victoria Street,** a 19th-century addition to the Old Town, leads to the George IV Bridge. Shops here sell antiques, designer clothing, and souvenirs. ✉ *Grassmarket, Edinburgh.*

The Greyfriars Kirkyard, part of the church Greyfriars Kirk, is allegedly one of the most haunted cemeteries in Europe.

★ Greyfriars Kirkyard

CEMETERY | This sprawling, hillside grave-yard, surely one of the most evocative in Europe (particularly at twilight), is a giddy mess of old, tottering tombstones that mark the graves of some of Scotland's most respected heroes and despised villains. Many of these inspired character names in the Harry Potter book series; fans can seek out Potters, McGonagalls, and Moodies, to name a few. Among the larger tombs arranged in avenues and the seemingly random assortment of grave markers, lie two rare surviving *mortsafes*: iron cages erected around graves in the early 1800s to prevent the theft of corpses for sale to medical schools.

At the southern end of the graveyard stands Greyfriars Kirk, the church where the National Covenant—a document declaring the Presbyterian Church in Scotland independent of the monarchy, and which plunged Scotland into decades of civil war—was signed in 1638. Nearby, at the corner of George IV Bridge and Candlemaker Row, stands one of Scotland's most photographed sites: the statue of Greyfriars Bobby, a Skye terrier who supposedly spent 14 years guarding the grave of his departed owner. ✉ *Greyfriars Pl., Old Town* ☎ *0131/225–1900* 🌐 *www.greyfriarskirk.com/visit-us/kirkyard* 💳 *Free.*

High Kirk of St. Giles (*St Giles' Cathedral*) **RELIGIOUS SITE** | St. Giles, which lies about one-third of the way along the Royal Mile from Edinburgh Castle, is one of the city's principal churches. It may not quite rival Paris's Notre Dame or London's Westminster Abbey—it's more like a large parish church than a great European cathedral—but it has a long and storied history. There has been a church here since AD 854, although most of the present structure dates from either 1120 or 1829, when the church was restored.

The tower, with its stone crown 161 feet above the ground, was completed between 1495 and 1500. Inside the church stands a life-size statue of the Scot whose spirit still dominates the place—the great religious reformer and preacher John Knox. But the most elaborate feature is the **Chapel of the Order of the Thistle,** built onto the southeast corner of the church in 1911 for the exclusive use of Scotland's only chivalric order, the Most Ancient and Noble Order of the Thistle. It bears the belligerent national motto *"nemo me impune lacessit"* ("No one provokes me with impunity"). Look out for the carved wooden angel playing bagpipes. ⊠ *High St., Old Town* ☎ *0131/225–9442* ⊕ *www.stgilescathedral.org.uk* ⌖ *Free, but donations welcome.*

High Street

NEIGHBORHOOD | The High Street (one of the five streets that make up the Royal Mile) is home to an array of impressive buildings and sights, including some hidden historic relics. Near Parliament Square, look on the west side for a **heart** mosaic set in cobbles. This marks the site of the vanished Old Tolbooth, which housed the Scottish parliament and a prison until it was demolished in 1817. The Mercat Cross (*mercat* means "market") is another great landmark of Old Town life, an old mercantile center, where royal proclamations were—and are still—read. Across High Street from the High Kirk of St. Giles stands the City Chambers, built by John Fergus and now the seat of local government; note how the building drops 11 stories to Cockburn Street on its north side. Finally, the Tron Kirk (named after a salt tron, or weight beam, that used to stand nearby) was built after 1633, when St. Giles's became an Episcopal cathedral for a brief time. ⊠ *Between Lawnmarket and Canongate, Old Town.*

Museum of Edinburgh

MUSEUM | A must-see if you're interested in the details of Old Town life, this bright yellow, 16th-century building is home to a fascinating museum of local history. It houses some of the most important artifacts in Scottish history—including the National Covenant, a document signed by Scotland's Presbyterian leadership in defiance of a reformed liturgy imposed by King Charles I of England that ignited decades of civil war—alongside Scottish pottery, silver, and glassware, as well as curios like Greyfriars Bobby's dog collar. ⊠ *142–146 Canongate, Old Town* ☎ *0131/529–4143* ⊕ *www.edinburghmuseums.org.uk.*

★ National Museum of Scotland

MUSEUM | FAMILY | This museum traces the country's fascinating story from the oldest fossils to the most recent popular culture, making it a must-see for first-time visitors to Scotland. Two of the most famous treasures are the Lewis Chessmen, 11 intricately carved 12th-century ivory chess pieces found on one of Scotland's Western Isles, and Dolly the sheep, the world's first cloned mammal and biggest ovine celebrity. A dramatic, cryptlike entrance gives way to the light-filled, birdcage wonders of the Victorian grand hall and the upper galleries. Other exhibition highlights include the hanging hippo and sea creatures of the Wildlife Panorama, beautiful Viking brooches, Pictish stones, and Queen Mary's *claisach* (harp). Take the elevator to the lovely rooftop terrace for spectacular views of Edinburgh Castle and the city below. ⊠ *Chambers St., Old Town* ☎ *0300/123–6789* ⊕ *www.nms.ac.uk* ⌖ *Free.*

★ Palace of Holyroodhouse

CASTLE/PALACE | Onetime haunt of Mary, Queen of Scots, with a long history of gruesome murder, destructive fire, and power-hungry personalities, the Palace of Holyroodhouse is now Queen Elizabeth's official residence in Scotland. A doughty, impressive palace standing at the foot of the Royal Mile, it's built around a graceful, lawned central court at the end of Canongate. And when royals are not in residence, you can take a tour. There's plenty to see here, so make sure you have at least two hours to tour the palace, gardens, and the ruins of the 12th-century abbey; pick up the free

The Grand Gallery of the National Museum of Scotland is reminiscent of a classic Victorian arcade mall.

audio guide for the full experience. The **King James Tower** is the oldest surviving section of the palace, containing Mary's rooms on the second floor and Lord Darnley's rooms below. The 150-foot-long **Great Picture Gallery,** on the north side, displays the portraits of 110 Scottish monarchs. ✉ *Canongate, Old Town* ☎ *0131/123–7306* ⊕ *www.rct.uk* 🎫 *£15; £25 includes Queen's Gallery and a garden history tour.*

The Real Mary King's Close

NEIGHBORHOOD | **FAMILY** | Buried beneath the City Chambers, this narrow, cobbled close (alleyway) provides a glimpse into a very different Edinburgh. It was once a busy open-air thoroughfare with hundreds of residents and a lively market, but in 1753 it was sealed off when the Royal Exchange (now the City Chambers) was built on top. Today costumed guides take you around the claustrophobic remains of the shops and houses, describing life here for the residents from plague and quarantine to rivers of sewage, as well as the odd murder mystery

and ghost story. But for all the (somewhat over-the-top) theatricality, the real highlights here are historical; the sealed-in street is a truly fascinating insight into 17th-century Edinburgh. ✉ *2 Warriston's Cl., Old Town* ☎ *0131/225–0672* ⊕ *www. realmarykingsclose.com* 🎫 *£16.50.*

The Scottish Parliament

GOVERNMENT BUILDING | Scotland's now-iconic Parliament building is starkly modernist, with irregular curves and angles that mirror the twisting shapes of the surrounding landscape. Stylistically, it is about as far removed from Westminster as can be. Originally conceived by the late Catalan architect Enric Miralles, and completed by his widow Benedetta Tagliabue, the structure's artistry is most apparent when you step inside. The gentle slopes, the forest's worth of oak, the polished concrete and granite, and the walls of glass create an understated magnificence. Take a free guided tour to see the main hall and debating chamber, a committee room, and other areas of the building, or choose a specialist subject for your tour, from history to literature to art. All tour reservations must be made online. Call well in advance to get a free ticket to view Parliament in action. ⊠ Horse Wynd, Old Town ☏ 0131/348–5000 ⊕ www.parliament.scot ⏱ Closed Sun.

Scotch Whisky Experience

MUSEUM | Transforming malted barley and spring water into one of Scotland's most important exports—that's the subject of this popular Royal Mile attraction. An imaginative approach to the subject has guests riding in low-speed barrel cars and exploring Scotland's diverse whisky regions and their distinct flavors. Sniff the various aromas and decide whether you like fruity, sweet, or smoky, and afterward experts will help you select your perfect dram. Your guide will then take you into a vault containing the world's largest collection of Scotch whiskies. Opt for one of the premium tours (from £28 to £75) for extras ranging from additional tastings to a Scottish dining experience. ⊠ 354 Castlehill, Old Town ☏ 0131/220–0441 ⊕ www.scotchwhiskyexperience.co.uk ⏱ From £16.

★ Scottish Storytelling Centre and John Knox House

ARTS VENUE | The stripped-down, low-fi, traditional art of storytelling has had something of a resurgence in Britain over the last decade or so, and there are few places better than this to experience a master storyteller in full flow. Housed in a modern building that manages to blend seamlessly with the historic structures on either side, the center hosts a year-round program of storytelling, theater, music, and literary events. A great little café serves lunch, tea, and home-baked cakes.

The center's storytellers also hold tours of John Knox House next door. It isn't certain that the religious reformer ever lived here, but there's evidence he died here in 1572. Mementos of his life are on view inside, and the distinctive dwelling

gives you a glimpse of what Old Town life was like in the 16th century—projecting upper floors were once commonplace along the Royal Mile. ⊠ 43–45 High St., Old Town ☏ 0131/556–9579 ⊕ www.scottishstorytellingcentre.com ⏱ Storytelling Centre free; John Knox House £6 ⏱ Closed Sun. Sept.–June.

Writers' Museum

MUSEUM | Situated down a narrow close off Lawnmarket is the 1662 Lady Stair's House, a fine example of 17th-century urban architecture. Inside, the Writers' Museum evokes Scotland's literary past with such exhibits as the letters, possessions, and original manuscripts of Sir Walter Scott, Robert Burns, and Robert Louis Stevenson. ⊠ Lady Stair's Close, Old Town ☏ 0131/529–4901 ⊕ www.edinburghmuseums.org.uk.

Restaurants

The most historic part of the city houses some of its grander restaurants (though, curiously, none of its current Michelin stars). It is also home to some of Edinburgh's oldest and most atmospheric pubs, which serve good, informal meals.

Checkpoint

$ | **INTERNATIONAL** | Originally run as a pop-up during the Festival Fringe, this supercool café-bar is now a permanent part of the Edinburgh dining scene. The coffee is sensational, but the comfort food is just as much of a draw. **Known for:** excellent coffee and hearty breakfasts; delicious light lunches; hip hangout in the evening. ⑤ Average main: £8 ⊠ 3 Bristo Pl., Old Town ☏ 0131/225–9352 ⊕ www.checkpointedinburgh.com.

★ Cannonball Restaurant

$$ | **ITALIAN** | The name refers to one of the most delightful quirks of Edinburgh's Old Town—the cannonball embedded in the wall outside, said to have been fired at the castle while Bonnie Prince Charlie was in residence (not true, but a good story). The atmosphere in this

three-story restaurant and whisky bar is casual and relaxed, despite the gorgeous art deco dining room with views of the castle esplanade. **Known for:** scrumptious Italian-Scottish cuisine; great views of the castle; bread-crumbed haggis cannonballs. $ Average main: £18 ⊠ 356 Castlehill, Old Town ☎ 0131/225–1550 ⊕ www.contini.com/cannonball.

David Bann
$ | VEGETARIAN | This hip eatery, situated just off the Royal Mile, serves exclusively vegetarian and vegan favorites, and its inventive dishes and modern interior make it a popular place with young locals. The menu changes constantly, but the invariably creative, flavorful dishes often leave carnivores forgetting they're eating vegetarian. **Known for:** superb vegetarian and vegan cuisine; very affordable; lovely setting. $ Average main: £13 ⊠ 56–58 St. Mary's St., Old Town ☎ 0131/556–5888 ⊕ www.davidbann.com.

Hanam's
$ | MIDDLE EASTERN | Kurdish food may not be as well known as other Middle Eastern cuisines, but dishes like *bay-engaan surocrau* (marinated slow-roasted eggplant) and lamb *tashreeb* (a flavorful casserole) are worth checking out. Hanam's proudly promotes Kurdish cuisine, but also serves more familiar and equally delicious Middle Eastern fare, from shish kebabs to falafel. **Known for:** traditional Kurdish cooking; BYOB policy; hookah on heated terrace. $ Average main: £14 ⊠ 3 Johnston Terr., Old Town ☎ 0131/225–1329 ⊕ www.hanams.com.

Howies
$ | BRITISH | The Victoria Street branch of this bistro chain is a good choice for contemporary Scottish fare, with lots of fresh local produce. Alongside the daily specials and quality Scottish steaks and salmon, there are some nicely inventive vegetarian options. **Known for:** quality Scottish menu; good value set-price lunch; can get very busy. $ Average main: £14 ⊠ 10–14 Victoria St., Old Town ☎ 0131/225–1721 ⊕ www.howies.uk.com.

La Garrigue
$$$ | FRENCH | Edinburgh is blessed with several excellent French bistros, and this is one of the best. Although the modern decor evokes Paris, the food has the rustic flavor of the southern Languedoc region. **Known for:** rustic French cuisine; attentive service; colorful crockery. $ Average main: £22 ⊠ 31 Jeffrey St., Old Town ☎ 0131/557–3032 ⊕ www.lagarrigue.co.uk.

★ Lovecrumbs
$ | CAFÉ | A bakery-café with an inordinately sweet tooth, Lovecrumbs joyously, deliciously, and unashamedly focuses on what *really* matters in life: cake. It serves delectable confections of all kinds, from sumptuous Victoria sponges to heavenly peanut-butter brownies to mouthwatering lemon tarts. **Known for:** extraordinary cakes galore; junk-shop-esque decor; large crowds despite unpredictable opening times. $ Average main: £4 ⊠ 155 W. Port, Old Town ☎ 0131/629–0626 ⊕ www.lovecrumbs.co.uk.

Michael's
$$ | MODERN BRITISH | Young chef Michael Neave delivers exceptional cuisine at affordable prices in his restaurant just off the Royal Mile. With a mission to "explore the best of Scotland's larder," quality Scottish produce is the star here, with meaty mains like Aberdeen Angus steaks, Perthshire venison, and Borders lamb appearing alongside Scottish seafood specialties like lobster and sea bream. **Known for:** superb Scottish cuisine; inventive sauces; great-value fixed-price menus. $ Average main: £19 ⊠ 21 Old Fishmarket Cl., Old Town ☎ 0131/226–4747 ⊕ www.michaelneave.co.uk ⊗ Closed Sun. and Mon.

★ Oink
$ | BRITISH | For a quick, cheap bite while wandering the Royal Mile, you can't beat Oink—possibly the best hog roast

The Palace of Holyroodhouse is the Queen's official residence in Scotland and the setting of a few key scenes in the television show *Outlander*.

(pulled pork) in Edinburgh. Located at the bottom of the Royal Mile (there are two other outlets, but this one is the best), it was founded by two farmers in 2008, and their high-quality, hand-reared pork has proved a huge hit ever since. **Known for:** unbelievable pulled pork; extra crackling on request; great-value lunch. $ *Average main: £6* ⊠ *82 Canongate, Old Town* ☎ *07584/637416* ⊕ *www.oink-hogroast.co.uk.*

Ondine

$$$ | SEAFOOD | This fabulous seafood restaurant just off the Royal Mile makes waves with its expertly prepared dishes from sustainable fishing sources. The menu is populated with Scottish seafood staples, from salmon and sea bream to lobster and langoustines, but these are often served in interesting and surprising ways. **Known for:** spectacular seafood; lavish decor; reservations usually needed for nights and weekends. $ *Average main: £25* ⊠ *2 George IV Bridge, Old Town* ☎ *0131/226–1888* ⊕ *www.ondinerestaurant.co.uk* ⊙ *Closed Sun.*

★ Timberyard

$$ | BRITISH | There are few restaurants that feel so wonderfully, well, *Edinburgh* as this one. The freshest seasonal ingredients, mostly sourced from small local producers, go into creating delicious, inventive fare. **Known for:** exciting dishes; hip interior; pricey multicourse menus. $ *Average main: £15* ⊠ *10 Lady Lawson St., Old Town* ☎ *0131/221–1222* ⊕ *www.timberyard.co* ⊙ *Closed Sun. and Mon.*

★ Wedgwood the Restaurant

$$$ | MODERN BRITISH | Rejecting the idea that fine dining should be a stuffy affair, owners Paul Wedgwood and Lisa Channon are in charge at this Royal Mile gem. Local produce and some unusual foraged fronds enliven the taste buds as Scottish and international influences are creatively fused together, from the starters (like the satisfyingly salty Scottish "miso" soup) to the desserts (such as the malt and whisky panna cotta). **Known for:** unfussy fine dining; delicious wild foraged salad; good three-course lunch deal. $ *Average main: £22* ⊠ *267 Canongate, Old Town*

☎ 0131/558–8737 ⊕ www.wedgwood-
therestaurant.co.uk.

Hotels

The narrow *pends* (alleys), cobbled
streets, and steep hills of the Old Town
remind you that this is a city with many
layers of history. From medieval to
modernist, these hotels all are within a
stone's throw of the action.

★ Hotel du Vin
$$ | **HOTEL** | Leave it to one of the United
Kingdom's most forward-thinking hotel
chains to convert a Victorian-era asylum
into this understated luxury property,
which combines a real sense of history
with contemporary decor and trappings.
Pros: unique and historic building; trendy
design; lively on-site dining and drink-
ing. **Cons:** quarter-mile walk to nearest
parking; neighborhood can be noisy;
service can be hit-and-miss. ⑤ *Rooms
from: £200* ✉ *11 Bristo Pl., Old Town*
☎ 0131/285–1479 ⊕ www.hotelduvin.
com ⤳ 47 rooms ¶◎¶ Free Breakfast.

The Inn on the Mile
$$$$ | **B&B/INN** | This chic and welcom-
ing boutique inn could hardly be more
central—some rooms even overlook the
Royal Mile. **Pros:** views of the Royal Mile;
excellent on-site bar; great design. **Cons:**
lots of steps and no elevator; sometimes
noisy; nearest parking at a public lot
(three-minute walk). ⑤ *Rooms from: £210*
✉ *82 High St., Old Town* ☎ 0131/556–
9940 ⊕ www.theinnonthemile.co.uk ⤳ 9
rooms ¶◎¶ Free Breakfast.

Radisson Collection Royal Mile Edinburgh
$$$ | **HOTEL** | The bright primary colors,
striking stenciled wallpapers, and bold,
eclectic furnishings inside this über-
trendy design hotel contrast with the
Gothic surroundings of the Royal Mile—
and yet, somehow, it works. **Pros:** perfect
location in the heart of the city; bold
and fashionable decor; complimentary
gin-and-tonic on arrival. **Cons:** decor a
little Austin Powers in places; expensive

during high season; street noise can leak
into rooms. ⑤ *Rooms from: £240* ✉ *1
George IV Bridge, Old Town* ☎ 0131/220–
6666 ⊕ www.radissonhotels.com/en-us/
hotels/radisson-collection-edinburgh-roy-
al-mile ⤳ 136 rooms ¶◎¶ Free Breakfast.

The Scotsman
$$$$ | **HOTEL** | This magnificent turn-of-
the-20th-century building, with its grand
marble staircase and its fascinating history—it was once the headquarters of the
Scotsman newspaper—now houses this
modern luxury hotel. **Pros:** gorgeous surroundings; personalized service; ideal Old
Town location. **Cons:** no air-conditioning;
spa can be noisy; could do with some
renovation. ⑤ *Rooms from: £270* ✉ *20
N. Bridge, Old Town* ☎ 0131/556–5565
⊕ scotsmanhotel.co.uk ⤳ 69 rooms
¶◎¶ Free Breakfast.

The Witchery by the Castle
$$$$ | **HOTEL** | Each suite within this lavish-
ly theatrical lodging has a theme—choices include the Library, the Guardroom,
and the Turret—and is appointed with
grand antiques, champagne chilling in an
immense bucket, and the finest-quality
bedding. **Pros:** Gothic drama and intriguing antiques; a truly romantic retreat;
sumptuous dining. **Cons:** can be noisy at
night; decor not for everybody; pricey.
⑤ *Rooms from: £395* ✉ *352 Castlehill,
Old Town* ☎ 0131/225–5613 ⊕ www.
thewitchery.com ⤳ 9 suites ¶◎¶ Free
Breakfast.

Nightlife

BARS AND PUBS
★ The Holyrood 9A
BARS/PUBS | This warm, wood-paneled
hipster hangout has a fine array of craft
beers on tap, as well as an impressive
whisky collection. It also serves some of
Edinburgh's best gourmet burgers. ✉ *9A
Holyrood Rd., Old Town* ☎ 0131/556–
5044 ⊕ www.theholyrood.co.uk.

The Last Drop

BARS/PUBS | There's plenty of atmosphere (and plenty of tourists) amid the nooks and crannies at The Last Drop. The name has a grim double meaning, as it was once the site of public hangings. ✉ 74–78 Grassmarket, Old Town ☎ 0131/225–4851 ⊕ www.nicholsonspubs.co.uk/restaurants/scotlandandnorthornireland/thelastdropgrassmarketedinburgh.

The Three Sisters

BARS/PUBS | This pub is a hive of activity during festival season, when the courtyard transforms into a beer garden with food stalls, and is packed wall-to-wall with revelers until the wee hours. Outside of the summer months, it remains a lively local favorite and the best place to watch live sports in Edinburgh. ✉ 139 Cowgate, Old Town ☎ 0131/622–6802 ⊕ www.thethreesistersbar.co.uk.

Under the Stairs

BARS/PUBS | As the name suggests, this shabby-chic cocktail bar-cum-bistro is tucked away below street level. A cozy, low-ceilinged place, full of quirky furniture and hip art exhibits, Under the Stairs serves specialty, seasonal cocktails, as well as superb bar food, to a mostly young crowd. ✉ 3A Merchant St., Old Town ☎ 0131/466–8550 ⊕ www.underthestairs.org.

★ Whiski Rooms

BARS/PUBS | This venerable establishment offers one of Old Town's most enjoyable whisky tastings: an informative and interactive experience with an expert guide. The 90-minute Premium Whisky Tasting features five unusual drams you'll almost certainly not have tasted before. When you're finished, either browse the shop stacked high with tempting bottles or head into the bar for another dram. ✉ 4–7 N. Bank St., Old Town ☎ 0131/225–7224 ⊕ www.whiskirooms.co.uk.

LIVE MUSIC

★ The Jazz Bar

MUSIC CLUBS | This basement music venue delivers exactly what the name promises: jazz, in all its many weird and wonderful forms. Blues, funk, acoustic, electric—there's something new to discover every night of the week. There's usually a small cover charge (cash only), but this all goes to musicians, not the venue. ✉ 1A Chambers St., Old Town ☎ 0131/220–4298 ⊕ www.thejazzbar.co.uk.

NIGHTCLUBS

Cabaret Voltaire

DANCE CLUBS | The vaulted ceilings of this subterranean club reverberate with dance music most nights, with an ever-changing lineup of cutting-edge DJs on the decks. The club also hosts regular live gigs and, during the Fringe, stand-up comedy shows. ✉ 36–38 Blair St., Old Town ☎ 0131/247–4704 ⊕ www.thecabaretvoltaire.com.

🎭 Performing Arts

Festival Theatre

MUSIC | This theater hosts regular concerts, as well as musical theater and Scottish Opera productions. ✉ 13–29 Nicolson St., Old Town ☎ 0131/529–6000 ⊕ www.capitaltheatres.com.

🛍 Shopping

BOOKS AND STATIONERY

Armchair Books

BOOKS/STATIONERY | Just a two-minute walk from Grassmarket, Armchair Books is a chaotic but characterful bookshop heaving with secondhand and antiquarian books. ✉ 72–74 W. Port, Old Town ☎ 0131/229–5927 ⊕ www.armchairbooks.co.uk.

Main Point Books

BOOKS/STATIONERY | This bibliophile's haven is stacked high with obscure first editions and bargain tomes. It also hosts regular literary events. ⊠ *77 Bread St., Old Town* ☎ *0131/228–4837* ⊕ *www.mainpointbooks.co.uk.*

CLOTHING
Bill Baber
CLOTHING | One of the more imaginative Scottish knitwear designers, Bill Baber's creative and colorful pieces are a long way from the conservative pastel woolies sold at some of the large mill shops. ⊠ *66 Grassmarket, Old Town* ☎ *0131/225–3249* ⊕ *www.billbaber.com.*

Ragamuffin
CLOTHING | First established on the Isle of Skye, Ragamuffin's Edinburgh outlet sells some of the funkiest, brightest, and most elegant knitwear produced anywhere in Scotland. ⊠ *278 Canongate, Old Town* ☎ *0131/557–6007.*

JEWELRY
Clarksons of Edinburgh
JEWELRY/ACCESSORIES | A family firm, Clarksons handcrafts a unique collection of jewelry, from Celtic to contemporary styles. The pieces here are made with silver, gold, platinum, and precious gems, with a particular emphasis on diamonds. ⊠ *87 W. Bow, Old Town* ☎ *0131/225–8141* ⊕ *www.clarksonsedinburgh.co.uk.*

SCOTTISH SPECIALTIES
★ Cadenhead's Whisky Shop
WINE/SPIRITS | Edinburgh's most iconic Scotch shop, Cadenhead's has an incredible selection of whisky to purchase (including rare bottles from closed distilleries), and also offers tasting sessions. The friendly and knowledgeable staff can help you pick out the perfect whisky to suit your palate. ⊠ *172 Canongate, Old Town* ☎ *0131/556–5864* ⊕ *www.cadenhead.scot.*

★ Cranachan & Crowdie
FOOD/CANDY | This lovely gourmet shop on the Royal Mile is brimming with the finest Scottish food and drink, from crunchy oatcakes to melt-in-the-mouth shortbread. There's even a chocolate counter for those with a particularly sweet tooth.

Staff are happy to put together hampers of food for any occasion—including an impromptu picnic back in your room. They also sell tweeds, handmade candles, and other gift-worthy knickknacks. ⊠ *263 Canongate, Old Town* ☎ *0131/556–7194* ⊕ *www.cranachanandcrowdie.com.*

Geoffrey Tailor Kiltmakers
LOCAL SPECIALTIES | This shop can clothe you in full Highland dress, with high-quality kilts made in its own workshops. ⊠ *57–59 High St., Old Town* ☎ *0131/557–0256* ⊕ *www.geoffreykilts.co.uk.*

New Town

It was not until the Scottish Enlightenment, a civilizing time of expansion in the 1700s, that the city's elite decided to break away from the Royal Mile's craggy slope and narrow closes to create a new neighborhood below the castle. This was to become the New Town, with elegant squares, classical facades, wide streets, and harmonious proportions. Clearly, change had to come. At the dawn of the 18th century, Edinburgh's unsanitary conditions—primarily a result of overcrowded living quarters—were becoming notorious. The well-known Scottish fiddle tune "The Flooers (flowers) of Edinburgh" was only one of many ironic references to the capital's unpleasant environment.

To help remedy this sorry state of affairs, in 1767 James Drummond, the city's lord provost (the Scottish term for mayor), urged the town council to hold a competition to design a new district for Edinburgh. The winner was an unknown young architect named James Craig (1744–95). His plan called for a grid of three main east–west streets, balanced at either end by two grand squares. These streets survive today, though some of the buildings that line them have been altered by later development. Princes Street is the southernmost, with Queen Street to the north and George Street as the axis, punctuated by St. Andrew and Charlotte squares. A look at the map will reveal a geometric symmetry unusual in Britain. Even the Princes Street Gardens are balanced by the Queen Street Gardens, to the north. Princes Street was conceived as an exclusive residential address, with an open vista facing the castle. It has since been altered by the demands of business and shopping, but the vista remains.

The New Town was expanded several times after Craig's death and now covers an area about three times larger than Craig envisioned. Indeed, some of the most elegant facades came later and can be found by strolling north of the Queen Street Gardens.

 ## Sights

Calton Hill

VIEWPOINT | Robert Louis Stevenson's favorite view of his beloved city was from the top of this hill, and it's easy to see why. Located in the heart of the city, Calton Hill offers stunning vistas of the Old and New Towns and out to the Firth of Forth, making it a popular setting for picnicking and watching festival fireworks. Great views aside, the hill is also home to a number of impressive monuments. The most notable is the so-called **National Monument,** also known as "Scotland's Disgrace," which was commissioned in 1822 and intended to mimic Athens's Parthenon. But after just 12 columns had been built, the money ran out, leaving the facade as a monument to high aspirations and poor fundraising. Nearby, the 100-foot-high **Nelson Monument,** completed in 1815 in honor of Britain's greatest naval hero, is topped with a "time ball" that is dropped at 1 pm every day. Other hillside monuments honor notable Scots ranging from mathematician John Playfair to philosopher Dugald Stewart.

The hill is also home to the **City Observatory,** which hosts regular contemporary art exhibitions, as well as upscale restaurant **The Lookout by Gardener's Cottage**. It also plays host to the **Beltane Fire Festival** every April 30. ⊠ *Bounded by Leith St. to the west and Regent Rd. to the south, New Town* ☎ *0131/529–5151* ⊕ *www. edinburgh.gov.uk* ⚑ *Nelson Monument £6.*

Princes Street

NEIGHBORHOOD | The south side of this dominant New Town street is occupied by the well-kept Princes Street Gardens, which act as a wide green moat to the castle on its rock. The north side is now one long sequence of chain stores with mostly unappealing modern fronts, with one or two exceptions: most notably the handsome Victorian facade that is home to Jenners department store. ⊠ *Waterloo Pl. to Lothian Rd., New Town.*

★ Royal Botanic Garden Edinburgh

GARDEN | FAMILY | Explore Britain's largest rhododendron and azalea gardens at this beautiful 70-acre botanical garden. Founded in 1670 as a physic garden, it now has a range of natural highlights such as soaring palms in the glass-domed Temperate House and the steamy Tropical Palm House, an extensive Chinese garden, and a pretty rock garden and stream. There's a visitor center with exhibits on biodiversity, a fabulous gift shop selling plants, books, and gifts, and two cafeterias. The handsome 18th-century Inverleith House hosts art exhibitions.

It's free to roam the gardens, though it costs extra for greenhouse admission, and you can splash out even more for guided garden walks and private tours. It takes 20 minutes to walk to the garden from Princes Street, or you can take a bus. ⊠ *Arboretum Pl., Inverleith* ☎ *0131/248–2909* ⊕ *www.rbge.org.uk* ⚑ *Free; Glasshouses £7.*

New Town

Sights ▼

1 Calton Hill............... **H5**
2 Princes Street........... **D6**
3 Royal Botanic Garden
 Edinburgh................ **C1**
4 Scott Monument........ **F6**
5 Scottish
 National Gallery......... **E6**

6 Scottish National
 Portrait Gallery.......... **F4**

Restaurants ▼

1 Contini George Street .. **D5**
2 Dishoom **F5**
3 Dusit..................... **E5**
4 Fhior..................... **F3**
5 Grazing by
 Mark Greenaway....... **C7**
6 The Honours............. **D5**

7 L'Escargot Bleu **F3**
8 Number One............. **F5**
9 The Pompadour......... **C6**
10 21212 .... **H4**

KEY

1 Exploring Sights
1 Restaurants
1 Hotels

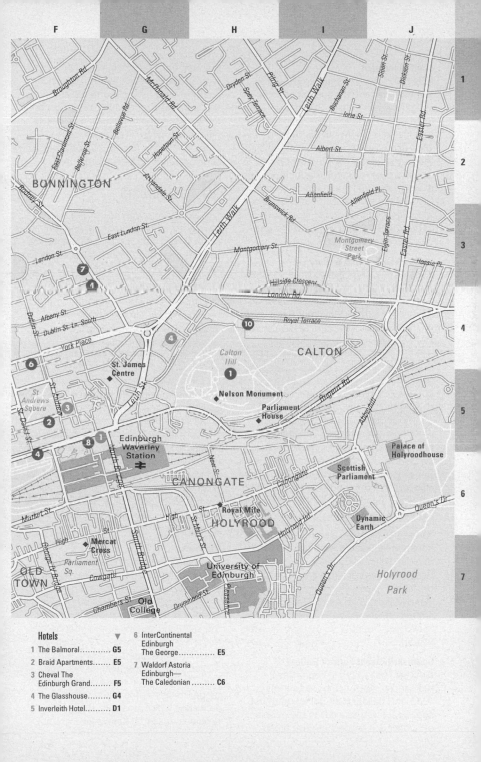

Hotels ▼

1 The Balmoral............. **G5**

2 Braid Apartments....... **E5**

3 Cheval The
  Edinburgh Grand........ **F5**

4 The Glasshouse......... **G4**

5 Inverleith Hotel.......... **D1**

6 InterContinental
  Edinburgh
  The George.............. **E5**

7 Waldorf Astoria
  Edinburgh—
  The Caledonian **C6**

Scott Monument

MEMORIAL | What appears to be a Gothic cathedral spire that's been chopped off and planted on Princes Street is in fact Scotland's tribute to one of its most famous sons, Sir Walter Scott. Built in 1844 and soaring to 200 feet, it remains the largest monument to a writer anywhere in the world. Climb the 287 steps to the top for a stunning view of the city and the hills and coast beyond. ✉ *E. Princes St. Gardens, New Town* ☎ *0131/529–4068* ⊕ *www.edinburghmuseums.org.uk* ✎ *£8; cash only.*

★ Scottish National Gallery

MUSEUM | Opened to the public in 1859, the Scottish National Gallery presents a wide selection of paintings from the Renaissance to the Postimpressionist period within a grand Neoclassical building. Most famous are the Old Master paintings bequeathed by the Duke of Sutherland, including Titian's *Three Ages of Man.* Works by Velázquez, El Greco, Rembrandt, Goya, Poussin, Turner, Degas, Monet, and van Gogh, among others, complement a fine collection of Scottish art, including Sir Henry Raeburn's *Reverend Robert Walker Skating on Duddingston Loch* and other works by Ramsay, Raeburn, and Wilkie. The gallery also has an information center, a quirky gift shop, and the excellent Scottish Cafe and Restaurant.

You can also hop on a shuttle bus (£1 donation requested) from here to the Scottish National Gallery of Modern Art, which has paintings and sculptures by Pablo Picasso, Georges Braque, Henri Matisse, and André Derain, among others. ✉ *The Mound, New Town* ☎ *0131/624–6200* ⊕ *www.nationalgalleries.org.*

Scottish National Portrait Gallery

MUSEUM | Set within a magnificent red-sandstone Gothic building from 1889, this gallery is an Edinburgh must-see. Conceived as a gift to the people of Scotland, it divides into five broad themes, from Reformation to Modernity, with special galleries for photography and contemporary art—all centered around the stunning Great Hall. It also plays host to regular temporary exhibitions, including the annual BP Portrait Award. ✉ *1 Queen St., New Town* ☎ *0131/624–6200* ⊕ *www.nationalgalleries.org.*

Restaurants

The New Town, with its striking street plan, ambitious architecture, and professional crowd, has restaurants where you can get everything from a quick snack to a more formal dinner.

Contini George Street

$$ | **ITALIAN** | Set within a grand former banking hall on George Street, this superb restaurant serves light but satisfying Italian favorites divided into *primi, secondi,* and *formaggi,* all within a light, airy setting of grand Corinthian columns, an open marble-topped bar, intricate wall hangings, and soft gray banquettes. The food choices are strictly seasonal, but regularly appearing favorites include the Scotch beef carpaccio and the housemade ravioli with ricotta and spinach. **Known for:** lovely, light Italian cuisine; grand but relaxed setting; Scotch beef carpaccio. ⑤ *Average main: £18* ✉ *103 George St., New Town* ☎ *0131/225–1550* ⊕ *www.contini.com/contini-george-street.*

Dishoom

$ | **INDIAN** | The city's most inventive Indian restaurant, Dishoom serves up an all-sensory experience, from the smells that greet you (delicious whiffs of incense mixed with aromatic spices) to the sight and sounds of the interior (the decor is all distressed-wood panels and chandeliers, inspired by Bombay's 1920 Iranian cafés) to the taste of the food itself. A tapas-style menu of deliciously tender meat, seafood, and vegetarian dishes welcomes you, along with delicious desserts. **Known for:** incredible

The Scottish National Gallery features a stunning collection of art, including many paintings from the Old Masters.

lamb salli boti; great cocktail and mocktail menu; unique Indian breakfast rolls. $ *Average main: £9* ✉ *3a St. Andrew Sq., Edinburgh* ☎ *0131/2026–406* ⊕ *www. dishoom.com.*

Dusit

$$ | THAI | Tucked down narrow Thistle Street, Dusit doesn't register on most travelers' radars, but it has been a local favorite since 2002. An authentic, contemporary Thai restaurant run by Bangkok-born Pom, the menu here delights with deliciously creamy curries, spicy stir-fries, and fragrant seafood specialties, all of which use a mix of fresh local produce and imported Thai vegetables. **Known for:** award-winning Thai food; local haunt; good value lunch menu. $ *Average main: £17* ✉ *49a Thistle St., New Town* ☎ *0131/220–6846* ⊕ *www.dusit.co.uk.*

Fhior

$$$$ | BRITISH | A relative newcomer to Edinburgh's dining scene, Fhior seems here to stay. Owner and chef Scott Smith, who previously ran the award-winning Norn, serves up seasonal, Scandinavian-inspired fare with rare Scottish ingredients, from beremeal (an ancient form of barley) bread to sea buckthorn. **Known for:** modernist decor; old-school Scottish dishes with a Scandinavian flair; multicourse menu options chosen by the chef. $ *Average main: £40* ✉ *36 Broughton St., Edinburgh* ☎ *0131/477–5000* ⊕ *www.fhior.com* ⊘ *Closed Sun.–Tues.*

Grazing by Mark Greenaway

$$$ | BRITISH | Despite the name and the smattering of shared plates on offer, Grazing is mostly about traditional, hearty bistro fare done brilliantly. Set within a lavish yet unstuffy dining room, the restaurant's menu of seasonal dishes with inventive twists adds a real sense of fun to this consistently excellent, if suprisingly high-priced, dining experience. **Known for:** fun and inventive dishes; attentive service; menu prices that tend to add up. $ *Average main: £25* ✉ *Waldorf Astoria Edinburgh—The Caledonian, Princes St., New Town* ☎ *0131/222–8857* ⊕ *www. markgreenaway.com.*

★ The Honours

$$$ | BISTRO | Run by Edinburgh restaurant grandee Martin Wishart, the Honours is a more relaxed (though almost as pricey) alternative to his eponymous flagship in Leith. Inside its gorgeous black-and-white, art deco interior, diners can enjoy a range of excellent Scottish seafood dishes; but those in the know order the meat, with extraordinary rare-breed sirloin and fillet beef steaks as well as delicious game like roe deer, guinea fowl, and rabbit. **Known for:** mouthwatering meat dishes; beautiful art deco decor; impeccable service. $ *Average main: £25* ✉ *58a North Castle St., New Town* ☏ *0131/220–2513* ⊕ *www.thehonours. co.uk* ⊙ *Closed Sun. and Mon.*

★ L'Escargot Bleu

$ | FRENCH | When it comes to quality at a good value, this pretty little French bistro, situated on one of Edinburgh's trendiest streets, is almost impossible to beat. You're warmly welcomed into an upscale but casual space of stripped wooden floors and period French posters, then shown a menu that seems to have a typo: £12.90 for a two-course lunch, or £14.90 for dinner of fine French cuisine as authentic as a withering stare on the Champs-Élysées. **Known for:** authentic French fare; hard-to-believe low prices; friendly service. $ *Average main: £13* ✉ *56 Broughton St., New Town* ☏ *0131/557–1600* ⊕ *www.lescargotbleu. co.uk* ⊙ *Closed Sun.*

Number One

$$$$ | BRITISH | Clublike but unstuffy, this outstanding basement restaurant, set within the Edwardian splendor of The Balmoral hotel, is made for intimate dining. The food is extraordinary, with a menu that highlights the best of Scottish seafood and meat in inventive fashion, but the prices make this a place for serious special occasions; the regular three-course prix-fixe is £90 per person (drinks not included) while the tasting menus will set you back even more. **Known for:** wonderfully intimate setting; inventive dishes; very expensive. $ *Average main: £90* ✉ *The Balmoral, 1 Princes St., New Town* ☏ *0131/557–6727* ⊕ *www.roccofortehotels.com* ⊙ *No lunch.*

★ The Pompadour

$$$$ | FRENCH FUSION | Sophisticated surroundings, spectacular views, and sumptuous cuisine make this restaurant, originally opened in 1925, one of Edinburgh's best spots for fine dining. Head chef Dan Ashmore uses his expertise in great Scottish produce, from venison to sea trout, to serve up a stunning, "mystery" seven-course tasting menu (it comes in a sealed envelope; it's up to you when, or if, you want to take a peek). **Known for:** beautiful pastel-floral dining room; subtly sumptuous flavors; gorgeous presentation. $ *Average main: £35* ✉ *Waldorf Astoria Edinburgh–The Caledonian, Princes St., New Town* ☏ *0131/222–8857* ⊕ *www.thepompadour.com* ⊙ *Closed Mon. and Tues.*

21212

$$$$ | MODERN FRENCH | Paul Kitching is one of Britain's most innovative chefs, and the theatrical dining experience at 21212 delivers surprises galore. Set within a Georgian town house, the Michelin-starred restaurant is sumptuously appointed while, behind a large glass screen, a small army of chefs is busy assembling the delicious and intricate dishes. **Known for:** contemporary Franco-Anglo-Scottish cuisine; atmospheric and romantic; enigmatic menu of two starters, two mains, and two desserts with soup and cheese courses in between. $ *Average main: £85* ✉ *3 Royal Terr., New Town* ☏ *0131/523–1030* ⊕ *www.21212restaurant.co.uk* ⊙ *Closed Sun.–Tues.*

Hotels

Calton Hill, which offers some of the best views of the city from its summit, is just one of the reasons to base yourself in the

New Town, filled with gorgeous 18th- and 19th-century architecture.

★ The Balmoral

$$$$ | HOTEL | The attention to detail in the elegantly appointed rooms and suites, where colors and patterns echo the country's heathers and moors, and the sheer Edwardian splendor of this grand, former railroad hotel make staying at The Balmoral a special introduction to Edinburgh. **Pros:** big and beautiful Edwardian building; top-hatted doorman; top-notch spa, restaurant, and whisky bar. **Cons:** small lap pool; spa books up fast; some rooms a little tiny. $ *Rooms from: £340* ✉ *1 Princes St., New Town* ☎ *0131/556–2414* ⊕ *www.roccofortehotels.com* ⤴ *188 rooms* ⦿ *Free Breakfast.*

Braid Apartments

$$ | RENTAL | This collection of chic, comfortable, and spacious self-service apartments is tucked away on quiet Thistle Street, meaning that guests can enjoy being in the heart of the New Town and yet out of sight (and sound) of the crowds. **Pros:** good modern facilities; quiet central location; friendly reception staff. **Cons:** no on-site parking; noisy water pumps; no access for people with disabilities. $ *Rooms from: £175* ✉ *27 Thistle St., New Town* ☎ *0800/304–7160* ⊕ *www.bymansley.com* ⤴ *20 rooms* ⦿ *No meals.*

Cheval The Edinburgh Grand

$$ | RENTAL | Despite all appearances—the classical Edinburgh exterior, the Corinthian-columned art deco lobby, the friendly and attentive concierges, and the in-house high-end restaurants—The Edinburgh Grand is not a swanky hotel, but rather a collection of grand and luxurious serviced apartments. **Pros:** beautiful apartments with supercomfy beds; ideal location for trams and trains; all amenities included. **Cons:** perilously dark corridors; no doors on some bathrooms; Register Club food disappointing and overpriced. $ *Rooms from: £200* ✉ *42 St. Andrew Sq., New Town*

☎ *0131/230–0570* ⊕ *www.lateralcity.com* ⤴ *50 apartments* ⦿ *No meals.*

★ The Glasshouse

$$$ | HOTEL | Glass walls extend from the 19th-century facade of a former church, foreshadowing the daring, modern interior of one of the city's original, and best, boutique hotels. **Pros:** truly stunning rooftop garden; very modern and stylish; near all the attractions. **Cons:** loud air-conditioning and toilet flushing; decor a little sterile for some; continental breakfast extra (hot breakfast even more). $ *Rooms from: £200* ✉ *2 Greenside Pl., New Town* ☎ *0131/525–8200* ⊕ *www.theglasshousehotel.co.uk* ⤴ *77 rooms* ⦿ *No meals.*

Inverleith Hotel

$ | B&B/INN | Across from the Royal Botanic Gardens, this renovated Victorian town house has cozy, well-lit rooms with velour bedspreads, dark-wood furniture, and pale-gold curtains—at an incredible value. **Pros:** quiet surroundings; knowledgeable staff; cheap parking nearby (free on weekends). **Cons:** some rooms are small; far from the Old Town; uphill walk to the city center. $ *Rooms from: £80* ✉ *5 Inverleith Terr., New Town* ☎ *0131/556–2745* ⊕ *www.inverleithhotel.co.uk* ⤴ *9 rooms* ⦿ *Free Breakfast.*

InterContinental Edinburgh The George

$$ | HOTEL | Built in 1775 for Edinburgh's elite, this row of five Georgian town houses in the heart of the New Town now hosts a luxury hotel. **Pros:** excellent central location; stylish and comfortable rooms; fast Wi-Fi throughout. **Cons:** regular wedding parties in reception area; service can be hit-and-miss; not all rooms have air-conditioning. $ *Rooms from: £200* ✉ *19–21 George St., New Town* ☎ *0131/225–1251* ⊕ *www.ihg.com/intercontinental/hotels/gb/en/edinburgh/edigs/hoteldetail* ⤴ *240 rooms* ⦿ *Free Breakfast.*

Waldorf Astoria Edinburgh—The Caledonian

$$$ | **HOTEL** | An imposing and ornate red-sandstone building situated at the west end of Princes Street Gardens, "The Caley" has dramatic Victorian decor, beautifully restored interiors, and more castle-view rooms than anywhere else—not to mention the best hotel dining in Edinburgh. **Pros:** impeccable service; not as pricey as some other grande dame hotels; outstanding restaurants. **Cons:** expensive parking (£25 per night); no wow factor for some; location a little away from the action. ⑤ *Rooms from: £250* ⊠ *Princes St., New Town* ☎ *0131/222–8888* ⊕ *waldorfastoria3.hilton.com* ⤴ *241 rooms* ❍❘ *Free Breakfast.*

Nightlife

BARS AND PUBS

Bramble Bar

BARS/PUBS | This easily walked-by basement bar on Queen Street—take the stairs down to a clothing-alteration shop and you'll see a small sign—is one of Edinburgh's great hidden gems. Expect superb cocktails, eclectic music (DJs spin most nights), young crowds, and lots of nooks and crannies. ⊠ *16A Queen St., New Town* ☎ *0131/226–6343* ⊕ *www.bramblebar.co.uk.*

★ Cafe Royal Circle Bar

BARS/PUBS | Famed for its atmospheric Victorian interiors—think ornate stucco, etched mirrors, tiled murals, stained glass, and leather booths—the Cafe Royal Circle Bar has been drawing a cast of Edinburgh characters since it opened in 1863. Regulars and newcomers alike pack in for the drinks (a host of real ales and malt whiskies) and tasty bar food—everything from yummy sandwiches and small plates to elaborate seafood platters. ⊠ *19 W. Register St., New Town* ☎ *0131/556–1884* ⊕ *www.caferoyaledinburgh.co.uk.*

Cask and Barrel

BARS/PUBS | A spacious, traditional pub on trendy Broughton Street, the Cask and Barrel serves hand-pulled ales from a horseshoe-shaped bar, ringed by a collection of brewery mirrors. ⊠ *115 Broughton St., New Town* ☎ *0131/556–3132* ⊕ *www.caskandbarrelbroughton.co.uk.*

Joseph Pearce's

BARS/PUBS | **FAMILY** | One of eight Swedish bars and restaurants in Edinburgh owned by the Boda group, Joseph Pearce's has a distinctly northern European feel, despite its solidly Edwardian origins. Scandi-themed cocktails are popular here, as are the meatballs, open sandwiches, and other Swedish dishes. There's a children's corner with toys to keep the little ones occupied, and a sunny outdoor space in summer. ⊠ *23 Elm Row, New Town* ☎ *0131/556–4140* ⊕ *www.bodabar.com.*

★ Juniper

BARS/PUBS | Situated right opposite Edinburgh Waverley Station, Juniper cultivates an air of glamorous fun, helped by its postcard-worthy views of the city and the castle. The wine list is good (if a little pricey), but it's the wildly imaginative cocktails that really make this place. A long-standing favorite is Strawberries and Steam, a strawberry-infused gin cocktail served in a teapot that's bubbling over with dry ice. You can soak up your drinks with nibbles from the modern Scottish "street food" menu. ⊠ *20 Princes St., New Town* ☎ *0131/652–7370* ⊕ *www.juniperedinburgh.co.uk.*

Kay's Bar

BARS/PUBS | Housed in a former Georgian coach house, this diminutive but friendly spot serves 50 single-malt whiskies, a range of guest ales, and decent bottled beers. Check out the cute little wood-paneled library room, with its tiny fireplace and shelves full of books. ⊠ *39 Jamaica St., New Town* ☎ *0131/225–1858* ⊕ *www.kaysbar.co.uk.*

Starbar

BARS/PUBS | Well worth seeking out, the tucked-away Starbar has a beer garden, table soccer, and—a rarity—a very good jukebox. It is also rumored to be haunted—get the owners to regale you with scary stories, including a specific clause in their lease that prevents them from removing a human skull from the building. ⊠ *1 Northumberland Pl., New Town* ☎ *0131/539–8070* ⊕ *www.starbar.co.uk.*

COMEDY CLUBS

The Stand

COMEDY CLUBS | Laugh until your sides split at The Stand, a legendary basement comedy club that hosts both famous names and up-and-coming acts all throughout the year, though it's particularly popular during the Fringe. There's a free improv show every Sunday lunchtime. ⊠ *5 York Pl., East End* ☎ *0131/558–7272* ⊕ *www.thestand.co.uk.*

LGBTQ BARS

CC Blooms

BARS/PUBS | Modern and colorful, CC Blooms is a club spread over two levels, playing a mix of musical styles and with regular cabaret nights. Open nightly, it's been a mainstay on the gay scene since the early '90s, and can now count several other gay-friendly bars and clubs as neighbors. ⊠ *23–24 Greenside Pl., New Town* ☎ *0131/556–9331* ⊕ *www. ccblooms.co.uk.*

Regent Bar

BARS/PUBS | Billing itself as "the best real ale gay pub in Edinburgh," this popular drinking hole is warm, homey, and welcoming—and it's dog-friendly, too. As advertised, the real ales selection is great. ⊠ *2 Montrose Terr., Abbeyhill* ☎ *0131/661–8198* ⊕ *www.theregentbar. co.uk.*

NIGHTCLUBS

The Liquid Room

DANCE CLUBS | Top indie bands and an eclectic mix of club nights (techno, hip-hop, and alternative, to name a few) have made the Liquid Room a favorite after-dark venue since 1997. ⊠ *9C Victoria St., New Town* ☎ *0131/225–2564* ⊕ *www. liquidroom.com.*

Performing Arts

Edinburgh Playhouse

THEATER | Big-ticket concerts and musicals, along with the occasional ballet and opera production, are staged at the popular Playhouse, with its enormous 3,000-seat auditorium. ⊠ *18–22 Greenside La., East End* ☎ *0844/871–3014* ⊕ *www. atgtickets.com.*

🛍 Shopping

ANTIQUES

★ Unicorn Antiques

ANTIQUES/COLLECTIBLES | This Victorian basement is crammed with fascinating antiques, including artworks, ornaments, silverware, and other such curios. ⊠ *65 Dundas St., New Town* ☎ *0131/556–7176* ⊕ *www.unicornantiques.co.uk.*

CLOTHING

Concrete Wardrobe

CLOTHING | For an eclectic mix of quirky knitwear and accessories, dive into Concrete Wardrobe. You can also find vintage furnishings and other crafty items. ⊠ *50a Broughton St., New Town* ☎ *0131/558–7130.*

Elaine's Vintage Clothing

CLOTHING | This wee boutique in trendy Stockbridge is crammed full of vintage threads for women and men. The finds span the 20th century, but most are from the '40s to the '70s. The friendly owner is happy to share her knowledge of the many elegant and quirky outfits on her rails. ⊠ *55 St. Stephen St., New Town* ☎ *0131/225–5783.*

DEPARTMENT STORES

★ Jenners

DEPARTMENT STORES | Jenners, a long-standing Edinburgh landmark that is now part of the U.K.-wide House of

Fraser chain, specializes in traditional china and glassware, as well as Scottish tweeds and tartans—though you'll find everything else you'd expect from a large department store, too. Its famous food hall, run by Valvona & Crolla, stocks traditional culinary delights including shortbread, marmalade, and honey. ⊠ *48 Princes St., New Town* ☎ *0343/909–2031* ⊕ *www.houseoffraser.co.uk.*

John Lewis

DEPARTMENT STORES | John Lewis specializes in furnishings and household goods, but also stocks designer clothes. It's part of the Edinburgh St. James shopping complex, which is currently closed for extensive redevelopment (due to finish in 2020), but John Lewis remains open as usual with access from Leith Street. ⊠ *Edinburgh St. James, Leith St., New Town* ☎ *0131/556–9121* ⊕ *www.johnlewis.com.*

JEWELRY

Hamilton & Inches

JEWELRY/ACCESSORIES | Established in 1866, this jeweler is worth visiting not only for its gold and silver pieces, but also for its late-Georgian interior. Designed by David Bryce in 1834, it's all columns and elaborate plasterwork. ⊠ *87 George St., New Town* ☎ *0131/225–4898* ⊕ *www.hamiltonandinches.com.*

Joseph Bonnar

JEWELRY/ACCESSORIES | Tucked behind George Street, Joseph Bonnar stocks Scotland's largest collection of antique jewelry, including 19th-century agate jewels. ⊠ *72 Thistle St., New Town* ☎ *0131/226–2811* ⊕ *www.josephbonnar.com.*

★ Sheila Fleet

JEWELRY/ACCESSORIES | As much art gallery as jewelry shop, designer Sheila Fleet's store in Stockbridge displays a variety of stunning jewelry inspired by her native Orkney, from wind and waves to Celtic spirals to island wildlife. ⊠ *18 St. Stephen St., Stockbridge* ☎ *0131/225–5939* ⊕ *www.sheilafleet.com.*

Haymarket

West of the Old Town and south of the West End is Haymarket, a district with its own down-to-earth character and well-worn charm. It offers varied shopping and dining options that become more upmarket as you head toward the West End and Leith.

Restaurants

This area has many restaurants that tend to be more affordable than those in the center of town.

First Coast

$$ | **INTERNATIONAL** | This laid-back bistro, just a few minutes from Haymarket Station, has a loyal following—and for good reason. Its multicultural menu has everything from Thai mango salads to Brazilian seafood stews to Korean rice cakes, as well as an unusually good selection of vegetarian options. **Known for:** great international fare; big on flavor; relaxing interior. Ⓢ *Average main: £15* ⊠ *97–101 Dalry Rd., Haymarket* ☎ *0131/313–4404* ⊕ *www.first-coast.co.uk* ⊗ *Closed Sun.*

Hotels

★ The Dunstane Houses

$$ | **HOTEL** | Set within two Victorian town houses that sit across the road from one another, with each offering a selection of beautifully appointed rooms and suites, this hotel is one of Edinburgh's most luxurious boutique options. **Pros:** beautifully decorated; excellent food and service; quiet, residential area. **Cons:** no elevator (and stairs to climb); a 20-minute walk to Princes Street; some traffic noise from outside. Ⓢ *Rooms from: £200* ⊠ *4 W. Coates, Haymarket* ☎ *0131/337–6169*

⊕ *www.thedunstane.com* ⇱ *35 rooms*
†◎| *Free Breakfast.*

The Victorian Town House

$ | **B&B/INN** | This handsome B&B,
situated in a quiet, leafy crescent but
within walking distance of Princes Street,
offers bright and spacious rooms with
a quirky mix of Edwardian and modern
furnishings. **Pros:** serene surroundings,
gracious staff; beautiful Water of Leith at
your doorstep. **Cons:** no parking nearby;
a little way from the Old Town. ⑤ *Rooms
from: £120* ⊠ *14 Eglinton Terr., Haymarket* ☏ *0131/337–7088* ⊕ *the-victori-
an-town-house.edinburgh-hotel.org* ⇱ *3
rooms* †◎| *Free Breakfast.*

West End

Handsome Georgian town houses give
this neighborhood a dignified feel. People
head here for the small boutiques and
cafés, as well as the wide range of cultural venues.

Sights

★ Dean Village

NEIGHBORHOOD | Founded as a milling
community in the 12th century, this
pretty residential area offers a pleasant
respite from the noise and crowds of
the city. Head down cobbled Bells Brae
Street and you'll be met by a charming
assortment of old mill buildings, stone
bridges, and lush greenery, all lining the
Water of Leith. Walk two minutes east
for a dramatic view of an imposing,
19th-century viaduct (Dean Bridge) or
a little farther west to visit the Scottish
National Gallery of Modern Art. ⊠ *Dean
Village, Dean Village* ⊕ *history.business.
site.*

★ Edinburgh Gin Distillery

WINERY/DISTILLERY | Whisky may be Scot-
land's most famous spirit, but gin also
has a long and storied history here and
as any visit to an Edinburgh bar will tell

you, it's currently all the rage. Edinburgh
Gin is a small distillery and visitor center
just off Princes Street, offering tours and
tastings that give a fascinating insight
into craft gin production. You'll see two
copper stills, Flora and Caledonia, which
helped kick-start the now award-winning
operation, and are still used to make
some of their experimental, small batch
gins. (Note that the main range, including
the navy-strength Cannonball Gin and the
coastal botanical-infused Seaside Gin, are
now produced at a larger facility in Leith).
Take a discovery tour (£10) or, if you'd like
a tasting too, a connoisseur tour (£25),
then head into the Heads & Tales bar to
sample some Scottish gin cocktails. ⊠ *1a
Rutland Pl., West End* ☏ *0131/656–2810*
⊕ *www.edinburghgin.com* ⊠ *£10.*

Edinburgh Zoo

ZOO | **FAMILY** | Home to star attractions
Tian Tian and Yang Guang, the Unit-
ed Kingdom's only two giant pandas,
Edinburgh's Zoo hosts more than 1,000
animals over 80 acres. Don't miss the
famous Penguin Parade, which takes
place every afternoon (as long as the
penguins are willing), or the ever-popular
Koala Territory, where you can get up
close to the zoo's four koalas—including joey Kalari, who was born in 2019.
Discounted tickets are available online.
⊠ *Royal Zoological Society of Scotland,
134 Corstorphine Rd., Corstorphine*
☏ *0131/334–9171* ⊕ *www.edinburghzoo.
org.uk* ⊠ *£19.95.*

🍴 Restaurants

Even after business hours, the city's
commercial center is a good place to find
a variety of international restaurants.

★ Bread Meats Bread

$ | **BURGER** | This family-run burger
joint has gained a nationwide reputation for its over-the-top add-ons like
bone-marrow butter, kimchi, 'Nduja
(spicy salami spread), and pomegranate
molasses. Take a seat inside the chic,

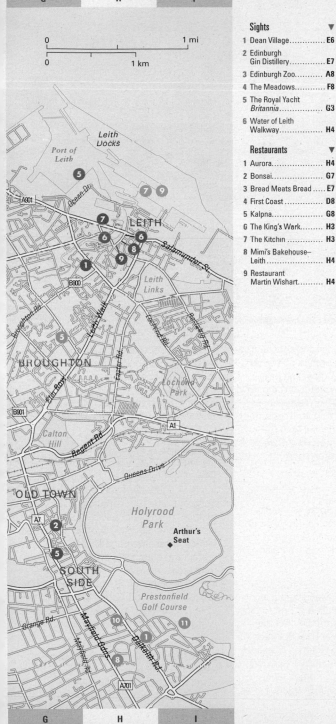

Sights ▼

1 Dean Village............... **E6**
2 Edinburgh
  Gin Distillery.............. **E7**
3 Edinburgh Zoo........... **A8**
4 The Meadows............ **F8**
5 The Royal Yacht
  Britannia................. **G3**
6 Water of Leith
  Walkway................. **H4**

Restaurants ▼

1 Aurora.................... **H4**
2 Bonsai.................... **G7**
3 Bread Meats Bread **E7**
4 First Coast **D8**
5 Kalpna.................... **G8**
6 The King's Wark......... **H3**
7 The Kitchin **H3**
8 Mimi's Bakehouse–
  Leith **H4**
9 Restaurant
  Martin Wishart.......... **H4**

Hotels ▼

1 AmarAgua **H9**
2 B+B Edinburgh.......... **E6**
3 The Bonham.............. **E6**
4 The Chester
  Residence **E7**
5 The Conifers............. **G5**
6 The Dunstane
  Houses................... **D7**
7 Fingal..................... **H3**
8 Glenalmond House **H9**
9 Malmaison................. **I3**
10 94DR..................... **H8**
11 Prestonfield House **I8**
12 Rutland Hotel............ **E7**
13 The Victorian
  Town House **D7**

The charming neighborhood of Dean Village is filled with old mill buildings and lush greenery.

reclaimed-wood interior and choose from a menu packed with amped-up burgers, as well as chicken, veggie, and halal options. **Known for:** signature Wolf of St. Vincent Street burger; no reservations so usually long waits; smart, modern interior. $ *Average main: £14* ✉ *92 Lothian Rd., West End* ☎ *0131/225–3000* ⊕ *www.breadmeatsbread.com.*

🛏 Hotels

With easy access to some of the city's trendiest shops and cafés, the West End has lodgings that take advantage of the neighborhood's handsome Georgian-style town houses.

B+B Edinburgh

$$ | **B&B/INN** | **FAMILY** | Standing out along an elegant and tranquil West End terrace, this excellent B&B is the first Scottish outpost of supertrendy B+B Belgravia of London; an imposing Victorian mansion that combines grand public spaces with affordable modern accommodation. **Pros:** fascinating building in tranquil area;

superb views; nice library and lounge bar. **Cons:** no night porter; hint of previous institutional use; basement rooms are dark. $ *Rooms from: £135* ✉ *3 Rothesay Terr., West End* ☎ *0131/225–5084* ⊕ *www.bb-edinburgh.com* ⇥ *27 rooms* ⦿ *Free Breakfast.*

The Bonham

$$$ | **HOTEL** | There's a clubby atmosphere throughout this hotel, where the typical high-ceilinged town-house rooms have gorgeous late-19th-century architectural features mixed with pastel-shade furnishings and distinctly Scottish patterned fabrics. **Pros:** smart and stylish; excellent restaurant; quiet location. **Cons:** few common areas; needs upgrading in places; no air-conditioning. $ *Rooms from: £165* ✉ *35 Drumsheugh Gardens, West End* ☎ *0131/226–6050* ⊕ *www.thebonham. com* ⇥ *49 rooms* ⦿ *Some meals.*

★ The Chester Residence

$$$ | **RENTAL** | A decadent hideaway located just off from the main drag, these elegant self-service apartments offer a lot of space and a plethora of peace in

a city where both can be hard to find. **Pros:** quiet but convenient location; well-stocked kitchens; beautiful gardens. **Cons:** lots of stairs and no elevators; no washing machines; no free on-site parking. $ *Rooms from: £225* ✉ *9 Rothesay Pl., West End* ☎ *0131/226–2075* ⊕ *www.chester-residence.com* ⇆ *23 apartments* ❄ *No meals.*

Rutland Hotel

$$ | HOTEL | Nominated for several style awards, this chic boutique hotel at the west end of Princes Street offers 12 guest rooms with flamboyant fabrics and classic furnishings, as well as eight stylish serviced apartments, a flexible option for a family or two couples traveling together. **Pros:** friendly staff; casual and unpretentious; great bar and restaurant. **Cons:** decor too loud and busy for some; no elevators to apartments; no free on-site parking. $ *Rooms from: £155* ✉ *1–3 Rutland St., West End* ☎ *0131/229–3402* ⊕ *www.therutlandhotel.com* ⇆ *20 rooms* ❄ *Free Breakfast* Ⓜ *West End-Princes St.*

Performing Arts

★ Filmhouse

FILM | Widely considered to be among the best independent cinemas in Britain, the excellent three-screen Filmhouse is the go to venue for modern, foreign-language, offbeat, and any other less-commercial films. It also holds frequent live events and mini-festivals for the discerning cinephile, and is the main hub for the International Film Festival each summer. The café and bar here are open late on weekends. ✉ *88 Lothian Rd., West End* ☎ *0131/228–2688* ⊕ *www.filmhousecinema.com.*

King's Theatre

THEATER | Built in 1906 and adorned with vibrant murals by artist John Byrne, the art nouveau King's Theatre has a great program of contemporary dramatic works. ✉ *2 Leven St., Tollcross*

☎ *0131/529–6000* ⊕ *www.capitaltheatres.com.*

The Lyceum

THEATER | Traditional plays and contemporary works, including previews or tours of London West End productions, are presented here. ✉ *30b Grindlay St., West End* ☎ *0131/248–4848* ⊕ *www.lyceum.org.uk.*

Traverse Theatre

THEATER | With its specially designed space, the Traverse Theatre has developed a solid reputation for new, stimulating plays by Scottish dramatists, as well as innovative dance performances. ✉ *10 Cambridge St., West End* ☎ *0131/228 1404* ⊕ *www.traverse.co.uk.*

Usher Hall

MUSIC | Edinburgh's grandest concert venue, Usher Hall hosts a wide range of national and international performers, from Kaiser Chiefs and Vampire Weekend to the Royal Scottish National Orchestra. ✉ *Lothian Rd., West End* ☎ *0131/228 1155* ⊕ *www.usherhall.co.uk.*

South Side

This residential district, which includes the suburbs of Morningside, Marchmont, and Newington (among others), offers a peek at the comings and goings of regular Edinburghers. Cost-conscious visitors can find lots of affordable restaurants and budget B&Bs here.

Sights

★ The Meadows

CITY PARK | FAMILY | Edinburgh's most popular green space, The Meadows is the first port of call for nearby workers, students, and families when the sun is out (or even when it isn't). You'll find people making the most of the grass here: picnicking, barbecuing, playing soccer, throwing frisbees, and flying kites. More formal sports facilities include tennis

564

courts, a small golf putting course, and the biggest kids' play area in Edinburgh. Come during one of the city's many cultural festivals and there's likely to be a show on, too. ⊠ *Melville Dr., South Side* ☎ *0131/529–5151* ⊕ *www.themeadowsofedinburgh.co.uk.*

Restaurants

Bonsai
$ | JAPANESE | The owners of Bonsai regularly visit Tokyo to research the casual dining scene, and their expertise is setting a high standard for Japanese cuisine in Edinburgh. The succulent *gyoza* (steamed dumplings) are pliant and tasty, while the wide variety of noodle, teriyaki, and sushi dishes balance sweet and sour deliciously. **Known for:** authentic sushi; great dragon gaijin-zushi (inside-out roll); friendly and informal vibe. $ *Average main: £6* ⊠ *46 W. Richmond St., South Side* ☎ *0131/668–3847* ⊕ *www.bonsaibarbistro.co.uk.*

★ Kalpna
$ | INDIAN | Amid an ordinary row of shops, the facade of this vegetarian Indian restaurant may be unremarkable, but the food is exceptional and a great value, too. You'll find south- and west-Indian specialties, including *dam aloo kashmiri* (a medium-spicy potato dish with a sauce made from honey, pistachios, and almonds) and *bangan achari* (super-spicy marinated eggplants). **Known for:** authentic veggie Indian fare; lively interior with exotic mosaics; great lunchtime buffet. $ *Average main: £10* ⊠ *2–3 St. Patrick Sq., South Side* ☎ *0131/667–9890* ⊕ *www.kalpnarestaurant.com.*

Hotels

AmarAgua
$ | B&B/INN | Four-poster beds, a tranquil location, and bountiful breakfasts set this Victorian town-house B&B apart. **Pros:** quiet setting; snug rooms; wonderful and varied breakfasts. **Cons:** far from the city

center; minimum two-night stay; early checkout (10 am) and late check-in (5 pm). $ *Rooms from: £105* ⊠ *10 Kilmaurs Terr., Newington* ☎ *0131/667–6775* ⊕ *www.amaragua.co.uk* ⊗ *Closed Jan* ⬓ *5 rooms* ⊚ *Free Breakfast.*

Glenalmond House
$ | B&B/INN | Elegantly furnished rooms, a friendly atmosphere, and a hearty breakfast are three big factors that make this town-house B&B a popular budget stay. **Pros:** knowledgeable owners; elegant furnishings; amazing sausages at breakfast. **Cons:** a 30-minute walk to the Royal Mile; some rooms small; street noise can be audible. $ *Rooms from: £100* ⊠ *25 Mayfield Gardens, South Side* ☎ *0131/668–2392* ⊕ *www.glenalmondhouse.com* ⬓ *9 rooms* ⊚ *Free Breakfast.*

94DR
$$ | B&B/INN | Like the infectiously optimistic owners, Paul and John, 94DR reaches for the stars with its stylish decor and contemporary trappings, while maintaining a comfortable, homey feel. **Pros:** warm welcome; gay-friendly vibe; smashing breakfast. **Cons:** 25-minute walk to the city center; some bathrooms small; a little pricey. $ *Rooms from: £175* ⊠ *94 Dalkeith Rd., South Side* ☎ *0131/662–9265* ⊕ *www.94dr.com* ⬓ *7 rooms* ⊚ *Free Breakfast.*

★ Prestonfield House
$$$ | HOTEL | The Highland "coos" (cows), peacocks, and grouse wandering around this hotel's 20-acre grounds transport you to a whole new world; one that's only five minutes by car from the Royal Mile. **Pros:** baroque grandeur; comfortable beds; extensive grounds. **Cons:** underwhelming showers; brooding decor can look gloomy; bit pretentious for some. $ *Rooms from: £260* ⊠ *Priestfield Rd., Prestonfield* ☎ *0131/225–7800* ⊕ *www.prestonfield.com* ⬓ *23 rooms* ⊚ *Some meals.*

The city's most popular green space, the Meadows, is especially lovely during cherry blossom season in the spring.

Nightlife

BARS AND PUBS
Cloisters

BARS/PUBS | Set within an old church parsonage, Cloisters now offers a very modern form of sanctuary: real ales, fine whisky, and good food at reasonable prices, with a total absence of music and game machines. ✉ *26 Brougham St., Tollcross* ☎ *0131/221–9997* ⊕ *www. cloistersbar.com.*

CEILIDHS AND SCOTTISH EVENINGS
★ Edinburgh Ceilidh Club

THEMED ENTERTAINMENT | One of Edinburgh's most popular ceilidhs, this traditional Scottish music and dance night is held each Tuesday at Summerhall. It's ideal for beginners, as a caller teaches the dance steps before the live band begins each song. The club also holds irregular nights at Assembly Roxy near South Bridge. ✉ *Summerhall, 1 Summerhall Pl., South Side* ☎ *0131/560–1580* ⊕ *www. edinburghceilidhclub.com* 🎟 *£7.*

Performing Arts

Church Hill Theatre

THEATER | The intimate, 335-seat Church Hill Theatre, managed by the city council, hosts high-quality productions by local amateur dramatic societies. ✉ *33 Morningside Rd., Morningside* ☎ *0131/220–4348* ⊕ *www.assemblyroomsedinburgh. co.uk.*

Leith

Just north of the city is Edinburgh's port, a place brimming with seafaring history and undergoing a supercharged revival after years of postwar neglect. It may not be as pristine as much of modern-day Edinburgh, but there are plenty of cobbled streets, dockside buildings, and bobbing boats to capture your imagination. Here along the lowest reaches of the Water of Leith (the river that flows through town), you'll find an ever-growing array of modish shops, pubs, and restaurants. Leith's major attraction is the Royal

Yacht *Britannia,* moored outside the huge Ocean Terminal shopping mall. You can reach Leith from the center by walking down Leith Walk from the east end of Princes Street (20 to 30 minutes)—or, better yet, walk along the beautiful Water of Leith Walkway (a great way to forget you're in a capital city). Alternatively, you can hop on a bus.

Sights

The Royal Yacht *Britannia*
LIGHTHOUSE | FAMILY | Moored on the waterfront at Leith is the Royal Yacht *Britannia*—launched in Scotland in 1953, retired in 1997, and now returned to her home country. A favorite of Queen Elizabeth II (she is reported to have shed a tear at its decommissioning ceremony), it is now open for the public to explore, from the royal apartments on the upper floors to the more functional engine room, bridge, galleys, and captain's cabin. The visitor center, based within the hulking, onshore Ocean Terminal shopping mall, has a variety of fascinating exhibits and photographs relating to the yacht's history. ⌂ *Ocean Dr., Leith* ☎ *0131/555–5566* ⊕ *www.royalyachtbritannia.co.uk* ✉ *£17.*

★ Water of Leith Walkway
TRAIL | The Water of Leith, Edinburgh's main river, rises in the Pentland Hills, skirts the edges of the city center, then heads out to the port at Leith, where it flows into the Firth of Forth. For a scenic stroll from the West End out to Leith, you can join this waterside walkway at the Scottish National Gallery of Modern Art, follow it through pretty Dean Village and Stockbridge, and continue past the Royal Botanic Garden, before emerging at The Shore. It takes about 90 minutes at a leisurely pace—and with all the tree-lined paths, pretty stone bridges, colorful wildflowers, and stunning birdlife (including herons, kingfishers, and buzzards) to see, we do suggest taking your time. Keep an eye out, too, for Anthony Gormley's "6 Times" artwork, a series of life-sized human sculptures dotted along the river. ⌂ *Leith* ☎ *0131/455–7367* ⊕ *www.waterofleith.org.uk.*

Restaurants

Seafood lovers are drawn to the old port of Leith to sample the freshest seafood amid the authentic seafaring setting. Some of Scotland's most renowned chefs have made Leith—and more specifically, The Shore, its upmarket waterfront—their home.

★ Aurora
$ | BRITISH | Probably the best quality-to-value dining option in Leith, Aurora offers deliciously inventive three-course lunch menus (with plenty of tasty sourdough bread) for the price of a pub main. This modern, Nordic-style bistro also serves heavenly brunches, as well as a varied dinner menu—choose anything from informal, tapas-style sharing plates to elaborate, six-course tasting menus with a wine pairing. **Known for:** high quality at a low cost; sumptuous braised pork cheeks; interior of reclaimed materials. ⑤ *Average main: £9* ⌂ *187 Great Junction St., Leith* ☎ *0131/554–5537* ⊕ *www.auroraedinburgh.co.uk* ⊗ *Closed Mon. and Tues.*

The King's Wark
$$ | BRITISH | This gastro-pub at The Shore in Leith combines a beautiful historic setting with great quality food and a wide selection of Scottish gins. At lunchtime, the dark-wood bar does a roaring trade in simple fare such as gourmet burgers, fish cakes, and haggis (traditional or vegetarian), but in the evening, the kitchen ups the ante with a chalkboard menu of locally caught seafood specialties, from hake to monkfish. **Known for:** affordable quality cuisine; atmospheric setting; Leith's best roast dinner. ⑤ *Average main: £16* ⌂ *36 The Shore, Leith* ☎ *0131/554–9260* ⊕ *www.kingswark.co.uk.*

The Kitchin

$$$$ | FRENCH | A perennially popular high-end dining option, Tom Kitchin's Michelin-starred venture packs in the crowds. Kitchin, who trained in France, runs a tight ship, and his passion for using seasonal and locally sourced produce to his own creative ends shows no sign of waning. **Known for:** nose-to-tail philosophy; lovely setting; very expensive dinners. $ *Average main: £35* ⊠ *78 Commercial Quay, Leith* ☎ *0131/555–1755* ⊕ *thekitchin.com* ⊘ *Closed Sun. and Mon.*

★ Mimi's Bakehouse—Leith

$ | BAKERY | FAMILY | Despite its large interior with acres of seating, this bakery-café still regularly has lines out the door. The reason is simple: it does the best cakes in Edinburgh, using everything from Oreos to Reese's Pieces to strawberries and cream. **Known for:** delicious and creative cakes; to-die-for breakfasts; fun and cheeky decor. $ *Average main: £10* ⊠ *63 The Shore, Leith* ☎ *0131/555–5908* ⊕ *www.mimisbakehouse.com* ⊘ *No dinner.*

★ Restaurant Martin Wishart

$$$$ | FRENCH | Leith's premier dining experience, this high-end restaurant combines imaginative cuisine, luxuriously understated decor, and a lovely waterfront location. Renowned Michelin-starred chef Martin Wishart woos diners with his inspired menu of artistically presented, French-influenced dishes. **Known for:** impeccable cuisine; beautiful location; multicourse tasting menus (with vegetarian versions of each). $ *Average main: £35* ⊠ *54 The Shore, Leith* ☎ *0131/553–3557* ⊕ *www.restaurantmartinwishart.co.uk* ⊘ *Closed Sun. and Mon.*

 ## Hotels

The Conifers

$ | B&B/INN | This small family-run guesthouse in a red-sandstone town house offers simple, traditionally decorated rooms and warm hospitality. **Pros:** nice mix of old and new; many original fittings; hearty breakfasts. **Cons:** a bit of a walk to the city center; just as far to The Shore; one bathroom not en suite. $ *Rooms from: £100* ⊠ *56 Pilrig St., Leith* ☎ *0131/554–5162* ⊕ *www.conifersguesthouse.com* ⇆ *4 rooms* ⦿ *Free Breakfast.*

Fingal

$$$ | HOTEL | For something completely different, step aboard this floating boutique hotel, permanently moored near the Royal Yacht *Britannia* in Leith, and discover 23 luxurious cabins and a chic restaurant and bar, all set above a lovingly preserved engine room. **Pros:** out-of-the-ordinary luxury; close to Leith's best bars and restaurants; quiet and peaceful. **Cons:** no room service; dinner is overpriced; a little way out of the center. $ *Rooms from: £220* ⊠ *Alexandra Dock, Leith* ☎ *0131/357–5000* ⊕ *www.fingal.co.uk* ⇆ *23 rooms.*

Malmaison

$$ | HOTEL | Once a seamen's hostel, this French-inspired boutique hotel, which is part of a pioneering U.K.-wide chain, draws a refined clientele to its superchic shorefront rooms. **Pros:** impressive building; elegant interiors; great waterfront location. **Cons:** price fluctuates wildly; bar sometimes rowdy at night; a long way from the center of town. $ *Rooms from: £135* ⊠ *1 Tower Pl., Leith* ☎ *0131/285–1478* ⊕ *malmaison.com-edinburgh.com* ⇆ *100 rooms* ⦿ *Free Breakfast.*

 ## Nightlife

BARS AND PUBS

The Lioness of Leith

BARS/PUBS | This historic pub has always been a popular Leith Walk haunt for locals, but recent acclaim for their gourmet, gargantuan Lioness Burgers has brought them wider attention. ⊠ *21–26 Duke St., Leith* ☎ *0131/629–0580* ⊕ *www.thelionessofleith.co.uk.*

Malt & Hops

BARS/PUBS | First opening its doors in 1749, Malt & Hops has a fine waterfront location and serves microbrewery cask ales—with a selection good enough to be endorsed by CAMRA (the Campaign for Real Ale). It also has a resident ghost. ⊠ *45 The Shore, Leith* ☎ *0131/555–0083.*

★ Teuchters Landing

BARS/PUBS | Tucked away down a side street near The Shore, Teuchters Landing is a perennially popular pub for its wide range of whiskies and beers, its excellent pub food (try the nachos with cheddar and haggis), and its pontoon for sunny days. It's also a great place for watching live sports. If you're feeling lucky, try the Hoop of Destiny game, for your chance to land a vintage dram for a fraction of its usual price. ⊠ *1c Dock Pl., Leith* ☎ *0131/554–7427* ⊕ *www.aroomin.co.uk.*

Shopping

SHOPPING CENTERS
Ocean Terminal

SHOPPING CENTERS/MALLS | As well as being home to the Royal Yacht *Britannia,* this on-the-water mall also has an impressive range of big-name brand stores and independent craft shops, as well as bars, restaurants, and a cinema. ⊠ *Ocean Dr., Leith* ☎ *0131/555–8888* ⊕ *www.oceanterminal.com.*

OUTDOOR SPORTS GEAR
Tiso Edinburgh Outdoor Experience

SPORTING GOODS | This sizable store stocks outdoor clothing, boots, and jackets ideal for hiking in the Highlands. It also sells tents and camping accessories for the truly hardy. There's a good little café inside, too. ⊠ *41 Commercial St., Leith* ☎ *0131/554–0804* ⊕ *www.tiso.com.*

The Lothians

The Lothians is the collective name given to the swath of countryside south of the Firth of Forth and surrounding Edinburgh. Many courtly and aristocratic families lived here, and the region still has the castles and mansions to prove it. And with the rich came deer parks, gardens in the French style, and Lothian's fame as a seed plot for Lowland gentility.

You can explore a number of historic houses and castles of West Lothian and the Forth Valley, and territory north of the River Forth, in a day or two, or you can just pick one excursion. Stretching east to the sea and south to the Lowlands from Edinburgh, Midlothian is no more than one hour from Edinburgh: Rosslyn Chapel is a highlight.

GETTING HERE AND AROUND

First Bus and Lothian Buses link most of this area. If you're planning to see more than one sight in the region by bus, it's worth planning an itinerary in advance. Dalmeny (for South Queensferry), Linlithgow, and Dunfermline all have rail stations and can be reached from Edinburgh stations.

The Queensferry Road, also known as the A90, is the main thoroughfare running through this region. After crossing the Forth Bridge, it joins the M90 heading north, with branches off to Culross (on the A985), Dunfermline (on the A823), and the Ochil Hills (on the A91).

South Queensferry

7 miles west of Edinburgh.

This pleasant little waterside community, a former ferry port, is completely dominated by the Forth Bridges, three dramatic structures of contrasting architecture (dating from the 19th, 20th, and 21st centuries) that span the Firth of Forth

The Lothians
and the Forth Valley

---

at this historic crossing point. It's near a number of historic and cultural sights.

GETTING HERE AND AROUND

The Queensferry Road, also known as the A90, is the main artery west from Edinburgh toward the Forth Bridge, Hopetoun House, the House of the Binns, and Blackness Castle.

Sights

Dalmeny House

HOUSE | The first of the stately houses clustered on the western edge of Edinburgh, Dalmeny House is the home of the Earl and Countess of Rosebery. This 1815 Tudor Gothic mansion displays among its sumptuous interiors the best of the family's famous collection of 18th-century French furniture. Highlights include the library, the Napoléon Room, the Vincennes and Sevres porcelain collections, and the drawing room, with its tapestries and intricately wrought French furniture. Admission is by guided tour in June and July only. ✉ *South Queensferry* ☎ *0131/331–1888* ⊕ *www. roseberyestates.co.uk* 💷 *£10* ⊕ *Closed Aug.–May and Thurs.–Sat. in June and July.*

Forth Bridge

BRIDGE/TUNNEL | Opened in 1890, when it was hailed as the eighth wonder of the world, this iconic red cantilevered rail bridge is a UNESCO World Heritage site. The extraordinary, 1½-mile-long crossing expands by another yard or so on a hot summer's day. The famous 19th-century bridge has since been joined by two neighbors; the 20th-century Forth Road Bridge (opened 1964) and the 21st-century Queensferry Crossing (opened 2017).

✉ *South Queensferry* ⊕ *www.theforth-bridges.org.*

Hopetoun House

HOUSE | The palatial premises of Hopetoun House are among Scotland's grandest courtly seats, and are now home to the Marquesses of Linlithgow. The enormous property was started in 1699 to the original plans of Sir William Bruce, then enlarged between 1721 and 1754 by William Adam and his sons Robert and John. The house has decorative work of the highest order and a notable painting collection, plus all the trappings to keep you entertained: a nature trail, a restaurant in the former stables, a farm shop, and a museum. The estate also specializes in clay pigeon shooting; groups of six or more can book an expert-led introductory session, with prices starting at £45 per person. ✉ *South Queensferry* ☎ *0131/331–2451* ⊕ *www. hopetoun.co.uk* 🖅 *£10.50; grounds only £4.75* ⊘ *Closed Oct.–Mar.*

★ Inchcolm Island

BOAT TOURS | Accessible by boat tour from South Queensferry, Inchcolm Island is home to a beautifully preserved 12th-century abbey, a First World War fortress, green cliffs, sandy beaches, and an abundance of wildlife, from playful gray seals to brightly colored puffins. Prepare to be dive-bombed by seagulls if you visit during nesting season. The island is run by Historic Scotland, which levies an entry fee of £6, but boat tours (run by Maid of the Forth and Forth Boat Tours) include this in the price of their tickets. ✉ *Inchcolm Island* ☎ *01383/823332* ⊕ *www.historicenvironment.scot* 🖅 *£20 (boat tour and island entry)* ⊂ *Closed Nov.–Mar.*

🍴 Restaurants

The Boat House

$$ | **MODERN BRITISH** | Scotland's natural larder is on display at this romantic restaurant on the banks of the Forth.

Seafood is the star of the show, and chef Paul Steward is the man behind the imaginative yet unfussy recipes. **Known for:** delicious seafood; freshly caught daily specials; spectacular views from the patio. ⑤ *Average main: £18* ✉ *22 High St.* ☎ *0131/331–5429* ⊕ *www.theboathouse-sq.co.uk.*

Jupiter Artland

10 miles west of Edinburgh.

For anyone drawn to interesting art and beautiful open spaces, a visit to this open-air collection of sculptures by world-renowned artists is a must.

GETTING HERE AND AROUND

To reach Jupiter Artland from Edinburgh, take the A71 southwest toward Kilmarnock. Just after Wilkieston, turn right onto the B7015. It's also easy to reach by bus: the X27 departs from Princes Street, while Bus 27 leaves from Dalry Road near Haymarket.

 Sights

★ Jupiter Artland

MUSEUM | The beautiful grounds of a Jacobean manor house have been transformed by an art-loving couple, Robert and Nicky Wilson, into an impressive sculpture park. With the aid of a map you can explore the magical landscapes and encounter works by renowned artists including Andy Goldsworthy, Anya Gallaccio, Jim Lambie, Nathan Coley, Ian Hamilton Finlay, and Anish Kapoor, among many others. A highlight is walking around Charles Jencks's *Cells of Life*, a series of shapely, grass-covered mounds. ✉ *Bonnington House Steadings, Wilkieston, Edinburgh* ☎ *01506/889900* ⊕ *www.jupiterartland.org* 🖅 *£9* ⊘ *Closed Oct.–mid May.*

Rosslyn Chapel's mention in *The Da Vinci Code* novel earned it international fame.

Culross

17 miles northwest of Edinburgh.

With its mercat cross, cobbled streets, tolbooth, and narrow *wynds* (alleys), seaside Culross is a picturesque little town. It's also a living museum of 17th-century Scottish life, with preserved historic properties open to the public. Culross once had a thriving industry and export trade in coal and salt (the coal was used in the salt-panning process), but as local coal became exhausted, the impetus of the Industrial Revolution passed Culross by, while other parts of the Forth Valley prospered. Culross became a backwater town, and the merchants' houses of the 17th and 18th centuries were never replaced by Victorian developments or modern architecture. In the 1930s the National Trust for Scotland started to buy up the decaying properties with a view to preservation. Today ordinary citizens live in many of these properties, but others are available to explore. Walking tours of the town are available for a small fee.

GETTING HERE AND AROUND

To get here by car, head north of the Forth Bridge on the A90, then westward on the A985. You can get here by bus (No. 8) from Dunfermline, which in turn is easily reached by train from Edinburgh.

Sights

★ Culross Palace

MUSEUM VILLAGE | Don't let the name fool you: this 16th-century merchant's house was never a royal residence, and lacks the ostentatious grandeur of a palace. It is, however, a fascinating slice of social history—the owner was a pioneer in local coal mining and salt production—and its interiors of Baltic pine, Dutch floor tiles, and Staffordshire pottery was pretty flashy for its time. It was also visited by King James VI in 1617. Today it retains its period charms, including a garden that grows herbs and vegetables typical of the period. ⊠ *Culross Palace* 🕿 *01383/880359* ⊕ *www.nts.org.uk* 🎫 *£10.50* ⊗ *Closed weekends Oct.–Mar.*

Roslin

7 miles south of Edinburgh.

It may be best known for its extraordinary chapel, but Roslin itself is a pleasant place to while away some time. There are some lovely walks from the village along the North River Esk.

GETTING HERE AND AROUND

By car take the A701 south from Edinburgh, turning off onto the B7006 just north of the town. Lothian Buses also shuttle passengers from Edinburgh: Bus 37 from North Bridge is the most direct way.

Sights

★ Rosslyn Chapel

RELIGIOUS SITE | This chapel has always beckoned curious visitors intrigued by the various legends surrounding its magnificent carvings, but today it pulses with tourists as never before. Much of this can be attributed to Dan Brown's best-selling 2003 mystery novel *The Da Vinci Code*, which featured the chapel heavily, claiming it has a secret sign that can lead you to the Holy Grail. Whether you're a fan of the book or not, this Episcopal chapel (services continue to be held here) remains an imperative stop on any traveler's itinerary. Originally conceived by Sir William Sinclair (circa 1404–80) and dedicated to St. Matthew in 1446, the chapel is outstanding for the quality and variety of the carving inside. Covering almost every square inch of stonework are human figures, animals, and plants. The meaning of these remains subject to many theories; some depict symbols from the medieval order of the Knights Templar and from Freemasonry. The chapel's design called for a cruciform structure, but only the choir and parts of the east transept walls were fully completed. Free talks about the building's history are held daily. ⊠ *Chapel Loan* ☎ *0131/440–2159* ⊕ *www.rosslynchapel.com* ⊠ *£9.*

Restaurants

The Original Rosslyn Inn

$ | **BRITISH** | This atmospheric inn, on the crossroads in the center of Roslin village, serves tasty, hearty pub grub, including fish-and-chips, burgers, and pies, plus good veggie options. The inn is very close to Rosslyn Chapel; walk past the car park for a few minutes and you'll see it on the other side of the main road. **Known for:** traditional Scottish pub; great steak-and-ale pie; convenient location. ⑤ *Average main: £9* ⊠ *2–4 Main St., Roslin* ☎ *0131/440–2384* ⊕ *www.theoriginalrosslyninn.co.uk.*

GLASGOW

Updated by
Mike Gonzalez

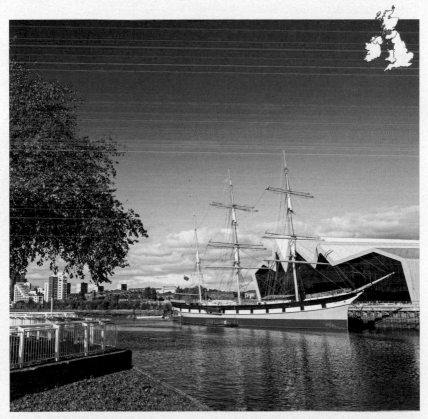

👁 **Sights**
★★★★☆

🍴 **Restaurants**
★★★★★

🛏 **Hotels**
★★★★☆

🛍 **Shopping**
★★★★★

🍸 **Nightlife**
★★★★☆

WELCOME TO GLASGOW

TOP REASONS TO GO

★ **Architecture:** The Victorians left a legacy of striking architecture, and Glasgow's buildings manifest the city's love of grand artistic statements—just remember to look up. The Arts and Crafts buildings by Charles Rennie Mackintosh are reason alone to visit.

★ **Art museums:** Some of Britain's best art galleries are in Glasgow. The Hunterian Art Gallery, the Kelvingrove Art Gallery and Museum, and the Gallery of Modern Art are worth a visit.

★ **Parks and gardens:** From Kelvingrove Park to the Glasgow Botanic Gardens, the city has more parks per square mile than any other in Europe. Stop by the Botanic Gardens for outdoor theatrical productions in summer or Glasgow Green for the annual piping festival.

★ **Food and drink:** Whether you fancy a Guinness in a traditional pub like the Scotia or a Pinot Noir in a fashionable wine bar, there's a place to quench all thirsts. Locals love their cafés and tearooms too.

1 City Centre. From Buchanan Street west to Hope Street and beyond, look up to see grand Victorian and neo-Gothic buildings expressing the confidence of an industrial capital. George Square's City Chambers are worth a visit before you trawl the shops, duck into one of the trendy eateries, or explore the bars and music venues.

2 Merchant City. In the Middle Ages, the city grew up around Glasgow Cathedral. As the city expanded along with the growing transatlantic trade, wealthy tobacco and cotton traders built palatial houses here. They were laid to rest in the glorious tombs of the Necropolis, which overlooks the city. Today the area is busy with restaurants, clubs, and high-end shops.

3 West End. In the quieter, slightly hillier western part of the city is Glasgow University and the more bohemian side of Glasgow. The West End's treasures include the Botanic Gardens, Kelvingrove Park, and the Kelvingrove Art Gallery and Museum. Along Byres Road, there are well-priced restaurants and lively bars that attract weekend revelers from across the city.

4 Finnieston. Once lined with shipyards, the River Clyde has been reborn as a relaxing destination that entrances visitors and locals. The Glasgow Science Centre and the Museum of Transport face each other across the water, while the Scottish Exhibition Centre and the SSE Hydro are major event venues. Argyle Street has been transformed into a

fashionable strip of
restaurants and bars.

5 East End. What was
once the poorest area of
Glasgow is being treated
to a major face-lift.
Glasgow Green's wonder-
ful People's Palace draws
visitors throughout the
year, and on weekends the
nearby Barras market is a
reminder of the area's
past. Its famous dance hall
has also been reborn as a
major arts center.

6 South Side. Often
overlooked, this less-
visited side of the city
includes beautiful Pollok
Park as well as Pollok
House, with its art collection and its elegant
gardens. Art-filled Mackintosh's House sits in Bellahouston Park.

**7 Side Trips from
Glasgow.** Just outside
Glasgow, you can find
Robert Owen's famous
community at New
Lanark, and in Ayrshire,
you'll find many
monuments to the life and
times of Scottish poet
Robert Burns.

Trendy stores, a booming cultural life, fascinating architecture, and stylish restaurants reinforce Glasgow's claim to being Scotland's most exciting city. After decades of decline, it finally experienced an urban renaissance uniquely its own. The city's grand architecture reflects a prosperous past built on trade and shipbuilding. Today buildings by Charles Rennie Mackintosh hold pride of place along with the Zaha Hadid–designed Riverside Museum.

Glasgow (the "dear green place," as it was known) was founded some 1,500 years ago. Legend has it that when the king of Strathclyde suspected his wife was being unfaithful, he threw a ring he had given her into the River Clyde. When he then accused her of having given the ring to another man, threatening her with execution if she couldn't prove she hadn't given the ring away, the distraught queen asked the advice of her confessor, St. Mungo. He suggested fishing for it—and the first salmon to emerge had the ring in its mouth. The moment is commemorated on the city's coat of arms.

The vast profits from American cotton and tobacco built the grand mansions of the Merchant City in the 18th century. The tobacco lords financed the building of wooden ships, and by the 19th century the River Clyde had become the center of a vibrant shipbuilding industry, fed by the city's ironworks and steelworks. The city grew again, but its internal divisions grew at the same time. The West End harbored the elegant homes of the newly rich shipyard owners. Down by the river, areas like the infamous Gorbals, with its crowded slums, or Govan, sheltered the laborers who built the ships. They came from the Highlands, expelled to make way for sheep, or from Ireland, where the potato famines drove thousands from their homes.

During the 19th century the city's population grew from 80,000 to more than a million. The new prosperity gave Glasgow its grand neoclassical buildings, such as those built by Alexander "Greek" Thomson, as well as the adventurous visionary buildings designed by Charles Rennie Mackintosh and others who produced Glasgow's Arts and Crafts movement.

The decline of shipbuilding and the closure of the factories in the later 20th century led to much speculation as to what direction the city would take. The curious thing is that, at least in part, the past gave the city its new lease on life. It was as if people looked at their city and saw Glasgow's beauty for the first time: its extraordinarily rich architectural heritage, its leafy parks, its artistic heritage, and its complex social history. Today Glasgow is a dynamic cultural center and a commercial hub, as well as a launching pad from which to explore the rest of Scotland, which, as it turns out, is not so far away. In fact, it takes only 40 minutes to reach Loch Lomond, where the other Scotland begins.

Planning

When to Go

The best times to visit Glasgow are spring and summer and into early fall. Although you may encounter crowds, the weather is more likely to be warm and dry. In summer the days can be long and pleasant—if the rain holds off—and festivals and outdoor events are abundant. Fall can be nice, although cold weather begins to set in after mid-September and the days grow shorter. From November to February it is cold, wet, and dark. Although thousands of people flock to Glasgow for New Year's celebrations, the winter months are relatively quiet in terms of crowds.

FESTIVALS
Aye Write
CULTURAL FESTIVALS | This highly successful literary festival brings together writers from Scotland and the world to discuss their work and exchange ideas. It is held in the Mitchell Library and other venues over one week in July. ✉ *Mitchell Library, North St., West End* ☎ *0141/287–2999* ⊕ *www.ayewrite.com* Ⓜ *St. George's Cross.*

★ Celtic Connections
FESTIVALS | Continually expanding, this music festival is held throughout the second half of January in venues across the city. Musicians from Scotland, Ireland, and other countries celebrate Celtic music, both traditional and contemporary. There are a series of hands-on workshops and a popular late-night club at the Royal Concert Hall. ✉ *Glasgow* ☎ *0141/353–8000* ⊕ *www.celticconnections.com.*

Glasgow Jazz Festival
CONCERTS | For five days in late June, Glasgow hosts jazz musicians from around the world in venues throughout the city, though mainly in the City Centre. ✉ *City Centre* ☎ *0141/552–3552* ⊕ *www.jazzfest.co.uk* ☞ *Tickets from Scottish Music Centre* Ⓜ *Buchanan St.*

Getting Oriented

Glasgow's layout is hard to read at a single glance. The River Clyde, around which Glasgow grew up as a trading city, runs through the center of the city—literally cutting it in two. To the north, the oldest part of Glasgow, the Merchant City, stretches from High Street (the heart of the medieval city) as far as Queen Street, bounded by George Square and Argyle Street to the north and south. Victorian Glasgow, which grew with the shipbuilding boom, extends as far as what is now the M8 motorway and the River Clyde to the south. Beyond the M8 is the West End, originally the wealthy area around Glasgow University. Its main street is Byres Road. Across Kelvingrove Park, what was once a fading and neglected area has sprung back to life; Finnieston is now the city's trendiest neighborhood, with shipbuilding giving way to riverside concerts and exhibition venues. The opposite bank of the river was the city's poorer quarter, where the workers lived, though beyond it are Pollok Park and

Pollok House, with its fine collection of art and furniture.

Planning Your Time

You could quite easily spend five comfortable days here, although in a pinch, two would do. The best strategy for seeing the city is to start at High Street on the east side of Merchant City and work your way west. On the first day explore the city's medieval heritage, taking in Glasgow Cathedral, the Museum of Religious Life, and Provand's Lordship, as well as the Necropolis with its fascinating crumbling monuments. The gentle walk west from here to the Merchant City is also a walk through time, to 17th- and 18th-century Glasgow, and George Square, around which spread the active and crowded shopping areas. For those interested in architect Charles Rennie Mackintosh, the Mackintosh Trail connects the many buildings designed by this outstanding Glasgow designer and architect. Full information on all his buildings can be found online at ⊕ *www.crmsociety.com*, where you can also purchase tickets, as well as at the individual sites. Another day could be well spent between the Kelvingrove Art Gallery (you can lunch here and listen to the daily concert on its magnificent organ) and the nearby Hunterian Museum and Gallery in the university. From here it's only minutes to lively Byres Road and its shops, pubs, and cafés or to the Finnieston strip along Argyle Street. The redevelopment of the riverside offers another route—to the Transport Museum and the Science Centre.

If you have a few extra days, head out to Robert Burns country and the extraordinary Burns Birthplace Museum in Ayrshire. It's a scenic 45-minute drive from Glasgow. Most destinations on the Clyde Coast are easily accessible from Glasgow. Direct trains from Glasgow Central station take you to Paisley, Irvine, and Lanark in less than an hour. These small towns need no more than a day to explore. To get a flavor of island life, take the hour-long train ride to Wemyss Bay and then the ferry to the Isle of Bute.

Getting Here and Around

AIR

Airlines flying from Glasgow Airport to the rest of the United Kingdom and to Europe include Aer Lingus, Air Canada, BMI Regional, British Airways, easyJet, Icelandair, Jet 2, and KLM. Several carriers fly from North America, including Air Canada, American Airlines, United, Westjet, and Icelandair (service via Reykjavík).

Ryanair and Vueling offer budget airfares between Prestwick and London and European destinations. Budget-minded easyJet has similar services from Glasgow Airport. Loganair flies to the islands.

Glasgow Airport (GLA) is about 7 miles west of the City Centre on the M8 to Greenock. The airport serves international and domestic flights, and most major European carriers have frequent and convenient connections to many cities on the continent; it closes overnight. There's a frequent shuttle service from London, as well as regular flights from Birmingham, Bristol, East Midlands, Leeds/Bradford, Manchester, Southampton, Isle of Man, and Jersey. There are also flights from Wales (Cardiff) and Ireland (Belfast, Dublin, and Londonderry). Local Scottish connections can be made to Aberdeen, Barra, Benbecula, Campbeltown, Inverness, Islay, Kirkwall, Shetland (Sumburgh), Stornoway, and Tiree.

Prestwick Airport (PIK), on the Ayrshire coast about 30 miles southwest of Glasgow, is known mainly as an airport for budget airlines like Ryanair and Vueling.

Although there's a railway station about 2 miles from Glasgow Airport (Paisley Gilmour Street), it is not very accessible. Transport to the City Centre is by bus or taxi and takes about 20 minutes. Metered taxis cost around £22. Express buses depart every 15 minutes from Glasgow Airport to Central and Queen Street stations and to the Buchanan Street bus station. The fare is £7.50 one way, £13.50 open round-trip per person.

The drive from Glasgow Airport into the City Centre via the M8 motorway (Junction 29) is normally quite easy. Most companies that provide chauffeur-driven cars and tours will also do limousine airport transfers. TBR Global Chauffeuring is a worldwide organization offering chauffeur-driven transport in Glasgow and across the United Kingdom.

There's a rapid half-hourly train service (hourly on Sunday) direct from Prestwick Airport's terminal to Glasgow Central. Strathclyde Passenger Transport and ScotRail offer a discount ticket that allows you to travel for half the standard fare; just show a valid airline ticket for a flight to or from Prestwick Airport. An hourly coach service makes the same trip but takes much longer than the train. Travelers arriving after 11 pm can take a late bus (X99); book this online with Dodds of Troon. The fare is £14.

The City Centre is reached by car from Prestwick via the fast M77 in about 40 minutes. Metered taxis are available at the airport. The fare to Glasgow is about £40.

AIRPORT CONTACTS Glasgow Airport.
✉ *Caledonia Way, Paisley* ☎ *0844/481–5555* ⊕ *www.glasgowairport.com.* **Prestwick Airport.** ✉ *A79, Prestwick* ☎ *0871/223–0700* ⊕ *www.glasgowprestwick.com.*

AIRPORT TRANSFER CONTACTS Dodds of Troon. ☎ *01292/288100* ⊕ *www.doddsoftroon.com.* **Little's Chauffeur Drive.** ☎ *0141/883–2111* ⊕ *www.littles.co.uk.* **Strathclyde Passenger Transport Travel Centre.** ✉ *Buchanan Street Bus Station, Killermont St., City Centre* ☎ *0141/332–6811* ⊕ *www.spt.co.uk* Ⓜ *Buchanan St..*

TBR Global Chauffeuring. ☎ *0141/280–4800* ⊕ *www.tbrglobal.com.*

BIKE

Increasingly bike-friendly, Glasgow has networks of off-road cycle paths. The city has a public bike-rental scheme run by nextbike; ranks of blue cycles at over 30 stations around the city are available for rent. You provide a credit card number and a £10 deposit on the smartphone app, over the phone, or on the on-bike computer, and give the cycle number. You'll be given the number for the combination lock and off you go. It's a great way to see the city, and you can return the bike at any station. Bikes cost £1 per 30 minutes up to 5 hours or £10 for 5–24 hours. The Glasgow Cycle Map available at information centers provides comprehensive route information, or see ⊕ *www.glasgow.gov.uk/cycling.* Companies like Glasgow Bike Tours also offer tours of the city on bike.

CONTACTS Glasgow Bike Tours. ☎ *7786/683445* ⊕ *www.glasgowbiketours.co.uk.* **nextbike.** ☎ *0208/166–9851* ⊕ *www.nextbike.co.uk.*

BUS

The main intercity operators are National Express, Scottish Citylink, and Megabus, which serve numerous towns and cities in Scotland, Wales, and England, including London and Edinburgh. Glasgow's bus station is on Buchanan Street, not far from Queen Street station.

When traveling from the City Centre to either the West End or the South Side, it's easy to use the city's integrated network of buses, subways, and trains. Service is reliable and connections are convenient from buses to trains and the subway. Many buses require exact fare, which is usually around £1.75.

Traveline Scotland provides information on schedules, fares, and route planning, as does the Strathclyde Passenger Transport Travel Centre, which has an information center.

CONTACTS Buchanan Street Bus Station. ✉ *Killermont St., City Centre* ☎ *0141/333–3708* ⊕ *www.spt.co.uk* Ⓜ *Buchanan St..* **Megabus.** ☎ *0141/352–4444* ⊕ *uk.megabus.com.* **National Express.** ☎ *0871/781–8181* ⊕ *www.nationalexpress.com.* **Scottish Citylink.** ☎ *0871/266–3333* ⊕ *www.citylink.co.uk.* **Traveline Scotland.** ☎ *0871/200–2233* ⊕ *www.travelinescotland.com.*

CAR

If you're driving to Glasgow from England and the south of Scotland, you'll approach the city via the M6, M74, and A74. From Edinburgh, the M8 leads to the City Centre. From the north, the A82 from Fort William and the A82/M80 from Stirling join the M8 in the City Centre.

You don't need a car in Glasgow, and you're probably better off without one. In the City Centre meters are expensive, running about £2.40 per hour during the day. In the West End they cost 80 pence per hour. Don't park illegally, as fines are upward of £30. Multistory garages are open 24 hours a day at Anderston Centre, George Street, Waterloo Place, Mitchell Street, Cambridge Street, and Concert Square. Rates run between £1 and £2 per hour. More convenient are the park-and-ride operations at some subway stations (Kelvinbridge, Bridge Street, and Shields Road).

SUBWAY

Glasgow's small subway system—it has 15 stations—is useful for reaching all the City Centre and West End attractions. Stations are signposted by a prominent letter "S." You can choose between a flat fare (£1.75) and a one-day pass (£4.20) that can be used after 9 am on weekdays and all day on weekends. A Smart Card, which you can get free online or at stations for £3, will give you reduced fares. A Roundabout ticket costs £7.20 a day and covers subway and trains. A Day Tripper ticket is well worth it for families, covering bus, subway, trains, and some ferries. It costs £12.70 for one adult and up to two children or £22.50 for two adults and up to four kids. The distance between many central stops is no more than a 10-minute walk. More information is available from Strathclyde Passenger Transport Travel Centre or its website, including transportation maps.

TAXI

Taxis are a fast and cost-effective way to get around. You'll find metered taxis (usually black and of the London sedan type) at stands all over the City Centre. Most have radio dispatch. Some have also been adapted to take wheelchairs. You can hail a cab on the street if its "for hire" sign is illuminated. A typical ride from the City Centre to the West End or the South Side costs around £7. Uber is also available in Glasgow.

CONTACTS Glasgow Taxis. ☎ *0141/429–7070* ⊕ *www.glasgowtaxis.co.uk.*

TRAIN

Glasgow has two main rail stations: Central and Queen Street. Central serves Virgin trains from London's Euston station (five hours). Trains for Ayr and to the south of Glasgow also depart from Central. East Coast trains run from London's Kings Cross (via Edinburgh) to Glasgow's Queen Street station. For details, contact National Rail. All routes heading north from Glasgow depart from Queen Street.

A regular bus service links the Queen Street and Central stations (although you can easily walk if you aren't too encumbered with bags). Queen Street is near the Buchanan Street subway station, and Central is close to St. Enoch. Taxis are available at both stations.

The Glasgow area has an extensive network of suburban railway services. Locals still call them the Blue Trains, even though most are now painted maroon and cream. For more information and a free map, contact the Strathclyde Passenger Transport Travel Centre or National Rail.

CONTACTS **National Rail.** ☎ *08457/484950* ⊕ *www.nationalrail.co.uk.* **Trainline.** ⊕ *www.thetrainline.com.*

Restaurants

Glasgow's vibrant restaurant culture is constantly renewing itself. More recently, the city has responded enthusiastically to the small-plate and sharing-platter trends, but there are still plenty of fine-dining options on the one hand, and steak houses and burger places on the other. The city continues to present the best that Scotland has to offer: grass-fed beef, free-range chicken, wild seafood, venison, duck, and goose, not to mention superb fruits and vegetables. The growing emphasis on organic food is reflected on menus that increasingly provide detailed information about the source of their ingredients. Around the city, an explosion of coffee shops offer artisanal macchiatos and mochas. And brunch is becoming an increasingly popular option.

You can eat your way around the world in Glasgow. A new generation of Italian restaurants serves updated versions of classic Italian dishes. Chinese, Indian, and Pakistani foods, longtime favorites, are now more varied and sophisticated, and Thai and Japanese restaurants have become popular. Spanish-style tapas are now quite common, and the small-plate trend has extended to every kind of restaurant. Seafood restaurants have moved well beyond the fish-and-chips wrapped in newspaper that were always a Glasgow staple, as langoustines, scallops, and monkfish appear on menus with ever more unusual accompaniments. And Glasgow has an especially good reputation for its vegan and vegetarian restaurants.

Eating in Glasgow can be casual or lavish. For inexpensive dining, consider the benefit of lunch or pretheater set menus. Beer and spirits cost much the same as they would in a bar, but wine is relatively expensive in restaurants. Increasing numbers of pubs offer food, but their kitchens usually close early. ■TIP→ **Some restaurants allow you to bring your own bottle of wine, charging just a small corkage fee. It's worth the effort.**

Hotels

Glasgow has a whole range of hotel options, from revamped grand hotels to basic budget options to stylish boutique properties. Glasgow's City Centre never sleeps, so downtown hotels may be noisier than those in the leafy and genteel West End or in fashionable Finnieston. Downtown hotels are within walking distance of all the main sights, while West End lodgings are more convenient for museums and art galleries.

Although big hotels are spread out all around the city, B&Bs are definitely a more popular, personal, and cheaper option. For country-house luxury you should look beyond the city—try Mar Hall, near Paisley. Regardless of the neighborhood, hotels are about the same in price. Some B&Bs as well as the smaller properties may also offer discounts for longer stays. Make your reservations in advance, especially when there's a big concert, sporting event, or holiday (New Year's Eve is popular). Glasgow is busiest in summer, but it can fill up when something special is going on. If you arrive in town without a place to stay, contact the Glasgow Tourist Information Centre.

It is always worthwhile to inquire about special deals or rates, especially if you book online and in advance. Another money-saving option is to rent an apartment. B&Bs are the best-priced short-term lodging option, and you're sure to get breakfast.

Most smaller hotels and all guesthouses include breakfast in the room rate. Larger hotels usually charge extra for breakfast. Also note that the most expensive hotels

15

Glasgow PLANNING

often exclude V.A.T. (Value-Added Tax, the sales tax) in the initial price quote but budget places include it.

Restaurant and hotel reviews have been shortened. For full information, visit Fodors.com. Restaurant prices are the average cost of a main course at dinner or, if dinner is not served, at lunch. Hotel prices are the lowest cost of a standard double room in high season, including 20% V.A.T.

WHAT IT COSTS in Pounds

	$	$$	$$$	$$$$
RESTAURANTS				
	under £15	£15–£19	£20–£25	over £25
HOTELS				
	under £125	£125–£200	£201–£300	over £300

Tours

City Sightseeing
TOUR—SIGHT | Daily hop-on, hop-off bus tours of Glasgow in open-topped double-decker buses are offered by City Sightseeing. The full tour lasts just under two hours, with an English-speaking guide aboard and a multilingual commentary. Tours begin at George Square. ✉ *City Centre* ☎ *0141/204–0444* ⊕ *www. citysightseeingglasgow.co.uk* ⤢ *From £16.*

Glasgow Street Art Tour
WALKING TOURS | A two-hour walking tour takes you around Glasgow to view its diverse and often surprising street murals. Tours occur on Friday, Saturday, and Sunday at 2 pm between June and October. ✉ *Entrance to the Lighthouse, Mitchell Ln.* ⊕ *www.walkingtoursin.com/ street-art-tour* ⤢ *From £10* Ⓜ *Buchanan Street.*

Rabbie's Trail Burners
TOUR—SIGHT | Choose from a range of well-regarded one-, two-, and three-day minibus tours with guides to Loch Lomond, Loch Ness, Stirling, and the Highlands. There is also a one-day Outlander tour from Glasgow. Glasgow-based tours depart from George Street beside the City Chambers, near George Square. ☎ *0131/226–3133* ⊕ *www.rabbies.com.*

Scottish Tourist Guides Association
TOUR—SIGHT | The association provides qualified and accredited Blue Badge Guides with specific areas of expertise; guides also speak a range of languages. Tours start at half a day, and driver guides are available. Book online in advance. ✉ *Glasgow* ☎ *01786/451953* ⊕ *www. stga.co.uk* ⤢ *From £150 for half-day tours.*

Visitor Information

The Glasgow Tourist Information Centre provides information about different types of tours and has an accommodations-booking service. Books, maps, and souvenirs are also available. There's a branch at Glasgow Airport, too. You can also find helpful information online at ⊕ *www.peoplemakeglasgow.com.*

CONTACT Visit Scotland icentre Glasgow. ✉ *156a/158 Buchanan Street, City Centre* ☎ *0141/566–4083* ⊕ *www.visitscotland. com/glasgow.*

 Activities

You can't go far these days in Glasgow without seeing a runner or cyclist; numerous parks provide plenty of opportunities, and the nextbike (⊕ *www.nextbike.co.uk*) public bike-rental program has been a boon to cyclists. It rains a lot in Glasgow, but don't let the weather stop you. It doesn't deter the locals who play soccer, tennis, hike, bike, run, swim, and walk in the rain.

Pretty George Square is the focal point of Glasgow.

FOOTBALL

The city has been sports mad, especially for football (soccer), for more than 100 years. The historic rivalry between its two main football clubs, Rangers and Celtic, is legendary, so the low-key club Partick Thistle is a less contentious alternative for football fans. Matches are held usually on Saturday or Sunday in winter. Admission prices start at about £20, and don't go looking for a family-day-out atmosphere. Football remains a fiercely contested game attended mainly by rowdy fans, though the stadiums at Ibrox and Celtic Park are becoming more family-friendly.

Celtic

SOCCER | This famous football club wears white-and-green stripes and plays in the east at Celtic Park, or Perkhead as it is know locally. Daily stadium tours must be booked ahead, and the Celtic Museum is also in the stadium. To get here, take a taxi from central Glasgow or a train from Central station to Dalmarnock (10-minute walk from station). Match tickets start at £90. ✉ Celtic Park, 18 Kerrydale St., East End ☎ 0871/226–1888 ⊕ www.celticfc. net ⌨ Stadium tours £15.

Partick Thistle

SOCCER | Soccer in Glasgow isn't just blue or green, nor is it dominated by international players and big money. Partick Thistle Football Club, known as the Jags, wears red and yellow, and its home field is Firhill Park. ✉ 80 Firhill Rd., West End ☎ 0141/579–1971 ⊕ www.ptfc.co.uk Ⓜ St. George's Cross.

Rangers

SOCCER | The Rangers wear blue and play at Ibrox, on the south side of the Clyde. Stadium tours are on Friday, Saturday, and Sunday; booking ahead is essential. ✉ 150 Edmiston Dr., South Side ☎ 0871/702–1972 ⊕ www.rangers.co.uk ⌨ Stadium tours £8 Ⓜ Ibrox.

City Centre

Some of the city's most important historical buildings are found in the City Centre close to George Square, many of them converted to very different purposes now. Along the streets of this neighborhood are some of the best examples of the architectural confidence and vitality that so characterized the burgeoning Glasgow of the turn of the 20th century. There are also plenty of shops, trendy eateries, and pubs.

Sights

Central Station

TRANSPORTATION SITE (AIRPORT/BUS/FERRY/ TRAIN) | It was the railways that first brought hordes of Victorian tourists to Scotland, and the great station hotels were places of luxury for those wealthier Victorian travelers; Central Station and its accompanying hotel are excellent examples of this. The Grand Central Hotel (once the Station Hotel) demonstrates how important this building was to the city. It remains a busy active train station from which to travel south to England or west to the Ayrshire coast and Prestwick Airport. The Champagne Bar in the Grand Central Hotel is a good vantage point for watching the station concourse and its comings and goings. The railway bridge across Argyll Street behind the station is known as the Highlandman's Umbrella because immigrants from the north once gathered there to look for work in the early 20th-century. ⊠ Gordon St., bounded by Gordon, Union, Argyle, Jamaica, Clyde, Oswald, and Hope Sts., City Centre.

★ City Chambers

BUILDING | Dominating the east side of George Square, this exuberant expression of Victorian confidence, built by William Young in Italian Renaissance style, was opened by Queen Victoria in 1888. Among the interior's outstanding features are the entrance hall's vaulted ceiling, sustained by granite columns topped with marble, the marble-and-alabaster staircases, and Venetian mosaics. The enormous banqueting hall has murals illustrating Glasgow's history. Free guided tours lasting about an hour depart weekdays at 10:30 and 2:30; tours are very popular, so pick up a ticket beforehand from the reception desk. The building is closed to visitors during civic functions. ⊠ 80 George Sq., City Centre ☎ 0141/287–2000 ⊕ www.glasgow.gov. uk ⊠ Free ⊙ Closed weekends Ⓜ Buchanan St.

Glasgow School of Art

BUILDING | Scotland's only public art school's main claim to fame used to be the iconic architecture of its main building, designed by architect Charles Rennie Mackintosh; sadly, the building was badly damaged by fires in 2014 and 2018. Glaswegians mourned its passing, but plans are in place to rebuild it, although officials have admitted that its restoration will be a long and complicated process. Fortunately, there are other wonderful Mackintosh buildings in and around the city. Stephen Holl's newer interpretation of the **Reid Building,** directly opposite the original, is a spectacular modern homage to it. ⊠ 164 Renfrew St., City Centre ☎ 0141/353–4526 ⊕ www.gsa.ac.uk/ tours Ⓜ Cowcaddens.

The Lighthouse

BUILDING | Charles Rennie Mackintosh designed these former offices of the Glasgow Herald newspaper, with the emblematic Mackintosh Tower, in 1893. On the third floor, the **Mackintosh Interpretation Centre** is a great place to start exploring this groundbreaking architect's work, which is illustrated in a glass wall with alcoves containing models of his buildings. From here you can climb the more than 130 steps up the tower and, once you have caught your breath, look out over Glasgow. (Alternatively, a viewing platform on the sixth floor can be reached by elevator.) Today the Lighthouse serves as Scotland's **Centre for Architecture, Design and the City,** celebrating all facets of architecture and design. The fifth-floor Doocot Café is a great place to take a break from sightseeing. ✉ *11 Mitchell La., City Centre* ☎ *0141/271–5365* ⊕ *www.thelighthouse. co.uk* ⊠ *Free* Ⓜ *St. Enoch.*

Mackintosh at the Willow

BUILDING | One of Charles Rennie Mackintosh's most admired commissions was the tearooms he designed in 1903 for Miss Cranston, whose tearooms across the city were a magnet for Glasgow's middle class. She commissioned the young Mackintosh for several projects; the Willow Tea Rooms were among the best known. The tearooms have now been restored to their 1903 state, with furniture to match Makintosh's design. You'll find other beautiful examples of his work in the building, too, including the Billiard Room, the Board Room, and the aptly named Salon de Luxe. An interactive exhibition focuses on the great artist in his time and place, together with his contemporaries, including the Glasgow Girls. ✉ *215-217 Sauchiehall St.* ☎ *141/204–1903* ⊕ *www.mackintoshatthewillow.com* Ⓜ *Buchanan Street.*

★ Tenement House

HOUSE | This ordinary first-floor apartment is anything but ordinary inside: it was occupied from 1937 to 1982 by Agnes Toward (and before that by her mother), both of whom seem never to have thrown anything away. Agnes was a dressmaker, and her legacy is this fascinating time capsule, painstakingly preserved with her everyday furniture and belongings. A small museum explores the life and times of its careful occupant. The red-sandstone building dates from 1892 and is in the Garnethill area near the Glasgow School of Art. ✉ *145 Buccleuch St., City Centre* ☎ *0141/333–0183* ⊕ *www.nts.org.uk* ⊠ *£7.50* ⊙ *Closed Nov.–Mar* Ⓜ *Cowcaddens.*

🍴 Restaurants

The City Centre has restaurants catering to the 9-to-5 crowd, meaning there are a lot of fine-dining establishments as well as good restaurants catching people as they leave work, drawing them in with pretheater menus.

Anchor Line

$$$ | **STEAKHOUSE** | Occupying the former headquarters of the Anchor Line, whose ships sailed from Scotland to America, this bar and restaurant near George Square has been impressively refurbished to create the sense of fine dining aboard a luxury ocean liner. The menu reflects the voyage, too, including Scottish seafood and lamb, and a full range of steaks and their sauces to represent America. **Known for:** high-end cocktails; luxurious fine dining; steak of all kinds. ⑤ *Average main: £20* ✉ *12 St. Vincent Pl., City Centre* ☎ *0141/248–1434* ⊕ *www. theanchorline.co.uk* Ⓜ *Buchanan St.*

The Butterfly and the Pig

$ | **BRITISH** | Down an innocuous-looking flight of stairs, this intimate restaurant is the type of place young locals love: flickering candles, mix-and-match crockery, and inventive, inexpensive food that offers new twists on the familiar. The menu reads like a comedic narrative, with descriptions like "traditional fish-and-chips, battered to death" or "Supreme Commander chicken." Although vegetarians are not well catered to, they at least can try the portobello-mushroom burgers with extra-thick potato chips. **Known for:** shabby chic atmosphere; quirky takes on familiar dishes; tea shop upstairs. ⑤ *Average main: £14* ✉ *153 Bath St., City Centre* ☎ *0141/221–7711* ⊕ *www.thebutterflyandthepig.com* Ⓜ *Buchanan St.*

★ Chaophraya

$ | **THAI** | You can experience dining at its most sumptuous and elegant for a good price in the grand surroundings of what was the Glasgow Conservatoire, where today golden Buddhas sit comfortably

Sights ▼

1 Central Station **D5**
2 City Chambers **F5**
3 Gallery of
   Modern Art **E5**
4 George Square **F4**
5 Glasgow Cathedral **I4**
6 Glasgow School
   of Art **C2**
7 The Lighthouse **E5**
8 Mackintosh at the
   Willow **C3**
9 Necropolis **J4**
10 St. Mungo Museum of
   Religious Life and Art **I4**
11 Tenement House **B2**

Restaurants ▼

1 Anchor Line **E4**
2 Babbity Bowster **G6**
3 The Butterfly and
   the Pig **C3**
4 Café Gandolfi **G6**
5 Chaophraya **E4**
6 Corinthian Club **F5**
7 Hutchesons City Grill ... **F5**
8 Kool Ba **G5**
9 Las Iguanas **E5**
10 Loon Fung **B2**
11 Macintosh
   at the Willow **C3**
12 Mussel Inn **D4**
13 Opium **D4**

City Centre and Merchant City

KEY

- ❶ Exploring Sights
- ❶ Restaurants
- ❶ Hotels

14 Rogano	E5	
15 Stereo	D4	
16 Two Fat Ladies	C3	
17 Where The Monkey Sleeps	C3	

Hotels ▼

1 Abode Glasgow	D3	
2 Apex City of Glasgow Hotel	D3	
3 Carlton George	E4	
4 citizenM Glasgow	D3	
5 Dakota Deluxe Glasgow	B3	
6 Grand Central Hotel	D5	

7 Hallmark Hotel Glasgow	B5	
8 Hotel Indigo Glasgow	C5	
9 Kimpton Blythswood Square	C4	
10 Malmaison Glasgow	B4	
11 Millennium Hotel Glasgow	F4	

12 Moxy Merchant City Hotel	H5	
13 Premier Inn Glasgow City Centre Buchanan Galleries	E3	
14 Victorian House	B2	
15 The Z Hotel Glasgow	F4	

beside busts of great composers. The delicate flavors of Thai cooking are at their finest here in the chef's wonderful signature Massaman lamb (and beef) curry, flavorsome Fisherman's Soup, and fusion dishes like scallops with black pudding. **Known for:** Massaman lamb curry; luxurious surroundings; extensive menu of Thai classics. $ *Average main: £14* ⊠ *The Town House, Nelson Mandela Pl., City Centre* ☎ *0141/332–0041* ⊕ *www.chaophraya.co.uk* Ⓜ *Buchanan St.*

Las Iguanas

$$ | **SOUTH AMERICAN** | The bright interior of this restaurant, part of a popular chain, echoes the Latin American–themed menu in its vibrant colors and decoration. The extensive menu features items like Argentine steak, Brazilian Xinxim (a type of curry stew), and classics like tapas and burritos. **Known for:** Xinxim, a stew of chicken and crayfish in a coconut sauce; colorful cocktails; equally colorful decor. $ *Average main: £15* ⊠ *15–20 W. Nile St., City Centre* ☎ *0141/248–5705* ⊕ *www.iguanas.co.uk* Ⓜ *Buchanan St.*

Loon Fung

$$ | **CANTONESE** | **FAMILY** | The friendly staff at this huge, popular Cantonese eatery guide you through the dishes here, including barbecued duck, deep-fried wontons with prawns, and more challenging dishes like pork with jellyfish or king prawn with salted egg. On most days you will see local Chinese families seated at the huge round tables enjoying the dim sum for which the restaurant is rightly famous. **Known for:** Glasgow's best dim sum; authentic Cantonese cuisine; lively family atmosphere. $ *Average main: £16* ⊠ *417–419 Sauchiehall St., City Centre* ☎ *0141/332–1240* ⊕ *www.loonfungglasgow.com/* Ⓜ *Cowcaddens.*

★ Macintosh at the Willow

$ | **BRITISH** | Miss Cranston's Willow Tea Rooms were the ultimate place to be seen in Glasgow in 1903, not only for the tasty tea but for the beautiful art nouveau decor and furniture designed by a young architect by the name of Charles Rennie Mackintosh. The original tearooms have now been fully restored here, and you can lunch on traditional Scottish cuisine or take an elegant high tea in the exquisite surroundings of the Salon de Luxe. **Known for:** traditional high tea in a stunning location; historic Mackintosh furniture; great steak pie and haggis. $ *Average main: £12* ⊠ *215–217 Sauchiehall St., City Centre* ☎ *0141/204–1903* ⊕ *www.mackintoshatthewillow.com/* ⊗ *No dinner* Ⓜ *Buchanan St.*

★ Mussel Inn

$$ | **SEAFOOD** | West-coast shellfish farmers own this sleek restaurant and feed their customers incredibly succulent oysters, scallops, and mussels. The pots of mussels, steamed to order and served with any of a number of sauces, are revelatory, and scallops, prawns, and oysters come together in a wonderful seafood pasta. **Known for:** delicious seafood pasta and chowder; famed Queenie oysters; mussels Moroccan style. $ *Average main: £18* ⊠ *157 Hope St., City Centre* ☎ *0141/572–1405* ⊕ *www.mussel-inn.com* Ⓜ *Buchanan St.*

★ Opium

$$ | **ASIAN** | This eatery has completely rethought Asian cuisine, taking Chinese, Malaysian, and Thai cooking in new directions and using sauces that are fragrant and spicy but never overpowering. Subdued lighting, neutral tones, and dark wood create a calm setting for specialties including superb dim sum and crisp wontons filled with delicious combinations of crab, shrimp, and chicken. **Known for:** creative Asian-fusion food; great cocktails; excellent dim sum. $ *Average main: £17* ⊠ *191 Hope St., City Centre* ☎ *0141/332–6668* ⊕ *www.opiumrestaurant.co.uk* Ⓜ *Buchanan St.*

★ Rogano

$$ | **MODERN EUROPEAN** | Two things have made the Rogano a Glasgow institution: its beautiful art deco decor, which

echoes the luxury Clyde-built oceanliners of the thirties, and its seafood menu, which has held its own despite the competition of the city's new generation of restaurants. The main restaurant is a formal affair, but the downstairs Café Rogano is more intimate and relaxed, serving oysters and a signature fish soup among many other options. **Known for:** gorgeous art deco bar; excellent old-school seafood options, including famed fish soup; exquisite cocktails. $ *Average main: £19* ⊠ *11 Exchange Pl., City Centre* ☎ *0141/248–4055* ⊕ *www.roganoglasgow.com* Ⓜ *Buchanan St.*

Stereo

$ | VEGETARIAN | Down a quiet lane near Glasgow Central station, this ultracool eatery dishes up a fantastic range of vegan food, from paella and gnocchi to a colorful platter with hummus, red-pepper pâté, and home-baked flatbread. The decor is homey and relaxed, and someone always seems to be nearby reading or writing. **Known for:** imaginative vegan food; hipster vibe with good art and music; perfect side dish of roasted sweet potato chips. $ *Average main: £10* ⊠ *20–28 Renfield La., City Centre* ☎ *0141/222–2254* ⊕ *www.stereocafebar.com* Ⓜ *Buchanan St.*

Two Fat Ladies

$$$ | SEAFOOD | From its start in 1989 in a tiny West End space, Two Fat Ladies raised the standards of seafood in the city well before the Finnieston revolution, and superb fish still dominates the limited menu. This City Centre branch retains a feeling of intimacy even if the decor and large window give off an airy vibe. **Known for:** some of the city's best seafood; intimate vibe; lamb shank with rosemary mash for non–fish lovers. $ *Average main: £20* ⊠ *118A Blythswood St., City Centre* ✢ *Just off Blythswood Sq.* ☎ *0141/847–0088* ⊕ *www.twofatladiesrestaurant.com* Ⓜ *Cowcaddens.*

Where the Monkey Sleeps

$ | CAFÉ | This quirky basement café, in a series of small rooms with brightly colored sofas, serves huge sandwiches with amusing names—the "Wytchfinder" has chorizo sausage and cheese, while the "Serious Operation" contains practically everything on the menu. Enjoy your choice with soup or one of the wonderful smoothies. **Known for:** brilliant sandwiches made-to-order (so expect a bit of a wait); atmosphere that invites hanging out; cheerful service. $ *Average main: £6* ⊠ *182 W. Regent St., City Centre* ☎ *0141/226–3406* ⊕ *www.monkeysleeps.com* ☉ *Closed weekends. No dinner* Ⓜ *Cowcaddens.*

Hotels

Here you'll be close to everything—the main sights, shops, theaters, restaurants, and bars—the pulse of the city. You don't have to worry about transportation in the center of town, but it can get noisy on weekend nights.

Abode Glasgow

$$ | HOTEL | Stylish and modern, this boutique hotel in an Edwardian building was once the grand home of a prime minister, hence the high ceilings and huge windows. **Pros:** stylish rooms; great location; echoes of Edwardian grandeur. **Cons:** limited public areas; some front rooms noisy; pricey parking. $ *Rooms from: £129* ⊠ *129 Bath St., City Centre* ☎ *0141/221–6789* ⊕ *www.abodeglasgow.co.uk* ⇄ *59 rooms* ⦿ *Free Breakfast* Ⓜ *Buchanan St.*

Apex City of Glasgow Hotel

$$ | HOTEL | The extraordinary floor-to-ceiling windows here set this modern chain hotel apart, providing a panoramic view over Glasgow and beyond from the upper floors (sixth and seventh). **Pros:** bright rooms; central location; awesome city views from higher floors. **Cons:** lower-floor rooms overlook other buildings; no parking facility and nearby lot

closes at night; corridors quite cramped. $ Rooms from: £127 ✉ 110 Bath St., City Centre ☎ 0141/375–3333 ⊕ www. apexhotels.co.uk ⌁ 106 rooms ⊙ Free Breakfast Ⓜ Buchanan St.

Carlton George
$ | HOTEL | A narrow revolving doorway, a step back from busy West George Street, creates the illusion of a secret passage-way leading into this lavish boutique hotel. **Pros:** near City Centre attractions and beside Queen Street station; nice resturant with stunning views; great val-ue. **Cons:** entrance very small and often crowded; area sometimes noisy at night; parking at nearby paid car park. $ Rooms from: £117 ✉ 44 W. George St., City Centre ☎ 0141/353–6373 ⊕ www.carlton. nl/george ⌁ 64 rooms ⊙ Free Breakfast Ⓜ Buchanan St.

★ citizenM Glasgow
$$ | HOTEL | There's no lobby at the futur-istic citizenM—no reception area at all, because you can only book online—but there are chic "living spaces" with ultra-modern furnishings where guests can congregate and streamlined rooms that are smartly designed. **Pros:** wonderful and creative design; central location; free Wi-Fi. **Cons:** not for the claustrophobic; breakfast costs more if you don't book ahead; the absence of reception staff can be confusing. $ Rooms from: £139 ✉ 60 Renfrew St., corner of Hope St., City Centre ☎ 01782/488–3490 ⊕ www. citizenm.com ⌁ 198 rooms ⊙ No meals Ⓜ Buchanan St.

★ Dakota Deluxe Glasgow
$$ | HOTEL | At this extremely stylish addition to Glasgow's hotel scene, the textured, neutral decor creates a restful, subdued atmosphere. **Pros:** relaxing public rooms; spacious, well-appointed bedrooms; lovely bathrooms. **Cons:** unex-citing views from hotel; not right in the middle of the action; slightly corporate feel. $ Rooms from: £145 ✉ 179 W. Regent St., City Centre ☎ 0141/404⌁3680

⊕ glasgow.dakotahotels.co.uk ⌁ 83 rooms ⊙ Free Breakfast Ⓜ Cowcaddens.

★ Grand Central Hotel
$$ | HOTEL | One of Europe's great Victorian hotels built when train travel was a luxury, this hotel located within Glasgow's historic train station deserves its name, as everything about it, from the magnificent marble-floor champagne bar to the ballroom fully restored to its original glory, is grand. **Pros:** a real air of luxury; generally spacious rooms; great champagne bar for lingering. **Cons:** occa-sional noise from street; parking a couple of blocks away; some small rooms. $ Rooms from: £125 ✉ 99 Gordon St., City Centre ☎ 0141/240–3700 ⊕ www. grandcentralhotel.com ⌁ 233 rooms ⊙ Free Breakfast Ⓜ Buchanan St.

Hallmark Hotel Glasgow
$$ | HOTEL | FAMILY | Behind a rather aus-tere exterior built on to what was once a mill, the Hallmark clearly sees itself as a family-oriented hotel, with the facilities of a large chain but decor and ambience that are unpretentious and comfortable. **Pros:** pleasant atmosphere; good spa and leisure center available to guests; close to City Centre. **Cons:** no views; some noise from nearby elevated motorway; hotel vehicle entrance not easy to find. $ Rooms from: £128 ✉ 27 Washing-ton St., City Centre ☎ 0141/222–2929 ⊕ www.hallmarkhotels.co.uk ⌁ 129 rooms ⊙ Free Breakfast Ⓜ St. Enoch.

Hotel Indigo Glasgow
$$ | HOTEL | In the center of the city, the fashionable Indigo is awash with bold colors and modern designs that empha-size comfort and calm. **Pros:** well-de-signed rooms; vivid colors, patterns, and lighting; good on-site dining. **Cons:** narrow corridors; only showers in the bathrooms; restaurant has an anonymous, corporate feel. $ Rooms from: £145 ✉ 75 Waterloo St., City Centre ☎ 0141/226–7700 ⊕ www.hinglasgow.co.uk ⌁ 94 rooms ⊙ No meals Ⓜ St. Enoch.

★ Kimpton Blythswood Square

$$ | **HOTEL** | History and luxury come together at this smart conversion of the former headquarters of the Royal Automobile Club of Scotland, which occupies a classical building on peaceful Blythswood Square. **Pros:** airy and luxurious; glorious bathrooms; great spa, restaurant, and bar. **Cons:** room lighting may be too dim for some, some street noise; the square itself is in need of some care and attention. ⑤ *Rooms from: £185* ✉ *11 Blythswood Sq., City Centre* ☎ *0141/248–8888* ⊕ *www.kimpton-blythswoodsquare.com* ⇩ *113 rooms* ⍾ *Free Breakfast* Ⓜ *Cowcaddens.*

Malmaison Glasgow

$$ | **HOTEL** | Housed in a converted church, this modern boutique hotel prides itself on personal service and outstanding amenities like plasma televisions and high-end stereo systems. **Pros:** stunning lobby; attention to detail; five-minute walk to Sauchiehall Street. **Cons:** bland views; dark hallways; no on-site parking. ⑤ *Rooms from: £129* ✉ *278 W. George St., City Centre* ☎ *0141/572–1000* ⊕ *www.malmaison.com* ⇩ *72 rooms* ⍾ *Free Breakfast* Ⓜ *Cowcaddens.*

Premier Inn Glasgow City Centre Buchanan Galleries

$ | **HOTEL** | It would be easy to miss the big City Centre branch of this popular budget hotel chain, since its entrance on Renfield Street is quite small, but it's worth seeking out for its winning location just around the corner from the pedestrian precinct in Sauchiehall Street. **Pros:** great location; bargain rates; modern rooms. **Cons:** some front rooms a bit noisy; entrance easily missed at street level; no parking facilities. ⑤ *Rooms from: £90* ✉ *Buchanan Galleries, 141 W. Nile St., City Centre* ☎ *0871/527–9360* ⊕ *www.premierinn.com* ⇩ *220 rooms* ⍾ *No meals* Ⓜ *Buchanan St.*

Victorian House

$ | **B&B/INN** | This unpretentious hotel sits on a quiet residential area above Sauchiehall Street but still close to Glasgow's Chinatown. **Pros:** appealing and quiet location; basement rooms very spacious; close to bars and restaurants. **Cons:** not all rooms are en-suite; no elevator; on-street parking sometimes difficult to find. ⑤ *Rooms from: £89* ✉ *212 Renfrew St., City Centre* ☎ *0141/332–0129* ⊕ *www.thevictorian.co.uk* ⇩ *58 rooms* ⍾ *Free Breakfast* Ⓜ *Cowcaddens.*

Nightlife

BARS AND PUBS

King Tut's Wah Wah Hut

MUSIC CLUBS | An intimate venue showcasing up-and-coming independent bands since 1990, King Tut's Wah Wah Hut claims to have been the venue that discovered the U.K. pop band Oasis. Indeed, the list of those who have played here reads like a catalog of indie music history. It's a favorite with students and hosts live music most nights, but the cozy and traditional pub setting draws people of all ages, and the refurbished bar is a pleasant and comfortable place for a drink or a meal. ✉ *227A St. Vincent St., City Centre* ☎ *0141/221–5279* ⊕ *www.kingtuts.co.uk* Ⓜ *Cowcaddens.*

La Cheetah

MUSIC CLUBS | A tiny club in the basement of Max's Bar, La Cheetah is popular precisely because it's small and intimate. It plays a variety of dance and electronic music, with some surprising well-known guests who just like the atmosphere. ✉ *73 Queen St., City Centre* ☎ *0141/221–1379* ⊕ *www.maxsbar.co.uk* Ⓜ *Buchanan St.*

★ Sloans

BARS/PUBS | One of Glasgow's oldest and most iconic pubs, the wood-paneled Sloans is always lively and welcoming; it serves traditional pub food like fish-and-chips throughout the day. The upstairs ballroom is a magnificent mirrored affair, and on the floor above there's dancing and a *ceilidh*—traditional music and dancing—every Friday night (booking essential). The pub has a good selection of beers and spirits, and the outdoor area is always lively when the weather cooperates. ✉ *108 Argyle St., City Centre* ✛ *Entrance during the day is through the Argyll Arcade, otherwise from a nearby alley off Argyle St. when the Argyll Arcade is closed.* ☎ *0141/221–8886* ⊕ *www.sloansglasgow.com* Ⓜ *St. Enoch.*

CLUBS

Argyle Street Arches

DANCE CLUBS | As the name suggests, this enormous and endlessly flexible space occupies the railway arches beneath Glasgow Central station. Most nights it's a popular music venue, but on weekends it becomes a street food market called Platform. Despite its appearance, this industrial space and its glass roof can be a surprisingly intimate place to see a show. ✉ *253 Argyle St., City Centre* ☎ *1345/6253* ⊕ *argylestarches.com* Ⓜ *St Enoch.*

Stereo

DANCE CLUBS | The small downstairs music venue gets crowded quickly when bands play Sunday to Thursday night, but that only adds to the electric atmosphere at Stereo. There's also a hopping nightclub where DJs spin on Friday and Saturday nights until the wee hours of the morning. Upstairs, the café-bar serves tasty vegan food and organic drinks. ✉ *20–28 Renfield La., City Centre* ☎ *0141/222–2254* ⊕ *www.stereocafebar.com* Ⓜ *Buchanan St.*

Sub Club

DANCE CLUBS | This atmospheric underground venue has staged cutting-edge music events since its jazz club days in the '50s. Legendary favorites like Saturday's SubCulture (House) and Sunday's Optimo (a truly eclectic mix for musical hedonists) pack in friendly and sweaty crowds on its large dance floor. ✉ *22 Jamaica St., City Centre* ☎ *0141/248–4600* ⊕ *www.subclub.co.uk* Ⓜ *St. Enoch.*

Performing Arts

Glasgow Royal Concert Hall

CONCERTS | The 2,500-seat Glasgow Royal Concert Hall is the venue for a wide range of concerts, from classical to pop. It also hosts the very popular late-night club during the annual Celtic Connections music festival. ✉ *2 Sauchiehall St., City Centre* ☎ *0141/353–8000* ⊕ *www.glasgowconcerthalls.com* Ⓜ *Buchanan St.*

King's Theatre

THEATER | Dramas, variety shows, and musicals are staged at the King's Theatre, open since 1904. Check ticket websites to see what's on. ✉ *297 Bath St., City Centre* ☎ *0141/240–1111* ⊕ *www.atgtickets.com* Ⓜ *Cowcaddens.*

Royal Scottish Conservatoire

CONCERTS | An important venue for music and drama, the Royal Scottish Conservatoire hosts regular concerts by well-known performers, as well as by its own students. The lunchtime concert series is popular. ✉ *100 Renfrew St., City Centre* ☎ *0141/332–4101* ⊕ *www.rcs.ac.uk* Ⓜ *Cowcaddens.*

Shopping

ARCADES AND SHOPPING CENTERS

Argyll Arcade

JEWELRY/ACCESSORIES | An interesting diversion off Argyle Street is the covered Argyll Arcade, the region's largest collection of jewelers under one roof. The L-shaped edifice, built in 1827, houses several locally based jewelers and a few shops specializing in antique jewelry, as well as the famed Sloans pub. ✉ *Buchanan St., City Centre* ⊕ *www.argyll-arcade.com* Ⓜ *St. Enoch.*

Buchanan Galleries

SHOPPING CENTERS/MALLS | Next to the Glasgow Royal Concert Hall, Buchanan Galleries houses the John Lewis department store and more than 80 high-quality shops. ✉ *220 Buchanan St., City Centre*

☏ 0141/333–9898 ⊕ www.buchanangal-leries.co.uk Ⓜ Buchanan St.

★ Princes Square
SHOPPING CENTERS/MALLS | The city's best shopping center is the art nouveau Princes Square, a lovely space filled with impressive shops and pleasant cafés and restaurants. A stunning glass dome was fitted over the original building, which dates back to 1841. ✉ 48 Buchanan St., City Centre ☏ 0141/221–0324 ⊕ www.princessquare.co.uk Ⓜ St. Enoch.

St. Enoch's Shopping Centre
SHOPPING CENTERS/MALLS | Eye-catching if not especially pleasing, this modern glass building resembles an over-grown greenhouse. It has dozens of stores, including the huge Hamley's toy store. ✉ 55 St. Enoch Sq., City Centre ☏ 0141/204–3900 ⊕ www.st-enoch.com Ⓜ St. Enoch.

BOOKS, PAPER, AND MUSIC
Cass Art Glasgow
CRAFTS | One of the country's largest suppliers of art and craft materials operates this store near the Glasgow Gallery of Modern Art. There's plenty to inspire your creativity, and good choices for kids as well. ✉ 63–67 Queen St., City Centre ☏ 0141/248–5899 ⊕ www.cassart.co.uk Ⓜ Buchanan St.

Monorail Music
MUSIC STORES | For the latest on the city's ever-thriving music scene, try this independent record store located within a café-bar called Mono, that is also an occasional music venue. The shop specializes in indie music and has a large collection of vinyl with everything from rock to jazz. ✉ 12 Kings Ct., City Centre ⊹ Close to the Tron Theatre ☏ 0141/552–9458 ⊕ www.monorailmusic.com Ⓜ St. Enoch.

Paperchase
BOOKS/STATIONERY | For everything that stationery has to offer—cards, notebooks, books—Paperchase is the place. And there's a café where you can ponder which notebook you want to buy. ✉ 185–221 Buchanan St., City Centre ☏ 0141/353–3491 ⊕ www.paperchase.co.uk Ⓜ Buchanan St.

Waterstones
BOOKS/STATIONERY | In an age of online sales, bookstores seem to be becoming scarcer. Waterstones remains the city's main bookshop, and it has an excellent selection throughout its four floors. There's also a good basement café. ✉ 153–57 Sauchiehall St., City Centre ☏ 0141/248–4814 ⊕ www.waterstones.com Ⓜ Buchanan St.

CLOTHING
Mr. Ben
CLOTHING | Here you'll find a large, funky selection of vintage and retro clothing for men and women. ✉ 6 King's Ct., City Centre ☏ 0141/553–1936 ⊕ mrbenretroclothing.com Ⓜ St. Enoch.

DEPARTMENT STORES
★ House of Fraser
DEPARTMENT STORES | A Glasgow institution, the House of Fraser stocks wares that reflect the city's material aspirations, including European designer clothing. There are also more locally produced articles, such as tweeds, tartans, glass, and ceramics. The magnificent interior is set off by a grand staircase rising to various floors and balconies. ✉ 21–45 Buchanan St., City Centre ☏ 0343/909–2025 ⊕ www.houseoffraser.co.uk Ⓜ St. Enoch.

John Lewis
DEPARTMENT STORES | This store is a favorite for its stylish mix of clothing, household items, electronics, and practically everything else. John Lewis claims to have "never been knowingly undersold" and prides itself on its customer service. It also has an elegant second-floor balcony café. ✉ Buchanan Galleries, 220 Buchanan St., City Centre ☏ 0141/353–6677 ⊕ www.johnlewis.com/glasgow Ⓜ Buchanan St.

SCOTTISH SPECIALTIES

Hector Russell Kiltmakers

CLOTHING | Primarily for men, this shop specializes in Highlands outfits, wool, and cashmere clothing. ✉ 110 Buchanan St., City Centre ☎ 0141/221–0217 ⊕ www. hector-russell.com Ⓜ Buchanan St.

Slanj Kilts

CLOTHING | For kilts, trews, and all things tartan, this shop offers a nice variety of traditional Scottish clothing to rent and for sale. ✉ 49 Bath St., City Centre ☎ 0333/320–1977 ⊕ www.slanjkilts.com Ⓜ Buchanan St.

SHOPPING DISTRICTS

Argyle Street

SHOPPING NEIGHBORHOODS | On the often-crowded pedestrian area of Argyle Street you'll find some of the more popular and less expensive chains like Gap, Next, and Schuh as well as Primark and H&M. There are current plans for the area to be extended and modernized starting in 2020 and lasting through 2021. ✉ City Centre Ⓜ St. Enoch.

Buchanan Street

SHOPPING NEIGHBORHOODS | This pedestrian-only street has become increasingly upmarket, with Monsoon, Topshop, Burberry, Jaeger, Pretty Green, and All Saints as well as House of Fraser and other chain stores along its length. Always crowded with shoppers, it has also become a mecca for the growing community of buskers in Glasgow's streets, playing every kind of music. ✉ City Centre Ⓜ Buchanan St.

Merchant City

Near the remnants of medieval Glasgow, around Glasgow Cathedral, is the Merchant City, with some of the city's most important 18th-century buildings. Many of them, like the great mansions along Ingram Street, were built by tobacco merchants with profits from the tobacco trade. Today those palatial homes hold restaurants and designer stores; one especially grand example houses the Gallery of Modern Art. Many of Glasgow's young and upwardly mobile have made their home here, in converted buildings ranging from warehouses to the old Sheriff's Court.

 Sights

Gallery of Modern Art (GoMA)

MUSEUM | One of Glasgow's boldest, most innovative galleries occupies the neoclassical former Royal Exchange building. The modern art, craft, and design collections include works by Scottish conceptual artists such as David Mach, and also paintings and sculptures from around the world, including Papua New Guinea, Ethiopia, and Mexico. Each floor of the gallery reflects one of the elements—air, fire, earth, and water—which creates some unexpected juxtapositions and also allows for various interactive exhibits. In the basement is a café, a tourist information center, and an extensive library. The building, designed by David Hamilton (1768–1843) and finished in 1829, was first a meeting place for merchants and traders; later it became Stirling's Library. It also incorporates the mansion built in 1780 by William Cunninghame, one of the city's wealthiest tobacco lords. ✉ Queen St., Merchant City ☎ 0141/287–3050 ⊕ www.glasgow-life.org.uk ⌲ Free Ⓜ Buchanan St.

George Square

PLAZA | The focal point of Glasgow is lined with an impressive collection of statues: Queen Victoria; Scotland's national poet, Robert Burns (1759–96); the inventor and developer of the steam engine, James Watt (1736–1819); Prime Minister William Gladstone (1809–98); and, towering above them all atop a column, Scotland's great historical novelist, Sir Walter Scott (1771–1832). That column was originally intended for George III (1738–1820), after whom the square is named, but when he was found to be insane toward the

One of the highlights of Glasgow Cathedral is its 20th-century stained glass windows.

end of his reign, a statue of him was never erected. On the square's east side stands the magnificent Italian Renaissance–style **City Chambers**; the handsome **Merchants' House** fills the corner of West George Street, crowned by a globe and a sailing ship. The fine old Post Office building, now converted into flats, occupies the northern side. There are plenty of benches in the center of the square where you can pause and contemplate. Glasgow's Queen Street Station is on the western corner. ⊠ *Merchant City* 🚇 *Free* Ⓜ *Buchanan St.*

★ Glasgow Cathedral

RELIGIOUS SITE | The most complete of Scotland's cathedrals (it would have been more complete had 19th-century vandals not pulled down its two rugged towers), this is an unusual double church, one above the other, dedicated to Glasgow's patron saint, St. Mungo. Consecrated in 1136 and completed about 300 years later, it was spared the ravages of the Reformation—which destroyed so many of Scotland's medieval churches—mainly

because Glasgow's trade guilds defended it. A late-medieval open-timber roof in the nave and lovely 20th-century stained glass are notable features.

In the lower church is the splendid crypt of St. Mungo, who was originally known as St. Kentigern (*kentigern* means "chief word"), but who was nicknamed St. Mungo (meaning "dear one") by his early followers. The site of the tomb has been revered since the 6th century, when St. Mungo founded a church here. Mungo features prominently in local legends; one such legend is about a pet bird that he nursed back to life, and another tells of a bush or tree, the branches of which he used to miraculously relight a fire. The bird, the tree, and the salmon with a ring in its mouth (from another story) are all found on the city's coat of arms, together with a bell that Mungo brought from Rome. ⊠ *Cathedral St., Merchant City* 🕾 *0141/552–6891* ⊕ *www.glasgowcathedral.org* 🚇 *Free* Ⓜ *Buchanan St.*

★ Necropolis

CEMETERY | A burial ground since the beginning of recorded history, the large Necropolis, modeled on the famous Père-Lachaise Cemetery in Paris, contains some extraordinarily elaborate Victorian tombs. A great place to take it all in is from the monument of John Knox (1514–72), the leader of Scotland's Reformation, which stands at the top of the hill at the heart of the Necropolis. Around it are grand tombs that resemble classical palaces, Egyptian tombs, or even the Chapel of the Templars in Jerusalem. You'll also find a smattering of urns and broken columns, the Roman symbol of a great life cut short. The Necropolis was designed as a place for meditation, which is why it is much more than just a graveyard. The main gates are behind the St. Mungo Museum of Religious Life and Art. The Friends of the Necropolis run regular and informative tours, but booking ahead is essential; the tours are free but donations are welcome. ✉ *2 Castle St., Merchant City* ☎ *0141/287–3961* ⊕ *glasgownecropolis. org* ✆ *Free* Ⓜ *Buchanan St.*

St. Mungo Museum of Religious Life and Art

MUSEUM | An outstanding collection of artifacts, including Celtic crosses and statuettes of Hindu gods, reflects the many religious groups that have settled throughout the centuries in Glasgow and the west of Scotland. A Zen garden creates a peaceful setting for rest and contemplation, and elsewhere stained-glass windows include a depiction of St. Mungo himself. Pause to look at the beautiful Chilkat Blanketwofven, made from cedar bark and wool by the Tlingit people of North America. ✉ *2 Castle St., Merchant City* ☎ *0141/276–1625* ⊕ *www. glasgowlife.org.uk* ✆ *Free* ☉ *Closed Mon.* Ⓜ *Buchanan St.*

🍴 Restaurants

Despite covering a relatively small area, the Merchant City has a wide variety of restaurants. The selection of cafés and eateries includes many budget-friendly options that cater to the working population.

★ Babbity Bowster

$$ | **MODERN EUROPEAN** | This warm and welcoming old merchant's house in the heart of the Merchant City offers excellent Scottish food, a barbecue menu, and a lively charming bar area. On Wednesday or Saturday traditional musicians gather for an impromptu session in the bar; the rest of the time there is just conversation. **Known for:** classy Scottish pub with rooms upstairs to stay the night; traditional Scottish food with a French twist including saddle of Highland deer; convivial bar atmosphere. Ⓢ *Average main: £18* ✉ *16–18 Blackfriars St.* ☎ *0141/552–5055* ⊕ *www.babbity-bowster.com* Ⓜ *Buchanan Street.*

Café Gandolfi

$$ | **MODERN BRITISH** | Occupying what was once the tea market, this trendy café draws a style-conscious crowd and can justly claim to have launched the dining renaissance of the Merchant City. The café opens early, serving its wonderful signature breakfasts, and the main menu is varied but resolutely Scottish; don't miss the scorched mackerel, the roast rack of Dornoch lamb, or the smoked haddie and Stornaway black pudding. **Known for:** Stornaway black pudding with mushrooms; unique, locally made furniture; intimate second-floor bar offering the same menu. Ⓢ *Average main: £15* ✉ *64 Albion St., Merchant City* ☎ *0141/552–6813* ⊕ *www.cafegandolfi. com* Ⓜ *Buchanan St.*

Corinthian Club

$$ | **MODERN BRITISH** | Inside what was once the mansion of tobacco merchant George Buchanan, the Corinthian Club includes two bars, a nightclub, and a casino in its maze of rooms. At the heart of the building, the main restaurant, the steak-and-seafood-focused Brasserie makes a dramatic first impression with its glass dome and statues. **Known for:** extravagant central restaurant; range of menus and spaces; spectacular columns under the roof. ⑤ *Average main: £17* ✉ *191 Ingram St., Merchant City* ☎ *0141/552–1101* ⊕ *www.thecorinthian-club.co.uk* Ⓜ *Buchanan St.*

Hutchesons City Grill

$$$ | BRITISH | Located in another of the Merchant City's iconic buildings, what was originally the 17th-century Hutchesons Hospital, is now an elegant restaurant specializing in steak and seafood. The steaks are sold by weight, while the main menu includes roast monkfish tail alongside an impressive array of beef. **Known for:** subdued elegance in an iconic building; one of Glasgow's best luxurious dining options; great Sunday roast with champagne. ⑤ *Average main: £20* ✉ *158 Ingram St., Merchant City* ☎ *0141/552–4050* ⊕ *www.hutchesonsglasgow.com* Ⓜ *Buchanan St.*

★ Kool Ba

$$ | ASIAN FUSION | Thick wooden tables, tapestries, and soft candlelight make you feel at home in the comfortable dining room of this atmospheric haven serving an intriguing mix of Indian and Persian fare. A family-owned restaurant, it's all about healthy, flavorful cooking; chicken tikka masala in a yogurt sauce or lamb korma with coconut cream and fruit or the Persian shashlik are good picks. **Known for:** Indian-Persian fusion cuisine; wide-ranging menu; weekend reservations a must. ⑤ *Average main: £16* ✉ *109–113 Candleriggs, Merchant City* ☎ *0141/552–2777* ⊕ *www.koolba.com* ⊙ *Closed Mon.* Ⓜ *Buchanan St.*

Hotels

Millennium Hotel Glasgow

$ | HOTEL | This huge hotel behind an original Georgian facade occupies almost a whole side of George Square and stretches above the rail station next door. **Pros:** central location; ample comfortable public areas; competitive prices. **Cons:** very long corridors; views of the square only from some (more expensive) rooms; can feel very anonymous. ⑤ *Rooms from: £90* ✉ *40 George Sq., City Centre* ☎ *0141/332–6711* ⊕ *www.millennium-hotels.co.uk* ⬩ *116 rooms* ⦿ *Free Breakfast* Ⓜ *Buchanan St.*

Moxy Merchant City Hotel

$ | HOTEL | With a youthful, defiantly anti-institutional vibe, the Moxy is perfect for those looking to capture Glasgow's lively energy. **Pros:** simple but comfortable rooms; relaxed informal environment; fun bar great for meeting new people. **Cons:** can get a little rowdy on weekends; surrounding area is a little shabby; grab-and-go food options a little sparse. ⑤ *Rooms from: £90* ✉ *210 High St.* ☎ *0141/846–0256* ⊕ *moxy-hotels.marriott.com/en/hotels/glasgow-merchant-city* ⬩ *81 rooms* ⦿ *Free Breakfast* Ⓜ *Buchanan Street.*

The Z Hotel Glasgow

$ | HOTEL | Just a few yards from George Square, this good-value modern hotel is one of the newer additions to Merchant City's accommodation options. **Pros:** central location close to Queen Street Station; good beds and bedding; great value. **Cons:** internal rooms have small (or no) windows; no restaurant; no parking facilities. ⑤ *Rooms from: £80* ✉ *36 N. Frederick St., Merchant City* ☎ *0141/212 4550* ⊕ *www.thezhotels.com* ⬩ *104 rooms* ⦿ *No meals.*

Nightlife

BARS AND PUBS

Arta

WINE BARS—NIGHTLIFE | Built on the site of Glasgow's traditional cheese market, Arta has transformed the place into what feels and looks like a Spanish hacienda. It is a labyrinth of different spaces and unexpected rooms on the ground and basement levels, where a live DJ, a salsa night, or a live band might be in action. You can also stay with the cocktails and tapas on the ground floor. ✉ *62 Albion St., Merchant City* ☎ *0141/552–2101* ⊕ *www.arta.co.uk* Ⓜ *Buchanan St.*

★ Scotia Bar

BARS/PUBS | This place is a survivor of a different, older city, but it offers a taste of an authentic Glasgow pub, with traditional folk music performances happening regularly. Dark wood, a wood-beamed ceiling, and a classic L-shaped bar set the mood. ✉ *112 Stockwell St., Merchant City* ☎ *0141/552–8681* ⊕ *www.scotia-bar-glasgow.co.uk* Ⓜ *St. Enoch.*

CLUBS

Polo Lounge

DANCE CLUBS | Oozing with Edwardian style, the Polo Lounge is Glasgow's largest gay club. Upstairs is a bar that resembles an old-fashioned gentlemen's club. On the two dance floors downstairs, the DJs spin something for everyone. ✉ *84 Wilson St., Merchant City* ☎ *0141/553–1221* ⊕ *www.pologlasgow. co.uk* Ⓜ *Buchanan St.*

🎭 Performing Arts

Old Fruitmarket

MUSIC CLUBS | A wonderful venue for almost every type of music, this was once the city's fruit and vegetable market. The first-floor balcony, with its intricate iron railings, still carries some of the original merchants' names. It's adjacent to City Halls in the heart of the Merchant City. ✉ *Candleriggs, Merchant*

City ☎ *0141/353–8000* ⊕ *www.glasgow-concerthalls.com* Ⓜ *Buchanan St.*

★ Sharmanka Kinetic Theatre

ART GALLERIES—ARTS | **FAMILY** | A unique spectacle, Sharmanka Kinetic Theatre is the brainchild of Eduard Bersudsky, who came to Glasgow from Russia in 1989 to continue making the mechanical sculptures that are his stock in trade. They are witty and sometimes disturbing, perhaps because they are constructed from scrap materials. They move in a kind of ballet to haunting, specially composed music punctuated by a light show. The shows are 45 or 70 minutes. ✉ *103 Trongate, Merchant City* ☎ *0141/552–7080* ⊕ *www. sharmanka.com* 🎟 *£8* Ⓜ *St. Enoch.*

Trongate 103

ART GALLERIES—ARTS | This vibrant contemporary arts center, housed in a converted Edwardian warehouse, is home base for diverse groups producing film, photography, paintings, and prints. It contains the Russian Cultural Centre and the Sharmanka Kinetic Theatre, as well as the Glasgow Print Studio, a well-established outlet for Glasgow artists; Street Level Photoworks, which aims at making photography more accessible; and the Transmission Gallery, a key exhibition space supporting nonconceptual art in the city. ✉ *103 Trongate, Merchant City* ☎ *0141/276–8380* Ⓜ *St. Enoch.*

🛍 Shopping

ANTIQUES AND FINE ART

★ Glasgow Print Studio

ART GALLERIES | Essentially an artists' cooperative, the Glasgow Print Studio's facilities launched a generation of outstanding painters, printers, and designers. The work of members past and present can be seen (and bought) at the Print Studio Gallery on King Street. ✉ *103 Trongate, Merchant City* ☎ *0141/552–0704* ⊕ *www.gpsart.co.uk* Ⓜ *St. Enoch.*

CLOTHING
Cruise
CLOTHING | As one of the first haute couture stores in central Glasgow, Cruise can claim to have launched a new commercial era in the city. It now has two stores in the Merchant City, where its high-fashion clothes and accessories for men and women are beautifully and characteristically displayed to those who can stretch their budgets to its levels. ✉ *180 Ingram St., Merchant City* ☎ *0141/332–5797* ⊕ *www.cruisefashion. com* Ⓜ *Buchanan St.*

JEWELRY
Orro
JEWELRY/ACCESSORIES | The beautiful and contemporary jewelry here uses modern designs and new materials in unexpected ways. The shop has a gallery feel, and you can browse uninterrupted. ✉ *12 Wilson St., Merchant City* ☎ *0141/552–7888* ⊕ *www.orro.co.uk* Ⓜ *Buchanan St.*

West End

Glasgow University dominates the West End, creating a vibrant neighborhood. Founded in 1451, the university is the third oldest in Scotland, after St. Andrews and Aberdeen. The industrialists and merchants who built their grand homes on Great Western Road and adjacent streets endowed museums and art galleries and commissioned artists to decorate and design their homes, as a stroll will quickly reveal. In summer the Glasgow Botanic Gardens, with the iconic glasshouse that is the Kibble Palace, becomes a stage for new and unusual versions of Shakespeare's plays. A fun way to save money is to picnic in the park; you can buy sandwiches, salads, and other portable items at shops on Byres Road. Alternatively, stroll past the university and down Gibson Street and Woodlands Road with their cafés and pubs.

⊙ Sights

★ Botanic Gardens
GARDEN | **FAMILY** | It is a minor Glasgow miracle how as soon as the sun appears, the Botanics (as they're known to locals) fill with people. Beautiful flower displays and extensive lawns create the feeling that this is a large back garden for the inhabitants of the West End's mainly apartment homes. At the heart of the gardens is the spectacular circular greenhouse, the **Kibble Palace,** a favorite haunt of Glaswegian families. Originally built in 1873, it was the conservatory of a Victorian eccentric. Kibble Palace and the other greenhouses contain tree ferns, palm trees, and the Tropicarium, where you can experience the lushness of a rain forest or see its world-famous collection of orchids. There is a tearoom, and in June and July the gardens host presentations of Shakespeare's plays (⊕ *www. bardinthebotanics.co.uk*). ✉ *730 Great Western Rd., West End* ☎ *0141/276–1614* ⊕ *www.glasgowbotanicgardens.com* 🎟 *Free* ⊗ *Closed dusk–7 am* Ⓜ *Hillhead.*

Glasgow University
COLLEGE | Gorgeous grounds and great views of the city are among the many reasons to visit this university. The Gilbert Scott Building, the university's main edifice, is a lovely example of the Gothic Revival style. **Glasgow University Visitor Centre,** near the main gate on University Avenue, has exhibits on the university and a small coffee bar; one-hour guided walking tours of the campus (Thursday–Sunday at 2) start here. A self-guided tour starts at the visitor center and takes in the east and west quadrangles, the cloisters, Professor's Square, Pearce Lodge, and the not-to-be-missed University Chapel. The university's Hunterian Museum and Art Gallery are also well worth a visit. ✉ *University Ave., West End* ☎ *0141/330–2000* ⊕ *www.glasgow. ac.uk* 🎟 *Free* Ⓜ *Hillhead.*

Hunterian Museum

MUSEUM | Set within Glasgow University, this museum, dating from 1807, showcases part of the collections of William Hunter, an 18th-century Glasgow doctor who assembled a staggering quantity of valuable material. Check out Hunter's hoards of coins, manuscripts, scientific instruments, and archaeological artifacts in this striking Gothic building. A permanent exhibit chronicles the building of the Antonine Wall, the Romans' northernmost defense. ✉ University Ave., West End ☎ 0141/330–4221 ⊕ www.gla.ac.uk/hunterian ➹ Free ⊘ Closed Mon. Ⓜ Hillhead.

★ Kelvingrove Art Gallery and Museum

MUSEUM | FAMILY | Worthy of its world-class reputation, the Kelvingrove Art Gallery and Museum attracts local families as well as international visitors. This combination of cathedral and castle was designed in the Renaissance style and built between 1891 and 1901. The stunning red-sandstone edifice is an appropriate home for works by Botticelli, Rembrandt, Monet, and others, not to mention the collection of arms and armor. The Glasgow Room houses extraordinary works by local artists. Whether the subject is Scottish culture, design, or storytelling, every room entices you to look deeper; labels are thought-provoking and sometimes witty. You could spend a weekend here, but in a pinch three hours would do one level justice—there are three. Leave time to visit the gift shop and the attractive basement restaurant. Daily free recitals on the magnificent organ (usually at 1) are well worth the trip. ✉ Argyle St., West End ☎ 0141/276–9599 ⊕ www.glasgowlife.org.uk ➹ Free (some special exhibitions require admission) Ⓜ Kelvinhall.

Kelvingrove Park

NATIONAL/STATE PARK | FAMILY | Both a peaceful retreat and a well-used playground, the park was purchased by the city in 1852. The River Kelvin flows through its green spaces. The park's numerous statues of prominent Glaswegians include one of Lord Kelvin (1824–1907), the Scottish mathematician and physicist remembered for his pioneering work in electricity. The shady park has a massive fountain commemorating a lord provost of Glasgow from the 1870s, a duck pond, two children's playgrounds, and a skateboard park. The An Clachan café beside the children's play area is an excellent daytime eatery and a boon to parents looking for a refuge. Public bowling and croquet greens are free, as are the tennis courts. The Bandstand, a 2,300-seat open-air theater, hosts major concerts in summer. ✉ Bounded by Sauchiehall St., Woodlands Rd., and Kelvin Way, West End ⊕ www.glasgowlife.org.uk ➹ Free Ⓜ Kelvinhall.

🍴 Restaurants

Balbir's

$$ | INDIAN | Don't let the tinted windows discourage you: this place is a temple for pure, healthy Indian food that's impressive in taste and presentation. Try the chicken tikka chasni (with mango chutney, lemon juice, and mint), lamb korma, or the traditional celebration dish of Goanese fish curry. **Known for:** healthy but delicious Indian food; multiple spice (and heat) combinations; everything on a grand scale. 💲 Average main: £17 ✉ 7 Church St., West End ☎ 0141/339–7711 ⊕ www.balbirs.co.uk ⊘ No lunch Ⓜ Kelvinhall.

Bay Tree

$ | MIDDLE EASTERN | This popular small café in the university area is unpretentious and quite cheap. It serves wonderful Middle Eastern food—mostly vegetarian dishes, but there are a few lamb and chicken creations as well. **Known for:** wide variety of meze; Turkish and Lebanese dishes; BYOB-policy (and a great wine store nearby). 💲 Average main: £11 ✉ 403 Great Western Rd., West End

The outstanding Kelvingrove Art Gallery and Museum presents engaging displays focusing on Scottish art, design, and culture.

☎ 0141/334–5898 ⊕ www.thebaytreew-estend.co.uk Ⓜ Kelvinbridge.

Bread Meats Bread

$ | BURGER | One of a new breed of burger joints that has emerged in the city, this casual spot with long wooden tables, stools, and benches is also a meeting place for coffee or a drink. The many creatively stuffed burgers and sauces are accompanied by different poutines and cheese toasties, a variation on the British classic known as rarebit. **Known for:** creative and delicious burgers; best poutines outside of Canada; cheerful sociable vibe. Ⓢ Average main: £10 ✉ 701 Great Western Rd., West End ☎ 0141/648⊠0399 ⊕ www.breadmeats-bread.com Ⓜ Hillhead.

Cafe Andaluz

$$ | TAPAS | With Iberian flair, this lively basement eatery is beautifully decorated using Spanish tiles throughout. The first tapas place to make an impact in Glasgow, it has been followed by others (and has opened a second location in the City Centre) but remains one of the most successful. **Known for:** nice Spanish wine selection; lively but intimate atmosphere; delicious paella. Ⓢ Average main: £15 ✉ 2 Cresswell La., West End ☎ 0141/339–1111 ⊕ www.cafeandaluz.com Ⓜ Hillhead.

Cafe Zique

$$ | BRITISH | This small but inviting café has a vibrant, bustling atmosphere while remaining unhurried. Its changing breakfast, lunch, and dinner menus of British fare are always fresh and exciting. **Known for:** wonderful breakfasts; tasty sobrasada (a chorizo spread); vibrant atmosphere. Ⓢ Average main: £15 ✉ 66 Hyndland St., West End ☎ 0141/339–7180 ⊕ www.cafezique.com Ⓜ Hillhead.

Hanoi Bike Shop

$$ | VIETNAMESE | Glasgow's first Vietnamese canteen offers a different style of dining, which is apparent from the moment you walk through the door and see the rustic setting, low tables, and stools. This is classic street food (all cooked on the premises and arriving when it is ready) and choices include blood sausage with razor clam salad, hot-and-sour fish soup,

and plenty of pho, the fragrant Vietnamese soup with noodles and sliced meat. **Known for:** excellent pho; street food in small plates; organic tofu options. ⓢ *Average main: £15 ⊠ 8 Ruthven La., West End ⊕ Down the alley opposite Hillhead subway station ☎ 0141/334–7165 ⊕ hanoibikeshop.co.uk Ⓜ Hillhead.*

The Left Bank

$$ | ECLECTIC | Close to Glasgow University, this popular bar and restaurant attracts a more mature student crowd. It's an airy spot with high ceilings, leather sofas, and wood floors, and the specialty is good, eclectic international food at reasonable prices. **Known for:** delicious small plates of varied cuisine; casual atmosphere; tasty brunch. ⓢ *Average main: £15 ⊠ 33–35 Gibson St., West End ☎ 0141/339–5969 ⊕ www.theleftbank. co.uk Ⓜ Kelvinbridge.*

Little Italy

$ | ITALIAN | FAMILY | Offering all things Italian, this constantly busy, noisy, and extremely friendly café sits in the heart of the West End. Its pizzas, made on the premises while you wait with a coffee or a glass of Italian wine, are probably the best around, and the house-made pastas are just as consistently good. **Known for:** perhaps Glasgow's best pizza; wide variety of Italian wines; perfect tiramisu for dessert. ⓢ *Average main: £14 ⊠ 205 Byres Rd., West End ☎ 0141/339–6287 ⊕ littleitalyglasgow.com Ⓜ Hillhead.*

Number Sixteen

$$ | BRITISH | This tiny, intimate restaurant serves only the freshest ingredients, superbly prepared, on a constantly changing menu. Halibut is served with choucroute and a passion-fruit dressing—a typically unpredictable meeting of flavors. **Known for:** excellent set menus; surprising flavor combinations; cozy interior, so reservations are a good idea. ⓢ *Average main: £18 ⊠ 16 Byres Rd., West End ☎ 0141/339–2544 ⊕ www. number16.co.uk Ⓜ Kelvin Hall.*

★ Stravaigin

$$$ | ECLECTIC | For many years Stravaigin has maintained the highest quality of cooking, creating adventurous dishes that often combine Asian and local flavors and unusual marriages of ingredients. You can try the *piri piri* quail (the seasoning is used in Africa) or the restaurant's famous haggis and neeps (turnips), symbolizing its commitment to local produce. **Known for:** buzzy bar with a quieter restaurant downstairs; classic haggis and neeps; daily-changing curry option. ⓢ *Average main: £20 ⊠ 28 Gibson St., West End ☎ 0141/334–2665 ⊕ www.stravaigin. co.uk Ⓜ Kelvinbridge.*

Ubiquitous Chip

$$$ | MODERN BRITISH | Occupying a converted stable behind the Hillhead subway station on busy Ashton Lane, this restaurant is a Glasgow institution, with an untarnished reputation for creative Scottish cooking. Its street-level restaurant is a beautiful courtyard protected by a glass roof, and the more informal brasserie upstairs also serves less expensive dishes like haggis with neeps and tatties or a plate of mussels. **Known for:** creative Scottish cuisine like venison haggis; popular upstairs bar great for socializing; lovely courtyard. ⓢ *Average main: £24 ⊠ 12 Ashton La., West End ☎ 0141/334–5007 ⊕ www.ubiquitous-chip.co.uk Ⓜ Hillhead.*

 # Hotels

Amadeus Guest House

$ | B&B/INN | This attractive Victorian town house has comfortably furnished rooms that are flooded with plenty of natural light. **Pros:** near West End attractions; two-minute walk from subway; kids under six free. **Cons:** some rooms small; finding parking sometimes difficult; a bit pricey for the location. ⓢ *Rooms from: £108 ⊠ 411 N. Woodside Rd., West End ☎ 0141/339–8257 ⊕ www.amadeus-guesthouse.co.uk ⇄ 9 rooms ⊙| Free Breakfast Ⓜ Kelvinbridge.*

Ambassador Hotel

$ | **HOTEL** | **FAMILY** | Opposite the West End's peaceful Glasgow Botanic Gardens, this hotel is within minutes of busy Byres Road yet well away from its noisy weekend activity. **Pros:** views of Botanic Gardens; great for families with kids; five-minute walk to public transportation and West End amenities. **Cons:** no elevator; on-street parking difficult after 6 pm; on the corner of a fairly busy road. ⑤ *Rooms from: £82* ✉ *7 Kelvin Dr., West End* ☎ *0141/946–1018* ⊕ *www.ambassador-hotel.net* ⌁ *26 rooms* ⦿ *Free Breakfast* Ⓜ *Hillhead.*

Clifton Hotel

$ | **HOTEL** | Occupying two of the grand houses along a collection of town houses above Great Western Road, this popular hotel offers wallet-friendly rates and simply furnished rooms done up in cheerful shades. **Pros:** conveniently located, free Wi-Fi; good budget option. **Cons:** basic amenities; no elevator; some rooms have a shared bathroom. ⑤ *Rooms from: £59* ✉ *26–27 Buckingham Terr., West End* ☎ *0141/334–8080* ⊕ *www.clifton-hotelglasgow.co.uk* ⌁ *26 rooms* ⦿ *Free Breakfast* Ⓜ *Hillhead.*

Heritage Hotel

$ | **HOTEL** | This small, unpretentious, but well-established hotel in a very central West End location has cozy, simply decorated rooms. **Pros:** very good location; lovely breakfast; on a quiet street. **Cons:** rooms quite small; no parking spaces and on-street parking is expensive; main road can get noisy. ⑤ *Rooms from: £80* ✉ *4/5 Albert Terr., West End* ⊹ *Entrance by Hillhead St.* ☎ *0141/339–6955* ⊕ *www. theheritagehotel.net* ⌁ *27 rooms* ⦿ *Free Breakfast* Ⓜ *Hillhead.*

★ Hotel du Vin Glasgow

$$ | **HOTEL** | Consisting of a group of Victorian houses on a tree-lined street, well away from the bustle of Byres Road, this hotel is all about elegance, from the sophisticated drawing room to the individually decorated guest rooms with flowing draperies, Egyptian linens, and mahogany furnishings like four-poster beds. **Pros:** stunning Scottish-style rooms; understated luxury; complimentary whisky on arrival. **Cons:** no elevator; on-street parking can be difficult after 6 pm; a little too much tartan in the decor. ⑤ *Rooms from: £146* ✉ *1 Devonshire Gardens, West End* ☎ *0330/016–0390* ⊕ *www.hotelduvin.com* ⌁ *49 rooms* ⦿ *Free Breakfast* Ⓜ *Hillhead.*

 Nightlife

BARS AND PUBS

Dram!

BARS/PUBS | With mismatched furnishings and the odd stag's head on the wall, the four large rooms here are decorated in a style that can only be described as "ultra eclectic." It's no place for a quiet, intimate evening, but Dram feels like a traditional bar while being brashly youthful and up-to-the-minute. There's a wide range of beers, and the place takes special pride in the 75 whiskies. On Thursday and Sunday, musicians gather in an informal jam session. Food is served every night until 9. ✉ *232–246 Woodlands Rd., West End* ☎ *0141/332–1622* ⊕ *www. dramglasgow.co.uk* Ⓜ *Kelvinbridge.*

Òran Mór

BARS/PUBS | At the top of Byres Road, Òran Mór has established itself as the heart of West End nightlife. Located in what was once a church, it still has beautiful stained-glass windows and a lovely nave gloriously decorated by outstanding Glasgow artist Alasdair Gray. The bar fills with different types of people at different times of day, but its late license means crowds surge Friday and Saturday nights. In the basement, the hugely successful lunchtime theater series "A Play, a Pie, and a Pint" plays to capacity crowds. It also houses a busy bistro, a brasserie, and an evening music venue, as well as a late-night club. The small beer garden fills up quickly in good weather. ✉ *731 Great Western Rd., West*

End ☎ 0141/357–6200 ⊕ www.oran-mor.
co.uk Ⓜ Hillhead.

Performing Arts

★ **A Play, a Pie, and a Pint**

THEATER | In a former church, Glasgow's
hugely successful lunchtime theater
series called "A Play, a Pie, and a Pint"
(and you do get all three) showcases new
writing from Scotland and elsewhere.
■ **TIP➔ Performances sell out quickly,
particularly late in the week, so book well
in advance on the website.** Doors open at
12:15 pm and shows begin at 1 pm Monday through Saturday. ⊠ Òran Mór, 731
Great Western Rd., Byres Rd. and Great
Western Rd., West End ☎ 0141/357–
6200 ⊕ www.playpiepint.com Ⓜ Hillhead.

🛍 Shopping

BOOKS, PAPER, AND MUSIC

Caledonia Books

BOOKS/STATIONERY | This well-organized
and well-stocked secondhand bookstore
fills the gap left by the departure of other
bookstores. The owners are knowledgeable and willing to search for even the
most obscure volumes. ⊠ 483 Great
Western Rd., West End ☎ 0141/334–
9663 ⊕ www.caledoniabooks.co.uk
Ⓜ Kelvinbridge.

Fopp

MUSIC STORES | This funky shop is an
extravaganza of music, books, and DVDs.
It's a small space, but the selection is
huge. The prices are a lot more reasonable than those at most other chain
stores. ⊠ 358 Byres Rd., West End
☎ 0141/222–2128 ⊕ www.fopp.com
Ⓜ Hillhead.

CLOTHING

Glasgow Vintage Co.

CLOTHING | You can find plenty of genuine
bargains here for upmarket vintage
clothes at down-market prices. There
are choices for men, women, and
children from the 1950s to the 1980s.

⊠ 453 Great Western Rd., West End
☎ 0141/338–6633 ⊕ www.glasgowvin-
tage.co.uk.

Strawberry Fields

CLOTHING | Designer clothing for children
is the specialty of Strawberry Fields.
⊠ 517 Great Western Rd., West End
☎ 0141/339–1121 Ⓜ Kelvinbridge.

FOOD

Demijohn

FOOD/CANDY | Specializing in infused
wines, spirits, oils, and vinegars, Demijohn calls itself a "liquid deli." ⊠ 382 Byres
Rd., West End ☎ 0141/337–3600 ⊕ www.
demijohn.co.uk Ⓜ Hillhead.

Iain Mellis Cheesemonger

FOOD/CANDY | This shop has a superb,
seemingly endless selection of fine Scottish cheeses, in addition to others from
England and across Europe, as well as
bread and olives. ⊠ 492 Great Western
Rd., West End ☎ 0141/339–8998 ⊕ www.
mellischeese.net Ⓜ Kelvinbridge.

HOME FURNISHINGS
AND TEXTILES

Nancy Smillie

HOUSEHOLD ITEMS/FURNITURE | Local to
the floorboards, Nancy Smillie is a
one-of-a-kind boutique that sells unique
glassware, jewelry, and furnishings. It
also runs a jewelry boutique at 425 Great
Western Road. ⊠ 53 Cresswell St., West
End ☎ 0141/334–0055 ⊕ www.nancys-
millieshop.com Ⓜ Hillhead.

Time and Tide

HOUSEHOLD ITEMS/FURNITURE | Loosely
described as a household goods store,
Time and Tide sells an eclectic mix of
lamps and candleholders and cushions
and things you never realized you needed
until you see them. ⊠ 398 Byres Rd.,
West End ☎ 0141/357–4548 ⊕ www.
timeandtidestores.co.uk Ⓜ Hillhead.

Finnieston

The River Clyde has long been the city's main artery, bearing Clyde-built ships, from warships to ocean liners, to the sea. Few of the yards remain open, and the Finnieston Crane, which once moved locomotives onto ships, is no longer active. But the area around it, bounded by the river on one side and Sauchiehall Street on the other, has undergone a great transformation since the 1990s. The riverside has been reborn, with Zaha Hadid's Transport Museum and the Tall Ship, as well as the Scottish Event Campus (SEC) occupying pride of place on the Finnieston bank and the Science Museum on the opposite side. The SSE Hydro, an ultramodern concert arena, has generated a new fashionable strip of bars and restaurants along Argyle Street as well as several new hotels.

⊙ Sights

Glasgow Science Centre
MUSEUM | FAMILY | Fun and engaging, this museum for children has three floors packed with games, experiments, and hands-on machines from pendulums to small-scale whirlpools, soundscapes to optical illusions. Its space-age home on the south side of the Clyde has a whole wall of glass looking out onto the river. The *BodyWorks* exhibition explores every aspect of our physical selves—you can even try and reconstruct a brain. There are daily events and science shows, a lovely play area for under-sevens, a planetarium, an IMAX theater, and the spectacular Glasgow Tower, 400 feet high, where you can survey the whole city from the river to the surrounding hills. All carry an additional charge. Always inquire whether the tower is open—even moderate winds will close it down. ■**TIP**➔ **Admission is expensive, but the tower and planetarium cost less if you buy all the tickets at the same time.** ✉ *50 Pacific Quay, Finnieston*

☎ *0141/420–5000* ⊕ *www.glasgowsciencecentre.org* 🎫 *£11.50; planetarium £2.70 with museum admission; Glasgow Tower £3.15 with museum admission; Tower only £6.50* ⊘ *Closed Mon., Tues., and Thurs. Nov.–Mar.* Ⓜ *Cessnock.*

★ Riverside Museum: Scotland's Museum of Transport and Travel
MUSEUM | FAMILY | Designed by Zaha Hadid to celebrate the area's industrial heritage, this huge metal structure with curving walls echoes the covered yards where ships were built on the Clyde. Glasgow's shipbuilding history is remembered with a world-famous collection of ship models. Locomotives built at the nearby St. Rollox yards are also on display, as are cars from every age and many countries. You can wander down Main Street, circa 1930, without leaving the building: the pawnbroker, funeral parlor, and Italian restaurant are all frozen in time. Relax with a coffee in the café, wander out onto the expansive riverside walk, or board the Tall Ship that is moored permanently behind the museum. Take Bus 100 from the City Centre, or walk from Partick subway station. ✉ *100 Poundhouse Pl., Finnieston* ☎ *0141/287–2720* ⊕ *www.glasgowlife.org.uk* 🎫 *Free* Ⓜ *Partick.*

Tall Ship at Riverside
LIGHTHOUSE | FAMILY | Built in 1896, this fine tall sailing ship now sits on the River Clyde immediately behind the Riverside Museum. The *Glenlee* once belonged to the Spanish Navy (under a different name), but carried cargo all over the world in her day. She returned to Glasgow and the River Clyde in 1993, and now forms part of the museum. You can wander throughout this surprisingly large cargo ship with or without an audio guide, peer into cabins and holds, and stand on the forecastle as you gaze down the river (but bring your own binoculars). Bus 100 from George Square brings you here, or you can walk from the Partick subway station in 10 minutes. ✉ *150*

West End and Finnieston

KEY
- **1** *Exploring Sights*
- **1** *Restaurants*
- **1** *Hotels*

Sights ▼
1 Botanic Gardens........ **E2**
2 Glasgow
  Science Centre **D7**
3 Glasgow University..... **F5**
4 Hunterian Museum..... **F4**
5 Kelvingrove Art Gallery
  and Museum **E6**

6 Kelvingrove Park........ **G6**
7 Riverside Museum:
  Scotland's Museum of
  Transport and Travel ... **B7**
8 Tall Ship at Riverside ... **B7**

Restaurants ▼
1 Baffo **E6**
2 Balbir's **D5**
3 Bay Tree **H4**
4 Bread Meats Bread **F3**
5 The Brunch Club........ **E6**
6 Butchershop
  Bar and Grill............. **F6**

7 Cafe Andaluz **E3**
8 Cafe Zique **C4**
9 Crabshakk **G7**
10 The Finnieston **G7**
11 Hanoi Bike Shop........ **E3**
12 The Left Bank **G4**
13 Little Italy **E4**
14 Mother India **G7**

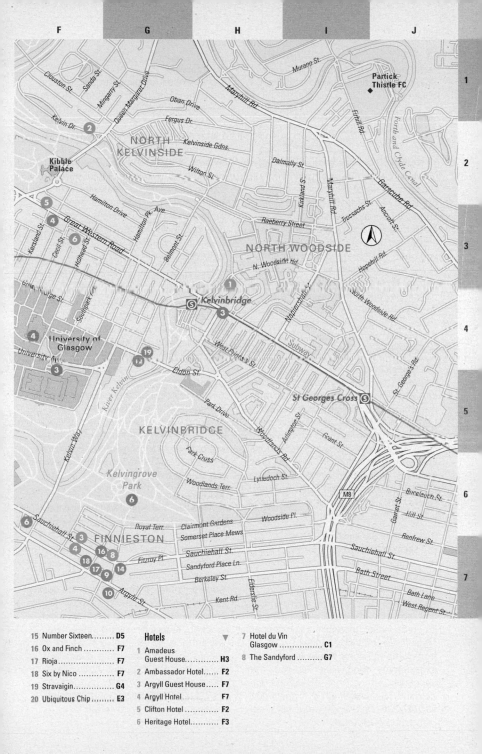

15	Number Sixteen	D5
16	Ox and Finch	F7
17	Rioja	F7
18	Six by Nico	F7
19	Stravaigin	G4
20	Ubiquitous Chip	E3

Hotels ▼

1	Amadeus Guest House	H3
2	Ambassador Hotel	F2
3	Argyll Guest House	F7
4	Argyll Hotel	F7
5	Clifton Hotel	F2
6	Heritage Hotel	F3
7	Hotel du Vin Glasgow	C1
8	The Sandyford	G7

Pointhouse Pl., Finnieston ☎ 0141/357–3699 ⊕ www.thetallship.com ⛾ Free Ⓜ Partick.

 Restaurants

Baffo

$ | **ITALIAN** | There has been something of an explosion of new pizzerias in Glasgow, many of them newer chains, but Baffo has made its mark and won approval from a demanding audience. Not only are the pizzas beautifully crispy and varied, they are also very large: if you need a half-meter of pizza (about 1½ feet), it's available as an economical choice. **Known for:** famous half-meter pizza; busy but friendly atmosphere; good pasta at decent prices. Ⓢ Average main: £10 ⊠ 1377 Argyle St., Finnieston ☎ 0141/583–0000 ⊕ www.baffo.co.uk Ⓜ Kelvin Hall.

The Brunch Club

$ | **CAFÉ** | The name says it all: this pleasant, airy café pays homage to all things brunch. There are eggs in every combination, decadent waffles and French toast, and a delicious array of classic brunch cocktails from Bloody Marys to mimosas. **Known for:** best brunch in Glasgow; great cocktails; relaxing vibe. Ⓢ Average main: £9 ⊠ 67 Old Dumbarton Rd., Finnieston ☎ 0141/237–7374 ⊕ www.thebrunchclub.co ⊗ No dinner Ⓜ Kelvin Hall.

Butchershop Bar and Grill

$$ | **STEAKHOUSE** | An early arrival in the redeveloping Finnieston area, Butchershop occupies what was once a pub and overlooks the bowling greens in Kelvingrove Park. Modern, open, and airy, it preserves the sociable atmosphere of its predecessor, though it is now a quality steak house offering a range of cuts from rump to T-bone. **Known for:** steaks of every variety; good value fixed-price menus; publike atmosphere. Ⓢ Average main: £19 ⊠ 1055 Sauchiehall St., Finnieston ☎ 0141/339–2999 ⊕ www.butchershop-glasgow.com Ⓜ Kelvin Hall.

★ Crabshakk

$$ | **SEAFOOD** | Anything but a shack, this intimate dining room has heavy wooden tables and chairs, an elegantly ornate ceiling, and a bar so shiny and inviting that it seems to almost insist you have a drink. The food comes from the sea—oysters, lobster, and squid—and you can have your choice served iced, grilled, roasted, or battered. **Known for:** local and sustainably sourced Scottish seafood; art deco decor; reservations essential. Ⓢ Average main: £15 ⊠ 1114 Argyle St., Finnieston ☎ 0141/334–6127 ⊕ www.crabshakk.com Ⓜ Kelvin Hall.

★ The Finnieston

$$ | **SEAFOOD** | A 19th-century inn turned into an elegant restaurant, the Finnieston retains the dark wood and narrow cubicles of earlier times, but today it is one of the new high-quality seafood restaurants that have transformed the faded Finnieston area into a fashionable district. The menu allows you to choose the fish and how it is prepared, the sauce, and salad or vegetable sides. **Known for:** impressive seafood cuisine; stunning array of cocktails; comfy wooden booths. Ⓢ Average main: £18 ⊠ 1125 Argyle St., Finnieston ☎ 0141/222–2884 ⊕ www.thefinnieston-bar.com Ⓜ Kelvin Hall.

Mother India

$$ | **INDIAN** | The brand known as Mother India really covers four adjacent restaurants rather than just one location, all highlighting small plates of impressive Indian cuisine. What makes this place across from Kelvingrove Art Gallery so popular is the combination of high-quality cooking and an extensive range of tastes, from the vegetarian dal to spicy ginger chicken. **Known for:** casual small-plate Indian food; no reservations, which means there are crowds and usually some wait; BYOB policy. Ⓢ Average main: £15 ⊠ 1355 Argyle St., Clyde ☎ 0141/339–9145 ⊕ www.motherindiaglasgow.co.uk Ⓜ Kelvin Hall.

★ Ox and Finch

$$$ | ECLECTIC | This immensely popular restaurant shines at every level—service, presentation, and taste. The stripped-back, rustic decor encourages chatter and the sharing of the eclectic small plates that are its specialty. **Known for:** small-plates dining with a wide variety of options; relaxed and buzzy atmosphere; huge wine list. $ *Average main: £20* ✉ *920 Sauchiehall St., Finnieston* ☎ *0141/339–8627* ⊕ *www.oxandfinch. com* Ⓜ *Kelvin Hall.*

Rioja

$$ | SPANISH | Rioja belongs to the second generation of tapas restaurants, combining classic small plates with new and innovative interpretations. At this dark, rustic spot with exposed brick, wood floors, and dark walls, *patatas riojanas* go a stage beyond *patatas bravas*, adding pork and chorizo, while the spring lamb with almond crust adds new flavors. **Known for:** contemporary take on tapas; good Spanish wines; late-night dining. $ *Average main: £15* ✉ *1116 Argyle St., Clyde* ☎ *0141/334–0761* ⊕ *www.riojafin-nieston.co.uk* Ⓜ *Kelvin Hall.*

Six by Nico

$$$ | BRITISH | In a street of adventurous eateries, Six by Nico adds a new dimension of fun and wit. The concept at this intimate, modern restaurant with black tile, wood floors and tables, and black chairs is a six-course tasting menu linked to a theme that changes every six weeks, whether it's fish-and-chips or Route 66, with dishes that deconstruct and reconstruct the familiar. **Known for:** highly original approach to a tasting menu; imaginative dishes (with wine-pairing option); reservations essential. $ *Average main: £25* ✉ *1132 Argyle St., Finnieston* ☎ *0141/334⬜5661* ⊕ *www.sixbynico.co.uk* ⊙ *Closed Mon.* Ⓜ *Kelvin Hall.*

Hotels

Argyll Guest House

$ | B&B/INN | In this budget-minded annex to the Argyll Hotel, across the road on Sauchiehall Street, the rooms are plainly furnished but scrupulously clean. **Pros:** close to Kelvingrove Park and public transportation; tasty breakfast; bargain prices. **Cons:** front rooms noisy on weekends; no elevator; basic amenities. $ *Rooms from: £65* ✉ *966–970 Sauchiehall St., Finnieston* ☎ *0141/357–5155* ⊕ *www.argyllhotelglasgow.co.uk* ⇌ *20 rooms* ⦿ *Free Breakfast* Ⓜ *Kelvin Hall.*

Argyll Hotel

$ | HOTEL | The tartan in the reception area reflects the clan theme throughout the hotel; each room is named after a clan, but each is also very different from the next. **Pros:** centrally located; comfortable rooms; reasonable prices. **Cons:** street can get noisy on weekends; metered parking on the street; downstairs breakfast area and bar need refurbishing. $ *Rooms from: £79* ✉ *973 Sauchiehall St., Finnieston* ☎ *0141/337–3313* ⊕ *www. argyllhotelglasgow.co.uk* ⇌ *38 rooms* ⦿ *Free Breakfast* Ⓜ *Kelvin Hall.*

The Sandyford

$ | HOTEL | The Victorian exterior of this hotel anticipates the colorful decor you'll find inside, where the large windows in the reception area let in lots of light. **Pros:** extremely well located; minutes from several good restaurants; very competitive prices. **Cons:** front rooms can get late-night noise; no elevator; parking on the street is metered. $ *Rooms from: £54* ✉ *904 Sauchiehall St., Finnieston* ☎ *0141/334–0000* ⊕ *www.sandyford-hotelglasgow.com* ⇌ *55 rooms* ⦿ *Free Breakfast* Ⓜ *Kelvin Hall.*

Nightlife

BARS AND PUBS

Ben Nevis

BARS/PUBS | A traditional pub still holding its own on the trendy Finnieston strip, this eccentric spot is full of Highland artifacts. There are more than 180 whiskies from which to choose and traditional live music on Wednesday, Thursday, and Sunday. ⊠ *1147 Argyle St., Finnieston* ☎ *0141/576–5204* ⊕ *www.thebennevis. co.uk* Ⓜ *Kelvinhall.*

78

BARS/PUBS | Enjoy cozy sofas, a real coal fire, and tasty vegan food throughout the day. There's live music every night, with jazz on Sunday. ⊠ *10–14 Kelvinhaugh St., Finnieston* ☎ *0141/576–5018* ⊕ *www. the78cafebar.com* Ⓜ *Kelvinhall.*

East End

Glasgow Green has always been the heart of Glasgow's East End, a formerly down-at-heel neighborhood that has seen many changes over time. One of the top attractions is the People's Palace, which tells the story of daily life in the city. On Sunday head to the nearby Barras market to hunt for bargains.

Sights

Glasgow Green

CITY PARK | **FAMILY** | Glasgow's oldest park has a long history as a favorite spot for public recreation and political demonstrations. Note the Nelson Column, erected long before London's; the McLennan Arch, originally part of the facade of the old Assembly Halls in Ingram Street; and the Templeton Business Centre, a former carpet factory built in the late 19th century in the style of the Doge's Palace in Venice. There is an adventure playground for kids and a small cycle track beside it, with children's bikes for rent. Don't miss the **People's Palace** and the Doulton

Fountain that faces it. The Green also hosts the World Piping Championship in summer and a major firework display for Guy Fawkes night (November 5). ⊠ *East End* ✛ *North side of River Clyde between Green St. and Saltmarket St.*

Hampden Park

SPORTS VENUE | **FAMILY** | A mecca for soccer enthusiasts who come from far and near to tread the famous turf, the home field for the country's national team was the largest stadium in the world when it was built in 1903. There are stadium tours on non-match days at 11, 12:30, 2, and 3. You can then visit the Scottish Football Museum, which traces the history of the game; the museum may close on game days. ⊠ *Letherby Dr., East End* ✛ *Nearest rail stations are Mount Florida and Kings Park. Buses from City Centre* ☎ *0141/616–6139* ⊕ *www.hampdenpark. co.uk* ✉ *Stadium tour £8, museum entrance £8, combined ticket £13.*

People's Palace and Winter Gardens

MUSEUM | **FAMILY** | The excited conversations among local visitors are the evidence that this museum tells the story of everyday lives in Glasgow. There is always something that sparks a memory: a photo, an object, a sound. Inside you'll find the writing desk of John McLean (1879–1923), the famous "Red Clydeside" political activist, and the banana boots worn onstage by Glasgow-born comedian Billy Connolly. On the top floor a sequence of fine murals by Glasgow artist Ken Currie tells the story of the city's working-class citizens. In contrast, the Doulton Fountain opposite the entrance celebrates the British empire. The museum is housed in a Victorian red-sandstone building at the heart of Glasgow Green, and behind it are the restored Winter Gardens (a Victorian conservatory) and a popular café. To get here from the St. Enoch subway station, walk along Argyle Street past Glasgow Cross. ⊠ *Glasgow Green, Monteith Row, East End* ☎ *0141/276–0788* ⊕ *www.*

glasgowlife.org.uk 🎫 *Free* ⊘ *Closed Mon.* Ⓜ *St. Enoch.*

Restaurants

A'Challtainn Fish Restaurant
$$ | SEAFOOD | A welcome addition for East End diners, A'Challtainn (which means "Hazel Wood," the area's original name) occupies the central courtyard space of the Barras Architecture and Design Centre within the heart of Glasgow's original flea market, the Barras. The menu showcases Scottish seafood, with both small plates and a fine dining menu. **Known for:** excellent seafood; nice selection of shared plates; great Sunday brunch. ⑤ *Average main: £16* ⊠ *Barras Architecture and Design Centre, 54 Calton Entry, East End* ☎ *0141/237–9220* ⊕ *www.achalltainn.com* ⊘ *Closed Mon.*

West on the Green
$ | GERMAN | This microbrewery serves beer brewed "according to German purity laws of 1516"—in other words, no additives to muddy the flavor. The German theme is continued with the slightly cavernous dining space dotted with large wooden tables, and the food, which includes wursts, Wiener schnitzel, and goulash. **Known for:** classic German cuisine like wurst and potato salad; variety of its own beer served in a popular beer garden; weekend brewery tours with tasting. ⑤ *Average main: £13* ⊠ *Templeton Bldg., Templeton St., East End* ☎ *0141/550–0135* ⊕ *www.westbeer. com* Ⓜ *St. Enoch.*

🛍 Shopping

★ Barras
OUTDOOR/FLEA/GREEN MARKETS | Scotland's largest indoor market—named for the barrows, or pushcarts, formerly used by the stallholders—prides itself on selling everything "from a needle to an anchor" and is a must-see for anyone addicted to searching through piles of junk for bargains. Open on weekends only, the atmosphere is always good-natured, and you can find just about anything here, in any condition, from dusty model railroads to antique jewelry. Haggling is mandatory. You can reach the Barras by walking along Argyle Street from the St. Enoch subway station. The Barrowland Ballroom, which forms part of the market, was once where Glaswegians went to dance; today it is a venue for concerts of every kind. ■TIP→ **Across the road is one of Glasgow's oldest pubs, the Saracen's Head; enter with caution—ghosts are said to abound.** ⊠ *Gallowgate, East End* ⊕ *www.theglasgowbarras.com.*

South Side

Just southwest of the City Centre in the South Side are two of Glasgow's dear green spaces—Bellahouston Park and Pollok Country Park—which have important art collections: Charles Rennie Mackintosh's House for an Art Lover in Bellahouston, and Pollok House in Pollok Country Park. A respite from the buzz of the city can also be found in the parks, where you can have a picnic or ramble through greenery and gardens. The famous Burrell Collection is also in the area, but the museum will be closed through 2020 for a substantial renovation.

Sights

House for an Art Lover
HOUSE | Within Bellahouston Park is a "new" Mackintosh house, based on a competition entry Charles Rennie Mackintosh submitted to a German magazine in 1901. The house was never built in his lifetime, but took shape between 1989 and 1996. It is home to Glasgow School of Art's postgraduate study center, and displays show designs for the various rooms and decorative pieces by Mackintosh and his wife, Margaret. The main lounge is spectacular. There's also a café

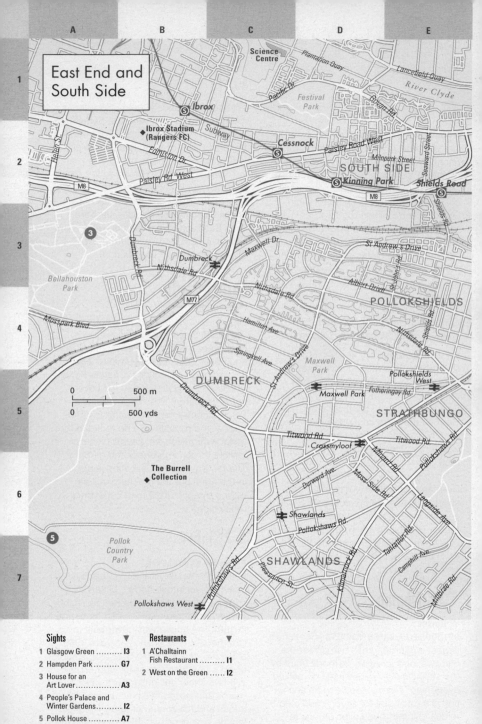

East End and South Side

Sights ▼

1 Glasgow Green I3
2 Hampden Park G7
3 House for an
   Art Lover A3
4 People's Palace and
   Winter Gardens.......... I2
5 Pollok House A7

Restaurants ▼

1 A'Challtainn
   Fish Restaurant I1
2 West on the Green I2

The "newest" Charles Rennie Mackintosh design is House for an Art Lover, which was designed in 1901, but completed in 1996, long after his death.

and shop filled with art. Buses 9, 53, and 54 from Union Street will get you here. Call ahead, as opening times can vary. ⊠ *Bellahouston Park, 10 Dumbreck Rd., South Side* ☎ *0141/353–4770* ⊕ *www.houseforanartlover.co.uk* ✉ *£6* ☉ *Closed weekdays Oct.–Mar.* Ⓜ *Ibrox.*

Pollok House

HOUSE | This classic Georgian house, dating from the mid-1700s, sits amid landscaped gardens and avenues of trees that are now part of Pollok Country Park. It still has the tranquil air of a wealthy but unpretentious country house. The Stirling Maxwell Collection includes paintings by Blake and a strong grouping of Spanish works by El Greco, Murillo, and Goya. Lovely examples of 18th- and early-19th-century furniture, silver, glass, and porcelain are also on display. The house has beautiful gardens that overlook the White Cart River. The downstairs servants' quarters include the kitchen, which is now a café-restaurant. The closest train station is Pollokshaws West, from Glasgow Central station; or you

can take Buses 45, 47, or 57 to the gate of Pollok County Park. ⊠ *Pollok County Park, 2060 Pollokshaws Rd., South Side* ☎ *0141/616–6410* ⊕ *www.nts.org.uk* ✉ *£7.50.*

Performing Arts

Tramway

ART GALLERIES—ARTS | **FAMILY** | South of the City Centre, this innovative arts center is well worth seeking out. It hosts regular exhibitions in its two galleries, and plays—often of a very experimental nature—in its flexible theater space. The city's famed Citizens Theatre Company is also currently performing here while its permanent space undergoes a major renovation. Tramway has a café and a more formal restaurant on the first floor. Don't miss the Hidden Garden, which has transformed an empty lot behind the building into a sculpture park. To get here, take the train from Glasgow Central station to Pollokshields East (one stop). ⊠ *25 Albert Dr., South Side* ☎ *0845/330–3501* ⊕ *www.tramway.org.*

Side Trips from Glasgow: Ayrshire, Clyde Coast, and Robert Burns Country

The jigsaw puzzle of firths and straits and interlocking islands that you see as you fly into Glasgow Airport harbors numerous tempting one-day excursion destinations. You can travel south to visit the fertile farmlands of Ayrshire or west to the Firth of Clyde. Besides the spots related to celebrated Scottish poet Robert Burns, key treasures in this area include Culzean Castle, as famous for its Robert Adam (1728–92) design as it is for its spectacular seaside setting and grounds.

For many people a highlight of this region is Robert Burns country, a 40-minute drive from Glasgow. The poet was born in Alloway, beside Ayr, and the towns and villages where he lived and loved make for an interesting day out. English children learn that Burns (1759–96) is a good minor poet, but Scottish children know that he's Shakespeare, Dante, Rabelais, Mozart, and Karl Marx rolled into one. As time goes by, it seems that the Scots have it more nearly right, as Burns increases in stature both as a poet and humanist. When you plunge into Burns country, don't forget that he's held in extreme reverence by Scots of all backgrounds. They may argue about Sir Walter Scott and Bonnie Prince Charlie, but there's no disputing the merits of the author of "Auld Lang Syne" and "A Man's a Man for A' That."

GETTING HERE AND AROUND
From Glasgow you can take the bus or train (from Glasgow Central station) to Ayr for the Burns Heritage Trail; and Troon, Prestwick, and Ayr to play golf. Bus companies also operate one-day guided excursions; for details, contact the tourist information center in Glasgow or the Strathclyde Passenger Transport Travel Centre. Traveline Scotland has helpful information.

If you're driving from Glasgow, there are two main routes to Ayr. The quickest is to take the M77 to the A77, which takes you to Ayr, where Alloway is well signposted. The alternative and much slower route is the coast road; take the M8 to Greenock and continue down the coast on the A78 until you meet the A77 and continue on into Burns Country.

Irvine

24 miles south of Glasgow.

Beyond Irvine's cobbled streets and grand Victorian buildings, look for a peaceful crescent-shaped harbor and fishermen's cottages huddled in solidarity against the Atlantic winds. The Scottish Maritime Museum pays homage to the town's seafaring past. Scotland's national poet, Robert Burns, lived here in 1781. Golf clubs Western Gailes and nearby Royal Troon make the area popular with golfers.

GETTING HERE AND AROUND
By car take the M8 from Glasgow, then the A726 and the A736 to Irvine. By rail it's a 40-minute journey from Glasgow Central station.

Sights

★ Scottish Maritime Museum
MUSEUM | FAMILY | On the waterfront in the coastal town of Irvine, this museum brings together ships and boats—both models and the real thing—to tell the tale of Scotland's maritime history, as well as chronicle the lives of its boatbuilders, fishermen, and sailors. The atmospheric Linthouse Engine Building, part of a former shipyard, hosts most of the displays. The museum also includes a shipyard worker's tenement home that you can

Ayrshire

explore. In Dumbarton, 35 miles to the north, you can visit the Denny Tank (part of the museum), where ship designs were tested. ■TIP→ **Children are admitted free.** ⊠ *6 Gottries Rd.* ☎ *01294/278283* 🌐 *www.scottishmaritimemuseum.org* 🎟 *£8.50.*

Activities

★ Western Gailes Golf Club
GOLF | Known as the finest natural links course in Scotland, Western Gailes is entirely nature-made, and the greens are kept in truly magnificent condition. This is the final qualifying course when the British Open is held at Royal Troon or Trump Turnberry. Tom Watson lists the par-5 6th hole as one of his favorites. Visitors can play during restricted hours through the week; reserve online. ⊠ *Gailes Rd.* ☎ *01294/311649* 🌐 *www.westerngailes.*

com 🖂 *Nov.–Feb £70 per round; Mar. £100 per round; Apr. and Oct. £140 per round; May–Sept. £175 per round* 🏌 *18 holes, 6640 yards, par 71.*

Ayr and Alloway

10 miles south of Irvine, 34 miles south of Glasgow.

The commercial port of Ayr is Ayrshire's chief town, a peaceful and elegant place with an air of prosperity. Poet Robert Burns was baptized in the Auld Kirk (Old Church) here and wrote a humorous poem about the Twa Brigs (Two Bridges) that cross the river nearby. Burns described Ayr as a town unsurpassed "for honest men and bonny lasses."

If you're on the Robert Burns trail, head for Alloway, on B7024 in Ayr's southern suburbs. A number of sights here are part of the **Burns National Heritage Park**, including the magnificent Robert Burns Birthplace Museum.

GETTING HERE AND AROUND

From Glasgow you can take the bus or train to Ayr; travel time is about an hour (a bit less by train). Drivers can use the A78 and A77 near the coast; a car would provide more flexibility to see the Burns sites around Alloway.

 Sights

Burns Cottage

HOUSE | In the delightful Burns Heritage Park, this thatched cottage is where Scotland's national poet lived for his first seven years. It has a living room, a kitchen, and a stable, one behind the other. The life and times of Burns, born in 1759, are beautifully and creatively illustrated in the fly-on-the-wall videos of daily life in the 18th century. The garden is lush with the types of vegetables the poet's father might have grown. From the cottage, take the Poet's Path through the village to the Robert Burns Birthplace Museum, the spooky churchyard where Tam o' Shanter faced fearsome ghosts, and the Brig o' Doon, all included in the museum entry ticket. ⊠ *Greenfield Ave., Alloway* ☎ *0844/493–2601* ⊕ *www.burnsmuseum.org.uk* ✉ *£10.50, includes Burns Monument and Robert Burns Birthplace Museum.*

Burns Monument

MEMORIAL | This neoclassical structure, built in 1823, overlooks the Brig o' Doon. You can climb to the top (with some care!). Entrance is included in the Burns Museum ticket. ⊠ *Murdoch's Lone, Alloway* ⊕ *www.burnsmuseum.org.uk* ✉ *Free; also included in £10.50 ticket to Burns Cottage and Robert Burns Birthplace Museum.*

★ Robert Burns Birthplace Museum

MUSEUM VILLAGE | Besides being a poet of delicacy and depth, Robert Burns was also a rebel, a thinker, a lover, a good companion, and a man of the countryside. This wonderful museum explains why the Scots so admire this complex "man o' pairts." The imaginative displays present each of his poems in context, with commentaries sensitively written in a modern version of the Scots language in which he spoke and wrote. Headsets let you hear the poems sung or spoken. The exhibits are vibrant and interactive, with touch screens that allow you to debate his views on politics, love, taxation, revolution, and Scottishness. An elegant café offers a place to pause, while the kids can play in the adjoining garden. Included in the ticket are the Burns Cottage, a few minutes' walk down a Burns-themed walkway, and the Burns Monument. ⊠ *Murdoch's Lone, Alloway* ☎ *01292/443700* ⊕ *www.burnsmuseum.org.uk* ✉ *£10.50, includes Burns Cottage and Burns Monument.*

🍽 Restaurants

Brig o' Doon House

$$ | BRITISH | Originally built in 1827, this attractive hotel restaurant often has a piper by the door to greet hungry travelers ready for a Scottish setting and some Scottish fare. Tartan carpets, dark-wood paneling, and buck heads mounted on the walls set the mood, and the bar is a shrine to Robert Burns. **Known for:** riverside location; Scottish food and decor; great venison casserole. ⑤ *Average main: £15* ⊠ *High Maybole Rd., Alloway* ☎ *01292/442466* ⊕ *www.brigodoonhouse.com.*

🏃 Activities

Prestwick Golf Club

GOLF | Tom Morris helped design this challenging Ayrshire coastal links course, which saw the birth of the British Open Championship in 1860. The first hole is reputed to be among the most challenging in Scotland, since the railway line runs along the length of the hole. But it doesn't get any easier after that. Some of its bunkers are especially threatening, and the bumps at the 5th are high enough to be called the Himalayas. Prestwick has excellent, fast rail links with Glasgow. There are a limited number of tee times on Saturday afternoon. ✉ *2 Links Rd., Prestwick ✛ 4 miles south of Ayr via the A79* ☎ *01292/477404* ⊕ *www.prestwickgc.co.uk* ✉ *Apr. and Oct., £160 weekdays, £210 weekends; May–Sept., weekdays £190, weekends £225; Nov.–Mar. Mon.–Sat. £110, Sun. £145* ⚑ *18 holes, 6544 yards, par 71.*

Culzean Castle and Country Park

12 miles south of Ayr, 50 miles south of Glasgow.

There's plenty to do at this popular spot between visiting the Robert Adam-designed house and touring the extensive grounds.

GETTING HERE AND AROUND

Stagecoach buses run from Ayr to the park entrance; the nearest train station from Glasgow is at Maybole, 4 miles to the east, but there is Stagecoach bus service to the park entrance. Note that the park entrance is a mile walk from the castle visitor center.

Sights

★ Culzean Castle and Country Park

CASTLE/PALACE | **FAMILY** | The dramatic cliff-top castle of Culzean (pronounced ku-*lain*) is quite a long drive from Glasgow, but it's the National Trust for Scotland's most popular property. Robert Adam designed the neoclassical mansion, complete with a walled garden, in 1777. The grounds are enormous and beautifully kept, combining parkland, forests, and a beach looking out over the Atlantic Ocean; the surprisingly lush shrubberies

reflect the warm currents that explain the mild climate. There are caves in the cliffs; tours are occasionally available. In the castle itself you can visit the armory, luxuriously appointed salons and bedchambers, and a nursery with its lovely cradle in a boat. Adam's grand double spiral staircase is the high point of its design. There's a free audio tour, and guided tours are available daily at 11 and 2:30. A short walk through the woods brings you to the visitor center with shops and a restaurant. ✉ *Culzean Castle, A719, Maybole* ☎ *01655/884455* ⊕ *www.nts.org.uk* ✉ *Park and castle £17, park only £11.50* ☉ *Castle closed Nov.–Mar.*

Hotels

Eisenhower Hotel

$$$ | **HOTEL** | It would be hard to imagine a more spectacular location for an overnight stay than the upper floors of Culzean Castle, which looks out toward Arran and the Atlantic Ocean. **Pros:** beautiful setting; luxurious lodging; a strong sense of history. **Cons:** a little remote; rather formal; not for minimalists. $ *Rooms from: £250* ✉ *Culzean Castle, A719, Maybole* ☎ *0844/493–2149* ⊕ *www.culzean-eisenhower.com* ⇆ *6 rooms* ❍❘ *Free Breakfast.*

Chapter 16

THE BORDERS AND THE SOUTHWEST

Updated by
Mike Gonzalez

⊙ Sights	🍴 Restaurants	🛏 Hotels	💼 Shopping	🍸 Nightlife
★★☆☆☆	★★☆☆☆	★☆☆☆☆	★☆☆☆☆	★☆☆☆☆

WELCOME TO THE BORDERS AND THE SOUTHWEST

TOP REASONS TO GO

★ **Ancient abbeys:** The great abbeys of the Border regions and the wonderful Sweetheart Abbey in the Southwest are mainly in ruins, but they retain an air of their former grandeur.

★ **Outdoor activities:** You can walk, bicycle, or even ride horses across Galloway or through the Borders. Abandoned railway tracks make good paths, and there are forests and moorlands if you prefer wilder country.

★ **Stately homes and castles:** Some of the landed aristocracy still lives in these grand mansions, and most of the homes are open to visitors, like Floors Castle, Threave, Drumlanrig, and the magical Caerlaverock Castle near Dumfries.

★ **Literary Scotland:** The Borders region has enough monuments dedicated to Sir Walter Scott to make him the focus of a visit. The poet Robert Burns spent much of his working life in Dumfries, and the Moat Brae Centre in Dumfries was where J. M. Barrie first came up with *Peter Pan*.

What was once for centuries a battleground region separating Scotland and England, today the Borders area is a bridge between the two countries. This is a place of upland moors and hills, farmland, and forested river valleys. Yet it also embraces the rugged coastline between Edinburgh and Berwick. It's rustic and peaceful, with textile mills, abbeys, castles, and gardens. The area is a big draw for hikers and walking enthusiasts, especially thanks to the lovely Tweed Valley Forest Park in the east and the Galloway Forest Park in the west. The Borders region is steeped in history, with Mary, Queen of Scots, a powerful presence despite the relatively short time she spent here. The moorlands of the Southwest feature dramatic art projects like the Striding Arches and *Crawick Multiverse* as well as peaceful seascapes like the Solway Firth and wilder ones on the Galloway coast.

1 Jedburgh. A pretty town dominated by a glorious abbey.

2 Kelso. A charming market town close to imposing Floors Castle.

3 Melrose. Home to a ruined abbey and the house once belonging to Sir Walter Scott.

4 Selkirk. Another small town with beautiful landscapes and Sir Walter Scott history.

5 Innerleithen. A former industrial boomtown of wool mills now popular for its outdoor activities.

6 Dumfries. A tranquil market town that was once home to Robert Burns and J. M. Barrie.

7 North of Dumfries. Where you'll find Drumlanrig Castle, *Crawick Multiverse*, and the Museum of Lead Mining.

8 Castle Douglas. A pleasant town specializing in local food products and home to Threave Castle.

9 Kirkcudbright. A lovely harbor town once a haven for artists, including one of the "Glasgow Boys."

10 Whithorn. Home to the historic early Christian settlement Whithorn Abbey.

11 Stranraer. Once the main ferry port for Ireland and now in the midst of redevelopment.

In the Borders region, south of Edinburgh, are more stately homes, fortified castles, and medieval abbeys than in any other part of Scotland. This is also Sir Walter Scott territory, including his pseudo-baronial home at Abbotsford.

The area embraces the whole 90-mile course of one of Scotland's great rivers, the Tweed. Passing woodlands luxuriant with game birds, the river flows in rushing torrents through this fertile land. To the west of the Borders is Dumfries and Galloway, an area of gentle coasts, forests, and lush hills, ideal country for walkers and cyclists.

For centuries the Borders was a battlefield, where English and Scottish troops remained locked in a struggle for its possession. At different times, parts of the region have been in English hands, just as slices of northern England (Berwick-upon-Tweed, for example) have been under Scottish control. The castles and fortified houses as well as the abbeys across the Borders are the surviving witnesses to those times. After the Union of 1707, fortified houses gradually gave way to the luxurious country mansions that pepper the area. And by the 19th century they had become grand country houses like Mellerstain House, built by fashionable architects.

All the main routes between London and Edinburgh traverse the Borders, whose hinterland of undulating pastures, woods, and valleys is enclosed within three lonely groups of hills: the Cheviots, the Moorfoots, and the Lammermuirs. Hamlets and prosperous country towns dot the

land, giving valley slopes a lived-in look, yet the total population is still sparse. The sheep that are the basis of the region's prosperous textile industry outnumber human beings by 14 to 1.

To the west is the region of Dumfries and Galloway, on the shores of the Solway Firth. It might appear to be an extension of the Borders, but the southwest has a history all its own. From its ports ships sailed to the Americas, carrying country dwellers driven from their land to make room for sheep. Inland, the earth rises toward high hills, forest, and bleak but captivating moorland, whereas nearer the coast you can find pretty farmlands, small villages, and unassuming towns. The shoreline is washed by the North Atlantic Drift (Scotland's answer to the Gulf Stream), and first-time visitors are always surprised to see palm trees and exotic plants thriving in gardens and parks along the coast.

At the heart of the region is Dumfries, the "Queen o' the South." Once a major port and commercial center, its glamour is now slightly faded. But the memory of poet Robert Burns, who spent several years living and working here and who is buried in the town, remains very much alive. In addition, Moat Brae can claim to be the location of Neverland, the imaginary world of *Peter Pan*, which was written there.

MAJOR REGIONS

The Borders. Borders towns cluster around and between two rivers—the Tweed and its tributary, the Teviot. Borders folk take great pride in the region's fame as Scotland's main woolen-goods manufacturing area. Its main towns— Jedburgh, Hawick, Selkirk, Peebles, Kelso, and Melrose—retain an air of prosperity and confidence with their solid stone houses and elegant town squares. Although many mills have closed since the 1980s, the pride in local identity is still evident in the fiercely contested Melrose Sevens rugby competition in April and the annual Common Ridings—local events commemorating the time when towns needed to patrol their borders—throughout June and July. A visit to at least one of the region's four great ruined abbeys makes the quintessential Borders experience. The monks in these powerful, long-abandoned religious communities were the first to work the fleeces of their sheep flocks, thus laying the groundwork for what is still the area's main manufacturing industry.

Although the Borders has many attractions, it's most famous for being the home base for Sir Walter Scott (1771–1832), the early-19th-century poet, novelist, and creator of *Ivanhoe*. Scott single-handedly transformed Scotland's image from that of a land of brutal savages to one of romantic and stirring deeds and magnificent landscapes. The novels of Scott are not read much nowadays— frankly, some of them are difficult to wade through—but the mystique that he created, the aura of historical romance, has outlasted his books. The ruined abbeys, historical houses, and grand vistas of the Borders provide a perfect backdrop.

Dumfries and Galloway. Galloway covers the southwestern portion of Scotland, west of the main town of Dumfries; it's a quiet and less-visited region of Scotland, in general. Here a gentle coastline gives way to farmland and then breezy uplands that gradually merge with coniferous forests. The region now claims two extraordinary public art projects—Charles Jencks's *Crawick Multiverse* and Andy Goldsworthy's *Striding Arches*. The Solway Firth is a vast nature preserve, and the climate of the west sustains the surprising tropical plants at the Logan Botanic Gardens and the gardens at Threave Castle. Even farther west, Galloway draws active visitors to its forests to hike or cycle.

Planning

When to Go

Because many lodgings and some sights are privately owned and shut down from early autumn until early April, the area is less suited to off-season touring than some other parts of Scotland. The best time to visit is between Easter and late September. The region does look magnificent in autumn, especially along the wooded river valleys of the Borders. Late spring is the time to see the rhododendrons in the gardens of Dumfries and Galloway.

FESTIVALS
Common Ridings
FESTIVALS | More than 10 Borders communities have reestablished their identities through the annual summer gatherings known as the Common Ridings. In medieval times it was essential that each town be able to defend its area by "riding the marches," or patrolling the boundaries. The Common Ridings that celebrate this history are more authentic than the Highland Games concocted by the Victorians. Although this is above all a celebration for native Borderers, you

will be welcome to share the excitement of clattering hooves and banners proudly displayed. ⊕ www.returntotheridings. co.uk.

Rugby Sevens

RUGBY | The Borders invented the fast-and-furious, cut-down version of rugby in 1883, though it has now spread worldwide. Teams are made up of 7 players rather than 15, and the matches are shorter. Although the population of the Borders is about 100,000, the region boasts a total of 17 clubs and some of Scotland's best players. Each spring, 10 teams compete for the Kings of the Sevens title. ⊕ www.kingsofthesevens.net.

Planning Your Time

The Borders Railway has opened the route between Edinburgh and the Borders, running from Edinburgh's Waverley Station to Tweedbank, in the heart of the Borders. Its 30-mile journey passes through Galashiels (for connections to Traquair House) and ends at Tweedbank, which is near Melrose and Walter Scott's home at Abbotsford. Beyond the Borders Railway, it is still more convenient to explore by car. If you're driving north along the A1 toward Edinburgh, it's easy to take a tour around the prosperous Borders towns. Turn onto the A698 at Berwick-upon-Tweed, which will take you along the Scottish–English border toward Kelso, Jedburgh, Dryburgh, and Melrose. It's 36 miles from Jedburgh to Peebles, a good place to stay overnight. Another day might begin with a visit to Walter Scott's lovely Abbotsford House, and then some shopping in any of these prosperous towns.

To the west, Dumfries and Galloway beckon. If you're traveling north toward Glasgow on the M6/A74, take the A70 west toward Dumfries. From the A1, on the east coast, travel west on the A708 to Moffat and pick up the A70 there. From Glasgow take the A74 south to Beattock and pick up the A701 there. Two days would give you time to explore Burns sites and more in Dumfries. From Dumfries you can visit Sweetheart Abbey (8 miles away), Caerlaverock Castle (9 miles away), and Threave Castle and Gardens (20 miles away). Castle Douglas is a good place to stop for lunch. The A710 and A711 take you along the dramatic coastline of the Solway Firth. Farther west along the A75 are the towns of Newton Stewart and Portpatrick, and on the A714, Glen Trool. The region does not have good rail links but there is good bus service, and by car it is a charming and compact region.

Getting Here and Around

AIR

The nearest Scottish airports are at Edinburgh, Glasgow, and Prestwick (outside Glasgow).

BOAT AND FERRY

P&O European Ferries and Stena Line operate from Larne, in Northern Ireland, to Cairnryan, near Stranraer, several times daily. The crossing takes one hour on the Superstar Express, two hours on other ferries.

CONTACTS P&O European Ferries. ☎ 0800/130–0030 ⊕ www.poferries.com. Stena Line. ☎ 08447/707070 ⊕ www. stenaline.co.uk.

BUS

If you're approaching from the south, check with Scottish Citylink, National Express, or First about buses from Edinburgh and Glasgow. In the Borders, Firstborders and Borders Buses offer service within the region. Stagecoach Western is the main bus company serving Dumfries and Galloway.

CONTACTS First Bus. ☎ 01224/650000 ⊕ www.firstgroup.com. Firstborders. ☎ 01896/754350 ⊕ www.firstborders. co.uk. National Express. ☎ 0871/781–8181 ⊕ www.nationalexpress.com.

Borders Buses. ☎ 01896/754350 ⊕ www. bordersbuses.co.uk. **Scottish Citylink.** ☎ 0871/266–3333 ⊕ www.citylink.co.uk. **Stagecoach Western.** ☎ 0141/552–4961 in Glasgow, 01387/253496 in Dumfries ⊕ www.stagecoachbus.com.

CAR

Traveling by car is the best and easiest way to explore the area, especially if you get off the main, and often crowded, arterial roads and use the little back roads. The main route into both the Borders and Galloway from the south is the M6, which becomes the M74 at the border. You can then take the scenic and leisurely A7 northwestward through Hawick toward Edinburgh, or the A75 and other parallel routes westward into Dumfries, Galloway, and the former ferry ports of Stranraer (nearby Cairnryan is an active ferry port) and Portpatrick.

There are several other possible routes: starting from the east, the A1 brings you from the English city of Newcastle to the border in about an hour. Moving west, the A697, which leaves the A1 north of Morpeth (in England) and crosses the border at Coldstream, is a leisurely back-road option. The A68 is probably the most scenic route to Scotland: after climbing to Carter Bar, it reveals a view of the Borders hills and windy skies before dropping into the ancient town of Jedburgh.

TRAIN

Apart from the main London–Edinburgh line, the Borders had no train service until 2015, when the rail link from Edinburgh to Tweedbank began service. The Borders Railway website has information about using it to explore the area. In the Southwest, trains headed from London's Euston to Glasgow stop at Carlisle, just south of the border, and some also stop at Lockerbie. Trains between Glasgow and Carlisle stop at Gretna Green, Annan, and Dumfries. From Glasgow there is service on the coastal route to Stranraer.

First Bus provides connections between Hawick, Selkirk, and Galashiels and train service at Carlisle, Edinburgh, and Berwick.

CONTACTS Borders Railway. ☎ 0344/811–0141 ⊕ www.scotrail.co.uk. **National Rail.** ☎ 03457/484950 ⊕ www.nationalrail.co.uk. **ScotRail.** ☎ 0344/811–0141 ⊕ www.scotrail.co.uk. **Trainline.** ☎ 0871/244–1545 ⊕ www.thetrainline.com.

Restaurants

Most good restaurants in the region used to be located in hotels, but today things are changing. Good independent eateries are popping up in small (and sometimes unlikely) towns and villages, and many new establishments specialize in fresh local ingredients. Seasonal menus are now popular. It is important to remember that restaurants here usually serve lunch between noon and 2 and dinner until 8:30 only.

Hotels

From top-quality, full-service hotels to quaint 18th-century drovers' inns to cozy bed-and-breakfasts, the Borders has all manner of lodging options. Choices in Dumfries and Galloway may be a little less expensive than in the Borders (with the same full range of services). These days many establishments are willing to lower their rates depending on availability.

Restaurant and hotel reviews have been shortened. For full reviews, see Fodors. com. Restaurant prices are the average cost of a main course at dinner or, if dinner is not served, at lunch. Hotel prices are the lowest cost of a standard double room in high season, including 20% V.A.T.

WHAT IT COSTS in Pounds			
$	$$	$$$	$$$$
RESTAURANTS			
under £15	£15–£19	£20–£25	over £25
HOTELS			
under £125	£125–£200	£201–£300	over £300

Visitor Information

Visit Scottish Borders has offices in Jedburgh, Hawick, and Peebles. The Dumfries & Galloway Tourist Board can be found in Dumfries and Stranraer. Seasonal information centers are at Castle Douglas, Eyemouth, Galashiels, Gretna Green, Kelso, Kirkcudbright, Langholm, Moffat, Sanquhar, and Selkirk. Liveborders provides online information on cultural and sporting activities in the Borders.

CONTACTS Liveborders. ✉ Melrose Rd., Galashiels 🕿 01896/661166 ⊕ www. liveborders.org.uk. **VisitScotland Dumfries iCentre.** ✉ 64 Whitesands, Dumfries 🕿 01387/253862 ⊕ www. visitscotland.com. **VisitScotland Jedburgh iCentre.** ✉ Murray's Green, Jedburgh 🕿 01835/863170 ⊕ www.visitscotland. com.

Jedburgh

50 miles south of Edinburgh, 95 miles southeast of Glasgow, 14 miles northeast of Hawick.

The town of Jedburgh (*burgh* is always pronounced *burra* in Scots) was for centuries the first major Scottish target of invading English armies. In more peaceful times it developed textile mills, most of which have since languished. The large landscaped area around the town's tourist information center was once a mill but now provides an encampment for the armies of modern tourists. The past still clings to this little town, however. The ruined abbey dominates the skyline, a reminder of the formerly strong governing role of the Borders abbeys.

GETTING HERE AND AROUND
By car from Edinburgh, you can take the A68 (about 45 minutes) or the A7 (about an hour). From Glasgow take the M8, then the A68 direct to Jedburgh (about two hours).

There are fairly good bus connections from all major Scottish cities to Jedburgh. From Edinburgh direct routes to Melrose take about two hours. From Glasgow it takes 3½ hours to reach Melrose. From Melrose it's just 20 minutes to Jedburgh.

The Borders Railway runs between Edinburgh and Tweedbank, about 15 miles northwest of Jedburgh.

ESSENTIALS
VISITOR INFORMATION VisitScotland Jedburgh iCentre. ✉ Murray's Green 🕿 01835/863170 ⊕ www.visitscotland. com.

 Sights

Harestanes Countryside Visitor Centre
MUSEUM | FAMILY | Housed in a former farmhouse 4 miles north of Jedburgh, this visitor center portrays life in the Scottish Borders through art exhibitions and natural history displays. Crafts such as woodworking and tile making are taught here, and finished projects are often on display. Outside are meandering paths, quiet roads for bike rides, and the biggest children's play area in the Borders. There's plenty for children, including a fascinating puzzle gallery full of sturdy wooden games. It is also on one of the best-known walking routes in the Borders, the St. Cuthbert's Path. ✉ Junction of A68 and B6400, 4 miles north of Jedburgh 🕿 01835/830306 ⊕ www.liveborders.org.uk 🎫 Free ⊙ Closed Nov.–Mar.

Hermitage Castle

CASTLE/PALACE | To appreciate the famous 20-mile ride of Mary, Queen of Scots, in 1566—she rushed to the side of her wounded lover, the Earl of Bothwell—travel southwest from Jedburgh to this, the most complete remaining example of the bare and grim medieval border castles. Restored in the early 19th century, it was built in the 13th century to guard what was at the time one of the important routes from England into Scotland. Local folklore maintains that the 14th-century Lord Soulis, a descendant of the original owner and notorious for diabolical excess, was captured by the local populace, who wrapped him in lead and boiled him in a cauldron—a much better story than the reality, which is that he died in Dumbarton Jail. ⊠ *Hawick ✢ 2 miles west of B6399, about 21 miles south of Jedburgh* ☎ *01387/376222* ⊕ *www.historicenvironment.scot* ⊠ *£6* ☯ *Closed Oct.–Mar.*

★ Jedburgh Abbey

RELIGIOUS SITE | The most impressive of the Borders abbeys towers above Jedburgh. Built by David I, king of Scots in the 12th century, the abbey was nearly destroyed by the English Earl of Hertford's forces in 1544–45, during the destructive time known as the Rough Wooing. This was English king Henry VIII's (1491–1547) armed attempt to persuade the Scots that it was a good idea to unite the kingdoms by the marriage of his young son to the infant Mary, Queen of Scots (1542–87); the Scots disagreed and sent Mary to France instead. The story is explained in vivid detail at the visitor center, which also has information about the ruins and an audio tour. The arched abbey walls, the nave, and the cloisters still give a sense of the power these buildings represented. ⊠ *High St.* ☎ *01835/863925* ⊕ *www.historicenvironment.scot* ⊠ *£6.*

Jedburgh Castle Jail and Museum

JAIL | **FAMILY** | This building might look like a castle, but it's actually a prison that sits where a castle originally once stood. Named for the prison reformer John Howard, who campaigned for improved prison conditions, today you can inspect prison cells, rooms with period furnishings, and costumed figures. The audio guide, which recounts the history of the prison and the town, is useful. In what was once the prison governor's house, you'll now find an exhibition about the town of Jedburgh. ⊠ *Castlegate* ☎ *01835/864750* ⊕ *www.scotborders.gov.uk/museums* ⊠ *Free* ☯ *Closed Nov.–Mar*

Mary, Queen of Scots Visitor Centre

HOUSE | This *bastel* (from the French *bastille*) was the fortified town house in which, as the story goes, Mary stayed before embarking on her famous 20-mile ride to Hermitage Castle to visit her wounded lover, the Earl of Bothwell (circa 1535–78) in 1566. Displays relate the tale and other episodes in her life, including her questionable choices of lovers and husbands and her own reflections on her life. Still, Mary's death mask suggests that she was serene at the end. There are tapestries and furniture of the period, and the house's ornamental garden has pear trees leading down to the river. ⊠ *Queen St.* ☎ *01835/863331* ⊕ *www.scotborders.gov.uk* ⊠ *Free* ☯ *Closed Dec.–Feb.*

🍴 Restaurants

Born in the Borders

$ | **BRITISH** | **FAMILY** | This family-friendly complex is built around a café and brewery producing Born in the Borders beer. The café serves breakfast and lunch while a shop sells the on-site brewed beer along with a "ginnery," where visitors can learn about how gin is made and sample a gin-and-tonic after a tour (£5). **Known for:** craft beer and gin; classic café cuisine; surrounding farmland in a remote location. ⑤ *Average main: £10* ⊠ *Lanton*

The Borders

Mill ⊕ Off the A78 near Jedburgh
☎ 01835/830495 ⊕ www.borninthebor-
ders.com ⊙ No dinner.

🛏 Hotels

Hundalee House

$ | **B&B/INN** | **FAMILY** | The richly decorated
Victorian-style rooms of this 18th-century
stone manor house have nice touches
such as four-poster beds and cozy fireplaces; 15 acres of gardens and woods
surround the B&B. **Pros:** fantastic views
of apple orchards; hearty breakfasts;
lovely views. **Cons:** farm aromas; far from
shops and restaurants; small rooms.
⑤ *Rooms from: £80* ⊠ *Off A68* ⊕ *1 mile
south of Jedburgh* ☎ *01835/863011*
⊕ *www.accommodation-scotland.org*
⊙ *Closed Jan.–Mar* ⇆ *5 rooms* ⊙ *Free
breakfast.*

Meadhon House

$ | **B&B/INN** | On a row of medieval
buildings in the heart of town, Meadhon
House is a charming 17th-century house
with a history to match; rooms are bright
and clean, with views onto the street
or over the large and fragrant garden
behind the house. **Pros:** central location;
pleasant rooms; welcoming atmosphere.
Cons: rooms on the small side; some
street noise; garden not open to guests.
⑤ *Rooms from: £75* ⊠ *48 Castlegate*
☎ *01835/862504* ⊕ *www.meadhon.co.uk*
▭ *No credit cards* ⇆ *5 rooms* ⊙ *Free
breakfast.*

🛍 Shopping

Edinburgh Woollen Mill

CLOTHING | The shelves at this shop burst
with sweaters, kilts, tartan knitwear, and
scarves. It's a good place to stock up on

gifts. ✉ *Bankend North, Edinburgh Rd.*
☎ *01835/863773* ⊕ *www.ewm.co.uk.*

Kelso

12 miles northeast of Jedburgh.

One of the most charming Borders burghs, Kelso is often described as having a Continental flavor—some people think its broad, paved square makes it resemble a Belgian market town. The community also has some fine examples of Georgian and Victorian Scots town architecture.

GETTING HERE AND AROUND

There are direct bus routes from Jedburgh to Kelso. Edinburgh has direct buses to Jedburgh; buses from Glasgow aren't direct. Your best option is to travel by car. From Jedburgh to Kelso take the A698, which is 12 miles, or about 20 minutes. Alternatively, the A699 is a scenic half-hour drive.

ESSENTIALS

VISITOR INFORMATION Kelso Tourist Information Centre. ✉ *Town House, The Square* ☎ *01573/221119* ⊕ *www.kelso.bordernet.co.uk.*

 Sights

★ Floors Castle

CASTLE/PALACE | The palatial Floors Castle, the largest inhabited castle in Scotland, is an architectural extravagance bristling with pepper-mill turrets. Not so much a castle as the ancestral seat of a wealthy and powerful landowning family, the Roxburghes, it stands on the "floors," or flat terrain, on the banks of the River Tweed. The enormous home was built in 1721 by William Adam (1689–1748) and modified by William Playfair (1789–1857), who added the turrets and towers in the 1840s. Rooms are crowded with valuable furniture, paintings, porcelain, and an eerie circular room full of stuffed birds; each room has a knowledgeable

guide at the ready. The surrounding 56,000-acre estate is home to more than 40 farms. Although the castle itself is closed to visitors in winter, the grounds and café are open year-round. ✉ *A6089* ☎ *01573/223333* ⊕ *www.floorscastle. com* 🖾 *Castle and grounds £11.50* ⊙ *Castle closed Nov.–Mar. and weekdays in Oct.*

Kelso Abbey

RELIGIOUS SITE | The least intact ruin of the four great abbeys, Kelso Abbey is just a bleak fragment of what was once the largest of the group. It was here in 1460 that the nine-year-old James III was crowned king of Scotland. On a main invasion route, the abbey was burned three times in the 1540s alone, on the last occasion by the English Earl of Hertford's forces in 1545, when the 100 men and 12 monks of the garrison were butchered and the structure all but destroyed. ✉ *Bridge St.* ☎ *0131/668–8600* ⊕ *www.historicenvironment. scot* 🖾 *Free* ⊙ *Closed Thurs. and Fri. Oct.–Mar.*

Mellerstain House and Gardens

HOUSE | One fine example of the Borders area's ornate country homes is Mellerstain House, begun in the 1720s and finished in the 1770s by Robert Adam (1728–92); it is considered one of his finest creations. Sumptuous plasterwork covers almost all interior surfaces, and there are outstanding examples of 18th-century furnishings, porcelain and china, and paintings and embroidery. The beautiful terraced gardens (open an hour before the house itself) are as renowned as the house. ✉ *Off A6089, Gordon* ✛ *7 miles northwest of Kelso* ☎ *01573/410636* ⊕ *www.mellerstain.com* 🖾 *Gardens £6, house and gardens £10* ⊙ *Closed Tues.–Thurs. and Oct.–Mar.*

★ Smailholm Tower

BUILDING | Standing uncompromisingly on top of a barren, rocky ridge in the hills south of Mellerstain, this 16th-century peel tower, characteristic of the Borders,

The grand Abbotsford House was once home to Sir Walter Scott.

was built solely for defense, and its unadorned stones contrast with the luxury of Mellerstain House. If you let your imagination wander at this windy spot, you can almost see the rising dust of an advancing raiding party. Sir Walter Scott found this spot inspiring, and he visited the tower often during his childhood. Anne Carrick's tableaux in the tower illustrate some of Scott's Borders ballads, and the ticket includes an audio tour of the building. ⊠ *Kelso* ✛ *Off B6404, 4½ miles south of Mellerstain House* ☎ *01573/460365* ⊕ *www.historicenvironment.scot* 🎫 *£6* ⏱ *Closed Oct.–Mar.*

🍴 Restaurants

The Cobbles

$$ | BRITISH | Just off the town's cobbled square, this well-established pub and restaurant with wooden tables and a bustling, cheerful atmosphere seems to be permanently busy. The extensive menu combines generously sized burgers, steaks, and meat pies with the ever-popular fish-and-chips. **Known for:** housemade desserts; craft beer menu; generous portions of classic Scottish cuisine. ⑤ *Average main: £16* ⊠ *7 Bowmont St.* ☎ *01573/223548* ⊕ *www.thecobbleskelso.co.uk.*

Hotels

★ Ednam House Hotel

$$ | HOTEL | This rather grand building on the banks of the River Tweed is close to Kelso's great abbey and sprawling market square. **Pros:** great outdoor activities; atmospheric lobby; impressive restaurant. **Cons:** some rooms need a makeover; popular for weddings and other events, so can be crowded; rooms with a river view cost more. ⑤ *Rooms from: £189* ⊠ *Bridge St.* ☎ *01573/224168* ⊕ *www.ednamhouse.com* ⏱ *Closed late Dec.–early Jan.* 🛏 *32 rooms* 🍴 *Free breakfast.*

Melrose

15 miles west of Kelso, 4 miles south-east of Galashiels.

Though it's small, there is nevertheless a bustle about Melrose, the perfect example of a prosperous Scottish market town and one of the loveliest in the Borders. It's set around a square lined with 18th- and 19th-century buildings housing myriad small shops and cafés. Despite its proximity to the much larger Galashiels, Melrose has rejected industrialization. You'll likely hear local residents greet each other by first name in the square.

GETTING HERE AND AROUND

Buses do go to Melrose, and the Borders Railway ends at Tweedbank, just 2 miles to the northwest. Driving remains the easiest way to get here from the south or east. From Galashiels, take the A6091 (10 minutes).

Sights

★ Abbotsford House

HOUSE | In this great house overlooking the Tweed, Sir Walter Scott lived, worked, and received the great and the good in luxurious salons. In 1811 the writer bought a farm on this site named Cartleyhole, which was a euphemism for the real name, Clartyhole (*clarty* is Scots for "muddy" or "dirty"). The romantic Scott renamed the property after a ford in the nearby Tweed used by the abbot of Melrose. Scott eventually had the house entirely rebuilt in the Scottish baronial style. It was an expensive project, and Scott wrote feverishly to keep his creditors at bay. John Ruskin, the art critic, disapproved, calling it an "incongruous pile," but most contemporary visitors find it fascinating, particularly because of its expansive views and delightful gardens.

A free audio tour guides you around the salon, the circular study, and the library with its 9,000 leather-bound volumes.

Perhaps more than anyone else, Scott redefined Scotland as a place of mystery and romance, and awoke the English, who read him avidly, to its natural beauty and its past—or at least a heavily dramatized version of it. The visitor center houses displays about Scott's life, a gift shop, and a restaurant serving lunch. To get here, take the A6091 from Melrose and follow the signs for Abbotsford. ⊠ *B6360* ✛ *Between Melrose and Tweedbank* ☎ *01896/752043* ⊕ *www.scottsabbotsford.co.uk* ✉ *House and gardens £11.20; gardens only £5.60* ⊘ *House closed Dec.–Feb.*

Dryburgh Abbey

RELIGIOUS SITE | The final resting place of Sir Walter Scott and his wife, and the most peaceful and secluded of the Borders abbeys, the "gentle ruins" of Dryburgh Abbey sit on parkland in a loop of the Tweed. The abbey, founded in 1150, suffered from English raids until, like Melrose, it was abandoned in 1544. The style is transitional, a mingling of rounded Romanesque and pointed early English. The north transept, where the Haig and Scott families lie buried, is lofty and pillared, and once formed part of the abbey church. ⊠ *St. Boswell's, B6404* ☎ *01835/822381* ⊕ *www.historicenvironment.scot* ✉ *£6.*

★ Melrose Abbey

RELIGIOUS SITE | Just off Melrose's town square sit the ruins of Melrose Abbey, one of the four Borders abbeys: "If thou would'st view fair Melrose aright, go visit it in the pale moonlight," wrote Scott in *The Lay of the Last Minstrel.* So many of his fans took the advice literally that a custodian begged him to rewrite the lines. Today the abbey is still impressive: a red-sandstone shell with slender windows, delicate tracery, and carved capitals, all carefully maintained. Among the carvings high on the roof is one of a bagpipe-playing pig. An audio tour is included in the admission price. The heart of 14th-century national hero Robert

Of the ruined abbeys in the Borders, Melrose is notable for its red-sandstone architecture and carvings.

the Bruce is rumored to be buried here. You can tour the on-site museum and its historical artifacts for free in July and August, but be sure to book in advance. ✉ *Abbey St.* ☎ *01896/822562* ⊕ *www. historicenvironment.scot* 🎫 *£6.*

Priorwood Garden and Harmony Garden

GARDEN | The National Trust for Scotland's Priorwood Garden, next to Melrose Abbey, specializes in flowers for drying, and dried flowers are on sale in the shop. Next to the gardens is an orchard with some old apple varieties. The walled Harmony Garden, belonging to the lovely Georgian house at its heart, sits nearby opposite the abbey. ✉ *Abbey St.* ☎ *01896/822493* ⊕ *www.nts.org.uk* 🎫 *Free* 🕐 *Closed Nov.–Mar.*

Restaurants

Hergés on the Loch

$$ | **ECLECTIC** | At this light and airy place, a wall of windows allows you to contemplate swans and ducks as they float serenely across Gunknowe Loch, and,

if the weather allows, you can dine on the terrace. The elegant but understated food, well presented and served in generous portions, includes familiar dishes like steak-and-ale pie, fish-and-chips, and steak. **Known for:** restful setting with loch views; reasonable prices; familiar food prepared imaginatively. ⑤ *Average main: £15* ✉ *Tweedbank Dr., Tweedbank* ☎ *01896/759909* ⊕ *www.hergesontheloch.com.*

🛏 Hotels

Burts Hotel

$$ | **HOTEL** | Dating from the 18th century, this charming whitewashed building in the center of Melrose has individually decorated and different rooms filled with floral pastels. **Pros:** walking distance to restaurants and pubs; good restaurant on-site; central location. **Cons:** rooms can be tiny; slightly overpriced for some rooms; bar can get noisy. ⑤ *Rooms from: £148* ✉ *Market Sq.* ☎ *01896/822285* ⊕ *www.burtshotel.co.uk* 🛏 *20 rooms* 🍽 *Free breakfast.*

Dryburgh Abbey Hotel

$ | HOTEL | Mature woodlands and verdant lawns surround this imposing, 19th-century mansion-turned-hotel, which is adjacent to the ruins of Dryburgh Abbey on a sweeping bend of the River Tweed. **Pros:** beautiful grounds; romantic setting; swimming pool, a rarity in this part of the country. **Cons:** some rooms need to be freshened up; service can be on the slow side; some (but not all) rooms look out onto the grounds. ⑤ *Rooms from: £114 ⊠ Off B6404, St. Boswells ☎ 01835/822261 ⊕ www.dryburgh.co.uk ↪ 38 rooms ⃝ Free breakfast.*

Shopping

Abbey Mill

CLOTHING | Take a break from sightseeing at Abbey Mill, where you'll find hand-woven knitwear as well as homemade jams and fudge. The wee tearoom is also popular. ⊠ *Annay Rd.* ☎ *01896/822138.*

Selkirk

6 miles south of Galashiels, 11 miles north of Hawick.

Selkirk is a hilly outpost with a smattering of antiques shops and an assortment of bakers selling Selkirk bannock (fruited sweet bread) and other cakes. It is the site of one of Scotland's iconic battles, Flodden Field, commemorated here with a statue in the town. Sir Walter Scott was sheriff (judge) of Selkirkshire from 1800 until his death in 1832, and his statue stands in Market Place. Selkirk is also near Bowhill, a stately home.

The town claims its Common Riding (⊕ *returntotheridings.co.uk*) is the largest mounted gathering anywhere in Europe. More than 400 riders take part in the event in June. It's also the oldest Borders festival, with roots back to the Battle of Flodden in 1513.

GETTING HERE AND AROUND

If you're driving, take the A7 south to Galashiels. The scenic journey is less than 7 miles and takes around 10 minutes. First Edinburgh Bus offers a regular service between Galashiels and Selkirk.

ESSENTIALS

VISITOR INFORMATION Selkirk Visitor Information Centre. ⊠ *Halliwell's House, Market Pl.* ☎ *01750/20054* ⊕ *www.visitscotland.com.*

Sights

Bowhill

HOUSE | Home of the Duke of Buccleuch, Bowhill dates from the 19th century and houses an outstanding collection of works by Gainsborough, Van Dyck, Canaletto, Reynolds, and Raeburn, as well as porcelain and period furniture. Although the grounds are mostly accessible from April through September, access to the house is only by guided tours on specific days in the summer; check the website for exact dates. There is an excellent adventure playground for the kids and a 57-mile country ride for those who prefer horseback riding. A local stable hires out horses. ⊠ *Off A708 ✛ 3 miles west of Selkirk* ☎ *01750/22204* ⊕ *www.bowhillhouse.co.uk* ⊠ *Grounds £5.50, house and grounds £11* ⊗ *Closed Oct.–Mar. and Mon.–Thurs. in June and Sept.*

Lochcarron Visitor Centre

FACTORY | You can take an informative guided tour of this world-renowned working textile mill and also purchase some of the best woolen goods on offer, from knitwear to tartans and tweeds. The shop also sells Scottish jewelry. ⊠ *Dinsdale Rd.* ☎ *01750/726100* ⊕ *www.lochcarron.com* ⊠ *Tour £9.95* ⊗ *Closed Sun.*

Sir Walter Scott's Courtroom

MUSEUM | The historic courtroom where Sir Walter Scott presided as sheriff from 1804 to 1832 contains a display examining his life, writings, and time on the bench. It uses models to re-create the atmosphere of a 19th-century Scottish court and includes an audio-visual presentation. A statue of the famous writer overlooks the comings and goings outside the court. ⊠ *Market Sq.* ☎ *01750/720761* ⊕ *www.scotborders. gov.uk* 🎟 *Free* ⊘ *Closed Nov.–Feb.*

Hotels

Best Western Philipburn House Hotel

$$ | HOTEL | West of Selkirk, this Alpine-style hotel enjoys a lovely setting among the woods and hills. **Pros:** pleasant rural setting; bright rooms; on-site parking. **Cons:** no elevator; restaurant closes rather early; breakfast is extra. ⑤ *Rooms from: £130* ⊠ *Linglie Rd.* ✛ *Opposite Salmon Viewing Centre* ☎ *01750/720747* ⊕ *www.bw-philipburnhousehotel.co.uk* ⇄ *24 rooms* ⎮⊙⎮ *No meals.*

Innerleithen

17 miles northwest of Hawick.

Innerleithen is one of the larger Borders towns; you'll feel that you've entered a hub of activity when you arrive. It's also dramatically beautiful. Surrounded by hills and glens, the town is where the Tweed and Leithen rivers join, then separate. Historically, Innerleithen dates back to pre-Roman times, and there are artifacts all around for you to see. Once a booming industrial town of wool mills, today it's a great destination for outdoor activities including hiking, biking, and fly-fishing.

GETTING HERE AND AROUND

To drive to Innerleithen, take the A7 north from Hawick and then the A707 north-west from Selkirk. There are no trains between the two towns.

Sights

Robert Smail's Printing Works

FACTORY | FAMILY | Try your hand at printing the way it used to be done: painstakingly setting each letter by hand. Robert Smail's print shop, founded in 1866 to produce materials for nearby factories, boat tickets, theater posters, and the local newspaper, is still a working print shop as well as a museum. Two great waterwheels once powered the presses, and they are still running. The guided tour, which includes making your own bookmark, takes 90 minutes. ⊠ *7–9 High St.* ☎ *01896/830206* ⊕ *www.nts. org.uk* 🎟 *£7* ⊘ *Closed Oct.–Mar. and Tues.–Thurs.*

★ Traquair House

HOUSE | Said to be the oldest continually occupied home in Scotland (since 1107), Traquair House has secret stairways and passages, a library with more than 3,000 books, and a bed said to be used by Mary, Queen of Scots in 1566. You can walk freely through the rooms, and each has an explanatory leaflet as well as helpful guides. The top floor of the house is an interesting small museum. Outside is a reasonably scary maze, an adventure playground, and some lovely woodland walks as well as pigs, goats, and chickens. The 18th-century brew house still makes highly recommended ale, and there's a café on the grounds near the beautiful walled garden. The Traquair Fair in August is the nearest you are likely to get to a medieval fair, and well worth the visit. You may even spend the night, if you wish. ⊠ *B709* ✛ *From the A70 some 6 miles south of Peebles, take the B709 for 7 miles; the car entrance into the house is in the village* ☎ *01896/830323* ⊕ *www.traquair.co.uk* 🎟 *Grounds £4, house and grounds £8.80, guided tours £10* ⊘ *Closed Dec.–Mar. and weekdays in Nov.*

With a history dating back to 1107, Traquair House is allegedly the oldest continually occupied house in Scotland.

Hotels

Traquair House

$$ | **B&B/INN** | Staying in one of the guest rooms in the 12th-century wing of Traquair House is to experience a slice of Scottish history. **Pros:** stunning grounds; spacious rooms; great breakfast. **Cons:** nearly 2 miles to restaurants and shops, rooms fill up quickly in summer; parking can be difficult in summer months. $ *Rooms from: £200* ✉ *B709* ☎ *01896/830323* ⊕ *www.traquair.co.uk* 🛏 *3 rooms* 🍽 *Free breakfast.*

Windlestraw Lodge

$$ | **HOTEL** | This elegant bed-and-breakfast and restaurant occupies a grand Edwardian country home surrounded by extensive gardens. **Pros:** beautifully designed rooms; excellent restaurant; lovely location. **Cons:** a bit expensive for what you get; not all rooms have Tweed views; restaurant is pricey. $ *Rooms from: £190* ✉ *9 Galashiels Rd., Walkerburn* ✛ *On the A72 between Galashiels and Innerleithen* ☎ *01896/870636* ⊕ *www.windlestraw. co.uk* 🛏 *6 rooms* 🍽 *Free breakfast.*

Dumfries

24 miles west of Gretna Green, 76 miles south of Glasgow, 81 miles southwest of Edinburgh.

The River Nith meanders through Dumfries, and the pedestrian-only center of this town of 31,000 makes wandering and shopping a pleasure. Author J. M. Barrie (1860–1937) spent his childhood in Dumfries, and the garden of Moat Brae House is said to have inspired his boyish dreams in *Peter Pan*. But the town also has a justified claim to Robert Burns, who lived and worked here for several years. His house and his favorite *howff* (pub), The Globe Inn, are here, too, as is his final resting place in St. Michael's Churchyard.

The Dumfries & Galloway Tourist Board has a lodging service and also sells golf passes for the region at £70 for three rounds.

GETTING HERE AND AROUND

Public transportation is a good option for reaching Dumfries—there's a good train station here, and most major Scottish cities have regular daily bus routes to the town. If you're driving from Gretna Green, take the A75; it's a 35-minute drive. From Glasgow take the M74 to the A701. From Edinburgh take the A701.

ESSENTIALS

VISITOR INFORMATION Dumfries & Galloway Tourist Board. ⊠ *64 Whitesands* ☎ *01387/253862* ⊕ *www.visitscotland. com.*

Sights

Dumfries Museum and Camera Obscura

MUSEUM | A camera obscura is essentially a huge reflecting mirror that projects an extraordinarily clear panoramic view of the surrounding countryside onto an internal wall. The one at the Dumfries Museum, which claims to be the oldest in the world, is housed in the old Windmill Tower, built in 1836. The museum itself covers the culture and daily life of the people living in the Dumfries and Galloway region from the earliest times. ⊠ *Rotchell Rd.* ☎ *01387/253374* ⊕ *www.dumgal.gov.uk/artsandmuseums* ⊠ *Museum free; Camera Obscura £3.60* ⊗ *Closed Nov.–Mar.*

Globe Inn

HISTORIC SITE | Poet Robert Burns spent quite a lot of time at the Globe Inn, where he frequently fell asleep in the tack room beside the stables; today it's still an active pub where you can eat and drink. Burns later graduated to the upstairs bedroom where he slept with his wife, Jean Armour, and scratched some lines of poetry on the window. The room is preserved (or at least partly re-created), and the bar staff will happily show you around if you ask. But beware, if you choose to sit in Burns's chair in the bar, tradition has it that you have to buy a round for the whole pub. ⊠ *56 High St.* ☎ *01387/252335* ⊕ *www.globeinndumfries.co.uk* ⊠ *Free.*

Gracefield Arts Centre

ARTS CENTERS | With galleries hosting changing exhibits of Scottish art mostly from the 1840s to today, Gracefield Arts Centre also has a well-stocked crafts shop. A café serves lunch and snacks. ⊠ *28 Edinburgh Rd.* ☎ *01387/262084* ⊕ *www.exploreart.co.uk* ⊠ *Free.*

Moat Brae and the Neverland Garden

HOUSE | FAMILY | Writer J.M. Barrie was a regular visitor to the Gordon family's grand Edwardian home at Moat Brae. The stories he told their children would eventually go on to become the tale of *Peter Pan*, and the house's on-site garden was the inspiration for Neverland. Today the garden has a replica of Captain Hook's ship, where kids can play. After coming perilously close to demolition, the house was saved and restored to its original state over several years, and the on-site center has been conceived as a National Storytelling Centre rather than simply a historical museum. It's meant to be a place where today's children can exercise their own imaginations. In the children's bedroom, Tinkerbell flies around the walls, and you can try to catch her. ⊠ *101 George St.* ☎ *01387/255549* ⊕ *www.peterpanmoatbrae.org* ⊗ *Closed Mon. Sept.–Apr.*

Robert Burns Centre

MUSEUM | Not surprisingly, Dumfries has its own Robert Burns Centre, housed in a sturdy 18th-century former mill overlooking the River Nith. The center has an audiovisual program and an extensive exhibit about the life of the poet. It also now houses Dumfries's only cinema. ⊠ *Mill Rd.* ☎ *01387/264808* ⊕ *www.dumgal.gov.uk/artsandmuseums* ⊠ *Free.*

Robert Burns House

HOUSE | Poet Robert Burns (1759–96) lived here, on what was then called Mill

Dumfries and Galloway

ENGLAND

Irish Sea

North Channel

Carlisle
Wigton
Maryport
Working-on
Silloth
Solway Firth

Langholm
Longtown
Gretna Green
Eastriggs
Ecclefechan
Annan
Lockerbie
Lochmaben
Moffat

Thornhill
Museum of Lead Mining
Crawick Multiverse
Sanquhar
Drumlanrig Castle
North of Dumfries
Striding Arches
Menaive
Carsphairn

Dumfries
Crocketford
New Abbey
Dalbeattie
Colvend
A710
ABBEY HEAD

DUMFRIES AND GALLOWAY

Corsock
Castle Douglas
Threave Garden and Estate
Threave Castle
Kirkcudbright
Borgue
Gatehouse of Fleet
A711

New Galloway
Creetown
EGGERNESS POINT
Wigtown Bay
Whithorn
Isle of Whithorn

EAST AYRSHIRE
New Cumnock
Dalmellington

SOUTH AYRSHIRE
Barr
Barrhill
Maybole
Turnberry
Girvan
Ballantrae

Newton Stewart
Wigtown
Port William
A747

Glenluce
Sandhead
Castle Kennedy Gardens
Stranraer
Loch Ryan
RHINNE OF GALLOWAY
Portpatrick
Port Logan
Drummore
MULL OF GALLOWAY
CRAMMAG HEAD
Luce Bay

AILSA CRAIG

10 mi
10 km
0

Street, for the last three years of his life, when his salary from the customs service allowed him to improve his living standards. Many distinguished writers of the day visited him here, including William Wordsworth. The house contains some of his writings and letters, a few pieces of furniture, and some family memorabilia. ⊠ *Burns St.* ☎ *01387/255297* ⊕ *www.dumgal.gov.uk/ artsandmuseums* ⊠ *Free.*

St. Michael's Churchyard

CEMETERY | When he died in 1796, Robert Burns was buried in a modest grave in St. Michael's Churchyard. English poet William Wordsworth, visiting a few years later, was horrified by the small gravestone and raised money to build the much grander monument that stands there today. ⊠ *39 Cardiness St.* ☎ *01387/253849* ⊕ *www.dumgal.gov.uk/ artsandmuseums* ⊠ *Free.*

Restaurants

Cavens Arms

$ | BRITISH | This lively, welcoming traditional pub in the center of town has a separate bar and dining area, comfortable seating, and a large selection of beers. It's a magnet for locals at dinnertime and always seems to be busy, a testimony to the quality of its food as well as the large portions. **Known for:** local beers; good food in generous pub portions; vibrant atmosphere. ⑤ *Average main: £13* ⊠ *20 Buccleuch St.* ☎ *01387/252896.*

The Stove Cafe

$ | BAKERY | In the very center of Dumfries, this café offers wholesome breakfasts, sandwiches, and cakes. It's also a blossoming arts center with music and other events throughout the year. **Known for:** good coffee; relaxed atmosphere good for hanging out; popular breakfasts and brunches. ⑤ *Average main: £10* ⊠ *100 High St.* ☎ *01387/252435* ⊕ *www. thestove.org* ⊗ *Closed Sun.*

Hotels

Cairndale Hotel

$ | HOTEL | Centrally located, the Cairndale has a Victorian Gothic appearance and spacious and comfortable rooms. **Pros:** central location; comfortable rooms; pool, sauna, and gym. **Cons:** generally old-fashioned feel; can get very crowded; small lobby. ⑤ *Rooms from: £93* ⊠ *132–6 English St.* ☎ *01387/354111* ⊕ *www. cairndalehotel.co.uk* ⊅ *91 rooms* ◉ *Free breakfast.*

Shopping

★ Loch Arthur Creamery and Farm Shop

FOOD/CANDY | Known for its high-quality dairy products, this lively and active farm run by the Camphill community in the charmingly named village of Beeswing has an expansive café and retail store selling a range of organic products. Much of what you eat or buy is produced on the farm, where they make their own bread, butcher their meat, and cook the delicious food served here. The building itself has large windows opening directly on to the fields beyond; on a nice day, you can eat outside. There's always freshly baked bread, cakes, cheeses, cold meats, and soups to choose from, all made on the farm. ⊠ *On A711, Beeswing* ✛ *6 miles south of Dumfries* ☎ *01387/259669* ⊕ *www.locharthur.org.uk.*

North of Dumfries

18 miles northwest of Dumfries.

Travel north along the A70 from Dumfries for a short trip through time at some very different attractions. Drumlanrig Castle is one of Scotland's grandest houses, set amid hills, moorland, and forest. In contrast, the world of lead miners, explored at the Museum of Lead Mining, was a great deal harsher. A spectacular modern addition to the area, the land artwork *Crawick Multiverse*, transforms the landscape into a mirror of the heavens. Sculptor Andy Goldsworthy's *Striding Arches* frame a natural space and invite the walker to explore them.

GETTING HERE AND AROUND

Trains run from Dumfries to Sanquhar, near *Crawick Multiverse*. You can get a bus from Dumfries to Drumlanrig and Sanquhar along the A701. For Ledhills and the mining museum, it's best to drive. The same is true for *Striding Arches*: Take the A76 from Dumfried to Thornhill, and then the A702 toward Monaive.

 ## Sights

★ *Crawick Multiverse*

PUBLIC ART | The extraordinary 2015 land artwork by Charles Jencks, 45 minutes north of Dumfries near the village of Sanquhar, must surely become a focus for visitors to the region for years to come. Jencks has transformed a 55-acre site, once an open-pit mine, into a beautiful and inspiring created landscape, at the heart of which are two grass spiral mounds that represent the Milky Way and the Andromeda Constellation. But they are simply the heart of a site where woodland, moor, mountain, and desert meet. Local rocks have been lifted to form avenues and labyrinths across the site. As you look across from its highest point, it is as if you were looking in a mirror in which the skies were reflected on the earth. Set aside two or three hours at least for the experience. ✉ *Crawick, Off B740, by Sanquhar* ✛ *Take the A75 toward Kirkconnel from Sanquhar, then turn on to the B740 (signposted Crawfordjohn)* ☎ *01659/50242* ⊕ *www.crawickmultiverse.co.uk* ✆ *£5.*

★ Drumlanrig Castle

CASTLE/PALACE | **FAMILY** | A spectacular estate, Drumlanrig Castle is as close as Scotland gets to the treasure houses of England—which is not surprising, since it's owned by the dukes of Buccleuch, one of the wealthiest British peerages.

Resplendent with romantic turrets, this pink-sandstone palace was constructed between 1679 and 1691 by the first Duke of Queensbury, who, after nearly bankrupting himself building the place, stayed one night and never returned. The Buccleuchs inherited the palace and filled the richly decorated rooms with paintings by Holbein, Rembrandt, and Murillo, among others. Because of the theft of a Leonardo da Vinci painting in 2003, all visits are conducted by guided tour. There is also a playground, a gift shop, and a tearoom. The grounds are varied and good for mountain biking; bikes can be rented at the castle. ✉ *Off A76, Thornhill* ✛ *18 miles northwest of Dumfries* ☎ *01848/600283* ⊕ *www.drumlanrig.com* ✆ *Park £6, castle and park £12* ⊘ *Closed Oct.–Mar.*

Museum of Lead Mining

MUSEUM | The Lochnell Mine was abandoned in 1861, after 150 years of operation, and the mine and miners' homes now form part of this museum re-creating their lives. The isolated village of Warnlockhead, where the mine was located, has not changed a great deal since then—there was little alternative employment for the miners and their families. The visitor center, housed in the old smithy, exhibits some of the minerals the mine yielded. The nearby Leadhills and Warnlockhead Narrow Gauge Railway runs on weekends throughout the summer and costs £4, with a 10% reduction for a joint ticket with the museum. ✉ *Off B797, Wanlockhead* ✛ *32 miles north of Dumfries* ☎ *01659/74387* ⊕ *www.leadminingmuseum.co.uk* ✆ *£12.95 for mine, cottages, and library; £5 mine only* ⊘ *Closed Oct.–Mar.*

Striding Arches

PUBLIC ART | British sculptor Andy Goldsworthy's extraordinary piece of public landscape art enriches the great natural amphitheater at Cairnhead in the southern uplands of Dumfries and Galloway. His three red-sandstone arches

Visits to Drumlanrig Castle are now by guided tour only, after a theft of a da Vinci painting occured here in 2003.

stand 13 feet high and mark out the area, "striding" across the landscape and symbolizing all those who have left the area and migrated in search of work or better lives. ✉ *Cairnhead Forest, near Moniaive* ⊹ *Take the A702 (off the A76 at Thornhill) to Moniaive, then the road to Benbuie until you reach The Byre. From there it is a walk to the viewpoint* ☏ *07801/232229* ⊕ *www.stridingarches.com* ✉ *Free.*

Castle Douglas

18 miles southwest of Dumfries, 25 miles west of Caerlaverock Castle, 84 miles south of Glasgow, 90 miles southwest of Edinburgh.

A quaint town that sits beside Carlingwark Loch, Castle Douglas is a popular base for exploring the surrounding countryside. The loch sets off the town perfectly, reflecting its dramatic architecture of sharp spires and soft sandstone arches. Its main thoroughfare, King Street, has unique shops and eateries.

GETTING HERE AND AROUND
There's no train station in Castle Douglas, and buses from Dumfries make several stops along the way. The best way to get here is by car. From Dalbeattie take the A711/A745 (10 minutes). From Glasgow take the A713 (just under two hours). From Edinburgh take the A70 (a little over 2 hours).

 Sights

★ Threave Castle
CASTLE/PALACE | Once home to the Black Douglases, who were the earls of Nithsdale and lords of Galloway, Threave's imposing towers reflect well the Lord of Galloway who built it, Archibald the Grim, in the 14th century. Not to be confused with the mansion in Threave Gardens, the castle was dismantled in the religious wars of the mid-17th century, though enough of it remained to have housed prisoners from the Napoleonic Wars two centuries later. It's a few minutes from Castle Douglas by car and is signposted from the main road. To get here, leave

your car in a farmyard and make your way down to the edge of the river. Ring the bell (loudly) and, rather romantically, a boatman will come to ferry you across to the great stone tower looming from a marshy island in the river. ⊠ *A75* ✛ *3 miles west of Castle Douglas* ☎ *07711/223101* ⊕ *www.historicenvironment.scot* ⊠ *£6 including ferry; buy tickets online or from the NTS Osprey Centre on the site (cash only)* ⊗ *Closed Nov.–Mar.*

Threave Garden and Estate
GARDEN | The National Trust for Scotland cares for the gently sloping parkland and gardens around an 1867 mansion built by William Gordon, a Liverpool business man. The house, fully restored in the 1930s, gives a glimpse into the daily life of a prosperous 19th-century family. The grounds demand an army of gardeners, and today many of them are students at the National Trust's School of Heritage Gardening, which has developed the variety of gardens here. Bats, ospreys, and other birds and animals share the space. Entry to the house is by timed guided tour, and it's wise to book ahead. There's an on-site restaurant. ⊠ *South of A75* ✛ *1 mile west of Castle Douglas* ☎ *01556/502575* ⊕ *www.nts.org.uk/Visits* ⊠ *Gardens £9, house and gardens £15, nature reserve free* ⊗ *Gardens closed Dec.–Feb. House closed Nov.–Apr.*

🍴 Restaurants

The Café at Designs Gallery
$ | CAFÉ | For a good balance of art and food, look no further than this café at a contemporary art and crafts gallery in the town center. You'll find the freshest ingredients here, from soup to salads, sandwiches to quiches; everything is made on-site, including the bread, and it's all organic. **Known for:** good lunch menu; housemade soups; lovely garden. ⑤ *Average main. £9* ⊠ *179 King St.* ☎ *01556/504552* ⊕ *www.designsgallery.co.uk* ⊗ *Closed Sun. No dinner.*

🛍 Shopping

By the Book
BOOKS/STATIONERY | This well-stocked and (more important) well-organized second-hand bookshop on Castle Douglas's main shopping street has large windows that invite you in to browse, which you can do without interruption—there's bound to be something you want, though it may be in a box or under the table. ⊠ *201 King St.* ☎ *01556/503338.*

Galloway Gems and Craft Centre and Outback Yarns
CRAFTS | In this glittery shop you can purchase mineral specimens, polished stone slices, and a range of Celtic and Nordic-inspired jewelry, as well as craft materials of every kind. For fiber artists and sewers, it's a real find. ⊠ *130–132 King St.* ☎ *01556/503254* ⊕ *www.outbackyarns.co.uk.*

Kirkcudbright

9 miles southwest of Castle Douglas, 89 miles south of Glasgow, 99 miles southwest of Edinburgh.

Kirkcudbright (pronounced kir-coo-bray) is an 18th-century town of Georgian and Victorian houses, some of them washed in pastel shades and roofed with the blue slate of the district. It sits on an inlet from the Solway Firth. In the early 20th century the town became a haven for artists, and its L-shaped main street is full of crafts and antiques shops.

GETTING HERE AND AROUND
Driving is your best and only real option. From Castle Douglas take the A711 (15 minutes). From Glasgow take the A713 (about two hours). From Edinburgh take the A701 (about 2½ hours).

ESSENTIALS

VISITOR INFORMATION VisitScotland
Kirkcudbright iCentre. ⊠ *Harbour Sq.*
☎ *01557/330494* ⊕ *www.visitscotland.
com.*

 Sights

★ Broughton House

HOUSE | The 18th-century Broughton
House was the home of the artist E. A.
Hornel from 1901 until his death in 1933
and remains largely as it was in his time.
Hornel was a member of the school of
painters called the "Glasgow Boys," who
were influenced by the Vienna Secession
and art nouveau. You can see many of
his paintings in the gallery Hornel built
onto the house to impress the guests
and buyers who came to see his work.
His use and love of color is obvious in
the beautiful garden, which combines
lawns, ponds, and formal and wildflower
beds. The knowledgeable guides will
gladly provide information about the
life and work of the painter. ⊠ *12 High
St.* ☎ *01557/330437* ⊕ *www.nts.org.uk*
⊠ *£8* ⊙ *House closed Nov.–Mar. Garden
closed Nov.–Jan.*

MacLellan's Castle

CASTLE/PALACE | Conspicuous in the
center of town are the stone walls of
MacLellan's Castle, a once-elaborate
castellated mansion dating from the 16th
century. You can walk around the interior,
still atmospheric even though the rooms
are bare. The "Lairds Lug," behind the
fireplace, allowed the *laird* (lord) to listen
in to what his guests were saying about
him. You can also get a glimpse of life
below stairs in the kitchen vaults beneath
the main staircase. The mansion has
lovely views over the town. ⊠ *Off High
St.* ☎ *01557/331856* ⊕ *www.histori-
cenvironment.scot* ⊠ *£4.80* ⊙ *Closed
Oct.–Mar.*

Tolbooth Arts Centre

ARTS VENUE | In the 17th-century
tolbooth (a combination town hall–
courthouse–prison), the Tolbooth Arts
Centre describes how the town attracted
famous artists, among them E. A. Hornel,
Jessie King, and Charles Oppenheimer.
Some of their paintings are on display,
as are works by contemporary artists.
⊠ *High St.* ☎ *01557/331556* ⊕ *www.
dumgal.gov.uk* ⊠ *Free* ⊙ *Closed Sun.
Oct.–May.*

 Restaurants

Artistas at the Selkirk Arms

$$ | **MODERN BRITISH** | Paintings of Scot-
land, starched white tablecloths, and
giant windows overlooking the well-
kept garden beckon you into this highly
praised eatery. Locals love that the food
on the bar and regular menus is locally
sourced and full of imagination. **Known
for:** local produce; both familiar and
more exotic dishes; charming location
in town. ⑤ *Average main: £16* ⊠ *Selkirk
Arms, High St.* ☎ *01557/330402* ⊕ *www.
selkirkarmshotel.co.uk.*

 Hotels

★ Selkirk Arms

$ | **HOTEL** | Bursting with charm, this
elegant 18th-century hotel has a lot going
for it, including spacious guest rooms
that are individually decorated with cozy
beds, contemporary wood furniture, and
soft lighting. **Pros:** free Wi-Fi; massive
breakfast; lively traditional pub. **Cons:**
rooms closest to restaurant can be noisy;
bar gets crowded during sporting events;
some rooms are small. ⑤ *Rooms from:
£99* ⊠ *High St.* ☎ *01557/330402* ⊕ *www.
selkirkarmshotel.co.uk* ⇆ *16 rooms*
⑩ *Free breakfast.*

Whithorn

17 miles south of Newton Stewart, 94 miles southwest of Glasgow, 121 miles southwest of Edinburgh.

Known for its early Christian settlement, Whithorn is full of history. The main street is notably wide, with pretty pastel buildings nestled up against each other, their low doorways and small windows creating images of years long past. It's still mainly a farming community but is fast becoming a popular tourist destination. Several scenes from the original *Wicker Man* (1973) were shot in and around the area. During the summer months, it's a popular place for festivals. The Isle of Whithorn, just beyond the town, is not an island at all but a fishing village of great charm.

GETTING HERE AND AROUND

There's no train station in Whithorn, and most of the buses are local (getting to main Scottish cities from Whithorn takes careful planning and several transfers). To drive from Newton Stewart, take the A714 and then A746. From Glasgow take the A77 (about 2½ hours). From Edinburgh take the A702 (about three hours).

Sights

Whithorn Priory and Museum

ARCHAEOLOGICAL SITE | The road that is now the A746 was a pilgrims' path that led to the royal burgh of Whithorn, where sat Whithorn Priory, one of Scotland's great medieval cathedrals, now an empty shell. It was built in the 12th century and is said to occupy the site of a former stone church, the Candida Casa, built by St. Ninian in the 4th century. As the story goes, the church housed a shrine to Ninian, the earliest of Scotland's saints, and kings and barons tried to visit the shrine at least once in their lives.

As you approach the priory, observe the royal arms of pre-1707 Scotland—that is, Scotland before the Union Act with England—carved and painted above the *pend* (covered walkway). The museum houses restored stonework from the period, including crosses. ⊠ *6 Bruce St.* ⊕ *www.historicenvironment.scot* ⊟ *£6 (includes the Whithorn Story and Visitor Centre)* ⊙ *Closed Nov.–Mar.*

🍴 Restaurants

Steam Packet Inn

$$ | BRITISH | Lovely and old-fashioned, this inn is always full, mainly because of its good beer and hearty, well-cooked food including fish-and-chips and lamb shanks. Located directly on the harbor, it has few local rivals, but customers come from far and wide to eat here and walk the headland behind the pub to the rocky shore of the Solway Firth. **Known for:** superior pub food; outstanding desserts; garden dining in nice weather. ⑤ *Average main: £15* ⊠ *Harbour Row, Isle of Whithorn* ☎ *01988/500334* ⊕ *www.thesteampacketinn.biz.*

Stranraer

31 miles northwest of Whithorn, 86 miles southwest of Glasgow via A77, 131 miles southwest of Edinburgh.

Stranraer was for more than a century the main ferry port between Scotland and Northern Ireland. Its closure, and the transfer of ferry traffic to nearby Cairnryan, continues to bring changes to the town. The city center has had a major face-lift, and there are plans to redevelop the harbor as a leisure center and transportation hub. Stranraer also has a lovely garden.

GETTING HERE AND AROUND

Stranraer's train station is directly accessible from Glasgow; bus services are also good (with many connections to smaller towns). If you're driving, take the A747 from Whithorn (about 45 minutes). From Glasgow take the M77/A77 (two hours), and from Edinburgh take the A77 (three hours).

 Sights

★ Castle Kennedy Gardens

GARDEN | The lovely Castle Kennedy Gardens surround the shell of the original Castle Kennedy, which burned down in 1716. Parks scattered around the property were built by the second Earl of Stair in 1733. The earl was a field marshal and used his soldiers to help with the heavy work of constructing banks, ponds, and other major landscape features. When the rhododendrons are in bloom (April through July, depending on the variety), the effect is kaleidoscopic. There's also a pleasant tearoom. ⊠ *, Sheuchan ✛ 3 miles east of Stranraer on the A875* ☎ *01776/702024* ⊕ *www.castlekenne-dygardens.co.uk* ☜ *£4.95* ⊙ *Closed Nov.– Jan. and weekdays in Feb. and Mar.*

THE CENTRAL HIGHLANDS, FIFE, AND ANGUS

Updated by Mike Gonzalez
and Nick Bruno

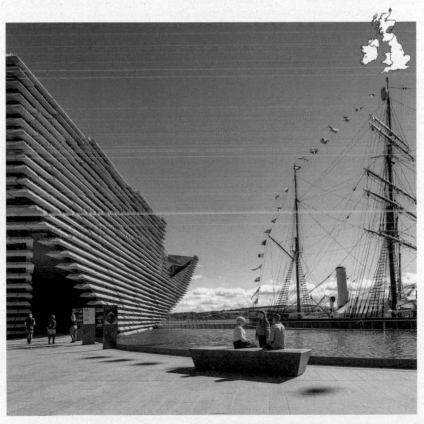

👁 Sights	🍴 Restaurants	🛏 Hotels	💼 Shopping	🍸 Nightlife
★★★★☆	★★★☆☆	★★★☆☆	★★☆☆☆	★★★☆☆

WELCOME TO THE CENTRAL HIGHLANDS, FIFE, AND ANGUS

TOP REASONS TO GO

★ **Loch Lomond:** You can see the sparkling waters of Scotland's largest loch by car, by boat, or on foot. A popular option is the network of bicycle tracks that creep around Loch Lomond and the Trossachs National Park, offering every conceivable terrain.

★ **Castles:** Choosing among Scotland's most splendid fortresses and mansions is a challenge. Among the highlights are Stirling Castle and Scone Palace.

★ **St. Andrews:** With its medieval streets, ruined cathedral and castle, and peculiarly posh atmosphere, St. Andrews is one of the most incongruous yet beguiling places in Scotland—even without its famous golf course.

★ **Great hikes:** The way to experience the Central Highlands is to head out on foot. The less-demanding woodland paths and gentle rambles of the Trossachs will stir even the least adventurous rambler.

The reference points for your trip are Stirling, an ancient historic town from whose castle you can see central Scotland laid out before you; Perth, 36 miles away, the gateway to the Highlands; the city of Dundee, on the river Tay; and the historic center and home of golf, St. Andrews, in Fife. North from Stirling, you cross the fertile open plain (the Carse of Stirling) dotted with historic cathedral towns. The Trossachs are the Scotland of the Romantic imagination, lochs and woodland glens, drovers' inns and grand country houses. The small towns of the region are bases from which to explore this varied countryside. To the west lies Loch Lomond, along whose banks the road leads from industrial Glasgow to the hills and glens of the Highlands.

1 Stirling. A historic town dominated by its castle.

2 Callander. The gateway to the Trossachs.

3 The Trossachs. A national park with every kind of landscape.

4 Aberfoyle. Easy access to Queen Elizabeth Forest Park and the eastern banks of Loch Lomond.

5 Loch Lomond. Scotland's largest and perhaps most famous loch.

6 Perth. Once Scotland's capital and now a gateway to the Highlands.

7 Dunkeld. The land of Beatrix Potter.

8 Pitlochry. An old Victorian spa town.

9 Blair Atholl. Home to Blair Castle, one of Scotland's great houses.

10 Auchterarder. A small Highland town dominated by a famous golf course.

11 St. Andrews. A university town famed for golfing.

12 Crail. A East Neuk fishing village.

13 Anstruther. A working port.

14 Falkland. A royal burgh.

15 Dundee. One of Scotland's most vibrant cities.

16 The Angus Glens. Rolling glens that cut into the Cairngorms.

17 Kirriemuir. Peter Pan's hometown.

18 Glamis. Home to a grand castle.

The Central Highlands are home to superb castles, moody mountains, and gorgeous glens that are best explored at a leisurely pace. The waters of Loch Lomond reflect the crags and dark woods that surround it, and attract those in search of a more romantic and nostalgic Scotland enshrined in the verses of the famous song that bears its name. When you finish a day of exploring, celebrate with a glass of one of the region's top-notch whiskies.

East of the Central Highlands, breezy cliff-top walkways, fishing villages, and open beaches characterize Fife and Angus. They sandwich Scotland's fourth-largest city, the rejuvenated city of Dundee. Scotland's east coast has only light rainfall throughout the year; northeastern Fife, in particular, may claim the record for the most sunshine and the least rainfall in Scotland, which all adds to the enjoyment when you're touring the coast or the famous golf center of St. Andrews.

North from Stirling, past Dunblane, are the birch-, oak-, and pine-covered Highland hills and valleys of the Trossachs, whose high peaks attract walkers and a tougher breed of cyclist. From Callander, a neat tourist town, the hills stretch westward to the "bonnie bonnie banks" of Loch Lomond. The Victorians were drawn here by the lyrical descriptions of the area by Romantic poets like Sir Walter Scott (1771–1832), who set his dramatic verse narrative of 1810, "The Lady of the Lake," in the landscape of the Trossachs. From the peaks of the Trossachs, on a good day, you can see Edinburgh Castle to the east and the tower blocks of Glasgow's housing projects to the west.

Farther north is Perth, once Scotland's capital; its wealthy mansions reflect the prosperous agricultural land that surrounds the city, and it is still an important market town today. Overlooking the River Tay, the city can reasonably claim to be the gateway to the Highlands, sitting as it does on the Highland Fault that divides Lowlands from Highlands. From Perth the landscape begins to change on the road to Pitlochry and the high, rough country of Rannoch Moor.

To the east, Fife proudly styles itself as a "kingdom," and its long history—which really began when the Romans went home in the 4th century and the Picts moved in—lends some substance to the boast. From medieval times its earls were first among Scotland's nobility and crowned her kings. For many, however, the most historic event in the region was the birth of golf, in the 15th century, which, legend has it, occurred in St Andrews, an ancient university town with stone houses and seaside ruins. The Royal & Ancient Golf Club, the ruling body of the game worldwide, still has its headquarters here.

North, across the Firth of Tay, lies the region of Angus, whose charm is its variety: in addition to its seacoast and pleasant Lowland market centers, there's also a hinterland of lonely rounded hills with long glens running into the typical Grampian Highland scenery beyond. One of Angus's interesting features, which it shares with the eastern Lowland edge of Perthshire, is its fruit-growing industry, which includes raspberries. Within it, you'll also find the city of Dundee, once a hub for textile industry based on jute and now seeking a new identity as a city of culture.

MAJOR REGIONS

Stirling. Famous for its castle and vibrant with history, Stirling has a small Old Town on the hill that is worth covering on foot. Look down from the Stirling Castle crag that dominates the plains below and you can see the stages of the city's growth descending from the hill. The town is a good center from which to explore the changing landscape of central Scotland.

The Trossachs and Loch Lomond. Immortalized by Wordsworth and Sir Walter Scott, the Trossachs (the name means "bristly country") contains some of Scotland's loveliest forest, hills, and glens, well justifying the area's designation as a national park. The area has a special charm, combining the wildness of the Highlands with the prolific vegetation of an old Lowland forest. Its open ground is a dense mat of bracken and heather, and its woodland is of silver birch, dwarf oak, and hazel—trees that fasten their

roots into the crevices of rocks and stop short on the very brink of lochs. There are also many small towns to visit along the way, some with their roots in a medieval world; others sprang up and expanded in the wake of the first tourists who came to Scotland in the late 19th century in search of wild country or healing waters. Dunblane has a magnificent cathedral, Doune's castle will make you stare in awe. This area is small but incredibly varied—from dramatic mountain peaks that attract walkers and climbers, to the gentler slopes and forests that stretch from Perth westward to Aberfoyle and the shores of Loch Lomond. The glens and streams that pepper the region create a romantic landscape that is a perfect habitat for the figure of Rob Roy McGregor—Robin Hood or bandit according to taste, but undeniably Scottish. Loch Lomond's western side is more accessible, if busier, than the east, but the views across the loch are spectacular.

The most colorful season is fall, particularly October, a lovely time when most visitors have departed, and the hares, deer, and game birds have taken over. Even in rainy weather the Trossachs of "darksome glens and gleaming lochs" are memorable: the water filtering through the rocks by Loch Lomond comes out so pure and clear that the loch is like a sheet of glass. The best way to explore this area is by car, by bike, or on foot; the latter two depend, of course, on the weather. Keep in mind that roads in this region of the country are narrow and winding, which can make for dangerous conditions in all types of weather.

Perthshire. The prosperous air of Perth, once the capital of Scotland, testifies to its importance as a port exporting wool, salmon, and whisky to the world. Scone Palace serves as a monument to that era. If Perthshire's castles invoke memories of past conflicts, the grand houses and spa towns here are testimony to the continued presence of a wealthy landed gentry. This is also a place for walking, cycling, and water sports. In some ways Perthshire is a crossing point where Lowlands and Highlands, two Scottish landscapes and two histories, meet. Perthshire itself is rural, agricultural Scotland, fertile and prosperous. Its woodlands, rivers, and glens (and agreeable climate and strategic position) drew the Romans and later the Celtic missionaries. In fact, the motto of the capital city, Perth, is "the perfect center." The route northward leads across the Highland Boundary and into the changing landscapes beyond Pitlochry to Rannoch Moor, where the wind sweeps across the hardy heather.

St. Andrews and East Neuk. In its western parts Fife still bears the scars of heavy industry, especially coal mining, but these signs are less evident as you move east. Northeastern Fife, around the town of St. Andrews, seems to have played no part in the Industrial Revolution; instead, its residents earned a living from the grain fields or from the sea. Fishing has been a major industry, and in the past a string of Fife ports traded across the North Sea. Today the legacy of Dutch-influenced architecture, such as crowstepped gables (the stepped effect on the ends of the roofs)—gives these East Neuk villages a distinctive character. St. Andrews is unlike any other Scottish town. Once Scotland's most powerful ecclesiastical center as well as the seat of the country's oldest university and then, much later, the very symbol and spiritual home of golf, the town has a comfortable, well-groomed air, sitting almost smugly apart from the rest of Scotland. Its latest cachet is being the place where the riveting 21st-century royal romance between Prince William and Kate Middleton began, which boosted university applications from around the world.

Dundee and Angus. The small, friendly city of Dundee sits near the mouth of the River Tay surrounded by the farms and glens of rural Angus and the coastal grassy banks and golf courses of northeastern Fife. A vibrant, industrious, and cultural city, it's undergoing a postindustrial renaissance of sorts, with the V&A museum as the centerpiece of the emerging waterfront regeneration. The first outpost of London's world-famous Victoria and Albert Museum, a repository of the decorative arts and design, is housed in a sculptural building jutting into Britain's most powerful river. Dundee is the United Kingdom's sole UNESCO City of Design, with a large student population, a lively arts and nightlife scene, and several historical and nautical sights. The tree-lined country roads of the Angus heartlands roll through strawberry and raspberry fields to busy market towns, wee villages, and Glamis Castle. Angus combines coastal agriculture on rich, red soils with dramatic inland glens that pierce their way into the foothills of the Grampian mountain range to the northwest. ■TIP➔ **The main road from Dundee to Aberdeen—the A90—requires special care with its mix of fast cars and unexpectedly slow farm traffic.**

Planning

When to Go

The Trossachs and Loch Lomond are in some ways a miniature Scotland, from the tranquil east shore of Loch Lomond to the hills and glens of the Trossachs and the mountains to the west—and all within a few hours' drive. In spring and summer, despite the erratic weather, the area is always crowded; this is a good time to go. However, the landscape is notably dramatic when the trees are turning red and brown in autumn, and evening skies are spectacular. Scotland in winter has a different kind of beauty, especially for skiers and climbers.

Planning Your Time

Scotland's beautiful interior is excellent touring country, though the cities of Stirling and Perth are worth your time, too; Stirling is a good starting point, and exploring its castle can take a half day. Two (slightly rushed) days would be enough to explore the Trossachs loop, to gaze into the waters of Loch Venachar and Loch Achray. The glens, in some places, run parallel to the lochs, including those along Lochs Earn, Tay, and Rannoch, making for satisfying loops and round trips. Loch Lomond is easily accessible from either Glasgow or Stirling, and is well worth exploring. Don't miss the opportunity to take a boat trip on a loch, especially on Loch Lomond or on Loch Katrine. St. Andrews, 52 miles from Edinburgh, is not to be missed, for its history and atmosphere as much as for the golf; allot an overnight stop and at least a whole day if you can. The nearby East Neuk of Fife has some of Scotland's finest coastline, now becoming gentrified by the Edinburgh second-home set but still evoking Fife's past. Dundee, with a rich maritime history and a grand museum, is an ideal base for a drive round the small towns of Angus; if you make a three-hour stop at Glamis Castle, this trip will take about a day.

Getting Here and Around

AIR

Perth and Stirling can be reached easily from the Edinburgh, Dundee, and Glasgow airports by train, car, or bus. There are handy flight options via Edinburgh and the small Dundee airport. For international flights, Edinburgh Airport is the easiest gateway into the region. The Dundee airport has twice daily connections with London Stansted.

CONTACTS Dundee Airport. ☎ *01382/662200* ⊕ *www.hial.co.uk/ dundee-airport.*

BUS

A good network of buses connects with this area via Edinburgh and Glasgow. For more information contact Scottish Citylink or National Express. The Perth and Kinross Council supplies a map (available in tourist information centers) showing all public transport routes in Perthshire, marked with nearby attractions. First, Scottish Citylink, and Stagecoach organize reliable local service on routes throughout the Central Highlands.

Among the various bus operators that serve much of the region, Stagecoach has the most coverage through Angus and Fife. Xplore Dundee serves the city and runs the airport transfer bus to and from Edinburgh Airport.

CONTACTS First Bus. ☎ *0345/646-0707* ⊕ *www.firstgroup.com.* **National Express.** ☎ *0871/781-8181* ⊕ *www.national- expressgroup.com.* **Scottish Citylink.** ☎ *0141/352-4444* ⊕ *www.citylink.co.uk.* **Stagecoach.** ☎ *0843/208-2338* ⊕ *www. stagecoachbus.com.*

CAR

It's easy to access the area from the central belt of Scotland via the motorway network. The M80 connects Glasgow to Stirling, and then briefly joins the M9 from Edinburgh, which runs within sight of the walls of Stirling Castle. From there the A9 runs from Stirling to Perth, and onward to Pitlochry; it is a good road but a little too fast (so take care). Perth can also be reached via the M90 over the Forth Bridge from Edinburgh. Three signed touring routes are useful: the Perthshire Tourist Route, the Deeside Tourist Route, and the Pitlochry Tourist Route, a beautiful and unexpected trip via Crieff and Loch Tay. Local tourist information centers can supply maps of these routes, or you can check online (⊕ *www. visitscotland.com*). Once you leave the major motorways, roads become narrower and slower, with many following the contours of the lochs. Be prepared for your journey to take longer than distances might suggest.

For seeing the most of Fife and Angus, car travel is basically essential, although there are some public transport alternatives. The major roads that span the region are not big motorways, but second-tier A roads; many of these roads are single-lane only, so be especially cautious when driving in this region.

TRAIN

The Central Highlands are linked to Edinburgh and Glasgow by rail, with through routes to England (some direct-service routes from London take fewer than five hours). Several discount ticket options are available, although in some cases on the ScotRail system a discount card must be purchased before your arrival in the United Kingdom. Note that families with children and travelers younger than 26 or older than 60 are eligible for significant discounts. Contact Trainline, Traveline Scotland, National Rail, or ScotRail for details.

The West Highland Line runs through the western portion of the area. Services also run to Stirling, Dunblane, Perth, and Gleneagles; stops on the Inverness–Perth line include Dunkeld, Pitlochry, and Blair Atholl.

The East Coast Main Line makes stops at Cupar, Leuchars (for St. Andrews), Dundee, Arbroath, and Montrose.

CONTACTS East Coast Main Line. ⊕ *www.scotrail.co.uk.* **National Rail Enquiries.** ☎ *03457/484950* ⊕ *www.nationalrail.co.uk.* **ScotRail.** ☎ *0344/811–0141* ⊕ *www.scotrail.co.uk.* **Trainline.** ☎ *0871/244–1545* ⊕ *www.thetrainline.com.* **Traveline Scotland.** ☎ *0871/200–2233* ⊕ *www.travelinescotland.com.*

Restaurants

Regional country delicacies—loch trout, river salmon, lamb, and venison—appear regularly on even modest menus in Central Highlands restaurants. In all the towns and villages in the area, you will find simple pubs, often crowded and noisy, many of them serving substantial food at lunchtime and in the evening until about 9 (eaten balanced on your knee, perhaps, or at a shared table). The more luxurious restaurants tend to be in upscale hotels, with prices to match. It can be difficult to find a place to eat later in the evening.

With an affluent population, St. Andrews supports several stylish hotel restaurants. Because it's a university town and popular tourist destination, there are also many good cafés and bistro-style restaurants. Bar lunches are the rule in large and small hotels throughout the region, and in seaside places the carry-*oot* (to-go) meal of fish-and-chips is an enduring tradition.

Hotels

A wide selection of accommodations is available throughout the region, especially in Stirling, Callander, and Pitlochry. They range from bed-and-breakfasts to private houses with a small number of rooms to rural accommodations (often on farms). The grand houses of the past—family homes to the landed aristocracy—have for the most part become country-house hotels. Their settings, often on ample grounds, offer an experience of grand living—but the area also has modern hotels, for those who prefer 21st-century amenities.

If you're staying in Fife, the obvious choice for a base is St. Andrews, with ample accommodations of all kinds. Dundee and its hinterlands have a number of diverse accommodations, including an influx of smart city center hotels, many of which offer good value.

Restaurant and hotel reviews have been shortened. For full information, visit Fodors.com. Restaurant prices are the average cost of a main course at dinner or, if dinner is not served, at lunch. Hotel prices are the lowest cost of a standard double room in high season, including 20% V.A.T.

WHAT IT COSTS in Pounds			
$	$$	$$$	$$$$
RESTAURANTS			
under £15	£15–£19	£20 £26	over £25
HOTELS			
under £125	£125–£200	£201 £300	over £300

Activities

Lowland-Highland Trail

BICYCLING | The region's big attraction for cyclists is the Lowland-Highland Trail, which stretches more than 60 miles and passes through Drymen, Aberfoyle, the Trossachs, Callander, Lochearnhead, and Killin. This route runs along former railroad-track beds, as well as private and minor roads, to reach well into the Central Highlands. Another almost completely traffic-free option is the roadway around Loch Katrine. Almost every town along the route has cycle-hire shops.

★ West Highland Way

HIKING/WALKING | The long-distance walkers' route, the West Highland Way, begins at Milngavie, outside Glasgow, running 96 miles from the Lowlands of central Scotland to the Highlands at Fort William. Along its course the landscape changes as you walk from the banks of Loch Lomond into the hills beyond, through the dramatic Glencoe, across Ranooch Moor and beyond it to Fort William and the heart of the Central Highlands. Nearly 50,000 people discover the glens each year, climbing the hills and listening to birds singing in the tree canopy. For the most part, this is not an especially difficult walk, though it can be demanding at moments, but keep Scotland's ever-changing weather in mind and go properly prepared. ⊕ *www.west-highland-way.co.uk.*

Stirling

26 miles northeast of Glasgow, 36 miles northwest of Edinburgh.

Stirling is one of Britain's great historic towns. An impressive proportion of the Old Town walls can be seen from Dumbarton Road, a cobbled street leading to Stirling Castle, built on a steep-sided plug of rock. From its esplanade there is a commanding view of the surrounding Carse of Stirling. The guns on the castle battlements are a reminder of the military advantage to be gained from its position.

GETTING HERE AND AROUND

Stirling's central position in the area makes it ideal for travel to and from Glasgow and Edinburgh (or north to Perth and the Highlands) by rail or bus. The town itself is compact and easily walkable, though a shuttle bus travels to and from the town center up the steep road to Stirling Castle every 20 minutes. You can stroll the Back Walk on a circuit around the base of the castle walls—set aside at least 30 minutes for a leisurely walk. The National Wallace Monument (2 miles away) is on the outskirts of the town and can be reached by taxi or on foot.

ESSENTIALS

VISITOR INFORMATION VisitScotland Stirling iCentre. ✉ *Old Town Jail, St. John St.* ☎ *01786/475019* ⊕ *my.stirling.gov.uk/tourism-visitors.*

Sights

★ Battle of Bannockburn Visitor Centre

MILITARY SITE | FAMILY | You can almost hear the trotting of horses' hooves and the zip of arrows in this 21st-century re-creation of the battle that changed the course of Scotland's history in 1314. Robert the Bruce's defeat of the armies of the English king, despite a 2-to-1 disadvantage, is the stuff of legend. Using 3-D technology, the visitor center allows you to see a battle raging across screens that ring the central hall. Participants on both sides speak directly to you, courtesy of holograms. Later you can play a role in a Bannockburn battle game (reservations essential; age seven and older only). Bruce pursued the Scottish crown, ruthlessly sweeping aside enemies; but his victory here was masterful, as he drew the English horses into marshy land (now the area around the new center), where they sank in the mud. A circular monument commemorates the battlefield. ■ TIP→ Book ahead; tickets are for timed entry. ✉ Glasgow Road, Bannockburn ☎ 01786/812664 ⊕ www.nts.org.uk/visit/places/bannockburn ☑ £11.50.

National Wallace Monument

MEMORIAL | This Victorian-era shrine to William Wallace (circa 1270–1305), the Scottish freedom fighter reborn as "Braveheart" in Mel Gibson's 1995 film of the same name, was built between 1856 and 1869. It sits on Abbey Craig, from which Wallace watched the English armies struggle across the old Stirling Bridge before attacking them and winning a major victory in 1297. A steep stone spiral staircase leads to the roof gallery, with views of the bridge and the whole Carse of Stirling. A less flamboyant version of Wallace's life is told in an exhibition and audiovisual presentation on the second floor. To reach the monument, follow the Bridge of Allan signs (A9) northward, crossing the River Forth by the New Bridge of 1832, next to the old one. The monument is signposted at the next traffic circle. From the car park a free shuttle will take you to the monument, or you can walk (15 minutes). ✉ Abbey Craig, Hillfoot Rd. ☎ 01786/472140 ⊕ www.nationalwallace-monument.com ☑ £10.50.

★ Stirling Castle

CASTLE/PALACE | FAMILY | Its magnificent strategic position on a steep-sided crag made Stirling Castle the grandest prize in the Scots Wars of Independence during the late 13th and early 14th centuries. Robert the Bruce's victory at Bannockburn won both the castle and freedom from English subjugation for almost four centuries. Take time to visit the **Castle Exhibition** beyond the lower gate to get an overview of its evolution as a stronghold and palace. ■ TIP→ It's a good idea to book tickets online before your visit.

The daughter of King Robert I (Robert the Bruce), Marjory, married Walter Fitzallan, the high steward of Scotland. Their descendants included the Stewart dynasty of Scottish monarchs (Mary, Queen of Scots, was a Stewart, though she preferred the French spelling, *Stuart*). The Stewarts were responsible for many of the works that survive within the castle walls. They made Stirling Castle their court and power base, creating fine Renaissance-style buildings that were never completely obliterated, despite reconstruction for military purposes.

You enter the castle through its outer defenses, which consist of a great curtained wall and batteries from 1708. From this lower square the most conspicuous feature is the **Palace,** built by King James V (1512–42) between 1538 and 1542. The decorative figures festooning the ornate outer walls show the influence of French masons. An orientation center in the basement, designed especially for children, lets you try out the clothes and musical instruments of the time. Across a terrace are the **Royal Apartments,** which re-create the furnishings and tapestries found here during the reign of James V and his French queen, Mary of Guise. The queen's bedchamber contains copies of the beautiful tapestries in which the hunt for the white unicorn is clearly an allegory for the persecution of Christ. Overlooking the upper courtyard is the **Great Hall,** built by King James IV (1473–1513) in 1503. Before the Union of Parliaments in 1707, when the Scottish aristocracy sold out to England, this building had been used as one of the seats of the Scottish Parliament.

Among the later works built for regiments stationed here, the **Regimental Museum** stands out, it's a 19th-century baronial revival on the site of an earlier building. Nearby the **Chapel Royal** is unfurnished. The oldest building on the site is the **Mint,** or **Coonzie Hoose,** perhaps dating as far back as the 14th century. Below it is an arched passageway leading to the westernmost ramparts, the **Nether Bailey,** with a view of the *carselands* (valley plain) of the Forth Valley.

To the castle's south lies the hump of the Touch and the Gargunnock Hills, which diverted potential direct routes from Glasgow and the south. For centuries all roads into the Highlands across the narrow waist of Scotland led through Stirling. If you look carefully northward, you can still see the Old Stirling Bridge, the site of William Wallace's most famous victory. ✉ *Castlehill* ☎ *01786/450000* ⊕ *www.stirlingcastle.gov.uk* 🎫 *£16.*

🍴 Restaurants

The Birds and the Bees

$$ | BRITISH | FAMILY | This lively pub is a little hard to find but worth the effort for the extensive menu—from burgers and steaks to jambalaya, curry and (this is, after all, Scotland) haggis "draped" in a whisky-and-mustard sauce. The feel is of good home cooking, without pretensions, and the servings are more than generous. **Known for:** hearty home-style cooking; delicious desserts; lovely

location. **⑤** *Average main: £15* ✉ *Easter Cornton Road, Causewayhead* ✢ *From the Wallace Monument head southeast on Hillfoots Road/B998 (if walking, you can take the Logie Road/B998 shortcut), then take the A9 toward Stirling. Make a right at Easter Cornton Road and follow it about one-half mile.* ☎ *01786/473663* ⊕ *www.thebirdsandthebees-stirling.com.*

Brea

$$ | BRITISH | This unpretentious and very popular place with wooden tables and chairs has a menu that celebrates Scottish food, though well-made burgers and steaks are also permanent features. The food offers some new takes on traditional favorites such as the rolled haddock with salmon, the Cullen skink soup, and haggis in various guises. **Known for:** burgers; good seafood; housemade desserts. **⑤** *Average main: £18* ✉ *5 Baker St.* ✢ *Down the hill from Stirling Castle* ☎ *01786/446277* ⊕ *www.brea-stirling. co.uk.*

Hotels

Friars Wynd

$ | HOTEL | This small boutique hotel in a restored townhouse is situated in the heart of Stirling. **Pros:** pleasant and relaxing atmosphere; tasteful decor; reasonably priced. **Cons:** Wi-Fi in public areas only; no parking; limited social space. **⑤** *Rooms from: £109* ✉ *17 Friars St.* ☎ *01786/447501* ⊕ *www.friarswynd. co.uk* 🛏 *8 rooms* ⏹ *Free breakfast.*

Portcullis Hotel

$$ | B&B/INN | This small hotel with a lively traditional pub scores above all on location: it is just outside the walls of Stirling Castle, and the views are spectacular, especially from the upper floors where the guest rooms are located. **Pros:** excellent location close to the castle; fine views; a distinctly local atmosphere. **Cons:** can get noisy; snug rooms; not cheap in high season. **⑤** *Rooms from: £145* ✉ *Castle Wynd* ☎ *01786/472290*

⊕ *www.theportcullishotel.com* 🛏 *4 rooms* †⊙† *Free breakfast.*

West Plean House

$ | **B&B/INN** | Dating from 1803, this handsome, rambling B&B with spacious rooms is part of a working farm. **Pros:** beautiful gardens; plenty of peace and quiet; huge and hearty breakfast. **Cons:** a little off the beaten track; a 3-mile walk to Stirling; occasional noise from the farm. ⑤ *Rooms from: £100* ⊠ *Denny Road* ☎ *01786/812208* ⊕ *www.westplean-house.com* ⊙ *Closed Dec.* 🛏 *4 rooms* †⊙† *Free breakfast.*

 Shopping

CLOTHING

House of Henderson

CLOTHING | A Highland outfitter of the old school, House of Henderson sells tartans, woolens, and accessories, and offers a made-to-measure kilt service. ⊠ *6–8 Friars St.* ☎ *01786/473681* ⊕ *www.houseofhenderson.co.uk.*

Mill Trail

CLOTHING | East of Stirling is Mill Trail country, along the foot of the Ochil Hills. As you travel from Stirling toward Tillicoutry, Alva, and Alloa, mill shops offer woolen clothing and cashmere at good prices.

GIFTS

Fotheringham Gallery

ART GALLERIES | This upscale gallery specializes in contemporary Scottish art as well as striking modern jewelry by Leigh Fortheringham. ⊠ *78 Henderson St., Bridge of Allan* ☎ *01786/832861* ⊕ *www.fotheringhamgallery.co.uk.*

Stirling Bagpipes

MUSIC STORES | This small shop sells bagpipes of every type and at every price, including antiques by legendary craftspeople that are displayed in glass cases. The owner, who tunes the chanters and drones in a room behind the shop, has been known to take time to walk shoppers through the history of these wonderful instruments, upon request. ⊠ *8 Broad St.* ☎ *01786/448886* ⊕ *www.stirlingbagpipes.com* ⊙ *Closed Sun. and Wed.*

Callander

8 miles northwest of Doune.

A traditional Highland-edge resort, the little town of Callander bustles throughout the year, largely with visitors and coach parties from Glasgow and Edinburgh. It is a gateway to the beauty of Loch Lomond and the Trossachs National Park, yet never too far from the cities of the central belt. There's plenty of window-shopping here, plus lively pubs and a selection of mainly bed-and-breakfast accommodations.

GETTING HERE AND AROUND

You can access Callander by bus from Stirling, Glasgow, or Edinburgh. If you're traveling by car from Stirling, take the M8 to Dunblane, then the A820 (which becomes the A84) to Callander. If you are coming from Glasgow, take the A81 through Aberfoyle to Callander; an alternative route (longer but more picturesque) is to take the A821 around Loch Venachar, then the A84 east to Callander.

ESSENTIALS

VISITOR INFORMATION Callander Visitor Information Centre. ⊠ *52–54 Main St.* ☎ *01877/330342* ⊕ *incallander.co.uk/visitorcentre.*

 Sights

Balquhidder Glen

VIEWPOINT | A 20-minute drive from Callander, through the Pass of Leny and beyond Strathyre, the lovely Balquhidder Glen (pronounced *bal*-kwidd- *er*) is a typical Highland glen, with a flat-bottom, U-shaped profile, indicating it was formed by prehistoric glaciers. This was MacGregor country, the most famous of whom was Rob Roy MacGregor, the Jacobite hero who is buried in the churchyard here. It is also walkers country, and several walkers routes pass through here. Gentler walks will take you to Kirkton Glen, past Monachyle Mhor, after the road ends. From there the view opens toward the mountain country around Ben More, where the hardier, well-equipped hillwalker may prefer to go. ⊠ Balquhidder ✛ From Callander take the A84 and turn left at Kingshouse; the road ends in the glen.

Hamilton Toy Museum

MUSEUM | FAMILY | This is one of those eccentric museums born of one person's (or one family's) passionate obsession. The small, crowded house and shop on Callander's main street contains one of the most extensive toy collections in Britain. The rooms throughout the house are crammed with everything from Corgi cars and an enormous number of toy soldiers, carefully organized by regiment, to Amanda Jane dolls and Beatles memorabilia. The collection of model railways has extended into tracks in the back garden. The museum is jammed and quirky, but full of reminders of everyone's childhood. ⊠ 111 Main St. ☏ 01877/330004 ⊕ www.thehamiltontoycollection.co.uk ⊠ £3 ◷ Closed Nov.–Mar.

 ## Restaurants

★ Venachar Lochside

$$ | MODERN BRITISH | All you see from the road is what seems to be a large shed, but inside is a busy restaurant. There's also a view—the restaurant's glass wall affords a lovely panorama of the water and surrounding hills. **Known for:** smoked-fish platter; fine seafood; lochside dining. ⑤ Average main: £15 ⊠ Loch Venachar ✛ On the A821 about 6 miles from Callander, at Brig o' Turk ☏ 01877/330011 ⊕ www.venachar-lochside.co.uk ◷ No dinner.

 ## Hotels

★ Monachyle MHOR

$$$$ | HOTEL | Splendidly isolated, this beautiful converted farmhouse with contemporary interiors is set amid forests and moorland, looking out onto Lochs Voil and Doine. **Pros:** stunning scenery; delicious food; complimentary salmon and trout fishing. **Cons:** remote location; rooms are on the small side; bar can get very crowded. ⑤ Rooms from: £325 ⊠ Off A84, Balquhidder ✛ From Callander, drive northwest 17 miles (40 minutes) ☏ 01877/384622 ⊕ www.mhor.net ⌁ 14 rooms ⑩ All-inclusive.

★ Roman Camp

$$ | B&B/INN | Within a hundred yards of Callander's main street, on the other side of an unpretentious arch, is this 17th-century hunting lodge hidden among ornate gardens. **Pros:** beautiful grounds; luxurious rooms; close to everything in town. **Cons:** restaurant is expensive; no Internet in rooms; much sought after for weddings, so could be busy. ⑤ Rooms from: £160 ⊠ Off Main Street ☏ 01877/330003 ⊕ www.romancamphotel.co.uk ⌁ 15 rooms ⑩ Free breakfast.

 ## Shopping

Trossachs Woollen Mill

CLOTHING | The Edinburgh Woollen Mill Group owns this mill shop in Kilmahog, a mile west of Callander. It has a vast selection of woolens on display, including luxurious cashmere and striking tartan throws, and will provide overseas mailing and tax-free shopping. The shop has a small café and a couple of resident animals. ⊠ Main St., Kilmahog ☏ 01877/330178 ⊕ www.ewm.co.uk.

The Trossachs

10 miles west of Callander.

The Trossachs has been a popular touring region since the late 18th century, at the dawn of the age of the romantic poets. Influenced by the writings of Sir Walter Scott, early visitors who strayed into the Highlands from the central belt of Scotland admired this as the first "wild" part of Scotland they encountered. Perhaps because the Trossachs represent the very essence of what the Highlands are supposed to be, the whole of this area, including Loch Lomond, is now protected as a national park. Here you can find birch and pine forests, vistas down lochs where the woods creep right to the water's edge, and, in the background, peaks that rise high enough to be called

mountains, though they're not as high as those to the north and west.

GETTING HERE AND AROUND

To reach the Trossachs, take the A84 from Callander through the Pass of Leny, then on to Crianlarich on the A85; from here you can continue down the western shore of Loch Lomond or carry on toward Fort William. Alternately, turn onto the A821 outside Callander and travel past Loch Katrine through the Duke's Pass to Aberfoyle.

Sights

Loch Achray

BODY OF WATER | Stretching west of the small community of Brig o' Turk, Loch Achray dutifully fulfills expectations of what a verdant Trossachs loch should be: small, green, reedy meadows backed by dark plantations, rhododendron thickets, and lumpy hills, thickly covered with heather. ⊠ *A821, Brig o'Turk.*

★ Loch Katrine
BODY OF WATER | FAMILY | This loch was a favorite among Victorian visitors—mysterious and wide and, at times, quite wild. Today it's the source of Glasgow's freshwater. Take a cruise around the loch if time permits, as the shores remain undeveloped and scenic. The steamship *Sir Walter Scott* and the motor launch *Lady of the Lake* sail from the lake's eastern end several times a day in season. You can make the round-trip journey around the loch, or head directly across to Stronachlachar, where you can pause for a coffee and to admire the beauty of the loch from the pier head and then return by bicycle on the lochside road. There are café facilities and cycle-hire shops at the head of the loch; reservations are required if you're taking a bike on the boat. Sailings continue through the year but are reduced in number between October and May. ⊠ *Trossachs Pier, Aberfoyle* ✛ *Off A821* ☎ *01877/376316* ⊕ *www.lochkatrine.com* ⌖ *Sir Walter Scott £17 round-trip, £14 one way; Lady of the Lake £14 round-trip, £10.50 one way. There are also shorter scenic cruises, £14 on the Sir Walter Scott, £10.50 on the Lady of the Lake.*

Trossachs National Park
NATIONAL/STATE PARK | Scotland's first national park, designated in 2002, the Trossachs were first discovered and developed as an area for Victorian tourists and visitors. It was Queen Victoria's fascination with the novels of Sir Walter Scott that stimulated an interest in the brooding glens and lochs of the area, as well as the healing qualities of its waters. The park sits on a geological fault that divides the fertile lowlands from the highlands and its hills and mountains, 21 of which are more than 3,000 feet (and known as "Munros"). For hikers there are woodland valleys for pleasant and leisurely walks, long-distance footpaths like the West Highland Rob Roy Ways for more determined walkers, and mountains like the demanding Cobbler and Ben Lomond, as well as shorter hikes on hills surrounding scenic lochs. For cyclists there are exciting routes, and for the nature lover there are many varieties of birds and animals in this protected habitat—capercaillie, golden eagles, red deer, and beavers among them. As the number of visitors has grown, lochside diners and charming country hotels have also multiplied. ⊕ *www.lochlomond-trossachs.org*

Aberfoyle

11 miles south of Loch Katrine, in the Trossachs.

This small tourist-oriented town has a somewhat faded air, but the surrounding hills (some snowcapped) and the green slopes visible from the town are the reason so many people pause here before continuing up to Duke's Pass or on to Inversnaid on Loch Lomond. Access to nearby Queen Elizabeth Forest Park and the Lodge Forest Centre is another reason to visit.

GETTING HERE AND AROUND
The main route out of Glasgow, the A81, takes you through Aberfoyle and on to Callander and Stirling. There are regular buses from Stirling and Glasgow to Aberfoyle.

ESSENTIALS
VISITOR INFORMATION VisitScotland Aberfoyle iCentre. ⊠ *Trossachs Discovery Centre, Main Street* ☎ *01877/381221.*

Sights

★ Inchmahome
ISLAND | The 13th-century ruined priory on the tiny island of Inchmahome, on the Lake of Menteith, is a lovely place for a picnic after you explore the building's

chapter house and other remains. It was a place of refuge in 1547 for the young Mary, Queen of Scots. In season, a seven-minute ferry takes passengers to the island, now owned by the National Trust for Scotland. The ferry jetty is just past the Port of Menteith (a village). ⊠ *Off A81* ⊹ *Take the A81 to the B8034; it's 4 miles east of Aberfoyle* ☎ *01786/385294* ⊕ *www.historicenvironment.scot* ⊠ *Ferry £9* ⊙ *Closed. Nov.–Mar.*

★ **Queen Elizabeth Forest Park**

NATURE PRESERVE | For exquisite nature, drive north from Aberfoyle on the A821 and turn right at signposts to Queen Elizabeth Forest Park. Along the way you'll be heading toward higher moorland blanketed with conifers. The conifers hem in the views of Ben Ledi and Ben Venue, which can be seen over the spiky green waves of trees as the road snakes around heathery knolls and hummocks. There's another viewing area, and a small parking lot, at the highest point of the road. Soon the road swoops off the Highland edge and leads downhill.

At the heart of the Queen Elizabeth Forest Park, the **Lodge Forest Visitor Centre** leads to four forest walks, a family-friendly bicycle route, and the 7-mile 3 Lochs Forest Drive, open April to October. Or you can sit on the terrace of the Bluebell Cafe and scan the forests and hills of the Trossachs. The visitor center has a wildlife-watch room, where you can follow the activities of everything from ospreys to water voles. ⊠ *Off A821* ⊹ *1 mile north of Aberfoyle* ☎ *01877/382383* ⊕ *forestryandland.gov.scot/visit/forest-parks/queen-elizabeth-forest-park* ⊠ *Free, but parking costs £3 for the day.*

Scottish Wool Centre

STORE/MALL | FAMILY | Besides selling a vast range of woolen garments and knitwear, the Scottish Wool Centre has a small café and some activities. Three times a day from April to September it presents an interactive "gathering" during which dogs herd sheep and ducks

in the large amphitheater, with a little help from the public. ⊠ *Off Main Street* ☎ *01877/382850* ⊕ *www.ewm.co.uk* ⊠ *Free.*

Restaurants

Pier Café

$ | **BRITISH** | At the historic Stronachlachar Pier, this light-filled coffee shop has a satisfying lunch menu (burgers and sandwiches) and a deck with expansive views over Loch Katrine. Cakes, scones, and soups are made on the premises. **Known for:** home baking; good coffee; loch views. $ *Average main: £10* ⊠ *B829, Stronachlachar* ☎ *01877/386374* ⊕ *www.thepiercafe.com* ⊙ *No dinner Sun.–Thur.*

Hotels

★ Lake of Menteith Hotel

$$ | **HOTEL** | At this beautifully located hotel overlooking the Lake of Menteith, muted colors and simple but elegant rooms create a restful atmosphere, enhanced, perhaps, by the silent hills that ring the hotel and the tranquil lake. **Pros:** elegant, unpretentious bedrooms; beautiful setting; lakeside seating at restaurant. **Cons:** not well signposted; not all rooms have lake views and those that do are more expensive; no elevator. $ *Rooms from: £160* ⊠ *Off A81* ☎ *01877/385258* ⊕ *www.lake-hotel.com* ⟿ *17 rooms* ⦿ *Free breakfast.*

Activities

GOLF
Aberfoyle Golf Club

GOLF | Queen Elizabeth Forest Park provides the backdrop for this hilly course. One of the area's many James Braid–designed parkland courses, it dates back to 1890. There are views of Ben Lomond and Stirling Castle from different points on the course, which is relatively short but varied and challenging even for quite experienced players, with several uphill

Some of the best hiking in Scotland is found in the hills around Loch Lomond.

shots and undulating ground. ⊠ *Braeval* ✛ *Off A821* ☎ *01877/382493* ⊕ *www. aberfoylegolf.co.uk* ⛳ *£20 weekdays, £25 weekends* ⚐. *18 holes, 5158 yards, par 66.*

HIKING
★ Ben A'an
VIEWPOINT | The climb up the steep, heathery Ben A'an requires a couple of hours and good lungs, but it's a worthwhile trip, providing you with some of the best Trossachs views, including those of Loch Achray and Loch Katrine. ⊠ *Off A821* ✛ *Access the beginning of the path near the Loch Achray parking lot.*

ZIPLINING
Go Ape High Wire Forest Adventure
CITY PARK | **FAMILY** | Near the Lodge Forest Visitor Centre in the Queen Elizabeth Forest Park, this is an exhilarating experience for thrill seekers age 10 and over. After a short orientation course, you can travel 40 feet above the forest via ziplines and rope ladders on a sort of midair assault course. ⊠ *Queen Elizabeth Forest Park, A821* ✛ *1 mile north of Aberfoyle*

☎ *0845/094–9032* ⊕ *www.goape.com* ⚐ *The Treetop Challenge (~2.5 hours), £33* ⊙ *Closed weekdays in Nov., Feb., and Mar.*

Loch Lomond

14 miles west of Aberfoyle.

The waters of Scotland's largest loch, which also happens to be one of its most beautiful, create a perfect reflection of the surrounding hills. You can cruise among its small islands or follow the low road that carries you from Glasgow to the beginning of the Highlands.

GETTING HERE AND AROUND
To reach Loch Lomond from Aberfoyle, take the A81 toward Glasgow, then the A811 to Drymen and then the B837 as far as it will take you. From Glasgow take the A82 to the Balloch roundabout, and either go right through Balloch for Drymen and the eastern shore, or continue along the A82 as it hugs the west bank all the way to Crianlarich.

You can drive, cycle, or walk along the 32 miles of Loch Lomond along its western shores, and watch the changing face of the loch as you go, or look up toward the shifting slopes of Ben Lomond.

ESSENTIALS
VISITOR INFORMATION Loch Lomond and the Trossachs National Park Headquarters. ✉ *Carrochan Road, Balloch* ☏ *01389/722600* ⊕ *www.lochlomond-trossachs.org.*

Sights

★ Loch Lomond
BODY OF WATER | Known for its "bonnie, bonnie banks," Loch Lomond is Scotland's most well-known loch and its largest in terms of surface area. Its waters reflect the crags that surround it.

On the western side of the loch, the A82 follows the shore for 24 miles, continuing a farther 7 miles to Crianlarich, passing picturesque Luss, which has a pier where you can hop aboard boats cruising along the loch, and Tarbert, the starting point for the *Maid of the Loch.* On the eastern side of the loch, take the A81 to Drymen, and from there the B837 signposted toward Balmaha, where you can hire a boat or take the ferry to the island of Inchcailloch. Once you're there, a short walk takes you to the top of the hill and a spectacular view of the loch. Equally spectacular, but not as wet, is the view from Conic Hill behind Balmaha, a short but exhilarating climb. The hill marks the fault that divides the Lowlands and Highlands. If you continue along the B837 beyond Rowardennan to where it ends at a car park, you can join the walkers at the beginning of the path up Ben Lomond. ⚠ **Don't underestimate this innocent-looking hill; go equipped for sudden changes in the weather.** Hikers can also try part of the 96-mile West Highland Way (⊕ *www.west-highland-way.co.uk*) that runs along the shore of Loch Lomond on its way north.

Restaurants

★ Coach House Coffee Shop
$ | **BRITISH** | With its over-the-top Scottishness, this lively restaurant and café serving Scottish classics fits perfectly into its surroundings. Long wooden tables, a large chimney with an open fire in the winter months, and a cabinet full of mouthwatering cakes baked by the owner create a cheerful atmosphere. **Known for:** teapots; stovies; Scottish style. $ *Average main: £12* ✉ *Church Road, Luss* ⊕ *Off A82* ☏ *01436/860341* ⊗ *No dinner.*

Drovers Inn
$ | **BRITISH** | Knowing its clientele, this quirky, noisy, friendly inn serves huge, hearty portions that are what you need after a day's walking on the nearby West Highland Way. Scottish staples like sausage and mash, minced beef, and haggis jostle for a place beside occasionally more adventurous dishes. **Known for:** big portions; old stuffed animals; good bar. $ *Average main: £12* ✉ *On A82 toward Crianlarich, Balloch* ⊕ *North of Ardlui, just north of Loch Lomond* ☏ *01301/704234* ⊕ *www.thedroversinn.co.uk.*

Hotels

Balloch House
$ | **HOTEL** | Cute, cozy, and very Scottish, this small hotel offers simple but clean rooms along with tasty breakfasts and good, hearty pub meals like fish-and-chips and local smoked salmon for reasonable prices. **Pros:** beautiful building; peat fires; near shopping. **Cons:** noisy pinball machine next to bar; not all rooms have views; has a busy pub. $ *Rooms from: £98* ✉ *Balloch Road, Balloch* ☏ *01389/752579* ⊕ *www.innkeeperslodge.com/loch-lomond* ⌁ *12 rooms* ❏ *Free breakfast.*

The Lodge on Loch Lomond
$$ | **HOTEL** | Known for its views, this hotel overlooking Loch Lomond sits beside the

picturesque village of Luss. **Pros:** wonderful setting; big and comfortable rooms; excellent restaurant with full loch views. **Cons:** not all rooms overlook the loch; can be busy with weddings and conferences; beach area is small and gets crowded in summer. *⑤ Rooms from: £174 ⊠ Luss, Alexandria ☎ 01436/860201 ⊕ www. loch lomond.co.uk ⇨ 48 rooms ⚍ Free Breakfast.*

Activities

BOATING
Cruise Loch Lomond

BOATING | FAMILY | You can take scenic boat tours of Loch Lomond year-round with this company. What you see on your journey depends on where you embark. From April to October boats depart from various ports around the loch, including Tarbet, Luss, Balmaha, and Inversnaid, while from November to March the boats operate on demand. During the warmer months there is also a Two-Loch Tour taking in Loch Lomond and Loch Katrine. *⊠ Tarbet ✛ Off A82 ☎ 01301/702356 ⊕ www.cruiselochlomond.co.uk ⚍ From £11.*

Macfarlane and Son

BOATING | At this longtime favorite, boats with outboard motors rent for £20 per hour or £50 per day. Rowboats rent for £10 per hour or £30 per day. From Balmaha, it is a short trip to the lovely island of Incailloch. Macfarlane's also runs a ferry to the island for £5 per person. *⊠ Balmaha Boatyard, B837, Balmaha ✛ From Drymen take the B837 ☎ 01360/870214 ⊕ www.balmahaboatyard.co.uk.*

Perth

36 miles northeast of Stirling, 43 miles north of Edinburgh, 61 miles northeast of Glasgow.

For many years Perth was Scotland's capital, and central to its history. One king (James I) was killed here, and the Protestant reformer John Knox preached in St. John's Kirk, where his rhetoric moved crowds to burn down several local monasteries. Perth's local whisky trade and the productive agriculture that surrounds the town have sustained it through the centuries. Its grand buildings, especially on the banks of the River Tay, testify to its continued wealth. The open parkland within the city (the Inches) gives the place a restful air, and shops range from small crafts boutiques to department stores. Impressive Scone Palace is nearby.

GETTING HERE AND AROUND
Perth is served by the main railway line to Inverness, and regular and frequent buses run here from Glasgow, Edinburgh, and Stirling. The central artery, the A9, passes through the city en route to Pitlochry and Inverness, while a network of roads opens the way to the glens and hills around Glen Lyon, or the road to Loch Lomond (the A85) via Crianlarich.

ESSENTIALS
VISITOR INFORMATION VisitScotland Perth iCentre. *⊠ 45 High St. ☎ 01738/450600 ⊕ www.visitscotland. com/info/services/perth-icentre-p234431.*

Sights

Elcho Castle

CASTLE/PALACE | Built around 1560 by the River Tay, the castle marks a transition period when these structures began to be built as grand houses rather than fortresses, and it's easy to see that Elcho was built for both comfort and defense. The well-preserved but uncluttered rooms let you imagine how life might have been here in the 17th century. The staircases still give access to all floors, and a flashlight is provided for the darker corners. From the battlements of the castle you can see the river stretching east and west. *⊠ Off A912 ✛ Close to Rhynd ☎ 01738/639998 ⊕ www.*

historicenvironment.scot/visit-a-place/
places/elcho-castle ⊠ £6 ⊙ Closed
Oct.–Mar.

★ Scone Palace

CASTLE/PALACE | FAMILY | The current
residence of the Earl of Mansfield, Scone
Palace (pronounced *skoon*) is much more
cheerful than the city's other castles.
Although it incorporates various earlier
works, the palace today has mainly a
19th-century theme, with mock castella-
tions that were fashionable at the time.
There's plenty to see if you're interested
in the acquisitions of an aristocratic Scottish family: magnificent porcelain, some
sumptuous furniture, a fine collection of
ivory, clocks, and 16th-century needle-
work. Each room has a guide who will
happily talk you through its contents and
their associations. In one bedroom hangs
a portrait of Dido Elizabeth Belle, a young
black slave adopted by the family, who
became a well-known society beauty in
the 1760s. (The 2013 film *Belle* is based
on her life). A coffee shop, restaurant,
gift shop, and play area are on-site. The
palace has its own mausoleum nearby,
on the site of a long-gone abbey on **Moot
Hill,** the ancient coronation place of the
Scottish kings. To be crowned, they sat
on the Stone of Scone, which was seized
in 1296 by Edward I of England, Scotland's greatest enemy, and placed in the
coronation chair at Westminster Abbey,
in London. The stone was returned to
Scotland in November 1996 and is now
on view in Edinburgh Castle. There is
a maze and a children's playground in
the grounds, which are free to enter.
⊠ Braemar Road ⊹ 2 miles north of Perth
☎ 01738/552300 ⊕ www.scone-palace.
co.uk ⊠ £12.50. Free for grounds only.

🕙 *House closed Nov.–Mar. Grounds closed Mon.–Thurs. Nov.–Mar.*

 Restaurants

Deans Restaurant

$$$ | BRITISH | The varied clientele reflects the broad appeal of noted chef Willie Deans's imaginative and satisfying cuisine, including a dinner menu with starters such as ceviche of sea bream, passion fruit, and lime, and Shetland fish curry and delicious Orkney steak for main courses. Deans is airy and pleasant, merging warm colors and light woods with comfortable sofas perfect for a pred-inner drink. **Known for:** pretheater menu; good lunch menu; Shetland fish curry. ⑤ *Average main: £23* ⊠ *77–79 Kinnoull St.* ☎ *01738/643377* ⊕ *www.letseatperth. co.uk.*

★ 63 Tay Street

$$$ | BRITISH | Dine looking out onto the River Tay in this elegant but relaxed restaurant with tall windows, gray-and-white walls, and wooden tables. Known for imaginative fare with an emphasis on seasonal and local produce, chef Graeme Pallister produces combinations that are adventurous, such as the "witch sole" with curry and sprouting broccoli or red deer with pear, parsnips, and licorice. **Known for:** imaginative use of seasonal ingredients; excellent tasting menu; wine list. ⑤ *Average main: £22* ⊠ *63 Tay St.* ☎ *01738/441451* ⊕ *www.63taystreet. com.*

 Hotels

Leonardo Boutique Hotel Huntingtower Perth

$$ | HOTEL | Less than 5 miles from Perth, this tranquil, traditional country hotel with an air of understated elegance has a spacious garden and trees that make it feel more rural than it really is. **Pros:** restful setting; amply sized rooms; dining room overlooks gardens. **Cons:** no elevator; perhaps a slight excess of tartan; no

air conditioning. ⑤ *Rooms from: £161* ⊠ *Crieff Road* ☎ *01738/583771* ⊕ *www. huntingtowerhotel.co.uk* ⤴ *34 rooms* ⦿⃝ *Free breakfast.*

Sunbank House Hotel

$ | B&B/INN | This handsome early-Victorian gray stone mansion near Perth's Branklyn Gardens overlooks the River Tay and the city of Perth. **Pros:** reasonably priced; friendly staff; delicious local cuisine. **Cons:** some rooms are very small; some traffic noise from the main road; 15 minutes' walk to town center. ⑤ *Rooms from: £105* ⊠ *50 Dundee Rd.* ☎ *01738/624882* ⊕ *www.sunbankhouse. com* ⤴ *9 rooms* ⦿⃝ *Free breakfast.*

 Shopping

Cairncross of Perth

JEWELRY/ACCESSORIES | The Romans coveted freshwater pearls from the River Tay. If you do, too, then head to Cairncross of Perth, where you can admire a display of some of the more unusual shapes and colors. Some of the delicate settings take their theme from Scottish flowers. ⊠ *18 St. John's St* ☎ *01738/624367* ⊕ *www. cairncrossofperth.co.uk.*

Whispers of the Past

JEWELRY/ACCESSORIES | This lovely shop has a collection of jewelry, china, and other gift items, some vintage and some new. ⊠ *15 George St.* ☎ *01738/635472* ⊕ *whispers-of-the-past.weebly.com.*

Dunkeld

14 miles north of Perth.

The historic town of Dunkeld remains intact and beautifully preserved with its rows of white houses around the town square. The original village was destroyed in 1689 in a ferocious battle during the Jacobite Rebellion and was rebuilt after its defeat by the Atholl family. Today it survives as part of the National Trust for Scotland's Little Houses Project, which helps maintain the houses. The town is overlooked by the grand but semiruined 12th-century cathedral (still used for services). Atholl Street, leading down to the River Tay, has several crafts shops and a hotel.

The bridge across the River Tay takes you to Birnam Wood, where Shakespeare's Macbeth met the three witches who issued the prophecy about his death. Witty wooden notices lead you to the right tree, a gnarled hollow oak.

GETTING HERE AND AROUND
Dunkeld is on the A9 between Perth and Pitlochry. The town is also on the main train line to Inverness.

 Sights

Beatrix Potter Exhibition and Garden
GARDEN | FAMILY | The interactive exhibition, specifically designed for children, celebrates the life and work of this much-beloved children's writer who, for many years, spent her family holidays in the area. You're free to walk around the enchanting garden where you can peep into the homes of Peter Rabbit and Mrs. Tiggy-Winkle, her best-known characters. The visitors center has a well-stocked shop and a small café serving breakfast, lunch, and coffee and cake. The garden is a mile south of Dunkeld, in Birnam. ✉ Birnam Arts Centre, Station Road, Birnam ☎ 01350/727674 ⊕ www.birnamarts.com ⊠ £3 exhibition, garden free.

Hermitage
FOREST | On the outskirts of Dunkeld, the Hermitage is a 1½-mile woodland walk that follows the River Braan. In the 18th century, the dukes of Atholl constructed two follies (fantasy buildings) here, **Ossian's Cave** and the awesomely decorated **Ossian's Hall**, above a spectacular—and noisy—waterfall. (Ossian was a fictional Celtic poet invented by James MacPherson in the 18th century for an era fascinated by the "primitive" past.) You'll also be in the presence of Britain's

tallest tree, a Douglas fir rising to 214 feet. ✉ Hermitage Car Park, Off A9 ✛ 2 miles west of Dunkeld ⊕ www.nts.org.uk ⊠ Free, parking lot £2.

 Restaurants

The Taybank
$$ | BRITISH | This lovely spot overlooking the River Tay is a musical meeting place once owned by Scottish singer and composer Dougie MacLean. It serves unpretentious but plentiful traditional pub food, like haggis, Cullen skink (fish soup), and stovies (a beef-and-potato dish) in the friendly, rough-and-ready bar. **Known for:** traditional Scottish fare; excellent music; beer garden. ⑤ Average main: £15 ✉ Tay Terrace ☎ 01350/727340 ⊕ www.thetaybankdunkeld.com.

 Shopping

Jeremy Law of Scotland
SHOES/LUGGAGE/LEATHER GOODS | At this family-owned business you can purchase deerskin shoes and moccasins, as well as leather items including jackets, gloves, shoes, and wallets. ✉ City Hall, Atholl Street ☎ 0800/146780 ⊕ www.moccasin.co.uk.

Pitlochry

15 miles north of Dunkeld.

In the late 19th century Pitlochry was an elegant Victorian spa town, famous for its mild microclimate and beautiful setting. Today it is a busy tourist town, with wall-to-wall gift shops, cafés, B&Bs, large hotels, and a huge golf course. The town itself is oddly nondescript, but it's a convenient base from which to explore the surrounding hills and valleys.

GETTING HERE AND AROUND
The main route through central Scotland, the A9, passes through Pitlochry, as does the main railway line from Glasgow/

Edinburgh to Inverness. From here the B8019 connects to the B846 west to Rannoch Moor or south to Aberfeldy.

ESSENTIALS

VISITOR INFORMATION VisitScotland Pitlochry iCentre. ⊠ 22 Atholl Rd. ☎ 01796/472215 ⊕ www. visitscotland.com/info/services/ pitlochry-icentre-p234421.

Sights

Edradour Distillery

WINERY/DISTILLERY | If you have a whisky-tasting bent, visit Edradour Distillery, which claims to be the smallest single-malt distillery in Scotland (but then, so do others). There's a fun, informative tour of the distillery where you get to see how the whisky is made; you also get to savor a free dram at the end of the tour. ⊠ Off A924 ⊕ 2½ miles east of Pitlochry ☎ 01796/472095 ⊕ www.edradour.com ⊠ Tours £12. There is a charge of £2 for using the toilet ⊗ Closed Sun. and Nov.–Mar.

★ Loch Rannoch

BODY OF WATER | With its shoreline of birch trees framed by dark pines, Loch Rannoch is the quintessential Highland loch, stretching more than 9 miles from west to east. Fans of Robert Louis Stevenson (1850–94), especially of *Kidnapped* (1886), will not want to miss the last, lonely section of road. Stevenson describes the setting: "The mist rose and died away, and showed us that country lying as waste as the sea, only the moorfowl and the peewees crying upon it, and far over to the east a herd of deer, moving like dots." ⊠ B846 ⊕ 20 miles west of Pitlochry.

Restaurants

Moulin Pub

$$ | **BRITISH** | At this traditional pub at the Moulin Hotel, you can eat in the pleasant dining room or at the lively bar, which has

dark, wooden interiors and some stuffed animals on the walls. Expect standard Scottish fare in generous quantities, including venison, scallops, and mussels; local produce is favored and the menu is spiced with some humorous naming. **Known for:** Scottish cuisine; ales made on-site; choice of lively or quiet dining. ⓢ Average main. £16 ⊠ 11–30 Kirkmichael Rd. ⊕ Between Pitlochry and Edradour ☎ 01796/472196 ⊕ www. moulinhotel.co.uk.

Hotels

★ Green Park Hotel

$$$ | **HOTEL** | Set among woods and on the shores of Loch Faskally, Green Park is a genuinely luxurious country-house hotel. **Pros:** great location; very attentive staff; country-house comfort. **Cons:** a slightly conservative feel; very popular, thus fills up far in advance; not as suitable for younger visitors. ⓢ Rooms from: £248 ⊠ Clunie Bridge Road ⊕ 5 mins north of Pitlochry center on A924 ☎ 01796/473248 ⊕ www.thegreenpark. co.uk ⊋ 51 rooms ⊗ All-inclusive.

Activities

GOLF

Blairgowrie Golf Club

GOLF | Well known to area golfers looking for a challenge, the Blairgowrie Golf Club's Rosemount Course is laid out on rolling land in the pine, birch, and fir woods, which bring a wild air to the scene. There are, however, wide fairways and at least some large greens. If Rosemount is hosting a tournament, you can play on Lansdowne, another 18-hole course, or Wee, a 9-hole course. ⊠ Golf Course Road, Blairgowrie ☎ 01250/872622 ⊕ www.theblairgowriegolfclub.co.uk ⊠ Rosemount/Lansdowne, May–Sept. £95, Apr. and Oct. £70, Nov.–Mar. £25; Wee, May–Sept. £20, Apr. and Oct. £17.50, Nov.–Mar. £7.50 ✗ Rosemount: 18 holes, 6630 yards, par 72;

Lansdowne: 18 holes, 6886 yards, par 72; Wee: 9 holes, 2327 yards, par 32.

Pitlochry Golf Course

GOLF | A decent degree of stamina is needed for the first three holes at Pitlochry, where steep climbs are involved. The reward is magnificent Highland scenery. Despite its relatively short length, this beautiful course has more than its fair share of surprises. The course offers golf with food packages. ⊠ *Golf Course Road* ☎ *01796/472792* ⊕ *www.pitlochry-golf.co.uk* ✉ *Apr.–Oct.: £42 weekdays, £50 weekends; Nov.–Mar. (restricted course) £10 weekdays, £20 weekends.* 🏌 *18 holes, 5681 yards, par 69.*

Blair Atholl

10 miles north of Pitlochry.

Located where the Tilt and Garry rivers flow together, this small town sits in the middle of the Grampian Mountains and is home to Blair Castle, one of Scotland's grandest of grand houses.

GETTING HERE AND AROUND

Popular Blair Castle is just off the A9 Pitlochry-to-Inverness road, beyond the village of Blair Atholl. The village has a railway station that is on the main Inverness line.

◉ Sights

★ Blair Castle

CASTLE/PALACE | Its setting among woodlands and gardens, together with its war-torn past, make Blair Castle one of Scotland's most highly rated sights. The turreted white castle was home to successive dukes of Atholl and their families, the Murrays, one of the most powerful in the land. During the Jacobite Rebellion of 1745, the loyalties of the Atholls were divided—a preserved piece of floor shows the marks of red-hot shot fired when the castle was under siege. In the end the supporters of the English king held off the rebels and were well rewarded for it. The dukes were allowed to retain a private army, the Atholl Highlanders. The castle entrance hall presents some of the dukes' collections of weapons, while a rich collection of furniture, china, and paintings occupies the family rooms. The grounds contain a 9-acre walled garden, an 18th-century folly, and a play area for children. ⊠ *Off B8079* ☎ *01796/481207* ⊕ *www.blair-castle.co.uk* ✉ *Castle and gardens £13, grounds only £7.70* ⊙ *Closed Nov.–Mar.*

Auchterarder

11 miles southeast of Crieff.

Famous for the Gleneagles Hotel (including its restaurant by Andrew Fairlie) and nearby golf courses, Auchterarder also has a flock of tiny antiques shops to amuse Gleneagles's golf widows and widowers.

GETTING HERE AND AROUND

Gleneagles station is on the main Inverness line, while the A9 gives direct access to Gleneagles and Auchterarder via the A823.

Restaurants

★ Andrew Fairlie at Gleneagles

$$$$ | **BRITISH** | Chef Andrew Fairlie established his restaurant in the Gleneagles Hotel in 2001, winning two Michelin stars for his elegant and restrained dishes. It is universally agreed that Fairlie set in motion a food revolution that changed Scottish cooking. **Known for:** two Michelin stars; cuisine marrying France and Scotland; a commitment to local produce. ⑤ *Average main: £110* ⊠ *Gleneagles Hotel, Off A823, Auchterarder* ☎ *01764/694267* ⊕ *www.andrewfairlie.co.uk* ⊙ *Closed Sun.*

🛏 Hotels

★ Gleneagles Hotel

$$$$ | HOTEL | One of Britain's most famous hotels, Gleneagles is the very essence of modern grandeur, a vast palace that stands hidden in breathtaking countryside amid its world-famous golf courses. **Pros:** luxurious rooms; famous Andrew Fairlie restaurant; the three courses are a golfer's paradise. **Cons:** quite conservative decor; restaurants get very crowded; nongolfers may feel out of place. ⑤ *Rooms from: £595* ✉ *Off A823* ☎ *01764/662231* ⊕ *www.gleneagles.com* 🛏 *258 rooms* ⦿⦿ *Free breakfast.*

🏃 Activities

GOLF

★ Gleneagles

GOLF | Its superb courses have made Gleneagles a part of golfing history. The 18 holes of the King's Course, designed by James Braid in 1919, have quirky names, such as the Warslin' Lea (Wrestling Ground)—the tough 17th hole that many golfers have grappled with. The Queen's Course mixes varied terrain, including woods and moors. Jack Nicklaus designed the PGA Centenary Course (host of the 2014 Ryder Cup), which sweeps into the Ochil Hills and has views of the Grampians. The 9-hole Wee Course provides challenges for beginners and pros. Gleneagles is also home to the PGA National Academy, a good place to improve your skills. ✉ *A823* ☎ *01764/662231* ⊕ *www.gleneagles. com* ⛳ *King's, Queen's, and PGA Centenary courses: May £150, June £180, July–Sept. 15 £220, Sept. 16–30 £250, Oct.1–15 £150, Oct.16–30 £99, Nov.– Mar. £80, Apr. £90* 🏌 *King's: 18 holes, 6790 yards, par 71; Queen's: 18 holes, 6790 yards, par 68; PGA Centenary: 18 holes, 6815 yards, par 72; Wee Course: 9 holes, 1418 yards, par 27.*

St. Andrews

52 miles northeast of Edinburgh, 83 miles northeast of Glasgow.

It may have a ruined cathedral and a grand university—the oldest in Scotland—but the modern claim to fame for St. Andrews is mainly its status as the home of golf. Forget that Scottish kings were crowned here, or that John Knox preached here and that Reformation reformers were burned at the stake here. Thousands flock to St. Andrews to play at the Old Course, home of the Royal & Ancient Club, and to follow in the footsteps of Hagen, Sarazen, Jones, and Hogan.

The layout is pure Middle Ages: its three main streets—North, Market, and South—converge on the city's earliest religious site, near the cathedral. Like most of the ancient monuments, the cathedral ruins are impressive in their desolation—but this town is no dusty museum. The streets are busy, the shops are stylish, the gray houses sparkle in the sun, and the scene is particularly brightened during the academic year by bicycling students in scarlet gowns.

GETTING HERE AND AROUND

If you arrive by car, be prepared for an endless drive round the town as you look for a parking space. The parking lots around Rose Park (behind the bus station and a short walk from the town center) are your best bet. If you arrive by local or national bus, the bus station is a five-minute walk from town. The nearest train station, Leuchars, is 10 minutes away by taxi (£15) or bus (£3.30), both of which can be found outside the station. St. Andrews can be fully enjoyed on foot without too much exertion.

ESSENTIALS

VISITOR INFORMATION St. Andrews. ✉ *70 Market St.* ☎ *01334/472021* ⊕ *www. visitscotland.com/destinations-maps/ st-andrews.*

◉ Sights

★ Bell Pettigrew Museum of Natural History

MUSEUM | Founded by Elsie Bell Pettigrew in memory of her husband, James, a former professor of medicine, this fascinating collection of zoological specimens takes you from sea to jungle, mountain to sky. The antiquated manner of their presentation reminds you of their significance in an age when most of these creatures were still unknown to most people. In the handsome 16th-century St. Mary's Quadrangle, home to the St. Andrews University's divinity and psychology departments, it is dominated by a holm oak and also contains a thorn tree supposedly planted by Mary, Queen of Scots. ✉ Bute Medical Bldg., Queens Gardens, off South St. ☎ 01334/461660 ⊕ www.st-andrews.ac.uk/museums/visit-us/bell-pettigrew ⊠ Free.

British Golf Museum

MUSEUM | Just opposite the Royal & Ancient Golf Club, this museum explores the centuries-old relationship between St. Andrews and golf and displays golf memorabilia from the 18th century to the 21st century. ✉ Bruce Embankment ☎ 01334/460046 ⊕ www.britishgolfmuseum.co.uk ⊠ £8.50.

St. Andrews Castle

ARCHAEOLOGICAL SITE | On the shore north of the cathedral stands ruined St. Andrews Castle, begun at the end of the 13th century. The remains include a rare example of a cold and gruesome bottle-shaped dungeon, in which many prisoners spent their last hours. Even more atmospheric is the castle's mine and countermine. The former was a tunnel dug by besieging forces in the 16th century; the latter, a tunnel dug by castle defenders in order to meet and wage battle belowground. You can stoop and crawl into this narrow passageway—an eerie experience, despite the addition of electric light. The visitor center has a good audiovisual presentation on the castle's history. In summer the beach below is popular with sunbathers and tide-pool investigators, weather permitting. ✉ N. Castle St. ☎ 01334/477196 ⊕ www.historicenvironment.scot ⊠ £6, £12 with St. Andrews Cathedral and St. Rule's Tower.

★ St. Andrews Cathedral

RELIGIOUS SITE | These are the poignant remains of what was once the largest and most magnificent church in Scotland. Work on it began in 1160, and after several delays it was finally consecrated in 1318. The church was subsequently damaged by fire and repaired but fell into decay during the Reformation. Only ruined gables, parts of the nave's south wall, and other fragments survive. The on-site museum helps you interpret the remains and gives a sense of what the cathedral must once have been like. ✉ Off Pends Rd. ☎ 01334/472563 ⊕ www.historicenvironment.scot ⊠ £6, includes St. Rule's Tower; £12 includes St. Andrews Castle.

St. Rule's Tower

VIEWPOINT | Local legend has it that St. Andrews was founded by St. Regulus, or Rule, who, acting under divine guidance, carried relics of St. Andrew by sea from Patras in Greece. He was shipwrecked on this Fife headland and founded a church. The holy man's name survives in the cylindrical tower, consecrated in 1126 and the oldest surviving building in St. Andrews. Enjoy dizzying views of town from the top of the 108-foot high tower, reached via a steep staircase. ✉ Off Pends Rd. ☎ 01334/472563 ⊕ www.historicenvironment.scot ⊠ £6, includes St. Andrews Cathedral; £12 includes St. Andrews Castle.

University of St. Andrews

COLLEGE | Scotland's oldest university is the alma mater of John Knox (Protestant reformer), King James II of Scotland, the Duke and Duchess of Cambridge (William and Kate), and Chris Hoy, Scotland's Olympic cyclist. Founded in 1411, the

Although it is considered to be in ruins, St. Andrews Castle is still one of the city's prettiest sites.

university's buildings pepper the town. For the quintessential University of St. Andrews experience, **St. Salvator's Quadrangle** reveals the magnificence of this historic institution. Looking out onto this impressive college green is the striking St. Salvator's Chapel, founded in 1450. It bears the marks of a turbulent past: the initials PH, carved into the paving stones under the bell tower, are those of Patrick Hamilton, who was burned alive outside the chapel for his Protestant beliefs. ⊠ *St. Mary's Pl.*

🍴 Restaurants

★ The Grange Inn

$$$$ | **CONTEMPORARY** | Fife foodies flock to this beautifully converted 17th-century farmhouse surrounded by verdant fields just 10 minutes outside town. The prix-fixe menus offer exquisitely crafted dishes using the best seasonal Scots produce such as beef, pork, mackerel, and wild sea trout. **Known for:** stunning location; great lunch deals; lovely views of St. Andrews. ⑤ *Average main: £30* ⊠ *Grange Rd.* ☎ *01334/472670* ⊕ *www.thegrange-inn.com* ⊘ *Closed Sun. and Mon.*

Tailend Restaurant

$ | **SEAFOOD** | The line of customers outside might be a bit off-putting, but just focus on the sweet smell of fish-and-chips from St. Andrews's best chipper. There's a busy light-filled dining room and modish seating area, or you can carry out and eat on the university grounds (though be wary of the dive-bombing gulls). **Known for:** the best fish-and-chips in St. Andrews; Arbroath smokies; fabulous starters and desserts. ⑤ *Average main: £14* ⊠ *130 Market St.* ☎ *01334/474070* ⊕ *www.thetailend.co.uk.*

The Saint

$ | **MODERN BRITISH** | **FAMILY** | Once local favorite the Westport, this reliable lunch and brunch stop has been revamped with swanky contemporary interiors complimented by a relaxed vibe, tasty cocktails, and excellent pub food. The reasonably priced menu offers everything from chunky gourmet sandwiches to seared scallops to heaped salads—all are best enjoyed in the flowery garden on sunny afternoons. **Known for:** gorgeous sun-draped beer garden; first-rate food from breakfast until late night; friendly youthful staff. $ *Average main: £14* ⊠ *170 South St.* ☎ *01334/473186* ⊕ *www.the-saint-bar.co.uk.*

 ## Hotels

Fairmont St Andrews

$$ | HOTEL | Two miles from St. Andrews, this modern hotel has spectacular views of the bay and two superb golf courses. **Pros:** spacious feel; spacious spa; golf at your doorstep. **Cons:** the huge atrium feels like a shopping center; paintings made to match the decor; food menu needs updating. $ *Rooms from: £199* ⊠ *A917* ☎ *01334/837000* ⊕ *www. fairmont.com/standrews* ⌁ *209 rooms* ❖ *Free breakfast.*

Old Course Hotel

$$$$ | HOTEL | Regularly hosting international golf stars and jet-setters, the Old Course Hotel has much-coveted guest room fairway views, grand public spaces, and fabulous facilities including a swanky spa. **Pros:** fabulous location and lovely views; unpretentious service; golfer's heaven. **Cons:** all the golf talk might bore nongolfers; standard rooms small and need an update; expensive. $ *Rooms from: £416* ⊠ *Old Station Rd.* ☎ *01334/474371* ⊕ *www.oldcoursehotel. co.uk* ⌁ *179 rooms* ❖ *Free breakfast.*

★ Rufflets St. Andrews

$$$ | HOTEL | Ten acres of formal and informal gardens surround this vine-covered country house with individually designed rooms, a wonderful restaurant, and a cozy lounge-bar with a handsome fireplace and terrace. **Pros:** attractive gardens; cozy drawing room; family-friendly lodges. **Cons:** too far to walk to St. Andrews; primarily venue for those celebrating, so can get noisy; no elevator in the main house. $ *Rooms from: £220* ⊠ *Strathkinness Low Rd.*

☎ *01334/472594* ⊕ *www.rufflets.co.uk* ⌁ *26 rooms* ❖ *Free breakfast.*

 ## Nightlife

Central Bar

BARS/PUBS | There are still some old-fashioned pubs to be found among the cocktail bars of St. Andrews, and this wood-and-leather-furnished haunt is a good bet for a friendly mingle with a pint in hand. You'll find a good range of beers (bottled and on tap) and decent pub food. ⊠ *77 Market St.* ☎ *01334/478296.*

 ## Shopping

Artery

CRAFTS | This well-curated shop sells work by local, Scottish, and British artists, including jewelry, ceramics, paintings, and intriguing handmade clocks. ⊠ *183 South St.* ☎ *01334/473153* ⊕ *arterygifts. com.*

Balgove Larder

FOOD/CANDY | Here you'll discover a huge selection of Scottish items, from spurtles (for stirring your porridge) to tablet (sugary toffee) to big, thick sausages made in its butchery. Foodies should check out the Farm Shop and monthly Night Market, while carnivores can follow their noses to the Steak Barn, where platters piled with huge hunks of beef and sausages are combined with twice-fried chips and onion rings. ⊠ *A91* ☎ *01334/898145* ⊕ *www.balgove.com.*

Mellis

FOOD/CANDY | This heady-smelling store is truly a cheese lover's mecca. Look for a soft, crumbly, and citrusy cheese (called Anster) made thanks to a local herd of Holstein-Friesians. ⊠ *149 South St.* ☎ *01334/471410* ⊕ *www.mellischeese. net.*

★ Topping and Company Booksellers

BOOKS/STATIONERY | This is a bibliophile's dream haunt, with high ceilings and alcoves lined with over 45,000 titles, knowledgeable staff, and frequent readings and literary events. ✉ *7 Greyfriars Garden* ☎ *01334/585111* ⊕ *www.topping-books.co.uk.*

Activities

GOLF

Eden Course

GOLF | The aptly named Eden Course, designed in 1914 by Harry S. Colt, winds through inland fields bordered with lovely foliage. It's a bit more forgiving compared to other St. Andrews courses. ✉ *West Sands Rd.* ⊕ *www.standrews. com* ⓢ *£25–£50* ⚐ *18 holes, 6250 yards, par 70*

★ Jubilee Course

GOLF | This windswept course offers quite a challenge even for experienced golfers. When it opened in 1897 it was intended for beginners, but the popularity of its seaside location encouraged the powers that be to convert it into a championship course. Many golfers say the 15th hole is one of the best in the sport. ✉ *West Sands Rd.* ⊕ *www.standrews.com* ⓢ *£40–£80* ⚐ *18 holes, 6742 yards, par 72.*

★ Old Course

GOLF | Believed to be the oldest golf course in the world, the Old Course was first played in the 15th century. Each year, more than 44,000 rounds are teed off, and no doubt most get stuck in one of its 112 bunkers. A handicap certificate and some very early morning waits for a possible tee-off are required. ✉ *West Sands Rd.* ⊕ *www.standrews.com* ⓢ *£90–£190* ⚐ *18 holes, 6721 yards, par 72.*

Crail

10 miles south of St. Andrews.

The oldest and most aristocratic of East Neuk burghs, pretty Crail is where many fish merchants retired and built cottages. The town landmark is a picturesque Dutch-influenced town house, or *tolbooth,* which contains the oldest bell in Fife, cast in Holland in 1520. Crail may now be full of artists, but it remains a working harbor; take time to walk the streets and beaches and to sample fish by the harbor. ■**TIP**➜ **As you head into East Neuk from this tiny port, look about for market crosses, merchant houses, and little doocots (dovecotes, where pigeons were kept)—typical picturesque touches of this region.**

GETTING HERE AND AROUND

Stagecoach bus No. 95 operates between Crail and St. Andrews. This service also takes you on to Anstruther, Pittenweem, St. Monans, and Lower Largo. Crail is about 15 minutes from St. Andrews by car via A917.

Sights

Crail Museum and Heritage Centre

MUSEUM | The story of this trading and fishing town can be found in the delightfully crammed Crail Museum and Heritage Centre, entirely run by local volunteers. There is a small tourist information desk within the center and fascinating guided walks start here Wedesday and Sunday from June through October. ✉ *62–64 Marketgate* ☎ *01333/450869* ⊕ *www.crailmuseum.org.uk* ⓢ *Free* ⊘ *Closed Oct.–Mar. Limited hrs Apr. and May.*

🍴 Restaurants

★ Reilly Shellfish Lobster Hut

$$ | **SEAFOOD** | This hut on the pier, a hidden gem, sells beautifully cooked lobsters for £12–£20 each (depending on size) and other items at times, including lobster rolls and dressed crab. They'll crack the lobster for you to allow for easy eating on a nearby bench; there is no seating, but the lobster is wonderful. **Known for:** freshest seafood; casual alfresco eating in a beach and harbor setting; varying, sometimes random hours.

St. Andrews and East Neuk

North Sea

Isle of May

Firth of Forth

$ *Average main: £15* ✉ *34 Shoregate*
☎ *01333/450476* ⊙ *Closed winter and
Mon. No dinner* ⊟ *No credit cards.*

 Hotels

The Hazelton
$ | **B&B/INN** | Beautifully polished wood,
exquisitely restored period features, and
gentle hues put the Hazelton head and
shoulders above the typical seaside B&B.
Pros: handsome building; central location
near pub and harbor; decent breakfast.
Cons: a couple of rooms on the small
side; unreliable communication via email;
intermittent traffic noise. $ *Rooms from:
£85* ✉ *29 Marketgate N* ☎ *01333/450250*
⊕ *www.thehazelton.co.uk* ⊙ *Closed Jan*
↪ *5 rooms* ⊙ *Free breakfast.*

Anstruther

4 miles southwest of Crail.

Anstruther, locally called Ainster, has
a lovely waterfront with a few shops
brightly festooned with children's pails
and shovels, a gesture to summer
vacationers.

GETTING HERE AND AROUND
Stagecoach bus No. 95 operates
between St. Andrews, Crail, Anstruther,
Pittenweem, St. Monans, and Lower Largo. By car Anstruther is 5 to 10 minutes
from Crail via A917.

 Sights

Isle of May Boat Trip
BOAT TOURS | Take to the waves (April
through September) on the compact *May*

Princess for a round-trip to the Isle of May, a rocky bird reserve near the mouth of the Forth. Measuring just under a mile long and a third of a mile wide, it harbors 14 species of breeding birds including arctic terns, guillemots, and puffins. The round-trip takes five hours, with three hours on shore to explore the island's history, monastery remains, and the breathtaking sights, sounds, and smells of the avian multitudes. ⊠ Middle Pier, Anstruther Harbour ☎ 07957/585200 ⊕ www.isleofmayferry.com ✆ £28.

★ **Scottish Fisheries Museum**

MUSEUM | FAMILY | Facing Anstruther Harbor, the Scottish Fisheries Museum is inside a colorful cluster of buildings, the earliest of which dates from the 16th century. A charming trail around the various buildings and odd spaces illustrates the life of Scottish fisherfolk; you can spend a couple of hours examining the many documents, artifacts, model ships, paintings, and displays (complete with the reek of tarred rope and net). There are floating exhibits at the quayside and a window onto a working boatyard. ⊠ Harbourhead ☎ 01333/310628 ⊕ www.scotfishmuseum.org ✆ £9.

🍴 Restaurants

★ **Anstruther Fish Bar and Restaurant**

$ | SEAFOOD | Next door to the Scottish Fisheries Museum, this popular fish-and-chips shop has a functional space to eat, but most people order takeout. Try local specialties including Pittenweem prawns in batter or the catch of the day, which could be mackerel (line caught by the owners), hake, or local crab. **Known for:** consistently excellent fish-and-chips; friendly staff; ice-cream counter with novel flavors. ⑤ Average main: £11 ⊠ 42–44 Shore St. ☎ 01333/310518 ⊕ www.anstrutherfishbar.co.uk.

The Cellar

$$$$ | EUROPEAN | Entered through a cobbled courtyard, this unpretentious,

atmospheric restaurant is run by talented head chef Billy Boyter and family. The three-course prix-fixe meals feature locally sourced seafood and meat such as crab, hake, mussels, beef, lamb, and quail. **Known for:** elegant yet informal dining; exquisite produce; wine-pairing option. ⑤ Average main: £70 ⊠ 24 E. Green ☎ 01333/310378 ⊕ www.thecellaranstruther.co.uk ☉ Closed Mon. and Tues. No lunch Wed.

🍸 Nightlife

★ **Dreel Tavern**

BARS/PUBS | A 16th-century coaching inn, the Dreel Tavern was resurrected and refurbished in 2017 by two young sisters who have built on the characterful stone building and added some tasteful improvements including an impressive food menu. Alongside decent draft beers, the excellent food showcases local produce such as lobster and smoked fish. The low-ceilinged wood-beamed bar makes for a lively atmosphere, especially during the occasional low-key musical gigs and gourmet events that happen here. A pretty beer garden overlooks the Dreel Burn and the family garden where much of the produce on the menu grows. ⊠ 16 High St. ☎ 01333/279238 ⊕ www.dreeltavern.co.uk.

Falkland

24 miles northwest of Pittenweem, 15 miles northwest of Elie.

One of the loveliest communities in Scotland, Falkland is a royal burgh of twisting streets and crooked stone houses.

GETTING HERE AND AROUND

Stagecoach bus No. 64 is the only direct service connecting Falkland to St. Andrews as well as Cupar and Ladybank (both of which are train stations on the Edinburgh to Dundee line). Falkland is about 15 minutes from Cupar and a half hour from St. Andrews by car via A91 and A912, or A91 to A914 to A912.

Sights

Falkland Palace

CASTLE/PALACE | A former hunting lodge of the Stuart monarchs, Falkland Palace dominates the town and is one of the country's earliest and finest examples of the French Renaissance style. Overlooking the main street is the palace's most impressive feature, the walls and chambers on its south side, all rich with buttresses and stone medallions, built by French masons in the 1530s for King James V (1512–42). He died here, and the palace was a favorite resort of his daughter, Mary, Queen of Scots (1542–87). The beautiful gardens behind Falkland Palace contain a rare survivor: a royal tennis court, built in 1539. In the gardens, overlooked by the palace turret windows, you may easily imagine yourself back at the solemn hour when James on his deathbed pronounced the doom of the house of Stuart: "It cam' wi' a lass and it'll gang wi a lass." ⊠ *Main St.* ☎ *01337/857397* ⊕ *www.nts.org.uk* ⊠ *£13* ⊘ *Closed Nov.–Feb.*

🍴 Restaurants

★ Pillars of Hercules

$ | VEGETARIAN | FAMILY | Head down a country lane to this organic farm and café-bistro for a tasty vegetarian meal made of produce grown in the wonderful gardens. On a sunny day take your crepe or heaped salad to a bench outside by the nursery, or grab some take-out deli foods from the shop. **Known for:** organic produce grown on-site; inventive dishes; beautiful grounds. ⑤ *Average main: £8* ⊠ *A912* ⊹ *1 mile northwest of Falkland* ☎ *01337/857749* ⊕ *www.pillars.co.uk* ⊘ *No dinner.*

Dundee

14 miles northwest of St. Andrews, 58 miles north of Edinburgh, 79 miles northeast of Glasgow.

Dundee makes an excellent base for a cultural stay and Fife and Angus exploration at any time of year. The Dundee Contemporary Arts center gave the city a much-needed boost in 1999; today artsy and foodie hangouts and a vibrant mix of student and creative life make it a beguiling stop. As you explore the streets and new waterfront, including the green expanse of Slessor Gardens, you may glimpse contrasting bold lines of the 2018 V&A Dundee museum of design, 1966 Tay Road Bridge, and 1888 Tay Rail Bridge. Those ever-changing views of the Tay led actor and wordsmith Stephen Fry to describe Dundee's setting as "ludicrously ideal." Heading southwest down cobbled Roseangle you reach Magdalen Green, where landscape artist James McIntosh Patrick (1907–98) found inspiration from the river and skyscapes. Dundonians' deadpan humor was distilled in the popular comic strips *The Beano* and *The Dandy,* first published here in the 1930s; statues by Scottish sculptors Tony and Susie Morrow depicting characters Desperate Dan, Dawg, and a catapult-wielding Minnie the Minx are in City Square.

GETTING HERE AND AROUND

The East Coast train line runs through the city, linking it to Edinburgh (and beyond, to London), Glasgow (and the West Coast of England), and Aberdeen, with trains to all every hour or half hour at peak times. Cheaper bus service is available to all these locations, as well as St. Andrews and several other towns in Fife and Angus.

If you're traveling by car, the A92 will take you north from Fife to Abroath and the Angus coast towns. The A90, from Perth, heads north to Aberdeen.

Most of the sights in Dundee are clustered together, so you can easily walk around the city. If the weather is bad or your legs are heavy, hail one of the many cabs on the easy-to-find taxi ranks for little more than a few pounds.

ESSENTIALS

VISITOR INFORMATION VisitScotland Dundee iCentre. ⊠ *16 City Sq.* ☎ *01382/527527* ⊕ *www.dundee.com.*

 ## Sights

Dundee Botanic Garden

GARDEN | FAMILY | This renowned botanical garden contains an extensive collection of native and exotic plants outdoors and in tropical and temperate greenhouses. There are some beautiful areas for picnicking, as well as a visitor center, an art gallery, and a coffee shop. ⊠ *Riverside Dr.* ☎ *01382/381190* ⊕ *www.dundee. ac.uk/botanic* ⊠ *£3.90.*

★ Dundee Contemporary Arts

MUSEUM | FAMILY | Between a 17th-century mansion and a cathedral, this strikingly modern building houses one of Britain's most exciting artistic venues. The two galleries house changing shows by internationally acclaimed contemporary artists. There are children's and adult's workshops, special events, and meet-the-artist events throughout the year. Two movie theaters screen mainly independent, revival, and children's films. There's also a craft shop and a buzzing café-bar that's open until midnight. ⊠ *152 Nethergate* ☎ *01382/432444* ⊕ *www.dca. org.uk* ⊠ *Free.*

★ McManus Galleries

MUSEUM | Dundee's principal museum and art gallery, housed in a striking Gothic Revival–style building, has an engaging collection of artifacts that document the city's history and the working, social, and cultural lives of Dundonians throughout the Victorian period and the 20th century. Its varied fine art collection includes paintings by Rossetti, Raeburn, and Peploe as well as thought-provoking yet accessible contemporary works and visiting exhibitions. ⊠ *Albert Sq.* ☎ *01382/307200* ⊕ *www.mcmanus.co.uk* ⊠ *Free.*

★ RRS *Discovery*

HISTORIC SITE | FAMILY | Dundee's urban-renewal program—the city is determined to celebrate its industrial past—was motivated in part by the arrival of the RRS (Royal Research Ship) *Discovery,* the vessel used by Captain Robert F. Scott (1868–1912) on his polar explorations. The steamer was originally built and launched in Dundee; now it's a permanent resident, sitting by the suitably clifflike V&A museum. At Discovery Point, under the handsome cupola, the story of the ship and its famous expedition unfold, you can even feel the Antarctic chill as if you were there. The ship, berthed outside, is the star: wander the deck, then explore the quarters to see the daily existence endured by the ship's crew and captain. ⊠ *Discovery Quay, Riverside Dr.* ☎ *01382/309060* ⊕ *www.rrsdiscovery.com* ⊠ *£11.50, £18.65 includes Verdant Works.*

★ V&A Dundee

MUSEUM | Opened to worldwide acclaim in 2018, the first outpost of the Victoria and Albert Museum of London is housed in an arresting riverside building by Japanese architect Kengo Kuma. Scotland's first-ever design museum contains seminal works and inspiring displays by Scots and international designers. The Scottish Design Galleries present the past, present, and future through the V&A collections and loans from around the world. Among the many highlights is Charles Rennie Mackintosh's Oak Room, unveiled for the first time in 50 years. Stellar shows, exclusively created for the new V&A galleries, spark inspiration among young and old. This "living room for the city," as Kuma described his design, is worth a visit for the building and setting alone: the vistas

Locke Hall

The acclaimed V&A Dundee features exhibits from designers across Scotland, including local legend Charles Rennie Mackintosh.

in and around its sea-cliff-like edges and perches provide places to linger, mingle, and reflect. If the weather is bad, the Living Room Café here is a great place to linger, refuel, and admire the views of the architecture and river, plus the gift shop has a wealth of quirky design gift ideas. ⊠ *Discovery Quay* ⊕ *www.vam. ac.uk* ⊠ *Free for permament collection; £12 for temporary exhibits.*

Verdant Works

MUSEUM | FAMILY | In a former jute mill, Verdant Works houses a multifaceted exhibit on the story of jute and the town's involvement in the jute trade. Restored machinery, audiovisual displays, and tableaux all bring to life the hard, noisy life of the jute worker. A light and airy café serves lovely little cakes. ⊠ *W. Hendersons Wynd* ☎ *01382/309060* ⊕ *www. verdantworks.com* ⊠ *£11.50, £18.65 includes RRS Discovery* ⊗ *Closed Mon. and Tues. Nov.–Mar.*

🍴 Restaurants

Boat Brae

$$ | BRITISH | Located within Newport's handsome former Victorian ferry terminal, this is a stunning spot to dine casually while spellbound by views of the Tay River and the Dundee skyline across the water. A versatile menu includes seafood shared platters and maritime mains, Scots steaks and lamb, and plenty of vegetarian options. **Known for:** historic building associated with the Thomas Telford-desgned pier; excellent breakfasts, sandwiches, and a cozy wood-filled bar; huge west-facing windows for sunset dining. ⑤ *Average main: £16* ⊠ *2–14 Boat Brae* ✛ *In Newport across the Tay; take bus 77 or X54* ☎ *01382/540540* ⊕ *www. boatbrae.com.*

★ Jute

$$ | BRITISH | Downstairs at Dundee Contemporary Arts, this lively eatery serves breakfast at the bar, cocktails and snacks on the terrace in fine weather, or dinner in the open-plan dining area with huge windows that offer views of artists at work in the printmakers studio. There are plenty of handsomely presented dishes featuring quality Scottish meat, fish, and vegetables. **Known for:** open-plan dining in artsy atmosphere; good for lunch and bar snacks; busy on weekends. $ *Average main: £16* ✉ *152 Nethergate* ☎ *01382/909246* ⊕ *www.jutecafebar. co.uk.*

★ Sol y Sombra Tapas Bar

$$$ | TAPAS | It looks like an old Scottish pub, and it is, but the vibrant ceramics, tapas, and sangria are so authentic they'll make you feel as if you're in España. Choose from the set menus, like a £10 lunch or £25 dinner, and you'll be served a steady stream of cracking little dishes. **Known for:** boisterous atmosphere; revelatory tapas; occasional live music. $ *Average main: £25* ✉ *27 Gray St., Broughty Ferry* ☎ *01382/776941* ⊕ *www. solysombratapasbar.co.uk.*

Hotels

Duntrune House

$ | B&B/INN | Set among acres of tidy lawns and rustling trees, this mansion is a genteel contrast to the city and even has a resident ghost. **Pros:** owners are keen genealogists and can offer advice to ancestor seekers; the house and gardens are full of interesting decor; self-catering flat available, too. **Cons:** might be too cluttered for some tastes; minimum two-night stay; five miles out of town. $ *Rooms from: £110* ✉ *Off A90, Duntrune* ✢ *5 miles northeast of Dundee* ☎ *01382/350239* ⊕ *duntrunehouse.co.uk* ☉ *Closed Nov.–Feb.* ⇆ *3 rooms* ◎ *Free breakfast.*

★ Shaftesbury Lodge

$ | HOTEL | Just off Perth Road, this Victorian-era villa set among well-tended shrubs is a find for those who like smaller, more intimate hotels. **Pros:** first-rate service; handsome Victorian details; close, but not too close, to the city. **Cons:** some

bathrooms are small; 15-minute walk into town; decor a tad dated. $ *Rooms from: £90* ✉ *1 Hyndford St.* ☎ *01382/669216* ⊕ *www.shaftesburylodge.co.uk* ⇆ *12 rooms* ◎ *Free breakfast.*

Nightlife

★ Clarks on Lindsay Street

MUSIC | This busy bar hosts live music until the early hours. Get in early to avoid the lines. ✉ *80 N. Lindsay St.* ☎ *01382/224925* ⊕ *www.clarksonlindsaystreet.com.*

Draffens

BARS/PUBS | Secreted down a wynd (alley), this small speakeasy has stylish, exposed-brick interiors, with decorative nods to the defunct Draffens department store and plenty of cocktail shaking going on. ✉ *Couttie's Wynd, Nethergate.*

Jute

BARS/PUBS | Better known as the bar at Dundee Contemporary Arts, this café-bar attracts film fans (the art-house cinema's entrance is next door), students, and the well-heeled for European beers, wine, cocktails, or coffee. It serves tasty bar snacks every night and hosts events related to the arts and cinema. ✉ *152 Nethergate* ☎ *01382/909246* ⊕ *www. jutecafebar.co.uk.*

★ Speedwell Bar

BARS/PUBS | Called Mennie's by locals, the Speedwell Bar is in a mahogany-paneled building brimming with Dundonian characters and architectural features. It's renowned for its superb cask beers, choice of malts, and Edwardian interior. ✉ *165–168 Perth Rd.* ☎ *01382/667783.*

Performing Arts

★ Dundee Repertory Theatre

THEATER | This is home to the award-winning Dundee Rep Ensemble and to Scotland's preeminent contemporary-dance group, Scottish Dance Theatre. Popular with locals, the restaurant and bar

Dundee and Angus

welcome late-night comedy shows and jazz bands. ⊠ *Tay Sq.* ☎ *01382/223530* ⊕ *www.dundeerep.co.uk.*

Shopping

Gallery Q
JEWELRY/ACCESSORIES | A compelling selection of jewelry, ceramics, textiles, sculptures, prints, and paintings by Scottish artists awaits at Gallery Q. ⊠ *160 Nethergate* ☎ *01382/220600* ⊕ *www. galleryq.co.uk.*

J. Allan Braithwaite
FOOD/CANDY | Established in 1868 and in its current home since 1932, this enticingly aromatic emporium has large old vats of many freshly roasted coffee blends and tea that you can pop into one of the quaint teapots you'll find here. ⊠ *6 Castle St.* ☎ *01382/322693.*

Activities

GOLF
★ Carnoustie Golf Links
GOLF | The venue for the British Open in 1999, 2007, and 2018, the coastal links around Carnoustie have challenged golfers since at least 1527. Winners here have included many of the sport's biggest names: Armour, Hogan, Cotton, Player, and Watson. There are three courses, the most famous of which is the breathtaking Championship Course, ranked among the very best in the world. The choice Burnside course is full of historical interest and local color, as well as being tough and interesting. The Buddon course, designed by Peter Allis and Dave Thomas, is recommended for links novices. ⊠ *20 Links Parade, Carnoustie* ☎ *01241/802270* ⊕ *www.carnoustiegolflinks.co.uk* ⊠ *Championship, £210; Buddon, £75;*

Burnside, £75 🏌. *Championship Course:*
18 holes, 6948 yards, par 72; Buddon
Course: 18 holes, 5921 yards, par 68;
Burnside Course: 18 holes, 6028 yards,
par 68 ⛳ *Reservations essential.*

transportation; bar and live-music nights
may be noisy; poor email communication. 💲 *Rooms from: £125* ✉ *B955, Glen*
Clova ☎ *01575/550350* ⊕ *www.clova.*
com ⟿ *10 rooms* ❮❷❯ *Free breakfast.*

The Angus Glens

25 miles northwest of Brechin.

You can rejoin the hurly-burly of the
A90 for the return journey south from
Montrose or Brechin; the more pleasant
route, however, leads southwester-
ly on minor roads (there are several
options) that travel along the face of the
Grampians, following the fault line that
separates Highlands and Lowlands. The
Angus Glens extend north from points on
A90. Known individually as the glens of
Isla, Prosen, Clova, and Esk, these long
valleys run into the high hills of the Grampians and some clearly marked walking
routes. Those in Glen Clova are especially
appealing.

Be aware that Thursday is a half day in
Angus; many shops and attractions close
at lunch.

GETTING HERE AND AROUND
You really need a car to reach the Angus
Glens and enjoy the gentle (and not so
gentle) inclines here. Glamis and Kirriemuir are both on the A928 (just off the
A90), and the B955—which loops round
at Glen Clova—is one of the loveliest
Scottish roads to drive along, especially
when the heather is blooming in late
summer.

Hotels

Glen Clova Hotel
$$ | HOTEL | Since the 1850s, the hospi-
tality of this hotel has lifted the spirits
of many a bone-tired hill walker, and it
remains as comfortable a spot as ever
today. **Pros:** stunning location; great base
for outdoor pursuits; spacious accommodations. **Cons:** lack of decent public

Kirriemuir

15 miles southwest of Brechin.

Kirriemuir stands at the heart of Angus's
red-sandstone countryside and was
the birthplace of the writer J. M. Barrie
(1860–1937), best known abroad as the
author of *Peter Pan* (a statue of whom
you can see in the town's square). *Kirrie,*
as it's known here, salutes favorite son
Bon Scott (1946–80)—the rasping AC/DC
vocalist—in a bronze-and-Caithness-rock
memorial statue at Bellies Brae. Metal pilgrims gather each springtime for Bonfest.

GETTING HERE AND AROUND
A number of roads lead to Kirriemuir,
but A928 (off A90), which also passes
Glamis Castle, is one of the loveliest.
Stagecoach Strathtay runs buses to this
area; Nos. 20 and 22 from Dundee are
the most regular.

Sights

Camera Obscura
VIEWPOINT | FAMILY | J. M. Barrie donated
this Camera Obscura to the town; located within a cricket pavilion, it magically
projects an image of the wonderful
landscape views onto the opposite wall.
It is one of only four in the country and
run by lovely volunteers. ✉ *Kirrie Hill*
☎ *01575/575885* ⊕ *www.kirriemuircam-*
eraobscura.com 💲 *Free (donations wel-*
come) 🕑 *Closed Nov.–Mar. and Tues.–Fri.*

J.M. Barrie's Birthplace
HOUSE | At J. M. Barrie's Birthplace, the
National Trust pays tribute to the man
who sought to preserve the magic of
childhood more than any other writer
of his age. The house's upper floors are
furnished as they might have been in

Barrie's time, complete with domestic necessities, while downstairs is his study, replete with manuscripts and personal mementos. The outside washhouse is said to have served as Barrie's first theater. ⊠ *9 Brechin Rd.* ☎ *01575/572646* ⊕ *www.nts.org.uk/Property/J-M-Barries-Birthplace/* ⊠ *£7* ⊘ *Closed Oct.–Mar. and Tues.–Fri.*

Kirriemuir Gateway to the Glens Museum

MUSEUM | As is the style in Angus, the local museum doubles as the visitor center, meaning you can get all the information you need and admire a few stuffed birds and artifacts at the same time. Rock fans will appreciate the exhibit celebrating local lad made good (or rather bad), the late Bon Scott, original lead singer of the rock band AC/DC. ⊠ *32 High St.* ☎ *01575/526006* ⊕ *archive.angus.gov. uk* ⊠ *Free* ⊘ *Closed Sun. and Mon.*

🍴 Restaurants

88 Espresso

$ | **CAFÉ** | **FAMILY** | If you're not in a rush (service can be slow), take time to savor excellent coffee, inventive sandwiches, pizzettes, cakes, and handmade chocolates at this appealing café and shop selling quality fare. If you're in a hurry, buy delicious cheese or chocolates to go or pick up a cheese and apple scone. **Known for:** creative house-baking including sourdough bread; handmade chocolates and truffles; cash-only policy. ⑤ *Average main: £8* ⊠ *17 High St.* ☎ *07449/345089* ⊘ *Closed Mon. and Tues. No dinner* ⊟ *No credit cards.*

Glamis

5 miles southwest of Forfar, 6 miles south of Kirriemuir.

Set in rolling countryside is the little village of Glamis (pronounced *glahms*), the highlight of which is nearby famous Glamis Castle.

GETTING HERE AND AROUND

The drive to Glamis Castle, along beech- and yew-lined roads, is as majestic as the castle itself. Take the A90 north from Dundee, then off onto the A928. The village of Glamis can be reached by the Stagecoach Strathtay No. 22, but service is rather infrequent.

👁 Sights

★ Glamis Castle

CASTLE/PALACE | One of Scotland's best known and most beautiful castles, Glamis Castle connects Britain's royalty through 10 centuries, from Macbeth (Thane of Glamis) to the late Queen Mother and her daughter, the late Princess Margaret, born here in 1930 (the first royal princess born in Scotland in 300 years). The property of the earls of Strathmore and Kinghorne since 1372, the castle was largely reconstructed in the late 17th century; the original keep, which is much older, is still intact. One of the most famous rooms in the castle is Duncan's Hall, the legendary setting for Shakespeare's *Macbeth*. Guided tours allow you to see fine collections of china, tapestries, and furniture. Within the castle is the delightful Castle Kitchen restaurant; the grounds contain a huge gift shop, a shop selling local produce, and a pleasant picnic area. ■**TIP→ If you are looking to hear the pipes and see some Highland dancing and games of strength, the Strathmore Highland Games are held here around the second weekend of June. See www.strathmorehighlandgames.co.uk for more information.** ⊠ *A94* ✛ *1 mile north of Glamis* ☎ *01307/840393* ⊕ *www. glamis-castle.co.uk* ⊠ *£15.50* ⊘ *Closed Nov.–Feb.*

Chapter 18

ABERDEEN AND THE NORTHEAST

Updated by
Robin Gauldie

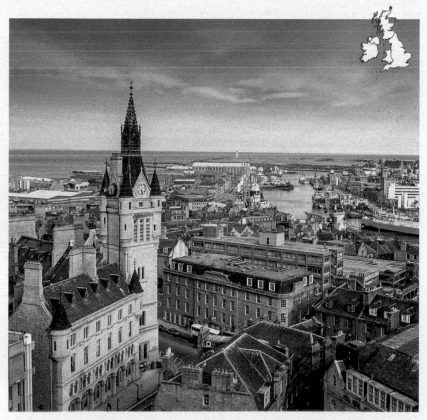

⊙ Sights	🍴 Restaurants	🛏 Hotels	🛍 Shopping	🍸 Nightlife
★★★☆☆	★★★☆☆	★★☆☆☆	★☆☆☆☆	★★☆☆☆

WELCOME TO ABERDEEN AND THE NORTHEAST

TOP REASONS TO GO

★ **Castles:** With more than 75 castles, some Victorian and others dating back to the 13th century, this area has everything from ravaged ruins like Dunnottar to opulent Fyvie Castle.

★ **Distilleries:** The valley of the River Spey is famous for its single-malt distilleries, including those connected by the signposted Malt Whisky Trail.

★ **Seaside cities and towns:** The fishing industry may be in decline, but the big-city port of Aberdeen and the colorful smaller fishing towns of Stonehaven and Cullen in the northeast are great (and very different) places to soak up the seagoing atmosphere—and some seafood.

★ **Walking:** There are all types of walking for all kinds of walkers, from the bracing but spectacular inclines of the Grampian Hills to the wooded gardens and grounds of Balmoral and Haddo House.

Aberdeen, on the North Sea in the eastern part of the region, is Scotland's third-largest city; many people start a trip here. Once you have spent time in the city, you may be inclined to venture west into rural Deeside, with its royal connections and looming mountain backdrop. To the north of Deeside is Castle Country, with many ancient fortresses. Speyside and the Whisky Trail lie at the western edge of the region and are equally accessible from Inverness. From Speyside you might travel back east along the pristine coastline at Scotland's northeastern tip.

1 Aberdeen. The gateway to the northeast.

2 Stonehaven. A seaside town with an iconic castle nearby.

3 Banchory. A popular stop on the way to Deeside.

4 Ballater. A handsome riverside town with royal connections.

5 Braemar. Home of the original Highland Games.

6 Alford. An unassuming village next to mighty Castle Fraser.

7 Dufftown. Speyside's whisky capital.

8 Craigellachie. An angler's delight located beside the River Spey.

9 Aberlour. A charming small town surrounded by distilleries.

10 Fochabers. A charming market town.

11 Cullen. Harbor village famed for seafood and white sands.

12 Banff. A fishing haven surrounded by Georgian houses.

13 Fyvie Castle. Grand Edwardian retreat with a superb art collection.

14 Ellon. A pretty suburb with magnificent gardens.

Here in this granite shoulder of Grampian, are some of Scotland's most enduring travel icons: Royal Deeside, the countryside that Queen Victoria made her own; the Castle Country route, where fortresses stand hard against the hills; and the Malt Whisky Trail, where peaty streams embrace the country's greatest concentration of distilleries.

The region's gateway is the city of Aberdeen. Once a prosperous merchant port, it became a boomtown in the 1970s with the discovery of oil beneath the North Sea, but as oil and gas reserves dwindle, the city is looking in new directions for its wealth.

More than 125 miles north of the central belt of Glasgow and Edinburgh, Aberdeen has historically been a fairly autonomous place. Even now it's perceived by many U.K. inhabitants as lying almost out of reach in the northeast. In reality it's a 90-minute flight from London or a little more than two hours by car from Edinburgh. Its 18th- and early-19th-century city center amply rewards exploration. Yet even if this popular base for travelers vanished from the map, an extensive portion of the northeast would still remain at the top of many travelers' wish lists.

Balmoral, the Scottish baronial–style house built for Queen Victoria as a retreat, is merely the most famous castle in the area, and certainly not the oldest. There are so many others that in one part of the region a Castle Trail has been established. In later structures, such as Castle Fraser, you can trace the changing styles and tastes of each of their owners over the centuries. Grand mansions such as 18th-century Haddo House, with its symmetrical facade and elegant interior, surrender any defensive role entirely.

A trail leading to a more ephemeral kind of pleasure can be found south of Elgin and Banff, where the glens embrace Scotland's greatest concentration of malt-whisky distilleries. With so many in Morayshire, where the distilling is centered on the valley of the River Spey and its tributaries, there's now a Malt Whisky Trail. Follow it, and visit other distilleries as well, to experience a surprising wealth of flavors.

The northeast's chief topographical attraction lies in the gradual transition from high mountain plateau—by a series of gentle steps through hill, forest, and farmland—to the Moray Firth and North Sea coast, where the word *unadulterated* is redefined. Here you'll find some of the United Kingdom's most perfect wild shorelines, both sandy and sheer cliff, and breezy fishing villages like Cullen on the Banffshire coast and Stonehaven, south of Aberdeen. The Grampian Mountains, to the west, contain some of the highest ground in the nation, in the area of the Cairngorms.

MAJOR REGIONS

Aberdeen. Family connections or Royal Deeside often take travelers to this part of Scotland, but many are surprised by how grand and rich in history Aberdeen is. The august granite-turreted buildings and rose-lined roads make this a surprisingly pleasant city to explore; don't miss Old Aberdeen in particular.

Royal Deeside and Castle Country. Deeside, the valley running west from Aberdeen down which the River Dee flows, earned its "royal" appellation when Prince Albert designed Balmoral Castle for Queen Victoria, and so began the royal family's love affair with Deeside—and Deeside's love affair with it. To this day, where royalty goes, lesser aristocracy and freshly minted millionaires follow. Many still aspire to own a grand shooting estate in Deeside, and you may appreciate this yearning when you see the piney hills, purple moors, and blue river intermingling. As you travel deeper into the Grampian Mountains, Royal Deeside's gradual scenic change adds a growing sense of excitement. This area has long been the retreat or the fortress of distinguished families, as the clutter of castles throughout the region shows. There are castles along the Dee as well as to the north in Castle Country, a region that illustrates the gradual geological change in the northeast: uplands lapped by a tide of farms. All the Donside and Deeside castles are picturesquely sited, with most fitted out with tall, slender turrets, winding stairs, and crooked chambers that epitomize Scottish baronial style. All have tales of ghosts and bloodshed, siege and torture. Many were tidied up and "domesticated" during the 19th century. Although best toured by car, much of this area is accessible either by public transportation or on tours from Aberdeen. The majesty of the countryside also guarantees a superlative stop for everyone interested in history and romance.

The Northeast and the Malt Whisky Trail. North of Deeside another popular area of this region lies inland, toward Speyside—the valley, or strath, of the River Spey—famed for its whisky distilleries, some of which it promotes in another signposted trail. Distilling Scotch is not an intrinsically spectacular process. It involves pure water, malted barley, and sometimes peat smoke, then a lot of bubbling and fermentation, all of which cause a number of odd smells. The result is a prestigious product with a fascinating range of flavors that you may either enjoy immensely or not at all. Unique in their architecture, their ingredients, and the end product, the distilleries of Speyside are keen to share with you their passion for "the water of life." This region also has rolling hills and, to the north, the beautiful, wild coastline of the North Sea. Instead of closely following the Malt Whisky Trail, dip into it and blend visits to distilleries with some other aspects of the county of Moray, particularly its coastline. Whisky notwithstanding, Moray's scenic qualities, low rainfall, and other reassuring weather statistics are worth remembering. You can also sample the northeastern seaboard, including some of the best but least-known coastal scenery in Scotland.

Planning

When to Go

May and June are probably the loveliest times to visit, but many travelers arrive from late spring to early fall. The National Trust for Scotland tends to close its properties in winter, so many of the northeast's castles are not open for off-season travel, though you can always see them from the outside. Many distilleries are open much of the year, but some close during winter months, so check before visiting.

Planning Your Time

How you allocate your time may depend on your special interests—castles or whisky, for example. But even if you can manage only a morning or an afternoon, do not miss a walk around the granite streets of Old Aberdeen, and take in St. Nicholas Kirk and a pint in the Prince of Wales pub. A trip southward to the fishing town of Stonehaven and the breathtaking cliff-top fortress of Dunnottar makes a rewarding afternoon. Royal Deeside, with a good sprinkling of castles and grandeur, needs a good two days; even this might be tight for those who want to lap up every moment of majesty at Balmoral, Crathes, Fraser, and Fyvie, the best of the bunch. A visit to malt-whisky country should include tours of Glenfiddich, Glenfarclas, Glenlivet, and Glen Grant distilleries, and although it's not technically a maker of malt whisky, Strathisla. Real enthusiasts should allot two days for the distilleries, and they shouldn't pass up a visit to Speyside Cooperage, one of the few remaining cooperages in Scotland. Cullen and Duff House gallery in Banff, on the coast, can be done in a day before returning to Aberdeen.

Getting Here and Around

AIR

The city is easy to reach from other parts of the United Kingdom as well as Europe. British Airways, EasyJet, Loganair, and Ryanair are some of the airlines with service to other parts of Britain. Aberdeen Airport—serving both international and domestic flights—is in Dyce, 7 miles west of the city center on the A96 (Inverness). The drive to the center of Aberdeen is easy via the A96 (which can be busy during rush hour).

CONTACTS Aberdeen Airport. ✉ Dyce Dr., Dyce ☎ 0344/481–6666 ⊕ www.aberdeenairport.com.

BOAT AND FERRY

Northlink Ferries has service between Aberdeen, Lerwick (Shetland), and Kirkwall (Orkney).

CONTACTS Northlink Ferries. ✉ Jamieson's Quay, Aberdeen ☎ 0845/600–0449 ⊕ www.northlinkferries.co.uk.

BUS

Long-distance buses run to Aberdeen from most parts of Scotland, England, and Wales. Contact Megabus, National Express, and Scottish Citylink for bus connections with English and Scottish towns. There's a network of local buses throughout the northeast run by Stagecoach, but they can take a long time and connections are not always well timed.

CONTACTS Megabus. ☎ 0900/160–0900 ⊕ uk.megabus.com. National Express. ☎ 08717/818181 ⊕ www.nationalexpress.com. Scottish Citylink. ☎ 0871/266–3333 ⊕ www.citylink.co.uk. Traveline. ☎ 0871/200–2233 ⊕ www.travelinescotland.com.

CAR

A car is the best way to see the northeast. If you are coming from the south, take the A90, continuing on from the M90 (from Edinburgh) or the M9/A9 (from Glasgow), which both stop at Perth. The coastal route, the A92, is a more leisurely alternative, with its interesting resorts and fishing villages. The most scenic route, however, is the A93 from Perth, north to Blairgowrie and into Glen Shee. The A93 then goes over the Cairnwell Pass, the highest main road in the United Kingdom. This route isn't recommended in winter, when snow can make driving difficult.

Around the northeast roads can be busy, with speeding and erratic driving a problem on the main A roads.

TRAIN

You can reach Aberdeen directly from Edinburgh (2½ hours), Inverness (2½ hours), and Glasgow (3 hours). ScotRail timetables have full details. There are also London–Aberdeen routes that go through Edinburgh and the east-coast main line connecting Aberdeen to all corners of the United Kingdom.

CONTACTS ScotRail. ⊠ *Aberdeen railway station, Guild St., Aberdeen* ☎ *0344/811–0141* ⊕ *www.scotrail.co.uk.*

Restaurants

As in much of the rest of Scotland, Aberdeen and the northeast have redis-covered the quality and versatility of the local produce. Juicy Aberdeen Angus steaks, lean lamb, and humanely reared pork appear on local menus, and there's a great choice of locally sourced seafood, from old-school fish-and-chips to dishes that fuse Mediterranean, Asian, and Latin influence. Traditional favorites like *Cullen skink* (a creamy smoked-fish soup) are on many menus.

Hotels

The northeast has some splendid country hotels with log fires and old Victorian furnishings, where you can also be sure of eating well. Many hotels in Aberdeen are in older buildings that have a baronial feel. The trend for serviced apartments has caught on here, with some extreme-ly modish and good-value options for those who want a bit more privacy. This trend is now extending into Deeside, where it's been notoriously difficult to find good accommodations beyond some country-house hotels, even though it's a popular tourist spot.

Restaurant and hotel reviews have been shortened. For full information, visit Fodors.com. Restaurant prices are the average cost of a main course at dinner or, if dinner is not served, at lunch. Hotel prices are the lowest cost of a standard double room in high season, including 20% V.A.T.

WHAT IT COSTS in Pounds			
$	$$	$$$	$$$$
RESTAURANTS			
under £15	£15–£19	£20–£25	over £25
HOTELS			
under £125	£125–£200	£201–£300	over £300

Visitor Information

The tourist information center in Aberdeen supplies information on all of Scotland's northeast. There are also year-round tourist information offices in Braemar and Elgin. In summer, also look for tourist information centers in Alford, Ballater, Banchory, Braemar, Elgin, and Stonehaven.

CONTACTS VisitScotland Aberdeen ICentre. ⊠ *23 Union St., Aberdeen* ☎ *01224/269180* ⊕ *www.visitscotland. com* ⊕ *www.visitabdn.com.*

Aberdeen

As a gateway to Royal Deeside and the Malt Whisky Trail, Aberdeen attracts visitors, though many are eager to get out into the countryside. Today, though, the city's unique history is finally being recognized as more impressive than many Scots had previously realized, and Aberdeen is being rediscovered. Distinc-tive architecture, some fine museums, universities, and good restaurants, nightlife, and shopping add to the appeal of Scotland's third-largest city (popula-tion 217,000). Union Street is the heart of the city, but take time to explore the university and the pretty streets of Old Aberdeen.

In the 18th century local granite quarrying produced a durable silver stone that would be used boldly in the glittering blocks, spires, columns, and parapets of Victorian-era Aberdonian structures. The city remains one of the United Kingdom's most distinctive, although some would say it depends on the weather and the brightness of the day. The mica chips embedded in the rock look like a million mirrors in the sunshine. In rain (and there is a fair amount of driving rain from the North Sea) and heavy clouds, however, their sparkle is snuffed out.

The city lies between the Dee and Don rivers, with a working harbor that has access to the sea; it has been a major fishing port and is the main commercial port in northern Scotland. The North Sea has always been important to Aberdeen. In the 1850s the city was famed for its sleek, fast clippers that sailed to India for cargoes of tea. In the 1970s exploitation of newly discovered offshore oil and gas turned Aberdeen into a world energy capital. As reserves dwindle and the oil industry winds down, the city is seeking new ways to diversify its economy.

GETTING HERE AND AROUND
AIR
Stagecoach Bluebird Jet Service 727 operates between the airport terminal in Dyce and Union Square in the center of Aberdeen. Buses (£3.40) run frequently at peak times, less often at midday and in the evening; the journey time is approximately 40 minutes.

Dyce is on ScotRail's Inverness–Aberdeen route. The rail station is a short taxi ride from the terminal building (£12). Trains run approximately every two hours.

BUS
First Aberdeen has easy and reliable service within the city of Aberdeen. Timetables are available from the tourist information center in Union Street.

CONTACTS First Aberdeen.
☎ *0345/6460707* ⊕ *www.firstgroup.com.*

CAR
Aberdeen is a compact city with good signage. Its center is Union Street, the main east–west thoroughfare, which tends to get crowded with traffic. Anderson Drive is an efficient ring road on the city's west side; be extra careful on its many traffic circles. It's best to leave your car in one of the parking garages (arrive early to get a space) and walk around, or use the convenient park-and-ride stop at the Bridge of Don, north of the city. Street maps are available from the tourist information center, newsstands, and booksellers.

TAXI
You can find taxi stands throughout the center of Aberdeen: at the railway station and at Back Wynd, Chapel Street, Dee Street, and Hadden Street. The taxis have yellow plates, meters, and might be saloon cars (sedans) or black cabs. They are great ways to travel between neighborhoods.

TRAIN
Aberdeen has good ScotRail service.

Sights

Aberdeen centers on Union Street, with its many fine survivors of the Victorian and Edwardian streetscape. Marischal College, dating from the late 16th century, is a city-center landmark, and has many grand buildings that are worth exploring.

Very much a separate area of the city, Old Aberdeen is north of the modern center, clustered around St. Machar's Cathedral and the many fine buildings of the University of Aberdeen. Take a stroll on College Bounds; handsome 18th- and 19th-century houses line this cobbled street in the oldest part of the city.

Aberdeen Art Gallery

MUSEUM | Northeast Scotland's most important art gallery reopened in November 2019 with the completion of its much-delayed renovation and expansion, giving it seven new exhibition spaces so that over 1,000 of its treasures can be displayed. There's also a penthouse gallery hosting three touring exhibitions each year. The collection contains excellent paintings, prints, drawings, sculptures, porcelain, costumes, and more, from 18th-century art to major contemporary British works by Lucien Freud and Henry Moore. Scottish artists are well represented in the permanent collection and special exhibits. Local stone has been used in the interior walls, pillars, and the central fountain, all designed by the acclaimed British sculptor Barbara Hepworth. ✉ *Schoolhill* ☎ *030000/200293* ⊕ *www.aagm.co.uk* ✉ *Free.*

★ Aberdeen Maritime Museum

MUSEUM | FAMILY | This excellent museum, which incorporates the 1593 Provost Ross's House, tells the story of the city's relationship with the sea, from early inshore fisheries to tea clippers and the North Sea oil boom. The information-rich exhibits include the bridge of a fishing boat and the cabins of a clipper, in addition to models, paintings, and equipment associated with the fishing, shipbuilding, and oil and gas industries. The Gateway to the North gallery on the top floor is a lively introduction to the archaeology of the region, with exhibits spanning the years 1136–1660. ✉ *Ship Row* ☎ *01224/337700* ⊕ *www.aagm. co.uk* ✉ *Free* ⊗ *Closed Mon.*

Cruickshank Botanic Garden

GARDEN | Built on land bequeathed by Miss Anne Cruickshank in memory of her beloved brother, Alexander, the 11-acre Cruickshank Botanic Garden at the heart

of Old Aberdeen has a peaceful water garden and lush greens ideal for lounging—when the weather allows—and beautifully tended subtropical and alpine collections. Botanical tours are available. ✉ *St. Machar Dr., at the Chanonry* ☎ *01224/272704* ⊕ *www.abdn.ac.uk/ botanic-garden* ✉ *Free.*

King's College

BUILDING | Founded in 1494, King's College is now part of the University of Aberdeen. Its **chapel**, built around 1500, has an unmistakable flying (or crown) spire. That it has survived at all was because of the zeal of the principal, who defended his church against the destructive fanaticism that swept through Scotland during the Reformation, when the building was less than a century old. Today the renovated chapel plays an important role in university life. Don't miss the tall oak screen that separates the nave from the choir, the ribbed wooden ceiling, and the stalls, as these constitute the finest medieval wood carvings found anywhere in Scotland. ✉ *25 High St.* ☎ *01224/272137* ⊕ *www.abdn. ac.uk* ⊗ *Closed weekends.*

King's Museum, Old Aberdeen Townhouse

COLLEGE | Across from the archway leading to King's College Chapel, this plain but handsome Georgian building was the center of all trading activity in the city before it became a grammar school, a Masonic lodge, and then a library. Now housing the university's museum, it hosts constantly changing exhibitions. It presents some impressive and often strange curiosities from the university's collection, from prehistoric flints to a tiger's penis. ✉ *17 High St.* ☎ *01224/274300* ⊕ *www.abdn.ac.uk/ kingsmuseum* ✉ *Free* ⊗ *Closed Sun. and Mon.*

Rosemount Viaduct

LOCAL INTEREST | Three silvery, handsome buildings on this bridge are collectively known by all Aberdonians as Education, Salvation, and Damnation. The **Central**

Perhaps Aberdeen's best museum, the Aberdeen Maritime Museum explores the city's history with the sea, from shipbuilding to fishing.

Library and **St. Mark's Church** date from the last decade of the 19th century, and **His Majesty's Theatre** (1904–08) has been restored inside to its full Edwardian splendor. If you're taking photographs, you can choose an angle that includes the statue of Scotland's first freedom fighter, Sir William Wallace (1270–1305), in the foreground pointing majestically to Damnation. ✉ *Aberdeen*.

★ St. Machar's Cathedral

RELIGIOUS SITE | It's said that St. Machar was sent by St. Columba to build a church on a grassy platform near the sea, where a river flowed in the shape of a shepherd's crook. This beautiful spot, now the still-beating heart of Old Aberdeen, fits the bill. Although the cathedral was founded in AD 580, most of the existing building dates from the 15th and 16th centuries. Built as a fortified kirk, its twin towers and thick walls give it a sturdy standing. The former can be seen up close by climbing the spiral staircases to the upper floors, which also affords an admirable view of the "body of the kirk" inside and graveyard outside. It lost its status as a cathedral during the Reformation and has since been part of the Church of Scotland. The stained-glass windows depicting the martyrdom of the saints and handsome heraldic ceiling are worth noting. ✉ *Chanonry* ☎ *01224/485988* ⊕ *www.stmachar.com.*

St. Nicholas Kirk

RELIGIOUS SITE | The original burgh church, the Mither Kirk, as this edifice is known, is not within the bounds of the early town settlement; that was to the east, near the end of present-day Union Street. During the 12th century the port of Aberdeen flourished, and there wasn't room for the church within the settlement. Its earliest features are its pillars—supporting a tower built much later—and its clerestory windows: both date from the 12th century. The East Kirk is closed for renovation work, which has been extended due to the discovery of numerous skeletons, mainly children, that date back to the 12th century; the post-excavation work can be viewed from a large window in the Drum's Aisle. In the chapel, look for Shona McInnes's stained-glass window commemorating the victims of the 1988 Piper Alpha oil-rig disaster and a glass case containing two books. One lists the names of all those who've lost their lives in the pursuit of oil exploration in the North Sea; the second is empty, a testament to the many "unknown" workers whose deaths were never officially recorded. ⊠ *Union St.* ☎ *01224/643494* ⊕ *www.kirk-of-st-nicholas.org.uk* ⊠ *Free, but donations welcome.*

Tolbooth Museum
MUSEUM | FAMILY | The city was governed from this 17th-century building, which was also the burgh court and jail, for 200 years. Now a museum of crime and punishment, its highly entertaining tour guides take you around its cells and dungeons and bring life and death to the various instruments of torture—including the "Maiden," a decapitating machine—making it a must-see for older kids. ⊠ *Castle St.* ☎ *01224/621167* ⊕ *www. aagm.co.uk* ⊠ *Free.*

Union Street
NEIGHBORHOOD | This great thoroughfare is to Aberdeen what Princes Street is to Edinburgh: the central pivot of the city plan and the product of a wave of enthusiasm to rebuild the city in a contemporary style in the early 19th century. ⊠ *Aberdeen.*

🍴 Restaurants

Ashvale
$ | BRITISH | FAMILY | Ask anyone about this long-established place and the response will probably be overwhelmingly positive. Fish-and-chips is the specialty, and the secret-recipe batter is now the stuff of legend. **Known for:** "The Whale," a giant 1-pound haddock fillet; tender locally sourced steaks; free meals for those under age five. ⑤ *Average main: £13* ⊠ *42–48 Great Western Rd.* ☎ *01224/575842* ⊕ *theashvale.co.uk.*

Foodstory
$ | VEGETARIAN | FAMILY | A bright, breezy vegetarian and vegan café-eatery, Foodstory pulls in a loyal crowd to graze on its healthy, freshly made breakfasts, lunches, and wonderful cakes. Expect organic breakfast and brunch choices such as superfood porridge, scones, and filling dishes such as vegetarian hot pot. **Known for:** oatmeal enriched with nuts, fruit, and berries; eco-friendly ethos; vegan breakfast and lunches. ⑤ *Average main: £7* ⊠ *13–15 Thistle St.* ☎ *01224/611717* ⊕ *www.foodstorycafe.co.uk.*

Moonfish
$$ | BRITISH | This elegant yet relaxed seafood restaurant can be found along a medieval lane next to St. Nicholas Kirk. Mains may include freshly caught sea trout, halibut, or hake served with imaginative accompaniments such as celeriac with seawood. **Known for:** halibut with roast chicory, leeks, and yeast crumble; craft gin cocktails; sophisticated setting. ⑤ *Average main: £16* ⊠ *9 Correction Wynd* ☎ *01224/644166* ⊕ *www.moonfishcafe.co.uk* ☉ *Closed Sun. and Mon.*

★ Silver Darling
$$$ | SEAFOOD | Huge windows overlook the harbor and beach at this quayside favorite in a former customhouse, long one of Aberdeen's most acclaimed restaurants. The French-inspired menu focuses on fish. Try the crab bisque with samphire to start, then move on to a lavish seafood platter of scallops, mussels, langoustes, prawns, and cockles. **Known for:** classic seafood platters; prawn and crab linguine; steak fillet with king prawns in garlic butter. ⑤ *Average main: £25* ⊠ *North Pier, Pocra Quay* ☎ *01224/576229* ⊕ *thesilverdarling.co.uk* ☉ *Closed Sun. No lunch Sat.*

Hotels

Atholl Hotel
$ | HOTEL | With its many turrets and gables, this granite hotel recalls a bygone

era but has modern amenities that now include an elevator and two rooms specially designed for people with disabilities. **Pros:** family-run establishment; outdoor garden seating for sunny days; private parking. **Cons:** rooms are blandly decorated; popular with locals for wedding and funeral receptions; unexciting bar. $ *Rooms from: £99* ⊠ *54 Kings Gate* ☎ *01224/323505* ⊕ *www.atholl-aberdeen. com* ➯ *34 rooms* ⏀ *Free breakfast.*

The Jays Guest House
$ | **B&B/INN** | Alice Jennings or her husband, George, will greet you at the front door of this granite house, a homey bed-and-breakfast they've run for more than 30 years. **Pros:** immaculate rooms; expert advice on city's sights; near Old Aberdeen and the university. **Cons:** no public areas; popular, so book ahead; not for those looking for a full-service hotel. $ *Rooms from: £80* ⊠ *422 King St.* ☎ *01224/612771* ⊕ *www.jaysguesthouse. co.uk* ➯ *10 rooms* ⏀ *Free breakfast.*

★ Malmaison
$$ | **HOTEL** | Part of a British minichain, this boutique hotel with fabulously comfy rooms and suites—some with terraces from which you can watch the sunset— sets the standard by which all rivals in Aberdeen are judged. **Pros:** stylish rooms; excellent restaurant; delightful staff. **Cons:** not very central; no pool; meat-heavy restaurant could do more for vegetarians. $ *Rooms from: £125* ⊠ *45–93 Queen's Rd.* ☎ *01224/507097* ⊕ *www.malmaison. com/locations/aberdeen* ➯ *77 rooms* ⏀ *All-inclusive.*

Marcliffe Hotel and Spa
$$ | **HOTEL** | Offering a perfect combination of town and country outside the city center, this elegant hotel stands on 11 acres of wooded grounds and combines old and new to impressive effect. **Pros:** the wooded environs means a stunning dawn chorus of birds; big rooms; well-regarded restaurant. **Cons:** if you struggle to sleep, the dawn chorus; a little out of town; popular with wedding parties.

$ *Rooms from: £170* ⊠ *N. Deeside Rd.* ☎ *01224/861000* ⊕ *www.marcliffe.com* ➯ *39 rooms* ⏀ *Breakfast.*

Nightlife

Aberdeen has a fairly lively nightlife scene revolving around pubs and clubs. Theaters, concert halls, arts centers, and cinemas are also well represented. The principal newspapers—the *Press and Journal* and the *Evening Express* can fill you in on what's going on anywhere in the northeast. Aberdeen's tourist information center has a monthly publication with an events calendar.

Although it can't hold a candle to Edinburgh or Glasgow when it comes to sophisticated nightlife, Aberdeen has a very lively, even sometimes raucous, clubbing scene with numerous venues that are popular with students and other young locals but are less appealing to more mature visitors or anyone over 30. Belmont Street is a lively bar-hopping neighborhood with bars to suit all tastes. Pubs close at midnight on weekdays and 1 am on weekends; clubs go until 2 or 3 am.

BARS AND PUBS
BrewDog
BREWPUBS/BEER GARDENS | Aberdeen's pioneering craft brewery–turned–global brand runs its flagship bar with suitable gusto and no lack of style. A bare-brick warehouse interior with lots of steel means there's lots of noise and chatter flying around the cavernous space, oiled by a choice of over 100 craft beers. ⊠ *17 Gallowgate* ☎ *01224/631223* ⊕ *www. brewdog.com.*

CASC Bar
BARS/PUBS | A fine selection of malt whiskies and Cuban cigars (which can be smoked in the outside seating area) makes this one of Aberdeen's more sophisticated watering holes. CASC, which stands for cigars, ale, Scotch, and coffee, is popular for its craft beers (more

than 150 of them) and cool industrial interior. It can seem a bit crowded and noisy on weekends. ✉ *7 Stirling St.* ☎ *01224/212373* ⊕ *www.cascbar.co.uk.*

Illicit Still

BARS/PUBS | The old-fashioned Illicit Still is named after the 18th-century practice of brewing your own beer to avoid the malt tax. A beautifully fitted-out drinking establishment, it's popular with local students and has live music on weekends. ✉ *Guest Row, Broad St.* ☎ *01224/623123* ⊕ *www.illicit-still.co.uk.*

The Prince of Wales

BARS/PUBS | Dating from 1850, the Prince of Wales has retained its paneled walls and wooden tables. Still regarded as Aberdeen's most traditional pub, it's hardly regal, but good-quality food and reasonable prices draw the regulars back. ✉ *7 St. Nicholas La.* ☎ *01224/640597* ⊕ *www.princeofwales-aberdeen.co.uk*

The Tippling House

BARS/PUBS | Youthful Aberdonian *bon viveurs* have taken this subterranean and sophisticated (by Belmont Street standards) late-night drinking den to their hearts and stomachs. It's a great place to escape and mingle and offers casual dining, innovative cocktails, craft beers, and spirits. ✉ *4 Belmont St.* ⊕ *www.thetipplinghouse.com.*

Shopping

Books and Beans

BOOKS/STATIONERY | This independent bookshop has its own Internet café (one of the few surviving such places in the city center) and sells a good range of flavored coffees. You're welcome to browse, sip, and surf the web at the same time. ✉ *22 Belmont St.* ☎ *01224/646438* ⊕ *www.booksandbeans.co.uk.*

Cocoa Ooze

FOOD/CANDY | Enjoy a cup of tea and a chocolate fondue before tasting and buying handmade chocolate gifts, such as chocolate-drenched cinder toffee and hand-rolled truffles. ✉ *24/28 Belmont St.* ☎ *01224/467212* ⊕ *www.cocoa-ooze.co.uk.*

Colin Wood Antiques

ANTIQUES/COLLECTIBLES | This shop is the place to go for small antiques, interesting prints, and regional maps. ✉ *25 Hose St.* ☎ *01224/643019* ⊕ *www.colinwood-antiques.com.*

Activities

GOLF

Murcar Links Golf Club

GOLF | Sea views and a variety of rugged terrain—from sand dunes to tinkling burns—are the highlights of this course, founded in 1909. It's most famous for breathtaking vistas at the 7th hole, appropriately called the Serpentine. Designer Archibald Simpson considered this course to be one of his finest. ✉ *Bridge of Don* ☎ *01224/704354* ⊕ *www.murcarlinks.com* 💷 *£110 weekdays, £135 weekends* 🏌 *18 holes, 6314 yards, par 73.*

★ Royal Aberdeen Golf Club

GOLF | This venerable club, founded in 1780, is the archetypal Scottish links course: tumbling over uneven ground, with the frequently added hazard of sea breezes. Prickly gorse is inclined to close in and form an additional hurdle. The two courses are tucked behind the rough, grassy sand dunes, and there are surprisingly few views of the sea. One historical note: in 1783 this club originated the five-minute-search rule for a lost ball. A handicap certificate and letter of introduction are required. Visitors are allowed only on weekdays. ✉ *Links Rd., Bridge of Don* ☎ *01224/702571* ⊕ *www.royalaberdeengolf.com* 💷 *Balgownie, £190; Silverburn, £70* 🏌 *Balgownie: 18 holes, 6900 yards, par 71; Silverburn: 18 holes, 4021 yards, par 64* ⚠ *Reservations essential.*

Stonehaven

15 miles south of Aberdeen.

Stonehaven's golden sands made this historic town near spectacular Dunnottar Castle a popular holiday destination, until Scots began vacationing in sunnier climates. The surrounding red-clay fields were made famous by Lewis Grassic Gibbon (real name James Leslie Mitchell), who attended school in the town and wrote the seminal Scottish trilogy *A Scots Quair,* about the people, the land, and the impact of World War I. Stonehaven is now famous for its Hogmanay (New Year's Eve) celebrations, where local men swing huge balls of fire on chains before tossing them into the harbor, and as the birthplace of a quirky Scots delicacy, the deep-fried Mars bar.

GETTING HERE AND AROUND

Most trains heading south from Aberdeen stop at Stonehaven; there's at least one per hour making the 15-minute trip. Stagecoach Bluebird runs bus services between Stonehaven and Aberdeen; the fastest, the X70, takes around 40 minutes. Drivers should take A90 south and turn off at A957.

Sights

★ Dunnottar Castle

CASTLE/PALACE | It's hard to beat the cinematic majesty of the magnificent cliff-top ruins of Dunnottar Castle, with its panoramic views of the North Sea. Building began in the 14th century, when Sir William Keith, Marischal of Scotland, decided to build a tower house to demonstrate his power. Subsequent generations added to the structure, and important visitors included Mary, Queen of Scots. The castle is most famous for holding out for eight months against Oliver Cromwell's army in 1651 and 1652, thereby saving the Scottish crown jewels, which had been stored here for safekeeping. Reach the castle via the A90; take the Stonehaven turnoff and follow the signs. Wear sensible shoes, and allow about two hours. ⊠ *Off A92* ☎ *01569/766320* ⊕ *www.dunnottarcastle. co.uk* ⌫ *£7.*

Stonehaven Tolbooth Museum

MUSEUM | Crime and punishment in days gone by are the central themes at this community-run museum in a 16th-century building that was once Stonehaven's jail and courthouse. Exhibits include the wooden stocks, where up to seven miscreants at a time could be publicly humiliated, and the crank, an appalling torture machine. There's also an eclectic collection of old farming tools and household utensils. ⊠ *Old Pier, Stonehaven Harbour* ⊕ *www.stonehaventolbooth. co.uk* ⌫ *Free* ⓢ *Closed Tues.*

Restaurants

The Ship Inn

$$ | SEAFOOD | This former coaching inn is exactly where you want to take nourishment after a bracing walk from Dunnottar Castle. Refurbishment has taken away much of the history, but wood paneling and rattan chairs make it comfortable, and huge new windows provide views of the harbor. **Known for:** traditional Cullen skink; nice views; splurge-worthy fritto misto. ⑤ *Average main: £16* ⊠ *5 Shore Head* ☎ *01569/762617* ⊕ *www.shipinn-stonehaven.com.*

Hotels

Bayview B&B

$$ | B&B/INN | This contemporary bed-and-breakfast couldn't be in a more convenient location or have better views. **Pros:** spic-and-span rooms; right on the beach; fresh, modern design. **Cons:** standard rooms are smallish; narrow driveway not great for larger cars; not all rooms have sea views. ⑤ *Rooms from: £125* ⊠ *Beachgate La.* ⌖ *On the beach, down the lane from the town square*

The gardens and trails of Crathes Castle are home to a wide variety of plants and flowers, as well as buzzards, herons, and kingfishers.

☎ *07791/224227* ⊕ *www.bayviewbandb. co.uk* ⇨ *7 rooms* ⏹ *Free breakfast.*

Shopping

Aunty Betty's

FOOD/CANDY | **FAMILY** | Even if the weather is lousy, this coffee, sweets, and ice-cream shop confirms you are on your summer holidays. Grown-ups will love the gin-and-tonic or champagne sorbets, kids the complimentary sprinkles. ⊠ *The Promenade* ☎ *01569/763656.*

Banchory

15 miles west of Stonehaven, 19 miles west of Aberdeen.

Banchory is an immaculate town filled with pinkish-granite buildings. It's usually bustling with ice-cream-eating strollers, out on a day trip from Aberdeen. Nearby are Crathes and Drum castles.

GETTING HERE AND AROUND

A car is by far the best way to get around the area; A93 is one of the main roads connecting the towns.

For those reliant on public transport, Stagecoach buses operate a number of services for towns along or just off A93 (Drum Castle, Banchory, Kincardine, Aboyne, Ballater, Balmoral, and Braemar).

Sights

★ Crathes Castle

CASTLE/PALACE | **FAMILY** | About 16 miles west of Aberdeen, Crathes Castle was once the home of the Burnett family and is one of the best-preserved castles in Britain. Keepers of the Forest of Drum for generations, the family acquired lands here by marriage and later built a castle, completed in 1596. The National Trust for Scotland cares for the castle, which is furnished with many original pieces and family portraits. The castle is open for guided tours only. Outside are grand yet lovingly tended gardens with calculated symmetry and flower-rich beds. Make sure you browse the Horsemill bookshop and sample the tasty baked goods in the tearoom. There's an adventure park for kids, and the staff organizes activities that are fun and educational. ⊠ *Off A93* ☎ *01330/844525* ⊕ *www.nts.org.uk* 🎫 *£13* ⊙ *Closed weekdays Nov.–Mar.*

★ Drum Castle
CASTLE/PALACE | This foursquare tower has an evocative medieval chapel that dates from the 13th century; like many other castles, it also has later additions up to Victorian times. Note the tower's rounded corners, said to make battering-ram attacks more difficult. Nearby, fragments of the ancient Forest of Drum still stand, dating from the days when Scotland was covered by great stands of oak and pine. The Garden of Historic Roses, open from April to October, lays claim to some old-fashioned roses not commonly seen today. ⊠ *Drumoak by Banchory* ✛ *Off the A93, 8 miles east of Banchory and 11 miles west of Aberdeen* ☎ *01330/700334* ⊕ *www.nts.org.uk* 🎫 *£13* ⊙ *Closed weekdays Oct.–Mar., closed Tues. and Wed. in Apr.–June and Sept.*

Royal Deeside Railway
SCENIC DRIVE | **FAMILY** | Built for Queen Victoria, this historic station and its railway line now serve passengers using veteran steam and diesel locomotives to haul vintage carriages along a short scenic route; the journey takes only 15–20 minutes. ⊠ *Milton of Crathes* ☎ *01330/844416* ⊕ *www.deeside-railway.co.uk* 🎫 *Round-trip £7.50.*

🛏 Hotels

★ Banchory Lodge
$$ | **HOTEL** | Right on the River Dee, this Georgian lodge offers the lovely touches you expect at a luxury hotel, but at a moderate cost. **Pros:** a warm welcome; great bar; excellent food and afternoon teas. **Cons:** popular for weddings; room sizes vary; no elevators so might be an issue for those with mobility issues. $ *Rooms from: £185* ⊠ *Dee St.* ☎ *01330/822625* ⊕ *www.banchorylodge. com* 🛏 *28 rooms* ⊚ *Free breakfast.*

Ballater

25 miles west of Banchory, 43 miles west of Aberdeen.

The handsome holiday resort of Ballater, once noted for the curative properties of its waters, has profited from the proximity of the royals nearby at Balmoral Castle. The Old Royal Station, purpose-built to pander to Victoria and her hangers-on, has been handsomely restored. You might be amused by the array of "by royal appointment" signs proudly hanging from many of its various shops (even monarchs need bakers and butchers).

The locals have long taken the town's royal connection in stride. To this day, the hundreds who line the road when the Queen and her family arrive for services at the family's parish church at Crathie are invariably visitors to Deeside—one of Balmoral's attractions for the monarch has always been the villagers' respect for royal privacy.

GETTING HERE AND AROUND
There's good train service to Aberdeen, but you'll need to catch a bus to get to this and other towns near A93. Stagecoach Bluebird Buses 201 and 202 operate hourly to all the main towns, including Ballater. Otherwise, it's an easy car trip.

ESSENTIALS
VISITOR INFORMATION Ballater Visitor Information Centre. ⊠ *Old Royal Station, Station Sq.* ☎ *01339/755306* ⊕ *www. visitscotland.com.*

Sights

★ **Balmoral Castle**

CASTLE/PALACE | The British royal family's favorite vacation spot is a fabulous fake-baronial pile, with emphasis on the "fake." Compared with Scotland's most authentic castles, Balmoral is a right royal upstart, designed in the 19th century by Queen Victoria's German-born consort, Prince Albert. That doesn't stop it being one of Scotland's most visited castles, though only the formal gardens, the ballroom, and the carriage hall, with their exhibitions of royal artifacts, commemorative china, and stuffed native wildlife, are on view.

When members of the royal family are in residence, usually from mid-August to the end of September, Balmoral is closed to visitors, including the grounds. You can take a guided tour in November and December; if the weather is crisp and bright, the estate is at its most dramatic and romantic. You're only allowed a peek inside, but the Royal Cottage is where Queen Victoria spent much of her time. You can see the table where she took breakfast and wrote her correspondence.

Around and about Balmoral are some notable spots—Cairn O'Mount, Cambus O'May, and the Cairngorms from the Linn of Dee—that are home to golden eagles, red squirrels, red deer, black and red grouse, snow bunting, and the United Kingdom's only free-roaming reindeer, some of which may be seen on the quintessentially royal Land Rover Safari Tour. Tempted by the setting? Balmoral Castle has a number of cottages (some very large) for rent by the week at certain times. These are atmospheric but can be basic (which, believe it or not, is how the royal family likes its holidays to be—though the late Diana, Princess of Wales, who vacationed here before the breakup of her marriage to Prince Charles, hated Balmoral's lack of luxury). ⊠ A93 ✢ 7

miles west of Ballater ☎ 01339/742534 ⊕ www.balmoralcastle.com ⌂ £15 ⊙ Closed when royals are in residence.

 Restaurants

The Carriage

$ | BRITISH | The Old Royal Station, built for Queen Victoria and restored after a disastrous fire in 2015, now houses this combination café, tearoom, and bistro. There's something here for everyone at almost any time of day, from coffee and cakes to high tea, lunch, and dinner. **Known for:** mushroom risotto with sage, squash, and ricotta; deep-fried haddock in Deeside batter; local regional produce. ⑤ Average main: £13 ⊠ Ballater Station, Station Square ☎ ⊕ www.thecarriageballater.co.uk ⊙ Closed Sun.–Tues.

 Hotels

★ **Hilton Grand Vacations at Craigendarroch Suites**

$$$ | HOTEL | FAMILY | This grand mansion has been turned into a resort with a luxury spa and country club, combining Victorian style with modern comforts. **Pros:** great pool and gym facilities; no smoking anywhere inside or out; rooms and suites have kitchenettes. **Cons:** if there's a conference, nonattending guests can feel lost among the crowds; incongruously corporate atmosphere; a bit pricey for this area. ⑤ Rooms from: £211 ⊠ Braemar Rd. ☎ 01339/755558 ⊕ www.hiltongrandvacations.com/scotland/hgvc-craigendarroch-suites ⇥ 51 suites ⍟ Free breakfast.

 Shopping

Deeside Books

BOOKS/STATIONERY | Beyond the gifts section, veer to the right and you will find an interesting collection of old, out-of-print, and hard-to-find books about Scotland, which make splendid gifts for lovers of all things Scottish. ⊠ *18–20 Bridge St.* ☏ *01339/754080* ⊕ *www.deesidebooks. com.*

McEwan Gallery

ART GALLERIES | A mile west of Ballater, the McEwan Gallery displays fine paintings, watercolors, prints, and books (many with a Scottish or golf theme) in an unusual house built by the Swiss artist Rudolphe Christen in 1902. ⊠ *A939* ☏ *01339/755429* ⊕ *www.mcewangallery. com.*

Braemar

17 miles west of Ballater. 60 miles west of Aberdeen, 51 miles north of Perth via A93.

Synonymous with the British monarchy, due to its closeness to Balmoral, and with the famous Highland Games, this village is popular year-round as a base for walkers and climbers enjoying the Grampian Mountains.

GETTING HERE AND AROUND

The town is on A93; there's bus service here and to other towns on the road.

Sights

Braemar Castle

CASTLE/PALACE | On the northern outskirts of town, Braemar Castle dates from the 17th century, although its defensive walls, in the shape of a pointed star, came later. At Braemar (the *braes,* or slopes, of the district of Mar), the standard, or rebel flag, was first raised at the start of the unsuccessful Jacobite rebellion of 1715. About 30 years later, during the last Jacobite rebellion, Braemar Castle was strengthened and garrisoned by government troops. From the early 1800s the castle was the clan seat of the Farquharsons, who hold their clan reunion here every summer.

Thanks to the commitment of local volunteers, a remarkable 2008 renovation restored Braemar to the home it would have been in the early 20th century, complete with all the necessary comforts and family memorabilia. A dozen rooms are on view, including the laird's day room with a plush daybed and the kitchen. ⊠ *Off A93* ☏ *01339/741219* ⊕ *www. braemarcastle.co.uk* 🏷 *£8* ⊘ *Closed Nov.–Easter. Closed Mon. and Tues. in Apr.–June, Sept., and Oct.*

Braemar Highland Gathering

FESTIVAL | **FAMILY** | The village of Braemar is associated with the Braemar Highland Gathering, held the first Saturday in September. Although there are many such gatherings celebrated throughout Scotland, this one is distinguished by the presence of the royal family. Competitions and events include hammer throwing, caber tossing, and bagpipe playing. If you plan to attend, book your accommodations months in advance and be sure to buy tickets and, if necessary, your car parking ticket about six months in advance, as they do sell out. ⊠ *Princess Royal and Duke of Fife Memorial Park, Broombank Terr.* ⊕ *www.braemar-gathering.org.*

🍴 Restaurants

Taste

$ | **CAFÉ** | Tasty and fresh soups and sandwiches made with local ingredients like venison pâté and Cambus O' May artisanal cheeses adorn the menu at this chalet-style café. You can order moist cakes and tasty lattes here, too. **Known for:** housemade soups; fresh-baked bread; artisan cheeses. ⓢ *Average main: £7* ⊠ *Auchendryne Sq.* ☏ *01339/741425* ⊕ *www.taste-braemar.co.uk* ⊘ *Closed Sun. and Mon. and two weeks in mid-July.*

Hotels

★ The Fife Arms

$$$$ | HOTEL | This opulently quirky, art-filled boutique hotel is a much-needed addition to Braemar's rather thin lodging portfolio. **Pros:** fabulous, art-filled rooms; locally sourced game, salmon, and seafood on the dining menu; great cocktails. **Cons:** very expensive; overwhelmingly arty; some may find taxidermied animals in rooms and public areas distasteful. ⑤ *Rooms from: £318* ⊠ *Mar Rd.* ☎ *01339/720200* ⊕ *www.fifearms.com* ⇴ *46 rooms* ⧉ *Free Breakfast.*

 ## Activities

GOLF
Braemar Golf Course

GOLF | It's worth playing the tricky 18-hole Braemar Golf Course if only to say you've played the highest 18-hole course in Scotland. Founded in 1902, it is laden with foaming water hazards. ⊠ *Cluny Bank Rd.* ☎ *01339/741618* ⊕ *www.braemargolfclub.co.uk* ⧉ *£25 weekdays, £30 weekends* ⅄ *18 holes, 4935 yards, par 65.*

Alford

28 miles west of Aberdeen, 41 miles northeast of Braemar.

A plain and sturdy settlement in the Howe (Hollow) of Alford, this town gives those who have grown somewhat weary of castle-hopping a break: it has a museum instead. Craigievar Castle and Castle Fraser are nearby, though.

GETTING HERE AND AROUND

The town is on A944.

 ## Sights

★ Castle Fraser

CASTLE/PALACE | The massive Castle Fraser is the ancestral home of the Frasers and one of the largest of the castles of Mar; it's certainly a contender as one of the grandest castles in the northeast. Although the well-furnished building shows a variety of styles reflecting the taste of its owners from the 15th through the 19th century, its design is typical of the cavalcade of castles in the region, and for good reason. This—along with many others, including Midmar, Craigievar, Crathes, and Glenbuchat—was designed by a family of master masons called Bell. There are plenty of family items, but don't miss the two Turret Rooms—one of which is the trophy room—and Major Smiley's Room. He married into the family but is famous for having been one of the escapees from Colditz (a high-security prisoner-of-war camp) during World War II. The walled garden includes a 19th-century knot garden, with colorful flower beds, box hedging, gravel paths, and splendid herbaceous borders. Have lunch in the tearoom or the picnic area. ⊠ *Off A944* ⊹ *8 miles southeast of Alford* ☎ *01330/833463* ⊕ *www.nts.org. uk* ⧉ *£12* ⊙ *Closed mid-Dec.–Feb. and weekdays in Mar. and Nov.–mid-Dec.*

Grampian Transport Museum

MUSEUM | FAMILY | The entertaining and enthusiastically run Grampian Transport Museum specializes in road-based means of locomotion, backed up by archives and a library. Its collection of buses and trams is second to none, but the Craigievar Express, a steam-driven creation invented by the local postman to deliver mail more efficiently, is the most unusual. Look out for the Hillman Imp: if Scotland has a national car, this is it. There's a small café that offers tea, baked goods, and ice cream. ⊠ *Montgarrie Rd.* ☎ *01975/562292* ⊕ *www.gtm.org.uk* ⧉ *£10 (includes two children)* ⊙ *Closed Nov.–Mar.*

Language and the Scots

Until quite recently, many Scots were made to feel uncomfortable—even within Scotland—about using their native regional dialects. After the Union of England and Scotland in 1707, Scotland's professional middle class, including its politicians, adopted an only mildly accented form of "standard English." Even today, the voices of the Scottish aristocracy—usually educated in elite English schools—are almost indistinguishable from those of their English counterparts. But in recent generations, Scots urban accents and rural dialects have become accepted once again. The creation of the post of Makar (first held by Edwin Morgan from 2004 to 2010 and now by Jackie Kay) signaled that Scots is once again to be taken seriously. Taking up the mantle of Robert Burns, whose poems drew on the *Lallans* (Lowlands) of his native southwest, contemporary authors such as Irvine Welsh and William McIlvanney and others write in the voices of working-class Scots city dwellers.

Lowland Scots

The Scots language (that is, Lowland Scots, not Gaelic), a northern form of Middle English influenced by Norse, Gaelic, French, and Dutch, was used in the court and in literature until the late 16th century. After the Scottish court moved to London in 1603 it declined as a literary or official language. But Scots survives in various forms, some of which—like the broadest urban accents of Dundee and Glasgow—are almost impenetrable to an ear used to "standard" English.

Some Scottish words are used and understood across the entire country (and world), such as *wee* (small), *aye* (yes), *lassie* (girl), and *bonny* (pretty). You may even find yourself exporting a few useful words, such as *dreich* (gloomy), *glaikit* (acting and looking foolish), or *dinna fash* (don't worry), all of which are much more expressive than their English equivalents. Doric, the regional dialect of Aberdeenshire, is the purest direct descendant of the old Scots tongue. It's loaded with borrowings from Norse, such as *quine* (a young woman) and *loon* (a young man), while "what" becomes "fit," "who" becomes "faa," and "which" becomes "fitna." The local version of "How do you do?" is "Fit like?" A country dweller might refer to an urban Aberdonian as a *toonser*; his city cousin might call him a *teuchter*. Neither term is entirely complimentary.

Gaelic

Scottish Gaelic—an entirely different language—is not, despite what many still think, Scotland's national tongue. This Celtic language is incomprehensible to 99% of Scots and spoken by fewer than 60,000 people. Most live in the Western Isles (*Eilean Siar* in Gaelic), with a handful in the Highlands and Argyll. All speak English as well as their mother tongue. Gaelic was frowned upon after the failure of the 1745 Jacobite rebellions, and numbers of Gaelic speakers have declined ever since, though the decline has slowed in recent years.

Dufftown

54 miles west of Aberdeen.

On one of the Spey tributaries, Dufftown was planned in 1817 by the Earl of Fife. Its simple cross layout with a square and a large clock tower (originally from Banff and now the site of the visitor center) is typical of a small Scottish town built in the 19th century. Its simplicity is made all the more stark by the brooding, heather-clad hills that rise around it. Dufftown is convenient to a number of distilleries.

GETTING HERE AND AROUND

To get here from Aberdeen, drive west on A90 and A920, then turn west at Huntly. It's not easy or quick, but you can take the train to Elgin or Keith and then the bus to Dufftown.

Sights

Balvenie Distillery

WINERY/DISTILLERY | As soon as you step into the old manager's office at Balvenie Distillery—now gently restored and fitted with knotted-elm furniture—you realize Balvenie wants to make sure that all visitors get to see, smell, and feel the magic of the making of this malt. Balvenie is unusual because it has its own cooperage with six coopers hard at work turning the barrels. Tours show the mashing, fermentation, and distillation process and end with a tasting. ■**TIP**➜ **Visitors must be 18 or older.** ⊠ *Balvenie St.* ☎ *01340/822210* ⊕ *www.thebalvenie. com* ✉ *£40* ⊙ *Closed weekends.*

★ Glenfiddich Distillery

WINERY/DISTILLERY | Many make Glenfiddich Distillery their first stop on the Malt Whisky Trail. The independent company of William Grant and Sons Limited was the first to realize the tourist potential of the distilling process. The company began offering tours around the typical pagoda-roofed malting buildings and subsequently built an entertaining visitor center. Besides a free 20-minute tour of the distillery there are various tours for more discerning visitors that include nosing and tasting sessions. Check out the Malt Barn Bar, serving a limited but tasty menu, and look out for viewings of the current Glenfiddich Distillery Artists in Residence's work. ⊠ *A941* ✛ *½ mile north of Dufftown* ☎ *01340/820373* ⊕ *www.glenfiddich.com* ✉ *Tours from £10.*

Strathisla Distillery

WINERY/DISTILLERY | Whisky lovers should take the B9014 11 miles northeast from Dufftown—or alternatively, ride the Keith Dufftown Railway—to see one of Scotland's most iconic distilleries, the Strathisla Distillery, with its cobblestone courtyard and famous double-pagoda roofs. Stretching over the picturesque River Isla, the Strathisla Distillery was built in 1786 and now produces the main component of the Chivas Regal blend. Guided tours, for those 18 and over only, take you to the mash house, tun room, and still house—all pretty much the same as they were when production began. The tour ends with a tasting session. ⊠ *Seafield Ave., Keith* ☎ *01542/783044* ⊕ *www.chivas.com* ✉ *£7.50* ⊙ *Closed weekends mid-Nov.–mid.-Mar.*

Hotels

The Fife Arms Hotel

$ | **B&B/INN** | This 18th-century coaching inn offers a whiff of atmosphere and acceptable accommodations for a one-night stay in motel-style rooms attached to an old-school pub popular with locals. **Pros:** great full Scottish breakfast; off-street parking; very central. **Cons:** some noise from adjoining pub; unexciting decor; basic amenities. ⑤ *Rooms from: £70* ⊠ *2 The Square* ☎ *01340/820220* ⊕ *www.fifearmsdufftown.co.uk* ⇌ *6 rooms* ❘⊙❘ *Free breakfast.*

Tours at Glenfiddich Distillery include older buildings and a modern visitor center—plus a wee dram.

Shopping

Collector's Cabin

ANTIQUES/COLLECTIBLES | Two adjoining shops—one with Scottish silver, fossils, and book illustrations, the other with kilts, ceramics, and other curiosities—are filled with conversation starters. This is truly a trove worth delving into. ✉ *22 and 24 Balvenie St.* ☎ *01340/821393* ⊕ *www. collectorscabin.vpweb.co.uk.*

Dufftown Glassworks

CRAFTS | This light and airy gallery sells interesting fused and painted glass, as well as prints and crafts by local makers. The adjoining café sells the best coffee in Dufftown, leaf tea, and a good selection of cakes from scones to lemon drizzle to gooey chocolate. ✉ *16 Conval St.* ☎ *01340/821534* ⊕ *dufftownglassworks. com.*

Craigellachie

4 miles northwest of Dufftown via A941.

Renowned as an angling resort, Craigellachie, like so many settlements on the River Spey, is sometimes enveloped in the malty reek of the local industry. Glen Grant is one of the distilleries nearby. The Spey itself is crossed by a handsome suspension bridge, designed by noted engineer Thomas Telford (1757–1834) in 1814 and now bypassed by the modern road.

GETTING HERE AND AROUND

The town is on A491; it's best to drive here, as public transportation is infrequent and complicated.

◉ Sights

★ Glen Grant Distillery & Garden

WINERY/DISTILLERY | This historic distillery on the northern edge of Rothes has been producing award-winning single malts since 1840, and it's still going strong today. An impressive visitor center provides guided tours of the distillery, revealing its distinctive blend of centuries-old traditions and cutting-edge technology, as well as offering private tastings. There's a shop and café, too. But the biggest draw here is the stunning Victorian gardens; walk along the snaking path and pass pristine lawns, rare blooming flowers, gently flowing streams, and pretty pagodas. On your walk look out for a small cave and a locked safe; these were used to store founder Major Grant's private whisky collection, so he could share a dram with his walking companions. ⊠ A941, Rothes ✠ North of town, left at junction of A941 and B9015 ☎ 01340/832118 ⊕ www.glengrant.com ⊠ £5 tour and tasting ⊙ Closed Sun. Nov.–Mar.

★ Macallan Distillery
WINERY/DISTILLERY | Beneath a vast, undulating, turf-covered roof that mimics the outlines of the surrounding moorland, the Macallan Distillery and Visitor Centre is now an exciting tourism hub for Speyside. The Six Pillars tour lasts around 90 minutes and includes nosing and tasting of some of the distillery's distinctively sherry-tinctured malts. ⊠ Easter Elchies ✠ About 1 mile west of Craigellachie, off B9102 ☎ 01304/318000 ⊕ www.themacallan.com ⊠ £15.

Speyside Cooperage and Visitor Centre
FACTORY | Situated four miles south of Rothes, this working cooperage is the only place left in the U.K. where you can see coopers hard at work making wooden whisky casks. Since 1947, coopers here have been using American oak, along with traditional tools and methods, to create the casks for distilleries across Scotland and beyond. This visitor center gives you the chance to see the coopers at work and learn more about the life cycle of a cask, with tours throughout the working week. There's also a well-stocked gift shop and barrel-themed café. ⊠ Dufftown Rd. ☎ 01340/871108 ⊕ www.speysidecooperage.co.uk ⊠ £4 ⊙ Closed weekends.

Restaurants

Copper Dog
$$ | BRITISH | With its reclaimed woodwork and mismatched wooden chairs, rows of malt whisky bottles, decorative oak barrel ends, and walls hung with prints, the Craigellachie Hotel's bar-restaurant is an edgy blend of cozy and shabby chic. The menu is equally relaxed, with dishes such as locally produced gourmet sausages, rumbledethumps (a casserole of baked potato, cabbage, and onions), and an outstanding platter of Scottish cheeses with housemade chutney, all of which can be matched with regional craft beers. **Known for:** Portsoy fish stew; local produce; local craft beers. Ⓢ Average main: £15 ⊠ Craigellachie Hotel, Victoria St. ☎ 01340/881204 ⊕ www.craigellachiehotel.co.uk.

🛏 Hotels

★ The Station Hotel
$$ | HOTEL | This historic yet contemporary hotel in the heart of Rothes is renowned for its luxury designer rooms and suites, its excellent café restaurant serving hearty pub grub, and its enormous selection of world whiskies and gins, to be enjoyed in the comfort of the stunning Spirit Safe bar. **Pros:** chic contemporary decor; incredible whisky selection; free car parking. **Cons:** breakfast buffet a little sparse; no elevator; expensive for the area. Ⓢ Rooms from: £170 ⊠ 51 New St. ☎ 01340/832200 ⊕ www.stationhotelspeyside.com ⤴ 14 rooms ⏺ Free Breakfast.

Aberlour

2 miles southwest of Craigellachie.

Aberlour, often listed as Charlestown of Aberlour on maps, is a handsome little burgh, essentially Victorian in style, though actually founded in 1812 by the local landowner. The names of the noted local whisky stills are Cragganmore, Aberlour, and Glenfarclas; Glenlivet and Cardhu are also nearby. Also in Aberlour is Walkers, famous for producing shortbread, tins of buttery, crumbly goodness, since 1898.

GETTING HERE AND AROUND
Aberlour is on A95; public transportation here is infrequent.

Sights

Ballindalloch Castle
CASTLE/PALACE | The family home of the Macpherson-Grants since 1546, Ballindalloch Castle is every visitor's idea of what a Scots laird's lair should look like. You can wander around the beautifully kept rooms and meticulously tended gardens at your leisure; you may even bump into the lord and lady of the manor, who live here all year. There's also a splendid tea shop offering large slices of cake. ⊠ *Off A95* ⊹ *8 miles southwest of Craigellachie* ☎ *01807/500205* ⊕ *www. ballindallochcastle.co.uk* ▨ *£12* ⊙ *Closed Oct.–Easter.*

Cardhu Distillery
WINERY/DISTILLERY | The striking outline of Cardhu Distillery, whose main product lies at the heart of Johnnie Walker blends, is set among the heather-clad Mannoch Hills. Established by John and Helen Cumming in 1811, it was officially founded in 1824 after distilling was made legal by the Excise Act of 1823. Guides take you to the mashing, fermenting, and distilling halls, and they explain the malting process, which now takes place on the coast at Burghead. ⊠ *B1902, Knockando* ⊹ *10 miles north of Glenlivet and 7 miles west of Aberlour* ☎ *01340/875635* ⊕ *www.discovering-distilleries.com/cardhu/find-us/* ▨ *£8* ⊙ *Closed Sun. Jan.–Mar. and Oct.–Dec. and Sat. Nov.–Dec.*

Glenfarclas
WINERY/DISTILLERY | Glenfarclas is one of Scotland's few remaining family-owned distilleries, passed down from father to son since 1865. That link to the past is most visible among its low buildings, where the retired whiskey-still sits outside: if you didn't know what it was, you could mistake it for part of a submarine. The tours end with tastings in the superlative Ship Room, the intact lounge of an ocean liner called the *Empress of Australia*. ⊠ *Off A95, Ballindalloch* ☎ *01807/500345* ⊕ *www.glenfarclas.com* ▨ *£7.50; tasting tours from £40* ⊙ *Closed weekends Oct.–June and Sun. July–Sept.*

Glenlivet
WINERY/DISTILLERY | The famous Glenlivet was the first licensed distillery in the Highlands, founded in 1824 by George Smith. Today it produces one of the best-known 12-year-old single malts in the world. The 75-minute Classic Tour offers an introduction to malt whisky making, explains the distillery's history, and includes a free dram; more in-depth tours are available. There's a coffee shop with baked goods and, of course, a whisky shop. Visitors must be 18 or over. ⊠ *Off B9008, Ballindalloch* ⊹ *10 miles southwest of Aberlour via A95 and B9008.* ☎ *01340/821720* ⊕ *www.glenlivet.com* ▨ *£12.50* ⊙ *Closed mid-Nov.–mid-Mar.*

Hotels

Mash Tun
$$ | B&B/INN | Curvy yet sturdy, this former station hotel, now a smart bed-and-breakfast with a popular restaurant, is the social hub of the village. **Pros:** superb accommodations; tasty meals; great

atmosphere in the restaurant and bar. **Cons:** often booked up in summer; small bedrooms; on the more expensive side for this area. ⑤ *Rooms from: £125* ⊠ *8 Broomfield Sq.* ☎ *01340/881771* ⊕ *www. mashtun aberlour.com* ⤙ *5 rooms* ⑪ *Free breakfast.*

Fochabers

9 miles east of Elgin.

With its hanging baskets of fuchsia in summer and its perfectly mowed village square, Fochabers has a cared-for charm that makes you want to stop here, even just to stretch your legs. Lying just to the south of the River Spey, the former market town was founded in 1776 by the Duke of Gordon. The duke moved the village from its original site because it was too close to Gordon Castle. Famous today for being home to the Baxters brand of soups and jams, Fochabers is near some of the best berry fields; come and pick your own in the summer months.

GETTING HERE AND AROUND
Fochabers is not on the Inverness-to-Aberdeen train line, but there is an hourly bus service (Stagecoach Bluebird No. 10) from Fochabers to Elgin. It's near the junction of A98 and A96.

Sights

Baxters Highland Village
STORE/MALL | Legendary Scottish food brand Baxters of Fochabers makes gourmet products here on the banks of the River Spey for worldwide export. From Tokyo to New York, upmarket stores stock the company's soups, jams, and chutneys. Watch cooking demonstrations, have a look at a re-creation of the Baxters' first grocery shop, or browse around the Best of Scotland, specializing in all kinds of Scottish products.

A restaurant serves up an assortment of delectables. ⊠ *A96* ☎ *01343/820666* ⊕ *www.baxters.com.*

Fochabers Folk Museum & Heritage Centre
MUSEUM | **FAMILY** | Once over the Spey Bridge and past the cricket ground (a very unusual sight in Scotland), you can find the symmetrical, 18th-century Fochabers village square. The old Pringle Church is now the home of the Fochabers Folk Museum, which boasts a fine collection of items relating to past life of all types of residents in the village and surrounding area. Exhibits include carts and carriages, farm implements, domestic labor-saving devices, and an exquisite collection of Victorian toys. ⊠ *High St.* ☎ *01343/821204* ⊕ *www. fochabers-heritage.org.uk* ✸ *Closed Mon. and Oct.–mid-May.*

Restaurants

Gordon Castle Walled Garden Cafe
$$ | **BRITISH** | With light streaming through the large windows onto the wooden tables and rattan chairs, there is an airiness and freshness to this eatery. Fish landed just a few miles away on the Moray coast is a good bet, as are the long-aged steaks. **Known for:** mushroom and rarebit toast; fresh summer fruit desserts; pretty walled garden. ⑤ *Average main: £15* ⊠ *Fochabers* ✛ *Just off A96, Fochabers Bypass Rd.* ☎ *01343/612317* ⊕ *www.gordoncastlescotland.com.*

⬤ Shopping

Watt's Antiques
ANTIQUES/COLLECTIBLES | This shop has small collectibles, jewelry, ornaments, and china. ⊠ *45 High St.* ☎ *01343/820077* ⊕ *www.wattsantiques.com.*

Cullen

21 miles east of Elgin, 13 miles east of Fochabers.

Look for some wonderfully painted homes at Cullen, in the old fishing town below the railway viaduct. The real attractions of this charming little seaside resort, however, are its white-sand beach (the water is quite cold, though) and the fine view west toward the aptly named Bowfiddle Rock. In summer Cullen bustles with families carrying buckets and spades and eating ice cream and chips.

A stroll past the small but once busy harbor reveals numerous fishers' cottages, huddled together with small yards where they dried their nets. Beyond these the vast stretch of beach curves gently round the bay. Above are the disused Victorian viaduct—formerly the Peterhead train line—and the 18th-century town.

GETTING HERE AND AROUND
Cullen is on A98, on Cullen Bay.

Sights

Seafield Street
NEIGHBORHOOD | The town has a fine *mercat* (market) cross and one main street—Seafield Street—that splits the town. It holds numerous specialty shops—antiques and gift stores, an ironmonger, a baker, a pharmacy, and a locally famous ice-cream shop among them—as well as several cafés. ✉ *Cullen.*

Restaurants

Linda's Fish & Chips
$ | **SEAFOOD** | **FAMILY** | This casual place serves the freshest fish, caught in nearby Buckie and cooked to crispy perfection (gluten-free batter is available, too). There's a seating area inside, but it's best for takeout. **Known for:** fish battered to perfection; crispy fries; deep-fried squid

rings. **$** *Average main: £10* ✉ *54 Seafield St.* ☎ *01542/840202.*

Hotels

Seafield Arms
$ | **HOTEL** | Built in 1822, this gallant old coaching inn has retained much of its period character through its rebirth as a modern boutique hotel. **Pros:** local atmosphere; excellent value; casual bar and elegant dining room. **Cons:** slightly pretentious; used for business meetings, so can feel a bit too businesslike; popular with wedding parties. **$** *Rooms from: £92* ✉ *17–19 Seafield St.* ☎ *01542/841604* ⊕ *www.seafieldarmscullen.co.uk* ➦ *16 rooms* ⊚ *No meals.*

Banff

36 miles east of Elgin, 47 miles north of Aberdeen.

Midway along the northeast coast, overlooking Moray Firth and the estuary of the River Deveron, Banff is a dour fishing town, huddled around a small harbor, with a bleak but sometimes lovely coastline of crags, cliffs, and sandy coves to either side. Sixteenth-century houses huddle around the harbor, while surprisingly grand Georgian streets are reminders of its glory years as a hub of the fishing industry.

GETTING HERE AND AROUND
Banff is on the A98 coastal road and at the end of the tree-lined A947 to Aberdeen. If you are relying on public transportation, Bus 325 from Aberdeen bus station takes two hours and gets you into Low Street, just five minutes from Duff House.

Fyvie Castle is one of Scotland's more complex constructions.

Sights

★ Duff House

HOUSE | The jewel in Banff's crown is the grand mansion of Duff House, a splendid William Adam–designed (1689–1748) Georgian mansion. It's now an annex of the National Galleries, housing works by El Greco, Sir Henry Raeburn, and Thomas Gainsborough. A good tearoom and a gift shop are on the ground floor. ⊠ Off A98 ☎ 01261/818181 ⊕ www.historicenviron-ment.scot ⊠ £9 ⊗ Closed Mon.–Thurs. Oct.–Mar.

Fyvie Castle

18 miles south of Banff.

This castle mixes ancient construction with Edwardian splendor and includes excellent art. The grounds are also worth exploring.

GETTING HERE AND AROUND

If you're driving from Banff, take the A947 south for 20 minutes or so until you see the turnoff.

Sights

★ Fyvie Castle

CASTLE/PALACE | In an area rich with castles, Fyvie Castle stands out as the most complex. Five great towers built by five successive powerful families turned a 13th-century foursquare castle into an opulent Edwardian statement of wealth. Some superb paintings are on view, including 12 works by Sir Henry Raeburn. There are myriad sumptuous interiors—the circular stone staircase is considered one of the best examples in the country—and delightfully laid-out gardens. A former lady of the house, Lillia Drummond, was apparently starved to death by her husband, who entombed her body inside the walls of a secret room. In the 1920s, when the bones were disrupted during renovations, a string of such terrible misfortunes followed that they were quickly returned and the room sealed off. Her name is carved into the windowsill of the Drummond Room. ✉ *Off A947, Turriff* ☎ *01651/819226* ⊕ *www.nts.org.uk* ✉ *£13* ⊘ *Closed mid-Dec.–Mar.*

Ellon

32 miles southeast of Banff, 14 miles north of Aberdeen.

Formerly a market center on what was then the lowest bridging point of the River Ythan, Ellon, a bedroom suburb of Aberdeen, is a small town at the center of a rural hinterland. It's also well placed for visiting Fyvie Castle and Haddo House.

GETTING HERE AND AROUND

To get to Ellon, take the A947 from Banff or the A90 from Aberdeen; both routes take half an hour.

⊙ Sights

Haddo House

HOUSE | Built in 1732, this elegant mansion has a light and graceful Georgian design, with curving wings on either side of a harmonious, symmetrical facade. The interior is late-Victorian ornate, filled with magnificent paintings (including works by Pompeo Batoni and Sir Thomas Lawrence) and plenty of objets d'art. Pre-Raphaelite stained-glass windows by Sir Edward Burne-Jones grace the chapel. Outside is a terrace garden with a fountain, and a few yards farther is Haddo Country Park, which has walking trails leading to memorials about the Gordon family. ■ **TIP→ Visits to the house are by prebooked tour only, which are held at 11 and 2.** ✉ *Off B999* ✛ *8 miles northwest of Ellon* ☎ *01651/851440* ⊕ *www.nts.org. uk* ✉ *£12* ⊘ *Closed mid-Dec.–mid-Jan.*

 ## Activities

GOLF

Cruden Bay Golf Club

GOLF | This historic golf course, sheltered among extensive sand dunes, offers a quintessential Scottish golf experience. Narrow channels and deep valleys on challenging fairways ensure plenty of excitement, making Cruden Bay one of the northeast's most outstanding courses. ✉ *Aulton Rd., Cruden Bay* ☎ *01779/812285* ⊕ *www.crudenbay-golfclub.co.uk* ✉ *Championship: £135; St. Olaf: weekdays £30, weekends £40* 🏌 *Championship: 18 holes, 6287 yards, par 70; St. Olaf: 9 holes, 2463 yards, par 32* ⚑ *Reservations essential* ☞ *Book months in advance for a round on weekends.*

Chapter 19

ARGYLL AND THE ISLES

Updated by
Robin Gauldie

👁 Sights	🍴 Restaurants	🛏 Hotels	💼 Shopping	🍸 Nightlife
★★★★☆	★★☆☆☆	★★★☆☆	★☆☆☆☆	★☆☆☆☆

WELCOME TO ARGYLL AND THE ISLES

TOP REASONS TO GO

★ **Whisky:** With 14 distilleries—9 on Islay, 1 each on Jura and Mull, and just 3 on the mainland—the region has been nicknamed Scotland's whisky coast.

★ **Iona and its abbey:** Maybe it's the remoteness that creates the almost mystical sense of history on Iona. From this early center of Scottish Christianity, evangelists traveled throughout Europe from the 6th century onward. It was also the burial place of Scottish kings, including Macbeth.

★ **The great outdoors:** Salmon and trout fill the lochs and rivers, while even bigger trophy fish await farther out to sea. Golfers have more than two dozen courses to choose from, and cyclists and walkers will find every kind of terrain at hand.

★ **Castles:** Often poised on cliffs overlooking the sea, the region's castles tell the story of eight centuries of occupations, sieges, and conflicts between warring clan chiefs and nobles.

With long sea lochs carved into its hilly, wooded interior, Argyll is a beguiling interweaving of water and land. The Mull of Kintyre, a narrow finger of land, points south towards nearby Ireland, separating the Firth of Clyde and its islands from the Atlantic and the isles of the Inner Hebrides. Arran, largest of the Clyde isles, looms near the mouth of the Clyde, separated from Kintyre by Kilbrannan Sound. Ferry services allow all kinds of interisland tours and can shorten mainland trips as well.

Linking the region with Glasgow, the A82 runs along the west shore of Loch Lomond to connect with the A83. That road follows the north shore of Loch Fyne, a long fjordlike inlet known for some of Scotland's finest seafood, all the way to Campbeltown near the tip of Kintyre. Along the way is Kennacraig, departure point for ferries to Islay and Jura. Coming from the east, the A85 runs through equally spectacular scenery between Perth and Oban, the main port for ferries to Mull

and other islands. From Oban the A828 runs north to Fort William and the Great Glen.

1 Oban. Argyll's gateway to the isles.

2 Appin. Remote, lovely, and steeped in clan history.

3 Loch Awe. Island-dotted and flanked by forested hills.

4 Inveraray. The storied seat of Campbell chieftains.

5 Kintyre Peninsula. A charming strip of land with beaches and wildlife.

6 Brodick. The largest town in Arran.

7 Machrie. A Moorland village surrounded by ancient stone circles.

8 Lochranza. Home to a renowned distillery and a castle that sheltered Robert the Bruce.

9 Islay and Jura. Islay is a place of pilgrimage for whisky connoisseurs while Jura is rugged, hilly, and perfect for walkers and whisky lovers alike.

10 Isles of Mull and Iona. The Isle of Mull has great fishing, a spectacular castle, and the colorful village of Tobermory. Iona is a tranquil isle with a famed ancient abbey.

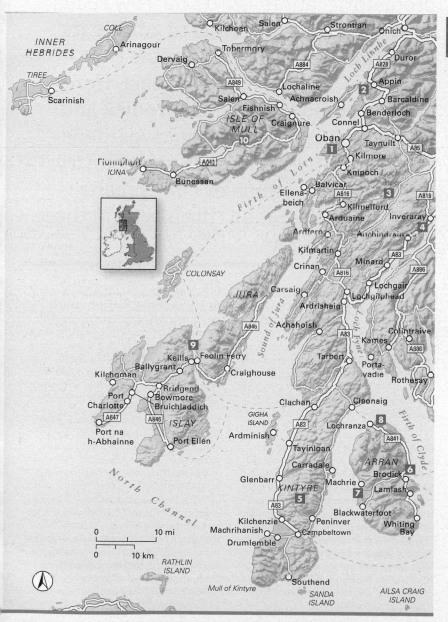

INNER HEBRIDES

COLL

Arinagour

TIREE

Scarinish

Kilchoan

Salen

Strontian

Onich

Tobermory

Dervaig

A884

A828

Duror

Appin

A849

Lochaline

Achnacroish

2

Barcaldine

Salen

Fishnish

Benderloch

ISLE OF MULL

Craignure

Connel

10

Oban

1

Taynuilt

A85

Kilmore

Fionnphort

A849

Knipoch

IONA

Bunessan

Balvicar

Firth of Lorn

Ellena-beich

A816

3

A819

Kilmelford

Arduaine

Inveraray

Ardfern

Auchindrain

4

COLONSAY

Kilmartin

A83

Minard

A886

Crinan

A816

JURA

Carsaig

Lochgair

Lochgilphead

Ardrishaig

Sound of Jura

A846

Achahoish

A83

Colintraive

Keills

Feolin Ferry

Tarbert

Kames

9

Porta-vadie

A886

Ballygrant

Craighouse

Rothesay

Kilchoman

Bridgend

Port Charlotte

Bowmore

Bruichladdich

Clachan

Claonaig

A847

A846

ISLAY

GIGHA ISLAND

A83

Lochranza

8

A841

Port na h-Abhainne

Ardminish

Tayinloan

Port Ellen

Carradale

ARRAN

Brodick

6

Glenbarr

Machrie

Lamlash

KINTYRE

7

North Channel

A83

5

Blackwaterfoot

Whiting Bay

Kilchenzie

Peninver

Machrihanish

Campbeltown

Drumlemble

Firth of Clyde

RATHLIN ISLAND

0   10 mi

0   10 km

Mull of Kintyre

Southend

SANDA ISLAND

AILSA CRAIG ISLAND

Argyll's rocky seaboard looks out onto islands that were once part of a single prehistoric landmass. Its narrow roads slow travel but give time to admire its lochs and woods, and the ruins that recall the region's dramatic past. Here, too, are grand houses like Brodick and Inveraray castles and elegant gardens such as Crarae. This is whisky country, too: the peaty aroma of Islay's malts is unmistakable. Yet all this is within three hours of Glasgow.

Western Scotland has a complicated, splintered coastline where you'll observe the interplay of sea, loch, and rugged green peninsula. The islands are breathtakingly beautiful, though they often catch the extremely wet weather arriving here from the Atlantic. It is common to experience four seasons in a day, as cliffs and woods suddenly and dramatically disappear in sea mists, then reappear just as suddenly.

Ancient castles like Dunstaffnage and the ruined towers on the islands of Loch Awe testify to the region's past importance. Prehistoric peoples left their mark here in the stone circles, carved stones, and Bronze and Iron Age burial mounds around Kilmartin and on Islay and Arran. The gardens of Inveraray and Brodick castles, nourished by the temperate west-coast climate, are the pride of Argyll, while the paths of Crarae's, south of Inveraray, wind through plantings of magnolias and azaleas.

The working people of Glasgow traditionally spent their family holidays on the Clyde estuary, taking day trips by steamer down the Firth, or making longer journeys to Rothesay on the Isle of Bute or to Arran and the Ayrshire coast. From Ardrossan, farther down the coast, ferries cruise to the prosperous and varied Isle of Arran.

Western Scotland's small islands have jagged cliffs or tongues of rock, long white-sand beaches, fertile pastures where sheep and cattle graze, fortresses, and shared memories of clan wars and mysterious beasts. Their cliff paths and lochside byways are a paradise for walkers and cyclists, and their whisky the ideal reward after a long day outside. While the islands' western coasts are dramatic, their more sheltered eastern seaboards are the location for pretty harbor towns like brightly painted Tobermory on Mull, or Port Ellen on Islay, with its neat rows of low whitewashed houses.

MAJOR REGIONS

Argyll. Topographical grandeur and rocky shores are what make Argyll special. Try to take to the water at least once, even if your time is limited. The sea and the sea lochs have played a vital role in the history of western Scotland since the time of the war galleys of the clans. Oban is the major ferry gateway and transport hub, with a main road leading south into the Kintyre Peninsula. The linked peninsulas of Knapdale and Kintyre—separated by the Crinan Canal at Tarbert—are areas of moorland and forest dotted with small lochs. From Inveraray at the head of Loch Fyne, you can take in Auchindrain's re-created fishing village on the way to the Arran ferry. Or turn west toward Crinan and the prehistoric sites around Kilmartin, then travel northward toward Loch Awe and its intriguing island ruins.

Arran. Touring this island will give you a glimpse in a day or two of the whole of Scotland in miniature. In the north the forbidding Goatfell (2,868 feet) is a challenge that draws walkers and climbers. The island's wilder west coast attracts bird-watchers and naturalists, while the fertile south of the island contains nine lovely golf courses, leisurely walks, and Brodick Castle. A temperate microclimate attracted ancient settlers whose stone circles still stand on the island. This weather also explains why it has long been a favorite getaway for Glaswegians, who come here to walk, climb Goatfell, or play golf.

Islay and Jura. The smell of peat that hangs in the air on Islay is bottled in its famous whiskies. Aside from distilleries, the island's historical sites evoke a past in which these islands were far less remote. The whitewashed cottages along the coast of Islay line clean and beautiful beaches, many of them visited by a variety of wildlife. Jura is wilder and more dramatic, its twin mountains (the Paps) dominating its infertile moorland.

Isle of Mull and Iona. The pretty harbor of Tobermory, with its painted houses, is a relaxing base from which to explore the varied and beautiful island of Mull. Along Mull's west coast, spectacular cliffs and rocky beaches look out onto the Atlantic. From Craignure the road crosses the sweeping green valleys of the Ross of Mull to Fionnphort and the ferry to the meditative island of Iona.

Planning

When to Go

This part of the mainland is close enough to Glasgow to make it accessible year-round. Oban is just over two hours from the city by car (three hours by bus), but getting to the isles via ferries takes longer, and the crossings are less frequent out of season. You can take advantage of quiet roads and plentiful accommodations in early spring and late autumn. The summer months of July and August can get very busy indeed; book accommodations and restaurants in advance during high season. In winter short daylight hours and winds can make island stays rather bleak, but add allure to the prospect of sipping malt whisky by a log fire. Birding enthusiasts can observe vast flocks of migrant Arctic wildfowl arriving and leaving Islay in autumn and spring. At any time come prepared with adequate clothing for fast-changing weather.

Planning Your Time

You could easily spend a week exploring the islands alone, so consider spending at least a few nights in this region. Argyll and some island excursions make pleasant and easy side trips from Glasgow and Loch Lomond. Driving anywhere here takes a little longer than you'd think, so allow ample travel time. A leisurely day will take you to Inveraray, its castle, and the surrounding gardens (don't miss the folk museum at Auchindrain) before driving on to Kennacraig to take the ferry for Islay and Jura. Two or three days here will give you a sense of the history and varied landscapes of these stunning islands—and time for a distillery or two. If you have time to visit just one island, sail from Oban to Mull, returning the same day or the next to take in the Scottish Sea Life Sanctuary. If you can, drive around beautiful Loch Awe on your way back to Glasgow. If time is really tight, consider flying from Glasgow to Islay or Tiree.

Plan ahead: car ferries fill up in the summer months (there is usually no problem for foot passengers), and some of the smaller islands are served only once or twice a week. Bear in mind that it is not easy to find places to eat after 9 pm at any time of year—though you can usually find a place that will sell you a whisky until much later.

Getting Here and Around

AIR
The closest major airport to Argyll and the Isles is Glasgow. Hebridean Air Services flies from Oban to Islay, Coll, Colonsay, and Tiree.

CONTACTS Hebridean Air Services.
☎ 0845/805–7465 ⊕ www.hebrideanair. co.uk.

BOAT AND FERRY
Caledonian MacBrayne (CalMac) operates car-ferry and passenger services to and from the main islands. It is important to plan ahead when traveling to the islands in order to coordinate the connecting ferries; CalMac can advise you on this. Multiple-island tickets are available and can significantly reduce the cost of island-hopping.

CalMac ferries run from Oban to Mull, Lismore, Coll, and Tiree; from Kennacraig to Islay, Jura, and Gigha; from Ardrossan to Arran; and from Port Askaig on Islay to Feolin on Jura; as well as a number of shorter routes. Western Ferries operate between Dunoon, in Argyll, and Gourock, west of Glasgow. The ferry passage between Dunoon and Gourock is one frequented by locals; it saves a lot of time, and you can take your car across as well. Jura Passenger Ferry operates between Tayvallich (on the mainland) and Craighouse on Jura.

Ferry reservations are needed if you have a car; passengers traveling by foot do not need to make reservations.

CONTACTS Caledonian MacBrayne.
(CalMac) ☎ 0800/066–5000 ⊕ www. calmac.co.uk. **Jura Passenger Ferry.** ☎ 07768/450000 ⊕ www.jurapassengerferry.com. **Western Ferries.** ☎ 01369/704452 ⊕ www.western-ferries. co.uk.

BUS
You can travel throughout the region by bus, but service here tends to be less frequent than elsewhere in Scotland. Scottish Citylink runs daily service from Glasgow's Buchanan Street station to the mid-Argyll region and Kintyre; the trip to Oban takes about three hours. Several other companies provide local services within the region.

CONTACTS Garelochhead Coaches.
☎ 01436/810200 ⊕ www.garelochheadcoaches.co.uk. **Islay Coaches.** ☎ 01496/840273 ⊕ www.bmundell. co.uk. **Scottish Citylink.** ☎ 0871/266–3333 ⊕ www.citylink.co.uk. **Stagecoach West Scotland.** ☎ 01770/302000 ⊕ www. stagecoachbus.com. **West Coast Motors.** ☎ 01586/552319 ⊕ www.westcoastmotors.co.uk.

CAR
Negotiating this area is easy except in July and August, when the roads around Oban may be congested. A number of single-lane roads, especially on the east side of the Kintyre Peninsula and on the

islands, require special care. Remember that white triangles indicate places where you can pass. You'll probably have to board a ferry at some point during your trip; nearly all ferries take cars as well as pedestrians.

From Glasgow take the A82 and the A85 to Oban, the main ferry terminal for Mull and the islands (about 2½ hours by car). From the A82 take the A83 at Arrochar; it rounds Loch Fyne to Inveraray. From there you can take the A819 from Inveraray around Loch Awe and rejoin the Glasgow–Oban road. Alternatively, you can stay on the A83 and head down Kintyre to Kennacraig, the ferry terminal for Islay. Farther down the A83 is Tayinloan, the ferry port for Gigha. You can reach Brodick on Arran by ferry from Ardrossan, on the Clyde coast (M8/A78 from Glasgow); in summer you can travel to Lochranza from Claonaig on the Kintyre Peninsula, but there are very few crossings.

TRAIN
Oban and Ardrossan are the main rail stations; it's a three-hour trip from Glasgow to Oban. For information call ScotRail. All trains connect with ferries.

CONTACTS ScotRail. ☎0871/200–2233 ⊕ www.scotrail.co.uk.

Restaurants

Argyll and the Isles have earned a reputation for excellent gastropubs and restaurants (many of which also offer accommodations) that use superb locally sourced produce, including luscious seafood, lamb, wild and farmed venison, and game of many kinds. Most hotels and many guesthouses offer evening meals, and it may often be your best option to look to hotel restaurants, though the quality can vary. Most restaurants and pubs stop serving food by 9 pm; lunch usually ends at 2:30.

Hotels

Accommodations in Argyll and on the Isles range from country-house hotels to private homes offering a bed and breakfast. Most small, traditional, provincial hotels in coastal resorts have been updated and modernized, while still retaining personalized service. And though hotels often have a restaurant offering evening meals, the norm is to offer breakfast only.

Restaurant and hotel reviews have been shortened. For full information, visit Fodors.com. Restaurant prices are the average cost of a main course at dinner or, if dinner is not served, at lunch. Hotel prices are the lowest cost of a standard double room in high season, including 20% V.A.T.

WHAT IT COSTS in Pounds			
$	$$	$$$	$$$$
RESTAURANTS			
under £15	£15–£19	£20–£25	over £25
HOTELS			
under £125	£125–£200	£201–£300	over £300

Tours

★ Sea Life Surveys
BOAT TOURS | FAMILY | Dolphins, seals, porpoises, and (if you're fortunate) minke whales and basking sharks are among the stars of the show on a Sea Life Surveys cruise from pretty Tobermory. Seabirds abound, too, and you may spot huge white-tailed eagles, once extinct here but reintroduced to this part of Scotland in recent years. Several cruises are offered: if time is short, choose the 90-minute Ecocruz. ⊠ A848, Tobermory ⊕ Cruises leave from floating pontoons opposite Mull Aquarium ☎ 01688/302916 ⊕ www.sealifesurveys.com ⊡ From £20.

As Argyll's biggest town, Oban greets visitors to the region with its seaside charm.

Staffa Tours

BOAT TOURS | **FAMILY** | This company organizes a number of tours to the smaller islands, with the emphasis on wildlife. Tours run from Mull, Ardnamurchan on the mainland, or from Iona. The three-hour trip to uninhabited Staffa includes Fingal's Cave, commemorated by Mendelssohn in his famous overture. With luck you may encounter dolphins on the way. Staffa also runs tours to the Treshnish islands, famous for the puffin colonies on Lunga. ✉ *The Boat Shed, Iona, Iona* ☎ *07732/912370* ⊕ *www. staffatours.com* ✉ *From £35.*

West Coast Tours

BUS TOURS | A range of bus tours in and around Oban and on Mull are available through West Coast Tours. The company can also arrange combined bus and boat tours. ✉ *George St., Oban* ☎ *01631/552319* ⊕ *www.westcoasttours. co.uk* ✉ *From £7.*

Visitor Information

The only year-round visitor information offices are in Bowmore, Craignure, and Oban.

Oban

96 miles northwest of Glasgow, 125 miles northwest of Edinburgh, 50 miles south of Fort William, 118 miles southwest of Inverness.

It's almost impossible to avoid Oban when touring the west. Its waterfront has some character, but the town's main role is as a launch point for excursions into Argyll and for ferries to the islands. A traditional Scottish resort town, Oban has many music festivals, *ceilidhs* with Highland dancing, as well as all the usual tartan kitsch and late-night revelry in pubs and hotel bars. The Oban Distillery offers tours and a shop. Still, there are more exciting destinations just over the horizon, on the islands, and down into Kintyre.

GETTING HERE AND AROUND

From Glasgow the A82 along Loch Lomond meets the A85 at Crianlarich. Turn left and continue to Oban. In summer the center of Oban can become gridlocked with ferry traffic, so leave yourself time for the wait. Alternatively, the A816 from Lochgilphead enters Oban from the less-crowded south. Train services run from Glasgow to Oban (ScotRail); Scottish Citylink runs buses from Glasgow to Oban several times a day.

ESSENTIALS

VISITOR INFORMATION Oban Tourist Information Centre. ⊠ *3 North Pier* ☎ *01631/563122* ⊕ *www.oban.org.uk.*

Sights

Dunstaffnage Castle

CASTLE/PALACE | Standing high atop volcanic rock, Dunstaffnage commands the hills and lochs that surround it. That is why this 13th-century castle was so strategic and contested by those battling for control of Argyll and the Isles. From the walk along the walls you have outstanding views across the **Sound of Mull** and the **Firth of Lorne**. A small well-illustrated guidebook (£2.50) lets you take your own guided tour, but there are storyboards throughout the building that give you a sense of how it was used across the ages. In the woods is the ruined chapel of St. Cuthbert, built by the Macdougall clan at the same time as the castle. ⊠ *Off A85* ☎ *01631/562465* ⊕ *www.historicenvironment.scot* ⊠ *£6* ☉ *Closed Thurs. and Fri. Oct.–Mar.*

Oban Distillery

WINERY/DISTILLERY | One of Scotland's oldest and smallest distilleries was founded in 1794, several years before the town where it now stands. It produces a well known 14 year old malt which, according to those who know, has a taste somewhere between the smoky

Islay whiskies and the softer, sweeter Highland varieties—a distinctive West Highland flavor. ⊠ *Stafford St.* ⊹ *Opposite North Pier* ☎ *01631/572004* ⊕ *www.obanwhisky.com* ⊠ *Basic tour £12* ☉ *Closed weekends in Dec.*

Oban War and Peace Museum

MUSEUM | FAMILY | This free museum recalls Oban's history through peace and war in photographs and other exhibits. Always a fishing harbor and a ferry port, during the Second World War the town became a key naval command center. ⊠ *Old Oban Times Building, Corran Esplanade* ☎ *01631/570001* ⊕ *www.obanmuseum.org.uk* ⊠ *Free* ☉ *Closed Nov.–Feb.*

Ocean Explorer Centre

MUSEUM | FAMILY | On the Firth of Lorn, this imaginative venture lets you get a look under the sea. Hands-on exhibits include microscopes where you can observe tiny algae and a live undersea camera where you can see what's happening below the waves. Part of a scientific research center, it's educational but also accessible and fun. There is a bright little café and a shop with books on marine science and other topics. It's 2 miles from Oban—follow the signs for nearby Dunstaffnage Castle. ⊠ *Kirk Rd.* ☎ *01631/559123* ⊕ *www.oceanexplorercentre.org* ⊠ *Free* ☉ *Closed weekends and late Dec.–early Jan.*

🍴 Restaurants

★ Ee-usk

$$$ | SEAFOOD | This clean-lined restaurant's name means "fish" in Gaelic, and it has earned quite a reputation for serving excellent dishes made with the freshest fish and shellfish delivered directly from Oban's harbor. The signature creations use appealingly simple sauces; try oven-baked wild halibut with creamed leeks or the full-scale seafood platter. **Known for:** Mull scallops; Loch Linnhe oysters and langoustines; island

views. $ *Average main: £25* ✉ *North Pier* ☎ *01631/565666* ⊕ *www.eeusk.com.*

Hawthorn Restaurant
$ | BRITISH | Fish shares the menu here with local lamb, pork, and game. Although it's just a few miles from Oban (whence it sources its seafood), the setting is rural, surrounded by crofts that are still working farms. **Known for:** freshly caught haddock; Argyll lamb; tasty steak pies. $ *Average main: £12* ✉ *Keil Crofts, Benderloch* ✛ *6 miles north of Oban off the main A816, after crossing the Connel Bridge* ☎ *01631/720777* ⊗ *Closed Mon. and Oct.–Mar.*

Oban Seafood Hut
$ | SEAFOOD | Serving arguably the best-value seafood in Oban, ex-fisherman John Ogden's quayside fish shack is a local legend. Look for a green-painted shed on the pier, then join the line of cognoscenti waiting for simply sautéed scallops, grilled langoustine and lobster, oysters, and mussels. **Known for:** king prawn sandwiches and scallops in garlic butter; cash or debit card only; only a few tables, so eating while standing a possibility. $ *Average main: £8* ✉ *CalMac Pier* ☎ *07881/418565* ⊗ *Closed Nov.–Apr.* ▭ *No credit cards.*

 Hotels

Glenburnie House
$ | B&B/INN | At this typical seafront guesthouse in a Victorian building with fine views over Oban Bay, most rooms are spacious and comfortable, if slightly overdecorated in traditional style. **Pros:** centrally located; good sea views; lots of local atmosphere. **Cons:** too many flowery fabrics for some tastes; no bar on-site; only meal available is breakfast. $ *Rooms from: £100* ✉ *Esplanade* ☎ *01631/562089* ⊕ *www.glenburnie.co.uk* ⊗ *Closed Dec.– Feb.* ⇆ *12 rooms* ⦿ *Breakfast.*

Kilchrenan House
$ | B&B/INN | Just a few minutes from the town center, this Victorian-era stone house has been transformed into a lovely bed-and-breakfast. **Pros:** great sea views; tasteful attention to detail; cozy rooms. **Cons:** some bedrooms may be too colorfully decorated for some tastes; attic rooms have a slanting roof; credit cards not accepted for one-night stays. $ *Rooms from: £80* ✉ *Corran Esplanade* ☎ *01631/562663* ⊕ *www.kilchrenan-house.co.uk* ⊗ *Closed Dec. and Jan* ⇆ *13 rooms* ⦿ *Free breakfast.*

★ Manor House Hotel
$$ | HOTEL | On the coast near Oban, this 1780 stone house—once the home of the Duke of Argyll—has sea views and a convenient location. **Pros:** excellent restaurant; complimentary golf at local course; free use of local gym. **Cons:** smallish bedrooms; no children under 12; pretty expensive by local standards. $ *Rooms from: £185* ✉ *Gallanach Rd.* ☎ *01631/562087* ⊕ *www.manorhouse-oban.com* ⇆ *11 rooms* ⦿ *Free Breakfast.*

Appin

17 miles north of Oban.

The little peninsula of Appin, a 20-minute drive from Oban, is a charming, well-kept secret. Just 2 miles along a narrow road from the main Fort William route (A828), the bay opens to Lismore and the sea. Castle Stalker, a privately owned castle on the water, sits magnificently in the center of the picture, a symbol of ancient coastal Scotland. This is an excellent, uncrowded base for walking, fishing, water sports, and cycling.

GETTING HERE AND AROUND
From Oban follow the A828 around Loch Creran and take the left turn to Port Appin just beyond Tynribbie. Continue for just over 2 miles to the old pier. From the port the passenger ferry runs to the island of Lismore throughout the year. Steamers once plied the waters of Loch Linnhe, but today the largest boats here

While you can't actually visit Appin's Castle Stalker, it makes for a lovely backdrop to a sunset.

are those taking workers to the quarries of Kingairloch.

Restaurants

★ Pierhouse Hotel and Restaurant

$$$ | SEAFOOD | The round towers of the old pier mark the entrance to this restaurant, appealingly situated on the water's edge. The restaurant serves the freshest seafood; try its signature platter of lobster, scallops, mussels, and langoustines. **Known for:** delicious lobster thermidor; rib-eye steak with langoustines; lively atmosphere. $ *Average main: £25* ⊠ *Port Appin* ☏ *01631/730302* ⊕ *www.pierhousehotel.co.uk.*

Hotels

★ Isle of Eriska

$$$$ | HOTEL | FAMILY | On one of Scotland's few private islands, this sybaritic enclave conceals luxury facilities like a spa, pool, gym, golf course, and a Michelin-starred restaurant behind a severe baronial facade. **Pros:** exceptional food; gorgeous views; superb leisure facilities. **Cons:** usually booked out at least one year ahead in high season; dining out not an easy option; very popular with wedding parties. $ *Rooms from: £300* ⊠ *Off A828, Benderloch* ✚ *Island signposted from Benderloch village and connected to mainland by short bridge* ☏ *01631/720371* ⊕ *www.eriska-hotel. co.uk* ⌁ *34 rooms* ℐ◯ℐ *Free breakfast.*

Loch Awe

18 miles east of Oban.

Measuring more than 25 miles long, Loch Awe is Scotland's longest stretch of freshwater. Its northwest shore is quiet; forest walks crisscross the Inverliever Forest here. At the loch's northern end, tiny islands, many with ruins, pepper the water. One, Inishail, is home to a 13th-century chapel.

GETTING HERE AND AROUND

From Oban the A85 will bring you to the head of Loch Awe and the small village of the same name. Turn onto the B845 at Taynuilt to reach the loch's northern shore, or continue through the forbidding Pass of Brander and turn onto the A819 to get to the southern shore. From here you can continue on to Inveraray, or drive along the loch on the B840.

Sights

★ Bonawe Iron Furnace

HISTORIC SITE | FAMILY | Seemingly out of place in this near-wilderness setting, Bonawe is a fascinating relic from the dawn of Britain's Industrial Revolution. In the mid-18th century, Argyll's virgin forests attracted ironmasters from England, where such valuable fuel sources were harder to find. Business boomed when wars with France boosted demand for pig iron and cannonballs, and in its heyday Bonawe employed up to 600 unskilled local wood gatherers and skilled southern foundrymen. ⊠ *Off B845, Bonawe* 🕾 *01866/822432* ⊕ *www. historicenvironment.scot* 🎫 *£6* 🕙 *Closed Sat.–Tues. and Oct.–Mar.*

Cruachan

FACTORY | FAMILY | Like the lair of a classic James Bond villain, this triumph of 20th-century British technology lurks deep within a vast man-made cavern. Hidden 3,000 feet beneath the slopes of Ben Cruachan, the colossal water-driven turbines of this subterranean power station, completed in 1965, supply clean energy to much of Scotland. The ½-mile bus ride from the surface to the generating hall is a surreal experience, made all the more so by the subtropical plants that thrive under artificial light in the warm, humid atmosphere. ⊠ *A85, Dalmally* 🕾 *01866/822618* ⊕ *www. visitcruachan.co.uk* 🎫 *£7.50* 🕙 *Closed weekends and Jan.*

Kilchurn Castle

ARCHAEOLOGICAL SITE | This is one of Argyll's most evocative ruins, with its crumbling lochside towers and high ramparts. Built by the Campbells in the 15th century, Kilchurn was rebuilt as a government garrison after the troubles of the late 17th century. The castle was abandoned after peace came to the Highlands following the final defeat of the Jacobite cause in 1746. ⊠ *Lochawe, Dalmally* ⊹ *2½ miles west of Dalmally* ⊕ *www.historic-scotland.gov.uk/places* 🕙 *Closed Oct.–Mar.*

Hotels

★ Taychreggan Hotel

$ | HOTEL | Peace and quiet are the big selling points of this lovely country-house hotel beside Loch Awe. Once a drovers' inn, the whitewashed building is surrounded by lawns and wooded gardens. **Pros:** lovely setting; activities including fishing and kayaking; wonderful meals. **Cons:** six miles from main road; limited restaurant menu; isolated location. 🛇 *Rooms from: £99* ⊠ *Off B845, Kilchrenan* 🕾 *01866/833211* ⊕ *www.tay-chregganhotel.co.uk* 🛌 *18 rooms* 🍴 *Free breakfast.*

Inveraray

21 miles south of Loch Awe, 61 miles north of Glasgow, 29 miles west of Loch Lomond.

Inveraray's star attraction is the grandiose seat of the Campbell Dukes of Argyll, for centuries the most powerful magnates of the Highlands. It's a trim little township, planned and built in the mid-18th century at the behest of the third duke. There are fine views of Loch Fyne, and there are gardens and museums to see nearby.

GETTING HERE AND AROUND

Driving from Oban take the A85 and the A819 beyond Loch Awe (the village). From Glasgow take the A82, turn onto the A83 at Arrochar, and make the long drive around Loch Fyne.

⊙ Sights

Ardkinglas Woodland Garden

GARDEN | Rambling over 12,000 acres, one of Britain's finest collections of conifers is set off by rhododendron blossoms in early summer. You can find the garden around the head of Loch Fyne, about 10 miles east of Inveraray. There's a wild woodland walk beyond the garden; both are open all year. The house, regarded as architect Sir Robert Lorimer's masterpiece, is open to visitors only on Fridays between April and October. ⊠ Ardkinglas Estate, Cairndow ☎ 01499/600261 ⊕ www.ardkinglas.com ⛁ £5.

★ Auchindrain Museum

MUSEUM VILLAGE | FAMILY | Step a few centuries back in time at this open-air museum, a rare surviving example of an 18th-century communal-tenancy farm. About 250 years ago, there were several thousand working communities like Auchindrain. Auchindrain was the last of them, its final tenant leaving in 1963. Today the bracken-thatch and iron-roof buildings, about 20 in all, give you a feel for early farming life in the Highland communities. Several houses are furnished and tell the story of their occupants. A tearoom is open morning to afternoon. ⊠ Auchindrain ✛ Off A83 about 6 miles south of Inveraray ☎ 01499/500235 ⊕ auchindrain.org.uk ⛁ £8 ⊙ Closed Nov.–Mar.

Crarae Garden

GARDEN | Exotic Himalayan plants flourish in the gentle microclimate of this 100-acre garden, where the Crarae Burn, a small stream, cascades through a rocky gorge. Rhododendrons, azaleas, and magnolias lend color, and native flowers and trees attract birds and butterflies. ⊠ A83 ✛ 10 miles southwest of Inveraray ☎ 01546/886614 ⊕ www.nts.org.uk ⛁ £7.50 ⊙ Closed Nov.–Mar.

Inveraray Castle

CASTLE/PALACE | The current seat of the Chief of the Clan Campbell is a smart, grayish-green turreted stone house with a self-satisfied air. Set among well-tended grounds, it contains displays of luxurious furnishings and interesting art, as well as a huge armory. Built between 1743 and 1789, the castle has spires on the four corner turrets that give it a vaguely French look. Tours of the castle follow the history of the powerful Campbell family and how it acquired its considerable wealth. There is a tearoom for snacks and light lunches. You can hike around the extensive estate grounds, but wear sturdy footwear. ⊠ Off A83 ☎ 01499/302203 ⊕ www.inveraray-castle.com ⛁ £12.50 ⊙ Closed Nov.–Mar.

Restaurants

★ Loch Fyne Oyster Bar and Restaurant

$$ | SEAFOOD | The legendary flagship of a chain of seafood restaurants that now stretches across the United Kingdom, this restaurant continues to please with its emphasis on ultrafresh, locally sourced seafood, simply prepared. Oysters, are, of course, a keynote, but the menu also features mussels, lobster, prawns, salmon, and much more from the sea, accompanied by perfect crunchy green vegetables such as peas, beans, and asparagus. **Known for:** plump oysters perfectly prepared; meltingly tender smoked salmon; seafood tapas. ⑤ Average main: £19 ⊠ Clachan Farm, A83, Cairndow ☎ 01499/600482 ⊕ www.lochfyne.com.

🛏 Hotels

★ The George Hotel

$ | HOTEL | The George has been Inveraray's social hub since the 18th century, when it was a coaching inn, and it still exudes history. **Pros:** excellent restaurant; atmospheric bars; live music on weekends. **Cons:** too much tartan for some; extra charge for child beds; live music makes some rooms noisy. $ *Rooms from: £90* ✉ *Main St. E* ☎ *01499/302111* ⊕ *www.thegeorgehotel. co.uk* ⊅ *25 rooms* ⦿ *Free breakfast.*

Kintyre Peninsula

57 miles south of Crinan (to Campbeltown).

Rivers and streams crisscross this long, narrow strip of green pasturelands and hills stretching south from Lochgilphead.

GETTING HERE AND AROUND

Continue south on the A83 (the road to Campbeltown) to Tarbert. Some 4 miles farther along the A83 is Kennacraig, where you catch the ferry to Islay. Beyond that is the pier at Tayinloan; CalMac ferries run from here to the Isle of Gigha.

ESSENTIALS

AIR TRAVEL CONTACT Campbeltown Airport. ✉ *Off A83, Campbeltown* ⚓ *At Machrihanish, 3 miles west of Campbeltown* ☎ *01586/553797* ⊕ *www.hial.co.uk.*

Sights

Isle of Gigha
ISLAND | Barely 7 miles long, this sheltered island between Kintyre and Islay has sandy beaches and rich wildlife. Ferries make the 20-minute trip from Tayinloan on the mainland. ✉ *Isle of Gigha* ☎ *01583/505390* ⊕ *www.gigha.org.uk.*

Activities

GOLF
Machrihanish Golf Club
GOLF | For many Scots golfers (and they should know) Machrihanish's out-of-the-way location makes it a place of

pilgrimage. Laid out in 1876, it's an intimidatingly memorable links course by a sandy bay. There is also a 9-hole course, The Pans. The historic clubhouse, devastated by fire in December 2018, is currently under restoration. ✉ *Off B843, Machrihanish* ☎ *01586/810213* ⊕ *www. machgolf.com* ⚑ *£75 Apr.–Oct., £30 Nov.–Mar.* ⚘ *Championship Course. 18 holes, 6235 yards, par 70; The Pans: 9 holes (out), 2376 yards, par 34* ⚓ *Reservations essential.*

Arran

Approaching Arran by sea, you'll first see forbidding Goatfell (2,868 feet) in the north, then the green fields of the south. These varied landscapes earn the island its sobriquet: "Scotland in Miniature." A temperate microclimate attracted ancient settlers whose stone circles still stand on the island. This weather also explains why it has long been a favorite getaway for Glaswegians, who come here to walk, climb Goatfell, or play golf.

GETTING HERE AND AROUND

Caledonian MacBrayne runs regular car and passenger ferries that cross the Firth of Clyde from Ardrossan (near Saltcoats) to Brodick throughout the year; crossing takes just under an hour. There is also a small ferry from Claonaig on the Kintyre Peninsula to Lochranza during the summer months.

Connecting trains run to the ferry at Ardrossan from Glasgow's Queen Street station. Stagecoach runs regular local bus services around the island. Exploring the island by car is easy, as the A841 road circles it.

Brodick

1 hour by ferry from Ardrossan.

Arran's largest village, Brodick, has a main street that is set back from the promenade and the lovely bay. Beyond that, it is really little more than a gateway to the rest of the island.

GETTING HERE AND AROUND
You can reach Brodick from Ardrossan by ferry. From Brodick the A841 circles the island; head south to reach Lamlash, north to reach Lochranza. The String Road crosses the island between Brodick and Machrie.

ESSENTIALS
The information center, opposite the landing point for the Ardrossan Ferry, has an accommodation desk as well as tourist information.

Sights

Brodick Castle and Country Park
CASTLE/PALACE | FAMILY | On the north side of Brodick Bay, this red-sandstone mansion with typical Scottish-baronial features was built in the 16th century and was the seat of the dukes of Hamilton, who added to it extensively throughout the 19th century. It reopened in 2019 after a £1.5 million renovation, and now features an adventure park and an exciting visitor experience where costumed performers bring the past to life. In summer the expansive gardens are ablaze with azalea and rhododendron blossoms.

The country park that surrounds the castle embraces Arran's most striking scenery, rising to the 2,867-foot summit of Goatfell, the island's highest peak. The beautiful upland landscape is more challenging to explore than it seems, so it's important to go prepared with sturdy footwear and waterproof clothing. From the summit there is a stunning panoramic view of the Firth, Kintyre, and the Ayrshire coast, and on a clear day you can just see Ireland. ⌧ Off A841, 1 mile north of Brodick Pier ☎ 01770/302202 ⊕ www. nts.org.uk ☯ Castle closed Jan.–Mar.

Isle of Arran Heritage Museum
MUSEUM | A typical Arran cottage, a re-created 1940s schoolroom, and farm buildings filled with antiquated implements that were in use within living memory make this lively little museum a must-see for anyone interested in the island's social history. ⌧ Rosaburn, A841 ☎ 01770/302636 ⊕ www.arranmuseum. co.uk ⌧ £4 ☯ Closed Nov.–Mar.

Restaurants

Brodick Bar and Brasserie
$$$ | BRITISH | This lively bar and restaurant serves fixed-price lunch and dinner menus featuring popular if unadventurous seafood favorites such as monkfish, halibut, and scallops, and adds spice to the mix with an array of Asian-influenced dishes. Like many places in the west of Scotland, hours are restricted, so it is well worth booking ahead. **Known for:** Sunday roast with all the trimmings; Brodick bouillabaisse of local langoustines and shellfish; Gigha halibut with roasted gnocchi. ⑤ Average main: £20 ⌧ Alma Rd. ☎ 01770/302169 ⊕ www. brodickbar.co.uk.

Hotels

★ Auchrannie Resort
$$$ | RESORT | FAMILY | With outstanding indoor and outdoor leisure facilities (including two pools and a spa), well-designed modern rooms, and three restaurants and bars, Auchrannie is by far the best place to stay on Arran. **Pros:** indoor leisure facilities including spa and pool; good for families; excellent outdoor activities. **Cons:** could-be-anywhere atmosphere; lacks character; not for anyone looking for peace and quiet. ⑤ Rooms from: £215 ⌧ Auchrannie Rd. ☎ 01770/30234 ⊕ www.auchrannie.co.uk ⌁ 115 rooms ⑩ Free breakfast.

Shopping

Arran Aromatics

PERFUME/COSMETICS | This is one of Scotland's best-known suppliers of scents, soaps, and perfumes of every kind. The shop is filled with pleasant smells, and between May and September a tour of the soap factory is available every Thursday evening. ✉ *Home Farm, A841* ☎ *01770/302595* ⊕ *www.arran.com.*

Isle of Arran Cheese Company

FOOD/CANDY | Arran is famous for its cheeses, especially its cheddar and its Arran blue; stop here to sample and buy handmade Scottish cheeses. ✉ *The Home Farm, A841* ☎ *01770/302788* ⊕ *www.arrancheeseshop.co.uk.*

Machrie

10 miles west of Brodick, 11 miles north of Lagg.

The area surrounding Machrie, home to a popular beach, is littered with prehistoric sites: chambered cairns, hut circles, and standing stones dating from the Bronze Age.

GETTING HERE AND AROUND

The quick route to Machrie is via the String Road (B880) from Brodick; turn off onto the Machrie Road 5 miles outside Brodick. A much longer but stunning journey will take you from Brodick, north to Lochranza, around the island to Machrie, and down the island's dramatic west coast, a distance of some 28 miles.

◉ Sights

Machrie Moor Stone Circles

ARCHAEOLOGICAL SITE | Six ancient circles of boulders and head-high sandstone pillars are scattered across Machrie Moor. These relics of a prehistoric culture are as old as Egypt's pyramids, if not quite as impressive, and the site evokes a dim and distant past. ✛ *1½ miles north*

of Machrie ⊕ *www.historicenvironment. scot.*

Restaurants

Cafe Thyme

$ | **TURKISH** | This bright and pleasant restaurant offers a combination of Scottish and Turkish flavors (an expression of the owners' backgrounds) as well as fine views out to sea. Look for meze as well as *pides* (Turkish pizza)—try the haggis-and-cheese or crayfish-and-olive combinations. **Known for:** Mediterranean meze; unusual East–West fusion dishes; Turkish-style haggis pizza. ⑤ *Average main: £13* ✉ *Machrie* ✛ *Next to Old Byre Visitor Centre* ☎ *01770/840608* ⊕ *www. oldbyre.co.uk/cafethyme.irs* ☾ *No dinner.*

Lochranza

13 miles north of Machrie, 14 miles north of Brodick.

Lochranza shows Arran's wilder northern side, with rocky seashores and sweeping slopes leading to the stark granite peaks of Goatfell and Caisteal Abahail (2,735 feet), which dominate the skyline.

The respected Isle of Arran Distillery nestles in the hills overlooking Lochranza Bay. Until recently, this was Arran's only distillery, but in 2019 it gained a baby sister, the Lagg Distillery at Kilmory; however, due to the length of time required for the distilling process, Lagg won't be producing its own malts until several years from now.

GETTING HERE AND AROUND

Lochranza is north of Brodick via the A841.

◉ Sights

★ Isle of Arran Distillery

WINERY/DISTILLERY | The open aspect and closeness to the sea explain the taste of Arran's well-respected single malt, light and airy and with the scent of sea and fields. The round white building housing the distillery sits comfortably among fields and hills in the northernmost part of the island. The tours take the visitor through the process of creating whisky, with a small or slightly larger tasting depending on the level. The basic tour ends with a dram. The CASKS café-restaurant is a comfortable place for a long lunch. ⊠ *Distillery Visitor Centre* ☎ *01770/830264* ⊕ *www.arranwhisky. com* ⊠ *Tours from £10.*

★ Lochranza Castle

CASTLE/PALACE | Perched above the bay, Lochranza is Arran's most picturesque ruin and occupies a special place in Scotland's history. It was here that Robert the Bruce, after years of dithering, returned from exile to commit himself to the war for Scotland's independence. ⊠ *Off A841* ☎ *0131/668–8800* ⊕ *www.historicenvironment.scot* ⊗ *Closed Oct.–Mar.*

Hotels

Butt Lodge

$ | B&B/INN | Set in 2 acres of private woods and gardens overlooking Kilbrannan Sound, this onetime Victorian shooting lodge offers a personalized welcome from owners who really make guests feel at home with hearty (but healthy) Scottish breakfasts and complimentary afternoon tea, served in a cozy lounge. **Pros:** peace and quiet; luxurious rooms and suites; great views. **Cons:** a little hard to find; no bar; up a winding farm road that can be tough on cars. ⑤ *Rooms from: £95* ⊠ *Off Newton Rd.* ✛ *½ mile east of Lochranza* ☎ *01770/830333* ⊕ *www.buttlodge.co.uk* ⊷ *6 rooms* ⏏ *Free breakfast.*

Islay and Jura

Islay is an island of rolling fields and pastures, heather-covered uplands where red deer roam and rutting stags clash antlers in spring, and white-sand beaches that on a summer day can look as enticing as any Caribbean strand. Huge flocks of Arctic wildfowl migrate to Islay in fall, leaving again in spring, when their wings literally darken the sunset sky. This was the long-ago seat of the Macdonald Lords of the Isles, a mongrel Celtic-Norse dynasty that held sway over the southern Hebrides for almost three centuries. Some of their heritage can still be seen. But it's a different inheritance that draws many visitors, namely the smoky, peaty malt whisky produced here by eight world-famous distilleries. Upstart Ardnahoe joined their ranks in 2018, with the stated aim of producing its own take on the classic Islay malt, but you won't be able to sample its wares for some years yet. In sharp contrast to Islay's gaggle of villages set among rolling moorland and fertile pastures, thinly populated Jura is ruggedly beautiful, with a hilly landscape dominated by twin summits, the Paps of Jura.

Bowmore

On Islay: 11 miles north of Port Ellen.

Bowmore, Islay's capital, is a good base for touring because it's central to Islay's main routes. A tidy town, its grid pattern was laid out in 1768 by local landowner Daniel Campbell, of Shawfield. Main Street stretches from the pier head to the commanding parish church, built in 1767 in an unusual circular design—so the devil could not hide in a corner.

GETTING HERE AND AROUND

Loganair flights from Glasgow and Edinburgh to Islay Airport take 40–50 minutes; the airport is 5 miles north of Port Ellen. Hebridean Air links Islay with

Colonsay and Oban. The trip by CalMac ferry from Kennacraig to Port Ellen takes about 2½ hours; ferries also travel less frequently to Port Askaig. From Port Ellen it is 10 miles on the A846 to reach Bowmore; drivers should use caution during the first mile out of Port Ellen, as the road is filled with sharp turns. The rest of the route is straight but bumpy, because the road is laid across peat bog.

Local bus services 450 and 451 connect the main island communities of Bowmore and Port Ellen with points around Islay. Timetables are available from the tourist information center.

ESSENTIALS
AIR TRAVEL CONTACT Islay Airport.
⊠ *A846, Glenegedale* ☎ *01496/302361*
⊕ *www.hial.co.uk.*

VISITOR INFORMATION Bowmore Visitor Information Centre. ⊠ *The Square* ☎ *01496/305165* ⊕ *www.visitscotland. com.*

👁 Sights

★ Bowmore Distillery
WINERY/DISTILLERY | Bowmore is the grand old lady of Islay's distilleries, and a tour is a must for any visitor. In business since 1779, the distillery, like all Islay whisky makers, stands by the sea. Standard tours include a walk around the malting areas and the stills, and connoisseurs can opt for in-depth tours that include tutored tastings. ⊠ *School St.* ☎ *01496/810441* ⊕ *www.bowmore.com* 🎟 *From £10* 🕐 *Closed Sun. Nov.–Mar.*

Islay Woollen Mill
FACTORY | Gorgeous tweed, plaid, and tartan clothing, wraps, and throws—woven at this historic mill and dyed in subtle, traditional tones—are sold here. ⊠ *A846* ✛ *4 miles outside Bowmore on the A846* ☎ *01496/810563* ⊕ *www.islaywoollen-mill.co.uk* 🎟 *Free* 🕐 *Closed Sun.*

🍴 Restaurants

★ Harbour Inn
$$$ | SEAFOOD | An adjunct of the Bowmore distillery, the Harbour Inn has a bar frequented by locals and a more upscale restaurant with a menu that emphasizes oysters, langoustines, mussels, and other local seafood. The elegant dining room looks out onto the water. **Known for:** classic Islay oysters; North African–influenced vegetarian dishes; seafood paired with malt whiskies. 💲 *Average main: £25* ⊠ *The Square* ☎ *01496/810330* ⊕ *www. bowmore.com/harbour-inn.*

👜 Shopping

Islay Whisky Shop
WINE/SPIRITS | If you don't have time to visit all of Islay's distilleries, let alone those elsewhere, you can do worse than visit this shop with its enormous collection of whiskies. ⊠ *Shore St.* ☎ *01496/810684* ⊕ *www.islaywhisky-shop.com.*

Port Charlotte

On Islay: 11 miles west of Bowmore.

Planned by a benevolent 19th-century laird (and named after his mom), Port Charlotte is an unusually (for Scotland) pretty village, with wild landscapes and sandy beaches nearby. South of the village, the A847 road leads to **Portnahaven** and **Port Wemyss**, where pleasing white cottages stand in a crescent around the headland.

GETTING HERE AND AROUND
To reach Port Charlotte from Bowmore, take the A846 via Bridgend and then the A847, Portnahaven Road. Local buses also connect Port Charlotte and Bowmore.

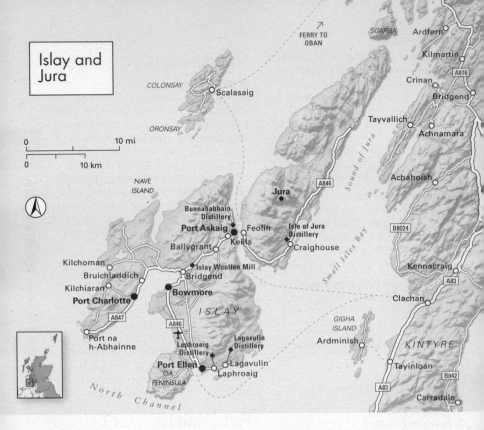

Islay and Jura

FERRY TO OBAN

SCARBA · Ardfern

Kilmartin

COLONSAY · Scalasaig

Crinan

A816

ORONSAY

Bridgend

Tayvallich

Achnamara

0 ——— 10 mi

0 ——— 10 km

NAVE ISLAND

Sound of Jura

Achahoish

Jura

A846

Bunnahabhain Distillery

Port Askaig · Feolin

Keills

Isle of Jura Distillery

B8024

Ballygrant

Craighouse

Small Isles Bay

Kilchoman

■ Islay Woollen Mill

Kennacraig

Bruichladdich

Bridgend

A83

Kilchiaran

Bowmore

Port Charlotte

Clachan

A847

I S L A Y

GIGHA ISLAND

A846

Ardminish

K I N T Y R E

Port na h-Abhainne

Laphroaig Distillery

Lagavulin Distillery

Tayinloan

B842

Port Ellen

Lagavulin

OA PENINSULA

Laphroaig

A83

N o r t h   C h a n n e l

Carradale

Sights

Museum of Islay Life

MUSEUM | A converted church is home to this local museum, a haphazard collection of local artifacts, photographs, and memorabilia. There is also a local history archive. ⊠ A847 ☎ 01496/850358 ⊕ www.islaymuseum.org ⊇ £4 ⊙ Closed weekends and Nov.–Mar.

Hotels

★ Port Charlotte Hotel

$$$ | HOTEL | Once a row of fishermen's cottages and with views over a sandy beach, this whitewashed Victorian hotel has been lovingly restored. **Pros:** beautiful location; lovely restaurant; views over the water. **Cons:** can be a little noisy from the bar; rooms are quite small;

not as luxurious as it claims. $ Rooms from: £250 ⊠ Main St. ☎ 01496/850360 ⊕ www.portcharlottehotel.co.uk ⇨ 10 rooms ⊙ Free breakfast.

Port Ellen

On Islay: 11 miles south of Bowmore.

Islay's sturdy community of Port Ellen was founded in the 1820s, and much of its architecture dates from the following decades. It has a harbor (ferries stop here), a few shops, and a handful of inns. The road traveling east from Port Ellen (the A846 to Ardbeg) passes three top distilleries and makes a pleasant afternoon's "whisky walk." All three distilleries offer tours, but you should call ahead for an appointment; there may be no tours on weekends at times. The last week in May, large numbers of whisky lovers descend on the island for the Islay Festival of Music and Malt, the heart of which is Port Ellen.

GETTING HERE AND AROUND
It is likely that Port Ellen will be your port of arrival on Islay. From here you can travel north to Bowmore, along the A846 before turning northwest towards Bridgend and Port Askaig.

Sights

Lagavulin Distillery
WINERY/DISTILLERY | Many malt whisky connoisseurs say the Lagavulin is the strongest nosed of all Islay's peaty malt whiskies. You can find out why, and how, with a distillery tour and tasting here. ✉ *A846* ☎ *01496/302400* ⊕ *www.malts. com* 🥃 *Tours from £6.*

Laphroaig Distillery
WINERY/DISTILLERY | Laphroaig (say la-*froig*) is Islay's most distinctive malt, redolent of peat, seaweed, and iodine. You can take a tour of the distillery, then settle in for a spell of sipping at the whisky bar. ✉ *A846* ☎ *01496/302418* ⊕ *www. laphroaig.com* 🥃 *From £10.*

🛏 Hotels

The Islay Hotel
$$ | HOTEL | This charming hotel overlooking Port Ellen's harbor has large, bright rooms decorated in muted contemporary colors. **Pros:** central location; bright, welcoming interior; good restaurant. **Cons:** can get crowded; some noise at weekends from live music in bar; no lounge or sitting area. ⑤ *Rooms from: £165* ✉ *Charlotte St.* ☎ *01496/300109* ⊕ *www.theislayhotel.com* 🛏 *13 rooms* 🍴 *Free Breakfast.*

Port Askaig

On Islay: 11 miles northeast of Bowmore.

Serving as the ferry port for Jura and receiving ferries from Kennacraig, Port Askaig is a mere cluster of cottages. Uphill, just outside the village, a side road travels along the coast, giving impressive views of Jura on the way. There are distilleries near here, too; make appointments for tours.

GETTING HERE AND AROUND
Traveling from Bowmore, you can reach Port Askaig (where the road ends) via A846. The village is also served by local buses.

Sights

★ Bunnahabhain Distillery
WINERY/DISTILLERY | Established in 1881, the Bunnahabhain (pronounced *Boon*-a-*ha*-bin) Distillery sits on the shore, with dramatic views across to the Paps of Jura. This is one of Scotland's most picturesque and evocative malt whisky distilleries, redolent of a preindustrialized era. ✉ *A846* ☎ *01496/840557* ⊕ *www. bunnahabhain.com* 🥃 *From £7* ⊗ *Closed Nov.–Mar.*

🛏 Hotels

Kilmeny Country House
$$ | B&B/INN | This luxurious bed-and-breakfast is on a 300-acre farm, but the rooms are so elegantly furnished that the place feels more like a hotel. **Pros:** elegant and quiet; great breakfast; afternoon tea tray on arrival. **Cons:** easy to miss; harsh cancellation policy; hotel prices but without all hotel facilities. ⑤ *Rooms from: £150* ✉ *A846, Ballygrant* ⊹ *Signposted off the A846 to Port Askaig, just before the village of Ballygrant* ☎ *01496/840668* ⊕ *www.kilmeny.co.uk* 🛏 *5 rooms* 🍴 *Free breakfast.*

Jura

5 minutes by ferry from Port Askaig.

The rugged, mountainous landscape of the island of Jura—home to only about 200 people—looms immediately east of Port Askaig, across the Sound of Islay: a perfect landscape for walkers. Jura has only one single-track road (the A846), which begins at Feolin, the ferry pier. It climbs across moorland, providing scenic views of the island's most striking feature, the Paps of Jura, three breast-shaped rounded peaks. The ruined Claig Castle, on an island just offshore, was built by the Lords of the Isles to control the sound. The island has no cash machines, so plan ahead.

GETTING HERE AND AROUND

The Port Askaig–Feolin car ferry takes five minutes to cross the Sound of Islay, and there is a passenger-only ferry during the summer from Tayvallich on Argyll to Craighouse. Bus service is also available from Craighouse and Inverlussa.

 Sights

Isle of Jura Distillery

WINERY/DISTILLERY | The community of Craighouse has the island's only distillery, producing malt whisky since 1810. Tours must be booked in advance by phone or online. ⊠ *Craighouse* ☎ *01496/820385* ⊕ *www.jurawhisky.com* 🗨 *Tours from £6* ☯ *Closed mid-July–mid-Aug., weekends in Oct.–Mar., and Sun. in Mar.–Oct.*

 Hotels

Jura Hotel

$ | **HOTEL** | Jura's only hotel, next to the island's renowned distillery, has simple but cozy no-frills rooms, and its pleasant gardens are attractive on a summer day. **Pros:** convenient location; good, unpretentious restaurant; lively bar. **Cons:** some shared bathrooms; no in-room TVs; the only hotel on the island, so almost always full. ⑤ *Rooms from: £110* ⊠ *A846, Craighouse* ☎ *01496/820243* ⊕ *www.jurahotel. co.uk* 🗨 *17 rooms* ⑩ *Free breakfast.*

Isle of Mull and Iona

Mull is one of the most beguiling of Scotland's isles, and happily it's also one of the easiest to get to. The island's landscapes range from the pretty harbor of Tobermory and the gentle slopes around Dervaig to dramatic Atlantic beaches on the west. In the south the long road past the sweeping green slopes of the Ross of Mull leads to Iona, Scotland's holy island and a year-round attraction.

GETTING HERE AND AROUND

Ferries to Mull are run by the ubiquitous Caledonian MacBrayne. Its most frequent car-ferry route to Mull is from Oban to Craignure (45 minutes). Two shorter routes are from Lochaline on the Morvern Peninsula to Fishnish (15 minutes), or Kilchoan (on the Adrnamurchan Peninsula) to Tobermory (15 minutes). The Kilchoan-Lochaline ferry is not bookable. West Coast Tours serves the east coast, running between Tobermory, Craignure, and Fionnphort (for the ferry to Iona).

Craignure

On Mull: 40-minute ferry crossing from Oban, 15-minute ferry crossing to Fishnish (5 miles northwest of Craignure) from Lochaline.

Craignure, little more than a pier and some houses, is close to the well-known Duart Castle. Reservations for the year-round ferries that travel from Oban to Craignure are advisable in summer. The ferry from Lochaline to Fishnish, just northwest of Craignure, does not accept reservations and does not run on Sunday.

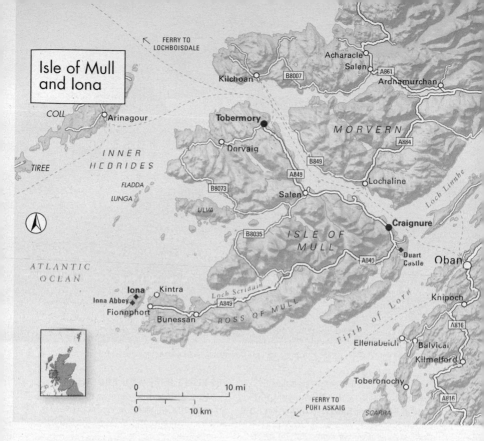

Isle of Mull and Iona

GETTING HERE AND AROUND

The arrival point for the 40-minute ferry crossing from Oban, Craignure is the starting point for further travel on Mull northwest toward Salen and Tobermory, or toward Fionnphort and the Iona ferry to the southwest.

ESSENTIALS

VISITOR INFORMATION Craignure Information Centre. ⊠ *The Pierhead* ☏ *01680/812377* ⊕ *www.visitscotland. com.*

 Sights

★ Duart Castle

CASTLE/PALACE | The 13th-century Duart Castle stands dramatically atop a cliff overlooking the Sound of Mull. The ancient seat of the Macleans, it was ruined by the Campbells, their archenemies, in 1691 but restored by Sir Fitzroy Maclean in 1911. Inside you can visit the dungeons and state rooms, then climb the keep for a view of the waterfront. Nearby stands the **Millennium Wood**, planted in 2000 with indigenous trees. To reach Duart by car, take the A849 and turn left around the shore of Duart Bay. From Craignure's ferry port, there is a direct bus that takes you to the castle in about 10 minutes. ⊠ *A849* ✛ *3 miles southeast of Craignure* ☏ *01680/812309* ⊕ *www.duartcastle.com* ⊠ *£6.50* ☉ *Closed Nov.–Mar.*

 Hotels

Craignure Inn

$ | **B&B/INN** | Snug bedrooms with exposed beams, polished wood furniture, and views of the Sound of Mull make

Once a key center of Christianity in Scotland, Iona Abbey still serves an ecumenical religious community.

this 18th-century inn very appealing. **Pros:** lively bar scene; hearty local food; expansive views. **Cons:** live music can get loud; bar can get very busy; rooms on the small size. $ *Rooms from: £95* ✉ *A849* ✛ *Near the ferry pier* ☎ *01680/812305* ⊕ *www.craignure-inn.co.uk* ⇝ *3 rooms* ⦿❘ *Free breakfast.*

Tobermory

On Mull: 5 miles northeast of Dervaig, 21 miles north of Craignure.

With its rainbow crescent of brightly painted harborside houses, Tobermory is the most photogenic village in the Isles and among the prettiest in all Scotland. Unsurprisingly, it's a lively tourist center and a popular base for exploring Mull, its smaller neighbors, and the sea-life-filled surrounding waters.

GETTING HERE AND AROUND
The most frequent service to Mull is via the Oban–Craignure ferry. Tobermory is 21 miles from Craignure along the A849/848 (via Salen).

ESSENTIALS
VISITOR INFORMATION Mull Information Centre. ✉ *Ledaig Car Park* ☎ *01683/302875* ⊕ *www.exploremull. com.*

 Sights

★ Tobermory Distillery
WINERY/DISTILLERY | Tobermory's cute little distillery has been making distinctive malts (the peaty Ledaig and the unpeated, lighter-tasting Tobermory) since 1798, though there have been intervening decades when it was "silent" and produced no whisky. It was relaunched in 1993, and a tour here is a more personal experience than is offered by some bigger, better-known distilleries. Starting in 2020, visitors will be able to

sample the distillery's newest product: its own gin. ⊠ *Bad-Daraich House, Ledaig* ✛ *Off Main St. on south side of harbor* ☎ *01688/302647* ⊕ *www.tobermorydistillery.com* 🎟 *Tours from £8.*

★ Whale Watch With Us

TOUR—SIGHT | High-speed boats carrying 12 passengers leave from Tobermory's harbor on scenic cruises, wildlife sea safaris, and whale-watching trips lasting up to four hours. You'll have a good chance of spotting dolphins, porpoises, and minke whales. If you're lucky, basking sharks and some of the sound's orcas may also put in an appearance. ⊠ *Raraig House, Raeric Rd.* ✛ *Ledaig pontoons, opposite car park and Tobermory Harbor Authority on Tobermory waterfront* ☎ *01688/302875* ⊕ *whalewatchwithus. com* 🎟 *From £30.*

🍴 Restaurants

★ Café Fish

$$$ | **SEAFOOD** | This restaurant's location has certainly contributed to its success—it's perched on the pier at the end of Tobermory. The owners pride themselves on the freshness of their fish; they have their own boat and bring in their own seafood each day. **Known for:** roast shellfish platters; Glengorm rib-eye steaks; Mull lobster grilled with garlic butter. ⑤ *Average main. £20* ⊠ *The Pier* ☎ *01688/301253* ⊕ *www.thecafefish.com* 🕙 *Closed Jan.–mid-Mar.*

🛏 Hotels

Tobermory Hotel

$$ | **HOTEL** | **FAMILY** | Made up of five former fishermen's cottages, this lodging on Tobermory's waterfront has a warm, intimate feel. **Pros:** adorable cottage setting with fireplace; good restaurant; very pet- and child-friendly. **Cons:** small rooms; tiny bathrooms; not all rooms have both shower and tub. ⑤ *Rooms from: £175* ⊠ *Main St.* ☎ *01688/302091* ⊕ *www.*

thetobermoryhotel.com 🕙 *Closed Nov.–Mar* 🛏 *18 rooms* ⏹ *Breakfast.*

Western Isles Hotel

$$ | **HOTEL** | This grand hotel from the Victorian era looks down on Tobermory from its idyllic location overlooking the Sound of Mull. **Pros:** brilliant views; spacious public rooms; great food. **Cons:** some rooms look onto the car park; rooms vary in size; overall lackluster atmosphere. ⑤ *Rooms from: £130* ⊠ *Off B882* ☎ *01688/302012* ⊕ *www.westernisleshotel.co.uk* 🛏 *26 rooms* ⏹ *Free breakfast.*

Iona

5 minutes by ferry from Fionnphort (Mull), which is 36 miles west of Craignure.

The ruined abbey on Iona gives little hint that this was once one of the most important Christian religious centers in the land. The priceless *Book of Kells* (now in Dublin) was illustrated here, and it was the monks of Iona who spread Christian ideas across Scotland and the north. The abbey was founded in the year 563 by the fiery and argumentative Columba (circa 521–97) after his expulsion from Ireland. Until the 11th century, many of Scotland's kings and rulers were buried here, their tombstones still visible inside the abbey. Although few visitors venture beyond the pier and the abbey, there are several tranquil paths around the island.

GETTING HERE AND AROUND

Caledonian MacBrayne's ferry from Fionnphort departs at regular intervals throughout the year (£4.50 round-trip). Timetables are available on the Caledonian MacBrayne website. Note that cars are not permitted; there's a parking lot by the ferry at Fionnphort.

Sights

★ Iona Abbey

RELIGIOUS SITE | Overseen by St. Columba, who traveled here from Ireland, Iona was the birthplace of Christianity in Scotland in the 6th century. It survived repeated Norse sackings before falling into disuse around the time of the Reformation. Restoration work began at the beginning of the 20th century. Today the restored buildings serve as a spiritual center under the jurisdiction of the Church of Scotland. Guided tours by the Iona Community, an ecumenical religious group, begin every half hour in summer and on demand in winter. ⊠ *Iona* ☎ *01681/700404* ⊕ *www.iona.org.uk* ✉ *£7.50.*

Hotels

St. Columba Hotel

$ | HOTEL | As befits a religious retreat, rooms in this 1846 minister's home are simple to the point of being spartan, but those in the front make up for it with glorious views across the Sound of Iona to Mull. **Pros:** impressive views; nice log fires; eco-friendly. **Cons:** no televisions; few home comforts; basic meals. ⑤ *Rooms from: £115* ⊠ *Next to cathedral* ✛ *About ¼ mile from the ferry pier* ☎ *01681/700304* ⊕ *www.stcolumba-hotel.co.uk* ☉ *Closed Nov.–Mar.* ⮡ *27 rooms* ⊘*Free breakfast.*

Chapter 20

INVERNESS, SKYE, AND THE NORTHERN HIGHLANDS

Updated by
Joseph Reaney

⊙ **Sights**
★★★★☆

🍴 **Restaurants**
★★★☆☆

🛏 **Hotels**
★★★☆☆

🛍 **Shopping**
★★☆☆☆

🍸 **Nightlife**
★☆☆☆☆

WELCOME TO INVERNESS, SKYE, AND THE NORTHERN HIGHLANDS

TOP REASONS TO GO

★ **Castles, fortresses, and battlefields:** Hear stories of the Highland people and famous figures like Bonnie Prince Charlie, and absorb the atmosphere of castles and battlefields, at Culloden Moor, Cawdor and Brodie castles, Fort George, and Glencoe.

★ **Outdoor activities:** The Great Glen is renowned for its hill walking. Some of the best routes are around Glen Nevis, Glencoe, and on Ben Nevis, the highest mountain in Britain.

★ **Whisky tours:** The two westernmost distilleries on the Malt Whisky Trail are in Forres. Benromach is the smallest distillery in Speyside and has excellent tours; Dallas Dhu is preserved as a museum.

★ **Isle of Skye:** Scotland in miniature, the landscape of Skye ranges from the lush, undulating hills and coastal tracks of Sleat to the deep glens and saw-toothed peaks of the Cuillin Mountains. Farther north are stunning geological features like the Old Man of Storr and Kilt Rock.

1 Inverness. The biggest city in the Highlands.

2 Culloden Moor. A famous battlesite.

3 Nairn. Home to Cawdor Castle.

4 Forres. A key stop on the Malt Whisky Trail.

5 Aviemore. The gateway to the Cairngorms.

6 Kingussie. A base for the Cairngorms.

7 Drumnadrochit and Loch Ness. Nessie's hometown.

8 Fort William. The Great Glen gateway.

9 Glenfinnan. Another town with history.

10 Arisaig. A gateway to the smaller Scottish isles.

11 Glencoe. A beautiful region.

12 Isle of Skye. The most popular of the Scottish isles.

13 Gairloch. Peaceful, picturesque, and warm.

14 Ullapool. A base for Lewis and Harris.

15 Lochinver. A shoreside community.

16 Scourie. An base for exploring Handa Island.

17 Durness. A remote village.

18 John O'Groats. Britain's northeastern tip.

19 Dornoch. Famed for its golf courses.

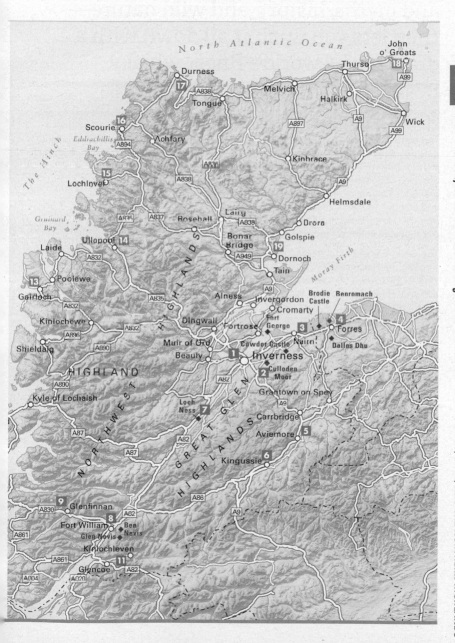

Defined by its striking topography, the Great Glen brings together mountains and myths, history and wild nature—then lets you wash it all down with a dram of the world's finest whisky.

Inverness is the gateway to an area in which the views from almost every twist and bend in the circuitous roads may take your breath away. Wild and remote, the Northern Highlands and the Western Isles of Scotland have a timeless grandeur. Dramatic cliffs, long beaches, and craggy mountains that rise up out of moorland like islands in a sea heighten the romance and mystery.

The Great Glen Fault runs diagonally through the Highlands of Scotland and was formed when two tectonic plates collided, shoving masses of the crust southwest toward the Atlantic Ocean. Over time the rift broadened into a glen, and a thin line of lochs now lies along its seam. The most famous of these is deep, murky Loch Ness, home to the elusive Loch Ness monster.

The city of Inverness has a growing reputation for excellent restaurants, and from here nearly everything in the Great Glen is an easy day trip. Just south of the city the 13th-century ruined Urquhart Castle sits on the shores of Loch Ness. In Fort Augustus, the Caledonian Canal joins Inverness to Fort William via a series of 29 locks. At the western end of the canal, Ben Nevis, Britain's highest mountain, rises sharply. The Nevis Range, like Cairngorms National Park to the east, is ideal for walking, climbing, and mountain biking through the hills and glens.

Impressive long, sandy beaches stretch out along the coast from the towns of Nairn and Findhorn. Finally, the Malt Whisky Trail begins in Forres and follows the wide, fast River Spey south until it butts against the Cairngorm Mountains and the old Caledonian forests, with their diverse and rare wildlife.

The Northern Highlands is a region where roads hug the coast, dipping down toward beaches and back up for stunning views over the clear ocean, across to the dramatic mountains, or along stunning heather moorland. These twisted, undulating roads—many of them single-track—demand that you shift down a gear, pause to let others pass, and take the time to do less and experience more of the rough-hewn beauty. If you're lucky, you may see a puffin fishing below the cliffs, an eagle swooping for a hare, or perhaps even a pod of dolphins or whales swimming off the coast. Adorable Highland *coos* (cows) are sure to make an appearance, too.

Sutherland was once the southern land belonging to the Vikings, and some names reflect this. Cape Wrath got its name from the Viking word *hvarth,* meaning "turning point," and Suilven translates as "pillar." The Isle of Skye and the Outer Hebrides are referred to as the Western Isles, and remain the stronghold of the Gaelic language. Skye is often called Scotland in miniature because the terrain shifts from lush valleys in the south, to the rugged girdle of the Cuillin Mountains, and then to the steep cliffs that define the northern coast. A short ferry journey away, the moody island of Lewis and Harris lays claim to the brilliant golden sands of Luskentyre and incredible prehistoric sites, from the lunar-aligned Calanais Standing Stones to the Iron Age Doune Broch.

MAJOR REGIONS

Inverness and Nearby. At the center of this region is Inverness, a small but appealing city that makes a useful gateway to the Great Glen. It has an increasingly strong range of restaurants and accommodations, but its cultural offerings remain more or less limited to what is happening at the Eden Court Theatre and the live music at a few good pubs. From Inverness just about anywhere in the Great Glen is a day trip. East of Inverness, the infamous Culloden Moor still looks desolate on most days, and you can easily imagine the fierce, brief, and bloody battle that took place here in 1746 that ended in final, catastrophic defeat for the Jacobites and their quest to restore the exiled Stewarts to the British throne. Because Jacobite tales are interwoven with landmarks throughout this entire area, you will get much more out of this storied landscape if you first learn something about this thorny but colorful period of Scottish history. The Morayshire coast boasts many long beaches and some refined castles (Cawdor and Brodie) that are definitely worth a visit. Moving east along the inner Moray Firth, you might be tempted by Benromach distillery in Forres, a taste of what you can find farther south if you follow the Malt Whisky Trail.

Speyside and the Cairngorms. Speyside is best known for its whisky distilleries, and those who enjoy a good dram often follow the Whisky Trail. The Spey is a long river, running from Fort Augustus to the Moray Firth, and its fast-moving waters make for excellent fishing at many points along the way. They also give Speyside malt whiskies a softer flavor than those made with peaty island water. The area's native and planted pine forests draw many birds each spring and summer,

and people come for miles to see the capercaillies and ospreys. Defining the eastern edge of the Great Glen, Cairngorms National Park provides sporty types with all the adventure they could ask for, including walking, kayaking, rock climbing, and even skiing, if the winter is cold enough. With craggy mountains, calm lochs, and swift rivers, the park has everything for lovers of the great outdoors. And while the towns and villages of Speyside and the Cairngorms are nothing special, they make great bases for heading out into nature.

Loch Ness, Fort William, and Nearby. Have a go trying to spot Nessie from the banks of Loch Ness. Compared with other lochs, Ness is not known for its beauty (although it's hardly a stain on the landscape). Instead, it draws attention for its infamous monster. Heading south from Inverness, you can travel along the loch's quiet east side or the more touristy west side. A pleasant morning can be spent at Urquhart Castle, in the tiny town of Drumnadrochit, or a bit farther south in the pretty town of Fort Augustus, where the Caledonian Canal meets Loch Ness. As you travel south and west, the landscape opens up and the Nevis Range comes into view. From Fort William you can visit the dark, cloud-laden mountains of Glencoe and the desolate stretch of moors and lochans at Rannoch Moor. Travelers drive through this region to experience the landscape, which changes at nearly every turn. It's a brooding, haunting area that's worth a visit in any season. If you dare, climb Britain's highest peak, Ben Nevis. The Road to the Isles, less romantically known as the A830, leads from Fort William to the coastal towns of Arisaig, Morar, and Mallaig, with access to the Small Isles of Rum, Eigg, Canna, and Muck.

Isle of Skye. Scotland's most famous island is home to the 11 peaks of the Cuillin Mountains, the quiet gardens of Sleat, and the dramatic peninsulas of

20

Inverness, Skye, and the Northern Highlands

Waternish and Trotternish. You can take a day trip to Skye, but it's worth spending a few days exploring its shores if you can.

The Northern Landscapes. The northernmost part of Scotland, from Inverness all the way up to John O'Groats in the east and Cape Wrath in the west, has some of the most distinctive mountain profiles and coastal stretches in all of Scotland. The rim roads around the wilds of Durness overlook rocky shores, and the long beaches are as dramatic as the awe-inspiring and desolate cross-country routes like Destitution Road in Wester Ross. To explore these landscapes most thoroughly, you should travel by car. You'll want to explore Stoer Point Lighthouse, the beaches north of Lochinver, and spectacular islandlike hills such as Suilven. Follow the North Coast 500 loop from Inverness to see the very best of the region. If you head counterclockwise up the east coast, along the north coast, and down the west coast, the spectacular landscape gets more and more dramatic at every turn. Travel clockwise, and you might find the east coast down from John O'Groats feels a bit anticlimactic.

Planning

When to Go

Late spring to early autumn is the best time to visit this region. If you catch good weather in summer, the days can be glorious. Unfortunately summer is also when you will encounter midges (tiny biting insects: keep walking, as they can't move very fast). The earlier in the spring or later in the fall you go, the greater the chances of your encountering the elements in their extreme form, and the fewer attractions and accommodations you will find open (even Skye closes down almost completely by the end of October.) Then again, you'll also find fewer tourists. Winter is best avoided

altogether, although many Scots value the open fires and the warming whisky that make the off-season so appealing

Planning Your Time

The Great Glen is an enormous area that can easily be broken into two separate trips. The first would be based in or near Inverness, allowing an exploration of Speyside, the Cairngorms, Cawdor and Brodie castles, and perhaps a few whisky-distillery tours. The second moves through the cloud-laden Glencoe and down through the moody Rannoch Moor, or toward the Road to the Isles; you could stay near Glencoe or in Fort William. To do the area justice you probably need at least three days.

The rough landscape of the Highlands and islands, as this region is sometimes called, means this isn't a place you can rush through. It could take eight busy days to do a coastal loop and also see some islands. Single-lane roadways, undulating landscapes, and eye-popping views will slow you down. You can base yourself in a town like Ullapool or Portree, or choose a B&B or hotel (of which there are many) tucked into the hills or sitting at the edge of a sea loch. If you have only a couple of days, head directly to the Isle of Skye and the other islands off the coast. They attract hordes of tourists, and for good reason, yet you don't have to walk far to find yourself in the wilderness. Sunday is a day of minimal activity here; restaurants, bars, and shops are closed, as are many sites.

Getting Here and Around

AIR
Inverness Airport has flights from London, Edinburgh, and Glasgow. Domestic flights covering the Highlands and islands are operated by LoganAir. Fort William has bus and train connections with

Glasgow, so Glasgow Airport can be a good access point.

CONTACTS Inverness Airport.
☎ 01667/464000 ⊕ www.invernessair-port.co.uk.

BOAT AND FERRY
Ferry services are generally reliable, weather permitting. Car and passenger ferries run from Ullapool to Stornoway (Lewis and Harris), from Oban to Castlebay (Barra), from Mallaig to Lochboisdale (South Uist), and from Uig (Skye) to Tarbert (Lewis and Harris) and Lochmaddy (North Uist). The Hopscotch planned-route ticket by Caledonian MacBrayne (known locally as CalMac) gives considerable reductions on interisland ferry fares; it is worth calling ahead and asking for the best route plan.

CONTACTS Caledonian MacBrayne. (CalMac) ☎ 0800/066–5000 ⊕ www.calmac. co.uk.

BUS
A long-distance Scottish Citylink service connects Glasgow and Fort William. Inverness is also well served from the central belt of Scotland. Discount carrier Megabus (book online to avoid phone charges) has service to Inverness from various U.K. cities. Traveling around the Great Glen area without a car is very challenging, and all but impossible in more rural areas. Stagecoach Highlands serves the Great Glen and around Fort William.

Scottish Citylink runs two main routes in the Northern Highlands; one heading west from Inverness to Ullapool and the other up the east coast to Scrabster (via Dornoch, Wick, and Thurso). It also has a route across the Isle of Skye to Uig. These buses can be a good way to see the region, but they don't run frequently. Once you're in the Northern Highlands, Stagecoach has some routes up the east coast of the mainland to Brora. It also has regular services on Skye.

CONTACTS Megabus. ☎ 0900/160–0900 ⊕ www.megabus.com. Scottish Citylink. ☎ 0871/266–3333 ⊕ www.citylink.co.uk. Stagecoach Highlands. ☎ 01463/233371 ⊕ www.stagecoachbus.com.

CAR
As in all areas of rural Scotland, a car is a great asset for exploring this region, especially because the best of the area is away from the main roads. The winding single-lane roads in the Northern Highlands demand a degree of driving dexterity, however. On good days, single-track driving can be relaxing, with a lovely pace of stopping, waving, moving on. Note that in this sparsely populated area distances between gas stations can be considerable, so it is wise to fill your tank when you see one. You can reach Inverness in 3½ hours from Edinburgh or Glasgow; it's around 4½ hours to Skye. You can use the main A82 from Inverness to Fort William, or use the smaller B862/B852 roads to explore the much quieter east side of Loch Ness. Mallaig, west of Fort William, is reached via a new road, but there are still a few narrow and winding single-lane roads, which require slower speeds and concentration.

TRAIN
ScotRail has connections from London to Inverness and Fort William (including an overnight sleeper service), as well as reliable links from Glasgow and Edinburgh. There's train service between Glasgow (Queen Street) and Inverness, via Aviemore, which gives access to the heart of Speyside.

Although there's no rail connection among towns within the Great Glen, this area has the West Highland Line, which links Fort William to Mallaig. This train, run by ScotRail, remains the most enjoyable way to experience the rugged hills and loch scenery between these two places. The Jacobite Steam Train is an exciting summer (late April to late October) option on the same route.

CONTACTS Jacobite Steam Train.
☎ 0844/850–4685 ⊕ www.westcoastrail-
ways.co.uk. **ScotRail.** ☎ 0344/811–0141
⊕ www.scotrail.co.uk.

Restaurants

Northern Scotland has many fine restaurants, where talented chefs use locally
grown produce. Most country-house inns
and pubs serve reliable, hearty seafood
and tasty meat-and-potatoes meals. The
Isle of Skye has the most—and the most
expensive—restaurants, many of them
exceptionally good, but you can find tasty
meals almost everywhere. In remote
regions you may just have to drive some
distance to find them. Remember that
locals eat early, so most restaurants stop
serving dinner at 9. Inverness, Aviemore,
and Fort William have plenty of cafés and
restaurants in all price ranges. Inverness
has particularly diverse dining options.
Outside the towns there are many country-house hotels serving superb meals.

Hotels

In the countryside, towns have accommodations ranging from cozy inns to
expansive hotels; in more remote areas
your choice will usually be limited to
smaller establishments. Book as far in
advance as you can, as the area is very
busy in the peak season and the best
places fill up early. In Inverness you may
find it more appealing to stay outside the
city center or in the pretty countryside
nearby. In the more remote parts of Scotland, your best lodging option may be to
rent a cottage or house. Besides allowing
you to make your own meals and to
come and go as you please, it can also
be less expensive. VisitScotland (⊕ www.
visitscotland.com), the official tourism
agency, lists many cottages and even
rates them with stars, just like hotels.

*Restaurant and hotel reviews have been
shortened. For full information, visit*
*Fodors.com. Restaurant prices are the
average cost of a main course at dinner
or, if dinner is not served, at lunch. Hotel
prices are the lowest cost of a standard
double room in high season, including
20% V.A.T.*

WHAT IT COSTS in Pounds			
$	$$	$$$	$$$$
RESTAURANTS			
under £15	£15–£19	£20–£25	over £25
HOTELS			
under £125	£125– £200	£201– £300	over £300

Tours

Inverness Tours

GUIDED TOURS | This outfitter runs the
occasional boat cruise, but it's mainly
known for very good tours around the
Highlands in well-equipped vehicles, led
by expert guides and heritage enthusiasts. Nevertheless, the price is per
minibus, not per person, so while it's
quite a bargain for parties of six or seven,
it's less appealing for small groups. It
may be possible to get single tickets if
another group will sell its unused space.
☎ 01667/455699 ⊕ www.invernesstours.
com ✉ From £150.

Rabbie's

BUS TOURS | This popular tour opera-
tor organizes tours of various lengths
throughout the Highlands, from half-day
trips to 17-day epics. Tours start from
Edinburgh, Glasgow, Aberdeen, or
Inverness, and travel is in comfortable
16-seater minibuses. ☎ 0131/226–3133
⊕ www.rabbies.com ✉ From £19.

Inverness

176 miles north of Glasgow, 109 miles northwest of Aberdeen, 161 miles northwest of Edinburgh.

It's not the prettiest or the most charming Scottish city, but with a few attractions and some reliably good hotels and restaurants, Inverness makes a practical base for exploring a region that has a lot to offer. From here you can fan out in almost any direction for interesting day trips: east to Moray and the distilleries near Forres, southeast to the Cairngorms, and south to Loch Ness. Throughout its past, the town was burned and ravaged by Highland clans competing for dominance.

GETTING HERE AND AROUND

You can easily fly into Inverness Airport, as there are daily flights from London, Bristol, Birmingham, Manchester, and Belfast; however, there are also easy train and bus connections from Glasgow Airport. Scottish Citylink has service here, and Megabus has long-distance bus service from Edinburgh and Glasgow. ScotRail runs trains here from London, Edinburgh, Glasgow, and other cities.

Once you're here, you can explore much of the city on foot. A rental car makes exploring the surrounding area much easier. But if you don't have a car, there are bus and boat tours from the city center to a number of places in the Great Glen.

An unusual option from Inverness is a day trip to Orkney. From June through August, John O'Groats Ferries runs daily tours from Inverness to Orkney. They cost £76 for a whole day, including a six-hour tour of the island.

ESSENTIALS

BOAT CONTACTS John O'Groats Ferries.
☎ *01955/611353* ⊕ *www.jogforry.co.uk.*

BUS CONTACTS Inverness Bus Station.
✉ *Margaret St.* ☎ *01463/233371.*

VISITOR INFORMATION Inverness—The City in the Highlands. ⊕ *www.inverness-scotland.com.*

Sights

★ Fort George

MILITARY SITE | After the fateful Battle of Culloden, the nervous government in London ordered the construction of a large fort on a promontory reaching into the Moray Firth. Fort George was started in 1748 and completed some 20 years later. It's one of the best-preserved 18th century military fortifications in Europe. At its height it housed 1,600 men and around 30,000 pounds of gunpowder; the on-site Highlanders Museum gives you a glimpse of the fort's history. The fort, 14 miles northeast of Inverness, is also a great base for spotting dolphins and whales out at sea. ✉ *Old Military Rd., Ardersier* ⊹ *Off B9006* ☎ *01667/460232* ⊕ *www.historicenvironment.scot* ✉ *£9.*

Inverness Castle

CASTLE/PALACE | One of Inverness's few historic landmarks is reddish-sandstone Inverness Castle (now the local Sheriff Court), nestled above the river off Castle Road on Castle Hill. The current structure is Victorian, built after a former fort was blown up by the Jacobites in the 1745 campaign. The castle isn't open to the public, but you are free to wander the grounds. ✉ *Inverness.*

St. Andrew's Cathedral

RELIGIOUS SITE | This handsome Victorian cathedral, dating from 1869, has two unique claims to fame: in addition to being the northernmost cathedral in the British Isles, it was, more significantly, the first cathedral to be built in Britain after the Reformation. The twin-turreted exterior of the building is made from characteristically reddish local Tarradale stone. Inside, it follows a medieval layout, with the addition of an unusual patterned wooden floor. Check out the

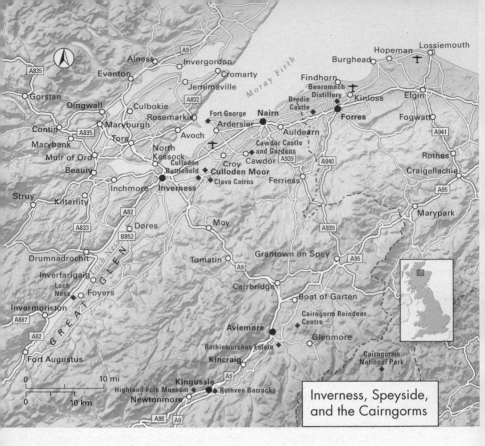

Inverness, Speyside,
and the Cairngorms

beautiful white marble font, carved in the shape of a seated angel. ☒ *Ardross St.* ☎ *01463/225553* ⊕ *www.morayepisco-palchurch.scot* ☒ *Free.*

 Restaurants

★ Café 1

$$ | **MODERN BRITISH** | Consistently recommended by locals as one of the best restaurants in the area, Café 1 really practices what it preaches in terms of sustainable, local produce. Taking inspiration from such big names as Blue Hill in New York, the restaurant rears its own herds to provide the Hebridean lamb and Highland beef on the menu, usually served with a simple order of chips (thick-cut fries) and rich garlic butter. **Known for:** castle views; melt-in-your-mouth lamb; ethically sourced ingredients. ⑤ *Average main: £19* ☒ *75 Castle St.* ☎ *01463/226200* ⊕ *www.cafe1.net* ⊘ *Closed Sun.*

River House

$$$ | **SEAFOOD** | Head chef and owner Alfie Little draws heavily on local inspiration to shape the menu at this tiny riverside seafood restaurant, which has an interior as stylish as its appealing gray-and-white exterior. Start with mussels or oysters from the Scottish islands, then take your pick from mains based on native fish such as Shetland halibut and Scrabster hake, and wash it all down with a local beer. **Known for:** intimate atmosphere; fresh, sustainable local seafood; riverside outdoor seating in summer. ⑤ *Average main: £23* ☒ *1 Greig St.* ☎ *01463/222033* ⊕ *www.riverhouseinverness.co.uk* ⊘ *Closed Sun. and Mon. No lunch.*

The sandstone structure known as Inverness Castle stands guard over the small city of Inverness.

★ Rocpool

$$ | BRASSERIE | Another perennial favorite, the Rocpool has a frequently changing menu of modern bistro classics, with a few international twists. Local seafood is a specialty, and the wine list is excellent. **Known for:** outstanding wine selection; contemporary twists on traditional dishes; quality meat and seafood. $ *Average main: £20* ✉ *1 Ness Walk* ☎ *01463/717274* ⊕ *www.rocpool-restaurant.com* ☾ *Closed Sun.*

★ Rocpool Reserve Restaurant

$$$ | MODERN BRITISH | The clean modern design is as sleek as the service at this restaurant in the Rocpool Reserve Hotel (not to be confused with the nearby Rocpool restaurant); think monochrome walls, straight lines, and a whole lot of upholstery in tasteful accent colors. As for the menu, expect creative, decadent dishes, including a signature soufflé that is far more filling than a lighter-than-air starter ought to be. **Known for:** inventive dishes; beautiful presentation; chic cocktail bar. $ *Average main: £26*

✉ *Rocpool Reserve Hotel, Culduthel Rd.* ☎ *01463/240089* ⊕ *www.rocpool.com.*

Hotels

Bluebell House

$ | B&B/INN | Each room at this traditional Scottish guesthouse has sturdy oak furnishings, including a downstairs bedroom with a full-curtained four-poster bed and a curved chaise lounge. **Pros:** large rooms; decadent furnishing; great hosts. **Cons:** smallish bathrooms; no windows in bathrooms; minimal technology. $ *Rooms from: £100* ✉ *31 Kenneth St.* ☎ *01463/238201* ⊕ *www.bluebell-house.com* ⇥ *4 rooms* ⦿ *Free breakfast.*

Bunchrew House Hotel

$$$$ | HOTEL | This 17th-century baronial mansion, its turrets reflected in a glassy lake, looks like something from a Scottish fairy tale. **Pros:** beautiful setting; atmospheric building; good restaurant. **Cons:** some rooms could do with refurbishment; quite expensive; a little out of town. $ *Rooms from: £345* ✉ *Off*

A862 ⊕ *About 3 miles west of Inverness* ☎ *01463/234917* ⊕ *www.bunchrewhousehotel.com* 🛏 *16 rooms* ❧ *Free breakfast.*

Moyness House

$$ | B&B/INN | On a quiet residential street with well-trimmed hedges a few minutes from downtown Inverness, this lovely Victorian villa was once the home of Scottish author Neil M. Gunn (1891–1973), known for short stories and novels that evoke images of the Highlands, such as *Morning Tide, Highland River,* and *Butcher's Broom.* **Pros:** beautiful building; lovely garden; great location near the river. **Cons:** public rooms a bit fussy for some; books up quickly; strict cancellation policy. $ *Rooms from: £95* ✉ *6 Bruce Gardens* ☎ *01463/233836* ⊕ *www.moyness.co.uk* 🛏 *7 rooms* ❧ *Free breakfast.*

★ Ness Walk

$$$ | HOTEL | This spot offers true five-star luxury in the form of spacious and stylish rooms, one of Inverness's best fine-dining restaurants (Torrish), and a verdant riverside location. **Pros:** beautiful riverside property; phenomenal afternoon tea; lounge check-in with champagne. **Cons:** walk from the city center; superattentive service can be stifling; very expensive. $ *Rooms from: £240* ✉ *12 Ness Walk* ☎ *01463/215215* ⊕ *www.nesswalk.com* 🛏 *47 rooms.*

Trafford Bank

$$ | B&B/INN | This former Bishop's home turned boutique B&B makes for a practical and stylish base, with owner Lorraine Freel's talent for interior design seen in the bespoke dining room chairs and handmade wallpaper—as well as in the eclectic array of art throughout. **Pros:** welcoming atmosphere; stylish rooms; relaxing vibe. **Cons:** some rooms on the small side; early checkout time; a walk from the city center. $ *Rooms from: £135* ✉ *96 Fairfield Rd.* ☎ *01463/241414*

⊕ *www.invernesshotelaccommodation. co.uk* 🛏 *5 rooms* ❧ *Free breakfast.*

 ## Nightlife

★ Hootananny

BARS/PUBS | An odd but much-loved combination of Scottish pub, concert hall, and Thai restaurant, Hootananny is one of the best places in the region to hear live music. The excellent pub has a warm atmosphere and serves food that comes highly recommended by locals. Several bands play each Saturday evening and a few during the week, too—check the website for listings. ✉ *67 Church St.* ☎ *01463/233651* ⊕ *www.hootanannyinverness.co.uk.*

 ## Shopping

Castle Gallery

ART GALLERIES | The excellent Castle Gallery sells contemporary paintings, sculpture, prints, and crafts. It also hosts frequently changing exhibitions by up-and-coming artists. ✉ *43 Castle St.* ☎ *01463/729512* ⊕ *www.castlegallery. co.uk.*

Duncan Chisholm

CLOTHING | This shop specializes in Highland dress and tartans. Mail-order and made-to-measure services are available. ✉ *47–51 Castle St.* ☎ *01463/234599* ⊕ *www.kilts.co.uk.*

Inverness Coffee Roasting Co

FOOD/CANDY | An ideal place to pick up a gift, this beautifully presented little coffee shop stocks a good selection of locally roasted beans to enjoy on the premises or take away with you. Indulgent handmade treats made in Inverness by luxury chocolatiers The Chocolate Place are also available here. ✉ *15 Chapel St.* ☎ *01463/242555* ⊕ *www.invernesscoffeeroasting.co.uk.*

Leakey's Bookshop

BOOKS/STATIONERY | This shop claims to be Scotland's largest secondhand bookstore. When you get tired of leafing through the 100,000 or so titles, climb to the mezzanine café and study the cavernous church interior, complete with wood-burning fire. Antique prints and maps are housed on the balcony. ✉ *Greyfriars Hall, Church St.* ☎ *01463/239947.*

Victorian Market

SHOPPING CENTERS/MALLS | Don't miss the colorful Victorian Market, built in 1870. The atmospheric indoor space houses more than 40 privately owned specialty shops. ✉ *Academy St.*

Activities

★ Castle Stuart Golf Links

GOLF | Opened in 2009, this course overlooking the Moray Firth is already considered one of Scotland's finest, hosting the Scottish Open in 2011. Expect undulating fairways and extensive bunkers that test your mettle. The 210-yard 17th hole provides perilous cliff-top play; the wind can defeat the canniest player. The art deco–inspired clubhouse offers stunning views of the water. ✉ *Off B9039* ☎ *01463/796111* ⊕ *www.castlestuartgolf.com* 🖺 *£210 May–Oct.; £155 Apr. and Nov.* 🏌 *18 holes, 6553 yards, par 72* ⟳ *Closed Dec.–Mar.*

Inverness Golf Club

GOLF | Established in 1883, and partly designed by famous British Open champion and course designer James Braid, Inverness Golf Club welcomes visitors to its parkland course 1 mile from downtown. The tree-lined course overlooking the Beauly Firth presents some unique challenges to keep even experienced golfers on their toes. ✉ *Culcabock Rd.* ☎ *01463/239882* ⊕ *www.invernessgolfclub.co.uk* 🖺 *£65 May–Aug.; £50 Apr., Sept., and Oct.; £25 Nov.–Mar.* 🏌 *18 holes, 6102 yards, par 69.*

Culloden Moor

8 miles east of Inverness.

Culloden Moor was the scene of the last battle fought on British soil—and to this day its name is enough to invoke raw and tragic feelings in Scotland. Austere and windswept, it's also a place of outstanding natural beauty.

GETTING HERE AND AROUND

Driving along the B9006 from Inverness is the easiest way to Culloden Battlefield, and there's a large car park to handle many visitors. Stagecoach Highlands Bus 5 also runs from Inverness to the battlefield.

Sights

Clava Cairns

ARCHAEOLOGICAL SITE | Not far from Culloden Moor, on a narrow road southeast of the battlefield, are the Clava Cairns, dating from the Bronze Age. In a cluster among the trees, these stones and monuments form a large ring with underground passage graves that are reached via a tunnel. Helpful placards put everything into historical context. ✉ *Off B851, Culloden* 🖺 *Free.*

★ Culloden Battlefield

MILITARY SITE | Here, on a cold April day in 1746, the hopelessly outgunned Jacobite forces of Bonnie Prince Charlie were destroyed by King George II's army. The victorious commander, the Duke of Cumberland (George II's son), earned the name of the Butcher of Cumberland for the bloody reprisals carried out by his men on Highland families, Jacobite or not, caught in the vicinity. In the battle itself, the duke's army—greatly outnumbering the Jacobites—killed up to 2,000 soldiers. The victors, by contrast, lost just 50. The National Trust for Scotland has re-created a slightly eerie version of the battlefield as it looked in 1746 that you can explore with a guided audio tour. An innovative visitor center enables you to get closer to the sights and sounds of the battle and to interact with the characters involved, while a viewing platform helps put things into perspective from on high (literally). Academic research and technology have helped recreate the Gaelic dialect, song, and music of the time. There's also a good on-site café. ⊠ Off B9006, Culloden ☎ 0844/493–2159 ⊕ www.nts.org.uk ⊠ £11.

Nairn

12 miles east of Culloden Moor, 17 miles east of Inverness, 92 miles west of Aberdeen.

This once-prosperous fishing village is now more likely to lure golfers than sailors. Nearby is Cawdor Castle, loaded with history. East of Nairn pier is a long beach, great for a stroll.

GETTING HERE AND AROUND
A car gives you the most flexibility, but Nairn is close to Inverness (via A96), and regular local buses serve the town.

 Sights

★ Cawdor Castle and Gardens
CASTLE/PALACE | FAMILY | Shakespeare's Macbeth was the Thane of Cawdor (a local officer of the crown), but the sense of history that exists within the turreted walls of Cawdor Castle is certainly more than fictional. Cawdor is a lived-in castle, not an abandoned, decaying structure. The earliest part is the 14th-century central tower; the rooms contain family portraits, tapestries, fine furniture, and paraphernalia reflecting 600 years of history. Outside the walls are sheltered gardens and woodland walks. Children will have a ball exploring the lush and mysterious Big Wood, with its wildflowers and varied wildlife. There are lots of creepy stories and fantastic tales amid the dank

dungeons and drawbridges. If the castle sounds appealing, keep in mind that the estate has cottages to rent. ⊠ B9090, Cawdor ✛ 5 miles southwest of Nairn ☎ 01667/404401 ⊕ www.cawdorcastle. com ⊠ Castle £12.50; grounds only £7.50 ⊙ Closed mid-Oct.–mid-Apr.

Phoenix Sea Adventures
TOUR—SIGHT | With one- and two-hour trips by boat from Nairn Harbour into the Moray Firth, Phoenix Sea Adventures offers you the chance to see seals, porpoises, and dolphins in their breeding areas. The daily departure times for the modern, ex-naval SWIFT vessels vary depending on the tides and the weather. Evening trips are offered on certain dates in summer. ⊠ Nairn Marina, Harbour St. ☎ 0770/316–8097 ⊕ www.phoenix-nairn. co.uk ⊠ Tours from £20.

 Hotels

★ Boath House
$$$$ | B&B/INN | Built in the 1820s and refurbished in 2017, this stunning Regency manor house offers elegant, spacious rooms (some with cast-iron bathtubs), a highly renowned fine-dining restaurant with local, ethically sourced ingredients, and a stunning setting within 20 acres of lovingly nurtured gardens. **Pros:** excellent dining; gorgeous 20-acre grounds; relaxed atmosphere. **Cons:** some airplane noise; no gym or spa facilities; very pricey. ⑤ Rooms from: £380 ⊠ Off A96, Auldearn ☎ 01667/454896 ⊕ www.boath-house.com ➵ 9 rooms ⦿ Free breakfast.

 Shopping

Auldearn Antiques
ANTIQUES/COLLECTIBLES | It's easy to spend an hour wandering around this old church, which is filled to the brim with furniture, fireplaces, architectural antiques, and linens. The converted farmsteads also have tempting antique chinaware and textiles. ⊠ Dalmore Manse,

Legend has it that Cawdor Castle was built around a thorn tree that can still be seen in the castle's dungeon today.

Lethen Rd., Auldearn ☎ *01667/453087*
⊕ *www.auldearnantiques.co.uk.*

🏃 Activities

Nairn Golf Club

GOLF | Highly regarded in golfing circles, the Nairn Golf Club dates from 1887 and is the regular home of Scotland's Northern Open. Huge greens, aggressive gorse, a beach hazard for five of the holes, a steady prevailing wind, and distracting views across the Moray Firth make play on the Championship Course unforgettable. The adjoining nine-hole Cameron Course is ideal for a warm-up or a fun round for the family. ⊠ *Seabank Rd.* ☎ *01667/453208* ⊕ *www.nairngolfclub. co.uk* ✉ *Championship Course: £160 (£110 off-peak) May–Sept.; £110 Apr. and Oct.; £50 Nov.–Mar.; Cameron Course: £20* 🏌 *Championship Course: 18 holes, 6774 yards, par 72; Cameron Course: 9 holes, 1634 yards, par 29* ⛳ *Reservations essential.*

Forres

10 miles east of Nairn.

The burgh of Forres is everything a Scottish medieval town should be, with a handsome tolbooth (the former courthouse and prison) and impressive gardens as its centerpiece. It's remarkable how well the old buildings have adapted to their modern retail uses. With two distilleries—one still operating, the other preserved as a museum—Forres is a key point on the Malt Whisky Trail. Brodie Castle is also nearby. Just 6 miles north you'll find Findhorn Ecovillage, and a sandy beach stretches along the edge of the semi-enclosed Findhorn Bay, which is excellent bird-watching territory.

GETTING HERE AND AROUND

Forres is easy to reach by car or bus from Inverness on the A96. Daily ScotRail trains run here from Inverness and Aberdeen.

Sights

Benromach Distillery

WINERY/DISTILLERY | The smallest distillery in Moray, Benromach was founded in 1898. It's now owned by whisky specialist Gordon and MacPhail, and produces an array of distinctive (often slightly peaty) malts, as well as the housemade gin Red Door. An informative hourly tour will lead you through the facilities, including seeing the poignant signatures of distillery managers before and after a 15-year closure in the late 20th century; tours end with a tutored nosing and tasting. ⊠ *Invererne Rd.* ☎ *01309/675968* ⊕ *www.benromach.com* ☜ *From £8.*

Brodie Castle

CASTLE/PALACE | A magnificent, medieval turreted fortification, Brodie Castle was rebuilt and extended in the 17th and 19th centuries. Consequently, there are fine examples of late-17th-century plasterwork preserved in the Dining Room and Blue Sitting Room, as well as a superb collection of artworks from the Old Masters up to the modern day. You'll also find an impressive library and beautiful gardens with over 400 varieties of daffodils. The castle is around 24 miles east of Inverness, making it a popular day trip. ⊠ *Off A96, Brodie* ☎ *01309/641371* ⊕ *www.nts.org.uk* ☜ *Castle and gardens £20, castle or gardens only £11.*

Dallas Dhu Historic Distillery

WINERY/DISTILLERY | The final port of call on the Malt Whisky Trail, the Dallas Dhu Historic Distillery was the last distillery built in the 19th century and was still in operation until the 1980s. Today its distillery rooms—from malt barn to still house to bonded warehouses—make up a fascinating exhibition that tells the story of Scotland's national drink. You'll be walked through the entire whisky-making process by an audio tour guide, before eventually arriving in the bar to taste a dram and watch an entertainingly dated video presentation. ⊠ *Mannachie Rd.*

☎ *01309/676548* ⊕ *www.historicenvironment.scot* ☜ *£6* ⊙ *Closed Thurs. and Fri. Oct.–Mar.*

Hotels

Cluny Bank Hotel

$$ | **HOTEL** | Take one look at any of this pretty Victorian hotel's unique bedrooms, filled with personal touches, and you could easily guess that this is a family-run venture. **Pros:** lovely hosts; tranquil residential area; award-winning restaurant. **Cons:** some bathrooms a bit small; a little out of town; decor tired in places. ⑤ *Rooms from: £130* ⊠ *69 St. Leonard's Rd.* ☎ *01309/674304* ⊕ *www.clunybankhotel.co.uk* ☜ *7 rooms* ⦿| *Free breakfast.*

Shopping

Brodie Countryfare

CLOTHING | Visit Brodie Countryfare only if you're feeling flush: you may covet the unusual knitwear, quality designer clothing and shoes, gifts, and toys, but they are *not* cheap. The excellent restaurant, on the other hand, is quite inexpensive. ⊠ *On A96, Brodie* ☎ *01309/641555* ⊕ *www.brodiecountryfare.com.*

Aviemore

6 miles southwest of Boat of Garten, 30 miles south of Inverness.

At the foot of the Cairngorms, once-quiet Aviemore now has all the brashness and boxiness of a year-round holiday resort. In the summer months it's filled with walkers, cyclists, and rock climbers, so it's a convenient place for stocking up on supplies. Nevertheless, many of the smaller villages nearby are quieter places to stay. ■**TIP→ Be forewarned: this region can get very cold above 3,000 feet, and weather conditions can change rapidly, even in the middle of summer.**

Rugged Cairngorms National Park features many lochs and beaches, including rocky Loch Morlich.

GETTING HERE AND AROUND

The A9, Scotland's major north–south artery, runs past Aviemore. From Boat of Garten take the A95. The town is serviced by regular trains and buses from Inverness, Edinburgh, and Glasgow.

ESSENTIALS

VISITOR INFORMATION VisitScotland Aviemore iCentre. ☒ *7 Grampian Rd.* ☎ *01479/810930* ⊕ *www.visitscotland. com.*

 Sights

Cairngorm Reindeer Centre

NATURE PRESERVE | FAMILY | On the high slopes of the Cairngorms, you may see the reindeer herd that was introduced here in the 1950s. The reindeer are docile creatures that seem to enjoy human company. Ranger-led visits to the herd are offered at least once a day from mid-February to December, weather permitting. In July and August you can also accompany rangers on gentle half-day treks through the mountains. From April

through December a small herd of young reindeer is cared for at a paddock near the visitor center; you can visit (and pet them) for a small fee. Bring waterproof gear, as conditions can be wet and muddy. ☒ *Reindeer House, Glenmore* ⊹ *6 miles east of Aviemore* ☎ *01479/861228* ⊕ *www.cairngormreindeer.co.uk* ☒ *£16; paddock £3.50* ⊘ *Closed Jan.–early Feb.*

★ Cairngorms National Park

NATIONAL/STATE PARK | A rugged wilderness of mountains, moorlands, glens, and lochs, the sprawling Cairngorms National Park, established in 2003, takes in more than 1,700 square miles. At the heart of Britain's largest national park (nearly 1,750 square miles of countryside) is a wild arctic landscape that sits on a granite plateau. Five of Scotland's nine 4,000-foot-high mountains are found in this range, and there are 13 more over 3,000 feet. These rounded mountains, including Cairn Gorm (meaning "blue hill" in Gaelic) and Ben Macdui, the second highest in Britain at 4,295 feet, were formed at the end of the last ice age. The

Lairig Ghru Pass, a stunning U-shaped glen, was carved by the retreating glacier.

Past Loch Morlich, at the high parking lot on the exposed shoulders of the Cairngorm Mountains, are dozens of trails for hiking and cycling. This is a massive park, encompassing small towns as well as countryside, but a good place to start exploring is the main visitor center in Aviemore. The staff can dispense maps, expert advice on the best trails, and also information on guided walks and other activities. Because much of the best scenery in the park is off-road—including ancient pine forests and open moorland—a particularly good way to cover ground in the park is on a pony trek. The **Rothiemurchus Estate** leads guided treks for riders of all ability levels.

The environment supports rare arctic-alpine and tundra plant and animal species (a full quarter of Britain's endangered species are found here) including flora such as the least willow and alpine blue-sow thistle, and birds such as the ptarmigan, dotterel, and Scottish crossbill—the only bird completely unique to Britain. Lower down the slopes, terrain that was once filled with woodland is now characterized by heather, cotton grass, and sphagnum moss. This open expanse allows visitors to glimpse animals such as the golden eagle, roe deer, or red deer. Fragments of the ancient Caledonian forest (largely Scots pine, birch, and rowan) remain, offering the ideal habitat for pine martens, red squirrels, and capercaillie (a large grouse). Studding these forests are dramatic glens and the Rivers Spey, Don, and Dee, which are home to Atlantic salmon, otters, and freshwater pearl mussels.

Weather conditions in the park change abruptly, so be sure to bring cold-weather gear, particularly if you plan on hiking long distance. ⊠ *Aviemore* ⊕ *cairngorms. co.uk.*

★ **Rothiemurchus Estate**

TOUR—SIGHT | FAMILY | This excellent activity center is among the best in the Cairngorms. It offers a host of organized outdoor diversions, including guided pony rides, mountain biking, fishing, gorge swimming, and white-water rafting. It also offers ranger-guided safaris to see the park's rare and endangered wildlife, including red squirrels and "hairy heilan coos" (Highland slang for Highland cattle—docile, yaklike creatures). The Rothiemurchus Centre is the best place to get oriented and book activities; it also has a handy restaurant and a well-stocked shop selling plenty of fresh produce from the estate. One of the most beautiful parts of the estate is a nature reserve called **Loch an Eilein.** There are great low-level paths around the tree-rimmed loch—perfect for bikes—or longer trails to Glen Einich. A converted cottage beside Loch an Eilein serves as a visitor center, art gallery, and craft store. ⊠ *Rothiemurchus Centre, B970, Inverdruie* ☎ *01479/812345* ⊕ *www.rothiemurchus.net* ◪ *Free.*

🍴 Restaurants

Old Bridge Inn

$$ | MODERN BRITISH | This old-style bar and conservatory restaurant serves what many locals call the best pub food in Aviemore. The menu changes with the seasons, but you can always expect simple dishes built around quality ingredients such as local lamb chops or Angus beef, as well as a variety of fresh fish. **Known for:** classic British fare; spirited live music; warm and welcoming vibe. ⑤ *Average main: £18* ⊠ *23 Dalfaber Rd.* ☎ *01479/811137* ⊕ *www.oldbridgeinn. co.uk.*

🛏 Hotels

★ Ravenscraig Guest House

$ | B&B/INN | Owned by Scottish-Swedish couple Scott and Helena, this charming little B&B offers a warm family welcome, modern rooms with bathrooms en suite, and a great location at the heart of Aviemore. **Pros:** fantastic breakfast; smart TVs in the rooms; free off-road parking. **Cons:** early checkout time; weak shower pressure; no dinner service. ⑤ *Rooms from: £95* ✉ *141 Grampian Rd.* ☎ *01479/810278* ⊕ *www.aviemoreonline. com* ⌁ *14 rooms* ⦵ *Free Breakfast.*

Rowan Tree Country Hotel
$ | **B&B/INN** | Hugging the quieter road from Aviemore to Kingussie, Rowan Tree offers a comfortable, traditional Highland stay and a practical base for exploring nature, from the on-the-doorstep Loch Alvie to the long-distance Speyside Way. The tartan-heavy, slightly gloomy lounge areas and the compact, vintage rooms won't be to everyone's taste. **Pros:** stunning countryside location; incredibly good value; delicious breakfast porridge with cream and Drambuie. **Cons:** very old-fashioned in places; 2 miles outside Aviemore; some rooms with shared bathrooms. ⑤ *Rooms from: £70* ✉ *B9152* ✛ *Near Alvie* ☎ *01479/810207* ⊕ *www. rowantreehotel.com* ⌁ *12 rooms* ⦵ *Free Breakfast.*

Activities

Glenmore Lodge
CLIMBING/MOUNTAINEERING | In Cairngorms National Park, this is a good center for day and residential courses on rock and ice climbing, hiking, kayaking, ski touring, mountain biking, and more. Some classes are aimed at under-18s. There are superb facilities, such as an indoor climbing wall. ✉ *Off B970, Glenmore* ✛ *About 9 miles east of Aviemore* ☎ *01479/861256* ⊕ *www.glenmorelodge. org.uk.*

G2 Outdoor
CLIMBING/MOUNTAINEERING | The wide range of adventures at G2 Outdoor includes white-water rafting, gorge walking, and rock climbing. The company offers a family float trip on the River Spey in summer, and in winter runs ski courses. ✉ *The Hatchery, Alvie Estate* ✛ *Off A9* ☎ *01540/651784* ⊕ *www.g2outdoor. co.uk.*

Kingussie

13 miles southwest of Aviemore.

Set in a wide glen, Kingussie is a pretty town east of the Monadhliath Mountains. With great distant views of the Cairngorms, it's perfect for those who would prefer to avoid the far more hectic town of Aviemore.

GETTING HERE AND AROUND
From Aviemore, Kingussie is easy to reach by car via the A9 and the A86. Although the slightly longer drive along the B9152 is generally quieter and more pleasant. There are also good bus and train services between the two towns.

Sights

★ Highland Folk Museum
MUSEUM | FAMILY | Explore reconstructed Highland buildings, including a Victorian-era schoolhouse, and watch tailors, clock makers, and joiners demonstrating their trades at this open-air museum. Walking paths (or old-fashioned buses) take you to the 18th-century township that was a setting for the hit TV show *Outlander* and includes a peat house made of turf, and a weaver's house. Throughout the museum there are hands-on exhibits like a working quern stone for grinding grain. ✉ *Aultlarie Croft, Kingussie Rd., Newtonmore* ☎ *01349/781650* ⊕ *www.highlifehighland. com* 🎫 *Free* 🕐 *Closed Nov.–Mar.*

Ruthven Barracks
MILITARY SITE | Looking like a ruined castle on a mound, Ruthven Barracks is redolent with tales of "the '45" (as the last Jacobite rebellion is often called). The defeated Jacobite forces rallied here after the Battle of Culloden, but then

abandoned and blew up the government outpost they had earlier captured. You'll see its crumbling, yet imposing, stone outline as you approach. ✉ *Off B970* ✛ ½ *mile southeast of Kingussie* ☎ ⊕ *www. historicenvironment.scot* ✇ *Free.*

Restaurants

★ The Cross at Kingussie

$$$$ | BRITISH | This former tweed mill, with a narrow river running alongside its stone walls, is a haven of wooden beams, whitewashed stone walls, and open fireplaces, all set within four acres of woodlands. The intimate dining room serves sumptuous Scottish produce, from duck and halibut to lamb and sea bass, each delicately prepared with an intimate knowledge of textures and flavors. **Known for:** perfectly curated set menus; stunning location; gorgeous desserts like passion fruit cheesecake. ⑤ *Average main: £55* ✉ *Tweedmill Brae, Ardbroilach Rd.* ☎ *01540/661166* ⊕ *www. thecross.co.uk* ⊗ *Closed Jan. No dinner Sun. and Mon.*

🛏 Hotels

Coig Na Shee

$ | B&B/INN | This century-old Highland lodge has a warm and cozy atmosphere, and each of its spacious bedrooms is unique, with well-chosen furnishings and soothing color schemes. **Pros:** quiet location; great walks from house; plenty of privacy. **Cons:** 3 miles outside Kingussie; hard to reach without a car; some rooms on the smaller side. ⑤ *Rooms from: £90* ✉ *Off Laggan Rd. (A86), Newtonmore* ☎ *01540/670109* ⊕ *www.coignashee. co.uk* ⇜ *5 rooms* ⑩ *Free breakfast* ⌲ *No children under eight.*

★ Sutherlands Guest House

$ | B&B/INN | Finding that sweet spot where contemporary meets cozy is no mean feat, but the husband-and-wife team behind this welcoming guesthouse make it look simple. **Pros:** lovely spacious bedrooms; stunning lounge views; great value. **Cons:** hilltop location best accessed by car; not licensed to sell alcohol; early checkout time. ⑤ *Rooms from: £110* ✉ *Old Distillery Rd.* ☎ *01540/661155* ⊕ *www.sutherlandskingussie.co.uk* ⇜ *5 rooms* ⑩ *Free breakfast.*

Drumnadrochit and Loch Ness

14 miles south of Inverness.

A tourist hub at the curve of the road, Drumnadrochit is not known for its style or culture, but it attracts plenty of people interested in searching for mythical monsters. There aren't many good restaurants, but there are some decent-enough hotels.

GETTING HERE AND AROUND

Drumnadrochit is an easy drive from Inverness (to the north) or Fort Augustus (to the south) on the A82. Buses run frequently, as this is a busy tourist destination.

Sights

Jacobite Cruises

TOUR—SIGHT | The company runs morning and afternoon cruises on Loch Ness to Urquhart Castle and other destinations throughout the region. Tours depart from either Clansman Harbour, 5 miles northeast of Drumnadrochit, or Dochgarroch Loch farther up the A82. ✉ *Barckla Harbour, A82* ☎ *01463/233999* ⊕ *www. jacobite.co.uk* ✇ *Tours from £15.*

Loch Ness

BODY OF WATER | From the A82 you get some spectacular views of the formidable Loch Ness, which has a greater volume of water than any other British lake, a maximum depth of more than 800 feet, and—perhaps you've already heard?—a

Loch Ness, Fort William
and Environs

famous monster. Early travelers who passed this way included General Wade (1673–1748), who, prior to destroying much of Hadrian's Wall in England, came to dig a road up the loch's eastern shore; English lexicographer Dr. Samuel Johnson (1709–84), who remarked at the time about the poor condition of the population and the squalor of their homes; and travel writer and naturalist Thomas Pennant (1726–98), who noted that the loch kept the locality frost-free in winter. None of these observant early travelers ever made mention of a monster. Clearly, they had not read the local guidebooks. From Easter to October, you can also take hourly cruises of the loch, leaving from the little craft store at the Loch Ness Lodge Hotel in Drumnadrochit, and try to spot Nessie yourself; pre-booking for the cruises is not available. ✉ Drumnadrochit.

Loch Ness Centre and Exhibition

MUSEUM | FAMILY | If you're in search of the infamous monster, the Loch Ness Centre and Exhibition walks you through the fuzzy photographs, the unexplained sonar readings, and the sincere testimony of eyewitnesses. It's an entertaining way to spend an hour, even if the boasts of "high tech" and "state-of-the-art" feel overly generous. It's said that the loch's huge volume of water has a warming effect on the local weather, making the loch conducive to mirages in still, warm conditions—but you'll have to make up your own mind about that explanation. ✉ A82 ☎ 01456/450573 ⊕ www.loch-ness.com 💷 £8.45.

★ Urquhart Castle

CASTLE/PALACE | About 2 miles southeast of Drumnadrochit, this castle is a favorite Loch Ness monster–watching spot. This romantically broken-down fortress stands on a promontory overlooking the loch, as it has since the Middle Ages. Because of its central and strategic position in the Great Glen line of communication, the castle has a complex history involving military offense and defense, as well as its own destruction and renovation. The castle was begun in the 13th century and was destroyed before the end of the 17th century to prevent its use by the Jacobites. A visitor center gives an idea of what life was like here in medieval times. ⊠ *Off A82* ☎ *01456/450551* ⊕ *www. historic-scotland.gov.uk* ⧫ *£12.*

 Hotels

Glengarry Castle Hotel

$$ | **HOTEL** | Tucked away in Invergarry, this rambling baronial mansion is 7 miles south of Fort Augustus and within easy reach of the Great Glen's most popular sights. **Pros:** atmospheric building and gardens; good-value take-out lunches; family rooms available. **Cons:** no elevator; a little way from Loch Ness; some may find it old-fashioned. ⑤ *Rooms from: £185* ⊠ *Off A82, Invergarry* ☎ *01809/501254* ⊕ *www.glengarry.net* ⊙ *Closed Nov.–Mar.* ⇨ *26 rooms* ⑩ *Free breakfast.*

★ Loch Ness Lodge

$$$ | **B&B/INN** | Run by siblings Scott and Iona Sutherland, Loch Ness Lodge is an elegant and exclusive lodging option offering a traditional Highland welcome; the formalities are kept to a minimum, but nice touches like the small decanter of sherry on arrival ensure you feel pampered. **Pros:** superb views of Loch Ness; lovely rooms; complimentary afternoon tea. **Cons:** near a busy road; no restaurant; easily confused with a (lesser) hotel of the same name in Drumnadrochit. ⑤ *Rooms from: £285* ⊠ *A82, Brachla* ☎ *01456/459469* ⊕ *www.loch-ness-lodge.com* ⇨ *9 rooms* ⑩ *Free breakfast.*

Fort William

32 miles southwest of Fort Augustus, 69 miles southwest of Inverness, 108 miles northwest of Glasgow, 138 miles northwest of Edinburgh.

As its name suggests, Fort William originated as a military outpost, first established by Oliver Cromwell's General Monk in 1655 and refortified by George I (1660–1727) in 1715 to help combat an uprising by the turbulent Jacobite clans. It remains the southern gateway to the Great Glen and the far west. It's not Scotland's most charming or authentic town, but it's got several good hotels and makes a convenient base for exploring the surrounding countryside.

GETTING HERE AND AROUND

From Glasgow (to the south) and Inverness (to the north), the A82 takes you the entire way. From Edinburgh take the M9 to the A84. This empties into the A85, which connects to the A82 that takes you to Fort William. Roads around Fort William are well maintained, but mostly one lane in each direction. They can be very busy in summer.

A long-distance Scottish Citylink bus connects Glasgow and Fort William. ScotRail has trains from London, as well as connections from Glasgow and Edinburgh. It also operates a train service three times a day between Fort William and Mallaig. For those who like to combine travel and accommodations, the Caledonian Sleeper (⊕ *www.sleeper.scot*) leaves most days from London Euston late in the evening, arriving at Fort William midmorning the following day.

The famous Jacobite Steam Train doubles as the Hogwarts Express in the Harry Potter films.

ESSENTIALS

VISITOR INFORMATION VisitScotland
Fort William iCentre. ✉ *15 High St.*
☎ *01397/701801* ⊕ *www.visitfortwilliam.*
co.uk ⊕ *www.visitscotland.com.*

 ## Sights

Ben Nevis

MOUNTAIN—SIGHT | The tallest mountain
in the British Isles, 4,411-foot Ben Nevis
looms over Fort William, less than 4 miles
from Loch Linnhe. A trek to its summit is
a rewarding experience, but you should
be fit and well prepared—food and water,
map and compass, first-aid kit, whistle,
hat, gloves, and warm clothing (yes, even
in summer), as well as insect spray for
midges—as the unpredictable weather
can make it a hazardous hike. Ask for
advice at the local tourist office before
you begin.

★ Jacobite Steam Train

**TRANSPORTATION SITE (AIRPORT/BUS/FERRY/
TRAIN)** | **FAMILY** | The most relaxing way
to take in the landscape of birch- and
bracken-covered wild slopes is by rail,
and the best ride is on the historic
Jacobite Steam Train, a spectacularly
scenic 84-mile round-trip that runs
between Fort William and Mallaig. You'll
see mountains, lochs, beaches, and
islands along the way. There are two
trips a day between mid-April and late
October (though weekend trips are only
in the height of summer). ✉ *Fort William
Travel Centre, Tom-na-Faire Station Sq.*
☎ *0844/850–4685* ⊕ *www.westcoas-
trailways.co.uk* ✉ *£59.95 round-trip*
⊕ *Closed late Oct.–mid-Apr.*

★ Nevis Range Mountain Experience

VIEWPOINT | Located 6 miles outside Fort
William, this fantastic outdoor center
offers a range of activities in all seasons,
from downhill skiing and snowboarding
to exhilarating mountain-biking trails,
treetop adventure obstacle courses, and
mountain-top paragliding. From June
to early September, you can also take a
gondola up to the 2,000-foot summit of
Aonach Mor, from which you can hike
and explore more of the mountain range

(and enjoy stunning views of Ben Nevis). There are also two good dining options; try Pinemarten Café at the foot of the gondola for its rich macaroni and cheese and local craft beer selection. ⊠ Off A82 ☎ 01397/705825 ⊕ www.nevisrange. co.uk 🎫 Gondola £19.50.

★ West Highland Museum

MUSEUM | In the town center, the small but fascinating West Highland Museum explores the history of Prince Charles Edward Stuart and the 1745 rebellion. Included in the museum's folk exhibits are a costume and tartan display and an excellent collection of Jacobite relics. One of the most intriguing objects here is a tray decorated with a distorted image of Bonnie Prince Charlie that only becomes visible when reflected in a wine glass or goblet. This elaborate ruse enabled clandestine supporters among the nobility to raise a (treasonous) toast without fear of discovery. ⊠ Cameron Sq. ☎ 01397/702169 ⊕ www.westhighlandmuseum.org.uk 🎫 Free ⊙ Closed Mon.–Sat. in July and Aug. and Sun. in Sept.–June.

 Restaurants

★ Crannog Seafood Restaurant

$$ | SEAFOOD | With a reputation for quality and simplicity, this restaurant on the town pier serves outstanding seafood. Fishing boats draw up on the shores of Loch Linnhe and deliver their catch straight to the kitchen. **Known for:** small but well-curated menu; idyllic lochside location; delicious Cullen skink. Ⓢ Average main: £19 ⊠ Town Pier ☎ 01397/705589 ⊕ www.crannog.net.

 Hotels

★ Crolinnhe

$$ | B&B/INN | An elegant old house with colorful gardens, this exceptionally comfortable B&B overlooks Loch Linnhe, yet is only a 10-minute walk from town. **Pros:**

stunning loch views; great breakfasts; comfortable rooms. **Cons:** final payment only by cash or check; short walk from town; grand decor not to everyone's tastes. Ⓢ Rooms from: £160 ⊠ Grange Rd. ☎ 01397/703795 ⊕ www.crolinnhe. co.uk ▭ No credit cards ⊙ Closed Nov.–Easter 🛏 3 suites ❖ Free breakfast.

Inverlochy Castle Hotel

$$$$ | HOTEL | A red-granite mansion turned luxury boutique hotel, Inverlochy Castle stands on 50 acres of woodlands in the shadow of Ben Nevis, with striking scenery on every side; prices are high, but you could have a meal here to take in the surroundings. **Pros:** spectacular setting; excellent restaurant; beautiful location. **Cons:** extremely expensive; must dress up for dinner; a little outside Fort William. Ⓢ Rooms from: £495 ⊠ Off A82 ☎ 01397/702177 ⊕ www.inverlochycastlehotel.com ⊙ Closed Jan. and Feb. 🛏 17 rooms ❖ Breakfast.

 Activities

This area—especially around Glen Nevis, Glencoe, and Ben Nevis—is popular with hikers; however, routes are not well marked, so contact the Fort William tourist information center before you go. The center will provide you with expert advice based on your interests, level of fitness, and hiking experience.

★ Glen Nevis

HIKING/WALKING | For a walk in Glen Nevis, drive north from Fort William on the A82 toward Fort Augustus. On the outskirts of town, just before the bridge over the River Nevis, turn right up the road signposted Glen Nevis. About 8 miles along this road is a parking lot (Upper Glen Nevis Car Park); from here, a footpath will lead you to a steel-cable bridge (1 mile), and then to Steall Waterfall. The ruined croft beside the boulder-strewn stream is a great picnic place. You can continue up the glen for some distance without any danger of becoming lost as long as you stay on the path and keep the river to your right. Watch your step going through the tree-lined gorge. The return route is simply back the way you came. ⊠ *Upper Glen Nevis Car Park.*

Glenfinnan

10 miles west of Fort William, 33 miles northwest of Glencoe.

Perhaps the most visitor-oriented stop on the route between Fort William and Mallaig, Glenfinnan has much to offer if you're interested in Scottish history. Here the National Trust for Scotland has capitalized on the romance surrounding the story of the Jacobites and their attempts to return a Stewart monarch and the Roman Catholic religion to a country that had become staunchly Protestant. It was at Glenfinnan that the rash adventurer Bonnie Prince Charlie gathered his meager forces for the final Jacobite rebellion of 1745–46.

GETTING HERE AND AROUND

If you're driving from Fort William, travel west via the A830. For great views, take a ride on the Jacobite Steam Train, which you can catch in Fort William.

 Sights

Glenfinnan Monument

MEMORIAL | One of the most striking monuments in Britain, the Glenfinnan Monument commemorates the place where Bonnie Prince Charlie raised his standard. The tower, which was built in 1815, overlooks Loch Shiel; note, however, that the figure on the top is a Highlander, not the prince himself. The story of his ill-fated campaign is told in the nearby visitor center. ■TIP→ **The view down Loch Shiel from the Glenfinnan Monument is one of the most photographed in Scotland.** ⊠ *Off*

A830 ☏ *01397/722250* ⊕ *www.nts.org. uk* ☞ *£4.*

Glenfinnan Viaduct

BRIDGE/TUNNEL | The 1,248-foot-long Glenfinnan Viaduct was a genuine wonder when it was built in 1897, and remains so today. The railway's contractor, Robert MacAlpine (known among locals as "Concrete Bob") pioneered the use of concrete for bridges when his company built the Mallaig extension, which opened in 1901. In more recent times the viaduct became famous for its appearance in the Harry Potter films. The viaduct can be seen on foot; about half a mile west of the railway station in Glenfinnan, on the A380 road, is a small parking lot. Take the footpath from here; you'll reach the viaduct in about ½ mile. If you time it right (usually at 11 am, 3 pm, and 7:30 pm, but you can confirm times at ⊕ *westcoastrailways.co.uk*), you'll see the iconic Jacobite Steam Train crossing the bridge. ⊠ *Glenfinnan Viaduct Car Park, Off A380.*

 Hotels

Glenfinnan House

$$ | **HOTEL** | This handsome hotel on the shores of Loch Shiel was built in the 18th century as the home of Alexander MacDonald VII of Glenaladale, who was wounded fighting for Bonnie Prince Charlie; it was transformed into an even grander mansion in the 19th century. **Pros:** fabulous setting; atmospheric dining experience; beautiful views. **Cons:** some shared bathrooms; a bit fussy for some; no air-conditioning. ⓢ *Rooms from: £145* ⊠ *Off A830* ☏ *01397/722235* ⊕ *www.glenfinnanhouse.com* ⊙ *Closed mid-Nov.–mid-Mar.* ⌑ *14 rooms* ⊙⊠ *Free breakfast.*

Arisaig

15 miles west of Glenfinnan.

Considering its small size, Arisaig, gateway to the **Small Isles,** offers a surprising choice of high-quality options for dining and lodging. To the north of Arisaig, the road cuts across a headland to reach a stretch of coastline where silver sands glitter with the mica in the local rock; clear water, blue sky, and white sand lend a tropical flavor to the beaches—when the sun is shining.

From Arisaig try to visit a couple of the Small Isles: **Rum, Eigg, Muck,** and **Canna,** each tiny and with few or no inhabitants. Rum serves as a wildlife reserve, while Eigg was the world's first community where electricity was produced off-grid, solely by wind, wave, and solar energy.

GETTING HERE AND AROUND

From Glenfinnan,you reach Arisaig on the A830, the only road leading west. The Fort William–Mallaig train also stops here.

 ## Sights

Arisaig Marine

TRANSPORTATION SITE (AIRPORT/BUS/FERRY/TRAIN) | Along with a host of wildlife excursions offering a chance to see minke whales, basking sharks, bottlenose dolphins, killer whales, porpoises, gray seals, and lots of sea birdlife (including cute puffins), Arisaig Marine runs a boat service from the harbor at Arisaig to the Small Isles from May to September. There's also a little tearoom and gift shop here. ⊠ *Arisaig Harbour* ☎ *01687/450224* ⊕ *www.arisaig.co.uk* ⊠ *Eigg £18 round-trip.*

Loch Morar

BODY OF WATER | Take the A830 north from Arisaig, turn right onto the B8008 before Morar, then turn right again onto an even smaller, unnamed side road, and you'll find yourself driving along the northern edge of Loch Morar, the deepest of all

the Scottish lochs (more than 1,000 feet). The next deepest point is miles out into the Atlantic, beyond the continental shelf. The beautifully atmospheric loch is said to have a resident monster, Morag, which undoubtedly gets less recognition than its famous cousin Nessie. Whether that means you have more chance of getting her to appear for a photograph, we can't say. ⊠ *Loch Morar, Off A830, Mallaig.*

 ## Restaurants

The Old Library

$$ | FRENCH | On the waterfront, this 1722 barn has been converted into a lovely, reasonably priced restaurant. Expect simple but tasty plates of local fish and meats, prepared in a French-bistro style—lamb shank, sirloin, or perhaps a fillet of buttery hake, served with seasonal veggies. **Known for:** hearty meals; ultra-fresh produce; local character. ⑤ *Average main: £18* ⊠ *B8008* ☎ *01687/450651* ⊕ *www.oldlibrary.co.uk.*

Hotels

★ Arisaig House

$$ | HOTEL | An open-arms welcome and stunning views of the Isle of Skye await you at this handsome stone mansion, built in the 1860s. **Pros:** beautiful views; lovely hosts; outstanding food. **Cons:** a bit isolated; expensive for the area; two-night minimum in summer. ⑤ *Rooms from: £195* ⊠ *Beasdale, Off A830* ☎ *01687/450730* ⊕ *www.arisaighouse.co.uk* ⊅ *12 rooms* ⑩ *Free breakfast.*

Glencoe

16 miles south of Fort William, 92 miles north of Glasgow, 44 miles northwest of Edinburgh.

Glencoe is both a small town and a region of stunning grandeur, with high peaks and secluded glens. Dramatic scenery is the main attraction here; it's as awesomely beautiful for a drive as it is for a hike. The A82—the main route through Glencoe—can get surprisingly crowded in high season, but it's one of the great scenic drives in Scotland. This area, where wild, craggy buttresses loom darkly over the road, has a special place in the folk memory of Scotland, as it was the site of an infamous 17th-century massacre.

GETTING HERE AND AROUND
Glencoe is easily accessed by car via the A82. ScotRail trains and regional buses arrive from most of Scotland's major cities.

 Sights

Glencoe Visitor Centre
INFO CENTER | This impressive visitor center tells the life story of Glencoe, from its volcanic origins to the MacDonald massacre to its current wildlife maintenance projects. There are fascinating exhibitions on the region, its landscape, and its people, as well as great hiking trails leaving from the center (you can get expert advice on longer hikes, too). There's also an excellent café and shop. ⋈ *Off A82 ✚ 1 mile south of Glencoe Village* 🕾 *01855/811307* ⊕ *www.glencoe-nts.org.uk* 🅿 *Parking £4* ⊗ *Closed Mar.–mid-Apr.*

 Hotels

★ Glencoe House
$$$$ | **B&B/INN** | Peaceful surroundings, arresting views, and the friendliest of welcomes await you at this former Victorian hunting lodge. **Pros:** beautiful landscape; superb restoration; lovely hosts. **Cons:** very expensive; limited facilities; breakfast a little underwhelming. 🟊 *Rooms from: £425* ⋈ *Glencoe Lochan* 🕾 *01855/811179* ⊕ *www.glencoe-house.com* 🛏 *14 suites* ⎰*O*⎱ *No meals.*

 Activities

★ Glencoe Activities
CLIMBING/MOUNTAINEERING | **FAMILY** | This popular outdoor center west of Ballachulish offers a long list of high-energy activities, from rock climbing to white-water rafting, and even hair-raising vertical canyon explorations complete with 600-foot descents. But there's a welcome twist here—it also caters to those with more limited mobility (or less adventurous souls). Guided Segway tours (£35) last 50 minutes and take you through some spectacular scenery, with stunning mountain views and even a trail along a stretch of Loch Leven. ⋈ *Dragon's Tooth Golf Course, Off A828 ✚ 4 miles west of Glencoe* 🕾 *01855/413200* ⊕ *www.glencoeactivities.com.*

Isle of Skye

The misty Isle of Skye is awash with romance and myth, lush green gardens, and steep, magnetic mountains. Its extraordinary natural beauty and royal connections see it rank highly on most visitors' must-see lists, while its proximity to the mainland makes it one of Scotland's most easily accessible islands.

Skye has a dramatic, mysterious, and mountainous landscape, where sunsets linger brilliantly until late at night and otherworldly mists roll gently through the valleys. Much photographed are the old crofts, one or two of which are still inhabited today. It also has an impressive range of accommodations, and restaurants that showcase the best of the island's produce and culinary talent.

To reach Skye, cross over the bridge spanning the narrow channel of Kyleakin, between Kyle of Lochalsh and Kyleakin. Or, if you're visiting in the summer, take a romantic boat trip between Mallaig and Armadale or between Glenelg and Kylerhea. You can tour comfortably around

Isle of Skye

the island in two or three days, but a bit longer will allow extra time for hiking or sea kayaking.

Orientation is easy: in the north, follow the roads that loop around the peninsulas of Waternish and Trotternish; in the south, enjoy the road running the length of the Sleat Peninsula. There are some stretches of single lane road, but for careful drivers these shouldn't pose a problem.

Kyle of Lochalsh

55 miles west of Inverness, 120 miles northwest of Glasgow.

The little town of Kyle of Lochalsh is the mainland gateway to Skye. Opened in 1995, the bridge transformed not only travel to Skye but the very seascape itself. The area's most notable—and most photographed—attraction is 8 miles farther east at Dornie—Eilean Donan Castle.

GETTING HERE AND AROUND

From the north you reach Kyle of Lochalsh via the A890; from the south take the A87. There are four direct trains a day from Inverness.

◉ Sights

★ Eilean Donan Castle

CASTLE/PALACE | Guarding the confluence of lochs Long, Alsh, and Duich stands the most picturesque of all Scottish fortifications. Eilean Donan Castle, perched on an islet connected to the mainland by a stone-arched bridge, dates from the 14th century and has all the dramatic stone walls, timber ceilings, and winding stairs you could possibly desire.

Just a glimpse at Eilean Donan Castle from a distance makes it clear why this is one of the most photographed castles in all of Scotland.

Empty and neglected for years after being bombarded by frigates of the Royal Navy during an abortive Spanish-Jacobite landing in 1719, this romantic Scottish icon was almost entirely rebuilt from a ruin in the early 20th century. The kitchen re-creates the busy scene before a grand banquet, and the upper floors show how the castle was transformed into a grand house. The picturesque cover of a thousand travel brochures, Eilean Donan has also appeared in a number of Hollywood movies and TV shows, from *The Wicker Man* to *Highlander*. There's a shop and a coffeehouse for the many visitors. ⊠ *Off A87, Dornie* ☎ *01599/555202* ⊕ *www. eileandonancastle.com* ⤳ *£10* ⊙ *Closed Jan.*

🍴 Restaurants

★ All the Goodness
$ | CAFÉ | This excellent little bakery-café serves housemade cakes, tray bakes, and pastries, along with artisan coffee and an array of tempting foodie gifts and souvenirs—all to be enjoyed with a stunning vista of Eilean Donan Castle. In summer the café also displays evocative works by local artist Lorraine Tolmie. **Known for:** delicious baked goods; superior tea and coffee; unbeatable castle views. ⑤ *Average main: £5* ⊠ *Off A87* ✢ *8 miles east of Kyle of Lochalsh* ☎ *01599/555221* ⊕ *www.allthegoodness. co.uk* ⊙ *Closed Mon.–Tues. No dinner.*

Broadford

8 miles west of Kyle of Lochalsh via Skye Bridge.

One of the larger of Skye's settlements, Broadford lies along the shore of Broadford Bay, which has been known to welcome whales to its sheltered waters.

GETTING HERE AND AROUND
Broadford is on the A87, the main road crossing the Isle of Skye.

TOURS
★ Misty Isle Boat Trips
TOUR—SIGHT | FAMILY | For fantastic views of the Cuillin Mountains and the Inner Hebrides, book a place on one of the Misty Isle Boat Trips. The expansive scenery around Loch Coruisk is some of the most spectacular in Scotland. Round-trip journeys depart from the town of Elgol, 15 miles southwest of Broadford, and booking ahead is essential. Prices vary, but a cruise to a seal colony costs £25. Private charters are also available. ⊠ *Elgol jetty, Sealladh na Mara, Elgol* ☎ *01471/866288* ⊕ *www.mistyisle-boattrips.co.uk* ⊠ *From £14* ⊙ *Closed Nov.–Mar.*

 Sights

Road to Elgol
SCENIC DRIVE | The B8083 leads from Broadford to one of the finest vistas anywhere in Scotland. This road passes by **Strath Suardal** and little **Loch Cill Chriosd** (Kilchrist), and also takes in breathtaking views of the mountain **Bla Bheinn** en route. As you near Elgol, look out for a gathering of traditional crofts that descends to a pier, then admire the heart-stopping profile of the Cuillin peaks from the shore. Seek out the path, around halfway down the hill, that leads across rough grasslands into the mountains. ⊠ *Elgol.*

 Hotels

Broadford Hotel
$$$ | HOTEL | Watch over Broadford Bay in comfort and style with a stay at this well-appointed hotel, which takes pride in being the place where Drambuie was invented. **Pros:** quintessentially Scottish; convenient location; Drambuie-colored tartan. **Cons:** no elevator; poorly lit public areas; breakfast underwhelming. ⑤ *Rooms from: £205* ⊠ *Torrin Road* ☎ *01471/822204* ⊕ *www.broadfordhotel.co.uk* ⇌ *11 rooms* �101 *Free breakfast.*

Armadale

17 miles south of Broadford, 43 miles south of Portree, 5 miles (ferry crossing) west of Mallaig.

Rolling moorlands, scattered with rivers and lochans, give way to enchanting hidden coves and scattered waterside communities. Welcome to **Sleat,** Skye's southernmost peninsula.

GETTING HERE AND AROUND
The Mallaig-Armadale ferry arrives here. There's a short (and beautiful) road to the southwest, while the main road heads east following the stunning coast.

 Sights

Armadale Castle, Gardens & Museum
CASTLE/PALACE | As the name suggests, this attraction has three distinct strings to its bow: a romantic, ruined castle; a lush, flower-filled estate; and a fascinating museum of local island history. The castle is a windswept 17th-century mansion house built by the influential Clan Donald, while the extensive gardens cover 40 acres, offering magnificent views across the Sound of Sleat to Knoydart and the Mallaig Peninsula. The highlight, however, is the fascinating museum, which tells the story of the clan and its proud title, the Lords of the Isles, with the help of an excellent audiovisual presentation. There's a gift shop, restaurant, library, and center for genealogy research. Also on the grounds are high-quality accommodations in the form of seven cottages, complete with kitchen facilities. Access is from Armadale Pier, where signs indicate the different forest walks that are available. ⊠ *Off A851* ☎ *01471/844305* ⊕ *www.armadalecastle.com* ⊠ *£8.75* ⊙ *Closed Weekends in Nov.–Mar.*

🛏 Hotels

Duisdale House Hotel
$$$ | HOTEL | Set in 35 acres of mature woodlands and gardens, this former mansion with a lovely hillside location and ocean views is boutique chic at its very best. **Pros:** finely furnished rooms; expansive views; attentive staff. **Cons:** nautical decor is an acquired taste; meals are expensive; some rooms are noisy. $ *Rooms from: £295* ✉ *Off A851, Isleornsay* ☎ *01471/833202* ⊕ *www.duisdale.com* ↪ *18 rooms* ⦿ *Breakfast.*

★ Kinloch Lodge
$$$$ | HOTEL | An upmarket hotel with an equally upmarket restaurant, Kinloch Lodge peacefully overlooks the tidal Loch na Dal. The historic buildings date from the 17th century, while the newer South House has the best views, built from the ground up with comfort and relaxation in mind. **Pros:** historic property; characterful interior; sublime afternoon tea. **Cons:** expensive dining; far from amenities; some of the old porcelain is stained. $ *Rooms from: £380* ✉ *Off A851, Isleornsay* ☎ *01471/833333* ⊕ *www.kinloch-lodge.co.uk* ↪ *19 rooms* ⦿ *Breakfast.*

🛍 Shopping

★ Ragamuffin
CLOTHING | This well stocked shop specializes in designer knitwear and has some of the nicest staff you could hope to meet. On cold winter days, they might make you coffee while you browse, then mail your purchases back home for you. ✉ *Armadale Pier, Off A851* ☎ *01471/844217.*

Portree

42 miles northwest of Armadale.

Portree, the population center of the island, is a pleasant place clustered around a small and sheltered bay. Although not overburdened by historical features, it's a fine touring base with a number of good shops.

GETTING HERE AND AROUND
The biggest town on Skye, Portree is well served by local buses and by a well-maintained road, the A87.

VISITOR INFORMATION VisitScotland
Portree iCentre. ✉ *Bayfield House, Bayfield Road* ☎ *01478/612992* ⊕ *www.visitscotland.com/info/services/portree-icentre-p333111.*

Sights

Aros
ARTS VENUE | On the outskirts of town, Aros is a community center that screens films, exhibits artworks, and hosts live music, dance, and theater productions. It's the cultural hub of the Isle of Skye. ✉ *Viewfield Road* ☎ *01478/613649* ⊕ *www.aros.co.uk* ✉ *Free.*

🍽 Restaurants

Café Arriba
$ | BRITISH | Up a steep flight of stairs, the laid-back café has window seats with great views over Portree Harbour. Using only local produce (whatever is "fresh, local, and available"), this is a good option for no-frills eating. **Known for:** delicious housemade cakes; mildly treacherous stairs; there are lines. $ *Average main: £9* ✉ *Quay Brae, Quay Street* ☎ *01478/611830* ⊕ *www.cafearriba.co.uk.*

Scorrybreac Restaurant
$$$$ | BRITISH | It may be tiny, but this 20-seater restaurant has made big waves since opening in 2013. The vibe is relaxed and informal, while the cooking is imaginative and varied, creating unexpected marriages such as coffee-crusted venison or hake with coconut. **Known for:** intimate dining; inventive dishes; gorgeous bay views. $ *Average main: £42* ✉ *7 Bosville Terr.* ☎ *01478/612069* ⊕ *www.scorrybreac.com* ⦿ *Closed Sun.–Mon. No lunch.*

Hotels

Cuillin Hills Hotel

$$$ | HOTEL | This delightful Victorian-era hunting lodge looks down on Portree and the brightly painted houses around the harbor. **Pros:** a short stroll from Portree; good breakfast menu; attentive service. **Cons:** rooms at back overpriced; restaurant can be full; no elevator. ⓢ *Rooms from: £245* ⊠ *Off A855* ☏ *01478/612003* ⊕ *www.cuillinhills-hotel-skye.co.uk* ↻ *34 rooms* ⓘⓄⓘ *Free breakfast.*

Shopping

Isle of Skye Soap Company

PERFUME/COSMETICS | This charming little shop handcrafts its own soaps, aromatherapy oils, candles, and other pleasingly fragranced gifts. Founder (and soap maker in chief) Fiona is an aromatherapist. ⊠ *Somerled Square* ☏ *01478/611350* ⊕ *www.skye-soap.co.uk.*

Trotternish Peninsula

16 miles north of Portree.

Travel north from Portree on the A855 and you'll see cliffs rising to the left. These are the closest edge of an ancient lava flow, set back from the road and running the length of the peninsula. Fossilized dinosaur bones have been uncovered at the base of these cliffs, while overhead you might just spot a sea eagle, identifiable by the flash of its white tail.

GETTING HERE AND AROUND

From Portree take the twisting, undulating A855 as it follows the coast.

Sights

★ Fairy Glen

NATURE SITE | What was once a hidden gem has now become just another stop on the ever-expanding Skye tourist trail. Still, come early or late to avoid the crowds and the Fairy Glen remains a magical place—an enchanting, otherworldly valley of strange green hillocks, eerily still pools, crumbling cottages, and roaming sheep. To get here, take a small road just south of Uig signed "Sheader and Balnaknock" and drive for a little over a mile. ⊠ *Free*

Kilt Rock

NATURE SITE | No drive between Portree and Staffin is complete without a sojourn at Skye's most famous sea cliff. Named for the shape of its sheer rock face, which is ridged like a pleated kilt and swoops out to sea at the "hem," soaring Kilt Rock (and its gushing waterfall) can be seen from a specially built viewing platform. ⊠ *Off A855, Staffin* ✛ *1½ miles south of Staffin.*

Old Man of Storr

NATURE SITE | Along the dramatic road around the Trotternish Peninsula, a gate beside a car park marks the beginning of the climb to the Old Man of Storr, one of Skye's most iconic landmarks. At 2,000 feet, this volcanic pinnacle is the highest point on the peninsula, so give yourself at least three hours to explore and enjoy the spectacular views from the top. ⚠ **The weather here changes very quickly, so be prepared.** ⊠ *Off A855.*

★ Quiraing

NATURE SITE | A spectacular geological formation of rocky crags and towering stacks, Quiraing dominates the horizon of the Trotternish Peninsula. It is situated about 5 miles beyond Kilt Rock, so for a closer look, make a left onto a small road at Brogaig by Staffin Bay. There's a parking lot near the point where this road breaches the ever-present cliff line. The road is very narrow and rough, so drive cautiously. The rambler's trail is on uneven, stony ground, and it's a steep scramble up to the rock formations. In ages past, stolen cattle were hidden deep within the Quiraing's rocky jaws.

The otherworldly Fairy Glen is one of the most magical places on the isle.

Skye Museum of Island Life

MUSEUM | Discover the old crofting ways of the local population at this museum, situated close to the tip of the Trotternish Peninsula. Informative displays and exhibits show life as it was on the island merely a century ago, from reconstructed interiors with traditional tools and implements to historical photographs and documents. ⊠ *Off A855, Kilmuir* ☎ *01470/552206* ⊕ *www.skyemuseum.co.uk* ✉ *£3* ⊙ *Closed Sun. and Oct.–Easter.*

Staffin Ecomuseum

MUSEUM VILLAGE | **FAMILY** | Billed as "a museum without walls," the Staffin Ecomuseum is a collection of 13 open-air geological and social exhibits dotted along the landscape of the peninsula. Follow the map along the coastal route and you will discover dinosaur footprints, a healing well, a deserted village, and more. This is not to be confused with Staffin Museum, Dugald Ross's nearby exhibition. ⊠ *Staffin Community Trust, 3 Ellishadder, Staffin* ⊕ *www.skyecomuseum.co.uk.*

Hotels

Corran House

$ | **B&B/INN** | Set back off the A87 near Kingsburgh, this cozy B&B is a convenient, good-value stay at the base of the Trotternish Peninsula, 8 miles northwest of Portree. **Pros:** great location between sights; splendid views; good value. **Cons:** not close to any one particular attraction; easy to miss; more expensive than it used to be. ⑤ *Rooms from: £100* ⊠ *1 Eyre, Portree* ⚓ *Set back from the road; look out for the small white sign* ☎ *01470/532699* ⊕ *www.corranhouseskye.co.uk* ✉ *6 rooms* ⦿ *Free breakfast.*

The Flodigarry Hotel

$$$ | **HOTEL** | With spectacular coastal views and antique furnishings throughout, the Flodigarry Hotel retains the feel of a grand country manor. **Pros:** spectacular views; a good base for walking; free

Wi-Fi. **Cons:** steep road down; expensive rooms; a long way from anywhere. ⑤ *Rooms from: £260* ⊠ *Off A855, Staffin* ☎ *01470/552203* ⊕ *www.hotelintheskye. co.uk* ⊅ *18 rooms* ⦿ *Free breakfast.*

Glendale

14 miles southwest of Waternish.

Glendale is a region rich in flora and fauna: otters, seals, and dolphins can be spotted off its rocky coast, while white-tailed sea eagles soar overhead. Dunvegan Castle is just at the region's eastern edge.

GETTING HERE AND AROUND
From the Waternish Peninsula, take the A850 southwest, turn onto the A863 southeast at Dunvegan, then follow the twisty, turny B884 west along the coast. It can feel rather isolated in bad weather or after dark.

Sights

Dunvegan Castle and Gardens
CASTLE/PALACE | In a commanding position looming over a sea loch, Dunvegan Castle has been the seat of the chiefs of Clan MacLeod for more than 700 years. Today it's a popular (if overpriced) tourist attraction. Step inside and into the clan's illustrious past through plush interiors, fascinating photos, and, most notably, the Fairy Flag—a silk banner, thought to be originally from Rhodes or Syria, which is credited with protecting the clan from danger. And make time to explore the gardens, with their water garden and falls, fern house, walled garden, and various viewing points. There's a café beside the car park. Boat trips from the castle to the nearby seal colony run April through September. ⊠ *Junction of A850 and A863, Dunvegan* ☎ *01470/521206* ⊕ *www.dunvegancastle.com* ⊿ *Castle and gardens £14; gardens only £12; seal trips £9.50.*

🍴 Restaurants

★ Three Chimneys
$$$$ | **MODERN BRITISH** | Perhaps the Isle of Skye's biggest culinary draw, this old stone-walled restaurant on the banks of Loch Dunvegan serves consistently daring, well-crafted food. The chef's belief in quality Scottish ingredients is evident in every dish, from the locally sourced game to the sublime Scottish seafood, and when aligned with the chic, minimalist interior—all crisp white walls and exposed brickwork—it makes for a luxury dining experience you won't soon forget. **Known for:** inventive seafood dishes; sublime haddock ravioli; faultless service. ⑤ *Average main: £69* ⊠ *B884, Colbost* ☎ *01470/511258* ⊕ *www.threechimneys. co.uk* ⊗ *Closed mid-Dec.–mid-Jan.* ⊕ *No children under eight at dinner.*

🛍 Shopping

Skye Silver
JEWELRY/ACCESSORIES | Distinctive gold and silver jewelry with Celtic themes is the bread and butter of Skye Silver. From pendants to rings, bracelets to earrings, the unique pieces here are inspired by the surrounding natural landscapes of sea and countryside, with motifs of island wildlife. ⊠ *The Old School, B884, Colbost* ☎ *01470/511263* ⊕ *www.skyesilver.com.*

Glen Brittle and the Cuillin Mountains

28 miles southeast of Glendale.

The gentle slopes of this valley are a gateway to the dramatic peaks and ridges of the Cuillin Mountains. Glen Brittle's lower slopes are fine for walkers and weekend climbers, but the higher ridges are strictly for serious mountaineers.

The Isle of Skye's most magical walk is to the Fairy Pools, rock pools of spring water fed by waterfalls from the Cuillin Mountains.

GETTING HERE AND AROUND

From Glendale follow the B884 east to Lonmore, turn south onto the A863, then after 16 miles head west on the B8009. Glen Brittle extends from here to cover the southwest corner of the island.

Sights

★ Fairy Pools

BODY OF WATER | One of the most magical sights in Scotland, the Fairy Pools are a spectacularly beautiful collection of waterfalls and plunge pools in the midst of Glen Brittle. The rocky gray landscape contrasts with the vivid blue-green of the pools, the colorful plant life, and visiting wildlife (including, occasionally, red deer) to give the environment a fairy-tale feel. You can walk to the pools from a parking lot 20 minutes away. Come at sunrise or sunset for smaller crowds and the opportunity for a truly enchanting swim—just don't expect the water to be warm. ⊠ *Glenbrittle* 🖾 *Free.*

Glen Brittle

MOUNTAIN—SIGHT | Enjoy spectacular mountain scenery in Glen Brittle, including some unforgettable views of the Cuillin Mountains (these are not for the casual walker, due to steep and dangerous cliff faces). The drive from Carbost along a single-track road is one of the most dramatic in Scotland and draws outdoorsy types from across the globe. At the southern end of the glen is a murky-colored beach, a campground, and gentle foothills that were made for strolling. ⊠ *Off A863 and B8009.*

Talisker Distillery

WINERY/DISTILLERY | The only distillery on the Isle of Skye is one of the best in Scotland. Talisker produces a sweet, light single malt that has the distinctive peaty aroma of island whiskies, yet with less intensity—making it a great introductory dram for newcomers to Scotch. Robert Louis Stevenson called Talisker "the king of drinks," and the inhabitants of Skye are very proud of it. Classic tours here take about 45 minutes, while tasting tours

The Northern Highlands

North Atlantic Ocean

North Sea

Dunnet Head

Strathy Point

Cape Wrath

Eddrachillis Bay

NORTHWEST HIGHLANDS

The Minch

ISLE OF LEWIS

ISLE OF SKYE

Sound of Raasay

Inner Sound

Gruinard Bay

Moray Firth

Duncansby Head
John o' Groats
Dunnet
Dunnet Head
Scrabster
Thurso
Wick
Watten
Halkirk
Reay
Crosskirk
Portskerra
Armadale
Bettyhill
Coldbackie
Tongue
Kinbrace
Kildonan
Helmsdale
Brora
Dunrobin Castle
Golspie
Portmahomack
Dornoch
Tain
Lairg
Rosehall
Invershin
Bonar Bridge
Evelix
Glenmorangie Distillery
Eddeiton
Alness
Invergordon
Cromarty
Fortrose Nairn
Inverness
Lossiemouth
Elgin
Rothes
Buckie
Portsoy
Keith
Dufftown
Huntly
Kinloss
Forres
Balnakeil Craft Village
Smoo Cave
Durness
Achfary
Kylesku
Eas a' Chual Aluinn Waterfall
Handa Island
Scourie
Drumbeg
Drumbeg Loop
Stoer
Lochinver
Assynt
Achmelvich
Achiltibuie
Coigach
Ullapool
Corrieshalloch Gorge
Garve
Gorstan
Strathpeffer
Contin
Dingwall
Muir of Ord
Beauly
Achnasheen
Kinlochewe
Destitution Road
Laide
Aultbea
Inverewe Gardens
Poolewe
Loch Maree
Gairloch
Torridon
Shieldaig
Applecross
Kinlochbervie
Sandwood Bay
Stornoway

A897
A9
A836
A838
A894
A835
A832
A836
A99
A838
A839
A949
A9
A835
A832
A896
A890
A95
A96
A9
A835
A855
A9
A838
A887

20 mi
20 km

(available weekdays) take between one-and-a-half and two hours. Book ahead, as tours are very popular. ✉ *B8009, Carbost* ☎ *01478/614308* ⊕ *www.malts.com* ✆ *Tours from £10.*

Gairloch

55 miles southwest of Ullapool.

Aside from its restaurants and lodgings, peaceful Gairloch has one further advantage: it often escapes the rain clouds that can cling to the high summits. You can enjoy a round of golf here and perhaps stay dry, even when the nearby Torridon Hills are deluged.

GETTING HERE AND AROUND

From Ullapool, head south down the A835 and, after 12 miles (just after Corrieshalloch Gorge), turn west onto the winding A832 (also known as "Destitution Road").

 ## Sights

Destitution Road
SCENIC DRIVE | The road south between **Corrieshalloch Gorge** (a very worthwhile stop) and Gairloch passes through wild woodlands around Dundonnell and Loch Broom, then takes in stunning coastal scenery with views of Gruinard Bay and its white beaches. Look out for the toothed ramparts of the mountain **An Teallach** (pronounced tyel-lack), visible on the horizon for miles. The moorland route you travel is officially called the A832, but is better (and more chillingly) known as Destitution Road; a holdover from the terrible potato famines of the 1840s.

★ Inverewe Garden
GARDEN | A highlight of the area, Inverewe Garden has lush plantings tucked away behind a dense barrier of trees and shrubs. This is all thanks to the warm North Atlantic Drift, which takes the edge off winter frosts. Inverewe is sometimes described as subtropical, but this inaccuracy irritates the head gardener; do not expect coconuts and palm trees here. Instead, look for rarities like the blue Himalayan poppy. ✉ *Off A832, Poolewe* ✚ *6 miles northeast of Gairloch* ☎ *01445/781229* ⊕ *www.nts.org.uk* ✆ *£12.50.*

★ Loch Maree
BODY OF WATER | Southeast of Gairloch stretches one of Scotland's most scenic lochs, Loch Maree. Its harmonious setting, with tall Scots pines and the mountain Slioch looming as a backdrop, is regularly visited by red deer, as well as the endangered pine marten (a member of the weasel family)—though they're just as likely to be hanging around the trash cans as in the trees. There are few official parking places along the loch, but those are nestled between the trees with limited views, so be prepared to park and climb to a better vantage point. ✉ *Gairloch.*

 ## Hotels

The Dundonnell
$ | HOTEL | Located along "Destitution Road," around 30 miles from Gairloch, this lovely family-run hotel sits on the edge of Little Loch Broom, with the mountains of An Leachall rising up behind. **Pros:** fabulous scenery; plenty of outdoor activities; good dining options. **Cons:** bland exterior; some outdated rooms; Wi-Fi only in public areas. ⑤ *Rooms from: £110* ✉ *A832, Dundonnell* ☎ *01854/633204* ⊕ *www.dundonnellhotel.com* ➲ *23 rooms* ⑩ *Free breakfast.*

Ullapool

35 miles south of Lochinver, 238 miles north of Glasgow, 57 miles northwest of Inverness.

Ullapool is an ideal base for hiking throughout Sutherland and taking wildlife and nature cruises, especially to the

Summer Isles. By the shores of salty Loch Broom, the town was founded in 1788 as a fishing station to exploit the local herring stocks. There's still a smattering of fishing vessels, as well as visiting yachts and foreign ships. When their crews fill the pubs, Ullapool has a surprisingly cosmopolitan feel. The harbor area comes to life when the Lewis and Harris ferry arrives and departs.

GETTING HERE AND AROUND
A desolate but well-maintained stretch of the A835 takes you from Inverness to Ullapool, with a connection to Torridon via the A832.

ESSENTIALS
VISITOR INFORMATION VisitScotland Ullapool iCentre. ⊠ *Argyle Street* ☎ *01854/612486.*

Sights

★ Assynt and Coigach
NATURE PRESERVE | To the east and south of Lochinver, on the way to Ullapool, lies a different kind of landscape: a vast region of brooding mountains and languid lochs, where peaks punch their way out of heathered terrain and appear to constantly shift positions. Even their names have a more mysterious air than those of the *bens* (mountain peaks or hills) elsewhere: Cul Mor, Cul Beag, Stac Pollaidh, Canisp, Suilven. Some hark back to Norse rather than to Gaelic—a reminder that Vikings used to sail this northern shore. The highlight of the region is the eerily pretty Loch Assynt, peppered with tiny wooded isles, but the Coigach peninsula northwest of Ullapool is equally dramatic.

The Ceilidh Place
ARTS VENUE | Ullapool's cultural focal point is The Ceilidh Place, an excellent venue for concerts and other events all through the year (*ceilidh* is a Scottish social gathering with traditional music and dance). It started out as a small café, but over the years it has added space for local performers, an excellent bookshop specializing in Scottish writing, and a handful of comfortable rooms (as well as a basic bunkhouse) for those who want to spend the night. It's a great place for afternoon coffee or a wee dram in the evening. ⊠ *14 W. Argyle St.* ☎ *01854/612103* ⊕ *www.theceilidhplace.com.*

Corrieshalloch Gorge
BODY OF WATER | For a thrilling touch of vertigo, don't miss Corrieshalloch Gorge, 12 miles south of Ullapool, just off the A835. Draining the high moors, the Falls of Measach plunge into a 200-foot-deep, thickly wooded gorge. There's a suspension-bridge viewpoint and a heady atmosphere of romantic grandeur, like an old Scottish print come to life. A short walk leads from a parking area to the viewpoint. ⊕ *www.nts.org.uk.*

🍴 Restaurants

The Arch Inn
$ | BRITISH | On the face of it, this popular restaurant isn't doing anything particularly remarkable; its simple pub-style menu of steaks, burgers, and fish-and-chips hardly pushes the envelope. But its use of fresh, local ingredients, its pretty presentation of dishes, and its appealing waterside seating make it a favorite dining spot among locals. **Known for:** fresh and tasty pub grub; waterside seating; always busy. ⑤ *Average main: £14* ⊠ *10–11 W. Shore St.* ☎ *01854/612454* ⊕ *www.thearchinn.co.uk.*

★ The West Coast Delicatessen
$ | CAFÉ | This charming family-run deli serves delicious housemade sandwiches, pies, soups, salads, and hummus to a long line of locals and tourists. It also has great cakes and baked goods. **Known for:** great housemade soups; excellent coffee; an array of artisanal products. ⑤ *Average main: £8* ⊠ *5 Argyle St.* ☎ *01854/613450* ⊕ *www.westcoastdeli.co.uk* ⊙ *Closed Sun. No dinner.*

Hotels

Tanglewood House

$ | **B&B/INN** | Sitting on a headland above a rocky beach, with spectacular views across Loch Broom toward Ullapool, one of Scotland's most unique and appealing B&Bs feels wonderfully remote while only being a short drive (or even a walk) into town. **Pros:** truly unique property; beautiful setting; fast and reliable Wi-Fi. **Cons:** steep drive down to the house; some fusty decor; a little remote. ⑤ *Rooms from: £99* ⊠ *Off A835* ☎ *01854/612059* ⊕ *www.tangle-woodhouse.co.uk* ⟿ *3 rooms* ⋈ *Free breakfast.*

★ Westlea House

$ | **B&B/INN** | This quaint, quirky boutique B&B is one of Ullapool's undoubted gems, with bedrooms themed around different natural features and cozy common rooms stuffed with comfy armchairs, colorful cushions, and off-the-wall artworks. **Pros:** wonderfully whimsical decor; superfriendly owners; great location. **Cons:** TVs are small; sea views limited, some low ceilings. ⑤ *Rooms from: £85* ⊠ *2 Market St.* ☎ *01854/612594* ⊕ *www.westlea-ullapool.co.uk* ⟿ *5 rooms.*

Kylesku

10 miles southeast of Scourie.

This tiny settlement once served as a ferry crossing, before being usurped by the (incredibly photogenic) Kylesku Bridge. Today it's a lovely stop for lunch, a boat trip along Loch Glendhu and Loch Glencoul, or even an overnight stay.

GETTING HERE AND AROUND

From Scourie head south on the A894.

 Sights

★ Drumbeg Loop

SCENIC DRIVE | Bold souls journeying from Kylesku to Lochinver may enjoy taking the interesting single-track B869 Drumbeg Loop. It has several challenging hairpin turns along with breathtaking views. Head 2 miles south of Kylesku on the A894 and hang a right when you see the brown sign to "An Druim Beag." Although it's only 20 miles to Lochinver, it will take around an hour without stops—but plan on longer, because you'll definitely want to stop. Just before the scattered community of Stoer, a road leads west to **Stoer Point Lighthouse.** If you're an energetic walker, you can hike across the short turf and heather along the cliff top for fine views west toward Lewis and Harris. There's also a red-sandstone sea stack: the **Old Man of Stoer** (not to be confused with the Old Man of Storr on Skye). This makes a pleasant excursion on a long summer evening.

Eas a' Chual Aluinn Waterfall

BODY OF WATER | With a drop of 685 feet, this is the longest waterfall in the United Kingdom. A rugged hike leads to the falls, which are at the head of Loch Glencoul. Start from the car park off the A894, on the bend of the road 4 miles south of Kylesku, just before you reach Loch na Gainmhich. Alternatively, between April and September, cruises from Kylesku Old Ferry Pier offer a less-taxing alternative (£30). ⊠ *Off A894, Lochinver.*

 Hotels

Kylesku Hotel

$$ | **HOTEL** | This charming hotel, looking out over Loch Glendhu and toward Eas Coul Aulin (Scotland's highest waterfall), has great service, excellent food, and a warm, relaxed atmosphere. **Pros:** stunning views; great staff; delicious food. **Cons:** some old-building quirks; two tiny (but cheap) attic rooms; 20-minute drive from Scourie. ⑤ *Rooms from: £130*

⊠ *Off A894* ✛ *10 miles south of Scourie*
☎ *01971/502231* ⊕ *www.kyleskuhotel.
co.uk* ⇆ *11 rooms* ⦿ *Breakfast.*

Scourie

27 miles southwest of Durness.

Scourie is a small coastal settlement
catering to visitors—particularly fisher-
folk—with a good range of accommodations. The bayside town makes a good
base for a trip to the bird sanctuary on
Handa Island.

GETTING HERE AND AROUND
From Durness head south on the A838,
turning onto the A894.

◉ Sights

★ Handa Island
ISLAND | Just off the coast of Scourie
is Handa Island, a bird sanctuary that
shelters huge seabird colonies, especially
impressive at nesting time. You can gaze
at more than 200,000 birds nesting on
dramatic cliffs here, including guillemots,
razorbills, great skuas, kittiwakes, and, of
course, crowd-pleasingly colorful puffins.
Sturdy boots, a waterproof jacket, and a
degree of fitness are needed to walk the
path around the island. This remarkable
reserve, administered by the Scottish
Wildlife Trust, is open only in spring and
summer, and can be reached by a small
open boat from Tarbert; contact the
Assynt Visitor Centre in Lochinver for
details. ■**TIP**→ **Note that ferries don't run
on Sunday.** ⊕ *scottishwildlifetrust.org.uk*
⊙ *Closed Oct.–Mar.*

⦿ Restaurants

★ Shorehouse Restaurant
$$ | **SEAFOOD** | If you're feeling peckish
after a trip to Handa Island, make a stop
at this exceptional seafood restaurant
overlooking Tarbet Harbor. It serves

freshly caught seafood specialties, from
hand-dived scallops and hot smoked
mackerel to whole lobsters, in a quaint,
maritime-themed setting. **Known for:**
spectacular seafood; gorgeous views;
friendly and attentive service. ⓢ *Average main: £17* ⊠ *Tigh Na Mara, Tarbet*
☎ *01971/502251* ⊙ *Closed Sun. and
Oct.–Easter.*

⦿ Hotels

★ Eddrachilles Hotel
$$ | **B&B/INN** | With one of the most spec-
tacular vistas of any hotel in Scotland—
out toward the picturesque islands of
Badcall Bay—Eddrachilles sits on a huge
plot of private moorland just south of the
Handa Island bird sanctuary. **Pros:** attractive garden; stunning shoreline nearby;
close to bird sanctuary. **Cons:** needs a lick
of paint; Wi-Fi limited to public areas; set
menus only. ⓢ *Rooms from: £145* ⊠ *Off
A894* ☎ *01971/502080* ⊕ *www.eddrachil-
les.com* ⊙ *Closed Nov.–mid-Mar.* ⇆ *10
rooms* ⦿ *Free breakfast.*

Durness

70 miles west of Thurso.

The sudden patches of green surrounding the village of Durness, on the north
coast, are caused by the richer limestone
outcrops among the acid moorlands. The
town is the jumping-off point for several
natural highlights, from a beautiful sandy
beach to the country's highest cliff.

GETTING HERE AND AROUND
From Tongue simply head west along the
A838.

◉ Sights

Balnakeil Craft Village
CRAFTS | Artisans sell pottery, leather,
weavings, paintings, and more from their
studios at Balnakeil Craft Village. It is a

charmingly odd place consisting of rows of shabby former military buildings located on an unnamed road running northwest from Durness and framed by dramatic views of Balnakeil Bay. The village is open during the summer, with most shops open daily from 10 to 5. ☒ Balnakeil ☎ 01971/511713 Nicola Poole's Wee Gallery ⊕ www.balnakeilcraftvillage.weebly.com ⊘ Closed Nov.–Mar.

Cape Wrath

VIEWPOINT | If you've made it this far north, you'll probably want to go all the way to Cape Wrath, a rugged headland at the northwest tip of Scotland. The white-sand beaches, impressive dunes covered in marram grass, and crashing seas of nearby Balnakeil Bay make it an exhilarating place to visit. As this land is owned by the Ministry of Defence (it is listed as an area for air force training), you can't drive your own vehicle. From May through September, a small boat ferries people here from Keoldale, 2 miles outside Durness. En route look out for Clo Mor; at 920 feet, they're the highest sea cliffs in mainland Britain. Once you're across the sea inlet, a minibus will take you to the lighthouse. Call ahead or check departure times on the board at the jetty. ☎ 01971/511284 ⊕ www.visitcapewrath.com 🎫 £20.50 boat/bus return ⊘ No boat mid-Oct.–mid-Apr.

★ Sandwood Bay

BEACH—SIGHT | The very definition of *off the beaten path*, Sandwood Bay is one of Scotland's most spectacular—and most isolated—beaches. The only way to reach it is to walk 4 miles each way across sheep fields and sand dunes. It's a lovely, fairly easy walk, which may just end with you having a long, sandy beach, with its dramatic sea stack Am Buachaille, all to yourself. To get here turn off the A838 onto the B801 at Rhiconich (14 miles southwest of Durness), then turn off at Kinlochbervie to Balchrick. Just before you reach the latter, look for a tiny white sign to "Sandwood," then follow this single-track lane to its end, where you can park and start walking. **Amenities:** parking (no fee). **Best for:** solitude; walking. ☒ Durness.

★ Sculpture Croft

ART GALLERIES | This odd garden of delights provokes a double-take from most drivers traveling along the A838, thanks to its incongruous ceramic-topped gates. Park opposite and take a stroll down into Danish artist Lotte Glob's pottery wonderland, where ceramic and metal sculptures are scattered across the gardens. Several paths lead down to the coast, and there are hundreds of pieces en route, including a library of ceramic books. Her work reflects and adds to the landscape, using natural shapes and forms and building patterns into the rocks themselves. End your visit with a trip to the studio and pottery shop. ☒ 105 Laid ☎ 01971/511727 ⊕ www.lotteglob.co.uk ⊘ Only open by appointment Oct.–mid-May.

★ Smoo Cave

CAVE | This atmospheric cavern, hollowed out of the limestone by rushing water, feels like something out of a fantasy novel. The combined sea-and-freshwater cave, complete with gushing waterfall, can be reached via a steep cliff stairway from the Smoo Cave car park. But don't start your descent before reading the explanatory boards at the top of the stairs, which tell the history of those who lived and used the caves in much earlier times. ☒ Off A838 🎫 Free.

🍴 Restaurants

Cocoa Mountain

$ | **CAFÉ** | A must for those with a sweet tooth, this "chocolate bar" within the Balnakeil Craft Village serves world-class truffles and stunningly rich hot chocolate made in its specialist "chocolate factory," which sources the beans from around the world. There are also sandwiches, cakes, and coffee available. **Known for:** sublime chocolate truffles; housemade hot chocolate; friendly service. ⑤ *Average main: £12* ✉ *Balnakeil Craft Village, Balnakeil* ☎ *01971/511233* ⊕ *www. cocoamountain.co.uk.*

Hotels

The Tongue Hotel

$ | HOTEL | With open fireplaces, tartan rugs, and floral wallpaper, this traditional Highland hotel is a great base for exploring the northern coast of the Scottish mainland. **Pros:** warm and friendly staff; beautiful location with stunning views; deliciously creamy porridge at breakfast. **Cons:** Wi-Fi only in public areas; TV sets from the '80s; food is hit and miss. ⑤ *Rooms from: £115* ✉ *Tongue* ☎ *01847/611206* ⊕ *www.tonguehotel. co.uk* ⇨ *19 rooms* ⦿ *Free breakfast.*

John O'Groats

15 miles north of Wick.

The windswept little outpost of John O'Groats is usually taken to be the northernmost point on the Scottish mainland, though that is not strictly true, as a short drive to Dunnet Head will reveal. From the harbor you can take a boat to see the dolphins and seals that live beneath the coastal cliffs—or head farther afield with a ferry to Orkney. The little town has charms of its own, including a row of colorful wooden houses (part of the Inn at John O' Groats) and a crafts center with high-quality shops selling knitwear, candles, and gifts.

GETTING HERE AND AROUND

Traveling north from Wick, take the A99. From the east, take the coast-hugging A836.

TOURS

John O'Groats Ferries

TOUR—SIGHT | Sailing from John O'Groats Harbor, this company offers 90-minute wildlife cruises past spectacular cliff scenery and birdlife into the Pentland Firth, to Duncansby Stacks, and to the island of Stroma. Trips cost £19 and are available daily at 2:30 between mid-June and August. The company also offers a Maxi Day tour of Orkney between May and September. It leaves at 8:45 am and costs £68. ✉ *Ferry Office, County Road, John O'Groats* ☎ *01955/611353* ⊕ *www. jogferry.co.uk* ⛴ *Tours from £19.*

Sights

Duncansby Head

VIEWPOINT | Head to this lighthouse for spectacular views of cliffs and sea stacks, as well as seabirds like guillemots and (if you're lucky) puffins. It's on the coastal road east of town. There are a few parking spaces there, or you can walk (about 30 minutes) from the main road. ✉ *John O'Groats* ⊕ *www.nlb.org. uk/lighthouses/duncansby-head* ⛴ *Free.*

Hotels

★ John O'Groats by Together Travel

$$$ | RENTAL | A local landmark in their own right, the brightly colored lodges here are the region's best self-catering accommodations—not to mention the most photogenic—and they provide stunning views out to sea (on a clear day, all the way to Orkney). **Pros:** very comfy beds; good Wi-Fi (a rarity here); natural light all day long. **Cons:** can feel understaffed; two nights minimum in high season; a little expensive. ⑤ *Rooms from: £210* ✉ *John O'Groats* ✛ *West of ferry terminal* ☎ *01625/416430* ⊕ *www. togethertravel.co.uk/destinations/scotland/john-ogroats* ⇨ *23 lodges* ⦿ *No meals.*

Dornoch

33 miles northeast of Dingwall.

A town of sandstone houses, tiny rose-filled gardens, and a 13th-century cathedral with stunning traditional and modern stained-glass windows, Dornoch is well worth a visit. It's noted for golf (you may hear it referred to as the "St. Andrews of the North"), but because of the town's location so far north, the golf courses here are delightfully uncrowded. Royal Dornoch is the jewel in its crown, praised by the world's top golfers.

GETTING HERE AND AROUND
From Dingwall or Inverness, take the A9 north to Dornoch. Note that this stretch of the road can get busy with ferry traffic.

ESSENTIALS
VISITOR INFORMATION Dornoch Visitors Centre. ☒ *The Carnegie Courthouse, Castle St.* ☎ *01862/810594* ⊕ *www.visitdornoch.com.*

Sights

Dunrobin Castle
CASTLE/PALACE | FAMILY | Situated 12 miles north of Dornoch, flamboyant Dunrobin Castle is an ancient seat that became the home of the dukes of Sutherland, at which point it was transformed into the 19th-century white-turreted behemoth you see today. As well as its grand palatial facade and lavish interiors, the property also has summer falconry demonstrations and Versailles-inspired gardens. The first duke, who was fascinated by trains, built his own railroad in the park and staffed it with his servants. Yet for all this frivolity, the duke has a controversial legacy; he was responsible for the Sutherland Clearances of 1810 to 1820, when people were forcibly removed from their farms to make room for sheep to graze. ☒ *Off A9, Golspie* ☎ *01408/633177* ⊕ *www.dunrobincastle.co.uk* ☒ *£12* ☉ *Closed Nov.–Mar.*

★ Glenmorangie Distillery
WINERY/DISTILLERY | The light color and delicate floral taste of the Speyside whiskies is exemplified in Glenmorangie, one of the best known of the Highland whiskies. The picturesque distillery in Tain, 8 miles south of Dornoch, offers fascinating tours that reveal how the taste is achieved (the secret's in the exceedingly tall stills). The Original Tour includes a dram, and the Signet Tour (£35) offers a chance to sample the rare, chocolatey Glenmorangie Signet in a unique audio tasting experience. ☒ *Off A9, Tain* ☎ *01862/892477* ⊕ *www.glenmorangie.com* ☒ *Tours from £8.*

Restaurants

★ Mac and Wild at Falls of Shin
$ | BRITISH | This upmarket café-restaurant, located 19 miles west of Dornoch in a modish wood-and-glass (and subtly salmon-shaped) building, serves deliciously meaty dishes, often using venison from deer hunted at the co-owner's nearby estate. It's also a two-minute stroll from the Falls of Shin, one of the Highlands' best spots to see wild salmon leaping upstream in the summer. **Known for:** fresh local produce; award-winning burgers; venison roast dinners. ⑤ *Average main: £13* ☒ *Achany Glen* ☎ *01549/402888* ⊕ *www.macandwild.com.*

Sutherland House
$ | BRITISH | Just off Dornoch's main square, Sutherland House restaurant has a feeling of intimacy in its two separate rooms, reinforced by the enthusiastic reception and delicious food. The menu is imaginative, with some unusual combinations dreamed up by the chef. **Known for:** imaginative seafood; chicken in Glenmorangie sauce; friendly service. ⑤ *Average main: £14* ☒ *Argyle St.* ☎ *01862/811023* ⊕ *www.sutherland-house.net.*

Hotels

★ Glenmorangie House

$$$$ | RESORT | Situated 10 miles southeast from the distillery, Glenmorangie House offers luxurious but casual stays in a spectacular 17th-century country home. **Pros:** wonderfully rural location; superb service; extensive whisky collection. **Cons:** puny showers take a while to heat up; need a car to get here; extremely expensive. $ *Rooms from: £405* ⊠ *Fearn by Tain, Tain* ☏ *01862/871671* ⊕ *www. theglenmorangiehouse.com* 🛏 *9 rooms* ❏ *Some meals.*

Shopping

Jail Dornoch

CLOTHING | It's rare for people to voluntarily walk into jail, but this place is the exception, as an old prison has been converted in a popular fashion store. The one-time cells are now home to a range of elegant clothes and accessories, toiletries, housewares, and interesting gifts. It's so popular that there's now a second outlet at Inverness Airport. ⊠ *Castle Street* ☏ *01862/810555* ⊕ *www. jail-dornoch.com.*

Activities

★ Royal Dornoch Golf Club

GOLF | The legendary Championship Course, laid out by Tom Morris in 1886, challenges even the very best golfers with its fast, raised greens. It also inspires them with views of white sandy beaches and tall mountains carpeted in wild yellow gorse each spring. The Struie Course provides even more sea views and demanding golf for players of every level. ⊠ *Golf Road* ☏ *01862/810219* ⊕ *www.royaldornoch.com* ⛳ *Championship: £180; Struie: £50* 🏌 *Championship: 18 holes, 6748 yards, par 70; Struie: 18 holes, 6265 yards, par 71* ⛳ *Reservations essential.*

Index

A

Abbey Road, 154
Abbotsford House, 631
Aberconwy House, 521
Aberdeen, 684–695
Aberdeen Art Gallery, 691
Aberdeen Maritime Museum, 691
Aberfoyle, 659–661
Abergavenny (Y Fenni), 485–488
Abergavenny Castle and Museum, 485
Abergavenny Food Festival, 474
Aberlour, 708–709
Aberystwyth, 504–507
Aberystwyth Castle, 505
Aberystwyth Cliff Railway, 505
Afternoon tea, 126
Air travel, 44–47, 67
Aberdeen and the Northeast, 688
Argyll and the Isles, 718
Bath, the Cotswolds, and Stratford-upon-Avon, 302–303
Borders and the Southwest, 624
Cambridge and East Anglia, 413
Canterbury and the Southeast, 190
Central Highlands, Fife, and Angus, 651
Cornwall and the West Country, 266
Edinburgh, 530–531
Glasgow, 578–579
Inverness, Skye, and the Northern Highlands, 744–745
Lake District, 388
London, 73
Manchester, Liverpool, and the Peak District, 350
Wales, 474–475
Yorkshire and the Northeast, 440
Aira Force, 404
Alain Ducasse at the Dorchester ✕, 92
Albert Dock, 364
Albert Hall (dance club), 361–362
Aldeburgh, 433–434
Aldeburgh Beach Lookout, 433
Aldeburgh Festival, 413
Aldeburgh Fish and Chip Shop ✕, 433
Aldeburgh Museum, 433
Alexander Keiller Museum, 247–248
Alford, 702
All Saints Church, 204
All the Goodness ✕, 767
Allan Bank, 397
Allium ✕, 244
Alloway, 616–618
Alnwick, 466–467
Alnwick Castle, 466–467
Alnwick Garden, 467
Amberley Castle 🏨, 223
Ambleside, 395–396
American Bar, 86–87

Andrew Fairlie at Gleneagles ✕, 668
Angel Hotel 🏨, 487
Anglesey (Ynys Môn), 519–520
Angus, 646–682
Angus Glens, 681
Anne of Cleves House, 213
Anne Hathaway's Cottage, 334
Anokaa ✕, 244
Another Place (statue), 364
Anstruther, 674–675
Anstruther Fish Bar and Restaurant ✕, 675
Apartment and house rentals, 53
Appin, 723–724
Apple Market, 98
Arden Hotel 🏨, 339
Ardkinglas Woodland Garden, 726
Arisaig, 764
Arisaig House 🏨, 764
Arisaig Marine, 764
Argyll and the Isles, 714–738
Arlington Row, 320
Armadale, 768–769
Armadale Castle, Gardens & Museum, 768
Armitt Museum, 395
Aros, 769
Arran, 727–730
Arthur's Seat, 535
Artist Residence 🏨, 85
Arundel, 222–223
Arundel Castle, 223
Ascot, 170
Ascot Racecourse, 170
Ashmolean Museum, 175
Assynt and Coigach, 776
Athelhampton House and Gardens, 255
Auchindrain Museum, 726
Auchrannie Resort 🏨, 728
Auchterarder, 668–669
Audley End House and Gardens, 416
Aurora ✕, 566
Austen, Jane, 237, 238, 302, 309
Avebury, 247–249
Avebury Stone Circles, 248
Aviemore, 754–757
Aylesbury, 182–183
Ayr, 616–618
Ayrshire, 615–618

B

Babbity Bowster ✕, 596
Baddesley Clinton, 341
Bakchich ✕, 368
Bakewell, 374–376
Bala Lake Railway, 512
Ballater, 699–701
Ballindalloch Castle, 708
Balmoral, The 🏨, 555
Balmoral Castle, 700
Balnakeil Craft Village, 778–779
Balquhidder Glen, 656–657

Balvenie Distillery, 705
Bamburgh, 468
Bamburgh Castle, 468
Banchory, 698–699
Banchory Lodge 🏨, 699
Bancone ✕, 102–103
Banff, 710–711
Bank Ground Farm 🏨, 401
Barbara Hepworth Museum and Sculpture Garden, 281
Barbican Centre, 122
Barras (market), 611
Barrie, J.M., 681–682
Bars
Aberdeen and the Northeast, 694–695
Bath, the Cotswolds, and Stratford-upon-Avon, 312–313
Canterbury and the Southeast, 196–197, 221
Central Highlands, Fife, and Angus, 679
Edinburgh, 546–547, 556–557
Glasgow, 598, 603–604
London, 86–87, 94–95, 106, 115, 127, 136, 147
Manchester, Liverpool, and the Peak District, 360–361, 370
Oxford and the Thames Valley, 179
Wales, 507
Bath, 237, 298–313
Bath Abbey, 305, 308
Bath Festival, 302
Bath Skyline Walk, 308
Battersea Arts Centre, 136
Battle Abbey, 211
Battle of Bannockburn Visitor Centre, 654
Baxters Highland Village, 709
Beach House ✕, 495
Beaches
Cornwall and the West Country, 282, 284
Edinburgh, 570
Inverness, Skye, and the Northern Highlands, 779
South, 257–258
Southeast, 217
Wales, 493–494, 498, 506, 514
Beamish, the Living Museum of the North, 457
Beaney House of Art & Knowledge, The, 192
Beatles, The, 154, 363, 364
Beatles' Childhood Homes, 364
Beatles Story, 364
Beatrix Potter Exhibition and Garden, 666
Beatrix Potter Gallery, 402
Beaulieu, 253
Beaulieu Abbey, 253
Beaumaris Castle, 520
Bed and breakfasts, 53
Bell Pettigrew Museum of Natural History, 670
Ben A'an, 661
Ben Nevis, 761
Benjamin Pollock's Toyshop, 109
Benromach Distillery, 754
Berkeley, The 🏨, 145

Berry Bros. & Rudd (shop), *88*
Betty's Cafe Tea Rooms ✕, *451*
Betws-y-Coed, *516–518*
Bibury, *326–327*
Bicycling, *56, 67*
Cambridge and East Anglia, *425*
Central Highlands, Fife, and Angus, *653*
Edinburgh, *534*
Glasgow, *579*
Lake District, *394, 403, 407–408*
London, *73*
South, *253*
Wales, *490, 491, 503*
Yorkshire and the Northeast, *461, 463*
Big Ben, *82*
Big Pit National Coal Museum, *486*
Birdoswald Roman Fort, *464*
Bishop's Palace, *271–272*
Blackfriar, The (pub), *121*
Blackwell, *392–393*
Blaenavon Ironworks, *486*
Blair Atholl, *668*
Blair Castle, *668*
Blenheim Palace, *181–182*
Blind Pit, The (bar), *106*
Bloody Tower, *117, 120*
Bloomsbury (London), *109–116*
Blue Dolphin Fish Bar ✕, *212*
Blue Mountain School (shop),
 127–128
Bluecoat (theater), *371*
Boath House 🍽, *752*
Boating and boat travel, *47–48, 56, 67*
Aberdeen and the Northeast, *688*
Argyll and the Isles, *718, 719–720, 737*
Borders and the Southwest, *624*
Cambridge and East Anglia, *431*
Central Highlands, Fife, and Angus, *663,
 674–675*
Edinburgh, *570*
Inverness, Skye, and the Northern High-
 lands, *745, 752, 758, 768, 780*
Lake District, *388, 401, 404, 406, 408*
London, *76*
Oxford and the Thames Valley, *167, 180*
Wales, *475, 510*
Bodiam Castle, *207–208*
**Bodleian Library and Radcliffe
 Camera**, *175*
Bodnant Garden, *521*
Bodnant Welsh Food Centre ✕,
 521–522
Bodysgallen Hall 🍽, *523*
Bonawe Iron Furnace, *725*
Books for Cooks (shop), *147–148*
Borders and the Southwest, *620–644*
Borough Market, *129, 132*
Borrowdale, *408*
Borrowdale Fells, *408*
Botanic Gardens (Glasgow), *599*
Bourton-on-the-Water, *323–324*
Bovey Castle 🍽, *292*
Bowhill, *633*
Bowmore, *730–731*
Bowmore Distillery, *731*
Bowness-on-Windermere, *392–394*

Braemar, *701–702*
Braemar Castle, *701*
Braemar Highland Gathering, *701*
Brantwood, *400*
Bread Meats Bread ✕, *559, 562*
Brecknock Museum & Art Gallery,
 488
Brecon (Aberhonddu), *488–491*
Brecon Beacons National Park,
 488–489
Brecon Cathedral, *489*
Brewery Arts Centre, *392*
Bridge Cottage (Dedham), *430*
Bridge House (Ambleside), *395*
Bridge of Sighs, *378*
Brighton, *216–221*
Brighton Beach, *217*
Brighton Fringe, *189*
Brighton Museum and Art Gallery,
 217
Brighton Pier, *217*
Brightonwave 🍽, *220*
Bristol, *268–271*
Britannia, *566*
British Film Institute Mediatheque,
 353
British Golf Museum, *670*
British Library, *109*
British Museum, *109–110*
Brixham, *295*
Broadford, *767–768*
Broadway, *318–319*
Broadway Market, *128*
Brockhole, *393*
Brodick, *727–729*
Brodick Castle and Country Park, *728*
Brodie Castle, *754*
Brontë Parsonage Museum, *455*
Brontë Waterfall, *455*
Broughton House, *642*
Bryn Celli Ddu, *520*
Buckingham Palace, *79*
Buckland-in-the-Moor, *289*
Bunnahabhain Distillery, *733*
Burford, *325–326*
Burns, Robert, *615–618, 636, 638*
Burns Cottage, *617*
Burns Monument, *617*
Bus tours, *76, 165, 174–175, 331, 334,
 533, 582, 720, 746*
Bus travel, *48–49, 66, 67*
Aberdeen and the Northeast, *688*
Argyll and the Isles, *718*
Bath, the Cotswolds, and Stratford-up-
 on-Avon, *303*
Borders and the Southwest, *624–625*
Cambridge and East Anglia, *414*
Canterbury and the Southeast, *190*
Central Highlands, Fife, and Angus, *651*
Cornwall and the West Country, *266*
Edinburgh, *531*
Glasgow, *579–580*
Inverness, Skye, and the Northern
 Highlands, *745*
Lake District, *388*
London, *73–74*

Manchester, Liverpool, and the Peak
 District, *350*
Oxford and the Thames Valley, *163–164*
Stonehenge and the South, *232*
Wales, *475*
Yorkshire and the Northeast, *440*
Butley Orford Oysterage ✕, *432*
Buxton, *372–374*
Buxton Country Park, *373*
Buxton Museum and Art Gallery, *373*
Buxton Opera House, *373*
Bwlch y Groes, *512*

C

Cabaret, *106, 221*
Cadenhead's Whisky Shop, *548*
Caernarfon Castle, *518*
Caerphilly Castle, *477*
Café Fish ✕, *737*
Cafe 1 ✕, *748*
Cafe Otto, *127*
Café Royal Circle Bar, *556*
Cairngorms National Park, *755–756*
Cairngorms Reindeer Centre, *755*
Calcot Manor 🍽, *330*
Caldey Island, *496*
Callander, *656–657*
Calton Hill, *549*
Cambridge, *410–426*
Cambridge Folk Festival, *424*
Camera Obscura (Aberystwyth), *505*
Camera Obscura (Dumfries), *636*
Camera Obscura (Kirriemuir), *681*
**Camera Obscura and World of
 Illusions** (Edinburgh), *538*
Cannonball Restaurant ✕, *543–544*
**Canongate Tolbooth and People's
 Story Museum**, *538*
Canterbury, *186–196*
Canterbury Cathedral, *192–193*
Canterbury Cathedral Lodge 🍽, *196*
Canterbury Roman Museum, *193*
Cape Wrath, *779*
Car travel, *49–51*
Aberdeen and the Northeast, *688*
Argyll and the Isles, *718–719*
Bath, the Cotswolds, and Stratford-up-
 on-Avon, *303*
Borders and the Southwest, *625*
Cambridge and East Anglia, *414*
Canterbury and the Southeast, *190*
Central Highlands, Fife, and Angus,
 651–652
Cornwall and the West Country, *266–267*
Edinburgh, *531–532*
Glasgow, *580*
Inverness, Skye, and the Northern
 Highlands, *745*
Lake District, *388*
London, *74–75*
Manchester, Liverpool, and the Peak
 District, *350–351*
Oxford and the Thames Valley, *164*
Stonehenge and the South, *232–233*
Wales, *475*
Yorkshire and the Northeast, *441*
Cardhu Distillery, *708*

Cardiff (Caerdydd), 477–485
Cardiff Bay, 477, 480
Cardiff Castle, 480
Carnoustie Golf Links, 680–681
Carreg Cennen Castle, 489
Casbah Coffee Club, 364
Casse-Croûte ✕, 134–135
Castell Coch, 481
Castell Dinas Brân, 508
Castle Combe, 313
Castle Cottage ✕, 515
Castle Douglas, 640–641
Castle Drogo, 292
Castle Fraser, 702
Castle Howard, 452
Castle Kennedy Gardens, 644
Castle Stuart Golf Links, 751
Castlefield Urban Heritage Park, 353
Castlerigg Stone Circle, 405
Castles
Aberdeen and the Northeast, 696, 698–699, 700, 701, 702, 706, 711 712
Argyll and the Isles, 721, 725, 726, 728, 730, 735
Bath, the Cotswolds, and Stratford-up-on-Avon, 316–317, 342–344
Borders and the Southwest, 627, 629, 639, 640 641, 642, 644
Central Highlands, Fife, and Angus, 654–655, 663–664, 668, 670, 682
Edinburgh, 539, 618
Inverness, Skye, and the Northern Highlands, 747, 752, 754, 760, 766–767, 768, 772, 781
Manchester, Liverpool, and the Peak District, 381
Oxford and the Thames Valley, 166
Southeast, 197, 198, 203, 206–208, 211–212, 214, 223
Stonehenge and the South, 234–235, 253 254, 255, 257
Wales, 477, 480–481, 485, 486–487, 489, 492, 496–497, 503, 505, 508, 509, 513 514, 518, 520, 521
West Country, 274–275, 278–279, 285, 292
Yorkshire and the Northeast, 452, 458, 466–467, 460
Catching Lives Charity Bookshop, 197
Cathedral Close (Salisbury), 242
Cathedral of St. Peter, 293
Caves, 278, 373, 489–490, 514, 779
Cawdor Castle and Gardens, 752
Ceilidh Place, 776
Ceilidhs, 565, 776
Celtic Connections, 577
Central Highlands, 646–682
Central Library (Manchester), 353
Central Station (Glasgow), 584
Ceredigion Museum, 505
Chagford, 289, 291–292
Channel Tunnel, 68
Chaophraya ✕, 585, 588
Chapel of the Order of the Thistle, 541
Chapter Arts Centre, 484
Charlecote Park, 334

Charles Dickens Museum, 110
Charleston, 213–214
Charlotte Street Hotel 🖭, 114
Chartwell, 203
Chastleton House, 322
Chatsworth House, 374–375
Chaucer Head Bookshop, 340
Chavenage, 329
Chawton, 236–238
Chawton House Library, 237–238
Chedworth Roman Villa, 326
Chelsea (London), 138–149
Cheltenham, 315–318
Chesil Beach, 257–258
Chester, 376–378
Chester Cathedral, 376–377
Chester Grosvenor Hotel 🖭, 378
Chester Residence, The 🖭, 562–563
Chester Rows, 377
Chesters Roman Fort, 462
Chichester, 223–226
Chichester Cathedral, 224–225
Chipping Campden, 319–321
Chirk Castle, 509
Christ Church, 175
Christ Church Picture Gallery, 177
Christ Church, Spitalfields, 122–123
Christchurch Gate, 193, 195
Christ's College, 416–417
Church of King Charles the Martyr, 200–201
Church of St. Mary, 208
Church of St. Mary Redcliffe, 268
Church of St. Peter and St. Paul, 429
Church Street Hotel 🖭, 135
Churchill Arms ✕, 320 321
Churchill War Rooms, 79
Circus (Bath), 308
Cirencester, 327–328
CitizenM Glasgow 🖭, 590
City, The (London), 116–122
City Centre (Glasgow), 584–594
City Chambers (Glasgow), 584, 595
City Cruises (London), 76
City of York Walls, 443
City Sightseeing (Stratford-upon-Avon), 331, 334
City walls (Canterbury), 195
City walls (Chester), 377–378
City walls (York), 443
Claridge's 🖭, 94
Clarks on Lindsay Street (bar), 679
Clava Cairns, 751
Clifton Suspension Bridge, 268–269
Climbing, 757, 765
Clink, The ✕, 483
Clipstone ✕, 111
Clive of India Museum, 503
Cliveden, 170–171
Cliveden House 🖭, 171
Clovelly, 276
Clovelly Visitor Centre, 2765
Clyde Coast, 615–618

Coach House Coffee Shop ✕, 662
Coast ✕, 497
Cobb, The, 259
Coigach and Assynt, 776
Coleridge Way, 275
Collegiate Church of St. Mary, 342
Columbia Road Flower Market, 128
Comedy clubs, 106, 557
Comedy Store, The, 106
Coniston, 400–402
Coniston Boating Centre, 401
Coniston Water, 401
Connaught, The 🖭, 94
Constitution Hill, 505
Contacts, 67–68
Conwy, 520–522
Conwy Castle, 521
Cookie Jar, The 🖭, 467
Corbridge Roman Town, 462
Corfe Castle, 253–254
Corinium Museum, 327
Corinthia, The 🖭, 86
Corner House, The ✕, 195
Cornerways 🖭, 282
Cornwall, 262 267, 277–286
Corrieshalloch Gorge, 776
Cotehele House and Quay, 290
Cotswold Motoring Museum and Toy Collection, 323
Cotswolds, 298–304
Cottage rentals, 53
Courtauld Gallery, 99
Covent Garden (London), 98–109
Covent Garden Hotel 🖭, 105
Covent Garden Piazza, 98
Covered Market, 180
COVID-19, 57
Coworth Park 🖭, 170
Crabshakk ✕, 608
Craignure, 734–736
Crail, 673–674
Crail Museum and Heritage Centre, 673
Cranachan & Crowdie (shop), 548
Crannog Seafood Restaurant ✕, 762
Craft in the Bay (shop), 485
Craigellachie, 706–707
Crarae Garden, 726
Crathes Castle, 698–699
Crawick Multiverse, 639
Criccieth Castle, 513
Crolinnhe 🖭, 762
Cross at Kingussie, The ✕, 758
Crown and Castle 🖭, 432
Crown Jewels, 117, 120
Cruachan, 725
Cruickshank Botanic Garden, 691
Cruises, 48, 167, 353, 758
Cuillin Mountains, 772–773, 775
Cuisine, 24–27
Culinary tours, 77
Cullen, 710
Culloden Battlefield, 751–752
Culloden Moor, 751–752

Culross, 571
Culross Palace, 571
Culzean Castle and Country Park, 618
Customs and duties, 56
Cutty Sark, 155

D

D-Day Story, The, 239
Dakota Deluxe Glasgow ⌘, 590
Dallas Dhu Historic Distillery, 754
Dalmeny House, 569
Dance, 107, 115–116
Dance clubs, 127, 361, 547, 557, 592, 598
Dartmoor National Park, 288–289
Dartmouth, 295–296
Deaf Institute, The (music club), 362
Deal, 197–198
Deal Castle, 197
Dean Village (Edinburgh), 559
Dedham, 430–431
Delaunay, The ✕, 111
Dennis Severs' House, 123
Depot at Mayfield (dance club), 361
Derwent Pencil Museum, 405
Derwentwater, 406
Destitution Road (Gairloch), 775
Devon Guild of Craftsmen, 292
Dickens House Museum, 197–198
DIG, 445
Dining, 53–55
price categories, 78, 164, 191, 233, 267, 304, 352, 390, 415, 442, 476, 533, 582, 626, 653, 689, 719, 746
Dinner by Heston Blumenthal ✕, 143
Dinosaurland Fossil Museum, 259
Discounts and deals, 49, 68, 351, 476
Dolgellau, 508
Dorchester, 254–256
Dorchester, The ⌘, 94
Dornoch, 781–782
Dorset Square Hotel ⌘, 94
Dove Cottage and Wordsworth Museum, 397–398
Dover, 198–200
Dover Castle, 198
Downing Street (London), 79, 82
Drakes ⌘, 220
Draycott, The ⌘, 145
Drum Castle, 699
Drumbeg Loop, 777
Drumlanrig Castle, 639
Drumnadrochit, 758–760
Drunken Duck Inn ⌘, 403
Dryburgh Abbey, 631
Duart Castle, 735
Duff House, 711
Dufftown, 705–706
Duke House ⌘, 423
Dumfries and environs, 635–638
Dumfries Museum and Camera Obscura, 636
Duncansby Head, 780
Dundee, 676–681

Dundee Botanic Garden, 677
Dundee Contemporary Arts, 677
Dundee Repertory Theatre, 679–680
Dunkeld, 665–666
Dunnottar Castle, 696
Dunrobin Castle, 781
Dunstaffnage Castle, 721
Dunstane Houses ⌘, 558–559
Dunster, 274–275
Dunster Castle, 274–275
Dunvegan Castle and Gardens, 772
Durham, 456–460
Durham Castle, 458
Durham Cathedral, 458
Durness, 778–780
Duties, 56
Dyffryn Arms, The (pub), 500
Dylan Thomas Centre, 493
Dynamic Earth, 538–539

E

Eas a' Chual Aluinn Waterfall, 777
East Anglia, 410–434
East End (Glasgow), 610–611
East London, 122–129
Eastgate Clock, 377–378
Eddrachilles Hotel ⌘, 778
Eden Project, 285–286
Edinburgh, 526–572
Edinburgh Castle, 539
Edinburgh Ceilidh Club, 565
Edinburgh Gin Distillery, 559
Edinburgh Festival Fringe, 529
Edinburgh Zoo, 559
Edinburgh's Hogmanay, 530
Ednam House Hotel ⌘, 630
Edradour Distillery, 667
Edwardian Manchester, a Radisson Collection Hotel ⌘, 359–360
Ee-usk ✕, 721, 723
Egerton House ⌘, 145–146
Egypt Centre, 493
Eilean Donan Castle 766–767
Elcho Castle, 663–664
Elizabethan Garden, 343–344
Ellon, 712
Elterwater, 399–400
Ely, 426–427
Ely Cathedral, 426
Elystan Street ✕, 144
Emmanuel College, 417
Eton, 169
Eton College, 169
Ettington Park Hotel ⌘, 339
Exeter, 292–294
Eyam Plague Village, 375

F

Fairy Glen, 770
Fairy Pools, 773
Falkland, 675–676
Falkland Palace, 676
Falmouth, 284–285

Farmhouse rentals, 53, 68
Fashion Museum and Assembly Rooms, 308
Fat Duck ✕, 168
Feathered Nest Inn ✕, 322
Felin Fach Griffin ✕, 491
Fellinis ✕, 395
Fellpack ✕, 406
Ferries, 475, 688, 718, 745, 780
Festivals and seasonal events, 59
Bath, the Cotswolds, and Stratford-up-on-Avon, 302
Borders and the Southwest, 623–624
Cambridge and East Anglia, 413, 424
Canterbury and the Southeast, 189, 212
Cornwall and the West Country, 265
Edinburgh, 529–530, 549
Glasgow, 577, 624
Manchester, Liverpool, and the Peak District, 350
Northeast, 701
Oxford and the Thames Valley, 163, 172, 173–174, 180
Stonehenge and the South, 232
Wales, 474, 491, 503
Yorkshire and the Northeast, 440
Ffestiniog Railway, 513
Fife, 646–682
Fife Arms, The ⌘, 702
Film, 353, 563
Filmhouse, 563
Finnieston, 605–610
Finnieston, The ✕, 608
Fishbourne Roman Palace, 225
Fishmore Hall ⌘, 382
Fitzwilliam Museum, 417, 420
5 Cwmdonkin Drive, 493
Flodden Wall, 539
Floors Castle, 629
Fochabers, 709
Fochabers Folk Museum & Heritage Centre, 709
Football, 137, 357, 362–363, 371–372, 534, 583, 610
Forres, 753–754
Fort George, 747
Fort William, 760–763
Forth Bridge, 569–570
Fortnum & Mason (shop), 88
Fowey, 285–286
Fox Talbot Museum, 315
Foyles (bookstore), 108
Fyvie Castle, 711–712

G

Gainsborough Bath Spa ⌘, 312
Gairloch, 775
Gallery of Modern Art, 594
Gardens
Aberdeen and the Northeast, 691, 706–707
Argyll and the Isles, 726
Bath, the Cotswolds, and Stratford-up-on-Avon, 309, 320, 328–330, 341–342, 343–344
Borders and the Southwest, 629, 632, 636, 641, 644

Cambridge and East Anglia, 416
Canterbury and the Southeast, 206–207
Central Highlands, Fife, and Angus, 666, 677
Cornwall and the West Country, 285–286
Edinburgh, 549
Glasgow, 599, 610–611, 618
Inverness, Skye, and the Northern Highland, 752, 768, 772, 775
Lake District, 390–391
London, 85, 89, 139, 151, 158
Manchester, Liverpool, and the Peak District, 350, 373
Oxford and the Thames Valley, 166, 177–178, 182–183
Stonehenge and the South, 249–251, 253, 255
Wales, 494, 521
Yorkshire and the Northeast, 450–451, 467
Gay bars, 557
Gelato Gusto ✕ , 219
George IV Bridge, 539
George Hotel, The ⬚ , 726–727
George Square (Glasgow), 594–595
Ghost tours, 443
Gidleigh Park ✕ , 292
Gilpin Hotel and Lake House ⬚ , 394
Gin, 559
Gladstone's Land, 539
Glamis, 682
Glamis Castle, 682
Glasgow, 574–618
Glasgow Cathedral, 595
Glasgow Print Studio, 598
Glasgow School of Art, 584
Glasgow Green, 610
Glasgow Science Centre, 605
Glasgow University, 599
Glasshouse, The ⬚ , 555
Glastonbury, 273–274
Glastonbury Abbey, 273–274
Glen Brittle, 772–773, 775
Glen Grant Distillery & Garden, 706–707
Glen Nevis, 762–763
Glencoe, 764–765
Glencoe Activities, 765
Glencoe House ⬚ , 765
Glencoe Visitor Centre, 765
Glendale, 772
Gleneagles (golf courses), 669
Gleneagles Hotel ⬚ , 669
Glenfarclas, 708
Glenfiddich Distillery, 705
Glenfinnan, 763
Glenfinnan Monument, 763
Glenfinnan Viaduct, 763
Glenlivet, 708
Glenmorangie Distillery, 781
Glenmorangie House ⬚ , 782
Globe Inn, 636
Gloucester Cathedral, 315–316
Glyndebourne Opera House, 215
Glynn Vivian Art Gallery, 493
Golf, 36–37
Aberdeen and the Northeast, 695, 702, 712

Argyll and the Isles, 727
Central Highlands, Fife, and Angus, 660–661, 667–668, 669, 670, 673, 680–681
Edinburgh, 534–535
Glasgow, 616, 617–618
Inverness, Skye, and the Northern Highland, 751, 753, 782
Gordon's Wine Bar, 87
Gospel Pass, 500
Gower Peninsula, 493–494
Gracefield Arts Centre, 636
Grampian Transport Museum, 702
Grand Central Hotel ⬚ , 590
Grange Inn, The ✕ , 671
Grasmere, 396–399
Grasmere Gingerbread Shop, 399
Grassmarket, 539
Gray's Restaurant ✕ , 468
Great Aberystwyth Camera Obscura, 505
Great Bath, 310
Great Hall (Winchester), 234
Groat House (Lavenham) ✕ , 429–430
Great Orme, 523
Great Orme Mines, 523
Great St. Mary's, 420
Green Park Hotel ⬚ , 667
Greenhead, 463–465
Greenway, 290
Greenwich, 155, 157
Greyfriars Kirkyard, 540
Grimspound, 289
Grosvenor Square (London), 89
Guild Chapel (Stratford upon Avon), 335
Guildhall (Exeter), 293
Gurnard's Head ✕ , 281
Gwydyr Forest and Swallow Falls, 516
Gymkhana ✕ , 93

H

Haddo House, 712
Haddon Hall, 375
Hadrian's Wall, 460–462
Hadrian's Wall environs 441–447
Hall's Croft, 335
Hamilton Toy Museum, 657
Hampden Park, 610
Hampstead (London), 149–154
Hampstead Heath, 150
Hampton Court Palace, 157
Handa Island, 778
Harbour Inn ✕ , 731
Harbourmaster Hotel ⬚ , 507
Hardy's Cottage, 255
Harestanes Countryside Visitor Centre, 626
Harlech Castle, 513–514
Harmony Garden, 632
Harrods (department store), 138
Harrogate, 450–452
Harry Potter Studio Tour, 184
Hastings, 210–213

Hastings Castle, 211
Hastings Contemporary Museum, 211
Hatchards (bookstore), 87
Hawkshead, 402–403
Haworth, 454–456
Haymarket (Edinburgh), 558–559
Hay-on-Wye (Y Gelli Gandryll), 500–503
Hazel Bank Country House ⬚ , 408
Hazlitt's ⬚ , 105
Heckfield Place ⬚ , 238
Heidi's Grasmere Lodge ⬚ , 398
Helvellyn, 404
Henley-in-Arden, 340–342
Henley-on-Thames, 172–174
Hermitage, 666
Hermitage Castle, 627
Herstmonceux Castle, 211–212
Hever, 202–204
Hever Castle, 203
Hexham, 462–463
Hexham Abbey, 462–463
Heywood Hill (bookstore), 96
Hidcote Manor Garden, 320
High Kirk of St. Giles, 540–541
High Street (Edinburgh), 541
Highclere Castle, 235
Highgate Cemetery, 150–151
Highgrove House, 329–330
Highland Folk Museum, 757
Hiking. ⇨ See Walking and hiking
Hill Top, 402–403
Hilton Grand Vacations at Craigendarroch Suites ⬚ , 700
Hispi Bistro ✕ , 358
Historic buildings, rentals of, 68
Hix Oyster & Fish House ✕ , 259
Hobsons Patisseries ✕ , 330
Hockney 1853 Gallery, 453
Holborn (London), 109–116
Holburne Museum, 308–309
Holy Trinity Church (Long Melford), 428
Holy Trinity Church (Stratford-upon-Avon), 335–336
Holyrood 9A, The (bar), 546
HOME (arts venue), 362
Honours, The ✕ , 554
Hootananny (pub), 750
Horn of Plenty, The ✕ , 290
Hopetoun House, 570
Hoppers ✕ , 103
Horse racing, 170
Horseback riding, 253, 756
Hotel du Vin (Bristol) ⬚ , 271
Hotel du Vin (Edinburgh) ⬚ , 546
Hotel du Vin (Exeter) ⬚ , 294
Hotel Endsleigh ⬚ , 290
Hotel 41 ⬚ , 86
Hotel Indigo Stratford-upon-Avon ⬚ , 339
Hotel Portmeirion ⬚ , 515
Hotels, 53, 68
price categories, 78, 164, 191, 233, 267, 304, 352, 390, 415, 442, 476, 533, 582, 626, 653, 689, 719, 746

Hours, The (shop), 491
House for an Art Lover, 611, 614
House of Agnes 🛏, 196
House of Fraser (department store), 593
House rentals, 53
Houses of Parliament, 82–83
Housesteads Roman Fort, 464–465
Howe Keld 🛏, 406–407
Hoxton Shoreditch, The 🛏, 126–127
Hunterian Museum, 600
Hyde Park, 138–139

I

Ightham Mote, 204–205
Imperial War Museum Duxford, 420
Inchcolm Island, 570
Inchmahome, 659–660
Innerleithen, 634–635
International Musical Eisteddfod, 474
International Slavery Museum, 365
Inveraray, 725–727
Inveraray Castle, 726
Inverewe Garden, 775
Inverness, 740–751
Inverness Castle, 747
Iona, 734, 737–738
Iona Abbey, 738
Ironbridge Gorge, 379–380
Ironbridge Gorge Museum, 379–380
Irvine, 615–616
Islay, 730–734
Islay Woollen Museum, 731
Isle of Arran Distillery, 729–730
Isle of Arran Heritage Museum, 728
Isle of Eriska 🛏, 724
Isle of Gigha, 727
Isle of Jura Distillery, 734
Isle of Mull, 734–738
Isle of Skye, 740–746, 765–775
Isles, The, 714–738
i360, 217
Itinerary recommendations, 60–66
Iveagh Bequest, 151
Ivy, The ✕, 103
IWM London, 132
IWM North, 353, 356

J

J.M. Barrie's Birthplace, 681–682
Jacobite Steam Train, 761
James Smith & Sons Ltd. (shop), 116
Jane Austen Centre, 309
Jane Austen's House Museum, 238
Jazz Bar, The, 547
Jedburgh, 626–629
Jedburgh Abbey, 627
Jedburgh Castle Jail and Museum, 627
Jenners (department store), 557–558
Jerusalem Tavern, 121–122
John Knox House, 543
John O'Groats, 780

John O'Groats by Together Travel 🛏, 780
John Rylands Library, 356
Jolyon's Boutique Hotel 🛏, 483–484
Jorvik Viking Centre, 445
Jubilee Course, 673
Jubilee Market, 98
Jumble Room, The ✕, 398
Juniper (bar), 556
Jupiter Artland, 570
Jura, 730, 734
Jute ✕, 678–679

K

Kalpna ✕, 564
Keighley and Worth Valley Railway, 456
Kelso, 629–630
Kelso Abbey, 629
Kelvingrove Art Gallery and Museum, 600
Kelvingrove Park, 600
Kendal, 390–392
Kenilworth Castle and Elizabethan Garden, 343–344
Kensington (London), 138–149
Kensington Gardens, 139
Kensington Palace, 139
Kenwood House, 151
Keswick, 405–408
Keswick Launch Company, 406
Kettle's Yard, 420
Kew, 158
Kew Gardens, 158
Kiftsgate Court Gardens, 320
Kilchurn Castle, 725
Kilt Rock, 770
Kimpton Blythswood Square 🛏, 591
King James Tower, 542
King's College (Aberdeen), 691
King's College (Cambridge), 420
King's College Chapel, 420–421
King's Gate, 235
King's Museum, Old Aberdeen Townhouse, 691
Kingussie, 757–758
Kinloch Lodge 🛏, 769
Kintyre Peninsula, 727
Kirkcudbright, 641–642
Kirriemuir, 681–682
Kirriemuir Gateway to the Glens Museum, 682
Kitsu ✕, 201
Knightsbridge (London), 138–149
Knole, 205–206
Kool Ba ✕, 597
Kyle of Lochalsh, 766–767
Kylesku, 777–778
Kynance Cove, 284

L

Lacock, 314–315
Lacock Abbey, 314–315

Lagavulin Distillery, 733
Lainston House 🛏, 236
Lake District, 384–408
Lake District National Park, 389
Lake of Menteith Hotel 🛏, 660
Lake Vyrnwy (Llyn Efyrnwy), 512–513
Lake Vyrnwy Hotel and Spa 🛏, 513
Lake Vyrnwy Nature Reserve, 512
Lakes Aquarium, 393
Lakeside & Haverthwaite Railway Company, 393
Lambs of Sheep Street ✕, 338
Land's End, 282
Lanes, The, 217
Langdales, The, 399–400
Langham, The 🛏, 94
Langley Castle 🛏, 463
Language, 509, 703
Laphroaig Distillery, 733
Last Invasion Tapestry, 498–499
Laugharne, 494
Lavenham, 428–430
Lavenham Guildhall, 429
Le Manoir aux Quat'Saisons ✕🛏, 178–179
Le Talbooth ✕, 431
LEAF on Bold Street (club), 371
Leeds Castle, 206
Leicester Square (London), 98
Leith, 565–568
L'Escargot Bleu ✕, 554
Levens Hall, 390–391
Lewes, 213–216
Lewes Castle, 214
Lewtrenchard Manor 🛏, 291
LGBTQ bars, 557
Liberty (department store), 108–109
Library House 🛏, 380
Lighthouse, The, 584–585
Lime Wood 🛏, 252
Lincoln's Inn, 110–111
Little Hall (Lavenham), 429
Liverpool, 346–352, 363–372
Liverpool One (shop), 371
Lizard Peninsula, 284
Llanberis, 518–519
Llanberis Pass, 518
Llandaff Cathedral, 481
Llandrindod Wells, 503–504
Llandudno, 522–523
Llanerchaeron, 505
Llangoed Hall 🛏, 501
Llangollen, 508–512
Llangollen Railway, 509
Llechwedd Slate Caverns, 514
Loch Achray, 658–659
Loch an Eilein, 756
Loch Arthur Creamery and Farm Shop, 638
Loch Awe, 724–725
Loch Fyne Oyster Bar and Restaurant ✕, 726
Loch Katrine, 659
Loch Lomond, 661–663

Loch Maree, 775
Loch Morar, 764
Loch Ness, 758–760
Loch Ness Centre and Exhibition, 759
Loch Ness Lodge 🖾, 760
Loch Rannoch, 667
Lochcarron Visitor Centre, 633
Lochranza, 729–730
Lochranza Castle, 730
Lodging, 53, 68
price categories, 70, 104, 101, 233, 267, 304, 352, 390, 415, 442, 476, 533, 582, 626, 653, 689, 719, 746
London, 70–158
London Edition, The 🖾, 114
London Eye, 132
London Food Lovers Food Tours, 77
London Transport Museum, 99
London Zoo, 153
Long Bridge, 242
Long Melford, 427–428
Longleat House, 249
Lost Gardens of Heligan, 286
Lothians, The, 568–572
Lovecrumbs ✕, 544
Lower Slaughter, 324
Lowry, The, 356
Ludlow, 381–382
Ludlow Castle, 381
Lumley Castle Hotel 🖾, 459
Lunya ✕, 368–369
Lydford, 290–291
Lydford Gorge, 291
Lyle's ✕, 125
Lyme Regis, 237, 258–260
Lyndhurst, 251–253
Lynmouth, 275–276
Lynton, 275–276
Lynton and Lynmouth Cliff Railway, 275

M

M Shed, 269
Mac and Wild at Falls of Shin ✕, 781
Macallan Distillery, 707
Machrie, 729
Machrie Moore Stone Circles, 729
Mackintosh, Charles Rennie, 584–585, 611, 614
Mackintosh Interpretation Centre, 584–585
Mackintosh at the Willow, 585
Mackintosh at the Willow ✕, 588
MacLellan's Castle, 642
MAD Museum, 336
Magdalen College, 177
Magna Carta, 109
Maiden Castle, 255
Main Street (Haworth), 456
Maison Talbooth 🖾, 431
Mallory Court Country House Hotel and Spa 🖾, 343
Malmaison 🖾, 694
Manchester, 346–363

Manchester Art Gallery, 356–357
Manchester Craft and Design Centre, 362
Manchester International Festival, 350
Manchester Museum, 357
Mandarin Oriental Hyde Park 🖾, 146
Manor House Hotel (Castle Combe) 🖾, 313
Manor House Hotel (Oban) 🖾, 723
Market Place (Coliabury), 242
Markets, 98, 128–129, 132, 142, 180, 242, 328, 425, 460, 494, 611
Marlow, 171–172
Mary, Queen of Scots Visitor Centre, 627
Mary Arden's Farm, 336
Mary Rose, The, 239–240
Mayfair and Marylebone (London), 88–97
Mayflower Museum, 287
McManus Galleries, 677
ME London 🖾, 105
Meadows, The, 563–564
Medieval city walls (Canterbury), 195
Melford Hall, 428
Mellerstain House and Gardens, 629
Melrose, 631–633
Melrose Abbey, 631–632
Melrose House 🖾, 274
Memsaab ✕, 430
Merchant City (Glasgow), 594–599
Merchants' House, 595
Merlin's Cave, 278
Mermaid Inn, The 🖾, 209
Mermaid Street (Rye), 208–209
Merseyside Maritime Museum, 365
Merthyr Mawr, 492
Midsummer House ✕, 422
Millennium Wood, 735
Mimi's Bakehouse–Leith ✕, 567
Mr Fogg's Residence (bar), 95
Misty Isle Boat Trips, 760
Moat Brae and the Neverland Garden, 636
Model Village, 323
Monachyle MHOR 🖾, 657
Moot Hall and Aldeburgh Museum, 433
Morgans 🖾, 496
More? The Artisan Bakers, 394
Mostyn Art Gallery, 523
Mount Edgcumbe, The 🖾, 202
Mowgli ✕, 369
Murrayfield Stadium, 535
Museum of Archaeology and Anthropology, 421
Museum of Bath Architecture, 309
Museum of Cardiff, 481
Museum of Edinburgh, 541
Museum of Islay Life, 732
Museum of Lead Mining, 639
Museum of Liverpool, 365
Museum of London, 117

Museum of Science and Industry, 353, 357
Music, 95, 147, 484, 485, 491, 547, 563, 592, 598, 776
Music clubs, 106–107, 147, 221, 361–362, 371, 484, 547, 591, 679, 750
Mussel Inn ✕, 588
Myddelton Grill on the Square, 524

N

Nairn, 752–753
Nant Gwrtheyrn, 514
Nantclwyd y Dre, 524
Nash Point, 492
National Botanic Garden of Wales, 494
National Cycle Museum, The, 503
National Football Museum, 357
National Gallery, 83
National Library of Wales, 505–506
National Maritime Museum, 155
National Maritime Museum Cornwall, 284
National Monument, 549
National Motor Museum, 253
National Museum Cardiff, 401
National Museum of Scotland, 541
National Museum of the Royal Navy, 240
National parks
Central Highlands, Fife, and Angus, 659
Inverness, Skye, and the Northern Highland, 755–756
Lake District, 389
Peak District, 375
South, 251
Wales, 488–489, 499, 516–517
West Country, 288–289
National Portrait Gallery, 83
National Railway Museum, 445
National Roman Legion Museum, 481
National Show Caves of Wales, 489–490
National Slate Museum, 518
National Theatre, 136–137
National Wallace Monument, 654
National Waterfront Museum, 494
Native 🖾, 360
Natural History Museum, 139
Necropolis, 596
Ned, The 🖾, 121
Nelson Monument, 549
Ness Walk 🖾, 750
Neverland Garden, 636
Nevis Range Mountain Experience, 761–762
New Forest, 251
New Forest Heritage Centre, 251
New Town (Edinburgh), 548–558
Newburgh Quarter (London), 99
Newquay, 280
Nightingale Cottage 🖾, 228
North of Dumfries, 638–640
Northeast (England), 436–468
Northeast (Scotland), 684–712

Northern Highlands, *740–782*
Notting Hill (London), *138–149*
Number 1 Royal Crescent, *309*
Number Sixteen 🔲, *146*

O

Oban, *720–721, 723*
Oban Distillery, *721*
Oban War and Peace Museum, *721*
Ocean Explorer Centre, *721*
Ogmore Castle, *492*
Oink ✕, *544–545*
Okehampton, *289*
Old Course, *673*
Old Gaol, *463*
Old Man of Coniston, *400, 402*
Old Man of Stoer, *777*
Old Man of Storr, *770*
Old Sarum, *242–243*
Old Stamp House ✕, *396*
Old Town (Edinburgh), *535–548*
1 Park Road 🔲, *394*
Opera, *107, 215, 373*
Opium ✕, *588*
Oriental Museum, *459*
Outdoor activities and sports, *36–37,
  55–56.* ⇨ *See also specific activities*
Ox and Finch ✕, *609*
Oxford, *160–164, 174–180*
Oxford Literary Festival, *163*
Oxford University Museum of Natu-
  ral History, *177*

P

Packwood House, *341–342*
Padella ✕, *135*
Padstow, *279–280*
Painswick, *328–329*
Painswick Rococo Garden, *328–329*
Palace House and Gardens (Beaulieu),
  253
Palace of Holyroodhouse, *541–542*
Palaces
  *Central Highlands, Fife, and Angus, 654,
    664–665, 676*
  Edinburgh, 541–542
  London, 79, 83, 139, 157
  Oxford and the Thames Valley, 181–182
  Southeast, 225
  West Country, 271–272
Pallant House Gallery, *225*
Pantiles, *201*
Park House ✕, *483*
Paul Ainsworth at no6 ✕, *279*
Paul Smith (shop), *108*
Pavilion Gardens, *373*
Peak District, *346–352*
Peak District National Park, *375*
Pembroke Castle, *496–497*
Pembrokeshire Coast National
  Park, *499*
Penally Abbey 🔲, *497*
Pendennis Castle, *285*
Pengwern Country House ✕, *517*

Penshurst Place, *203–204*
Penzance, *282–283*
People's History Museum (Manches-
  ter), *357*
People's Palace and Winter Gardens
  (Glasgow), *610–611*
People's Story Museum (Edinburgh),
  538
Perth, *663–665*
Pettigrew Tea Rooms ✕, *483*
Petworth House and Park, *225*
Philip Treacy (shop), *95*
Phoenix Sea Adventures, *752*
Photographers' Gallery, The, *99*
Pierhead, *481–482*
Pierhouse Hotel and Restaurant
  ✕, *724*
Pig, The ✕, *251–252*
Pig Near Bath, The ✕, *311*
Pig on the Beach, The 🔲, *254*
Pillars of Hercules ✕, *676*
Pistyll Rhaeadr, *509*
Pitlochry, *666–668*
Pitt Rivers Museum, *177*
Plantagenet House ✕, *497*
Plas Mawr, *521*
Plas Newydd (Anglesey), *520*
Plas Newydd (Llangollen), *509–510*
Play, a Pie, and a Pint (theater), *604*
Plymouth, *287–288*
Plymouth Gin Distillery, *287*
Polar Museum, *421–422*
Pollok House, *614*
Pompadour, The ✕, *554*
Pontcysyllte, *510*
Poole's Cavern and Buxton Country
  Park, *373*
Port Askaig, *733*
Port Charlotte, *731–732*
Port Charlotte Hotel 🔲, *732*
Port Ellen, *732–733*
Portobello Market, *142*
Porthdinllaen, *514*
Porthmadog, *513–516*
Portmeirion, *514*
Portsmouth, *238–241*
Portsmouth Historic Dockyard, *240*
Portree, *769–770*
Potter, Beatrix, *393–394, 402–403, 666*
Powis Castle, *503*
Prehistoric sites and artifacts
  Argyll and the Isles, 729
  Cambridge and East Anglia, 432
  *Inverness, Skye, and the Northern
    Highlands, 751*
  Lake District, 405
  *Manchester, Liverpool, and the Peak
    District, 373*
  Stonehenge and the South, 245–248, 255
  Wales, 520, 523
Prestonfield 🔲, *564*
Price categories
  Aberdeen and the Northeast, 689
  Argyll and the Isles, 719

  *Bath, the Cotswolds, and Stratford-up-
    on-Avon, 304*
  Borders and the Southwest, 626
  Canterbury and the Southeast, 191
  Cambridge and East Anglia, 415
  Central Highlands, Fife, and Angus, 653
  Cornwall and the West Country, 267
  *dining, 78, 164, 191, 233, 267, 304, 352,
    390, 415, 442, 476, 533, 582, 626, 653,
    689, 719, 746*
  Edinburgh, 533
  Glasgow, 582
  *Inverness, Skye, and the Northern
    Highlands, 746*
  Lake District, 390
  *lodging, 78, 164, 191, 233, 267, 304, 352,
    390, 415, 442, 476, 533, 582, 626, 653,
    689, 719, 746*
  London, 78
  *Manchester, Liverpool, and the Peak
    District, 352*
  Oxford and the Thames Valley, 164
  Stonehenge and the South, 233
  Wales, 476
  Yorkshire and the Northeast, 442
Princes Square (Glasgow), *593*
Princes Street (Edinburgh), *549*
Princess Diana Memorial Fountain,
  139
Prior Park Landscape Garden, *309*
Priorwood Garden and Harmony
  Garden, *632*
Pubs, *55*
  Aberdeen and the Northeast, 695
  *Bath, the Cotswolds, and Stratford-up-
    on-Avon, 312, 313*
  Cambridge and East Anglia, 424
  *Central Highlands, Fife, and Angus,
    672, 675*
  *Edinburgh, 546–547, 556–557, 565,
    567–568*
  Glasgow, 591–592, 598, 610
  *Inverness, Skye, and the Northern
    Highlands, 750*
  London, 106, 115, 121–122
  *Manchester, Liverpool, and the Peak
    District, 361*
  *Oxford and the Thames Valley, 197,
    210, 215*
  Wales, 484, 498, 500, 507
  Yorkshire and the Northeast, 449, 459
Pulteney Bridge, *309–310*
Pump Room (Bath), *310*
Punting, *180, 425–426*

Q

Queen Elizabeth Forest Park, *660*
Queen Elizabeth Olympic Park, *123*
Queens' College, *422*
Quiraing, *770*

R

Radcliffe Camera and Bodleian
  Library, *175*
Radnorshire Museum, *503*
Raffles 🔲, *294*
Ragamuffin (shop), *769*
Raglan Castle, *486–487*

Railroads. ⇨ See Train travel and railroads
Raoul's (bar), 179
Ravenscraig Guest House ⌂, 756–757
Real Mary King's Close, The, 542
Refuge by Volta, The ✕, 359
Regency, 219
Regent's Canal, 123, 125
Regent's Park (London), 149–154
Regimental Museum of the Royal Welsh, 490–491
Reilly Shellfish Lobster Hut ✕, 673–674
Residence, The ⌂, 370
Restaurant Martin Wishart ✕, 567
Restaurants, 53–55
price categories, 78, 164, 191, 233, 267, 304, 352, 390, 415, 442, 476, 533, 582, 626, 653, 689, 719, 746
RHS Garden Bridgewater, 358
Richard Booth Books (shop), 502–503
Richmond, 157–158
Richmond Park, 157–158
Rick Stein, Winchester ✕, 236
Riddle and Finns The Lanes ✕, 219–220
River & Rowing Museum, 173
River Cam, 426
Riverside Museum: Scotland's Museum of Transport and Travel, 605
Riverstation ✕, 270
Road to Elgol, 768
Robert Burns Birthplace Museum, 617
Robert Burns Centre, 636
Robert Burns Country, 615–618
Robert Burns House, 636, 638
Robert Smail's Printing Works, 634
Rochester, 206–207
Rocpool ✕, 749
Rocpool Reserve Restaurant ✕, 749
Rodmarton Manor, 330
Rogano ✕, 588–589
Roman Army Museum, 465
Roman artifacts
Bath, the Cotswolds, and Stratford-up-on-Avon, 310, 326
Canterbury and the Southeast, 193, 199, 225
Manchester, Liverpool, and the Peak District, 353
Wales, 481
Yorkshire and the Northeast, 460–462, 464–465
Roman Baths and the Pump Room, 310
Roman Camp ⌂, 657
Roman Painted House, 199
Rookery, The ⌂, 114
Rose & Crown ✕, 343
Rosemount Viaduct, 691–692
Roslin, 572
Rosslyn Chapel, 572
Rothay Manor ⌂, 396

Rothiemurchus Estate, 756
Rowing, 173–174
Royal Aberdeen Golf Club, 695
Royal Academy of Arts, 89
Royal Albert Hall, 147
Royal Albert Memorial Museum, 293
Royal Botanic Garden Edinburgh, 549
Royal Castle Hotel ⌂, 290
Royal Deeside Railway, 699
Royal Dornoch Golf Club, 782
Royal Exchange Theatre, 362
Royal Liver Building, 385
Royal Navy Submarine Museum, 240
Royal Observatory, 155, 157
Royal Opera House, 107
Royal Pavilion, 219
Royal Pump Room Museum (Harrogate), 450
Royal Seven Stars Hotel ⌂, 295
Royal Shakespeare Company, 340
Royal Shakespeare Theatre, 336
Royal Tunbridge Wells, 200–202
Royal Welsh Show, 503
Royal Yacht Britannia, 566
RRS Discovery, 677
Rufflets St. Andrews ⌂, 672
Rugby, 535
Ruskin Museum, 401
Ruthin (Rhuthun), 523–524
Ruthin Gaol, 524
Ruthven Barracks, 757–758
Rye, 207–210
Rye Waterways (pub), 210
Rye Windmill ⌂, 209–210

S

Sadler's Wells, 116
Safety, 56–57
St. Albans, 183–184
St. Andrews, 669–673
St. Andrews Castle, 670
St. Andrew's Cathedral (Inverness), 747–748
St. Andrews Cathedral (St. Andrews), 670
St. Brides Spa Hotel ⌂, 498
St. Davids (Tyddewi), 498–500
St. Davids Cathedral, 499
St. Fagans National Museum of History, 482
St. Ives, 281–282
St. James (Chipping Campden), 320
St. James's (London), 78–88
St. James's Palace, 83
St. James's Park, 83–84
St. John ✕, 114
St. John the Baptist (Burford), 325
St. John the Baptist (Cirencester), 327
St. John's College (Oxford), 177
St. Machar's Cathedral, 692
St. Mary's Church, 173
St. Mary-the-Virgin, 431
St. Michael's Churchyard, 638

St. Michael's Mount, 283
St. Mungo Museum of Religious Life and Art, 596
St. Nicholas Kirk, 692–693
St. Oswald's, 398
St. Pancras Renaissance ⌂, 115
St. Paul's Cathedral, 117
St. Rule's Tower, 670
Salisbury, 241–245
Salisbury Cathedral, 243
Salisbury Museum, 243–244
Salt House Bacaro ✕, 389
Saltaire, 452–453
Saltram, 287
Sandwood Bay, 779
Savill Garden, 166
Savoy, The ⌂, 105
Scafell Pike, 408
Scarlet, The ⌂, 280
Science Museum, 142–143
Scone Palace, 664–665
Scotch Whisky Experience, 543
Scotia Bar, 598
Scott, Sir Walter, 633–634
Scott Monument, 552
Scottish evenings, 565
Scottish Fisheries Museum, 675
Scottish languages, 703
Scottish Maritime Museum, 615–616
Scottish National Gallery, 552
Scottish National Portrait Gallery, 552
Scottish Parliament, 542–543
Scottish Storytelling Centre and John Knox House, 543
Scottish Wool Centre, 660
Scourie, 778
Scudamore's Punting Co., 425–426
Sculpture Croft, 779
Sea Life Surveys, 719
Seafield Street (Cullen), 710
Seafood Restaurant, The ✕, 279
Selfridges (department store), 97
Selkirk, 633–634
Selkirk Arms ⌂, 642
Serpentine Lido, 139
Shaftesbury, 256
Shaftesbury Lodge ⌂, 679
Shakespeare Birthday Celebrations, 302
Shakespeare Bookshop, 340
Shakespeare's Birthplace, 336–337
Shakespeare's Birthplace Trust, 334
Shakespeare's Globe, 132–133
Shakespeare's New Place, 337
Shakespeare's Schoolroom and Guildhall, 337
Shambles, The, 445
Shangri-La Hotel at The Shard ⌂, 135
Sharmanka Kinetic Theatre, 598
Sheila Fleet (shop), 558
Sheldonian Theatre, 177
Sherborne, 256–257

Sherborne Abbey, *256–257*
Sherborne Castle, *257*
Sherlock Holmes Museum, *89*
Shopping, *28–29*
Shorehouse Restaurant ✕, *778*
Silver Darling ✕, *693*
Silver Mountain Experience, *506*
Sir John Soane's Museum, *111*
Sir Walter Scott's Courtroom, *633–634*
Sissinghurst Castle Farmhouse
⬚, *207*
Sissinghurst Castle Garden, *206–207*
Six Portland Road ✕, *144*
63 Tay Street ✕, *665*
Skye Museum of Island Life, *771*
Sloans (pub), *591–592*
Smailholm Tower, *629–630*
Smallest House in Great Britain, *521*
Smoo Cave, *779*
Snape Maltings (cultural center), *434*
Snowdon Mountain Railway, *518–519*
Snowdonia National Park, *516–517*
Snowshill Manor, *319*
Soccer, *137, 357, 362–363, 371–372,
534, 583, 610*
Soho (London), *98–109*
Sol y Sombra Tapas Bar ✕, *679*
Somerset House, *99*
Somerset Rural Life Museum, *274*
South, The, *228–260*
South Devon Railway, *295*
South of the Thames (London), *129–138*
South Side (Edinburgh), *563–565*
South Side (Glasgow), *611–614*
South Queensferry, *568–570*
Southbank Centre, *137*
Southeast, *186–226*
Southwark Cathedral, *133–134*
Southwest, *620–644*
Speedwell Bar, *679*
Speyside Cooperage and Visitor
Centre, *707*
Spinnaker Tower, *240–241*
Spring ✕, *104–105*
SS *Great Britain*, *269–270*
Staffin Ecomuseum, *771*
Stafford London, The ⬚, *86*
Station Hotel, The ⬚, *707*
Stevenson, Robert Louise, *549*
Stirling, *653–656*
Stirling Castle, *654–655*
Stoer Point Lighthouse, *777*
Stoke Park ⬚, *168*
Stonegate, *445*
Stonehaven, *696, 698*
Stonehaven Tolbooth Museum, *696*
Stonehenge, *228–234, 245–247*
Stourhead, *249–251*
Stow-on-the-Wold, *321–323*
Stowe Landscape Gardens, *182–183*
Stranraer, *643–644*
Stratford-upon-Avon, *298–304,
331–340*

Stratford-upon-Avon Butterfly
Farm, *337*
Strathisla Distillery, *705*
Stravaigin ✕, *602*
Stray, The, *450*
Striding Arches, *639–640*
Subway travel, *75–76, 580*
Sudeley Castle, *316–317*
Sundial ✕, *212*
Surfing, *276, 280, 522*
Sutherlands Guest House ⬚, *758*
Sutton Hoo (Woodbridge), *432*
Swallow Falls, *516*
Swan House ⬚, *212–213*
Swan-Upping, *172*
Swanage Railway, *254*
Swansea (Abertawe), *492–496*
Swansea Market, *494*
Swansea Museum, *494–495*
Swim the Lakes (tours), *389*

T

Talisker Distillery, *773, 775*
Tall Ship at Riverside, *605, 608*
Tartan Bicycle Company, The, *534*
TAST ✕, *359*
Tate Britain, *84*
Tate Liverpool, *365*
Tate Modern, *134*
Tate St. Ives, *281*
Tavistock and environs, *289–290*
Taxes, *57–58, 68*
Taxis, *75, 532, 580*
Taychreggan Hotel ⬚, *725*
Tea, *126*
Tenby (Dinbych-y-Pysgod), *496–498*
Tenby Museum and Art Gallery, *497*
Tenement House, *585*
Tennis, *137*
Tetbury, *329–331*
Teuchter's Landing (pub), *568*
Thackeray's ✕, *222*
Thames River, *154–158, 167*
Thames Valley, *160–184*
Theater, *66*
    Bath, the Cotswolds, and Stratford-up-
        on-Avon, *336, 340*
    Canterbury and the Southeast, *189, 226*
    Central Highlands, Fife, and Angus,
        679–680
    Edinburgh, *529, 557, 563, 565*
    Glasgow, *592, 598, 604, 614*
    Inverness, Skye, and the Northern
        Highlands, *769*
    Lake District, *392, 407*
    London, *87, 115, 122, 132–133, 136–138,
        147, 154*
    Manchester, Liverpool, and the Peak
        District, *356, 362, 371, 373*
    Wales, *484–485, 507*
    West Country, *283*
Thermae Bath Spa, *310*
33 The Scullery ✕, *338*
Thomas, Dylan, *493*
Thornbury Castle ⬚, *271*

Threave Castle, *640–641*
Threave Garden and Estate, *641*
Three Chimneys ✕, *772*
Timberstone ⬚, *382*
Tintagel, *277–279*
Tintagel Castle, *278–279*
Tintern Abbey, *487*
Tipping, *58*
Tobermory, *736–737*
Tobermory Distillery, *736–737*
Tolbooth Arts Centre (Kirkcudbright),
642
Tolbooth Museum (Aberdeen), *693*
Tonbridge, *204–206*
Top Withens, *456*
Topping and Company Booksellers,
672–673
Totnes, *294–295*
Tours
    Argyll and the Isles, *719–720, 737*
    Bath, the Cotswolds, and Stratford-up-
        on-Avon, *305, 308, 331, 334*
    Cambridge and East Anglia, *416*
    Canterbury and the Southeast, *192*
    Central Highlands, Fife, and Angus,
        674–675
    Edinburgh, *533–534, 570*
    Glasgow, *582*
    Inverness, Skye, and the Northern High-
        lands, *746, 752, 758, 768, 780*
    Lake District, *389, 406*
    London, *76–77, 154*
    Manchester, Liverpool, and the Peak
        District, *353, 363*
    Oxford and the Thames Valley, *165,
        174–175, 184*
    Stonehenge and the South, *233*
    Wales, *476–477, 497*
    Yorkshire and the Northeast, *443*
Tower Bank Arms ✕, *403*
Tower Bridge, *117*
Tower of London, *117, 120*
Town House, The (Arundel) ✕, *223*
Town Trails of Tenby, *497*
Townhouse, The (Stratford-upon-Avon)
✕, *338*
Trafalgar Square (London), *84*
Train travel and railroads, *51–52,
66, 68*
    Aberdeen and the Northeast, *689, 699*
    Argyll and the Isles, *719*
    Bath, the Cotswolds, and Stratford-up-
        on-Avon, *303*
    Borders and the Southwest, *625*
    Cambridge and East Anglia, *414*
    Canterbury and the Southeast, *190*
    Central Highlands, Fife, and Angus, *652*
    Cornwall and the West Country, *267,
        275, 295*
    Edinburgh, *532*
    Glasgow, *580–581*
    Inverness, Skye, and the Northern High-
        lands, *745–746, 761*
    Lake District, *388–389, 393*
    London, *75*
    Manchester, Liverpool, and the Peak
        District, *351*
    Oxford and the Thames Valley, *164*
    Stonehenge and the South, *233, 254*

Wales, 475, 505, 506, 509, 512, 513, 515, 518–519
Yorkshire and the Northeast, 441, 445, 456
Tram travel, *532*
Transportation, *44–52, 66*
Traquair House, *634*
Tredegar House, *482*
Treehouse, The ✕ **,** *467*
Tremadog, *515*
Tre'r Ceiri, *514–515*
Trotower Court, *487*
Trinity College, *422*
Trossachs, The, *658–659*
Trossachs National Park, *659*
Trotternish Peninsula, *770–772*
Tube travel, *75–76*
Tudor Merchant's House, *497*
Tunbridge Wells, *200–202*
Turkish Baths Harrogate, *450*
2 Blackburne Terrace 🛏 **,** *370*
Two Brewers ✕ **,** *168*
Twr-Y-Felin Hotel 🛏 **,** *500*
Ty Castell 🛏 **,** *519*
Ty Siamas, *508*
Tyntesfield, *270*

U

Ullapool, *775–777*
Ullswater, *404–405*
Ullswater Steamers, *404*
Underground Passages, *293*
Underground tube travel, *75–76*
Unicorn Antiques (shop), *557*
Union Street (Aberdeen), *693*
University of Oxford Botanic Garden, *177–178*
University of St. Andrews, *670–671*
Upper Slaughter, *324*
Urquhart Castle, *760*

V

V&A Dundee, *677–678*
Vale of Ceiriog, *510*
Vale of Rheidol Railway, *506*
Valle Crucis Abbey, *510*
Valley Gardens, *450–451*
Varsity, The 🛏 **,** *424*
Venachar Lochside ✕ **,** *657*
Verdant Works, *678*
Victoria & Albert Museum, *143*
Victorian Festival, *474*
View from the Shard, *134*
Vindolanda, *405*
Visitor information, *58, 67–68*

W

Waddesdon Manor, *183*
Wales, *470–524*
Wales Millennium Centre, *482*
Walker Art Gallery, *365, 368*
Walking and hiking, *56, 67*
Bath, the Cotswolds, and Stratford-up-on-Avon, 305, 308
Cambridge and East Anglia, 416
Canterbury and the Southeast, 192
Central Highlands, Fife, and Angus, 661
Edinburgh, 533–534
Glasgow, 582
Inverness, Skye, and the Northern Highlands, 762–763
Lake District, 396, 399, 400, 402
London, 77, 154
Manchester, Liverpool, and the Peak District, 353
South, 256, 260
Wales, 480, 487, 507, 512, 520
West Country, 280, 289
Yorkshire and the Northeast, 443, 461–462
Wallace, William, *654*
Wallace Collection, *89, 92*
Walnut Tree, The ✕ **,** *487*
Wardens' Way, *324*
Warner Bros. Harry Potter Studio Tour, *104*
Warwick, *342–343*
Warwick Castle, *342–343*
Water of Leith Walkway, *555*
Water sports, *408*
We The Curious, *270*
Weald and Downland Open Air Museum, *225–226*
Webbes at the Fish Café ✕ **,** *209*
Wedgewood the Restaurant ✕ **,** *545, 546*
Wellington Arch, *92*
Wells, *271–273*
Wells Cathedral, *272–273*
Welsh Highland Heritage Railway (Porthmadog), *515*
Welsh Highland Railway (Llanberis), *519*
Welsh language, *509*
West Coast Delicatessen, The ✕ **,** *776*
West Country, *262–296*
West End (Edinburgh), *559–563*
West End (Glasgow), *599–604*
West Highland Museum, *762*
West Highland Way, *653*
West Kennett Long Barrow, *248*
Western Gailes Golf Club, *616*
Westgate Towers, *195*
Westlea House, The 🛏 **,** *777*
Westminster (London), *78–88*
Westminster Abbey, *84–85*
Westonbirt National Arboretum, *330*
Weymouth, *257–258*
Whale Watch With Us, *737*
Where the Light Gets In ✕ **,** *359*
Whiski Rooms (bar), *547*
Whisky
Aberdeen and the Northeast, 705, 706–708
Argyll and the Isles, 721, 729–731, 733, 734, 736–737
Central Highlands, Fife, and Angus, 667
Edinburgh, 543
Inverness, Skye, and the Northern Highlands, 754, 773, 775, 781
Whispering Gallery, *117*
White Cliffs, *199*
White Swan 🛏 **,** *340*
White Tower, *117, 120*
Whitechapel Gallery, *125*
Whithorn, *643*
Whithorn Priory and Museum, *643*
Whitworth Art Gallery, *358*
Widecombe-in-the-Moor, *289*
Wigmore Hall, *95*
Willy Lott's House, *431*
Wilson, Cheltenham Art Gallery and Museum, *317*
Wilton House, *244*
Winchester, *234–236, 237*
Winchester Cathedral, *235*
Windermere, *392–394*
Windermere Jetty, *393*
Windsor, *164–169*
Windsor Castle, *166*
Windsor Great Park, *166, 168*
Winter Gardens, *610–611*
Woodbridge, *432*
Woodstock, *180–182*
Wordsworth Museum, *397–398*
World of Beatrix Potter, *393–394*
World of Illusions, *538*
World Museum Liverpool, *360*
Wreckfish ✕ **,** *369*
Writers' Museum, *543*

Y

Yewfield Vegetarian Guesthouse 🛏 **,** *403*
Ynyshir Restaurant and Rooms ✕ **,** *506*
Ynyslas Beach, *506*
York, *442–450*
York Minster, *445, 447*
Yorke Arms, The ✕ **,** *451*
Yorkshire and the Northeast, *436–468*
Yorkshire Air Museum, *447*
Yorkshire Museum, *447*
Ypres Tower, *209*

Z

Zetter, The 🛏 **,** *115*
Ziplining, *516, 661*
Zipworld, *516*
Zoos/safari parks, *153, 249, 559*
ZSL London Zoo, *153*

Photo Credits

Notes

Notes

Notes

Fodor's ESSENTIAL GREAT BRITAIN

Publisher: Stephen Horowitz, *General Manager*

Editorial: Douglas Stallings, *Editorial Director*; Jill Fergus, Jacinta O'Halloran, Amanda Sadlowski, *Senior Editors*; Kayla Becker, Alexis Kelly, *Editors*

Design: Tina Malaney, *Director of Design and Production*; Jessica Gonzalez, *Graphic Designer*; Mariana Tabares, *Design and Production Intern*

Production: Jennifer DePrima, *Editorial Production Manager*; Elyse Rozelle, *Senior Production Editor*; Monica White, *Production Editor*

Maps: Rebecca Baer, *Senior Map Editor*; Mark Stroud (Moon Street Cartography), *Cartographer*

Photography: Viviane Teles, *Senior Photo Editor*; Namrata Aggarwal, Ashok Kumar, Carl Yu, *Photo Editors*; Rebecca Rimmer, *Photo Intern*

Business and Operations: Chuck Hoover, *Chief Marketing Officer*; Robert Ames, *Group General Manager*; Devin Duckworth, *Director of Print Publishing*; Victor Bernal, *Business Analyst*

Public Relations and Marketing: Joe Ewaskiw, *Senior Director Communications and Public Relations*

Fodors.com Jeremy Tarr, *Editorial Director*; Rachael Levitt, *Managing Editor*

Technology: Jon Atkinson, *Director of Technology*; Rudresh Teotia, *Lead Developer*; Jacob Ashpis, *Content Operations Manager*

Writers: Rob Andrews, Nick Bruno, Jo Caird, Rhonda Carrier, Sally Coffey, Robin Gauldie, Michael Gonzalez, Sophie Ibbotson, James O'Neill, Toby Orton, Joseph Reaney, Ellin Stein, Victoria Trott, Alex Wijeratna

Editors: Amanda Sadlowski

Production Editor: Monica White

3rd Edition

ISBN 978-1-64097-324-4

ISSN 2373–9169

Library of Congress Control Number 2018950372

All details in this book are based on information supplied to us at press time. Always confirm information when it matters, especially if you're making a detour to visit a specific place. Fodor's expressly disclaims any liability, loss, or risk, personal or otherwise, that is incurred as a consequence of the use of any of the contents of this book.

SPECIAL SALES

This book is available at special discounts for bulk purchases for sales promotions or premiums. For more information, e-mail SpecialMarkets@fodors.com.

PRINTED IN THE UNITED STATES OF AMERICA

10 9 8 7 6 5 4 3 2 1

About Our Writers

Longtime contributor **Robert Andrews** updated the Cornwall and the West Country chapter this edition.

Based in Dundee, **Nick Bruno** is a travel writer, journalist, and a Fodor's contributor for over a decade. For this edition, he updated the Fife and Angus content.

Jo Caird is a travel and arts journalist who writes on theater, visual arts, film, literature, and food and drink. For this edition, she updated several neighborhoods in the London chapter.

A leading family travel expert, Manchester-based writer **Rhonda Carrier** writes for publications such as *National Geographic Traveller*, the *Guardian*, and *Condé Nast Traveller*. She updated the Manchester, Liverpool, and the Peak District content this edition.

Sally Coffey is a journalist who specializes in British travel and tourism. She updated the Stratford-upon-Avon content and select towns in the Heart of England this edition.

Robin Gauldie is a freelance journalist specializing in travel and the tourism industry, and is the author of more than 30 travel guidebooks. Robin updated the Aberdeen and the Northeast and the Argyll and the Isles chapters this edition.

Mike Gonzalez is emeritus professor of Latin American Studies at Glasgow University and also writes regularly for the *Herald* and other publications on politics and culture. He updated the Glasgow and the Borders and the Southwest chapters along with the Central Highlands content.

Sophie Ibbotson is a writer, entrepreneur, and lover of wild places, which means updating the Lake District chapter and the Bath and the Cotswolds content was right up her alley.

James O'Neill loves London and—as his work updating several neighborhoods for this edition proves—loves rediscovering it, too.

Having studied in London and never left—aside from a brief sojourn in Madrid—**Toby Orton** has experienced everything in the capital from Hackney to Notting Hill, Highgate to Peckham, and still finds it the most inspiring city in the world. He updated several neighborhoods in the London chapter this edition, along with the Oxford and the Thames Valley and Cambridge and East Anglia chapters.

Joseph Reaney is an experienced travel writer and editor, born in England and currently based part-time in Scotland and part-time in the Czech Republic—and regularly writes about all his homes. This edition, he updated the Experience, Travel Smart, Canterbury and the Southeast, Edinburgh, and Inverness, Skye, and the Northern Highlands chapters, along with the Northeast England content.

About Our Writers

Ellin Stein has written for publications on both sides of the Atlantic, including the *New York Times*, the *Times of London*, and *InStyle*. For this edition, Ellin updated several neighborhoods in the London chapter along with the Stonehenge and the South chapter and the Yorkshire content.

Victoria Trott is a Wales-based freelance writer who updated the Wales chapter this edition.

London restaurant maven **Alex Wijeratna** is always amazed by the capital's rocket-fueled restaurant scene. He updated the Soho and Convent Garden section of the London chapter.